For Reference

Not to be taken from this room

A CENTURY OF
POPULATION GROWTH

১

1790-1900

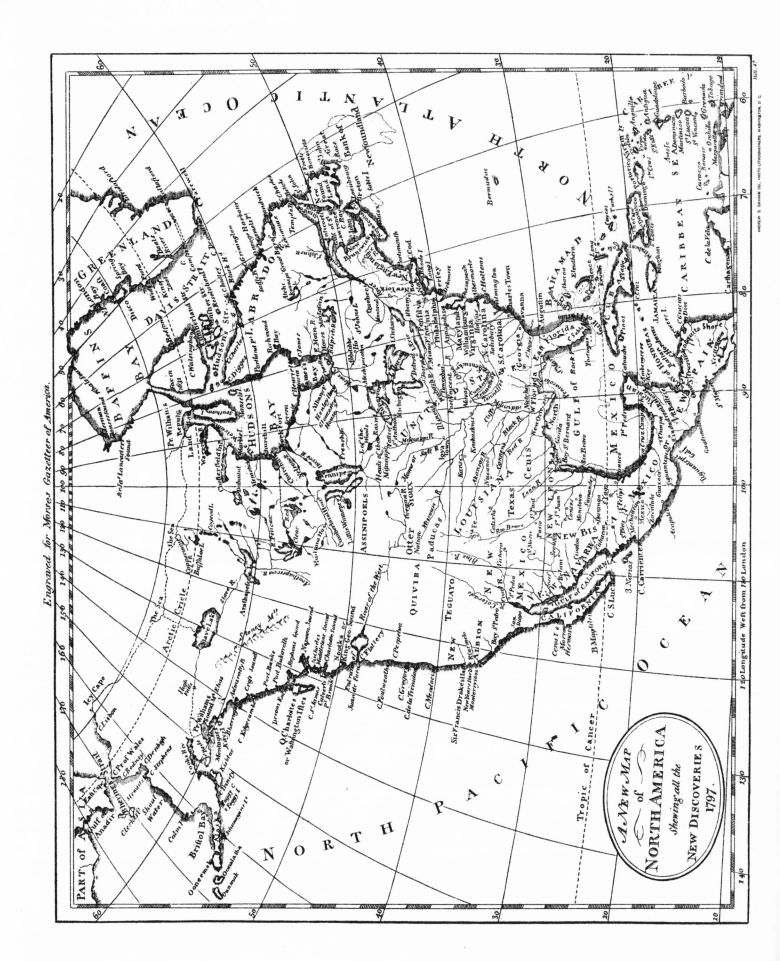

A New Map of NORTH AMERICA Shewing all the NEW DISCOVERIES 1797.

A CENTURY OF
POPULATION GROWTH

FROM THE FIRST CENSUS OF
THE UNITED STATES TO
THE TWELFTH
1790—1900

GENEALOGICAL PUBLISHING COMPANY

Baltimore, 1989

Originally Published

WASHINGTON

GOVERNMENT PRINTING OFFICE

1909

Reprinted

Genealogical Publishing Company

Baltimore, 1967, 1969, 1970, 1989

Library of Congress Catalog Card Number 67-25405

International Standard Book Number 0-8063-0332-8

Made in the United States of America

CONTENTS.

———

(v)

GENERAL TABLES.

ENUMERATIONS OF POPULATION IN NORTH AMERICA PRIOR TO 1790.

CONTENTS.

GENERAL TABLES DERIVED FROM THE FIRST AND SUBSEQUENT CENSUSES: 1790–1900.

MAPS, DIAGRAMS, AND ILLUSTRATIONS.

LETTER OF TRANSMITTAL.

DEPARTMENT OF COMMERCE AND LABOR,
BUREAU OF THE CENSUS,
Washington, D. C., April 15, 1909.

SIR:

In accordance with an act of Congress passed in 1903, the Department of the Interior transferred to the custody of the Director of the Census the records relating to the successive censuses of the United States. Among these records were the original schedules of the First Census for 11 of the 17 states and territories comprised in the United States in 1790.

The schedules of the First Census were prepared by underpaid assistant marshals, who furnished their own stationery, and naturally gave no thought to the permanent preservation of the manuscript, which to them merely represented the fulfilling of their task. In consequence, after the lapse of more than a century, the remaining schedules of the First Census show evidences of serious deterioration. This has been increased by the wear and tear resulting from frequent use for reference.

The states for which the schedules still exist are Maine, New Hampshire, Vermont, Massachusetts, Rhode Island, Connecticut, New York, Pennsylvania, Maryland, North Carolina, and South Carolina. The states and territories for which the schedules are lacking are New Jersey, Delaware, Virginia, Georgia, Kentucky, and the Southwest Territory (Tennessee). It is possible that some of the missing schedules were never in the custody of the Federal Government; others doubtless were obtained during the first half of the nineteenth century, and were either destroyed during the invasion of Washington by the British or in the Patent Office fire, which subsequently occurred, or were lost or mislaid during a period when the Federal records did not receive the intelligent care now accorded them.

In order permanently to preserve the valuable but vanishing census records which still remain, relating to the first year of constitutional government, and in response to urgent requests from many patriotic societies and public-spirited individuals, Congress authorized, in the sundry civil appropriation bill for the fiscal year 1907, the publication, by the Director of the Census, of the names of heads of families returned at the First Census. The Director was instructed to sell these publications at such price as in his opinion was just, and to report to Congress the proceeds. In accordance with the authority thus granted (and subsequently renewed), as the resources available for the printing requirements of the Bureau of the Census permitted, the Director of the Census published, from time to time during the succeeding year and a half, a part, or volume, for each of the states for which the schedules are in existence. For Virginia it was found that partial returns were available from the state enumerations of 1782, 1783, 1784, and 1785. These lists, which comprise most of the names of heads of families for nearly half of the state, were therefore included as a part, or volume, uniform with the returns of the Federal census for the other states.

After the publication of these volumes, the sale of which had been considerable, it became evident that this unique series (which is not included among the regular publications of the Census) would not be complete without a final section, or volume, discussing the historical aspects of the First Census and presenting such statistics as could be compiled from the limited returns of the first enumeration of the population. The results of the First Census were originally published in summarized form in a small volume, and it was recalled that no attempt had ever been made to present returns of that census in full detail, nor had the Federal Census Office ever attempted to analyze the returns, or to compare them with the corresponding figures at later censuses. The Director accordingly assigned to Mr. W. S. Rossiter, chief clerk of the Census, the task of compiling a report which should meet the requirements above noted. The results are embodied in the following pages.

Systematic inspection and analysis of the returns of the First Census revealed the fact that some of the tabulations would result in the presentation of figures basic in their relation to statistical science. Other statistical information proved to be available—in some instances easily deducible from the returns of the First Census, and in others resulting from assumptions believed to be justifiable, and for which the reasons

(ix)

are fully stated.   A second and perhaps more important series of tables resulted from an inspection of the names of the heads of families at the First Census. The tables thus secured present many facts—with respect to both nomenclature and nationality—that are of great interest to persons descended from the population enumerated in 1790. It is also hoped that this publication will prove of equal interest to those who have not the personal interest resulting from the enumeration of their ancestors at the First Census. In these pages will be found tabular analysis and discussion indicating the two great streams of population which have united to form the population of the Republic at the beginning of the twentieth century.

As work on this publication progressed it became evident that the scope had broadened and that it should constitute a review of the growth of the population during the century of census taking.   Some changes were made, therefore, in the form of presentation and the volume thus became more general in character than was first intended.

Acknowledgment is made of the faithful and efficient work of Miss Martha W. Williams in the construction of tables, of Miss Joyce Lee in the formation of tables and in criticism, and of Mr. Charles P. Smith in extended historical research and criticism.   I desire also to make grateful acknowledgment of the valuable assistance rendered this Office by Mr. William Nelson, secretary of the Historical Society of New Jersey, in clearing up many doubtful points in connection with a state for which no census returns exist; by Mr. Joseph Fornance, president, Historical Society of Montgomery county, Pa.; by Judge Harman Yerkes, Doylestown, Bucks county, Pa.; by Thomas L. Montgomery, state librarian, Harrisburg, Pa.; by Mr. Boyd Crumrine, Washington county, Pa.; by Rev. Horace Edw. Hayden, corresponding secretary and librarian, Wyoming Historical and Geological Society, Wilkes-Barre, Pa.; and of assistance in the preparation of the lists of minor civil divisions at the date of the First Census, rendered by Mr. William G. Stanard, corresponding secretary and librarian of the Virginia Historical Society; by Prof. Charles Lee Raper, president of the Historical Society of North Carolina; by Mr. Robert T. Quarles, state archivist of Tennessee; by Mrs. Jennie C. Morton, secretary of the Kentucky State Historical Society; by Mr. Henry C. Conrad, president of the Historical Society of Delaware; and by Mr. Richard H. Spencer, corresponding secretary of the Maryland Historical Society.

Very respectfully,

Director.

Hon. CHARLES NAGEL,
    Secretary of Commerce and Labor.

A CENTURY OF POPULATION GROWTH.

FROM THE FIRST TO THE TWELFTH CENSUS OF THE UNITED STATES: 1790–1900.

By W. S. Rossiter, Chief Clerk of the Bureau of the Census.

INTRODUCTION.

The results of a modern census have been accurately defined as a national account of stock. Early censuses were merely counts of inhabitants; additional facts relating to population were next secured; and the most recent step in census taking, especially in the United States, has been to include practically all lines of human activity. The modern census is thus the result of evolution.

In this evolution, however, civilized nations have not advanced equally. A decided and rather significant difference of opinion exists as to the practical value of census taking. Some nations attach great importance to statistics, and take accurate and detailed censuses at frequent and regular intervals; others manifest little interest, and make their enumerations at irregular intervals, with the result that such statistics as are obtained are neither comparable nor satisfactory.

The attitude of a nation toward a census is largely the result of education. A considerable element in every community fails to perceive the influence exerted by statistics upon legislation, and even morals; and it is only when a sufficient number of the citizens of a country have become educated to the value of accurate statistical information, either by their own national requirements or by observation of valuable results which have followed census taking in other countries, that periodic enumerations of population are instituted. It does not always happen, however, that nations composed of highly educated, methodical, and businesslike communities reach the greatest perfection in census taking, and obtain the most accurate and illuminating statistics.

The marked differences in the attitude of communities toward the systematic collection of statistics are well illustrated by the various states of the United States. Some maintain statistical bureaus and take a state census for the quinquennial year in each decade, while others depend entirely upon the Federal census for such statistical information as they require. Massachusetts, Rhode Island, and New York have taken state censuses for many years; certain neighboring states, as Connecticut and Pennsylvania, have

never done so. At the present time the state censuses of Massachusetts and Rhode Island are elaborate, scientific, and accurate, and in some of their details surpass the Federal census. Although eleven other states [1] make an intercensal enumeration, with varying degrees of accuracy and detail, no other state approaches these two in the amount and variety of information secured.

In view of the great importance to which statistical science has attained in nearly all civilized nations at the present time, it is interesting to note that the practice of making periodic censuses, or enumerations, of population is of comparatively recent origin. Except in Sweden (where a count of inhabitants has been made at stated intervals since the middle of the eighteenth century), accurate and periodic enumerations of population were practically unknown, alike upon the continent of Europe and in the British Isles, until the nineteenth century. [2]

In both France and Great Britain, the first census was taken in 1801. It is probable, in view of the supremacy of Napoleon at that time, that in France the motive for making an enumeration was principally to determine the military resources of the French nation. In Great Britain, however, while the census was in some degree the result of a demand for definite information of value to the military authorities, it was also the result of the great interest in the study of statistics aroused by the results of important economic researches described in publications that had appeared toward the

---

[1] Florida, Iowa, Kansas, Minnesota, New Jersey, New York, North Dakota, Oregon, South Dakota, Wisconsin, and Wyoming.

[2] "We know also that the three Scandinavian countries have been making enumerations ever since those of 1750 and 1769; that the United States of America, which began the series of their decennial enumerations in 1790, also preceded France in this respect; and that England commenced these enumerations the same year as France. Other nations have followed the example little by little, and the subject-matter has increased. There are only a very small number of civilized countries which do not undertake at a fixed time, or which have not undertaken at least once, the enumeration of their population; and almost all, in Europe at least, publish statements of the movement of their population. We recall that the first census having a really scientific character is that of Belgium in 1846, and that it is due in large measure to Quetelet and Heuschling. The first census of the same kind taken in Germany is that of 1871." *Levasseur, La Population Française, vol. 1, page 292.*

close of the eighteenth century. The most important of these were Adam Smith's Inquiry into the Nature and Sources of the Wealth of Nations, which appeared in 1776, and Malthus's Essay on the Principle of Population, which appeared in 1798. These two books raised new problems as to the increase or decrease in wealth and in population, which could not be intelligently discussed without the aid of accurate statistics.

The enumerations of 1801 in France and Great Britain undoubtedly formed an object lesson to the other nations of Europe and served to turn their attention to the importance of obtaining precise statistical information. There were also other factors at work. The beginning of the nineteenth century was marked by extraordinary military activity; changes in the boundaries of countries resulted, and consequently great changes in national population—on the one hand by loss through war, and on the other by gain through the acquisition of new territory. Statesmen began to appreciate the value of having definite information concerning military strength and national resources. Moreover, the marked increase in population and the industrial awakening which were concurrent early in the century made the estimates with which previous generations had been content increasingly unreliable. As all these factors operated over a large area, it is not surprising that several countries entered upon an era of census taking at nearly the same period.

The dates at which various European countries made the first complete enumeration of their inhabitants were as follows:

Sweden	1749
Spain	1798
France	1801
Great Britain	1801
Prussia	1810
Norway	1815
Saxony	1815
Baden	1816
Austria	1818
Bavaria	1818
Greece	1836
Switzerland	1860
Italy	1861
Russia	1897

The first census of the entire United States was taken in 1790, or nearly ten years before the first census in any European country, except Sweden. Because of this fact the United States has received much credit. The French statistician, Moreau de Jonnés, declared that the United States presents a phenomenon without a parallel in history—"that of a people who instituted the statistics of their country on the very day when they founded their government, and who regulated by the same instrument the census of inhabitants, their civil and political rights, and the destinies of the nation."

Against such a position, it has frequently been claimed that the United States did not undertake a systematic periodic enumeration with a deliberate statistical purpose; that, on the contrary, the statistical results of Federal census taking were merely a by-product of an enumeration of population provided for in the Constitution for purposes of apportionment, as a prerequisite to representative government. From this, it is claimed, resulted the statistics of population which accidentally placed the United States in the position of having led the way in the most important economic evolution of the age—periodic census taking.

While there is an element of truth in this contention, it is significant that several of the states composing the young Republic had formed the habit of making frequent enumerations of their inhabitants during their existence as colonies. It is probable that none of these enumerations was made for purposes of apportionment. At many of them the information secured was as full as at the first Federal census, and at several the statistics obtained were far more complete and significant. It was reasonable to expect, therefore, that consideration of the earlier censuses taken in America should lead the representatives of the states in the Constitutional Convention of 1787 to incorporate in the organic law of the nation a requirement for a periodic census. It was equally consistent that the members of the First Congress, in providing for the first Federal enumeration, influenced by the earlier practice of census taking, should require more than the mere count of inhabitants specified by the Constitution.

James Madison, who was instrumental in securing the expansion of census inquiry under the first act from a mere count of inhabitants to a schedule covering name of head of family, two age groups of white males, and freedom or servitude of the colored population, was an influential member of the Constitutional Convention, and the author of the Madison papers, which are accepted as the most authoritative record of the deliberations of that convention. It is reasonable to suppose that the enlightened and statesmanlike position assumed by Mr. Madison in the congressional debates upon the First Census act reflected convictions held and possibly expressed by him during the deliberations of the Constitutional Convention.

The influence of pre-Constitutional censuses upon the subsequent statistical history of the United States is a subject that hitherto has received but little consideration. So far as the present Census authorities are aware, the subject has never been discussed in the report of any census except that of 1850. In view of their peculiar historical significance, and their evident influence and bearing upon the beginnings of census taking in the United States, it is believed that a discussion of pre-Constitutional enumerations, with reproductions of all the authentic returns of such enumerations, forms a fitting introduction to a discussion of the history and statistics of the first Federal census, and the growth of national population.

I. POPULATION IN THE COLONIAL AND CONTINENTAL PERIODS.

CENSUS PROCEDURE IN COLONIAL AND CONTINENTAL PERIODS—POPU-
LATION PRIOR TO 1790—RECENT ESTIMATES OF EARLY POPULATION—
POPULATION OF CITIES—CHANGES IN URBAN POPULATION 1710 TO 1900.

Enumerations of population, more or less accurate, were made in nearly all the Northern colonies during the Colonial period, and several of the states took one or more censuses during the Continental period. Nearly all of these enumerations were more than a simple numbering of the people; in some instances, the inhabitants were classified by race, sex, age, and marital condition.

Colonial period (prior to 1774).—Most of the enumerations of the Colonial period were made at the instance of the British Board of Trade—which at this period exercised many of the functions now vested in a colonial office—in order to obtain information which would be of value in the administration of the affairs of the colonies. Thus, in a sense, the British Board of Trade was the originator of census taking in America.

These enumerations were made under the immediate supervision of the colonial governors, by sheriffs, justices of the peace, and other county or town officers. No enumeration embracing all the colonies was ever made, and in some of the colonies no accurate count of population occurred during the entire Colonial period. At times the board experienced great difficulty in getting the information desired. Its demands were often but partially complied with by the colonies, were sometimes entirely ignored, and were generally a source of friction. In consequence, the population statistics given out were not always reliable. Indeed, the colonial governors encountered so many obstacles in their attempts to make the required enumerations, that in many cases the tables prepared by them to supply the information demanded were based on muster rolls and lists of taxables, rather than on actual counts. Even when actual enumerations were made, they were often incomplete or inaccurate. The small population dispersed over large areas, the difficulties of travel, the independent spirit of the people, and the fact that in many instances the sheriffs and other officers charged with the enumeration received no compensation for their services, were all factors opposed to completeness and accuracy. "Superstition also was an influence opposed to census taking. In 1712 Governor Hunter undertook an enumeration of the inhabitants of New York. In writing to the home government he excused the imperfection of the returns in part by saying that 'the people were deterred by a simple superstition and observation that sickness followed upon the last numbering of the people.' Governor Burnett, of New Jersey, in a communication to the British board in 1726, alluding to an enumeration made in New York three years before, said, 'I would have then ordered the like accounts to be taken in New Jersey, but I was advised that it might make the people uneasy, they being generally of a New England extraction, and thereby enthusiasts; and that they would take it for a repetition of the same sin that David committed in numbering the people, and might bring on the same judgments. This notion put me off at that time, but, since your lordships require it, I will give the orders to the sheriffs that it may be done as soon as may be.'" [1]

Continental period (1774–1789).—The Colonial period in North America had covered more than a century and a half, and the policy of the board of trade in demanding exact returns of population at frequent intervals during this period doubtless had great weight in educating the people of the colonies to an appreciation of the value of accurate statistical information. It is significant, at least, that the states which took censuses in the Continental period upon their own initiative, after having thrown off the yoke of Great Britain, were those in which, as colonies, enumerations had been made by British authority; while those states which made no such enumerations were in the main those in which no colonial enumerations had been made. The Continental censuses are of great interest, and, so far as accuracy and completeness are concerned, probably compare well with the first Federal census. Especially to be noted is the Rhode Island census of 1774, in which the schedule of enumeration is almost identical with that of the Federal census of 1790.

The necessity for a national census, comprehending all the states, became apparent early in the Continental period. During the War of the Revolution, the Continental Congress had authorized and directed the issue of $3,000,000 in bills of credit. It had also resolved that the credit of the Thirteen United Colonies should be pledged for the redemption of these bills; that each colony should provide ways and means to redeem its proportion in such manner as it should see fit; that the proportion of each colony should be determined by the number of its inhabitants

---

[1] Johnston's New Universal Encyclopaedia, vol. 1, page 845.

of all ages, including negroes and mulattoes; and that it should be recommended to the colonial authorities to ascertain in the most confidential manner their respective populations, and to send the returns, properly authenticated, to Congress. Massachusetts and Rhode Island took a census upon this recommendation in 1776, but most of the colonies failed to comply. In November, 1781, a resolution was introduced in Congress recommending to the several states that they make an enumeration of their white inhabitants pursuant to the ninth article of the Confederation. The resolution failed to pass and the article was inoperative. Several of the states, however, made an enumeration about this time. The question of a settlement of the national debt became continually more serious, and the unwillingness of some of the states to order a general census and assume their equitable proportion made it apparent that a complete enumeration of the inhabitants of the country could never be made except by a central directing authority. Hence, when the Constitutional Convention met, all members seem to have been agreed that a provision for a Federal census at stated intervals should be incorporated in the Constitution.

CENSUSES PRIOR TO 1790.

The following table shows the number of official censuses of the inhabitants, of which record has been found, made in each of the colonies before 1790:

COLONY.	Total.	NUMBER OF CENSUSES.				
		Colonial period.				Continental period.
		1600 to 1649.	1650 to 1699.	1700 to 1749.	1750 to 1773.	1774 to 1789.
All colonies..............	38	1	1	14	11	11
New England colonies.........	20	....	....	3	8	9
Maine..................	2	....	....	....	[1]1	[1,2]1
New Hampshire...........	4	....	....	....	2	[1,2]2
Vermont................	1	....	....	....	[3]1	....
Massachusetts...........	2	....	....	....	1	[2]1
Rhode Island...........	7	....	....	3	1	3
Connecticut.............	4	....	....	....	2	2
Middle colonies..............	14	....	1	10	2	1
New York................	11	....	1	[4]7	2	1
New Jersey..............	3	....	....	3	....	....
Pennsylvania............						
Delaware...............						
Southern colonies..............	4	1	....	1	1	1
Maryland................	2	....	....	1	1	....
Virginia................	2	1	....	....	....	[2,5]1
North Carolina..........						
South Carolina..........						
Georgia.................						

[1] Taken as part of a census of Massachusetts.
[2] Partly estimated.
[3] Taken as part of a census of New York.
[4] Of these, 2 were partly estimated.
[5] Census of polls and taxable property. There are four incomplete lists of polls made during this period and still in existence, but only one appears to have been used as a basis for an estimate of population.

The table shows that 38 censuses of various colonies were taken, within the area of the original thirteen states, before the first enumeration was made in Great Britain. Apparently the British Government desired more definite statistical information regarding its colonies than it required concerning the British Isles.

New York and Rhode Island developed the greatest aptitude for census taking; of the total of 38 enumerations made before the date of the first Federal census, 18, or more than half, were made in these two colonies—11 in the former and 7 in the latter. The people of Massachusetts and Connecticut manifested considerable opposition to census taking, seeing no advantage in it to themselves, and fearing that in some way the information obtained would be used by the British authorities to their disadvantage. The first census embracing all the inhabitants of Connecticut was taken in 1756, and the first in Massachusetts not until 1764—when the general court, after continued demands from the governor, and fearing longer to irritate British authority, ordered a general census. Pennsylvania and Delaware, as well as the Southern colonies, present a marked contrast to New York; so far as appears, the Federal census of 1790 was the first thorough enumeration ever made within the borders of any of them, except Virginia.

The records of enumerations before 1790 are in many cases fragmentary; often totals only are given, and in some instances the results of the same enumeration are reported differently by different authorities. It must be remembered, however, that correct enumeration of any community is at best a difficult task, and the results of early censuses in every country have been inaccurate and disappointing. The later censuses in the Colonial period and most of those of the Continental period, were more accurate, and compare well with the first Federal census.

The following paragraphs present, for each of the colonies in turn, the general results of all known enumerations up to 1790, together with the estimates made by colonial governors and other officials which appear to possess a fair degree of accuracy, and also certain estimates by modern students of Colonial population. The results of all pre-Constitutional censuses are presented in detail on pages 149 to 185. In the summaries and more extended tables which follow, the population as shown by the first Federal census, 1790, is included for comparison.

New Hampshire.—None of the figures given below include the Vermont towns.

YEAR.	Estimates.	Censuses.
1641..	1,000	....
1675..	4,000	....
1689..	6,000	....
1716..	9,000	....
1721..	9,500	....
1732..	12,500	....
1742..	24,000	....
1749..	30,000	....
1761..	38,000	....
1767..	....	52,700
1773..	....	72,092
1775..	....	81,000
1786..	....	95,755
1790..	....	141,899

The census of 1775 was taken in order to ascertain the quantity of arms and ammunition in the province, and to correct the wild estimate made by Congress of 102,000 inhabitants, exclusive of slaves.

Massachusetts (including Maine).—The first census in Massachusetts was one of the "negro slaves, both males and females, 16 years old and upward," ordered in 1754, and finished in the beginning of 1755. The earliest recorded movement for a census of all the inhabitants was begun in 1760, and the resulting census was taken in 1764-65. This census was comprehensive in its scope, and the schedule of information strikingly resembles that of the first Federal census. It was ordered in 1764, and by the terms of the act was to have been completed by the last of that year; but the selectmen in some of the towns were negligent and dilatory, and did not send in their returns as required. On March 5, 1765, an act was approved by the governor by which the selectmen were required to complete the census and make their returns before May 25 following, under a penalty of £50. But even then, either some towns failed to make returns or else the returns have been lost.[1]

This census was taken according to the following schedule:

White people, under 16 years {Male. Female.

White people, above 16 years {Male. Female.

Families.

Houses.

Negroes and mulattoes {Males. Females.

Indians {Males. Females.

The following are contemporary estimates of the combined population of Massachusetts and Maine (including New Hampshire in 1665):

1632	2,300
1643	16,000 to 17,000
1665	30,000
1675	33,000
1692	60,000
1721	94,000
1735	145,000
1742	165,000
1751	165,000
1755	200,000

The estimate given for 1735 includes 2,600 negroes, and that for 1755 includes from 4,000 to 5,000. The fact that the population remained stationary during the nine years from 1742 to 1751 is ascribed to "a great depopulation by smallpox and war."

The totals reported at the three pre-Constitutional censuses of Massachusetts and Maine are compared below with the results of the Federal census of 1790. The census of 1784 was a count of polls only. The

population figures given are estimates by Doctor Chickering,[2] based on the results of the count.

CENSUS.	Both colonies.	Massa-chusetts.	Maine.
1764-65	269,711	245,718	23,993
1776	338,667	291,147	47,520
1784	408,059	346,653	61,406
1790	475,199	378,556	96,643

Rhode Island.—Of the seven pre-Constitutional censuses of Rhode Island, that of 1774 was particularly elaborate, giving the names of the heads of families, white males and white females over and under 16 years, negroes, and Indians. The results of this census were published in detail in 1858. Because of Rhode Island's share in the slave trade, the proportion of colored persons in the population was large— one person in every nine being either a negro or an Indian.

YEAR.	Estimates.	Censuses.
1658	1,200	
1663	2,000	
1675	3,000	
1689	5,000	
1708		7,181
1730		17,935
1742	30,000	
1748		34,000
1755		40,636
1774		59,707
1776		55,011
1782		52,400
1790		69,112

Of the population at the census of 1730, 985 were Indians. The decreases in population from 1774 to 1782 were directly due to the war, during which a large portion of the state was in the possession of the British forces. Indeed, the census of 1782 specifically excluded one whole town which was still in the enemy's hands.

Connecticut.—The number of official enumerations was much smaller in Connecticut than in Rhode Island. The growth of population, however, was more regular. The information desired by the British Board of Trade was furnished more often from estimates than from enumerations.

YEAR.	Estimates.	Censuses.
1643	5,500	
1665	9,000	
1679	14,000	
1689	20,000	
1713	34,000	
1730	51,000	
1749	100,000	
1756		130,612
1761		146,520
1774		196,088
1782		208,870
1790		237,655

Of the population reported at the census of 1761, 930 were Indians. The stunted growth in the later years appears to have been due to the heavy emigration from Connecticut to New York and to the West.

---

[1] Dr. J. Belknap (Mass. Hist. Soc. Collections, Vol. LV, page 198) says that this census, being an unpopular measure, was not accurately taken.

[2] Statistical View of the Population of Massachusetts from 1763 to 1840, page 7.

New York and Vermont.—Eleven enumerations were made in New York prior to 1790—a larger number than in any other colony. The first of these, made in 1698, was the first census of any magnitude on the continent. There is no evidence that Vermont was included in any of the colonial censuses of New York, except that of 1771.

YEAR.	Estimates.	Censuses.
1664	7,000	
1673	10,500	
1689	20,000	
1698		18,067
1703		20,748
1712	28,000	22,608
1715	31,000	
1723		40,564
1731		50,289
1737		60,437
1746		70,000
1749		73,448
1756		96,790
1771		168,006
1775	190,000	
1786		238,895
1790		340,241

The date of the first estimate, 1664, is the year of the British Conquest. Governor Hunter's census, in 1712, met with so much opposition, from a superstitious fear that it would breed sickness, that only partial returns were obtained. The census of 1746 also was incomplete; Albany county was reported as "not possible to be numbered on account of the enemy." The census of 1749 was taken by Governor Clinton, who volunteered the information that the returns, in common with those of preceding censuses, might not be strictly accurate, since the officers received no pay for this service, and it was performed reluctantly and carelessly.

Of the population reported at the census of 1771, 163,337 was reported for New York and 4,669 specifically for certain Vermont towns. At the Federal census of 1790 the population of New York was 340,241 and that of Vermont was 85,341.

New Jersey.—There is very little information concerning the population of the colony of New Jersey, only three enumerations having been made before the first Federal census. Census taking was unpopular, because of the religious prejudices and superstition of the people.

YEAR.	Estimates.	Censuses.
1702	15,000	
1726		32,442
1737		47,369
1745		61,383
1749	60,000	
1754	78,500	
1774	120,000	
1784	149,434	
1790		184,139

Of the population reported at the census of 1745, 4,606 were slaves. The estimate for 1749 is for whites only; the estimates for 1754 and 1784 include 5,500 and 10,500 blacks, respectively.

Pennsylvania and Delaware.—The census of 1790 appears to have been the first thorough enumeration ever attempted in either Pennsylvania or Delaware. Accordingly estimates of the population are subject to a large margin of error. In the case of some of the estimates given below, for years prior to 1770, it is uncertain whether the inhabitants of Delaware are included.

1681	500
1685	7,200
1700	20,000
1715	45,800
1730	49,000
1731	69,000
1740	100,000
1750	150,000
1757	200,000
1760	220,000

The 500 inhabitants given as the estimate for 1681—before the arrival of Penn's settlers—were whites, and mainly Swedes, on the banks of the Delaware. The 1730 estimate, made by Governor Gordon, is probably too small.

The following are estimates made separately for the two colonies of Pennsylvania and Delaware, together with the returns of the Federal census of 1790:

YEAR.	Pennsylvania.	Delaware.
1770	250,000	25,000
1775	302,000	
1780		37,000
1782	350,000	
1790	433,611	59,046

Maryland.—Maryland presents, throughout its colonial history, a uniform and gradual growth, which strikingly resembles that of Connecticut.

YEAR.	Estimates.	Censuses.
1660	8,000	
1676	16,000	
1701	32,258	
1712		46,073
1715	50,200	
1719	61,000	
1748	130,000	
1755		153,564
1761	164,007	
1775	200,000	
1783	254,000	
1790		319,728

The population reported at the census of 1712 included 8,330 negroes, and the total reported for 1755 was composed of 107,208 whites, 42,764 negroes, and 3,592 mulattoes. The estimates for 1719, 1748, and 1761 include 11,000, 36,000, and 49,675 blacks, respectively.

Virginia.—The first of all the colonies to be founded, Virginia, had a feeble growth at the start, but soon became the leader in population.

YEAR.	Estimates.	Censuses.
1616	351	
1620	2,400	
1628	3,000	
1635		5,119
1640	7,647	
1648	15,000	
1659	30,000	
1671	40,000	
1689	60,000	
1717	100,000	
1754	284,000	
1772	475,000	
1775	550,000	
1782		567,614
1790		747,610

For the four years 1782 to 1785, inclusive, there are in existence lists of polls in some of the Virginia counties. The population given above for 1782 is the estimate made by Thomas Jefferson, based on the list for that year.[1]

The meager data on which Mr. Jefferson's estimate was based were that in 1782, in all but 8 of the Virginia counties, there were 53,289 free males 21 years of age and over, 211,698 slaves (of both sexes and all ages), and 23,766 "tithable slaves" (apparently slaves 16 years of age and over); and that in the 8 counties not included in the list of polls there were, in 1779 and 1780, 3,161 militia.

Mr. Jefferson made five assumptions: (1) That the number of persons under 16 years of age equaled the number 16 years and over; (2) that the number of males from 16 to 20 years of age, inclusive, was equal to the number of unmarried men in the militia (males between 16 and 50 years), which was one-third of the total number in the militia, or about one-fourth of all males 16 years and over; (3) that the number of females equaled the number of males; (4) that the number of free males 16 years of age and over in 1782, in the 8 counties not included in the list of polls, was equal to the number of the militia in those counties in 1779 and 1780; (5) that the ratio of free to slave population was the same in these 8 counties as in the rest of the state.

With the facts and the basis outlined above, Mr. Jefferson evolved the following data:

Population of Virginia in 1782.

POPULATION.	The state.	Counties included in list of polls.	Other counties.
Total population	567,614	543,438	24,176
Free population	296,852	284,208	12,644
Males	148,426	142,104	6,322
Under 16 years	74,213	71,052	3,161
16 years and over	74,213	71,052	3,161
16 to 20 years	18,553	17,763	790
21 years and over	55,660	53,289	2,371
Females	148,426	142,104	6,322
Slave population	270,762	259,230	11,532

It will be observed that Mr. Jefferson's estimate is smaller than either the population at the Federal

[1] Thomas Jefferson: Notes on the State of Virginia, pages 94 and 95.

census of 1790 or the estimate for 1775 would indicate. He made the very conservative assumption, in (4), that the number of the militia (males between 16 and 50) equaled the number of free males 16 years of age and over; had he assumed that the number of the militia equaled the number of free males 21 years of age and over—in accordance with the proportions which can readily be obtained by analyzing (2)—his estimate would have been increased to 301,068 free persons and 274,608 slaves, or a total of 575,676.

North Carolina, South Carolina, and Georgia.—No thorough enumeration was ever made in these colonies during the Colonial or the Continental period. Accordingly all of the population figures given below, except for the Federal census of 1790, are estimates.

North Carolina.

YEAR.	Estimated population.
1677	4,000
1701	5,000
1711	7,000
1717	10,000
1732	36,000
1754	90,000
1764	135,000
1774	260,000
1790	[1] 395,005

[1] Census.

The estimate given for 1732 includes 6,000 negroes, and that for 1754 includes 20,000 negroes.

South Carolina.

YEAR.	ESTIMATED POPULATION.		
	Total.	White.	Negro.
1682	2,200	[1]	[1]
1708	9,500	4,000	5,500
1714	16,300	6,300	10,000
1720	20,828	9,000	11,828
1749	64,000	25,000	39,000
1763	105,000	35,000	70,000
1773	175,000	65,000	110,000
1790	[2] 249,073	[2] 140,178	[2] 108,895

[1] Not estimated separately.   [2] Census.

The decrease in the number of negroes between 1773 and 1790—which was accompanied by a marked decrease in the proportion they formed of the total population—was due to a large deportation of negroes by British authority during the War of the Revolution.

Georgia.

YEAR.	ESTIMATED POPULATION.		
	Total.	White.	Negro.
1752	5,000	[1]	[1]
1760	9,000	6,000	3,000
1766	18,000	10,000	8,000
1773	33,000	18,000	15,000
1776	50,000	[1]	[1]
1790	[2] 82,548	[2] 52,886	[2] 29,662

[1] Not estimated separately.   [2] Census.

RECENT ESTIMATES OF POPULATION PRIOR TO 1790.

Attention has already been called to the fact that at no time prior to 1790 was there a simultaneous enumeration of all the colonies. Estimates for various years have been made, however, by a number of historians and statisticians. In the preparation of this report valuable assistance was obtained from the exhaustive study made by Prof. Franklin Bowditch Dexter, of Yale University, of population in the several American colonies. Estimates in Bancroft's History of the United States also proved helpful. Mr. Bancroft, however, says of one of his estimates that it "rests on the consideration of many details and opinions of that day, private journals and letters, reports to the board of trade, and official papers of the provincial governments." Professor Dexter apparently depended less on British sources of information, and put more credence in official enumerations and in estimates based on militia rolls and lists of polls.

It is interesting to compare the estimates of the two authorities mentioned above with the estimates prepared by Mr. J. B. D. De Bow, Superintendent of the Seventh Census (1850), and published in the report of that census. Accordingly the various estimates obtainable from these three sources are summarized in the following statement:

Estimates of colonial population: 1640 to 1780.

YEAR.	Dexter.	Bancroft.	De Bow.
1640	25,000		
1660	80,000		
1688		200,000	
1701			262,000
1721	500,000		
1743	1,000,000		
1749			1,046,000
1750	1,207,000	1,260,000	
1754	1,360,000	1,428,500	
1760	1,610,000	1,695,000	
1767	2,000,000		
1770	2,205,000	2,312,000	
1775			2,803,000
1780	2,580,000	2,945,000	

Professor Dexter's first estimate relates to the period when Parliament gained the ascendency in England; at that time, he states, "60 per cent of the inhabitants were in New England and most of the remainder in Virginia." His second estimate indicates that at the time of the Restoration the population had more than trebled, "the greatest gain being in the most loyal divisions, Virginia and Maryland, which now comprehended one-half the whole." Concerning a group of his later estimates Professor Dexter says: "A round half million appears to have been reached about 1721, with the Middle colonies showing again the largest percentage of growth and New England the least. A million followed in twenty-two years more, or in 1743, this figure being doubled in turn twenty-four years later, or in 1767, the latter reduplication being delayed a little, doubtless by the effect of intervening wars."

Mr. Bancroft says, concerning his estimate for 1754: "The board of trade reckoned a few thousand more and revisers of their judgment less." He also makes a subdivision by color for each of his estimates, except that for 1688, as follows:

Bancroft's estimate of population, by color.

YEAR.	Total.	White.	Black.
1750	1,260,000	1,040,000	220,000
1754	1,428,500	1,165,000	263,500
1760	1,695,000	1,385,000	310,000
1770	2,312,000	1,850,000	462,000
1780	2,945,000	2,383,000	562,000

For two years, 1688 and 1754, Mr. Bancroft presented estimates for each of the colonies. These are deemed of sufficient interest and importance to be presented in full.

Bancroft's estimates of population, by colonies.

COLONY.	1688[1]	1754[2] Total.	1754[2] White.	1754[2] Black.
All colonies	200,000	1,428,500	1,165,000	263,500
New Hampshire	6,000	} 263,000	} 50,000	} 6,000
Massachusetts and Maine	44,000		207,000	
Rhode Island	6,000	39,500	35,000	4,500
Connecticut	19,000	136,500	133,000	3,500
New York	20,000	96,000	85,000	11,000
New Jersey	10,000	78,500	73,000	5,500
Pennsylvania and Delaware	12,000	206,000	195,000	11,000
Maryland	25,000	148,000	104,000	44,000
Virginia	50,000	284,000	168,000	116,000
North Carolina	}	90,000	70,000	20,000
South Carolina	} 8,000	80,000	40,000	40,000
Georgia	}	7,000	5,000	2,000

[1] History of the United States, Vol. I, page 602.
[2] History of the United States, Vol. II, page 389.

Concerning the estimates for 1754, Mr. Bancroft says: "Nearly all are imperfect. The greatest discrepancy in judgments relates to Pennsylvania and the Carolinas."

Mr. De Bow's estimates for the several colonies in 1701, 1749, and 1775—which, it will be remembered, are the only statements concerning pre-Constitutional population hitherto published in a Federal census report—are as follows:

De Bow's estimates of population, by colonies.

COLONY.	1701	1749	1775
All colonies	262,000	1,046,000	2,803,000
Slaves, estimated			500,000
New Hampshire	10,000	30,000	102,000
Massachusetts (including Maine)	70,000	220,000	352,000
Rhode Island	10,000	35,000	58,000
Connecticut	30,000	100,000	262,000
New York (including Vermont)	30,000	100,000	238,000
New Jersey	15,000	60,000	138,000
Pennsylvania and Delaware	20,000	250,000	378,000
Maryland	25,000	85,000	174,000
Virginia	40,000	85,000	300,000
North Carolina	5,000	45,000	181,000
South Carolina	7,000	30,000	93,000
Georgia		6,000	27,000

The estimates given above were made by the colonists at the dates referred to, and at the time Mr. De Bow wrote were the most reliable in existence. When

BOSTON,
with its Environs.

British Statute Miles.

NANTASKET ROAD

Gallop's Island

Nicke Mate

Rainford or Hospital Island

Nahant Bay

Phillips Point Gut

Sucking Island

Shirley Point

Pulling Point

Deer Island

Apple Island

Bird Islᵈ

NODLE'S ISLAND

HOG ISLAND

CHELSEA

Governor's Island

CASTLE ISLAND

Dorchester Point

Spectacle

Long Island

Western Channel

THOMPSON'S ISLAND

Winnesimet

Malden R.

Kipsmimet

Penny Ferry

Whitinsimet

Charles River

CHARLES TOWN

Bridge erected 1786

Mill Pond

North Battery

Hancock's Wharf

Long Wharf

BOSTON

South Battery

Dorchester Flats

DORCHESTER

Mill Pond

CAMBRIDGE

Little Cove

Charles River

Muddy River

BOSTON NECK

ROXBURY

Roxbury Fort

Road to Providence & Rhode Islᵈ

Brookline Fort

Brookline

Plowd Hill

Cobble Hills

References to Boston &c.
1 State (form'ly King) Street.
2 Faneuil Hall, & Dock Square.
3 Old South Meeting House.
4 Beacon Hill.
5 Fort Hill.
6 Copse alias Cops Hill.
7 Fort on Noddles Islᵈ raised after the Town was evacuated.

T. Conder Sculp. t Londo.

WASHINGTON, D.C.

they are considered, however, in the light of accepted investigations and discussions in progress during the last half century, they prove to be in many cases much too generous. It seems advisable, therefore, after the lapse of more than half a century since this subject was discussed in a Census report, to present a new series of estimates, based upon the best information now obtainable. Indeed, it is unlikely that another publication will be issued by the Federal Census Office in which a discussion of this character will be so appropriate as in connection with the reproduction of the returns of the First Census. Moreover, unless some future discovery is made of enumerations or of extensive statistical material, at present unknown, there is little probability that the figures given below will be materially changed hereafter.

The following tables represent the first attempt, within the knowledge of the Census authorities, to trace the population of the colonies by decades, upon the basis of enumerations and contemporary and other estimates.[1] In all consideration of these tables (with the exception of the actual returns for 1790) it must, of course, be remembered that the population shown for each colony is in nearly every case merely an estimate.

These estimates are derived from enumerations at neighboring dates, or from the nearest enumeration or estimate of that period;[2] they must be accepted, therefore, simply as approximations in the absence of definite returns. They can be defended, however, not only as being the closest approximations to the population of that period which it is possible to secure after a careful consideration of many authorities, but also on the ground that they are probably more accurate than earlier estimates. Study by many distinguished students of history and statistics has resulted in much discussion; many old records have been examined, and comparisons have been made between the population estimates of early writers and those of modern experts, so that extreme or unreasonable estimates, which in some cases stood for many years, have been eliminated. In consequence, the estimates of early population presented in the following tables may be accepted as expressing the best judgment of students of history and statistics at the present period.

[1] The free population of 1790 was 3,250,000. In 1688 the whole population is estimated by Mr. Bancroft to have been 200,000. If we take the free population of that day at 185,000 and add thereto one-third for each decennial period, we shall obtain the amount given by the census in 1790, as follows:

YEAR.	Population.	YEAR.	Population.
1690	185,000	1750	1,035,000
1700	246,000	1760	1,380,000
1710	328,000	1770	1,840,000
1720	437,000	1780	2,453,000
1730	582,000	1790	3,270,000
1740	776,000		

—H. C. Carey, Principles of Political Economy (1840), Part III, pages 25 and 26.

[2] See tables 76 to 103, pages 149 to 185.

TABLE 1.—ESTIMATED POPULATION DURING COLONIAL AND CONTINENTAL PERIODS: 1610 TO 1790.

STATE.	1610	1620	1630	1640	1650	1660	1670	1680	1690
Total	210	2,499	5,700	27,947	51,700	84,800	114,500	155,600	213,500
Maine				400	700	1,000	[1]	[1]	[1]
New Hampshire				500	800	1,400	[1] 2,300	[1] 3,000	[1] 4,000	[1] 5,000
Vermont									
Massachusetts		99	1,300	14,000	18,000	[1] 25,000	[1] 30,000	[1] 40,000	[1] 54,000
Rhode Island					300	800	1,500	2,500	4,000	5,000
Connecticut					2,000	6,000	8,000	10,000	13,000	18,000
New York				500	1,000	3,000	6,000	9,000	14,000	20,000
New Jersey								2,500	6,000	9,000
Pennsylvania										[2] 12,000
Delaware									500	[2]
Maryland				1,500	4,500	8,000	15,000	20,000	25,000
Virginia	210	2,400	3,000	7,647	17,000	33,000	40,000	49,000	58,000
North Carolina						1,000	2,500	4,000	3,000
South Carolina								1,100	4,500
Georgia									
Kentucky									
Tennessee									

STATE.	1700	1710	1720	1730	1740	1750	1760	1770	1780	1790
Total	275,000	357,500	474,388	654,950	889,000	1,207,000	1,610,000	2,205,000	2,781,000	3,929,625
Maine	[1]	[1]	[1]	[1]	[1]	[1]	[1]	34,000	55,500	96,643
New Hampshire	6,000	7,500	9,500	12,000	22,000	31,000	38,000	60,000	84,500	141,899
Vermont				[3]	[3]	[3]	[3]	25,000	40,000	85,341
Massachusetts	[1] 70,000	[1] 80,000	[1] 92,000	[1] 125,000	[1] 158,000	[1] 180,000	[1] 235,000	265,000	307,000	378,556
Rhode Island	6,000	8,000	11,000	16,950	24,000	35,000	44,000	55,000	52,000	69,112
Connecticut	24,000	31,000	40,000	55,000	70,000	100,000	142,000	175,000	203,000	237,655
New York	19,000	26,000	36,000	[3] 49,000	[3] 63,000	[3] 80,000	[3] 113,000	160,000	200,000	340,241
New Jersey	14,000	20,000	26,000	37,000	52,000	66,000	91,000	110,000	137,000	184,139
Pennsylvania	[2] 20,000	[2] 35,000	[2] 48,000	[2] 65,000	[2] 100,000	[2] 150,000	[2] 220,000	250,000	335,000	433,611
Delaware	[2]	[2]	[2]	[2]	[2]	[2]	[2]	25,000	37,000	59,096
Maryland	31,000	43,000	62,000	82,000	105,000	137,000	162,000	200,000	250,000	319,728
Virginia	72,000	87,000	116,000	153,000	200,000	275,000	346,000	[4] 450,000	520,000	747,610
North Carolina	5,000	7,000	13,060	30,000	50,000	80,000	115,000	230,000	300,000	395,005
South Carolina	8,000	13,000	20,828	30,000	45,000	68,000	95,000	140,000	160,000	249,073
Georgia						5,000	9,000	26,000	55,000	82,548
Kentucky								[4]	45,000	73,677
Tennessee										35,691

[1] Maine included with Massachusetts.   [3] Vermont included with New York.
[2] Delaware included with Pennsylvania.   [4] Kentucky included with Virginia.

TABLE 2.—PER CENT OF INCREASE OF ESTIMATED POPULATION DURING COLONIAL AND CONTINENTAL PERIODS: 1610 TO 1790.

STATE.	1610 to 1620	1620 to 1630	1630 to 1640	1640 to 1650	1650 to 1660	1660 to 1670	1670 to 1680	1680 to 1690	1690 to 1700	1700 to 1710	1710 to 1720	1720 to 1730	1730 to 1740	1740 to 1750	1750 to 1760	1760 to 1770	1770 to 1780	1780 to 1790
Total	1,090.0	128.1	390.3	85.0	64.0	35.0	35.9	37.2	28.8	30.0	32.7	38.1	35.7	35.8	33.4	37.0	26.1	41.3
Maine			75.0	42.9													63.2	74.1
New Hampshire			60.0	75.0	64.3	30.4	33.3	25.0	20.0	25.0	26.7	26.3	83.3	40.9	22.6	57.9	40.8	67.9
Vermont																	60.0	113.4
Massachusetts		1,213.1	976.9	28.6	38.9	20.0	33.3	35.0	29.6	14.3	15.0	35.9	26.4	13.9	30.6	12.8	15.8	23.3
Rhode Island			166.7	87.5	66.7	60.0	25.0	20.0	20.0	33.3	37.5	54.1	41.6	45.8	25.7	25.0	[1]5.5	32.9
Connecticut				200.0	33.3	25.0	30.0	38.5	33.3	29.2	29.1	37.5	27.3	42.9	42.0	23.2	16.0	17.1
New York			100.0	200.0	100.0	50.0	55.6	42.9	[1]5.0	36.8	38.5	36.1	28.6	27.0	41.3	41.6	25.0	70.1
New Jersey							140.0	50.0	55.6	42.9	30.0	42.3	40.5	26.9	37.9	20.9	24.6	34.4
Pennsylvania									66.7	75.0	37.1	35.4	53.8	50.0	46.7	13.6	34.0	29.4
Delaware																	48.0	59.7
Maryland				200.0	77.8	87.5	33.3	25.0	24.0	38.7	44.2	32.3	28.0	30.5	18.2	23.5	25.0	27.9
Virginia	1,042.9	25.0	154.9	122.3	94.1			18.4	24.1	20.8	33.3	31.9	30.7	37.5	25.8	30.1	15.6	43.8
North Carolina						150.0	60.0	[1]25.0	66.7	40.0	86.6	129.7	66.7	60.0	43.8	100.0	30.4	31.7
South Carolina								309.1	77.8	62.5	60.2	44.0	50.0	51.1	39.7	47.4	14.3	55.7
Georgia															80.0	188.9	111.5	50.1
Kentucky																		63.7
Tennessee																		

[1] Decrease.

These tables comprehend approximately two-thirds of the period which has elapsed since the establishment of English settlements upon the North Atlantic coast of America. They begin with the population of Virginia in 1610—the first population in a decennial year forming part of a continuous series—consisting of 210 souls maintaining a precarious foothold upon an unexplored continent; and end, after the lapse of approximately two centuries, with an aggregate population of 3,929,625 inhabitants, possessing more than 800,000 square miles of territory, as shown by the Federal census of 1790.

While percentages of increase in population can be accepted only as suggestions of approximate growth, it will be observed that those which are shown in Table 2 tend to confirm the impression concerning the growth of population natural under the conditions which prevailed at this period.[1] For the first half century, or until the middle of the seventeenth century, percentages obviously have little significance as indicating normal growth, because they were violently affected by every shipload of colonists that arrived. From 1660 to the close of the century, as the population began to assume greater proportions and to extend over larger areas of territory, the percentages of increase, both in individual colonies and in the aggregate for all the colonies, tend to become more uniform, and thus to reflect the influence of natural increase as compared with artificial increase by additions from Europe.[2] In the eighteenth century there was a noteworthy uniformity of percentages of increase, with the exception of the reduced increase shown for the decade from 1770 to 1780, a variation which unquestionably reflects the period of warfare and privation through which the colonists were then passing.

Incidentally it should be stated that in the making of these tables the population assigned at each decade to each of the colonies has been computed without the least regard to the total population or the percentage of increase in total population which would be shown; the result for each colony has been prepared independently, from the historical sources previously mentioned, so as to reflect as closely as possible the population conditions actually prevailing at the dates specified. Hence the interesting uniformity of increase from decade to decade shown by the aggregate for all colonies tends to strengthen confidence in the accuracy of the estimates presented. Moreover, it will be noted that the similarity in percentages of increase remains practically the same from decade to decade during the first half century of actual enumeration (1790 to 1840), as during the latter half of the period covered by the above tables.

It is of additional interest to observe the geographic grouping of population during the early history of the colonies. The following table shows the number and the proportion of inhabitants in each of the three geographic groups of colonies at the beginning and the end of the pre-Constitutional period, and at half century intervals:

[1] "He who will construct retrospectively general tables (of Colonial population) from the rule of increase in America, since 1790, will err very little."—Bancroft: History of the United States, ed. 1852, Vol. IV, page 128, note.

[2] "In the Northern states of America, where the means of subsistence have been more ample, the manners of the people more pure, and the checks to early marriages fewer than in any of the modern states of Europe, the population has been found to double itself, for above a century and a half successively, in less than each period of twenty-five years.

"In the back settlements, where the sole employment is agriculture, and vicious customs and unwholesome occupations are little known, the population has been known to double itself in fifteen years. * * *

"It appears from some recent calculations and estimates that from the first settlement of America to the year 1800 the periods of doubling have been but very little above twenty years."—Malthus: Essay on the Principle of Population, vol. 1, pages 6 and 7: London, Edition 1806.

MAP
of
NEW YORK I.
with the adjacent Rocks
and other remarkable
Parts of
HELL-GATE.
By Thos. Kitchin Senr.
Hydrographer to his
Majesty.

b.b. Barracks built for American Winter
Quarters, and burnt when the King's
Troops landed at Frogs Point.

NEW JERSEY

NORTH or HUDSONS RIVER

Tide of Flood

WEST CHESTER COUNTY

Road to Albany
Kings Bridge
Road to East Chester
Road to West Chester & Frogs Pt.

Spiting Devil
Redoubt
Batt.
Dartmans

Ft. Washington
now Kniphausen
Redoubt
Jeffery's Hook
Ft. Lee
Battery
The Blue Bell
Morris
Batt.
Batterys
Rebel Entrenchm.
Batt.
Batt.

YORK ISLAND

Harlem Creek
Snake Hill
Harlem Ch.

Salt Meadows
Morrisena
Montresor I.
Two Brothers
Buhanna or Buchannans I.
House
Salt House

The Mill Rock

Part of the SOUND

McGowens Pass
Batt.
Batt.
Walderons Tavern
Horns Hook
Waltons Batt.

Hell Gate
Rock
Hogs Back
Flying Pan
The Ships Course
The Pott
Pinfolds
Huliths I.
Flushing Bay

Blomingdale
Turtle Creek
Kings Br.
Hancock Rock
Hallets Cove
Mills
Otters Point
Mill

NEW YORK

Scott
Clark
Morians
Inclenburg
Road
Beekman
Blackwell
Kings B.
Watts
Kettelas
Stuyvesant

EAST RIVER

Newtown
Newtown Creek

Hobocken
Hoboken Cr.
Ol. Delancy
Kennedy
Paulus Hook
Ol. Delancy
L. Warren
Mortier
L. Lispenard
Foundry
Bowry lane
Salt Meadows
Corlears Hook
Ship Yards

NEW YORK
Ferry
Fort
Ferry

Bushwick
Bushwick Cr.
Flushing

NASSAU or LONG IS:

Oyster Bank
a Bergen
Flood Ebb
Bucking I.
Governors I.
Still H.
Bedloes or Kennedys I.
Mill
Red Hook
Mill

Brookland
Mill
Walabout Bay
Houses
Pirington
Brookland
Bedford
to Jamaica
passroy road

British Statute Miles
¼ ½ ¾ 1   2   3

40 Deg. 40 Min Nth. Latitude

74° 6′ W. Long. fr. London

TABLE 3.—ESTIMATED POPULATION IN THE PRE-CONSTITUTIONAL PERIOD, OF THE AREA ENUMERATED IN 1790, BY GEOGRAPHIC GROUPS.

GEOGRAPHIC GROUP.	1610		1650		1700		1750		1790	
	Population.	Per cent.	Population.	Per cent.	Population.	Per cent.	Population.	Per cent.	Population.	Per cent.
Area enumerated in 1790	210	100.0	51,700	100.0	275,000	100.0	1,207,000	100.0	3,929,625	100.0
New England			27,200	52.6	106,000	38.5	346,000	28.7	1,009,206	25.7
Middle colonies			3,000	5.8	53,000	19.3	296,000	24.5	1,017,087	25.9
Southern colonies	210	100.0	21,500	41.6	116,000	42.2	565,000	46.8	1,903,332	48.4

In 1610 the total white population in the original area of the United States was located in the single colony of Virginia; but in 1650 more than half of all the colonists were located in New England, and most of the remainder in Virginia. From that date the proportion in the New England colonies steadily declined, and the proportion in the Southern colonies steadily increased. The remarkable increase in the proportion in the Middle colonies during the period from 1650 to 1700 was due to the settlement of Pennsylvania and extensive immigration into that colony.

POPULATION OF CITIES.

Three cities which have continued to the present time to be leaders in population were preeminent during the Colonial and Continental periods, not only in the number of their inhabitants, but also in prosperity and influence. These cities were New York, Philadelphia, and Boston. From its foundation, in 1630, until the middle of the eighteenth century, Boston was the most populous town in the American colonies. Philadelphia (including suburbs) then took the lead, which it retained until it in turn was passed by New York, in 1810. Hence, each of these three cities has been the leader in population at some period.

The two tables which follow present the population, from the earliest records up to 1790, of the 7 cities which had acquired a population of 8,000 inhabitants prior to the Federal census of 1790, or which reported a population of approximately that figure in that year. The first table gives the results of censuses, contemporary estimates, and modern estimates based on contemporary data—as poll lists or counts of dwellings. The second table gives, for each decennial year from 1710 to 1790, the population of all cities which had reached, or practically reached, the minimum of 8,000 inhabitants. Figures given in the second table, but not in the first, are estimates based on the most reliable sources of information.

The most significant facts reflected by the following tables are the continual uncertainty concerning increase or decrease of population during the whole of the eighteenth century and the insignificant increase recorded in each of the 7 cities during the entire period from 1710 to 1790. The variations in population which are shown during different periods for each of these cities are frequently violent.

Population of cities of the United States to and including 1790.

YEAR.	Philadelphia (including suburbs).	New York.	Boston.	Charleston.	Baltimore.	Salem.	Newport.
1656		1,000					
1680			4,500				
1683	[1] 500						
1690			7,000				
1698			4,937				
1700	[1] 4,400		6,700				
1703			4,436				
1708							2,203
1710			9,000				
1712		5,840					
1720			11,000				
1722			10,567				
1723		7,248					
1730			13,000				4,640
1731		8,622					
1737		10,664					
1740			17,000				
1742			16,382				
1746		11,717					
1748							6,508
1749	[1] 13,000	13,294					
1750			15,731				
1752					200		
1753	14,563						
1755							6,753
1756		13,040					
1760	18,756		15,631				
1765			15,520			4,427	
1769	28,042						
1770		21,863	15,520	10,863			
1771							
1773				12,000			
1774							9,209
1775					5,934		
1776	[1] 34,400					5,337	5,299
1777	[2] 25,600						
1780			10,000				
1782							5,530
1783	[1] 37,800						
1786		23,614					
1787					15,000		
1790	42,444	33,131	18,038	16,359	13,503	7,921	6,716

[1] Estimated on the assumption that the number of persons to each dwelling, as shown on page 13, was 6.3.
[2] Estimated from Lord Howe's census.

Population of cities having at least 8,000 inhabitants, for each decennial year from 1710 to 1790.

YEAR.	Philadelphia (including suburbs).	New York.	Boston.	Charleston.	Baltimore.	Salem.	Newport.
1710			9,000				
1720			11,000				
1730	8,500	8,500	13,000				
1740	10,500	11,000	17,000				
1750	13,400	13,300	15,731				
1760	18,756	14,000	15,631	8,000			
1770	28,000	21,000	15,520	10,863			9,000
1780	30,000	18,000	10,000	10,000	8,000		
1790	42,444	33,131	18,038	16,359	13,503	7,921	

Changes, whether of increase or decrease, were generally due to local conditions, explained by the historians of the time. The lack of sanitary appliances and of skillful physicians exposed the American cities, especially in the eighteenth century, to attacks of contagious maladies, which in several instances greatly reduced the population, either by death or by enforced removal of citizens. Such fluctuations of population must be regarded as incidents inseparably connected with the early life of urban communities in which the inhabitants are engaged in a hand-to-hand struggle for existence.

DIAGRAM 1.—POPULATION OF THE PRINCIPAL CITIES OF THE UNITED STATES BEFORE 1790.

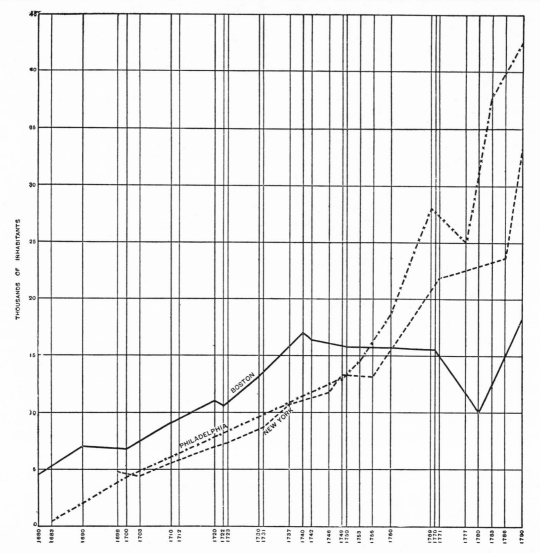

It will be observed that the maximum population of the city of Newport prior to 1790 was reached in 1774; and that the population of Salem even in 1790 had not attained the minimum city population of 8,000—falling short of that number by 79 souls. But as it has been the custom of previous Census authorities to include Salem in the list of cities having a distinctly urban population in 1790, it is here included in the list of those having a population of 8,000 inhabitants.

Four out of the 6 cities having a population of 8,000 or more in 1790 were located in the Northern states; Baltimore was upon the edge of the Northern states; and only one city—Charleston—was situated in the distinctly Southern states. In Virginia, the oldest of the colonies, no city possessed in 1790 a population greater than 4,000. Indeed, with the exception of the city of Charleston, above noted, all of the great area lying south of the Potomac must be regarded as distinctly rural at that period. The marshal who supervised in 1790 the taking of the Federal census for North Carolina, in making his returns, accompanied them with the observation that in that large commonwealth there was no community the population of which exceeded 2,000 inhabitants.

In 1700 the aggregate population of the 3 leading cities—Boston, New York, and Philadelphia—was approximately 15,500. Ninety years later the aggregate population of these 3 cities was 95,000, having increased sixfold. The striking change which has taken place since 1790 in all the conditions which tend to increase urban population is illustrated by the fact that in 1900, or at the close of the succeeding century, the population of these 3 cities was 5,291,791, having increased more than fiftyfold in the second period of one hundred and ten years. The rates of increase

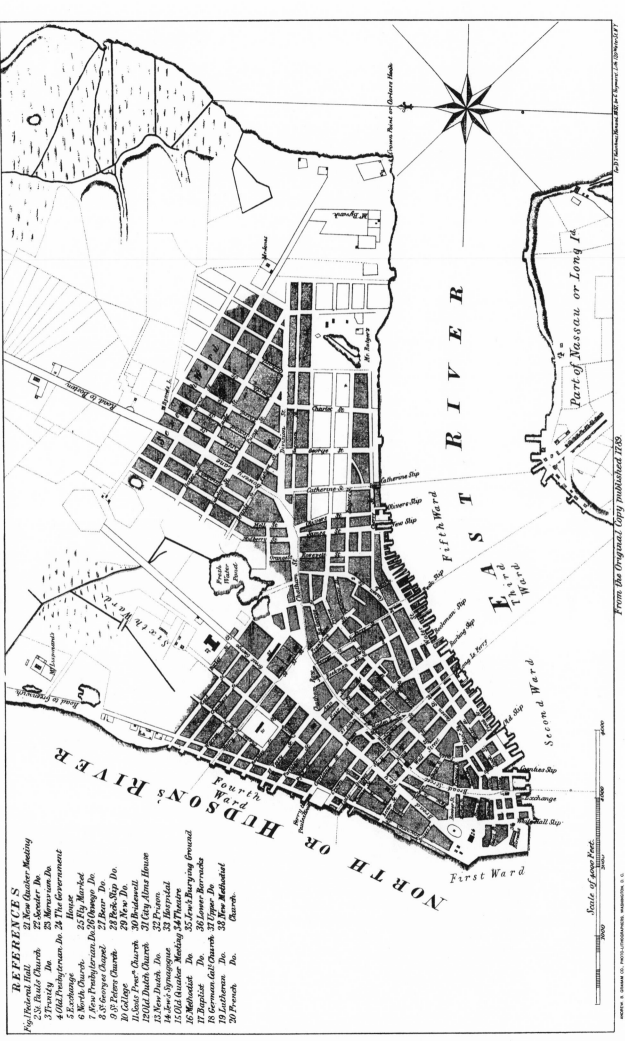

PLAN OF THE CITY OF NEW YORK

REFERENCES

Fig.1 Federal Hall	21 New Quaker Meeting
2 S.t Pauls Church	22 Seeder Do.
3 Trinity Do.	23 Moravian Do.
4 Old Presbyterian Do.	24 The Government
5 Exchange	House
6 North Church	25 Fly Market
7 New Presbyterian Do.	26 Oswego Do.
8 S.t Georges Chapel	27 Bear Do.
9 S.t Peters Church	28 Peck-Slip Do.
10 College	29 New Do.
11 Scots Pres.n Church	30 Bridewell.
12 Old Dutch Church	31 City Alms House
13 New Dutch. Do.	32 Prison.
14 Jew's Synagogue	33 Hospital
15 Old Quaker Meeting	34 Theatre
16 Methodist Do.	35 Jews Burying Ground
17 Baptist Do.	36 Lower Barracks
18 German Cal.t Church	37 Upper Do
19 Lutheran Do.	38 New Methodist
20 French Do.	Church.

From the Original Copy published 1789.

Scale of 4000 Feet.

here noted reflect the differing tendencies of the two centuries under consideration. Rapid increase in urban population is generally regarded as one of the results of the unprecedented growth in commercial and industrial activity, characteristic of the nineteenth century.

The proportion of the population living in cities showed a significant uniformity from the beginning of the eighteenth century to 1820. Indeed, the proportion in 1730 was almost precisely the same as that shown for 1820—nearly a century later. The low proportion shown for 1780 was obviously the result of the Revolutionary War, in which practically all the principal cities suffered from the ravages of war or pestilence, or both. The movement of population toward the cities, a movement which gathered momentum after 1830, may be regarded primarily as the result of industrial expansion. From that date the growth of population in manufacturing centers uninterruptedly kept pace with the growth in number of industries and in value of products.

The principal facts regarding the early population of the cities shown in the tables on page 11, including reference to some of the causes which led to violent increase or decrease, will be found in the following summaries.

Philadelphia.—The colonial population of Philadelphia can not be stated with precision. Dr. James Mease, in his "Picture of Philadelphia," gives the following table:

YEAR.	Dwelling houses.	Population.
1683	80	
1700	700	
1749[1]	2,076	
1753	2,300	14,563
1760	2,960	18,756
1769	4,474	28,042
1776	5,460	
1783	6,000	
1790	6,651	

[1] "The enumeration of 1749 was made by citizens of the first respectability. Mulberry ward, by Doctor Franklin; Dock ward, Joseph Shippen; Lower Delaware, William Allen (Chief Justice); Upper Delaware, Thomas Hopkinson; South ward and Southern suburbs, Edward Shippen; High street, Thomas Lawrence, jr.; Walnut, William Humphreys; Chestnut, Joseph Turner; North ward and Northern suburbs, Dr. William Shippen; Middle ward, William Coleman. The alteration of the division of the wards in 1800 renders it impossible to judge of the comparative increase of population in the several quarters of the city."—*James Mease, M. D.: The Picture of Philadelphia (1811), pages 31 and 32.*

The data given for 1760 are confirmed by a passage from "Burnaby's Travels," written in 1759. Mr. Burnaby visited Philadelphia in that year, and reported that it contained about 3,000 houses and from 18,000 to 20,000 inhabitants.

The only census before 1790 was taken about October, 1777, for Lord Howe, when he held possession of the city; it yielded 5,470 dwellings (587 of which were empty) and 21,767 inhabitants, exclusive of the army and strangers. At all times when both the number of houses and inhabitants were given, except during the Revolution, the number of inhabitants bore to the number of houses a ratio of from 6.2 to 6.4. The population figures omitted from Mease's table have been computed for the tables of pre-Constitutional population of cities, on page 11, by applying to Doctor Mease's data as to number of dwellings a ratio of 6.3.

New York.—Twelve censuses of the city of New York were taken prior to 1790, the first being taken in 1656. Hence, the population figures for New York as shown on page 11 may all be accepted as accurate.

Boston.—From the time of its founding until about 1755, Boston was the most populous town in the American colonies. The first recorded enumeration of the inhabitants of Boston was made in 1722, during a pestilence of smallpox; the population was found to be 10,567. A second census was taken in 1742 and a third in 1765. In connection with a report on a census of Boston taken in 1845, Mr. Lemuel Shattuck made a very thorough study of the early population of that city,[1] from which he deduced the figures given for decennial years in the table on page 11.

The decrease in the population from 1740 to 1750 was due to depopulation by smallpox and war. The decrease from 1770 to 1780 was due to the occupation of Boston by the British; according to Mr. Shattuck, in 1776 Boston contained only 2,719 white inhabitants, many of the former inhabitants having been dispersed in the country. In 1777 there were 2,863 males 16 years of age and over—"of whom," says the record, "11 were Quakers, 7 belonged to the castle, 188 were colored, 36 in Charlestown, Falmouth, and Newport, 200 at sea, and 543 in the army." The number of males 16 years of age and over actually living in Boston was therefore only 1,878; and of these, many were said to be old, infirm, and decrepit.

Charleston.—The fourth city in size in 1790 was Charleston, S. C. Before the Revolution this was an important commercial center. Lieutenant-Governor Bull reported that on November 30, 1770, the number of houses in Charleston was 1,292, and its population was 10,863—5,030 whites and 5,833 blacks (domestic servants and mechanics). De Brahm, three years later, reported that the city contained about 1,500 houses and more than 12,000 souls, more than half of whom were negroes and mulattoes. The Revolution seriously affected the prosperity and the population of the city. Morse's Gazetteer, published in 1789, says that in 1787 the city contained 1,600 houses and a population of 15,000—9,600 white inhabitants and 5,400 negroes.

Baltimore.—An inventory of this town in 1752 indicated 25 houses and 200 inhabitants. In 1775 a census showed 564 houses and 5,934 inhabitants. Brissot de Warville, who passed through the city in 1788, states that it "was but a village before the war; but during that period a considerable portion of the commerce of Philadelphia was removed to this place."

Salem.—Founded in 1628, Salem had a slow growth during the first century of its existence. There were

[1] "Report by the committee of the city council," appointed to obtain the census of Boston for the year 1845, page 5.

two censuses before 1790; the population in 1765 was 4,427, and in 1776 it was 5,337. A somewhat accelerated growth after the war, due to the importance of Salem's foreign commerce, brought the population in 1790 up to 7,921.

Newport and Providence.—It is easy to trace the population of the city of Newport and of the town of Providence from the summaries of the censuses given for Rhode Island in Table 85. The population of Newport in 1774 was 9,209—a figure which it did not attain again until the census of 1850. The city never recovered its commercial prosperity lost at the time of the Revolution.

New Haven, New London, and Norwich.—These Connecticut towns were populous and prosperous during the latter half of the eighteenth century, and carried on an important coastwise and West Indian commerce. The commerce of all three, however, was greatly injured during the Revolutionary War, and New Haven, at least, never fully regained her former rank as a shipping center.

YEAR.	New Haven.	New London.	Norwich.
1756	5,085	3,171	5,540
1774	8,295	5,888	7,327
1782		5,688	7,325

The city of New Haven was incorporated on January 8, 1783; in 1787 its population was 3,364.[1] Scott's United States Gazetteer, published in 1795, states that the city of New London contained 340 dwellings and the city of Norwich 450 dwellings; this would indicate a population of about 2,000 for New London and about 3,000 for Norwich.

COMPARISON OF URBAN AND RURAL POPULATION.

While the population figures shown in Table 1 are to some extent based upon estimates, they may be accepted as reasonably accurate for the purpose of making a general separation of the inhabitants of the colonies in early years into the two main classes of urban and rural. Even at the close of the eighteenth century the urban communities were merely country towns as compared with the urban communities of the present time. Nevertheless, it is not to be doubted that the distinction between the dwellers in the cities, small as they were, and the dwellers in the strictly rural districts, was clearly marked. By adopting the community of 8,000 as a minimum, the following table has been constructed for a period covering two

[1] "There are between 300 and 400 neat dwelling houses in the city, principally of wood. The streets are sandy but clean. Within the limits of the city are 4,000 souls."—*Morse: Gazetteer of the United States, 1797.*

DIAGRAM 2.—PER CENT OF TOTAL POPULATION OF UNITED STATES IN CITIES OF 8,000 POPULATION AND OVER.

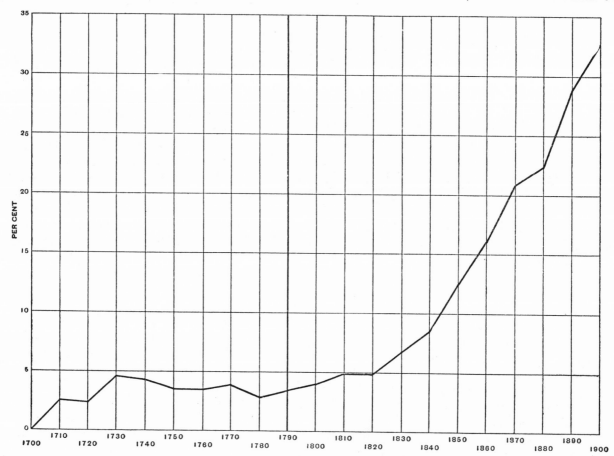

the Constitution. Precedent was being made at every step. No office of the Government, not even the Presidency, had been in existence long enough to command any respect, except such as was imparted by the personality of the official himself. Political party lines, which became clearly defined by 1792, had not yet appeared. Many divisions of sentiment, however, had already developed, especially in connection with the interpretation of the Constitution. Every freeholder was deeply interested in such questions as slavery, Federal assumption of state debts, and the taxation necessary for raising the revenues required to conduct the National Government.

No service performed by General Washington in the successful prosecution of the Revolutionary War compared with that which he rendered in saving the Republic from itself during the early days of his administration.[1] The operation of the Government under the new Constitution had thus far proceeded without serious friction, but with considerable criticism and unrest. Popular confidence in and respect for President Washington, the hero of the Revolution, was probably the principal factor which prevented the early occurrence of serious disagreements. While the success of the struggle for liberty in America had profoundly impressed the nations of Europe, on the other hand the theories proclaimed by the radicals in France had already attracted attention in the United States and seriously affected a large element of the population. Indeed, French revolutionary ideas were destined to become of some political importance during the administration of President Washington, a consideration which doubtless caused the patient and sagacious President periods of grave anxiety. In fact, in 1790 problems arose on all sides. It appears to have been an open question, at times, whether a dozen self-willed commonwealths, having different views upon many questions of public policy, and great independence of thought and action, ever could be brought to bend submissively to the control of a constitution created for the good of all, but requiring of necessity many mutual concessions and considerable breadth of view.

BOUNDARIES AND AREA.

In 1790 the Union consisted of 13 states—Rhode Island, the last of the original 13 to enter the Union, being admitted on May 29. Vermont, the first addi-

tion, was admitted in 1791, before the census had been completed. Massachusetts included Maine, Virginia included West Virginia and nominally included Kentucky. Georgia included parts of Alabama and Mississippi. The present state of Tennessee, formed out of territory ceded to the Union by North Carolina, was known as the Territory South of the Ohio River, or Southwest Territory. The vast area between the Ohio and Mississippi rivers and the Great Lakes—comprising the present states of Ohio, Indiana, Illinois, Michigan, and Wisconsin, with part of Minnesota—was called the Territory Northwest of the Ohio River, or Northwest Territory.

The United States in 1790 was bounded on the west by the Mississippi river, beyond which stretched a vast unexplored territory claimed by the Spanish king. On the south was the Spanish colony of Florida, of which the northern boundary was in dispute, but between which and the settlements in Georgia stretched an uninhabited region containing vast swamps. The northern boundary also was in dispute for long distances; the boundary between Maine and the Dominion of Canada was a fertile source of contention; as a result of the fact that the water line through the St. Lawrence river and the Great Lakes was undefined, some of the islands in those waters were claimed by both the United States and Great Britain; and the discovery that the Mississippi river did not extend as far north as the Lake of the Woods revealed a gap in the boundary line of the Northwest. It was not until more than fifty years later, by the Ashburton treaty, that the boundary of Maine was fully determined and the boundary through Lake Superior and thence to the Lake of the Woods agreed upon.

The gross area of the United States in 1790 was 820,377 square miles, but the settled area was only 239,935 square miles, or about 29 per cent of the total. The thickly populated areas were along the seaboard and in the valleys of the larger rivers. Western New York was a wilderness; rude frontier forts occupied the present sites of Oswego and Utica; and Binghamton and Elmira were outposts of civilization, the former having been settled in 1787 and the latter in 1788. Much of western Pennsylvania, also, was a wilderness.

At the time of the Declaration of Independence only 6 of the 13 American states—New Hampshire, Rhode Island, New Jersey, Pennsylvania, Delaware, and Maryland—had definite boundaries. Each of the others laid claim, on the strength of early and often very conflicting grants of territory, to large and ill-defined areas in the vast unexplored region west of the Appalachian mountains.

The ownership of these western lands by individual states was opposed by those states which did not share in their possession, mainly on the ground that the resources of the General Government, to which all contributed, should not be taxed for the protection and development of this region, while its advantages would inure

---

[1] "While the American Union was forming itself, some of the worst symptoms of social and political dissolution were manifesting themselves * * *. The greatest revelation rendered to all subsequent generations by these opening years of the American Republic is in the constant proof they exhibit of the prevailing power of the people for self-government * * *. It was reserved for the sagacity of Hamilton—an alien genius, a rare creation independent of race or time—to see through to the end, to uphold the possibilities of an empire. But the man of the time, the concrete actual personification of these godlike faculties, inchoate and dimly perceived in common men, was George Washington."—*Weeden: Economic and Social History of New England, Vol. II, pages 864 to 967.*

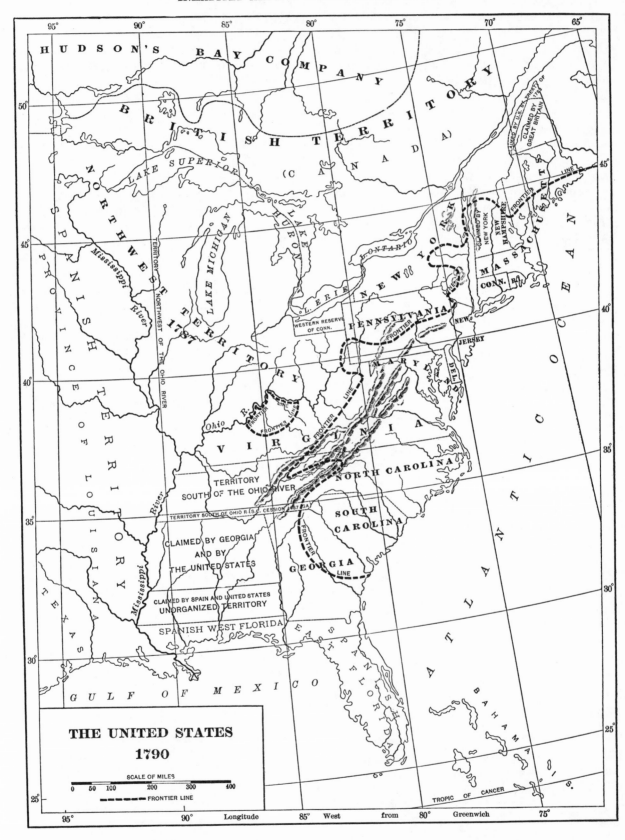

THE UNITED STATES
1790

SCALE OF MILES

0   50   100   200   300   400

- - - - - - - FRONTIER LINE

to the benefit of but a favored few. On this ground several of the states refused to ratify the Constitution until this matter had been settled by the cession of these tracts to the General Government.

Moved by these arguments, as well as by the consideration of the conflicting character of the claims, which must inevitably lead to trouble among the states, Congress passed, on October 30, 1779, the following act:

Whereas the appropriation of the vacant lands by the several states during the present war will, in the opinion of Congress, be attended with great mischiefs. Therefore,

Resolved, That it be earnestly recommended to the state of Virginia to reconsider their late act of assembly for opening their land office; and it be recommended to the said state, and all other states similarly circumstanced, to forbear settling or issuing warrants for unappropriated lands, or granting the same during the continuance of the present war.[1]

By 1790 Massachusetts, Connecticut, New York, and Virginia had ceded to the Federal Government all right and title to lands claimed by them in the Northwest Territory, with the exception of what was known as the "Connecticut Reserve;" North Carolina and South Carolina had yielded up their claims to territory extending to the Mississippi; and Maine, Vermont, and Kentucky were sufficiently distinct to be reported separately at the First Census. Georgia still held out, but Georgia's western territory was practically a wilderness, the enumerated area being merely that part of the present state which lies along the seacoast.

In 1790 the claim of the Federal Government to ownership of the vast areas between the Appalachian mountains and the Mississippi river was still subject, to some extent, to the rights of the Indians; but such rights had never been seriously regarded in the past, and in fact subsequently proved of little consequence in the settlement of the territory.

The greatest length of the Northwest Territory was about 900 miles, and its greatest breadth, approximately 700. It was bounded on the east by Pennsylvania, on the southeast by the Ohio river, and on the north and west by the international boundary. By contemporary writers it was estimated to contain 220,000,000 acres of land surface. This land, with the exception of a few tracts, was held by the Federal Government, to be sold for the discharge of the national debt. One exception was the narrow strip known as the "Connecticut Reserve," bordering on Lake Erie and stretching 120 miles west of the western boundary of Pennsylvania. This tract belonged to the state of Connecticut. Title to about one-sixth of it was given to citizens of Connecticut who had lost property in the Revolution, and the remainder was sold by the state, in 1795-96, to the Connecticut Land Company, for $1,200,000, the proceeds being used for the support of schools and colleges in that state. It was not until the year 1800 that Connecticut relinquished jurisdiction over this region in favor of the Federal Government.

By an act of Congress passed on the 13th of July, 1787, the Northwest Territory was erected, for the pur-

poses of temporary government, into one district— subject, however, to a division when circumstances should make it expedient. The fifth article of this act provided that there should be formed in the territory not less than 3 nor more than 5 states. Under its terms tentative state boundaries appear to have been constructed for the maximum number, which are shown upon contemporary maps as First State, Second State, etc. The First State roughly coincided with the present state of Ohio, the Second with a part of the present state of Indiana, the Third with a part of Illinois, the Fourth with a part of Michigan, and the Fifth with more than the present state of Wisconsin. In 1790, therefore, the foundations of 5 great states may be said to have been laid.

Beginning on the meridian line which forms the western boundary of Pennsylvania, seven ranges of townships had been surveyed and laid off by order of Congress. In a portion of the territory the Indian title had been extinguished and 4 counties had been laid off by June, 1790—Washington, erected on July 26, 1788; Hamilton, January 2, 1790; St. Clair, April 27, 1790; and Knox, June 20, 1790. Of these, Washington and Hamilton counties were located in the present state of Ohio, Knox county in Indiana (north of Vincennes), and St. Clair county in Illinois.

The Northwest Territory contained but a few thousand inhabitants, nearly all of whom were in the fertile valley of the Ohio. Bands of marauding savages contested the advance of settlers and made the life of the pioneers hazardous and often tragic. Cincinnati was settled in 1780 and Marietta in 1788; but for years Cincinnati was only a garrison, and the first white child was not born there until 1790. The westernmost settlement on the Ohio was at Louisville. All of the Great Lake ports were in the hands of the British. Across the mountains, south of the Ohio, the only considerable settlements were in Kentucky and western Tennessee, whither settlers had been led by Daniel Boone and other hardy hunters, to make homes for themselves in the fertile blue grass regions. Only about one-twentieth of the people of the country lived west of the crest of the Appalachian mountains. The western country was so vast, and the facilities for transportation and communication so meager, that Jefferson predicted it would be a thousand years before the country as far west as the Mississippi would be thickly settled.

Local organization.—The states differed widely in local government, and hence in the geographic subdivision of their counties. In New England the county was a corporation which existed for judicial rather than for political purposes. The political unit was the town, which received its charter from the state legislature, elected its own officers, and managed its local affairs in its own way.

In the Middle states—New York, New Jersey, Pennsylvania, and Delaware—the county was of much

---

[1] Henry Gannett, United States Geological Survey, "Boundaries of the United States," third edition, page 30.

greater importance than in New England; on the other hand, the subdivision of the county called the township (except in Delaware, where it is called the hundred), was of less importance than the New England town. In New York the township was created by the county board; in New Jersey, by the state legislature; in Pennsylvania, by the county court of quarter sessions; in Delaware there appears not to have been any definite and systematic subdivision of the counties. New York adjoined New England, and a large part of the population of the state were persons who had migrated from that section, and naturally had carried with them the idea of the town system of local government; consequently, in 1790, the township limits in New York were better defined than those in any other state outside of New England, with the possible exception of New Jersey, the only Middle state in which the township was created by the state. In Pennsylvania the township, as a geographic area, was less important than in New York. The principal maps of Pennsylvania at the period under consideration show the location of mountains and rivers in detail, the names of counties, and the names of the more prominent towns and cities, but do not define the township boundaries. Population was increasing and extending with great rapidity, existing townships were being subdivided, and new ones were being created. Under these conditions the boundaries of the townships in the more thinly settled portions were very unstable.

In the Southern states the county was the political unit, fulfilling all the functions of both the county and town in New England. Subdivision into townships was made for administrative purposes only;[1] in some instances these subdivisions corresponded to the election precincts of the present day.

CURRENCY.

The close of the War of the Revolution found the finances of the country in almost hopeless confusion, and affairs had improved but little by 1790. There was no mint, and but little specie, and much of the trade, especially in the interior, was carried on by barter. All the coins in circulation were foreign, and many were badly worn and mutilated.

The commonest coin was the Spanish "milled dollar," or "piece of eight," which was obtained in trade from the West Indies; after the Revolution this coin, with its subdivisions, was the recognized unit of account. The coins of Great Britain were in limited circulation in all the states, and reckoning was often in pounds, shillings, and pence; but because of the

[1] In most of the county-system states the local subdivisions, by whatever name known, are created by the county authorities. They are but skeletons and exist only for convenience as districts for holding elections, for fixing the jurisdiction of the justice of the peace, or for determining the militia-company organization. Justices of the peace and constables are found in these districts, but the districts are in no sense political organs. (Hinsdale: The American Government, page 404.)

limited supply of English coins, and from other causes, the value of the pound and shilling differed materially in the different states. Hence it was often necessary, in business transactions, to name the state of exchange. The principal gold coins in use, other than the British pieces, were the French guinea and pistole, the Portuguese moidores and johannes, or "joe," and the Spanish doubloon and pistole; but the number of these was small. The silver coins in circulation, besides British pieces and the Spanish dollar, were chiefly the crown and livre of France. The copper coins were principally those of Great Britain. The supply of fractional currency was inadequate to the demand, and silver pieces were often cut into halves and quarters in order to make change.

In 1785 Congress adopted as the currency basis the silver dollar, on a decimal system, as exemplified in the Spanish dollar; and by 1790, in making exchanges, the value of all coins was quite generally referred to this standard. The system of reckoning in shillings and pence, however, persisted in some places and with some people. The equivalent of the dollar in New England and Virginia was 6 shillings; in New York and North Carolina, 8 shillings; in South Carolina, 32½ shillings; in Georgia, 5 shillings; and in the four other colonies, 7½ shillings.

In addition to specie, there was a large amount of paper money in circulation. During the Revolution, and in the succeeding years of the Continental period, both the Confederation and the individual states had made large issues of paper money, and, being unable to redeem it, had refunded now and then by new issues. This was never worth its face value, and steadily depreciated from the date of issue. In March, 1780, the Continental currency had fallen to such a point that one dollar in silver was worth 65 dollars in paper. "Not worth a continental" came to be the phrase used for anything practically worthless. There can be no doubt that this paper money had much to do with the demoralization of industry during the Continental period. A contemporary writer and close observer of the times—Peletiah Webster, of Philadelphia—says: "We have suffered more from this cause than from any other cause of calamity. It has killed more men, perverted and corrupted the choicest interests of our country more, and done more injustice, than even the arms and artifices of our enemies." And again he says: "If it saved the state, it has violated the equity of our laws, corrupted the justice of our public administration, enervated the trade, industry, and manufactures of our country, and gone far to destroy the morality of our people." M. de Warville, in his travels in America in 1788, inveighed against the paper money of Rhode Island and New Jersey in tones no less uncertain. As a climax to the whole, Congress even refused to accept its own paper money in payment of postage.

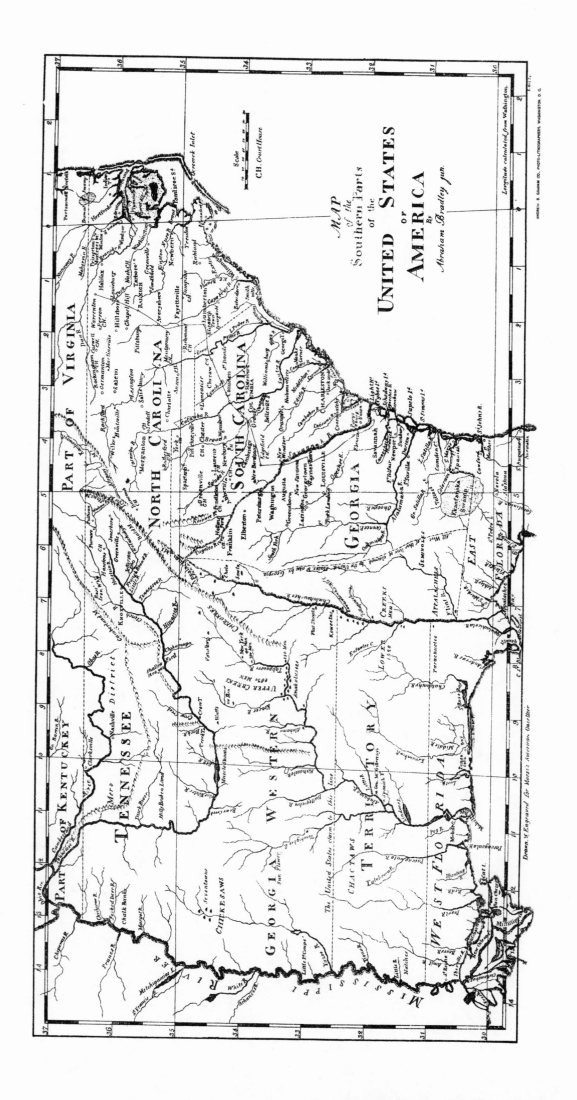

MAP
of the
Southern Parts
of the
UNITED STATES
or
AMERICA
By
Abraham Bradley jun.

Scale

CH. Court House

ANDREW B. GRAHAM CO. PHOTO-LITHOGRAPHERS, WASHINGTON, D. C.

Longitude calculated from Washington.

Drawn & Engraved for Morse's American Gazetteer.

PART OF VIRGINIA

NORTH CAROLINA

SOUTH CAROLINA

GEORGIA

EAST FLORIDA

PART OF KENTUCKY

TENNESSEE

WESTERN TERRITORY

GEORGIA WESTERN TERRITORY

WEST FLORIDA

CHEROKEES

UPPER CREAG MEN

CREEKS

CHACTAWS

CHICKESAWS

MISSISSIPPI RIVER

In Virginia the lack of specie was supplied largely by paper currency called "tobacco money." This was a genuine asset currency, the notes being simply the public warehouse receipts for the tobacco placed therein. They circulated freely in the state, according to the known value of the tobacco.

In 1790 there were but three banks in the United States: The Bank of North America, established in the city of Philadelphia; the Bank of New York; and the Bank of Massachusetts, in Boston. Of these three, the first-named is the only one which had at any time a direct relation with the Federal Government.

TRANSPORTATION.

The common mode of travel before the Revolution was by boat or horse. The river valleys are usually the portions of a country first settled, and in the newer portions of America travel was often by river routes. Many persons did not own carriages or wagons; in consequence, a considerable proportion of the population had no requirement for wagon roads. This was particularly the case in the South, where the plantations were situated along the banks of navigable streams and products were marketed by boat.

With the growth of the colonies, and an increasing requirement for intercommunication, the extension of stagecoach systems was very rapid, and became especially marked after the Revolution. As might be expected, such extension was coincident with the opening of many new roads and the improvement of existing highways. In 1790, however, there remained many sections of the country in which there were no roads. On the maps of the states published during the last decade of the eighteenth century, no highways are shown in the eastern part of Maine, and but few in northern New England, northern and western New York, northwestern Pennsylvania, and throughout the mountainous regions of the South. Many highways were such in name only—often little more than bridle paths or blazed trails running through otherwise unbroken wildernesses. Even the more pretentious roads were poor, and often impassable. Bridges were all but unknown in the thinly settled portions; and in the fall and spring, when the rivers were covered with unsafe ice or were full of floating ice, travel was extremely dangerous.

Between important towns, especially in New England, better conditions prevailed. From Boston, roads branched off in many directions. A broad highway extended westward through Marlboro, Worcester, Spencer, and Springfield; another passed through Lynn, Salem, Portsmouth, and Portland, to the headwaters of the Kennebec; other roads led to Providence, Lowell, and Concord. Roads followed both banks of the Merrimac and Connecticut rivers; and an important road ran from Concord and Ashburnham, Mass., through Rutland, Vt., and along the

eastern shore of Lake Champlain. Over these highways the products of the surrounding country for long distances were brought to Boston for export.

The maps of Rhode Island and Connecticut at this period present a network of highways. From Providence a road skirted the western coast of Narragansett bay and followed the Sound to New York. In the Connecticut valley, also, there were many important roads.

In New York the Albany post road ran from New York city along the eastern bank of the Hudson river to Albany, and thence northward to Plattsburg and into Vermont. Through Albany passed the western highway from Massachusetts to the Mohawk valley, over which, in 1790, numbers of emigrants journeyed daily. In the wilds of western New York this road dwindled to a trail, and as such continued to Fort Niagara.

Across the state of New Jersey there were many roads, but the principal highway extended from New York through Newark, Elizabethtown, and Brunswick to Trenton. Another road skirted the eastern and southern shores of New Jersey. From Trenton a road passed through Burlington, Philadelphia, Chester, Wilmington, Elkton, Havre de Grace, Baltimore, Alexandria, and then southward.

Philadelphia was a common center of highways for a wide radius. This city was a great market for the sale of farm produce; in the autumn and winter the highways were filled with heavily loaded wagons from the surrounding farms, bound for Philadelphia. The main road from Philadelphia westward passed through Lancaster, Harrisburg, Carlisle, Shippensburg, Bedford, and Pittsburg. Several other roads crossed or nearly crossed the state, converging at the mountain passes and centering upon Pittsburg.

The maps of the Southern states show many roads, but the most important were along the seacoast. Leaving Alexandria, an important road ran through Fredericksburg and Jamestown, Va., Hertford, Newbern, and Wilmington, N. C., Charleston, S. C., and Savannah, Ga., thus completing a chain of highways from the Kennebec river to Georgia.

Several roads crossed the mountain barriers of Virginia and North Carolina to the West, those that were not lost on the banks of rivers being centered upon Lexington, Danville, Clarksville, Knoxville, and Nashville. One of the most famous of these was the "Wilderness road," which passed through the Cumberland Gap. It was the only direct overland route into Kentucky, and was marked out by Daniel Boone. Not until 1795 was this road widened into a wagon track.

Bridges over even the larger rivers were not common, and the smaller streams were usually forded; but by 1790 many bridges had been built near the large cities and on the principal roads. The greatest engineering feat in the Republic was the bridge over the Charles river, connecting Boston and Charlestown. This bridge was built in 1786, and was then the longest bridge in the world. The Charles river was about as wide at that point as the Thames river at the famous London bridge.

Stagecoaching days had not arrived at their zenith by 1790, but the stagecoach was fast coming to be the common mode of inland travel. The system was developed to the greatest extent in New England, where the population was comparatively dense. As early as 1765 there were two stage routes between Providence and Hartford. In 1769 a coach was announced between Hartford and Norwich, "a day's journey only," and two coaches a week between Providence and Boston, which journey also was accomplished in a day. In 1793 there were daily stages between Boston and Providence, the fare being but a dollar. In 1790 stages ran between Newburyport and Boston three times a week in summer and twice a week in winter; between Boston and New York, by the way of Worcester, Springfield, and Hartford, three times a week in summer and twice a week in winter; between New York and Philadelphia, five times a week; between Philadelphia and Baltimore, and between Baltimore and Alexandria, three times a week; and between many other cities at less frequent intervals.

Mr. Levi Pease started the first line of stages between Boston and New York shortly after the conclusion of peace in 1783.[1] He also obtained the first government contract within the United States for carrying the mails by stage, and the first mail in this new service passed through Worcester on January 17, 1786.[2]

The distance between Boston and New York was covered under ordinary conditions in four days, and the time of the "diligence" between New York and Philadelphia was two days. Intelligence of Washington's election to the Presidency of the United States, in New York, on April 7, 1789, was conveyed to him at Mt. Vernon by Charles Thomson, the clerk of Congress, on April 14. Washington died on December 14, 1799, and news of an event of such great interest was probably forwarded with all possible dispatch; yet this news did not reach Boston until December 24.

The most traveled road in the country was doubtless the highway across New Jersey connecting New York and Philadelphia. For most of the distance this road was kept in excellent repair. For part of the distance, from New York to Newark, it represented considerable engineering enterprise, being built wholly of wood in the midst of water and "on a soil that trembled when stepped upon." The stagecoach used was a kind of open wagon, hung with curtains of leather and woolen, which could be raised or lowered at pleasure. It had four benches and would seat twelve persons. Light baggage was put under the benches, and the trunks were attached behind.

The highway from Philadelphia to Baltimore was less traveled, and, because of the character of the soil, was often in an almost impassable condition.[3]

Samuel Breck, speaking of travel between New York and Boston in 1787, says:

In those days there were two ways of getting to Boston: One way by a clumsy stage that travels about 40 miles a day, with the same horses the whole day; so that rising at 3 or 4 o'clock and prolonging the day's ride into the night, one made out to reach Boston in six days; the other route was by packet-sloop up the Sound to Providence and thence by land to Boston. This was full of uncertainty, sometimes being traveled in three and sometimes in nine days. I myself have been that length of time (nine days) going from New York to Boston.

---

[1] Stages from Portsmouth in New Hampshire, to Savannah in Georgia:

There is now a line of stages established from New Hampshire to Georgia, which go and return regularly, and carry the several mails, by order and permission of Congress.

The stages from Boston to Hartford in Connecticut set out, during the winter season, from the house of Levi Pease, at the sign of the New York Stage, opposite the Mall, in Boston, every Monday and Thursday morning, precisely at 5 o'clock, go as far as Worcester on the evenings of those days, and on the days following proceed to Palmer, and on the third day reach Hartford; the first stage reaches the city of New York on Saturday evening following.

The stages from New York for Boston set out on the same days, and reach Hartford at the same time as the Boston stages.

The stages from Boston exchange passengers with the stages from Hartford at Spencer, and the Hartford stages exchange with those from New York at Hartford. Passengers are again exchanged at Stratford ferry, and not again until their arrival in New York.

By the present regulation of the stages it is certainly the most convenient and expeditious way of traveling that can possibly be had in America, and in order to make it the cheapest, the proprietors of the stages have lowered their prices from four pence to three pence a mile, with liberty to passengers to carry fourteen pounds baggage.

In the summer season the stages are to run with the mail three times in a week instead of twice, as in the winter, by which means those who take passage at Boston, in the stage which sets off on Monday morning, may arrive at New York on the Thursday evening following, and all the mails during that season are to be but four days going from Boston to New York, and so from New York to Boston.

Those who intend taking passage in the stages must leave their names and baggage the evening preceding the morning that the stage sets off, at the several places where the stages put up, and pay one-half of their passage to the place where the first exchange of passengers is made, if bound so far, and if not, one-half of their passage so far as they are bound.

N. B.—Way passengers will be accommodated when the stages are not full, at the same rate, viz, 3 pence only per mile.

Said Pease keeps good lodging, etc., for gentlemen travelers, and stabling for horses.

Boston, January 2, 1786.—*Massachusetts Spy, or the Worcester Gazette, January 5, 1786.*

[2] Alice Morse Earle: Stage Coach and Tavern Days, pages 295 to 297.

[3] A Frenchman who made a journey from Philadelphia to Baltimore in November, 1788, thus describes a portion of his trip: "From thence (Havre de Grace) to Baltimore are reckoned 60 miles. The road in general is frightful, it is over a clay soil, full of deep ruts, always in the midst of forests; frequently obstructed by trees overset by the wind, which obliged us to seek a new passage among the woods. I can not conceive why the stage does not often overset. Both the drivers and their horses discover great skill and dexterity, being accustomed to these roads."—*Brissot de Warville: Travels in the United States of America (1788).*

At that time there was scarcely a town along the coast of Rhode Island, Connecticut, and New Jersey that was not connected by sailing sloops with New York. The fare from Providence to New York by packet was $6. From ports in New England, sloops made frequent trips to Boston; and from the southern ports, to the nearest principal cities. All through the advertisements in the newspapers of that period were notices of the regular or occasional sailings of sloops to different seacoast towns. These sloops had accommodations for passengers, and were generally comfortable, but with head winds the time of arrival was very uncertain. Meals were charged for at high rates—sometimes in excess of the fare; and it was often claimed that the skipper delayed the voyage when there were many passengers, in order to profit at their expense.

THE POSTAL SERVICE.

The post office system established during the Continental period was continued when the Federal Government was established. This system was based upon an "Ordinance for Regulating the Post Office of the United States of America," passed by the Continental Congress, October 18, 1782. In 1790 there were 75 post offices and 1,875 miles of post roads; for the first quarter of that year the receipts were $37,935 and the expenditures $32,140, which left a surplus of $5,795.

The main post road ran from Wiscasset, Me., through Boston, Springfield, Hartford, New York, Philadelphia, Baltimore, Alexandria, Wilmington, and Charleston, to Savannah. With this as a main system, crossroads branched off, connecting the principal settlements; but a large number of important towns, and even entire states, had no communication by post. Many of the post roads were marked by milestones, set up when Franklin was Postmaster-General, to assist the postmasters in ascertaining the postage. Indeed, some of these milestones are still in existence.

Most of the mail was carried by stages, the Postmaster-General being instructed to favor stage lines in awarding contracts.[1] The only portions of the main system served by postriders were from Wiscasset, Me., to Newburyport, Mass., and from Georgetown, S. C., to Charleston, S. C. Postriders still rode, however. on several of the crossroads.

[1] "The mail is now carried in stagecoaches in which there are generally several passengers, sometimes as many as six, and it is supposed that many more letters go by the passengers than by the mail; it is to be supposed that most persons would wish to be excused from the trouble of carrying these letters, and if this section passes they will be furnished with an excuse for not taking them; and it appears very unreasonable and absurd that the public should pay the proprietors of the stages for transporting the mail, and in this way be defrauded out of that revenue which they are undoubtedly entitled to receive."—*Mr. Livermore, of House of Representatives, June, 1790.*

At this time there were about twenty different contracts for carrying the mail, and this had a tendency to confuse the system.[2] The Postmaster-General states, in a report submitted to Congress in 1790, that "every contractor consults his own interest as to the days and hours of arrival and departure of the mail, without having a due regard to the necessary connection of the post office. A regular system of days and hours of departure has never been established farther southward than Alexandria."

The revenue of the post office at this period arose "principally from letters passing from one seaport to another." The amount of postage depended upon the distance the letter was to be carried. The postage on letters was usually collected at the place of delivery, but the postmaster had authority to collect it at the place of posting if he desired to do so.

In 1787 the postage on letters established in the ordinance of 1782 was reduced 25 per cent, and the Postmaster-General was instructed to fix such rates for the carriage of large packages as he judged would be most likely to induce persons to patronize the post. These rates continued in force until 1792.

It has been asserted by many historians that newspapers were not sent by post at this period, but the ordinance quoted seems to make provision for them to be so sent. Moreover, the Postmaster-General states that "newspapers, which have hitherto passed free of postage, circulate extensively through the post offices; one or two cents upon each would probably amount to as much as the expense of transporting the mail."

By a law approved February 20, 1792, the following rates of postage went into effect: For the postage of every single letter—under 30 miles, 6 cents; 30 to 60 miles, 8 cents; 60 to 100 miles, 10 cents; 100 to 150 miles, 12½ cents; 150 to 200 miles, 15 cents; 200 to 250 miles, 17 cents; 250 to 350 miles, 20 cents; 350 to 450 miles, 22 cents; over 450 miles, 25 cents. "And every double letter shall pay double the said rates; every triple letter, triple; every packet weighing one ounce avoirdupois, to pay at the rate of four single letters for

[2] "No letters from the northward or eastward of this, bearing date between the 15th and 30th of May, have come to my hands; and having abundant evidence, before I reached Charleston, of the slow movement of the mail, through the three southernmost states, I did, before I left that place, on the 9th of that month, direct that all letters which might be for and following me, be returned to Fredericksburg, as the first place I should touch the post line upon my return. But, these directions not arriving in Richmond in time, as I conjecture, the letters of that interval agreeably to the superscriptions, which I am informed were on them, were forwarded from that place to Taylor's Ferry in expectation of meeting me there. But to this circumstance, which was unknown to me, and to finding from better information than I set out with, that it would be more convenient to cross James river higher up than at Taylor's, is to be ascribed my missing the communications, which were made between the 15th and 30th of May, as mentioned before. These dispatches I may be long without, and perhaps never get; for there are no cross posts in those parts, and the letters, which will have to pass through many hands, may find some who are not deficient in curiosity."—*The Writings of George Washington, Vol. XII, page 45.*

POST OFFICES IN THE UNITED STATES, 1790.

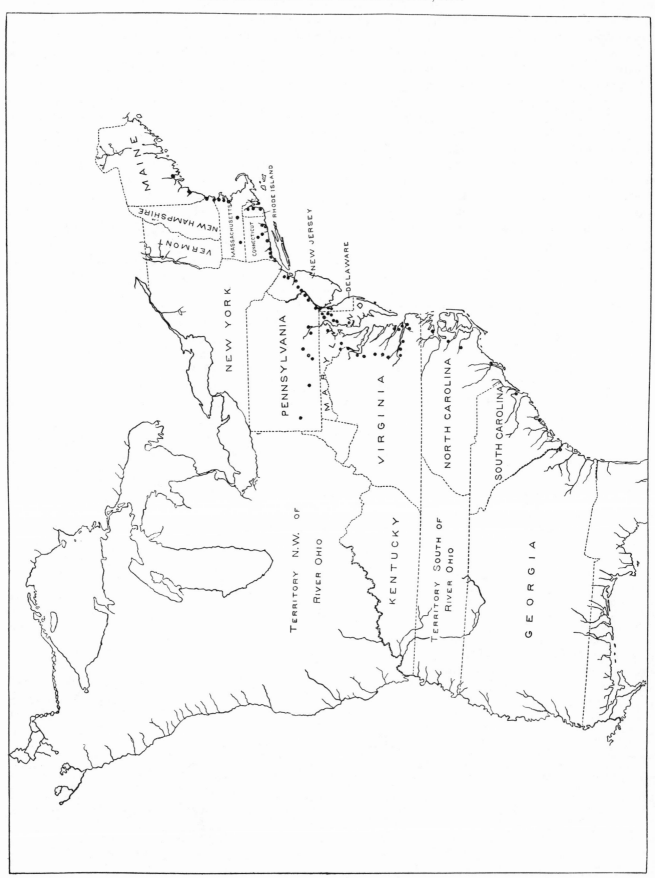

each ounce, and in that proportion for any greater weight."

The rate on newspapers was fixed at one cent for carriage under 100 miles, and one and one-half cents for a greater distance. But every printer of newspapers was allowed to send one paper free to each and every other printer of newspapers within the United States, subject to such regulations as the Postmaster-General should provide. These rates continued until 1816. The franking privilege at this time was quite extensive, and undoubtedly made serious inroads upon the revenue.

Postage could not be paid in paper currency; specie alone was receivable. As the coins in the different states varied, the payment was attended with some confusion. The Postmaster-General, in his report to Congress in 1790, states that "the postage on a single letter from New York to Philadelphia is one penny-weight eight grains, or sixpence two-thirds Pennsylvania currency. This can not be made out in any pieces of coin current in the United States. The letters are charged with seven pence, which is right; for if there must be a fraction, it ought always to be taken in favor of the post office." He further stated that the postage on letters probably averaged about fifteen cents.

The 75 post offices which had been established up to 1790 were distributed as follows:

Maine.—Wiscasset, Portland.
New Hampshire.—Portsmouth.
Massachusetts.—Newburyport, Ipswich, Salem, Boston, Worcester, Springfield.
Rhode Island.—Providence, Newport, East Greenwich, South Kingstown.
Connecticut.—Hartford, Middletown, New Haven, Stratford, Fairfield, Norwalk, Stamford, New London, Norwich.
New York.—New York.
New Jersey.—Newark, Elizabethtown, Brunswick, Princeton, Trenton.
Pennsylvania.—Bristol, Philadelphia, Chester, Lancaster, Yorktown, Carlisle, Shippensburg, Chambersburg, Bedford, Pittsburg.
Delaware.—Wilmington, Duck Creek, Dover.
Maryland.—Elkton, Charlestown, Havre de Grace, Harford, Baltimore, Bladensburg, Georgetown, Warwick, Georgetown Cross Roads, Chestertown, Chester Mills, Easton.
Virginia.—Alexandria, Colchester, Dumfries, Fredericksburg, Bowling Green, Hanover Court House, Richmond, Petersburg, Cabinpoint, Smithfield, Suffolk, Williamsburg, Yorktown, Hampton, Norfolk.
North Carolina.—Edenton, Washington, Newbern, Wilmington.
South Carolina.—Georgetown, Charleston.
Georgia.—Savannah.

It appears from this analysis that the state of Vermont, the district of Kentucky, and the Southwest Territory (Tennessee) possessed no postal facilities whatever; and that three states, including the prominent state of New York, had but one post office each. It is evident, however, that the postal conditions at the date of the First Census were generally regarded as inadequate and unsuited to the requirements of the country. The act of 1792, which was an attempt to

effect a material improvement in the postal conditions, resulted in the prompt increase in the number of post offices. The number reported by the Post Office Department in 1796 was 503.

Analysis of the geographic location of the post offices in existence in 1790.

United States	75
New England states	22
Maine	2
New Hampshire	1
Vermont	
Massachusetts	6
Rhode Island	4
Connecticut	9
Middle states	19
New York	1
New Jersey	5
Pennsylvania	10
Delaware	3
Southern states	34
Maryland	12
Virginia	} 15
West Virginia	
North Carolina	4
South Carolina	2
Georgia	1
Kentucky	
Southwest Territory	

It will be observed that in 1790 just about half of the post offices were situated in the Southern states. An analysis of the larger number reported in 1796 shows a similar proportion, suggesting an apparent desire on the part of the Federal Government to maintain equal postal facilities in the various sections of the Republic.

INDUSTRIES.

During the period of constitutional government in the United States the inhabitants of the Republic have derived their support, and individuals and communities have accumulated wealth, principally from three main classes of industries—agriculture, manufactures, and mining. To these should be added the fisheries, and also commerce—both interstate and foreign; the last-named class, however, depends largely upon the products of the other callings.

The conditions which prevailed in 1790 in connection with each of these great industries were the beginnings of the operations which, steadily increasing in magnitude during the nineteenth century, have attained proportions that have attracted the attention and admiration of other nations.

Problems which were confronted at that period in connection with marketing foodstuffs and merchandise were entirely different from those which prevailed after the lapse of a few decades. In the interior, laborious journeys by horse or in stage or wagon, along newly broken highways, formed the sole means of communication by land. Water transportation was afforded by sailing vessels making trips which were usually without schedule and almost always uncertain. Hence, each state depended principally upon its own products not only for food, but for most of the other requirements of its communities.

Merchandise and produce that could not stand a freight charge of $15 per ton could not be carried overland to a consumer 150 miles from the point of production; as roads were, a distance of 50 miles from market often made industrial independence expedient. Where the produce of the farms could not be sold, where wood and lumber were not marketable, the people had no resource but to raise their own wool and flax, and spin and weave and make their own clothing. Other crafts felt these influences, although the working of wood and metals and leather fell to skilled artisans in the villages rather than to the household. The local store had a small traffic in articles that could not be produced, and in luxuries. Salt fish was widely distributed; rum went everywhere; salt was a universal necessity; tools and utensils and furniture were imported; a few articles of dress carried the style of the city to the hamlet, so insignificant was the traffic uniting the country town to the great world.[1]

In all callings the changes which have been in progress from 1790 to 1900 have been in the direction of the utilization of the services of others and the employment of labor saving machinery to increase product and the profit of the employer. These changes have been particularly marked in connection with manufacturing and mining enterprises. In commerce—a calling in which the services of others were freely employed at the close of the eighteenth century—the change in this particular has been much less pronounced.

Although the commerce of the United States has assumed enormous proportions during the century or more which has elapsed since 1790, the greatest development of the nation has been in the three main classes of occupations—agriculture, manufactures, and mining. In fact, analysis of the population statistics of the United States in 1900 shows that of the 30,000,000 persons engaged in gainful occupations, approximately 20,100,000, or 67 per cent, claimed some connection with one of these three classes.

It is unfortunate that there are no industrial statistics for 1790. It is possible, however, to sketch with some degree of accuracy the relative importance to the community of each of the industries mentioned as a source of subsistence and wealth.

Agriculture.—The economic conditions which prevailed in 1790 present a marked contrast with those which have developed since and which prevailed universally in 1900. In 1900 the proportion of those engaged in agriculture was only about one-third of all persons gainfully employed. At the close of the eighteenth century the greater part of the inhabitants of the United States derived their support from this industry. It is probable that nine out of every ten breadwinners were engaged in some form of agriculture during the greater part of the year; indeed, in the Southern states the proportion was somewhat larger.

Horses, cattle, and swine, in numbers proportionate to the needs of the population, were raised in every

state. Sheep were raised principally in the New England and Middle states. The principal wheat producing state was Pennsylvania. The staple crop of Maryland, Virginia, and North Carolina was tobacco, and that of South Carolina was rice. Cotton was but little cultivated. Some hemp and flax were raised in the New England and Middle states.

The more thrifty and capable citizens engaged in agriculture in 1790 were doubtless obtaining a modest return, but it is unlikely that any large fortunes were being amassed from distinctly agricultural operations. In the South, it is true, some planters owned very large plantations and large numbers of slaves; but it is probable that few individuals had acquired great wealth. In the North slave labor was unprofitable for numerous reasons; thus it came about that in the Northern states nearly every farmer tilled his own land, and, not being able to secure labor when he wanted it, was unable to accumulate wealth by utilizing systematically the services of others.

Manufactures.—During the Colonial period the mother country had discouraged the ambitions of the colonists in the direction of manufactures. At that time Great Britain was upon the threshold of the extraordinary industrial activity which developed during the nineteenth century; it was obviously to her advantage to prevent the colonies from securing independence in manufactures, in order to maintain and extend the market for her own products. During the Revolution this source of supply was suddenly cut off, and under the pressure of necessity many manufacturing enterprises sprang up in the rebellious colonies. Upon the conclusion of peace in 1783, however, the English manufacturers flooded the American market with their manufactured products. This state of affairs for a time embarrassed and discouraged native manufacturers.

At the period under consideration manufactures in the United States consisted almost entirely of neighborhood industries, or hand trades. The modern factory system, involving division of labor and the employment of labor saving machinery, was practically unknown. In several of the shoe shops of Lynn and other New England cities, some division of labor had been introduced, but for the most part each workman made an entire shoe. Practically the same conditions obtained in other branches of manufacture.

In January, 1790, when President Washington delivered his first annual message to Congress, he was clad in a suit made of broadcloth woven at Hartford, Conn. In this message the subject of the promotion of manufactures in the young Republic was commended to the attention of Congress, and in pursuance of this suggestion Congress requested the Secretary of the Treasury to prepare a report upon the state of manufacturing industries, in order to render the United States industrially independent of other nations, so

---

[1] Wilbert Lee Anderson: The Country Town, page 20.

far as practicable. In accordance with this request Alexander Hamilton, Secretary of the Treasury, in the following year (1791) submitted to Congress a report which added materially to his reputation as a statesman. This report was twice reprinted by order of Congress.

Already the ingenuity of the citizens of the United States had created, here and there in the New England and Middle states, infant industries which subsequently developed far beyond the dreams of that period. Indeed, the number of specific industries noted as in existence in 1790 was more than double the number of those which were known to have existed prior to the Revolution.

Mr. Tench Coxe, the Assistant Secretary of the Treasury, estimated the value of manufactures in the United States in 1790 at more than $20,000,000. Three years later he reported that the value of manufactures was, in his opinion, double the value of the exports of native commodities, and much greater than the value of all imports.[1]

A large proportion of the manufactured goods included by Secretary Hamilton and Mr. Coxe was produced in households. In many villages and upon farms, during periods of the year in which their services were not actively required in agricultural pursuits, entire families devoted their time to spinning, weaving, and making up coarse cloths. It was estimated that in many localities from two-thirds to four-fifths of the clothing of the inhabitants was made by themselves. The primary demand for such products was of course domestic, but a large surplus found its way into the markets.

The textile industry had made but a small beginning in 1790. Because of competition with the factory product of England, where the making of textiles had already reached a high degree of perfection, the progress of the manufacturers in the young Republic was slow and discouraging. A cotton mill was established at Beverly, Mass., in 1787, but did not long survive. In Rhode Island, however, Samuel Slater, who had emigrated from England, constructed at Pawtucket a factory with machinery on the English plan. This establishment was a success from the outset, and formed the first successful cotton mill in the United States. Thereafter the growth of textile industries was steadily away from household toward factory product.

In 1790 the shipbuilding industry had attained considerable proportions. The success of this industry was, in large measure, due to the facilities for the construction of vessels and ships of all sizes, resulting from excellent harbors, with timber growing to the water's edge. Mr. Coxe observed in 1793 that the shipbuilding industry in the United States had grown more rapidly in 1792 than in any prior year since the settlement of the country. Generally speaking, shipbuilding had

never been better understood and had never been carried to greater perfection, than at that period and in the early decades of the nineteenth century.

Manufactures of iron, also, were of considerable importance. In 1790 this industry centered in the Middle states and Virginia, though considerable quantities of manufactured iron were produced in Massachusetts, where in 1784 there were 76 iron works—most of which, however, were small. In a debate in the House of Representatives in the First Congress, while a tariff upon spikes, nails, etc., was under consideration, Representative Ames, of Massachusetts, said: "This manufacture, with very little encouragement, has grown up remarkably. It has become common for the country people in Massachusetts to erect small forges in their chimney corners, and in winter, and on evenings when little other work can be done, great quantities of nails are made, even by children. These people take the rod iron of the merchant and return him the nails, and in consequence of this easy mode of barter the manufacture is prodigiously great. These advantages are not exclusively in the hands of the people of Massachusetts. The business might be prosecuted in a similar manner in every state exerting equal industry."

Paper making was pursued extensively in several of the states. In 1790 there were 53 paper mills within range of the Philadelphia market. In the First Congress it was stated in debate that the paper mills of Pennsylvania produced annually 70,000 reams of various kinds of paper, which competed favorably with the imported product.

Glass was manufactured in considerable quantities in several of the states, among which Virginia was prominent. The manufacture of boots and shoes, the curing and dressing of fish, the production of soap, of tobacco products, and of various articles of necessity, utility, or comfort were well under way. But at that period little or nothing was manufactured in the United States solely for luxury or elegance.

Mining.—At the close of the eighteenth century the mineral resources of the United States, as they are known to-day and have been known for many years, were practically unsuspected. Probably no section of the continent is richer in mineral resources than that including Pennsylvania, West Virginia, and portions of contiguous states; yet the inhabitants of the United States in 1790 had no knowledge of the great natural wealth of these areas. The existence of petroleum in Pennsylvania and of extensive deposits of coal and iron in that state and in Virginia was known, and iron works were numerous in many states; but little of the coal was mined, and the use and value of petroleum were unknown.

This ignorance concerning the mineral resources of the country, however, is not surprising; the territory containing the greatest mineral wealth was either thinly settled or an unexplored wilderness. Nor is it surprising that the mineral resources known to exist

---

[1] First Century of the Republic (Harper's), page 161.

were not developed. Mining operations as understood to-day were unknown, and the mining and treatment of ores was conducted in the most primitive fashion. The steam engine had not yet become the servant of the miner, either at the mine or upon rails. Indeed, the cost of transportation was so great that mining was unprofitable unless conducted near large cities or waterways.

Coal was consumed in the United States in very small quantities. Ignorant of the vast stores of this mineral which underlie entire counties, those who required coal imported it. The quantity brought into the country during the year ending September 30, 1790, was 183,677 bushels. But bituminous coal was being mined at Spottsylvania, in the Richmond basin, in Virginia, and by 1789 some of this found its way into the northern markets; in 1789 Virginia coal sold in Philadelphia at 1s. 6d. a bushel. Bituminous coal was mined, or rather shoveled, from the earth, also, in the Pittsburg district in Pennsylvania; but none of this found its way across the mountains. Seams of anthracite had been discovered at Wilkes-Barre, Plymouth, Kingston, and Exeter, in Luzerne county, and at several places in Schuylkill county, Pa., and along the Hudson river, in New York. Some smiths are said to have used this material in their forges, but the value of anthracite as a fuel was practically unknown.[1] A newspaper of the time stated that these seams might some day become valuable on account of the possible existence of fossils embedded in them.

Iron ore was mined in the American colonies as early as the seventeenth century. Practically all of the American product was made with charcoal. In 1790 the production of iron in this country appeared to be fully equal to the consumption. The exports of pig iron in that year amounted to 3,555 tons.

Iron was mined in nearly every state. Bog and pond ores were obtained in eastern Massachusetts; rich iron ore was mined at Cumberland Hill, R. I., at Lime Rock and other places in Connecticut, in Orange county, N. Y., and in many places in New Jersey, Pennsylvania, Maryland, and Virginia.

Morris county, N. J., was particularly prominent in the production of iron. Mr. J. M. Swank quotes from Jedediah Morse the following record of iron enterprises which were in existence in New Jersey between 1790 and 1795:

The iron manufactories are, of all others, the greatest source of wealth to the state. Iron works are erected in Gloucester, Burlington, Morris, and other counties. The mountains in the county of Morris give rise to a number of streams necessary and convenient for these works, and at the same time furnish a copious supply of wood and ore of a superior quality. In this county alone are no less than seven rich iron mines, from which might be taken ore suffi-

cient to supply the United States; and to work it into iron, are two furnaces, two rolling and slitting mills, and about thirty forges, containing from two to four fires each. These works produce annually about 540 tons of bar iron, 800 tons of pigs, besides large quantities of hollow ware, sheet iron, and nail rods. In the whole state it is supposed there is yearly made about 1,200 tons of bar iron, 1,200 ditto of pigs, 80 ditto of nail rods, exclusive of hollow ware and various other castings, of which vast quantities are made. Steel was manufactured at Trenton in time of the war, but not considerably since.[2]

In Pennsylvania rich deposits of iron were known to exist in at least 11 of the 22 counties, and considerable quantities of pig iron were produced in Berks, Chester, Dauphin, Franklin, Lancaster, Mifflin, and Washington counties.

In "Notes on the State of Virginia," written in 1781 and 1782, Thomas Jefferson mentioned several iron mines on the south side of the James river and at other places in the state, and estimated the annual output of the mines of that state at approximately 5,000 tons.

Lead was found in Herkimer county, N. Y., and in the mountains of Virginia, but the quantity produced was small. The area which is now southwestern Missouri, but which in 1790 was not a part of the United States, contained lead mines of considerable importance at that period; from about the middle of the eighteenth century to the year 1800 the output of these mines is said to have aggregated 8,000 tons.

Several attempts had been made to mine gold, silver, and copper in different states; but for the most part they were financial failures and were soon abandoned. Copper mines in Connecticut, New Jersey, and Maryland had been worked intermittently during the eighteenth century; but none were in operation in 1790, with the possible exception of one at Belleville, N. J.

Montgomery county, N. Y., supplied small amounts of sulphur, and caves of Virginia considerable quantities of saltpeter.

Fisheries.—In 1790 the United States had 539 vessels and 3,287 seamen engaged in the cod fishery, all in Massachusetts—Marblehead and Gloucester being the leading towns in this industry.

The whaling industry, also, was confined almost entirely to Massachusetts. Whaling operations were carried on principally in the waters of the North Atlantic, as far as Greenland. The sperm whale of the South Atlantic was but little hunted at this period. It was not, indeed, until a few years later that the whaling industry assumed large proportions

Only about 40 whaling vessels were fitted out each year, most of them from Dartmouth (which then included New Bedford), Wellfleet and other Cape Cod ports, and Nantucket. Probably less than 1,000 seamen were employed; but the industry gave rise to dependent industries, which afforded employment to a considerable number in addition.

---

[1] "In 1812 Col. George Shoemaker, of Pottsville, Pa., loaded nine wagons with coal from his mines at Centreville and hauled it to Philadelphia, where with great difficulty he sold two loads at the cost of transportation and gave the other seven loads away. He was by many regarded as an impostor for attempting to sell stone as coal."—*J. M. Swank: Iron in All Ages, page 474.*

[2] J. M. Swank, Iron in All Ages, page 162.

The cod and whale fisheries represented almost the whole fishing industry in 1790, though herring were caught on the New England coast, and oysters were gathered in the South for local consumption.

The total tonnage of the fishing vessels of each state is given in Table 5, on page 30.

Commerce.—Attention has already been called to the fact that by 1790 the shipbuilding industry had attained considerable proportions in the United States. At first the ships constructed were disposed of in England. In time, however, the colonies awoke to the possibilities of profitable trade, and a maritime class arose, bringing about an extensive interchange of products between the inhabitants of North America and those of other lands.

In 1790 commerce offered the most promising field for the profitable investment of capital, and was the chief outlet for business ability and capacity. It also afforded the principal opportunity for the accumulation of great individual wealth. John Jacob Astor had already acquired, in the fur trade, a fortune (amounting to $1,000,000) of great magnitude for that period. In all the large seaboard towns were to be found merchants who owned vessels plying to foreign ports. In these ships they transported merchandise, either on their own account or on that of others. Many of the merchants in Boston, New York, and Philadelphia had amassed fortunes which enabled them to live in a style of luxury and elegance; John Hancock, of Boston, and Stephen Girard, of Philadelphia, were examples of this class of citizens.

The prosperity of the mercantile and commercial interests of the colonies had not been viewed with favor in England. Many restrictions were placed by the British Government upon the commerce of the colonies. But in the face of these restrictions—many of which were often disregarded—the colonies had succeeded in maintaining a considerable commerce up to the beginning of the Revolutionary War. This contest brought disaster to the commercial interests of the country, especially to the commercial state of Rhode Island and to many ports in other New England states. After the conclusion of peace, the volume of commerce grew rapidly, but the centers of commercial prosperity did not continue the same as they were before the war.

By the close of the eighteenth century the commerce of the young Republic had greatly increased. American vessels had pushed to the Orient and to the coasts of Africa, and had established a profitable trade with those regions.

The following extract affords an idea of the commercial activities of the time:

Our public papers vaunt the magnificence of the European nations, who make discoveries and voyages round the world; the Americans do the same thing; but they boast not of their exploits with so much emphasis. In September, 1790, the ship *Columbia*, Captain Gray, sailed to discover the northwest of this continent; this is his second voyage round the world; the brig *Hope* has sailed for the same object. Our papers have resounded with the quarrels of the English and Spaniards for the commerce of Nootka Sound. The Americans make no quarrels; but they have already made a considerable commerce on the same coast in furs and peltry. They were there trading in the year 1789, in good intelligence with both parties. In the same year no less than forty-four vessels were sent from the single town of Boston to the northwest of America, to India, and to China. They bound not their hopes here; they expect, one day, to open a communication more direct to Nootka Sound. It is probable that this place is not far from the headwater of the Mississippi; which the Americans will soon navigate to its source, when they shall begin to people Louisiana and the interior of New Mexico.[1]

According to American State Papers, the imports into and exports from the United States for the fiscal year ending September 30, 1790, were each valued at a little over $20,000,000, or about $5 per capita. Exports to the value of $6,888,978.50 were sent to Great Britain and Ireland; to the value of $2,077,757.50, to the British West Indies; and to the value of $3,284,656, to the French West Indies.

The principal imports into the country subject to duty during the same period, in order of value, were distilled spirits, wines, molasses, sugar, coffee, tea, salt, nails and spikes, steel (unwrought), candles, cheese, and soap.

The principal articles of export for that year, arranged according to value, were flour, tobacco, rice, wheat, corn, dried fish, potash, indigo, staves and heading, horses, meal, beef, and boards.

The changes in the value of foreign commerce between 1790 and 1907 are indicated in the following table:

YEAR.	IMPORTS.		EXPORTS.	
	Total.	Per capita.	Total.	Per capita.
1790[1]	[2]$20,000,000	$5.09	[3]$20,205,156	$5.14
1907	1,434,421,425	16.55	1,880,851,078	21.60

[1] August, 1789, to September 30, 1790.

[2] The value of imports subject to ad valorem duties was $15,388,409.11. The American State Papers do not give the value of those which were subject to specific duties and those which were free, but responsible historians have stated that the value of the total imports for 1790 was slightly in excess of $20,000,000.

[3] Tench Coxe, the Assistant Secretary of the Treasury under Washington, in making his report on the value of the exports for the fiscal year 1790, says: "In addition to the foregoing, a considerable number of packages have been exported from the United States, the value of which, being omitted in the returns from the custom-houses, could not be introduced into this abstract."

It will be observed that the changes in per capita averages in a century amounted to a threefold increase in imports and more than a fourfold increase in exports.

The following data as to the tonnage of American and foreign vessels entering the ports of the United States in 1790 are taken from Burnaby's Travels:[2]

---

[1] M. de Warville, Travels in North America, 1791.

[2] Burnaby's Travels through North America, third edition, Appendix No. 2.

TABLE 5.—TONNAGE OF VESSELS WHICH ENTERED THE PORTS OF THE UNITED STATES DURING THE YEAR ENDING SEPTEMBER 30, 1790, BY STATE OF ENTRY.

STATE.	Principal ports.	All nations.	TONNAGE OF VESSELS BELONGING TO—								
			United States.					United States with some foreign country.	Foreign countries.		
			Total.	Vessels in the over-sea trade.	Coasting vessels of over 20 tons.	Fishing vessels.			Total.	Great Britain and Ireland.	All other.
United States.........		766,091	502,526	363,093	113,181	26,252		651	262,914	225,495	37,419
New Hampshire.............	Portsmouth................	17,011	13,519	11,376	1,670	473	....		3,492	3,459	33
Massachusetts.............	Boston, Salem............	197,368	177,022	99,123	53,073	24,826	....		20,346	19,493	853
Rhode Island[1]............	Newport..................	9,842	9,526	7,062	1,626	838	....		316	96	220
Connecticut...............	New Haven, New London..	33,173	30,617	24,287	6,330	....	....		2,556	2,556	....
New York.................	New York................	92,114	48,274	42,071	6,203	....	....		43,840	36,917	6,923
New Jersey................		5,861	5,514	2,085	3,429	....	....		347	267	80
Pennsylvania.............	Philadelphia.............	109,918	56,997	50,942	6,055	....	651		52,270	42,604	9,666
Delaware.................		5,924	4,142	2,681	1,461	....	....		1,782	1,782	....
Maryland.................	Baltimore................	88,255	55,431	39,272	16,099	60	....		32,824	23,340	9,484
Virginia..................	Norfolk, Alexandria........	103,893	43,529	33,560	9,914	55	....		60,364	56,273	4,091
North Carolina[2]........	Wilmington, Newbern.....	35,126	29,941	24,218	5,723	....	....		5,185	4,942	243
South Carolina[3]........	Charleston...............	40,361	17,380	16,872	508	....	....		22,981	18,725	4,256
Georgia..................	Savannah................	27,245	10,634	9,544	1,090	....	....		16,611	15,041	1,570

[1] Returns from June 21, 1790.
[2] Returns from March 11, 1790.
[3] Returns for Charleston are for three-fourths of the year only.

The ports of Massachusetts show a larger total tonnage and also a larger tonnage of United States vessels (both over-sea and coastwise) than those of any other state; and to this large proportion should be added nearly all the vessels engaged in the fisheries.

The countries owning the foreign vessels for which the tonnage is included in Table 5, and the tonnage brought in the vessels of the different countries, arranged in the order of their importance, were as follows:

COUNTRY.	Total tonnage.
All foreign countries..............................	262,914
Great Britain...................................	222,347
Ireland..	3,148
France...	13,435
Netherlands....................................	8,815
Spain..	8,551
Portugal.......................................	2,925
Denmark.......................................	1,619
Germany.......................................	1,369
Prussia..	394
Sweden..	311

Most of the imports and exports were landed in or sent from a few ports. The most important of these were Salem, Boston, New York, Philadelphia, Baltimore, and Charleston. About one-fifth of the value of imports was landed in New York, while about one-third of that of exports was shipped from Philadelphia.

Salem was the headquarters for the Pacific ocean and East Indian trade. More than forty ships were employed in this trade, principally from that port. The exports were ginseng, shipped direct to China, and beef, pork, flour, and wheat, generally disposed of at intermediate ports, on the outward passage.

From Boston the principal articles of export were rum, potash, pearlash, lumber, fish, and the products of the fisheries, particularly whale oil, whalebone,

soap, and candles. Rum was sent everywhere, but principally to Africa and its islands; most of the potash and pearlash, to Great Britain; lumber, principally to Great Britain and the West Indies; dried and pickled fish, to the French and Dutch West Indies; and whale oil, principally to France.

The shipping from Newport, New Haven, and New London was carried on principally with the West Indies, and was not extensive. The exports were lumber, live stock, grain, and other farm produce. From New Haven occasional cargoes of flaxseed were sent to Ireland.

Much of the commerce of New York was carried on with the West Indies. The principal exports from this city were wheat, flour, lumber, beef, pork, and live stock.

The exports from Philadelphia exceeded in value those from any other port, largely because of the great quantities of flour and wheat exported. The West Indies afforded the principal market for flour, most of which was carried in American bottoms; Great Britain, France, Spain, and Portugal consumed the greater part of that sent to Europe. Nearly all of the wheat was sent to Europe. Other important exports were Indian corn, meal, live stock, beef, and pork.

The chief exports from Baltimore were tobacco, Indian corn, wheat, and flour. The tobacco trade was conducted principally by foreign agents, with European capital, and largely in foreign shipping; most of the tobacco was sent to Great Britain and Holland. Wheat went in large quantities, in foreign vessels, to Spain and Portugal. Indian corn went chiefly to Portugal, though much of the corn was sent in American craft to the Eastern and Southern states.

Charleston was by far the most important port of the South. The foreign commerce was large, and about three-fifths of it was carried in foreign vessels. From Charleston was sent nearly all the rice and indigo exported. Great Britain, Germany, Holland, France, and the West Indies took most of the rice, and Great Britain and Holland nearly all the indigo. Other exports were tar, pitch, turpentine, tobacco, lumber, and cotton.

The exports from Savannah were much the same as those from Charleston, and were carried principally in foreign vessels.

The following table, from American State Papers, shows whence the incoming tonnage came. The data do not agree with those shown in Table 5—Burnaby's table having been compiled later, and probably from revised figures.

TABLE 6.—TONNAGE OF VESSELS WHICH ENTERED THE PORTS OF THE UNITED STATES DURING THE YEAR[1] ENDING SEPTEMBER 30, 1790, CLASSIFIED ACCORDING TO COUNTRY BY WHICH OWNED AND TRADE IN WHICH EMPLOYED.

OWNED BY—	Total tonnage.	TONNAGE IN OVER-SEA TRADE, FROM PORTS IN—							TONNAGE OF COASTERS.			Tonnage of foreign vessels (included in the foregoing) from ports into which vessels of the United States are not admitted.
		All foreign countries.	Europe and its islands.[2]	Asia and its islands.[3]	Africa and its islands.[2,3]	Foreign America.			Total.	Licensed.	Unlicensed.	
						South of the United States.		North of the United States.				
						West Indies.	All other.					
All countries...................	726,561	542,962	240,485	4,842	384	268,735	4,632	23,884	183,599	113,181	70,418	115,428
United States....................	457,468	287,616	113,203	4,667	305	167,400	281	1,760	169,852	113,181	56,671	....
United States with some foreign country..	964	964	964	....	....	....	....	....	....	....	....	....
Foreign countries................	268,129	254,382	126,318	175	79	101,335	4,351	22,124	13,747	....	13,747	115,428
United Kingdom..................	229,893	220,116	103,993	....	....	92,876	1,260	21,987	9,777	....	9,777	110,952
Great Britain....................	226,747	217,183	101,605	....	....	92,331	1,260	21,987	9,564	....	9,564	110,407
Ireland.........................	3,146	2,933	2,388	....	....	545	....	....	213	....	213	545
France..........................	13,802	11,875	7,512	175	79	4,075	....	34	1,927	....	1,927	34
Netherlands.....................	6,941	6,332	4,568	....	....	1,764	....	....	609	....	609	....
Spain...........................	8,772	8,582	3,996	....	....	1,565	2,918	103	190	....	190	4,269
Portugal........................	2,850	2,850	2,432	....	....	245	173	....	....	....	....	173
Denmark.........................	2,416	1,749	1,067	....	....	682	....	....	667	....	667	....
Hanse towns.....................	1,948	1,948	1,948	....	....	....	....	....	....	....	....	....
Prussia.........................	394	....	....	....	....	....	....	....	394	....	394	....
Sweden..........................	311	128	....	....	....	128	....	....	183	....	183	....
All other.......................	802	802	802	....	....	....	....	....	....	....	....	....

[1] Returns for North Carolina, from March 11, 1790; those for Rhode Island, from June 21, 1790.
[2] Madeira, Canary, and Cape Verde islands are included with Europe, instead of with Africa.
[3] Cape of Good Hope and islands of Bourbon, Mauritius, and St. Helena are included with Asia, instead of with Africa.

The countries shown in the foregoing table as owners of the foreign shipping are the same, and are in the same order, as those given in the tabular statement on page 30, except that Germany in the statement mentioned is replaced by the Hanse towns in Table 6. Of the over-sea commerce of 542,962 tons, more than half was carried in ships belonging to the United States (most of them being owned in Massachusetts), and the bulk of the remainder in British vessels. Nearly one-half of the imports from Europe were brought in vessels belonging to the United States.

Particularly noticeable is the fact that nearly one-half of all imports were from the West Indies, and that much more than one-half of the West Indian imports were brought in vessels belonging to the United States, chiefly from the French West Indies. Most of the remainder was brought in British vessels, from British West Indian ports into which the ships of the United States were not allowed to enter; it was in consequence of this fact that in 1790 measures were being agitated in Congress with a view to discriminating duties on cargoes of British vessels.

EDUCATION.

In all of the Northern states, laws were in force in 1790 which provided for the education of children in the rudiments of knowledge. In New England nearly everyone possessed a common school education, and a person of mature years who could not read and write was rarely to be found. Every Massachusetts town having 50 householders or more was required to maintain a schoolmaster to teach children and youth to read and write; and every town that had 100 families was required to maintain a grammar school.[1]

In the Middle states there were fewer state laws relating to compulsory education, but public schools were common. There were very few freeborn illiterates in these states. In Pennsylvania and parts of New Jersey there were large numbers of Germans, and in isolated localities the German language was in com-

[1] "A few academies with limited resources prepared lads for Harvard or Yale. The great body of the people were educated in the district school, two months in the winter by a man, two months in summer by a woman. The three R's were taught there by a poor scholar generally, or by a youth who was earning means to complete his own education. The range of books was very limited. Stout old Ezekiel Cheever's Latin Accidence had held the ground during the century for the upper class of pupils. Noah Webster's spelling book was just coming into use, with Webster's Selections, Morse's Geography, and the Youth's Preceptor. The Bible was the groundwork of all reading. The helps to the pupils being few in comparison with modern resources and methods, the self-help and reliance developed by this crude system of education was something remarkable. This appeared in average characters and ordinary minds."—*Weeden: Economic and Social History of New England, 1620–1789, Vol. II, page 861.*

mon use and was taught in the schools. It would appear, however, that the literacy was quite as high among the Germans as among the English.

In the Southern states there were but few free public schools, because of the dispersed situation of the inhabitants; and in the larger towns there were but few academies. Education was confined largely to the wealthier classes. Wealthy men were accustomed to send their sons to the colleges in the Northern states or to Europe to complete their education. In the thinly settled western sections a large proportion of the people were illiterate. Among the slaves, illiteracy was almost the universal condition.

Higher education in the United States in 1790 consisted largely in the study of the classics. The graduating classes of 1789 in all the colleges aggregated only about 170. The following list shows the most important colleges and universities in the United States in 1790, and in most instances gives the approximate number of students.

INSTITUTION.	Location.	Date of founding.	Students in 1790.
Dartmouth College	Hanover, N. H	1769	152.
Harvard University	Cambridge, Mass.	1636	120 to 150.
Rhode Island College (Brown University).	Providence, R. I	1764	About 60.
Yale College	New Haven, Conn	1700	150 to 250.
Columbia College	New York, N. Y	1754	30 to 40.
Nassau Hall (Princeton University).	Princeton, N. J	1746	About 70.
Queens (Rutgers) College	Brunswick, N. J	1766	30 to 40.
University of Pennsylvania	Philadelphia, Pa.	1740	
Dickinson College	Carlisle, Pa	1783	About 80.
Franklin College	Lancaster, Pa	1787	
Washington College	Chestertown, Md	1782	
St. Johns College	Annapolis, Md	1784	
Georgetown University	Georgetown, Md	1789	
William and Mary College	Williamsburg, Va	1693	About 30.

Law, theology, and medicine were about the only professions in the United States in 1790. New England was the seat of learning in law and theology; and Philadelphia—through the influence of Franklin—in medicine [1] and science. Some of the colleges doubtless offered professional courses; but there were only two medical schools in the country, and no regular school of law. At that period it was customary to acquire a professional education by a period

[1] "The physician had not then become the priest and natural confessor of the American household, as he is to-day; but he was of great importance in the social system. His education through books was scanty, judged by modern standards, while a large knowledge of human kind drawn from direct observation served to bring him into close accord with his patients. Apothecaries were hardly known outside the largest towns; for the doctors' saddlebags carried the simple pharmacy to the remotest hut. Cheerfully those public servants toiled over the hardest roads, in every season and in all weather, to attend rich and poor alike; the country doctor could not choose his patients if he would. A rigid standard of custom gave his services to all who needed them, fees being hardly considered when anyone needed medical attendance.

"The fees were very modest. Even in Boston, prior to 1782, the ordinary visit was charged at 1 shilling 6 pence to 2 shillings. Half a dollar was only charged 'such as were in high life.' In that year a club of the leading physicians fixed the common fee at 50 cents, in consultation at $1. Night visits were doubled; midwifery was at $8; capital operations in surgery, at £5 lawful money; medicines were charged at very high prices, comparatively."— Weeden: Economic and Social History of New England, 1620–1789, Vol. II, page 863.

of study in the office of some one who had become eminent in law or medicine, as the case might be.

NEWSPAPERS AND PERIODICALS.

The newspapers and periodicals known to have been published in the United States during some part of the year 1790 number 103. This number comprises those publications which are fully authenticated, and of which a complete list will be found on page 33. It is believed to include all publications issued in several of the states, and the more influential and important newspapers and periodicals published in the remaining states. The list, however, is probably incomplete. It is not to be doubted that there were a considerable number of publications of which, after the lapse of more than a century, all record has vanished. In some instances, indeed, references are made by local historians to publications which were evidently in existence in 1790, but of which no further trace can be found.

The following table analyzes, by period of issue, the publications in each state in 1790:

Newspapers and periodicals published in the United States in 1790, classified by period of issue.

STATE.	Total.	Daily.	Semiweekly.	Weekly.	Monthly.	Bimonthly.	Unknown.
United States	103	8	12	73	6	1	3
New England states	37		3	32	2		
Maine	2			2			
New Hampshire	6		1	5			
Vermont	2			2			
Massachusetts	14		2	10	2		
Rhode Island	4			4			
Connecticut	9			9			
Middle states	42	7	6	22	4	1	2
New York	14	3	4	4	1		2
New Jersey	3			2		1	
Pennsylvania	23	4	2	14	3		
Delaware	2			2			
Southern states	24	1	3	19			1
Maryland	9		2	7			
Virginia	9			9			
North Carolina	1						1
South Carolina	2	1	1				
Georgia	2			2			
Kentucky	1			1			

Of the 103 publications reported, 96 were newspapers and 7 were periodicals. More than one-third of the whole number were published in New England, and two-fifths in the Middle states. Most of the newspapers published south of the Potomac are credited to Maryland and Virginia.

An examination of the proportions of daily, semiweekly, weekly, and monthly publications in 1790 naturally suggests the following comparison with the corresponding proportions of the immense volume of publications issued in 1900. The most striking fact revealed by this comparison is the growth of the daily paper and the monthly periodical at the expense of weekly and semiweekly papers.

PERIOD OF ISSUE.	1790	1900
Daily	7.8	13.2
Semiweekly	13.6	2.5
Weekly	68.9	34.9
Monthly	5.8	34.6
All other	3.9	14.8

In 1790 the contents of newspapers were chiefly advertisements, notices of auction sales, shipping news, short clippings from papers in other states, letters from places in the West and from the West India Islands, and extracts from European newspapers. There were also a few broad jokes and anecdotes scattered through the pages. Events of local interest were seldom published, and editorial remarks were few in number, although sometimes vigorous in expression.

During the sessions of Congress the debates were published at length in all the daily papers, and important bills were given in full, even to the signatures of the President and Vice-President. But there were no news collecting agencies, and little of the news published seems to have come to the knowledge of the editors through any systematic efforts of their own. Very few, if any, of the papers had correspondents in different sections of the country.

The weekly paper was in many cases the only outlet for literary activity. There were long disquisitions on religious and political topics, and essays after the manner of the Spectator were frequent. There were also numerous communications from local writers. These were never signed by the writer, but with some such classical pseudonym as Publicola, Nestor, or Cicero; they usually abounded in classical allusions and quotations, and were on all subjects— religion, politics, law, medicine, and morals.

In no instance was the circulation of a newspaper published in 1790 very large; it probably did not exceed 1,000 copies per issue in the case of the most prosperous publication. In 1789 not less than 30,000 copies of newspapers were printed every week in New England;[1] they circulated in almost every town and village.

Newspapers were usually distributed by newsboys, or by postboys who made long trips through the rural districts on horseback, performing other errands along their routes. Drivers of stagecoaches sometimes received subscriptions for papers, and distributed them on regular trips.

Some of the newspapers published in 1790 have survived to the present time; but most of those which are still published are issued under names which have been partially or completely changed, and some have been merged in other publications.

[1] Gazetteer of the United States, Jedediah Morse.

Newspapers and periodicals published in 1790.

PLACE OF PUBLICATION AND TITLE IN 1790.	Period of issue in 1790.	Date when established.	First publisher.	Publisher in 1790.	Remarks.
MAINE.					
Portland:					
The Cumberland Gazette	Weekly	Jan. 1, 1785	Benjamin Titcomb and Thomas B. Wait.	Thomas B. Wait	Consolidated Sept. 3, 1796; in existence in 1895.
Gazette of Maine	Weekly	Oct. 1, 1790	Benjamin Titcomb	Benj. Titcomb	
NEW HAMPSHIRE.					
Concord:					
The Concord Herald and New-hampshire Intelligencer.	Weekly	Jan. 6, 1790	George Hough	George Hough	Discontinued Oct. 30, 1805.
Dover:					
Political and Sentimental Repository, or Strafford Recorder.	Weekly	July 15, 1790	Eliphalet Ladd	Eliphalet Ladd	Discontinued in 1829.
Exeter:					
New Hampshire Gazetteer	Weekly	Aug. —, 1789	Henry Ranlet	Henry Ranlet	Discontinued in 1797.
Keene:					
The New Hampshire Recorder and the Weekly Advertiser.	Weekly	Aug. 7, 1789	James D. Griffith	James D. Griffith	Discontinued in 1792.
Portsmouth:					
The New-Hampshire Gazette, and the General Advertiser.	Weekly	Oct. 7, 1756	Daniel Fowle	John Melcher	Became weekly edition of Daily Chronicle in 1861. In existence in 1895.
Osborne's New Hampshire Spy	Semiweekly	Oct. 24, 1786	Geo. Jerry Osborne	Geo. Jerry Osborne	Discontinued in 1793.
VERMONT.					
Bennington:					
The Vermont Gazette	Weekly	June 5, 1783	Anthony Haswell and David Russell.	Anthony Haswell and David Russell.	In existence in 1879.
Windsor:					
Vermont Journal and Universal Advertiser.	Weekly	Aug. 7, 1783	George Hough and Alden Spooner.	George Hough (?) and Alden Spooner.	Vermont Journal in 1900.
MASSACHUSETTS.					
Boston:					
The Boston Gazette and the Country Journal.	Weekly	Apr. 7, 1755	Benjamin Edes and John Gill.	Benjamin Edes and Benj. Edes, jr.	Discontinued Sept. 17, 1798.
Independent Chronicle and the Universal Advertiser.[1]	Weekly	Aug. 2, 1768	Samuel Hall	Thomas Adams	Merged in Boston Daily Advertiser in 1831.
American Herald: And The Washington Gazette.	Weekly	Oct. 27, 1781	Edward E. Powars	Edward E. Powars	Probably consolidated with the Herald of Freedom in 1791 or 1792.
The Columbian Centinel	Semiweekly	Mar. 24, 1784	William Warden and Benjamin Russell.	Benjamin Russell	Merged in Boston Daily Advertiser, May 1, 1840.

[1] Established at Salem.

Newspapers and periodicals published in 1790—Continued.

PLACE OF PUBLICATION AND TITLE IN 1790.	Period of issue in 1790.	Date when established.	First publisher.	Publisher in 1790.	Remarks.
MASSACHUSETTS—continued.					
Boston—Continued.					
The Gentlemen and Ladies' Town and Country Magazine.	Monthly	May, 1784	Job Weeden and William Barrett.	Nathaniel Coverley	Discontinued in December, 1790.
The Herald of Freedom	Semiweekly	Sept. 15, 1788	Edmund Freeman and Loring Andrews.	Edmund Freeman	In existence June 28, 1793.
The Massachusetts Magazine, Or Monthly Museum.	Monthly	Jan. —, 1789	Isaiah Thomas and Ebenezer T. Andrews.	Isaiah Thomas and Ebenezer T. Andrews.	Discontinued in December, 1796.
Newburyport:					
The Essex Journal and New Hampshire Packet.	Weekly	Dec. 1, 1773	Isaiah Thomas and Henry W. Tinges.	John Mycall	Became the Morning Star in April, 1794. Discontinued before 1800.
Northampton:					
The Hampshire Gazette	Weekly	Sept. 6, 1786	William Butler	William Butler	Berkshire County Eagle in 1900.
Pittsfield:					
Berkshire Chronicle and Massachusetts Intelligencer.	Weekly	May 8, 1788	Roger Storrs	Roger Storrs	In existence in 1900.
Salem:					
The Salem Gazette	Weekly	Oct. 14, 1786	John Dabney and Thomas C. Cushing.	Thomas C. Cushing	In existence in 1895.
Springfield:					
The Hampshire Chronicle	Weekly	Mar. 1, 1787	Zephaniah Webster	Ezra Waldo Weld	In existence in 1795.
Stockbridge:					
The Western Star	Weekly	Nov. —, 1789	Loring Andrews	Loring Andrews	In existence in 1898.
Worcester:					
Thomas's Massachusetts Spy; or The Worcester Gazette.[1]	Weekly	July 17, 1770	Isaiah Thomas	Isaiah Thomas	The Massachusetts Spy in 1900.
RHODE ISLAND.					
Newport:					
The Newport Mercury	Weekly	Sept. —, 1758	James Franklin, jr	Henry Barber	In existence in 1900.
Newport Herald	Weekly	Mar. 1, 1787	Peter Edes	Peter Edes	Discontinued in 1791.
Providence:					
The Providence Gazette and Country Journal.	Weekly	Oct. 20, 1762	William Goddard	John Carter	Merged in Rhode Island American in October, 1825.
United States Chronicle	Weekly	Jan. 1, 1784	Bennett Wheeler	Bennett Wheeler	Discontinued in 1802.
CONNECTICUT.					
Danbury:					
The Farmer's Journal	Weekly	Mar. 18, 1790	Nathan Douglas and Edwards Ely.	Nathan Douglas and Edwards Ely.	Republican Farmer (Bridgeport) in 1900.
Hartford:					
The Connecticut Courant and Weekly Intelligencer.	Weekly	Oct. 29, 1764	Thomas Green	Barzillai Hudson and Geo. Goodwin.	In existence in 1900.
The American Mercury	Weekly	July 12, 1784	Joel Barlow and Elisha Babcock.	Elisha Babcock	Merged in the Independent Press in 1833.
Litchfield:					
The Weekly Monitor; and American Advertiser.	Weekly	Dec. 21, 1784	Thomas Collier and Copp	Thomas Collier	Discontinued in 1806.
Middletown:					
Middlesex Gazette or Federal Adviser.	Weekly	Nov. 8, 1785	Woodward and Green	Moses H. Woodward	Discontinued in May, 1834.
New Haven:					
Connecticut Journal	Weekly	Oct. 23, 1767	Thomas and Samuel Green	Thomas and Samuel Green	Connecticut Herald and Weekly Journal in 1900.
The New Haven Gazette	Weekly	Jan. 5, 1790			Discontinued June 29, 1791.
New London:					
Connecticut Gazette	Weekly	Aug. 8, 1758	Timothy Green	Timothy Green	Discontinued in 1844.
Norwich:					
The Norwich Packet and the Connecticut, Massachusetts, New Hampshire, and Rhode Island Weekly Advertiser.	Weekly	Dec. 16, 1773	Alexander Robertson & James Robertson and John Trumbull.	John Trumbull	Discontinued in 1804.
NEW YORK.					
Albany:					
The Albany Gazette	Semiweekly	May 28, 1784	Charles R. Webster	Charles R. Webster	Discontinued Apr. 14, 1845.
The Albany Register	(2)	— —, 1788	Robert Barber	John and Robert Barber	Merged in New York Standard.
Goshen:					
The Goshen Repository		— —, 1788	David Mandeville		Discontinued in 1804.
Hudson:					
Hudson Gazette	Weekly	Apr. 7, 1785	Charles R. Webster and Ashbel Stoddard.	Charles R. Webster and Ashbel Stoddard.	In existence in 1900.
Lansingburg:					
Federal Herald	Weekly	May 5, 1788	Babcock and Hickok	Babcock and Hickok	In existence in 1890.
New York:					
The New York Journal and Patriotic Register.	Semiweekly	May 29, 1766	John Holt	Thomas Greenleaf	Discontinued in 1810.
The Argus, or Greenleaf's New Daily Advertiser.	Daily	May 29, 1766	John Holt	Thos. Greenleaf	Discontinued in November, 1810.
New York Packet	Semiweekly	Jan. 4, 1776	Samuel Loudon	Samuel Loudon	In existence in 1835.
The Daily Advertiser	Daily	Mar. 1, 1785	Francis Childs	Philip Freneau	Merged in Express in 1836.
The New York Daily Gazette	Daily	Dec. 29, 1788	John and Archibald M'Lean	Archibald M'Lean	In existence in 1828.
Gazette of the United States[3]	Semiweekly	Apr. 15, 1789	John Fenno	John Fenno	Merged in North American in 1847.
New York Magazine	Monthly	Jan., 1790	Thomas and James Swords	Thos. and Jas. Swords	Discontinued in 1797.
Weekly Museum	Weekly				In existence in 1816.
Poughkeepsie:					
Poughkeepsie Journal[4]	Weekly	— —, 1734	John Holt	Nicholas Power	United with Poughkeepsie Eagle in 1844. In existence in 1850.
NEW JERSEY.					
New Brunswick:					
The Brunswick Gazette	Weekly	Sept. —, 1786	Shelly Arnett	Abraham Blauvelt	In existence in 1816.
Elizabethtown:					
New Jersey Journal, and Political Intelligencer.	Weekly	— —, 1779	Shepard Kollock	Shepard Kollock	Elizabeth Daily Journal in 1900.
The Christian's, scholar's, and farmer's magazine.	Bimonthly	Apr. — '789	Shepard Kollock	Shepard Kollock	Discontinued in March, 1791.

[1] Established at Boston.   [2] Weekly in 1792.   [3] Removed to Philadelphia Oct. 13, 1790.   [4] Established in New York City.

Newspapers and periodicals published in 1790—Continued.

PLACE OF PUBLICATION AND TITLE IN 1790.	Period of issue in 1790.	Date when established.	First publisher.	Publisher in 1790.	Remarks.
PENNSYLVANIA.					
Carlisle:					
The Carlisle Gazette, & the Western Repository of Knowledge.	Weekly	Aug. 10, 1785	Kline and Reynolds	Kline and Reynolds	In existence June 9, 1790.
Chambersburg:					
Western Advertiser and Chambersburg Weekly.	Weekly	June —, 1790	William Davison	Wm. Davison	Franklin Repository in 1900.
Germantown:					
Die Germantauner Zeitung	Weekly	Aug. 20, 1739	Christopher Saur	Michael Billmeyer	Discontinued in 1809.
Harrisburg:					
The Oracle of Dauphin	Weekly	— —, 1789	T. Roberts and Co	T. Roberts and Co	Discontinued about 1832.
Lancaster:					
Neue Unpartheyische Lancäster Zeitung und Anzeigs-Nachrichten.	Weekly	Aug. 8, 1787	Stiemer, Albrecht, and Lahn	Johann Albrecht & Co	Discontinued in 1794.
Philadelphia:[1]					
The Pennsylvania Gazette	Weekly	Dec. 24, 1728	Samuel Keimer	David Hall and William Sellers.	Became Saturday Evening Post in 1821. In existence in 1900.
The Pennsylvania Journal and Weekly Advertiser.	Semiweekly	Dec. 2, 1742	William Bradford	William and Thos. Bradford.	Discontinued in 1797.
The Pennsylvania Packet and Daily Advertiser.	Daily	Oct. 28, 1771	John Dunlap	John Dunlap and David C. Claypoole.	Merged in the North American in 1840. In existence in 1900.
The Arminian Magazine	Monthly	Jan. —, 1778	Prichard and Hall		In existence in 1790.
The Freeman's Journal, or the North American Intelligencer.	Weekly	Apr. 25, 1781	Francis Bailey	Francis Bailey	Discontinued in 1792.
Gemeinnützige Philadelphische Correspondenz.	Weekly	May 21, 1781	Melchior Steiner	Melchior Steiner	Discontinued in 1810.
Independent Gazetteer, or the Cronicle of Freedom.	Daily	Apr. 13, 1782	Eleazer Oswald	Eleazer Oswald	Discontinued in 1799.
Pennsylvania Mercury and The Universal Advertiser.	Weekly	Aug. 20, 1784	Daniel Humphreys	Daniel Humphreys	
Universal Asylum and Columbian Magazine.	Monthly	Sept. —, 1786	Matthew Carey, T. Siddons, C. Talbot, W. Spotswood, & J. Trenchard.		Discontinued in December, 1792.
The American Museum; or Universal Magazine.	Monthly	Jan. —, 1787	Matthew Carey	Matthew Carey	Discontinued Dec. 31, 1792.
The Federal Gazette and Philadelphia Daily Advertiser.	Daily	Mar. 8, 1788	Andrew Brown	Andrew Brown	Merged in North American in 1840.
Der General - Postbothe an die Deutsche Nation.	Semiweekly	Nov. 27, 1789	Melchior Steiner	Melchior Steiner	Discontinued about July, 1790.
Die Chesnuthiller Wochenschrift	Weekly	Oct. 8, 1790	Samuel Saur	Samuel Saur	In existence in 1794.
The General Advertiser and Political, Commercial, Agricultural and Literary Journal.	Daily	Oct. —, 1790	Benjamin Franklin Bache	Benjamin Franklin Bache.	Merged in Pennsylvania Gazette in 1828.
Farmers' Weekly Museum	Weekly	— —, 1790			In existence in 1790.
Pittsburg:					
Pittsburg Gazette	Weekly	July 29, 1786	John Scull and Joseph Hall		Commercial Gazette in 1900.
Reading:					
Neue Unpartheyische Readinger Zeitung und Anzeigs-Nachrichten.	Weekly	Feb. 18, 1789	Johnson, Barton, and Jungmann.	Barton and Jungmann	Discontinued in 1816.
York:					
Pennsylvania Herald and York General Advertiser.	Weekly	Jan. 7, 1789	James Edie, John Edie, and Henry Wilcocks.	James Edie, John Edie, and Henry Wilcocks.	In existence in 1799.
DELAWARE.					
Wilmington:					
Wilmington Gazette	Weekly	— —, 1784			In existence in 1880.
The Delaware Gazette	Weekly	Mar. —, 1785	Peter Brynberg and Samuel Andrews.	Peter Brynberg and Samuel Andrews.	In existence in 1894.
MARYLAND.					
Annapolis:					
Maryland Gazette	Weekly	Jan. 17, 1745	Jonas Green	Frederick and Samuel Green.	Discontinued in 1839.
Baltimore:					
The Maryland Journal and Baltimore Advertiser.	Semiweekly	Aug. 20, 1773	William Goddard	Wm. Goddard and James Angell.	Baltimore American in 1900.
The Maryland Gazette; or the Baltimore Advertiser.	Semiweekly	May 16, 1783	John Hayes	John Hayes	In existence in 1791.
Easton:					
Maryland Herald and Eastern Shore Intelligencer.	Weekly	May 16, 1790	James Cowan	James Cowan	In existence in 1804.
Frederick:					
The Maryland Chronicle and the Universal Advertiser.	Weekly	Jan. 4, 1786	Matthias Bartgis	Matthias Bartgis	In existence in 1824.
The Maryland Gazette and Frederick Weekly Advertiser.	Weekly	Mar. 1, 1790	John Winter	John Winter	In existence in 1791.
Georgetown:[2]					
The Times and the Patowmack Packet.	Weekly	Feb. —, 1789	Charles Fierer	Charles Fierer and Thos. N. Fosdick.	In existence in 1791.
Georgetown Weekly Ledger	Weekly	Mar. —, 1790	Day and Hancock	Day and Hancock	In existence in 1793.
Hagerstown:					
Washington Spy	Weekly	Jan. 1, 1790	Stewart Herbert	Stewart Herbert	In existence in 1797.
VIRGINIA.					
Fredericksburg:					
The Virginia Herald and Fredericksburg Advertiser.	Weekly	— —, 1787	Timothy Green	Timothy Green	In existence in 1836.
Martinsburg:					
Potomak Guardian and Berkeley Advertiser.	Weekly	Nov. —, 1790	Nathaniel Willis	Nathaniel Willis	In existence in 1896.
Norfolk:					
The Norfolk and Portsmouth Chronicle.	Weekly	Aug. 29, 1789	Prentis and Baxter	Prentis and Baxter	In existence in 1793.
Petersburg:					
The Virginia Gazette and Petersburg Intelligencer.	Weekly	July —, 1786	Miles Hunter & William Prentis.	William Prentis	In existence in 1800.

[1] See also Gazette of the United States, which was published in New York city until Oct. 13, 1790, when it was removed to Philadelphia.
[2] Now in the District of Columbia.

Newspapers and periodicals published in 1790—Continued.

PLACE OF PUBLICATION AND TITLE IN 1790.	Period of issue in 1790.	Date when established.	First publisher.	Publisher in 1790.	Remarks.
VIRGINIA—continued.					
Richmond:					
Virginia Gazette and Independent Chronicle.[1]	Weekly	Aug. 6, 1736	William Parks	John Dixon	In existence in 1793.
The Virginia Gazette and Weekly Advertiser.	Weekly	— —, 1782	Thomas Nicolson and William Prentiss.	Thomas Nicolson	In existence in 1793.
The Virginia Independent Chronicle and General Advertiser.	Weekly	— —, 1786	Augustine Davis	Augustine Davis	Discontinued in 1809.
Winchester:					
The Virginia Gazette, and Winchester Advertiser.	Weekly	July 11, 1787	Bartgis & Willcocks	Bartgis & Co	In existence in 1790.
The Virginia Centinel; or the Winchester Mercury.	Weekly	Apr. 2, 1788	Richard Bowen and Co	Richard Bowen and Co	In existence in 1800.
NORTH CAROLINA.					
Fayetteville:					
The Fayetteville Chronicle or North Carolina Gazette.					In existence in 1790.
SOUTH CAROLINA.					
Charleston:					
The State Gazette of South Carolina.	Semiweekly	Apr. —, 1777	Peter Timothy	Ann S. Timothy	Discontinued in 1800.
The City Gazette or Daily Advertiser.	Daily	Mar. —, 1783	John Miller	Markland and M'Iver	In existence in 1817.
GEORGIA.					
Augusta:					
The Augusta Chronicle and Gazette of the State.	Weekly	Oct. 2, 1786	John E. Smith	John E. Smith	In existence in 1900.
Savannah:					
Georgia Gazette	Weekly	Apr. 17, 1763	James Johnston	James and Nicholas Johnston.	Discontinued in 1802.
KENTUCKY.					
Lexington:					
Kentucke Gazette	Weekly	Aug. 11, 1787	John Bradford	John Bradford	Discontinued in 1848.

[1] Established at Williamsburg.

SLAVERY.

Slavery was introduced into the colonies in August, 1619, when 20 African negroes were brought to Jamestown by Dutch traders and sold to the planters of Virginia. At that time the sale of Africans who had been captured or purchased was sanctioned by the leading European nations, and formed a very profitable business. The slave traders, taking advantage of the new field opened to them by the colonization of the coast of North America, introduced slavery into most of the colonies soon after they were founded. The only colony established with ordinances against this institution was Georgia; and this state also was soon forced, by social contact and business competition with the neighboring settlements, to legalize the holding of slaves.

The actual importations of slaves can only be estimated. Mr. Carey, author of a work on the slave trade, is the authority for the following estimate of the number of slaves imported:

PERIOD.	Number of slaves.
Total	333,000
Prior to 1715	30,000
1715 to 1750	90,000
1751 to 1760	35,000
1761 to 1770	74,000
1771 to 1790	34,000
1791 to 1808	70,000

It is claimed, however, that this total is too small, and that a closer estimate would bring the number to 370,000 or even 400,000. Mr. Carey's figures indicate that the average annual importation was about 2,500 between 1715 and 1750, and 3,500 for the period from 1751 to 1760. The following decade was the period of greatest activity, the importation reaching an average of 7,400 a year. For the twenty years from 1771 to 1790 the average fell to 1,700, but for the period immediately preceding the legal abolition of the slave traffic in the United States it was more than double that number. By 1790 the survivors and descendants of the African slaves imported numbered 757,208, according to the Federal census of that year.

Early in the history of the Southern colonies the planters realized that slave labor could be utilized to good advantage in the cultivation of tobacco and some other crops.[1] At the beginning of the eighteenth century negro slavery was considered by the settlers of all of the colonies as a usual and routine matter, and in the New England and Middle colonies, as well as in the South, the possession of slaves was generally

[1] The cotton crop, which later furnished an extensive field for slave labor, did not assume great importance until the invention of the cotton gin in 1793. After that date the employment of slaves in the cultivation of cotton became especially profitable, since this crop furnishes work for a considerable portion of the year, and makes it possible to utilize to advantage the services of women and children.

accepted as an evidence of wealth and of importance in the community.

By 1750 negro slavery was recognized by law in every North American colony. At the time of the Declaration of Independence the British possessions had local enactments protecting slave property and providing special codes and tribunals for slaves. Some of the slave codes were extremely severe, because of the fear of negro insurrections.

Although slavery became the presumptive status of every negro, most of the colonies recognized the status of free negroes. But the presence of a free negro was believed to have an unfavorable influence on the slaves in the neighborhood, and hence many of the colonies made the conditions surrounding manu-mission so exacting that slave owners seldom took advantage of the legal right to free their slaves. There are, however, numerous instances of negroes who were freed by their masters, and some cases of negroes who were given their freedom by the state on account of some public service performed by them; but no data are available as to the aggregate number of slaves manumitted.

Free negroes were allowed property rights, and consequently some of them became slave owners. Often a manumitted negro would purchase the freedom of the members of his family or of friends, and unless he went through the formality of manumission these persons were legally his slaves.

The growth of the antislavery movement forms an interesting phase of the history of the Colonial, Continental, and early Federal periods. The antislavery sentiment which existed in the Southern colonies in the early part of the eighteenth century was, as a rule, the result of economic causes; when these colonies feared the growth in the number of negroes, or desired more revenue, attempts were made by the legislatures to cut off or to tax the importation of slaves. On the other hand, in the North the feeling of antagonism toward human slavery, which grew rapidly and was voiced by men of high principle and strong religious belief, was based largely on moral grounds. The claim is often made that this attitude of the Northern colonies in connection with the slave problem did not become general until after these communities had disposed of all of their slaves. But, while there is an element of truth in this, the fact remains that from a condition of dependence upon slaves for menial services of various kinds, the people of the New England and Middle states steadily and completely changed their point of view, taking the position that slavery was both unwise and immoral, and disposed of their slaves. The demand for labor was supplied mainly by apprentices and by "redemptioners"—men and women who, being unable to pay the expenses of their passage to this country, were "bound" to persons buying their services for a period usually lasting from three to five years.

The first petition against slavery recorded in American history was made in 1688, by Friends, in Germantown, Pa. The agitation against slavery was continued by other Quakers, by the Puritans, and by groups of individuals here and there. As the direct result of this movement, prohibitive duties on the importation of slaves were imposed by Pennsylvania in 1712, and also by other colonies from time to time.[1]

Since the slave trade was a source of revenue to British merchants, and even to the Crown, legislation against it was distasteful to the British Government, and objections were raised on account of the legislative action of the colonies. The governors sent to South Carolina in 1756 and 1761 bore instructions prohibiting the enactment of any law imposing duties on imported negroes.

By 1778 legislative measures prohibiting the slave trade had been passed by all of the New England and Middle states, and by Maryland and Virginia; by 1798, similar action had been taken by every other state, although the trade was afterwards revived in South Carolina.

The first assumption of national control of the slave trade came in 1774, when the Continental Congress passed a resolution to abolish it. In 1789 the convention that framed the Constitution made plans for the abolition of this traffic in 1808, and later the first day of 1808 was chosen as the time when the slave trade should become illegal.

The first action against the ownership of slaves was taken by Vermont. In its Declaration of Rights, in 1777, this colony declared for the freedom of all persons at the age of maturity; a few years later it took a more definite stand, abolishing slavery outright. By 1783 slavery had been prohibited in Massachusetts and New Hampshire. Gradual emancipation was provided for in acts passed by Pennsylvania in 1780 and by Connecticut and Rhode Island in 1784. In 1787 slavery was forbidden in the Northwest Territory by congressional legislation, although the courts held that the ordinance did not free the slaves already held in the territory. By the date of the first Federal census laws providing for the extinction of slavery had been put into operation in all states north of Maryland, with the exception of New York and New Jersey.

INDIANS.

In 1790 the Indian had ceased to be a factor of any consequence in the affairs of the states enumerated at the First Census. The Indians living in the area enumerated consisted of a few scattered remnants of once powerful tribes. Frequent conflicts

[1] In some colonies the duty on a slave brought from another colony was several times that on a slave imported directly from Africa or from the West Indies; the impression appears to have existed that slaves were sent from one colony to another because of undesirable qualities, or because they had committed crimes, and that the colony which deported them was taking this way of ridding itself of their presence.

LOCATION OF INDIAN TRIBES: 1790.

[The heavy line marks the division between the area free from hostile Indians and that still in possession of Indians.]

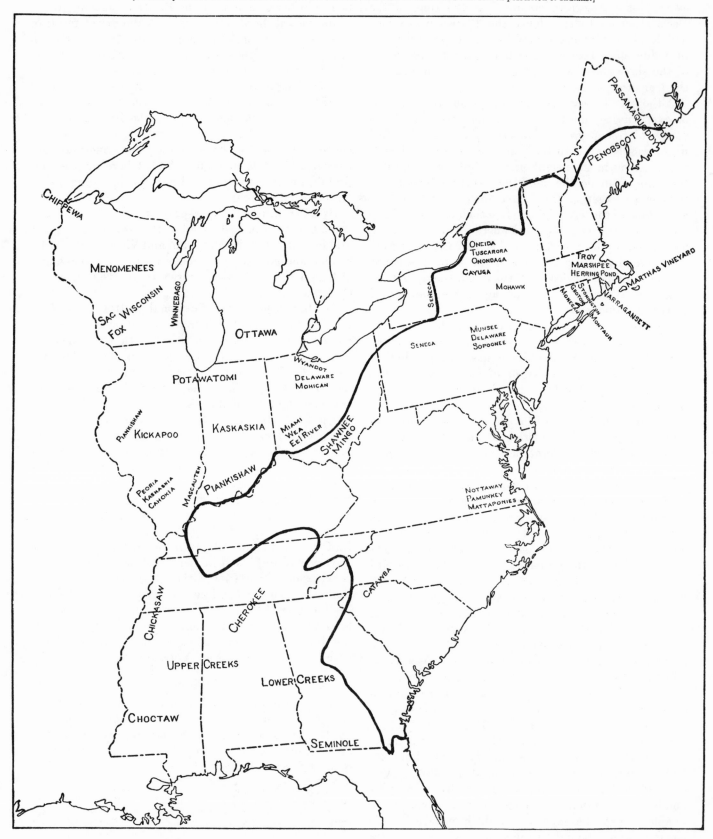

with the white settlers, and the adoption of all of the vices and few, if any, of the virtues of the newcomers upon their soil, had reduced the number of Indians east of the Allegheny mountains to a few thousands. Remnants of the original tribes still remained in 4 New England states, and in New York, Pennsylvania, Virginia, and South Carolina; but in most instances— especially in New England—they were reduced to small villages or even to a few wanderers (for the most part half-breeds), whose numbers may be accepted as almost a negligible quantity. Only in New York and Pennsylvania—upon reservations established in those states—and in the lands to the west of the frontier settlements, were the Indians still sufficiently numerous to maintain tribal relations or to occupy any considerable extent of territory.

From time to time futile attempts were made to civilize and educate the Indians in the East. Indeed, provision was made for their education at Harvard University early in its history. Several Indians entered that institution, but nearly all of them died before they had been long in attendance.

West of the Alleghenys the white man had established a few settlements, especially in Kentucky and eastern Tennessee; but for the most part the country was a wilderness, still in the undisputed possession of Indian tribes. In this area the Indians still maintained their independence and a considerable strength in numbers—sufficient, indeed, to present to the officials of the young Republic a problem of some magnitude, and to exercise a decidedly deterrent effect upon immigration. But since, in the desultory warfare which they maintained against the whites, the Indians were the principal sufferers, their numbers were constantly diminishing.

Only a small part of the territory occupied by white men had been acquired from the Indians by actual purchase. In the early history of the colonies, purchases of land from the Indians, and treaties made with them, appear to have resulted from a desire to obtain immunity from the uncertainties of Indian warfare and depredation, rather than from any recognition of the right of the Indians to the soil of which they were being deprived. The pioneer settlers habitually disregarded Indian treaties, and in general the Indians derived little benefit from them; even where purchases of land were negotiated by treaty, in many cases this action was not taken until after the land had been settled. In general, the Indian had received but small consideration from the white man during the entire Colonial period, being regarded merely as a dangerous incumbrance upon fair regions which it was the purpose of the white man to occupy as speedily as his numbers permitted.

In 1795, shortly after the First Census, in an attempt to put an end to the continued warfare with the Federal Government and doubtless also for the purpose of encouraging settlements in that region, General Wayne negotiated a treaty with the Indians living in what was then called the Northwest Territory.[1] The developments resulting from this policy were similar to what had previously occurred east of the Alleghenys—the Indians retreated step by step before the advancing pioneers, more and more of their territory was occupied by white settlements, and their numbers were constantly decreased by contact with the whites and by warfare among themselves.

Indians in the United States in 1790.

STATE OR TERRITORY AND TRIBE.	Number.	Place of residence.
Maine:		
Passamaquoddy		Near the waters of Passamaquoddy bay.
Penobscot	400	On Penobscot river, from head of tide water northward.
Massachusetts:		
Herring Pond	[1] 120	Sandwich, on Cape Cod, 59 miles south of Boston.
Wampanoag	[2] 280	Troy, Bristol county, 50 miles south of Boston.
		Marshpee, on Cape Cod, 78 miles southeast of Boston.
	400	Marthas Vineyard Island.
Rhode Island:		
Narragansett	500	Charlestown, 40 miles southwest of Providence.
Connecticut:		
Mohegan and other tribes		Stonington, southeast corner of Connecticut.
		Groton, adjoining Stonington.
		Between Norwich and New London.
New York:		
Montauk		Montauk Point, east end of Long Island.
Six Nations—		
Cayuga	500	Reservation of 1,000 square miles at northern end of Cayuga Lake.
Mohawk	([3])	Fort Hunter, on Mohawk river.
Oneida	700	Oneida reservation.
Onondaga	500	Reservation of over 100 square miles on Onondaga Lake.
Seneca	2,000	Chiefly on Genesee river; also a town on Buffalo creek, and 2 small towns on Allegheny river.
Tuscarora [4]	400	On Tuscarora or Oneida creek.
Pennsylvania:		
Delaware, Munsee, and Sopoonee.	1,300	On north branch of Susquehanna river.
Virginia:		
Mattaponi, Nottaway, and Pamunkey.	100	Southampton county, southeastern Virginia.
Seneca	150	Two towns on French creek.
South Carolina:		
Catawba	450	At Catawba, on Catawba river, on the boundary line between North Carolina and South Carolina.
Northwest Territory:		
Chippewa		Coasts of Lake Superior.
Delaware, Mohican, and Wyandot.		Northern Ohio.
Illinois, Kaskaskia, and Peoria.		Near Kaskaskia river, Illinois.
Kickapoo		Central Illinois.
Mascauten		Neighborhood of Piankashaws.
Menomenee		Around Green bay.
Miami, Wea, and Eel River Indians.		Vicinity of Miami river.
Ottawa		Southern peninsula of Michigan.
Piankashaw		Wabash river and branches, and Illinois river.
Potawatomi		Southern shores of Lake Michigan.
Sac and Fox		Mouth of Wisconsin river.
Shawnee		Southern Ohio, on Scioto river and a branch of the Muskingum.
Winnebago		Around Winnebago bay.
Wisconsin		On Wisconsin river.
Southwest Territory:[5]		
Cherokee	3,000	Northern Georgia and southern Tennessee.
Chickasaw		Western Tennessee.
Choctaw		Between Alabama and Mississippi rivers.
Creek nation	22,000	
Upper Creek	11,000	On upper waters of Alabama river.
Lower Creek	11,000	On Apalachicola river and its two branches—the Chattahoochee and the Flint.
Seminole		

[1] Half were of mixed blood.
[2] Only about 40 or 50 were pure Indian.
[3] Only one family in the United States.
[4] Migrated from North Carolina in 1715, and adopted by the Oneidas, a related tribe.
[5] Including the area of Alabama and Mississippi.

[1] The Indian tribes with whom this treaty was negotiated were the Wyandots, Delawares, Shawnees, Ottawas, Chippewas, Potawatomis, Miamis, Eel River Indians, Weas, Kickapoos, Piankashaws, and Kaskaskias.

The names of the Indian tribes in each state and territory in 1790, together with the approximate numbers in the various tribes, so far as they can be determined, are shown in the list on page 39.

The law authorizing the first Federal census made no provision for the enumeration of any Indians except those who were taxed; and there were probably but few who were included in that category. The best information available concerning the number of Indians within the United States in 1790 is the estimate of Gen. Henry Knox, Secretary of War under President Washington, who placed the total Indian population in 1789 at 76,000. Of this number he located 20,000 between the Great Lakes and the Ohio river, and 56,000 south of the Ohio and east of the Mississippi. The warriors—or gun men, as they were termed at that time—were assumed to represent one-fourth of the total Indian population.

The following paragraphs present, for some of the states and territories, facts which are of interest but could not readily be incorporated in the foregoing list:

Maine.—The Provincial Congress of Massachusetts had reserved to the Penobscot tribe a tract of land 12 miles wide, intersected by the Penobscot river. The tribe, numbering about 100 families, was settled along the banks of the river from the head of tide water northward. Their principal town was Indian Old Town, situated on an island of about 200 acres in the Penobscot river, 12 miles north of Bangor. It is probable that the vast wilderness in that part of Maine north and west of the narrow inhabited strip along the coast supported numbers of Indians, many of whom doubtless roamed at will across the Canadian border, as whim or scarcity of food determined.

Massachusetts.—In this state there were still a few hundred Indians. Along the coast of Cape Cod they remained, notwithstanding their small numbers, in comparatively undisturbed possession of considerable areas.

New York.—From the Mohawk valley westward, some remnants remained of the once powerful Six Nations of the Iroquois. The state authorities of New York had made treaties with these Indians, and had reserved to them certain restricted areas. The Oneidas were located on Oneida creek, 21 miles west of Fort Stanwix; with them resided the remnants of the Tuscaroras and Mohegans. Most of the Senecas dwelt along the Genesee river. One family only of the Mohawks was known to be living in New York in 1790, the remainder of the tribe having migrated to Canada. The Onondagas were located on Onondaga Lake, the Cayugas on Cayuga Lake, while the Delawares, like the Mohawks, were practically extinct in this state.

New Jersey.—In this state there were probably not more than one hundred Indians all told. About half of these were located on a state reservation at Evesham, called "Brotherton;" the remainder were scattered through the state, many of them being held as slaves. In 1801 the Brotherton Indians were invited by the Mohegans to locate with them at Stockbridge, near Oneida Lake, New York, and the invitation was accepted.[1]

Pennsylvania.—In addition to the remnants of three tribes living on the north branch of the Susquehanna river, there were probably roving bands from the Iroquois tribes in the northwestern portion of the state.

South Carolina.—The Catawbas, descendants of a once powerful tribe, had become degenerate from contact and association with the whites. They owned a tract 15 miles square, lying on both sides of the Catawba river; a part of this land they had leased to the whites for a period of ninety-nine years.

Northwest Territory.—W. Winterbotham, in a "View of the United States of America" (1796), estimated the number of Indians in this territory in 1792 at 65,000. The tribes inhabiting the territory he enumerated as "the Piantias, on both sides of the Mississippi; the Casquerasquias, on the Illinois; the Piankashaws and other tribes, on the Wabash; the Shawanese, on the Scioto; the Delawares, the Miamis, the Ouiscons, Mascoutens, Sakies, Sioux, Mekekonakis, Pilans, Powtowatamis, Messaques, Ottawas, Chipewas, and Wiandots."

Incited by the British and French on the north, these Indians kept up almost continual warfare against the settlers. In the vicinity of the Wabash were several warlike tribes which made frequent incursions across the Ohio into Kentucky, killing cattle and horses and murdering the inhabitants; by their hostile attitude these Indians deflected southward, to the valley of the Ohio and especially to Kentucky, the stream of migration from New York and Pennsylvania to the West.

Southwest Territory (including area of Alabama and Mississippi).—As already stated, the tribes of greatest numerical importance in 1790 inhabited the southern and southwestern portion of the Republic. Among these were the Creeks, Cherokees, Choctaws, and Chickasaws.

The Upper Creeks dwelt principally on the upper waters of the Alabama and the Lower Creeks on the Apalachicola and on its two branches, the Chattahoochee and the Flint; the Seminoles, a branch of the Lower Creeks, extended into Florida. In 1789 the number of warriors in the whole Creek nation was estimated not to exceed 4,500, and the number of women, children, and old men 18,000; the Lower Creeks were rather more numerous than the related Seminole tribe, and these two together about equaled the Upper Creeks in number. The towns or subtribes of the Creeks, including both divisions of the nation, were about eighty in number, but differed widely in population and importance. A few towns,

---

[1] William Nelson: Indians of New Jersey, pages 118 and 119.

called "mother towns," had the principal direction of affairs.

Though the Creeks were in a great measure hunters, they possessed cattle, horses, and a few slaves, cultivated some Indian corn and potatoes, and in some instances had introduced the plow. Being nearer to the settlers in the Southern states than any other tribe, they had awakened to the value of their lands, and under the leadership of a shrewd half-breed, Alexander McGillivray, they kept up a fitful war against the advance of the settlers. On August 7, 1790, they concluded a treaty with the United States which clearly defined the boundary of the Indian lands, beyond which the white settlers should not pass. Article 6 of this treaty reads:

If any citizen of the United States or other person, not being an Indian, shall attempt to settle on any of the Creeks' land, such person shall forfeit the protection of the United States, and the Creeks may punish him or not, as they please.

North of the Creeks were the Cherokees. They were located principally on the headwaters of the Tennessee river, but their hunting grounds extended from the Cumberland river along the frontiers of Virginia, North Carolina, South Carolina, and part of Georgia. Commissioners sent to treat with them in 1785 estimated that they could muster 2,000 warriors. In 1789 the number had decreased to about 600, undoubtedly as a result of wars with the whites.

West of the Creeks, and within the confines of the present state of Mississippi, was the populous nation of the Choctaws. Being far removed from the settlements on the Atlantic, they were of little concern to the white inhabitants. In 1789 they were estimated to number about 15,000, as compared with nearly 30,000 a few years earlier.

The Chickasaws, in western Tennessee, numbered about 3,500.

III. THE FIRST CENSUS OF THE UNITED STATES.

THE FIRST CENSUS ACT—DEBATES IN THE CONGRESS—PRO-
VISIONS OF THE ACT—EXECUTION OF THE LAW—THE ENU-
MERATION—THE RETURNS—THE ENUMERATORS' SCHEDULES.

The provision under which the Federal census is taken is contained in Article I, section 2, of the Constitution of the United States, which directs that—

Representatives and direct taxes shall be apportioned among the several states which may be included within this Union according to their respective numbers, which shall be determined by adding to the whole number of free persons, including those bound to service for a term of years, and excluding Indians not taxed, three-fifths of all other persons. The actual enumeration shall be made within three years after the first meeting of the Congress of the United States, and within every subsequent term of ten years, in such manner as they shall by law direct.

The debates in the Constitutional Convention do not afford any evidence that the scope of the census was seriously considered. There is reason to believe, however, that many members of the convention had in mind more than a mere count of the inhabitants. Several of them contended that representatives and direct taxes should be apportioned according to wealth as well as population. Mr. Ellsworth introduced a motion "that the rule of contribution by direct taxation, for the support of the Government of the United States, shall be the number of white inhabitants, and three-fifths of every other description in the several states, until some other rule, that shall more accurately ascertain the wealth of the several states, can be devised and adopted by the legislature." [1] Mr. Williamson introduced a motion "that, in order to ascertain the alterations that may happen in the population and wealth of the several states, a census shall be taken of the free white inhabitants, and three-fifths of those of other descriptions," etc. [2]

THE FIRST CENSUS ACT.

The provision of the Constitution quoted above does not clearly define the scope of the census, and the question whether it is restrictive—that is, whether the words "actual enumeration" apply exclusively to the objects mentioned—has never been considered judicially. But the provision has often been interpreted as restrictive, and the question has been raised whether Congress has not transcended its constitutional pow-ers in authorizing purely statistical inquiries other than those for the single purpose of apportioning representatives and direct taxes. [3] In this connection the debates in Congress on the bill providing for the First Census are of especial interest.

On May 18, 1789, soon after the convening of the First Congress, a committee was appointed in the House of Representatives to prepare and bring in a bill providing for the "actual enumeration of the inhabitants of the United States, in conformity with the Constitution;" this committee never reported. On January 11, 1790, another committee, consisting of ten members (one from each state), was appointed for the same purpose; it reported a bill on January 19.

The House debates on this bill are reported in the Annals of Congress, First Congress, second session. From Mr. Madison's remarks it is evident that the schedule reported by the committee provided for only a bare enumeration of the inhabitants.

Mr. Madison observed that they had now an opportunity of obtaining the most useful information for those who should hereafter be called upon to legislate for their country, if this bill was extended so as to embrace some other objects besides the bare enumeration of the inhabitants; it would enable them to adapt the public measures to the particular circumstances of the community. In order to know the various interests of the United States, it was necessary that the description of the several classes into which the community is divided should be accurately known. On this knowledge the legislature might proceed to make proper provision for the agricultural, commercial, and manufacturing interests, but without it they could never make their provisions in due proportion.

This kind of information, he observed, all legislatures had wished for, but this kind of information had never been obtained in any country. He wished, therefore, to avail himself of the present opportunity of accomplishing so valuable a purpose. If the plan was pursued in taking every future census, it would give them an opportunity of marking the progress of the society and distinguishing the growth of every interest. This would furnish ground for many useful calculations, and at the same time answer the purpose of a check on the officers who were employed to make the enumeration, for as much as the aggregate number is divisible into parts, any imposition might be discovered with proportionable ease. If these ideas meet the approbation of the House, he hoped they would pass over the schedule in the second clause of the bill, and he would endeavor to prepare something to accomplish this object.

The House granted Mr. Madison's request, and he formulated a more elaborate schedule. Just what his

---

[1] The Madison Papers, page 1082.
[2] Elliott's Debates on the Federal Constitution, vol. 5, page 295.

[3] Encyclopaedia Brittanica, vol. 5, page 339.

plan was in detail is not stated in the Annals of Congress, but the issue of the Boston Gazette and the Country Journal for February 8, 1790, in its report of the proceedings of Congress, contains the following:

Mr. Madison proposed the following as the form of a general schedule, in lieu of that in the bill, viz:

Free white males under 16.
Free white males above 16.
White females.
Free blacks.
Slaves.

He then proposed that a particular schedule should likewise be included in the bill, specifying the number of persons employed in the various arts and professions carried on in the United States.

When the bill again came up for discussion, on February 2—

Mr. Livermore apprehended this (Madison's) plan was too extensive to be carried into operation and divided the people into classes too minute to be readily ascertained. For example, many inhabitants of New Hampshire pursued two, three, or four occupations, but which was the principal one depended upon the season of the year or some other adventitious circumstance; some followed weaving in the spring and summer, but the making of shoes was the most predominant in the fall and winter; under what class are these people to be thrown, especially if they joined husbandry and carpenter's work to the rest? He was confident the distinction which the gentlemen wished to make could not be performed. He was therefore against adding additional labor, and consequently incurring additional expense, whether the work was executed or not. Besides this, he apprehended that it would excite the jealousy of the people; they would suspect that the Government was too particular, in order to learn their ability to bear the burden of direct or other taxes, and under this idea they may refuse to give the officer such a particular account as the law requires, by which means you expose him to great inconvenience and delay in the performance of his duty. * * *

Mr. Page thought this particular method of describing the people would occasion alarm among them; they would suppose the Government intended something, by putting the Union to this additional expense, besides gratifying an idle curiosity; their purposes can not be supposed the same as the historian's or philosopher's—they are statesmen, and all their measures are suspected of policy. If he had not heard the object so well explained on this floor, as one of the people, he might have been jealous of the attempt, as it could serve no real purpose, for, he contended, if they were now acquainted with the minutiae they would not be benefited by it. He hoped the business would be accomplished in some other way. * * *

Mr. Madison thought it was more likely that the people would suppose the information was required for its true object, namely, to know in what proportion to distribute the benefits resulting from an efficient General Government.

It is significant that in the discussion of Madison's schedule there is no suggestion recorded in the Annals of Congress that it was unconstitutional; but the Boston newspaper quoted above has this paragraph:

Mr. White said that tho' he should be pleased with obtaining an enumeration on the gentleman's plan, he rather supposed that Congress is not authorized by the Constitution to call for so particular an account. The Constitution refers only to a census for the more perfectly equalizing the representation.

This objection had apparently little weight, and the bill passed with Madison's schedule and all of his amendments.

In the Senate the provision for ascertaining the occupations of the people was rejected—on what grounds is not known, for the debates of that body at that time were behind closed doors.

In the debate in the House with regard to the time to be allowed for completing the enumeration, six, four, and three months were proposed. Mr. Sedgwick, of Massachusetts, believed that since so long a time was to elapse before the assistants were to enter upon their duties the work of preparation should be completed in two or three months, and possibly one month would be sufficient. It was argued that the longer the time allowed the less accurate would be the returns.

Mr. Madison observed that the situation of the several states was so various that the difficulty of adopting a plan for effecting the business upon terms that would give general satisfaction could only be obviated by allowing sufficient time. Some of the states have been accustomed to take the enumeration of their citizens; others have never done it at all. To the former the business will be easy, and may be completed within the shortest period; in the others it will be attended with unforeseen difficulties.

Six months was agreed upon by the House, but in the Senate this was changed to nine months. The bill passed the Senate on February 22 and was approved by the President on March 1, 1790.

Provisions of the act.—By the First Census act the marshals of the several judicial districts of the United States were authorized and required to cause the number of the inhabitants within their respective districts to be taken, "omitting Indians not taxed, and distinguishing free persons, including those bound to service for a term of years, from all others; distinguishing also the sexes and colors of free persons, and the free males of 16 years and upward from those under that age." The inquiries regarding the color of free persons, the sex of the whites, and the separation of white males into those above and those below 16 years of age were outside of the constitutional requirement of the enumeration, and reflect the efforts of Madison to obtain a comprehensive census. The last inquiry was undoubtedly instituted for the purpose of ascertaining the industrial and military strength of the country.

For the purpose of this enumeration, which was to be commenced on the first Monday in August, 1790, and completed within nine calendar months, the marshals were empowered to appoint within their respective districts as many assistants or enumerators as should appear to them necessary, assigning to each a certain division of his district, which "shall consist of one or more counties, cities, towns, townships, hundreds, or parishes, or of a territory plainly and distinctly bounded by water courses, mountains, or public roads."

In the case of Rhode Island and Vermont subsequent legislation was had July 5, 1790, and March 2, 1791, respectively, by which the terms of the act providing for the first enumeration were extended to these two districts. The enumeration in Vermont was to commence on the first Monday in April, 1791, and to close within five calendar months thereafter. By an act of November 8, 1791, the time for the completion of the census in South Carolina was extended to March 1, 1792.

Before entering upon the discharge of their duties, the marshals and assistant marshals were required to take an oath to cause to be made, or to make, as the case might be, "a just and perfect enumeration and description of all persons" residing within their several districts.

For the purpose of settling all doubts which might arise respecting the persons to be returned and the manner of making the returns, it was provided that every person whose usual place of abode was in any family on the aforesaid first Monday in August should be returned as in such family; that any person without any "usual place of abode" was to be enumerated in the district in which he was on the first Monday in August; and that any person who at the time of the enumeration was temporarily absent from his usual place of abode should be returned as belonging to that place in which he usually resided. The act further provided that every person 16 years of age and over who refused or failed to render a true account when required by the enumerator to answer questions in contemplation of the act, was liable to a fine of $20. Penalties were prescribed also for the failure of an enumerator or marshal to comply with the provisions of the act.

The amount of compensation prescribed for the marshals of the districts varied from $100 to $500, as follows:

$100—Rhode Island, Delaware.
  200—Maine, New Hampshire, Vermont, Connecticut, New Jersey.
  300—Massachusetts, New York, Pennsylvania, Maryland, South Carolina.
  350—North Carolina.
  500—Virginia.

The rate of compensation allowed the assistants was $1 for every 300 persons in cities and towns containing more than 5,000 persons, and $1 for every 150 persons in country districts; but in those districts where, "from the dispersed situation of the inhabitants," $1 for 150 persons should seem inadequate, the marshals were authorized, subject to the approval of the judges of their respective districts, to increase the compensation to $1 for not less than 50 persons returned.

One of the peculiar provisions of the law, worthy of notice, was that each assistant, before making his return to the marshal, was required to "cause a correct copy, signed by himself, of the schedule containing the number of inhabitants within his division to be set up at two of the most public places within the same, there to remain for the inspection of all concerned," for which work, upon satisfactory proof, he was entitled to receive $4.

Each assistant was required to make his returns to his marshal within the allotted time, on a properly ruled schedule "distinguishing the several families by the names of their master, mistress, steward, overseer, or other principal person therein," and showing for each family the number of free white males 16 years and upward, including heads of families, free white males under 16 years, free white females, including heads of families, all other free persons, and slaves.

The marshals were required to transmit to the President of the United States on or before September 1, 1791, "the aggregate amount of each description of persons within their respective districts," and to file the original returns of their assistants with the clerks of their respective district courts, "who are hereby directed to receive and carefully preserve the same." The total cost of the First Census was $44,377.28.

EXECUTION OF THE LAW.

Upon the President, whose duties at that period included active supervision of all the routine affairs of government, devolved the task of making the first enumeration. Just what method he followed in putting the First Census law into operation is not definitely known. It is generally supposed that he or the Secretary of State dispatched copies of the law to the different marshals, with orders to take the census; but a search of the correspondence files of the State Department, made to ascertain whether this theory could be substantiated, did not reveal any record of correspondence with the marshals for 1790 other than that in connection with the transmission of their commissions.

It has been suggested by some writers that the marshals may have received their instructions through the governors of the several states. During the early years of the country's history it was customary to transmit to the governor of each state, to be communicated to the legislature, copies of all important Federal laws. In the files of the State Department there is a record that in March, 1790, a circular letter containing two copies of the census act was sent to the governors of the several states, and it has been suggested that this letter may have contained directions to the governors to issue instructions to the marshals; but the fact that no such instructions are included in the list of inclosures given in the following copy of this letter, which was published in the Archives of Pennsylvania,[1] seems inconsistent with this theory:

OFFICE OF SECRETARY OF STATE,
March 31st, 1790.

SIR:

I have the honor to send you, herewith enclosed, two copies, duly authenticated, of the Act providing for the enumeration of the Inhabitants of the United States; also of the Act to establish an uniform rule of naturalization; also of the Act making appropriations for the support of the Government for the year 1790, and of being, with sentiments of the most perfect respect.

Your Excellency's most obed't & most h'ble servant,

TH. JEFFERSON.

His Excellency The President of Pennsylvania.

---

[1] Vol. II, page 679.

This letter does not conclusively disprove the theory, for other letters containing the instructions may have been sent to the governors; but all of the important correspondence of the governor of Pennsylvania for the year 1790 is apparently published in the Archives, and although other letters from Jefferson are included, in none is the subject of the census mentioned. In short, there is little reason to doubt that the Federal Government dealt directly with Federal representatives in the several states and territories.

The First Census law omitted to make provision for an enumeration of the inhabitants in the Northwest and Southwest territories. There is no record of any enumeration of the Northwest Territory in 1790. At that time the governor was actively engaged in Indian warfare, and doubtless it was impossible for him to undertake a census. At any rate, so far as is known there was no correspondence between Secretary Jefferson and Governor St. Clair relative to the subject.

In the case of the Southwest Territory, which was fast being settled, it seems to have occurred to Secretary Jefferson, as an afterthought, that an enumeration of the inhabitants would be of value, and he accordingly sent the following letter to Governor Blount:

PHILADELPHIA, *March 12, 1791.*

SIR:

I am honored with your favor of February 17, as I had been before with that of November 26, both of which have been laid before the President.

Within a few days the printing of the laws of the 3d. session of Congress will be completed, and they shall be forwarded to you as soon as they are so.

As the census of all the rest of the Union will be taken in the course of this summer, and will not be taken again under ten years, it is thought extremely desirable that that of your Government should be taken also, and arranged under the same classes as prescribed by the Act of Congress for the general census. Yet that act has not required it in your Territory, nor provided for any expense which might attend it. As, however, you have Sheriffs who will be traversing their Districts for other purposes, it is referred to you whether the taking of the census on the general plan, could not be added to their other duties, and as it would give scarcely any additional trouble, whether it would require any additional reward, or more than some incidental accommodation or advantage, which, perhaps, it might be in your power to throw in their way. The returns by the Sheriffs should be regularly authenticated first by themselves, and then by you, and the whole sent here as early in the course of the summer as practicable. I have the honor to be with great esteem and respect, Sir, &c

TH. JEFFERSON.

As there was no marshal for this territory, for the purpose of this enumeration Governor Blount was virtually both governor and marshal. Hence this letter can hardly be accepted as throwing any light on the question whether the marshals received their instructions from the Secretary of State or from the state governors.

The suggestion has been advanced that the First Census act was considered self-explanatory. The above letter affords no evidence that Governor Blount received any instructions regarding the enumeration other than those contained in the census act. It is probable that the marshals and assistant marshals were allowed to interpret the act for themselves. The form of the returns and of the marshals' summaries is all but conclusive on this point, since there is no uniformity among them. The census act indicated the form of schedule which should be used by the enumerators, and so far as known all the returns were made in accordance with this form, except those for Maine and the Southwest Territory. It also instructed the marshal to show in his summary the aggregate number of each description of persons within his district, but it did not indicate what subdivisions of the district should be made. Some of the returns give only the information required by the census act, while others give much additional information, such as the number of houses and of families, the excess of males or of females, and the population of towns, townships, and principal places.

The enumeration.—The enumeration was ordered to commence on August 2, 1790, and to close within nine calendar months. The census law did not require, however, that the enumerators should prosecute their work continuously to completion. The dates upon which the assistants swore to their returns indicate that many must have worked intermittently; some of the returns were attested only a few weeks after August 2, but the majority bear dates several months later.

Although the area enumerated at the census of 1790 was only a fraction of the area of enumeration at the present time, it presented serious difficulties for the enumerator. The boundaries of towns and other minor civil divisions, and in some cases of counties, were ill defined, so that the enumerator must often have been uncertain whether a family resided in his district or in an adjoining district. This condition existed particularly in the newly settled portions of the country, where the local government had not been fully organized. In many sections the danger from hostile Indians doubtless made travel unsafe for the enumerator.

The pay allowed the enumerator for his work was very small, the highest rate under any conditions being only $1 for 50 persons, out of which the enumerator had to furnish schedules properly ruled. In some cases this was barely enough to pay the expenses of the enumerator, and in at least one state the marshal had difficulty in getting enumerators at the established rates of pay. Under these circumstances, it is reasonable to suppose that many of the isolated households of pioneers were not enumerated.

One difficulty encountered by the enumerators in certain sections of the country was the unwillingness of the people to give the information required. Many persons had never before been enumerated. Some were superstitious regarding a census. An early colonial enumeration in New York had been followed by much sickness; and the people, recalling that a similar experience had befallen the children of Israel as the result of an enumeration made by King David, ascribed this sickness directly to the census. But a very much more potent factor in arousing opposition to the enumeration was the belief that the census was in some way connected with taxation.

As predicted in the debate which preceded the adoption of the census act in the House of Representatives, the enumeration proceeded more rapidly in those states which had already taken a census than in those which had not. Samuel Bradford, the enumerator for the city of Boston and some outlying districts, began work on August 2, 1790, and on August 21 had completed the enumeration of the city. His notebook shows that the work required seventeen working days, and that he enumerated on an average more than one thousand persons per day. As his compensation was $1 for every 300 persons enumerated, his earnings amounted to more than $3 per day—compensation about equal to that of enumerators to-day, and, with few if any exceptions, greatly in excess of that earned by the other enumerators at the First Census.

The enumerators published the results for their districts as soon as their work was completed, and many of the newspapers of that period contained frequent statements concerning the population of different places. The population for the whole of the state of Massachusetts was first published in the Columbian Centinel of February 26, 1791. The population of several towns in Rhode Island was published early in October, 1790, and the population of the city of Charleston, S. C., appeared in the Pennsylvania Packet for November 12 of that year.

It is probable that in all the states, except Vermont and South Carolina, the enumeration was completed within the nine months allowed by the census act. In Vermont the enumeration did not commence until the first Monday in April, 1791, and was not required to be completed for five months.

In South Carolina the marshal experienced difficulty in getting assistants at the lawful rate of pay, and the enumeration met with some opposition from the people. In September, 1791, the grand jury of the Federal district court for Charleston made a presentment against six persons for refusing to render an account of persons in their families as required by the census act, and also a presentment against one of the enumerators for neglect of duty in not completing his district in conformity with the act.[1] In October of that year the Representatives of South Carolina in Congress stated that the census in that state had been nearly completed, but that the rate of pay was so small and the conditions such that for certain sections of the state the marshal had been unable to secure enumerators; an extension of time and a higher rate

of pay were asked for. An extension of time to March 1, 1792, was readily granted, but a higher rate of pay was refused. It was stated that as the marshals of some other states, who had complained of the inadequacy of the compensation allowed, had nevertheless contrived to get the work done at the prescribed rates, it would be inequitable for Congress to make an exception in the case of South Carolina. The marshal's return for this state is dated February 5, 1792, which was eighteen months and three days after the date when the enumeration was scheduled to commence.[2]

The census in the Southwest Territory was taken by the captains of the militia, apparently without compensation, on the last Saturday of July, 1791, and Governor Blount dated his return for the territory September 19, 1791, stating that five of the captains had not then reported. From this it would appear that the census was taken with more dispatch in this territory than in some of the organized states.

THE RETURNS.

The returns of the enumerators were made to the marshals. These officials, after having made a summary showing the "aggregate amount of each description of persons within their respective districts," as required by law, deposited them, as directed, with the clerks of the district courts for safe-keeping. The marshals' summaries were sent direct to the President, by whom they were turned over to the Secretary of State, who made or caused to be made copies thereof, which were sent to the ministers of the United States abroad. The President also sent to Congress, on October 27, 1791, a tabular statement of the results of the census in each of the states except South Carolina, where the enumeration had not then been completed. The return for this state was subsequently communicated on March 3, 1792.

The First Census report contained a return of population for all the states by counties; in the returns for North Carolina, South Carolina, Georgia, and the Southwest Territory, the counties were grouped under districts. For some states the population was given also by minor civil divisions. Detailed information of this character was printed wherever the return was made in detail by the marshal to the Department of State. In many instances, however, the marshal did not furnish the Federal Government with the details which had been supplied to him by the enumerators under his supervision; consequently, for a large part of the territory enumerated, no detailed information was published—nor, indeed, has the population of the minor civil divisions within the states for which such

---

[1] New York Daily Advertiser, November 1, 1791.

[2] The enumeration, therefore, must have included some persons not in existence in 1790. It is probable, however, that the delayed schedules were from the more remote and sparsely settled sections of the state and added but little to the total population. Thus to a very small extent the census of 1790 perhaps overstates the population, with the result that the census of 1800 fails to show the actual decennial increase.

EARLY CENSUS SCHEDULES

information existed but was not published, been available heretofore to students, except by consulting the original schedules.

In Table 104, page 188, is published for the first time a complete return of the population, at the First Census, of all the states and territories by counties and minor civil divisions, so far as the schedules still in existence permit.

The published returns.—The results of the census, exclusive of the returns for South Carolina, were first published in book form in 1791, in what is now a very rare little octavo volume of 56 pages; later editions, published in 1793 and 1802, included the report for South Carolina. For the preparation of this volume little tabulation was required, and no extra clerical force was employed; the marshals' summaries were sent direct to the printer, and published in the form in which they were received, with a summary showing the population of the United States by states.

For the district of Maine the returns relate only to the total population, without any of the subdivisions required by the act. In the returns for the Southwest Territory, the white males are divided into those 21 (instead of 16) years and over and those under 21 years. The printed returns of the marshals of all the other states cover the details required by the census act as to the number of each class of persons enumerated, but do not present these details by cities and towns, except for the states of Maine, New Hampshire, Vermont, Massachusetts, Rhode Island, New York, and part of New Jersey. The printed results for the remaining districts are confined to the counties and a few of the larger cities and towns.

In addition to the information prescribed by the census act, the marshal for the district of Massachusetts gave the number of dwelling houses and of families in each city and town covered by the report. The marshal for the district of New York included in his returns the excess of males or females among the white population of each city and town for which report was made. In Pennsylvania the enumerators of the city of Philadelphia furnished the occupations of all heads of families enumerated.[1]

---

[1] Clement Biddle, the marshal for the state of Pennsylvania, published in 1791 a directory of the city of Philadelphia, in which the names and occupations of many, if not all, of the inhabitants of the city proper are the same as those of the heads of families shown in the census schedules. It is possible and perhaps probable that the occupations of the heads of families were obtained in the census enumeration for use in this directory.

TABLE 7.—POPULATION OF THE UNITED STATES AS RETURNED AT THE FIRST CENSUS, BY STATES: 1790.

DISTRICT.	Free white males of 16 years and upward, including heads of families.	Free white males under 16 years.	Free white females, including heads of families.	All other free persons.	Slaves.	Total.
Vermont	22,435	22,328	40,505	255	[1] 16	[2] 85,539
New Hampshire	36,086	34,851	70,160	630	158	141,885
Maine	24,384	24,748	46,870	538	None.	96,540
Massachusetts	95,453	87,289	190,582	5,463	None.	378,787
Rhode Island	16,019	15,799	32,652	3,407	948	68,825
Connecticut	60,523	54,403	117,448	2,808	2,764	237,946
New York	83,700	78,122	152,320	4,654	21,324	340,120
New Jersey	45,251	41,416	83,287	2,762	11,423	184,139
Pennsylvania	110,788	106,948	206,363	6,537	3,737	434,373
Delaware	11,783	12,143	22,384	3,899	8,887	[3] 59,094
Maryland	55,915	51,339	101,395	8,043	103,036	319,728
Virginia	110,936	116,135	215,046	12,866	292,627	747,610
Kentucky	15,154	17,057	28,922	114	12,430	73,677
North Carolina	69,988	77,506	140,710	4,975	100,572	393,751
South Carolina	35,576	37,722	66,880	1,801	107,094	249,073
Georgia	13,103	14,044	25,739	398	29,264	82,548
Total number of inhabitants of the United States exclusive of Southwest and Northwest territories	807,094	791,850	1,541,263	59,150	694,280	3,893,635

	Free white males of 21 years and upward.	Free males under 21 years of age.	Free white females.	All other persons.	Slaves.	Total.
Southwest Territory	6,271	10,277	15,365	361	3,417	35,691
Northwest Territory						

[1] The census of 1790, published in 1791, reports 16 slaves in Vermont. Subsequently, and up to 1860, the number is given as 17. An examination of the original manuscript returns shows that there never were any slaves in Vermont. The original error occurred in preparing the results for publication, when 16 persons, returned as "free colored," were classified as "slave."

[2] Corrected figures are 85,425, or 114 less than figures published in 1790, due to an error of addition in the returns for each of the towns of Fairfield, Milton, Shelburne, and Williston, in the county of Chittenden; Brookfield, Newbury, Randolph, and Strafford, in the county of Orange; Castleton, Clarendon, Hubbardton, Poultney, Rutland, Shrewsbury, and Wallingford, in the county of Rutland; Dummerston, Guilford, Halifax, and Westminster, in the county of Windham; and Woodstock, in the county of Windsor.

[3] Corrected figures arc 59,096, or 2 more than figures published in 1790, due to error in addition.

The varied form of the summaries was probably due to the fact that the marshals received no instructions as to the form the summaries should take, other than a copy of the census act. Most of the variations which occurred could have been overcome readily by correspondence and judicious editing, but the Secretary of State appears to have accepted the marshals' summaries as final, making no attempt to secure uniformity. Moreover, little attention seems to have been given to the preparation of the printed report of the First Census, for in some instances the columns of figures are added incorrectly, indicating either errors in proof reading or—more probably—inaccuracies in the manuscript delivered to the State Department and lack of editorial examination.

Attention is especially invited to the fact that for some unexplained reason the age classification specified under the act authorizing the census—the subdivision of white males into those 16 years of age and over and those under 16 years—was varied in the enumeration of the Southwest Territory, the total number of white males being divided into those 21 years of age and over and those under 21 years. This fact makes it impossible to classify the total white population of the nation by sex and age.

The total population reported by the First Census caused considerable disappointment. The following quotations from Jefferson clearly reflect the confident expectation of the people that a decidedly larger figure would be realized.

Under date of January 23, 1791, Jefferson wrote:

The census has made considerable progress, but will not be completed till midsummer. It is judged at present that our numbers will be between four and five millions. Virginia, it is supposed will be between 7 and 800,000.[1]

On August 24, 1791, he wrote to William Carmichael as follows:

I enclose you a copy of our census, which, so far as it is written in black ink, is founded on actual returns, what is in red ink being conjectured, but very near the truth. Making very small allowance for omissions, which we know to have been very great, we may safely say we are above four millions.[2]

And again, on August 29, 1791, to William Short he wrote the following:

I enclose you also a copy of our census, written in black ink so far as we have actual returns, and supplied by conjecture in red ink, where we have no returns; but the conjectures are known to be very near the truth. Making very small allowance for omissions, which we know to have been very great, we are certainly above four millions, probably about four millions one hundred thousand.[3]

It is interesting to note that Washington shared

Jefferson's views as to the incompleteness of the returns. Under date of July 28, 1791, he wrote to Gouverneur Morris as follows:

In one of my letters to you, the account of the number of inhabitants which would probably be found in the United States on enumeration was too large. The estimate was then founded on the ideas held out by the gentlemen in Congress of the population of the several states, each of whom (as was very natural), looking through a magnifier, would speak of the greatest extent to which there was any probability of their numbers reaching. Returns of the census have already been made from several of the states, and a tolerably just estimate has been now formed in others, by which it appears that we shall hardly reach four millions; but this you are to take along with it, that the real number will greatly exceed the official return, because, from religious scruples, some would not give in their lists; from an apprehension that it was intended as the foundation of a tax, others concealed or diminished theirs; and from the indolence of the mass and want of activity in many of the deputy enumerators, numbers are omitted. The authenticated number will, however, be far greater, I believe, than has ever been allowed in Europe, and will have no small influence in enabling them to form a more just opinion of our present growing importance than have yet been entertained there.[4]

The enumerators' schedules.—It is impossible to trace clearly the history of the original, or enumerators', schedules. The census act states that the marshals shall deposit them, under a heavy penalty for failure to do so, with the clerks of the district courts of their respective districts. The acts for the censuses of 1800, 1810, and 1820 contained the same provisions. By an act of Congress approved May 28, 1830, the clerks of the several district courts of the United States were directed to transmit to the Secretary of State such schedules of the first four censuses as were in their respective offices.[5] The schedules were kept in the custody of the Secretary of State until the organization of the Interior Department, in 1849, when they were transferred, together with the returns of the succeeding censuses, to the custody of the Secretary of the Interior. They were kept in a fireproof vault in the Patent Office until June, 1904, when they were transferred to the Census Office, where they have since remained.

Some of the volumes appear not to have been as carefully preserved as the census acts required; from some volumes sheets have been torn out and lost, while others are stained, illegible, and partly burned. In 1897 the schedules for all censuses prior to 1890 were carefully examined, and it was ascertained that for the censuses of 1790 to 1820, inclusive, the files were incomplete. The missing schedules for the states and

---

[1] The Writings of Thomas Jefferson, Vol. VIII, page 122.
[2] Ibid., page 229.
[3] Ibid., page 236.

[4] The Writings of Washington, Vol. X, pages 176 and 177.
[5] It is not certain that the first four census acts had been observed by the marshals and that this resolution was complied with in all cases by the clerks of the district courts. The schedules for the census of 1790 for Rhode Island, however, were forwarded to the Secretary of State at Washington in compliance with the resolution, for bound in the schedules is the affidavit dated June 22, 1830, of the clerk of the district court of that state to the effect that he is forwarding the said schedules.

territories included in the area of the United States in 1790 are indicated by asterisks in the following table:

STATE OR TERRITORY.	1790	1800	1810	1820
Rhode Island				*
New Jersey	*	*	*	*
Delaware	*			
Virginia	*	*		
South Carolina				*
Georgia (including Alabama[1] and Mississippi)	*	*	*	
Kentucky	*	*		
Southwest Territory (Tennessee)	*	*	*	
Northwest Territory[2] (Ohio,[3] Indiana, Illinois, Michigan, Wisconsin)	*	*	*	*

[1] The schedules for Alabama in 1820 are not in existence.
[2] There is no evidence of any enumeration of Northwest Territory in 1790.
[3] The schedules for Ohio in 1820 are in existence.

Of the schedules for all the remaining states and organized territories, those for Arkansas in 1820 alone are missing.

With a view to ascertaining the whereabouts of the missing volumes, the Department of the Interior conducted a correspondence with the heads of the several Executive Departments at Washington, with the governors of the several states, and, through the Department of Justice, with the clerks of the courts in said states. None of them could be recovered, however, nor was it possible to procure any information regarding them.

There is a record that the 1790 returns for Virginia were destroyed when the British burned the Capitol at Washington during the War of 1812. But it is a question whether anything more than the marshal's summary was burned; if the First Census law was complied with, the original returns must have been in the custody of the clerk of the district court of Virginia.

Doctor Chickering, in his "Statistical View of the Population of Massachusetts,"[1] published in 1846, states that a copy of the 1790 schedules for Massachusetts was lost in the destruction of the Patent Office by fire on December 15, 1836, and that soon afterwards the original schedules in the district clerk's office in Massachusetts were ordered to be sent to Washington to replace the copy destroyed. But the Patent Office fire here referred to was not discovered until it had gained such great headway that the persons in the building barely escaped with their lives. It is probable that all the census returns were kept together; and, if so, the burning of any of the returns would doubtless have meant the destruction of the entire series. Moreover, a report made to Congress by the Commissioner of Patents, December 28, 1836, giving what purports to be a complete list of everything lost in the fire, makes no mention of any census schedules being burned.

Fortunately, the 1790 schedules for the states which were most populous at that period, with the exception of Virginia, are still in existence; and the place of those for Virginia is taken in some measure by lists of inhabitants at state enumerations made near the close

[1] Page 5.

of the Revolutionary War. As shown by the aggregate returns for the six inquiries at the First Census, the relative importance of the omitted states (including Virginia) is as follows:

ELEMENTS OF THE POPULATION.	Total returns.	RETURNS FOR WHICH SCHEDULES ARE—		
		Preserved.	Lost.	
			Number.	Per cent of total returns.
Total population	3,929,625	2,684,499	1,245,126	31.7
White population	3,172,444	2,327,262	845,182	26.6
Free white males 16 years and upward, including heads of families	815,098	600,926	214,172	26.3
Free white males under 16 years	800,663	580,114	220,549	27.5
Free white females, including heads of families	1,556,683	1,146,222	410,461	26.4
All other free persons	59,557	38,253	21,304	35.8
Slaves	697,624	318,984	378,640	54.3

For each of the inquiries relating to white persons, the proportion represented by the lost schedules is about one-fourth; for free negroes, one-third; and for slaves, slightly more than one-half. Most of the slaves for which the schedules are lost were reported by Virginia.

The schedules of the First Census on file in the Census Office are as follows:

Maine	1 volume.
New Hampshire	2 volumes.
Vermont	2 volumes.
Massachusetts	1 volume.
Rhode Island	1 volume.
Connecticut	3 volumes.
New York	4 volumes.
Pennsylvania	8 volumes.
Maryland	2 volumes.
North Carolina	2 volumes.
South Carolina	1 volume.
Total	27 volumes.

These volumes differ widely in shape and size. The paper for the schedules was furnished by the enumerators themselves, and is of many different kinds. It varies from 4 to 36 inches in length, the longer sheets requiring several folds. Many enumerators used merchants' account books, journals, or ledgers; others used large sheets of paper, neatly ruled and folded. The headings were generally written in by hand, but printed headings were used on the schedules for Massachusetts and for one district of New York. All of the schedules for Massachusetts are on printed blanks of uniform size, a fact which suggests that the blanks were furnished or sold to the enumerators by the marshal. Most of the volumes contain the schedules of several enumerators, though a few enumerators handed in schedules sufficient to fill a whole volume. For a binding sometimes an old newspaper, heavy wrapping paper, or a piece of wall paper was used.

In 1897 the 1790 schedules were paged, arranged, and indexed by the Department of the Interior, and carefully repaired with transparent silk to prevent further deterioration.

In the returns of some of the enumerators the names of heads of families are arranged alphabetically, indicating that they were copied from preliminary notes gathered while making the enumeration. In many cases the name of a minister, as being the chief personage in a town, heads the list, regardless of alphabetical or other arrangement. Many of the entries are picturesque. Few men had more than one Christian name; hence, in order to make it clear what person was meant, additional information was often given, as "Leonard Clements (of Walter)," "Sarah Chapman, (Wid. of Jno.)," "Walter Clements (Cornwallis Neck)." In the Southern states there were many plantations whose owners were absent at the time of the enumeration; frequently the name of the owner was given, with large holdings of slaves, but not one white person enumerated. Some slaves who were living apart from their owners, either alone or as heads of households, were entered separately, as "Peter, negro (Chas. Wells property)." Heads of free colored families were often stated to be "free," as "Ruth, Free negro," "Brown, John (free mulatto)." Some enumerators obtained the number of free colored males, as well as of free whites, above and below 16 years of age.

IV. AREA AND TOTAL POPULATION.

AREA—POPULATION—POPULATION BY AREAS
OF ENUMERATION—BY STATES AND TER-
RITORIES—DENSITY OF POPULATION.

In the preceding pages of this publication the origin of census operations has been pointed out from the historical point of view, and there have been successively considered the population of the several colonies in the Colonial and Continental periods, the extent and the material condition of the Republic in the year in which the First Census was taken, and the enactment and operation of the First Census legislation.

The tables and text in this chapter and in those which follow are based upon analysis and inspection of census returns, and constitute the first systematic discussion of the results of the First Census. In many instances the figures presented may be accepted as basic, and thus as furnishing data by which can be measured the changes that have occurred during more than a century of American census taking, in connection with the subjects considered; in others they are offered frankly as approximations, substantially accurate, and bearing upon economic subjects which are of great importance but for which no figures of any kind have ever before been presented.

Prior to 1850 census reports contained no analysis of census returns. The officials of the Department of State, who were charged with the taking and publishing of the Federal census, were content to present tabulations without making any attempt to point out the most important results. A period of more than half a century elapsed after the First Census before the economic significance of census returns—the importance of which had been pointed out by Mr. Madison in the debate in the First Congress upon the act providing for the enumeration—was even partially appreciated.

Under the most favorable conditions, however, comparatively little could have been written in 1792 concerning the results of the First Census. The science of statistics was in its infancy, and analysis and interpretation of statistics were nowhere attempted. Moreover, had the officials of the Federal Government presented an analysis of the returns, the entire discussion necessarily would have been confined to pointing out the more noteworthy facts indicated by the actual census data derived from the five inquiries comprising the schedule. The chief value of census statistics lies in a comparison of the returns of one period with those of another; but as this was the first census of the United States, no comparable figures existed by which to measure change, unless the partial enumerations and the estimates of population available from the later Colonial and Continental periods be regarded as roughly comparable.

It is clear, therefore, that an analysis and comparison of the meager information secured at the First Census can be made most effective after the lapse of at least a century of periodic census taking. Hence such conclusions as can be drawn from the studies which appear in this publication probably possess greater value, because they cover an entire century of perspective, than conclusions which might have been drawn at some earlier period.

Consideration of the basic facts relating to population which were secured at the First Census confirms the belief that the returns obtained, when carefully tested and examined, supply practically all the statistical information that reasonably could have been expected of that period. In 1790 the United States was a sparsely settled country, and great value attached even to a mere count of population. But as social and economic problems grew more complex with the increase of population, the importance of detailed knowledge concerning the human units comprising the nation became much greater. Moreover, increase in wealth and political influence has created economic problems which were unknown in 1790.

AREA.

The Republic began its career as a nation nominally possessing an area of 843,246 square miles, of which 820,377 square miles constituted land area. Of the latter total, however, only 417,170 square miles are included within the limits of the states and territories which were enumerated in 1790. The total area of the United States in 1900 was more than four times, and that of continental United States was nearly four times, the total area in 1790. The enumerated area within

(51)

CHANGES IN AREA FOR ONE HUNDRED AND TEN YEARS.

CHANGES IN AREA FOR ONE HUNDRED AND TEN YEARS.

continental United States increased more than seven-fold during the century.

According to the Twelfth Census Statistical Atlas, the "settled" area of the country in 1790—that is, the area having a population density of at least 2 persons per square mile—comprised 239,935 square miles, while in 1900 the settled area of continental United States was 1,925,590 square miles. Deducting 1,000 square miles for settled areas in the Northwest Territory, which was not enumerated in 1790, it appears that areas having a density of less than 2 persons per square mile formed nearly 43 per cent of the enumerated area in 1790, and but little over 35 per cent of the enumerated area within continental United States in 1900.

The following table embodies the result of an attempt to estimate the area of enumeration within continental United States at each census:

TABLE 8.—LAND AREA OF CONTINENTAL UNITED STATES, OF AREA OF ENUMERATED IN 1790 AND OF ADDED AREA: 1790 TO 1900.

CENSUS YEAR.	LAND AREA (SQUARE MILES) OF CONTINENTAL UNITED STATES.									
	Total.	Enumerated.								Unenumerated.
		Continental United States.			Enumerated in 1790.[2]		Added to area of enumeration since 1790.			
		Total.	Settled (at least 2 persons per square mile).[1]	Unsettled.	Settled (at least 2 persons per square mile).	Unsettled.	Total.	Settled (at least 2 persons per square mile).	Unsettled.[3]	
1790	820,377	[4]417,170	[5]238,935	178,235	[5]238,935	178,235	....	....	....	403,207
1800	820,377	434,670	305,708	128,962	295,708	121,462	17,500	10,000	7,500	385,707
1810	1,699,761	556,010	407,945	148,065	329,945	87,225	138,840	78,000	60,840	1,143,751
1820	1,754,622	688,670	508,717	179,953	358,717	58,453	271,500	150,000	121,500	1,065,952
1830	1,754,622	877,170	632,717	244,453	382,717	34,453	460,000	250,000	210,000	877,452
1840	1,754,622	1,183,870	807,292	376,578	397,292	19,878	766,700	410,000	356,700	570,752
1850	2,943,142	1,519,170	979,249	539,921	399,249	17,921	1,102,000	580,000	522,000	1,423,972
1860	2,974,159	1,951,520	1,194,754	756,766	399,754	17,416	1,534,350	795,000	739,350	1,022,639
1870	2,974,159	2,126,290	1,272,239	854,051	400,239	16,931	1,709,120	872,000	837,120	847,869
1880	2,974,159	2,727,454	1,569,565	1,157,889	403,565	13,605	2,310,284	1,166,000	1,144,284	[6]246,705
1890	2,974,159	2,974,159	1,947,280	1,026,879	407,280	9,890	2,556,989	1,540,000	1,016,989	....
1900	2,974,159	2,974,159	1,925,590	1,048,569	410,590	6,580	2,556,989	1,515,000	1,041,989	....

[1] Twelfth Census Statistical Atlas, Plates 2 to 13 and pages 26 to 36. The separation into the area enumerated in 1790 (column 5) and the added area (column 8) is estimated.
[2] For each census, the sum of columns 5 and 6 is 417,170. See footnote 4.
[3] Estimated from the settled area (column 8) by the use of a graduated series of percentages—from 75 per cent in 1800 to 96 per cent in 1870.
[4] The land area shown as enumerated in 1790 includes an estimate of 17,841 for those counties of Georgia which were enumerated in that year; for all other states and territories included in the area of enumeration the total land area is used, because some portion of every county was enumerated.
[5] Excluding an estimate of 1,000 square miles for the settled area in the Northwest Territory, which was not enumerated in 1790.
[6] Land area of Indian Territory and Oklahoma—69,414 square miles, according to Census Bulletin 71—together with the area of Indian reservations in states and organized territories added to the area of enumeration since 1790—amounting to 177,291 square miles, according to the Report of the Commissioner of Indian Affairs for 1880.

POPULATION.

March 3, 1792, President Washington reported to Congress that the population of the Republic was 3,929,214. A recount in 1908 of the population enumerated at the First Census, from all those schedules in which the handwriting remains sufficiently legible to indicate that no error of tabulation need occur because of mutilation or age, shows that the official figures reported to Congress and published in 1792 should have been increased by at least 411 persons. It was possible to revise accurately the returns of only nine of the states, since, as it will be remembered, the schedules for New Jersey, Delaware, Virginia, Georgia, Kentucky, and the Southwest Territory are no longer in existence. Those for Maryland and South Carolina, although for the most part in existence, are in some cases mutilated or illegible, making it impossible to attempt revision of the returns for those states.

So far as is now known, no enumeration was made in the territory northwest of the Ohio river; in fact, an historian of a little later period declares that "the number of inhabitants in this large tract of country has never been ascertained."[1] Governor St. Clair estimated that in 1790 the territory contained only about 4,000 inhabitants, widely scattered in detached settlements between which there was but little communication, and which were so hedged about by hostile Indians that for many years their chief concern was to protect themselves against uprisings and massacres. Jedediah Morse estimated the white pop-

[1] Winterbotham: View of the United States of America (1796), Vol. II, page 487.

ulation of the territory in 1792 at 7,820,[1] scattered among a few frontier settlements and outposts.

---

[1] From the best data the author has received, the population may be estimated, five years ago, as follows:

Indians (supposed)...	65,000
Ohio Company purchase.......................................	2,500
Colonel Symmes's settlements................................	2,000 }1792
Galliopolis (French settlements opposite Kanhaway river)...........	1,000
Vincennes and its vicinity, on the Wabash.....................	1,500
Kaskaskias and Cahokia......................................	680 }1790
At Grand Ruisseau, village of St. Philip, and Prairie-du-rochers......	240
Total...	72,820

In 1790 there were in the town of Vincennes about 40 American families and 31 slaves, and on the Mississippi, 40 American families and 73 slaves, all included in the above estimate. On the Spanish or western side of the Mississippi there were in 1790 about 1,800 souls, principally at Genevieve and St. Louis. The lands on the various rivers which water this territory are interspersed with all the variety of soil which conduces to pleasantness of situation and lays the foundation for the wealth of an agricultural and manufacturing people.—*Jedediah Morse: American Gazetteer, Boston, 1797.*

Accepting Governor St. Clair's conservative estimate of 4,000 inhabitants in the Northwest Territory, allowing a population of 1,000 for the five districts of the Southwest Territory—three in Greene county, one in Davidson county, and one south of the French Broad river—for which no returns were ever received, and correcting the known shortage of 411, the total population of the United States in 1790 was 3,934,625.

Population by areas of enumeration.—The advance of population with each decade, as, little by little, vast areas of territory were added to the national domain, is shown in the following table:

TABLE **9.**—POPULATION OF THE UNITED STATES, CLASSIFIED BY AREAS OF ENUMERATION: 1790 TO 1900.[1]

AREA ENUMERATED—	1790	1800	1810	1820	1830	1840	1850	1860	1870	1880	1890 [2]	1900 [2]
In 1900............												[3]76,303,387
In 1890............											62,979,766	76,058,167
In 1880............										50,189,209	62,721,109	75,267,776
In 1860 and 1870...								31,443,321	38,558,371	50,155,783	62,689,057	75,204,184
In 1850............							23,191,876	31,260,793	37,929,731	48,222,957	58,904,079	70,867,006
In 1840............						[4]17,069,453	22,800,466	30,079,246	36,247,709	45,212,662	54,320,914	64,806,614
In 1830............					[5]12,866,020	17,019,890	22,602,175	29,232,310	34,613,983	42,807,274	51,008,334	60,823,367
In 1810 and 1820...			7,239,881	9,638,453	12,825,972	16,965,413	22,514,730	29,091,886	34,426,235	42,537,781	50,706,912	60,294,825
In 1800............		5,308,483	7,142,480	9,404,187	12,439,390	16,131,726	21,105,027	26,766,422	31,493,554	38,626,930	45,780,928	54,494,971
In 1790............	3,929,625	5,247,355	6,779,308	8,293,869	10,240,232	11,781,231	14,569,584	17,326,157	19,687,504	23,925,639	28,188,321	33,553,630
Total added area...	....	61,128	460,573	1,344,584	[5]2,625,788	[4]5,288,222	8,622,292	14,117,164	18,870,867	26,263,570	34,791,445	[3]42,749,757
First in 1800........		61,128	363,172	1,110,318	2,199,158	4,350,495	6,535,443	9,440,265	11,806,050	14,701,291	17,592,607	20,941,341
First in 1810........		....	97,401	234,266	386,582	833,687	1,409,703	2,325,464	2,932,681	3,910,851	4,925,984	5,799,854
First in 1830........				....	[5]40,048	54,477	87,445	140,424	187,748	269,493	391,422	528,542
First in 1840........					....	[4]49,563	198,291	846,936	1,633,726	2,405,388	3,222,580	3,983,247
First in 1850........						....	391,410	1,181,547	1,682,022	3,010,295	4,583,165	6,060,392
First in 1860........							....	182,528	628,640	1,932,826	3,784,978	4,337,178
First in 1880........									....	33,426	32,052	63,592
First in 1890........										....	[2]258,657	[2]790,391
First in 1900........											....	[3]245,220

[1] In compiling this table it was first determined what states, or parts of states, were included within the area of enumeration added to continental United States during each decade. The population of each added area was then compared with the total population of the same states at each succeeding census. The area added during each decade is briefly described in the following paragraphs:

1790 to 1800: The five states entirely within the limits of the Northwest Territory—Ohio, Indiana, Illinois, Michigan, and Wisconsin—together with western Georgia, Alabama, and Mississippi. Practically all of this area was within the limits of the United States in 1790, but was not enumerated.

1800 to 1810: Louisiana, Arkansas, and Missouri. The rest of the Louisiana Purchase (1803) was not enumerated in 1810.

1810 to 1820: There was no new state or territory added to the area of enumeration. Florida was purchased in 1819, but was not enumerated in 1820.

1820 to 1830: Florida.

1830 to 1840: Minnesota and Iowa.

1840 to 1850: Texas, New Mexico, Arizona, Utah, Washington, Oregon, and California. Beginning with 1860, the population of the Gadsden Purchase (1853) is included with this area because it could not be obtained separately.

1850 to 1860: North Dakota, South Dakota, Nebraska, Kansas, Montana, Idaho, Wyoming, Colorado, and Nevada.

1860 to 1870: There was no new state or territory added to the area of enumeration. Alaska was purchased in 1867, but was not enumerated in 1870.

1870 to 1880: Alaska.

1880 to 1890: Indian Territory and Oklahoma.

1890 to 1900: Hawaii.

[2] The population of Indian reservations, which were first enumerated in 1890, is here included with that of the areas in which located.

[3] Including 91,219 persons stationed abroad, in the military and naval service of the United States.

[4] Including 6,100 persons stationed abroad, in the military and naval service of the United States.

[5] Including 5,318 persons stationed abroad, in the military and naval service of the United States.

Upon comparing the growth, in extent and in population, of the area enumerated in 1790 with that of continental United States as a whole, it appears that the gradual decline in the proportionate extent and population of the original area, as compared with the whole of continental United States, is merely a reflection of the growth of the added area in extent and population.

The added area had outstripped the original area in extent by 1830, but its population did not pass that of the original area until 1880. Increase in the younger states continued to outstrip increase in the older states, so that in 1900 the original area formed less than one-seventh of the area of continental United States, and its population was less than half of the total. In 1900 the total population of the added area exceeded that of the original area by more than nine millions, the excess being more than one-third of the total population of the original states at the Twelfth Census, and almost three times the entire white population of the Republic in 1790.

TABLE **10.**—COMPARISON OF GROWTH IN AREA AND POPULATION, FOR THE TOTAL AREA OF CONTINENTAL UNITED STATES AND FOR THE AREA ENUMERATED IN 1790: 1790 TO 1900.

YEAR.	AREA OF ENUMERATION.		POPULATION.			INCREASE OF POPULATION OVER PRECEDING CENSUS.			PER CENT OF INCREASE OF POPULATION OVER PRECEDING CENSUS.		
	Square miles.	Per cent area enumerated in 1790 forms of total area enumerated at each census.	Total.	Of area enumerated in 1790.		Total.	For area enumerated in 1790.		Total.	For area enumerated in 1790.	For added area.
				Number.	Per cent of total.		Number.	Per cent of total.			
1790	417,170	100.0	3,929,625	3,929,625	100.0						
1800	434,670	96.0	5,308,483	5,247,355	98.8	1,378,858	1,317,730	95.6	35.1	33.5	
1810	556,010	75.0	7,239,881	6,779,308	93.6	1,931,398	1,531,953	79.3	36.4	29.2	653.5
1820	688,670	60.6	9,638,453	8,293,869	86.0	2,398,572	1,514,561	63.1	33.1	22.3	191.9
1830	877,170	47.6	12,866,020	10,240,232	79.6	3,227,567	1,946,363	60.3	33.5	23.5	95.3
1840	1,183,870	35.2	17,069,453	11,781,231	69.0	4,203,433	1,540,999	36.7	32.7	15.0	101.4
1850	1,519,170	27.5	23,191,876	14,569,584	62.8	6,122,423	2,788,353	45.5	35.9	23.7	63.0
1860	1,951,520	21.4	31,443,321	17,326,157	55.1	8,251,445	2,756,573	33.4	35.6	18.9	63.7
1870	2,126,290	19.6	38,558,371	19,687,504	51.1	7,115,050	2,361,347	33.2	22.6	13.6	33.7
1880	2,727,454	15.3	50,189,209	23,925,639	47.7	11,630,838	4,238,135	36.4	30.2	21.5	39.2
1890	2,974,159	14.0	62,979,766	28,188,321	44.8	12,790,557	4,262,682	33.3	25.5	17.8	32.5
1900	2,974,159	14.0	76,303,387	33,553,630	44.0	13,323,621	5,365,309	40.3	21.2	19.0	22.9

For every decade the percentage of increase in number of inhabitants was less for the area enumerated in 1790 than for the United States as a whole. During the first half of the century, with one exception, the increase in the area enumerated in 1790 was approximately from one-fourth to one-third. Since that period it has exceeded 20 per cent only once—in 1880. The effects of the Civil War and of migration to the West and Southwest are shown by an increase of but 13.6 per cent for 1870. The percentage of increase for 1900, however, was higher than that shown for 1890, and was close to the percentage for 1880—the highest percentage shown during the last half century. This fact suggests certain comparatively recent causes of increase in the original area, some of which are alluded to elsewhere in this report.[1]

Up to 1860 the increase in the population of the added area is not significant, because the continual accessions of territory affect the comparability of the returns. Since that year large areas nominally included within the territory enumerated have been opened up to settlement, but the only definite geographic area added to the area of enumeration is that comprised in Indian Territory and Oklahoma. Since 1860 the percentage of increase in the population of the added area has not reached 40 per cent; from 1880 to the Twelfth Census the percentage steadily diminished until, converging from widely separated extremes in the earlier decades of the century, in 1900 the percentage of increase in both sections had become nearly the same. This fact reflects the rapid settlement of continental United States, and the disappearance of any considerable areas which could be regarded as unsettled regions. At the close of the century every portion of the national domain had been erected into states, or into territories the boundaries of which are not likely to change materially upon acquiring statehood; and these were again fully subdivided into counties, cities, and towns. In consequence, toward the close of the century conditions in the added area tended to resemble more and more closely those long existing in the original area.

Population by states and territories.—Table 11 presents the marvelous growth in population, during the one hundred and ten years which have elapsed, of the states and territories enumerated in 1790.

Attention has already been called, in a preceding chapter, to the significant constancy in the percentage of increase in the population of the colonies for nearly a century and a half prior to the First Census of the United States. The accompanying diagram illustrates this fact and the continuance of practically uniform percentages from 1660 to 1860.

From the First Census to the Twelfth the aggregate population of the states enumerated in 1790 increased almost tenfold. This increase resulted both from the contributions of the original elements (those persons, both white and negro, enumerated at the First Census) and from the addition of large numbers of foreigners arriving after 1790 and locating in the New England and Middle states. In view of the generous contributions which the original states of the Union were making toward the development and peopling of the vast areas opened to settlement (and for the most part erected into states) since 1790—nearly eight times as great as the entire area actually enumerated in 1790—this achievement, during the brief period of one century, must be regarded as a remarkable one.

[1] See page 127.

TABLE **11.**—POPULATION OF THE UNITED STATES AND OF EACH STATE OR TERRITORY ENUMERATED IN 1790: 1790 TO 1900.

STATE OR TERRITORY.	1790	1800	1810	1820	1830	1840	1850	1860	1870	1880	1890	1900
United States..............	3,929,625	5,308,483	7,239,881	9,638,453	12,866,020	17,069,453	23,191,876	31,443,321	38,558,371	50,189,209	62,979,766	76,303,387
Area enumerated in 1790.........	3,929,625	5,247,355	6,779,308	8,293,869	10,240,232	11,781,231	14,569,584	17,326,157	19,687,504	23,925,639	28,188,321	33,553,630
New England................	1,009,206	1,233,011	1,471,973	1,660,071	1,954,717	2,234,822	2,728,116	3,135,283	3,487,924	4,010,529	4,700,749	5,592,017
Maine....................	96,643	151,719	228,705	298,335	399,455	501,793	583,169	628,279	626,915	648,936	661,086	694,466
New Hampshire.........	141,899	183,858	214,460	244,161	269,328	284,574	317,976	326,073	318,300	346,991	376,530	411,588
Vermont.................	85,341	154,465	217,895	235,981	280,652	291,948	314,120	315,098	330,551	332,286	332,422	343,641
Massachusetts...........	378,556	422,845	472,040	523,287	610,408	737,699	994,514	1,231,066	1,457,351	1,783,085	2,238,947	2,805,346
Rhode Island............	69,112	69,122	76,931	83,059	97,199	108,830	147,545	174,620	217,353	276,531	345,506	428,556
Connecticut..............	237,655	251,002	261,942	275,248	297,675	309,978	370,792	460,147	537,454	622,700	746,258	908,420
Middle states...............	1,017,087	1,466,838	2,087,376	2,772,594	3,664,412	4,604,345	5,990,267	7,571,201	8,935,821	10,643,486	12,874,713	15,639,413
New York................	340,241	589,051	959,049	1,372,812	1,918,608	2,428,921	3,097,394	3,880,735	4,382,759	5,082,871	6,003,174	7,268,894
New Jersey...............	184,139	211,149	245,562	277,575	320,823	373,306	489,555	672,035	906,096	1,131,116	1,444,933	1,883,669
Pennsylvania............	433,611	602,365	810,091	1,049,458	1,348,233	1,724,033	2,311,786	2,906,215	3,521,951	4,282,891	5,258,113	6,302,115
Delaware................	59,096	64,273	72,674	72,749	76,748	78,085	91,532	112,216	125,015	146,608	168,493	184,735
Southern states..............	1,903,332	2,547,506	3,219,959	3,861,204	4,621,103	4,942,064	5,851,201	6,619,673	7,263,759	9,271,624	10,612,859	12,322,200
Maryland and District of Columbia..............	319,728	355,641	404,569	440,389	486,874	513,731	634,721	762,129	912,594	1,112,567	1,272,782	1,466,762
Virginia and West Virginia..................	747,610	880,200	974,600	1,065,366	1,211,405	1,239,797	1,421,661	1,596,318	1,667,177	2,131,022	2,418,774	2,812,984
North Carolina..........	395,005	478,103	555,500	638,829	737,987	753,419	869,039	992,622	1,071,361	1,399,750	1,617,949	1,893,810
South Carolina..........	249,073	345,591	415,115	502,741	581,185	594,398	668,507	703,708	705,606	995,577	1,151,149	1,340,316
Georgia.................	82,548	161,414	201,937	226,739	233,831	231,681	272,151	299,411	327,490	441,659	526,052	640,538
Kentucky................	73,677	220,955	406,511	564,317	687,917	779,828	982,405	1,155,684	1,321,011	1,648,690	1,858,635	2,147,174
Tennessee...............	35,691	105,602	261,727	422,823	681,904	829,210	1,002,717	1,109,801	1,258,520	1,542,359	1,767,518	2,020,616
Added area...............	....	61,128	460,573	1,344,584	2,625,788	5,288,222	8,622,292	14,117,164	18,870,867	26,263,570	34,791,445	42,749,757

DIAGRAM **3.**—PER CENT OF INCREASE IN POPULATION BY DECADES FROM 1650 TO 1900.

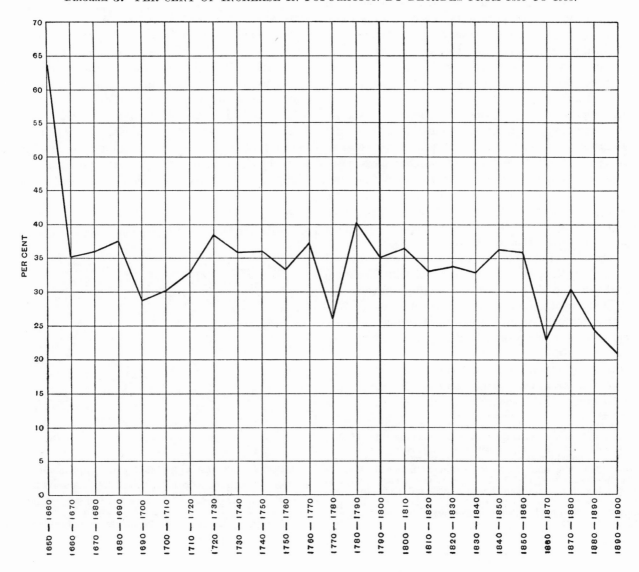

Dividing the area enumerated in 1790 into three geographic groups, it is found that between 1790 and 1900 the population of the New England states increased slightly more than fivefold; that of the Middle states, more than fifteenfold; and that of the Southern states, more than sixfold. This record of population change suggests that the most striking increase has taken place in the two states which are the greatest centers of commerce, mining, and manufacturing—New York and Pennsylvania.

The per cent of decennial increase in the total population of the United States from 1790 to 1900 was as follows:

1790 to 1800	35.1
1800 to 1810	36.4
1810 to 1820	33.1
1820 to 1830	33.5
1830 to 1840	32.7
1840 to 1850	35.9
1850 to 1860	35.6
1860 to 1870	22.6
1870 to 1880	30.1
1880 to 1890	25.5
1890 to 1900	21.2

It is significant that from 1790 to 1860, a period of seventy years, the percentages of decennial increase in total population remained reasonably constant. This is illustrated by the fact that the increase of population for the first decade, 1790 to 1800, was 35.1 per cent, while the increase for the seventh decade, 1850 to 1860, was 35.6 per cent.

Such noteworthy uniformity of increase naturally led to opinions and prophecies concerning the future population of the Republic which proved to be erroneous. President Lincoln, in his annual message to Congress in 1862,[1] fell into the error of assuming that the increase of population, because constant for more than half a century, would so continue, and upon that assumption predicted for 1900 a population much greater than was actually realized.

From 1850 to 1900 the decennial percentage of increase for the total population steadily declined, except for the decade 1870 to 1880, following the Civil War; for the last decade of the century only 21.2 per cent increase was shown. It is probable, moreover, that the downward tendency here shown has not been arrested.

Density of population.—In 1790 the density of the enumerated area was a little less than 10 persons per square mile. With the passage of the century the

[1] "At the same ratios of increase which we have maintained, on an average, from our first national census of 1790 until that of 1860, we should in 1900 have a population of 103,208,415 (in 1910, 138,-918,526). And why may we not continue that ratio far beyond that period? Our abundant room—our broad, natural homestead—is our ample resource. * * * Our country may be as populous as Europe now is at some point between 1920 and 1930—say about 1925—our territory, at 73⅓ persons to the square mile, being of capacity to contain 217,186,000"—*Messages of the Presidents, Vol. VI, pages 138, 139.*

density of the same area has increased practically ninefold, and that of continental United States as a whole has nearly trebled.

TABLE 12.—*Density of population per square mile: 1790 and 1900.*

	1790	1900
Continental United States	9.4	25.6
Area enumerated in 1790	9.4	80.4
New England states	16.3	90.2
Maine	3.2	23.2
New Hampshire	15.8	45.7
Vermont	9.3	37.6
Massachusetts	47.1	348.9
Rhode Island	63.4	407.0
Connecticut	49.1	187.5
Middle states	10.0	153.2
New York	7.1	152.6
New Jersey	24.7	250.3
Pennsylvania	9.6	140.1
Delaware	30.2	94.3
Southern states	7.5	49.4
Maryland and District of Columbia	32.2	147.9
Virginia and West Virginia	11.5	43.4
North Carolina	8.1	39.0
South Carolina	8.3	44.4
Georgia[1]	4.6	35.9
Kentucky	1.8	53.7
Tennessee	0.9	48.4
Added area[1]	....	16.7

[1] Georgia counties covering an area of 17,841 square miles were enumerated in 1790. The rest of the state is included in the added area.

In 1790 Rhode Island, the smallest state enumerated, reported the largest number of inhabitants per square mile, and in 1900 it still retained first position. But the density of this state increased less than sevenfold during the century; and that of Massachusetts, which was second in rank in 1900, increased less than eightfold. The great increase in density shown during the century for the entire area enumerated in 1790 was contributed principally by those portions of New York, Pennsylvania, and the Southern states which were sparsely populated in 1790. For example, Kentucky increased thirtyfold and Tennessee fiftyfold.

States showing density, in 1900, less than average for U. S. in 1790.

Upon inspecting the density of population in the states comprising the Union in 1900, as shown in the Population Reports of the Twelfth Census,[2] it becomes

[2] Twelfth Census, Report on Population, Part I, page xxxiii.

evident that no states except Florida, North Dakota, South Dakota, and the Western states now have a density of less than 10 persons per square mile, or, in other words, a density as low as the density of popula- tion for the entire area enumerated in 1790. Applying to the population of the different areas of enumeration in continental United States the land area of the states and territories included, the following figures result:

TABLE 13.—DENSITY OF POPULATION IN SPECIFIED AREAS OF ENUMERATION WITHIN CONTINENTAL UNITED STATES: 1790 TO 1900.

AREA ENUMERATED—	1790	1800	1810	1820	1830	1840	1850	1860	1870	1880	1890	1900
In 1890 and 1900											21.2	25.6
In 1860, 1870, and 1880								10.8	13.3	17.3	21.6	25.9
In 1850							11.3	15.2	18.4	23.4	28.6	34.4
In 1840						14.7	19.7	26.0	31.3	39.0	46.9	55.9
In 1830					12.6	16.6	22.1	28.6	33.8	41.9	50.0	59.5
In 1810 and 1820			7.5	10.0	13.3	17.5	23.3	30.1	35.6	44.0	52.4	62.3
In 1800		6.6	8.9	11.7	15.5	20.1	26.3	33.4	39.3	48.2	57.2	68.0
In 1790	9.4	12.6	16.3	19.9	24.5	28.2	34.9	41.5	47.2	57.4	67.6	80.4
Total added area		0.2	0.8	2.4	4.3	7.1	5.3	5.7	7.6	10.6	13.6	16.7
First in 1800		0.2	0.9	2.9	5.7	11.3	17.0	24.6	30.8	38.3	45.8	54.6
First in 1810			0.6	1.4	2.3	5.0	8.5	14.0	17.6	23.5	29.6	34.8
First in 1830					0.6	1.0	1.6	2.6	3.4	4.9	7.1	9.6
First in 1840						0.3	1.5	6.2	12.0	17.6	23.6	29.2
First in 1850							0.4	1.3	1.9	3.3	5.1	6.7
First in 1860								0.2	0.7	2.3	4.5	5.1
First in 1890											2.0	8.3

DIAGRAM 4.—*Increase in density in original and added area: 1790 to 1900.*

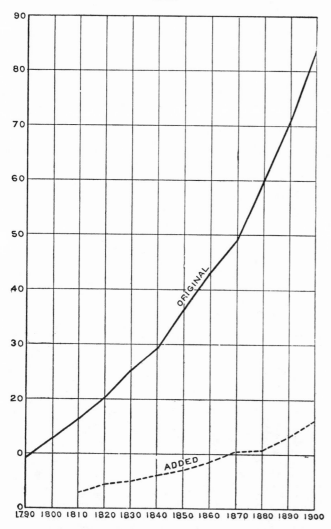

Between 1790 and 1900 the density of population in the area enumerated in 1790 increased nearly nine- fold. In the same period the density of the added area as a whole increased from nothing to 16.7, so that in 1900 it was about one-fifth as great as that of the original area.

The above table shows very clearly that detailed comparisons between the original and the added area are likely to be misleading, because of the composite character of the latter. The areas added in 1800, 1810, and 1840, which together comprise practically all of the states lying in the fertile valley of the Mississippi and east of that river, had attained in 1900 a density of from 30 to 50 persons per square mile. In Florida, which includes large areas of swamp land, the density after seventy years was only 9.7 persons per square mile. West of the Mississippi the density is not very great; but it has doubled in the twenty years since 1880, and will doubtless continue to increase.

The changes in density during the century illustrate effectively the influence of industrial development upon the growth and the movement of population. In several states of the original area this influence has produced conditions, and resulting densities, which approximate those of some of the countries of Europe. Thus, the density of Rhode Island (407.0) in 1900 was nearly the same as that of Holland (406.4) in 1899; the density of Massachusetts (348.9) corresponded with that of the United Kingdom (341.6) in 1901; and the density of Connecticut (187.5) corresponded with that of France (190.7) in 1901. Had the density of continental United States been as great as that of Russia in Europe (50.3) in 1897 the population of continental United States in 1900 would have been approximately 150,000,000; had it been as great as that of France, the population would have been more than 500,000,000.

V. POPULATION OF COUNTIES AND THEIR SUBDIVISIONS.

COUNTY AREAS MADE COMPARABLE—POPULATION OF MINOR
CIVIL DIVISIONS—NAMES OF TOWNS NOT RETURNED
SEPARATELY AT THE FIRST CENSUS—POPULATION OF CITIES.

POPULATION OF COUNTIES.

In 1790 there were 292 counties in the area enumerated; in 1900 there were 784 counties in the same area. Of the 292 counties enumerated in 1790, however, few were even approximately the same in area as the counties bearing the same name a century later. In order, therefore, to determine what changes have occurred in county population, it is necessary first to ascertain, as accurately as possible, the 1900 areas comparable with those which existed under the same county names in 1790.[1]

The population in 1900 of the counties included in the area enumerated in 1790 is presented in Table 105 (page 201), in comparison with the returns for 1790. As this adjustment has been made in connection with the classification of population by color, sex, and age, some reference to the more important facts indicated will be found in the section dealing with that classification.

The statement has frequently been made that many of the counties in the area enumerated in 1790 have decreased in population during the nineteenth century. The following analysis of county areas in the several states enumerated in 1790, according to the amount of increase or decrease, is based upon the comparable areas presented in Table 105:

TABLE **14.**—*Counties enumerated in 1790, classified according to the amount of increase or decrease of population within their boundaries from 1790 to 1900.*

STATE OR TERRITORY.	Total number of counties.	Number of counties decreasing.	NUMBER OF COUNTIES INCREASING—			
			Less than 25 per cent.	From 25 to 100 per cent.	From 100 to 500 per cent.	Over 500 per cent.
Area enumerated in 1790.....	292	10	15	51	122	94
New England......................	41	1	....	10	16	14
Maine........................	5	....	....	....	1	4
New Hampshire...............	5	....	....	2	3	....
Vermont.....................	7	....	....	2	3	2
Massachusetts...............	11	1	....	2	3	5
Rhode Island................	5	....	....	1	2	2
Connecticut.................	8	....	....	3	4	1
Middle states...................	52	....	....	2	23	27
New York....................	15	....	....	1	5	9
New Jersey..................	13	....	....	....	9	4
Pennsylvania................	21	....	....	....	7	14
Delaware....................	3	....	....	1	2	....
Southern states..................	199	9	15	39	83	53
Maryland....................	19	1	3	6	6	3
Virginia[1]..................	78	8	11	23	24	12
North Carolina..............	54	....	....	6	34	14
South Carolina..............	20	....	1	4	9	6
Georgia.....................	11	....	....	....	4	7
Kentucky....................	9	....	....	....	2	7
Tennessee...................	8	....	....	....	4	4

[1] Includes West Virginia.

---

[1] The changes in most cases have been in the direction of organizing new counties from the area existing under the county name in 1790; in Maine, for example, 5 counties only had been erected in 1790, as compared with 16 in 1900. Wherever a 1790 county line passed through a town having over 500 inhabitants in 1900, estimated parts of such population were assigned to the counties on each side of the line.

For determining the changes in county areas which have occurred during the century, three general sources of information are available: (1) The statutes of the several states; (2) maps made in 1790, or sufficiently near that year to show with reasonable accuracy the counties as they were at the time; and (3) gazetteers, yearbooks, and state histories and manuals. Beginning with the Ninth Census (1870) the Federal census reports upon population have recorded the changes made in the area of counties during the decade preceding the publication of the report. This material was useful to supplement similarly detailed information for the period from 1790 to 1860, when the latter could be secured.

The statutes of the several states must be accepted as the most reliable source of information for this analysis. In cases where natural boundaries, such as rivers, bays, mountain ridges, etc., are specified as county limits, these can be readily located upon recent maps, and hence the county boundaries as they existed in 1790 can easily be determined. Such natural features bounded in whole or in part the counties of Maryland and Kentucky at the close of the eighteenth century. For these states, therefore, little evidence was required in addition to that derived from state statutes. In most instances, however, the statutes in defining county lines refer to landmarks which have long since vanished, such as "a stick and stones," or "three trees," or to the property of persons long since deceased, which can not now be easily identified. Determination of the exact location of such landmarks would have required much detailed research, involving great expense, and was obviously impracticable. Hence, in such cases it has been necessary to rely

upon maps of the 1790 period and upon the secondary sources of information above mentioned.

Maps for 1790, or for years close to that date, are available for most of the states enumerated in 1790. But the best maps of the period are to some extent incorrect both in boundaries and in areas; few of them indicate the boundaries of counties, and even these sometimes proved useless on account of inaccuracy. For the states of Virginia and Georgia no maps containing the county lines could be found, and it is probable that none are in existence. It is curious that Virginia, in which the oldest settlements and the largest population existed at the First Census, should be one of the states for which such important information is entirely lacking.

Gazetteers, yearbooks, and state histories and manuals proved useful as guides and as a secondary source of information, and data thus secured were freely used as a basis for constructing county lines where more direct evidence was lacking or could not be secured without great expenditure of clerical labor. A few of the state manuals contain carefully compiled data recording all changes in the areas of counties; for example, the manual of the state of Massachusetts specifies the date of transfer of all towns or parts of towns from one county to another. But in general, publications of this character contain merely a list of the counties, with the date of formation and the county or counties from which formed. Such information proved helpful, however, because it facilitated the work of combining the 1900 counties, or parts of counties, which were formed from any county enumerated in 1790. It was also useful in verifying the boundaries shown in maps and in making clear some of the lines specified in the statutes.

From this explanation of the method of procedure adopted, it is obvious that absolute accuracy has not been secured in the attempt to obtain comparable areas at the first and last censuses. But for the desired purpose—that of establishing a reasonable basis of comparison—the county lines, as shown in the accompanying maps and utilized in the tables, are without question sufficiently accurate.

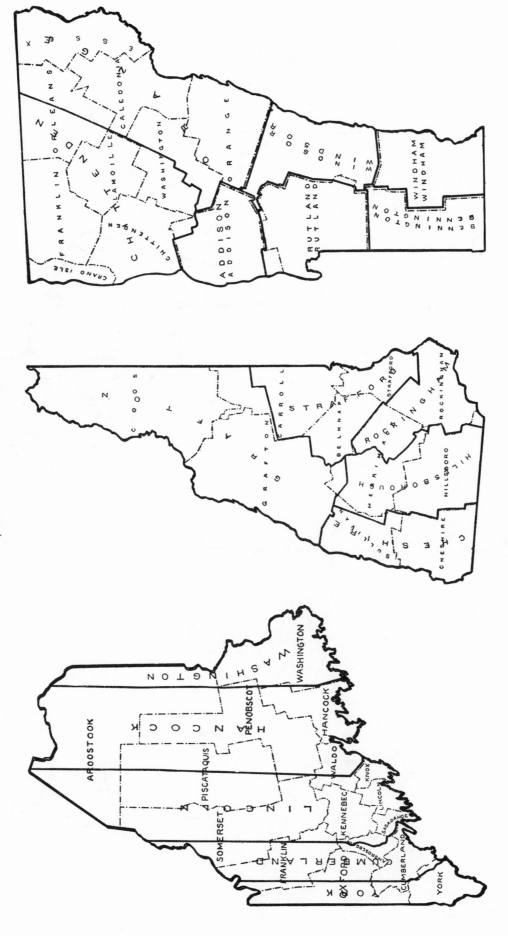

MAINE, NEW HAMPSHIRE, AND VERMONT—CHANGES IN COUNTY LINES: 1790 AND 1900.

(Solid lines indicate 1790 boundaries.)

MASSACHUSETTS, CONNECTICUT, AND RHODE ISLAND—CHANGES IN COUNTY LINES: 1790 AND 1900.

(Solid lines indicate 1790 boundaries.)

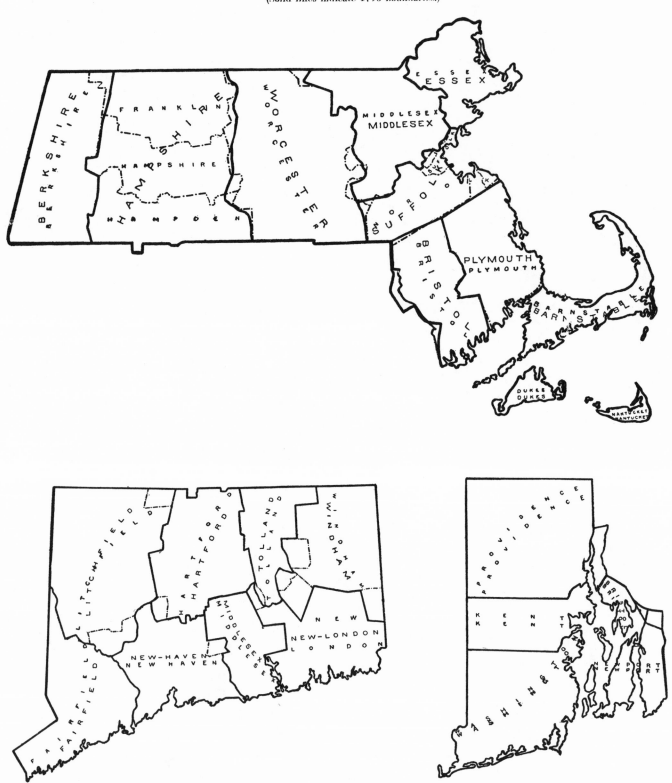

NEW YORK—CHANGES IN COUNTY LINES: 1790 AND 1900.

(Solid lines indicate 1790 boundaries.)

CLINTON

FRANKLIN

CLINTON

ESSEX

ST. LAWRENCE

WARREN

WASHINGTON

WASHINGTON

SARATOGA

RENSSELAER

HAMILTON

FULTON

MONTGOMERY

SCHENECTADY

ALBANY

COLUMBIA

COLUMBIA

GREENE

RENSSELAER

JEFFERSON

HERKIMER

LEWIS

ONEIDA

MONTGOMERY

SCHOHARIE

DELAWARE

ULSTER

PUTNAM

DUTCHESS

WESTCHESTER

WESTCHESTER

ROCKLAND

SULLIVAN

ORANGE

ORANGE

OSWEGO

MADISON

ONONDAGA

CORTLAND

CHENANGO

OTSEGO

BROOME

TIOGA

CAYUGA

TOMPKINS

SCHUYLER

CHEMUNG

SENECA

YATES

WAYNE

ONTARIO

STEUBEN

MONROE

LIVINGSTON

ORLEANS

GENESEE

WYOMING

ALLEGANY

NIAGARA

ERIE

CATTARAUGUS

MONTGOMERY

CHAUTAUQUA

SUFFOLK

SUFFOLK

NASSAU

QUEENS

QUEENS

NEW YORK

NEW YORK

KINGS

KINGS

RICHMOND

RICHMOND

NEW JERSEY—CHANGES IN COUNTY LINES: 1790 AND 1900.

(Solid lines indicate 1790 boundaries.)

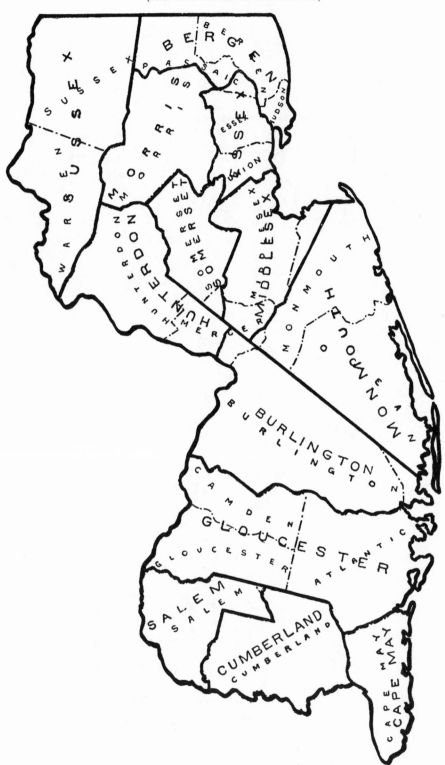

PENNSYLVANIA—CHANGES IN COUNTY LINES: 1790 AND 1900.

(Solid lines indicate 1790 boundaries.)

MARYLAND AND DELAWARE—CHANGES IN COUNTY LINES: 1790 AND 1900.

(Solid lines indicate 1790 boundaries.)

VIRGINIA AND WEST VIRGINIA—CHANGES IN COUNTY LINES: 1790 AND 1900.

(Solid lines indicate 1790 boundaries.)

NORTH CAROLINA AND SOUTH CAROLINA—CHANGES IN COUNTY LINES: 1790 AND 1900.

(Solid lines indicate 1790 boundaries.)

GEORGIA—CHANGES IN COUNTY LINES: 1790 AND 1900.

(Solid lines indicate 1790 boundaries.)

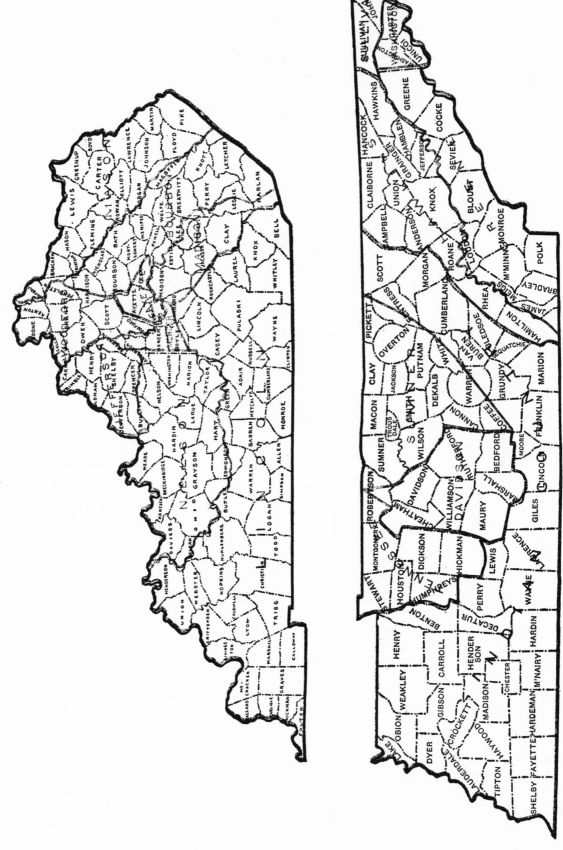

KENTUCKY AND TENNESSEE—CHANGES IN COUNTY LINES: 1790 AND 1900.

(Solid lines indicate 1790 boundaries.)

Upon this basis, which is obviously the only correct method of analysis, decreases are shown for only 1 county in New England (Nantucket Island), 1 in Maryland, and 8 in Virginia. In other words, of the county areas enumerated in 1790 only about 3 per cent showed a decrease during the century which has elapsed since the First Census. On the other hand, approximately three-fourths of the entire number have increased much more than 100 per cent, and about one-third showed a population increase of over 500 per cent.

One hundred and forty-eight counties in the area enumerated in 1790 reported a maximum population at some year since 1850 but prior to 1900, without having undergone any change of area sufficient to explain the lower figure. The following table shows that in the aggregate the maximum population of these counties exceeded their population in 1900 by 244,763, or 7.8 per cent. This fact is shown graphically in the map on the next page.

TABLE 15.—NUMBER OF COUNTIES IN AREA ENUMERATED IN 1790 REACHING MAXIMUM POPULATION PRIOR TO 1900, WITH THE POPULATION IN 1900, AND THE AGGREGATE MAXIMUM POPULATION OF SUCH COUNTIES.

STATE OR TERRITORY.	Number of counties.	Population in 1900.	Aggregate maximum population.	NUMBER OF COUNTIES REACHING MAXIMUM POPULATION IN—				
				1850	1860	1870	1880	1890
Area enumerated in 1790	148	3,152,070	3,396,833	11	15	9	66	47
New England	24	564,738	637,605	5	6	4	3	6
Maine	8	216,362	244,613		3	3	2	
New Hampshire	3	54,430	60,161	1	1			1
Vermont	10	238,591	263,308	3	1	1	1	4
Massachusetts	2	30,832	44,442	1	1			
Rhode Island								
Connecticut	1	24,523	25,081					1
Middle states	43	1,467,648	1,571,390	3	2	3	24	11
New York	25	958,851	1,032,815	3	2	3	13	4
New Jersey	1	34,507	38,570				1	
Pennsylvania	16	441,528	467,131				9	7
Delaware	1	32,762	32,874				1	
Southern states	81	1,119,684	1,187,838	3	7	2	39	30
Maryland	5	99,180	104,444				4	1
Virginia	29	339,716	366,970	2	7		15	5
West Virginia								
North Carolina	9	145,881	153,874				2	7
South Carolina								
Georgia	16	168,184	177,852	1		1	8	6
Kentucky	13	188,678	198,094			1	5	7
Tennessee	9	178,045	186,604				5	4

The preponderance of maximum population at the Tenth Census was probably due to the fact that the agricultural prosperity of the original area of the United States reached its highest point about 1880; after that date the competition of the West in agricultural products became rapidly greater, thus increasing the problems of the eastern farmer, and offering added inducements for removal to more favored sections or for migration to cities.

The following table presents a classification of counties by specified sizes at intervals of practically half a century:

TABLE 16.—COUNTIES IN THE UNITED STATES GROUPED ACCORDING TO SIZE AS MEASURED BY POPULATION, WITH NUMBER AND PROPORTION OF POPULATION IN EACH GROUP: 1790, 1850, AND 1900.[1]

LIMITS OF POPULATION.	1790			1850						1900					
				For total area.			For area enumerated at First Census.			For total area.			For area enumerated at First Census.		
	Counties.	Population.		Counties.	Population.		Counties.	Population.		Counties.	Population.		Counties.	Population.	
		Number.	Per cent of total.		Number.	Per cent of total.		Number.	Per cent of total.		Number.	Per cent of total.		Number.	Per cent of total.
All counties	292	3,929,625	100.0	1,621	23,191,876	100.0	749	15,203,618	100.0	2,713	72,682,620	100.0	784	32,423,487	100.0
Less than 5,000	42	136,755	3.5	436	1,149,920	5.0	71	257,604	1.7	375	979,745	1.3	18	77,237	0.2
5,000 to 10,000	106	779,720	19.8	428	3,130,978	13.5	214	1,596,663	10.5	397	3,072,602	4.2	107	845,122	2.6
10,000 to 15,000	56	690,538	17.6	303	3,748,171	16.2	168	2,086,184	13.7	417	5,210,957	7.2	127	1,579,431	4.9
15,000 to 20,000	38	662,499	16.9	150	2,604,223	11.2	76	1,310,572	8.6	459	7,990,377	11.0	141	2,450,495	7.6
20,000 to 25,000	14	312,774	8.0	91	2,011,408	8.7	59	1,307,537	8.6	304	6,784,301	9.3	83	1,862,318	5.7
25,000 to 30,000	11	310,250	7.9	66	1,801,368	7.8	39	1,061,812	7.0	219	6,002,795	8.3	67	1,831,416	5.6
30,000 to 40,000	15	509,681	13.0	62	2,133,465	9.2	45	1,574,383	10.4	224	7,613,744	10.5	80	2,709,902	8.4
40,000 to 50,000	5	222,741	5.7	29	1,272,263	5.5	24	1,050,065	6.9	99	4,426,865	6.1	37	1,655,711	5.1
50,000 and over	5	304,667	7.8	56	5,340,080	23.0	53	4,958,798	32.6	219	30,601,234	42.1	124	19,411,855	59.9

[1] Limited to areas having organized county government. Not including the District of Columbia, cities independent of county organization, Indian reservations, the districts of Alaska, or the islands of Hawaii.

COUNTIES IN AREA ENUMERATED IN 1790, WHICH HAD LESS POPULATION IN 1900 THAN AT SOME PREVIOUS
CENSUS SINCE 1850 WITHOUT CORRESPONDING CHANGE IN AREA.

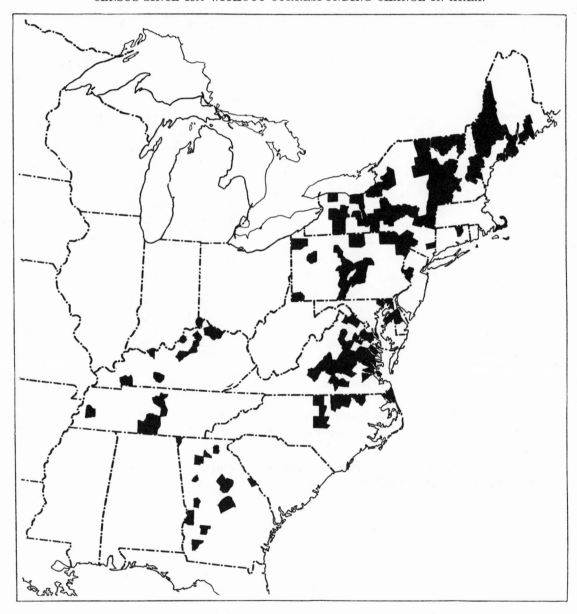

The population conditions prevailing in the United States in 1790—when the two groups of counties having between 5,000 and 20,000 inhabitants included more than half of the population and two-thirds of the counties—had changed materially by 1850, and by 1900 the class which preponderated in 1790 had become comparatively insignificant. On the other hand, the group which preponderated in 1900—that having a population of 50,000 or over, which included 219 counties and two-fifths of the population—in 1790 included but 5 counties and less than 10 per cent of the population.

In 1900 the area enumerated in 1790 contained 784 counties. A comparison of the population of these counties from decade to decade shows in many instances apparent decrease in inhabitants, but in a large proportion of these cases such decrease is the result of changes in county areas—the tendency, as population grew denser, being to subdivide large counties.

POPULATION OF MINOR CIVIL DIVISIONS.

Local organization within counties in 1790 has already been described briefly in Chapter II, in connection with the subjects of boundaries and area of the United States in 1790. Minor civil divisions (subdivisions of the counties) were returned separately at the census of 1790 for the New England states and for a portion of the Middle states, but not for any Southern state. This makes the county the smallest unit available for comparison when the entire Republic is considered.

In 1790, in all settled portions of New England, the boundaries of the towns were specified in the charters, and were well defined. It was therefore natural to expect that the enumerators and marshals would make their returns by towns. All returns were by towns, except for New London county, Conn. The summary of the marshal for Connecticut, however, did not give the population of minor civil divisions in any county.

In the Middle states, except in the more thickly settled sections, the boundaries of the minor civil divisions were less clearly defined than in New England, and more unstable. The county was the important subdivision, and doubtless many of the enumerators, in the absence of definite instructions, considered a return of the minor subdivisions of small consequence even where practicable.

All the enumerators for New York showed the population of the townships under the counties. In the Census report, however, the population of Ontario county—which included all the western portion of the state—is not shown by townships.

The 1790 schedules for New Jersey are not in existence. The marshal for New Jersey included in his summary the names of the townships in the 13 counties which composed the state, but reported the population of individual townships for only 5 counties,

or scarcely more than one-third of the total number. If the enumerators in the remaining 8 counties—which were not confined to any one section of the state—were required to ascertain the population by townships, they probably succeeded in doing so with little or no difficulty. Hence the responsibility for inconsistent returns must have rested with the marshal.

Of the 21 counties in Pennsylvania in 1790, only 9 of the older settled counties were returned by townships or minor civil divisions. For 5 other counties the returns were partly by minor civil divisions and partly grouped under such phrases as "remainder of county" or "eastern (or western) portion of county." For the remaining 7 counties, which were practically unsettled, and might be termed frontier counties, the population was given for the county only, with the comment "not returned by townships."

The returns for Delaware and for all the Southern states were presented by counties only. In the South the roads were poor, even in the more thickly settled districts, and at a distance from the coast they degenerated into trails or ceased entirely, so that the geographers of that period found it difficult to construct maps which would present the physical formation with accuracy; it was not to be expected that an enumeration made under such difficulties could present accurately the population by divisions smaller than counties, even where such divisions existed. In the returns for Virginia and South Carolina the population of the most important places was appended; the returns for the District of Kentucky gave separately the population of 5 towns. Villages existed within the counties, and the boundaries of the larger villages were probably well defined. But inasmuch as they were subject to change by the local authorities at pleasure, it is probable that little importance attached to them as separate units. This is indicated by the fact that in 1790 many villages had two names, as Waltham, or Westham, in Henrico county, Va.; and also by the fact that in many cases the same village is designated by different names on different maps published about that time.

Attempts to ascertain from outside sources the names of townships and of villages or other settlements which existed in 1790 but were not reported at the First Census, made it evident that complete lists of minor civil divisions are not available for any of the Southern states. For Virginia it was possible to compile from a contemporary history a reasonably accurate list of settlements which were in existence in 1790; but the lack of such lists for other states, and the difficulty in securing information upon this subject, justify the inclusion in this publication of the following lists of minor civil divisions, which were compiled, after considerable inquiry and research, from the principal gazetteers, maps, etc., of the period, and from lists of post offices as they existed in 1796. After having been prepared with care, these lists were submitted to officials of state historical societies in Pennsylvania,

Delaware, Maryland, Virginia, North Carolina, South Carolina, Georgia, Kentucky, and Tennessee, respectively. Thus they have received the consideration and revision of the most competent authorities in the states considered.

No definite information exists as to the exact legal status of the 436 communities or settlements in the Southern states which possessed sufficient importance to appear in the records of the states, thus justifying inclusion below. Some of them doubtless had a municipal form of government, however small their population; others may have been townships in the geographic sense, possibly without population; still others may have been settlements without any township formation below the county.

PENNSYLVANIA.

[Those counties for which minor civil divisions are not given in the census returns, or are given in part only.]

Allegheny county:
 Deer.
 Depreciation tract.[1]
 Elizabeth.
 Fayette.
 Indiana.
 Mifflin.
 Moon.
 Ohio.
 Pine.
 Pitt.
 Pittsburgh town.
 Plum.
 Robinson.
 Ross.
 St. Clair.
 Versailles.
Bedford county:
 Bedford.
 Belfast.
 Bethel.
 Brothers Valley.
 Colerain.
 Cumberland Valley.
 Dublin.
 Elk Lick.
 Hopewell.
 Londonderry.
 Millford.
 Providence.
 Turkey Foot.
 Woodberry.
Bucks county:
 Bedminster.
 Bensalem.
 Bristol.
 Buckingham.
 Durham.
 Falls.
 Haycock.
 Hilltown.
 Lower Makefield.
 Lower Milford.
 Middletown.
 New Britain.
 Newtown.
 Nockamixon.
 Northampton.

Bucks county—Continued.
 Oxford.
 Plumstead.
 Rockhill.
 Solebury.
 Southampton.
 Springfield.
 Tinicum.
 Upper Makefield.
 Warminster.
 Warrington.
 Warwick.
 Wrightstown.
Cumberland county:
 Allen.
 Carlisle.
 East Pennsborough.
 Hopewell.
 Middletown.
 Newton.
 Rye.
 Tyborn.
 Tyrone.
 Westpensboro.
Dauphin county:
 Bethel.
 Derry.
 East Hanover.
 Harrisburgh town.
 Heidleberg.
 Lebanon.
 Londonderry.
 Lower Paxtang.
 Upper Paxtang.
 West Hanover.
Franklin county:
 Antrim.
 Fannet.
 Greene.
 Guildford.
 Hamilton.
 Letterkenney.
 Lurgau.
 Montgomery.
 Peters.
 Southampton.
 Washington.

Huntingdon county:
 Barree.
 Dublin.
 Frankstown.
 Hopewell.
 Huntingdon.
 Shirley.
 Woodberry.
Luzerne county:
 Exeter.
 Hanover.
 Kingston.
 Lachawanock.
 Newport.
 Pittston.
 Plymouth.
 Salem.
 Tunkahannock.
 Tyoga.
 Wilkesbarre.
 Willingborough.
 Wyalusing.
Mifflin county:
 Armagh.
 Derry.
 Fermanagh.
 Greenwood.
 Lack.
 Lewistown.
 Milford.
 Upper Bald Eagle.
 Wayne.
Montgomery county:
 Abington.
 Cheltenham.
 Douglass.
 Franconia.
 Frederick.
 Gynned.
 Hatfield.
 Horsham.
 Limerick.
 Lower Merion.
 Lower Salford.
 Marlborough.
 Montgomery.
 Moreland.
 New Hanover.
 Norriton.
 Perkiomen.
 Plymouth.
 Providence.
 Springfield.
 Toamencing.

Montgomery county—Cont'd.
 Upper Dublin.
 Upper Hanover.
 Upper Merion.
 Upper Salford.
 Whitemarsh.
 Whitepaine.
 Worcester.
Northumberland county:
 Augusta.
 Bald Eagle.
 Beaver Dam.
 Buffaloe.
 Catawessy.
 Chilisquaque.
 Derry.
 Fishing Creek.
 Loyalsock.
 Lycoming.
 Mahoning.
 Mahonoy.
 Muncy.
 Nepanese.
 Penn's.
 Pine Creek.
 Point.
 Potters.
 Shamokin.
 Turbut.
 Washington.
 Whitedeer.
Washington county:
 Amyell.
 Chartier.
 Coecil.
 Cross Creek.
 Cumberland.
 Donegal.
 East Bethlehem.
 Fallowfield.
 Findlay.
 Franklin.
 Greene.
 Hanover.
 Hopewell.
 Morgan.
 Morris.
 Nottingham.
 Peters.
 Smiths.
 Strabane.
 Summerset.
 Washington.
 West Bethlehem.

DELAWARE.

Kent county:
 Dover.
 Duck Creek.
 Frederica.
 Milford.
Newcastle county:
 Christiana.
 Middletown.
 Newark.
 Newcastle.
 Newport.

Newcastle county—Continued.
 St. Georges.
 Stanton.
 Wilmington.
Sussex county:
 Dagsboro.
 Georgetown.
 Lewes.
County not specified:
 Cantwell's Bridge.

MARYLAND.

Allegany county:
 Cumberland.
 Old Town.
Ann-Arundel county:
 Annapolis.
 Elkridge.
 Hitton.
 London.
Baltimore county:
 Gotham.
 Hookstown.
 Reistertown.

Baltimore town and precincts:
 Baltimore.
Calvert county:
 Hunting Town.
 Lower Marlborough.
 Prince Frederick.
 St. Leonards.
Caroline county:
 Denton.
 Federalsburg.
 Greensborough.
 Hillsborough.

---

[1] Lands north of the Ohio river and west of the Allegheny river, ordered to be sold by the state at public auction and to be paid for by certificates issued by the state and representing the depreciation of the currency theretofore paid out by the state.

MARYLAND—continued.

Cecil county:
  Charlestown.
  Elkton.
  Frederick.
  French Town.
  Warwick.
Charles county:
  Allan's Fresh.
  Benedict.
  Bristol.
  Byran Town.
  Cedar Point.
  Newport.
  Port Tobacco.
Dorchester county:
  Bucktown.
  Cambridge.
  Hunting-Creek-town.
  Indian-Town.
  Newmarket.
  Vienna.
Frederick county:
  Emmitsburgh.
  Fredericktown.
  Leesburg.
  Liberty-Town.
  Newmarket.
  Taneytown.
  Westminster.
Harford county:
  Abingdon.
  Bellaire.
  Coopstown.
  Harford.[1]
  Havre de Gras.
  Joppa.
Kent county:
  Bridgetown.
  Chester.
  Georgetown.
  Massy's Cross Roads.
  St. James.
  Sassafras.

Kent county—Continued.
  Swantown.
Montgomery county:
  Montgomery C. H.
  Unity town.
Prince Georges county:
  Bladensburg.
  Nottingham.
  Piscataway.
  Queen Anne.
  Upper Marlborough.
Queen Anns county:
  Bridgetown.
  Centreville.
  Church Hill.
  Mount Pleasant.
  Queenstown.
  Ruthsborough.
St. Marys county:
  Chaptico.
  Leonardstown.
Somersett county:
  Princess Ann.
  Salisbury.
  Trap.
Talbot county:
  Easton.
  Hole-in-the-Wall.[2]
  Hooktown.
  Kingston.
  Oxford.
  Williamsburg.
  Trappe.
Washington county:
  Elizabeth.[3]
  Hancock.
  Jerusalem.[4]
  Margarettsville.
  Sharpsburg.
  Williamsport.
Worcester county:
  Snowhill.

VIRGINIA.

Accomack county:
  Accomac (Court House).[5]
  Horntown.
Albemarle county:
  Charlottesville.
  Milton.
  Warren.
Amelia county:
  Winterham.
Amherst county:
  Cabellsburg.
  New Glasgow.
  Warminster.
Augusta county:
  Staunton.
Bedford county:
  Liberty.
  New London.
Berkley county:
  Bath (Court House).
  Bucklestown.
  Charlestown.
  Gerardstown.
  Martinsburg.
  Middletown.
  Shepherdstown.[6]
Botetourt county:
  Fincastle.
  Pattonsburg.
Buckingham county:
  Greensville.
  New Canton.

Campbell county:
  Lynchburgh.
Caroline county:
  Bowling Green.[7]
  North Wales.
  Port Royal.
Charlotte county:
  Charlotte (Court House).[8]
  Jefferson.
Chesterfield county:
  Bermuda Hundred.
  Gatesville.
  Manchester.
  Pocahantas.
  Warwick.
Culpeper county:
  Culpeper (Court House).[9]
  Stevensburg.
Cumberland county:
  Cartersville.
  Chester.
  Cumberland (Court House).
  Effingham.
Dinwiddie county:
  Petersburg.
Elizabeth City county:
  Hampton.
Essex county:
  Beaufort.
  Botetourt.
  Laytons.
  Tappahannock.

VIRGINIA—continued.

Fairfax county:
  Alexandria.
  Colchester.
  Matildaville.
  Philee.
  Salisbury.
  Shippandstown.
Fauquier county:
  Carolandsville.
Fluvanna county:
  Columbia.
Franklin county:
  Rocky Mount.
Frederick county:
  Frontroyal.
  Stevensburg.[10]
  Winchester.
Gloucester county:
  Gloucester.
Goochland county:
  Goochland (Court House).
Greenbrier county:
  Lewisburg.
Greensville county:
  Hicksford.
Halifax county:
  Halifax (Court House).[11]
  Peytonsburg.
Hampshire county:
  Frankford.
  Romney.
  Watson.
Hanover county:
  Hanover (Court House).
  Hanover-Town.[12]
  New Castle.
Hardy county:
  Moorefields.
Harrison county:
  Clarksburg.
Henrico county:
  Richmond.
  Westham.[13]
Isle of Wight county:
  Smithfield.
James City county:
  Jamestown.
  Williamsburg.
Jefferson county:
  Charlestown.
Kanawha county:
  Kanawha (Court House)[14]
King George county:
  New Marlborough.
King William county:
  Delaware.[15]
Lancaster county:
  Gordonsville.
  Lancaster (Court House).
Loudon county:
  Leesburg.
  Middleburg.
Lunenburg county:
  Dalstonburg.
Mecklenburg county:
  Mecklenburg.[16]
Middlesex county:
  Urbanna.
Monongalia county:
  Morgantown.
Montgomery county:
  Montgomery (Court House).
Nansemond county:
  Suffolk.

New Kent county:
  New Kent (Court House).
Norfolk county:
  Norfolk.
  Portsmouth.
Northampton county:
  Northampton.[17]
Northumberland county:
  Northumberland (Court House).
Ohio county:
  West Liberty.
  Wheeling.
Orange county:
  Orange (Court House).
Pendleton county:
  Franklin.
Pittsylvania county:
  Cooksburg.
  Pittsylvania (Court House).[18]
Powhatan county:
  Scottville.
Prince Edward county:
  Prince Edward (Court House).
Prince George county:
  Blandford.
  Port Conway.
Prince William county:
  Carrborough.
  Dumfries.
  Newport.
Princess Anne county:
  Kempsville.
Richmond county:
  Leeds.
  Richmond (Court House).[19]
Rockbridge county:
  Lexington.
Rockingham county:
  Rockingham (Court House).[20]
Shenandoah county:
  Chester.
  Miller's Town.
  New Market.
  Strasburg.
  Woodstock.
Southampton county:
  Jerusalem.[21]
Spotsylvania county:
  Fredericksburg.
Stafford county:
  Falmouth.
  Leesville.
Surry county:
  Cabbin Point.
  Cobham.
Washington county:
  Abingdon.
Westmoreland county:
  Kinsale.
  Westmoreland (Court House).
Wood county:
  Belleville.
York county:
  York Town.
County not specified:
  Goldson's.
  Harris's.
  Sweet Springs.[22]
  Todds.

[1] Also called Bush Town.
[2] Now Hambleton.
[3] Also called Hagerstown.
[4] Also called Funk's town.
[5] Also called Drummondstown.
[6] Also called Mecklenburg.
[7] Originally called New Hope.
[8] Also called Marysville.
[9] Formerly called Fairfax.

[10] Also called Newtown.
[11] Also called Banister.
[12] Once called Page's Warehouse.
[13] Also called Waltham.
[14] County seat was later Charleston.
[15] Also called West Point.

[16] Now Boydton.
[17] Now called Eastville.
[18] Now Chatham.
[19] Now Warsaw.
[20] Now Harrisonburg.
[21] Now Courtland.
[22] Later called Fontville.

NORTH CAROLINA.

Anson county:
  Anson C. H.
  Wadesborough.
Beaufort county:
  Washington.
  Woodstock.
Bertie county:
  Windsor.
Bladen county:
  Elizabeth-Town.
Brunswick county:
  Brunswick.
  Charlotteburg.
  Clarendon.
  Old Town.
  Smithville.
Burke county:
  Morganton.
Camden county:
  Indian Town.
  Jonesborough.
  Sawyer's Ferry.
Carteret county:
  Beaufort.
Caswell county:
  Leesburg.
Chatham county:
  Campbelltown.
  Chatham C. H.
  Pittsborough.
Chowan county:
  Edenton.
Craven county:
  Newbern.
Cumberland county:
  Averysborough.
  Fayetteville.
Currituck county:
  Currituck C. H.
Dobbs county:
  Kingston.
Duplin county:
  Cross-Roads.
  Duplin C. H.
  Sarecto.
Edgecombe county:
  Tarborough.
Franklin county:
  Louisburg.
Granville county:
  Oxford.
  Williamsborough.
Guilford county:
  Bells Mills.
  Martinville.
  New Garden.
Halifax county:
  Blountsville.
  Halifax.
  Scotland Neck.
Hertford county:
  Murfreesborough.
  Princeton.
  Winton.
Iredell county:
  Iredell C. H.
Johnston county:
  Smithfield.
Jones county:
  Trenton.
Lincoln county:
  Lincolnton.

Martin county:
  Williamston.
Mecklenburg county:
  Charlotte C. H.
Montgomery county:
  Montgomery C. H.
  Stokes.
Moore county:
  Alfordstown.
  Moore C. H.
Nash county:
  Nash C. H.
New Hanover county:
  Exeter.
  South Washington.
  Wilmington.
Onslow county:
  Swannsborough.
Orange county:
  Chapel-Hill.
  Hillsborough.
Pasquotank county:
  Nixonton.
Perquimans county:
  Hertford.
Pitt county:
  Greenville.
  Martinsborough.
Randolph county:
  Randolph C. H.
Richmond county:
  Richmond C. H.
Robeson county:
  Lumberton.
Rockingham county:
  Rockingham C. H.
Rowan county:
  Salisbury.
Rutherford county:
  Rutherford.
Sampson county:
  Sampson C. H.
Stokes county:
  Bethabara.
  Bethania.
  Friedburg
  Friedland.
  Germanton.
  Salem.
  Unitas (at head of Gargal's Creek).
Surry county:
  Hope.
  Huntsville.
  Rockford.
Tyrrell county:
  Plymouth.
Wake county:
  Raleigh.
Warren county:
  Warrenton.
Wayne county:
  Waynesborough.
Wilkes county:
  Wilkes.
County not specified:
  Hogantown.
  Mount Tizrah.
  Richland.

SOUTH CAROLINA.

Abbeville county:
  Abbeville Court House.
Beaufort district:
  Beaufort.
  Coosawatchie.
  Purysburg.
  Union.

Berkley county:
  St. Johns Parish.
Camden district:
  Camden.
  Columbia.
  Cowpens.
  Rugeley's Mills.

SOUTH CAROLINA—continued.

Charleston district:
  Charleston.
  Jacksonborough.
  Middleton.
  Monks Corner.
  Wilsons Ferry.
  Wilton.
Cheraw district:
  Cheraw Court House.
Chester county:
  Chester Court House.
Chesterfield county:
  Chatham.
Claremont county:
  Statesburg.
Dorchester county:
  Dorchester.
Edgefield county:
  Edgefield Court House.
Fairfield county:
  Winnsborough.
Georgetown district:
  Georgetown.
  Kingston.
  Williamsburg.
Greenville county:
  Greenville Court House.

Lancaster county:
  Lancaster.
Laurens county:
  Laurens Court House.
Newberry county:
  Newberry Court House.
Ninety-six district:
  Cambridge.
  Duetts Corner.
  Londonderry.
  New Bordeaux.
  New Windsor.
Orangeburgh district:
  Belleville.
  Granby.
  Orangeburg.
Pendleton county:
  Pendleton Court House.
Spartanburgh county:
  Spartan Court House.
Union county:
  Pinckneyville.
Not specified by county:
  Clermont.
  Hatton's Ford.
  Radnor.
  Saxegotha.

GEORGIA.

Burke county:
  Fort Telfair.[1]
  Louisville.
  New Gottingen.
  New Savannah village.
  Waynesborough.
Camden county:
  Colerain.
  St. Mary's.
  St. Patricks.
Chatham county:
  Savannah.
Effingham county:
  Ebenezer.
Elbert county:
  Dartmouth.
  Elberton.
  Petersburg.
Franklin county:
  Carnesville.
  Eastanallee.
  Franklin c. h.
Glyn county:
  Brunswick.
  Frederica.
Greene county:
  Greensborough.

Liberty county:[2]
  Barrington.[3]
  Darien.[3]
  Medway village.
  New Inverness.
  Newport Bridge.
  Sapelo village.
  Sunbury.
Oglethorpe county:
  Georgetown.
  Lexington.
Richmond county:
  Augusta.
  Bedford.
Washington county:
  Golphington.[4]
  Oconee.
Wilkes county:[5]
  Washington.
  Wrightsborough.
County not specified:
  Abercorn.
  Hardwick.
  Old Town.
  St. Savilla.
  Talassee.

KENTUCKY.[6]

Bourbon county:
  Bourbonton.[7]
Fayette county:
  Lexington.
Jefferson county:
  Bullitt's Lick.
  Campbelltown.[8]
  Louisville.

Lincoln county:
  Crab Orchard.
  Knob Lick.
  Lincoln.
  Russellville.
  St. Asaph's.[9]
  Stanford.

[1] Now Telfairville.
[2] Part shown in 1900 as McIntosh.
[3] Now shown in McIntosh county.
[4] Not shown on 1900 maps.
[5] Now McDuffie county.
[6] Does not include 99 pioneer stations, known to have been settled before 1790; nor several others probably settled before that date, for which no data could be found.
[7] Established in 1789 as Hopewell; later called Bourbonton; now Paris.
[8] Incorporated in 1785; name changed before 1806 to Shippingport; now part of Louisville.
[9] Called also Logan's Fort.

KENTUCKY—continued.

Madison county:
Boonesborough.
Milford.
Richmond.
Mason county:
Charlestown.
Limestone.[1]
Lower Blue Licks.
May's Lick.
Washington.
Mercer county:
Boiling Spring.
Danville.

Mercer county—Continued.
Harrodstown.[2]
Warwick.
Nelson county:
Bairdstown.[3]
Bealsborough.
Hardinsburg.
Hartford Station.[4]
Woodford county:
Frankfort.
Georgetown.[5]
Leestown.
Petersburg.[6]

TENNESSEE.

Davidson county:
Nashville.
Greene county:
Greeneville.
Hawkins county:
Rogersville.
Knox county:
Knoxville.
Tennessee county:
Clarksville.

Washington county:
Jonesborough.
County not specified:
Brass Town.
Chissel.
Coyan.
Hawkins Court House.
Holston.

[1] Now Maysville.
[2] Later Oldtown; now Harrodsburg.
[3] Now Bardstown.
[4] Now Hartford.
[5] Originally called McClelland's Station; later Lebanon. Present name dates from 1790.
[6] Originally Tanner's Station.

For the northern portion of the country, it is possible to present accurately the total and average population of minor civil divisions at the First and Twelfth censuses. This is done in the next tabular statement.

A threefold increase in the number of minor civil divisions enumerated in 1900, as compared with the number enumerated in 1790, has been attended by practically a threefold increase in the population of such divisions. The average population of minor civil divisions in New England has increased more than threefold, while that of the Middle states has more than doubled. The proportionate change thus favorable to New England is explained by the fact that the population of the states in that group is much denser than elsewhere in the United States, and as the geographic area is small, and was practically all settled in 1790, the increase in the average population of minor civil divisions represents principally the effect of a moderate increase of population within a limited geographic area. In the Middle states the existence of much larger areas, portions of which were entirely unsettled in 1790, has resulted in a much smaller increase in the average.

STATE.	1790			1900			Per cent increase, 1790 to 1900, in number of minor civil divisions.
	Number of minor civil divisions.	Population.		Number of minor civil divisions.	Population.		
		Total.	Average per minor civil division.		Total.	Average per minor civil division.	
Total	1,591	2,026,293	1,273	5,500	21,231,430	3,860	245.7
New England	937	1,009,206	1,077	1,687	5,592,017	3,315	80.0
Maine	153	96,643	632	631	694,466	1,101	312.4
New Hampshire	197	141,899	720	245	411,588	1,680	24.4
Vermont	188	85,341	454	252	343,641	1,364	34.0
Massachusetts	279	378,556	1,357	353	2,805,346	7,947	26.5
Rhode Island	30	69,112	2,304	38	428,556	11,278	26.7
Connecticut	90	237,655	2,641	168	908,420	5,407	86.7
Middle states	654	1,017,087	1,555	3,813	15,639,413	4,102	483.0
New York	137	340,241	2,484	974	7,268,894	7,463	610.9
New Jersey	94	184,139	1,959	424	1,883,669	4,443	351.1
Pennsylvania	407	433,611	1,065	2,382	6,302,115	2,646	485.3
Delaware	16	59,096	3,694	33	184,735	5,598	106.3

The list of 436 minor civil divisions in the Southern states approximates, so far as it is possible at the present time to secure such information, to the actual number of towns or settlements included within the counties composing the states in question. Utilizing the figures for the Southern states thus obtained, the following results appear:

STATE OR TERRITORY.	1790			1900			Per cent increase, 1790 to 1900, in number of minor civil divisions.
	Number of minor civil divisions.	Population.		Number of minor civil divisions.	Population.		
		Total.	Average per minor civil division.		Total.	Average per minor civil division.	
Southern states	436	1,903,332	4,365	6,167	13,897,993	2,254	1,314.4
Maryland and District of Columbia	88	319,728	3,633	273	1,466,762	5,373	210.2
Virginia and West Virginia	134	747,610	5,579	801	2,812,984	3,512	497.8
North Carolina	88	395,005	4,489	958	1,893,810	1,977	988.6
South Carolina	45	249,073	5,535	434	1,340,316	3,088	864.4
Georgia	39	82,548	2,117	1,457	2,216,331	1,521	3,635.9
Kentucky	31	73,677	2,377	693	2,147,174	3,098	2,135.5
Tennessee	11	35,691	3,245	1,551	2,020,616	1,303	14,000.0

Accepting the number of minor civil divisions shown for 1790 as substantially accurate, between 1790 and 1900 the number increased approximately thirteenfold. This, if it represents actual increase, results not merely from the subdivision of existing minor civil divisions, but principally from the establishment of new communities. In 1790 much of the territory included in the Southern states was a wilderness. Kentucky did not reach the dignity of statehood until two years after the census had been taken; Tennessee, then known as the Southwest Territory, was still farther from admission to the Union.

It is probable, however, that the list of minor civil divisions in the South, while fairly accurate so far as the larger settlements are concerned, is very incomplete for the smaller villages, and especially for townships and other rural subdivisions.

It will be observed that the change in average population indicated for the Southern states—a decrease from 4,365 in 1790 to 2,254 in 1900—differs widely from the change shown by the actual figures for the New England and Middle states. In the Southern states the center of activity in 1790 was the plantation, while the economic changes during the century have been continually away from the plantation and toward communities. But if the number of minor civil divisions shown for 1790 is too small, the average population for that year is correspondingly too large.

POPULATION OF CITIES.

In 1790 there were but 5 cities having a population of 8,000 inhabitants or more—Boston, New York, Philadelphia, Baltimore, and Charleston. In 1900 the number of cities included within the area enumerated in 1790 and having a population of 8,000 or more was 286, an increase of more than fiftyfold. Indeed, so great has been the increase of communities of this size that Rhode Island—smallest of all the states— had more cities of 8,000 inhabitants or over in 1900 than were found in the entire Republic in 1790.

The limit of size above established for 1790 admits so many communities in 1900 that it seems best to consider this subject from a different point of view. The following table presents the population of the 47 cities in the area enumerated in 1790 which had in 1900 a population of 50,000 or more, in comparison with the population of the same places at the First Census, so far as the earlier figures are obtainable. Of these 47 cities, 39 were located in the New England and Middle states and 8 in the Southern states. The population in 1790 of 32 of these cities can be presented approximately; 5 did not exist even as independent townships in 1790, but were formed later from parts of other townships and subsequently became cities; 9 appear not to have had any population at the date of the First Census.

Cities having a population of 50,000 or over in 1900 in area covered by enumeration of 1790, by states.

CITY.	POPULATION.	
	1790	1900
Total..................	158,535	10,259,186
Maine:		
Portland....................	2,239	50,145
New Hampshire:		
Manchester....................	362	56,987
Massachusetts:		
Fall River....................	(1)	104,863
New Bedford....................	3,298	62,442
Lawrence....................	(1)	62,559
Lynn....................	2,291	68,513
Springfield....................	1,574	62,059
Cambridge....................	2,109	91,886
Lowell....................	(2)	94,969
Somerville....................	(3)	61,643
Boston....................	[4] 18,038	560,892
Worcester....................	2,095	118,421
Rhode Island:		
Providence....................	[4] 6,371	175,597
Connecticut:		
Bridgeport....................	[5] 100	70,996
Hartford....................	4,072	79,850
New Haven....................	4,487	108,027
New York:		
Albany....................	3,494	94,151
Buffalo....................		352,387
New York....................	[4] 32,305	3,437,202
Rochester....................	1,628	162,608
Utica		56,383
Syracuse....................		108,374
Troy....................	[6] 100	60,651
New Jersey:		
Camden....................		75,935
Newark....................	1,000	246,070
Hoboken....................		59,364
Jersey City....................		206,433
Trenton....................	1,946	73,307
Paterson....................	500	105,171
Elizabethtown....................	1,000	52,130
Pennsylvania:		
Allegheny....................		129,896
Pittsburg....................	[4] 376	321,616
Reading....................	2,225	78,961
Harrisburg....................	880	50,167
Erie....................		52,733
Scranton....................		102,026
Wilkes-Barre	300	51,721
Philadelphia....................	[4] 28,522	1,293,697
Delaware:		
Wilmington....................	[7] 600	76,508
Maryland:		
Baltimore....................	[8] 13,503	508,957
Virginia:		
Richmond....................	3,761	85,050
South Carolina:		
Charleston....................	[9] 16,359	55,807
Georgia:		
Savannah....................	2,300	54,244
Atlanta....................		89,872
Kentucky:		
Louisville....................	200	204,731
Tennessee:		
Nashville....................	500	80,865
Memphis....................		102,320

[1] Not returned separately.
[2] Part of Chelmsford, total population 1,144.
[3] Part of Charlestown, total population 1,583.
[4] Original city area only.
[5] Formed in 1821 of parts from Fairfield and Stafford.
[6] Morse's Gazetteer.
[7] Estimated.
[8] Town and precincts.
[9] St. Phillips and St. Michael parishes.

It must not be overlooked, in studying tables of this character, that the results are seldom entirely comparable. In nearly all of the 47 cities included in the above table the area has changed materially since 1790, and tends to change from decade to decade, as increasing population requires an extension of municipal boundaries to meet industrial and residential requirements.

Of the 5 cities having the largest population at the First Census—Boston, New York, Philadelphia, Baltimore, and Charleston—Charleston, the fourth city in population in 1790, alone of the 5 has failed to maintain its importance as a center of population. The other 4 cities remained leaders in population a century later, with only two rivals—both located outside of the area enumerated in 1790. Chicago, a remote wilderness in 1790 and for nearly half a century afterwards, in 1900 exceeded in population Philadelphia, Boston, and Baltimore; while St. Louis, in 1790 a small frontier settlement not even within the boundaries of the United States, at the last census slightly exceeded in population Boston and Baltimore.

Although the total population of the United States increased rapidly from 1790 to 1900, the increase of the 4 early leaders in urban population—New York, Philadelphia, Boston, and Baltimore—was relatively even more rapid. In 1790 their combined population was less than 100,000, forming but 2.4 per cent of the population of the Republic; in 1900 it was 5,800,748—nearly 58 times as great as in 1790—and formed 7.5 per cent of the national population, or more than three times the proportion for 1790.

The population reported under the names of these 4 cities, at the beginning and at the end of the century, can not be regarded as strictly comparable, because the limits of each have expanded so that they now include large areas which in 1790 were independent and unconnected. While principally open country at that time, these areas nevertheless supported a population which, if it had been included as urban population at the First Census, would have altered materially the totals reported in 1790. Elsewhere in these pages (see Table 21, page 84) will be found the population in 1900, classified as white and colored, for the cities of New York, Philadelphia, Boston, and Baltimore, computed for the areas of these cities as they existed in 1790.

VI. WHITE AND NEGRO POPULATION.

SURVIVORS OF 1790—WHITES AND NEGROES IN TOTAL
POPULATION—IN FOUR PRINCIPAL CITIES—COMPARI-
SON OF INCREASE IN THE UNITED STATES AND
EUROPE—INCREASE BY IMMIGRATION—NATURAL
INCREASE—OF WHITES—OF NEGROES—SUMMARY.

The population of the earliest English settlements in America was composed of two elements, white and negro; these two elements, though subject to entirely different conditions, continue to compose the population of the Republic, and since 1790 have recorded roughly comparable rates of increase. The following table presents the classification, by color, for continental United States at each census from 1790 to 1900, thus indicating the changes which have occurred in the two racial elements of population during the period of Federal census taking:

TABLE 17.—POPULATION OF CONTINENTAL UNITED STATES, CLASSIFIED BY COLOR, WITH PER CENT OF INCREASE: 1790 TO 1900.

CENSUS YEAR.	TOTAL POPULATION.		WHITE POPULATION.		COLORED POPULATION.								
					Negro.						Indian and Mongolian.	
					Total.		Free.		Slave.			
	Number.	Per cent of increase over preceding census.	Number.	Per cent of increase over preceding census.	Number.	Per cent of increase over preceding census.	Number.	Per cent of increase over preceding census.	Number.	Per cent of increase over preceding census.	Number.	Per cent of increase over preceding census.
1790	3,929,625	....	3,172,444	....	757,181	....	59,557	....	697,624	....	....	....
1800	5,308,483	35.1	4,306,446	35.7	1,002,037	32.3	108,435	82.1	893,602	28.1	....	....
1810	7,239,881	36.4	5,862,073	36.1	1,377,808	37.5	186,446	71.9	1,191,362	33.3	....	....
1820	¹9,638,453	33.1	7,862,166	34.1	1,771,656	28.6	233,634	25.3	1,538,022	29.1	....	....
1830	12,866,020	33.5	10,537,378	34.0	2,328,642	31.4	319,599	36.8	2,009,043	30.6	....	....
1840	17,069,453	32.7	14,195,805	34.7	2,873,648	23.4	386,293	20.9	2,487,355	23.8	....	....
1850	23,191,876	35.9	19,553,068	37.7	3,638,808	26.6	434,495	12.5	3,204,313	28.8	....	....
1860	31,443,321	35.6	26,922,537	37.7	4,441,830	22.1	488,070	12.3	3,953,760	23.4	78,954	....
1870	38,558,371	22.6	33,589,377	24.8	4,880,009	9.9	4,880,009	899.9	....	....	88,985	12.7
1880	50,155,783	30.1	43,402,970	29.2	6,580,793	34.9	6,580,793	34.9	....	....	172,020	93.3
1890	62,947,714	25.5	55,101,258	27.0	7,488,676	13.8	7,488,676	13.8	....	....	357,780	108.0
1900	75,994,575	20.7	66,809,196	21.2	8,833,994	18.0	8,833,994	18.0	....	....	351,385	²1.8

¹ Includes 4,631 persons returned as "all other persons, except Indians not taxed."   ² Decrease.

The total increase from 1790 to 1900 in the aggregate population of continental United States was 1,833.9 per cent. The white population increased 2,005.9 per cent; the negro, 1,066.7 per cent. The changes which are shown in the decennial increase of the white population conform in general with those for the total population, but the fluctuations are not so wide. Obviously, therefore, the changes in the negro population were more decided than those in the white element; the increase in the negro population from 1800 to 1810 was more than twice the increase from 1890 to 1900.

A further distribution of population, by color, for the states and territories both of the area enumerated in 1790 and of the added area, is presented in Table 108, on page 222. In order to illustrate more effectively the changes occurring in the two main elements of the population in the parent states as compared with the younger portions of continental United States, the increase in the succeeding table is shown for thirty-year intervals.

In both areas each element of the population showed, with a single exception, a diminishing increase. In continental United States both elements more than doubled in each thirty-year period from 1790 to 1850; but from 1850 to 1880 the increase in the negro element was only 80.9 per cent; and in the succeeding period the increase of the white population was but one-half and that of the negro population but one-third.

Both the white and the negro elements of the population increased more rapidly in the added area than in the original area during the period from 1790 to 1880, but during the last twenty years the total population and both elements have shown a tendency toward similarity of increase in the two areas.

TABLE 18.—PER CENT OF INCREASE, DURING SPECIFIED PERIODS, IN THE WHITE AND NEGRO POPULATION OF THE AREA ENUMERATED IN 1790, AND OF THE ADDED AREA WITHIN CONTINENTAL UNITED STATES: 1790 TO 1900.

GEOGRAPHIC DIVISION.	1790 TO 1820				1820 TO 1850				1850 TO 1880		1880 TO 1900	
	White.	Colored.			White.	Colored.			White.	Negro.	White.	Negro.
		Total.	Free.	Slave.		Total.	Free.	Slave.				
Continental United States	147.8	134.0	292.3	120.5	148.7	105.4	86.0	108.3	122.0	80.9	53.9	34.2
Area enumerated in 1790	112.2	105.6	260.8	92.3	83.6	41.6	68.3	37.3	67.3	46.8	42.9	22.3
New England	65.1	24.4	59.1	[1]96.1	65.1	10.0	10.8	[1]100.0	46.7	73.4	39.3	48.0
Middle states	179.1	70.0	375.0	[1]50.5	119.5	37.1	70.3	[1]88.7	78.4	46.8	46.4	65.2
Southern states	98.4	110.9	281.5	103.4	56.9	42.4	77.6	39.5	64.7	46.5	39.5	18.8
Added area					536.8	564.5	271.9	593.7	216.1	146.9	63.9	45.8
Northern states[2]					526.6	640.6	562.0	671.7	222.0	184.4	52.0	28.6
Southern states[2]					504.9	559.4	90.8	588.9	138.0	127.0	67.0	47.7
Western states[2]									807.9	855.0	140.2	155.3

[1] Decrease.   [2] For states included, see Table 36, page 105.

DIAGRAM 5.—INCREASE OF TOTAL POPULATION AND OF WHITE AND NEGRO POPULATION: 1790 TO 1900.

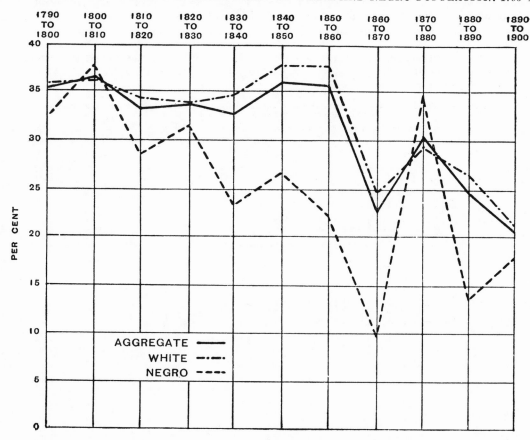

SURVIVORS OF 1790.

Of the white population enumerated at the First Census of the United States, some individuals survived to be enumerated successively at each of the censuses to and including that of 1900. Analysis of the age periods shown at each census, with adjustments eliminating persons born after 1790, results in the following record of persons enumerated at subsequent censuses and reporting an age which implied that they were born in 1790 or before:

TABLE **19.**—*White population enumerated at the census of 1790 surviving at each census year: 1790 to 1900.*

CENSUS YEAR.	WHITE POPULATION SURVIVING.		DIED OR DEPARTED DURING FOLLOWING DECADE.	
	Number.	Per cent of number in 1790.	Number.	Per cent of number living in year specified.
1790	3,172,444	100.0	380,116	12.0
1800	2,792,328	88.0	392,143	14.0
1810	2,400,185	75.7	340,685	14.2
1820	2,059,500	64.9	474,178	23.0
1830	1,585,322	50.0	455,702	28.7
1840	1,129,620	35.6	309,749	27.4
1850	819,871	25.8	418,161	51.0
1860	401,710	12.7	300,804	74.9
1870	100,906	3.2	89,428	88.6
1880	11,478	0.4	10,887	94.9
1890	591	(1)	568	96.1
1900	23	(1)	....	....

1 Less than one-tenth of 1 per cent.

The foregoing analysis possesses a sentimental rather than a statistical interest. It is impossible to present with entire accuracy the exact number surviving and thus enumerated at each census, because of inability to segregate, for any census prior to the Twelfth, those inhabitants (of an age which would have entitled them to be enumerated at the First Census, had they been present at that time) who were acquired by accessions of territory, or those who immigrated to the United States after 1790.

Since the United States antedates in periodic census taking all other civilized nations, with one exception, the fact that the lifetime of even a few persons spanned the one hundred and ten years elapsing between the First and the Twelfth censuses reflects in a striking manner the brevity of the period during which census taking has been a stated function of government.

PROPORTION OF WHITES AND NEGROES IN THE TOTAL POPULATION.

A study of the changes in the proportions of whites and negroes in the total population of the states, both of the area enumerated in 1790 and of the added area, develops some significant facts.

TABLE **20.**—PER CENT OF WHITE AND COLORED IN THE TOTAL POPULATION AT THE CENSUSES OF 1790, 1820, AND 1850, COMPARED WITH THE PER CENT OF WHITES AND NEGROES IN THE TOTAL POPULATION AT THE CENSUSES OF 1880 AND 1900.

[The free colored reported in 1790, 1820, and 1850 include Indians, but it is believed that the numbers are too small to invalidate the comparison between the negro element in 1880 and 1900 and the total colored at the earlier censuses.]

STATE OR TERRITORY.	1790				1820				1850				1880 [1]		1900 [1]	
	White.	Colored.			White.	Colored.			White.	Colored.			White.	Negro.	White.	Negro.
		Total.	Free.	Slave.		Total.	Free.	Slave.		Total.	Free.	Slave.				
Continental United States	80.7	19.3	1.5	17.8	81.6	18.4	2.4	16.0	84.3	15.7	1.9	13.8	86.5	13.1	87.8	11.6
Enumerated at First Census	80.7	19.3	1.5	17.8	81.2	18.8	2.6	16.2	84.9	15.1	2.5	12.6	86.5	13.5	88.1	11.8
New England	98.3	1.7	1.3	0.4	98.7	1.3	1.3	(2)	99.2	0.8	0.8	....	99.0	1.0	98.9	1.1
Maine	99.4	0.6	0.6	....	99.7	0.3	0.3	....	99.8	0.2	0.2	....	99.8	0.2	99.8	0.2
New Hampshire	99.4	0.6	0.4	0.1	99.6	0.3	0.3	....	99.8	0.2	0.2	....	99.8	0.2	99.8	0.2
Vermont	99.7	0.3	0.3	....	99.6	0.4	0.4	....	99.8	0.2	0.2	....	99.7	0.3	99.8	0.2
Massachusetts	98.6	1.4	1.4	....	98.7	1.3	1.3	....	99.1	0.9	0.9	....	99.0	1.0	98.9	1.1
Rhode Island	93.6	6.4	5.0	1.4	95.6	4.4	4.3	0.1	97.5	2.5	2.5	....	97.7	2.3	97.9	2.1
Connecticut	97.7	2.3	1.2	1.1	97.1	2.9	2.9	(2)	97.9	2.1	2.1	....	98.2	1.9	98.3	1.7
Middle states	93.8	6.2	1.8	4.4	96.0	3.9	3.1	0.8	97.5	2.5	2.4	....	97.9	2.0	97.6	2.3
New York	92.4	7.6	1.4	6.2	97.1	2.9	2.1	0.7	98.4	1.6	1.6	....	98.7	1.3	98.6	1.4
New Jersey	92.3	7.7	1.5	6.2	92.7	7.2	4.5	2.7	95.1	4.9	4.9	....	96.6	3.4	96.3	3.7
Pennsylvania	97.6	2.4	1.5	0.9	96.9	2.9	2.9	(2)	97.7	2.3	2.3	....	98.0	2.0	97.5	2.5
Delaware	78.4	21.6	6.6	15.0	76.0	24.0	17.8	6.2	77.8	22.2	19.7	2.5	82.0	18.0	83.4	16.6
Southern states	64.4	35.6	1.5	34.1	63.0	37.0	2.8	34.2	65.2	34.8	3.3	31.5	67.8	32.2	71.2	28.7
Maryland and District of Columbia	65.3	34.7	2.5	32.2	64.2	35.8	9.9	25.8	71.8	28.2	13.4	14.8	75.8	24.3	78.1	21.9
Virginia and West Virginia	59.1	40.9	1.7	39.1	56.6	43.4	3.5	39.9	62.9	37.1	3.8	33.3	69.2	30.9	75.0	25.0
North Carolina	73.2	26.8	1.3	25.5	65.6	34.4	2.3	32.1	63.6	36.4	3.2	33.2	62.0	38.0	66.9	33.0
South Carolina	56.3	43.7	0.7	43.0	47.2	52.8	1.4	51.4	41.1	58.9	1.3	57.6	39.3	60.7	41.6	58.4
Georgia (eastern part)	64.1	35.9	0.5	35.5	50.8	49.2	0.7	48.5	44.3	55.7	0.8	54.9	44.9	55.1	46.4	53.6
Kentucky	83.0	17.0	0.2	16.9	77.0	22.9	0.5	22.5	77.5	22.5	1.0	21.5	83.5	16.5	86.7	13.3
Tennessee	89.4	10.6	1.0	9.6	80.4	19.6	0.6	18.9	75.5	24.5	0.6	23.9	73.9	26.1	76.2	23.8
Added to area of enumeration since 1790					83.9	16.0	1.4	14.6	83.4	16.6	0.8	15.8	86.5	12.7	87.6	11.4
Added to area of enumeration, 1790 to 1820					85.7	14.2	1.5	12.7	84.9	15.1	0.9	14.2	86.9	13.0	87.3	12.6
Ohio					99.2	0.8	0.8	....	98.7	1.3	1.3	....	97.5	2.5	97.7	2.3
Indiana					99.0	1.0	0.8	0.1	98.9	1.1	1.1	....	98.0	2.0	97.7	2.3
Illinois					97.4	2.5	0.8	1.7	99.4	0.6	0.6	....	98.5	1.5	98.2	1.8
Michigan					97.9	0.3	0.3	....	99.4	0.6	0.6	....	99.1	0.9	99.3	0.7
Wisconsin					89.8	10.2	10.2	....	99.8	0.2	0.2	....	99.8	0.2	99.9	0.1
Alabama					66.8	33.2	0.4	32.7	55.3	44.7	0.3	44.4	52.6	47.5	54.8	45.2
Mississippi					55.9	44.1	0.6	43.5	48.8	51.2	0.2	51.0	42.4	57.5	41.4	58.5
Louisiana					47.8	51.8	6.8	45.0	49.3	50.7	3.4	47.3	48.4	51.5	52.9	47.1
Arkansas					88.1	11.7	0.4	11.3	77.3	22.7	0.3	22.4	73.7	26.3	72.0	28.0
Missouri					84.1	15.9	0.5	15.4	86.8	13.2	0.4	12.8	93.3	6.7	94.8	5.2
Georgia (western part)					65.1	34.9	0.2	34.7	44.3	55.7	0.7	55.0	56.2	43.8	56.1	43.9

1 The proportion which the colored population, other than negro, forms of the total population is not presented here, because there was no similar element at the earlier censuses with which to draw comparisons.

2 Less than one-tenth of 1 per cent.

TABLE **20.**—PER CENT OF WHITE AND COLORED IN THE TOTAL POPULATION AT THE CENSUSES OF 1790, 1820, AND 1850, COMPARED WITH THE PER CENT OF WHITES AND NEGROES IN THE TOTAL POPULATION AT THE CENSUSES OF 1880 AND 1900—Continued.

STATE OR TERRITORY.	1790				1820				1850				1880 [1]		1900 [1]	
	White.	Colored.			White.	Colored.			White.	Colored.			White.	Negro.	White.	Negro.
		Total.	Free.	Slave.		Total.	Free.	Slave.		Total.	Free.	Slave.				
Added to area of enumeration, 1820 to 1850........									85.2	14.8	0.4	14.4	88.2	9.5	90.0	8.4
Minnesota............									99.4	0.6	0.6	....	99.5	0.2	99.2	0.3
Iowa................									99.8	0.2	0.2	....	99.4	0.6	99.4	0.6
Florida..............									54.0	46.0	1.1	44.9	52.9	47.0	56.3	43.7
Texas...............									72.5	27.5	0.2	27.3	75.2	24.7	79.6	20.4
New Mexico..........									100.0	....			90.9	0.8	92.3	0.8
Arizona.............									100.0	....			86.9	0.4	75.6	1.5
Utah................									99.6	0.4	0.2	0.2	98.9	0.2	98.5	0.2
Washington..........									87.3	12.7	12.7	....	89.5	0.4	95.8	0.5
Oregon..............									99.5	0.5	0.5	....	93.3	0.3	95.4	0.3
California...........									99.0	1.0	1.0	....	88.7	0.7	94.5	0.7
Added to area of enumeration, 1850 to 1880........													94.8	2.5	96.1	1.6
North Dakota South Dakota........													98.5	0.3	96.1	0.1
Nebraska............													99.4	0.5	99.1	0.6
Kansas..............													95.6	4.3	96.3	3.5
Montana.............													90.4	0.9	93.0	0.6
Idaho...............													89.0	0.2	95.5	0.2
Wyoming............													93.5	1.4	96.2	1.0
Colorado............													98.4	1.3	98.0	1.6
Nevada..............													86.0	0.8	83.6	0.3
Added to area of enumeration since 1880............													....	....	79.3	6.0
Indian Territory......													....	....	77.2	9.4
Oklahoma............													....	....	92.3	4.7
Persons stationed abroad....													....	....	92.3	7.0

[1] The proportion which the colored population, other than negro, forms of the total population is not presented here, because there was no similar element at the earlier censuses with which to draw comparisons.

In 1790 the white population formed 80.7 per cent and the negro population—both free and slave—19.3 per cent of the total. Since 1790 there has been a steady advance in the proportion which the white race has formed of the total population of continental United States, with a corresponding decline in the proportion of negroes; in 1900 the whites formed 87.8 per cent, and the negroes only 11.6 per cent of the total population.

DIAGRAM **6.**—*White and colored in the total population of the original and added area.*

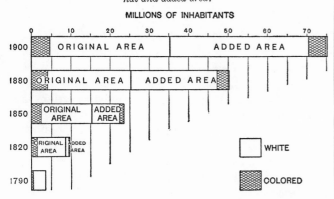

In the area enumerated in 1790 the changes were similar to those outlined for continental United States. In New England the changes were very slight, and in the Middle states they were not much greater. The Southern states of the original area, however, have changed considerably in this respect. In the contiguous states of Maryland (including the District of Columbia), Virginia (including West Virginia), and Kentucky, the proportion of whites decreased and that of negroes increased from 1790 to 1820, after which the conditions were reversed; in North Carolina, South Carolina, and Tennessee, the proportion of whites decreased and that of negroes increased until 1880, after which there was a very slight movement in the opposite direction; in Georgia there was no sustained tendency in either direction.

By applying the proportion formed by the negro element in the total population in 1790 to the combined white and negro population of continental United States in 1900, and the proportion which the negro element formed of the combined white and negro population in 1900 to the population in 1790, the following results are obtained:

RACE.	1790		1900	
	Actual number.	Number on basis of proportion shown in 1900.	Actual number.	Number on basis of proportion shown in 1790.
White..................	3,172,444	3,469,859	66,809,196	61,044,054
Negro..................	757,181	459,766	8,833,994	14,599,136

WHITE AND COLORED POPULATION IN FOUR PRINCIPAL
CITIES.

The difficulty which is confronted upon attempting to compare the population of cities enumerated in 1790 with the population of the same areas in 1900, arises principally from the fact that in 1900 the oldest sections had become almost exclusively devoted to business purposes, and therefore reported but a small proportion of the total city population. Persons who now reside in such sections are in most instances the residents of tenement houses, janitors of large buildings and their families, custodians, watchmen, and persons whose work connects them so closely with commercial and manufacturing plants as to necessitate residence in or near their places of employment.

DIAGRAM 7.—COMPARISON OF AREA OF CITIES.

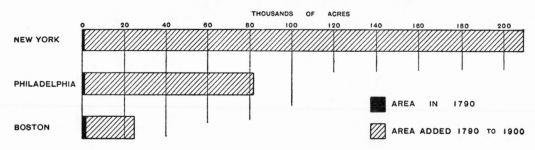

TABLE 21.—POPULATION, CLASSIFIED BY COLOR, FOR EACH LARGE CITY REPORTED IN 1790, COMPARED WITH
THAT REPORTED IN 1900, BOTH FOR THE SAME AREA AND UNDER THE SAME NAME.

CITY.	1790					1900											
			Colored.			Reported for same area.						Reported under same name.				
	Total.	White.	Total.	Free.	Slave.	Total.	White.	Colored.				Total.	White.	Colored.			
								Total.	Negro.	In-dian.	Mongo-lian.			Total.	Negro.	In-dian.	Mongo-lian.
POPULATION.																	
New York city.....	32,305	29,043	3,262	1,078	2,184	238,296	233,918	4,378	1,667	5	2,706	3,437,202	3,369,898	67,304	60,666	31	6,607
Philadelphia.......	28,522	26,892	1,630	1,420	210	155,691	135,879	19,812	19,213	107	492	1,293,697	1,229,673	64,024	62,613	234	1,177
Boston.............	18,038	17,277	761	761	....	168,552	160,849	7,703	7,091	2	610	560,892	548,083	12,809	11,591	3	1,215
Baltimore..........	13,503	11,925	1,578	323	1,255	28,160	21,826	6,334	6,260	......	74	508,957	429,218	79,739	79,258	......	481
PER CENT OF POPULATION.																	
New York city.....	100.0	89.9	10.1	3.3	6.8	100.0	98.2	1.8	0.7	(1)	1.1	100.0	98.0	2.0	1.8	(1)	0.2
Philadelphia.......	100.0	94.3	5.7	5.0	0.7	100.0	87.3	12.7	12.3	0.1	0.3	100.0	95.1	4.9	4.8	(1)	0.1
Boston.............	100.0	95.8	4.2	4.2	....	100.0	95.4	4.6	4.2	(1)	0.4	100.0	97.7	2.3	2.1	(1)	0.2
Baltimore..........	100.0	88.3	11.7	2.4	9.3	100.0	77.5	22.5	22.2	......	0.3	100.0	84.3	15.7	15.6	......	0.1

[1] Less than one-tenth of 1 per cent.

The sevenfold increase in the population of the original area of New York represents principally tenement house population, since the city limits in 1790 extended but little beyond the present City Hall square. In Boston the population of the original area increased ninefold, in Philadelphia fivefold, and in Baltimore it but little more than doubled.

Probably the most significant feature of the table is the illustration of the inevitable tendency of population to move away from the older centers as the number of inhabitants increases and city limits expand, which is afforded by the degree to which the inhabitants of the 4 cities have abandoned, for residence purposes, the areas which comprised these cities in 1790. This tendency is more pronounced in New York (doubtless because of physical formation) and Baltimore than in either Philadelphia or Boston. In New York less than 7 per cent of the population now reside within the limits of the city as it existed at the First Census; in Baltimore less than 6 per cent; in Philadelphia 12 per cent; and in Boston 30 per cent.

INCREASE IN THE UNITED STATES COMPARED WITH THAT IN EUROPE.

The nineteenth century is probably the most noteworthy century with respect to the growth of the population of civilized nations. In the United States in 1800 the conditions were of course exceptional. A wealth of opportunity existed in connection with natural resources: mines discovered but still unworked, agricultural and forest resources of infinite variety and richness, and opportunities for industrial development beyond the dreams of the most imaginative, demanded population and encouraged increase at the rapid rate that Malthus, at the close of the eighteenth century, asserted to be possible only in the United States, where unlimited opportunities for support existed. In Europe, also, new demands for population, unknown at the period when Malthus wrote, were about to arise, by reason of the creation of industrial activities and the enormous extension of commerce. Hence, at the close of the eighteenth century the inhabitants both of the United States and of Europe stood upon the threshold of a development and opportunity latent in previous centuries, but already becoming active.

At the outset it will be of interest to consider the increase of population in the United States in comparison with increase in the principal countries of Europe. Since the First Census of the United States antedates census taking in Europe by at least a decade, only the nineteenth century should be considered.

COUNTRY.	Increase from 1800 to 1900.
United States	1,331.6
Belgium	204.3
Denmark	163.4
United Kingdom	155.9
Norway	154.6
Germany	143.2
Holland	143.1
Sweden	118.6
Italy	88.4
Portugal	85.1
Switzerland	84.1
Austria	81.6
Spain	76.6
France	42.5

With the exception of France, all the nations of Europe approximately doubled or more than doubled their population during the nineteenth century; a threefold increase appeared for Belgium alone. During the same period the population of continental United States increased more than fourteenfold; indeed, it had more than doubled by 1820—after only twenty years. This surprising growth, however, is in reality in no way comparable with the natural increase shown by the nations of Europe. The total population of approximately 76,000,000 in 1900 resulted from a generous natural increase of persons enumerated in 1790, from additions acquired by accessions of territory, and from an unparalleled immigration movement, substantially unchecked for more than half a century.

Hence natural growth, which in other nations is practically the only source of population increase, in the United States is but one of several factors. In consequence, the increase shown from 1790 to 1900 is merely a gross increase, depending on other than normal causes, and possessing comparatively little significance until analyzed.

INCREASE THROUGH IMMIGRATION.

The extraordinary additions to the population of the United States through immigration are shown in the following:

1790 to 1820	[1] 250,000
1821 to 1850	2,455,815
1851 to 1880	7,725,229
1881 to 1900	9,090,972

The immigration in the twenty years from 1880 to 1900 nearly equals the total for the sixty years from 1820 to 1880. Prior to 1820 there were very few immigrants; most of these came to the United States after 1810, and the number arriving prior to 1800 is so small as to be negligible.

In 1820 the foreign stock—that is, the immigrants with their children and grandchildren—could hardly have exceeded 350,000; and if this be deducted from the total population (9,638,453) for 1820, the remainder will still be more than twice the population in 1790. "If the population reported at the First Census, 3,929,214, had been doubled only once in thirty years, the result in 1910 would have been 62,867,424. In the theoretical doubling process the increase during the last thirty-year period (1880 to 1910) is equivalent to approximately 1,000,000 persons a year. Upon that basis, in 1900 the native population would have amounted to about 50,000,000 (including negroes); whereas the actual population in 1900 was 76,000,000. Thus the total population at the last census exceeded the theoretical figure for the same year by about 50 per cent. Hence, if we accept this comparison as possessing an approximate value, that part of the growth of the United States which has resulted from immigration is possibly about equal to the progress which has actually occurred from 1880 to 1900 in population, and thus presumably in wealth, amounting in the former to from 25,000,000 to 30,000,000 souls, and in the latter to more than $40,000,000,000.''[2]

NATURAL INCREASE.

Effective discussion of increase of population must be based upon some separation, necessarily very general in character, of the nativity and parentage of the

[1] This estimate has the sanction of several Census reports and other authorities, but is regarded by many as too high. The Census report for 1850 gives the total immigration for the period mentioned as 234,000; that for 1860 as 274,000.

[2] North American Review, September, 1908, page 365.

two principal elements, white and negro, which have contributed the great aggregate reported in 1900. It is important to determine the natural increase, in order to measure the growth and influence of native stock in the United States, and for purposes of comparison with the growth of population in foreign countries.

The distribution of population in the United States in 1900, by its various elements, is shown in the following table:

TABLE 22:—WHITE AND COLORED POPULATION OF CONTINENTAL UNITED STATES, CLASSIFIED BY NATIVITY OF PARENTS AND AS NATIVE AND FOREIGN ELEMENTS: 1900.

ELEMENT OF THE POPULATION.	Total.	CLASSIFIED BY NATIVITY OF PARENTS.			CLASSIFIED BY ELEMENT.			
		Both parents native.	One parent native and the other foreign born.	Both parents foreign born.	Native.		Foreign.	
					Number.	Per cent of total.	Number.	Per cent of total.
Total population.........................	75,994,575	49,965,636	5,109,052	20,919,887	52,520,162	69.1	23,474,413	30.9
White population..........................	66,809,196	40,958,216	5,075,093	20,775,887	43,495,762	65.1	23,313,434	34.9
Native................................	56,595,379	40,949,362	5,013,737	10,632,280	43,456,230	76.8	13,139,149	23.2
Foreign born..........................	10,213,817	8,854	61,356	10,143,607	39,532	0.4	10,174,285	99.6
Colored population........................	9,185,379	9,007,420	33,959	144,000	9,024,400	98.2	160,979	1.8
Negro................................	8,833,994	8,779,805	26,300	27,889	8,792,955	99.5	41,039	0.5
Indian and Mongolian.................	351,385	227,615	7,659	116,111	231,445	65.9	119,940	34.1

In the above table the native and foreign elements were determined by adding to the numbers having both parents native and both parents foreign born, respectively, one-half of the number having one parent native and the other foreign born. But the distribution here shown is obviously unsatisfactory, since the term "native," according to modern census usage, includes all persons born in the United States, and thus not only persons descended from distinctly native stock, but also the descendants, in the third and subsequent generations, of persons born in foreign countries. In consequence of this fact, upon analysis the census classification proves entirely unsuited to a determination of normal increase, and it becomes necessary to approximate the number of the descendants of the white and negro population enumerated at the First Census.

Increase of white population.—The white population in 1790 and 1800 was both sturdy and prolific, and until about 1830 it contributed a decennial increase of approximately one-third, practically unaided by immigration. After 1830, an increasing number of white foreign born persons added not only themselves but their progeny to the white element. The second, third, and even the fourth generations of foreign stock have now added their increment, so that it is impossible to determine accurately the number of persons in the United States in 1900 who were directly descended from the population enumerated at the beginning of the nineteenth century. Yet practically all of the increase during the nineteenth century in the population of European nations was derived from the native stock, residing within their national boundaries in 1800, and not from immigration.

At the census of 1900 the white foreign element in the United States—that is, the number of white persons having both parents foreign born, together with one-half the number having one parent foreign born and the other native—aggregated 23,313,434 persons. Discarding this class of inhabitants from the total white population of 66,809,196, the remaining 43,495,762 obviously comprise the descendants of the white population enumerated in 1790 (and also in 1800, since no appreciable addition from other nations occurred during the decade), augmented by the descendants, in the third and subsequent generations, of white persons who migrated to the United States, especially from Great Britain and Germany,[1] after 1800, and also by persons added to the white native element through annexations of territory in the first half of the century. Additions of the latter class can not be accurately measured, but should be regarded as a part of the native stock.

In the remainder of 43,495,762 above specified, what was the contribution of the elements enumerated in 1800, and what the contribution, in the third and subsequent generations, of persons arriving in the United States after the beginning of the century?

It is here that exact figures in the process of separation fail, and hypothesis and approximation, however ingenious, begin. Yet, since this analysis deals with the comparative growth of population in America and Europe, it is clearly within the bounds of scientific discussion to point out some of the simpler methods by which approximations of the growth of native stock can be made: (1) By elimination of all foreign stock from the native element; (2) by applying the rate of increase for the Southern states to the rest of the country; and (3) by applying the proportion of persons in Massachusetts having

[1] Natives of Great Britain and Germany constituted 85.7 per cent of all the foreign born in the United States in 1850. (Tenth Census, Population, page 461.)

native grandfathers to the rest of the country. Should a reasonable harmony appear in the results secured, that fact would tend to justify acceptance of the approximate percentage of increase secured.

1. *Elimination of foreign stock from native element.*— The character of the data which are available renders it necessary to consider the native descendants of the foreign born (in the third and subsequent generations) in three groups, as descendants of the immigrants arriving prior to 1853, between 1853 and 1870, and between 1870 and 1880; naturally, grandchildren of immigrants arriving after 1880 need not be considered.

At the census of 1850 the foreign born were returned separately for the first time, and were found to number 2,244,602, of whom 2,240,535 were white; the number of foreign born colored persons was so small as to be negligible. In the Compendium of the Seventh Census (1850) the number of foreign born and the progeny of foreigners arriving after 1790 is estimated at 3,000,000 or 3,200,000 in 1853.[1] On the basis of this approximation (obviously made at a period when a reasonable approximation should have been possible), the descendants of white immigrants arriving subsequent to 1790 or 1800 and prior to 1853 must have numbered about 1,000,000 in that year; and it is probable that of this total about one-half were native white of foreign parentage and the other half native white of native parentage.[2] It is reasonable to assume that since the white population of the United States more than trebled between 1850 and 1900, the group of native white of native parentage at least trebled during the same period, thus contributing about 1,500,000 to the native white of native parentage in 1900. The 500,000 native white of foreign parentage in 1850 were very young, and probably did not contribute to a great extent to the native white population of native parentage before 1870. The estimate of the contribution by the immigrants arriving between 1790 and 1850 is doubtless liberal enough to counterbalance this omission.

---

[1] "Estimating the survivors in 1850 of the foreigners who had arrived in the United States since the census of 1790 upon the principle of the English life tables, and making the necessary allowance for the less proportion of the old and very young among them, and for reemigration, etc., their number is stated in the abstract of the census published in 1853, page 15, at 2,460,000. From this, a deduction is then made of 10 per cent, on account of the greater mortality of emigrants and their lower expectation of life, which brings the actual survivors very nearly to the figures of the census. The deduction of 10 per cent seems hardly sufficient, and does not accord with the deductions that are generally made in the reasonings of vital statisticians. It would be safer to assume 15 per cent than 10, which would reduce the survivors to a little more than 2,000,000. To this add 50 per cent for the living descendants of foreigners who have come into the country since 1790 (observing that nearly four-fifths of the number have arrived since 1830, and could not have both children and grandchildren born in the country, and more than half have arrived since 1840, and must have had comparatively few native born children, it would not be safe to add any more), and the number of foreigners and their descendants in 1853 is not likely to exceed 3,000,000 or 3,200,000."—*Compendium of the Seventh Census, page 119.*

[2] The native whites of native parentage were probably for the most part not the children of the living native whites of foreign parentage, but the descendants of immigrants who arrived before the War of 1812.

In 1870 there were 4,167,616 native inhabitants both of whose parents were foreign born, and 1,157,170 native persons having one parent native and the other foreign born. Hence, the foreign element within the native population comprised 4,746,201 persons; native colored persons—negroes, Indians, and Mongolians—of foreign parentage were so few in number as to be practically negligible. Since the total population of the United States doubled between 1870 and 1900, and the birth rate is generally accepted as being higher for the foreign than for the native population, it is reasonable to assume that the foreign element within the native white population doubled, or a little more than doubled, during the period under consideration. In the process of doubling, however, it must be remembered that the increment will be greater than the base, which is being constantly reduced by death; hence the native white of foreign parentage and their offspring, which together evidently amounted to approximately 10,000,000 in 1900, were composed of two unequal parts, the native white of foreign parentage contributing approximately 4,000,000, and their offspring—classified as native white of native parentage—approximately 6,000,000.

The contribution to the native white of native parentage made by native whites of foreign parentage born after 1870 can not be determined with any degree of accuracy. The total number of native white persons of foreign parentage born between 1870 and 1880 and surviving in 1900 was 3,067,062. It is possible that this element may have contributed 500,000 persons to the native whites of native parentage.

The above computations indicate that in 1900 the contributions of the foreign stock to the so-called native element had reached the following approximate total:

Contribution of immigrants arriving—

Between 1790 and 1853	1,500,000
Between 1853 and 1870	6,000,000
Between 1870 and 1880	500,000
Total	8,000,000

In 1900 the native element in the United States was 43,495,762. Eliminating the 8,000,000 persons above determined, the white population enumerated in 1800 appears to have increased to 35,495,762.

2. *Growth of white native stock, at rate of increase for Southern states.*—At the census of 1850, when the classification by nativity was introduced, the white population of 12 Southern states—Virginia, Kentucky, Tennessee, North Carolina, South Carolina, Georgia, Florida, Alabama, Mississippi, Louisiana, Texas, and Arkansas—included in the aggregate less than 4 per cent who were foreign born. The proportion of foreign born in this group of states increased but little during the half century, and even at the census of 1900 the white population was composed almost entirely of the descendants of persons enumerated in 1790 and 1800.

This suggests utilizing the increase of white population shown by the Southern states as a basis from which to compute the increase in the distinctly native stock of the white population residing in the other states and territories; after 1870, however, only one-half of the rate of increase should be used, because of the fact, generally known and admitted, that the rate of increase of the native stock of the white population in the Northern and many of the Western states has been very low since 1870. The accuracy of such a computation is increased by discarding the foreign element of the white population in 1870 and 1880, and the total foreign white and the native white of foreign parentage in 1890 and 1900. Upon making such an analysis the following figures result:

CENSUS YEAR.	ACTUAL WHITE POPULATION OF SPECIFIED ELEMENT.					ESTIMATED NATIVE STOCK OF THE WHITE POPULATION.	
	In continental United States.	In 13 Southern states.		In remainder of continental United States.		For "remainder of continental United States" based on white population in 1820, by applying per cent of increase in Southern states to 1870 and half of decennial percentages after that year.	For continental United States.
		Number.	Per cent of increase over preceding census.	Number.	Per cent of increase over preceding census.		
			TOTAL WHITE POPULATION.				
1820	7,862,166	2,437,451	....	5,424,715	....	....	....
			NATIVE ELEMENT OF THE WHITE POPULATION.[1]				
1870	23,374,577	6,518,012	167.4	16,856,565	210.7	14,505,688	21,023,700
1880	29,621,812	8,843,928	35.7	20,777,884	23.3	17,102,206	25,946,134
			NATIVE WHITE POPULATION OF NATIVE PARENTAGE.				
1890	34,358,348	10,884,524	23.1	23,473,824	13.0	19,086,062	29,970,586
1900	40,949,362	13,328,329	22.5	27,621,033	17.7	21,242,787	34,571,116

[1] Obtained by subtracting from the total native element the native born negroes.

Upon replacing the native white population of native parentage living, in 1890 and 1900, in the Southern states and in the remainder of continental United States by the native whites of native parentage born in the Southern states and in the remainder of continental United States, the native stock of the white population appears to be as follows:

CENSUS YEAR.	ACTUAL NATIVE WHITE POPULATION OF NATIVE PARENTAGE.					ESTIMATED NATIVE STOCK OF THE WHITE POPULATION.	
	Living in continental United States.	Born in 13 Southern states.		Born in remainder of continental United States.		For "remainder of continental United States."	For continental United States.
		Number.	Per cent of increase over preceding census.	Number.	Per cent of increase over preceding census.		
1890	34,358,348	11,262,307	[1]27.3	23,096,041	[1]11.2	19,445,208	30,707,515
1900	40,949,362	13,903,622	23.5	27,045,740	17.1	21,739,743	35,643,365

[1] Increase over the native element of the white population.

The theoretical number shown as the native stock of the white population in 1870 for the country exclusive of the Southern states (14,505,688) must be very near the true figure; the excess of the native element over the native stock of the white population of this area was only 2,350,877, and it may safely be assumed that of this number the offspring of immigrants arriving between 1790 and 1853 (who numbered 1,000,000, according to the Compendium of the Seventh Census) contributed at least 2,000,000, leaving only 350,877 to represent the offspring of immigrants arriving between 1853 and 1870.

Only one-half of each percentage of increase shown for the Southern states in 1880, 1890, and 1900 was employed in computing the native stock of the white population in the rest of the country. It is worthy of note that, if the entire percentage be employed, the resulting figure for 1900 (30,946,644) approximately equals the native element of the white population (29,995,187) in the same area; in other words, the use of the entire percentage produces a figure large enough to include the entire contribution made to the native element by the descendants of the foreign white in the third and subsequent generations. This result may be merely a coincidence, but it recalls a theory advanced by Gen. Francis A. Walker, Superintendent of the Tenth Census, that the advent of large numbers of foreigners affects unfavorably the birth rate of the native element of a community.[1] This theory has been opposed by many statisticians of prominence.

3. *Growth of white population of native stock, measured by proportion of persons in Massachusetts having native grandfathers.*—As already pointed out, the classification of parentage by the Federal census stops with native white of native parentage. For this analysis the essential fact is the number of native white persons having native grandparents, and the problem which is confronted by the inquirer is to determine the percentage which would be deducted from the native white population of native parentage if it were statistically possible to segregate the native white persons having native grandparents.

The classification of the population of Massachusetts by nativity of grandfathers was made at the state census of 1905. It is doubtful whether any attempt to ascertain nativity of grandparents can ever be entirely successful, because of the likelihood of error concerning this subject, on the part of persons responding to the enumerators' questions; but if the returns of Massachusetts be accepted as approximately correct, they offer an opportunity to advance one generation beyond the Federal census, and thus to secure, for one state at least, the proportion of white persons who, besides being native born, possessed native grandfathers. Of the entire population of Massachusetts in 1905, slightly less than one-third reported native birth and native grandfathers. Upon eliminating the colored, it is found that the native white population reported as having both native fathers and native grandfathers formed 79.1 per cent of the total native white having native fathers.[2] It is obvious that if it

were possible to determine accurately the number of native white persons having native grandfathers in 1900, a close approximation would be reached concerning the increase in the white population of the native stock, since this classification reaches back to the period when immigration had not yet become an important factor, and hence to the period when practically all the population was composed of persons enumerated in 1800 or their progeny. Assuming that the proportion shown by the state census of Massachusetts is applicable to the other states, the total number of white persons in 1900 descended from the white population enumerated in 1800 numbered 33,729,282.

The results of the three computations described above are summarized in the following statement:

ELEMENTS OF THE POPULATION.	WHITE POPULATION: 1900.			
	First computation—elimination of the foreign stock from the native element.	Second computation—growth of native stock at rate of increase for Southern states.	Third computation—growth of native stock measured by proportion of persons in Massachusetts having native grandfathers.	Average.
Total	66,809,196	66,809,196	66,809,196	66,809,196
Native element	43,495,762	43,495,762	43,495,762	43,495,762
Native stock	35,495,762	35,643,365	33,729,282	34,956,136
Foreign stock	8,000,000	7,852,397	9,766,480	8,539,626
Foreign element	23,313,434	23,313,434	23,313,434	23,313,434
Total foreign stock	31,313,434	31,165,831	32,404,047	31,853,060

The three computations show a range of nearly 2,000,000 (between 33½ and 35½ millions). Utilizing the average of the three, it appears that in 1900 the white population of continental United States contributed by persons enumerated at the Second Census was approximately 35,000,000; while the contribution to the native whites of native parentage made by the third and subsequent generations descended from immigrants arriving after 1800 numbered approximately 8,500,000. Adding the latter figure to the known foreign element in 1900, it is found that the contribution of the foreign stock to the white population was 31,853,060. Hence, at the Twelfth Census the total white population of continental United States appears to have been divided between the descendants of persons enumerated at the Second Census and of persons who became inhabitants of the United States after 1800, in the proportion of about 35 to 32.

The white population shown at the Second Census, 1800, was 4,306,446. To this number should be added 100,000 persons, as the approximate number acquired by accessions of territory early in the century, who must be regarded as a part of the native

---

[1] "The access of foreigners at the time and under the circumstances constituted a shock to the principle of population among the native element. That principle is always acutely sensitive, alike to sentimental and to economic conditions. And it is to be noted, in passing, that not only did the decline in the native element as a whole, take place in singular correspondence with the excess of foreign arrivals, but it occurred chiefly in just those regions to which the newcomers most freely resorted. * * * If the foregoing views are true, or contain any considerable degree of truth, foreign immigration into this country has, from the time it first assumed large proportions, amounted not to a reenforcement of our population, but to a replacement of native by foreign stock. That if the foreigners had not come, the native element would long since have filled the places the foreigners usurped, I entertain not a doubt."—*Discussions in Economics and Statistics, vol. 2, page 422.*

[2] In making this computation, it was assumed that all native colored persons had native grandfathers, and also that all native white persons having native grandfathers had native fathers.

stock.[1] Upon this basis the increase from 1800 to 1900 in the native white stock of continental United States was 694.3 per cent.

It is not surprising that the increase of inhabitants upon both continents is one of the most noteworthy developments of the century; but the great excess of increase of population in the United States over that of the nation of Europe showing the largest percentage illustrates, and to some extent measures, the wealth of opportunity in the young Republic and the unusual virility of the population.

The largest percentage of increase during the century from 1800 to 1900, shown by the table on page 85, for any European nation, was that reported for Belgium— 204 per cent. Had the percentage of increase of the native stock of the white population of the United States enumerated in 1800 been only as great as that shown by Belgium, the white population of the United States in 1900 would have been as follows:

Native element of the white population:
    Descendants of white native stock................. 13,395,596
    Descendants of white immigrants arriving after
        1790, as above computed........................ 8,539,626
Foreign element of the white population 23,313,434

        Total.. 45,248,656

This total approximates the white population of the United States in 1880. Thus the greater fertility of the native white stock of the United States, as compared with fertility in the countries of Europe showing the largest increase, has resulted in a white population in 1900 which is twenty years in advance of what it would have been if computed on the slower rate of increase shown for Belgium. It would be difficult to suggest more vividly the great fecundity during the nineteenth century of the white population inhabiting the United States in 1800.[2]

It is probable that a readjustment of population increase is now in progress, and that the steady diminution in the rate of increase shown for both Europe and the United States in the later decades of the nineteenth century affords confirmation of the general accuracy of the theory advanced by Malthus, long

discredited, because it happened to be put forward at a period when newly awakened national development on both continents seemingly disproved it.

Increase of white population of native parentage in the states enumerated in 1790.—The methods outlined above for determining the increase in the native stock of the white population are too detailed, and the results too imperfect, to justify computation for individual states. Since the Census classification which most closely approximates the native stock is the native white of native parentage, in the following summary the white population in 1800 of the states enumerated in 1790 is compared with the native white population of native parentage in the same area in 1900, for the purpose of illustrating the tendency to comparatively small increase exhibited by the native element of the white population in the older states of the original area.

TABLE **23.**—*White population in 1800 of each state and territory enumerated in 1790, compared with the native white population of native parentage in the same area in 1900.*

STATE.	White population, 1800.	Native white population of native parentage, 1900.	INCREASE.	
			Amount.	Per cent.
Area enumerated in 1790....	4,250,896	18,926,020	14,675,124	345.2
New England..................	1,214,359	2,511,110	1,296,751	106.8
Maine.......................	150,901	493,082	342,181	226.8
New Hampshire..............	182,998	242,614	59,616	32.6
Vermont....................	153,908	225,381	71,473	46.4
Massachusetts..............	416,393	1,032,264	615,871	147.9
Rhode Island...............	65,438	144,986	79,548	121.6
Connecticut................	244,721	372,783	128,062	52.3
Middle states..............	1,388,003	7,524,608	6,136,605	442.1
New York...................	557,731	2,851,513	2,293,782	411.3
New Jersey.................	194,325	825,973	631,648	325.0
Pennsylvania...............	586,095	3,729,093	3,142,998	536.3
Delaware...................	49,852	118,029	68,177	136.8
Southern states............	1,648,534	8,890,302	7,241,768	439.3
Maryland and District of Columbia..................	226,392	814,122	587,730	259.6
Virginia and West Virginia...	514,280	1,985,194	1,470,914	286.0
North Carolina.............	337,764	1,250,811	913,047	270.3
South Carolina.............	196,255	540,766	344,511	175.5
Georgia[1]..................	102,261	1,144,360	1,042,099	1,019.1
Kentucky...................	179,873	1,673,413	1,493,540	830.3
Tennessee..................	91,709	1,481,636	1,389,927	1,515.6

[1] Entire state.

Upon comparing the white population in 1800 in the area enumerated in 1790 with the native white population of native parentage in the same area in 1900, the increase during the century is shown to be less than 350 per cent. As already pointed out, the population even as thus classified has been reenforced during the century by the third and subsequent generations of the descendants of immigrants. The significance of the table therefore lies principally in the comparatively moderate increase which appears upon withdrawing from the total population even part of the increase due to immigration.

This summary is presented by the 3 general geographic divisions, in order to indicate the differences in increase which appeared in these sections. In none of the New England states was there a large

---

[1] The insignificance of the original white population of added areas is strikingly illustrated by the fact that at the first census taken after the acquisition of the Louisiana Purchase (seven years later), the white population enumerated in what are now the states of Louisiana, Arkansas, and Missouri formed only nine-tenths of 1 per cent of the total white population of the United States in 1810. Similarly, the white population of Florida was but two-tenths of 1 per cent of the total white population in 1830, and that of the vast regions acquired between 1840 and 1850 was but 1.7 per cent of the total in the latter year.

[2] "Their numbers are not augmented by foreign emigrants; yet from their circumscribed limits, compact situation, and natural population, they are filling the western parts of the state of New York and the country on the Ohio with their own surplusage." (Washington to Sir John Sinclair, 1796.) "It is worth remarking that New England, which has sent out such a continued swarm to other parts of the Union for a number of years, has continued at the same time, as the census shows, to increase in population, although it is well known that it has received but comparatively few emigrants from any quarter." (James Madison, 1821)—*Bancroft, 3, 213; Tenth Census, Population, page 457.*

increase during the century in the number of native whites of native parentage. This fact is indicative of heavy emigration, and doubtless also of a very low birth rate. The immense increase shown for Georgia, Kentucky, and Tennessee can not be regarded as especially important, because at the beginning of the century these areas were just being settled, and 2 of the 3 were merely territories or districts. During the earlier decades of the century, when the older states were to a great extent distributers of population, these 3 states were distinctly the recipients of immigration; obviously, therefore, the growth of population in all 3 was contributed largely by persons of native stock.

Growth of the British race.—Elsewhere in these pages will be found a discussion of nationality at the First Census, indicating that much the larger part of the white inhabitants of the United States were natives, or the offspring of natives, of Great Britain, and principally of England.[1] The population of Great Britain in 1712 is estimated to have been but 9,000,000. During the succeeding century (the eighteenth) Great Britain contributed from this small population the stock which formed the larger part of the white population of the United States in 1790, and which, as already pointed out, increased by 1900 to approximately 35,000,000 souls. In 1801 the population of the United Kingdom was 16,200,000; by 1900 it had increased to 41,000,000. But during the nineteenth century the mother country also contributed, even more freely than she had contributed during the eighteenth century to North America, to the population of the United States and to that of a score of younger colonies. The spectacle is thus presented of a nation which not only increased during the century more generously than did any of its rivals, but at the same time created other nations, one of which alone produced within the century a native population nearly equal to that of the mother country. It is possible that a racial growth similar in character may have occurred upon a small scale in connection with some of the colonies established by ancient cities along the Mediterranean, but in magnitude there appears to be no parallel in history for this population achievement of the British race from 1700 to 1900.

Increase of negro population.—In comparing the increase of population in the United States with that of the nations of Europe, attention has thus far been directed to the changes in white population, since the white race only can be considered in comparison with Europe. It must be remembered, however, that the negro has always constituted an important part of the population of the United States, and also that the negro element must be classed as distinctly native. From 1,002,037 negroes in the United States in 1800 the number increased to 8,833,994 in continental United States in 1900, of whom 8,792,955 belonged to the native element.

It must not be overlooked that the negroes enumerated in 1800 received accessions between 1800 and 1808, and possibly surreptitious additions later, through further importation of slaves. Since this enforced immigration occurred at the beginning of the century under consideration, the total increase from this source should be included in the total negro population existing at the beginning of the century. This addition was more than 70,000,[2] probably about 100,000, and there should be added also approximately 50,000 negroes acquired by accession of territory. With this adjustment, the increase from 1800 to 1900 in the native element of the negro population of the United States was 663.3 per cent.

The increase of negroes, however, presents an entirely different problem from that presented by the increase of whites. The negro race is very prolific, and possibly would have accomplished, unaided, the increase shown. But it is impossible even to estimate what influence the white race has exerted upon the increase of what is classed as negro population. There were many mulattoes in the United States even before 1800; by a census of Maryland in 1755, 8.0 per cent of the negroes were returned as mulattoes. Attempts were made at the censuses of 1870 and 1890 to measure the strain of white blood in persons classed as negroes, and the returns, while regarded as very inaccurate, supplied at least an approximate measurement, where before none had existed. The negroes reported as partly white formed 12 per cent of the total number in 1870 and 15.2 per cent of the total in 1890. It is probable that this proportion is increasing; even upon the basis of the proportion shown for 1890, however, in 1900 the number of persons in continental United States classed as negroes, but containing some white blood, would have been at least 1,342,767. Part of this number might be regarded as outside of normal increase, and as bearing to the natural increase of negroes enumerated in 1800 a relation somewhat similar to the increase contributed to the white inhabitants of the Republic by immigrants and children of immigrants. It is more probable, however, that the contribution of the white race to negro increase should be regarded as a substitute for increase which otherwise would have been furnished by the negro race itself.

Summary of increase in total population.—From the foregoing analysis of the increase of the native white and negro elements composing the population of the United States, the total number of persons enumerated (and included) in both elements in 1800 (5,558,483) increased to 43,749,091 in 1900, an increase of 687.1 per cent. During the century, therefore, the population of the United States, including both white and negro, unaided by immigration, increased nearly sevenfold, while during the same period the population of Europe, exclusive of Russia, Turkey, and Greece, increased 119.4 per cent. The largest increase shown

---

[1] Chapter XI, page 116.

[2] Seventh Census, Compendium, page 83.

by any nation of Europe was 204 per cent, or less than one-third as great.

The similarity here shown in the increase during the nineteenth century of the whites and negroes enumerated at its beginning, possesses especial significance when it is remembered that during the greater part of the century the conditions under which the two races existed were radically different. The white race possessed all the advantages of unlimited resources and complete independence, and of a strict observance of the family relation. In marked contrast, during much more than half of the period under consideration the negro race was for the most part in a state of bondage, and the family relation was doubtless frequently subordinated to the exigencies of ownership.

TABLE **24.**—*White, negro, Indian, and Mongolian population, with number and per cent of increase, for continental United States: 1800 and 1900.*

	1800 [1]	1900	INCREASE.	
			Number.	Per cent.
Total population	5,558,483	75,994,575	70,436,092	1,267.2
White	4,406,446	66,809,196	62,402,750	1,416.2
Native stock	4,406,446	34,956,136	30,549,690	693.3
Foreign stock		31,853,060	31,853,060	
Negro	1,152,037	8,833,994	7,681,957	666.8
Native stock	1,152,037	8,792,955	7,640,918	663.3
Foreign stock		41,039	41,039	
Indian and Mongolian		351,385	351,385	

[1] Including an estimate of 100,000 white persons and 50,000 negroes as the population in 1800 of areas added after that year, and an estimate of 100,000 negroes as the number of slaves imported after 1800.

APPORTIONMENT.

The Constitution contained the following provision:

Representatives and direct taxes shall be apportioned among the several states which may be included within this Union, according to their respective numbers, which shall be determined by adding to the whole number of free persons, including those bound to service for a term of years, and excluding Indians not taxed, three-fifths of all other persons.[1]

The same paragraph further stipulated that, until an enumeration should be made, each state should be entitled to a specified number of representatives, the total being 65.

The population required for one representative has increased from 33,000 in 1790 to nearly 200,000 in 1900, or six times the number of citizens represented at the outset. With the basis of apportionment at the last census the same as at the first, the membership in the House of Representatives, instead of being 386, as determined by the apportionment act under the Twelfth Census, would have been 2,259. On the other hand, were the ratio which was employed in 1900 applied to the states in 1790, the largest delegation in the House of Representatives would have been 3 members; only 4 states would have had 2 members; the remaining states would have had but 1; and the total

[1] Since superseded by the Fourteenth Amendment.

membership of the House of Representatives would have been 19.

The change in the apportionment of representatives in Congress which has been in progress during the century from the First Census to the Twelfth is indicated by the following summary:

Apportionment of congressional representation: 1790 to 1900.

CENSUS YEAR.	Population to each representative.	REPRESENTATIVES.				
		Total number.	Area enumerated in 1790.		Added area.	
			Number.	Per cent of total.	Number.	Per cent of total.
1790	33,000	105	105	100.0		
1800	33,000	141	141	100.0		
1810	35,000	181	175	96.7	6	3.3
1820	40,000	213	187	87.8	26	12.2
1830	47,700	240	199	82.9	41	17.1
1840	70,680	223	161	72.2	62	27.8
1850	93,423	234	154	65.8	80	34.2
1860	127,381	241	139	57.7	102	42.3
1870	131,425	292	156	53.4	136	46.6
1880	151,911	325	153	47.1	172	52.9
1890	173,901	356	168	47.2	188	52.8
1900	194,182	386	179	46.4	207	53.6

This comparison affords an effective and final illustration of the extraordinary change which has occurred during the first century of population growth in the United States.

VII. SEX AND AGE OF THE WHITE POPULATION.

DECREASE IN PROPORTION OF MALES—IN PROPOR-
TION OF EACH SEX UNDER 16 YEARS—INFLUENCE
OF IMMIGRATION—OF MODERN SANITARY SCIENCE.

At the First Census a complete classification of sex and a partial classification of age were obtained for the entire white population. The three questions under which these items were secured were as follows:

1. Free white males of 16 years and upward, including heads of families.
2. Free white males under 16 years.
3. Free white females, including heads of families.

Sex.—Discussion of the proportions of the sexes in the United States has been presented from time to time in reports of the Federal census. Such change as has occurred in the proportion of the sexes is best illustrated by computing the number of males in each 1,000 of population in 1790 and 1900 and midway, in 1850.

TABLE 25.—*Proportion of males in the white population, by states and territories: 1790, 1850, and 1900.*

STATE OR TERRITORY.	NUMBER OF MALES PER 1,000 OF WHITE POPULATION.		
	1790	1850	1900
Continental United States	509	513	513
Area enumerated in 1790	509	504	502
New England	498	498	494
Maine	511	510	505
New Hampshire	503	491	499
Vermont	526	509	509
Massachusetts	490	491	487
Rhode Island	492	489	489
Connecticut	495	495	500
Middle states	514	506	502
New York	516	507	497
New Jersey	510	501	500
Pennsylvania	514	506	508
Delaware	517	502	510
Southern states	515	506	506
Maryland and District of Columbia	514	504	495
Virginia and West Virginia	514	504	510
North Carolina	511	494	500
South Carolina	523	502	504
Georgia	513	510	504
Kentucky	527	516	509
Tennessee	519	505	508
Added area		529	521

The proportion of males in the white population shows a more marked decrease from 1790 to 1900 in the Middle and Southern states than in New England. In 1790 the only states reporting an excess of females were Massachusetts, Rhode Island, and Connecticut.

In 1900 such excess was reported not only by Massachusetts and Rhode Island, but also by New Hampshire, New York, and Maryland. Had the proportions been the same in 1790 as in the original area in 1900, there would have been 23,194 fewer white males than were reported at the First Census. If, on the other hand, the proportion of males in the area enumerated in 1790 had been the same in 1900 as in 1790, the number of males reported would have been greater by 216,826.

Age.—The age classification secured at the First Census separated white males into age groups above and under the age of 16 years, without a similar separation for females. In any attempt to analyze the age figures thus presented, it becomes necessary to estimate the same classification with respect to females. The defect noted in the enumeration of 1790 was corrected at the census of 1800. Hence, within a decade of 1790 the exact proportion of females in the age groups specified were definitely known. This fact suggests the practicability of utilizing the well-known and fairly constant statistical ratio between the numbers of males and females, and the probably similar ratios for the principal age groups.

Before utilizing such proportions, it was of course necessary to demonstrate that the results would be substantially accurate. If from the Second to the Third Census no marked variation is found in the proportion formed of all white females by white females under 16 years of age, either in the total or in the returns for the same states, the proportion from 1790 to 1800 is likely to have been fairly constant; furthermore, if the proportion formed of all white males by white males under 16 in 1790, as compared with the similar proportion shown in 1800, varied little, it would then be established beyond reasonable doubt that the proportion of white females in the same age groups, though unascertained, must have differed but little in 1790 from the proportions actually shown in 1800. Hence, the application of the proportion shown for white females under 16 years of age in the various states in 1800, to obtain the number of females in the same age group in 1790, would be fully justified. What are the results of an analysis concerning the constancy of such ratios?

(93)

The proportion which the white females under 16 years of age in the year 1800 formed of all white females amounted to about one-half. It varied less than one-twentieth of 1 per cent from 1800 to 1810. The percentages for the United States and for the New England states, Middle states, and Southern states at both censuses were:

	1800	1810
United States	49.7	49.7
New England	46.3	46.4
Middle states	50.2	50.3
Southern states	51.6	51.4

For the most part the range among individual states is very narrow. In 8 out of 17 states the difference in proportion is less than 1 per cent, and in no instance does it exceed 3 per cent.

The proportion in 1800 for males under 16 years of age is substantially the same as for females, being:

	1800	1810
United States	50.4	50.3
New England	48.9	47.9
Middle states	50.0	50.2
Southern states	51.8	51.8

The important question, however, is obviously the confirmation which may or may not be afforded by the similarity of the proportion shown for white males under 16 years of age at the Second Census as compared with the First. The proportions of males in this age group at the First and Second censuses were as follows:

	1790	1800
United States	49.6	50.4
New England	48.4	48.9
Middle states	48.7	50.0
Southern states	51.1	51.8

In short, the uniformity in the proportion of white females under 16 years of age among all white females in 1810 as compared with 1800, the similarity in the proportion of white males under 16 and white females under 16 in 1800 as compared with 1810, and the similarity of the proportion of all white males formed by those under 16 years of age in 1800 as compared with 1790, appear to justify the use of the proportion of females under 16 years of age returned in 1800 by the several states, to compute the number of females in the same age group in 1790. Accordingly, in Table 106, on page 208, will be found the probable number of females under and over the age of 16, determined in accordance with the proportions shown by the various states in 1800.

SEX AND AGE.	WHITE POPULATION IN 1790.	
	Number.	Per cent.
Total	3,172,444	....
16 years and over	1,619,184	51.0
Under 16 years	1,553,260	49.0
Males	1,615,761	....
16 years and over	815,098	50.4
Under 16 years	800,663	49.6
Females	1,556,683	....
16 years and over	804,086	51.7
Under 16 years	752,597	48.3

The proportions of white persons of both sexes who were under 16 years of age in 1790 are compared with the corresponding proportions in 1900 in the following summary:

Per cent white persons under 16 years of age form of total white population, and per cent white males and females of the same age group form of all white males and females, respectively: 1790 and 1900.

STATE OR TERRITORY.	BOTH SEXES.		MALES.		FEMALES.	
	1790	1900	1790	1900	1790	1900
Continental United States	49.0	35.6	49.6	35.2	48.3	36.1
Area enumerated in 1790	49.0	34.1	49.6	34.3	48.3	33.9
New England	47.0	29.1	48.4	29.6	45.6	28.7
Maine	50.7	29.0	50.4	29.0	51.1	29.0
New Hampshire	48.6	27.5	49.1	27.5	48.0	27.5
Vermont	51.3	29.4	49.9	29.2	52.8	29.6
Massachusetts	45.5	29.0	47.8	29.6	43.4	28.3
Rhode Island	46.4	30.5	49.5	31.7	43.3	29.3
Connecticut	45.4	29.7	47.2	29.8	43.7	29.7
Middle states	49.4	32.6	48.7	32.6	50.2	32.5
New York	49.3	30.9	48.3	31.2	50.5	30.6
New Jersey	48.7	32.7	47.8	32.7	49.6	32.6
Pennsylvania	49.8	34.5	49.2	34.2	50.4	34.8
Delaware	49.4	32.7	50.8	32.6	48.0	32.9
Southern states	50.2	40.0	51.1	40.2	49.2	39.7
Maryland and District of Columbia	45.0	33.3	47.9	33.9	41.9	32.8
Virginia and West Virginia	49.7	40.0	51.1	40.0	48.1	40.1
North Carolina	51.9	42.8	52.5	43.6	51.1	42.0
South Carolina	52.2	41.8	51.5	42.5	53.0	41.1
Georgia	53.1	41.6	51.7	41.8	54.5	41.4
Kentucky	54.5	40.4	53.0	40.3	56.3	40.4
Tennessee	55.0	41.1	52.9	41.4	57.2	40.8
Added area	......	36.9	......	35.8	......	38.0

The summary indicates that the proportion of each sex under 16 years of age was materially less for the United States in 1900 than in 1790, and slightly less in the area enumerated in 1790 than for the entire nation. The most decided changes in this respect appear in the New England states. In some of these the proportion in 1900 was little more than one-half of that shown in 1790. The change is least marked in the Southern states, where the white population has maintained a much larger proportion of increase than in other portions of the country, and has been but little affected by immigration during the century. In 1790 7 out of the 17 states and territories enumerated showed a proportion of more than one-half under 16 years of age; the lowest proportion shown by any state or territory at that census was that of Maryland, in which 45 per cent of the inhabitants were under 16 years of age. In 1900, however, no state reported a proportion as high as the lowest reported for 1790.

The question at once presents itself, whether a large part of the decided reduction shown in this summary is not attributable to the arrival in the last decade of the nineteenth century of great numbers of immigrants, a very large proportion of whom were over 16 years of age. Such an influx would seemingly tend to augment the proportion of the population in the higher age group at the expense of that in the lower. To measure the influence of this element, two computations were made to determine the proportion which in 1900 (1) the native white of native parentage under 16 years of age and (2) the native white of foreign parentage and the foreign white in the same age period, formed of the total produced by adding to their number the number of persons available for their support. The first computation gave the proportion which the native white of native parentage under 16 years of age formed of the total obtained by adding to their number the total native white of native parentage above 16, and the married, widowed, and divorced native white of foreign parentage in this same age period; the second gave the proportion which the total of the foreign white under 16 years of age and the native white of foreign parentage in the same age period formed of the aggregate produced upon adding to their number the foreign white above 16 years and the single native white of foreign parentage in the same age period. For the United States as a whole, the proportions obtained by these two computations were 35.5 and 35.9 per cent, respectively, as compared with 35.6 in the preceding summary. It thus appears that the

influence of the large influx of adult immigrants upon the proportions shown in the summary has been practically offset by a higher birth rate among these immigrants, and that the proportion shown for 1900 in the preceding summary has not been materially affected by immigration.

While the increase or decrease in the birth rate between the First and Twelfth censuses is the principal factor in determining the proportions above and below the age of 16 years, increased longevity is another possible factor which might exert some influence upon the proportions. The average age of the population has unquestionably increased materially since 1790, because of improved sanitary conditions, the advance in medical and surgical skill, and doubtless also the greater intelligence of the community with respect to the preservation of health; it is not probable, however, that the last-named factor would materially affect the percentage here shown. The advance in medical skill and sanitary appliances since 1790 has tended to preserve infant life perhaps even more than adult life, and the increase in the average age is due rather to the preservation of life among young people who are crippled, deformed, or weak, than to the actual lengthening of life to old age.

The argument has frequently been advanced that the important point to be considered is the number of survivors in the young population, since the number of survivors from a high birth rate attended by a high death rate may perhaps be no greater than the number from low birth and death rates. The statistics under consideration relate to living children under 16 years of age; and, whatever the mortality may have been, the fact remains that at the period of the First Census the survivors were so numerous as to increase the population with almost unexampled rapidity.

VIII. ANALYSIS OF THE FAMILY.

AVERAGE SIZE OF PRIVATE FAMILIES—SLAVE-
HOLDING AND NONSLAVEHOLDING FAMILIES—
PROPORTION OF CHILDREN—DWELLINGS.

NUMBER OF FAMILIES.

In the preceding chapters analysis has been confined principally to tabulations of data secured from the report of the First Census and thus available for all the states. In this and in several of the succeeding chapters the statistics presented are derived principally from the schedules. This fact obviously precludes detailed consideration of returns for the states of New Jersey, Delaware, and Georgia, and for the districts of Kentucky and Tennessee. While the schedules for Virginia also are missing, their place is supplied in a measure by lists of inhabitants at state enumerations made near the close of the Revolution. For the other states and territories mentioned, facts in some instances, can be approximated with reasonable accuracy from the returns for adjoining states.

Size of families.—In tabulating families as reported at the First Census only private families were considered—in other words, all households which were obviously institutions, or of a public or semipublic character, were excluded. The following table affords a comparison of the average size of private families in 1790 and 1900:

TABLE **26.**—AVERAGE SIZE OF PRIVATE FAMILIES, BY STATES AND TERRITORIES: 1790 AND 1900.

STATE OR TERRITORY.	TOTAL FREE POPULATION IN FAMILIES.		NUMBER OF FAMILIES.		AVERAGE NUMBER OF PERSONS IN EACH FAMILY.	
	1790	1900	1790	1900	1790	1900
Continental United States	3,199,784	73,410,992	557,889	15,963,965	5.7	4.6
Area enumerated in 1790	3,199,784	32,435,715	557,889	7,036,638	5.7	4.6
New England	998,879	5,351,133	174,017	1,236,929	5.7	4.3
Maine	96,089	670,067	17,009	161,588	5.6	4.1
New Hampshire	141,500	394,378	24,065	96,534	5.9	4.1
Vermont	85,239	332,800	14,992	80,559	5.7	4.1
Massachusetts	375,779	2,672,527	65,779	604,873	5.7	4.4
Rhode Island	66,533	409,713	11,296	92,735	5.9	4.4
Connecticut	233,739	871,648	40,876	200,640	5.7	4.3
Middle states	962,032	15,009,190	166,762	3,359,344	5.8	4.5
New York	315,409	6,922,931	54,878	1,608,170	5.7	4.3
New Jersey	172,716	1,819,831	[1]29,779	408,993	5.8	4.4
Pennsylvania	423,698	6,086,595	73,874	1,303,174	5.7	4.7
Delaware	50,209	179,833	[1]8,231	39,007	6.1	4.6
Southern states	1,238,873	12,075,392	217,110	2,440,365	5.7	4.9
Maryland and District of Columbia	202,966	1,414,205	[2]36,228	295,302	5.6	4.8
Virginia and West Virginia	454,983	2,747,856	[1]75,830	544,529	6.0	5.0
North Carolina	292,554	1,871,311	[2]52,613	367,565	5.6	5.1
South Carolina	141,565	1,322,918	25,872	267,859	5.5	4.9
Georgia [3]	53,284	624,244	[1]9,867	131,865	5.4	4.7
Kentucky	61,247	2,112,452	[1]10,937	434,228	5.6	4.9
Tennessee	32,274	1,982,406	[1]5,763	399,017	5.6	5.0
Added area	....	40,975,277	....	8,927,327	....	4.6

[1] Estimated.   [2] Estimated for 3 counties.   [3] Part enumerated in 1790.

In the foregoing table the average number of persons per private family for 1790 is necessarily computed for the free population only, while the average for 1900 is computed for the total population. Had the computation at the Twelfth Census been made for white and colored separately, greater accuracy could have been secured by using the return for the white element alone for comparison with the returns for 1790; but such classification was not made. A study was made, however, during the preparation of the Twelfth Census reports, to determine whether such a classification was advisable by reason of apparent difference in size of family in the two elements; and it was found that, in spite of popular impression to the contrary, the difference was so small as to be negligible.

The average size of family in 1790 was 5.7 persons for the entire area covered; for the several states it ranged from 5.4 in Georgia to 6.1 in Delaware. In 1900 the average size of family, both for continental United States as a whole and for the area covered in 1790, had decreased by more than 1 person (5.7 to 4.6); for the states covered in 1790 it ranged from 4.1 in Maine, New Hampshire, and Vermont to 5.1 in North Carolina.

DIAGRAM 8.—CHANGE IN AVERAGE SIZE OF FAMILIES: 1790 TO 1900.

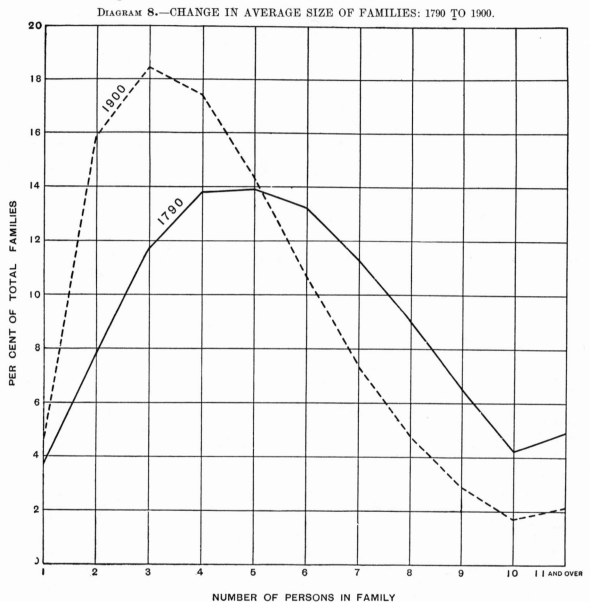

NUMBER OF PERSONS IN FAMILY

This table furnishes another instance in which analysis of the returns of 1790, when compared with similar analysis for the returns of 1900, shows the minimum in 1790 to be larger than the maximum in 1900. At the Twelfth Census 73,410,992 persons in continental United States, out of an entire population of approximately 76,000,000, were returned as living in 15,963,965 private families. If this number of persons (both white and colored) had reported families of the size shown in 1790, the total number of families in 1900 would have been 12,879,121; in other words, in 1900, had the size of family remained the same as in 1790, the number of persons who composed the 15,963,965 families would have been grouped in 3,084,844 fewer families than were actually reported. On the other hand, if the average size of the 15,963,965 families reported in 1900 had been as great as the average shown in 1790, the population in 1900 would have been increased by nearly 20,000,000. This comparison suggests the increase which has been in progress in number of households, without corresponding increase in the number of members. The greater part of this change is doubtless the result of the decreased proportion of children.

The following tables show a distribution, according to size, of the number of private families in 1790 and of the total number of families in 1900:

TABLE 27.—PRIVATE FAMILIES, CLASSIFIED ACCORDING TO SIZE, BY STATES AND TERRITORIES:[1] 1790.

STATE OR TERRITORY.	Total number of families.	NUMBER OF FAMILIES CONTAINING—										
		1 person.	2 persons.	3 persons.	4 persons.	5 persons.	6 persons.	7 persons.	8 persons.	9 persons.	10 persons.	11 persons and over.
Area covered by 1790 schedules in existence	410,636	15,353	31,979	48,116	56,615	57,171	54,052	46,172	36,932	26,687	17,356	20,203
New England	174,017	5,134	13,564	20,428	23,857	24,240	23,247	19,944	15,979	11,600	7,542	8,482
Maine	17,009	1,109	1,115	1,978	2,201	2,223	2,175	1,886	1,531	1,129	784	878
New Hampshire	24,065	814	1,502	2,669	3,282	3,392	3,109	2,855	2,301	1,732	1,131	1,278
Vermont	14,992	505	1,060	1,734	2,146	2,139	2,040	1,781	1,400	895	638	654
Massachusetts	65,779	1,393	5,754	7,990	8,999	9,224	8,709	7,490	5,971	4,380	2,791	3,078
Rhode Island	11,296	231	865	1,387	1,523	1,472	1,551	1,221	1,028	810	510	698
Connecticut	40,876	1,082	3,268	4,670	5,706	5,790	5,663	4,711	3,748	2,654	1,688	1,896
Middle states	128,752	3,669	9,716	15,152	17,916	18,388	17,211	14,695	11,654	8,412	5,440	6,499
New York	54,878	1,123	3,909	6,560	7,945	8,197	7,466	6,330	4,918	3,555	2,233	2,642
Pennsylvania	73,874	2,546	5,807	8,592	9,971	10,191	9,745	8,365	6,736	4,857	3,207	3,857
Southern states	107,867	6,550	8,699	12,536	14,842	14,543	13,594	11,533	9,299	6,675	4,374	5,222
Maryland [2]	33,294	1,687	2,696	3,890	4,619	4,588	4,204	3,640	2,827	1,952	1,326	1,865
North Carolina [3]	48,701	3,519	3,754	5,483	6,482	6,491	6,083	5,162	4,326	3,134	2,038	2,229
South Carolina	25,872	1,344	2,249	3,163	3,741	3,464	3,307	2,731	2,146	1,589	1,010	1,128

[1] Data not available for New Jersey, Delaware, Virginia, Georgia, Kentucky, or Southwest Territory.
[2] Data not available for Allegany, Calvert, or Somersett county.
[3] Data not available for Caswell, Granville, or Orange county.

TABLE 28.— PRIVATE FAMILIES IN 1790, AND ALL FAMILIES IN 1900, CLASSIFIED ACCORDING TO SIZE, BY STATES AND TERRITORIES.[1]

STATE OR TERRITORY, AND CENSUS YEAR.	PER CENT OF FAMILIES CONTAINING—										
	1 person.	2 persons.	3 persons.	4 persons.	5 persons.	6 persons.	7 persons.	8 persons.	9 persons.	10 persons.	11 persons and over.
Continental United States:											
1790	3.7	7.8	11.7	13.8	13.9	13.2	11.2	9.0	6.5	4.2	4.9
1900	5.1	15.0	17.6	16.9	14.2	10.9	7.7	5.2	3.2	1.9	2.2
Area covered by 1790 schedules in existence:											
1790	3.7	7.8	11.7	13.8	13.9	13.2	11.2	9.0	6.5	4.2	4.9
1900	4.4	15.9	18.4	17.4	14.3	10.7	7.4	4.8	2.9	1.7	2.1
New England—											
1790	3.0	7.8	11.7	13.7	13.9	13.4	11.5	9.2	6.7	4.3	4.9
1900	4.9	17.6	19.6	17.7	13.9	9.9	6.5	4.1	2.4	1.4	2.0
Maine—											
1790	6.5	6.6	11.6	12.9	13.1	12.8	11.1	9.0	6.6	4.6	5.2
1900	5.3	19.0	21.0	18.2	13.4	9.1	5.7	3.5	2.1	1.2	1.6
New Hampshire—											
1790	3.4	6.2	11.1	13.6	14.1	12.9	11.9	9.6	7.2	4.7	5.3
1900	6.6	20.4	20.5	17.3	12.7	8.5	5.4	3.4	2.1	1.3	2.0
Vermont—											
1790	3.4	7.1	11.6	14.3	14.3	13.6	11.9	9.3	6.0	4.3	4.4
1900	5.2	18.5	21.0	18.3	13.9	9.5	5.8	3.5	1.9	1.0	1.3
Massachusetts—											
1790	2.1	8.7	12.1	13.7	14.0	13.2	11.4	9.1	6.7	4.2	4.7
1900	4.5	16.8	19.0	17.7	14.2	10.3	6.8	4.3	2.6	1.5	2.2
Rhode Island—											
1790	2.0	7.7	12.3	13.5	13.0	13.7	10.8	9.1	7.2	4.5	6.2
1900	4.4	17.7	18.8	17.4	13.8	10.0	6.9	4.5	2.8	1.6	2.2
Connecticut—											
1790	2.6	8.0	11.4	14.0	14.2	13.9	11.5	9.2	6.5	4.1	4.6
1900	4.8	17.3	19.2	17.7	14.0	10.3	6.8	4.3	2.5	1.3	1.8
Middle states—											
1790	2.8	7.5	11.8	13.9	14.3	13.4	11.4	9.1	6.5	4.2	5.0
1900	4.0	16.0	18.8	17.9	14.7	10.8	7.3	4.5	2.7	1.5	1.8
New York—											
1790	2.0	7.1	12.0	14.5	14.9	13.6	11.5	9.0	6.5	4.1	4.8
1900	4.6	17.5	19.5	18.0	14.3	10.3	6.7	4.1	2.3	1.2	1.5
Pennsylvania—											
1790	3.4	7.9	11.6	13.5	13.8	13.2	11.3	9.1	6.6	4.3	5.2
1900	3.3	14.1	18.0	17.7	15.1	11.5	8.0	5.2	3.2	1.8	2.1
Southern states—											
1790	6.1	8.1	11.6	13.8	13.5	12.6	10.7	8.6	6.2	4.1	4.8
1900	4.9	13.1	15.6	15.4	13.8	11.5	8.9	6.6	4.4	2.7	3.1
Maryland and District of Columbia—											
1790	5.1	8.1	11.7	13.9	13.8	12.6	10.9	8.5	5.9	4.0	5.6
1900	4.1	13.7	16.7	16.6	14.7	11.7	8.5	5.8	3.6	2.1	2.5
North Carolina—											
1790	7.2	7.7	11.3	13.3	13.3	12.5	10.6	8.9	6.4	4.2	4.6
1900	4.6	12.1	14.9	15.1	13.7	11.7	9.4	7.2	5.0	3.1	3.3
South Carolina—											
1790	5.2	8.7	12.2	14.5	13.4	12.8	10.6	8.3	6.1	3.9	4.4
1900	6.2	13.8	15.2	14.7	12.9	10.9	8.7	6.7	4.6	3.0	3.4
Added area:											
1900	5.4	14.6	17.2	16.7	14.2	11.0	7.9	5.4	3.4	2.0	2.2

[1] Data for 1790 not available for New Jersey, Delaware, Virginia, Georgia, Kentucky, or Southwest Territory.

In each class of families having less than 6 members, the proportion of the total number of families was less in 1790 than in 1900 both for the United States as a whole and for the area for which the 1790 schedules are in existence. For families having 6 members and over, the reverse was true. It is significant that in 1900 the proportion of families having 2, 3, 4, and 5 members was smaller, while the proportion in each class having more than 5 members was larger, in the added area than in the area for which the 1790 schedules are in existence. This doubtless reflects the influence of dense population, and especially of urban population, upon the size of family. For the area enumerated in 1790 the proportion of families having only 2 members was twice as large in 1900 as in 1790, while the proportion of those having 9 persons or more was only half as large in 1900. These facts emphasize the decided reduction in the size of families which occurred during the course of the century.

In 1900, as compared with 1790, New England showed a greater decrease in the size of family than the other sections of the original area;[1] the proportion of families having 8 members was less than one-half as great in 1900 as in 1790, and the proportion having 10 members less than one-third as great in the later year. In the state of Vermont the proportion of families having 10 members dropped to one-fourth.

In the Southern states the decline in the size of the family was less marked.

Upon arranging the total number of families in four general groups according to size, it is found that in 1790 approximately one-third of all families had less than 5 members, while in 1900 this group included considerably more than one-half of all families. Contrast between the classification of families by size in 1790 and in 1900 is equally marked in the remaining groups, the larger families showing a much greater proportion in 1790 than in the later year.

[1] Of economic and social conditions in New England at the close of the eighteenth century, W. B. Weeden writes as follows: "A controlling feature of our society was in the rapid and easy growth of the family out of the conditions prevailing in all the towns. The common people created self-sustaining families as readily as the banyan tree spreads a grove around the parent trunk. New land was easily obtained. A thrifty farmer could buy acres enough on which to settle his sons from the savings of a few years. The ax could create the log house anywhere, and in most places sawmills gave a cheap supply of planks and deals. The splitting of shingles was an accomplishment almost as common as whittling. The practice of making this cheap and excellent roofing material was carried into the Middle states by the New England emigrants. The homestead was often given to the younger son, who provided for the parents in their old age, the elder brothers having acquired settlements of their own. Thus the teeming social soil was ready for the family roots, which were constantly extending. Unmarried men of thirty were rare in country towns. Matrons were grandmothers at forty; mother and daughter frequently nursed their children at the same time. Father, son, and grandson often worked together in one field; and the field was their own."—Economic and Social History of New England, 1620–1789, Vol. II, page 860.

TABLE 29.—*Private families in 1790 and all families in 1900, classified according to size, with per cent distribution.*

| SIZE OF FAMILY. | Private families in 1790. | ALL FAMILIES IN 1900. | |
		In continental United States.	In area for which 1790 schedules are in existence.
		NUMBER.	
All families	[1] 410,636	16,187,715	5,108,092
Less than 5 persons	152,063	8,832,364	2,865,677
5 to 8 persons	194,327	6,171,689	1,902,366
9 or 10 persons	44,043	830,616	235,217
11 persons and over	20,203	353,046	104,832
		PER CENT DISTRIBUTION.	
All families	100.0	100.0	100.0
Less than 5 persons	37.0	54.6	56.1
5 to 8 persons	47.3	38.1	37.2
9 or 10 persons	10.7	5.1	4.6
11 persons and over	4.9	2.2	2.1

[1] Incomplete owing to loss of schedules.

The progress of the nation from 1790 to 1900 has involved far-reaching social changes, during which the inhabitants have gathered from farm and frontier into densely settled industrial centers. The effect of this change on the size of family and on family environment has been very marked; it is probable that no statistical change recorded in these pages as having occurred during the century is more decided or possesses greater economic significance.

SLAVEHOLDING AND NONSLAVEHOLDING FAMILIES.

A subdivision of the white and free colored families reported at the First Census into two general classes, slaveholding and nonslaveholding, is presented in Table 30.

The average size of white slaveholding families was slightly greater than the average for white nonslaveholding families. Of the total number of families under consideration, little more than 10 per cent were classed as slaveholding. Approximately one-fourth of the slaveholding families reported were located in New England and the Middle states. Those in New England were reported principally by Rhode Island and Connecticut; and of the 2 Middle states represented, New York contributed much the larger number of slaveholders.

Table 114, page 276, presents the information summarized in Table 30, extended to counties and minor civil divisions so far as they were returned separately.

TABLE 30.—NUMBER OF PRIVATE FAMILIES, CLASSIFIED AS SLAVEHOLDING AND NONSLAVEHOLDING WHITE AND FREE COLORED, WITH PER CENT FAMILIES OF EACH CLASS FORM OF ALL PRIVATE FAMILIES, BY STATES AND TERRITORIES:[1] 1790.

STATE OR TERRITORY.	Total number.	PRIVATE FAMILIES. Slaveholding. White. Number of families.	Total.	Average per family.	Slaveholding. Free colored. Number of families.	Total.	Average per family.	Nonslaveholding. White. Number of families.	Total.	Average per family.	Nonslaveholding. Free colored. Number of families.	Total.	Average per family.	PER CENT. Slaveholding. White.	Free colored.	Nonslaveholding. White.	Free colored.
Area covered by 1790 schedules in existence..............	410,636	47,664	280,345	5.9	195	652	3.3	357,811	2,032,768	5.7	4,966	19,533	3.9	11.6	(2)	87.1	1.2
New England...............	174,017	2,141	13,522	6.3	6	23	3.8	170,242	978,684	5.7	1,628	6,650	4.1	1.2	(2)	97.8	0.9
Maine..................	17,009	....	....	......	......	......	......	16,972	95,953	5.7	37	136	3.7	....	......	99.8	0.2
New Hampshire........	24,065	123	760	6.2	......	......	......	23,859	140,428	5.9	83	312	3.8	0.5	......	99.1	0.3
Vermont...............	14,992	....	....	......	......	......	......	14,969	85,154	5.7	23	85	3.7	....	......	99.8	0.2
Massachusetts.........	65,779	....	....	......	......	......	......	65,149	373,187	5.7	630	2,592	4.1	....	......	99.0	1.0
Rhode Island.........	11,296	461	2,993	6.5	......	......	......	10,393	61,590	5.9	442	1,950	4.4	4.1	......	92.0	3.9
Connecticut...........	40,876	1,557	9,769	6.3	6	23	3.8	38,900	222,372	5.7	413	1,575	3.8	3.8	(2)	95.2	1.0
Middle states...............	128,752	9,638	60,437	6.3	16	63	3.9	117,869	674,120	5.7	1,229	4,487	3.7	7.5	(2)	91.5	1.0
New York.............	54,878	7,787	47,495	6.1	9	40	4.4	46,398	265,430	5.7	684	2,444	3.6	14.2	(2)	84.5	1.2
Pennsylvania..........	73,874	1,851	12,942	7.0	7	23	3.3	71,471	408,690	5.7	545	2,043	3.7	2.5	(2)	96.7	0.7
Southern states.............	107,867	35,885	206,386	5.8	173	566	3.3	69,700	379,964	5.5	2,109	8,396	4.0	33.3	0.2	64.6	2.0
Maryland[3].............	33,294	12,142	71,168	5.9	84	211	2.5	19,870	109,577	5.5	1,198	4,572	3.8	36.5	0.3	59.7	3.6
North Carolina[4]........	48,701	14,945	87,121	5.8	28	119	4.3	33,076	178,077	5.4	652	2,902	4.5	30.7	0.1	67.9	1.3
South Carolina..........	25,872	8,798	48,097	5.5	61	236	3.9	16,754	92,310	5.5	259	922	3.6	34.0	0.2	64.8	1.0

[1] Data not available for New Jersey, Delaware, Virginia, Georgia, Kentucky, or Southwest Territory.
[2] Less than one-tenth of 1 per cent.
[3] Data not available for Allegany, Calvert, or Somersett county.
[4] Data not available for Caswell, Granville, or Orange county, except the total number of families.

NUMBER OF CHILDREN PER WHITE FAMILY.

In the preceding chapter the number of white females under 16 years of age was determined with reasonable accuracy. Hence it is possible to consider the total number of children (under 16 years) per white family in 1790 in the area for which schedules are still in existence, as compared with the number shown by the census returns in 1900.

The number of private white families included in the schedules of the First Census which are still in existence is slightly more than 400,000. In the course of a century the number of private white families in the same area increased more than tenfold, but the number of white children under 16 years of age in the same area increased during the same period little more than sixfold. From the returns for the first and last censuses of record, it is possible to show that in the area included the average number of children under 16 years of age per family was nearly twice as great in 1790 as in 1900. Moreover, it will be observed from the table that the number varied but little (from 2.6 to 2.9) in 1790, while in 1900, although the averages returned were in general reduced about one-half, the range was much wider. Both at the beginning and at the close of the century the lowest average was shown for New England. In 1900 the highest average was shown for the Southern states.

TABLE 31.—Average number of white children under 16 years per private white family, by states: 1790 and 1900.[1]

STATE OR TERRITORY.	PRIVATE WHITE FAMILIES. 1790	1900	WHITE CHILDREN UNDER 16 YEARS OF AGE. 1790	1900	AVERAGE NUMBER OF WHITE CHILDREN UNDER 16 YEARS OF AGE PER FAMILY. 1790	1900
Area for which schedules are in existence........	412,850	4,661,504	1,149,001	7,095,506	2.8	1.5
New England............	172,383	1,221,856	466,290	1,610,495	2.7	1.3
Maine.................	16,972	161,041	48,753	200,792	2.9	1.2
New Hampshire......	23,982	96,354	68,564	112,987	2.9	1.2
Vermont.............	14,969	80,388	43,632	100,857	2.9	1.3
Massachusetts........	65,149	596,611	169,869	786,349	2.6	1.3
Rhode Island.........	10,854	90,458	29,987	144,163	2.8	1.6
Connecticut..........	40,457	197,004	105,485	265,347	2.6	1.3
Middle states............	127,507	2,855,574	365,764	4,330,159	2.9	1.5
New York............	54,185	1,584,311	155,090	2,212,213	2.9	1.4
Pennsylvania........	73,322	1,271,263	210,674	2,117,946	2.9	1.7
Southern states..........	112,960	584,074	316,947	1,154,852	2.8	2.0
Maryland and District of Columbia[2]..	35,052	232,270	93,843	381,253	2.7	1.6
North Carolina[3]......	52,356	244,524	149,942	540,543	2.9	2.2
South Carolina.......	25,552	107,280	73,162	233,056	2.9	2.2

[1] Data not available for New Jersey, Delaware, Virginia, Georgia, Kentucky, or Southwest Territory.
[2] Includes an estimate for Allegany, Calvert, and Somersett counties.
[3] Includes an estimate for Caswell, Granville, and Orange counties.

In the foregoing table the number of white children per private family has been considered only for the states for which schedules are in existence. For the entire United States in 1900 the average was 1.7, and for the area added after the First Census the average was 1.8. The highest proportions (2.3) were shown for Texas and Mississippi.

Had the ratio of children to private white families been the same in 1790 as it was in 1900, the number of children in 1790 would have been less than half the number actually reported at the First Census. It would be idle to speculate upon the effect which so low a proportion in 1790 and at subsequent early censuses would have wrought upon the nation; but without question had the proportion which now actually exists appeared at the beginning of the century, the history of the Republic would have been materially altered.

On the other hand, the application of the generous proportion of children shown for 1790 to the number of private white families reported in 1900 (which averaged less than 2 children each) results in a theoretical increase in the number of young children so great as to be astonishing. In short, had the households into which the white inhabitants of the United States were divided in 1900 been as prolific as were the households of the wh. citizens of the Republic at the beginning of Constitutional Government, the population of the United States in 1900 would have been greater by 15,500,000 children, regardless of the cumulative effect of the maintenance of the higher ratio at previous censuses.

FAMILIES AND DWELLINGS.

The printed schedules used by the enumerators for Massachusetts at the First Census included an inquiry regarding the number of dwellings within their respective districts, probably instituted as a result of a similar inquiry at the Colonial census of Massachusetts in 1764–65. The returns secured afford a basis for an interesting study concerning the average number of families and of persons to a dwelling in urban and in rural communities.

By Census definition in 1900, a dwelling is a place in which, at the time of the census, one or more persons regularly sleep; hence uninhabited houses were not counted as dwellings at the Twelfth Census. The same was true of the First Census, since no vacant houses were returned on the schedules.

Inasmuch as tenement and apartment houses were returned as dwellings in 1900, it would be natural (especially in a commonwealth conspicuous for its industrial interests and dense population) to expect that in 1900 the number of families per dwelling would be larger than in 1790, when there were few tenement houses and no apartment houses. The figures, however, clearly show that the average has not materially increased.

The following table shows the number of dwellings and private families, the total population, and the average number of families and of persons per dwelling, for each county of Massachusetts enumerated in 1790, and for the same areas in 1900:

TABLE 32.—*Dwellings and private families in the counties of Massachusetts reported in 1790, and in the same areas [1] in 1900.*

COUNTY.	Dwell-ings.	PRIVATE FAMILIES.		POPULATION.	
		Total.	Average per dwelling.	Total.	Average per dwelling.
1790					
The state............	54,377	65,779	1.2	378,556	7.0
Barnstable..............	2,343	2,889	1.2	17,342	7.4
Berkshire..............	4,476	4,899	1.1	30,263	6.8
Bristol..............	4,514	5,541	1.2	31,696	7.0
Dukes and Nantucket......	1,013	1,430	1.4	7,810	7.7
Essex..............	7,644	10,883	1.4	57,879	7.6
Hampshire..............	9,181	9,617	1.0	59,656	6.5
Middlesex..............	5,998	7,580	1.3	42,769	7.1
Plymouth..............	4,240	5,173	1.2	29,512	7.0
Suffolk..............	6,355	8,038	1.3	44,865	7.1
Worcester..............	8,613	9,729	1.1	56,764	6.6
1900					
The state............	451,362	604,373	1.3	2,805,346	6.2
Barnstable..............	7,678	7,911	1.0	27,826	3.6
Berkshire..............	18,257	20,530	1.1	95,774	5.2
Bristol..............	34,451	53,856	1.6	251,229	7.3
Dukes and Nantucket......	2,209	2,332	1.1	7,567	3.4
Essex..............	61,004	79,664	1.3	356,569	5.8
Hampshire..............	46,393	58,640	1.3	275,028	5.9
Middlesex..............	108,206	133,991	1.2	628,097	5.8
Plymouth..............	22,358	26,330	1.2	108,114	4.8
Suffolk..............	97,439	147,443	1.5	708,324	7.3
Worcester..............	53,367	74,176	1.4	346,818	6.5

[1] Except that no adjustment has been made for changes since 1790 in the boundary line between Massachusetts and Rhode Island.

The average number of persons per dwelling in the state decreased from 7 in 1790 to 6.2 in 1900. In only 2 counties, Bristol and Suffolk, did the average increase; this increase was undoubtedly due to the influence of tenement and apartment house population, though it should be borne in mind that in these counties in 1900 were large numbers of foreign born, whose families were much larger than the average native family. The reduction in the average number of persons to a dwelling in the remaining counties is undoubtedly the result of the decreased size of family. It will be remembered that in this state, as in the other New England states, low average size of family was shown, and the influence of the great change recorded appears to have been such as to overcome the opposite tendency of occupancy of a dwelling or building by a considerable number of families.

The counties having the largest average number of persons to a dwelling in 1790 (Dukes and Nantucket and Essex) had very small averages in 1900. The explanation of the large averages for 1790 lies partly in the fact that these same counties showed the largest average numbers of families per dwelling. The very small averages shown for 1900 for these counties, and also for Barnstable county, undoubtedly reflect the fact that the population of these counties is exceptional in several particulars. It is principally native white of native parents—in which element the average size of family is very small—and, as shown by the state census of 1905, is still decreasing.

Inspection of the average number of persons per dwelling in the Massachusetts counties in 1790, as compared with similar figures for 1900, shows that the range of variation was more than three times as great at the Twelfth Census as it was at the First. The relative uniformity shown in 1790, and the fact that nearly all the population of the country was engaged in agriculture, go far to justify the presumption that, at the time of the First Census, the conditions of population in one state closely resembled those in the other states of the limited area covered by the census. On this basis the approximate number of dwellings in the United States may reasonably be computed by employing as a ratio the number of families per dwelling in Massachusetts.

The number of dwellings occupied in 1900 by families, other than private, can not be deducted from the total number; but it is doubtful whether such a deduction, if it could be made, would affect appreciably the average number of private families per dwelling. It was found by computation that the ratio of all families to all dwellings in Massachusetts differed from the ratio of private families to all dwellings by only one one-hundredth of a family per dwelling.

Since in Massachusetts the proportion of colored families was so small that their effect on the ratio of all families to all dwellings may be disregarded, it was deemed more accurate to apply the ratio for this state to the white population of the other states (in many of which the colored population was relatively very numerous), rather than to their total population, and thus to obtain the number of dwellings of white persons only.

The increase during the century in the number of dwellings in the area enumerated in 1790 was nearly twelvefold. This table further illustrates the tendency toward large families in 1790, offsetting, in the averages, the small families and large buildings (such as the apartment and tenement houses) in 1900. As previously suggested, the effect of the former overcomes the latter, with the rather unexpected result that the average of 7 white persons per dwelling in 1790 declined to 5.7 in 1900, and in 4 out of the 17 states presented the average was less than 5. Had the average number of white persons to a dwelling which appeared in 1900 prevailed in 1790, there would have been approximately 100,000 more dwellings of white persons in the Republic. On the other hand, had the average which prevailed in 1790 prevailed also in 1900, the number of dwellings would be reduced approximately 1,000,000—the equivalent of all the dwellings in New York, the most populous state in the Union. These comparisons, however, possess value only as measuring vividly the change which has occurred in the proportions.

TABLE 33.—*Estimated average number of white persons per dwelling, for each state and territory enumerated in 1790, and for the same areas [1] in 1900.*

STATE OR TERRITORY.	1790			1900		
	White population.	Number of dwellings of white persons.[2]	Average number of persons to a dwelling.	White population.	Number of dwellings of white persons.[3]	Aver age number of persons to a dwelling.
Area enumerated in 1790	3,172,444	454,309	7.0	29,564,821	5,209,847	5.7
New England	992,384	140,742	7.1	5,527,026	978,140	5.7
Maine	96,107	14,218	6.8	692,226	148,028	4.7
New Hampshire	141,112	19,986	7.1	410,791	86,467	4.8
Vermont	85,072	12,467	6.8	342,771	74,831	4.6
Massachusetts	373,187	53,312	7.0	2,769,764	445,637	6.2
Rhode Island	64,670	9,045	7.1	419,050	66,312	6.3
Connecticut	232,236	31,714	7.3	892,424	156,865	5.7
Middle states	954,003	136,477	7.0	15,264,839	2,564,696	6.0
New York	314,366	45,158	7.0	7,156,881	1,019,228	7.0
New Jersey	169,954	24,279	7.0	1,812,317	308,872	5.9
Pennsylvania	423,373	61,103	6.9	6,141,664	1,204,764	5.1
Delaware	46,310	5,937	7.8	153,977	31,832	4.8
Southern states	1,226,057	177,090	6.9	8,772,956	1,667,011	5.3
Maryland and District of Columbia	208,649	26,677	7.8	1,143,956	211,429	5.4
Virginia and West Virginia	442,117	61,405	7.2	2,108,088	395,596	5.3
North Carolina	289,181	40,018	7.2	1,263,603	240,530	5.3
South Carolina	140,178	21,293	6.6	557,807	107,915	5.2
Georgia[4]	52,886	12,507	4.2	297,007	58,580	5.1
Kentucky	61,133	10,233	6.0	1,862,309	359,052	5.2
Tennessee	31,913	4,957	6.4	1,540,186	293,909	5.2

[1] Except that no adjustment has been made for changes since 1790 in the boundary line between Massachusetts and Rhode Island.
[2] Estimated on the basis of the ratio of white and free colored families to all dwellings in Massachusetts.
[3] Estimated.
[4] Part enumerated in 1790.

IX. PROPORTION OF CHILDREN IN WHITE POPULATION.

RATIO OF WHITE ADULTS OF SELF-SUPPORTING AGE TO WHITE
CHILDREN—OF WHITE CHILDREN TO ADULT WHITE FEMALES—
EFFECT OF CHANGES IN THE PROPORTION OF CHILDREN.

It is probable that no change in the composition of the white population of the United States possesses greater interest, or is more important to the future welfare of the nation, than the proportion of the total constituted by children. It is clear that upon the changes in this respect, occurring from census to census, in the Republic and in individual states and communities, depends practically all economic readjustment. What proportion of the white population was formed by children under 16 years of age at the First Census, and at the Twelfth? And, if a marked change has occurred during the period under consideration, what are some of the possible causes?

In the following table comparison is made of the proportion of children per 1,000 of the total white population at intervals from 1790 to 1900. It is necessary to accept the age period under 16 years as a limitation of "children," because of the use of that age period at the earlier censuses.

TABLE 34.—*Number of children per 1,000 of the white population, by states and territories: 1790, 1820, 1850, 1880, and 1900.*

STATE OR TERRITORY.	NUMBER OF WHITE PERSONS UNDER 16 YEARS OF AGE PER 1,000 OF ALL AGES.				
	1790	1820	1850	1880	1900
United States	490	489	431	390	356
Area enumerated in 1790	490	483	414	373	344
New England	470	443	358	309	291
Maine	507	485	404	318	290
New Hampshire	486	447	342	281	275
Vermont	513	463	378	324	294
Massachusetts	455	420	338	305	290
Rhode Island	464	429	349	315	305
Connecticut	454	422	340	315	297
Middle states	494	485	405	358	326
New York	493	484	385	336	309
New Jersey	487	472	410	361	327
Pennsylvania	498	489	429	385	345
Delaware	494	479	431	367	327
Southern states	502	508	464	431	402
Maryland and District of Columbia	450	457	414	377	333
Virginia and West Virginia	497	487	451	434	400
North Carolina	519	507	455	429	428
South Carolina	522	503	456	433	418
Georgia [1]	531	519	493	442	421
Kentucky	545	533	474	439	404
Tennessee [2]	[3] 550	551	488	449	411
Added area	....	526	463	406	368

[1] Entire state.
[2] Southwest Territory in 1790.
[3] Basic figures obtained from ratios existing in Tennessee in 1800.

The change which occurred in the original area during the first thirty-year period—from 1790 to 1820—

was so slight as to possess little significance. During this period there was, indeed, a slight increase in the proportion shown in the Southern states. The decline in the succeeding periods was—1820 to 1850, 69; 1850 to 1880, 41; 1880 to 1900 (twenty years), 29; hence, the decline in the proportion of white children under 16 in each 1,000 white persons of all ages was 7 during the first thirty years of Federal census taking and 139 in the succeeding eighty years.

It will be observed that the Southern states, although little affected since the First Census by additions to population through immigration, have, by maintaining a higher birth rate than the New England and Middle states, increased their numbers from distinctively native population at a rate approximating, or possibly exceeding, the rate attained by other portions of the country with the assistance of immigrants and their descendants.

RATIO OF WHITE ADULTS OF SELF-SUPPORTING AGE TO WHITE CHILDREN.

The changes between the First and Twelfth censuses in the average number of white adults available for the support of each white child are shown in the following table. Since children do not, as a rule, pass suddenly into the adult class with respect to ability to support young persons, for the purposes of this study twenty years is set as the minimum age at which persons are capable of supporting children.

TABLE 35.—*Ratio of white adults of self-supporting age to white children: 1790 to 1900.*

CENSUS YEAR.	White persons 20 years and over.	White children under 16 years.	Ratio of persons 20 years and over to all children under 16 years.
1790	1,214,388	1,553,260	0.78
1800	1,832,375	2,156,357	0.85
1810	2,485,176	2,933,211	0.85
1820	3,395,467	3,843,680	0.88
1830	4,626,290	4,970,210	0.93
1840	6,440,054	6,510,878	0.99
1850	9,421,637	8,428,458	1.12
1860	13,310,660	11,329,812	1.17
1870	17,070,373	13,719,431	1.24
1880	22,928,219	16,919,639	1.36
1890	30,263,755	20,154,222	1.50
1900	37,748,491	23,846,473	1.58

For the censuses from 1790 to 1850, inclusive, some minor adjustments of age periods for this table proved to be necessary in order to secure comparable figures; in some instances these adjustments were for the period under 16 years of age, and in others for the period 20 years of age and over. They were not sufficient, however, to affect to any appreciable degree the percentages which appear in the table, even though it be conceded that some errors may exist in the computations required to be made from the nearest age group.

DIAGRAM 9.—*Ratio of white adults of self-supporting age to white children under 16 years.*

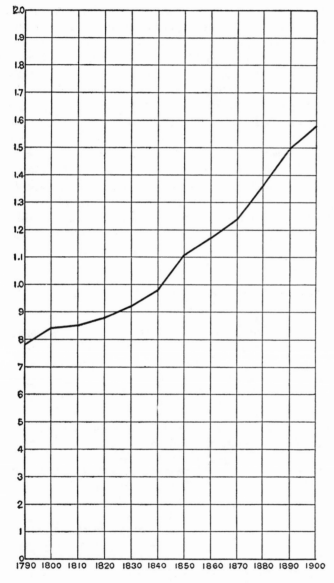

The proportion for 1900 is practically double that for 1790. The uninterrupted increase shown in the proportion of white adults of self-supporting age to white children proves exceedingly suggestive. At the First Census 780 adults contributed to the maintenance and rearing of 1,000 children in the United States; but in 1900 the relationship of adults to children had

changed so greatly that the ratio became 1,580 adults to each 1,000 children.[1]

The ratios of adults to children at the most recent censuses of the principal nations of Europe were as follows:

COUNTRY.	Census year.	Ratio of adults of self-supporting age (20 years and over) to children under 16 years.
France	1901	2.4
Ireland	1901	1.8
England and Wales	1901	1.7
Scotland	1901	1.6
Italy	1901	1.6
Austria-Hungary	1900	1.5
Germany	1900	1.5
United States	1900	1.6

In 1790 the ratios of white adults of self-supporting age to white children were practically uniform throughout the area enumerated. This fact suggests that in 1790 similar conditions prevailed generally throughout the country in connection with domestic and family affairs. In 1900 the ratios varied widely in different states, and in some instances—especially in New England and in some of the other older settled states—attained a high figure. The analysis is presented in full in the following table. In order to show the effect of locality, the states are grouped under main and minor geographic divisions.

In the different divisions and states of continental United States the number of white adults available in 1900 for the support of each 1,000 white children varied from 1,060 in Indian Territory to 2,400 in Nevada. Within the area enumerated in 1790 the extremes were 1,130 for North Carolina and (disregarding the District of Columbia) 2,390 for New Hampshire.

When the states of the area enumerated in 1790 are grouped by geographic divisions it is found that in both 1790 and 1900 the Southern states showed the smallest proportion of white adults of self-

---

[1] " No great power of imagination is needed in order to perceive the enormous effect of these (European population) changes, * * * and if at the present moment yearly 20 young persons out of a population of 1,000 enter life as full grown members of society, it will make a great difference if this number is reduced—say to 15. Everywhere in offices and shops the number of juveniles will be on the decrease, whereas gray-haired officials will be more abundant, and if it is true that all new ideas are born in young brains, then this distribution of age is identical with a serious loss for the population. * * *

In a stagnant population, according to the life tables for males, about 26 per cent would be under 15 years old, but if all the principal causes of death disappear the number would sink to 23 per cent. In the former case 74 adults would bring up 26 children; in the latter the numbers would be 77 and 23; consequently there would, in the case of the higher, accordingly be 2.8 adults to 1 child, in the other, 3.3."—*Westergaard, Proceedings of the International Institute of Statistics, 1907, page 113.*

supporting age to white children, and the New England states showed the largest. In 1900, however, the two extremes had grown so far apart that the Southern states, although nearly doubling their proportion during the century, showed a ratio scarcely more than one-half of that indicated for New England. The difference between the ratios per 1,000 children for the two sections had advanced from 700 and 800 adults, respectively, in 1790, to 1,280 and 2,190 in 1900.

TABLE 36.—*Ratio of white adults of self-supporting age to white children, by states and territories: 1900.*

STATE OR TERRITORY.	White population under 16 years.	White population 20 years and over.	Ratio of white population 20 years and over to white population under 16 years.
Continental United States [1]	23,846,473	37,748,491	1.58
Area enumerated in 1790	10,464,298	17,663,445	1.69
New England	1,610,495	3,531,973	2.19
Maine	200,792	441,215	2.20
New Hampshire	112,987	269,686	2.39
Vermont	100,857	217,746	2.16
Massachusetts	804,542	1,774,910	2.21
Rhode Island	125,970	262,269	2.08
Connecticut	265,347	566,147	2.13
Middle states	4,972,312	9,179,888	1.85
New York	2,212,213	4,438,326	2.01
New Jersey	591,730	1,092,418	1.85
Pennsylvania	2,117,946	3,557,203	1.68
Delaware	50,423	91,941	1.82
Southern states	3,881,491	4,951,584	1.28
Maryland and District of Columbia	381,253	674,660	1.77
Virginia and West Virginia	844,206	1,084,553	1.28
North Carolina	540,543	613,164	1.13
South Carolina	233,056	273,618	1.17
Georgia [2]	497,862	580,671	1.17
Kentucky	751,566	953,950	1.27
Tennessee	633,005	770,968	1.22
Added area	13,382,175	20,085,046	1.50
Northern states	9,222,868	14,510,777	1.57
Ohio	1,335,964	2,406,258	1.80
Indiana	847,755	1,410,271	1.66
Illinois	1,660,114	2,715,180	1.64
Michigan	813,188	1,401,750	1.72
Wisconsin	780,664	1,113,736	1.43
Minnesota	668,183	935,121	1.40
Iowa	802,660	1,236,108	1.54
Missouri	1,095,731	1,605,117	1.46
North Dakota	128,739	160,507	1.25
South Dakota	155,250	195,142	1.26
Nebraska	408,226	561,678	1.38
Kansas	526,394	769,909	1.46
Southern states	2,898,532	3,232,544	1.12
Florida	121,473	151,885	1.25
Alabama	431,494	480,601	1.11
Mississippi	276,328	307,476	1.11
Louisiana	307,120	361,674	1.18
Texas	1,057,904	1,160,016	1.10
Indian Territory	134,300	141,961	1.06
Oklahoma	154,435	183,954	1.19
Arkansas	415,478	444,977	1.07
Western states	1,260,775	2,341,725	1.86
Montana	69,674	143,887	2.07
Wyoming	28,843	54,107	1.88
Colorado	169,736	324,184	1.91
New Mexico	74,124	93,918	1.27
Arizona	31,307	55,314	1.77
Utah	118,758	130,847	1.10
Nevada	9,689	23,262	2.40
Idaho	60,508	82,975	1.37
Washington	162,542	300,219	1.85
Oregon	131,768	232,065	1.76
California	403,826	900,947	2.23

[1] Excluding persons stationed abroad.   [2] Entire state.

The marked difference in the ratio shown by the group of Southern states, in comparison with some other sections, suggests a tabulation of the South in comparison with the rest of the country; and upon making such analysis it appears that the ratio of white adults of self-supporting age to each 1,000 white children in 1900 was 1,210 in the South and 1,730 in the remainder of the country.

It must not be overlooked that the ratios here shown are based upon the entire white population, native and foreign. It was impossible to secure an analysis for the native and foreign elements separately; but attempts to secure such separation indicated that the native element tended to record a much higher ratio of adults to children than the foreign element—in some instances, indeed, probably exceeding 3,000 adults to each 1,000 children.

RATIO OF WHITE CHILDREN TO ADULT WHITE FEMALES.

The relative importance of children in the white population has already been measured by considering the proportion children form of the total and the ratio of adults of self-supporting age to children. Another standpoint from which to view this subject consists in a consideration of the ratio of white children (under 16 years of age) to white females 16 years of age and over.

TABLE 37.—*Ratio of white children to adult white females in each state and territory enumerated in 1790 and in the same areas in 1900.*

STATE OR TERRITORY.	RATIO OF WHITE CHILDREN UNDER 16 TO ALL WHITE FEMALES 16 YEARS AND OVER.	
	1790	1900
Area enumerated in 1790	1.9	1.0
New England	1.7	0.8
Maine	2.1	0.8
New Hampshire	1.9	0.8
Vermont	2.3	0.9
Massachusetts	1.6	0.8
Rhode Island	1.6	0.8
Connecticut	1.6	0.8
Middle states	2.0	1.0
New York	2.1	0.9
New Jersey	2.0	1.0
Pennsylvania	2.1	1.1
Delaware	2.0	1.0
Southern states	2.0	1.3
Maryland and District of Columbia	1.6	1.0
Virginia and West Virginia	2.0	1.4
North Carolina	2.2	1.5
South Carolina	2.3	1.4
Georgia	2.4	1.4
Kentucky	2.6	1.4
Tennessee	2.7	1.4

Comparison of the ratios shown in this table for 1790 and 1900 reveals a variation comparable in extent with that shown in Table 35. An average of nearly 2 children to every white female of mature years in 1790 declined to an average of 1 in 1900, or half as great for the entire area considered. In all the New England states, and in New York, the average was less than 1 in 1900.

The significance of this subject is so great that it will be appropriate to point out the conditions which prevailed in 1850 and 1900 in continental United States and in individual states.

TABLE 38.—RATIO OF WHITE CHILDREN TO ALL WHITE FEMALES 16 YEARS OF AGE AND OVER, BY STATES AND TERRITORIES: 1850 AND 1900.

STATE OR TERRITORY.	1850			1900 [1]		
	White females 16 years and over.[2]	White children under 16 years.[2]	Ratio of white children to white females 16 years and over.	White females 16 years and over.	White children under 16 years.	Ratio of white children to white females 16 years and over.
Continental United States	5,376,497	8,428,458	1.6	20,822,625	23,846,473	1.1
Area enumerated in 1790	3,620,445	5,088,903	1.4	9,735,972	10,090,044	1.0
New England	878,777	968,798	1.1	1,993,736	1,610,495	0.8
Maine	169,536	234,873	1.4	243,124	200,792	0.8
New Hampshire	107,780	108,632	1.0	149,330	112,987	0.8
Vermont	95,547	118,583	1.2	118,318	100,857	0.9
Massachusetts	335,407	332,988	1.0	1,019,195	804,542	0.8
Rhode Island	48,332	50,270	1.0	150,094	125,970	0.8
Connecticut	122,175	123,452	1.0	313,675	265,347	0.8
Middle states	1,714,728	2,364,449	1.4	5,127,096	4,972,312	1.0
New York	920,783	1,173,119	1.3	2,496,517	2,212,213	0.9
New Jersey	137,787	190,801	1.4	610,528	591,730	1.0
Pennsylvania	635,840	969,870	1.5	1,969,432	2,117,946	1.1
Delaware	20,318	30,659	1.5	50,619	50,423	1.0
Southern states	1,026,940	1,755,656	1.7	2,615,140	3,507,237	1.3
Maryland and District of Columbia	132,474	188,663	1.4	388,125	381,253	1.0
Virginia and West Virginia	245,388	403,250	1.6	618,013	844,206	1.4
North Carolina	156,758	251,542	1.6	366,471	540,543	1.5
South Carolina	75,367	125,113	1.7	162,973	233,056	1.4
Georgia (eastern part)	32,028	56,521	1.8	86,277	123,608	1.4
Kentucky	191,611	361,111	1.9	545,038	751,566	1.4
Tennessee	193,314	369,456	1.9	448,243	633,005	1.4
Added area	1,756,052	3,339,555	1.9	11,086,653	13,756,429	1.2
Northern states	1,316,612	2,459,118	1.9	7,916,781	9,222,868	1.2
Ohio	512,296	889,640	1.7	1,347,828	1,335,964	1.0
Indiana	237,871	476,641	2.0	785,402	847,755	1.1
Illinois	204,097	402,665	2.0	1,483,102	1,660,114	1.1
Michigan	100,334	176,868	1.8	759,528	813,188	1.1
Wisconsin	75,585	133,184	1.8	609,341	780,664	1.3
Minnesota	1,213	2,291	1.9	482,631	668,183	1.4
Iowa	44,933	94,532	2.1	672,837	802,660	1.2
Missouri	140,283	283,297	2.0	890,534	1,095,731	1.2
North Dakota	([3])	([3])	....	74,807	128,739	1.7
South Dakota	([3])	([3])	....	98,724	155,250	1.6
Nebraska	([3])	([3])	....	295,832	408,226	1.4
Kansas	([3])	([3])	....	416,215	526,394	1.3
Southern states	413,463	836,759	2.0	2,065,284	3,272,786	1.6
Georgia (western part)	97,533	200,412	2.1	256,699	374,254	1.5
Florida	10,771	22,098	2.1	83,066	121,473	1.5
Alabama	104,534	208,287	2.0	282,156	431,494	1.5
Mississippi	67,725	146,893	2.2	179,268	276,328	1.5
Louisiana	63,289	102,964	1.6	207,418	307,120	1.5
Texas	33,783	73,142	2.2	639,303	1,057,904	1.7
Indian Territory	([3])	([3])	....	73,702	134,300	1.8
Oklahoma	([3])	([3])	....	93,012	154,435	1.7
Arkansas	35,828	82,963	2.3	250,660	415,478	1.7
Western states	25,977	43,678	1.7	1,104,588	1,260,775	1.1
Montana	([3])	([3])	....	52,580	69,674	1.3
Wyoming	([3])	([3])	....	19,217	28,843	1.5
Colorado	([4])	([4])	....	155,298	169,736	1.1
New Mexico and Arizona	16,973	25,956	1.5	69,940	105,431	1.5
Utah	[4] 2,749	[4] 5,163	1.9	74,735	118,758	1.6
Nevada	([4])	([4])	....	9,318	9,689	1.0
Idaho	([3])	([3])	....	36,346	60,508	1.7
Oregon and Washington	2,234	5,538	2.5	239,741	294,310	1.2
California	4,021	7,021	1.7	447,413	403,826	0.9

[1] Excluding persons stationed abroad.
[2] Subdivision of group 15 to 19 years estimated.
[3] Not enumerated.
[4] Enumerated as part of Utah territory if at all.

No state of the Union enumerated in 1850 showed an increase, during the half century which elapsed to 1900, in the ratio of children to adult white females. Within this short period the ratio of children to each 1,000 females declined from 1,600 to 1,100 for the entire United States, and from 1,400 to 1,000 in the area enumerated in 1790. The two preceding tables, therefore, reveal the fact that the ratio of 1,900 children to each 1,000 white women for the United States in 1790 declined 300 (to 1,600) in the sixty years elapsing to 1850, and 500 (to 1,100) in the succeeding half century.

How great has been the change during the century

in the proportion of children in the white population can best be realized by applying the ratio shown in 1900 to the number of white females above the age of 16 in 1790, and the ratio shown in 1790 to the number of white females 16 years of age and over in 1900.

AREA.	NUMBER OF WHITE CHILDREN UNDER 16 YEARS OF AGE.			
	1790		1900	
	Actual number.	On basis of ratio shown for continental United States in 1900, number would have been—	Actual number.	On basis of ratio shown in 1790, number would have been—
Continental United States..............	1,553,260	884,495	23,846,810	39,563,953
Area enumerated in 1790......	1,553,260	884,495	10,090,044	18,498,347
Added area................	....	....	13,756,766	21,065,606

Changes in the ratio of white children to adult white females, during the eighteenth and nineteenth centuries.—The enumeration of the inhabitants of New York city in 1703 specified the number of white females and the number of white children of both sexes. This fact makes possible a computation, for one representative community, of the proportion of children to white females at one of the earliest enumerations made in British North American territory. The ratio of white children of both sexes to white females 16 years of age and over, as indicated by this census, was 1.9.

Of even greater interest is the partial enumeration of New York colony made in 1712–1714. The returns of this census cover all counties except Queens, although the returns for Kings and Richmond counties give only the total population, and Albany, Dutchess, and Ulster counties were not returned at all until 1714. The detailed returns of this census cover the entire white population in even greater detail than was shown at the First Census of the United States. The proportion of white children under 16 years of age to white females 16 years of age and over, for the counties reported in detail, is given in Table 39.

The results of the New York censuses of 1703 and 1712 lead to the conclusion that at this period in the history of the colony there were about 2 white children to each adult white female. It is probable that at this early period there was little variation in the conditions prevailing in the different colonies; most of the inhabitants were engaged in agricultural pursuits, and there was practically no urban population in the modern sense of the term. This uniformity of conditions, together with the fact that even as late as 1790 the ratio of white children to white women varied but little in the different states and geographic divisions, suggests the inference that throughout the eighteenth century, and in all the British American colonies, there were approximately 2 white children to each adult

white female. This inference accords with the fact that the economic and social conditions of the colonies remained substantially unchanged during that period. It also serves to emphasize strikingly, by contrast, the change which occurred in the United States during the nineteenth century in the ratio of white children to adult white females.

TABLE **39.**—*Ratio of white children under 16 years of age to white females 16 years of age and over in New York, by counties: 1712.*

COUNTY.	White females 16 years and over.	WHITE CHILDREN UNDER 16 YEARS.			Ratio of white children under 16 years to white females 16 years and over.
		Both sexes.	Males.	Females.	
Total................	4,317	8,450	4,389	4,061	2.0
Albany [1]..................	725	1,404	753	651	....
Dutchess [1]................	98	218	120	98	....
New York	1,365	2,379	1,197	1,182	1.7
Orange	96	187	105	82	1.9
Suffolk	990	2,136	1,092	1,044	2.2
Ulster [1]...................	442	877	450	427	....
Westchester	601	1,249	672	577	2.1

[1] Returns not received until 1714.

Ratios of children to adult females in the native and the foreign stock of the white population.—It will be recalled that in a preceding chapter the contributions of the two main elements of the white population—descendants of persons enumerated in 1790 and of persons who came to the United States after the First Census—were estimated to represent approximately 35,000,000 and 32,000,000, respectively, of the total white population in 1900. Which of these two elements is the more liberal contributor of population increase at the present time? If the second, or foreign element, is the larger contributor what share is being borne in such contribution by the various nationalities which compose it? It is clear that the answers to these questions are of great importance to the Republic, since the ideals and policies of the nation must depend upon the characteristics of its citizens. Unfortunately, however, census publications can give no answer to questions concerning the fecundity of the various elements of the population.

There is a widespread opinion among students of population statistics that the white native stock, represented by the 35,000,000 of persons in 1900, is now increasing at a very slow rate, if at all; in all probability it is barely maintaining itself.[1] This point of view appears to be confirmed by many of the facts which are presented in this report. If this be true, or even

[1] "As a general proposition it will hold true that the absolute and relative fecundity of the native born element is less throughout the country than that of the foreign born. There are differences, of course, in the degree of fecundity, and fortunately the native birth rate is still comparatively normal in the Southern and Western states; but there can be no doubt that throughout the country the foreign element is reproducing itself much more rapidly than the native, with probably four generations to a century, against less than three among the natives."—*F. L. Hoffman, North American Review, May, 1909, page 675.*

partially true, then the other, or foreign, element of the white population, represented in 1900 by 32,000,000 persons, of whom more than 20,000,000 were either foreign born or the children of persons born abroad, is now contributing the bulk of population increase. There is no reason to doubt, however, that within this element the different nationalities differ widely in their percentages of increase.

In order to determine whether differences of this character actually exist, a test was made by analyzing the names appearing upon the Twelfth Census schedules for 2 counties which remained practically unchanged in area during the century—Hartford county,

Conn., and Columbia county, N. Y. Hartford county, Conn., was selected partly because in 1790 its population was exclusively British, and practically all English, so that the changes, if any, occurring during the century, could be clearly marked in connection with that nationality; and partly because in 1900 it was a typical county. The population had increased sixfold during the century; it was partly urban and partly rural; it was exceedingly prosperous, and obviously had fully participated in the growth and progress of the nation. Columbia county, N. Y., was a distinctly rural county in 1790, and largely rural also in 1900. The tabulations resulted as follows:

TABLE **40.**—RATIO OF ADULT WHITE FEMALES TO WHITE CHILDREN, FOR EACH NATIONALITY AS INDICATED BY NAMES OF HEADS OF FAMILIES IN HARTFORD COUNTY, CONN.: 1790 AND 1900.

NATIONALITY.	1790					1900				
	White females 16 years and over.		White children under 16 years.			White females 16 years and over.		White children under 16 years.		
				Number.					Number.	
	Number.	Per cent distribution.	Total.	Average to each female 16 years and over.	Per cent distribution.	Number.	Per cent distribution.	Total.	Average to each female 16 years and over.	Per cent distribution.
Total.	10,614	100.0	17,076	1.6	100.0	66,517	100.0	55,653	0.8	100.0
British.	10,594	99.8	17,042	1.6	99.8	52,500	78.9	36,576	0.7	65.7
English.	10,236	96.4	16,516	1.6	96.7	32,159	48.3	17,916	0.6	32.2
Scotch.	303	2.9	416	1.4	2.4	2,798	4.2	2,094	0.7	3.8
Irish.	55	0.5	110	2.0	0.6	17,543	26.4	16,566	0.9	29.8
Dutch.	6	0.1	10	1.7	0.1	151	0.2	127	0.8	0.2
French.	11	0.1	22	2.0	0.1	1,781	2.7	2,173	1.2	3.9
German.						6,375	9.6	7,752	1.2	13.9
All other [1].	3	(2)	2	0.7	(2)	5,710	8.6	9,025	1.6	16.2

[1] Includes Hungarian, Italian, Roumanian, Russian, Scandinavian, etc.   [2] Less than one-tenth of 1 per cent.

TABLE **41.**—RATIO OF ADULT WHITE FEMALES TO WHITE CHILDREN, FOR EACH NATIONALITY AS INDICATED BY NAMES OF HEADS OF FAMILIES IN COLUMBIA COUNTY, N. Y.: 1790 AND 1900.

NATIONALITY.	1790					1900				
	White females 16 years and over.		White children under 16 years.			White females 16 years and over.		White children under 16 years.		
				Number.					Number.	
	Number.	Per cent distribution.	Total.	Average to each female 16 years and over.	Per cent distribution.	Number.	Per cent distribution.	Total.	Average to each female 16 years and over.	Per cent distribution.
Total.	6,203	100.0	13,054	2.1	100.0	15,542	100.0	11,205	0.7	100.0
British.	4,980	80.3	10,646	2.1	81.6	11,713	75.4	7,673	0.7	68.5
English.	4,815	77.6	10,344	2.1	79.2	8,644	55.6	5,490	0.6	49.0
Scotch.	137	2.2	230	1.7	1.8	516	3.3	340	0.7	3.0
Irish.	28	0.5	72	2.6	0.6	2,553	16.4	1,843	0.7	16.4
Dutch.	1,148	18.5	2,290	2.0	17.5	985	6.3	633	0.6	5.6
French [1].	30	0.5	60	2.0	0.5	241	1.6	226	0.9	2.0
German.	37	0.6	42	1.1	0.3	2,343	15.1	2,163	0.9	19.3
All other [2].	8	0.1	16	2.0	0.1	260	1.7	510	2.0	4.6

[1] Practically all French Canadians in 1900.   [2] Includes Hungarian, Italian, Roumanian, Russian, Scandinavian, etc.

In 1900 the British stock was making a comparatively meager contribution to the population of both counties. The 1790 ratios of 1.6 children under 16 years of age to each female 16 years and over in the Connecticut county and 2.1 in the New York county, by 1900 had shrunk one-half in the former and one-third in the latter. Since in 1790 the British element was composed almost exclusively of English, it is in this nationality that most of the descendants of persons· enumerated in 1790 in these 2 counties are to be found. It will be observed that in both instances the ratio for the English is even lower than that for the remainder of the British element.

The other than British elements show in each county, in 1900, a more liberal ratio of children to women. Both the French Canadian and the German nationalities show a ratio which, while much less than that shown for 1790, is nevertheless higher than that of the British element. The increase in the ratio is greatest, however, for the nationalities analyzed upon the schedule and grouped in the table under the head of "all other." This term includes principally Italians, Hungarians, Russians, and Scandinavians—nationalities which are included in the most recent immigration movement. In both counties the contribution of this element, in 1900, greatly exceeds that of any other, approaching the very liberal proportion of children to adult females shown for the total white population at the First Census of the United States.

The foregoing analysis is presented merely as an illustration of the significant variation in the contribution of various racial elements to the increase of population in the United States. The labor involved in a complete tabulation of this kind is so great that it could not be attempted except at a decennial census, and it is doubtful if facilities would exist at that time. But the test tabulations here presented tend to confirm the impression that during the eighteenth century practically no change occurred in the social and economic structure of the colonies which subsequently became parts of the United States, while during the nineteenth century a very marked readjustment has been in progress, resulting in a striking change in the ratio of children to adult females.

Comparison of the United States with Europe.—Consideration of the changes shown to have occurred in the United States during the century, in the ratio of white children to adult white females, is aided by making a study of the corresponding ratios for the four principal nations of Europe.

COUNTRY.	Census year.	Females 16 years and over.	Children under 16 years.	Ratio of children under 16 to females 16 years and over.
United Kingdom	1901	14,251,030	14,211,381	1.0
France	1901	14,190,357	10,684,083	0.8
Germany	1900	18,293,000	20,722,000	1.1
Italy	1901	10,549,684	11,722,730	1.1
United States	1900	20,822,625	23,846,473	1.1

The above table indicates that the proportion of children to adult females was practically the same in the United States in 1900 as in Great Britain, Germany, and Italy at the corresponding enumerations in those countries; hence it appears that population conditions in the Republic are tending to become more in harmony with those obtaining in other civilized countries. It should be noted that although the ratio shown for France is considerably less than those for Great Britain, Germany, Italy, and the United States, it is identical with that shown for 5 of the New England states, and but one-tenth less than that shown for New York.

EFFECT OF CHANGES IN THE PROPORTION OF CHILDREN.

There are many standpoints from which to view this subject. From one, it might be claimed that the people of the United States, taking all into account, have concluded that they are only about one-half as well able to rear children—at any rate without personal sacrifice—under the conditions prevailing in 1900 as their predecessors proved themselves to be under the conditions which prevailed in 1790. It is possible also to claim that at the period of the First Census the simple living characteristic of a new country, the simple wants supplied by neighborhood industries, and the self-dependence of the family due to sparseness of population, all tended toward large families.

In 1900 the resources of the nation were developed to the point of fruition. From various causes the population had become very large. Wealth had increased to a degree unparalleled elsewhere in the world or in any age. At the present time the complexity of living, congestion of population, dependence on foreign help, and especially the innumerable wants fostered by machine-made goods, manufactured upon an enormous scale and ever tempting to greater expenditure, all tend toward restriction of size of families.

At the beginning of the nineteenth century a vast continent, with untold resources, awaited development and created what might be termed a population hunger. In Europe, at the same period, the creation of unexampled industrial activity produced, though to a lesser degree, a somewhat similar condition. The close of the nineteenth century finds the insistent demand for population practically satisfied, and in some instances more than satisfied, both in the United States and in Europe. The degree to which this demand is occurring in different sections of the United States is suggested by the wide variations in the proportions of white children to white adults in the various states and geographic divisions. The older communities, having already acquired dense population, resulting in a more severe struggle for existence, show the highest proportion of adults to children; while in the younger or more sparsely settled states, and in those in which wide opportunity for the individual still exists, the proportion of children to adults is much greater. It must be remembered, however, that in communities which have been in existence less than fifty years the birth rates, as reflected by the proportion of children in the white population, may be abnormally high, because of the abnormal age distribution of the population of such sections.

It would be idle to attempt to point out the social and economic results likely to occur in the future from the changes here shown to have taken place, even were such a discussion appropriate in these pages. A century hence the student of population changes will be able to measure, in the same manner as the significance of population changes from 1790 to 1900 is here measured, but in abler and more accurate fashion, the effect—economic loss, or possibly, indeed, economic gain—upon the United States of failure of the white population to contribute (on the basis of the 1790 proportion) many millions of young people to the activities of the Republic. He will confront the fact that in the early life of the Republic there appeared in the total population a very large proportion of young persons, but that after the expiration of a century, as the population approached 100,000,000 and all the activities of the nation were developed and expanded to a marvelous degree, the proportion of young persons decreased to such an extent as to create a remarkable contrast between the conditions which prevailed at the beginning and at the end of the nineteenth century. It is probable that against such a background the economic history of the coming century will be written.

X. SURNAMES OF THE WHITE POPULATION IN 1790.

APPROXIMATE NUMBER—NOMENCLATURE—PREPONDERANCE OF
ENGLISH AND SCOTCH NAMES—UNUSUAL AND STRIKING SUR-
NAMES—DISTRIBUTION OF SURNAMES—CONCENTRATION OF POP-
ULATION UNDER CERTAIN NAMES—ABSENCE OF MIDDLE NAMES.

In the states for which the schedules of the First Census still exist there were 27,337 surnames in 1790. It is impossible to compute from this figure the number of surnames in the entire United States at the date of the First Census, but the fact that the states for which the schedules are lacking, with the exception of New Jersey, were settled largely by English immigrants, suggests the probability that the names in addition to those appearing upon the existing schedules were comparatively few in number. It is thus probable that the entire number of surnames in the United States at that period did not much exceed 30,000.

The tables which follow present some classification of nomenclature resulting from an inspection of the names of heads of families as they appear upon the schedules. This classification has been made because of the historical value which attaches to such analysis. The heads of families enumerated at the First Census were practically the founders of the Republic; it was they who adopted the Constitution which made the Republic permanent. Furthermore, the constant increase of interest in genealogy makes this analysis of especial interest.

A large preponderance of English and Scotch names appears upon the schedules of the First Census. The proportion, indeed, is so large that these two nationalities embrace substantially the entire population, with the exception of that of certain sections, principally in New York, Pennsylvania, and North Carolina. Moreover, inspection of the names, conveys the impression that they were largely of Anglo-Saxon origin.

Many of the names upon the schedules probably have now passed out of existence, because of an increasing tendency on the part of the public to avoid striking or fantastic names. Most of those names which tended to cause a distinct loss of dignity to the bearer have, in the course of a century, been so modified, with the social advance of the possessors, as to lose unpleasant characteristics. Many Christian names which were of frequent occurrence in the seventeenth and eighteenth centuries, and indeed in the early part of the nineteenth century, have become obsolete. Their use by the present generation would be regarded as an absurdity. Inspection of the city directories for several of the larger municipalities

shows that many of the more peculiar and eccentric names reported at the First Census still continue to be borne; but it is a fact, also, that such names are by no means so conspicuous at the present time as at the earlier period. The addition of a great body of names originating in countries other than Great Britain tends to reduce the prominence of English names, as the proportion contributed by such names decreases. It is true that many of the names so added may be formed of the parts of speech of other languages, but this fact is concealed by their occurrence in a foreign tongue.

Those who study the names upon the schedules of the First Census are impressed by the fact that a large proportion of the total number are derived from common nouns or other parts of speech related to the daily affairs, occupations, events, and surroundings of the individual and the community. Tests were made of the names returned for 3 states, to determine the proportion of families bearing names of this class. It was found that of all families reported in these 3 states about 30 per cent derived their names from parts of speech.

Of the 27,337 different surnames for which the 1790 schedules are in existence, 9.4 per cent were derived from parts of speech. Upon making a classification of the names so derived, according to the meaning of the words, they fall into the following general classes:[1]

Household and domestic affairs—food and eating, drink, clothing, and sewing materials.

Nations and places.

Human characteristics—nationality, kinds of men, condition, appearance or state, bathing, ailments and remedies, parts and actions of the body, relationship.

Games, religion, music, and literature.

Property—kind of house and building material and belongings, surroundings, furniture and tableware, merchandise and commodities, and money.

Nature—color, objects of nature or features of landscape, trees, plants and flowers, fruits, nuts, weather, beasts, birds, insects and creeping creatures.

The ocean and maritime subjects.

War.

Death and violence.

Time.

Unusual and ludicrous combinations of common nouns and of Christian names and surnames.

---

[1] Classification of the surnames shown upon the census schedules, according to their meaning as parts of speech, proves of so much interest that, while not properly a part of a report of this character, some of the more noteworthy names are given in the following classified list:

HOUSEHOLD AND DOMESTIC AFFAIRS.

Food and eating.—Soup, Oyster, Fish, Trout, Salmon, Haddock, Shad, Crab; Veal, Lamb, Pork, Savory, Stew; Fowl, Duck, Quail, Goose, Gravy; Tripe, Tongue, Kidney, Liver, Hash, Ham, Eggs;

Two facts are of especial interest in connection with an analysis of names. The parts of speech which are represented are almost entirely Anglo-Saxon. They are derived from the most common events of life, conditions, places, or things, and it may be said that they represent almost one-third of the population of the United States in 1790. The prevalence of biblical given names reflects the religious feeling of the period. The absence of those names which were offensive from the standpoint of politics, on the other hand, reflects the political prejudices prevailing at that date. For example, the name "Charles" is found rather infrequently. Indeed, in the entire state of Massachusetts, one of the most populous states of that period, it occurs less than 250 times on the schedules.

A classification of the total number of names represented upon the schedules (27,337), according to frequency of occurrence, as, for example, the number of names which appear but once, the number which appear but twice, etc., show the following interesting results:

NUMBER OF TIMES NAMES APPEAR UPON SCHEDULES, BY GROUPS.	Number of names.	Per cent each class forms of all names.
Total..	27,337	100.0
1..	11,934	43.7
2..	3,609	13.2
3 to 4..	3,235	11.8
5 to 9..	3,105	11.4
10 to 24..	2,564	9.4
25 to 49..	1,244	4.6
50 to 99..	744	2.7
100 to 199..	511	1.9
200 to 299..	154	0.6
300 to 399..	84	0.3
400 to 499..	55	0.2
500 to 749..	53	0.2
750 to 999..	12	(1)
1,000 to 1,499....................................	19	0.1
1,500 to 1,999....................................	6	(1)
2,000 to 2,999....................................	6	(1)
3,000 and over...................................	2	(1)

¹ Less than one-tenth of 1 per cent.

Goodbread, Butter, Olives, Radish, Mustard, Cress, Vinegar; Corn, Beets, Onions, Beans, Collard, Carrott, Peas, Squash, Brownrice, Sago; Waffle, Honey, Pancake, Jam, Mush, Treacle; Cake, Custard, Tart, Cheese, Almond, Dates, Shaddock, Melon; Mints, Fudge; Coffee, Tea, Sugar, Milk; Hunger, Food, Meal, Diet, Slice, Broil, Boiling, Ginger, Greens, Alspice, Lard, Pepper.

Drink.—Brandy, Goodrum, Grog, Grapewine, Redwine, Punch, Cider, Port, Negus, Freshwater, Beer, Booze, Goodwine, Wine.

Clothing.—Dress, Raiment, Gowns, Frocks, Petticoat, Bloomer, Scarf, Redsleeves, Frill, Shawl, Bonnet, Feather, Boas, Mitts, Beads, Spangle, Shoe, Highshoe, Stockings, Coats, Shirts, Waistcoat, Jumpers, Smock, Overall, Collar, Lightcap, Mitten, Boots, Socks, Brogan, Cap.

Sewing materials.—Linen, Silk, Poplin, Crape, Lace, Wool, Buttons; Machine, Needles, Pattern, Pin, Bodkin, Spool; Threadcraft, Mendingall, Patching, Whitecotton.

NATIONS AND PLACES.

England, Ireland, Hungary, Germany, Holland, Spain, Poland, Athens, Boston, Canada, Bohemia, Venice, Parliament, Paradise, Bedlam.

HUMAN CHARACTERISTICS.

Nationality.—English, Irish, French, German, Prussian, Poles, Spaniard, Malay, Tartar, Dago, Mussulman, Dutch.

Kinds of men.—Beeman, Councilman, Countryman, Iceman, Ploughman, Sickman, Shortman, Smallman, Toughman, Tidyman, Weatherman, Weedingman, Peacemaker, Houselighter, Woolweaver, Landmiser, Pioneer, Pilgrim, Pagan, Pettyfool, Passenger, Grooms, Biters, Fakes, Equals, Drinker, Dancer, Kicker, Cusser, Spitter, Booby, Dunce, Gump, Boor, Crank, Crook, Rascal, Swindle, Knave, Outlaw, Madsavage, Coward, Hero, Double, Goodfellow.

Condition.—Hunger, Thirst, Smell, Taste, Anger, Laughter, Comfort, Reason, Clemency, Justice, Care, Pride, Wit, Pluck, Faith, Devotion, Goodcourage, Fuss, Flurry, Fury, Thrift, Doubt, Piety.

Appearance or state.—Short, Shorter, Plump, Comely, Sallow, Supple, Bony, Barefoot, Allred, Busy, Idle, Careless, Strict, Calm, Gushing, Dumb, Howling, Daft, Looney, Dowdy, Neat, Empty, Greedy, Fearing, Fearless, Faithful, Fickle, Forward, Humble, Gadding, Sober, Maudlin, Gaudy, Quaint, Harsh, Jolly, Kind, Severe, Literal, Final, Wealthy, Miserly, Naughty, Toogood, Sullen, Sanguine, Proud, Prudent, Rough, Tough, Hasty, Weary, Old, Oider, Wordly, Witty, Allright, Proper, Lazy, Lucky, Upright, Underhand, Measley, Rude, Toobald, Cacklin.

Bathing.—Coldbath, Towel, Soap.

Ailments and remedies.—Fatyouwant, Gout, Fever, Crampeasy, Boils, Measles, Swelling, Corns, Rickets, Gripe, Ache, Cough, Sliver, Blackhead, Warts, Tetter, Fits; Surgeon, Quack; Balm, Physic, Salts, Mixture, Blister, Pellet, Pill.

Parts and actions of the body.—Head, Brains, Forehead, Cheeks, Nose, Ears, Chin, Beard, Lips, Tongue, Shoulders, Wrists, Hands, Fingers, Thumbs, Hips, Side, Knee, Leg, Foot, Heel, Bones, Gullets, Hearts, Kidneys, Bowels, Livers, Glands, Breaths, Voices, Whisper, Murmurs, Grunts, Howls, Yells, Smack, Caress.

Relationship.—Brother, Sister, Couples, Husbands, Son, Daughter, Uncles, Cousins, Neighbors.

GAMES, RELIGION, MUSIC, AND LITERATURE.

Games.—Clubs, Cards, Chess, Faro, Dice, Dance, Waltz.

Religion.—Preacher, Rector, Church, Chapel, Steeples, Spires, Bell, Clapper, Organ, Pew, Sermon, Creed, Bible, Psalms, Psalter, Sinners, Blessing, Miracle, Angels, Heavens, Hell.

Music and literature.—Music, Chord, Harmony, Overture, Christian, Singer, Duett, Harp, Fiddle, Fife, Cornet; Poet, Rymes, Jingles, Ballad, Parody.

PROPERTY.

Kind of house, building material, and belongings.—House, Lot, Brickhouse, Acres, Greathouse, Marble, Mahogany, Oldhouse, Halfacre, Stonehouse, Longhouse, Newhouse, Laughinghouse, Roof, Brickroof, Shingle, Gambrel, Gable, Gutters, Spout, Lumber, Brick, Wooden, Plank, Scantling, Lath, Crack, Cranny, Door, Latch, Knob, Lockkey, Kitchen, Buttery, Shelf, Furnace, Heater, Register, Porch, Shed, Pump, Corners.

Surroundings.—Stable, Barns, Trough, Manger, Coolyard, Brickwell, Coldwell, Cornhouse, Woodhouse, Milkhouse, Warehouse, Millhouse, Wharf.

Furniture and tableware.—Table, Curtain, Vase, Clocks, Desk, Chairs, Cushion, Pillow, Bolster, Box, Broom, Bucket, Candle, Snuffer, Plate, Platter, Bowls, Newbowl, China, Silver, Knife, Forks, Spoons, Pitcher, Mug, Saucer.

Merchandise and commodities.—Stove, Wood, Coke, Oven, Coal, Fender, Auction, Wondersale, Shovel, Poker, Hammock, Pickett, Tubs, Ax, Ladder, Mallet, Nuthammer, Hatchet, Wrench, Level, Nipper, Whetstone, Gouge, Nail, Tack, Awl, Oats, Bran, Shorts, Husks, Wheat, Mash, Bags, Balloon, Barley, Barrels, Basket, Bench, Bike, Boiler, Bomb, Brass, Buckhorn, Camphor, Cane, Cap, Chalk, Chopper, Coin, Coldiron, Combs, Compass, Coop, Coopernail, Copper, Cork, Cowhorn, Cradle, Cutwork, Dipper, Divans, Files, Filters, Grater, Gravel, Gum, Hammers, Hassock, Hogshead, Hornbuckle, Hose, Inks, Iron, Irons, Ivory, Junk, Kettle, Kite, Leeks, Lightwood, Locket, Maize, Tenpenny, Oldshoe, Paste, Pearl, Pen, Pencil, Pipes, Plough, Powder, Primer, Rags, Rakes, Rattle, Razor, Rivets, Rockets, Rope, Rug, Satchel, Screws, Sequin, Shot, Sickle, Silkrags, Silver, Slate, Smallcorn, Snuff, Spikes, Sticks, Stilts, Straw, Tallow, Tarbox, Ticket, Tiles, Tool, Trap, Trucks, Trunk, Tubes, Turnipseed, Twine, Twist, Varnish, Wafer, Washer, Weights, Whips, Whitehorn, Wigs, Wire, Yarn, Yoke, Harness, Hames, Reins, Sulkey, Surrey, Coltrider, Heldebridle.

Money.—Purse, Money, Cash, Dollar, Milldollar, Penny, Thickpenny, Shilling, Dimes, Nickles, Pence.

NATURE.

Color.—Colour, Black, White, Gray, Green, Brown, Red, Ruby, Pink, Purple, Seagray, Nile, Orange, Tan, Olive, Lavender, Carmine, Blue, Scarlet.

Objects of nature or features of landscape.—Mountain, Tallhill, Widedale, Lakes, Meadows, Parks, Pastures, Rivers, Woodsides, Roads, Bridges, Bogs, Forest, Chestnutwood, Hazelgrove, Wood-

The most significant fact which appears in the preceding table is the large proportion of the total number of names which is formed by names represented by one family only, and the rapid decrease as the groups include more frequent occurrence of names. For example, of the names which appear between 1,000 and 1,500 times—in other words, are represented by that number of families—there are but 19; while, in the highest class, but 2 names are represented by 3,000 or more families.

It is important to remember that a comparatively small part of the total number of surnames in the United States in 1790 includes practically the entire white population. Eleven thousand nine hundred and thirty-four names represent but one-half of 1 per cent of the white population, hence the 99.5 per cent were represented by 15,403 surnames.

The number of times surnames appear in the various states and their classification into groups, according to frequency of occurrence, is shown in the following table:

TABLE 42.—NUMBER OF NAMES REPORTED FOR WHITE FAMILIES, CLASSIFIED ACCORDING TO THE NUMBER OF FAMILIES RECORDED UNDER SUCH NAMES, BY STATES: 1790.

NUMBER OF WHITE FAMILIES.	United States.	Maine.	New Hampshire.	Vermont.	Massachusetts.	Rhode Island.	Connecticut.	New York.	Pennsylvania.	Maryland.	Virginia.	North Carolina.	South Carolina.
Total	27,337	2,640	2,588	2,469	4,452	1,396	3,412	7,462	13,383	6,552	5,355	6,777	5,391
1	11,934	1,052	917	928	1,641	578	1,363	3,419	6,661	3,239	2,038	2,696	2,613
2	3,609	362	325	345	536	191	389	989	1,984	973	838	1,025	825
3 to 4	3,235	373	350	352	487	175	357	890	1,844	891	788	978	757
5 to 9	3,105	398	404	420	563	187	426	931	1,457	732	802	928	635
10 to 24	2,564	312	337	315	550	147	435	731	905	477	597	729	391
25 to 49	1,244	107	167	81	347	76	233	324	311	166	189	252	117
50 to 99	744	30	69	25	220	35	152	130	151	59	73	105	40
100 to 199	511	6	16	2	77	7	49	39	49	13	24	51	10
200 to 299	154		2	1	21		6	6	13	1	3	6	2
300 to 399	84		1		6			2	5	1	2	4	1
400 to 499	55				2		1	1	1		1	1	
500 to 749	53				1							1	
750 to 999	12							1		2			1
1,000 to 1,499	19				1								
1,500 to 1,999	6												
2,000 and over	8												

land, Woodyfield, Wilderness, Fountain, Middlebrook, Marsh, Pool, Pond, Gully, Ditch, Farm, Taterfield, Bars, Garden, Grass, Longwall, Tanyard, Market, Maypole, Lowbridge, Drawbridge, Woodendyke, Saltmarsh, Oysterbanks, Sharpstone, Redstone, Mud, Soot, Smoke, Blaze, Fires, Sparks.

Trees.—Maples, Oaks, Greenoak, Chestnut, Walnut, Pine, Bay, Willow, Tumbletree, Redwood, Roots, Sap, Acorn.

Plants and flowers.—Plants, Weeds, Vines, Shrub, Mallow, Primrose, Calls, Ivy, Pinks, Parsley, Marjoram, Wormwood, Fennel, Caraway, Bramble, Brier, Thistle, Barnthistle, Toadvine, Ragbush, Clover, Seeds, Pollen.

Fruits.—Fruit, Apple, Pippin, Currants, Cherry, Blackheart, Grapes, Lemons, Peach, Plum, Quince, Pears, Limes, Berry, Mayberry, Appleberry, Bilberry, Touchberry, Thornberry, Dewberry, Fortuneberry, Flyberry, Huckelberry, Rasberry, Winterberry, Wineberry, Rottenberry.

Nuts.—Nut, Chestnut, Walnut, Hickrynut.

Weather.—Weathers, Dry, Damp, Pleasant, Dismal, Sprinkle, Shower, Rains, Storms, Gales, Simoon, Hail, Slush, Freeze, Blizzard, Coldair.

Beasts.—Horse, Hoss, Hossies, Colts, Trotter, Mules, Kicks, Ox, Bulls, Cows, Heifer, Redheifer, Calf, Middlecalf, Goats, Sheep, Lamb, Cats, Leathercat, Mouser, Pup, Shoat, Squirrel, Beavers, Mink, Coons, Seals, Sealion, Bear, Bruin, Cub, Leopard, Tiger, Moose, Lions, Panther, Flippers, Claws, Hoofs, Horns, Tails, Clatter, Canter, Gallop.

Birds.—Eagle, Canary, Lark, Woodpicker, Parrot, Peacock, Raven, Sparrow, Starling, Skyhawk, Stork, Swan, Buzzard, Crows, Snipes, Robins, Hawks, Pheasants, Rocks, Fowls, Chick, Bantam, Gosling, Geese, Pigeon, Dove, Birdsong, Birdwhistle.

Insects and creeping creatures.—Ant, Beetle, Fly, Bees, Hornet, Roach, Locust, Snails, Grubs, Maggot, Worm, Snake, Turtle, Frog.

THE OCEAN AND MARITIME SUBJECTS.

Seas, Billows, Bays, Breeze, Ship, Sloop, Barge, Bigraft, Anchor, Shoals, Sails, Bunks, Commodore, Mariner, Shipboy, Swab.

WAR.

War, Battle, Campaign, Fight, Fightmaster, Cannon, Boom, Guns, Trigger, Shots, Pistol, Shoots, Swords, Banner, Bugle, Bugler, Fort, Officer, Booty, Treason, Prison.

DEATH AND VIOLENCE.

Death, Deadman, Hearse, Vaults, Tombs, Moregraves, Duel, Murder, Demon, Ghost, Mummy.

TIME.

Months, Weeks, Shortday, Nights, Hour, Winter, Midwinter, August, Yesterday, Tewday, Allday, Always, Friday, Sunday, Monday, Lunch, Supper, Goodnight, Clock, Bells, Christmas, Easter.

UNUSUAL COMBINATIONS OF COMMON NOUNS.

Beersticker, Cathole, Churning, Clampit, Clapsaddle, Clinkscales, Cockledress, Coldflesh, Crackbone, Drips, Flybaker, Fryover, Gallivant, Getstrap, Goodbit, Goosehorn, Graytracks, Hogmire, Honeycomb, Hungerpealer, Huntsucker, Icebrass, Liptrot, Livergall, Lookinbill, Milksack, Moonshine, Partneck, Pockerpine, Reedhovel, Scoot, Shamback, Sharpneck, Silvernail, Slappy, Spitsnoggle, Splitstone, Stophell, Straddle, Sunlighter, Sydebottom, Sydersticker, Tallowback, Threewits, Trueluck, Wallflour, Willibother, Witchwagon.

STRIKING OR LUDICROUS COMBINATIONS OF CHRISTIAN NAMES AND SURNAMES.

Joseph Came, Peter Wentup, Joseph Scolds, John Sat, Thomas Simmers, John Smothers, Sarah Simpers, Ruth Shaves, Barbary Staggers, William Sorrows, Joseph Rodeback, Christy Forgot, Agreen Crabtree, Christian Bonnet, Truelove Sparks, Snow Frost, Preserved Taft, Wanton Bump, Adam Hatmaker, Darling Whiteman, Mourning Chestnut, River Jordan, Moses Rainwater, Christian Shelf, Sermon Coffin, Boston Frog, Jedediah Brickhouse, Jemima Crysick, Bachelor Chance, Susannah Boots, Britain Spelling, History Gott, Anguish Lemmon, Thomas Gabtale, Unity Bachelor, Web Ashbean, Booze Still, Over Jordan, Thomas Purify, Constant Gallneck, Pleasant Basket, Hannah Petticoat, Balaam Bell, Abraham Bokay, Cutlip Hoof, Comfort Clock, Jonah Hatchet, Noble Gun, Hardy Baptist, Sillah Jester, Jacob Worm, Hannah Cheese, Henry Callico, Abraham Singhorse, Sharp Blount, Mercy Pepper.

Of the total number of surnames reported in the United States, almost exactly half were returned for Pennsylvania. This was nearly double the number returned for any other state—probably because of the large proportion of Germans composing the population of that state. It is clear that the occurrence of more than one nationality as an element of population tends to increase greatly the number of surnames. In general, the number of surnames was smallest in the New England states, where the proportion of British stock was greatest. In South Carolina, with a population no larger than that of Maine, the number of surnames was more than double the number reported upon the Maine schedules. In all the states the number of surnames occurring but once—that is, as represented by but 1 family—was very much greater than the occurrence of surnames represented by even two families. In New England the number of single surnames was almost exactly three times as great in each state as the number represented by 2 families. In the other states a slightly smaller proportion appeared, except in the case of Virginia and North Carolina. In but 4 states—Massachusetts, Connecticut, Pennsylvania, and North Carolina—did any surname occur more than 500 times. The names so represented were Brown and Smith in Massachusetts; Smith in Connecticut; Smith and Williams in Pennsylvania; and Smith and Jones in North Carolina. But 1 surname occurred more than 1,000 times in any one state—the name of Smith in Massachusetts.

When analysis is made of the number of persons comprising the families shown in the previous table, the following results appear:

TABLE **43.**—NUMBER OF NAMES REPORTED FOR WHITE FAMILIES, CLASSIFIED ACCORDING TO THE NUMBER OF WHITE PERSONS IN ALL HOUSEHOLDS RECORDED UNDER SUCH NAMES, BY STATES: 1790.

NUMBER OF WHITE PERSONS.	United States.	Maine.	New Hampshire.	Vermont.	Massachusetts.	Rhode Island.	Connecticut.	New York.	Pennsylvania.	Maryland.	Virginia.	North Carolina.	South Carolina.
Total	27,337	2,640	2,588	2,469	4,452	1,396	3,412	7,462	13,383	6,552	5,355	6,777	5,391
1	710	81	40	27	62	18	59	106	301	155	200	389	189
2 to 9	11,727	1,045	890	932	1,685	595	1,292	3,419	6,585	3,202	2,029	2,656	2,570
10 to 49	9,162	1,012	1,008	1,051	1,399	495	1,074	2,486	4,928	2,408	2,173	2,608	2,043
50 to 99	2,055	261	276	267	450	117	365	674	779	448	520	571	335
100 to 199	1,463	162	201	137	358	92	310	447	463	203	271	316	160
200 to 299	639	47	94	30	185	38	114	164	114	78	70	100	47
300 to 399	343	15	34	17	106	25	78	69	81	27	38	52	22
400 to 499	220	9	14	4	65	5	39	36	43	12	14	19	8
500 to 749	354	6	20	2	74	5	51	34	50	9	22	35	10
750 to 999	187	1	7	1	26	3	19	15	12	5	10	17	3
1,000 to 1,499	197	1	2	1	26	3	7	9	17	5	5	7	3
1,500 to 1,999	95		1		9		2		4		2	2	
2,000 to 2,999	97		1		5		1	3	4		1	4	1
3,000 to 3,999	37				1						1	1	
4,000 to 4,999	16						1		2				
5,000 to 7,499	19				1								
7,500 to 9,999	8												
10,000 to 14,999	6												
15,000 and over	2												

While the number of names represented by 1 family is exceedingly large, the number of names represented by only 1 person is very small. In all the states, the proportion of surnames represented by from 2 to 50 persons includes the greater number; in Pennsylvania, for example, all but 1,870 names out of 13,383 were represented by from 2 to 50 people. Such an analysis brings out the fact of the very wide distribution of names, and the small number of persons appearing under a surname in any one state.

Table 44 shows that the average number of persons per name for the area covered was between 90 and 100, while the proportion varied in the different states from 25 to 83. It is a significant fact, suggested both by this table and by Table 43 that Massachusetts, the population of which was almost exclusively of British extraction, closely followed by most of the New England states, reports the highest proportion of families per name and consequently of persons per name. Table 44 reflects, in general, the tendency of the homogeneous population to show a smaller proportion of surnames to population than does a mixed population, such as that of Pennsylvania and South Carolina.

TABLE **44.**—*Average number of white families per name, and average number of white persons per name and family, by states: 1790.*

STATE.	Number of names.	Number of families.	Number of persons.	AVERAGE NUMBER OF— Families per name.	Persons— Per name.	Per family.
United States	27,337	443,726	2,505,371	16.2	91.6	5.6
Maine	2,640	16,972	95,334	6.4	36.1	5.6
New Hampshire	2,588	23,982	140,479	9.3	54.3	5.9
Vermont	2,469	14,969	84,772	6.1	34.3	5.7
Massachusetts	4,452	65,149	371,770	14.6	83.5	5.7
Rhode Island	1,396	10,854	64,988	7.8	46.6	6.0
Connecticut	3,412	40,457	232,641	11.9	68.2	5.8
New York	7,462	54,190	308,404	7.3	41.3	5.7
Pennsylvania	13,383	73,323	419,917	5.5	31.4	5.7
Maryland	6,562	32,012	179,283	4.9	27.3	5.6
Virginia	5,355	38,245	203,502	7.1	38.0	5.3
North Carolina	6,777	48,021	265,006	7.1	39.1	5.5
South Carolina	5,381	25,552	139,275	4.7	25.9	5.5

In Table 111, which appears upon page 227, will be found a list of 3,661 names, comprising all those represented by at least 100 white persons. These names have been correlated, and the total number of families bearing such names in the United States and in each of the several states (in 1790) is shown, with the approximate number of persons comprised in such families. Reference has already been made to the dissimilarity between the number of surnames in the United States at the period of the First Census and the number of persons represented by names. The tendency of the population at that period to group under surnames of frequent occurrence is indicated by the fact that 11,934 names represent less than 1 per cent of the white population; 11,742 represented 15.7 per cent and the remaining 3,661 names specified in Table 111 represented 83.8 per cent.

The total number of names comprised in this table approximates 13 per cent of the entire number of names recorded upon the schedules for the area covered, and eight-tenths of 1 per cent of all the families in the same area.

A conclusion to be drawn from this analysis is that at the beginning of Constitutional Government approximately 800 surnames—practically all of which were of English or British origin—contributed about one-third of the entire population of the United States, while all the remaining population was distributed among a great variety of surnames, 38 per cent of which were represented by one family only.

The number of heads of families with approximate total number of persons, under a few of the names of more frequent occurrence, were:

NAME.	Number of families.	Total persons.
Smith	5,932	33,245
Brown	3,358	19,175
Davis	2,575	14,300
Jones	2,561	14,300
Johnson	2,646	14,004
Clark	2,242	13,766
Williams	2,283	12,717
Miller	2,225	12,694
Wilson	1,765	9,797

These 9 names represented about 4 per cent of the total white population in 1790.

The absence of middle names or initials from the schedules of the First Census is so noticeable as to suggest the practical growth of this custom after the beginning of the nineteenth century. The carelessness of enumerators might, in many instances, explain the failure to include middle names or initials upon some of the schedules, but defects of enumeration in this particular would not be so general as to result in almost complete absence of such names. Upon a document of such momentous importance as the Declaration of Independence, signed by the most distinguished men of the period, complete signatures were of course to be expected; yet it will be remembered that upon this document appear the names of but 3 persons having middle names—Robert Treat Paine, Richard Henry Lee, and Francis Lightfoot Lee.

It would be of the utmost interest to compare statistics of surnames at the Twelfth Census with those here presented for the First, but no such information is available. Meager as are the statistical data yielded by the First Census, it is probable that it will long stand as the only census for which statistics of nomenclature exist.

XI. NATIONALITY AS INDICATED BY NAMES OF HEADS OF FAMILIES REPORTED AT THE FIRST CENSUS.

NATIONALITY IN STATES FOR WHICH SCHEDULES EXIST—IN THOSE FOR WHICH SCHEDULES ARE MISSING—COMPOSITION OF POPULATION OF TYPICAL COUNTIES IN 1900—SLAVEHOLDING BY NATIONALITY.

In modern census taking nationality is determined by the response of the individual to the question concerning place of birth or the place of birth of parents. Such a classification is obviously impossible in connection with the First Census; as the only means of determining the nationalities of whole families at that census is by inspection of the names of the heads of families as they appear upon the existing schedules. If this be remembered, so that no confusion shall arise through an attempt to force comparisons, the results attained from inspection of the First Census schedules present a very interesting and doubtless a reasonably accurate analysis of the nationality of the population at the time. Such classification, however, is obviously in the nature of an indication of blood, or what may be termed nationality strain, since it takes no account of the actual place of birth or parentage of the individual, or of the length of time which the bearers of the name may have been absent from the mother country. The ancestors of

the bearer of an Irish or Dutch name may have arrived in the first shipload of immigrants who landed on the shores of Virginia, Manhattan, or New England, so that at the time of the First Census the descendant enumerated possessed few or none of the characteristics of the nationality indicated. On the other hand, the individual may have arrived in the United States alone or with his family but a few weeks prior to the enumeration.

Emphasis is laid upon the above facts in order that no misunderstanding may arise concerning the analysis of nationality here presented. While, therefore, it can not be regarded as possessing the least value from the standpoint of modern classification by place of birth, such an analysis, especially for the period under consideration, possesses great value as indicating the proportions contributed by the different nationalities, to the population at the time the First Census was taken.

TABLE 45.—PER CENT DISTRIBUTION OF THE WHITE POPULATION OF EACH STATE ACCORDING TO NATIONALITY AS INDICATED BY NAMES OF HEADS OF FAMILIES: 1790.

NATIONALITY AS INDICATED BY NAME.	AREA COVERED.		MAINE.		NEW HAMPSHIRE.		VERMONT.		MASSACHUSETTS.		RHODE ISLAND.		CONNECTICUT.	
	Number.	Per cent.	Number.	Per cent.	Number.	Per cent.	Number.	Per cent.	Number.	Per cent.	Number.	Per cent.	Number.	Per cent.
All nationalities	2,810,248	100.0	96,107	100.0	141,112	100.0	85,072	100.0	373,187	100.0	64,670	100.0	232,236	100.0
English	2,345,844	83.5	89,515	93.1	132,726	94.1	81,149	95.4	354,528	95.0	62,079	96.0	223,437	96.2
Scotch	188,589	6.7	4,154	4.3	6,648	4.7	2,562	3.0	13,435	3.6	1,976	3.1	6,425	2.8
Irish	44,273	1.6	1,334	1.4	1,346	1.0	597	0.7	3,732	1.0	459	0.7	1,589	0.7
Dutch	56,623	2.0	279	0.3	153	0.1	428	0.5	373	0.1	19	(1)	258	0.1
French	13,384	0.5	115	0.1	142	0.1	153	0.2	746	0.2	88	0.1	512	0.2
German	156,457	5.6	436	0.5			35	(1)	75	(1)	33	0.1	4	(1)
Hebrew	1,243	(1)	44	(1)					67	(1)	9	(1)	5	(1)
All other	3,835	0.1	230	0.2	97	0.1	148	0.2	231	0.1	7	(1)	6	(1)

NATIONALITY AS INDICATED BY NAME.	NEW YORK.		PENNSYLVANIA.		MARYLAND.		VIRGINIA.[2]		NORTH CAROLINA.		SOUTH CAROLINA.	
	Number.	Per cent.	Number.	Per cent.	Number.	Per cent.	Number.	Per cent.	Number.	Per cent.	Number.	Per cent.
All nationalities	314,366	100.0	423,373	100.0	208,649	100.0	442,117	100.0	289,181	100.0	140,178	100.0
English	245,901	78.2	249,656	59.0	175,265	84.0	375,799	85.0	240,309	83.1	115,480	82.4
Scotch	10,034	3.2	49,567	11.7	13,562	6.5	31,391	7.1	32,388	11.2	16,447	11.7
Irish	2,525	0.8	8,614	2.0	5,008	2.4	8,842	2.0	6,651	2.3	3,576	2.6
Dutch	50,600	16.1	2,623	0.6	209	0.1	884	0.2	578	0.2	219	0.2
French	2,424	0.8	2,341	0.6	1,460	0.7	2,653	0.6	868	0.3	1,882	1.3
German	1,103	0.4	110,357	26.1	12,310	5.9	21,664	4.9	8,097	2.8	2,343	1.7
Hebrew	385	0.1	21	(1)	626	0.3			1	(1)	85	0.1
All other	1,394	0.4	194	(1)	209	0.1	884	0.2	289	0.1	146	0.1

[1] Less than one-tenth of 1 per cent.   [2] Source of data explained on page 119.

The analysis by nationality as shown by names indicates that the English stock composed 83.5 per cent of all the white population at the period of the First Census, and if the Scotch and the Irish be added, the British stock represented a little more than 90 per cent; while the Germans contributed slightly less than 6 per cent, and the Dutch 2 per cent. This fact is not surprising; the colonies had been under English rule for more than a century, the last to submit being the Dutch colony of New Amsterdam, from which New York and New Jersey were created in 1664.

Virginia, settled by the British in 1609, had at the First Census but 6 per cent non-English population, and of these 5 per cent were what are known as "Valley Dutch," that is, Germans who had migrated through Maryland from Pennsylvania.

New England was almost as English as old England, the lowest proportion (93.1) being in Maine and the highest (96.2) in Rhode Island.

Were it feasible to make an analysis of the population of the Southern states in 1900 similar to that made from the schedules of the First Census, it is probable that little change would be noted from the proportions shown in 1790. In that section there has been a noteworthy preservation of the purity of the stock enumerated in 1790, contrasted with the extraordinary change in the composition of the population which has taken place in the remainder of the nation.

DIAGRAM 10.—PROPORTION OF TOTAL POPULATION FORMED BY EACH NATIONALITY: 1790.

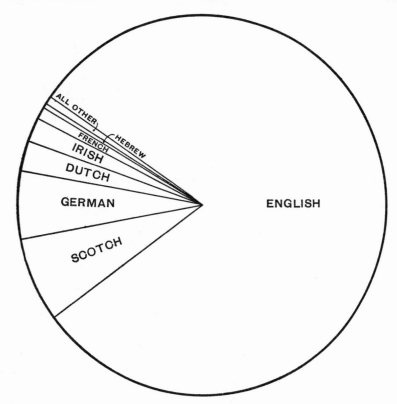

TABLE 46.—PER CENT DISTRIBUTION OF THE WHITE POPULATION OF EACH NATIONALITY AS INDICATED BY NAMES OF HEADS OF FAMILIES, ACCORDING TO STATE OF RESIDENCE: 1790.

STATE.	ALL NATIONALITIES.		ENGLISH.		SCOTCH.		IRISH.		DUTCH.		FRENCH.		GERMAN.		HEBREW.		ALL OTHER.	
	Number.	Per cent.	Number	Per cent.	Number.	Per cent.	Number.	Per cent.	Number.	Per cent.	Number.	Per cent.	Number.	Per cent.	Number.	Per cent.	Number.	Per cent.
Area covered..	2,810,248	100.0	2,345,844	100.0	188,589	100.0	44,273	100.0	56,623	100.0	13,384	100.0	156,457	100.0	1,243	100.0	3,835	100.0
Maine..............	96,107	3.4	89,515	3.8	4,154	2.2	1,334	3.0	279	0.5	115	0.9	436	0.3	44	3.5	230	6.0
New Hampshire.....	141,112	5.0	132,726	5.7	6,648	3.5	1,346	3.0	153	0.3	142	1.1	......	......	......	......	97	2.5
Vermont...........	85,072	3.0	81,149	3.5	2,562	1.4	597	1.3	428	0.8	153	1.1	35	(¹)	......	......	148	3.9
Massachusetts.......	373,187	13.3	354,528	15.1	13,435	7.1	3,732	8.4	373	0.7	746	5.6	75	(¹)	67	5.4	231	6.0
Rhode Island.......	64,670	2.3	62,079	2.6	1,976	1.0	459	1.0	19	(¹)	88	0.7	33	(¹)	9	0.7	7	0.2
Connecticut.........	232,236	8.3	223,437	9.5	6,425	3.4	1,589	3.6	258	0.5	512	3.8	4	(¹)	5	0.4	6	0.2
New York..........	314,366	11.2	245,901	10.5	10,034	5.3	2,525	5.7	50,600	89.4	2,424	18.1	1,103	0.7	385	31.0	1,394	36.3
Pennsylvania.......	423,373	15.1	249,656	10.6	49,567	26.3	8,614	19.5	2,623	4.6	2,341	17.5	110,357	70.5	21	1.7	194	5.1
Maryland...........	208,649	7.4	175,265	7.5	13,562	7.2	5,008	11.3	209	0.4	1,460	10.9	12,310	7.9	626	50.4	209	5.4
Virginia ²..........	442,117	15.7	375,799	16.0	31,391	16.6	8,842	20.0	884	1.6	2,653	19.8	21,664	13.8	......	......	884	23.1
North Carolina......	289,181	10.3	240,309	10.2	32,388	17.2	6,651	15.0	578	1.0	868	6.5	8,097	5.2	1	0.1	289	7.5
South Carolina......	140,178	5.0	115,480	4.9	16,447	8.7	3,576	8.1	219	0.4	1,882	14.1	2,343	1.5	85	6.8	146	3.8

¹ Less than one-tenth of 1 per cent.   ² Source of data explained on page 119.

Diagram 11.—DISTRIBUTION OF POPULATION OF STATES ACCORDING TO NATIONALITY: 1790.

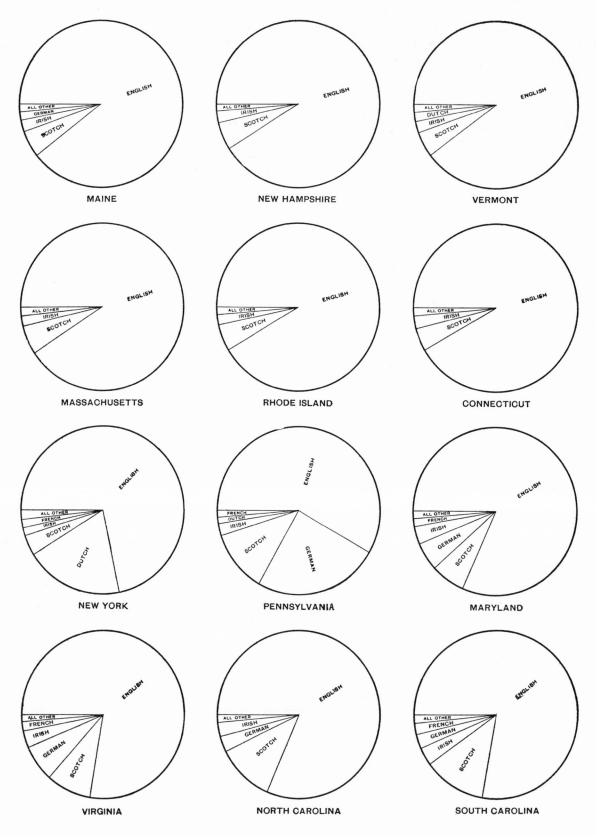

NATIONALITY IN THE STATES AND TERRITORIES FOR WHICH SCHEDULES ARE MISSING.

Reference has already been made to the fact that analysis of nationality at the First Census is necessarily limited to the schedules which are still in existence. In the case of Virginia, proportions of the population represented by the different nationalities were obtained by utilizing the returns of the state enumerations made in 1782 to 1785 (covering 38 counties), and applying the results thus obtained to the population of the entire state as returned at the census of 1790. For Delaware the schedules of the Second Census are available. As there was but little change in the total population of the state, or its composition, during the decade, the percentages shown at the Second Census doubtless reflect accurately the nationality of the population of the state reported ten years earlier. This analysis shows the following result:

Nationalities of the population of Delaware, on the basis of the 1800 proportions: 1790.

NATIONALITY.	Proportion shown from schedules of 1800.	Distribution of population in 1790 on the 1800 proportions.
All nationalities	100.0	46,310
British	97.7	45,245
English	86.3	39,966
Scotch	7.5	3,473
Irish	3.9	1,806
Dutch	1.0	463
French	0.5	232
German	0.4	185
All other	0.4	185

The earliest schedules for the state of New Jersey which are in existence are those for the Fifth Census (1830), which was so far distant from 1790 that the later census obviously could not be regarded as reflecting conditions which prevailed in 1790. With the assistance of the Historical Society of New Jersey, a list of the freeholders of Somerset county in the year 1790 was secured, and an analysis was made of these names—obviously those of all of the representative or property

holding citizens of the county, embracing more than two-thirds of the entire number of heads of families as reported at the First Census. This analysis showed the following result:

Nationalities of the population of Somerset county, N. J., as indicated by the surnames of freeholders: 1790.

TOWN.	Total.	English.	Scotch.	Irish.	Dutch.	French.	German.	All other.
The county	1,277	755	65	12	383	24	7	31
Per cent	100.0	59.1	5.1	0.9	30.0	1.9	0.5	2.4
Bernards town	307	243	34	5	22	3	......	......
Bedminster town	139	96	8	2	28	3	2	......
Bridgewater town	271	170	8	5	57	9	5	17
Eastern town	187	71	6	....	102	3	......	5
Hillsborough town	216	92	2	....	108	6	......	8
Western town	157	83	7	....	66	....	......	1

If it were an assured fact that Somerset county was representative in the composition of its population, it is obvious that the percentages here shown might, with some propriety, be applied to the remaining 12 counties. Unfortunately this method of procedure is not feasible. The composition of the population by nationality varied greatly in the counties of New Jersey. The proportion shown in Somerset is therefore no guide to the proportions which actually existed elsewhere.

An analysis of the population of the various counties of New Jersey has been furnished, at the request of the Director of the Census, by Mr. William Nelson, corresponding secretary of the New Jersey Historical Society, after consultation with Dr. Austin Scott, of New Brunswick, N. J., and Dr. E. S. Sharpe, president of the Salem County Historical Society.[1] Such an analysis is necessarily merely an approximation, but it represents the painstaking estimates of the leading authorities in the state upon New Jersey history, and the figures resulting from an application of the percentages to the population of the state in 1790 are doubtless sufficiently accurate to indicate the distribution by nationality. Upon the basis of this analysis the following tables result:

[1] *Bergen.*—This county was originally settled by Dutch, with a very small admixture of Danes. Prior to 1680 there was a strong infusion of French settlers from Harlem. There was at no time any independent immigration from France. Some of the families having Dutch names, as the "Van Buskirks," were of German origin, and for more than a century were almost exclusively connected with the German Lutheran Church. As early as 1700 there was a considerable infusion of German population from New York city and from German settlements north of New Jersey. About 1765 there was a considerable importation of German miners, principally from Bavaria, who settled in the upper part of the county, working in the iron mines of Bergen county and Morris county. There were Scotch settlers also at a very early period, say 1725 and later, who perhaps worked in the Dutch flax industry, and through affiliations with or acquaintance with Dutch settlers came to this country. I would say that in 1790 the population was about as follows: French, 15 per cent; Germans, 20 per cent; Scotch, 5 per cent; Irish (principally in the iron mines), 5 per cent; English, 15 per cent; Dutch, 40 per cent.

Burlington.—This county was almost exclusively settled from England, or by English capitalists, who, however, induced some settlement from the Friends of Ireland; also Friends from Wales. There was a small admixture of Swedes, who had previously settled in the southern part of the state. I would approximate the percentages of nationality in 1790 as follows: Welsh, 5 per cent; Swedes, 5 per cent; Irish, 10 per cent, English, 80 per cent.

Cape May.—This county was originally settled by Swedes and Finns, but soon there was an influx of English from Long Island and New England. In 1790 the percentages of nationality were as follows: Swedes, 40 per cent; Finns, 10 per cent; English, 50 per cent.

Cumberland.—This county was principally settled by the English from Long Island, New England, and the mother country, with a slight admixture of Finns. In 1790 the percentages of nationality were as follows: Swedes, 10 per cent; Finns, 2 per cent; Welsh, 3 per cent; Germans (employed in the iron works and glass works), 10 per cent; Irish (employed in the iron works and glass works), 10 per cent; English, 65 per cent.

Essex.—This county was originally settled from New England and Long Island and was exclusively English. By 1790 a considerable

Estimated per cent of the population of New Jersey contributed by specified nationalities: 1790.

COUNTY.	English and Welsh.	Scotch.	Irish.	Dutch.	French.	German.	Hebrew.	Swedish and Finnish.	All other.
The state.............................	58.0	7.7	7.1	12.7	2.1	9.2	....	2.9	0.1
Bergen......	15.0	5.0	5.0	40.0	15.0	20.0			
Burlington.......	85.0	....	10.0					5.0	
Cape May......	50.0							50.0	
Cumberland......	68.0		10.0			10.0		12.0	
Essex......	60.0	10.0	10.0	15.0	5.0				
Gloucester......	80.0	....	5.0			5.0		10.0	
Hunterdon......	30.0	10.0	10.0	25.0		25.0			
Middlesex......	38.0	32.0	4.0	20.0	4.0	2.0			
Monmouth......	75.0	15.0	5.0		3.0	2.0			
Morris......	55.0	5.0	10.0	10.0		20.0			
Salem......	83.0	....	10.0					7.0	
Somerset......	59.1	5.1	0.9	30.0	1.9	0.5			2.4
Sussex......	55.0	5.0	5.0	15.0		20.0			

Total number of persons in families in New Jersey of which the names of heads indicate specified nationality, computed upon the basis of estimated proportions in 1790.

COUNTY.	Total.	English and Welsh.	Scotch.	Irish.	Dutch.	French.	German.	Hebrew.	Swedish and Finnish.	All other.
The state..........................	169,954	98,620	13,156	12,099	21,581	3,565	15,678	....	5,006	249
Bergen...........	10,108	1,516	506	505	4,043	1,516	2,022			
Burlington...........	17,270	14,679	....	1,727					864	
Cape May...........	2,416	1,208	....						1,208	
Cumberland...........	7,990	5,433	.I........	799			799		959	
Essex...........	16,454	9,873	1,645	1,645	2,468	823				
Gloucester...........	12,830	10,264	....	642			641		1,283	
Hunterdon...........	18,661	5,599	1,866	1,866	4,665	....	4,665			
Middlesex...........	14,498	5,509	4,639	580	2,900	580	290			
Monmouth...........	14,969	11,227	2,245	749		449	299			
Morris...........	15,532	8,543	777	1,553	1,553	....	3,106			
Salem...........	9,891	8,210	....	989					692	
Somerset...........	10,339	6,111	528	94	3,103	197	57			249
Sussex...........	18,996	10,448	950	950	2,849	....	3,799			

The estimates referred to place the percentage of Dutch in the total population of New Jersey higher than actually existed in 1790 anywhere else in the United States, even in New York. This, however, does not discredit the estimate as New Jersey was part of the early Dutch settlement.

immigration of other nationalities had set in, and in that year the population was approximately as follows: French, 5 per cent; Scotch, 10 per cent; Irish, 10 per cent; Dutch, 15 per cent; English, 60 per cent.

Gloucester.—This county was settled originally by the Swedes. Afterwards there was an influx, principally of English, with some slight admixture of Welsh. In 1790 the population was approximately as follows: Swedes, 10 per cent; Welsh, 5 per cent; Germans, 5 per cent; Irish, 5 per cent; English, 75 per cent.

Hunterdon.—This county was originally settled by English from Burlington county. About 1715 there was a considerable immigration of Germans, who came from the Palatinate and elsewhere in Germany, being members of the Lutheran Church. There was also a considerable immigration from northern New Jersey, principally Bergen county, and also from Monmouth and Somerset counties, and from Long Island. In 1790 the population was approximately as follows: Germans, 25 per cent; Dutch, 25 per cent; Irish (working in the mines and on farms), 10 per cent; Scotch, 10 per cent; English, 30 per cent.

Middlesex.—This county was settled originally by the English. About 1685 there was a considerable importation of Scotch. About 1690–1730, the Dutch came in. In 1790 the population was made up about as follows: Dutch, 20 per cent; Scotch, 20 per cent; Germans, 5 per cent; Irish, 5 per cent; French, 2 per cent; English, 48 per cent.

Monmouth.—This county was originally settled by the English, but before the end of the seventeenth century there was a considerable influx of Dutch, principally from Long Island. Some of the Scotch settlers of Middlesex also drifted in. In 1790 the population was approximately as follows: Scotch, 15 per cent; Irish, 5 per cent; French, 3 per cent; Germans, 2 per cent; English, 75 per cent.

Morris.—This county was settled early in the eighteenth century, say 1710–1720, by English and Germans in almost equal proportions. Afterwards Dutch drifted in. About 1765 there was a further influx of German miners from Bavaria, and from then on Irish workmen were attracted to the mines. In 1790 the population was approximately as follows: Irish, 10 per cent; Scotch, 5 per cent; Dutch, 10 per cent; Germans, 20 per cent; English, 55 per cent.

Salem.—This county was originally settled, about 1675, by English, with a slight infusion from Ireland and Wales. There were also some Swedes and Finns from the original settlers, about 1635. The population underwent very slight changes until 1790, when it stood about as follows: Finns, 2 per cent; Swedes, 5 per cent; Irish, 10 per cent; Welsh, 5 per cent; English, 78 per cent.

Somerset.—This county was analyzed by the Census Office from the list of freeholders in 1790. I would have said that Somerset had: Scotch, 10 per cent; Irish, 3 per cent; French, 2 per cent; Germans, 5 per cent.

Sussex.—This county was originally settled early in the eighteenth century, or perhaps late in the seventeenth century, by Dutch from New York state. Then English settlers came in from Burlington and Hunterdon counties; also Germans from Hunterdon county; about 1765 German miners from Bavaria, and Irish laborers in the mines, with some slight infusion of Scotch also. In 1790, I should say the population was about as follows: Irish, 5 per cent; Scotch, 5 per cent; Germans, 20 per cent; Dutch, 15 per cent; English, 55 per cent.

WILLIAM NELSON.

The composition of the white population of Georgia, Kentucky, and of the district subsequently erected into the state of Tennessee, is also unknown; but in view of the fact that Georgia was a distinctly English colony, and that Tennessee and Kentucky were settled largely from Virginia and North Carolina, the application of the North Carolina proportions to the white population of these three results in what is doubtless an approximation of the actual distribution.

Utilizing for the states and territories for which the 1790 schedules are missing, the proportions secured as above indicated, the following summary results:

TABLE 47.—COMPUTED DISTRIBUTION OF THE WHITE POPULATION OF EACH STATE FOR WHICH SCHEDULES ARE MISSING, ACCORDING TO NATIONALITY: 1790.

NATIONALITY.	NEW JERSEY.		DELAWARE.		GEORGIA.		KENTUCKY.		TENNESSEE.	
	Number.	Per cent.	Number.	Per cent.	Number.	Per cent.	Number.	Per cent.	Number.	Per cent.
All nationalities	169,954	100.0	46,310	100.0	52,886	100.0	61,133	100.0	31,913	100.0
English	98,620	58.0	39,966	86.3	43,948	83.1	50,802	83.1	26,519	83.1
Scotch	13,156	7.7	3,473	7.5	5,923	11.2	6,847	11.2	3,574	11.2
Irish	12,099	7.1	1,806	3.9	1,216	2.3	1,406	2.3	734	2.3
Dutch	21,581	12.7	463	1.0	106	0.2	122	0.2	64	0.2
French	3,565	2.1	232	0.5	159	0.3	183	0.3	96	0.3
German	15,678	9.2	185	0.4	1,481	2.8	1,712	2.8	894	2.8
All other [1]	5,255	3.1	185	0.4	53	0.1	61	0.1	32	0.1

[1] Includes Hebrew.

NATIONALITY OF TOTAL WHITE POPULATION IN 1790 AND OF WHITE NATIVE STOCK IN 1900.

The above figures may be accepted as representing the actual proportions with sufficient accuracy to justify computing the distribution by nationality for the total white population of the United States as it existed in 1790. The result is as follows:

TABLE 48.—*Number and per cent distribution of the white population according to nationality: 1790.*

NATIONALITY AS INDICATED BY NAME.	AREA COVERED.	
	Number.	Per cent.
All nationalities	3,172,444	100.0
English	2,605,699	82.1
Scotch	221,562	7.0
Irish	61,534	1.9
Dutch	78,959	2.5
French	17,619	0.6
German	176,407	5.6
All other	10,664	0.3

In a preceding chapter the number of descendants of white persons enumerated at the First Census has been established as approximately 35,000,000 in 1900. While it is not to be expected that the exact proportions of nationalities indicated above as existing in 1790 have been maintained in the native population, it is interesting to note that were the proportions contributed by the different nationalities composing the native population the same in 1900 as they were in 1790, the 35,000,000 would have been distributed as shown in Table 49.

As a matter of fact it is probable that the native population in recording an increase of nearly 700 per cent during the century has departed somewhat from the proportions shown at the outset. It will be remembered that the analysis in a preceding chapter showed the addition in 1900 of 32,000,000 of white persons arriving after the First Census, either foreign born themselves or of foreign parentage. It has also been pointed out that the foreign stock is probably increasing with greater rapidity than the native. Whatever the proportionate increase may be, however, between the two elements, it is of these two rather diverse strains that the white population of the United States is at present composed.

TABLE 49.—*White native stock in 1900 distributed by nationality according to proportions shown for 1790.*

NATIONALITY.	Population.
All nationalities	35,000,000
English	28,735,000
Scotch	2,450,000
Irish	665,000
Dutch	875,000
French	210,000
German	1,960,000
All other	105,000

NATIONALITY IN 1900 IN TYPICAL COUNTIES.

In order to illustrate the change which has been in progress during the century, an analysis was made by nationality of the names upon the 1900 schedules of Hartford county, Conn.,[1] and of Columbia county, N. Y., which were regarded as typical urban and rural counties, respectively. Both remained practically unchanged in boundary from 1790 to 1900. By applying the same method of analysis to the names upon the schedules of the Twelfth Census as was applied to those upon the schedules of 1790, and by which the results presented in the preceding tables were secured, the nationality of the white population of the 2 counties mentioned was composed in 1900 as is shown in Table 50:

[1] See page 123.

DISTRIBUTION OF DIFFERENT NATIONALITIES IN 1790, BY STATES.

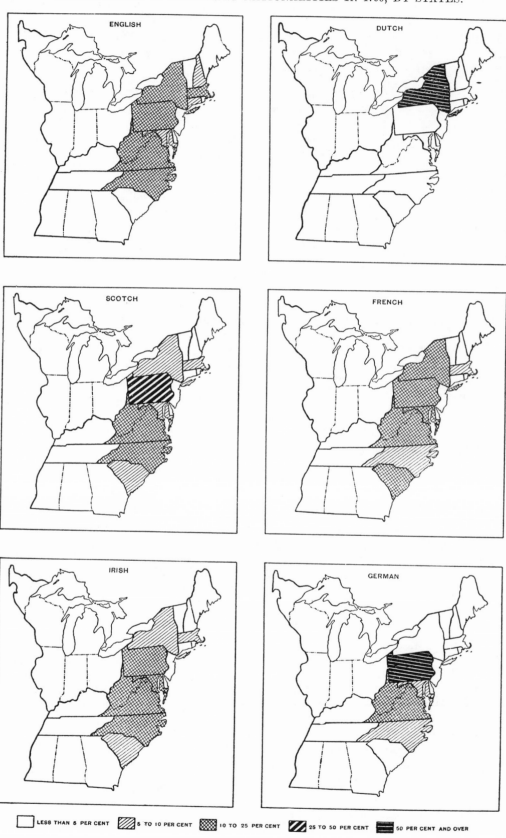

LESS THAN 5 PER CENT   5 TO 10 PER CENT   10 TO 25 PER CENT   25 TO 50 PER CENT   50 PER CENT AND OVER

TABLE 50.—WHITE POPULATION OF HARTFORD COUNTY, CONN., AND OF COLUMBIA COUNTY, N. Y., CLASSIFIED BY NATIONALITY AS INDICATED BY NAMES OF HEADS OF FAMILIES: 1790 AND 1900.

| NATIONALITY. | HARTFORD COUNTY, CONN. | | | | COLUMBIA COUNTY, N. Y. | | | |
| | 1790 | | 1900 | | 1790 | | 1900 | |
	Population.	Per cent distribu-tion.	Population.	Per cent distribu-tion.	Population.	Per cent distribu-tion.	Population.	Per cent distribu-tion.
All nationalities	37,498	100.0	192,108	100.0	25,811	100.0	41,779	100.0
British	37,429	99.8	134,860	70.2	20,847	80.8	29,852	71.4
English	36,239	96.6	75,691	39.4	20,183	78.2	22,998	55.0
Scotch	956	2.5	7,300	3.8	521	2.0	1,337	3.2
Irish	234	0.6	51,869	27.0	143	0.6	5,517	13.2
Dutch	21	0.1	576	0.3	4,710	18.2	2,642	6.3
French	42	0.1	[1] 6,532	3.4	118	0.5	752	1.8
German			23,437	12.2	102	0.4	7,196	17.2
All other[2]	6	([3])	26,703	13.9	34	0.1	1,337	3.2

[1] Principally French Canadian.   [2] Includes Hungarians, Italians, Roumanians, Russians, Scandinavians, etc.   [3] Less than one-tenth of 1 per cent.

In Hartford county the population, which in 1790 was almost exclusively British, shows a reduction in that respect of nearly one-third in 1900 in favor of other nationalities; while within the British element the English stock, which completely overshadowed the other two elements in 1790 has shrunk to scarcely more than one-third, but the Irish has greatly increased. Indeed, the increase in the latter element represents a change from not more than 500 in 1790 (including the Scotch-Irish) to more than 50,000 in 1900. It is worthy of note also that the British element, which in 1790 was much greater in Hartford county than in Columbia, has decreased to approximately 70 per cent in both; and other changes, such as the increase in German and other nationalities in the community at the expense of the British element as a whole, and increase in the Irish stock at the expense of the English or original stock, have also been characteristic of both counties.

The changes indicated in these 2 counties are interesting, and probably are typical of the changes which have been in progress in all the Northern states in the original area.

SLAVEHOLDING, BY NATIONALITY.

The average number of slaves per family for the several nationalities is shown in the following table:

TABLE 51.—NUMBER OF WHITE FAMILIES, SLAVEHOLDING AND NONSLAVEHOLDING, CLASSIFIED ACCORDING TO NATIONALITY, WITH NUMBER OF WHITE PERSONS AND OF SLAVES REPORTED FOR SUCH FAMILIES: 1790.

| NATIONALITY. | WHITE FAMILIES. | | | | WHITE PERSONS. | | SLAVES. | | |
	Total number.	Slave-holding.	Nonslave-holding.	Per cent slaveholding families formed of all families.	Total number.	Average number per family.	Total number.	Average number per slave-holding family.	Number per 100 of all families.
All nationalities	405,475	47,664	357,311	11.8	2,324,339	5.7	311,919	6.5	77
English and Welsh	336,651	38,146	298,505	11.3	1,933,218	5.7	258,684	6.8	77
Scotch	27,250	4,362	22,888	16.0	153,458	5.6	27,570	6.3	101
Irish	6,285	962	5,323	15.3	34,589	5.5	6,578	6.8	105
Dutch	9,399	2,625	6,774	27.9	55,666	5.9	8,906	3.4	95
French	1,913	589	1,324	30.8	10,444	5.5	6,567	11.1	343
German	23,300	871	22,429	3.7	133,032	5.7	3,079	3.5	13
Hebrew	213	33	180	15.5	1,198	5.6	157	4.8	74
All other	464	76	388	16.4	2,734	5.9	378	5.0	81

It is necessary, in consulting the foregoing table, to bear in mind the fact that in some instances the proportions are misleading. It will be observed that the average number of slaves per family are largest for families of French origin. This is accounted for by the fact that the total number of families of obviously French origin in the United States was small, and that a large proportion of such families were located in South Carolina, the state in which the average number of slaves per family was highest. It is not surprising, therefore, that the French families led in the proportion which slaveholding families formed of total families—nearly one-third were slaveholders. This nationality, however, was closely followed by the old Dutch families of New York, who still continued to possess slaves at the period under consideration. It is significant that the smallest proportion is shown by the Germans, who even at this early period were obviously opposed to slave ownership.

Had the proportion of slaves for the entire white population of the United States in 1790 been the same as it was for the German element, the aggregate number of slaves at the First Census would have been but 52,520, instead of approximately 700,000.

XII. INTERSTATE MIGRATION.

ANALYSIS OF POPULATION ACCORDING TO GEOGRAPHIC DIVI-
SION OF RESIDENCE AND OF BIRTH—DECREASE IN CONTRIBU-
TION OF ORIGINAL AREA TO POPULATION OF ADDED AREA.

Facilities for transportation to all parts of the Union are so great that the inhabitants of one section are able to migrate to another, even at great distance, with comparatively small expenditure, inconvenience, or delay. In consequence many persons change their place of abode so freely that in every state reside natives of practically every other state of the Union.

Classification of the white population, by nativity and parentage is possible only for 1890 and 1900; but the returns, though covering only one decade, prove of interest when further classified as for the area enumerated in 1790 and the added area. The following summary analyzes the native white population of native parentage in continental United States according to areas of residence and of birth:

AREA OF RESIDENCE.	NATIVE WHITE POPULATION OF NATIVE PARENTAGE BORN IN SPECIFIED AREA.			
	United States.[1]	Area enumerated in 1790.	Added area.[1]	State or territory of birth unknown.
1890				
Continental United States..	34,358,348	18,884,378	15,217,257	256,713
Area enumerated in 1790..........	16,458,185	16,077,268	287,409	93,508
Added area......................	17,900,163	2,807,110	14,929,848	163,205
1900				
Continental United States..	40,949,362	21,037,083	19,772,003	140,276
Area enumerated in 1790..........	18,926,020	18,435,940	440,927	49,153
Added area......................	22,023,342	2,601,143	19,331,076	91,123

[1] Including persons born in Alaska, Hawaii, Philippine Islands, and Porto Rico; persons born at sea under the United States flag; and American citizens born abroad.

The natives of the original area outnumbered those of the added area by more than 3,500,000 persons in 1890, and by about 1,250,000 in 1900. The natives of the two sections are thus tending toward equality in numbers. Of greater significance is the change apparently in progress in the number of persons born in one area and resident in the other. The heavy contribution of the original area to the population of the added area decreased, while the much smaller contribution of the added area to the original area increased, and by approximately the same number as the falling off shown by the original area.

It can not be assumed that the change here noted as in progress in 1900, in comparison with similar returns for 1890, has been of long duration; the large number of persons shown in 1900 as born in the older states and resident in the newer is the living aggregate of the generous decennial contribution by the original states to the upbuilding of innumerable communities in the South and Southwest. This contribution must have increased, with little interruption, for many years; while, on the other hand, the number of persons born in the added area and resident in the original area must have been almost negligible in number even so late as 1880. The rather significant change here indicated prompts further analysis by geographic divisions in Tables 52 and 53.

In 1890 approximately one-tenth as many persons born in the added area were resident in the area enumerated in 1790 as were born in the latter area and resided in the former; by 1900 the ratio had changed to approximately one-sixth, as a result of marked increase (amounting to nearly one-half) in the number of persons born in the added area and residing in the original area. All of the 3 geographic divisions of the added area contributed increasingly of their native born to the population of the original area.

The change here shown is confirmed by an examination of the per cent distribution of the residents of each area according to birthplace. The proportion of the native whites of native parentage born in each division of the area enumerated in 1790 and living in each division of the added area was less in 1900 than in 1890; on the other hand, the proportion living in each division of the area enumerated in 1790 and born in the Northern states of the added area increased, and the corresponding proportions for the Southern and Western states of the added area either increased or remained stationary.

In observing the percentages of increase given below, it should be remembered that the increase of population born in the area of residence is natural increase, while the only source of increase of migrant population is continued immigration. The larger the number of persons already in the class, the larger must be the loss through death and the consequent requirement for new arrivals to make good the decrease thus occasioned.

TABLE 52.—NATIVE WHITE POPULATION OF NATIVE PARENTAGE LIVING IN SPECIFIED GEOGRAPHIC DIVISIONS OF THE AREA ENUMERATED IN 1790, DISTRIBUTED ACCORDING TO GEOGRAPHIC DIVISION OF BIRTH: 1890 AND 1900.

GEOGRAPHIC DIVISION OF BIRTH.	NATIVE WHITE POPULATION OF NATIVE PARENTAGE LIVING IN SPECIFIED GEOGRAPHIC DIVISIONS OF THE AREA ENUMERATED IN 1790.							
	Number.				Per cent distribution.			
	Area enumerated in 1790.	New England.	Middle states.	Southern states.	Area enumerated in 1790.	New England.	Middle states.	Southern states.
	1890							
United States	16,364,677	2,422,429	6,508,486	7,433,762	100.0	100.0	100.0	100.0
Continental United States	16,362,866	2,421,697	6,507,517	7,433,652	100.0	100.0	100.0	100.0
Area enumerated in 1790	16,077,268	2,400,690	6,422,837	7,253,741	98.2	99.1	98.7	97.6
Added area	285,598	21,007	84,680	179,911	1.7	0.9	1.3	2.4
Northern states	211,295	17,299	76,285	117,711	1.3	0.7	1.2	1.6
Southern states	67,409	1,720	5,110	60,579	0.4	0.1	0.1	0.8
Western states	6,894	1,988	3,285	1,621	(1)	0.1	0.1	(1)
Outlying districts	1,811	732	969	110	(1)	(1)	(1)	(1)
	1900							
United States	18,876,867	2,500,345	7,498,970	8,877,552	100.0	100.0	100.0	100.0
Continental United States	18,862,177	2,493,559	7,491,938	8,876,680	99.9	99.7	99.9	100.0
Area enumerated in 1790	18,435,940	2,460,114	7,347,966	8,627,860	97.7	98.4	98.0	97.2
Added area	426,237	33,445	143,972	248,820	2.3	1.3	1.9	2.8
Northern states	313,784	27,474	128,784	157,526	1.7	1.1	1.7	1.8
Southern states	98,822	2,464	8,298	88,060	0.5	0.1	0.1	1.0
Western states	13,631	3,507	6,890	3,234	0.1	0.1	0.1	(1)
Outlying districts	14,690	6,786	7,032	872	0.1	0.3	0.1	(1)

1 Less than one-tenth of 1 per cent.

TABLE 53.—NATIVE WHITE POPULATION OF NATIVE PARENTAGE LIVING IN SPECIFIED GEOGRAPHIC DIVISIONS OF THE ADDED AREA WITHIN CONTINENTAL UNITED STATES, DISTRIBUTED ACCORDING TO GEOGRAPHIC DIVISION OF BIRTH: 1890 AND 1900.

GEOGRAPHIC DIVISION OF BIRTH.	NATIVE WHITE POPULATION OF NATIVE PARENTAGE LIVING IN SPECIFIED GEOGRAPHIC DIVISIONS OF THE ADDED AREA WITHIN CONTINENTAL UNITED STATES.							
	Number.				Per cent distribution.			
	Added area within continental United States.	Northern states.	Southern states.	Western states.	Added area within continental United States.	Northern states.	Southern states.	Western states.
	1890							
United States	17,736,958	12,148,750	4,131,477	1,456,731	100.0	100.0	100.0	100.0
Continental United States	17,733,492	12,146,159	4,131,309	1,456,024	100.0	100.0	100.0	100.0
Area enumerated in 1790	2,807,110	1,859,533	645,750	301,827	15.8	15.3	15.6	20.7
New England	311,811	222,608	11,287	77,916	1.8	1.8	0.3	5.3
Middle states	1,172,475	998,878	31,518	142,079	6.6	8.2	0.8	9.8
Southern states	1,322,824	638,047	602,945	81,832	7.5	5.3	14.6	5.6
Added area	14,926,382	10,286,626	3,485,559	1,154,197	84.2	84.7	84.4	79.2
Outlying districts	3,466	2,591	168	707	(1)	(1)	(1)	(1)
	1900							
United States	21,932,219	14,094,381	5,840,231	1,997,607	100.0	100.0	100.0	100.0
Continental United States	21,914,451	14,082,591	5,839,063	1,992,797	99.9	99.9	100.0	99.8
Area enumerated in 1790	2,601,143	1,568,299	721,626	311,218	11.9	11.1	12.4	15.6
New England	245,609	161,991	10,411	73,207	1.1	1.1	0.2	3.7
Middle states	999,810	818,685	35,864	145,261	4.6	5.8	0.6	7.3
Southern states	1,355,724	587,623	675,351	92,750	6.2	4.2	11.6	4.6
Added area	19,313,308	12,514,292	5,117,437	1,681,579	88.1	88.8	87.6	84.2
Outlying districts	17,768	11,790	1,168	4,810	0.1	0.1	(1)	0.2

1 Less than one-tenth of 1 per cent.

The percentages of increase from 1890 to 1900 in the native white persons of native parentage living in the area enumerated in 1790 and in the added area, are as follows:

GEOGRAPHIC DIVISION OF BIRTH.	PER CENT OF INCREASE, 1890 TO 1900, FOR NATIVE WHITE POPULATION OF NATIVE PARENTAGE LIVING IN THE AREA ENUMERATED IN 1790.			
	Total.	New England.	Middle states.	Southern states.
United States	15.4	3.2	15.2	19.4
Continental United States	15.3	3.0	15.1	19.4
Area enumerated in 1790	14.7	2.5	14.4	18.9
Added area	49.2	59.2	70.0	38.3
Northern states	48.5	58.8	68.8	33.8
Southern states	46.6	43.3	62.4	45.4
Western states	97.7	76.4	109.7	99.5
Outlying districts	711.2	827.0	625.7	692.7

GEOGRAPHIC DIVISION OF BIRTH.	PER CENT OF INCREASE, 1890 TO 1900, FOR NATIVE WHITE POPULATION OF NATIVE PARENTAGE LIVING IN ADDED AREA WITHIN CONTINENTAL UNITED STATES.			
	Total.	Northern states.	Southern states.	Western states.
United States	23.7	16.0	41.4	37.1
Continental United States	23.6	15.9	41.3	36.9
Area enumerated in 1790	[1] 7.3	[1] 15.7	11.8	3.1
New England	[1] 21.2	[1] 27.2	[1] 7.8	[1] 6.0
Middle states	[1] 14.7	[1] 18.0	13.8	2.2
Southern states	2.5	[1] 7.9	12.0	13.3
Added area	29.4	21.7	46.8	45.7
Outlying districts	412.6	355.0	595.2	580.3

[1] Decrease.

Inspection of the first of the foregoing summaries shows that the percentage of increase in the number of white persons of native parentage born and living in the New England states is practically negligible, while the corresponding percentage for the number born and living in the Southern states is almost as great as the percentage of increase in the total population of the United States during the decade. In marked contrast to the small native increase shown in the New England and Middle states is that of persons born in the added area and resident in the two sections specified. Continuance of such large percentages would represent a significant population change. On the other hand, the changes indicated by the second summary prove to be the reverse of those shown by the first.

A class of citizens aggregating nearly 3,000,000, as does the great body of natives born in the original area but living in the added area, will lose, in a decade, not less than 400,000 of their number through death; in addition, a number—possibly not large, but sufficient to exert some influence—will return to their native area or depart from the country. Hence, in order merely to maintain the exact number previously enumerated, by making good the loss, approximately 500,000 persons must remove from the original area to the added area. Additions beyond this number would constitute increase in the class; the decline during the decade from 1890 to 1900 was due to the fact that the additions were not sufficient to make good the losses, from whatever cause.

There are doubtless other factors at work in connection with migration back and forth between the original area and the added area. Attention has already been called to the remarkable decrease in the fecundity of the native stock in the original area. A decreasing proportion in this class must necessarily lead to a decrease in the departures. Furthermore, some influence is exerted by the tendency toward equilibrium of opportunity between the West and the East, now resulting from the general settlement of those areas in the West and Northwest that formerly offered unlimited opportunity and attraction to the more venturesome and ambitious among the natives of the older states.

The changes here pointed out are doubtless contrary in part to those which are popularly believed to be in progress. They are further confirmed by the known fact that there is an increasing tendency, on the part of natives of the newer states of the West and Southwest who have accumulated large fortunes, to seek the financial and business centers of the East for residence and investment. Accessibility to the seaboard—an important consideration in the establishment of early settlements—is doubtless still an influential factor, as facilitating travel and quick communication with other parts of the world.

XIII. FOREIGN BORN POPULATION.

PROPORTIONS CONTRIBUTED BY ORIGINAL AND ADDED AREAS—
CHANGE IN CHARACTER OF POPULATION—SMALL PROPORTION
OF FOREIGN BORN IN SOUTHERN STATES—COUNTRY OF BIRTH.

Attention has thus far been directed to the distribution of the native white population, especially persons of native parentage. Analysis of the changes which have occurred, as indicated in the previous pages, shows that the total population of the original area has increased steadily since the First Census, to a total of approximately 35,000,000; while that of the added area increased during the earlier periods at a much more rapid rate, but in the last decade tended to become uniform with the original area in percentage of increase. The aggregate population of the added area in 1900 was 41,000,000; hence there was a general similarity both in total population and in the percentage of increase between the older and newer sections of the country.

It will be of interest at this point to consider the contribution of the foreign element in each of the two areas.

TABLE 54.—FOREIGN BORN POPULATION IN EACH STATE OF THE AREA ENUMERATED IN 1790, AND IN THE ADDED AREA OF CONTINENTAL UNITED STATES: 1850 TO 1900.

STATE.	1850[1]	1860[1]	1870	1880	1890[2]	1900
Continental United States	2,244,602	4,138,697	5,567,229	6,679,943	9,249,547	10,341,276
Area enumerated in 1790	1,466,806	2,264,121	2,765,197	3,055,088	4,153,155	5,022,989
New England	306,249	469,330	648,001	793,612	1,142,432	1,445,237
Maine	31,825	37,453	48,881	58,883	78,961	93,330
New Hampshire	14,265	20,938	29,611	46,294	72,340	88,107
Vermont	33,715	32,743	47,155	40,959	44,088	44,747
Massachusetts	164,024	260,106	353,319	443,491	657,137	846,324
Rhode Island	23,902	37,394	55,396	73,993	106,305	134,519
Connecticut	38,518	80,696	113,639	129,992	183,601	238,210
Middle states	1,024,547	1,563,740	1,881,741	2,030,376	2,758,906	3,331,369
New York	655,929	1,001,280	1,138,353	1,211,379	1,571,050	1,900,425
New Jersey	59,948	122,790	188,943	221,700	328,975	431,884
Pennsylvania	303,417	430,505	545,309	587,829	845,720	985,250
Delaware	5,253	9,165	9,136	9,468	13,161	13,810
Southern states	136,010	231,051	235,455	231,100	251,817	246,383
Maryland and District of Columbia	58,176	90,013	99,666	99,928	113,066	114,053
Virginia and West Virginia	22,985	35,058	30,845	32,961	37,257	41,912
North Carolina	2,581	3,298	3,029	3,742	3,702	4,492
South Carolina	8,707	9,986	8,074	7,686	6,270	5,528
Georgia[3]	6,488	11,671	11,127	10,564	12,137	12,403
Kentucky	31,420	59,799	63,398	59,517	59,356	50,249
Tennessee[4]	5,653	21,226	19,316	16,702	20,029	17,746
Added area	777,796	1,874,576	2,802,032	3,624,855	5,096,392	5,318,287

[1] Corrected figures as given in Ninth Census Report on Population, Table IV.
[2] Exclusive of Indian Territory and Indian reservations.
[3] Entire state.
[4] Designated as "Southwest Territory" in 1790 Census Report.

Beginning with a total foreign born population of approximately 2,250,000 in 1850, the number had more than quadrupled by 1900. Approximately two-thirds of the foreign born enumerated at the census of 1850 were reported as residing in the area enumerated at the First Census, the remaining one-third being scattered in the great extent of country comprised in the newer states and territories. The relationship thus indicated changed with great rapidity at the succeeding censuses.

YEAR.	DISTRIBUTION OF THE TOTAL FOREIGN BORN.	
	Original area.	Added area.
1850	65.3	34.7
1860	54.7	45.3
1870	49.7	50.3
1880	45.7	54.3
1890	44.9	55.1
1900	48.6	51.4

By 1870 the added area contained a slight majority of all the foreign born reported at that census. This proportion increased during the next twenty years. In 1890 the number of foreign born persons in the added area exceeded the number in the original area by more than 900,000, but the proportions for 1900 suggest that a decided change was in progress. Should the Thirteenth Census show the same rates of change for both areas as were shown from 1890 to 1900, the area enumerated in 1790 will once more report an excess of the foreign born population.

DIAGRAM **12.**—*Foreign born population of area enumerated in 1790 and of added area: 1850 to 1900.*

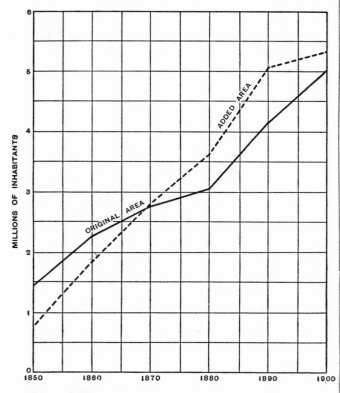

Table 54 offers clear evidence of the change in the character of population which is in progress in the area enumerated at the First Census. Although the increase maintained is apparently gratifying, much of it is due to accessions of foreigners. Large numbers of immigrants arriving in the United States remain in the seaboard cities or in the older states, attracted by the magnitude of industrial operations and the dense population. It has already been shown that the proportion of children in the older sections of the Republic is lower than elsewhere; hence, while the inhabitants of the older states continue to increase in number to a degree which gratifies local pride, the composition of the population appears to be undergoing a comparatively rapid change.

There is another aspect of this subject, however, which in some respects is even more significant. The Southern states forming a part of the original area, as already pointed out for the entire group, have been practically silent partners so far as the subject of foreign born population is concerned. In 1850, out of a total foreign element in the area enumerated in 1790 of approximately 1,500,000, but 133,961 were reported by the Southern states. Thus practically the entire contribution of foreign born at the census mentioned was made by the New England and Middle states. Fifty years later, in 1900, persons of foreign birth continued practically a negligible element in the Southern states, while in the centers of population which had reported them at the earlier period their number had increased to nearly 5,000,000. Therefore the comparison made in the previous pages is in reality a comparison not of the contribution of foreign born residing in the original area, but of the number residing in a portion of that area, with the number reported by all of the states and territories erected after the First Census. Subdivision of the original area into 3 geographic divisions reveals the following proportions at 3 census periods:

AREA.	PER CENT DISTRIBUTION OF THE FOREIGN BORN POPULATION.		
	1850	1880	1900
United States	100.0	100.0	100.0
Area enumerated in 1790	65.3	45.7	48.6
New England	13.6	11.9	14.0
Middle states	45.6	30.4	32.2
Southern states	6.1	3.4	2.4
Added area	34.7	54.3	51.4

In each of the 2 decades here shown the Southern states have reported a very small and decreasing proportion of the total foreign element. On the other hand, the New England and Middle states together reported 59.3 per cent of all the foreign born in the United States in 1850, 42.3 per cent of all in 1880, and 46.2 per cent of all in 1900. It must be remembered that these proportions relate to a total foreign born population which quadrupled in the half century under consideration.

TABLE **55.**—*Number of foreign born in every 1,000 of the total white population: 1850 to 1900.*

YEAR.	ORIGINAL AREA.			Added area.[1]
	Total.	New England and Middle states.	Southern states.	
1850	115	155	32	115
1860	147	193	47	160
1870	156	207	43	172
1880	143	196	33	159
1890	163	225	31	169
1900	164	229	25	143

[1] Computed on the basis of the total white population of that part of continental United States not included in the original area; population of Indian Territory and Indian reservations included for 1900 only.

It is significant that the number of foreign born in every 1,000 of white population has shown practically continuous increase in the New England and Middle states. The number of native born of foreign parentage by geographic divisions, a classification possible for the years 1870, 1890, and 1900, was as follows:

TABLE 56.—*Number of native born of foreign parentage[1] in each 1,000 of the total white population: 1870, 1890, and 1900.*

YEAR.	ORIGINAL AREA.			Added area.[2]
	Total.	New England and Middle states.	Southern states.	
1870	150	193	52	169
1890	190	253	55	225
1900	214	289	54	251

[1] This designation comprehends, for 1890 and 1900, all native white persons having either one or both parents foreign born; and for 1870 all native born of foreign parents (obtained by deducting the foreign born from the total number of persons having one or both parents foreign). It is assumed that in 1870 the native born of foreign parents were white.
[2] Computed on the basis of the total white population of that part of continental United States not enumerated in 1790; population of Indian Territory and Indian reservations included for 1900 only.

Upon combining the number of foreign born and their native children, who comprise what may be termed the distinctly foreign element, the following proportion in each 1,000 of white population appears:

TABLE 57.—*Number of persons of foreign birth and of native birth and foreign parentage, in each 1,000 of the white population: 1870, 1890, and 1900.*

YEAR.	ORIGINAL AREA.				Added area.
	Total.	New England.	Middle states.	Southern states.	
1870	306	331	427	94	340
1890	352	477	479	85	393
1900	378	546	507	79	394

It will be recalled that, in 1900, the number of foreign born in every 1,000 of the white population was greater in the original area than in the added area, the former having passed the latter between 1890 and 1900. Upon extending the classification of the foreign element to include the native born of foreign parents, as shown above, the added area continues to present a larger proportion of persons classed as of foreign parentage than the original area, but the increase from 1890 to 1900 was but 1 per 1,000 in the added area, while in the original area the increase was 26 per 1,000. Consequently the difference in the proportion of the foreign element in every 1,000 decreased materially, and the same decrease, continued in 1910, would show a larger proportion of the foreign element in each 1,000 of the white population in the original area than in the added area. It is significant that the Southern states thus far have shown a decreasing rather than an increasing proportion, and it is thus evident that

a comparison between the foreign element per 1,000 of population in the original and added areas is greatly affected, in the original area, by the small proportion shown in the Southern states. In both New England and the Middle states, more than half of each 1,000 of the white population in 1900 were of foreign parentage. It appears, moreover, from the preceding summary, that in these 2 sections of the country the proportion is increasing with great rapidity. During the twenty years from 1870 to 1890 this element increased in New England 146 and in the Middle states 52 per 1,000 of population, while during the decade from 1890 to 1900 the increase in the New England states was 69 and in the Middle states 28. From this analysis it appears that not only were more than half of the entire white population in these sections persons of foreign parentage, but the rapidity of increase in the proportion showed no diminution.

DISTRIBUTION BY COUNTRY OF BIRTH.

In Table 110, which appears on page 226, is presented the foreign born population of continental United States and of the area enumerated in 1790, by country of birth. The earliest date for which the segregation of foreign born by country of birth is obtainable was the census of 1850. Variations in classification have made the preparation of this table a task of some difficulty. It is believed, however, to be substantially accurate. The significant movement of foreign born population in the United States, with relation to the older and the newer areas, is reflected by the following percentage table:

TABLE 58.—*Per cent distribution of foreign born, by country of birth: 1850 and 1900.*

NATIONALITY.	CONTINENTAL UNITED STATES.		AREA ENUMERATED IN 1790.		ADDED AREA.	
	1850	1900	1850	1900	1850	1900
Total	100.0	100.0	100.0	100.0	100.0	100.0
Canada and Newfoundland	6.6	11.4	6.8	13.1	6.1	9.8
All other North America	0.9	1.3	0.3	0.3	2.0	2.2
England and Wales	13.7	9.0	13.4	10.1	14.4	8.0
Ireland	42.8	15.6	53.1	23.2	23.4	8.5
Scotland	3.1	2.3	3.3	2.5	2.9	2.0
Germany	26.0	25.8	18.4	19.7	40.3	31.6
Norway and Sweden	0.7	8.8	0.1	3.1	1.8	14.1
Denmark	0.1	1.5	0.1	0.4	0.1	2.5
Austria-Hungary	(1)	5.6	(1)	6.2	0.1	5.0
Italy	0.2	4.7	0.1	7.2	0.2	2.3
Russia, including Finland	0.1	4.7	0.1	6.2	0.1	3.3
Poland		3.7		4.1		3.4
Switzerland	0.6	1.1	0.3	0.7	1.2	1.5
Netherlands	0.4	1.0	0.3	0.4	0.8	1.6
France	2.4	1.0	1.5	0.9	4.1	1.1
Spain and Portugal	0.2	0.4	0.1	0.4	0.3	0.3
Belgium	0.1	0.3	(1)	0.2	0.1	0.4
Turkey and Greece	(1)	0.2	(1)	0.2	(1)	0.1
Europe not specified		0.2		0.3		0.1
China	(1)	0.8	(1)	0.3	0.1	1.2
Japan		0.2		(1)		0.5
All other Asia	(1)	0.1	(1)	0.2	(1)	0.1
Oceania	(1)	0.1	(1)	(1)	(1)	0.1
South America	0.1	(1)	(1)	(1)	0.1	(1)
Africa	(1)	(1)	(1)	(1)	(1)	(1)
All other	1.9	0.2	1.9	0.2	1.8	0.2

[1] Less than one-tenth of 1 per cent.

While this table indicates the proportion which each principal element of the foreign born forms of the total foreign born in the United States and in the original and added areas, it does not throw light upon the proportion of each nationality residing in each of the two areas. Selecting the principal nations, the proportions shown are as follows:

TABLE **59.**—PER CENT DISTRIBUTION, BY GEOGRAPHIC AREAS, OF NATIVES OF SPECIFIED FOREIGN COUNTRIES: 1850 AND 1900.

AREA.	NORTH AMERICA.		ENGLAND, SCOTLAND, AND WALES.		IRELAND.		GERMANY AND AUSTRIA-HUNGARY.		SCANDINAVIA.		ITALY.		RUSSIA, FINLAND, AND POLAND.		ALL OTHER COUNTRIES.	
	1850	1900	1850	1900	1850	1900	1850	1900	1850	1900	1850	1900	1850	1900	1850	1900
United States...........	100.0	100.0	100.0	100.0	100.0	100.0	100.0	100.0	100.0	100.0	100.0	100.0	100.0	100.0	100.0	100.0
Area enumerated in 1790.......	62.4	51.2	64.5	54.4	81.1	71.8	46.3	39.9	16.4	17.0	49.6	74.9	68.8	58.9	48.0	33.7
New England.............	29.8	39.1	10.8	15.8	20.4	23.9	1.2	2.8	4.0	6.7	7.2	12.7	3.3	9.8	8.3	8.8
Middle states..............	31.5	11.4	48.8	35.9	55.1	45.2	36.1	33.7	10.5	10.0	28.2	60.3	55.1	46.4	33.3	22.5
Southern states............	1.1	0.7	4.9	2.7	5.6	2.7	9.0	3.4	1.8	0.3	14.2	2.0	10.4	2.7	6.5	2.5
Added area...................	37.6	48.8	35.5	45.6	18.9	28.2	53.7	60.1	83.6	83.0	50.4	25.1	31.2	41.1	52.0	66.3

A smaller proportion of the natives of nearly every foreign country were residents of the original area in 1900 than in 1850. The natives of Italy form an exception to this rule; for, whereas in the earlier year more than half of them were located in the added area, in 1900, as a result of the great immigration from that country in the latter part of the century, nearly three-fourths of all were located in the area enumerated in 1790. The decreased proportion of the foreign born in the Southern states of the original area is noticeable. Nearly one-seventh of the Italians in the country were residents of these states in 1850, while in 1900 the proportion was negligible.

XIV. STATISTICS OF SLAVES.

NUMBER OF SLAVES IN UNITED STATES — IN ORIGINAL AND
ADDED AREAS — SLAVEHOLDING FAMILIES — NUMBER OF WHITE
PERSONS DIRECTLY OR INDIRECTLY CONNECTED WITH SLAVE-
HOLDING—RATIO OF SLAVES TO WHITES—VALUE OF SLAVES.

Slavery existed in all the states and territories which were enumerated in 1790, with the exception of Vermont, Massachusetts, and the district of Maine. Comparatively few slaves, however, were held in the Northern states; more than nine-tenths of all slaves at the First Census were reported from the Southern states. Virginia ranked first in number of slaves, reporting 292,627. The second in rank was South Carolina, closely followed by Maryland and North Carolina; but the total number of slaves in these 3 states only slightly exceeded the number in Virginia alone. The number of slaves in the United States in 1790 is shown by states in the following summary:

United States	697,624
New Hampshire	157
Rhode Island	958
Connecticut	2,648
New York	21,193
New Jersey	11,423
Pennsylvania	3,707
Delaware	8,887
Maryland	103,036
Virginia	292,627
North Carolina	100,783
South Carolina	107,094
Georgia	29,264
Kentucky	12,430
Southwest Territory	3,417

The number of slaves at each census from 1790 to 1860, with the percentage of decennial increase, was as follows:

CENSUS YEAR.	Number of slaves.	Per cent of increase.
1790	697,624	
1800	893,602	28.1
1810	1,191,362	33.3
1820	1,538,022	29.1
1830	2,009,043	30.6
1840	2,487,355	23.8
1850	3,204,313	28.8
1860	3,953,760	23.4

The percentages of increase remained remarkably uniform from 1790 to 1830. Indeed, no violent fluctuations occurred during the entire slaveholding period.

The higher percentage shown for the decade 1800 to 1810 reflects the large importation of negroes during the years immediately preceding January 1, 1808, after which date the trade in slaves was prohibited. It has been noted that there was little difference between the rate of increase in the white and the negro population in the early part of the century; since nearly all the negroes were slaves, it of course follows that there was little difference prior to 1830 in the rate of increase in slaves as compared with that of whites. After that date, however, the rate of slave increase tended to diminish.

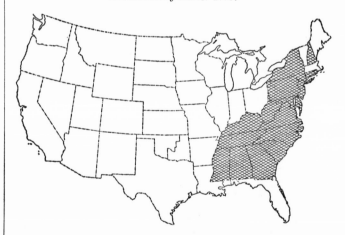

States holding slaves: 1790.

Marked changes appear from decade to decade in the rate of increase for slaves in the different states, although for the entire United States, as already pointed out, it remained reasonably uniform.

The extension of slavery from 1790 to 1860 by annexation of territory, and especially by settlement and the transfer of slaves from the older to the newly settled areas in the South and Southwest, is clearly indicated in the following table.

In the 3 slave states of Delaware, Maryland, and Virginia, at the period under consideration slaves were employed principally in the cultivation of tobacco. The soil was rapidly impoverished by this crop, however, and as a result the center of tobacco culture tended to move farther westward, into new and more favorable sections in Kentucky and Tennessee.

TABLE **60.**—NUMBER OF SLAVES IN THE AREA ENUMERATED IN 1790 AND IN THE ADDED AREA, BY STATES AND TERRITORIES: 1790 TO 1860.

STATE OR TERRITORY.	1790	1800	1810	1820	1830	1840	1850	1860
United States	697,624	893,602	1,191,362	1,538,022	2,009,043	2,487,355	3,204,313	3,953,760
Enumerated in 1790	697,624	889,804	1,122,110	1,341,718	1,577,105	1,609,105	1,842,570	1,975,802
New England	3,763	1,339	418	145	48	23		
Maine					2			
New Hampshire	157	8			3	1		
Vermont								
Massachusetts					1			
Rhode Island	958	380	108	48	17	5		
Connecticut	2,648	951	310	97	25	[1]17		
Middle states	45,210	41,184	30,840	22,365	6,024	3,347	2,526	1,816
New York	21,193	20,903	15,017	10,088	75	4		
New Jersey	11,423	12,422	10,851	7,557	2,254	674	236	[2]18
Pennsylvania	3,707	1,706	795	211	403	64		
Delaware	8,887	6,153	4,177	4,509	3,292	2,605	2,290	1,798
Southern states	648,651	847,281	1,090,852	1,319,208	1,571,033	1,605,735	1,840,044	1,973,986
Maryland and District of Columbia	103,036	[3]107,707	[3]115,056	[3]111,917	[3]107,499	[3]93,057	94,055	90,374
Virginia[4]	287,959	[3]339,796	[3]383,521	[3]411,886	[3]453,698	[3]431,873	452,028	472,494
West Virginia[4]	4,668	7,172	10,836	15,119	17,673	18,488	20,500	18,371
North Carolina	100,783	133,296	168,824	204,917	245,601	245,817	288,548	331,059
South Carolina	107,094	146,151	196,365	258,475	315,401	327,038	384,984	402,406
Georgia (eastern part)	29,264	59,232	91,154	110,055	124,345	124,145	149,489	158,080
Kentucky	12,430	40,343	80,561	126,732	165,213	182,258	210,981	225,483
Tennessee	3,417	13,584	44,535	80,107	141,603	183,059	239,459	275,719
Added area		3,798	69,252	196,304	431,938	878,250	1,361,743	1,977,958
First enumerated in 1800		3,798	31,581	115,401	277,182	605,890	884,915	1,175,829
Northern states		135	429	1,107	788	348		
Ohio					6	3		
Indiana		28	237	190	3	3		
Illinois		[5]107	168	917	747	331		
Michigan			24		1			
Wisconsin						[6]31	11	
Southern states		3,663	31,152	114,294	276,394	605,542	884,915	1,175,829
Georgia (western part)		174	14,064	39,601	93,186	156,799	232,193	304,118
Alabama		[7]494	[8]2,565	41,879	117,549	253,532	342,844	435,080
Mississippi		2,995	14,523	32,814	65,659	195,211	309,878	436,631
First enumerated in 1810			37,671	80,903	139,255	246,627	379,331	557,772
Louisiana[9]			34,660	69,064	109,588	168,452	244,809	331,726
Arkansas			[10]136	1,617	4,576	19,935	47,100	111,115
Missouri			[11]2,875	10,222	25,091	58,240	87,422	114,931
First enumerated in 1830					15,501	25,717	39,310	61,745
Florida					15,501	25,717	39,310	61,745
First enumerated in 1840						16		
Iowa						16		
First enumerated in 1850							58,187	182,595
Utah territory							26	29
Texas							58,161	182,566
First enumerated in 1860								17
Nebraska								15
Kansas								2

[1] Exclusive of 37 slaves captured in the slaver Amistad.
[2] Colored apprentices for life, by the act to abolish slavery passed April 18, 1846.
[3] Alexandria county, which from 1800 to 1840, inclusive, formed a part of the District of Columbia, is here included with Virginia, for comparative purposes.
[4] The totals for the counties which in 1863 and 1866 were set off from Virginia to form West Virginia are here shown separately, because of the marked difference between the 2 states with respect to slavery.
[5] Reported as for Randolph county, Indiana territory.
[6] Reported as for Brown, Crawford, and Iowa counties, Michigan territory.
[7] Reported as for Washington county, Mississippi territory.
[8] Reported as for Baldwin, Madison, and Washington counties, Mississippi territory.
[9] In 1810 Louisiana was called "Orleans territory," and the name "Louisiana territory" was applied to the remainder of the Louisiana Purchase, which was unorganized.
[10] Reported as for "settlements of Hope Field and St. Francis" and for "settlements on the Arkansas" in the unorganized territory then called "Louisiana territory." Compare with note 9.
[11] Reported as for Cape Girardeau, New Madrid, St. Charles, St. Louis, and St. Geneviève districts in the unorganized territory then called "Louisiana territory." Compare with note 9.

As the cultivation of tobacco by slave labor became somewhat less profitable in the older states, the acquisition of territory in the far South and Southwest and the introduction and rapid expansion of cotton growing in that section made slave labor highly profitable in connection with this important crop. After the further importation of slaves was prohibited in 1808, the market price of negroes advanced rapidly, because of the increasing demand for their services in the cotton fields. Planters in Maryland and Virginia found it to their pecuniary advantage either to sell slaves or to move with them farther south or into

Kentucky or Tennessee. These changes resulted in a shifting of the slave population in the Southern states.

In Delaware the number of slaves was greatest at the First Census, but declined steadily (except during the decade 1810 to 1820) until 1860. In Maryland the number decreased at each census but one from 1810 to 1860. The number in Virginia increased but 4 per cent from 1830 to 1860; in North Carolina, during the same period, the increase was 35 per cent, or about 1 per cent per annum. For that part of Georgia enumerated in 1790 the increase was 27.1 per cent, but the whole state showed an increase of more than 100 per cent.

As reflected by percentage of increase from decade to decade, the area showing liberal increase of slave population tended to become more restricted. In 1850 and 1860 decided increase in number of slaves was practically confined to the lower South. In 1860 only Georgia, the Gulf states, Missouri, and Arkansas showed an increase exceeding 20 per cent in the number of slaves.

In forty years, from 1820 to 1860, both Alabama and Mississippi recorded a tenfold increase in slave population, while the white population increased but sixfold in Alabama and eightfold in Mississippi. The number of slaves in Louisiana increased with similar rapidity; and in the decade from 1850 to 1860 the slave population of Texas trebled.

In the following table, which presents the percentages of increase in slaves in all the so-called slave states during the period of slavery, the shifting of slave property to the lower South and Southwest is clearly indicated:

TABLE 61.—*Per cent increase of the slave population of the slave states at each census: 1790 to 1860.*

STATE OR TERRITORY.	1790 to 1800	1800 to 1810	1810 to 1820	1820 to 1830	1830 to 1840	1840 to 1850	1850 to 1860
Delaware	[1]30.8	[1]32.1	7.9	[1]27.0	[1]20.9	[1]12.1	[1]21.5
Maryland[2]	4.5	6.8	[1]2.7	[1]3.9	[1]13.4	1.1	[1]3.9
Virginia	18.6	13.7	8.3	10.4	[1]4.5	4.9	3.9
North Carolina	32.3	26.7	21.4	19.9	0.1	17.4	14.7
South Carolina	36.5	34.4	31.6	22.0	3.7	17.7	4.5
Georgia[3]	103.0	77.1	42.2	45.4	29.2	35.9	21.1
Florida					65.9	52.9	57.1
Kentucky	224.6	99.7	57.3	30.4	10.3	15.8	6.9
Tennessee	297.5	227.8	79.9	76.8	29.3	30.8	15.1
Alabama[4]		419.2	1,532.7	180.7	115.7	35.2	26.9
Mississippi		384.9	125.9	100.1	197.3	58.7	40.9
Louisiana[5]			99.3	58.7	53.7	45.3	35.5
Arkansas[6]			1,089.0	183.0	335.6	136.3	135.9
Texas							213.9
Missouri[7]			255.5	145.5	132.1	50.1	31.5

[1] Decrease.
[2] Includes District of Columbia.
[3] Entire state.
[4] Reported as for Washington county, Mississippi territory, in 1800, and as for Baldwin, Madison, and Washington counties, Mississippi territory, in 1810.
[5] Called "Orleans territory" in 1810. See Table 60, note 9.
[6] Reported in 1810 as for "settlements of Hope Field and St. Francis" and for "settlements on the Arkansas" in the unorganized territory then called "Louisiana territory."
[7] Reported in 1810 as for Cape Girardeau, New Madrid, St. Charles, St. Louis, and St. Genevieve districts, in the unorganized territory then called "Louisiana territory."

Comparison of the increase in the number of slaves in the original and added area and the proportion con- tributed by each, reflects the progress of settlement of the younger slave states, and their constant increase in proportionate importance as slaveholders.

TABLE 62.—*Per cent increase and proportion of slaves reported in area enumerated in 1790 and in added area: 1790 to 1860.*

YEAR.	ORIGINAL AREA.		ADDED AREA.	
	Per cent of increase.	Proportion of total slaves.	Per cent of increase.	Proportion of total slaves.
1790		100.0		
1800	27.5	99.6		0.4
1810	26.1	94.2	1,723.4	5.8
1820	19.6	87.2	183.5	12.8
1830	17.5	78.5	120.0	21.5
1840	2.0	64.7	103.3	35.3
1850	14.5	57.5	55.1	42.5
1860	7.2	50.0	45.3	50.0

The decennial rate of increase in the number of slaves in the original area was noticeably uniform for forty years after the First Census, but from 1830 to 1840 the increase declined to 2 per cent, a rate so small as to be practically negligible. In 1850 a considerable increase was reported, but in 1860 there was again an insignificant percentage. In general, therefore, the uniform increase of one-fourth or one-sixth shown in the original area to 1830 declined during the final thirty years of slavery to a small and wavering increment. Meantime the relative rank of the two areas in slaveholding was steadily changing and the Southern states in the added area were becoming more and more important as slaveholding communities. The proportion of 99.6 per cent of all slaves shown by the original area in 1800 had dropped to one-half by 1860. Such changing proportions manifest a much greater relative increase in the number of slaves in the added area than in the original area. The large earlier percentages were of course devoid of significance as indicative of natural increase, since they were principally the result of acquisition of new slave territory and the rapid settlement therein of a considerable slaveholding population. The rate of increase, however, although it declined sharply after 1830, continued very high in the added area to the close of the slaveholding period. The changes here shown in the total added area suggest analysis of the increase in the number of slaves in the area added at each census after 1790. The percentages in the following summary, like those which precede, are computed from Table 60:

DECADE.	DECENNIAL PER CENT OF INCREASE IN NUMBER OF SLAVES IN AREA FIRST ENUMERATED IN—						
	1800	1810	1820	1830	1840	1850	1860
1790 to 1800							
1800 to 1810	731.5						
1810 to 1820	265.4	114.8					
1820 to 1830	140.2	72.1					
1830 to 1840	118.6	77.1		65.9			
1840 to 1850	46.1	53.8		52.9			
1850 to 1860	32.9	47.0		57.1		213.8	

SLAVEHOLDING FAMILIES.

In a preceding chapter which treats of families (see page 96), a presentation is made of slaveholding families in 1790, white and colored, in which the number of members and the average size of such families are given. The following table presents the number of slaveholding families, the total number of slaves, and the average number per family, by states and territories in 1790 and 1850:

TABLE 63.—NUMBER OF SLAVEHOLDING FAMILIES AND AVERAGE NUMBER OF SLAVES PER FAMILY, BY STATES AND TERRITORIES: 1790 AND 1850.

STATE OR TERRITORY.	1790					1850				
	Slaveholding families.		Slaves.			Slaveholding families.[1]		Slaves.		
			Number.		Per cent of total population.			Number.		Per cent of total population.
	Number.	Per cent of all families.	Total.	Average per slaveholding family.		Number.	Per cent of all families.	Total.	Average per slaveholding family.	
United States................	96,168	17.2	697,624	7.3	17.8	347,725	9.7	3,204,313	9.2	13.8
Area enumerated in 1790...................	96,168	17.2	697,624	7.3	17.8	214,799	9.3	1,842,570	8.6	12.6
New England................	2,147	2.8	3,763	1.8	0.4	....	....	....	....	....
Maine......										
New Hampshire............	123	0.5	157	1.3	0.1					
Vermont......										
Massachusetts......										
Rhode Island............	461	4.1	958	2.1	1.4					
Connecticut............	1,563	3.8	2,648	1.7	1.1					
Middle states	16,265	9.8	45,210	2.8	4.4	1,009	0.1	2,526	2.5	(2)
New York................	7,796	14.2	21,193	2.7	6.2	....	....	....	....	....
New Jersey................	[3]4,760	16.0	11,423	2.4	6.2	200	0.2	236	1.2	(2)
Pennsylvania............	1,858	2.5	3,707	2.0	0.9	....	....	....	....	....
Delaware................	[3]1,851	22.5	8,887	4.8	15.0	809	5.2	2,290	2.8	2.5
Southern states	77,756	35.8	648,651	8.3	34.1	213,790	30.3	1,840,044	8.6	31.4
Maryland and District of Columbia..........	[4]13,777	38.0	103,036	7.5	32.2	17,517	18.3	94,055	5.4	14.8
Virginia and West Virginia............	[3]34,026	44.9	292,627	8.5	39.1	55,063	32.9	472,528	8.6	33.2
North Carolina............	[5]16,310	31.0	100,783	6.7	25.5	28,303	26.8	288,548	10.2	33.2
South Carolina............	8,859	34.2	107,094	12.1	43.0	25,596	48.4	384,984	15.0	57.6
Georgia................	[3]2,419	24.5	29,264	12.1	35.5	[6]15,062	70.3	[6]149,489	9.9	54.9
Kentucky................	[3]1,855	17.0	12,430	6.7	16.9	38,385	28.9	210,981	5.5	21.5
Tennessee[7]................	[3]510	8.8	3,417	6.7	9.6	33,864	26.0	239,459	7.1	23.9
Added area................	....	....	....	....	....	132,926	10.3	1,361,743	10.2	15.8

[1] Given in the Compendium of the Seventh Census, Table xc, as "slaveholders."
[2] Less than one-tenth of 1 per cent.
[3] Estimated. See page 138.
[4] Allegany, Calvert, and Somersett counties estimated.
[5] Caswell, Granville, and Orange counties estimated.
[6] Figures are for part enumerated in 1790.
[7] The figures shown as for Tennessee in 1790 were reported as for the Southwest Territory, which had an area slightly greater than that of Tennessee.

In 1790 the proportion which slaveholding families formed of all families exceeded 20 per cent in Delaware, Maryland, Virginia, North Carolina, South Carolina, and Georgia, but was less than 20 per cent in Kentucky and much less in Tennessee. Even in New York the proportion was but little smaller than in Kentucky. In 1850 the number of slaveholding families had become less than 20 per cent of all families in Delaware and Maryland, whereas the proportion exceeded that figure in Kentucky and Tennessee. In only 2 states, North Carolina and South Carolina, was the increase in the average number of slaves per family worthy of note.

Slaveholding families classified by size of holdings.— But one classification of slaveholding families according to the number of slaves held has heretofore been made at a Federal census. At the Seventh Census (1850) a tabulation of this character was prepared and printed in the Compendium, and this affords an interesting analysis of slaveholders at that period. In the following table a similar classification is made for 1790 for all states for which the schedules are still in existence. An estimate is included for Virginia, based on figures of 1782 and 1783. (See pages 137 and 138.)

TABLE **64.**—SLAVEHOLDING FAMILIES, CLASSIFIED ACCORDING TO NUMBER OF SLAVES HELD, BY STATES AND TERRITORIES: 1790 AND 1850.

STATE OR TERRITORY.	Total number of slave-holding families.	NUMBER OF FAMILIES HOLDING—									
		1 slave.	2 to 4 slaves.	5 to 9 slaves.	10 to 19 slaves.	20 to 49 slaves.	50 to 99 slaves.	100 to 199 slaves.	200 to 299 slaves.	300 slaves and over.	Number of slaves unknown
					1790						
Area for which 1790 schedules exist [1]	81,885	20,047	24,912	18,017	11,735	5,274	813	198	38	7	844
New England	2,147	1,332	689	113	12	1					
New Hampshire	123	97	24	2							
Rhode Island	461	255	160	45	1						
Connecticut	1,563	980	505	66	11	1					
Middle states	9,654	4,119	3,534	1,310	193	2					496
New York	7,796	3,088	2,867	1,165	181	1					494
Pennsylvania	1,858	1,031	667	145	12	1					2
Southern states	70,084	14,596	20,689	16,594	11,530	5,271	813	198	38	7	348
Maryland [2]	12,226	2,841	3,617	2,807	1,796	713	96	16	3	1	336
Virginia [3]	34,026	5,785	9,510	8,559	6,745	2,998	342	75	12		
North Carolina [2]	14,973	4,040	4,959	3,375	1,788	701	90	11	2		7
South Carolina	8,859	1,930	2,603	1,853	1,201	859	285	96	21	6	5
					1850						
United States	347,725	68,998	105,703	80,767	54,595	29,733	6,196	1,479	187	67	
Area comparable with that shown in 1790	127,488	22,164	37,624	31,052	22,190	11,565	2,194	572	89	38	
New England											
Middle states [4]	1,009	498	372	119	20						
Southern states	126,479	21,666	37,252	30,933	22,170	11,565	2,194	572	89	38	
Maryland and District of Columbia	17,517	5,585	5,870	3,463	1,861	657	73	7		1	
Virginia	55,063	11,385	15,550	13,030	9,456	4,880	646	107	8	1	
North Carolina	28,303	1,204	9,668	8,129	5,898	2,828	485	76	12	3	
South Carolina	25,596	3,492	6,164	6,311	4,955	3,200	990	382	69	33	
Remainder of area enumerated in 1790	87,311	19,427	28,455	20,909	12,416	5,380	628	82	11	3	
Added area	132,926	27,407	39,624	28,806	19,989	12,788	3,374	825	87	26	

[1] Data not available for New Jersey, Delaware, Georgia, Kentucky, and Tennessee. An estimate has been made for Virginia. (See page 137.)
[2] Data not available for 3 counties.
[3] Estimated. See page 137.
[4] As there were no slaves reported in New York or Pennsylvania in 1850, the number reported in Delaware and New Jersey is given, for purposes of comparison with the Middle states.

The changes which are recorded in the interesting comparisons shown in Table — are made clear upon inspection of the changes in proportions shown in the following table:

TABLE **65.**—PER CENT DISTRIBUTION OF SLAVEHOLDING FAMILIES ACCORDING TO NUMBER OF SLAVES HELD: 1790 AND 1850.

OWNERS OF—	TOTAL COMPARABLE AREA. [1]		MARYLAND AND DISTRICT OF COLUMBIA.		VIRGINIA.		NORTH CAROLINA.		SOUTH CAROLINA.	
	1790	1850	1790	1850	1790	1850	1790	1850	1790	1850
1 slave	24.5	17.4	23.2	31.9	17.0	20.7	27.0	4.3	21.8	13.6
2 and under 5 slaves	30.4	29.5	29.6	33.5	27.9	28.2	33.1	34.2	29.4	24.1
5 and under 10 slaves	22.0	24.4	23.0	19.8	25.2	23.7	22.5	28.7	20.9	24.7
10 and under 20 slaves	14.3	17.4	14.7	10.6	19.8	17.2	11.9	20.8	13.6	19.4
20 and under 50 slaves	6.4	9.1	5.8	3.8	8.8	8.9	4.7	10.0	9.7	12.5
50 and under 100 slaves	1.0	1.7	0.8	0.4	1.0	1.2	0.6	1.7	3.2	3.9
100 and under 200 slaves	0.2	0.4	0.1	(2)	0.2	0.2	0.1	0.3	1.1	1.5
200 and under 300 slaves	(2)	0.1	(2)		(2)	(2)	(2)	(2)	0.2	0.3
300 slaves and over	(2)	(2)	(2)	(2)					0.1	0.1
Unknown	1.0		2.7				(2)		0.1	

[1] Comprises in each year the New England and Middle states for which data are available and the Southern states here specified.
[2] Less than one-tenth of 1 per cent.

This analysis shows that in the comparable area practically the same proportion of owners held from 2 to 4 slaves in 1850 as in 1790. There was a considerable decrease, however, in the proportion of families having only 1 slave in 1850 as compared with 1790, and an increase in the proportions in the groups into which those holding between 5 and 300 slaves were divided.

The changes recorded by individual states for which data are available for both censuses were more marked than those for the entire area. The economic conditions which prevailed in Maryland and Virginia are clearly reflected in the percentages shown in the table. During the period under consideration the proportion of slaveholders owning but 1 slave increased in these states and decreased in North Carolina and South Carolina. In 3 of the 4 states an increase appeared in the proportion of persons holding from 2 to 4 slaves. In the fourth, South Carolina, a decrease appeared. In general the percentages shown reflect the tendency in Maryland and Virginia to reduce slaveholdings, either because of changing industrial conditions demanding less slave labor or because of an increasing number of more highly skilled white laborers better adapted to the increasingly exacting demands. In North and South Carolina the changes tend in the other direction, and are clearly the result of increasing dependence upon slave labor and of expansion of industries in which large numbers of slaves were essential to the prosperity of the community.

Slaveholding families in states for which schedules are missing.—The total number of slaveholding families shown upon the schedules of the First Census which are still in existence is 47,859. The total number of slaves owned by these families was 318,984, or slightly less than one-half the entire slave population of the United States in 1790. The average number of slaves held by the families reported on existing schedules as slaveholding was 6.7. If this average were applied to the total number of slaves reported, 378,640, upon the schedules which are not now in existence, the number of slaveholding families upon those schedules would appear to be 56,513.

The impression at once arises that this figure is too large, for the average by which it is secured includes all the Northern states. The slave owners of that section of the Republic required slaves principally as household servants, and the number owned by individuals was almost always small. Only 3 persons in the Northern states owned over 20 slaves each (Elijah Mason, sr., 28 slaves, Lebanon town, Windham county, Conn.; Robert Livingston, 44 slaves, Livingston town, Columbia county, N. Y.; and Margaret Hutton, 24 slaves, Washington township, Fayette county, Pa.).

The average number of slaves per slaveholding family, for each state for which records are still available, was as follows:

STATE.	Average number of slaves per slaveholding family.
New Hampshire	1.3
Rhode Island	2.1
Connecticut	1.7
New York	2.7
Pennsylvania	2.0
Maryland	7.5
North Carolina	6.7
South Carolina	12.1

If slaveholding families in New Jersey, which lay between New York and Pennsylvania and was probably subject to the same local influences, are assumed to have held an average of 2.4 slaves (the mean between the average in New York and that in Pennsylvania) then the total number of slaveholding families in New Jersey approximated 4,760. Doubtless this figure is close to the actual number.

In Delaware it is probable that conditions relating to slave ownership resembled more closely those which existed in Maryland than those to the northward, in Pennsylvania. If, however, the mean between the average in these 2 states, 4.8, be accepted and utilized as the probable average in Delaware, there were in that state approximately 1,851 slaveholding families.

For Virginia it would not be just to estimate the number of slaves per slaveholding family from the numbers for neighboring states, since the conditions prevailing in Maryland and North Carolina differed widely from each other, and doubtless differed as widely from those in Virginia, which was generally regarded at that period as the wealthiest state in the Union. Fortunately, another method is available by which the average number of slaves per slaveholding family in Virginia may be determined with reasonable accuracy.

It has already been explained that the partial lists of heads of families in existence for several counties of Virginia for 1782, 1783, 1784, and 1785 have been published by the Director of the Census in the series of Census publications containing the names of heads of families at the First Census. Inspection of these lists shows that the number of negroes connected with white households was reported in 1782 and 1783 for a total of 32 counties. While it is true that for some counties all white households are not reported upon these schedules, it is probable that the lists include, for the portions of the counties covered, all property owners, and hence represent the actual conditions of slave ownership. The counties for which lists exist, though located largely in the older settled areas, are not confined strictly to any one section, but are reasonably representative of the state. The total number of slaveholding families for the two years shown in the two returns above given was 10,806, and the total number of negroes, 91,768.

Analysis of the number of slaves per slaveholding family shows a county variation in 1782 from 2.9 in Pittsylvania to 11 or more in Amelia, Cumberland, Hanover, and New Kent. The average for the 19 counties for which returns for 1782 exist is 8.3 slaves per slaveholding family; for the 13 counties enumerated in 1783 and for which returns exist, the average is 8.8. The general average secured by combining the returns for both years as though reported at one census, is 8.5 slaves per slaveholding family. The detailed returns upon which these averages were computed are as follows:

TABLE **66.**—*Number of slaveholding families, number of slaves, and average number of slaves per slaveholding family in Virginia: 1782 and 1783.*

COUNTY.	1782			COUNTY.	1783		
	Slave-holding families.	Ne-groes.	Average number of slaves per family.		Slave-holding families.	Ne-groes.	Average number of slaves per family.
Total....	6,635	55,242	8.3	Total....	4,171	36,526	8.8
Amelia.........	794	8,749	11.0	Amherst.......	494	3,852	7.7
Charlotte.......	410	3,442	8.4	Chesterfield....	589	5,961	10.1
Cumberland....	346	3,882	11.2	Essex.........	347	2,817	8.1
Fairfax.........	420	3,609	8.6	Gloucester.....	325	2,764	8.5
Fluvanna......	157	1,330	8.5	Greensville....	257	2,691	10.5
Frederick......	229	767	3.3	Lancaster......	282	2,567	9.1
Halifax........	464	3,290	7.1	Middlesex.....	180	2,282	12.7
Hampshire.....	156	513	3.3	Nansemond...	463	2,567	5.5
Hanover........	464	5,184	11.2	Powhatan.....	227	2,669	11.8
Mecklenburg....	566	4,927	8.7	Prince Edward	165	1,468	8.9
Monongalia.....	23	81	3.5	Princess Anne.	432	2,656	6.1
New Kent......	260	2,957	11.4	Richmond.....	300	3,885	13.0
Northumber-land......	472	3,925	8.3	Shenandoah...	110	347	3.2
Orange........	319	2,848	8.9				
Pittsylvania....	628	1,835	2.9				
Surry.........	278	2,729	9.8				
Sussex.........	418	3,696	8.8				
Warwick.......	91	776	8.5				
City of Williamsburg (James City and York counties.)	140	702	5.0				

There is no reason to doubt that the average thus secured reflects accurately the proportion of slaves to owners which existed throughout Virginia about the period of the First Census, and it is therefore accepted and utilized as such. The fact that the general average of slaves per slaveholding family in the distinctly slave states for which schedules exist is 8.1 tends to confirm this conclusion. Upon the basis of the average of 8.5 slaves thus established, there were 34,026 slaveholding families in Virginia in 1790.

The average in South Carolina may fairly be applied to Georgia, inasmuch as economic conditions in the 2 states resembled each other closely. The number of slaveholding families in Georgia, obtained in this way, is 2,419. In Kentucky and Tennessee the conditions were doubtless similar to those which existed in North Carolina. The use of the average number of slaves per slaveholding family in that state makes the number of such families in Kentucky 1,855, and in Tennessee, 510. As thus computed, the total number of slaveholding families in the states of New Jersey, Delaware, Virginia, Georgia, and the districts of Kentucky and Tennessee was 45,421. If this be accepted as a just approximation, the total number of slaveholding families in the United States in 1790 was 96,168.[1]

Proportion of the white population connected with slave ownership.—Consideration of the total number of slaveholding families in the United States in 1790 suggests an analysis of the proportion of the white population who were members of such families. From a computation based on the average size of white slave-

[1] Including an estimate of 2,888 for 6 counties—3 in Maryland and 3 in North Carolina—for which the schedules are missing.

holding families, already presented for the slaveholding states, the following results appear:

TABLE **67.**—*Proportion of the white population connected with slave ownership: 1790.*

STATE OR TERRITORY.	Average size of white slaveholding families.	Number of white persons in white slaveholding families.	Per cent of total white population.
United States....................	5.9	563,699	17.8
New England.....................	6.3	13,522	1.4
Maine........................	....	....	....
New Hampshire..............	6.2	760	0.5
Vermont.....................	....	....	....
Massachusetts...............	....	....	....
Rhode Island................	6.5	2,993	4.6
Connecticut.................	6.3	9,769	4.2
Middle states...................	6.3	101,961	10.7
New York....................	6.1	47,495	15.1
New Jersey[1]................	6.3	29,938	17.6
Pennsylvania................	7.0	12,942	3.1
Delaware[1]..................	6.3	11,586	25.0
Southern states.................	5.8	448,216	36.6
Maryland[2]..................	5.9	80,724	38.7
Virginia[1]..................	5.8	197,351	44.6
North Carolina[2]............	5.8	94,418	32.7
South Carolina..............	5.5	48,097	34.3
Georgia[1]...................	5.8	13,932	26.3
Kentucky[1].................	5.8	10,742	17.6
Southwest Territory[1].......	5.8	2,952	9.3

[1] Estimated.   [2] Estimated for 3 counties.

At the Seventh Census (1850) it was computed by the Superintendent, Mr. De Bow, that the population connected with slave ownership in 1850 numbered approximately 2,000,000. The average number of persons in slaveholding families was placed at 5.7. If this proportion be utilized for the purpose of ascertaining the distribution of the number of persons above mentioned, the following table results:

TABLE **68.**—*Proportion of the white population connected with slave ownership: 1850.*

STATE.	Number of white persons in white slaveholding families.[1]	Per cent of total white population.
United States.........................	1,982,033	10.1
New England.........................	....	....
Maine............................	....	....
New Hampshire...................	....	....
Vermont..........................	....	....
Massachusetts....................	....	....
Rhode Island.....................	....	....
Connecticut......................	....	....
Middle states........................	5,751	0.1
New York.........................	....	....
New Jersey.......................	1,140	0.2
Pennsylvania.....................	....	....
Delaware.........................	4,611	6.5
Southern states......................	1,976,282	32.1
Maryland and District of Columbia....	99,847	21.9
Virginia..........................	313,859	35.1
North Carolina....................	161,327	29.2
South Carolina....................	145,897	53.1
Georgia...........................	219,199	42.0
Florida...........................	20,064	42.5
Kentucky.........................	218,795	28.7
Tennessee.........................	193,025	25.5
Alabama..........................	166,982	39.2
Mississippi.......................	131,761	44.6
Louisiana.........................	117,819	46.1
Texas.............................	44,158	28.7
Arkansas..........................	34,194	21.1
Missouri..........................	109,355	18.5

[1] Estimated.

The proportion of the white population of the United States formed by members of slaveholding families declined from 17.8 in 1790 to 10.1 in 1850; in other words, 178 persons out of every 1,000 of the white population were directly or indirectly connected with slave ownership in 1790 and 101 out of every 1,000 in 1850. In 1790 approximately one-fifth of the total white population of the slave states and more than one-third of the white population of all the Southern states were members of slaveholding families. In 1850 the decline in the proportion of such persons was apparent in every geographic division. Slavery had disappeared in the New England states. In the Southern states as a whole there was a decrease from 36.6 to 32.1. Some of the states in the lower South, however, showed an increase.

In 1850 the number of persons in white slaveholding families formed about one-third of the total white population of the slave states. In South Carolina, Alabama, Mississippi, and Louisiana, exclusive of the largest cities, the proportion reached one-half of the whole population.[1]

The proportion of persons in the entire white population either directly or indirectly connected with slave ownership, as shown in the following table, declined slightly from 1790 to 1850. In the 2 Middle states in which slavery still existed in the later year, the decline was very marked, while in the Southern states it amounted to about one-ninth. The real explanation of this table lies in the fact that the movement of slaves was steadily toward the lower South and Southwest, where the proportion in the entire population, as will be perceived from Table 20, was becoming very large,

[1] Seventh Census Compendium, page 94.

and also in the fact that the proportion of those who either owned slaves or were in some manner identified with slaveholding was slowly but steadily declining.

TABLE **69.**—*Proportion of the white population connected with slave ownership in states which reported slaves at both censuses: 1790 and 1850.*

	1790		1850	
STATE.	Number of persons in white slaveholding families.	Per cent of total white population.	Number of persons in white slaveholding families.[1]	Per cent of total white population.
Area covered...............	489,740	34.0	1,357,700	28.6
Middle states...............	41,524	[2]19.2	5,751	[2]1.1
New Jersey...............	[1]29,938	17.6	1,140	0.2
Delaware...............	[1]11,586	25.0	4,611	6.5
Southern states...............	448,216	36.6	1,351,949	32.1
Maryland[3]...............	[4]80,724	38.7	99,847	21.9
Virginia...............	[1]197,351	44.6	313,859	35.1
North Carolina[3]...............	[4]94,418	32.7	161,327	29.2
South Carolina...............	48,097	34.3	145,897	53.1
Georgia...............	[1]13,932	26.3	219,199	42.0
Kentucky...............	[1]10,742	17.6	218,795	28.7
Tennessee...............	[1]2,952	9.3	193,025	25.5

[1] Estimated.
[2] Computed on the basis of the combined white population of New Jersey and Delaware.
[3] Includes District of Columbia.
[4] Estimated for 3 counties.

RATIO OF SLAVES TO WHITE PERSONS.

In the Southern states as they existed at the time of the First Census, the slaves numbered 648,651 and the whites, 1,226,057. Therefore, for every 100 whites there were 53 slaves. This proportion varied considerably in the 7 states and territories included in this group. The proportions of slaves to whites in 1790 and 1850, and that of negroes to whites in 1900, were as follows:

TABLE **70.**—RATIO OF SLAVES TO EVERY 100 WHITE PERSONS IN 1790 AND 1850, AND OF NEGROES TO EVERY 100 WHITE PERSONS IN 1900.

STATE OR TERRITORY.	1790			1850			1900		
	White persons.	Slaves.	Number of slaves to every 100 white persons.	White persons.	Slaves.	Number of slaves to every 100 white persons.	White persons.	Negroes.	Number of negroes to every 100 white persons.
Continental United States...............	3,172,444	697,624	22	19,553,068	3,204,313	16	66,809,196	8,833,994	13
Area enumerated in 1790...............	3,172,444	697,624	22	12,365,444	1,842,570	15	29,564,821	3,956,864	13
New England...............	992,384	3,763	[1]	2,705,095	....	....	5,527,026	59,099	1
Maine...............	96,107	....	....	581,813	....	....	692,226	1,319	[1]
New Hampshire...............	141,112	157	[1]	317,456	....	....	410,791	662	[1]
Vermont...............	85,072	....	....	313,402	....	....	342,771	826	[1]
Massachusetts...............	373,187	....	....	985,450	....	....	2,769,764	31,974	1
Rhode Island...............	64,670	958	1	143,875	....	....	419,050	9,092	2
Connecticut...............	232,236	2,648	1	363,099	....	....	892,424	15,226	2
Middle states...............	954,003	45,210	5	5,843,163	2,526	[1]	15,264,839	356,618	2
New York...............	314,366	21,193	7	3,048,325	....	....	7,156,881	99,232	1
New Jersey...............	169,954	11,423	7	465,509	236	[1]	1,812,317	69,844	4
Pennsylvania...............	423,373	3,707	[1]	2,258,160	....	....	6,141,664	156,845	3
Delaware...............	46,310	8,887	19	71,169	2,290	3	153,977	30,697	20

[1] Less than 1.

TABLE 70.—RATIO OF SLAVES TO EVERY 100 WHITE PERSONS IN 1790 AND 1850, AND OF NEGROES TO EVERY 100 WHITE PERSONS IN 1900—Continued.

STATE OR TERRITORY.	1790			1850			1900		
	White persons.	Slaves.	Number of slaves to every 100 white persons.	White persons.	Slaves.	Number of slaves to every 100 white persons.	White persons.	Negroes.	Number of negroes to every 100 white persons.
Area enumerated in 1790—Continued.									
Southern states...............................	1,226,057	648,651	53	3,817,186	1,840,044	48	8,772,956	3,541,147	40
Maryland[1]....................	208,649	103,036	49	455,884	94,055	21	1,143,956	321,706	28
Virginia[2]....................	442,117	292,627	66	894,800	472,528	53	2,108,088	704,221	33
North Carolina..............	289,181	100,783	35	553,028	288,548	52	1,263,603	624,469	49
South Carolina..............	140,178	107,094	76	274,563	384,984	140	557,807	782,321	140
Georgia (eastern part).......	52,886	29,264	55	120,662	149,489	124	297,007	343,421	116
Kentucky....................	61,133	12,430	20	761,413	210,981	28	1,862,309	284,706	15
Tennessee...................	31,913	3,417	11	756,836	239,459	32	1,540,186	480,243	31
Added area....................	....	....	....	7,187,624	1,361,743	19	37,244,375	4,877,130	13
Northern states..............	....	....	....	5,267,988	87,422	2	25,775,870	495,751	2
Ohio.......................	....	....	....	1,955,050	....	....	4,060,204	96,901	2
Indiana....................	....	....	....	977,154	....	....	2,458,502	57,505	2
Illinois...................	....	....	....	846,034	....	....	4,734,873	85,078	2
Michigan...................	....	....	....	395,071	....	....	2,398,563	15,816	1
Wisconsin..................	....	....	....	304,756	....	....	2,057,911	2,542	([3])
Minnesota..................	....	....	....	6,038	....	....	1,737,036	4,959	([3])
Iowa.......................	....	....	....	191,881	....	....	2,218,667	12,693	1
Missouri...................	....	....	....	592,004	87,422	15	2,944,843	161,234	5
North Dakota...............	....	....	....	....	....	....	311,712	286	([3])
South Dakota...............	....	....	....	....	....	....	380,714	465	([3])
Nebraska...................	....	....	....	....	....	....	1,056,526	6,269	1
Kansas.....................	....	....	....	....	....	....	1,416,319	52,003	4
Southern states..............	....	....	....	1,742,059	1,274,295	73	7,595,037	4,351,125	57
Georgia (western part)......	....	....	....	400,910	232,193	58	884,287	691,392	78
Florida....................	....	....	....	47,203	39,310	83	297,333	230,730	78
Alabama....................	....	....	....	426,514	342,844	80	1,001,152	827,307	83
Mississippi................	....	....	....	295,718	309,878	105	641,200	907,630	142
Louisiana..................	....	....	....	255,491	244,809	96	729,612	650,804	89
Texas......................	....	....	....	154,034	58,161	38	2,426,669	620,722	26
Indian Territory...........	....	....	....	....	....	....	302,680	36,853	12
Oklahoma...................	....	....	....	....	....	....	367,524	18,831	5
Arkansas...................	....	....	....	162,189	47,100	29	944,580	366,856	39
Western states..............	....	....	....	177,577	26	([3])	3,873,468	30,254	1
Montana....................	....	....	....	....	....	....	226,283	1,523	1
Wyoming....................	....	....	....	....	....	....	89,051	940	1
Colorado...................	....	....	....	....	....	....	529,046	8,570	2
New Mexico.................	....	....	....	61,359	....	....	180,207	1,610	1
Arizona....................	....	....	....	166	....	....	92,903	1,848	2
Utah.......................	....	....	....	11,330	26	([3])	272,465	672	([3])
Nevada.....................	....	....	....	....	....	....	35,405	134	([3])
Idaho......................	....	....	....	....	....	....	154,495	293	([3])
Washington.................	....	....	....	1,049	....	....	496,304	2,514	1
Oregon.....................	....	....	....	12,038	....	....	394,582	1,105	([2])
California.................	....	....	....	91,635	....	....	1,402,727	11,045	1
Total for slave states[4]	1,272,367	657,538	52	6,222,418	3,204,051	51	18,796,609	8,028,519	43

[1] Includes District of Columbia.
[2] Includes West Virginia.
[3] Less than 1.
[4] Delaware, Maryland (including District of Columbia), Virginia (including West Virginia), North Carolina, South Carolina, Georgia, Florida, Kentucky, Tennessee, Alabama, Mississippi, Louisiana, Texas, Missouri, and Arkansas.

There were fewer slaves to every 100 white persons in 1850 than in 1790 in the United States and in every state north of North Carolina; but in the other states of the original area the proportion increased. The increase was particularly heavy in South Carolina, where there were nearly twice as many slaves to every 100 of the white population in 1850 as in 1790. In this state and in Mississippi are found the highest proportions of negroes to whites in 1900.

For the slave states as a whole the number of slaves to every 100 white persons was slightly smaller in 1850 than in 1790. The proportion was higher in the Southern states of the added area than in the group of Southern states enumerated at the First Census.

VALUE OF SLAVES.

Statistics relating to slaves in the United States in 1790 would not be complete without reference to the property value which they represented. Writers upon this subject have estimated that at the period of taking the First Census the average price of negroes in the United States varied from $150 to $200. It must be remembered that a comparison of values, whether of slaves, real estate, or other property, at that period with the present one is comparatively unsatisfactory, owing to the change which has occurred during the century in the relative value of money. Such valuations should be considered only in relation to the valuation of other property at that period; or, if they are considered in terms of money in 1900, not less than double the figure specified should be allowed.

Considered in terms of money values at that period, the slaves in New England in 1790 had a value of more than $500,000 and those in the Middle states a value of approximately $7,000,000. Hence about 6 per cent of the total value of slaves was contributed by the Northern states.

In view of the large total represented by the preceding computation, there can be no doubt that at the date of the First Census slaves represented a large proportion (possibly larger than at any subsequent period) of the total property value of the United States.

Upon the basis of an average price of negroes of $150,[1] the wealth of the United States in slaves in 1790 was as follows:

[1] Political Science Quarterly, Vol. XX, pages 264–267.

TABLE **71.**—*Number and value of slaves held, by states and territories: 1790.*

STATE OR TERRITORY.	Number.	Value.
United States	697,624	$104,643,600
New England	3,763	564,450
Maine		
New Hampshire	157	23,550
Vermont		
Massachusetts		
Rhode Island	958	143,700
Connecticut	2,648	397,200
Middle states	45,210	6,781,500
New York	21,193	3,178,950
New Jersey	11,423	1,713,450
Pennsylvania	3,707	556,050
Delaware	8,887	1,333,050
Southern states	648,651	97,297,650
Maryland	103,036	15,455,400
Virginia	292,627	43,894,050
North Carolina	100,783	15,117,450
South Carolina	107,094	16,064,100
Georgia	29,264	4,389,600
Kentucky	12,430	1,864,500
Southwest Territory	3,417	512,550

XV. OCCUPATIONS AND WEALTH.

OCCUPATIONS — OF HEADS OF FAMILIES IN PHILA-
DELPHIA AND SOUTHWARK IN 1790 — IN UNITED
STATES IN 1850 AND 1900 — APPROXIMATE WEALTH
IN 1790 — INDUSTRY AND WEALTH, 1850 AND 1900.

Population change in the United States is closely connected with national prosperity. Throughout the century the citizens of the Republic, whether native or foreign, have continually expanded their enterprises, and created and maintained an insistent demand for labor. This in turn, as pointed out by Malthus at the close of the eighteenth century, stimulated population increase at certain periods, and in many localities.

OCCUPATIONS.

The character of the occupations in which the people of a community are engaged affects to some degree the increase of population, through exerting a direct influence upon the health, vitality, temperament, and happiness of the active workers. During at least the first half century of the existence of the Republic, and possibly longer, the occupations of the people were conducive to health and industrial independence, and therefore in general tended to encourage population increase.

It is unfortunate that none of the earlier censuses afford any satisfactory returns from which to compute the number of persons engaged even in the principal callings. Except for Southwark and part of Philadelphia, the schedules of the First Census contain no information upon this important subject. Such information as is presented for these two relates only to heads of families. The fact that the enumerator, soon after completing his work, published a city directory in which he utilized the information contained upon the schedules, suggests that the gratuitous information there shown was obtained with the intention of ultimate use in this directory, rather than for census purposes. After the passage of a century, however, the Philadelphia and Southwark returns possess some interest, in that they reflect the activities of the metropolis of the Republic in 1790, as shown by the callings of heads of households.

Occupations of heads of families in Philadelphia and Southwark in 1790.—At the First Census the population of Philadelphia and of Southwark was returned as follows:

CITY.	Heads of families.	Total population.
Philadelphia	4,312	28,522
Northern district (between Vine and Race streets)	878	3,938
Middle district (from the north side of Chestnut street to the south side of Race street)	1,930	13,674
Southern district (from the south side of Chestnut street to the north side of South street)	1,504	10,910
Southwark	970	5,663

The occupations of the heads of families were returned for the middle and southern districts, comprising 3,434 heads of families (79.6 per cent of the total number) and 24,584 population, and for the whole of Southwark. A classification of the occupations shown results as follows:

TABLE **72.**—*Heads of families in the middle and southern districts of Philadelphia, and in Southwark, classified according to occupation: 1790.*

OCCUPATION.	Middle and southern districts of Philadelphia.	South-wark.
All heads of families	3,434	970
Returned with occupation	2,758	827
Agricultural pursuits	15	3
Professional service	220	35
Artists	2	1
Attorneys at law	25	2
Clergymen	11	4
Doctors of physic, surgeons, dentists, etc	27	4
Officials (government)	79	10
Schoolmasters and professors	71	14
All other professional services	5	.....
Domestic and personal service	443	236
Barbers and hairdressers	59	3
Boarding and lodging house keepers	17	9
Inn and tavern keepers	128	22
Laborers, porters, helpers, etc	239	200
Nurses and midwives	.....	2
Trade and transportation	934	183
Bankers and brokers	27	1
Clerks and accountants	20	5
Draymen and carters	14	3
Hucksters and peddlers	26	1
Merchants and dealers	779	57
Sea captains, mariners, mates, etc	68	116

TABLE **72.**—*Heads of families in the middle and southern districts of Philadelphia, and in Southwark, classified according to occupation: 1790*—Continued.

OCCUPATION.	Middle and southern districts of Philadelphia.	Southwark.
Returned with occupation—Continued.		
Manufacturing and mechanical pursuits.................	1,146	370
Bakers and confectioners...........................	88	21
Blacksmiths....................................	58	31
Brewers......................................	15	2
Brickmakers and potters........................	11	1
Bricklayers...................................	18	8
Butchers.....................................	30	5
Cabinetmakers................................	17	8
Carpenters and joiners:		
House....................................	166	43
Ship.....................................	3	76
Clock and watch makers........................	12	1
Coopers......................................	35	27
Goldsmiths and silversmiths....................	20	3
Harness and saddle makers.....................	30	1
Leather curriers and tanners....................	27	1
Mantuamakers and seamstresses.................	....	7
Metal workers................................	34	1
Painters, glaziers, etc.........................	31	7
Plasterers....................................	11	4
Printers, bookbinders, etc......................	40	2
Ropemakers..................................	5	16
Shoemakers..................................	165	42
Stonecutters.................................	8	4
Tailors......................................	186	28
Textile workers...............................	37	2
Tinmen......................................	17	2
Weavers.....................................	2	17
Wheelwrights................................	13	3
Miscellaneous industries......................	67	7
Returned without occupation.....................	[1] 676	[2] 143

[1] Includes 51 reported as "gentlemen."
[2] Includes 9 reported as "gentlemen."

The above table indicates that about four-fifths of the heads of families in the two districts of Philadelphia under consideration, and a slightly larger proportion of those in Southwark, were gainfully employed. The classification of the 1790 returns available for Philadelphia and Southwark under the 5 main occupation groups employed by the Census results as follows:

OCCUPATION GROUP.	PHILADELPHIA.		SOUTHWARK.	
	Heads of families.	Per cent distribution.	Heads of families.	Per cent distribution.
All occupations..................	2,758	100.0	827	100.0
Agricultural pursuits.................	15	0.5	3	0.4
Professional service..................	220	8.0	35	4.2
Domestic and personal service..........	443	16.1	236	28.5
Trade and transportation..............	934	33.9	183	22.1
Manufacturing and mechanical pursuits.	1,146	41.6	370	44.7

From the proportions indicated for the different groups, it is clear that Southwark, like many towns on the outskirts of large cities at the present time, included a large proportion of persons who were wage-earners or followed the humbler callings.

The proportions shown for Philadelphia can not be compared with the occupation returns secured at recent censuses, because these include the occupations of all persons gainfully employed, whether heads of families or not. The number and proportion of persons above the age of 10 reported in each occupation group in Philadelphia in 1900 were as follows:

OCCUPATION GROUP.	PERSONS GAINFULLY EMPLOYED.	
	Number.	Per cent distribution.
All occupations...........................	568,923	100.0
Agricultural pursuits......................	5,642	1.0
Professional service.......................	28,071	4.9
Domestic and personal service.............	123,751	21.8
Trade and transportation..................	152,262	26.8
Manufacturing and mechanical pursuits.....	259,197	45.6

Occupations in the United States in 1850 and 1900.— The first reasonably complete return of the occupations of individuals was that of 1850. Some comparisons can be made of proportions shown in that year with similar proportions in 1900. Even for so brief a period as the half century which elapsed from 1850 to 1900, however, comparisons can not be entirely satisfactory. The activities of the community have been in a state of continual expansion. While certain occupations, such as agriculture, have remained the same, or so nearly the same that comparison can readily be made, other lines of activity have changed so greatly as to make comparisons misleading, and in many instances impossible. From year to year new occupations are created, drawing some of the activities of the community from the older callings, and these in turn are surpassed in importance by others. Thus, even though a standard occupation, or group of occupations, may have grown steadily and perhaps to a remarkable degree, the proportionate part which it forms of all callings may have tended to become less.

In 1850, 90.8 per cent of all white males 15 years of age and over were gainfully employed; in 1900 the corresponding percentage was 87.6. The distribution of this element of the population in 5 occupation groups is as follows:

TABLE **73.**—*Number and per cent distribution of white males 15 years of age and over engaged in 5 main groups of occupations: 1850 and 1900.*

OCCUPATION GROUP.	1850		1900	
	Number.	Per cent distribution.	Number.	Per cent distribution.
All occupations..............	5,210,047	100.0	19,981,794	100.0
Agricultural pursuits..............	[1] 2,298,870	44.1	7,195,521	36.0
Professional service...............	159,430	3.1	793,180	4.0
Domestic and personal service......	978,131	18.8	2,689,133	13.4
Trade and transportation...........	481,741	9.3	3,949,262	19.8
Manufacturing and mechanical pursuits..................	1,291,875	24.8	5,354,698	26.8

[1] Not including 42,370 students and cadets and 119,459 free colored males.

Possibly the most significant fact shown by the foregoing table is the marked increase during the last half century in the relative importance of trade and transportation, at the expense of agricultural pursuits and of domestic and personal service. While in 1900, as in 1850, agriculture gave employment to a larger number than any other class, the proportion in this group decreased during the half century.

INDUSTRY AND WEALTH.

No reliable statistics either of the industry or of the wealth of the nation at the beginning of Constitutional Government can be obtained.[1] Attention has already been directed, however, to the fact that in 1790 the population was almost entirely agricultural. Moreover, it has been shown that at the period under consideration urban population was almost a negligible quantity, and that the variations in social and economic conditions were much less marked than they are to-day. Hence there is some justification for the belief that property, limited in amount though it was, was much more evenly distributed in 1790 than at the present time. The total lack of statistics upon this subject justifies some computation, provided a reasonable basis can be found.

Approximate wealth in 1790.—It has already been shown that in 1790 the population of the Republic was engaged principally in agricultural pursuits; indeed, it has been estimated that agriculture supported 90 per cent of the people. If it be granted that at least a very large proportion of the people were so engaged, it may be assumed that in most instances a dwelling represented a farm, so that the number of houses must roughly indicate the number of farms, or of buildings of similar average value in villages and towns. To this number should be added the business properties which existed in all fair-sized communities.

The number of dwellings in the United States in 1790 has been established with reasonable accuracy in a preceding chapter as 464,309. Dr. James Mease states, in A Picture of Philadelphia, published in 1811, that in 1790 the city contained 6,651 dwelling houses and 415 stores and workshops. It thus appears that in Philadelphia, at the period of the First Census, the number of buildings other than dwellings (and the outhouses connected with or dependent upon dwellings) was equivalent to approximately 7 per cent of all dwellings. If the proportion here shown for Philadelphia be assumed to be correct for the country as a whole, the entire number of stores, factories, workshops, churches, and public buildings was 32,501. This, added to the number of dwellings, makes a total of 496,810 buildings, most of which, as already suggested, were houses upon farms.

In 1900 the average value of farms was $2,200. If about one-third of this figure, or $700, be accepted as representing an approximate average value for all real estate holdings, and to this figure be added the approximate value of slaves as already established,[2]

and an allowance for all other values, including farm animals, the following results appear:

Buildings and real estate	$347,767,000
Slaves	104,643,600
All other property, including farm animals	100,000,000
Total	552,410,600

As admitted at the outset, no accurate measurement of the wealth of the nation at the beginning of Constitutional Government has been or can be made; but the foregoing analysis serves at least to indicate that in 1790 the value of all property could not greatly have exceeded $500,000,000 according to the standards of value at that time.

If the total here shown is accepted as representing a fair approximation of the value existing at the period under consideration, the per capita value, based upon the free population shown in 1790, was $171. It will be remembered, however, that standards of value at the close of the eighteenth century were much lower than at the present time, so that in present day terms the values above shown would probably be represented by not less than twice the figures stated. Hence, if computed according to the standards of 1900, a total valuation of $552,410,600 in 1790 would represent not less than $1,000,000,000 in 1900, and a per capita valuation of between $300 and $400.

Upon the basis of wealth as outlined above, the aggregate and per capita wealth of the United States in 1790, by specified geographic divisions, was as follows:

TABLE **74.**—*Aggregate and per capita wealth of the free population, by geographic divisions: 1790.*

GEOGRAPHIC DIVISION.	Aggregate.	Per capita.
United States	$552,410,600	$170.92
New England	138,731,444	137.98
Middle states	141,320,642	145.41
Southern states	272,358,514	217.07

From this computation it appears probable that at the period of the First Census the per capita wealth of the free population was greatest in the Southern states. The known facts undoubtedly serve to substantiate this conclusion. In the Southern states the population was comparatively small considering the area; the farms had become plantations, in connection with which the value not only of the real property, improvements, and live stock, but also of slaves, was to be considered. The leadership of the South in wealth is further indicated by the fact that in the Constitutional Convention of 1787 the Southern states demanded representation according to their free population and three-fifths of the number of their slaves, on the ground that they possessed larger property interests than the Northern states, so that, if direct taxes on property were imposed by the Federal

---

[1] Mulhall places the aggregate wealth of the United States in 1790 at $620,000,000, divided as follows: Lands, $479,000,000; houses, etc., $141,000,000.

[2] See page 141.

Government, they would have to pay larger amounts in proportion to their representation.

The great wealth which the New England and Middle states have acquired during the century following the first enumeration has resulted principally from extraordinary industrial development. In 1790 the inhabitants of the New England states were engaged almost exclusively in agriculture; with the meager agricultural resources existing in that section it could not be expected that, even with the highest development, farm values and farm products would prove proportionately large when compared with those in portions of the Republic more highly favored by climate and fertility of soil. Practically the same conditions prevailed in the Middle states, although somewhat greater natural resources, and the increased values resulting from such cities as New York and Philadelphia, served to make the per capita value of property slightly greater than that of New England.

Comparison of 1850 with 1900.—The following table presents such comparisons as are possible concerning the material resources of continental United States, and also of the area enumerated in 1790, at the censuses from 1850 to 1900:

TABLE **75.**—COMPARISON OF GROWTH IN AREA, POPULATION, AGRICULTURE, MANUFACTURES, AND NATIONAL WEALTH, FOR THE TOTAL AREA OF CONTINENTAL UNITED STATES AND FOR THE AREA ENUMERATED IN 1790: 1850 TO 1900.

CENSUS YEAR.	CONTINENTAL UNITED STATES.						
	Area enumerated.		Population.	Agriculture.		Manufactures—value of products.	National wealth—value of all property.
	Square miles.	Per cent area enumerated in 1790 forms of total area enumerated at each census.		Acres of improved land.	Value of farm property.[1]		
1850	1,519,170	27.5	23,191,876	113,032,614	$3,967,343,580	$1,019,106,616	[2]$7,135,780,228
1860	1,951,520	21.4	31,443,321	163,110,720	7,980,493,063	1,885,861,676	[2]16,159,616,068
1870	2,126,290	19.6	38,558,371	188,921,099	8,944,857,749	4,232,325,442	[2]24,054,814,806
1880	2,727,454	15.3	50,155,783	284,771,042	[3]12,180,501,538	5,369,579,191	43,642,000,000
1890	2,974,159	14.0	62,947,714	357,616,755	[3]16,082,267,689	9,372,378,843	65,037,091,197
1900	2,974,159	14.0	75,994,575	414,498,487	20,439,901,164	13,010,036,514	88,517,306,775
Increase:							
1850 to 1860	432,350	....	8,251,445	50,078,106	4,013,149,483	866,755,060	9,023,835,840
1860 to 1870	174,770	....	7,115,050	25,810,379	964,364,686	2,346,463,766	7,895,198,738
1870 to 1880	601,164	....	11,597,412	95,849,943	3,235,643,789	1,137,253,749	19,587,185,194
1880 to 1890	246,705	....	12,791,931	72,845,713	3,901,766,151	4,002,799,652	21,395,091,197
1890 to 1900	....	....	13,046,861	56,881,732	4,357,633,475	3,637,657,671	23,480,215,578

CENSUS YEAR.	AREA ENUMERATED IN 1790.									
	Population.		Agriculture.				Manufactures—value of products.		National wealth—value of all property.	
			Acres of improved land.		Value of farm property.[1]					
	Number.	Per cent of total.	Number.	Per cent of total.	Amount.	Per cent of total.	Amount.	Per cent of total.	Amount.	Per cent of total.
1850	14,569,584	62.8	70,223,511	62.1	$2,613,595,463	65.9	$835,489,765	81.2	[2]$4,930,793,981	69.1
1860	17,326,157	55.1	81,933,952	50.2	4,195,624,939	52.5	1,407,690,264	74.6	[2]9,102,463,876	56.3
1870	19,687,504	51.6	80,672,316	42.7	4,136,676,463	34.0	2,967,465,381	70.0	[2]14,725,586,812	61.2
1880	23,925,639	47.7	95,001,365	33.4	4,738,167,384	38.9	3,559,794,469	66.3	22,348,012,800	51.2
1890	28,188,321	44.8	97,235,805	27.2	4,828,788,468	30.0	5,563,835,986	59.4	27,632,937,998	42.5
1900	33,553,630	44.2	99,947,259	24.1	5,000,462,719	24.4	7,487,459,407	57.4	40,296,048,530	45.5
Increase :										
1850 to 1860	2,756,573	33.4	11,710,441	23.4	1,582,029,476	39.4	572,200,499	66.0	4,171,669,895	46.2
1860 to 1870	2,361,347	33.2	[4]1,261,636	(4)	[4]58,948,476	(4)	1,559,775,117	66.5	5,623,122,936	71.2
1870 to 1880	4,238,135	36.5	14,329,049	14.9	601,490,921	18.6	592,329,088	52.1	7,622,425,988	38.9
1880 to 1890	4,262,682	33.3	2,234,440	3.1	90,621,084	2.3	2,004,041,517	50.1	5,284,925,198	24.7
1890 to 1900	5,365,309	41.1	2,711,454	4.7	171,674,251	3.9	1,923,623,421	52.5	12,663,110,532	53.9

CENSUS YEAR.	PER CENT OF INCREASE.									
	Population—		Agriculture.				Manufactures—value of products—		National wealth—value of all property—	
			Acres of improved land—		Value of farm property—					
	Of total area.	Of area enumerated in 1790.	In total area.	In area enumerated in 1790.	In total area.	In area enumerated in 1790.	In total area.	In area enumerated in 1790.	In total area.	In area enumerated in 1790.
1850 to 1860	35.6	18.9	44.3	16.7	101.2	60.5	85.1	68.5	126.5	84.6
1860 to 1870	22.6	13.6	15.8	[4]1.5	12.1	[4]1.4	124.4	110.8	48.9	61.8
1870 to 1880	30.1	21.5	50.7	17.8	36.2	14.5	26.9	20.0	81.4	51.8
1880 to 1890	25.5	17.8	25.6	2.4	32.0	1.9	74.5	56.3	49.0	23.6
1890 to 1900	20.7	19.0	15.9	2.8	27.1	3.6	38.8	34.6	36.1	45.8

[1] The value of farm property is included as a part of the national wealth.
[2] Taxable property only.
[3] Including estimated value of range animals.
[4] Decrease.

As shown by the table, the growth of the added area reduced the proportion which the area enumerated in 1790 formed of the total area by approximately one-half—from two-sevenths in 1850 to one-seventh in 1900. During the same period the proportion which the population, value of manufactured products, and national wealth in the original area formed of the corresponding totals for the United States, declined only about one-third. These changes reflect a noteworthy growth in the original area. On the other hand, the relative importance of agricultural operations in the original area, as measured both by the acreage of improved land and by the value of farm property, was only one-third as great in 1900 as in 1850—a fact which reflects the rapid development of the fertile areas in the West and Southwest.

When the changes in proportions outlined above are considered by decades, it is found that the changes in population, acreage of improved agricultural land, and value of manufactured products were progressive. It is significant that the decrease in the relative importance of the original area was more rapid during the early part of the half century than at its close. During the last decade the proportion of population decreased less than 1 per cent and that of manufactures but 2 per cent, while the proportion of national wealth showed an increase of 3 per cent. Only in the agricultural operations was a marked decreas estill evident in the proportion contributed by the older area as compared with that of the newer.

The above analysis of proportions shown for the original area receives further confirmation upon examining the percentages of increase in Table 75. In every instance, except for the national wealth in the decades 1860 to 1870 and 1890 to 1900, the percentage of increase was higher for the country as a whole—and hence, obviously for the added area—than for the original area. Both areas showed marked increases in the value of manufactured products and in aggregate wealth. In the case of the two items used as a measure of changes in agriculture, however, the difference between the two areas is very striking—the original area showing relatively small increases, and in one decade, 1860 to 1870, a decrease.

The marked differences in the contributions of different sections to the national resources are clearly indicated by the following per capita values:

GEOGRAPHIC DIVISION.	VALUE OF FARM PROPERTY.		VALUE OF MANUFACTURED PRODUCTS.		AGGREGATE WEALTH.	
	1850 [1]	1900 [2]	1850 [1]	1900 [2]	1850 [1]	1900 [2]
Continental United States.	$202.90	$305.94	$52.12	$194.73	$364.94	$1,324.93
Area enumerated in 1790......	204.72	164.22	65.44	245.90	386.23	1,323.39
New England and Middle states...................	199.58	143.87	84.29	314.71	368.74	1,563.99
Southern states...........	215.16	208.05	27.26	97.75	421.69	805.39
Added area.................	199.47	424.63	27.06	151.89	324.90	1,326.21

[1] Computed on basis of free population.
[2] Computed on basis of white population.

Discussion of the aggregate wealth of the original and added areas necessitates some reference to the value of slaves in 1850. Writers of that period [1] estimated the average value per slave, for all ages, at $400. Accepting this as an approximate figure, the total value of slaves was $828,336,000 in the original area and $451,809,600 in the added area, or about twice as great in the original slave states as in those erected from territory added after 1790. Out of a total valuation of the real and personal property in the slaveholding states amounting to nearly $2,000,000,000, the value of slaves formed 43.5 per cent.

If the total wealth of the United States in 1790 (on the basis of the present standard of values) be accepted as approximately $1,000,000,000, the increase from 1790 to 1900 approaches ninetyfold. During the period mentioned, the population of the United States increased fourteenfold; hence, while the population increased at a rate far in advance of that shown by any other civilized nation during the same period, the increase of wealth in the United States far outstripped that of population.

[1] The total value of all slaves in 1850 was $1,280,145,600, computed upon the average value of $400 per head (Hinton Helper: The Impending Crisis, page 306, Table 58, N. Y., 1860). The average value of boys and girls, men and women between the ages of about 15 and 25, as recorded by Mr. Frederick Law Olmsted (A Journey in the Seaboard Slave States, page 38), was $739 in Virginia in 1853. If young children and men and women above the age of 25 be included to old age, it is probable that a general average of not more than $400, as quoted by Helper, would result.

ENUMERATIONS OF POPULATION
IN NORTH AMERICA
PRIOR TO 1790

NEW HAMPSHIRE.

TABLE 76.—A GENERAL ACCOUNT OF THE NUMBER OF INHABITANTS OF THE SEVERAL TOWNS IN THE PROVINCE OF NEW HAMPSHIRE, AS APPEARS BY THE RETURNS OF THE SELECTMEN FROM EACH PLACE, IN THE YEAR 1767.[1]

NAME OF THE TOWNS.	Unmarried men from 16 to 60.	Married men from 16 to 60.	Boys from 16 years & under.	Men 60 years & above.	Females unmarried.	Females married.	Male slaves.	Female slaves.	Widows.	Total.
Greenland	75	98	184	23	271	117	8	9	20	805
Rochester	86	142	257	26	280	166	3	2	22	984
Gosport	27	37	79	12	59	47	2	2	19	284
Winchester	35	64	107	10	132	74	1	1	4	428
Sandown	42	81	123	8	156	89	1	0	9	509
Somersworth	87	125	299	30	291	144	19	10	39	1,044
Chesterfield	30	56	107	4	104	60	0	0	4	365
Richmond	36	54	95	1	92	52	0	0	3	333
Hinsdale	18	23	36	2	50	24	0	1	4	158
Plymouth	31	31	62	0	72	31				227
Dunstable	32	69	151	10	169	78	2	2	7	520
Portsmouth	440	641	900	61	1,340	677	124	63	220	4,466
Hopkinton	37	75	141	4	132	75	0	0	9	473
New Durham	11	25	42	2	49	26	0	0	2	157
Dover	186	217	347	39	500	239	19	9	58	1,614
Parish of Madbury	54	95	162	29	220	119	1	2	13	695
Charlestown	31	44	86	4	114	48	1	0	6	334
Hampton	72	120	195	40	263	146	0	0	30	866
Candia	27	68	99	0	100	68	0	0	1	363
Londonderry	235	272	571	85	799	342	13	10	62	2,389
New Castle	50	83	146	21	167	98	11	8	22	606
Exeter	151	241	384	37	507	262	28	22	58	1,690
Walpole	24	52	104	1	72	52	0	0	3	308
Plainfield	10	20	36		26	20				112
Cornish	17	21	36		37	22	0	0	0	133
Alstead	15	25	30		35	25	0	0	0	130
Clarmont	13	27	50		40	27	0	0	0	157
Marlow	8	15	19		20	15	0	0	0	77
Newport	16	5	3			5	0	0	0	29
Hanover	11	26	16		13	26				92
Canaan	10	2	3		2	2				19
Lebanon	12	30	50		40	30				162
Kingston	73	133	245	23	333	160	3	1	28	999
Swanzy	23	49	82	7	96	54	1	0	8	320
Westmoreland	28	71	112	3	103	71	0	0	3	391
Keene	51	66	84	4	149	68	0	0	8	430
Monadnock, No. 4, Stoddarts To	14	20	25		14	20				93
Marlboro' No. 5	9	16	25	1	26	16	0	0	0	93
Gilsum	7	22	36	1	39	23	0	0	0	128
Croydon	16	9	7		10	9				51
Poplin	36	79	155	6	153	84	0	0	8	521
Newington	41	59	105	11	180	70	17	14	17	514
Dunbarton	25	39	70	6	80	45	2	0	4	271
Rye	46	109	159	16	223	126	11	7	39	736
Concord (formerly Rumford)	62	125	189	18	204	126	9	4	15	752
Kensington	62	107	166	28	250	118		2	24	755
Newtown	58	69	119	15	170	83	0	2	13	529
Newmarket	120	182	288	23	407	198	13	16	34	1,286
Boscawen	17	45	77	8	83	52	0	0	3	285
Stevenstown	18	36	55	0	62	36	1	0	2	210
Hillsboro'	3	16	27	0	3	15	0	0	0	64
New Boston	25	41	92	6	80	47	1	1	3	296
Barrington	66	161	272	18	292	170	4	0	18	1,001
Hawk	30	74	109	6	178	80	1	1	9	488
Nottingham West	49	75	155	16	176	92	1	1	18	583
Holles	81	117	223	12	227	127	1	1	20	809
Township No. 1	20	47	80	1	79	47	0	0	4	278
Miles Slip, between Holles & No. 1	4	12	15	1	24	12	0	0	0	68
Durham	104	166	272	38	386	192	21	11	42	1,232
Parish of Lee	63	147	198	19	269	143	3	1	18	861
Weare Town	8	50	80	2	78	50	0	0	0	268
Chester	116	168	289	31	357	190	3	1	34	1,189
Stratham	73	132	196	24	295	153	7	2	34	916
South Hampton	51	68	98	18	154	85	1	2	14	491
Wilton	27	62	100	3	92	63	0	0	3	350
Raymond	21	78	132	3	134	81	0	0	6	455
Bedford	30	43	93	13	117	51	6	3	6	362
Derryfield	9	31	59	7	81	38	0	0	5	230
Plastow	59	71	119	23	192	92	1	1	18	576
Atkinson	51	73	92	12	143	85	4	3	13	476
Nottingham	35	107	195	10	219	116	6	6	14	708
Epsom	15	40	71	5	66	40	0	0	2	239
Gilmanton	18	47	73	0	67	44	0	0	1	250
Pembroke	49	85	134	16	169	97	0	2	5	557
Bow	17	33	50	2	50	33	0	0	2	187
Litchfield	27	20	67	13	74	33	3	9	8	[2] 254
Pelham	37	81	154	18	158	81	0	1	13	543
Salem	63	138	239	16	204	155	2	2	28	847
Windham	19	50	117	15	120	66	1	3	11	402
Hampstead	48	96	162	10	197	105	1	0	25	644
North Hampton	28	93	142	18	189	96	0	1	16	583
East Kingston	50	58	100	20	127	81	3	0	12	451
Epping	99	205	378	21	464	214	6	3	20	1,410
Brentwood	86	142	271	22	345	163	1	1	33	1,064
Canterbury	42	82	138	11	140	83	3	0	4	503

[1] Provincial Papers of New Hampshire, Vol. VII, pages 168 to 170.   [2] Corrected figures.

NEW HAMPSHIRE—Continued.

TABLE 76.—A GENERAL ACCOUNT OF THE NUMBER OF INHABITANTS OF THE SEVERAL TOWNS IN THE PROVINCE OF NEW HAMPSHIRE, AS APPEARS BY THE RETURNS OF THE SELECTMEN FROM EACH PLACE, IN THE YEAR 1767—Continued.

NAME OF THE TOWNS.	Unmarried men from 16 to 60.	Married men from 16 to 60.	Boys from 16 years & under.	Men 60 years & above.	Females unmarried.	Females married.	Male slaves.	Female slaves.	Widows.	Total.
Haverhill	21	32	43	1	43	29	2	1	0	172
Orford	12	14	18	1	18	12	0	0	0	75
Peterborough	33	64	113	13	149	68	1	0	2	443
Hampton Falls	127	188	313	33	457	208	3	3	49	1,381
Lynesborough	26	43	76	4	71	50	0	0	2	272
Monson	21	46	68	5	101	49	0	0	3	293
Amherst	63	135	200	17	270	147	6	2	18	858
Merrimac	31	65	98	8	121	65	2	1	9	400
Rindge	18	54	84	4	82	54	0	1	1	298
Total	4,510	[1]7,670	[1]12,924	[1]1,160	[1]15,992	[1]8,467	384	249	1,364	[1]52,720

[1] Corrected figures.

TABLE 77.—FREE AND SLAVE POPULATION OF NEW HAMPSHIRE, BY COUNTIES AND TOWNS: CENSUS OF 1773.[1]

COUNTIES AND TOWNS.	Unmarried men from 16 to 60.	Married men from 16 to 60.	Boys 16 years and under.	Men 60 years and upwards.	Females unmarried.	Females married.	Widows.	Male slaves.	Female slaves.	Total.
Total	6,263	10,604	18,334	1,538	22,228	11,887	1,569	379	295	73,097
Rockingham county	3,132	4,835	8,363	943	11,239	5,695	1,034	260	206	[2]35,707
Allenstown	8	17	39	4	49	21	4		1	143
Atkinson	39	73	132	16	170	87	13	2	3	535
Bow	5	58	84	2	101	58				308
Brentwood	78	146	261	28	365	175	33	2	1	1,089
Candia	52	111	182	2	200	112	4			663
Canterbury	66	96	150	10	164	104	5	5	0	600
Chichester	29	44	77	2	75	46				273
Chester	151	229	355	53	453	261	43	5	2	1,552
Concord	96	151	260	30	283	154	12	8	9	1,003
Deerfield	68	143	238	8	290	151	10	2	1	[2]911
Epping	121	225	406	31	571	246	31	10	7	1,648
Epsom	18	53	86	1	109	53	4	1	1	[2]326
Exeter	129	252	366	50	539	270	59	24	25	1,714
East Kingston	29	54	93	20	118	72	13	3		402
Greenland	70	85	178	16	242	103	20	6	11	731
Hampstead	58	106	181	24	219	125	14	1	0	728
Hampton	80	120	203	36	291	151	33	2	1	917
Hampton Falls	44	146	99	21	218	96	22	1	1	648
Hawke[3]	25	71	110	8	172	81	10	1	0	478
Kensington	65	107	182	34	265	141	28			822
Kingston	110	142	201	41	295	172	23	3	2	989
Londonderry	228	299	587	84	833	357	58	12	13	2,471
Loudon	12	36	58	2	54	38	3		1	204
New Castle	58	89	128	24	167	100	22	7	6	601
Newington	46	62	114	20	172	77	21	21	15	548
Newmarket	113	178	341	22	435	188	43	8	16	1,344
Newtown	52	74	118	24	189	95	18	0	2	572
North Hampton	47	96	172	25	228	116	16	0	2	702
Northwood	9	49	58	2	77	51	4	0	0	250
Nottingham	49	139	251	14	283	139	19	5	5	904
Pelham	49	95	198	21	193	114	12	1	1	684
Pembrook	45	110	176	12	186	119	12	5	1	666
Plaistow	49	78	125	23	194	101	17	3	1	591
Poplin[4]	35	83	156	10	178	91	10		1	564
Portsmouth	617	371	868	93	1,346	682	235	100	60	4,372
Raymond	44	98	189	11	222	107	12			683
Rye	69	113	190	24	259	132	36	12	7	842
Sandown	54	81	148	15	182	95	14	1	0	590
South Hampton	39	67	96	18	153	81	17	1	1	473
Seabrook	48	94	153	17	156	103	25			596
Stratham	77	138	234	27	382	161	45	3	1	1,068
Windham	51	56	120	18	161	69	14	5	8	502
Strafford county	932	1,599	2,742	223	3,221	1,775	232	64	38	10,826
Barnstead	12	26	41	3	41	29				152
Barrington	110	223	350	7	397	223	26	4	1	1,341
Dover	172	220	393	43	514	255	42	15	11	1,665
Durham	108	138	266	52	336	183	42	15	9	1,149
East Town[5]	20	49	65	1	64	48			1	248
Gilmanton	49	105	180	2	188	105	5	1		635
Leavitts Town[6]	6	20	30	0	34	21				111
Lee	58	142	257	18	309	157	13	5	1	960
Madbury	34	84	154	29	199	107	15		3	625
Meredith	23	37	57	0	64	37	0	0	0	218
Moultonborough	28	46	68	2	68	49	2	0	0	263
New Durham	30	42	72	1	88	42	4	1	0	280
Rochester	123	210	346	26	437	241	34	2	1	1,420

[1] Provincial Papers of New Hampshire, Vol. X, pages 625 to 636.
[2] Corrected figures.
[3] Now Danville.
[4] Now Fremont.
[5] Now Wakefield.
[6] Now Effingham.

NEW HAMPSHIRE—Continued.

Table **77.**—FREE AND SLAVE POPULATION OF NEW HAMPSHIRE, BY COUNTIES AND TOWNS: CENSUS OF 1773—Con.

COUNTIES AND TOWNS.	Unmarried men from 16 to 60.	Married men from 16 to 60.	Boys 16 years and under.	Men 60 years and upwards.	Females unmarried.	Females married.	Widows.	Male slaves.	Female slaves.	Total.
Strafford county—Continued.										
Sandwich	9	35	64	0	61	35	0	0	0	204
Somersworth	106	140	246	34	278	161	42	20	11	1,038
Sandbornton	28	57	104	3	100	57	2	1	0	352
Wolfborough	16	25	49	2	43	25	5	....	....	165
Hillsborough county	976	2,112	3,683	207	4,016	2,243	200	39	38	13,514
Amherst	109	237	330	13	412	245	19	3	2	1,370
Bedford	54	62	121	15	49	72	7	4	4	388
Boscawen	34	76	140	11	147	90	6	0	0	504
Camden[1]	11	21	40	....	37	21	2	....	....	132
Derryfield[2]	28	30	77	7	92	40	3	1	1	279
Dunbarton	26	73	148	6	128	78	4	1	....	464
Dunstable	51	71	156	18	213	89	5	1	6	610
Goffstown	67	101	195	11	237	107	9	3	2	732
Henniker	19	60	93	2	96	62	5	0	1	338
Hillsborough	16	27	34	3	44	29	....	....	....	153
Hollis	104	180	287	18	355	190	25	2	1	1,162
Hopkinton	43	151	297	10	267	156	17	2	0	943
Litchfield	26	35	68	13	95	43	12	2	5	299
Mason	32	77	136	4	125	81	7	1	....	463
Merrimac	50	82	129	8	170	89	11	8	5	552
New Almsbury[3]	10	36	62	4	59	38	4	....	....	213
New Boston	23	61	137	6	110	64	5	2	2	410
New Britain[4]	9	26	36	2	36	26	....	....	....	135
New Ipswich	48	165	232	5	277	139	12	2	2	882
Nottingham W'st[5]	41	88	150	14	179	100	16	2	2	592
Peterborough	44	66	131	12	172	72	11	3	3	514
Peterborough-Slip	7	14	22	1	23	14	0	0	0	81
Salisbury	20	70	111	5	130	76	3	1	0	416
Temple	28	74	121	2	115	76	2	0	0	418
Weare	39	138	262	10	280	147	7	....	1	884
Wilton	37	91	168	7	168	99	8	1	1	580
Cheshire county	793	1,473	2,626	126	2,812	1,568	86	7	2	[6]9,493
Alstead	24	37	66	4	59	42	1	....	....	[6]233
Charlestown	69	83	151	3	191	85	8	....	....	590
Chesterfield	55	109	224	12	220	120	7	0	0	747
Claremont	41	66	121	2	125	66	2	0	0	423
Cornish	28	36	52	1	60	35	1	....	....	213
Croydon	13	16	21	1	23	16	1	....	....	91
Dublin	16	45	74	1	71	46	1	1	0	255
Fitzwilliam	18	44	55	....	53	44	....	....	....	214
Gilsom	17	21	32	4	37	22	2	0	0	[6]135
Hinsdale	28	28	48	5	70	31	8	1	1	220
Jaffrey	13	50	89	2	92	52	5	0	0	303
Keene	65	96	140	11	217	105	10	1	....	645
Lempster	11	13	16	....	17	9	....	....	....	66
Limerick[7]	16	43	62	2	49	43	....	....	....	215
Marlow	11	29	43	....	40	32	1	....	....	156
Monadnock, No. 5[8]	17	39	88	1	89	40	1	....	....	275
Monadnock, No. 6[9]	12	23	32	0	27	23	0	0	0	117
Newport	14	23	40	2	54	23	....	....	....	156
Plainfield	32	40	65	6	85	43	4	....	....	275
Richmond	32	112	257	5	218	115	6	....	....	745
Rindge	42	99	170	11	166	109	5	2	0	604
Saville[10]	8	16	15	0	16	16	1	0	0	72
Surry	22	30	52	2	70	32	0	0	0	208
Swanzey	42	74	148	13	164	85	9	1	0	536
Unity	7	18	32	....	32	17	....	....	....	106
Walpole	48	81	157	11	160	87	5	....	....	549
Westmoreland	50	109	206	13	198	117	5	0	0	698
Winchester	42	93	170	14	209	113	3	1	1	646
Grafton county	430	585	920	39	940	606	17	9	11	[6]3,557
Apthorp[11]	1	3	4	0	2	3	1	0	0	14
Bath	18	25	46	0	36	25	0	0	0	150
Campton	14	22	39	1	40	22	1	....	....	139
Canaan	12	11	16	....	11	12	....	....	....	62
Conway	40	42	39	4	37	40	1	....	....	203
Cockermouth[12]	11	22	24	....	28	22	....	....	....	107
Dorchester	23	13	33	....	38	14	....	....	....	121
New Grantham[13]	7	10	12	2	17	11	0	1	0	60
Hanover	58	49	86	7	80	54	....	4	4	342
Haverhill	30	66	107	1	112	66	3	1	1	387
N'w Holderness[14]	9	21	45	6	41	25	0	0	0	147
Lancaster	3	6	8	2	10	7	1	0	0	37
Lebanon	44	50	62	4	79	54	2	0	0	295
Lime	29	37	53	5	71	39	3	2	2	241
New Chester[15]	5	31	63	2	46	32	0	0	0	179
Northumberland	10	9	8	....	11	8	0	0	0	46
Orford	17	39	60	3	63	43	1	....	2	228
Plymouth	29	57	90	1	107	57	2	1	2	345
Stewartstown[16]	24	14	17	....	19	14	....	....	....	88
Rumney	21	31	61	1	47	29	2	0	0	192
Thornton	16	13	18	1	12	14	....	....	....	74
Trecothick[17]	8	8	16	....	18	8	....	....	....	[6]58
Wentworth	1	6	13	....	15	7	....	....	....	42

[1] Now Washington.
[2] Now Manchester.
[3] Now Warner.
[4] Now Andover.
[5] Now Hudson.
[6] Corrected figures.
[7] Now Stoddard.
[8] Now Marlborough.
[9] Now Nelson.
[10] Now Sunapee.
[11] Now Dalton.
[12] Now Groton.
[13] Now Grantham.
[14] Now Holderness.
[15] Now Hill.
[16] Including Cockburn and Colbrook.
[17] Now Ellsworth.

A CENTURY OF POPULATION GROWTH.

NEW HAMPSHIRE—Continued.

TABLE 78.—RETURN OF THE NUMBER OF INHABITANTS IN THE SEVERAL TOWNS AND PLACES IN NEW HAMPSHIRE, TAKEN BY ORDER OF THE CONVENTION, WITH THE NUMBER OF FIRE ARMS, THE POWDER, &c.: 1775.[1]

COUNTIES AND TOWNS.	Males under 16.	Males from 16 to 50 not in the Army.	Males above 50.	Persons in the Army.	Females.	Negroes and Slaves for life.	Total.	Fire arms fit for use.	Fire arms wanting.	Public stock of Powder.	Powder in private hands.
Rockingham county:											
Portsmouth	1,013	823	191	50	2,373	140	4,590				
Hampton	190	147	62	20	440	3	862	192			94
Exeter	401	273	86	51	892	38	1,741	193	150	50	80
Londonderry	618	404	157	66	1,316	29	2,590	283	183		132
New-Castle	101	85	33		221	9	449	63		68	
Rye	206	146	47	15	442	14	870	170			101
Kingston	214	155	67	27	491	7	961		127		35
Newington	97	90	34	6	266	39	532	93	20	60	
Stratham	252	183	58	17	622	5	1,137				
Greenland	169	136	42	10	381	21	759	108	33	45	61
New-Market	322	212	50	30	658	17	1,289				
South-Hampton	109	92	27	10	259	1	498	66	31		58
Plaistow	129	85	35	33	288	5	575	46	39		10
Hampstead	182	106	44	35	398	3	768	51	75		32
Salem	296	151	49	47	539	2	1,084	104		43	71
Pelham	206	112	10	29	362	0	749	110	40		28
Chester	384	273	101	51	787	3	1,599	175	112		30
Hampton-Falls	151	91	42	19	339	3	645	80	15	30	71
Nottingham	268	165	26	22	502	11	[2] 994	101	68	53	42
Brentwood	253	174	57	35	577	4	1,100	113	68	40	160
North-Hampton	153	97	39	24	335	4	652	122		50	86
East-Kingston	114	63	29	9	210	3	428	65			31
Newtown	121	96	30	8	283	2	540	46	41		
Kensington	172	122	49	39	413	2	797	100			83
Windham	120	86	33	15	262	13	529	69	17		16
Bow	88	47	11	17	187	0	350	33	14		13
Epping	377	242	77	61	793	19	1,569				
Epsom	110	57	15	15	189	1	387	44	26		28
Pembroke	179	114	33	23	388	7	744				
Sandown	120	87	12	20	219	1	459	68	39	103	
Hawke	129	76	26	13	260	0	504	52			9
Concord	280	186	36	46	490	14	1,052	98			
Canterbury	199	124	30	35	331	4	723	45	109	80	
Candia	232	120	19	27	346		744	72	48		
Raymond	187	120	24	18	334		683				
Poplin	153	92	24	7	274	2	552				
Deerfield	250	204	26	30	418	1	929	120	68		51
Atkinson	145	91	30	18	286	5	575	62	49		36
Chichester	117	187	13	4	197		[2] 518	47	31	42	
Allenstown	39	18	7	1	82	2	149	11			
Seabrook	144	109	39	11	304		607	74			24
Northwood	85	57	6	10	155		313	36	16		10
Loudon	90	85	9	3	161	1	349	49	36		
Gosport											
Hillsborough county:											
Amherst	343	240	53	81	707	4	1,428	121		41	55
Litchfield	62	44	19	13	136	10	284	39	8	0	28
Boscawen	162	91	33	17	281	1	585	58	65		7
Bedford	109	93	28	14	241	10	495		37	0	11
Derryfield	68	41	15	16	142	3	285	20	20	0	0
Goffstown	215	138	21	40	411	6	831				
Nottingham-West	168	100	36	22	319	4	649	66	32	0	25
Salisbury	142	92	15	6	242	1	498	47	45		
Peterborough	135	77	23	25	277	8	546	23			
Dunbarton	144	92	14	14	232	1	497				
Hopkinton	332	160	30	42	519	2	1,085		56		6
Wilton	162	102	17	26	314	2	623	72		47	40
Peterborough-Slip	31	17	1	6	52		107	7			
Dunstable	215	88	30	40	325	7	705	46	42	36	41
New-Boston	164	98	27	20	256	4	569				
Weare	248	177	18	32	421	1	[2] 897	72			10
Hollis	306	174	71	60	640	4	1,255	131	92	0	111
New-Ipswich	268	246	26	42	475	3	[2] 1,060	105	48	74	87
Merrimack	127	110	32	19	305	13	606	79	36		9½
Lyndeborough	201	103	34	27	348	0	713				
Henniker [3]	117	67	15	9	158	1	367	40		0	0
Hillsborough											
Raby [4]											
Mason	148	86	12	27	227	1	501	48	49	0	14
Temple	143	94	6	18	230	0	491	66		112	45
Francestown	55	37	7	9	92	0	200	0	11		
Society Land	42	36	8	9	82	0	177				
Warner	78	45	6	6	126	1	262	21	26	0	0
New-Britain [5]	56	38	5	3	77	0	179	27		0	0
Perry's-Town [6]	39	22	5	4	60	0	130	12	17	0	0
Mile Slip [7]	20	15	3	3	42	0	83				
Deering											
Fishersfield [8]											

[1] New Hampshire Historical Collections, 1824, Vol. I. (Census incomplete; several towns not reported.)
[2] Corrected figures.
[3] Hillsborough, Antrim, and Hancock were joined with Henniker in this enumeration.
[4] Joined with Mason.
[5] Now (1824) Andover.
[6] Now (1824) Sutton.
[7] Including Duxbury farm.
[8] Joined with Sutton in this enumeration.

NEW HAMPSHIRE—Continued.

TABLE 78.—RETURN OF THE NUMBER OF INHABITANTS IN THE SEVERAL TOWNS AND PLACES IN NEW HAMPSHIRE, TAKEN BY ORDER OF THE CONVENTION, WITH THE NUMBER OF FIRE ARMS, THE POWDER, &c.: 1775—Continued.

COUNTIES AND TOWNS.	Males under 16.	Males from 16 to 50 not in the Army.	Males above 50.	Persons in the Army.	Females.	Negroes and Slaves for life.	Total.	Fire arms fit for use.	Fire arms wanting.	Public stock of powder.	Powder in private hands.
Strafford county:											
Dover	410	342	74	28	786	26	1,666	180		60	
Durham	286	185	68	57	593	25	1,214	222		200	76
Lee	236	147	58	12	497	4	954	119	51	24	51
Somersworth	245	129	36	46	479	30	965		184		
Barrington	464	245	72	23	848	3	1,655	184			
Gilmanton	238	151	16	12	357	1	775	99	46	44	5
Sandbornton	120	87	12	20	219	1	459				
Rochester	396	303	61	26	759	3	1,548	206		36	36
Madbury	164	117	38	7	345	6	677	78	62	60	60
Barnstead	82	53	4	2	111		252	28	25		
New-Durham	70	50	15	6	144	1	286	27	20		3
Do. Gore	35	20	1	0	44		100		10		
Middleton	72	40	7	6	108		233	27	20		4
Eastown[1]	86	70	10	4	149	1	320				
Leavitts-Town[2]	23	16	2	3	39		83	11	5		2
Wolfeborough	57	53	4	4	91	2	211	34	25	25	5
Moultonborough	76	61	9	4	122		272	31			
Sandwich	81	45	9	1	109		245	27		36	
Holderness	49	36	7	0	80		172	25	10		1
Meredith	70	50	7	10	122		259	30	26	50	
Campton	57	44	5	1	83		190				
Tamworth	50	32	2	3	64		151	17			
Gore	4	6	3		13		26	4	2		1
Cheshire county:											
Swanzey	168	118	25	20	316	0	647	72	50	0	16
Walpole	214	100	26	33	283	2	658			21	
Rindge	135	108	12	35	250	2	542		21		
Westmoreland	213	127	23	38	357	0	758	63	67		
Winchester	207	112	30	18	354	2	723	68			18
Hinsdale										0	0
Gilsum	45	32	10	7	84	0	178	15		0	20
Cornish	83	77	9	4	136	0	309	53	33	0	5
Surry	59	37	8	7	104	0	215	23	22		
Plainfield	78	83	13	0	134	0	308	36	49		
Charlestown	158	94	17	22	303		594				9
Dublin	88	54	9	10	143	1	305	32	31		
Claremont	148	125	18	1	231	0	523	60	65		
Alstead	88	79	5	4	141	0	317	18		0	0
Marlow	56	45	6	9	91	0	207		26		
Newport	46	39	4	1	67	0	157	14			2
Croydon	37	34	2	3	67	0	143			0	5
Acworth											
Saville	15	14	4	3	29	0	65	5			
Unity	39	35	3	7	62	0	146	13	25	0	0
Jaffrey	90	72	8	16	165	0	351				
Fitzwilliam[3]											
Marlborough	104	54	2	14	148	0	322	26	28		5
Packersfield	52	34	4	13	83	0	186	23	10		6
Stoddard	75	38	7	11	93	0	224	14	24	0	0
Chesterfield	241	155	30	36	412	0	874	86	99	0	0
Washington	47	29	4	6	77	0	163	13		0	6
Lempster	43	31	4	1	49	0	128	17	18	0	0
Richmond	280	143	16	26	395	0	860	56	88		5
Keene	174	140	24	31	387	0	756	72	92	90	22
Grafton county:											
Haverhill	97	69	9	17	169	4	365			50	5
Plymouth	93	83	15	8	178	5	382				6
Lebanon	86	91	13	2	155	0	347			60	
New-Chester	66	32	5	5	88	0	196	26	11	0	2
Hanover	98	108	12	22	184	10	434	45	177	48	
Canaan	16	17	3	3	28	0	67	17	0	0	0
Cockermoth	35	23	2	5	53	0	118	18	27	0	3
Lyme	57	61	10	8	116	0	252	30	31	38	0
Orford	60	42	7	5	106	2	222	13	29	0	30
Rumney	77	41	4	11	104	0	237				0
Piermont	52	28	4	15	69	0	168	1	31	16	0
Bath	47	25	5	10	57	0	144	8	24	15	8
Gunthwaite	14	6	2	5	20	0	47		6	14	
Lancaster	17	15	0	2	27	0	61	8	7	0	11
Alexandria	38	26	7	8	58	0	137	18		0	0
Northumberland	16	20	2	0	19	0	57	7	15	0	70
Thornton	26	26	5	8	52	0	117	6	25	0	3
Lyman											
Conway	79	51	6	18	117	2	273	40	44	25	
Grantham	11	20	4	1	37	1	74	2	18	0	0

[1] Now (1824) Wakefield.   [2] Now (1824) Effingham.   [3] Joined with Swanzey in this enumeration.

NEW HAMPSHIRE—Continued.

TABLE **78.**—RETURN OF THE NUMBER OF INHABITANTS IN THE SEVERAL TOWNS AND PLACES IN NEW HAMPSHIRE, TAKEN BY ORDER OF THE CONVENTION, WITH THE NUMBER OF FIRE ARMS, THE POWDER, &c.: 1775—Continued.

COUNTIES AND TOWNS.	Males under 16.	Males from 16 to 50 not in the Army.	Males above 50.	Persons in the Army.	Females.	Negroes and Slaves for life.	Total.	FIRE ARMS & POWDER.			
								Fire arms fit for use.	Fire arms wanting.	Public stock of Powder.	Powder in private hands.
Grafton county—Continued.											
Grafton											
Trecothick											
Fairfield											
Coventry											
Landaff	14	8	2	1	15	0	40	1			8
Morristown	10	5	0	1	13	0	29	3	0	0	3
Apthorp											
Dartmouth								4			
Stratford	15	14	0	2	10	0	41	7	7	0	12
Colebrook	0	1	0	0	3	0	4	1			
Cockburne	5	5	0	1	3	0	14	3	2	0	3
Stewart-Town											
Enfield	15	17	1	0	17	0	50	10	7	0	0
Wentworth [1]											
Warren [2]											

[1] Joined with Orford.   [2] Joined with Piermont in this enumeration.

TABLE **79.**—FREE AND SLAVE POPULATION OF NEW HAMPSHIRE, BY COUNTIES AND TOWNS: CENSUS OF 1786.[1]

[In this census the selectmen of the different towns were directed to ascertain "the whole number of white and other free citizens, inhabitants of every age, sex, and condition, including those bound to servitude for a term of years; and also in a separate column, or class, all other persons not comprehended in the foregoing description, except Indians not paying taxes."]

COUNTIES AND TOWNS.	Whole number.	Slaves.	Other persons.
Rockingham county:			
Allenstown	175		
Atkinson	500		
Candia	959		23 "not free citizens."
Canterbury	857	3	
Chester	1,757	2	
Concord	1,397		5 "other persons."
Deerfield	1,283		
East Kingston	420		
Epping	1,340		7 blacks.
Exeter	1,592		
Greenland	655	7	
Hampton	866		1 black.
Hampton Falls	569		
Hawke (Danville)	301		
Kensington	798		
Loudon	822		"No blacks to be numbered."
Newington	456		20 blacks.
New Market	1,172	2	
Newtown	343		
Northfield	349		
Northwood	575		
North Hampton	659		
Nottingham	1,015		11 negroes.
Pelham	875		
Pembroke	991		3 blacks.
Pittsfield	598		
Plaistow	551		
Poplin	500		
Portsmouth—"whites"	4,133		89 blacks.
Raymond	786		
Rye	653		2 "other persons."
Salem	1,075	7	
Sandown	521		
Seabrook	668		
South Hampton	450		2 blacks.
Stratham—"whites"	894		13 blacks.
Windham	583		9 blacks living with their masters.
Total	32,138	21	185
Hillsborough county:			
Acworth	482		1 black.
Alstead	943		
Amherst	1,912		
Andover	410		
Antrim	289		
Bedford	778		7 "of the other class."
Boscowen	827		4 negroes.
Charlestown	968		
Chesterfield	1,535		
Cornish	605		

[1] Provincial Papers of New Hampshire, Vol. X, page 689.

NEW HAMPSHIRE—Continued.

TABLE 79.—FREE AND SLAVE POPULATION OF NEW HAMPSHIRE, BY COUNTIES AND TOWNS: CENSUS OF 1786—
Continued.

COUNTIES AND TOWNS.	Whole number.	Slaves.	Other persons.
Hillsborough county—Continued.			
Derryfield	338	....	
Dunbarton	741	....	
Dunstable.....................................	554	....	"other sex's none."
Duxbury and Mile-Slip....................	140	....	
Fisherfield (now Newbury)	217	....	
Goffstown....................................	1,048	....	15 blacks.
Hancock......................................	291	....	
Henniker.....................................	858	....	4 "black servants."
Hollis..	1,421	2	
Hopkinton....................................	1,536	....	1 "other person."
Mason..	866	....	
Merrimack....................................	692	....	9 blacks.
New Bradford................................	128	....	2 negroes.
New Ipswich..................................	1,049	....	
New London...................................	219	....	
Nottingham West.............................	1,010	....	
Peterborough-Slip...........................	175	....	"none bound to servitude."
Peterborough.................................	824	7	
Rahy..	262	....	
Salisbury....................................	1,045	....	
Society Land.................................	157	....	
Sutton.......................................	337	....	
Temple.......................................	701	....	
Weare..	1,574	....	
Wilton.......................................	1,001	....	5 blacks.
Total................................	25,933	9	48
Strafford county:			
Barnstead....................................	568	1	
Barrington...................................	990	....	
Burton.......................................	74	....	
Dover..	1,427	4	
Durham.......................................	1,230	3	
Eaton..	138	....	1 negro girl—"cripel."
Effingham....................................	54	....	1 aged gentleman—town charge. 3 blacks.
Gilmanton....................................	1,636	....	
Lee..	956	....	
Madbury......................................	585	....	
Meredith.....................................	572	....	
Moultonborough..............................	400	....	
New Durham...................................	242	....	3 negroes.
Rochester....................................	2,453	....	
Sanbornton...................................	1,107	....	
Sandwich.....................................	653	....	
Tamworth.....................................	287	1	
Wakefield....................................	505	....	
Total................................	13,877	9	8
Cheshire county:			
Claremont....................................	914	3	48 "transcint persons."
Croydon......................................	381	....	
Dublin.......................................	658	....	
Fitzwilliam..................................	870	....	
Gilsum.......................................	304	....	1 black.
Hinsdale.....................................	326	4	
Keene..	1,122	....	
Lempster.....................................	322	....	
Marlborough..................................	618	....	
Marlow.......................................	252	....	
New Grantham.................................	201	....	
Newport......................................	552	....	2 blacks.
Packersfield.................................	567	....	
Plainfield...................................	580	....	
Protectworth.................................	127	....	
Richmond.....................................	1,250	....	
Rindge.......................................	759	....	
Stoddard.....................................	563	....	
Swanzey......................................	1,000	....	
Unity..	404	....	
Washington...................................	474	....	
Westmoreland.................................	1,621	....	
Wendell......................................	195	....	
Winchester...................................	1,100	....	3 blacks.
Total................................	15,160	7	54
Grafton county:			
Alexandria...................................	291	....	
Bath...	335	....	
Campton......................................	307	....	
Canaan.......................................	253	....	
Cardigan.....................................	80	....	

NEW HAMPSHIRE—Continued.

TABLE 79.—FREE AND SLAVE POPULATION OF NEW HAMPSHIRE, BY COUNTIES AND TOWNS: CENSUS OF 1786—Continued.

COUNTIES AND TOWNS.	Whole number.	Slaves.	Other persons.
Grafton county—Continued.			
Cockermouth	281		
Gunthwaite	152		
Dorchester	116		
Enfield	484		
Grafton	350		4 servants bound out for a term of time.
Hanover	866		4 "not comprehended" in other classes.
Haverhill	458		
Lancaster	102		
Lebanon	841		2 "not included," etc.
Lyman	116		
Lyme	490		12 "not included."
New Chester	496		
New Holderness	260		7 transient persons.
Orford	363		5 negroes, 8 transient persons.
Piermont	353		3 male negroes.
Plymouth	528		4 others.
Rumney	359		
Thornton	295		7 other persons.
Wentworth	168		
Total	8,344	0	56

Summary of the census of 1786, by counties.

COUNTIES.	No. of towns.	Free inhabitants.	Slaves.	Others.	Total population.
Rockingham	37	32,138	21	185	32,344
Strafford	18	13,877	9	8	13,894
Hillsborough	35	25,933	9	48	25,990
Cheshire	24	15,160	7	6	15,173
Grafton	24	8,344	0	56	8,400
Total	138	95,452	46	303	95,801

MASSACHUSETTS.

TABLE 80.—MALE AND FEMALE NEGRO SLAVE POPULATION OF MASSACHUSETTS, BY COUNTIES AND TOWNS: CENSUS OF 1754.[1]

COUNTIES AND TOWNS.	NEGRO SLAVES.			COUNTIES AND TOWNS.	NEGRO SLAVES.		
	Male.	Female.	Total.		Male.	Female.	Total.
Suffolk county	798	424	1,274	Essex county—Continued.			
				Boxford	4	4	8
Boston	647	342	989	Methuen			
Dorchester	18	13	31	Middleton	9	3	12
Roxbury	38	15	53	Danvers	9	12	21
Weymouth	12	11	23				
Hingham			[2]17	Middlesex county	210	123	361
Dedham							
Braintree	20	16	36	Charlestown			
Hull:				Watertown	7	5	12
In the town	7	4		Medford	27	7	34
At the lighthouse	3 10	1 5	15	Cambridge	33	23	56
Medfield	3	1	4	Concord	10	5	15
Milton	15	4	19	Sudbury	9	5	14
Wrentham	13	3	16	Woburn	9	8	17
Brookline	10	7	17	Reading	14	6	20
Needham	1	0	1	Malden	16	5	21
Medway	4	3	7	Groton	7	7	14
Bellingham	1	1	2	Billerica	3	5	8
Walpole	0	1	1	Chelmsford			[2]8
Stoughton	6	2	8	Marlborough	3	3	6
Chelsea			[2]35	Dunstable			
				Sherburne	3		3
Essex county	178	122	439	Stow			
				Newton	10	3	13
Salem	47	36	83	Framingham			
Ipswich			[2]62	Dracut			
Newbury	34	16	50	Weston	8	2	10
Lynn				Lexington	13	11	24
Gloucester			[2]61	Littleton	3	5	8
Rowley	10	2	12	Hopkinton			[2]15
Salisbury	6	1	7	Holliston			
Wenham			[2]16	Stoneham	6	2	8
Manchester	1	5	6	Westford			[2]5
Haverhill	8	8	16	Bedford	2	4	6
Andover	28	14	42	Wilmington	4	3	7
Marblehead				Townsend	2	1	3
Topsfield	4	1	5	Tewksbury	1	1	2
Amesbury	3	2	5	Acton	1		1
Beverly	12	16	28	Waltham	2	2	4
Bradford	3	2	5				

[1] J. H. Benton, jr.: "Early Census Making in Massachusetts, 1643 to 1765," pages 12 to 17.　　　　[2] Not returned by sex.

MASSACHUSETTS—Continued.

TABLE **80.**—MALE AND FEMALE NEGRO SLAVE POPULATION OF MASSACHUSETTS, BY COUNTIES AND TOWNS: CENSUS OF 1754—Continued.

COUNTIES AND TOWNS.	NEGRO SLAVES.			COUNTIES AND TOWNS.	NEGRO SLAVES.		
	Male.	Female.	Total.		Male.	Female.	Total.
Middlesex county—Continued.				Plymouth county—Continued.			
Shirley	1		1	Pembroke	6	4	10
Pepperell				Abington	5	2	7
Natick		3	3	Kingston	3	3	6
Lincoln	16	7	23	Hanover:			
				Nathaniel Sylvester	1		
Worcester county	47	22	88	David Stockbridge, Esq	1	1	
				Rev. Mr. Benjamin Bass	1	1	
Lancaster	4	1	5	Job Tilden	1	1	
Mendon			¹8	Capt. Ezekiel Turner	1		
Brookfield				Samuel House		1	
Oxford	3	1	4	Joshua Barstow		1	
Worcester	4	4	8	Matthew Estes		2	
Leicester	5	1	6	Caleb Barker		1	
Rutland	1	2	3	Amos Sylvester		1	
Sutton			¹3	John Bailey	1		
Westborough	4	2	6	Richard Curtis	1		
Uxbridge:				Isaac Turner	7	1 10	17
Rev. Mr. Webb	2			Halifax	2	2	4
Deacon Read	1			Wareham			
John Elleson	4		7				
Southborough:				Bristol county	39	22	122
Rev. Mr. Nathan Stone		1	1				
Shrewsbury	3	1	4	Taunton			¹27
Lunenburgh	6	2	8	Rehoboth			
Dudley	1	1	2	Dartmouth			¹34
Harvard				Swanzey			
Grafton			¹6	Freetown	14	7	21
Upton				Attleborough	7	3	10
Hardwick				Norton			
Bolton	2	1	3	Dighton	9	9	18
Sturbridge	2	2	4	Easton	2	1	3
Holden				Raynham			
Western	2	1	3	Berkley	7	2	9
Douglass							
N. Braintree				Nantucket county			
Spencer:							
Rev. Mr. Joshua Eaton	2	1	3	Sherburne			₄
Leominster	1	1	2				
Rutland District			¹2	Barnstable county	36	30	76
Hampshire county	56	18	74	Barnstable	18	15	33
				Sandwich	4	4	8
Springfield	22	5	27	Yarmouth			
Hadley	13	5	18	Eastham	6	5	11
Westfield	15	4	19	Falmouth			¹10
Hatfield	5	4	9	Chatham			
Deerfield				Truro			
Northampton				Provincetown			
Northfield				Harwich	8	6	14
Sunderland							
Brimfield				Dukes county	3	4	7
Blandford							
Pelham				Edgarton			
Palmer	1		1	Tisbury			
Southampton				Chilmark	3	4	7
South Hadley							
Greenfield				York county	75	41	147
New Salem							
Montague				York			¹24
Granville				Kittery	18	17	35
Greenwich				Wells	12	4	16
Sheffield				Falmouth	16	5	21
Stockbridge				Scarborough	7	4	11
				Berwick	14	8	22
Plymouth county	²63	49	²124	Biddeford			
				Arundel	2	1	3
Plymouth			₄	N. Yarmouth	2	1	3
Scituate	22	21	43	Brunswick	2	1	3
Duxborough				Georgetown			¹7
Marshfield:				Newcastle			
Kenelm Winslow, Esq	3	4		Gorhamtown	2		2
John Winslow, Esq		1					
Mr. Jedediah Bourn	3	1		Total for colony	²1,505	855	², ³2,712
Deacon Israel Thomas	1						
Thomas Foord	1			Suffolk county	798	424	1,274
Anthony Thomas	1			Essex county	178	122	439
Thomas Foster	2			Middlesex county	210	123	361
Capt. Abijah White		1		Worcester county	47	22	88
John Little, Esq	3			Hampshire county	56	18	74
Edward Oaksman	1			Plymouth county	²63	49	²124
Widow Jude Clift	1			Bristol county	39	22	122
Mr. Nath. Ray Thomas	1	²18 7	²25	Nantucket county			
Bridgewater				Barnstable county	36	30	76
Middleborough			¹12	Dukes county	3	4	7
Rochester				York county	75	41	147
Plympton							

¹ Not returned by sex.　　　² Corrected figures.　　　³ Includes 352 not returned by sex.

MASSACHUSETTS—Continued.

MASSACHUSETTS (INCLUDING MAINE): CENSUS OF 1784.[1]

NOTE.—By multiplying the total number of polls by 4, Dr. Felt computes the population of Massachusetts in 1784 at 310,968, and that of Maine at 55,216. Dr. Chickering, by multiplying only the number of rateable and not rateable polls by 4½, obtains for the population of Massachusetts 346,653, and for Maine 61,406.

Recapitulation.

COUNTIES.	NUMBER OF POLLS.[2]		COUNTIES.	NUMBER OF POLLS.[2]	
	Rateable and not rateable.	Supported by the town.		Rateable and not rateable.	Supported by the town.
Barnstable	3,148	88	Worcester	12,263	86
Berkshire	5,892	15	Cumberland[3]	3,708	
Bristol	6,197	83	Lincoln[3]	5,071	35
Dukes	718	4	York[3]	4,944	46
Essex	11,023	115			
Hampshire	11,497	34		90,757	789
Middlesex	9,691	76		789	
Nantucket	813	21			
Plymouth	6,425	47		91,546×4=366,184	
Suffolk	9,367	139			

[1] Collections of the Am. Stat. Association, vol. 1, page 170.   [2] Includes all male persons between 16 and 100 years of age.   [3] In the district of Maine.

TABLE 81.—WHITE, NEGRO, INDIAN, AND FRENCH NEUTRAL POPULATION OF MASSACHUSETTS, BY COUNTIES AND TOWNS: CENSUS OF 1764.[1]

COUNTIES AND TOWNS.	Houses.	Families.	WHITES UNDER 16 YEARS.		WHITES ABOVE 16 YEARS.		NEGROES & MULATTOES.		INDIANS.		FRENCH NEUTRALS.				Total.
											Under 16 years.		Above 16 years.		
			Male.	Female.	Male.	Female.	Male.	Female.	Male.	Female.	Male.	Female.	Male.	Female.	
Suffolk county:															
Boston	1,676	2,069	4,109	4,010	2,941	3,612	510	301	21	16					15,520
Roxbury	212	212	291	324	371	421	47	33			1	3	1	1	1,493
Dorchester	204	245	292	284	343	404	23	14							1,360
Milton	124	141	215	222	214	245	31	16			2	1	1	1	948
Braintree	327	357	571	590	555	651	31	35	1	1	1	3	3	3	2,445
Weymouth	203	248	275	294	315	347	13	14							1,258
Hingham	375	426	594	539	555	702	38	39			7	11	9	12	2,506
Hull	31	33	31	27	39	57	9	7							170
Stoughton	265	424	593	555	567	580	9	17	9	10					2,340
Dedham	239	309	417	441	484	531	21	15	3	3		1	2	1	1,919
Medfield	113	121	111	126	176	211	3	1	2	4	1	2	1	1	639
Wrentham	293	347	464	463	514	551	18	12	1		4	1	1	1	2,030
Medway	123	138	165	178	215	210	10	7	1		1	1	2	3	793
Bellingham	72	82	119	111	116	108	8								462
Needham	129	168	209	226	246	250	8	6							945
Brookline	53	53	68	62	97	93	13	5							338
Chelsea	54	70	110	85	99	125	20	13							452
Walpole	100	106	188	177	207	209	2	2				1	3	3	792
Total	4,593	5,549	8,822	8,714	8,054	9,307	814	537	38	34	17	24	23	26	36,410
Essex county:															
Salem	509	923	884	985	1,050	1,335	117	56			8	3	13	18	4,469
Danvers	288	381	458	468	501	634	37	35			2	8	5	3	2,151
Ipswich	531	670	791	801	931	1,119	60	40			6	6	7	9	3,770
Newbury	401	489	622	605	819	872	21	17			1	1	1	1	2,960
Newburyport	357	546	613	566	739	837	35	29			15	11	14	23	2,882
Marblehead	519	935	1,189	1,031	1,199	1,435	71	29							4,954
Lynn	275	388	489	481	531	648	31	18			3	5	1	1	2,208
Andover	360	438	533	558	565	700	56	30			7	7	3	3	2,462
Beverly	307	404	495	482	472	635	37	42	1				2	5	2,171
Rowley	239	290	222	329	411	493	11	11				2	1	1	1,481
Salisbury	201	240	280	322	354	366	5	2			3	4	4	4	1,344
Haverhill	304	350	494	469	505	487	13	12			3	3	2	4	1,992
Glocester	404	677	865	841	887	1,061	57	52			1	1	4	3	3,772
Topsfield	105	130	160	141	183	219	12	4							719
Boxford	128	149	200	194	220	227	5	5							851
Almsbury	242	264	351	366	389	444	8	9							1,567
Bradford	173	192	257	238	281	384	9	6			2	2	1	1	1,181
Wenham	72	95	125	120	120	166	13	15	3	2					564
Middleton	83	97	125	121	140	160	14	21							581
Manchester	103	155	159	163	183	203	10	13	1		1	4	1	1	739
Methuen	158	158	250	194	247	239	2			1					933
Total	5,759	7,971	9,562	9,475	10,727	12,664	624	446	5	3	52	57	59	77	43,751
Middlesex county:															
Cambridge	237	257	311	286	374	510	47	43			2	2	4	3	1,582
Charlestown	289	375	369	392	486	648	84	52			2	2	6	7	2,048
Watertown	103	117	172	136	179	195	5	6							693
Woburn	228	287	365	314	373	424	20	19							1,515
Concord	244	265	335	389	381	432	15	12							1,564

[1] Early Census Making in Massachusetts 1643 to 1765. Corrections in additions have been made where necessary.

MASSACHUSETTS—Continued.

TABLE 81.—WHITE, NEGRO, INDIAN, AND FRENCH NEUTRAL POPULATION OF MASSACHUSETTS, BY COUNTIES AND TOWNS: CENSUS OF 1764—Continued.

COUNTIES AND TOWNS.	Houses.	Families.	WHITES UNDER 16 YEARS. Male.	Fe-male.	WHITES ABOVE 16 YEARS. Male.	Fe-male.	NEGROES & MULATTOES. Male.	Fe-male.	INDIANS. Male.	Fe-male.	FRENCH NEUTRALS. Under 16 years. Male.	Fe-male.	Above 16 years. Male.	Fe-male.	Total.
Middlesex county—Continued.															
Newton	174	222	304	316	322	348	10	7		1					1,308
Sudbury	263	316	422	416	436	471	15	12	1						1,773
Marlboro	183	213	307	255	348	356	10	11							1,287
Billerica	189	223	312	235	313	360	8	6							1,234
Framingham	205	234	325	302	306	347	14	11			1	1	2	4	1,313
Lexington	126	142	210	189	228	241	26	18							912
Chelmsford	133	176	224	227	246	304	7	4							1,012
Sherborn	106	113	172	140	156	187	4	8	2	1		2	1		673
Reading	224	296	335	339	400	422	25	9				1	3	3	1,537
Malden	144	174	206	210	230	289	27	21			4	3	1	1	992
Weston	105	126	195	175	196	184	10	8							768
Medford	104	147	161	150	207	223	29	18				2			790
Littleton	122	143	160	175	212	209	8	9							773
Hopkinston	135	154	242	274	223	271	9	7				1			1,027
Westford	143	169	231	217	233	269	5	7							962
Waltham	94	107	145	162	169	174	8	5							663
Wilmington	94	97	166	159	164	174	6	4							673
Groton	174	242	365	365	340	358	8	7							1,443
Shirley	41	72	122	102	90	110	4	2							430
Ston	121	135	196	191	194	204	6	3							794
Townsend	94	97	166	151	137	136	4	4							598
Stoneham	54	59	56	77	77	98	14	18							340
Natick	71	91	109	120	99	122	10	14	13	24					511
Dracut															
Bedford	67	72	101	116	100	124	9	7							457
Lincoln	84	99	153	170	145	153	20	5							646
Tewksbury	103	147	191	198	184	203	2	3							781
Holliston	103	115	168	170	183	176	5	3							705
Acton	96	100	142	147	160	159	1	2							611
Dunstable	90	98	140	122	138	143	9	7							559
Pepperrell	117	130	193	200	189	172	1	3							758
Total	[1]4,860	[1]5,810	7,771	7,587	8,218	9,196	485	375	16	29	9	11	17	18	33,732
Hampshire county:															
Springfield	404	477	641	608	697	770	27	12							2,755
Northampton	188	203	314	285	341	334	5	6							1,285
Southampton	66	76	92	100	117	127	1								437
Southadley	133	142	193	213	202	209									817
Hadley	89	99	125	127	150	151	13	7							573
Amherst	96	104	167	160	150	162	5	1							645
Hatfield	126	132	192	177	204	209	14	7			2	4	2	4	815
Westfield	191	195	341	328	318	296	23	18							1,324
Deerfield	85	123	188	157	193	182	11	6							737
Greenfield	45	58	106	79	95	87	1								368
Montague	49	64	97	99	95	100		1							392
Northfield	60	60	105	97	103	104	3	3							415
Brimfield	121	130	198	161	207	203	2	2							773
South Brimfield	90	91	142	130	151	147	2	2							574
Monson	68	69	107	79	101	95	3	4							389
Pelham	57	57	87	87	84	111	2								371
New Salem	62	69	99	87	99	89	1								375
Blanford	68	68	116	90	99	99	1	1							406
Palmer	74	88	123	110	133	140	2								508
Granville	100	123	197	149	180	152	3	1							682
Belchertown	61	68	112	99	99	108									418
Colrain	45	48	76	65	74	82									297
Ware	74	76	127	122	109	126		1							[1]545
Chesterfield	30	30	39	41	46	35									161
Bernardstown	38	40	56	68	54	53									231
Roxbury Canady, or Warwick	36	36	57	43	51	40									191
Shutesbury	56	59	76	98	82	73	1								330
Wilbraham	74	82	119	118	129	123	1	1							491
Sunderland															
Greenwich															
Huntstown															
Total	2,586	2,867	4,292	3,977	[1]4,423	4,407	121	73			2	4	2	4	[1]17,305
Worcester county:															
Worcester	204	229	376	350	370	357	11	5	4	5					1,478
Lancaster	301	328	514	421	505	532	12	14	1						1,999
Sutton	294	370	558	497	510	555	6	11							2,137
Mendon	284	336	466	425	441	497	5	4			1	2	1	1	1,843
Brookfield	267	283	493	412	439	452	10	5							1,811
Shrewsbury	199	223	367	319	339	360	7	8		1					1,401
Uxbridge	186	211	283	308	305	304	6	7							1,213
Westborough	163	181	278	218	277	324	4	5	1	3					1,110
Southboro	110	126	160	161	184	216	5	5							731
Rutland	166	182	275	244	281	273	9	8							1,090

¹ Corrected figures.

MASSACHUSETTS—Continued.

TABLE 81.—WHITE, NEGRO, INDIAN, AND FRENCH NEUTRAL POPULATION OF MASSACHUSETTS, BY COUNTIES AND TOWNS: CENSUS OF 1764—Continued.

COUNTIES AND TOWNS.	Houses.	Families.	WHITES UNDER 16 YEARS.		WHITES ABOVE 16 YEARS.		NEGROES & MULATTOES.		INDIANS.		FRENCH NEUTRALS.				Total.
											Under 16 years.		Above 16 years.		
			Male.	Female.	Male.	Female.	Male.	Female.	Male.	Female.	Male.	Female.	Male.	Female.	
Worcester county—Continued.															
Rutland district	118	118	187	192	177	159	10	9							734
Oxford	128	148	247	206	214	217	4	2							890
Charlton	114	124	191	164	195	188	1				1		1		741
Leicester	119	146	187	170	210	196	4	3							770
Spencer	100	111	174	173	160	152	2	3							664
New Braintree	94	98	152	146	152	141	2	1							594
Oakham	41	41	73	78	60	58	1								270
Lunenburg	145	175	220	136	237	221	5	2							821
Bolton	145	155	234	225	225	239	1	1			1	5	1	1	933
Sturbridge	136	136	212	240	218	219	3	1	2	1	1		1	1	899
Hardwick	153	161	259	256	239	251	3		1	1					1,010
Grafton	109	109	178	175	193	196	5	2	6	8					763
Upton	94	104	158	159	135	157	3	2					3	2	619
Leominster	104	107	186	199	173	180	2	3							743
Holden	62	75	161	116	109	107	1	1							495
Western	92	100	138	148	155	138	3	1							583
Douglass	90	97	142	139	111	129									521
Harvard	153	173	276	270	272	296	7	5							1,126
Dudley															
Petersham	100	115	202	186	166	145	3	5							707
Templetown	65	64	95	84	88	81									348
Westminster	86	86	133	108	112	113									466
Athol	41	60	88	81	103	85	2								359
Princetown	57	55	82	65	72	65									284
Fitchburgh	43	43	70	66	61	60	1	1							259
Total	¹4,563	5,070	7,815	7,137	7,488	7,663	138	114	15	19	4	7	7	5	30,412
Plymouth county:															
Plymouth	256	373	488	475	532	605	38	39	23	25	3	2	9	7	2,246
Bridgewater	571	630	964	932	910	1,042	45	49	8	15	8	9	3	5	3,990
Middleboro'	498	577	855	841	804	880	17	15	8	18					3,438
Scituate	348	431	516	520	603	742	55	52	4	9					2,501
Rochester	272	326	470	442	485	520	12	10	10	27	1	2	3	3	1,985
Pembroke	210	283	315	290	357	425	14	8	7	21	5	2	1	1	1,446
Duxborg'	154	197	238	220	273	311	3	5	1	5			1	4	1,061
Marshfield	150	168	287	218	274	328	25	15	1	4	2		1	4	1,159
Plimpton	186	232	352	236	328	362	9	3	7	13	3	1	2	1	1,317
Kingston	110	131	194	162	196	196	6	5			4		5	6	774
Abington	174	217	323	308	300	311	11	10							1,263
Hallifax	85	97	122	130	127	166	6	5		1					557
Wareham	57	81	123	119	116	140	2	3	6	10					519
Hanover															
Total	3,071	3,743	5,247	4,893	5,305	6,028	243	219	75	148	26	16	25	31	22,256
Barnstable county:															
Barnstable	325	361	474	432	524	622	36	20	6	7	6	6	3	2	2,138
Yarmouth	255	295	400	405	427	486	11	11	12	19	3	2	3	1	1,780
Sandwich	200	245	313	317	346	368	18	14	30	43					1,449
Harwich	235	283	398	386	420	454	12	11	35	56					1,772
Eastham	182	237	292	267	342	415	5	6	1	3					1,331
Wellfleet	129	157	243	217	216	227	9	5	3	8					928
Falmouth	145	182	266	266	266	234	19	12	35	27					1,125
Truro	107	134	225	230	241	222	3	3		1					925
Chatham	105	127	145	153	173	202	4	1							678
Mashpee	82	85	23	19	15	20	18	13	101	129					338
Total	1,765	¹2,106	2,779	2,692	2,970	3,250	135	96	223	293	9	8	6	3	12,464
Bristol county:															
Taunton	397	493	651	617	678	734	26	29	1	8					2,744
Dartmouth	679	790	1,103	965	1,129	1,248	37	24	35	40					4,581
Rehoboth	498	617	964	901	818	954	28	25	1	5					3,696
Swanzey															
Attleboro'	266	301	461	419	422	422	13	2							1,739
Norton	295	343	477	447	460	528	19	11							1,942
Dighton	148	198	276	269	273	297	31	28	2	1					1,177
Easton	134	154	219	172	222	220	2	2	2	3					842
Raynham	100	109	170	146	181	184	3	3			1	1	2	3	694
Berkley	94	110	165	153	150	181	6	4		2					661
Freeton															
Total	2,611	3,115	4,486	4,089	4,333	4,768	165	128	41	59	1	1	2	3	18,076
York county:															
York	272	397	496	486	568	671	36	20			6	5	4	6	2,298
Kittery	288	372	489	490	551	766	31	31			3	3	2	2	2,368
Berwick	222	364	664	552	567	547	20	24							2,374
Wells	219	251	427	382	363	357	21	13			3	1	1	1	1,569

¹ Corrected figures.

MASSACHUSETTS—Continued.

TABLE 81.—WHITE, NEGRO, INDIAN, AND FRENCH NEUTRAL POPULATION OF MASSACHUSETTS, BY COUNTIES AND TOWNS: CENSUS OF 1764—Continued.

COUNTIES AND TOWNS.	Houses.	Families.	WHITES UNDER 16 YEARS.		WHITES ABOVE 16 YEARS.		NEGROES & MULATTOES.		INDIANS.		FRENCH NEUTRALS.				Total.
											Under 16 years.		Above 16 years.		
			Male.	Female.	Male.	Female.	Male.	Female.	Male.	Female.	Male.	Female.	Male.	Female.	
York county—Continued.															
Arundel	124	138	216	228	190	194	2	3			1	1	1	1	837
Biddeford	87	116	182	186	178	179	8	14			1	3	1	1	753
Pepperelboro	66	96	140	126	145	125	2						2		540
Narraganset No. 1															
Total	1,278	1,734	2,614	2,450	2,562	2,839	120	105			14	13	11	11	10,739
Cumberland county:															
Falmouth	160	585	969	918	964	875	30	14			2	7		4	3,783
North Yarmo	154	188	251	277	278	255	8	10							1,079
Scarborough	200	210	353	281	319	304	10	5							1,272
Harpswell	55	111	224	224	188	186	4	10							836
Brunswick	73	73	139	114	149	98	3	1							504
Gorham															
Windham															
Pearson town															
Total	642	1,167	1,936	1,814	1,898	1,718	55	40			2	7		4	7,474
Lincoln county:															
Pownalboro'	161	175	210	223	225	232	6	3							899
Georgetown	180	184	388	325	317	287	8	4							1,329
Newcastle	69	69	127	117	100	109	1								454
Topsham	54	52	78	85	85	78	1								327
Woolwich	64	63	116	110	92	97									415
Bowdoinham	38	37	63	53	59	44	1								220
Total	566	580	982	913	878	847	17	7							3,644
Dukes county:															
Edgartown	128	150	234	209	233	248	12	8	37	49					1,030
Chilmark	90	114	152	156	159	179	9	8	72	116					851
Tisbury	110	100	165	166	226	233	4	5	15	24					838
Total	328	364	551	531	618	660	25	21	124	189					2,719
Nantucket county:															
Sherburne	413	602	776	758	904	882	24	20	83	66	13				3,526
Berks county:															
Great Barrington	87	91	127	121	149	134	9	10							550
Sheffield	126	172	250	276	272	249	16	10							1,073
Sandisfield	66	69	126	93	105	81	2	2							409
Tyringham	51	55	95	85	77	66	2								325
Pittsfield	39	70	110	114	105	89	6	4							428
Egremont															
Stockbridge	34	34	50	46	64	57	15	12	108	113					465
New Marlboro															
No. 4															
Total	403	491	758	735	772	676	50	38	108	113					3,250
Total for colony	31,707	43,483	52,859	50,588	53,752	59,501	2,824	2,067	728	953	133	128	141	167	223,841

Summary of white, negro, Indian, and French neutral population of Massachusetts, by counties: census of 1764.

COUNTIES.	Houses.	Families.	WHITES.				NEGROES AND MULATTOES.		INDIANS.		FRENCH NEUTRALS.				Total population.
			Under 16 years.		Above 16 years.						Under 16 years.		Above 16 years.		
			Male.	Female.	Male.	Female.	Male.	Female.	Male.	Female.	Male.	Female.	Male.	Female.	
Total for state	31,707	43,483	52,859	50,588	53,752	59,501	2,824	2,067	728	953	133	128	141	167	223,841
Barnstable	1,765	2,286	2,779	2,692	2,970	3,250	135	96	223	293	9	8	6	3	12,464
Berks	403	491	758	735	772	676	50	38	108	113					3,250
Bristol	2,611	3,115	4,486	4,089	4,333	4,768	165	128	41	59	1	1	2	3	18,076
Dukes	328	364	551	531	618	660	25	21	124	189					2,719
Essex	5,759	7,971	9,562	9,475	10,727	12,664	624	446	5	3	52	57	59	77	43,751
Hampshire	2,586	2,867	4,292	3,977	4,363	4,407	121	73			2	4	2	4	17,245
Middlesex	5,618	11,425	7,771	7,587	8,218	9,196	485	375	16	29	9	11	17	18	33,732
Nantucket	413	602	776	758	904	882	24	20	83	66	13				3,526
Plymouth	3,071	3,743	5,247	4,893	5,305	6,028	243	219	75	148	26	16	25	31	22,256
Suffolk	4,593	5,549	8,822	8,714	8,054	9,307	·814	537	38	34	17	24	23	26	36,410
Worcester	4,560	5,070	7,815	7,137	7,488	7,663	138	114	15	19	4	7	7	5	30,412

MASSACHUSETTS—Continued.

Summary of white, negro, Indian, and French neutral population of Maine, by counties: census of 1764.

COUNTIES.	Houses.	Families.	WHITES.				NEGROES AND MULATTOES.		INDIANS.		FRENCH NEUTRALS.				Total population.
			Under 16 years.		Above 16 years.						Under 16 years.		Above 16 years.		
			Male.	Female.	Male.	Female.	Male.	Female.	Male.	Female.	Male.	Female.	Male.	Female.	
Total for state...............	2,486	3,481	5,532	5,177	5,338	5,404	192	152	....	....	16	20	11	15	21,857
Cumberland.......................	642	1,167	1,936	1,814	1,898	1,718	55	40	....	....	2	7	....	4	7,474
Lincoln.........................	566	580	982	913	878	847	17	7	....	....	....	....	....	....	3,644
York............................	1,278	1,734	2,614	2,450	2,562	2,839	120	105	....	....	14	13	11	11	10,739

RHODE ISLAND.

TABLE **82.**—A LIST OF THE NUMBER OF FREEMEN AND MILITIA, WITH THE SERVANTS, WHITE AND BLACK, IN THE RESPECTIVE TOWNS; AS ALSO THE NUMBER OF INHABITANTS IN HER MAJESTY'S COLONY OF RHODE ISLAND, &c., DECEMBER THE 5TH, 1708.[1]

TOWNS.	Freemen.	Militia.	White Servants.	Black Servants.	Total No. of inhabitants.
Newport...	190	358	20	220	2,203
Providence...	241	283	6	7	1,446
Portsmouth...	98	104	8	40	628
Warwick..	80	95	4	10	480
Westerly...	95	100	5	20	570
New Shoreham...	38	47	....	6	208
Kingstown..	200	282	....	85	1,200
Jamestown..	33	28	9	32	206
Greenwich..	40	65	3	6	240
Total..	1,015	1,362	55	426	7,181

[1] Rhode Island Colonial Records, vol. 4, page 59.

It is to be understood that all men within this colony, from the age of sixteen to the age of sixty years, are of the militia, so that all freemen above and under said ages are inclusive in the abovesaid number of the militia.

As to the increase or decrease of the inhabitants within five years last past, we are not capable to give an exact account, by reason there was no list ever taken before this (the militia excepted), which hath increased since the 14th of February, 1704-5 (at which time a list was returned to your Lordships) the number of 287.

SAMUEL CRANSTON, Governor.

Newport, on Rhode Island, December the 5th, 1708.

TABLE **83.**—WHITE, NEGRO, AND INDIAN POPULATION OF RHODE ISLAND: 1748.[1]

TOWNS.	Whites.	Negroes.	Indians.	TOWNS.	Whites.	Negroes.	Indians.
Total......................	15,302	1,648	985	Westerly...............................	1,620	56	250
				North-Kingston........................	1,875	165	65
Newport....................	3,843	649	148	South-Kingston........................	965	333	225
Providence.................	3,707	128	81	East-Greenwich........................	1,149	40	34
Portsmouth.................	643	100	70	Jamestown.............................	222	80	19
Warwick....................	1,028	77	73	New-Shoreham..........................	250	20	20

[1] Callender's Historical Discourse, page 94.

TABLE **84.**—WHITE, NEGRO, AND INDIAN POPULATION OF THE COLONY OF RHODE ISLAND, ACCORDING TO THE OFFICIAL CENSUS OF 1774.[1]

TOWNS.	Families.	WHITES.				Total whites.	Indians.	Blacks.	Total of each town.
		Males.		Females.					
		Above 16.	Under 16.	Above 16.	Under 16.				
Total	9,450	14,032	12,731	15,349	12,348	54,460	1,479	3,668	[2]59,607
Newport.........................	1,590	2,100	1,558	2,624	1,635	7,917	46	1,246	9,209
Providence......................	655	1,219	850	1,049	822	3,950	68	303	4,321
Portsmouth......................	220	343	341	400	285	1,369	21	122	1,512
Warwick.........................	353	569	512	615	465	2,161	88	89	[2]2,338
Westerly........................	257	421	441	443	401	1,706	37	69	1,812
New Shoreham....................	75	109	119	121	120	469	51	55	575
East Greenwich..................	275	416	345	464	338	1,563	31	69	1,663
North Kingstown.................	361	538	497	595	552	2,182	79	211	2,472
South Kingstown.................	364	550	554	597	484	2,185	210	440	2,835
Jamestown.......................	69	110	90	118	82	400	32	131	563

[1] Census of Rhode Island, 1774 (printed in detail with the names of all heads of families in 1858), page 239.　　　[2] Corrected figures.

RHODE ISLAND—Continued.

TABLE 84.—WHITE, NEGRO, AND INDIAN POPULATION OF THE COLONY OF RHODE ISLAND, ACCORDING TO THE OFFICIAL CENSUS OF 1774—Continued.

TOWNS.	Families.	WHITES. Males. Above 16.	Males. Under 16.	Females. Above 16.	Females. Under 16.	Total whites.	Indians.	Blacks.	Total of each town.
Smithfield	476	742	665	769	638	2,814	23	51	2,888
Scituate	564	909	879	933	817	3,538	8	55	3,601
Glocester	525	743	724	740	719	2,926	....	19	2,945
West Greenwich	304	429	395	465	456	1,745	....	19	1,764
Charlestown	307	312	315	350	264	1,241	528	52	1,821
Coventry	274	474	555	493	470	1,992	11	20	2,023
Exeter	289	441	415	478	446	1,780	17	67	1,864
Middletown	123	210	179	259	156	804	13	64	881
Bristol	197	272	232	319	256	1,079	16	114	1,209
Tiverton	298	418	500	438	434	1,790	71	95	1,956
Warren	168	237	251	255	185	928	7	44	979
Little Compton	218	304	254	382	220	1,160	25	47	1,232
Richmond	189	286	316	324	287	1,213	20	24	1,257
Cumberland	264	400	408	478	450	1,736	3	17	1,756
Cranston	340	476	399	517	390	1,782	19	60	1,861
Hopkinton	299	427	420	477	415	1,739	21	48	1,808
Johnston	167	242	227	254	234	957	9	65	1,031
North Providence	138	193	172	230	197	792	7	31	830
Barrington	91	142	118	162	120	542	18	41	601

TABLE 85.—POPULATION OF RHODE ISLAND AT DIFFERENT DATES, FROM 1708 TO 1860, INCLUSIVE, BY COUNTIES AND TOWNS.[1]

COUNTIES AND TOWNS.	Date of incorporation or settlement.	1708	1730	1748	1755	1774	1776	1782	1790	1800	1810	1820	1830	1840	1850	1860
State total	1636	7,181	17,935	32,773	40,414	59,707	55,011	52,347	68,825	69,122	77,031	83,059	97,210	108,830	147,545	174,620
Bristol county	1747			1,749	2,005	2,789	2,610	2,471	3,211	3,801	5,072	5,637	5,446	6,476	8,514	8,907
Barrington	1770					601	538	534	683	650	604	634	612	549	795	1,000
Bristol	1747			1,069	1,080	1,209	1,067	1,032	1,406	1,678	2,693	3,197	3,034	3,490	4,616	5,271
Warren	1747			680	925	979	1,005	905	1,122	1,473	1,775	1,806	1,800	2,437	3,103	2,636
Kent county	1750	720	2,401	4,384	5,502	7,888	7,993	7,526	8,848	8,487	9,834	10,228	12,788	13,083	15,068	17,303
Coventry	1741			792	1,178	2,023	2,300	2,107	2,477	2,423	2,928	3,139	3,851	3,433	3,620	4,247
East Greenwich	1677	240	1,223	1,044	1,167	1,663	1,664	1,609	1,824	1,775	1,530	1,519	1,591	1,509	2,358	2,882
West Greenwich	1741			766	1,246	1,764	1,653	1,698	2,054	1,757	1,619	1,927	1,817	1,415	1,350	1,258
Warwick	1643	480	1,178	1,782	1,911	2,438	2,376	2,112	2,493	2,532	3,757	3,643	5,529	6,726	7,740	8,916
Newport county	1703	3,245	6,064	11,092	12,284	15,928	11,699	11,677	14,300	14,845	16,294	15,771	16,535	16,874	20,007	21,896
Fall River	1856															3,377
Jamestown	1678	206	321	420	517	563	322	345	507	501	504	448	415	365	358	400
Little Compton	1747			1,152	1,170	1,232	1,302	1,341	1,542	1,577	1,553	1,580	1,378	1,327	1,462	1,304
Middletown	1743			680	778	881	860	674	840	913	976	949	915	891	830	1,012
Newport	1639	2,203	4,640	6,508	6,753	9,209	5,299	5,530	6,716	6,739	7,907	7,319	8,010	8,333	9,563	10,508
New Shoreham	1672	208	290	300	378	575	478	478	682	714	722	955	1,185	1,069	1,262	1,320
Portsmouth	1638	628	813	992	1,363	1,512	1,347	1,350	1,560	1,684	1,795	1,645	1,727	1,706	1,833	2,048
Tiverton	1747			1,040	1,325	1,956	2,091	1,959	2,453	2,717	2,837	2,875	2,905	3,183	4,699	1,927
Providence county (towns)	1703			3,690	7,788	14,912	14,124	13,230	18,011	18,240	20,798	23,969	30,184	34,901	46,013	57,133
Burrillville	1806										1,834	2,164	2,196	1,982	3,538	4,140
Cranston	1754				1,460	1,861	1,701	1,589	1,877	1,644	2,161	2,274	2,652	2,901	4,311	7,500
Cumberland	1747			806	1,083	1,756	1,686	1,548	1,964	2,056	2,210	2,653	3,675	5,225	6,661	8,339
East Providence	1862															
Foster	1781							1,763	2,268	2,457	2,613	2,900	2,521	2,181	1,932	1,935
Glocester	1731			1,202	1,511	2,945	2,832	2,791	4,025	4,009	2,310	2,504	2,521	2,304	2,872	2,427
Johnston	1759					1,031	1,022	996	1,320	1,364	1,516	1,542	2,115	2,477	2,937	3,440
North Providence	1765					830	813	698	1,071	1,067	1,758	2,420	3,503	4,207	7,680	11,818
Pawtucket	1862															
Scituate	1731			1,232	1,813	3,601	3,289	1,628	2,315	2,523	2,568	2,834	3,993	4,090	4,582	4,251
Smithfield	1731			450	1,921	2,888	2,781	2,217	3,171	3,120	3,828	4,678·	6,857	9,534	11,500	13,283
Providence city	1636	1,446	3,916	3,452	3,159	4,321	4,355	4,310	6,380	7,614	10,071	11,767	16,836	23,172	41,513	50,666
Washington county	1729	1,770	5,554	8,406	9,676	13,869	14,230	13,133	18,075	16,135	14,962	15,687	15,421	14,324	16,430	18,715
Charlestown	1738			1,002	1,130	1,821	1,835	1,523	2,022	1,454	1,174	1,160	1,284	923	994	981
Exeter	1743			1,174	1,404	1,864	1,982	2,058	2,495	2,476	2,256	2,581	2,383	1,776	1,634	1,741
Hopkinton	1757					1,808	1,845	1,735	2,462	2,276	1,774	1,821	1,777	1,726	2,477	2,738
North Kingstown	1674	1,200	2,105	1,935	2,109	2,472	2,761	2,328	2,907	2,794	2,957	3,007	3,036	2,909	2,971	3,104
South Kingstown	1723		1,523	1,978	1,913	2,835	2,779	2,675	4,131	3,438	3,560	3,723	3,663	3,717	3,807	4,717
Richmond	1747			508	829	1,257	1,204	1,094	1,760	1,368	1,330	1,423	1,363	1,361	1,784	1,964
Westerly	1669	570	1,926	1,809	2,291	1,812	1,824	1,720	2,298	2,329	1,911	1,972	1,915	1,912	2,763	3,470

[1] Census of Rhode Island, 1865, page xxxii, prepared by Edwin M. Snow

CONNECTICUT.

TABLE 86.—WHITE, NEGRO, AND INDIAN POPULATION OF THE COLONY OF CONNECTICUT, BY COUNTIES AND TOWNS: CENSUS OF 1756.[1]

COUNTIES AND TOWNS.	Whites.	Negroes.	Indians.	COUNTIES AND TOWNS.	Whites.	Negroes.	Indians.
Hartford county:				Fairfield county—Continued.			
Bolton	755	11		Reading			
Colchester	2,228	84		Ridgfield	1,069	46	
East-Haddam	1,913	65		Stanford	2,648	120	
Enfield	1,050			Stratford	3,508	150	
Farmington	3,595	112					
Glastenbury	1,091	24		Total	19,849	711	
Haddam	1,223	18					
Hartford	2,926	101		Windham county:			
Hebron	1,855			Canterbury	1,240	20	
Middletown	5,446	218		Coventry	1,617	18	
Symsbury	2,222	23		Pomphret	1,677	50	
Somers	900			Killingly	2,100		
Stafford	1,000			Lebanon	3,171	103	
Suffield	1,414	24		Mansfield	1,598	16	
Tolland	902	15		Plainfield	1,751	49	
Wethersfield	2,374	109		Ashford	1,245		
Willington	650			Voluntown	1,029	19	
Windsor	4,170	50		Union	500		
				Windham	2,406	40	
Total	35,714	854		Woodstock	1,336	30	
New-Haven county:							
Branford	1,694	106		Total	[2]19,670	345	
Derby	1,000						
Durham	765	34		Litchfield county:			
Guilford	2,263	59		Barkhemsted	18		
Milford	1,633			Canaan	1,100		
New-Haven	5,085			Colebrook			
Wallingford	3,713			Cornwall	500		
Waterbury	1,802	27		Goshen	610		
				Hartland	12		
Total	17,955	226		Harwinton	250		
				Kent	1,000		
New-London county:				Litchfield	1,366		
Groton	2,532	179	158	New-Hartford	260		
Lyme	2,762	100	94	New-Milford	1,121	16	
Killingsworth	1,442	16		Norfolk	84		
New-London	3,171			Salisbury	1,100		
Norwich	5,317	223		Sharon	1,198	7	
Preston	1,940	78		Torrington	250		
Saybrook	1,898	33		Winchester	24		
Stonington	2,953	200	365	Woodbury	2,880	31	
Total	22,015	829	617	Total	11,773	54	
Fairfield county:				Hartford county	35,714	854	
Danbury	1,509	18		New-Haven county	17,955	226	
Fairfield	4,195	260		New-London county	22,015	829	617
Greenwich	2,021			Fairfield county	19,849	711	
New-Fairfield	713			Windham county	19,670	345	
New-Town	1,230	23		Litchfield county	11,773	54	
Norwalk	2,956	94					
				Total for colony	126,976	3,019	617

[1] Connecticut Colony Public Records, Vol. XIV, page 492.　　　　　　[2] Corrected figures.

A CENTURY OF POPULATION GROWTH.

CONNECTICUT—Continued.

TABLE **87.**—WHITE, NEGRO, AND INDIAN POPULATION OF THE COLONY

| | COUNTIES AND TOWNS. | Males under ten years. | Females under ten years. | MALES BETWEEN TEN AND TWENTY YEARS, MARRIED OR SINGLE. | | FEMALES BETWEEN TEN AND TWENTY YEARS. | | MALES BETWEEN TWENTY AND SEVENTY | | FEMALES BETWEEN TWENTY AND SEVENTY. | |
				Married.	Single.	Married.	Single.	Married.	Single.	Married.	Single.
	Hartford county:										
1	Bolton	154	162		121	2	105	154	48	159	59
2	Chatham	420	392		276	2	276	349	129	350	127
3	Colchester	530	477		389	6	344	442	139	430	165
4	East-Haddam	447	457	4	348	9	334	412	123	429	134
5	East-Windsor	481	443		353	2	332	439	178	433	217
6	Enfield	213	225	1	131	14	126	191	91	193	120
7	Farmington	965	1,007	1	736	10	616	958	295	965	292
8	Glastenbury	331	337	1	275	8	248	283	76	293	90
9	Haddam	294	286		224	9	187	241	89	251	104
10	Hartford	770	753	11	583	11	515	715	307	715	363
11	Hebron	360	375	2	316	8	308	312	122	307	123
12	Middletown	717	766	6	591	19	529	677	276	695	316
13	Simsbury	671	609	6	406	12	439	591	120	597	118
14	Somers	146	156		133	2	130	158	51	159	56
15	Stafford	223	199		199	9	162	201	59	197	48
16	Suffield	330	331	9	244	6	212	279	101	283	143
17	Tolland	200	193		150	1	157	101	86	161	171
18	Wethersfield	490	494	5	407	18	361	492	216	493	285
19	Willington	178	157		119	10	122	155	39	146	46
20	Windsor	299	302	7	242	7	219	319	134	310	157
21	Total	8,219	8,121	53	6,243	165	5,722	7,469	2,679	[2]7,616	3,134
	New-Haven county:										
22	Branford	284	309		224		215	317	81	322	148
23	Derby	289	289	2	252	10	205	270	106	277	83
24	Durham	166	148	2	141	2	124	149	69	154	56
25	Guilford	396	372		362		286	462	170	471	237
26	Milford	279	289	10	241	7	214	322	110	329	100
27	New-Haven	1,309	1,213	1	902	25	829	1,246	618	1,246	467
28	Wallingford	824	799	3	623	17	544	726	189	737	217
29	Waterbury	619	609	5	422	19	361	568	132	569	138
30	Total	4,166	4,028	23	3,167	80	2,778	4,060	1,475	4,105	1,446
	New-London county:										
31	Groton	574	570	10	441	22	390	538	142	532	200
32	Lyme	597	601	1	430	14	422	515	448	519	231
33	Killingworth	311	301		247	4	249	272	120	278	122
34	New-London	935	917	21	599	33	593	806	207	817	343
35	Norwich	1,099	1,054		916	8	741	1,056	412	1,069	505
36	Preston	401	405	16	291	16	244	295	99	306	128
37	Saybrook	432	461	1	284	10	275	411	107	410	171
38	Stonington	913	818	4	651	16	622	714	151	721	262
39	Total	5,262	5,127	53	3,859	123	3,536	4,607	1,686	4,652	1,962
	Fairfield county:										
40	Danbury	425	387	2	302	12	282	416	103	424	81
41	Fairfield	774	689	2	557	12	519	741	228	739	183
42	Greenwich	496	420	12	333	24	287	403	114	404	112
43	New-Fairfield	199	204		170	8	182	207	51	199	44
44	Newtown	357	357	1	277	8	281	324	103	324	67
45	Norwalk	754	700		544		486	638	173	638	217
46	Redding	208	189		152	2	121	196	46	206	46
47	Ridgfield	299	269	1	214	4	189	276	59	281	57
48	Stamford			13	1,008	7	909	561	244	562	199
49	Stratford	806	795	2	655	33	618	830	292	812	240
50	Total	4,318	4,010	33	4,212	110	3,874	4,592	1,413	4,589	1,246
	Windham county:										
51	Canterbury	438	374	3	330	3	242	356	114	358	123
52	Coventry	340	290		234		259	307	97	315	137
53	Pomfret	334	325	2	276	5	286	314	154	320	177
54	Killingly	582	521		461	2	372	530	152	542	168
55	Lebanon	590	552	4	515	26	460	540	208	549	285
56	Mansfield	354	382	2	307	14	305	353	142	353	165
57	Plainfield	254	241	1	168	3	177	215	73	217	83
58	Ashford	421	375	3	277	13	263	330	67	339	93
59	Voluntown	242	245		202	4	156	231	57	235	45
60	Union	97	67		68		61	83	14	83	16
61	Windham	532	533	1	482	7	387	476	173	491	267
62	Woodstock	320	333		230	1	234	243	119	243	195
63	Total	4,504	4,238	16	3,550	78	3,202	3,978	1,370	4,045	1,754
	Litchfield county:										
64	Barkhemsted										
65	Canaan	258	273	2	194	9	190	263	63	254	47
66	Colebrook										
67	Cornwall	190	160		130	1	107	152	30	155	20
68	Goshen	202	193		138	4	113	171	59	172	29
69	Hartland										
70	Harwinton	179	163		115		119	161	50	161	50
71	Kent	384	352	11	176	17	166	313	141	262	78
72	Litchfield	428	435	1	304	7	266	399	150	403	83
73	New-Hartford	176	158		119	4	116	146	49	155	45

[1] Connecticut Colony Public Records, Vol. XIV, pages 485 to 491.

CONNECTICUT—Continued.

OF CONNECTICUT, BY COUNTIES AND TOWNS: CENSUS OF 1774.[1]

MALES ABOVE SEVENTY.		FEMALES ABOVE SEVENTY.		Negro males under twenty.	Negro females under twenty.	Negro males above twenty.	Negro females above twenty.	Indian males under twenty.	Indian females under twenty.	Indian males above twenty.	Indian females above twenty.	Total whites.	Total blacks.	
Married.	Single.	Married.	Single.											
11	5	5	9	3	....	4	....	....	....	....	....	994	7	1
20	10	11	7	5	4	15	2	1	1	2	11	2,369	28	2
29	7	18	31	41	44	61	27	8	7	2	11	3,057	201	3
20	5	6	15	21	18	13	6	1	1	3	2	2,743	65	4
37	8	16	22	9	8	9	6	2	1	1	2	2,961	38	5
21	5	13	9	....	3	4	....	....	....	....	....	1,353	7	6
35	17	19	47	16	14	26	7	8	9	14	12	5,963	106	7
3	17	7	23	18	19	13	13	3	9	1	3	1,992	79	8
10	3	6	9	4	4	5	....	....	....	....	....	1,713	13	9
42	20	42	34	28	29	51	37	3	2	....	....	4,881	150	10
15	8	16	13	12	10	19	11					2,285	52	11
23	10	16	39	45	46	61	46					4,680	198	12
39	8	35	20	9	6	10	4					3,671	29	13
14	3	8	8	....	1	2	....					1,024	3	14
15	5	10	6	....	....	....	1					1,333	1	15
12	6	7	17	5	6	16	6	1	....	2	1	1,980	37	16
13	3	5	6	5	2	2	1	3	....	1	1	1,247	15	17
28	13	17	28	44	26	44	28					3,347	142	18
13	3	11	1	....	....	1	....					1,000	1	19
22	19	22	14	9	8	14	6	2	2	....	2	²2,073	43	20
422	175	290	358	274	248	370	201	32	32	24	34	²50,666	1,215	21
13	5	7	13	28	27	35	21	2	....	1	1	1,938	113	22
12	6	6	12	11	15	12	12	5		.5	5	1,819	70	23
6	4	3	7	7	10	16	11	1	....	....	....	1,031	45	24
35	9	29	17	13	14	20	14	8	10	2	3	2,846	84	25
15	10	11	28	41	35	52	30	....	....	1	3	1,965	162	26
48	44	24	50	66	70	70	56	7	2	....	2	8,022	273	27
33	10	24	31	27	28	48	31	2	1	....	1	4,777	138	28
20	6	9	21	6	7	15	6	2	1	....	1	3,498	38	29
182	94	113	179	199	206	²268	²181	27	19	9	16	25,896	925	30
19	8	13	29	51	39	42	42	55	36	39	56	3,488	360	31
34	5	17	26	36	26	35	27	21	18	23	42	3,860	228	32
14	6	12	21	4	6	6	3	6	2	4	2	1,957	33	33
49	13	15	18	70	79	89	78	64	48	35	59	5,366	522	34
55	23	38	56	62	54	69	49	16	14	11	20	7,032	295	35
21	11	7	15	5	11	25	12	11	9	1	9	2,255	83	36
26	5	20	15	15	12	20	8	3	....	1	....	2,628	59	37
22	13	21	28	85	49	49	36	73	80	28	56	4,956	456	38
240	84	143	208	328	276	335	255	249	207	142	244	31,542	2,036	39
14	6	7	12	15	13	15	7	....	....	2	1	2,473	53	40
30	11	20	39	83	75	91	66	....	....	2	2	4,544	319	41
19	9	10	11	35	25	34	20	....	3	2	3	2,654	122	42
9	3	6	6	5	4	6	5	....	....	....	....	1,288	20	43
20	6	20	23	12	20	18	9	1	1	....	....	2,168	61	44
43	8	25	17	37	25	43	31	....	2	4	3	4,243	145	45
10	4	6	3	9	14	17	5	....	....	....	....	1,189	45	46
7	4	6	7	9	9	9	8	....	....	....	....	1,673	35	47
....	....	....	....	12	18	17	13					3,503	60	48
38	14	19	47	69	72	108	70	7	12	9	7	5,201	354	49
190	65	119	165	286	275	358	234	8	18	19	16	28,936	1,214	50
19	5	10	17	6	4	22	9	1	1	7	2	2,392	52	51
21	1	14	17	4	6	7	5	....	....	2	....	2,032	24	52
17	8	7	16	22	11	13	7	2	4	3	3	2,341	65	53
36	14	22	37	12	2	14	7	2	4	1	5	3,439	47	54
43	9	25	35	30	19	22	27	9	5	4	3	3,841	119	55
17	13	11	25	3	1	4	3	3	6	1	2	2,443	23	56
13	4	12	18	18	9	18	13	9	8	3	5	1,479	83	57
17	8	7	15	2	2	7	2	....	....	....	....	2,228	13	58
26	2	22	9	9	3	9	8	2	3	....	1	1,476	35	59
8	5	6	4	....	....	1	1					512	2	60
35	3	18	32	18	10	15	29	2	7	3	7	3,437	91	61
11	13	11	21	3	14	15	10	13	9	7	9	1,974	80	62
263	85	165	246	127	81	147	121	43	47	31	37	27,494	634	63
....	....	....	....	....	....	....	....					³250	....	64
7	1	6	6	16	16	17	13					1,573	62	65
....	....	....	....									³150	....	66
3	3	3	3	2	2	5	1	1	4	2	....	957	17	67
7	....	4	6	3	....	9	1	....	....	....	....	1,098	13	68
....	....	....	....									³500		69
7	....	4	6	1	....	1	1	....	....	....	....	1,015	3	70
9	1	7	5	3	3	4	2	18	20	11	13	1,922	74	71
10	5	4	14	8	15	7	7	1	1	1	5	2,509	45	72
8	2	2	5	....	....	3	....	4	3	1	5	985	16	73

² Corrected figures.   ³ Not distributed by sex.

A CENTURY OF POPULATION GROWTH.

CONNECTICUT—Continued.

Table **87.**—WHITE, NEGRO, AND INDIAN POPULATION OF THE COLONY

	COUNTIES AND TOWNS.	Males under ten years.	Females under ten years.	MALES BETWEEN TEN AND TWENTY YEARS, MARRIED OR SINGLE.		FEMALES BETWEEN TEN AND TWENTY YEARS.		MALES BETWEEN TWENTY AND SEVENTY.		FEMALES BETWEEN TWENTY AND SEVENTY.	
				Married.	Single.	Married.	Single.	Married.	Single.	Married.	Single.
	Litchfield county—Continued.										
74	New-Milford	490	497	15	325	27	254	482	83	460	61
75	Norfolk	156	151	....	109	3	110	155	30	155	27
76	Salisbury	347	358	....	240	7	224	278	111	271	70
77	Sharon	343	342	....	259	11	236	307	77	303	56
78	Torrington	132	134	....	99	....	75	139	56	146	54
79	Westmoreland	384	352	11	176	17	166	313	141	262	78
80	Winchester	55	69	....	34	1	19	60	18	56	11
81	Woodbury	921	889	4	600	33	587	821	260	795	235
82	Total	4,645	4,526	44	3,018	141	2,748	4,160	1,318	4,010	944
83	Hartford county	8,219	8,121	53	6,243	165	5,722	7,469	2,679	[1]7,616	3,134
84	New-Haven county	4,166	4,028	23	3,167	80	2,778	4,060	1,475	4,105	1,446
85	New-London county	5,262	5,127	53	3,859	123	3,536	4,607	1,686	4,652	1,962
86	Fairfield county	4,318	4,010	33	4,212	110	3,874	4,592	1,413	4,589	1,246
87	Windham county	4,504	4,238	16	3,550	78	3,202	3,978	1,370	4,045	1,754
88	Litchfield county	4,645	4,526	44	3,018	141	2,748	4,160	1,318	4,010	944
89	Total for colony	31,114	30,050	222	24,049	697	21,860	28,866	9,941	[1]29,017	10,486

[1] Corrected figures.

CONNECTICUT—Continued.

OF CONNECTICUT, BY COUNTIES AND TOWNS: CENSUS OF 1774—Continued.

MALES ABOVE SEVENTY.		FEMALES ABOVE SEVENTY.		Negro males under twenty.	Negro females under twenty.	Negro males above twenty.	Negro females above twenty.	Indian males under twenty.	Indian females under twenty.	Indian males above twenty.	Indian females above twenty.	Total whites.	Total blacks.	
Married.	Single.	Married.	Single.											
19	6	11	6	12	8	8	6	....	....	....	....	[1]2,736	34	74
4	1	1	4	1	2	....	....	....	....	....	....	[1]906	3	75
11	1	9	9	8	7	10	10	5	2	1	1	1,936	44	76
19	9	12	12	5	6	8	6	....	....	1	....	1,986	26	77
3	5	5	....	....	....	1	1	....	....	....	....	[1]848	2	78
9	1	7	5	....	....	....	....	....	....	....	....	1,922	....	79
1	....	1	2	7	1	2	2	....	....	....	....	327	12	80
22	16	16	25	26	19	24	11	3	2	2	2	5,224	89	81
139	51	92	108	92	79	99	61	32	32	19	26	[1,2]26,844	440	82
422	175	290	358	274	248	370	201	32	32	24	34	[1]50,666	1,215	83
182	94	113	179	199	206	[1]268	[1]181	27	19	9	16	25,896	925	84
240	84	143	208	328	276	335	255	249	207	142	244	31,542	2,036	85
190	65	119	165	286	275	358	234	8	18	19	16	28,936	1,214	86
263	85	165	246	127	81	147	121	43	47	31	37	27,494	634	87
139	51	92	108	92	79	99	61	32	32	19	26	[1]26,844	440	88
1,436	554	922	1,264	1,306	1,165	[1]1,577	[1]1,053	391	355	244	373	[1,2]191,378	6,464	89

[2] Includes 900 not distributed by sex.

NEW YORK.

TABLE 88.—POPULATION OF THE COLONY OF NEW YORK, BY COUNTIES: 1698.[1]

COUNTIES.	Men.	Women.	Children.	Negroes.	Total.
Albany	380	270	803	23	1,476
Dutchess and Ulster	248	111	869	156	1,384
Kings	308	332	1,081	296	2,017
New-York	1,019	1,057	2,161	700	4,937
Orange	29	31	140	19	219
Queens	1,465	1,350	551	199	3,565
Richmond	328	208	118	73	727
Suffolk	973	1,024	124	558	2,679
Westchester	316	294	307	146	1,063
Total	5,066	4,677	6,154	2,170	18,067

[1] Census of the State of New-York, 1855, page iv.

TABLE 89.—MALE AND FEMALE POPULATION OF THE COLONY OF NEW YORK, IN CERTAIN AGE GROUPS, BY COUNTIES: 1703.[1]

COUNTIES.	Males from 16 to 60.	Females.	Male children.	Female children.	Male negroes.	Female negroes.	Male negro children.	Female negro children.	All above 60.	Total.[2]
Albany	510	385	515	605	83	53	36	28	58	2,273
Kings	345	304	433	487	135	75	72	61	....	1,912
New-York	813	1,009	934	989	102	288	131	109	....	4,375
Orange	49	40	57	84	13	7	7	6	5	268
Queens	952	753	1,093	1,170	117	114	98	95	(3)	4,392
Richmond	176	140	42	49	60	32	4	1	....	504
Suffolk	787	756	818	797	60	52	38	38	(3)	3,346
Ulster	383	305	436	357	63	36	31	15	23	1,649
Westchester	472	469	382	386	74	45	50	29	39	1,946
Total	4,487	4,161	4,710	4,924	707	702	467	382	125	20,665

[1] Census of the State of New-York, 1855, page iv.
[2] In a subsequent communication to the Lords of Trade in 1712 (Colonial History of New-York, Vol. V, page 339) the totals of the census of 1703 are quoted differently from those in the above table. There are no means for determining whether this difference arose from a subsequent correction of errors, or from mistakes in copying. As given in the latter, the totals were as follows: New York, 4,436; Kings, 1,915; Richmond, 503; Orange, 268; Westchester, 1,946; Queens, 4,392; Suffolk, 3,346; Albany, 2,273; Ulster and Dutchess, 1,669.
[3] Included in first column.

TABLE 90.—NAMES OF MASTERS OF FAMILIES IN THE CITY OF NEW YORK, BY WARDS, ACCORDING TO THE ENUMERATION MADE ABOUT THE YEAR 1703.[1]

MASTERS OF FAMILYS.	Males from 16 to 60.	females.	Male Children.	female Children.	Male Negros.	female Negros.	Male Negro Children.	female Negro Children.	all above 60.
Total for city	780	985	903	924	298	276	124	[2] 101	55
EAST WARD.									
Ebenezr Wilson	3	4	1	3	1	1	....	....	....
Mr Leuis	....	1	4	2	....	1	....	....	....
Mr Everson	....	2	2	......	1	....	....	....	....
Mrs Vantyle	....	1	1	1	....	....	....	....	....
Mr Haris	2	1	....	1	....	2	3	1	....
Thoms Dyer	1	....	....	....	....	....	....	....	....
Mrs Smith	....	3	4	....	....	....	....	....	....
Garot Haier	2	2	2	....	....	....	....	....	....
Frances Coderos	....	2	1	3	....	1	....	....	....
John Lasly	1	1	....	....	....	....	....	....	....
Thoms Evens	1	1	1	....	....	....	....	....	....
*—— Hendrick	1	3	....	....	....	....	....	....	....
Peter Vantilbry	2	1	1	....	....	1	....	....	....
Frances Wessells	2	2	....	5	5	....	....	....	....
Mrs Basset	....	1	1	2	....	....	....	....	....
Capt Novered	....	1	2	1	....	1	....	....	....
John Morthouse	1	....	....	....	....	....	....	....	....
Beverly Latham	1	1	3	1	....	....	....	....	....
Mrs Rabi	1	2	2	....	....	....	....	....	....
Capt Morris	1	1	....	3	1	2	1	....	....
Peter Mountu	1	3	1	....	....	....	....	....	....
Hendrick Mayr	1	1	2	....	....	....	....	....	....
John Stephens	1	1	2	3	....	....	....	....	....
Capt Tudor	2	5	2	4	....	....	1	1	....
Stuen Volo	1	2	1	3	....	....	....	....	....
Fany ye Doctr	1	3	....	1	....	....	....	....	....
Abraham Brazier	1	1	1	1	....	....	....	....	....
Mr Sinkeler	2	1	0	1	1	1	1	1	....
Mr Lees	2	1	....	....	....	2	....	....	....
Capt Forkell	1	1	1	2	....	1	1	3	....
Peter Thouet	1	2	....	....	....	....	1	1	....

[1] New York Documentary History, pages 395 to 405.   [2] Corrected figures.   * Illegible.

NEW YORK—Continued.

TABLE **90.**—NAMES OF MASTERS OF FAMILIES IN THE CITY OF NEW YORK, BY WARDS, ACCORDING TO THE ENUMERATION MADE ABOUT THE YEAR 1703—Continued.

MASTERS OF FAMILYS.	Males from 16 to 60.	females.	Male Children.	female Children.	Maie Negros.	female Negros.	Male Negro Children.	female Negro Children.	all above 60.
EAST WARD—continued.									
James pencer		1		2					
Margrett Briges		1							
Doctr Defany	1	1		2					
Mr Sellwood	1								
Widd Brown		2	1						
Mr Cholwell	1	1	2	1		2	1		
John Ledham	1	1	1	1					
Andrew Gravenrod	1	1	2	3	1	1			
William Apell	1	1							
James Blower	1	1							
John Vanderspeygel	2	1	1	3				1	
John Bures	1	1		1					
Mrs Blackgrove		1	3	1	2	2	2	1	
Mrs Byner	2	2			1	1		1	
Doctr Peters	1	1		1					
John Devi	1	1	2	3		1			
Mr Burger	2	1	3	2	2	1			
John Brockman	1	1		1					
John Bason	1	1	1						
John Dyer	1	2	1	1					
Capt Borditt	2	1	2		1				
Capt Baker	1					1		1	
James Emmett	1	2	3	1	1	1			
Samson Boutons	4		2	1					
James Bouloro	1	1							
Evert Pelts	1	1		3					
Mr Carter		2							
Joseph Isacks	1	1	1	3	1				
John Theobalds	1		2	3	2	1			
Mr Rinderson	1	1		1	1	1			
Widd Smith		1	3		1				
Leend Hewsen	1		1	2	1	1			
Benj Druelef	3	1	2			1	1	2	
Mr Waters	1	1	2	1		2			
Mr Lysoner	1			2		2			1
Mr Hardinburg	1	1	3	2	1	1			
Paul Myler	1	1	3			1			
Capt Vancrouger	1	1	1	1				1	
Mrs Clobery		1		2		1		1	
John Marteris	1		1						
Georg Stanton	2	1	2	2	4	2	2		
Daniel Janden	2	1	3	1					
Abraham Vanhorn	1	1		1	1	1	1		
Abraham Abranson		2	2	1			1		
Andries Abrahamse	1	1		1					
Derick Adolph	1	1	3						
John Manbruitts	1	1	1	1					
Garott Van Caver	1	1	1	1		1			
*—— Hogland	1	1	1	4	2	1		1	
Mr Read	1	1	1	1		1			
Mr Monsett	1	2	2	1					
Thoms Caroll	1	2	2	1		1			
Widd Petersebants	1	2	1	2				1	
Aaron Bloom	1	2	2	4		1	1		
Mr Toy	1	1	1						
Georg Maynard	1	1							
Abraham Wandell	1	2							
John Tomson	1	2	2	3					
Benj Barns	1	1							
Capt Cragror	1	2		2		1			
Wm Nasroses		1	1	4					
Wm Shickles		1		3					
Nicholas Dauly	1	1	1						
Caston Lusen	1	1		1					
Johnas Longstrauts	1	1	2	1					
Abraham Molts	1	1		1					
Capt Trevett	1	2							
Georg Elesworth	1	1	4	2	2				
Colonl Depyster	1	2	1	3	5	2		2	
Georg Dunken	1	1	1	1		2			
Widd Decay		1	3	2	1	1	1		
Meyer Merett	1	2		3					
Capt Shelly	1	2			1	1	1		
Peter Morrayn	1	1		6	1				
Thoms Adams	1	0	2	1					
Widd Kidd		2							
Widd Vanbroug		1			1				
Widd Proost		1	2	4	2				
Jacobus Vanderspegle	1	1	4	3			1		

*Illegible.

A CENTURY OF POPULATION GROWTH.

NEW YORK—Continued.

TABLE **90.**—NAMES OF MASTERS OF FAMILIES IN THE CITY OF NEW YORK, BY WARDS, ACCORDING TO THE ENUMERATION MADE ABOUT THE YEAR 1703—Continued.

MASTERS OF FAMILYS.	Males from 16 to 60.	females.	Male Children.	female Children.	Male Negros.	female Negros.	Male Negro Children.	female Negro Children.	all above 60.
EAST WARD—continued.									
Doct Stets	1		2	7		1			
Elyes Now	1	3	2	2	1				
Widd Van Vous		1	1	2	1		1	2	
John Davi	1	1	2					1	
Abraham Johns	2					1	1		
Simon Bonan	1	1							
Widd Vanbusing		1			1				
Widd Adolph	1	3	1					1	
Thoms Child	1	1	1		2	1	1	1	
Saml Phillips	1	1	1		1				
Amon Bonan	1		1			1			
Johanes D. Wandler	1		1	4					
Joseph Smith	1	2	4						
Johanes Dohneare	1	1	1	4	1	1	2	1	
John Godfry	1	1	1	1		1			
Barnardus Smith	1	1	1	1		0			
Elyes Rambert	1	1	4						
Jacob Brant	1	1		2	1				
Peter Rous	1		2	1					
Widd Jordan		1	2	4	1	1	1		
Thoms Sanderson	1	1	1	1			1		
Michell									
Denes Rishey	1	1	2						
Andrew Larrance	1	1	5	1					
Agustous Loukes	1		1		1			1	
Cornelius Joussos	1	1	3						
John Poulee	1	2	4						
Mr Funnell	1	1	3				2	1	
Mr D Romer	1	1	2		1		1	1	
Capt Peneson	1	1	1		1				
James Turse	1	1	2	1					
James Turse									
Michael Slevett	2	2		1		1			
Peter Baunt	1	1	1	1					
Widd Ellworth		1	1	2					
Capt Wilson	1	1	3	2	1				
Boult Leire	1	1							
Benj Bill	1	1	1	1		1			
Danl Fargoe	1			1					
Danl Devous	1	1	2	1					
Arthr Williams	1	1		2					
Georg Brass	1	1	4	2					
Wm Elcworth	1	1	1	3					
Joshuah David	1	1	4	1					
Widd Vandewater		1	2	1					
Cornelius Bolson	1	1	1						
Danl Mynard	1	1	1	1					
John Mambroits	1	1	1	1					
Mr Cromlin	1			1					
Lucas Tinhoven	1	1		2					
Johanes Urielant	1	1		1					
Pete Newcurk	1	1	0	5	0	2			
Gabriell Ludlow	1	1	1	5	1	1			
Canny Flower	1	1	1	2					
Mr Slay	1	1	2	2					
Wm Bikman	0	0	0	1	2	1			1
James Debross	1	0	0	0	1				
Wm Anderson	1	1	2	0	2	0	1		
Peter Rightman	1	1	3	2					
Capt Tuder	1	1	1	4	0	1			
Wm Fardnandus	1	1							
Hendrick Carkman	1	1	1	1	0	1			
John Lastly	1	1	1						
Widd Vontylborough	0	1	1	2					
Wm Pell	1	1	1	3					
Thoms Huck	2	0	0	0	1				
Widd Peterow	0	1	3	3	1				
Robert Pudenton	1	2							
Wm Shackerly	1	1	0	1	1				
Mr Huddleston	1	1	2	1	0	2			
Nichol Debower	1	1	1	1					
Johanes D payster	1	1	1	3	1	2	0	2	
Wm White	1	1	1						
Widd Nanclaft	0	1		3		1	1	1	
Abraham Moll	1	1		1					
Levenus Deuind	1	1					1		
Richd Sackett	1	1	2	2	3	1			
Elener Eleworth	1		2	3	2	1			
Soffell Seeworth					1	1			1
Isaac Dinell	1	1	4	1					

NEW YORK—Continued.

TABLE **90.**—NAMES OF MASTERS OF FAMILIES IN THE CITY OF NEW YORK, BY WARDS, ACCORDING TO THE ENUMERATION MADE ABOUT THE YEAR 1703—Continued.

MASTERS OF FAMILYS.	Males from 16 to 60.	females.	Male Children.	female Children.	Male Negros.	female Negros.	Male Negro Children.	female Negro Children.	all above 60.
EAST WARD—continued.									
Isaac Ferbergin	1	1	4						
Johanes Jooston	1	1	2						
Widd Lees		1		1					
Mrs Mussett	1	1							
Wm Naseros	1	1	1	4					
Loud Leuis	1	1	2	5	1	1	1		
Thoms Roberts	1								
Roger Britt	1								
Thoms Hams	1	1							
Robt Walls	1								
Giddeon Vergeren	1	0					1		
Evert Dicken									
John Nanfan	1				1				
Claud Bouden									
Hendrick Vandespegle	1								
Mr Gleencross	1	1							
Dan Thwaictes	1	1		2					
Widd Petrer Bond		2		2			1		
Charl Bakeman	1								
Johanes Banker	1								
Harma Louricar	1	1	1						
Jos Carlsee									2
Simeon Shumoine	1	0	2	2					
SOUTH WARD.									
Danill Roberts	3	1							
Mr Ling	2	0	0	0	0	3			
John & Elias Petram	2	1	4	2	1	1	0	1	
Hendrick Kellison	1	1	3	0	0	0	0	0	
Archibald Morris	1	1	0	1	0				
Jurian Bush	1	1	1	2					
Victor Bicker	1	2	0	1					
Elizabeth Eliot	0	1							
Sarah Scouton	1	2	1	4					
Saml Sokane	1	2	1	3					
Jacobus Cornelius	1	1	1	2	0	0	0	1	
Peter Wesels	1	1	3	1	0	1			
Jacobus Morrisgreen	1	1	0	1	1				
William Syms	1	1	0	3					1
John Wattson	0	1	1	1	1				1
William Haywood	2	1	2	2				1	1
John Canoon	2	1	0	1			1		
Thomas Elison	1	4	1	3					
Widdow Bush	1	2	1	1					1
William Kage	1	2	0			1			
Widdow Wessells	2	3							
William Jackson	4	1	1	1	1	1			
Johannes Van Geser	2	3							
Willelmus Neuenhousen	1	2						1	
William Taylor	1	1	3	1	2	1			
Michael Hardin	2	3						1	
Thomas Hardin	2	1	1	2	0	1			
Anna Smith	0	1	1			1			
Mr Shaepass	1	1	0	1	1	1			1
Capt Debrouts					0				3
Madam Duboise	0	3							
Cornelius Depeyster	1	2	1	3	0	1	1		
Widdow ffrouse		2	3	1					
Thomas Roberts	1	1	2	3	3	1			
John Elison	2	1	3	0	1	2	1		
Isaac Depeyster	1	1	3	3				3	
Widdow Howard		3		1				4	1
Nicholas Tinoven	1	1				1	1	1	
Mr Davenport	2	1					1		
Giles Gaudenoa		1						1	1
Widdow Stokes	1	1		1					
Robert Elison	1	2				2			
Andreas Maer	2	2	2			1			
Benjamin Winecope	2	1	1						
Widdow Stukey	1	2	2						
Madm Weaver		2	1	2	1	2		1	
Thomas Ives	2	1			1	1			
Derick Ten Eyck	3	1	2		12	1			
John Peroe	1	3							
Thos Gleaves	1	1	3	2	2	2	1		
*—— Pasco	1	1					1	1	
Mr Cosens	1	1	2	2		2	1		
Andrew Law	2	3	2	2					
Widdow Bassett		1	2	1					
William Lloyd		1	2						

*Illegible.

NEW YORK—Continued.

TABLE 90.—NAMES OF MASTERS OF FAMILIES IN THE CITY OF NEW YORK, BY WARDS, ACCORDING TO THE ENUMERATION MADE ABOUT THE YEAR 1703—Continued.

MASTERS OF FAMILYS.	Males from 16 to 60.	females.	Male Children.	female Children.	Male Negros.	female Negros.	Male Negro Children.	female Negro Children.	all above 60.
SOUTH WARD—continued.									
Adrian Man	4	01	3	1					
Widdow Lysenner	0	2		1					
Mr Van Dam	2	2	3	2	3	2	1		
Widdow Cloper	2	1	1	1				1	
John Pitt	1	1	1	1					
Robert Deintant	1	1		1					
Widdow Dikey		2	1	7	4	1	1	1	
Widdow van Scarck		6	1	2	1	1	1	1	
Capt Corbutt	3	3		2	2	2			
Delancena Jew	1	1	1	1		1		1	
Anthony Farmer	1	1	1	2		1	1	2	
Gilbert Vanimbrough	1	1	1	3	1				
Abraham Vanderell	1	1							
Lawrence Heading	1	2						1	
Widdow Symonse Janson		1							1
Widdow Hallgrave	0	1	0	1					
Widdow Phillips		1	1		1	2	2	1	
Stephen Richards	1	2	1	2		1			
Mr Rossoll	1	1	2	1		1	1		
Widdew Seiler		1	1		3	1	1		
John Wansart	1	1						1	
Herman Rutgese	2	1		1	2				
Widdow Nespot	1	1		1					
Widdow Deforest	1	1	2	5					
Justus Jay	1	2		3	1				
Widdow Brown		1	1	3					
Peter Myir	1	1	1	4					
Widdow Doweher	1	1	1	2					
John Kingstone	1	1							
Nicholas Lorteen	1	1							
Capt Matthews		1	3	2		1	1		
Johannes Johnson	1	1	2	2					
John Petraaslot	1	1	1	1					
James Many	1	3							
Samll Burges		1			3	1			
Mr Cooper	1	2	2	2			1	1	
Johannes Vanrost	1	1	2	3			1		
Mr Vangoson	1	2	1						
Mr Vangoson	1	2	1	1					
Capt Tinoven	1	1				1	1	1	
Christophr Hogland	1	1	2						
Widdow van plank		3	2	3		1			
Johannes Vanderhield	1	1	1		1	1			
Widdow Keisted		2	5	1	1				
Andreas Breestad	2	4	4	2	2	1			
Widdow Deshamp	1	2	1			4		2	
Mr Antill	1	1	2	2		2		2	
Wilellmus Navensusen	2	2						1	
Francis Vincent	2	1	1	2	1	1	1		
Peter Kip	1	1	1				1		
Gre Robertson		2							
Jacob Maurice	2	1	1		1				
Garrett Vesey	1	1	1	3	1				
Widdow Bush	1	2							
Johannes Craft	1	1							
Samll Beckman	1	1	2	4					
Mr Honan	1	2		1		1			
Widdow Cortland	2	2		3	5	2	1	1	
Widdow Keisteed	1	1		1				1	
Hendrick Mester	1	1							
Abraham Webrana	1	1	2						
Edward Blagg	1		1			2			
Capt ffinch	1	1		2					
NORTH WARD.									
Isaac Stoutenbrough	1	1	2	0					1
Lydiah Rose	0	3	1						
Johannes Veckden	1	1	1	2					
Gerrard Grans	1	1	4	1					
Jeemz Lie	1	1		1					
Freerick Bloom	1	1	2	1					
Wm Ockton	1	1							
Gerret De Boogh	1	1	1						
Mangell Ransen	1	1	2	2	2				1
Danl Domskon	1	1	1	1					
Jacob Van Direse	1	1	1	3					
Eleazer Bogert	1	1	4						
Joriz Breger	1	1	2						
Jasbuz Boz	1	1	2		1				
Johannes Bogert	1	1		0					

NEW YORK--Continued.

TABLE 90.—NAMES OF MASTERS OF FAMILIES IN THE CITY OF NEW YORK, BY WARDS, ACCORDING TO THE ENUMERATION MADE ABOUT THE YEAR 1703—Continued.

MASTERS OF FAMILYS.	Males from 16 to 60.	females.	Male Children.	female Children.	Male Negros.	female Negros.	Male Negro Children.	female Negro Children.	all above 60.
NORTH WARD—continued.									
Wm Waderson	1	2							
Johannes Proovoos	1			1					
Joseph Waderson	1	1	2	3					
Henry Coleman	1	1		1	1				
Philip Bellenz	1	1		1					
Joseph Bresser	1	1		1					
Ratie Vanderbeeck		1	2						
Johannes Bant	1	1	2						
Jacob Balck	1	1	0	1					
Saml Marten	1	1							
Jo Dicker	1	1		2					
John Terree	1	1		1					
Kuijbert Vandenberg	1	1		3					
John Bentell		3							
Joseph Paling	1	1	1	3	1	1			
Mr Evert	1	1	0	3	0	1			
Jacob Swart	1	1	2	1					
Bartholemew Vonol	1	1	1						
Edwd Lock	1	1	2	1					
Marre Quick		1	1						
Isaac Juter	1	1	2	1					
Mr Floran	1	1	0	1					
Danl Travore	1	1	1						
Mr Ritvire	1	1							
Henderick Drimiez	1	1	1	1					
Derick Ritenbogert	1	1	1	1					
Abraham Vanaren	1	1	2	2	1	1	1	1	1
Jan Karelse	1	1		1					
Janetie degraus		2	0	1					
Harmen degraus	1	1	3	2					
Andrew Douwe	1	1		2					
Aijs Van Velsen	1	1	2	2					
Yochem Lotyer	1	1	2	1					
Mr Hooper		1	0	2					
Hendrick Oostrom									
Yan Heslook	1	1		1					
Jan Beadre	1	1	2						
Christian Lowrier	1	1	2						
Annetie Lowrier		1							
Wm Visser	1	1	2	4	1				
Robt Milre									2
Stoffel Pelz			2	2	1	1	1		
Aijme Vandyck	1	1	2	2					
Peter Van Waggele	1	1		2	1				
Susanna Tocter		1		1					
Evert Bressen	1	1	2	5					
Johannes P Cavice	1	1		1					
Hanz Kierstede	1	1	2	1					
Wyburgh Vanbos		1		1					
Direck Slick	1	1	2	1					
Enoch Kill	1	1							
Danl Barteloo	1	1		2					
Reyere Martese	1	1	2	1					
Abraham Vandurse	1	1	3	2					
Danl Walderon	1	1		5					
*—— Morott		1	0	2					
Tam Fell	1	1		2					
Alexander Lam	1	1	2	4					
Wm Attell	1	1	2	3					
Mrs Ameker									1
Peter Burger	1	1	2	2					
Wm Mandriese	1	1	1	1					
Onerre Obee		5							
Catherine Kip		1	4	4	2	2		1	
Wm Vaneckt	1	1	3	1					
Isaack Kip	1	2	5	1	2	2			
Orseltie Vandyck		2	1						
Jacob Boele	1	1	4	1	0	1	2	1	
Engletre Mol		1	1	2					
Wm Rooseboom	1	1		3					
Abraham Vangeldere	1	1	1	3					
Yoost Heyresse	1	1	3						
Antre Vanoorstrant		1	2	2	1				
Johannes Kenne	1								
Nicholas Delaplyne									1
Jacob Carrebill	1	1							
Wier Boergeran	1	1	1						
Abraham Keteltaz	1	1	1	1					
Antiene Yellerton		1	2	1					
Bnej Proovoost	1	0	5	6					

*Illegible.

A CENTURY OF POPULATION GROWTH.

NEW YORK—Continued.

TABLE **90.**—NAMES OF MASTERS OF FAMILIES IN THE CITY OF NEW YORK, BY WARDS, ACCORDING TO THE ENUMERATION MADE ABOUT THE YEAR 1703—Continued.

MASTERS OF FAMILYS.	Males from 16 to 60.	females.	Male Children.	female Children.	Male Negros.	female Negros.	Male Negro Children.	female Negro Children.	all above 60.
NORTH WARD—continued.									
Denis Sweetman	1	1	1						
Hendrick Boz	1	1	3	1					
Garret Lansen	1	1	2	3					
Annetie Henne		1		1					
Mr Vandrick		1		1					
Abraham Kip	1	1	1	1	1	1	1	1	
ffrans Vandyck	1	1	3						
Robert Podventon	1								
Aaron Vanvlarden	1	1	4	1					
John Van strijp	1	1							
Hathman Wessels	1	1		1					
Peter Yaaokse	1	1	2	1	1	1			
Mattyz Boeckout	1	1							
Peter Saryo	1	1	1	1					
Yan Sivvere	1								
Yan Hille	1	2	3	3					
Yan Yonz	1								
Stijntie Yoris		1							
Anenez Tiebout	1	1	3	2					
Wm Yorster	1	1	3	2					
Wm Proovoost	1	1	2	2					
Mr Kinning		1	7	1					
Catharina Selecoat		1							
Fillet Sweer	1	1							
Wm Pell	1	1	2	3					
Cornelia Vandervoers	1	1							
Yan Meet	1	1	4	2					
Barent Vantilburgh	1		1	1					
Wm Stenton	1	1	0	2					
Loo Witten	1	1		2					
Nieste Viene		2	1			1			
Yan Devenne	1	1		1	1				
Cornelia Maruz		1	2	3					
Doreman Stor	1	1			1				
Mrs Lindslee		1							
Swerez Hendricks	2			1					
David Hoesaert	1	1	2	1					
Ante Burgers	0	1	3	3					
Ysack Brat	1	1		2					
Elsie Sippie		3	4						
Yohanniz Vandewater	1	2	2						
Nelte Plaurere	2	2	1	4					1
Garret Hallaer	1	1		1	1				
Hardmen Holduz	1								
Solomon Vanderboogh	1	1	3						
Allebertuz Ringo	1	1	3	2					
Vansent Tielo	1	1	2	3					
Hester Montaine		1	3	1					
David Christeaense	2	1	1	2					
Yan Keoeck	1	1	5	1	1	1			
Sarebz Loeter	1	4	1	1					
Mrs Stevez		2			4	1			2
Anderiez Marschalock	1	2	5	1					
Yacob Bennett	1	2	3	1					
Wm Bogaert	1	1	1	1					
Yan Vanhorn	1	1							
Aennez Ynick	1	1	2	2			1		
Garret Wouterse	1	1	1	1					
Hatie Provoost		1	2	4	2				
Martie Vandeheyden	0	1	1	1					
Barent Lool	1	1	2	2					
Yannez Laegerau	1	1		1	1				
Garret Onckelback	1	1	1	2					
Yan Vantilburgh	1	1							
Saml Lockeriest	1	1	3		1	1			1
Barnarduz Smit	1	1	9	1					2
Yan Pieterse Boz									2
Caterina Bootz									1
Barnardus Hardebroer	1		1	4	1				
Corneliz Loris	1	1	4		1				
Peter Boz	1	1	1	2					
Mrs Monvel		1	1				2		
Garret Burger	1	1	2	2					
Yan Herrick	1	1	0	2					
Garret Wynanse	1	1							
Lavie Vandmirse		1	2	2					
Sijmon Breeste	1	1	2	3	1				
Yannetre Wande Watte		1							
Am Reijt	1	1	1	1					
Yacob deportee	1	1	2	1					
Yan Narbree	1	1	1						
Yohannez Vantiburgh	1	1	2						

NEW YORK—Continued.

TABLE **90.**—NAMES OF MASTERS OF FAMILIES IN THE CITY OF NEW YORK, BY WARDS, ACCORDING TO THE ENUMERATION MADE ABOUT THE YEAR 1703—Continued.

MASTERS OF FAMILYS.	Males from 16 to 60.	females.	Male Children.	female Children.	Male Negros.	female Negros.	Male Negro Children.	female Negro Children.	all above 60.
NORTH WARD—continued.									
Yan Konce	1								
Mrs Boseit		1							
Wessell Eversee	1	1	2	2					
Bettie Rammesen		2	1						
WEST WARD.									
Peter Bayard	1	1		2		1			
Garret Vantright	0	2		1					1
Cornelius Lodge	1	1		1					
Wm Smith Aldermn	1	1			2	1	4	2	
Ball: Bayard	4	1			1	1	3	1	1
Matt: De Hart	2	2	1	2					
Jacob Vansune	1	2					1		
Catherine Rolegome		2			1			1	
Charles Denisoe	1	1				1			
Robt Darkins	2	2	1	1	1	2			
Derus Vandinbrough	1	1	1	1	2	1			
Bar: Laroox	2	1	3	3	0	1			
John Barbarie	2	1	3	3	0	3			
James Colett	1	1	4						
John Dublett		2							1
Peter Munvil	1	1				1			
Isaac De Boogh	1	1							
Peter Pieret	2	2	1	2	11	1	1	1	
Mrs Rumboll		3	0			1	0	2	0
Evert Van Howk	1	1	3	2					
Robt White	1	1	1	2					
Margrett Hudson		1	1	1					
Catherine White		2		2					
Wm Walch	1	2	3						
Johan: Van Gelder	1	1	5	2					
Isaac Anderson	1	1	3	1		1			
John Hutchins	1	1				2	1		
Susannah Wells		1	1	1					
Deborah Symcom				1					1
Cornelius Clopper	1	1	1	2					
And: Faucout	1	1							
Augustus Grassett	1	1				1			
Jacobus Berry	1	1	1	2					
Coll: Peartree	1	1	1		2	2	1	1	
Urian Blank	1								
Mary Blank		1		1					
Robt Edwards	1	1		2					
Rebekah Adams		1	1	1					
George Williams	1	1							
Wm Stoks	1	1	1	1					
Francis Bocketts	1	1	2	2					
Tobias Stoutenbrough	2	2	4		1	1			
Agnes Davis		1		2					
Daniel Ebbetts	2	1							
Eliz: Plumley		2	1				1		
Samp: Shilton Braughton	2	4			1				
Han: Tenijck	2	3	1	1					
Robt Anderson	1	1	1						
Peter Johnson	1	1			1				
Abra: Masiear	1	1	3	2	1	1			
John Anen	1	2		2					
Wm Arison	1	1		2	1	1			
David Mackdugell	1	1	1						
Isaac Garners	1	1	1						
Will: Shullwood	1	1		1					
Laynard D Graw	1	3	4	2					
Jores Riersie	1	2	4	4	2		1		
John Cure	1	1		1					
Archibald Reed	1	1							
Hanna Tinbrook	2	1	1						
Andrew Lamarue	1	1	1	1					
Michael Harring	1			1					
Edwd Burley	1	1	1						
Lieft Buckley		1		4					
Rinear Risoe	2	2	1	1					
Walter D Boise	1	1		1			1		
Garret Cosyn	1	1	1	1					
Pietr Parmyter	1	2	1	1					
Alberts Laynderts									1
Paul Tuk		1							1
Peter Marks	1	1		1					
Armanus Van Geldr	1	1	2	3					
Phill: Doley	1	1	1						
Jno D. Le ffountaine	1	1	3	2					
Jacob Kuwning	1	1	2	2					

NEW YORK—Continued.

TABLE **90.**—NAMES OF MASTERS OF FAMILIES IN THE CITY OF NEW YORK, BY WARDS, ACCORDING TO THE ENUMERATION MADE ABOUT THE YEAR 1703—Continued.

MASTERS OF FAMILYS.	Males from 16 to 60.	females.	Male Children.	female Children.	Male Negros.	female Negros.	Male Negro Children.	female Negro Children.	all above 60.
WEST WARD—continued.									
Joseph Wright	1	1	4	1					
Peter Willtrans Roome	1	1	4	4					
Wm Moss	1	2	2	2					
Nicholas Blachford	1	1							
Will: Robinson	1	1							
Mary Collum		1		2	1				
Garret Blank		1	2	2	1				
Margaret Van D: Schuyer		1							
Peter Do	1	1	4	2					
John French	1	2		3					
Mary Harks		2							
Edmund Thomas	1	1	1						
Francis Cowenhoaf	2								
Margrett Markner		4							
John Swere	1	1	2	1					
Eliz: Collier		1							
Cor: Garretts	1	1	1	1					
John Harris	1	1	1	1					
Alford Suerts	1	1	1	4	1		1	3	
Will: Hagers	1	1	2						
Walter Hagers	1	1		1					
Johannes Ebon	2	1	2	2					
Garret Ketteltass									
James Beard									
Cornelius Quick	1	1	4	2		1			
Jacob Naoms	1		1			1			
John Windefort	1	1	2	1					
Bernard Bush	1	1	1	2					
Jocum Robeson	1	1	2						
John Vanderbeck	1	1	1	1					
Conradus Do:	1	1	1	1					
William Pearce	1	3	2	3					
Robt Crannell	1	1	2	2					
Anne Marie		1		1					
John Thorn	1	1							
Richard Fleming	1	1		1					
Margt: ffordiz		2							
John Williams Romiere	1	1	1	1					
*—ies Dolse	1	1	1						
Jacob Hases	1	1	1						
John Peake	1	2	4	3					
John Leathing	1	1	1						
Edwd Anderson	1	1		1					
Peter Low	2					1			
Alida Wright		1		2					
Griffin Jones	1	1							
Powels Turke Junr	1	1		2					
Hendrick Johnson	1	1		3					1
Eliz: Wackham		4							
Thomas Coburn	1	1							
Richard Green	1	1		1					
John Lucas	1	1		1					
Sergeant Smith	1	1							
John Bowring	1	1		1					
Peter Fauconnier	1	3	2	2	1	1			
DOCK WARD.									
Phillip ffrench	1	1	1	2	3	2	1	1	
Mrs Mogon		1	2	2		1			
Zacharie Angeum	1	1		3					
Anthony Davis		1	1	1					
Elias Budinot	1	1		1		1		1	
Johan Hardenbrok	1	1	1	2				1	
John Parmiter	1	1	1	1					
Samuel Bayard	1	1	1	2	1	1			
Nicholas Jamin		1				5	1		
Jno Casall	1	1				2			1
Johannes Hoglandt	1	2	1		1	1			
Widow Alkfield		1	1	1					
Garret Dyking	1	1	2	2	1	1	1	1	
Catharin Potter		1		2		1			
David Jameson	1	1	1	2	1	2			
Moses Levey	3	2	1	1		1	1		
Robert Lurting	2	3	3	3		1	1		
Samuel Veach	1	2		1				2	
Widow Taylor	0	1	2	1	1	1		2	
David Villat	1	1	1	1					
Mrs Allie		1	2			1	1		
David Logall	1	1	1			1			
Thos Burrough	1	1	1	2		1			
Capt Simes	1	2	2	1	1	1		1	
Robt Skelton	1	2		1	1				

* Illegible.

NEW YORK—Continued.

TABLE **90.**—NAMES OF MASTERS OF FAMILIES IN THE CITY OF NEW YORK, BY WARDS, ACCORDING TO THE ENUMERATION MADE ABOUT THE YEAR 1703—Continued.

MASTERS OF FAMILYS.	Males from 16 to 60.	females.	Male Children.	female Children.	Male Negros.	female Negros.	Male Negro Children.	female Negro Children.	all above 60.
DOCK WARD—continued.									
Charles Wooley	3				1				
Garret Vanhorne	1	1	1	2	2	1			
Paul Drulett	1	1	2	4		2			
Lewis ffarree	1	3	2	2		1	1		
Stephen D'lancey	1	1	2		3	2	1	1	
Jno James Vanveale	1	1				1		1	
Widdow ffaget		3							
Hendrick Vand:Hull	1	1	1	1					
John Shackmaple	1	2							
Peter Hemoims	2	1		1					
John Van horne	1	1	2	01	3	01	1		
Jacobus vancourtlandt	1	1	1	2	2	2	1		
Jacobus Decay	1	1	2	1	4	3	1	1	
Mrs Cuylar	1	2	1		1	1			
Jacob Ten Eyck	2	2		1			1		
Abraham Governere	1	1	1	1				1	
English Smith		2	1						1
Cornelius Jacobs		2	1	5		1		1	
David Provost Junr	1		2	3	2	1			
Widdow Sanders		3				1	3		
Affey Tuder		1	1			1			
Widdow D Roblus		4	3	1		1			
Widdow Dillies & Nathaniel Masston in Ditto	3	4	1	5		1			1
Widdow Vanhorne	1	3				1			
Abraham Sanford	1	1	3	2					
William Walton	1	2	1		1		1		
Christopher Gillin	1	1	1	2					
William Chambers	1	2	3		1				
Johannes outman	1	2	1		1				
Issac D Markeys	1	2	1	1	1	2		1	
Widdow Lawrence		1	3	2					
Peter Lakerman	1	1	1		1	1	1		1
John Gurney	1	1		1	1	1			
Widdow Sowalls	1	2							
Coll. Nich: Bayard		1	1		2			1	
ffrancis Garrabrant	1	2		2	2				
William Barkely	1	3	1	1		1			
Nicholas ffieldon	1	1	2	2					
Bartholomew Hart	1	1		1	2	1			
*—— Overin	1								
Thomas Wenham	1	1	1	1	2	3			
*—— Hibon	2	1		2	1				
*—— Vandemar	1	2	1						
* ——iv Cookers		2		1					
John Scott	1	2	1				1		
Widdow D. Pyster		1		2	1	1			
John Lorring	1	1		1		2			
Nicholas Garretts		3	2	2	1	0		1	
Abraham V: D: waters	1	1							
Harmanes Burger	1	1	1	1					
Martines Criger	1	1	1						
Andris Tenbrook	1	1	1	1					
Rugert Waldron	3	1	1	1					
John Davis	1	1	1	1	2	1	1	2	
Widdow Buddinot	1	4	2		1	2			
Richard Willit	2	1				1	1		
* ——vis Gomas	2	2	3	1	1	1			
John Harperding		1		1				1	1
Avert Elberseye	1	3	4		1				
Roger Jones	2								
Johannes Thiebout	1	1	1						
Martin Coock	1	1		1		2			
Albert Coock	2	1	3	2	1	1			
Lawrence Vanhock	2	2	2	2	1				
Cornelius Veilin	2	1	1	2				1	
Abrahm Mettelares	2	1	5	1	1	1			
John Lansing									
Evert Van D. watr	1	1		1				1	
William Echeles	1	1		1	2				
Edward Marshall	1	1	1			1			
John Wanshares	1	1		1					
John Vansent	2	1			2	1			
William Bradford	2	1	3	2		2			
Conrad Ten Eyke	4	3	1		1				
* ——rd Provost Sear	1	2		2		1			
John Everts	1	1		1	1				
Geesje ten Eges		1				1			
Hugh Crow	1	1	1					1	
Anthony Rutgers	1	1	2			1			
John Whitt	1	0	1	2					

*Illegible.

NEW YORK—Continued.

TABLE **90.**—NAMES OF MASTERS OF FAMILIES IN THE CITY OF NEW YORK, BY WARDS, ACCORDING TO THE ENUMERATION MADE ABOUT THE YEAR 1703—Continued.

MASTERS OF FAMILYS.	Males from 16 to 60.	females.	Male Children.	female Children.	Male Negros.	female Negros.	Male Negro Children.	female Negro Children.	all above 60.
DOCK WARD—continued.									
Mr Legrand	1								
Nicholas Materbe	1	1							
Samll Leveridg	1	3	4		2	1			1
William White Junr	2	1							
Mary Wakham		4						1	
Henry Money	2	1							
John Stephens	2								
Richd Green	1	1							
*——n Varickbookhouse	2	3	1	3					
*——rence Vessells	1	1	2	2	3	1			
*——aham Lawkerman	1	1	1		3	2	1	1	
Everdas Bogardus	1	2							
William Bickley	2					1	1	1	
Jannetie Van briekelen		3							
Abraham Splinter	2	1		2				1	
Gabrll Thiebod	1	1	2						
Widdow Colie	2								
Mrs. Mashett		1	1						
Johannes Burger	1	2	4						
OUT WARD.									
*—— Ritman	2	2	2	1	1		2		
*—— Kip	2	2		1	5	2	1		
*——elus Bak	1	1	1	1					
*——ids Widd		1	2	3					
Peter Bokho	1	1							
John Barr	2	1	1	3					
*—— Solomon	1	2	2						1
*——hn Peter	1	1	1	2					
*——nl Carpenter	2	2	1						1
Abraham Brimer	1	1	4						
*—— Gunoson	1	1		1					
John Dikman	1	1							
*—— Tunsedes	2	4		2	1		3	2	1
John Devor	2		3	3					
Cornelius Drk	2	1	2	2					1
Cornelius Aker	1	1	4				1		
Tuns Cornelius	2	1	3	1	1		2		
Oranout Waber		1	1	1					1
Wolford Waber	1	1	1	1					
*—— Solomon	1	1	2						
Will Da	1	1		1					
Hendrick Bordis	1	1	4	2	1				
*—— Moor	2	1	1	2	1				
*—— Griggs	1	1		2					
*—— Thomas	1	1		3	1			1	
*—— Gracklin									
Sam'l Mountaine	1	2	6	2	1				
Capt Sidmen	2	1	1	1	4	2	2	2	0
John Bronod	1	1	2	1	1		1	1	1
Rebeccah Van Scyock	1	1			2	1			
Wases Peterson	1	1	2	2	1				
Thoms Akerson	1	1	2	1					
Solomon Widdow	1	1	1	2					
Amanuel Franson	2	2		1					
Jacob Cornelius	2	1		2				0	1
Thomas Sekls	1	1							
John Clapp	1	1	2			2	1		
Abraham Bolt	1	1	3	6		1	1		
Capt Lock	1	1		1	1				
Hendrick Van Scoyock		1	2						1
Philip Minthorne	1	1	3						
*——ou	1	1	1	1	1	1	1		
*——eabor		1				1		1	1
*——way	1	1	1	1	5	1	1		
*—— —		3	1	1	2		1		
*——noute	1		1	2		1			
*—— Thomas	2	2	1	1					2
Walter Lamas				1					1
David Minvel	1	2	1		1	1			
*——lin Pierson	2	1	2	4	1	1			
Agar Harman	2	2	1	4				2	
Jacob Conant	1	1		1				1	

* Illegible.

NEW YORK—Continued.

TABLE 91.—WHITE AND SLAVE POPULATION OF NEW YORK, IN CERTAIN AGE GROUPS, BY SEX, ACCORDING TO THE PARTIAL CENSUS OF 1712.[1]

[The returns of this census are imperfect, "the people being deterred by a simple superstition, and observation that sickness followed upon the last numbering of the people."[2] The results here given are compiled from the original returns.[3]]

COUNTIES.	WHITES.						SLAVES.				Total.
	Males under 16.	Males between 16 and 60.	Males over 60.	Females under 16.	Females 16 to 60.	Females over 60.	Males under 16.	Males over 16.	Females under 16.	Females over 16.	
Albany[4]	753	688	54	651	676	49	98	155	83	122	3,329
Dutchess[4]	120	89	11	98	97	1	6	12	4	7	445
Kings[2]											1,925
New York	1,197	1,062	60	1,182	1,268	97	155	321	179	320	5,841
Orange	105	98	4	82	91	5	9	21	11	12	438
Richmond											1,279
Suffolk	1,092	929	114	1,044	926	64	26	116	32	70	4,413
Ulster[4]	450	424	44	427	406	36	68	148	39	78	2,120
Westchester	672	560	75	577	539	62	72	127	62	72	2,818
Total	4,389	3,850	362	4,061	4,003	314	434	900	410	681	22,608

[1] Census of the State of New-York, 1855, page 5.
[2] Colonial History of New-York, Vol. V, page 339
[3] New-York Colonial MSS., Vol. LVII, Secretary's office.
[4] Returns not received until 1714.

TABLE 92.—WHITE AND NEGRO POPULATION OF THE PROVINCE OF NEW YORK, DISTINGUISHED AS CHILDREN AND ADULTS, BY SEX: 1723.[1]

[Lond. Doc. XXII.]

NAME OF THE COUNTY.	WHITE.					NEGROES AND OTHER SLAVES.					Totall of Persons.
	Men.	Women.	Male Children.	Female Children.	Totall of White Persons.	Men.	Women.	Male Children.	Female Children.	Totall of Negroes & other Slaves.	
New York	1,460	1,726	1,352	1,348	5,886	408	476	220	258	1,362	7,248
Richmond	335	320	305	291	1,251	101	63	49	42	255	1,506
Kings	490	476	414	394	1,774	171	123	83	67	444	2,218
Queens	1,568	1,599	1,530	1,371	6,068	393	294	228	208	1,123	7,191
Suffolk	1,441	1,348	1,321	1,156	5,266	357	367	197	54	975	6,241
West Chester	1,050	951	1,048	912	3,961	155	118	92	83	448	4,409
Orange	309	245	304	239	1,097	45	29	42	31	147	1,244
Dutchess	276	237	259	268	1,040	22	14	2	5	43	1,083
Ulster	642	453	563	699	2,357	227	126	119	94	556	2,923
Albany	1,512	1,408	1,404	1,369	5,693	307	200	146	155	808	6,501
Totall	9,083	8,763	8,500	8,047	34,393	2,186	1,810	1,178	997	6,171	40,564

[1] New York Documentary History, page 471.

TABLE 93.—MALE AND FEMALE POPULATION OF THE PROVINCE OF NEW YORK, ABOVE AND UNDER 10 YEARS OF AGE, BY COLOR, FOR CITIES AND COUNTIES, NOVEMBER 2, 1731.[1]

[MS. in Sec's Off.]

CITYS AND COUNTIES.	Sheriffs.	Whites males above 10 years old.	Whites females above 10.	Whites males under 10.	Whites females under 10.	blacks males above ten.	blacks females above ten.	Blacks males under 10.	Blacks females under 10.	The amount in each county.
City and County of New York	Henry Beekman	2,628	2,250	1,143	1,024	599	607	186	185	8,622
City & County of Albany	Gosen Van Schick	2,481	1,255	2,352	1,212	568	185	346	174	8,573
Queens County	Thos Hicks	2,239	2,175	1,178	1,139	476	363	226	199	7,995
Suffolk County	David Corey 715 Indians	2,144	1,130	2,845	955	239	83	196	83	7,675
West Chester County	Gilbert Willet	1,879	1,701	1,054	707	269	96	176	151	6,033
Ulster County	John Wyncoop	990	914	577	515	321	196	124	91	3,728
Kings County	Domini Van Der Veer	629	518	243	268	205	146	65	76	2,150
Orange County	William Pullen	627	534	325	299	85	47	19	33	1,969
Richmond County	Charles Garritson	423	571	263	256	111	98	51	44	1,817
Dutchess County	William Squire	570	481	263	298	59	32	13	8	[2]1,724
Total		[2]14,610	11,529	10,243	6,673	2,932	1,853	1,402	1,044	[2]50,286
		11,529							1,402	
		10,243							1,853	
		6,673							2,932	
		[2]43,055	Whites.						7,231	blacks.

[1] New York Documentary History, page 471.
[2] Corrected figures.

NEW YORK—Continued.

TABLE 94.—A LIST OF THE NUMBER OF INHABITANTS, BOTH WHITES AND BLACKS OF EACH SPECIES, WITHIN THE PROVINCE OF NEW YORK, ABOVE AND UNDER THE AGE OF TEN YEARS, TAKEN IN THE YEAR 1737.[1]

[Lond. Doc. XXVI.]

COUNTIES.	White Males above 10 years.	White Females above 10 years.	White Males under 10 years.	White Females under 10 years.	Black Males above 10 years.	Black Females above 10 years.	Black Males under 10 years.	Black Females under 10 years.	Total of each county.	Total in 1731.	Since increased.
New York	3,253	3,568	1,088	1,036	674	609	229	207	10,664	8,622	2,042
Albany	3,209	2,995	1,463	1,384	714	496	223	197	10,681	8,573	2,108
West Chester	2,110	1,890	950	944	304	254	153	140	6,745	²6,033	712
Orange	860	753	501	433	125	95	38	35	2,840	1,969	871
Ulster	1,175	1,681	541	601	378	260	124	110	4,870	3,728	1,142
Dutchess	940	860	710	646	161	42	37	22	3,418	²1,724	²1,694
Richmond	488	497	289	266	132	112	52	53	1,889	1,817	72
Kings	654	631	235	264	210	169	84	101	2,348	2,150	198
Queens	2,407	2,290	1,395	1,656	400	370	254	227	9,059	7,995	1,064
Suffolk	2,297	2,353	1,175	1,008	393	307	203	187	7,923	7,675	248
Total	17,393	17,518	8,347	8,238	3,551	2,714	1,397	1,279	60,437	²50,286	²10,151

[1] New York Documentary History, page 472.   ² Corrected figures.

TABLE 95.—AN ACCOUNT OF THE NUMBER OF INHABITANTS OF THE PROVINCE OF NEW YORK, TAKEN 4 JUNE, 1746, BY ORDER OF HIS EXCELLENCY GOVERNOUR CLINTON.[1]

[London Doc., XXVIII.]

CITIES AND COUNTIES.	Males white under 16.	Males white 16 & under 60.	Males white above 60.	Females white under 16.	Females white 16 and upwards.	Males black under 60.	Males black 16 & under 60.	Males black above 60.	Females black under 16.	Females black 16 & upwards.	Total number.
City & Co. of N. Y.	2,117	2,097	149	2,013	2,897	419	645	76	735	569	²11,717
Kingston county	350	435	71	366	464	140	167	32	154	152	2,331
Albany county³											
Queens county	1,946	1,826	233	2,077	1,914	365	466	61	391	361	9,640
Dutchess county	2,200	2,056	200	2,100	1,750	106	160	26	108	100	8,806
Suffolk county	1,887	1,835	226	1,891	2,016	329	393	52	315	310	9,254
Richmond county	445	376	35	421	414	92	88	13	95	94	2,073
Orange county	536	763	67	871	721	82	99	34	51	44	3,268
Westchester county	2,435	2,090	303	2,095	1,640	187	180	27	138	140	9,235
Ulster county	1,022	1,044	116	972	1,000	244	331	43	229	264	5,265
Total	12,938	12,522	1,400	12,806	12,816	1,964	2,529	364	2,216	2,034	61,589

Total white ²52,482.

[1] New York Documentary History, O'Callaghan, page 472.   ²Corrected figures.   ³Not possible to be numbered on account of the enemy.

TABLE 96.—AN ACCOUNT OF THE NUMBER OF INHABITANTS IN THE PROVINCE OF NEW YORK, TAKEN 10TH MAY, 1749, BY ORDER OF HIS EXCELLENCY THE HONOURABLE GOVERNOUR CLINTON.[1]

[Lond. Doc., XXIX.]

CITIES AND COUNTIES.	Males white under 16 y'rs.	Males white 16 & under 60.	Males white above 60.	Fem'ls white under 16.	Fem'ls white 16 & upwards.	Total white.	Males black under 16.	Males black 16 & under 60.	Males black 60 & upwards.	Fem'ls black under 16.	Fem'ls black 16 & upwards.	Total black.
City & Co. of N. Y.	2,346	2,765	183	2,364	3,268	10,926	460	610	41	556	701	2,368
King's county	288	437	62	322	391	1,500	232	244	21	137	149	783
Albany county	2,249	2,359	322	2,137	2,087	9,154	309	424	48	334	365	1,480
Queens county	1,630	1,508	151	1,550	1,778	6,617	300	386	43	245	349	²1,323
Dutchess county	1,970	1,820	160	1,790	1,751	7,491	103	155	21	63	79	421
Suffolk county	2,058	1,863	248	1,960	1,969	8,098	305	355	41	292	293	1,286
Richmond county	431	420	36	424	434	1,745	88	110	20	93	98	409
Orange county	1,061	856	66	992	899	3,874	62	95	16	84	103	360
Westchester county	2,511	2,312	228	2,263	2,233	9,547	303	270	66	238	279	1,156
Ulster county	913	992	110	810	979	3,804	217	301	50	198	240	1,006
	Total number of whites					62,756	Total number of blacks					²10,592

Total number of Inhabitants, white and black, ²73,348.   G. CLINTON.

[1] New York Documentary History, O'Callaghan, page 473.   ²Corrected figures.

NEW YORK—Continued.

TABLE 97.—GENERAL LIST OF INHABITANTS IN THE PROVINCE OF NEW YORK, EXTRACTED FROM THE RETURNS OF THE SHERIFFS OF THE SEVERAL COUNTIES, IN PURSUANCE OF WARRANTS TO THEM, DATED 16TH FEBRUARY, 1756.[1]

CITIES AND COUNTIES.	WHITES.						BLACKS.					
	Males under 16.	Males above 16 & under 60.	Males 60 and upwards.	Females under 16.	Females above 16.	Total.	Males under 16.	Males above 16 & under 60.	Males 60 and upwards.	Females under 16.	Females above 16.	Total.
City and County of New York............	2,260	2,308	174	2,359	3,667	10,768	468	604	68	443	695	[2]2,278
City and County of Albany...............	3,474	3,795	456	3,234	3,846	14,805	658	786	76	496	403	[2]2,419
Ulster County.........................	1,655	1,687	156	1,489	1,618	6,605	328	437	49	326	360	1,500
Dutchess County.......................	3,910	2,873	203	3,530	2,782	[2]13,298	211	270	53	163	162	859
Orange County........................	1,213	1,088	74	1,083	998	[2]4,456	103	116	24	93	94	430
Westchester County....................	3,153	2,908	1,039	2,440	2,379	11,919	296	418	77	267	280	1,338
Kings County.........................	417	467	84	358	536	1,862	212	214	21	201	197	845
Queens County........................	1,900	2,147	253	1,892	2,365	8,617	581	563	55	500	470	2,169
Suffolk County........................	2,283	2,141	221	2,265	2,335	9,245	278	297	40	194	236	1,045
Richmond County......................	344	411	107	334	471	1,667	145	92	30	97	101	465

Whites, [2]83,242.

Blacks, [2]13,348.

Total, [2]96,590.

[1] New York Documentary History, O'Callaghan, page 473.   [2] Corrected figures.

TABLE 98.—LIST OF INHABITANTS IN THE SEVERAL COUNTIES IN THE PROVINCE OF NEW YORK, TAKEN IN THE YEAR 1771.[1]

NAMES OF THE SEVERAL COUNTIES.	WHITES.						BLACKS.						Total of whites and blacks.
	Males under 16.	Males above 16 & under 60.	Males 60 and upwards.	Females under 16.	Females above 16.	Total of whites in each county.	Males under 16.	Males above 16, and un-der 60.	Males 60 and upwards.	Females under 16.	Females above 16.	Total of blacks in each county.	
City & Co. of New York........	3,720	5,083	280	3,779	5,864	18,726	568	890	42	552	1,085	3,137	21,863
Albany..........................	9,740	9,822	1,136	9,086	9,045	38,829	876	1,100	250	671	980	3,877	42,706
Ulster..........................	2,835	3,023	262	2,601	3,275	11,996	518	516	57	422	441	1,954	13,950
Dutchess.......................	5,721	4,687	384	5,413	4,839	21,044	299	417	34	282	328	1,360	22,404
Orange.........................	2,651	2,297	167	2,191	2,124	9,430	162	184	22	120	174	662	10,092
Westchester....................	3,813	5,204	549	3,483	5,266	18,315	793	916	68	776	887	[2]3,440	[2]21,755
Kings..........................	548	644	76	513	680	2,461	297	287	22	261	295	1,162	3,623
Queens.........................	1,253	2,083	950	2,126	2,332	8,744	374	511	271	546	534	2,236	10,980
Suffolk.........................	2,731	2,834	347	2,658	3,106	11,676	350	389	59	320	334	1,452	13,128
Richmond.......................	616	438	96	508	595	2,253	177	152	22	106	137	594	2,847
Cumberland.....................	1,071	1,002	59	941	862	3,935	....	6	1	1	2	[2]10	[2]3,945
Gloucester......................	178	185	8	193	151	715	2	4	....	3	....	[2]9	[2]724
Totals..................	[2]34,877	37,302	4,314	33,492	38,139	148,124	4,416	5,372	848	[2]4,060	5,197	[2]19,893	[2]168,017

WM TYRON.

Estimated amount of population in 1774.

[Lond. Doc. XLIV.]

Whites..	161,098
Blacks..	21,149
Total estimated Population in 1774................................	182,247

[1] New York Documentary History, O'Callaghan, page 474.   [2] Corrected figures.

TABLE 99.—WHITE AND SLAVE POPULATION, AND INDIANS TAXED, IN NEW YORK, IN CERTAIN AGE GROUPS, BY SEX: 1786.[1]

COUNTIES.	WHITES.					SLAVES.		Indians who pay taxes.	Total.
	Males under 16 years.	Males above 16 and under 60 years.	Males above 60 years.	Females under 16 years.	Females above 16 years.	Male negroes.	Female negroes.		
Albany...................................	17,703	15,866	1,364	16,644	16,093	2,335	2,355	....	72,360
Dutchess.................................	8,209	6,973	628	7,700	7,481	830	815	....	32,636
Kings....................................	542	776	66	519	766	695	622	....	3,986
Montgomery..............................	3,564	3,487	342	3,844	3,415	217	188	....	15,057
New York................................	4,360	5,742	399	4,260	6,746	896	1,207	4	23,614
Orange...................................	3,382	3,182	247	3,206	3,187	442	416	....	14,062
Queens..................................	2,441	2,717	295	2,308	3,140	1,160	1,023	....	13,084
Richmond................................	616	622	43	540	638	369	324	....	3,152
Suffolk..................................	2,917	3,141	334	2,700	3,633	567	501	....	13,793
Ulster...................................	4,971	4,792	464	4,381	4,865	1,353	1,309	8	22,143
Washington..............................	1,130	1,152	58	1,118	983	8	7	....	4,456
Westchester.............................	4,972	4,477	491	4,546	4,818	649	601	....	20,554
Total..............................	54,807	52,927	4,731	51,766	55,765	9,521	9,368	12	238,897

[1] Census of the State of New York, 1855.

NEW JERSEY.

TABLE **100.**—AN ACCOUNT OF THE INHABITANTS OF THE PROVINCE OF NEW JERSEY, DISTINGUISHING THEIR AGE, SEX, AND COLOUR, TAKEN IN THE YEAR 1726.[1]

[From P. R. O. B. T. New Jersey, Vol. III, E 32, and N. Y. Col. Docts., Vol. V, page 819.]

NAMES OF COUNTYS.	WHITES.					NEGROES.					Total of both.
	Males above 16.	Females above 16.	Males under 16.	Females under 16.	Total of whites.	Males above 16.	Females above 16.	Males under 16.	Females under 16.	Total of negroes.	
Middlesex	953	878	1,016	859	3,706	90	73	73	67	303	4,009
Essex	992	1,021	983	926	3,922	92	78	70	68	308	4,230
Monmouth	1,234	1,061	1,095	1,056	4,446	170	90	88	85	433	4,879
Somerset	582	502	403	405	1,892	126	96	87	70	379	2,271
Bergen	569	509	556	547	2,181	173	121	100	98	492	2,673
Burlington	1,080	983	965	844	3,872	86	63	53	55	257	4,129
Hunterdon	892	743	851	750	3,236	43	45	32	21	141	3,377
Glocester	608	462	526	529	2,125	32	21	24	27	104	[2]2,229
Salem	1,060	861	1,015	891	3,827	52	38	35	25	150	3,977
Cape May	209	156	148	141	654	8	5	1	....	14	668
Total	8,179	7,176	7,558	6,948	29,861	872	630	563	516	2,581	32,442

Sent to the Lords of Trade by Gov. Burnet May 9th, 1727. "I now send Your Lordships an account of all the Inhabitants of New Jersey, as they were taken by the Sheriffs of the severall Countys. They are about three-quarters of the Inhabitants of New York."—ED.

[1] New Jersey Archives, Vol. V, page 164.   [2] Corrected figures.

TABLE **101.**—WHITE AND SLAVE POPULATION OF NEW JERSEY, ABOVE AND UNDER 16 YEARS OF AGE, BY SEX: 1737–38.

COUNTIES.	WHITES.					NEGROES & OTHER SLAVES.					Total of Both in each county.
	Males above 16.	Females above 16.	Males under 16.	Females under 16.	Total of Whites.	Males above 16.	Females above 16.	Males under 16.	Females under 16.	Total of Slaves.	
Middlesex	1,134	1,085	1,086	956	[2]4,261	181	124	91	107	503	4,764
Essex	1,118	1,720	1,619	1,494	[2]5,951	114	114	84	63	375	[2]6,326
Bergen	939	822	820	708	3,289	256	203	187	160	806	4,095
Somersett	967	940	999	867	3,773	255	175	170	132	732	4,505
Monmouth	1,508	1,339	1,289	1,295	5,431	233	152	129	141	655	6,086
Burlington	1,487	1,222	1,190	996	4,895	134	87	58	64	343	5,238
Gloucester	930	757	782	676	3,145	42	24	32	24	122	3,267
Salem	1,669	1,391	1,313	1,327	5,700	57	56	40	31	184	5,884
Cape May	261	219	271	211	962	12	10	9	11	42	1,004
Hunterdon	1,618	1,230	1,270	1,170	5,288	75	53	49	42	219	5,507
Total	[2]11,631	10,725	10,639	9,700	[2]42,695	1,359	998	849	775	3,981	[2]46,676

[1] New Jersey Archives, Vol. VI, page 244.   [2] Corrected figures.

TABLE **102.**—POPULATION OF NEW JERSEY IN 1737–38 AND IN 1745.[1]

[From P. R. O. B. T., New Jersey, Vol. V, F. 77.]

The Number of People in the Western Division of the Province of New Jersey taken by order of His Excellency Lewis Morris Esq'r Captain General & Commander in Chief of the Province of New Jersey &c. in the Year of our Lord 1745.

COUNTIES.	Males above 16 Years.	Males under 16 Years.	Females above 16 Years.	Females under 16 Years.	Quakers or Reputed Quakers.	SLAVES.		Whole Number of Inhabitants.	Increase since 1737–8.	Decrease since 1737–8.
						Males.	Females.			
Morris	1,109	1,190	957	1,087	22	57	36	4,436	8,080	....
Hunterdon	2,302	2,182	2,117	2,090	240	244	216	9,151		....
Burlington	1,786	1,528	1,605	1,454	3,237	233	197	6,803	1,565	....
Gloucester	913	786	797	808	1,436	121	81	3,506	239	....
Salem	1,716	1,746	1,603	1,595	1,090	90	97	6,847	963	....
Cape May	306	284	272	274	54	30	22	1,188	184	....
Total	8,132	7,716	[2]7,351	7,308	6,079	775	649	[2]31,931	11,031	....

The Number of People in the Eastern Division of the Province of New Jersey taken per order as on preceding table.

COUNTIES.	Males above 16 Years.	Males under 16 Years.	Females above 16 Years.	Females under 16 Years.	Quakers or Reputed Quakers.	SLAVES.		Whole Number of Inhabitants.	Increase since 1737–8.	Decrease since 1737–8.
						Males.	Females.			
Bergen	721	494	590	585	....	379	237	3,006	....	1,089
Essex	1,694	1,652	1,649	1,548	35	244	201	6,988	....	31
Middlesex	1,728	1,651	1,659	1,695	400	483	396	7,612	2,848	....
Monmouth	2,071	1,975	1,783	1,899	3,131	513	386	8,627	2,541	....
Somersett	740	765	672	719	91	194	149	3,239	....	....
Total	6,954	6,537	6,353	6,446	[2]3,657	1,813	1,369	29,472	5,389	1,120
Total in both Divisions	15,086	14,253	[2]13,704	13,754	[2]9,736	2,588	2,018	[2]61,403	16,420	....

[1] New Jersey Archives, Vol. VI, pages 242, 243.   [2] Corrected figures.

MARYLAND.

TABLE **103.**—AN ACCOUNT OF THE NUMBER OF SOULS IN THE PROVINCE OF MARYLAND, IN THE YEAR 1755.[1]

	TAXABLE PERSONS 16 YEARS OF AGE.											PERSONS NOT TAXABLE.								
	Whites.			Mulattoes.				Blacks.				Whites.			Servants, women.		Mulattoes. Past labor or cripples.		Blacks. Past labor or cripples.	
	Free.	Servants.		Free.		Slaves.		Free.		Slaves.		Free.								
NAME OF THE COUNTY.	Men.	Men, hired or indented.	Men, convicts.	Men.	Women.	Men.	Women.	Men.	Women.	Men.	Women.	Clergy.	Men, poor.	Women.	Hired or indented.	Convicts.	Free.	Slaves.	Free.	Slaves.
Baltimore	2,630	595	472	36	21	25	16	2	2	1,144	833	4	58	2,587	200	87	14	4	8	47
Ann Arundell	1,534	438	184	16	22	25	11	8	4	1,472	1,060	3	64	1,539	93	51	4	15	6	92
Calvert	609	124	......	24	8	......	4	......	1	550	519	2	20	639	61	......	2	15	7	39
Prince George	1,515	255	73	17	21	37	43	3	3	1,278	151	3	44	1,080	55	27	8	7	2	88
Frederick	2,775	216	94	23	4	10	24	45	26	437	314	1	45	2,213	163	32	6	2	4	13
Charles	1,929	173	205	60	36	48	33	3	1	1,196	950	4	51	1,777	106	78	17	5	2	32
St. Mary's	1,561	194	29	16	17	38	27	16	5	822	761	3	61	1,806	164	13	16	14	3	49
Worcester	1,768	45	1	31	32	3	7	1	2	401	359	1	57	1,964	37	1	1	10	7	44
Somerset	1,348	31	1	23	16	15	15	4	3	637	571	3	61	1,446	37	......	......	1	2	37
Dorset	1,950	172	7	9	7	9	22	7	3	624	514	3	44	2,097	126	......	8	8	2	44
Talbot	1,223	294	25	24	18	72	63	12	3	647	595	2	34	1,296	160	4	10	1	4	30
Queen Anne's	1,745	284	287	18	20	33	32	8	9	643	572	3	31	1,843	159	73	3	6	3	32
Kent	1,454	365	82	8	13	7	9	10	5	691	523	2	34	1,448	181	12	6	9	6	35
Cecil	1,345	390	47	2	12	120	86	......	2	286	216	1	33	1,186	282	8	......	2	2	13
Total	23,386	3,576	1,507	307	247	442	392	119	69	10,828	[2]7,938	35	637	23,521	1,824	386	95	99	58	595

	PERSONS UNDER 16 YEARS OF AGE.														AGGREGATE.			
	Whites.						Mulattoes.				Blacks.							
	Free.		Servants hired, or indented.		Servants, convicts.		Free.		Slaves.		Free.		Slaves.					
NAME OF THE COUNTY.	Boys.	Girls.	Boys.	Girls.	Boys.	Girls.	Boys.	Girls.	Boys.	Girls.	Boys.	Girls.	Boys.	Girls.	Whites.	Mulattoes.	Blacks.	Total.
Baltimore	3,115	2,951	126	49	6	6	63	62	28	43	3	1	959	1,041	12,886	312	4,040	17,238
Ann Arundell	1,913	1,705	82	26	16	......	28	35	31	23	10	5	1,314	1,321	7,648	210	5,292	13,150
Calvert	861	745	48	28	......	......	30	31	15	17	......	......	671	645	3,137	146	2,432	5,715
Prince George	1,840	1,674	33	10	1	......	42	26	46	55	......	......	1,340	1,239	7,210	302	4,104	11,616
Frederick	3,246	3,105	80	56	9	1	22	23	19	19	3	1	465	473	12,036	152	1,781	13,969
Charles	1,681	1,799	228	41	16	7	69	57	52	51	7	......	1,145	1,197	8,095	428	4,533	13,056
St. Mary's	1,845	1,764	29	24	5	3	24	22	94	98	13	17	862	839	7,501	366	3,387	11,254
Worcester	2,067	2,083	28	12	......	......	28	29	7	8	13	6	561	511	8,064	156	1,905	10,125
Somerset	1,330	1,232	12	......	......	......	24	19	21	25	1	1	875	891	5,501	159	3,022	8,682
Dorset	2,347	2,222	54	17	......	2	12	22	35	32	6	1	666	681	9,041	164	2,548	11,753
Talbot	1,322	1,197	57	9	......	......	20	19	74	81	......	1	579	657	5,623	382	2,528	8,533
Queen Anne's	2,037	1,864	82	44	9	......	31	24	57	58	2	4	621	603	8,461	282	2,497	11,240
Kent	1,527	1,423	134	76	4	1	16	19	9	20	8	3	650	653	6,743	116	2,584	9,443
Cecil	1,506	1,372	55	20	1	1	10	4	89	108	5	......	275	252	6,247	433	1,051	7,731
Total	26,637	25,136	1,048	412	67	21	419	392	577	638	71	40	10,983	11,003	108,193	3,608	41,704	153,505

[1] Gentleman's Magazine, Vol. XXXIV, page 261. [2] Corrected figures.

GENERAL TABLES
DERIVED FROM THE FIRST AND
SUBSEQUENT CENSUSES

1790-1900

TABLE **104.**—POPULATION AS REPORTED AT THE FIRST CENSUS, BY COUNTIES AND MINOR CIVIL DIVISIONS: 1790.

MAINE.

COUNTY AND TOWN.	Total.	White Population in 1790. Males. 16 years and over.	Males. Under 16 years.	Females.	All other free persons.	Slaves.
Cumberland county	25,530	6,208	6,624	12,519	179	
Bakerstown plantation	1,270	289	370	611		
Bridgton	329	100	81	147	1	
Brunswick	1,387	355	332	662	38	
Bucktown plantation	453	96	146	211		
Butterfield plantation	189	49	55	85		
Cape Elizabeth	1,356	341	324	683	8	
Durham	722	161	215	343	3	
Falmouth	2,995	648	815	1,504	28	
Flintstown plantation	190	54	48	88		
Freeport	1,327	333	342	650	2	
Gorham and Scarborough	4,476	1,108	1,134	2,187	47	
Gray	577	148	139	290		
Harpswell	1,071	253	268	539	11	
New Gloucester	1,358	320	338	694	6	
North Yarmouth	1,923	464	488	957	14	
Otisfield plantation	197	56	46	95		
Plantation No. 4	344	89	101	154		
Portland	2,239	564	537	1,122	16	
Raymondtown plantation	345	81	92	170	2	
Rusfield gore	102	22	30	50		
Scarborough (see Gorham and Scarborough).						
Shepardsfield plantation	528	126	140	261	1	
Standish	705	181	182	341	1	
Turner	349	87	104	158		
Waterford plantation	160	55	32	73		
Windham	938	228	265	444	1	
Hancock county	9,542	2,435	2,529	4,540	38	
Barrettstown	173	61	44	68		
Belfast	245	64	55	126		
Bluehill	274	69	79	125	1	
Camden	331	93	85	153		
Canaan	132	34	39	59		
Conduskeeg plantation	567	145	170	249	3	
Deer Isle	683	175	182	318	8	
Ducktrap	278	78	82	118		
Eastern River township No. 2	240	59	63	118		
Eddy township	110	19	32	59		
Frankfort	891	235	235	419	2	
Gouldsborough	267	78	64	116	9	
Isleborough	382	90	114	177	1	
Mount Desert	744	191	207	345	1	
Orphan Island	124	33	31	60		
Orrington	477	114	128	234	1	
Penobscot	1,040	248	248	538	6	
Sedgwick	569	144	155	270		
Small islands not belonging to any town	66	19	17	30		
Sullivan	504	126	123	254	1	
Trenton (including township No. 1, east side of Union river)	312	75	92	144	1	
Township No. 1 (Bucks)	316	85	81	148	2	
Township No. 6 (west side of Union river)	239	69	49	120	1	
Vinalhaven	578	131	154	292	1	
Lincoln county	29,733	7,668	7,679	14,245	141	
Balltown	904	228	251	425		
Bath	943	233	259	444	7	
Boothbay	998	247	248	499	4	
Bowdoin	970	235	261	459	15	
Bowdoinham	455	109	127	218	1	
Bristol	516	115	143	257	1	
Canaan	446	99	132	215		
Carratunk	105	31	35	39		
Carrs plantation, or Unity	127	32	33	62		
Chester plantation	70	24	19	27		
Cushing	942	256	235	451		
Edgecomb	843	182	259	402		
Fairfield	453	122	114	217		
Georgetown	1,327	342	320	654	11	
Great Pond plantation	164	43	52	69		
Greene	372	101	99	172		
Hallowell	1,189	330	281	566	12	
Hancock	278	83	64	130	1	
Hunts Meadow	68	15	21	32		
Jones plantation	244	62	63	119		
Lewistown and gore adjoining	526	127	140	259		
Little River	64	17	15	32		
Littleborough plantation	270	71	69	123	7	
Livermore, east side of Androscoggin river	44	15	8	21		
Meduncook	321	89	79	153		
New Castle	898	226	221	448	3	
Lincoln county—Continued.						
New Sandwich	296	91	65	140		
Nobleborough	1,310	316	348	642	4	
Norridgewock	332	91	89	152		
Norridgewock, settlement east of	43	11	12	20		
Pittston	603	182	133	281	7	
Pownalborough	2,043	535	535	969	4	
Prescotts and Whitchers plantation	32	12	8	11	1	
Rockmeeko, east side of river	59	28	7	24		
Sandy river, first township	493	141	127	223	2	
Sandy river, from its mouth to Carrs plantation	324	78	93	152	1	
Sandy river, middle township	65	17	15	33		
Sandy river, upper township	60	18	17	25		
Seven Mile Brook	138	41	34	62	1	
Smithtown plantation	512	142	129	240	1	
Starling plantation	168	60	31	77		
Thomaston	799	207	209	379	4	
Titcomb	147	34	36	77		
Topsham	826	215	203	398	10	
Twenty-five Mile Pond	119	33	27	59		
Union	200	53	50	94	3	
Vassalborough	1,246	301	311	623	11	
Waldoborough	1,720	429	454	824	13	
Wales plantation	440	115	120	205		
Warren	646	178	148	307	13	
Washington	612	166	138	308		
Winslow, with its adjacents	798	203	223	371	1	
Winthrop	1,227	304	328	593	2	
Woolwich	791	205	195	390	1	
Between Norridgewock and Seven Mile Brook	147	28	46	73		
Washington county	2,760	754	708	1,278	20	
Bucks Harbor Neck	61	14	18	29		
Machias	818	229	210	372	7	
Plantations east of Machias:						
No. 1	66	18	16	32		
No. 2	144	41	30	67	6	
No. 4	54	16	13	25		
No. 5	84	24	26	34		
No. 8	244	75	60	109		
No. 9	29	9	7	13		
No. 10	42	14	5	23		
No. 11	37	8	10	19		
No. 12	54	13	15	26		
No. 13	7	1	5	1		
Plantations west of Machias:						
No. 4	233	71	59	103		
No. 5	177	45	49	83		
No. 6	209	56	55	98		
No. 11	95	22	24	49		
No. 12	8	4	1	3		
No. 13	223	51	61	105	6	
No. 22	175	43	44	87	1	
York county	29,078	7,276	7,193	14,451	158	
Arundel	1,461	367	375	708	11	
Berwick	3,890	978	920	1,950	42	
Biddeford	1,018	273	233	506	6	
Brownfield township	146	39	37	68	2	
Brownfield township—in the gore adjoining	20	6	5	9		
Buxton	1,508	357	402	746	3	
Coxhall	761	164	235	362		
Francisborough plantation	409	98	101	210		
Fryeburgh	549	142	138	268	1	
Hiram	92	22	29	41		
Kittery	3,205	765	696	1,705	39	
Lebanon	1,276	310	344	622		
Limerick	409	98	110	200	1	
Little Falls	607	159	147	301		
Little Ossipee	663	144	200	318	1	
New Penacook	77	23	13	41		
Parsonsfield	654	174	169	311		
Pepperellborough	1,343	339	358	646		
Porterfield	71	23	14	34		
Sanford	1,798	449	473	876		
Shapleigh	1,319	310	370	630	9	
Sudbury-Canada	324	82	89	153		
Sudbury, settlements adjoining	51	17	13	21		
Suncook	85	22	25	38		
Washington plantation	261	72	51	138		
Waterborough	968	229	276	463		
Waterford	154	45	35	74		
Wells	3,061	819	733	1,494	15	
York	2,898	750	602	1,518	28	

TABLE **104.**—POPULATION AS REPORTED AT THE FIRST CENSUS, BY COUNTIES AND MINOR CIVIL DIVISIONS: 1790—Continued.

NEW HAMPSHIRE.

COUNTY AND TOWN.	Total.	White population in 1790. Males. 16 years and over.	Under 16 years.	Females.	All other free persons.	Slaves.
Cheshire county	28,753	7,008	7,567	14,090	70	18
Acworth	705	160	197	348		
Alstead	1,112	268	285	558	1	
Charlestown	1,094	307	254	531	1	1
Chesterfield	1,903	441	532	928	2	
Claremont	1,423	348	389	682	2	2
Cornish	982	238	258	484	1	1
Croydon	536	121	150	262	3	
Dublin	899	227	223	444	5	
Fitzwilliam	1,038	255	278	505		
Gilsom	298	70	64	164		
Hinsdale	524	127	142	251		4
Jaffrey	1,238	285	336	606	11	
Keene	1,307	319	318	663	5	2
Langdon	244	58	76	108	2	
Lempster	415	110	95	207	3	
Marlborough	786	175	219	392		
Marlow	319	73	90	156		
New Grantham	333	90	88	153	1	1
Newport	779	187	198	389	4	1
Packersfield	724	170	208	343	3	
Plainfield	1,024	259	277	486	2	
Protectworth	210	56	49	104		1
Richmond	1,380	332	368	680		
Rindge	1,143	276	306	554	7	
Stoddard	701	162	194	344		1
Sullivan	220	48	68	103	1	
Surry	448	117	111	220		
Swanzey	1,155	291	286	572	6	
Unity	538	133	139	265	1	
Walpole	1,254	327	335	589	1	2
Washington	545	137	135	273		
Wendell	267	70	64	133		
Westmoreland	2,000	473	524	998	4	1
Winchester	1,209	298	311	595	4	1
Grafton county	13,468	3,768	3,311	6,340	28	21
Alexandria	297	79	87	131		
Bartlett	248	55	57	135		1
Bath	493	117	136	239		1
Bridgewater	281	84	62	134		1
Burton	141	34	45	62		
Cambridge (not inhabited)						
Campton	395	113	79	202		1
Canaan	483	137	123	223		
Chatham	58	17	13	28		
Cockburn	26	9	5	12		
Cockermouth	373	94	104	175		
Colburne	29	10	6	13		
Concord (alias Gunthwaite)	313	91	75	147		
Coventry	88	21	20	47		
Dalton	14	3	4	7		
Dame's Location	21	4	8	9		
Dartmouth	111	34	25	52		
Dorchester	175	48	45	82		
Dummer (not inhabited)						
Enfield (alias Relhan)	724	188	173	361	2	
Errol (not inhabited)						
Franconia	72	22	18	32		
Grafton	403	99	110	194		
Hale's Location	9	3	2	4		
Hanover (including 152 students at Dartmouth College)	1,379	476	297	596	8	2
Hart's Location	12	3	4	5		
Haverhill	552	163	118	266	1	4
Kilkenny (not inhabited)						
Lancaster	161	45	45	71		
Landaff	292	75	80	137		
Lebanon	1,180	375	282	515	8	
Lincoln	22	8	5	9		
Littleton	96	28	26	42		
Lyman	202	57	39	106		
Lyme	816	231	189	392	4	
Millfield (not inhabited)						
New Chester	312	70	103	139		
New Holderness	329	96	73	160		
Northumberland	117	34	27	56		
Orange	131	32	37	61		1
Orford	540	140	125	272		3
Peeling (not inhabited)						
Percy	48	14	11	23		
Piermont	426	103	113	206	1	3
Plymouth	625	182	142	297		4
Rumney	411	97	113	201		
Senter's Location	8	5		3		
Shelburne	35	12	5	18		
Stark's Location	29	8	5	16		
Sterling's Location	9	3	2	4		
Stratford	144	44	35	65		

COUNTY AND TOWN.	Total.	White population in 1790. Males. 16 years and over.	Under 16 years.	Females.	All other free persons.	Slaves.
Grafton county—Continued.						
Success (not inhabited)						
Thornton	385	96	98	191		
Trecothick (not inhabited)						
Wales's Location	6	1	3	2		
Warren	206	52	64	86	4	
Wentworth	241	56	73	112		
Hillsborough county	32,883	8,145	8,392	16,170	176	
Amherst	2,369	571	575	1,205	18	
Andover	645	166	167	312		
Antrim	526	138	144	244		
Bedford	897	210	240	440	7	
Boscawen	1,108	282	274	551	1	
Bradford	217	56	60	101		
Campbell's Gore	120	28	35	57		
Dearing	938	213	264	459	2	
Derryfield	362	92	95	175		
Derryfield Gore	30	10	4	16		
Dunbarton	921	209	244	448	20	
Dunstable	634	179	146	308	1	
Duxbury Mile-slip	169	39	45	85		
Fishersfield	325	68	105	152		
Francestown	983	232	234	517		
Goffstown	1,275	324	303	614	34	
Hancock	634	156	160	315	3	
Heniker	1,124	266	325	525	8	
Hillsborough	798	193	211	393	1	
Hollis	1,441	340	378	723		
Hopkinton	1,715	445	417	852	1	
Kersarge Gore	103	27	27	49		
Litchfield	369	99	87	166	17	
Lyndborough	1,280	313	349	618		
Lyndborough Gore	38	11	8	19		
Mason	922	215	242	462	3	
Merrimac	819	209	207	393	10	
New Boston	1,204	313	303	578	10	
New Ipswich	1,241	338	285	614	4	
New London	311	69	90	152		
Nottingham West	1,064	267	246	544	7	
Peterborough	861	221	213	423	4	
Raby	338	86	89	160	3	
Salisbury	1,362	335	385	640	2	
Sharon	260	68	63	129		
Society Land	329	84	89	156		
Sutton	520	132	122	266		
Temple	747	177	196	368	6	
Warner	863	220	195	448		
Weare	1,924	491	500	931	2	
Wilton	1,097	253	270	562	12	
Rockingham county	43,184	11,141	9,667	21,987	292	97
Allenstown	255	68	63	123	1	
Atkinson	480	129	102	247	2	
Bow	566	147	151	268		
Brintwood	976	255	224	490	6	1
Candia	1,040	246	273	521		
Canterbury	1,048	295	223	526	1	3
Chester	1,899	490	448	960	1	
Chichester	492	137	118	237		
Concord	1,738	494	405	828	7	4
Deerfield	1,613	444	358	808	1	2
East Kingston	358	90	87	179	2	
Epping	1,255	338	256	654	2	5
Epsom	830	200	203	427		
Exeter	1,722	437	343	859	81	2
Gosport (on Star Island)	93	32	22	39		
Greenland	634	170	141	309	12	2
Hampstead	725	195	157	370	2	1
Hampton	852	238	174	436	3	1
Hampton Falls	540	150	96	291	3	
Hawke	422	101	95	225		1
Kensington	804	222	147	435		
Kingston	905	244	188	470	3	
Londonderry	2,604	676	573	1,325	25	5
Loudon	1,074	272	274	521	5	2
Newcastle	534	125	117	292		
Newington	542	132	109	285	2	14
Newmarket	1,137	284	235	610	7	1
Newtown	530	126	132	271		1
Northampton	657	184	138	333	2	
Northfield	606	154	155	295	2	
Northwood	746	188	181	376		1
Nottingham	1,069	275	249	530	4	11
Peiham	794	216	193	385		
Pembrook	962	239	247	474		2
Pittsfield	872	204	220	444	4	
Plaistow	516	134	123	259		
Poplin	493	136	104	251	1	1
Portsmouth	4,720	1,158	973	2,487	76	26

TABLE 104.—POPULATION AS REPORTED AT THE FIRST CENSUS, BY COUNTIES AND MINOR CIVIL DIVISIONS: 1790—Continued.

NEW HAMPSHIRE—Continued.

COUNTY AND TOWN.	Total.	Males. 16 years and over.	Males. Under 16 years.	Females.	All other free persons.	Slaves.
Rockingham county—Cont'd.						
Raymond	727	177	181	361	8	......
Rye	865	226	189	439	8	3
Salem	1,218	287	294	626	9	2
Sandown	562	138	115	309	......	......
Seabrook	715	178	178	357	2	......
South Hampton	449	125	82	241	1	......
Stratham	832	229	158	486	8	1
Windham	663	156	173	328	1	5
Strafford county	23,611	6,012	5,918	11,596	64	21
Barnstead	807	192	214	400	......	1
Barrington	2,481	608	650	1,221	2	......
Conway	574	149	146	279	......	......
Dover	1,996	547	418	1,005	18	8
Durham	1,246	336	271	634	2	3
Eaton	254	60	72	122	......	......
Effingham	153	42	43	67	......	1
Gilmantown	2,610	615	682	1,290	22	1

COUNTY AND TOWN.	Total.	Males. 16 years and over.	Males. Under 16 years.	Females.	All other free persons.	Slaves.
Strafford county—Continued.						
Lee	1,036	277	224	533	2	......
Madbury	592	167	126	295	4	......
Merideth	882	248	211	419	4	......
Middleton	617	151	162	304	......	......
Moultonborough	565	133	148	283	......	1
New Durham	554	139	140	275	......	......
New Durham Gore	445	108	118	212	7	......
New Hampton	652	171	173	306	2	......
Ossipee	339	86	82	171	......	......
Rochester	2,852	728	740	1,383	......	1
Sanborntown	1,587	415	424	748	......	......
Sandwich	905	216	243	446	......	......
Somersworth	945	248	211	481	1	4
Stark's Location	3	2	......	1	......	......
Sterling's Location	48	10	13	25	......	......
Tamworth	266	67	72	126	......	1
Tuftonborough	109	29	20	60	......	......
Wakefield	646	158	195	293	......	......
Wolfborough	447	110	120	217	......	......

VERMONT.

COUNTY AND TOWN.	Total.	Males. 16 years and over.	Males. Under 16 years.	Females.	All other free persons.	Slaves.
Addison county	6,420	1,768	1,656	2,959	37	......
Addison	402	108	106	186	2	......
Bridport	450	123	122	205	......	......
Bristol	211	53	57	101	......	......
Cornwall	825	214	218	333	......	......
Ferrisburg	481	137	119	213	12	......
Hancock	56	18	11	27	......	......
Kingston	101	26	31	44	......	......
Leicester	344	94	81	169	......	......
Middlebury	395	125	92	176	2	......
Monkton	449	122	134	193	......	......
New Haven	717	180	218	319	......	......
Panton	220	57	66	97	......	......
Salisbury	444	122	107	215	......	......
Shoreham	701	198	161	337	5	......
Vergennes	201	73	35	79	14	......
Weybridge	174	48	41	84	1	......
Whiting	249	70	57	121	1	......
Bennington county	12,206	3,103	3,205	5,865	33	......
Arlington	992	252	252	488	......	......
Bennington	2,350	628	601	1,101	20	......
Bromley	71	21	19	31	......	......
Dorsett	957	240	230	487	......	......
Glastonbury	34	6	11	17	......	......
Landgrove	31	7	4	20	......	......
Manchester	1,278	338	339	596	5	......
Pownal	1,732	418	498	815	1	......
Reedsborough	63	16	15	32	......	......
Rupert	1,034	251	289	494	......	......
Sandgate	773	198	189	386	......	......
Shaftsbury	1,990	491	528	967	4	......
Stamford	272	69	65	137	1	......
Sunderland	414	113	101	199	1	......
Winhall	155	39	46	69	1	......
Woodford	60	16	18	26	......	......
Chittenden county	7,287	2,251	1,761	3,252	23	......
Alburgh	446	147	106	189	4	......
Bakersfield	13	4	4	5	......	......
Bolton	88	21	26	41	......	......
Burlington	330	108	68	151	3	......
Cambridge	359	108	84	167	......	......
Cambridge Gore	15	3	6	6	......	......
Charlotte	635	189	142	301	3	......
Colchester	137	42	40	55	......	......
Duxbury	39	9	18	12	......	......
Elmore	12	7	1	4	......	......
Essex	354	118	76	160	......	......
Fairfax	254	85	61	108	......	......
Fairfield	126	43	28	55	......	......
Fletcher	47	13	14	20	......	......
Georgia	340	105	80	155	......	......
Highgate	103	26	31	45	1	......
Hinesburgh	454	127	115	212	......	......
Hungerford	40	16	8	11	5	......
Huntsburgh	46	25	10	11	......	......
Hydespark	43	10	12	18	3	......
Isle Mott	47	18	13	16	......	......
Jerico	381	115	90	176	......	......
Johnson	93	31	16	46	......	......
Middlesex	60	16	19	25	......	......
Milton	283	90	65	128	......	......
Minden	18	6	6	6	......	......

COUNTY AND TOWN.	Total.	Males. 16 years and over.	Males. Under 16 years.	Females.	All other free persons.	Slaves.
Chittenden county—Cont'd.						
Moretown	24	10	6	8	......	......
Morristown	10	6	......	4	......	......
New Huntington	136	34	40	62	......	......
New Huntington Gore	31	10	7	14	......	......
North Hero	125	40	25	57	3	......
St. Albans	256	89	61	105	1	......
St. George	57	14	17	26	......	......
Shelburne	387	108	103	176	......	......
Smithfield	70	28	14	28	......	......
South Hero	537	164	128	245	......	......
Starksborough	40	15	6	19	......	......
Swanton	74	22	25	27	......	......
Underhill	59	16	12	31	......	......
Waitsfield	61	21	16	24	......	......
Waterbury	93	22	27	44	......	......
Westford	63	23	8	32	......	......
Williston	469	136	120	213	......	......
Wolcott	32	11	7	14	......	......
Orange county	10,526	2,873	2,765	4,847	41	......
Barnet	477	137	132	207	1	......
Barton (not inhabited)	......	......	......	......	......	......
Berlin	134	38	33	63	......	......
Billymead (not inhabited)	......	......	......	......	......	......
Bradford	654	158	176	313	7	......
Braintree	221	61	66	89	5	......
Brookfield	419	113	116	189	1	......
Brownington (not inhabited)	......	......	......	......	......	......
Brunswick	66	15	15	36	......	......
Burke (not inhabited)	......	......	......	......	......	......
Cabot	122	33	37	52	......	......
Calais	45	14	11	20	......	......
Caldersburgh (not inhabited)	......	......	......	......	......	......
Canaan	19	4	5	10	......	......
Chelsea	239	77	62	100	......	......
Concord	49	18	12	19	......	......
Corinth	578	147	156	275	......	......
Danville	574	165	139	270	......	......
Dewey's Gore	48	12	18	18	......	......
Fairley	463	132	120	210	1	......
Ferdinand (not inhabited)	......	......	......	......	......	......
Glover (not inhabited)	......	......	......	......	......	......
Granby (not inhabited)	......	......	......	......	......	......
Greensborough	19	9	4	6	......	......
Groton	45	15	9	21	......	......
Guildhall	158	55	41	62	......	......
Hardwick	3	3	......	......	......	......
Harris Gore (not inhabited)	......	......	......	......	......	......
Hopkins Grant (not inhabited)	......	......	......	......	......	......
Lemington	31	12	7	12	......	......
Lewis (not inhabited)	......	......	......	......	......	......
Littleton	63	16	14	33	......	......
Lunenburgh	119	30	29	60	......	......
Lyndon	59	29	10	20	......	......
Maidstone	125	34	36	55	......	......
Marshfield (not inhabited)	......	......	......	......	......	......
Minehead (not inhabited)	......	......	......	......	......	......
Montpelier	118	55	19	44	......	......
Navy (not inhabited)	......	......	......	......	......	......
Newark (not inhabited)	......	......	......	......	......	......
Newbury	872	225	222	413	12	......
Northfield	40	10	10	20	......	......
Orange (not inhabited)	......	......	......	......	......	......
Peachum	365	102	90	173	......	......
Randolph	893	227	237	429	......	......
Random (not inhabited)	......	......	......	......	......	......

TABLE **104.**—POPULATION AS REPORTED AT THE FIRST CENSUS, BY COUNTIES AND MINOR CIVIL DIVISIONS: 1790—Continued.

VERMONT—Continued.

COUNTY AND TOWN.	Total.	Males. 16 years and over.	Under 16 years.	Females.	All other free persons.	Slaves.
Orange county—Continued.						
Roxbury	14	6	2	6		
Ryegate	187	46	54	87		
St. Andrews (not inhabited)						
St. Johnsbury	143	54	34	55		
Sheffield (not inhabited)						
Strafford	844	213	228	403		
Thetford	862	211	218	419	14	
Topsham	162	36	56	70		
Tunbridge	487	121	147	219		
Vershire	439	117	118	204		
Victory (not inhabited)						
Walden	11	3	3	5		
Walden's Gore	32	9	9	14		
Washington	72	26	13	33		
Westmore (not inhabited)						
Wheelock	33	14	7	12		
Wildersburgh	76	30	16	30		
Williamstown	146	41	34	71		
Winlock (not inhabited)						
Woodbury (not inhabited)						
Rutland county	15,590	3,990	4,098	7,470	32	
Benson	658	185	182	290	1	
Brandon	637	154	168	314	1	
Castleton	809	210	222	376	1	
Chittenden	159	38	49	72		
Clarendon	1,480	343	397	740		
Danby	1,206	276	333	589	8	
Fair Haven	545	174	121	250		
Harwich	165	38	49	78		
Hubbardton	410	120	94	196		
Ira	312	77	82	153		
Killington	32	11	10	11		
Middletown	699	169	172	358		
Midway	34	7	9	18		
Orwell	778	215	218	341	4	
Pawlet	1,458	348	399	709	2	
Philadelphia	39	12	9	18		
Pittsfield	49	13	12	24		
Pittsford	850	219	208	422	1	
Poultney	1,120	282	292	539	7	
Rutland	1,417	396	351	668	2	
Shrewsbury	382	98	101	183		
Sudbury	258	67	69	122		
Tinmouth	935	247	244	442	2	
Wallingford	538	142	131	262	3	
Wells	620	149	176	295		
Windham county	17,572	4,416	4,672	8,426	58	
Athens	450	103	138	209		
Brattleborough	1,589	381	426	758	14	
Dummerston	1,490	362	394	724	10	
Guilford	2,422	586	646	1,177	13	
Hallifax	1,209	302	342	561	4	
Hinsdale	482	118	142	221	1	
Jamaica	263	71	66	126		
Johnson's Gore	49	15	13	21		
Londonderry	362	90	99	172	1	
Marlborough	629	149	176	304		
New Fane	660	163	177	320		
Putney	1,848	438	492	906	12	
Rockingham	1,235	327	319	587	2	
Somerset	111	26	35	50		
Stratton	95	27	22	46		
Thomlinson	561	143	165	253		
Townsend	678	192	171	315		
Wardsborough, North District	483	128	126	229		
Wardsborough, South District	270	72	69	129		
Westminster	1,599	429	387	782	1	
Whitingham	442	114	119	209		
Wilmington	645	180	138	327		
Windsor county	15,740	4,004	4,148	7,543	45	
Andover	275	75	74	126		
Barnard	673	177	167	329		
Bethel	473	126	118	229		
Bridgwater	293	68	78	147		
Cavendish	491	126	125	240		
Chester	981	265	255	457	4	
Hartford	988	248	250	489	1	
Hartland	1,652	415	442	789	6	
Ludlow	179	43	57	79		
Norwich	1,158	280	322	556		
Pomfret	710	177	209	319	5	
Reading	747	171	211	359	6	
Rochester	215	62	47	106		
Royalton	748	195	190	363		
Saltash	106	29	35	42		
Sharon	569	147	147	275		
Springfield	1,097	289	289	516	3	
Stockbridge	100	32	25	43		
Weathersfield	1,146	294	285	560	7	
Windsor	1,542	395	406	732	9	
Woodstock	1,597	390	416	787	4	

MASSACHUSETTS.

COUNTY AND TOWN.	Total.	Males. 16 years and over.	Under 16 years.	Females.	All other free persons.	Slaves.
Barnstable county	17,342	4,200	4,093	8,677	372	
Barnstable	2,610	631	623	1,301	55	
Chatham	1,134	266	290	575	3	
Eastham	1,834	426	431	974	3	
Falmouth	1,639	420	365	816	38	
Harwich	2,392	545	593	1,243	11	
Marshpee plantation	308	35	27	72	174	
Province Town	454	142	99	211	2	
Sandwich	1,991	460	469	1,015	47	
Truro	1,193	324	279	586	4	
Wellfleet	1,115	301	252	560	2	
Yarmouth	2,672	650	665	1,324	33	
Berkshire county	30,263	7,356	7,790	14,794	323	
Adams	2,041	473	561	1,003	4	
Adams and Windsor—in the gore adjoining	425	102	121	191	11	
Alford	577	142	173	262		
Becket	751	195	187	362	7	
Bethlehem	261	62	73	125	1	
Dalton	554	129	134	283	8	
Egremont	759	187	191	376	5	
Great Barrington	1,373	328	335	664	46	
Hancock	1,204	295	322	586	1	
Lanesborough	2,142	522	547	1,058	15	
Lee	1,170	286	310	571	3	
Lenox	1,169	279	299	574	17	
Loudon	344	96	84	164		
Mount Washington	261	57	78	126		
Mount Washington (Boston Corner)	67	13	21	33		
New Ashford	464	93	126	243	2	
New Marlborough	1,550	395	400	742	13	
Partridgefield	1,041	250	279	509	3	
Pittsfield	1,982	491	497	949	45	
Richmond	1,255	336	291	624	4	
Berkshire county—Continued.						
Sandisfield	1,571	379	379	804	9	
Sandisfield—south 11,000 acres adjoining	161	37	43	81		
Sheffield	1,893	467	462	932	32	
Stockbridge	1,336	311	322	639	64	
Tyringham	1,397	337	368	683	9	
Washington	588	143	160	283	2	
West Stockbridge	1,113	260	298	545	10	
Williamstown	1,769	445	454	865	5	
Williamstown—in the gore adjoining	51	8	22	21		
Windsor	916	222	233	454	7	
Zoar plantation[1]	78	16	20	42		
Bristol county	31,696	7,956	6,939	16,071	730	
Attleborough	2,167	565	451	1,133	18	
Berkley	850	213	179	446	12	
Dartmouth	2,500	645	541	1,231	83	
Dighton	1,793	416	409	879	89	
Easton	1,466	366	379	704	17	
Freetown	2,206	565	465	1,121	55	
Mansfield	983	271	198	509	5	
New Bedford	3,298	854	720	1,686	38	
Norton	1,428	376	309	730	13	
Raynham	1,095	301	222	543	29	
Rehoboth	4,710	1,151	1,063	2,405	91	
Somerset	1,151	270	234	585	62	
Swanzey	1,782	429	369	912	72	
Taunton	3,804	922	864	1,928	90	
Westport	2,463	612	536	1,259	56	
Dukes county	3,255	823	711	1,696	25	
Chilmark	771	199	157	405	10	
Edgartown	1,344	336	318	682	8	
Tisbury	1,140	288	236	609	7	

[1] Schedules missing.

TABLE 104.—POPULATION AS REPORTED AT THE FIRST CENSUS, BY COUNTIES AND MINOR CIVIL DIVISIONS: 1790—Continued.

MASSACHUSETTS—Continued.

COUNTY AND TOWN.	Total.	White Population in 1790. Males. 16 years and over.	Under 16 years.	Females.	All other free persons.	Slaves.
Essex county	57,879	14,258	12,567	30,182	872	....
Amesbury	1,801	470	384	944	3	....
Andover	2,862	741	612	1,415	94	....
Beverly	3,295	748	739	1,750	58	....
Boxford	925	247	191	481	6	....
Bradford	1,371	378	263	725	5	....
Danvers	2,424	625	486	1,279	34	....
Gloucester	5,317	1,267	1,218	2,791	41	....
Haverhill	2,404	612	535	1,250	7	....
Ipswich	4,563	1,151	920	2,414	78	....
Lynn	2,291	625	514	1,132	20	....
Lynnfield	491	119	108	261	3	....
Manchester	959	233	202	515	9	....
Marblehead	5,661	1,265	1,327	2,982	87	....
Methuen	1,295	338	293	663	1	....
Middleton	682	164	140	362	16	....
Newbury	3,970	1,038	844	2,047	41	....
Newburyport	4,817	1,153	1,072	2,525	67	....
Rowley	1,772	453	366	944	9	....
Salem	7,917	1,846	1,707	4,104	260	....
Salisbury	1,779	457	381	931	10	....
Topsfield	781	214	156	398	13	....
Wenham	502	114	109	269	10	....
Hampshire county	59,656	15,109	15,009	29,087	451	....
Amherst	1,233	335	287	609	2	....
Ashfield	1,458	354	369	734	1	....
Belchertown	1,485	370	396	713	6	....
Bernardston	690	175	172	343	....	....
Blandford	1,416	345	359	703	9	....
Brimfield	1,213	318	309	584	2	....
Buckland	718	164	191	363	....	....
Charlemont	665	166	173	326	....	....
Chester	1,119	285	300	527	7	....
Chesterfield	1,183	283	317	581	2	....
Colrain	1,418	348	371	688	11	....
Conway	2,093	500	558	1,022	13	....
Cummington	873	237	212	419	5	....
Deerfield	1,328	352	306	646	24	....
Easthampton	457	127	108	221	1	....
Goshen	681	161	185	327	8	....
Granby	596	164	154	276	2	....
Granville	1,980	497	501	969	13	....
Greenfield	1,498	391	390	714	3	....
Greenwich	1,045	271	265	504	5	....
Hadley	882	240	187	436	19	....
Hatfield	703	199	147	343	14	....
Heath	379	86	105	188	....	....
Holland	428	115	97	204	12	....
Leverett	524	126	129	268	1	....
Leyden	989	209	297	481	2	....
Longmeadow	744	200	182	356	6	....
Ludlow	560	134	158	266	2	....
Middlefield	603	154	172	277	....	....
Monson[1]	1,331	336	324	653	18	....
Montague	908	236	219	451	2	....
Montgomery	449	110	116	221	2	....
New Salem	1,543	390	387	765	1	....
Northampton[1]	1,628	498	341	771	18	....
Northfield	868	224	224	415	5	....
Norwich	737	186	197	350	4	....
Orange	784	186	203	395	....	....
Palmer	809	215	186	396	12	....
Pelham	1,040	246	277	517	....	....
Plainfield	443	106	118	214	5	....
Plantation No. 7	540	135	156	249	....	....
Rowe	443	119	122	202	....	....
Shelburne	1,183	300	273	598	12	....
Shutesbury	674	160	196	315	3	....
South Brimfield	606	144	171	291	....	....
South Hadley	759	209	181	359	10	....
Southampton	829	226	178	418	7	....
Southwick	841	215	217	397	12	....
Springfield	1,574	415	359	787	13	....
Sunderland	462	123	101	237	1	....
Ware	773	189	205	378	1	....
Warwick	1,244	277	308	657	2	....
Wendell	519	130	147	242	....	....
West Springfield	2,367	630	525	1,160	52	....
Westfield	2,205	527	565	1,055	58	....
Westhampton	682	162	185	333	2	....
Whately	735	184	199	351	1	....
Wilbraham	1,553	380	393	755	25	....
Williamsburgh	1,049	258	261	520	10	....
Worthington	1,117	287	278	547	5	....

COUNTY AND TOWN.	Total.	White Population in 1790. Males. 16 years and over.	Under 16 years.	Females.	All other free persons.	Slaves.
Middlesex county	42,769	11,071	9,620	21,486	592	....
Acton	853	216	204	427	6	....
Ashby	751	187	194	369	1	....
Bedford	523	150	117	254	2	....
Billerica	1,191	335	256	595	5	....
Boxborough	412	100	86	217	9	....
Cambridge	2,109	534	454	1,063	58	....
Carlisle	555	149	99	305	2	....
Charlestown	1,589	395	360	809	25	....
Chelmsford	1,144	327	233	572	12	....
Concord	1,585	414	312	830	29	....
Dracut	1,217	310	284	584	39	....
Dunstable	380	107	79	193	1	....
East Sudbury	801	206	176	410	9	....
Framingham	1,598	394	350	828	26	....
Groton	1,840	477	429	929	5	....
Holliston	874	236	199	424	15	....
Hopkinton	1,316	310	329	665	12	....
Lexington	941	251	212	470	8	....
Lincoln	740	180	184	370	6	....
Littleton	854	223	177	438	16	....
Malden	1,032	239	214	559	20	....
Marlborough	1,552	431	335	778	8	....
Medford	1,036	262	215	525	34	....
Natick	610	141	133	300	36	....
Newton	1,354	332	301	696	25	....
Pepperell	1,132	286	245	581	20	....
Reading	1,802	480	386	905	31	....
Sherburn	858	249	211	392	6	....
Shirley	677	166	155	354	2	....
Stoneham	381	108	83	182	8	....
Stow	800	205	195	397	3	....
Sudbury	1,288	324	287	675	2	....
Tewksbury	955	237	231	480	7	....
Townsend	993	273	244	472	4	....
Tyngsborough on north side of Merrimack	181	44	50	87	....	....
Tyngsborough on south side of Merrimack	202	52	46	87	17	....
Waltham	880	232	207	431	10	....
Watertown	1,091	319	250	511	11	....
Westford	1,229	301	306	618	4	....
Weston	1,009	256	226	504	23	....
Wilmington	710	181	172	345	12	....
Woburn	1,724	452	394	855	23	....
Nantucket county	4,555	1,201	1,017	2,303	34	....
Sherburn	4,555	1,201	1,017	2,303	34	....
Plymouth county	29,512	7,493	6,536	14,984	499	....
Abington	1,453	357	339	742	15	....
Bridgewater	4,953	1,250	1,121	2,457	125	....
Carver	847	214	214	407	12	....
Duxborough	1,457	378	322	747	10	....
Halifax	664	178	155	329	2	....
Hanover	1,084	268	235	546	35	....
Kingston	1,006	261	222	505	18	....
Marshfield	1,269	386	210	645	28	....
Middleborough	4,524	1,165	1,051	2,284	24	....
Pembroke	1,954	480	433	998	43	....
Plymouth	2,995	749	646	1,546	54	....
Plympton	956	233	220	499	4	....
Rochester	2,642	680	606	1,302	54	....
Scituate	2,854	692	554	1,543	65	....
Wareham	854	202	208	434	10	....
Suffolk county	44,865	11,366	9,333	23,104	1,062	....
Bellingham	735	187	184	362	2	....
Boston	18,038	4,325	3,376	9,576	761	....
Boston, islands in the harbor	282	192	25	60	5	....
Braintree	2,775	687	640	1,430	18	....
Brookline	484	152	94	225	13	....
Chelsea	469	133	94	221	21	....
Cohasset	817	188	212	417	....	....
Dedham	1,659	438	300	844	17	....
Dorchester	1,722	488	345	859	30	....
Dover	482	119	112	247	4	....
Foxborough	683	166	169	348	....	....
Franklin	1,101	305	235	558	3	....
Hingham	2,085	505	454	1,102	24	....
Hull	120	24	31	63	2	....
Medfield	731	201	120	395	15	....
Medway	1,040	285	208	521	26	....

[1] Schedules missing.

TABLE **104.**—POPULATION AS REPORTED AT THE FIRST CENSUS, BY COUNTIES AND MINOR CIVIL DIVISIONS: 1790—Continued.

MASSACHUSETTS—Continued.

COUNTY AND TOWN.	Total.	White pop. 1790 — Males 16 years and over.	Males Under 16 years.	Females.	All other free persons.	Slaves.
Suffolk county—Continued.						
Milton	1,039	271	205	536	27	......
Needham	1,109	272	269	555	13	......
Roxbury	2,224	618	459	1,107	40	......
Sharon	1,034	256	258	515	5	......
Stoughton	1,994	484	477	1,012	21	......
Walpole	1,007	254	251	497	5	......
Weymouth	1,469	346	368	747	8	......
Wrentham	1,766	470	387	907	2	......
Worcester county	56,764	14,600	13,664	28,091	409	......
Ashburnham	956	212	260	475	9	......
Athol	848	219	205	419	5	......
Barre	1,613	426	401	748	38	......
Berlin	512	129	138	245	......	1
Bolton	856	237	171	447	1	......
Boylston	841	227	183	416	15	......
Brookfield	3,103	784	765	1,547	7	......
Charlton	1,963	501	490	970	2	......
Douglas	1,079	267	264	548	......	......
Dudley	1,101	265	275	549	12	......
Fitchburgh	1,151	265	300	585	1	......
Fitchburgh—in the gore adjoining	14	2	6	6	......	......
Gardner	531	121	156	253	1	......
Gerry	739	177	182	379	1	......
Grafton	872	241	210	421	......	......
Hardwick	1,722	459	393	857	13	......
Harvard	1,387	362	298	716	11	......
Holden	1,077	278	267	532	......	......
Hubbardston	933	221	257	440	15	......
Lancaster	1,460	387	313	737	23	......
Leicester	1,079	286	248	537	8	......
Leominster	1,189	314	254	613	8	......
Leominster—in the gore adjoining	27	5	10	12	......	......
Worcester county—Continued.						
Lunenburgh	1,277	302	310	663	2	......
Mendon	1,556	389	369	795	3	......
Middlesex gore (adjoining Sturbridge)	64	15	20	29	......	......
Milford	839	225	175	427	12	......
New Braintree	939	254	188	483	14	......
Northborough	619	161	152	302	4	......
Northbridge	569	137	140	287	5	......
Oakham	772	191	197	383	1	......
Oxford	995	271	234	485	5	......
Oxford, north gore	74	19	18	37	......	......
Oxford, south gore	163	34	43	86	......	......
Paxton	558	140	139	271	8	......
Petersham	1,560	397	377	781	5	......
Princeton	1,016	258	251	504	3	......
Princeton—in the gore adjoining	26	5	6	15	......	......
Royalston	1,130	275	282	571	2	......
Rutland	1,071	294	243	526	8	......
Shrewsbury	963	269	209	473	12	......
Southborough	837	205	189	442	1	......
Spencer	1,321	338	316	661	6	......
Sterling	1,428	377	350	687	14	......
Sturbridge	1,703	445	400	854	4	......
Sutton	2,627	666	652	1,297	12	......
Templeton	950	232	226	492	......	......
Upton	830	210	199	392	29	......
Uxbridge	1,308	344	311	636	17	......
Ward	473	128	118	227	......	......
Westborough	929	239	256	430	4	......
Western	898	246	227	414	11	......
Westminster	1,176	310	277	585	4	......
Winchendon	945	238	250	455	2	......
Worcester	2,095	601	494	949	51	......

RHODE ISLAND.

COUNTY AND TOWN.	Total.	Males 16 years and over.	Males Under 16 years.	Females.	All other free persons.	Slaves.
Bristol county	3,211	778	677	1,558	100	98
Barrington	683	165	144	330	32	12
Bristol	1,412	327	292	677	52	64
Warren	1,116	286	241	551	16	22
Kent county	8,851	2,158	2,128	4,153	349	63
Coventry	2,483	645	633	1,165	35	5
East Greenwich	1,826	428	393	920	72	13
Warwick	2,490	566	516	1,151	222	35
West Greenwich	2,052	519	586	917	20	10
Newport county	14,351	3,256	2,856	7,062	805	372
Jamestown	507	100	91	232	68	16
Little Compton	1,529	357	356	771	22	23
Middletown	840	214	161	424	26	15
New Shoreham	681	154	133	290	56	48
Newport	6,744	1,460	1,244	3,393	421	226
Portsmouth	1,600	402	350	792	37	19
Tiverton	2,450	569	521	1,160	175	25
Providence county	24,376	6,155	5,486	11,877	777	81
Cranston	1,877	444	408	942	73	10
Cumberland	1,966	503	485	970	8	......
Foster	2,268	528	603	1,118	15	4
Glocester	4,016	986	995	2,012	22	1
Johnston	1,320	333	280	633	71	3
North Providence	1,071	270	237	509	50	5
Providence	6,371	1,709	1,249	2,939	427	47
Scituate	2,316	563	548	1,170	29	6
Smithfield	3,171	819	681	1,584	82	5
Washington county	18,323	3,709	4,598	8,219	1,453	344
Charlestown	2,023	345	445	815	406	12
Exeter	2,496	583	613	1,176	87	37
Hopkinton	2,464	522	685	1,178	72	7
North Kingstown	2,904	601	667	1,341	199	96
Richmond	1,769	366	510	815	76	2
South Kingstown	4,369	832	999	1,813	545	180
Westerly	2,298	460	679	1,081	68	10

CONNECTICUT.

COUNTY AND TOWN.	Total.	Males 16 years and over.	Males Under 16 years.	Females.	All other free persons.	Slaves.
Fairfield county	36,290	9,149	8,394	17,630	318	799
Brookfield	1,012	267	219	516	7	3
Danbury	3,032	781	704	1,504	20	23
Fairfield	4,010	1,028	896	1,869	14	203
Greenwich	3,175	798	698	1,559	38	82
Huntington	2,742	671	625	1,278	48	120
New Fairfield	1,572	401	404	754	4	9
Newtown	2,788	720	637	1,350	10	71
Norwalk } Stamford	8,810	2,187	2,099	4,324	83	117
Reading	1,501	390	327	735	17	32
Ridgefield	1,947	488	461	989	4	5
Stratford	3,222	799	724	1,552	49	98
Weston	2,479	619	600	1,200	24	36
Hartford county	38,149	9,808	8,844	18,846	395	256
Berlin	2,496	632	562	1,288	12	2
Bristol	2,468	592	615	1,242	17	2
East Hartford	3,012	787	668	1,519	7	31
East Windsor	2,581	712	561	1,274	26	8
Enfield	1,805	476	393	923	......	13
Hartford county—Continued.						
Farmington	2,683	678	676	1,283	39	7
Glastenbury	2,732	639	672	1,323	71	27
Granby	2,611	680	672	1,250	9	......
Hartford	4,072	1,056	858	2,032	79	47
Simsbury	2,679	687	663	1,316	11	2
Southington	2,104	540	502	1,033	18	11
Suffield	2,485	645	594	1,190	28	28
Wethersfield	3,790	953	818	1,909	51	59
Windsor	2,631	731	590	1,264	27	19
Litchfield county	38,635	10,135	9,237	18,747	313	203
Bethlem	1,056	275	243	534	......	4
Cornwall	1,475	396	318	715	27	19
Harwinton	1,367	354	334	673	......	6
Kent	1,317	348	317	635	11	6
Litchfield	20,278	5,302	4,914	9,782	191	89
New Milford	3,170	855	733	1,518	39	25
Southbury	1,734	485	367	847	14	21
Warren	775	195	205	364	5	6
Washington	1,677	442	405	814	11	5
Watertown	3,143	799	783	1,547	3	11
Woodbury	2,643	684	618	1,318	12	11

TABLE **104.**—POPULATION AS REPORTED AT THE FIRST CENSUS, BY COUNTIES AND MINOR CIVIL DIVISIONS: 1790—Continued.

CONNECTICUT—Continued.

COUNTY AND TOWN.	Total.	White population in 1790. Males. 16 years and over.	Under 16 years.	Fe-males.	All other free persons.	Slaves.	COUNTY AND TOWN.	Total.	White population in 1790. Males. 16 years and over.	Under 16 years.	Fe-males.	All other free persons.	Slaves.
Middlesex county	18,828	4,730	4,140	9,622	144	192	Tolland county	13,251	3,449	3,138	6,524	94	46
Chatham	3,218	810	729	1,642	21	16	Bolton	1,360	376	323	655	4	2
East Haddam	2,740	702	589	1,396	34	19	Coventry	2,125	513	509	1,080	16	7
Haddam	2,197	576	476	1,140	2	3	Ellington	1,059	286	220	533	16	4
Killingworth	2,147	586	452	1,087	11	11	Hebron	2,313	639	526	1,104	25	19
Middletown	5,298	1,238	1,199	2,695	57	109	Somers	1,220	322	300	591	2	5
Saybrook	3,228	818	695	1,662	19	34	Stafford	1,859	475	454	928		2
							Tolland	1,484	387	361	717	14	5
New Haven county	30,703	7,843	6,841	15,198	434	387	Union	630	150	162	317		1
							Willington	1,201	301	283	599	17	1
Branford	2,227	558	496	1,086	40	47							
Cheshire	2,332	591	504	1,193	31	13	Windham county	28,881	7,436	6,547	14,373	341	184
Derby	2,960	744	722	1,399	52	43							
Durham	1,071	315	214	526	7	9	Ashford	2,582	661	643	1,250	21	7
East Haven	1,026	235	225	524	7	35	Brooklyne	1,327	352	302	633	30	10
Guilford	3,439	951	713	1,727	23	25	Canterbury	1,885	501	391	975	16	2
Hamden	1,421	374	321	718	4	4	Hampton	1,333	339	303	680	10	1
Milford	2,087	537	432	984	69	65	Killingley	2,162	541	544	1,048	20	9
New Haven city	4,487	1,127	931	2,233	125	71	Lebanon	4,156	1,042	930	2,080	53	51
North Haven	1,235	323	272	626	8	6	Mansfield	2,635	689	610	1,320	9	7
Wallingford	3,355	842	783	1,659	26	45	Plainfield	1,711	468	356	817	60	10
Waterbury	2,932	733	717	1,458	14	10	Pomfret	1,760	461	375	885	20	19
Woodbridge	2,131	513	511	1,065	28	14	Thompson	2,270	563	555	1,140	5	7
							Voluntown	1,865	485	433	912	14	21
New London county [1]	32,918	8,189	7,148	16,268	732	581	Windham	2,764	670	580	1,422	64	28
							Woodstock	2,431	664	525	1,211	19	12

NEW YORK.

COUNTY AND TOWN.	Total.	White population in 1790. Males. 16 years and over.	Under 16 years.	Fe-males.	All other free persons.	Slaves.	COUNTY AND TOWN.	Total.	White population in 1790. Males. 16 years and over.	Under 16 years.	Fe-males.	All other free persons.	Slaves.
Albany county	75,980	18,684	18,960	34,443	171	3,722	Dutchess county—Continued. Philipstown	2,079	517	593	942	2	25
Albany city	3,494	803	652	1,442	26	571	Poughkeepsie	2,529	617	573	1,092	40	207
First ward	1,612	392	329	672	5	214	Rhinebeck	3,662	875	756	1,544	66	421
Second ward	878	206	171	383	18	100	Southeast	921	231	241	433	3	13
Third ward	1,004	205	152	387	3	257	Washington	5,190	1,267	1,295	2,495	55	78
Ballstown	7,316	1,893	2,014	3,317	23	69							
Cambridge	5,009	1,246	1,312	2,408		43	Kings county	4,549	903	703	1,415	46	1,482
Catskill	1,980	475	357	835	8	305							
Coxsackie	3,401	796	821	1,474	8	302	Brooklyn	1,656	362	260	565	14	455
Duanesburgh	1,469	410	369	684	1	5	Bushwick	540	123	69	172	5	171
Easton	2,547	569	718	1,203		57	Flatbush	941	160	153	238	12	378
Freehold	1,821	529	425	861	1	5	Flatlands	423	72	71	143		137
Halfmoon	3,609	865	948	1,666	7	123	Gravesend	426	88	69	129	5	135
Hoosick	3,031	693	839	1,454	18	27	New Utrecht	563	98	81	168	10	206
Pittstown	2,458	567	700	1,158		33							
Rensselaerville	2,776	712	740	1,311		13	Montgomery county	28,852	7,866	7,205	13,152	41	588
Rensselaerwick	8,305	2,024	2,087	3,632		562							
Saratoga	3,071	738	867	1,405	8	53	Canajoharie	6,155	1,647	1,538	2,868	6	96
Schaghticoke	1,650	409	387	711		143	Caughnawaga	4,261	1,128	1,068	1,928	4	133
Schenectady	756	180	170	328		78	Chemung	2,396	649	648	1,091	1	7
Schenectady, south of the Mohawk	3,475	899	678	1,483	34	381	Chenango	45	13	12	20		
Schoharie	2,074	542	435	936	9	152	German Flatts	1,307	354	301	630	2	20
Stephentown	7,209	1,819	1,943	3,420	1	26	Harpersfield	1,726	524	424	772		6
Stillwater	3,078	770	796	1,441	10	61	Herkimer	1,525	406	388	722	1	8
Watervliet	7,422	1,739	1,694	3,265	17	707	Mohawk	4,440	1,088	1,141	2,092	8	111
Island in the river not included in any town	29	6	8	9		6	Otsego	1,702	563	427	698	6	8
							Palatine	3,404	805	815	1,582	10	192
Clinton county	1,615	545	356	682	16	16	Whites	1,891	689	443	749	3	7
Champlain	575	187	124	247	15	2	New York city and county	33,111	8,482	5,900	15,237	1,119	2,37
Crown Point	203	73	38	91	1		New York city	32,305	8,310	5,790	14,943	1,078	2,184
Plattsburgh	458	153	108	184		13	Dock ward	1,895	455	307	854	45	234
Wellsburgh	379	132	86	160		1	East ward	3,766	966	593	1,611	82	514
							Montgomery ward	6,825	1,764	1,248	3,159	281	373
Columbia county	27,496	6,554	6,739	12,518	52	1,633	North ward	5,557	1,407	955	2,632	252	311
							Out ward	5,651	1,484	1,092	2,629	178	268
Canaan	6,670	1,707	1,702	3,220	5	36	South ward	1,767	451	324	822	55	115
Claverack	3,257	739	747	1,419	11	341	West ward	6,844	1,783	1,271	3,236	185	369
Clermont	862	186	207	357		112	Harlem division	806	172	110	294	41	189
Germantown	512	117	128	227		40							
Hillsdale	4,454	1,054	1,223	2,140	4	33	Ontario county	1,074	524	192	342	6	10
Hudson	2,585	616	589	1,155	26	199							
Kinderhook	4,667	1,035	1,031	1,956	6	639	Canandaigua	464	291	60	111	1	1
Livingston	4,489	1,100	1,112	2,044		233	Erwin	168	56	36	69		7
							Genesee	343	140	74	122	5	2
Dutchess county	45,276	10,972	11,069	20,940	431	1,864	Jerusalem	99	37	22	40		
Amenia	3,078	768	780	1,449	29	52	Orange county	18,477	4,596	4,334	8,385	201	961
Beekman	3,600	850	951	1,682	11	106							
Clinton	4,607	1,173	1,113	2,115	30	176	Goshen	2,447	616	518	1,042	59	212
Fishkill	5,941	1,366	1,290	2,643	41	601	Haverstraw	4,824	1,190	1,173	2,207	16	238
Frederickstown	5,932	1,428	1,540	2,850	41	63	Minisink	2,216	552	546	1,050	17	51
Northeast	3,401	839	863	1,597	22	80	New Cornwall	4,228	1,081	1,030	1,908	42	167
Pawling	4,336	1,031	1,074	2,098	91	42	Orange	1,163	288	175	476	26	198
							Warwick	3,599	869	892	1,702	41	95

[1] Not returned by towns.

TABLE **104.**—POPULATION AS REPORTED AT THE FIRST CENSUS, BY COUNTIES AND MINOR CIVIL DIVISIONS: 1790—Continued.

NEW YORK—Continued.

COUNTY AND TOWN.	Total.	WHITE POPULATION IN 1790.			All other free persons.	Slaves.
		Males. 16 years and over.	Males. Under 16 years.	Females.		
Queens county	16,013	3,555	2,863	6,468	819	2,308
Flushing	1,608	325	229	587	127	340
Jamaica	1,674	397	294	697	65	221
Newtown	2,109	421	353	748	54	533
North Hempstead	2,697	550	442	1,026	172	507
Oyster Bay	4,097	949	756	1,707	304	381
South Hempstead	3,828	913	789	1,703	97	326
Richmond county	3,827	747	753	1,445	127	755
Castleton	804	178	172	314	26	114
Northfield	1,021	223	226	402	35	135
Southfield	865	151	139	306	35	234
Westfield	1,137	195	216	423	31	272
Suffolk county	16,546	3,787	3,294	7,229	1,131	1,105
Brookhaven	3,227	727	617	1,375	275	233
Easthampton	1,497	354	272	673	99	99
Huntington	3,366	791	763	1,518	75	219
Islip	607	132	126	246	68	35
Shelter Island	201	39	38	77	23	24
Smithtown	1,024	195	179	371	113	166
Southampton	3,402	781	653	1,542	280	146
Southold	3,222	768	646	1,427	198	183
Ulster county	29,370	7,050	6,783	12,462	161	2,914
Hurley	847	166	129	306	1	245
Kingston	3,923	902	742	1,549	9	721
Manakating	1,763	436	491	780	5	51
Marbletown	2,190	492	469	840	15	374
Middletown	1,019	293	259	460	1	6
Montgomery	3,564	898	834	1,578	18	236
New Marlborough	2,246	539	607	1,027	15	58
New Paltz	2,304	512	519	959	12	302
New Windsor	1,819	463	417	805	17	117
Newburgh	2,347	610	585	1,083	12	57
Rochester	1,628	374	321	638	14	281
Ulster county—Continued.						
Shawangunk	2,123	483	452	818	21	349
Wallkill	2,571	604	690	1,166	9	102
Woodstock	1,026	278	268	453	12	15
Washington county	14,077	3,616	3,789	6,623	3	46
Argyle	2,350	625	660	1,051	......	14
Granville	2,242	583	566	1,093	......	....
Hampton	463	108	131	224	......	....
Hebron	1,703	406	479	818	......	....
Kingsbury	1,120	299	291	529	1	......
Queensbury	1,080	261	275	543	......	1
Salem	2,198	582	573	1,021	1	21
Westfield	2,111	543	600	959	......	9
Whitehall	810	209	214	385	1	1
Westchester county	23,978	5,934	5,318	10,952	358	1,416
Bedford	2,470	618	622	1,182	10	38
Cortlandt	1,932	484	452	905	25	66
Eastchester	741	174	161	319	12	75
Greenburgh	1,367	324	312	601	9	121
Harrison	1,007	242	220	453	38	54
Mamaroneck	452	108	98	171	18	57
Morrisania	133	43	17	41	2	30
Mt. Pleasant	1,926	501	422	911	8	84
New Rochelle	690	170	130	277	26	87
North Castle	2,470	607	591	1,200	43	29
North Salem	1,060	268	239	509	16	28
Pelham	199	45	31	84	1	38
Poundridge	1,072	247	270	548	7	......
Rye	986	258	164	427	14	123
Salem	1,453	366	326	728	14	19
Scarsdale	281	73	53	116	11	28
Stephen	1,297	343	297	612	7	38
Westchester	1,203	279	212	421	49	242
White Plains	505	130	100	218	8	49
Yonkers	1,125	265	220	458	12	170
York	1,609	389	381	771	28	40

NEW JERSEY.

COUNTY AND TOWN.	Total.	WHITE POPULATION IN 1790.			All other free persons.	Slaves.
		Males. 16 years and over.	Males. Under 16 years.	Females.		
Bergen county	12,601	2,865	2,299	4,944	192	2,301
Bergin, Franklin, Hackinsack, Harrington, N. Barbadoes, Saddle River	12,601	2,865	2,299	4,944	192	2,301
Burlington county	18,095	4,625	4,164	8,481	598	227
Burlington, Chester, Chesterfield, Evansham, Little Egghar, Mansfield, New Hanover, Northampton, Notingham, Springfield, Willingboro'	18,095	4,625	4,164	8,481	598	227
Cape-May county	2,571	631	609	1,176	14	141
Lower Precinct, Middle Precinct, Upper Precinct	2,571	631	609	1,176	14	141
Cumberland county	8,248	2,147	1,966	3,877	138	120
Deerfield, Downs, Fairfield, Greenwich, Hopewell, Maurice River, Stowenuk	8,248	2,147	1,966	3,877	138	120
Essex county	17,785	4,339	3,972	8,143	160	1,171
Acquacknack, Elizabethtown, Newark	17,785	4,339	3,972	8,143	160	1,171
Gloucester county	13,363	3,287	3,311	6,232	342	191
Deptford, Eggharbor, Galloway, Glou town, Glou. townsh, Greenwich, Newtown, Waterford, Woolwich	13,363	3,287	3,311	6,232	342	191
Hunterdon county	20,153	4,966	4,379	9,316	191	1,301
Alexandria	1,503	377	401	685	......	40
Amwell	5,201	1,249	1,173	2,480	16	283
Bethleham	1,335	331	329	643	1	31
Hopewell	2,320	579	448	1,041	19	233
Kingwood	2,446	603	574	1,161	4	104
Maidenhead	1,032	237	189	432	14	160
Lebanon, Readington, Tewksbury	4,370	1,092	919	2,033	58	268
Trenton	1,946	498	346	841	79	182
Middlesex county	15,956	3,995	3,375	7,128	140	1,318
Amboy	582	149	108	246	31	48
North Brunswick	2,312	638	456	1,010	3	205
Piscataway	2,261	537	514	982	10	218
South Amboy	2,626	642	597	1,196	8	183
South Brunswick	1,817	439	361	789	10	218
Windsor	2,838	719	565	1,318	46	190
Woodbridge	3,520	871	774	1,587	32	256
Monmouth county	16,918	3,843	3,678	7,448	353	1,596
Dover	910	237	231	422	6	14
Lower Freehold	3,785	819	778	1,549	12	627
Middletown	3,225	711	618	1,343	62	491
Shrewsbury	4,673	1,094	1,041	2,161	165	212
Stafford	883	219	221	441	......	2
Upper-Freehold	3,442	763	789	1,532	108	250

TABLE **104.**—POPULATION AS REPORTED AT THE FIRST CENSUS, BY COUNTIES AND MINOR CIVIL DIVISIONS: 1790—Continued.

NEW JERSEY—Continued.

COUNTY AND TOWN.	Total.	White population in 1790. Males. 16 years and over.	Males. Under 16 years.	Fe-males.	All other free persons.	Slaves.
Morris county	16,216	4,092	3,938	7,502	48	636
Hanover						
Mendham						
Morristown	16,216	4,092	3,938	7,502	48	636
Pequanack						
Roxbury						
Salem county	10,437	2,679	2,396	4,816	374	172
Elsingborough						
Lo Penn's Neck						
Low Aloway Cr						
Mannington						
Piles Grove	10,437	2,679	2,396	4,816	374	172
Pitts grove						
Salem						
Up Aloway's Cr						
Up Penn's Neck						
Somerset county	12,296	2,819	2,390	5,130	147	1,810
Bedminster	1,197	275	260	489	4	169
Bernardstown	2,377	601	560	1,115	8	93

COUNTY AND TOWN.	Total.	White population in 1790. Males. 16 years and over.	Males. Under 16 years.	Fe-males.	All other free persons.	Slaves.
Somerset county—Continued.						
Bridgewater	2,578	586	462	1,119	34	377
Eastern Precinct	2,068	481	298	795	26	468
Hillsborough	2,201	463	465	868	19	386
Western Precinct	1,875	413	345	744	56	317
Sussex county	19,500	4,963	4,939	9,094	65	439
Greenwich	2,035	507	510	944	10	64
Hardwicke						
Independance	6,490	1,641	1,681	3,023	16	129
Newton						
Hardyston	2,393	610	637	1,110	10	26
Knowlton	1,937	488	490	935	11	13
Mansfield	1,482	377	368	700	2	35
Montague	543	150	124	241	3	25
Oxford	1,905	471	468	892	9	65
Sandyston	519	131	122	239	1	26
Wallpack	496	129	102	233	1	30
Wantage	1,700	459	437	777	1	26

PENNSYLVANIA.

COUNTY AND TOWN.	Total.	White population in 1790. Males. 16 years and over.	Males. Under 16 years.	Fe-males.	All other free persons.	Slaves.
Allegheny county	10,203	2,524	2,745	4,763	12	159
Depreciation tract	206	50	59	97	......	21
Elizabeth	1,498	368	398	711	......	21
Pitt	1,468	380	365	681	2	40
Pittsburgh town	376	100	80	195	1	......
Plum	402	104	105	192	......	1
Versailles	414	94	114	203	......	3
That part of Allegheny county taken from Washington county	5,839	1,428	1,624	2,684	9	94
Bedford county [1]	13,132	2,887	3,840	6,325	34	46
Berks county	30,189	7,711	7,551	14,666	201	60
Albany	773	191	180	402	......	......
Alsace	836	207	226	400	3	......
Amity	869	229	215	413	11	1
Bern	2,268	528	651	1,069	18	2
Bethel	950	234	234	481	1	......
Brecknock	324	78	85	161	......	......
Brunswick and Manheim	1,504	368	399	736	......	1
Caernarvon	509	137	123	240	5	4
Colebrookdale	553	149	135	265	4	......
Cumru	1,450	371	363	706	10	......
Douglass	480	123	120	230	6	1
Earl	527	136	136	252	2	1
East District	634	150	166	313	5	......
Exeter	893	236	215	432	3	7
Greenwich	724	187	164	373	......	......
Heidelberg	2,095	528	511	1,026	24	6
Hereford	969	240	236	489	3	1
Longswamp	739	185	194	359	1	......
Maiden Creek	735	205	168	353	9	......
Manheim (see Brunswick and Manheim).						
Maxatany	1,022	274	241	498	9	......
Oley	973	267	217	469	16	4
Pinegrove	900	214	251	435	......	......
Reading borough	2,225	583	512	1,118	3	9
Richmond	654	190	160	291	9	4
Robeson	1,088	289	276	514	8	1
Rockland	744	199	184	358	3	......
Ruscomb	472	119	121	228	4	......
Tulpehocken	2,315	603	553	1,123	21	15
Union	704	182	169	334	16	3
Windsor	1,260	309	346	598	7	......
Bucks county [1]	25,216	6,529	5,894	11,951	581	261
Chester county	27,829	7,486	6,590	13,065	544	144
Birmingham	221	58	53	109	1	......
Brandywine	740	214	178	343	5	......
Charlestown	1,260	319	312	582	40	7
Coventry	1,168	308	271	545	43	1
East Bradford	836	221	226	378	11	......
East Caln	702	191	158	329	21	3
East Fallowfield	517	141	136	239	1	......
East Marlborough	811	226	183	388	14	......
East Nantmill	1,154	281	298	546	21	8

COUNTY AND TOWN.	Total.	White population in 1790. Males. 16 years and over.	Males. Under 16 years.	Fe-males.	All other free persons.	Slaves.
Chester county—Continued.						
East Nottingham	820	221	195	390	12	2
East Town	423	113	111	197	......	2
East Whiteland	491	136	114	219	20	2
Fallowfield	792	229	159	384	11	9
Goshen	1,272	359	272	604	33	4
Honeybrook	794	193	205	380	3	13
Kennet	658	180	164	298	14	2
London Britain	247	70	50	107	12	8
Londonderry	588	163	132	282	4	7
Londongrove	786	203	203	370	5	5
New Garden	742	191	186	349	15	1
New London	746	211	164	333	18	20
Newlin	534	120	147	260	7	......
Oxford	1,004	277	226	465	16	20
Pennsbury	595	145	150	286	14	......
Pikeland	817	185	221	392	19	......
Sadsbury	607	168	143	281	8	7
Thornbury	123	40	27	51	5	......
Trediffrin	988	277	217	466	25	3
Uwchland	976	258	221	465	28	4
Vincent	1,230	339	274	609	7	1
West Bradford	723	182	195	337	9	......
West Caln	840	229	214	394	3	......
West Marlborough	678	208	144	309	16	1
West Nantmill	903	294	177	414	11	7
West Nottingham	432	102	110	197	20	3
West Town	366	95	74	179	18	......
West Whiteland	457	118	106	213	16	4
Willistown	788	221	174	375	18	......
Cumberland county	18,208	4,816	4,514	8,449	206	223
Hopewell						
Newton						
Tyborn	7,599	1,991	1,867	3,550	93	98
Westpensboro						
Eastern portion of county	10,609	2,825	2,647	4,899	113	125
Dauphin county	18,155	4,651	4,434	8,801	59	210
Harrisburgh town	880	259	184	411	1	25
Lebanon town	960	245	240	471	2	2
Remainder of county	16,315	4,147	4,010	7,919	56	183
Delaware county	9,469	2,530	2,109	4,494	287	49
Ashton	444	114	107	210	13	......
Bethel	224	50	67	99	7	1
Birmingham	428	98	109	202	15	4
Chester	673	200	128	323	22	......
Concord	674	168	160	305	35	6
Darby	641	168	137	313	15	8
Edgmont	437	104	106	213	9	5
Haverford	465	130	102	218	6	9
Lower Chichester	501	135	94	257	15	......
Lower Providence	216	68	50	97	1	......
Marple	471	120	105	235	11	......
Middletown	582	167	127	265	20	3
Newtown	451	126	101	218	5	1
Radnor	681	191	164	320	4	2
Ridley	502	137	106	229	29	1

[1] Not returned by townships.

TABLE **104.**—POPULATION AS REPORTED AT THE FIRST CENSUS, BY COUNTIES AND MINOR CIVIL DIVISIONS: 1790—Continued.

PENNSYLVANIA—Continued.

COUNTY AND TOWN.	Total.	Males. 16 years and over.	Males. Under 16 years.	Females.	All other free persons.	Slaves.
Delaware county—Continued.						
Springfield	335	89	72	142	28	4
Thornbury	401	99	92	198	12	......
Tinicum	158	46	27	58	24	3
Upper Chichester	265	66	63	132	3	1
Upper Darby	571	164	113	282	12	......
Upper Providence	349	90	79	178	1	1
Fayette county	13,318	3,415	3,420	6,155	46	282
Bullskin	754	192	186	356	1	19
Franklin	1,854	443	488	881	11	31
Georges	1,371	350	359	658	......	4
German	1,299	319	355	622	......	3
Luzerne	1,113	285	281	515	5	27
Menallen	1,668	439	442	737	7	43
Springhill	1,321	325	330	626	2	38
Tyrone	730	210	183	316	......	21
Union	1,538	424	360	717	9	28
Washington	1,241	319	311	532	11	68
Wharton	429	109	125	195	......	......
Franklin county	15,662	4,021	3,874	7,162	279	326
Fannet } Hamilton } Letterkenney } Montgomery } Peters }	7,212	1,862	1,838	3,230	134	148
Remainder of county	8,450	2,159	2,036	3,932	145	178
Huntingdon county[1]	7,558	1,871	2,089	3,531	24	4?
Lancaster county	36,081	9,714	8,067	17,411	542	347
Bart	873	214	218	421	15	5
Brecknock	636	142	161	326	7	......
Caernarvon	766	168	185	348	36	29
Cocalico	3,023	767	714	1,539	3	......
Colerain	665	196	145	321	3	......
Conestogo	1,031	236	284	514	7	......
Donegal	533	155	111	247	10	10
Drumore	1,025	316	189	466	20	34
Earl	3,050	670	717	1,506	137	20
Elizabeth	546	147	120	273	5	1
Elizabeth town	196	52	42	102	......	......
Heidelberg	69	21	19	29	......	......
Hempfield	1,605	440	378	776	7	4
Lampeter	1,541	447	356	730	7	1
Lancaster	297	93	63	139	1	1
Lancaster borough	3,762	1,049	790	1,830	36	57
Leacock	1,405	395	296	683	13	18
Little Britain	1,291	357	271	589	32	42
Manheim	780	215	192	372	......	1
Manheim town	367	108	75	184	......	......
Manor	1,635	414	380	798	43	......
Martick	1,290	374	280	614	13	9
May town	1,134	314	256	521	20	23
Mountjoy	849	230	172	436	4	7
Rapho	1,606	469	306	784	26	11
Sadsbury	720	203	151	340	15	11
Salisbury	1,368	367	291	612	52	46
Strasburg	1,689	510	376	781	16	6
Warwick	2,269	595	519	1,130	14	11
Luzerne county[1]	4,892	1,237	1,328	2,303	13	11
Mifflin county	7,562	1,954	1,955	3,552	42	59
That portion south of the river Juniata	2,187	586	557	1,030	5	9
Remainder of county	5,375	1,308	1,398	2,522	37	50
Montgomery county	22,918	6,001	5,382	10,982	440	113
Abington	881	265	177	424	10	5
Cheltenham	620	103	138	272	45	2
Manor of Moreland	1,283	345	273	588	60	17
Springfield	446	121	95	222	8	......
Remainder of county	19,688	5,107	4,699	9,476	317	89
Northampton county	24,238	6,007	6,404	11,675	132	20
Allen	1,456	382	352	717	5	......
Bethlehem	960	258	160	537	4	1
Chestnut Hill	709	150	222	337	......	......
Cosikton District	327	99	88	139	1	......
Delaware	421	110	104	201	6	......
Easton town	708	173	170	349	11	5
Forks	741	175	217	343	4	2
Hamilton	595	143	179	272	1	......

COUNTY AND TOWN.	Total.	Males. 16 years and over.	Males. Under 16 years.	Females.	All other free persons.	Slaves.
Northampton county—Cont'd.						
Heidelberg	962	244	254	464	......	......
Lehigh	626	146	181	299	......	......
Lower Mount Bethel	896	230	211	453	1	1
Lower Saucon	997	268	222	489	18	......
Lower Smithfield	1,436	359	364	647	59	7
Lowhill	419	97	115	206	1	......
Lynn	1,016	225	308	483	......	......
Macunge	1,263	335	330	596	1	1
More	752	200	170	382	......	......
Nazareth	889	252	231	403	3	......
Penn	607	151	167	287	2	......
Plainfield	886	193	245	448	......	......
Salisbury	1,010	257	248	505	......	......
Towamensink	395	102	97	195	......	1
Upper Milford	1,149	273	279	597	......	......
Upper Mount Bethel	1,040	254	301	478	6	1
Upper Saucon	851	200	255	396	......	......
Upper Smithfield	352	101	94	155	1	1
Wallen Papack	170	44	43	82	1	......
Weisenbergh	626	133	195	297	1	......
Whitehall	1,253	266	394	593	......	......
Williams	726	187	208	325	6	......
Northumberland county[1]	17,147	4,191	4,729	8,051	89	87
Philadelphia county	54,388	14,497	10,896	26,523	2,099	373
Blockley	883	244	179	434	22	4
Bristol	723	191	179	331	19	3
Byberry	586	148	141	278	13	6
Germantown town	2,769	752	597	1,394	21	5
Kingsessing	542	149	107	225	54	7
Lower Dublin	1,267	318	263	610	57	19
Manor of Moreland	376	93	79	181	15	8
Moyamensing and Passyunk	1,393	377	299	682	27	8
Northern Liberties town	9,907	2,537	2,206	4,884	219	61
Oxford	979	258	215	463	26	17
Passyunk. (See Moyamensing and Passyunk.)						
Roxborough	778	205	220	350	2	1
Southwark	5,663	1,486	1,141	2,808	204	24
Philadelphia city	28,522	7,739	5,270	13,883	1,420	210
Northern district (between Vine and Race streets from the Delaware to the Schuylkill)	3,938	1,048	733	2,045	85	27
Middle district (from the north side of Chestnut street to the south side of Race street from the Delaware to the Schuylkill)	13,674	3,655	2,623	6,713	612	71
Southern district (from the south side of Chestnut street to the north side of South street from the Delaware to the Schuylkill)	10,910	3,036	1,914	5,125	723	112
Washington county[1]	23,892	5,333	7,279	11,005	12	263
Westmoreland county	16,019	4,013	4,359	7,480	39	128
Armstrong	1,452	389	403	647	8	5
Derry	1,623	399	434	778	6	6
Donegal	727	191	183	352	1	......
Fairfield	639	147	170	311	3	8
Franklin	778	207	210	360	1	......
French Creek	93	56	13	24	......	......
Hempfield	2,200	534	621	1,032	7	6
Mount Pleasant	1,059	272	304	474	......	9
North Huntingdon	1,581	372	428	763	1	17
Rostraver	1,087	253	290	495	......	49
Salem	795	203	197	387	4	4
South Huntingdon	1,647	390	467	772	4	14
Unity	1,246	305	352	579	1	9
Washington	706	197	184	323	1	1
Wheatfield	386	98	103	183	2	......
York county	37,535	9,171	9,469	17,542	850	503
Chanceford	1,690	457	399	772	35	27
Codorus	1,485	359	390	707	17	12
Dover	1,478	330	377	756	15	......
Fawn	1,307	342	299	610	13	43
Hellam	769	183	176	365	38	7
Hopewell	1,184	292	323	540	18	11
Manchester	1,686	381	428	835	29	13
Monaghan	1,463	343	374	673	61	12
Newberry	2,216	521	631	1,051	13	......
Paradise	1,179	263	307	575	30	4
Reading	978	219	247	435	52	25
Shrewsbury	1,258	300	337	579	27	15

[1] Not returned by townships.

TABLE **104.**—POPULATION AS REPORTED AT THE FIRST CENSUS, BY COUNTIES AND MINOR CIVIL DIVISIONS: 1790—Continued.

PENNSYLVANIA—Continued.

COUNTY AND TOWN.	Total.	Males. 16 years and over.	Males. Under 16 years.	Females.	All other free persons.	Slaves.	COUNTY AND TOWN.	Total.	Males. 16 years and over.	Males. Under 16 years.	Females.	All other free persons.	Slaves.
York county—Continued.							*York county—Continued.*						
Warrington	1,469	342	374	702	43	8	Berwick, Cumberland, Franklin, Germany, Hamiltonban, Heidelberg, Mount Pleasant, Mountjoy, and Straban	9,800	2,551	2,376	4,359	269	245
Windsor	1,447	336	395	705	8	3							
York	1,381	288	385	664	34	10							
York borough	2,076	462	451	1,008	125	30							
Huntington, Manallen, Manheim, and Tyrone	4,669	1,202	1,200	2,206	23	38							

DELAWARE.

COUNTY AND TOWN.	Total.	Males. 16 years and over.	Males. Under 16 years.	Females.	All other free persons.	Slaves.	COUNTY AND TOWN.	Total.	Males. 16 years and over.	Males. Under 16 years.	Females.	All other free persons.	Slaves.
Kent	18,920	3,705	3,467	6,878	2,570	2,300	Sussex	20,488	4,105	3,929	7,739	690	4,025
New-Castle	19,688	3,973	4,747	7,767	639	2,562							

MARYLAND.

COUNTY AND TOWN.	Total.	Males. 16 years and over.	Males. Under 16 years.	Females.	All other free persons.	Slaves.	COUNTY AND TOWN.	Total.	Males. 16 years and over.	Males. Under 16 years.	Females.	All other free persons.	Slaves.
Western shore	212,089	38,573	35,748	69,187	4,136	64,445	*Western shore—Continued.*						
Allegany county	4,809	1,068	1,283	2,188	12	258	Washington county	15,822	3,738	3,863	6,871	64	1,286
Ann-Arundel county	22,598	3,142	2,850	5,672	804	10,130	Eastern shore	107,639	17,342	15,591	32,208	3,907	38,591
Baltimore county	25,434	5,184	4,668	9,101	604	5,877							
Baltimore town and precincts	13,503	3,866	2,556	5,503	323	1,255	Caroline county	9,506	1,812	1,727	3,489	421	2,057
Calvert county	8,652	1,091	1,109	2,011	136	4,305	Cecil county	13,625	2,847	2,377	4,831	163	3,407
Charles county	20,613	2,565	2,399	5,160	404	10,085	Dorchester county	15,875	2,541	2,430	5,039	528	5,337
Frederick county	30,791	7,010	7,016	12,911	213	3,641	Kent county	12,836	1,876	1,547	3,325	655	5,433
Harford county	14,976	2,872	2,812	5,100	775	3,417	Queen Anns county	15,463	2,158	1,974	4,039	618	6,674
Montgomery county	18,003	3,284	2,746	5,649	294	6,030	Somersett county	15,610	2,185	1,908	4,179	268	7,070
Prince Georges county	21,344	2,653	2,503	4,848	164	11,176	Talbot county	13,084	1,938	1,712	3,581	1,076	4,777
St. Marys county	15,544	2,100	1,943	4,173	343	6,985	Worcester county	11,640	1,985	1,916	3,725	178	3,836

VIRGINIA.

COUNTY AND TOWN.	Total.	Males. 16 years and over.	Males. Under 16 years.	Females.	All other free persons.	Slaves.	COUNTY AND TOWN.	Total.	Males. 16 years and over.	Males. Under 16 years.	Females.	All other free persons.	Slaves.
Accomack	13,959	2,297	2,177	4,502	721	4,262	James City	4,070	395	359	765	146	2,405
Albemarle	12,585	1,703	1,790	3,342	171	5,579	King George	7,366	757	781	1,585	86	4,157
Amelia, including Nottoway, a new county	18,097	1,709	1,697	3,278	106	11,307	King & Queen	9,377	995	1,026	2,138	75	5,143
Amherst	13,703	2,056	2,235	3,995	121	5,296	King William	8,128	723	732	1,438	84	5,151
Augusta, the part east of the North mountain	10,886	2,048	1,665	3,438	40	1,222	Lancaster	5,638	535	542	1,182	143	3,236
Part west of do		551	572	986	19	345	Loudon	18,962	3,677	3,992	7,080	183	4,030
Bedford	10,531	1,785	2,266	3,674	52	2,754	Louisa	8,467	957	1,024	1,899	14	4,573
Berkley	19,713	4,253	4,547	7,850	131	2,932	Lunenburg	8,959	1,110	1,185	2,252	80	4,332
Botetourt, as it stood previous to the formation of Wythe from it & Montg'ry	10,524	2,247	2,562	4,432	24	1,259	Mecklenburg	14,733	1,857	2,015	3,683	416	6,762
Brunswick	12,827	1,472	1,529	2,918	132	6,776	Middlesex	4,140	407	370	754	51	2,558
Buckingham	9,779	1,274	1,537	2,685	115	4,168	Monongalia	4,768	1,089	1,345	2,168	12	154
Campbell	7,685	1,236	1,347	2,363	251	2,488	Montgomery, as it stood previous to the formation of Wythe from it and Botetourt	13,228	2,846	3,744	5,804	6	828
Caroline	17,489	1,799	1,731	3,464	203	10,292	Nansemond	9,010	1,215	1,167	2,331	480	3,817
Charles-City	5,588	532	509	1,043	363	3,141	New-Kent	6,239	605	587	1,199	148	3,700
Charlotte	10,078	1,285	1,379	2,535	63	4,816	Norfolk	14,524	2,650	1,987	4,291	251	5,345
Chesterfield	14,214	1,652	1,557	3,149	369	7,487	Northampton	6,889	857	743	1,581	464	3,244
Culpeper	22,105	3,372	3,755	6,682	70	8,226	Northumberland	9,103	1,046	1,137	2,323	197	4,460
Cumberland	8,153	885	914	1,778	142	4,434	Ohio	5,212	1,222	1,377	2,308	24	281
Dinwiddie	13,934	1,790	1,396	2,853	561	7,334	Orange	9,921	1,317	1,426	2,693	64	4,421
Elizabeth-City	3,450	390	388	778	18	1,876	Pendleton	2,452	508	686	1,124	1	73
Essex	9,122	908	869	1,766	139	5,440	Pittsylvania	11,579	2,008	2,447	4,083	62	2,979
Fairfax	12,320	2,138	1,872	3,601	135	4,574	Powhatan	6,822	623	548	1,115	211	4,325
Fauquier	17,892	2,674	2,983	5,500	93	6,642	Prince Edward	8,100	1,044	1,077	1,961	32	3,986
Fluvanna	3,921	589	654	1,182	25	1,466	Prince George	8,173	965	822	1,600	267	4,519
Franklin	6,842	1,266	1,629	2,840	34	1,073	Princess Anne	7,793	1,169	1,151	2,207	64	3,202
Frederick division	19,681	1,757	1,653	3,041	49	1,319	Prince William	11,615	1,644	1,797	3,303	167	4,704
Ditto		2,078	2,517	4,269	67	2,931	Randolph	951	221	270	441		19
Gloucester	13,498	1,597	1,523	3,105	210	7,063	Richmond	6,985	704	697	1,517	83	3,984
Goochland	9,053	1,028	1,059	2,053	257	4,056	Rockbridge	6,548	1,517	1,552	2,756	41	682
Greenbrier, including Kanawa, a new county	6,015	1,463	1,574	2,639	20	319	Rockingham	7,449	1,816	1,652	3,209		772
Greensville	6,362	669	627	1,234	212	3,620	Russell	3,328	734	969	1,440	5	190
Halifax	14,722	2,214	2,320	4,397	226	5,565	Shannandoah	10,510	2,409	2,779	4,791	19	512
Hampshire	7,346	1,662	1,956	3,261	13	454	Southampton	12,864	1,632	1,546	3,134	559	5,993
Hanover	14,754	1,637	1,412	3,242	240	8,223	Spotsylvania	11,252	1,361	1,278	2,532	148	5,933
Hardy	7,336	1,108	2,256	3,192	411	369	Stafford	9,588	1,341	1,355	2,769	87	4,036
Harrison	2,080	487	579	947		67	Surry	6,227	732	651	1,379	368	3,097
Henrico	12,000	1,823	1,170	2,607	581	5,819	Sussex	10,549	1,215	1,174	2,382	391	5,387
Henry	8,479	1,523	1,963	3,277	165	1,551	Warwick	1,690	176	158	333	33	990
Isle of Wight	9,028	1,208	1,103	2,415	375	3,867	Washington	5,625	1,287	1,440	2,440	8	450
							Westmoreland	7,722	815	754	1,614	114	4,425
							York	5,233	530	461	1,124	358	2,760

TABLE **104.**—POPULATION AS REPORTED AT THE FIRST CENSUS, BY COUNTIES AND MINOR CIVIL DIVISIONS: 1790—Continued.

NORTH CAROLINA.

DISTRICT, COUNTY, AND TOWN.	Total.	WHITE POPULATION IN 1790. Males. 16 years and over.	Under 16 years.	Females.	All other free persons.	Slaves.
Edenton district	53,769	8,405	8,653	16,510	1,048	19,153
Bertie county	12,462	1,719	1,802	3,442	378	5,121
Camden county	4,022	725	754	1,475	30	1,038
Chowan county, excluding Edenton town	3,413	457	438	865	7	1,646
Edenton town	1,575	181	113	306	34	941
Currituck county	5,220	1,018	1,024	1,960	115	1,103
Gates county	5,386	790	772	1,514	93	2,217
Hertford county	5,949	813	824	1,632	232	2,448
Pasquotank county	5,477	951	1,035	1,804	87	1,600
Perquimans county	5,439	884	921	1,714	37	1,883
Tyrrell county	4,826	867	970	1,798	35	1,156
Fayette district	34,393	7,111	7,324	13,677	608	5,673
Anson county	5,235	1,035	1,183	2,147	41	829
Cumberland county, excluding Fayetteville town	7,195	1,458	1,366	2,656	49	1,666
Fayetteville town	1,535	394	195	398	34	514
Moore county	3,870	850	965	1,672	12	371
Richmond county	5,053	1,096	1,205	2,114	55	583
Robeson county	5,343	1,132	1,138	2,263	277	533
Sampson county	6,162	1,146	1,272	2,427	140	1,177
Halifax district	64,848	9,215	10,130	18,610	1,364	25,529
Edgecombe county	10,265	1,663	1,878	3,487	70	3,167
Franklin county	7,502	1,076	1,381	2,307	37	2,701
Halifax county, including Halifax town	14,310	1,873	1,826	3,471	443	6,697
Martin county	6,010	1,067	1,010	2,008	96	1,829
Nash county	7,390	1,134	1,434	2,621	193	2,008
Northampton county	9,992	1,335	1,283	2,502	458	4,414
Warren county	9,379	1,067	1,318	2,214	67	4,713
Hillsborough district	59,971	10,937	12,903	21,980	702	13,449
Caswell county[1]	10,096	1,801	2,110	3,377	72	2,736
Caswell district						
Gloucester district						
Nash district						
Richmond district						
St. David's district						
St. James district						
St. Lawrence district						
St. Lukes district						
Chatham county	9,161	1,761	2,168	3,664	10	1,558
Granville county[1]	10,982	1,581	1,873	3,050	315	4,163
Abraham's Plains district						
Beaver Dam district						
Dutch district						
Epping Forest district						74
Fishing Creek district						
Fort Creek district						
Goshen district						
Henderson district						
Island Creek district						
Knap of Leeds district						
Oxford district						182
Ragland district						
Tabb's Creek district						
Tar River district						
Orange county[1]	12,216	2,433	2,709	4,913	101	2,060
Caswell district						
Chatham district						
Hillsboro district						
Hillsboro town						
Orange district						
St. Asaph's district						
St. Mark's district						
St. Mary's district						
St. Thomas' district						
Randolph county	7,318	1,590	1,952	3,292	24	460
Wake county	10,198	1,771	2,091	3,684	180	2,472
Morgan district	33,317	6,953	8,773	14,961	13	2,617
Burke county	8,106	1,705	2,108	3,684	9	600
First company	833	169	216	356		92
Second company	525	90	148	263		24
Third company	607	120	156	248	7	76
Fourth company	441	99	129	203		10
Fifth company	596	124	146	275		51
Sixth company	677	141	169	306	2	59
Seventh company	631	124	152	268		87
Eighth company	685	150	183	324		28

DISTRICT, COUNTY, AND TOWN.	Total.	WHITE POPULATION IN 1790. Males. 16 years and over.	Under 16 years.	Females.	All other free persons.	Slaves.
Morgan district—Continued. Burke county—Continued.						
Ninth company	677	147	187	317		26
Tenth company	459	99	126	213		21
Eleventh company	559	133	119	266		41
Twelfth company	481	94	155	217		15
Thirteenth company	935	215	222	428		70
Lincoln county	9,246	2,057	2,293	4,041		855
First company	492	110	124	215		43
Second company	509	114	127	229		39
Third company	503	118	146	221		18
Fourth company	733	166	180	349		38
Fifth company	602	130	167	289		16
Sixth company	1,099	250	261	494		94
Seventh company	735	170	174	281		110
Eighth company	653	148	184	303		18
Ninth company	1,427	318	308	610		191
Tenth company	718	145	189	333		51
Eleventh company	1,010	202	227	351		230
Twelfth company	765	186	206	366		7
Rutherford county	7,808	1,576	2,119	3,502	2	609
First company	573	105	110	218		140
Second company	581	110	147	244		80
Third company	390	70	110	150		60
Fourth company	361	70	99	168		24
Fifth company	603	121	163	291		28
Sixth company	686	127	192	323		44
Seventh company	514	111	138	230		35
Eighth company	527	103	154	248	2	20
Ninth company	584	119	167	287		11
Tenth company	598	114	165	259		60
Eleventh company	955	186	287	431		51
Twelfth company	692	139	209	305		39
Thirteenth company	358	93	93	163		9
Fourteenth company	386	108	85	185		8
Wilkes county	8,157	1,615	2,253	3,734	2	553
First company	535	111	132	237		55
Second company	609	101	164	268		76
Third company	505	100	134	233	2	36
Fourth company	541	106	157	265		13
Fifth company	466	88	145	222		11
Sixth company	601	121	169	291		20
Seventh company	392	76	100	162		54
Eighth company	319	76	105	128		10
Ninth company	631	118	150	297		66
Tenth company	488	109	132	224		23
Eleventh company	600	109	149	246		96
Twelfth company	443	88	122	199		34
Thirteenth company	723	152	205	332		34
Fourteenth company	377	75	96	188		18
Fifteenth company	369	78	114	173		4
Sixteenth company	558	107	179	269		3
Newbern district	55,683	9,595	9,876	19,329	841	16,042
Beaufort county	5,405	910	924	1,821	128	1,622
Carteret county	3,734	718	709	1,505	93	709
Craven county, including Newbern town	10,474	1,710	1,538	3,226	337	3,663
Dobbs county	6,994	1,164	1,293	2,479	46	2,012
Hyde county	4,204	792	714	1,518	37	1,143
Johnston county	5,691	1,040	1,177	2,081	65	1,328
Jones county	4,796	736	794	1,541	70	1,655
Pitt county	8,270	1,461	1,508	2,912	25	2,364
Wayne county	6,115	1,064	1,219	2,246	40	1,546
Salisbury district	66,927	14,003	15,932	28,490	249	8,253
Guilford county	7,300	1,615	1,807	3,235	27	616
Iredell county	5,430	1,118	1,218	2,223	3	868
Mecklenburg county	11,360	2,364	2,563	4,758	67	1,608
Montgomery county	5,039	942	1,220	2,029	11	837
Rockingham county	6,211	1,188	1,411	2,489	10	1,113
Rowan county, including Salisbury town	15,972	3,399	3,828	6,902	102	1,741
Stokes county	8,423	1,846	2,122	3,665	12	778
Surry county	7,192	1,531	1,763	3,189	17	692
Wilmington district	26,097	3,953	4,062	7,799	216	10,067
Bladen county	5,100	837	834	1,685	58	1,686
Brunswick county	3,070	380	398	778	3	1,511
Duplin county	5,663	1,035	1,187	2,052	3	1,386
New Hanover county, including Wilmington town	6,837	834	702	1,496	68	3,737
Onslow county	5,427	867	941	1,788	84	1,747

[1] Names taken from county tax lists.

TABLE 104.—POPULATION AS REPORTED AT THE FIRST CENSUS, BY COUNTIES AND MINOR CIVIL DIVISIONS: 1790—Continued.

SOUTH CAROLINA.

DISTRICT, COUNTY, AND PARISH.	Total.	Males. 16 years and over.	Males. Under 16 years.	Females.	All other free persons.	Slaves.
Beaufort district[1]	18,753	1,266	1,055	2,043	153	14,236
Camden district	38,265	6,941	8,694	13,607	158	8,865
Chester county	6,866	1,446	1,604	2,831	47	938
Claremont county	4,548	517	841	1,080	....	2,110
Clarendon county	2,392	444	516	830	....	602
Fairfield county	7,623	1,335	1,874	2,929	....	1,485
Lancaster county	6,302	1,253	1,537	2,074	68	1,370
Richland county	3,930	596	710	1,173	14	1,437
York county	6,604	1,350	1,612	2,690	29	923
Charleston district	66,985	5,060	3,177	7,165	950	50,633
Berkley county, St. Johns parish	5,922	209	152	331	60	5,170
Colleton county, St. Johns parish	5,312	209	104	272	22	4,705
Dorchester county, St. Georges parish	4,299	337	311	604	25	3,022
Christ Church parish	2,954	156	138	272	11	2,377
St. Andrews parish	2,947	125	71	174	31	2,546
St. Bartholomes parish	12,606	625	491	1,017	135	10,338
St. James Goose Creek parish	2,787	158	79	202	15	2,333
St. James Santee parish	3,797	140	110	187	15	3,345
St. Pauls parish	3,433	65	48	103	15	3,202
St. Phillips and St. Michaels parish	16,359	2,810	1,561	3,718	586	7,684
St. Stephens parish	2,733	81	45	100	1	2,506
Charleston district—Cont'd. St. Thomas parish	3,836	145	67	185	34	3,405
Cheraw district[1]	10,706	1,779	1,993	3,646	59	3,229
Georgetown district	22,122	2,356	2,467	4,055	113	13,131
All Saints parish	2,225	104	102	223	1	1,795
Prince Fredericks parish	8,135	907	915	1,596	32	4,685
Prince Georges parish	11,762	1,345	1,450	2,236	80	6,651
Ninety-six district	73,729	14,973	17,165	30,324	198	11,009
Abbeville county	9,197	1,904	1,948	3,653	27	1,665
Edgefield county	13,289	2,333	2,571	4,701	65	3,619
Greenville county	6,503	1,400	1,627	2,861	9	606
Laurens county	9,337	1,969	2,270	3,971	7	1,120
Newberry county	9,342	1,992	2,232	3,962	12	1,144
Pendleton county	9,568	2,007	2,535	4,189	3	834
Spartanburgh county	8,800	1,868	2,173	3,866	27	866
Union county	7,693	1,500	1,809	3,121	48	1,215
Orangeburgh district	18,513	3,201	3,171	6,040	170	5,931
North part	11,281	1,780	1,693	3,258	21	4,529
South part	7,232	1,421	1,478	2,782	149	1,402

GEORGIA.

DISTRICT, COUNTY, AND PARISH.	Total.	Males. 16 years and over.	Males. Under 16 years.	Females.	All other free persons.	Slaves.
Lower district	19,266	2,050	1,160	2,637	158	13,261
Camden	305	81	44	96	14	70
Chatham	10,769	846	480	1,130	112	8,201
Effingham	2,424	627	336	711	....	750
Glyn	413	70	36	87	5	215
Liberty	5,355	426	264	613	27	4,025
Middle district	25,336	4,649	4,790	8,643	52	7,202
Burke	9,467	1,808	1,841	3,415	11	2,392
Middle district—Continued. Richmond	11,317	1,894	1,925	3,343	39	4,116
Washington	4,552	947	1,024	1,885	2	694
Upper district	37,946	6,404	8,094	14,459	188	8,801
Franklin	1,041	225	243	417	....	156
Greene	5,405	1,027	1,111	1,882	8	1,377
Wilks	31,500	5,152	6,740	12,160	180	7,268

KENTUCKY.

DISTRICT, COUNTY, AND PARISH.	Total.	Males. 16 years and over.	Males. Under 16 years.	Females.	All other free persons.	Slaves.
Beards Town, in Nelson county	216	52	49	85	1	29
Bourbon	7,837	1,645	2,035	3,249	....	908
Danville, in Mercer county	150	49	28	51	....	22
Fayette county	17,576	3,241	3,878	6,738	30	3,689
Jefferson	4,565	1,008	997	1,680	4	876
Lexington, in Fayette county	834	276	203	290	2	63
Lincoln	6,548	1,375	1,441	2,630	8	1,094
Louisville, in Jefferson county	200	49	44	79	1	27
Madison	5,772	1,231	1,421	2,383	....	737
Mason	2,267	431	676	952	....	208
Mercer	6,941	1,411	1,515	2,691	7	1,317
Nelson	11,099	2,456	2,746	4,644	34	1,219
Washington, in Mason county	462	163	95	183	....	21
Woodford	9,210	1,767	1,929	3,267	27	2,220

[1] Not returned by counties.

TABLE 105.—WHITE AND COLORED POPULATION OF EACH COUNTY REPORTED IN 1790, COMPARED WITH THAT OF THE SAME AREA IN 1900, TOGETHER WITH THE NUMBER OF COLORED PER 1,000 WHITES.

MAINE.

COUNTY.	POPULATION IN 1790.					POPULATION IN 1900.						Number of colored persons per 1,000 whites, 1790.	Number of negroes per 1,000 whites, 1900.
			Colored.					Colored.					
	Total.	White.	Total.	Free.	Slave.	Total.	White.	Total.	Negro.	Indian.	Mongolian.		
The state	96,643	96,107	536	536	....	694,466	692,226	2,240	1,319	798	123	6	2
Cumberland [1]	25,530	25,351	179	179	....	175,900	175,364	536	488	2	46	7	3
Hancock [2]	9,542	9,504	38	38	....	162,135	161,503	632	283	333	16	4	2
Lincoln [3]	29,733	29,592	141	141	....	200,626	200,152	474	387	50	37	5	2
Washington [4]	2,760	2,740	20	20	....	79,640	79,126	514	94	411	9	7	1
York [5]	29,078	28,920	158	158	....	76,165	76,081	84	67	2	15	5	1

NEW HAMPSHIRE.

COUNTY.	POPULATION IN 1790.					POPULATION IN 1900.						Number of colored persons per 1,000 whites, 1790.	Number of negroes per 1,000 whites, 1900.
	Total.	White.	Total.	Free.	Slave.	Total.	White.	Total.	Negro.	Indian.	Mongolian.		
The state	141,899	141,112	787	630	157	411,588	410,791	797	662	22	113	6	2
Cheshire [6]	28,753	28,665	88	70	18	48,334	48,255	79	58	10	11	3	1
Grafton [7]	13,468	13,419	49	28	21	74,771	74,673	98	81	3	14	4	1
Hillsborough [8]	32,883	32,707	176	176	....	129,068	128,881	187	141	....	46	5	1
Rockingham [9]	43,184	42,795	389	292	97	85,034	84,835	199	179	6	14	9	2
Strafford [10]	23,611	23,526	85	64	21	74,381	74,147	234	203	3	28	4	3

VERMONT.

COUNTY.	POPULATION IN 1790.					POPULATION IN 1900.						Number of colored persons per 1,000 whites, 1790.	Number of negroes per 1,000 whites, 1900.
	Total.	White.	Total.	Free.	Slave.	Total.	White.	Total.	Negro.	Indian.	Mongolian.		
The state	85,341	85,072	269	269	....	343,641	342,771	870	826	5	39	3	2
Addison [11]	6,420	6,383	37	37	....	19,650	19,648	2	2	....	....	6	([12])
Bennington [13]	12,206	12,173	33	33	....	21,705	21,536	169	165	....	4	3	8
Chittenden [14]	7,287	7,264	23	23	....	107,008	106,724	284	275	....	9	3	3
Orange [15]	10,526	10,485	41	41	....	90,824	90,774	50	38	4	8	4	([12])
Rutland [16]	15,590	15,558	32	32	....	45,120	44,898	222	211	1	10	2	5
Windham [18]	17,572	17,514	58	58	....	26,660	26,593	67	64	....	3	3	2
Windsor [17]	15,740	15,695	45	45	....	32,674	32,598	76	71	....	5	3	2

MASSACHUSETTS.

COUNTY.	POPULATION IN 1790.					POPULATION IN 1900.						Number of colored persons per 1,000 whites, 1790.	Number of negroes per 1,000 whites, 1900.
	Total.	White.	Total.	Free.	Slave.	Total.	White.	Total.	Negro.	Indian.	Mongolian.		
The state	378,556	373,187	5,369	5,369	....	2,751,852	2,716,096	35,756	32,192	587	2,977	14	12
Barnstable [13]	17,342	16,970	372	372	....	27,826	26,971	855	615	231	9	22	23
Berkshire [18]	30,263	29,940	323	323	....	95,774	94,400	1,374	1,305	3	66	11	14
Bristol [19]	31,696	30,966	730	730	....	197,735	194,556	3,179	2,958	86	135	24	15
Dukes [13]	3,255	3,230	25	25	....	4,561	4,256	305	150	154	1	8	35
Essex [20]	57,879	57,007	872	872	....	356,569	354,298	2,271	1,945	3	323	15	6
Hampshire [21]	59,656	59,205	451	451	....	275,028	273,043	1,985	1,807	15	163	8	7
Middlesex [22]	42,769	42,177	592	592	....	628,097	618,867	9,230	8,546	36	648	14	14
Nantucket [13]	4,555	4,521	34	34	....	3,006	2,958	48	46	....	2	8	16
Plymouth [23]	29,512	29,013	499	499	....	108,114	166,983	1,131	1,040	10	81	17	10
Suffolk [24]	44,865	43,803	1,062	1,062	....	708,324	695,047	13,277	11,959	15	1,303	24	17
Worcester [25]	56,764	56,355	409	409	....	346,818	344,717	2,101	1,821	34	246	7	5

RHODE ISLAND.

COUNTY.	POPULATION IN 1790.					POPULATION IN 1900.						Number of colored persons per 1,000 whites, 1790.	Number of negroes per 1,000 whites, 1900.
	Total.	White.	Total.	Free.	Slave.	Total.	White.	Total.	Negro.	Indian.	Mongolian.		
The state	69,112	64,670	4,442	3,484	958	482,050	472,718	9,332	8,874	35	423	69	19
Bristol [13]	3,211	3,013	198	100	98	13,144	12,975	169	158	4	7	66	12
Kent [13]	8,851	8,439	412	349	63	29,976	29,634	342	335	....	7	49	11
Newport [26]	14,351	13,174	1,177	805	372	137,462	135,085	2,377	2,268	2	107	89	17
Providence [27]	24,376	23,518	858	777	81	277,314	271,817	5,497	5,179	27	291	36	19
Washington [13]	18,323	16,526	1,797	1,453	344	24,154	23,207	947	934	2	11	109	40

[1] Area covered in 1900 by parts of Franklin, Somerset, York, Cumberland, Androscoggin, and Oxford counties.
[2] Area covered in 1900 by Hancock county, and by parts of Waldo, Penobscot, Piscataquis, and Aroostook counties.
[3] Area covered in 1900 by Lincoln, Knox, Kennebec, and Sagadahoc counties, and by parts of Waldo, Androscoggin, Somerset, Piscataquis, Franklin, Aroostook, and Penobscot counties.
[4] Area covered in 1900 by Washington county, and by parts of Penobscot and Aroostook counties.
[5] Area covered in 1900 by parts of York, Cumberland, Oxford, and Franklin counties.
[6] Area covered in 1900 by Cheshire county, and by part of Sullivan county.
[7] Area covered in 1900 by Grafton and Coos counties, and by parts of Carroll and Merrimack counties.
[8] Area covered in 1900 by Hillsboro county (except Pelham, which was in Rockingham county in 1790), and by parts of Merrimack and Sullivan counties.
[9] Area covered in 1900 by Rockingham county, part of Merrimack county, and the town of Pelham (now in Hillsboro county).
[10] Area covered in 1900 by Strafford and Belknap counties, and by parts of Carroll and Merrimack counties.
[11] Area covered in 1900 by part of Addison county.
[12] Less than one.
[13] Area covered in 1900 coextensive with that of 1790.
[14] Area covered in 1900 by Franklin, Grand Isle, Lamoille, and Chittenden counties, and by parts of Orleans, Addison, and Washington counties.
[15] Area covered in 1900 by Essex, Caledonia, and Orange counties, and by parts of Orleans and Washington counties.
[16] Area covered in 1900 by parts of Rutland and Addison counties.
[17] Area covered in 1900 by Windsor county, and by part of Rutland county.
[18] Area covered in 1900 by Berkshire county, and by part of Franklin county.
[19] Area covered in 1900 by parts of Bristol and Norfolk counties, and by part of Providence county, R. I.
[20] Area covered in 1900 by part of Essex county.
[21] Area covered in 1900 by parts of Hampshire, Hampden, Franklin, and Worcester counties.
[22] Area covered in 1900 by parts of Middlesex, Suffolk, and Worcester counties.
[23] Area covered in 1900 by parts of Plymouth and Bristol counties.
[24] Area covered in 1900 by parts of Suffolk, Norfolk, Essex, Plymouth, Middlesex, and Worcester counties.
[25] Area covered in 1900 by parts of Worcester, Hampden, Hampshire, and Middlesex counties.
[26] Area covered in 1900 by Newport county, and by part of Bristol county, Mass.
[27] Area covered in 1900 by part of Providence county.

TABLE 105.—WHITE AND COLORED POPULATION OF EACH COUNTY REPORTED IN 1790, COMPARED WITH THAT OF THE SAME AREA IN 1900, TOGETHER WITH THE NUMBER OF COLORED PER 1,000 WHITES—Continued.

CONNECTICUT.

COUNTY.	POPULATION IN 1790.					POPULATION IN 1900.						Number of colored persons per 1,000 whites, 1790.	Number of negroes per 1,000 whites, 1900.
	Total.	White.	Colored.			Total.	White.	Colored.					
			Total.	Free.	Slave.			Total.	Negro.	Indian.	Mongo-lian.		
The state	237,655	232,236	5,419	2,771	2,648	908,420	892,424	15,996	15,226	153	617	23	17
Fairfield [1]	36,290	35,173	1,117	318	799	184,203	180,839	3,364	3,227	9	128	32	18
Hartford [2]	38,149	37,498	651	395	256	195,147	191,776	3,371	3,190	5	176	17	17
Litchfield [3]	38,635	38,119	516	313	203	66,238	65,182	1,056	998	33	25	14	15
Middlesex [4]	18,828	18,492	336	144	192	40,876	40,405	471	450	1	20	18	11
New Haven [5]	30,703	29,882	821	434	387	267,492	262,221	5,271	5,056	2	213	27	19
New London [6]	32,918	31,605	1,313	732	581	81,183	79,421	1,762	1,641	83	38	42	21
Tolland [7]	13,251	13,111	140	94	46	22,203	22,130	73	66	1	6	11	3
Windham [8]	28,881	28,356	525	341	184	51,078	50,450	628	598	19	11	19	12

NEW YORK.

COUNTY.	Total.	White.	Total.	Free.	Slave.	Total.	White.	Total.	Negro.	Indian.	Mongo-lian.	per 1,000 whites, 1790.	per 1,000 whites, 1900.
The state	340,241	314,366	25,875	4,682	21,193	7,268,894	7,156,881	112,013	99,232	5,257	7,524	82	14
Albany [9]	75,980	72,087	3,893	171	3,722	428,417	424,404	4,013	3,889	16	108	54	9
Clinton [10]	1,615	1,583	32	16	16	210,073	208,408	1,665	335	1,272	58	20	2
Columbia [11]	27,496	25,811	1,685	52	1,633	43,211	41,779	1,432	1,417		15	65	34
Dutchess [12]	45,276	42,981	2,295	431	1,864	95,457	93,093	2,364	2,335	1	28	53	25
Kings [11]	4,549	3,021	1,528	46	1,482	1,166,582	1,146,909	19,673	18,367	6	1,300	506	16
Montgomery [13]	28,852	28,223	629	41	588	1,127,730	1,119,761	7,969	7,236	616	117	22	6
New York city and county [14]	33,111	29,619	3,492	1,119	2,373	1,850,093	1,808,968	41,125	36,246	21	4,858	118	20
Ontario [15]	1,074	1,058	16	6	10	1,234,365	1,225,283	9,082	5,796	3,115	171	15	5
Orange [16]	18,477	17,315	1,162	201	961	142,157	137,256	4,901	4,837		64	67	35
Queens [17]	16,013	12,886	3,127	819	2,308	208,447	203,328	5,119	4,921	1	197	243	24
Richmond [11]	3,827	2,945	882	127	755	67,021	65,863	1,158	1,072		86	299	16
Suffolk [11]	16,546	14,310	2,236	1,131	1,105	77,582	74,298	3,284	3,035	168	81	156	41
Ulster [18]	29,370	26,295	3,075	161	2,914	157,428	155,638	1,790	1,768	1	21	117	11
Washington [19]	14,077	14,028	49	3	46	75,567	75,228	339	290	37	12	3	4
Westchester [20]	23,978	22,204	1,774	358	1,416	384,764	376,665	8,099	7,688	3	408	80	20

NEW JERSEY.

COUNTY.	Total.	White.	Total.	Free.	Slave.	Total.	White.	Total.	Negro.	Indian.	Mongo-lian.	per 1,000 whites, 1790.	per 1,000 whites, 1900.
The state	184,139	169,954	14,185	2,762	11,423	1,883,669	1,812,317	71,352	69,844	63	1,445	83	39
Bergen [21]	12,601	10,108	2,493	192	2,301	505,412	497,571	7,841	7,379		462	247	15
Burlington [22]	18,095	17,270	825	598	227	104,373	100,586	3,787	3,723	22	42	48	37
Cape-May [11]	2,571	2,416	155	14	141	13,201	12,328	873	869		4	64	70
Cumberland [11]	8,248	7,990	258	138	120	51,193	48,785	2,408	2,403		5	32	49
Essex [23]	17,785	16,454	1,331	160	1,171	572,685	554,107	18,578	18,022	6	550	81	33
Gloucester [24]	13,363	12,830	533	342	191	185,950	168,239	17,711	17,561	7	143	42	104
Hunterdon [25]	20,153	18,661	1,492	191	1,301	77,412	74,415	2,997	2,934	17	46	80	39
Middlesex [26]	15,956	14,498	1,458	140	1,318	90,882	88,050	2,832	2,782	1	49	101	32
Monmouth [27]	16,918	14,969	1,949	353	1,596	92,158	85,636	6,522	6,457	3	62	130	75
Morris [11]	16,216	15,532	684	48	636	65,156	63,503	1,653	1,618		35	44	25
Salem [11]	10,437	9,891	546	374	172	25,530	22,493	3,037	3,029		8	55	135
Somerset [28]	12,296	10,339	1,957	147	1,810	37,802	35,225	2,577	2,540	7	30	189	72
Sussex [29]	19,500	18,996	504	65	439	61,915	61,379	536	527		9	27	9

[1] Area covered in 1900 coextensive with that of 1790.
[2] Population of Wolcott town added to, and that of Hartland town and Marlboro town subtracted from, 1900 figures to make areas comparable.
[3] Population of Southbury town, Hartland town, and Middlebury town added to 1900 figures to make areas comparable.
[4] Population of Durham town subtracted from 1900 figures to make areas comparable.
[5] Population of Middlebury town, Southbury town, and Wolcott town subtracted from, and that of Durham town added to, 1900 figures to make areas comparable.
[6] Population of Columbia town and part of Marlboro town added to, and that of Lebanon town and Voluntown town subtracted from, 1900 figures to make areas comparable.
[7] Population of Columbia town and Mansfield town subtracted from, and part of Marlboro town added to, 1900 figures to make areas comparable.
[8] Population of Mansfield town, Lebanon town, and Voluntown town added to 1900 figures to make areas comparable.
[9] Area covered in 1900 by Albany, Rensselaer, Saratoga, and Schenectady counties, and by parts of Greene and Schoharie counties.
[10] Area covered in 1900 by Clinton, Franklin, Essex, and St. Lawrence counties.
[11] Area covered in 1900 coextensive with that of 1790.
[12] Area covered in 1900 by Dutchess and Putnam counties.
[13] Area covered in 1900 by Chemung, Montgomery, Fulton, Herkimer, Hamilton, Otsego, Jefferson, Tioga, Broome, Chenango, Oneida, Lewis, Madison, Cortland, Oswego, Onondaga, Cayuga, Seneca, and Tompkins counties, and by parts of Delaware, Schoharie, Schuyler, and Wayne counties.
[14] Area covered in 1900 by Manhattan borough.
[15] Area covered in 1900 by Chautauqua, Cattaraugus, Allegany, Erie, Niagara, Wyoming, Genesee, Orleans, Monroe, Livingston, Ontario, Yates, and Steuben counties, and by parts of Wayne and Schuyler counties.
[16] Area covered in 1900 by Orange and Rockland counties.
[17] Area covered in 1900 by Queens and Nassau counties.
[18] Area covered in 1900 by Ulster and Sullivan counties, and by parts of Greene and Delaware counties.
[19] Area covered in 1900 by Washington and Warren counties.
[20] Area covered in 1900 by Westchester county, and by part of New York county.
[21] Area covered in 1900 by Bergen and Hudson counties, and by part of Passaic county.
[22] Area covered in 1900 by Burlington county, and by parts of Mercer and Ocean counties.
[23] Area covered in 1900 by Essex and Union counties, and by part of Passaic county.
[24] Area covered in 1900 by Gloucester, Atlantic, and Camden counties.
[25] Area covered in 1900 by Hunterdon county, and by part of Mercer county.
[26] Area covered in 1900 by Middlesex county, and by parts of Mercer and Monmouth counties.
[27] Area covered in 1900 by parts of Mercer, Monmouth, and Ocean counties.
[28] Area covered in 1900 by Somerset county, and by part of Mercer county.
[29] Area covered in 1900 by Warren and Sussex counties.

Table 105.—WHITE AND COLORED POPULATION OF EACH COUNTY REPORTED IN 1790, COMPARED WITH THAT OF THE SAME AREA IN 1900, TOGETHER WITH THE NUMBER OF COLORED PER 1,000 WHITES—Continued.

PENNSYLVANIA.

COUNTY.	POPULATION IN 1790.					POPULATION IN 1900.						Number of colored persons per 1,000 whites, 1790.	Number of negroes per 1,000 whites, 1900.
	Total.	White.	Colored.			Total.	White.	Colored.					
			Total.	Free.	Slave.			Total.	Negro.	Indian.	Mongolian.		
The state	433,611	423,373	10,238	6,531	3,707	6,302,115	6,141,664	160,451	156,845	1,639	1,967	24	26
Allegheny [1]	10,203	10,032	171	12	159	1,217,750	1,186,717	31,033	30,615	79	339	17	26
Bedford [2]	13,132	13,052	80	34	46	196,533	195,203	1,330	1,314	4	12	6	7
Berks [3]	30,189	29,928	261	201	60	316,005	315,081	964	940		24	9	3
Bucks [4]	25,216	24,374	842	581	261	71,190	68,788	2,402	2,200	185	17	35	32
Chester [4]	27,829	27,141	688	544	144	95,695	86,391	9,304	9,242	39	23	25	107
Cumberland [5]	18,208	17,779	429	206	223	76,607	73,690	2,917	1,900	1,015	2	24	26
Dauphin [6]	18,155	17,886	269	59	210	168,270	161,579	6,691	6,668	6	17	15	41
Delaware [4]	9,469	9,133	336	287	49	94,762	84,815	9,947	9,894	8	45	37	117
Fayette [4]	13,318	12,990	328	46	282	110,412	105,442	4,970	4,952		18	25	47
Franklin [4]	15,662	15,057	605	279	326	54,902	52,944	1,958	1,954		4	40	37
Huntingdon [7]	7,558	7,491	67	24	43	135,803	134,628	1,175	1,168		7	9	9
Lancaster [8]	36,081	35,192	889	542	347	159,241	156,761	2,480	2,461	1	18	25	16
Luzerne [9]	4,892	4,868	24	13	11	562,463	560,417	2,046	2,004		42	5	4
Mifflin [10]	7,562	7,461	101	42	59	82,108	81,387	721	716	2	3	14	9
Montgomery [4]	22,918	22,365	553	440	113	138,995	134,436	4,559	4,503	19	37	25	33
Northampton [11]	24,238	24,086	152	132	20	314,685	313,535	1,150	1,116	4	30	6	4
Northumberland [12]	17,147	16,971	176	89	87	697,909	694,059	3,850	3,733	32	85	10	5
Philadelphia [4]	54,388	51,916	2,472	2,099	373	1,293,697	1,229,673	64,024	62,613	234	1,177	48	51
Washington [13]	23,892	23,617	275	12	263	121,107	116,393	4,714	4,690		24	12	40
Westmoreland [14]	16,019	15,852	167	39	128	243,032	240,845	2,187	2,149		38	11	9
York [15]	37,535	36,182	1,353	850	503	150,909	148,880	2,029	2,013	11	5	37	14

DELAWARE.[4]

COUNTY.	Total.	White.	Total.	Free.	Slave.	Total.	White.	Total.	Negro.	Indian.	Mongolian.	1790.	1900.
The state	59,096	46,310	12,786	3,899	8,887	184,735	153,977	30,758	30,697	9	52	276	199
Kent	18,920	14,050	4,870	2,570	2,300	32,762	25,017	7,745	7,738		7	347	309
New-Castle	19,688	16,487	3,201	639	2,562	109,697	93,406	16,241	16,197	9	35	194	173
Sussex	20,488	15,773	4,715	690	4,025	42,276	35,504	6,772	6,762		10	299	190

MARYLAND.[16]

COUNTY.	Total.	White.	Total.	Free.	Slave.	Total.	White.	Total.	Negro.	Indian.	Mongolian.	1790.	1900.
The state	319,728	208,649	111,079	8,043	103,036	1,466,762	1,143,956	322,806	321,766	25	1,015	532	281
Allegany [17]	4,809	4,539	270	12	258	71,395	69,594	1,801	1,795		6	59	26
Ann-Arundel [18]	22,598	11,664	10,934	804	10,130	56,325	36,545	19,790	19,772		18	937	541
Baltimore [19]	25,434	18,953	6,481	604	5,877	144,933	125,446	19,487	19,447		40	342	155
Baltimore town and precincts [20]	13,503	11,925	1,578	323	1,255	469,116	396,324	72,792	72,337		455	132	183
Calvert [4]	8,652	4,211	4,441	136	4,305	10,223	5,080	5,143	5,143			1,055	1,012
Caroline [21]	9,506	7,028	2,478	421	2,057	16,248	12,009	4,239	4,237		2	353	353
Cecil [4]	13,625	10,055	3,570	163	3,407	24,662	20,850	3,812	3,805	3	4	355	183
Charles [4]	20,613	10,124	10,489	404	10,085	17,662	8,014	9,648	9,648			1,036	1,204
Dorchester [22]	15,875	10,010	5,865	528	5,337	27,962	18,476	9,486	9,484		2	586	513
Frederick [23]	30,791	26,937	3,854	213	3,641	71,443	64,193	7,250	7,247		3	143	113
Harford [4]	14,976	10,784	4,192	775	3,417	28,269	22,411	5,858	5,854		4	389	261
Kent [4]	12,836	6,748	6,088	655	5,433	18,786	11,343	7,443	7,442		1	902	656
Montgomery [24]	18,003	11,679	6,324	294	6,030	45,000	30,387	14,613	14,584	1	28	541	480
Prince Georges [25]	21,344	10,004	11,340	164	11,176	294,067	199,448	94,619	94,157	21	441	1,134	472
Queen Anns [4]	15,463	8,171	7,292	618	6,674	18,364	11,991	6,373	6,372		1	892	531
St. Marys [4]	15,544	8,216	7,328	343	6,985	17,182	8,926	8,256	8,256			892	925
Somersett [26]	15,610	8,272	7,338	268	7,070	38,997	26,126	12,871	12,867		4	887	493
Talbot [4]	13,084	7,231	5,853	1,076	4,777	20,342	12,875	7,467	7,466		1	809	580
Washington [4]	15,822	14,472	1,350	64	1,286	45,133	42,642	2,491	2,488		3	93	58
Worcester [27]	11,640	7,626	4,014	178	3,836	30,643	21,276	9,367	9,365		2	526	440

[1] Area covered in 1900 by Allegheny, Butler, Crawford, Erie, Mercer, and Lawrence counties, and by parts of Armstrong, Beaver, Venango, Warren, and Forest counties.
[2] Area covered in 1900 by Bedford, Somerset, and Fulton counties, and by parts of Cambria and Blair counties.
[3] Area covered in 1900 by Berks county, and by part of Schuylkill county.
[4] Area covered in 1900 coextensive with that of 1790.
[5] Area covered in 1900 by Perry and Cumberland counties.
[6] Area covered in 1900 by Dauphin county, and by part of Lebanon county.
[7] Area covered in 1900 by Huntingdon county, and by parts of Center, Cambria, Clearfield, and Blair counties.
[8] Area covered in 1900 by Lancaster county, and by part of Lebanon county.
[9] Area covered in 1900 by Luzerne, Susquehanna, Wyoming, and Lackawanna counties, and by part of Bradford county.
[10] Area covered in 1900 by Mifflin and Juniata counties, and by part of Center county.
[11] Area covered in 1900 by Northampton, Wayne, Lehigh, Pike, Monroe, and Carbon counties, and by part of Schuylkill county.
[12] Area covered in 1900 by Northumberland, Lycoming, Jefferson, McKean, Potter, Tioga, Columbia, Union, Clarion, Clinton, Elk, Sullivan, Montour, Snyder, and Cameron counties, and by parts of Armstrong, Center, Venango, Warren, Indiana, Clearfield, Bradford, and Forest counties.
[13] Area covered in 1900 by Washington and Greene counties, and by part of Beaver county.
[14] Area covered in 1900 by Westmoreland county, and by parts of Armstrong and Indiana counties.
[15] Area covered in 1900 by York and Adams counties.
[16] Includes population of the District of Columbia in 1900.
[17] Area covered in 1900 by Allegany and Garrett counties.
[18] Area covered in 1900 by Anne Arundel and Howard counties.
[19] Area covered in 1900 by Baltimore county, and by parts of Carroll county and Baltimore city.
[20] Area covered in 1900 by part of Baltimore city.
[21] Area covered in 1900 by Caroline county, and by part of Dorchester county.
[22] Area covered in 1900 by part of Dorchester county.
[23] Area covered in 1900 by Frederick county, and by part of Carroll county.
[24] Area covered in 1900 by Montgomery county, and Georgetown, D. C.
[25] Area covered in 1900 by Prince Georges county, and the District of Columbia, exclusive of Georgetown.
[26] Area covered in 1900 by Somerset county, and by part of Wicomico county.
[27] Area covered in 1900 by Worcester county, and by part of Wicomico county.

TABLE **105.**—WHITE AND COLORED POPULATION OF EACH COUNTY REPORTED IN 1790, COMPARED WITH THAT OF THE SAME AREA IN 1900, TOGETHER WITH THE NUMBER OF COLORED PER 1,000 WHITES—Continued.

VIRGINIA.[1]

COUNTY.	POPULATION IN 1790.					POPULATION IN 1900.						Number of colored persons per 1,000 whites, 1790.	Number of negroes per 1,000 whites, 1900.
	Total.	White.	Colored.			Total.	White.	Colored.					
			Total.	Free.	Slave.			Total.	Negro.	Indian.	Mongolian.		
The state	747,610	442,117	305,493	12,866	292,627	2,812,984	2,108,088	704,896	704,221	366	309	691	334
Accomack	13,959	8,976	4,983	721	4,262	32,570	20,743	11,827	11,825	....	2	555	570
Albemarle	12,585	6,835	5,750	171	5,579	34,922	21,969	12,953	12,950	....	3	841	589
Amelia (including Nottoway Co.)	18,097	6,684	11,413	106	11,307	21,403	8,018	13,385	13,385	....	....	1,708	1,669
Amherst[2]	13,703	8,286	5,417	121	5,296	33,939	21,210	12,729	12,729	....	....	654	600
Augusta[3]	10,886	9,260	1,626	59	1,567	50,662	41,919	8,743	8,738	....	5	176	208
Bedford	10,531	7,725	2,806	52	2,754	30,356	20,617	9,739	9,739	....	....	363	472
Berkley[4]	19,713	16,650	3,063	131	2,932	40,065	34,218	5,847	5,847	....	....	184	171
Botetourt[5]	10,524	9,241	1,283	24	1,259	76,940	58,791	18,149	18,139	....	10	139	309
Brunswick	12,827	5,919	6,908	132	6,776	18,217	7,375	10,842	10,842	....	....	1,167	1,470
Buckingham[6]	9,779	5,496	4,283	115	4,168	20,634	10,599	10,035	10,035	....	....	779	947
Campbell[7]	7,685	4,946	2,739	251	2,488	44,832	25,871	18,961	18,961	....	....	554	733
Caroline	17,489	6,994	10,495	203	10,292	16,709	7,667	9,042	9,042	....	....	1,501	1,179
Charles-City	5,588	2,084	3,504	363	3,141	5,040	1,344	3,696	3,696	....	....	1,681	2,750
Charlotte[8]	10,078	5,199	4,879	63	4,816	15,879	7,116	8,763	8,763	....	....	938	1,231
Chesterfield	14,214	6,358	7,856	369	7,487	28,519	17,481	11,038	11,037	....	1	1,236	631
Culpeper[9]	22,105	13,809	8,296	70	8,226	33,182	20,885	12,297	12,296	....	1	601	589
Cumberland	8,153	3,577	4,576	142	4,434	8,996	2,791	6,205	6,205	....	....	1,279	2,223
Dinwiddie	13,934	6,039	7,895	561	7,334	37,184	16,931	20,253	20,251	....	2	1,307	1,196
Elizabeth-City	3,450	1,556	1,894	18	1,876	19,460	10,757	8,703	8,582	108	13	1,217	798
Essex	9,122	3,543	5,579	139	5,440	9,701	3,576	6,125	6,125	....	....	1,575	1,713
Fairfax[10]	12,320	7,611	4,709	135	4,574	31,089	20,465	10,624	10,614	....	10	619	519
Fauquier	17,892	11,157	6,735	93	6,642	23,374	15,074	8,300	8,298	....	2	604	550
Fluvanna	3,921	2,430	1,491	25	1,466	9,050	5,039	4,011	4,011	....	....	614	796
Franklin	6,842	5,735	1,107	34	1,073	25,953	20,005	5,948	5,947	....	1	193	297
Frederick[11]	19,681	15,315	4,366	116	4,250	31,248	26,342	4,906	4,903	....	3	285	186
Gloucester[12]	13,498	6,225	7,273	210	7,063	21,071	12,068	9,003	9,003	....	....	1,168	746
Goochland	9,053	4,140	4,913	257	4,656	9,519	3,961	5,558	5,558	....	....	1,187	1,403
Greenbrier (including Kanawa)[13]	6,015	5,676	339	20	319	406,338	387,036	19,302	19,295	1	6	60	50
Greensville	6,362	2,530	3,832	212	3,620	9,758	3,402	6,356	6,356	....	....	1,515	1,868
Halifax	14,722	8,931	5,791	226	5,565	37,197	17,922	19,275	19,275	....	....	648	1,075
Hampshire[14]	7,346	6,879	467	13	454	27,322	26,116	1,206	1,205	1	....	63	46
Hanover	14,754	6,291	8,463	240	8,223	17,618	9,696	7,922	7,898	24	....	1,345	815
Hardy[15]	7,336	6,556	780	411	369	15,724	15,015	709	709	....	....	119	47
Harrison[16]	2,080	2,013	67	....	67	149,276	146,447	2,829	2,805	7	17	33	19
Henrico	12,000	5,600	6,400	581	5,819	115,112	70,044	45,068	45,046	1	21	1,143	643
Henry[17]	8,479	6,763	1,716	165	1,551	34,667	24,660	10,007	10,007	....	....	254	406
Isle of Wight	9,028	4,786	4,242	375	3,867	13,102	6,833	6,269	6,268	....	1	886	917
James City	4,070	1,519	2,551	146	2,405	5,732	2,712	3,020	3,020	....	....	1,679	1,114
King & Queen	9,377	4,159	5,218	75	5,143	9,265	4,006	5,259	5,259	....	....	1,255	1,313
King George	7,366	3,123	4,243	86	4,157	6,918	3,596	3,322	3,322	....	....	1,359	924
King William	8,128	2,893	5,235	84	5,151	8,380	3,266	5,114	4,962	152	....	1,810	1,519
Lancaster	5,638	2,259	3,379	143	3,236	8,949	4,058	4,891	4,891	....	....	1,496	1,205
Loudon[18]	18,962	14,749	4,213	183	4,030	30,398	23,139	7,259	7,257	....	2	286	314
Louisa	8,467	3,880	4,587	14	4,573	16,517	7,896	8,621	8,621	....	....	1,182	1,092
Lunenburg	8,959	4,547	4,412	80	4,332	11,705	5,133	6,572	6,572	....	....	970	1,280
Mecklenburg	14,733	7,555	7,178	416	6,762	26,551	10,353	16,198	16,198	....	....	950	1,565
Middlesex	4,140	1,531	2,609	51	2,558	8,220	3,684	4,536	4,536	....	....	1,704	1,231
Monongalia[19]	4,768	4,602	166	12	154	80,015	78,800	1,215	1,206	....	9	36	15
Montgomery[20]	13,228	12,394	834	6	828	174,225	152,327	21,898	21,894	....	4	67	144
Nansemond	9,010	4,713	4,297	480	3,817	23,078	10,115	12,963	12,962	....	1	912	1,281
New Kent	6,239	2,391	3,848	148	3,700	4,865	1,660	3,205	3,204	1	....	1,609	1,930
Norfolk	14,524	8,928	5,596	251	5,345	114,831	57,212	57,619	57,455	52	112	627	1,004
Northampton	6,889	3,181	3,708	464	3,244	13,770	6,141	7,629	7,627	....	2	1,166	1,242
Northumberland	9,163	4,506	4,657	197	4,460	9,846	5,680	4,166	4,166	....	....	1,034	733
Ohio[21]	5,212	4,907	305	24	281	133,162	130,672	2,490	2,470	....	20	62	19

[1] Area covered in 1900 by Virginia and West Virginia. Independent cities are included in county totals for 1790 and 1900.
[2] Area covered in 1900 by Amherst and Nelson counties.
[3] Area covered in 1900 by Augusta county, and by parts of Bath, Pocahontas, and Highland counties.
[4] Area covered in 1900 by Berkeley and Jefferson counties, and by part of Morgan county.
[5] Area covered in 1900 by Botetourt, Alleghany, and Roanoke counties, and by parts of Craig, Monroe, and Bath counties.
[6] Area covered in 1900 by Buckingham county, and by part of Appomattox county.
[7] Area covered in 1900 by Campbell county, and by part of Appomattox county.
[8] Area covered in 1900 by Charlotte county, and by part of Appomattox county.
[9] Area covered in 1900 by Culpeper, Madison, and Rappahannock counties.
[10] Area covered in 1900 by Alexandria county, and by part of Fairfax county.
[11] Area covered in 1900 by Frederick and Clarke counties, and by part of Warren county.
[12] Area covered in 1900 by Gloucester and Mathews counties.
[13] Area covered in 1900 by Greenbrier, Boone, Cabell, Clay, Fayette, Jackson, Kanawha, Lincoln, Logan, Mason, Mingo, Nicholas, Putnam, Raleigh, Roane, Wayne, and Wyoming counties, and by parts of Braxton, Calhoun, Gilmer, McDowell, Monroe, Pocahontas, Summers, Webster, Wirt, and Wood counties.
[14] Area covered in 1900 by Hampshire and Mineral counties, and by part of Morgan county.
[15] Area covered in 1900 by Hardy and Grant counties.
[16] Area covered in 1900 by Harrison, Doddridge, Lewis, and Ritchie counties, and by parts of Barbour, Braxton, Calhoun, Gilmer, Marion, Taylor, Upshur, Webster, Wirt, Wood, and Pleasants counties.
[17] Area covered in 1900 by Henry and Patrick counties.
[18] Area covered in 1900 by Loudoun county, and by part of Fairfax county.
[19] Area covered in 1900 by Monongalia county, and by parts of Preston, Marion, and Taylor counties.
[20] Area covered in 1900 by Montgomery, Bland, Carroll, Floyd, Giles, Grayson, Mercer, Pulaski, and Wythe counties, and by parts of Craig, McDowell, Monroe, Smyth, Summers, and Tazewell counties.
[21] Area covered in 1900 by Ohio, Brooke, Hancock, Marshall, Tyler, and Wetzel counties, and by part of Pleasants county.

TABLE **105.**—WHITE AND COLORED POPULATION OF EACH COUNTY REPORTED IN 1790, COMPARED WITH THAT OF THE SAME AREA IN 1900, TOGETHER WITH THE NUMBER OF COLORED PER 1,000 WHITES—Continued.

VIRGINIA [1]—Continued.

COUNTY.	POPULATION IN 1790.					POPULATION IN 1900.						Number of colored persons per 1,000 whites, 1790.	Number of negroes per 1,000 whites, 1900.
	Total.	White.	Colored.			Total.	White.	Colored.					
			Total.	Free.	Slave.			Total.	Negro.	Indian.	Mongolian.		
Orange [2]	9,921	5,436	4,485	64	4,421	18,785	11,833	6,952	6,950	....	2	825	587
Pendleton [3]	2,452	2,378	74	1	73	12,045	11,730	315	315	....	....	31	27
Pittsylvania	11,579	8,538	3,041	62	2,979	63,414	35,607	27,807	27,804	....	3	356	781
Powhatan	6,822	2,286	4,536	211	4,325	6,824	2,343	4,481	4,481	....	....	1,984	1,913
Prince Edward [4]	8,100	4,082	4,018	32	3,986	16,118	5,912	10,206	10,206	....	....	984	1,726
Prince George	8,173	3,387	4,786	267	4,519	7,752	2,886	4,866	4,858	8	....	1,413	1,683
Prince William	11,615	6,744	4,871	167	4,704	11,112	8,240	2,872	2,871	1	....	722	348
Princess Anne	7,793	4,527	3,266	64	3,202	11,192	5,505	5,687	5,687	....	....	721	1,033
Randolph [5]	951	932	19	....	19	48,876	47,292	1,584	1,579	3	2	20	33
Richmond	6,985	2,918	4,067	83	3,984	7,088	4,159	2,929	2,929	....	....	1,394	704
Rockbridge	6,548	5,825	723	41	682	24,187	19,693	4,494	4,494	....	....	124	228
Rockingham [6]	7,449	6,677	772	....	772	38,139	34,909	3,230	3,228	....	2	116	92
Russell [7]	3,338	3,143	195	5	190	115,100	108,258	6,842	6,842	....	....	62	63
Shannandoah [8]	10,510	9,979	531	19	512	33,351	31,209	2,142	2,142	....	....	53	69
Southampton	12,864	6,312	6,552	559	5,993	22,848	9,165	13,683	13,683	....	....	1,038	1,493
Spotsylvania	11,252	5,171	6,081	148	5,933	14,307	8,799	5,508	5,507	....	1	1,176	626
Stafford	9,588	5,465	4,123	87	4,036	8,097	6,489	1,608	1,608	....	....	754	248
Surry	6,227	2,762	3,465	368	3,097	8,469	3,286	5,183	5,183	....	....	1,255	1,577
Sussex	10,549	4,771	5,778	391	5,387	12,082	4,121	7,961	7,961	....	....	1,211	1,932
Warwick	1,690	667	1,023	33	990	24,523	13,948	10,575	10,527	....	48	1,534	755
Washington [9]	5,625	5,167	458	8	450	48,895	44,469	4,426	4,417	7	2	89	99
Westmoreland	7,722	3,183	4,539	114	4,425	9,243	4,381	4,862	4,861	....	1	1,426	1,110
York	5,233	2,115	3,118	358	2,760	7,482	3,401	4,081	4,081	....	....	1,474	1,200

NORTH CAROLINA.

COUNTY.	Total.	White.	Total.	Free.	Slave.	Total.	White.	Total.	Negro.	Indian.	Mongolian.	1790.	1900.
The state	395,005	289,181	105,824	5,041	100,783	1,893,810	1,263,603	630,207	624,469	5,687	51	366	494
Edenton district	53,769	33,568	20,201	1,048	19,153	110,615	56,455	54,160	54,147	8	5	602	959
Bertie [10]	12,462	6,963	5,499	378	5,121	20,538	8,717	11,821	11,821	....	....	790	1,356
Camden [10]	4,022	2,954	1,068	30	1,038	5,474	3,283	2,191	2,191	....	....	362	667
Chowan [10]	4,988	2,360	2,628	41	2,587	10,258	4,406	5,852	5,850	....	2	1,114	1,328
Currituck [11]	5,220	4,002	1,218	115	1,103	8,413	6,409	2,004	2,004	....	....	304	313
Gates [10]	5,386	3,076	2,310	93	2,217	10,413	5,609	4,804	4,804	....	....	751	856
Hertford [10]	5,949	3,269	2,680	232	2,448	14,294	5,895	8,399	8,391	8	....	820	1,423
Pasquotank [10]	5,477	3,790	1,687	87	1,600	13,660	6,630	7,030	7,027	....	3	445	1,060
Perquimans [10]	5,439	3,519	1,920	37	1,883	10,091	5,088	5,003	5,003	....	....	546	983
Tyrrell [12]	4,826	3,635	1,191	35	1,156	17,474	10,413	7,056	7,056	....	....	328	677
Fayette district	34,393	28,112	6,281	608	5,673	196,881	112,522	84,359	80,347	4,012	....	223	714
Anson [13]	5,235	4,365	870	41	829	35,897	20,092	15,805	15,805	....	....	199	787
Cumberland [11]	8,730	6,467	2,263	83	2,180	44,067	26,810	17,257	17,256	1	....	350	644
Moore [10]	3,870	3,487	383	12	371	23,622	15,773	7,849	7,849	....	....	110	498
Richmond [15]	5,053	4,415	638	55	583	28,408	13,801	14,607	14,473	134	....	145	1,049
Robeson [10]	5,343	4,533	810	277	533	40,371	19,577	20,794	16,917	3,877	....	179	864
Sampson [16]	6,162	4,845	1,317	140	1,177	24,516	16,469	8,047	8,047	....	....	272	489
Halifax district	64,848	37,955	26,893	1,364	25,529	184,929	83,827	101,102	101,095	1	6	709	1,206
Edgecombe [17]	10,265	7,028	3,237	70	3,167	38,474	16,904	21,570	21,567	....	3	461	1,276
Franklin [18]	7,502	4,764	2,738	37	2,701	25,116	12,678	12,438	12,438	....	....	575	981
Halifax [10]	14,310	7,170	7,140	443	6,697	30,793	11,060	19,733	19,733	....	....	996	1,784
Martin [10]	6,010	4,085	1,925	96	1,829	15,383	8,056	7,327	7,327	....	....	471	910
Nash [19]	7,390	5,189	2,201	193	2,008	32,419	18,887	13,532	13,529	....	3	424	716
Northampton [10]	9,992	5,120	4,872	458	4,414	21,150	9,031	12,119	12,118	1	....	952	1,342
Warren [20]	9,379	4,599	4,780	67	4,713	21,594	7,211	14,383	14,383	....	....	1,039	1,995
Hillsborough district	59,971	45,820	14,151	702	13,449	242,575	148,918	93,657	93,652	....	5	309	629
Caswell [21]	10,096	7,288	2,808	72	2,736	31,713	16,491	15,222	15,222	....	....	385	923
Chatham [10]	9,161	7,593	1,568	10	1,558	23,912	15,573	8,339	8,339	....	....	207	535
Granville [22]	10,982	6,504	4,478	315	4,163	37,504	17,176	20,328	20,328	....	....	688	1,184
Orange [23]	12,216	10,055	2,161	101	2,060	64,584	43,593	20,991	20,987	....	4	215	481
Randolph [10]	7,318	6,834	484	24	460	28,232	24,560	3,672	3,672	....	....	71	150
Wake [24]	10,198	7,546	2,652	180	2,472	56,630	31,525	25,105	25,104	....	1	351	796

[1] Area covered in 1900 by Virginia and West Virginia. Independent cities are included in county totals for 1790 and 1900.
[2] Area covered in 1900 by Orange and Greene counties.
[3] Area covered in 1900 by Pendleton county, and by part of Highland county.
[4] Area covered in 1900 by Prince Edward county, and by part of Appomattox county.
[5] Area covered in 1900 by Randolph and Tucker counties, and by parts of Barbour, Pocahontas, Preston, Upshur, and Webster counties.
[6] Area covered in 1900 by Rockingham county, and by part of Page county.
[7] Area covered in 1900 by Russell, Buchanan, Dickenson, Lee, and Wise counties, and by parts of McDowell, Scott, and Tazewell counties.
[8] Area covered in 1900 by Shenandoah county, and by parts of Page and Warren counties.
[9] Area covered in 1900 by Washington county, and by parts of Scott and Smyth counties.
[10] Area covered in 1900 coextensive with that of 1790.
[11] Area covered in 1900 by Currituck county, and by part of Dare county.
[12] Area covered in 1900 by Tyrrell and Washington counties, and by part of Dare county.
[13] Area covered in 1900 by Anson county, and by part of Union county.
[14] Area covered in 1900 by Harnett county, and by part of Cumberland county.
[15] Area covered in 1900 by Richmond and Scotland counties.
[16] Area covered in 1900 by Sampson county, with the exception of a small section.
[17] Area covered in 1900 by Edgecombe county, and by part of Wilson county.
[18] Area covered in 1900 by part of Franklin county.
[19] Area covered in 1900 by Nash county, and by part of Wilson county.
[20] Area covered in 1900 by Warren county, and by part of Vance county.
[21] Area covered in 1900 by Caswell and Person counties.
[22] Area covered in 1900 by Granville county, and by parts of Vance and Franklin counties.
[23] Area covered in 1900 by Orange and Alamance counties, and by part of Durham county.
[24] Area covered in 1900 by Wake county, and by part of Durham county.

TABLE **105.**—WHITE AND COLORED POPULATION OF EACH COUNTY REPORTED IN 1790, COMPARED WITH THAT OF THE SAME AREA IN 1900, TOGETHER WITH THE NUMBER OF COLORED PER 1,000 WHITES—Continued.

NORTH CAROLINA—Continued.

COUNTY.	POPULATION IN 1790.					POPULATION IN 1900.						Number of colored persons per 1,000 whites, 1790.	Number of negroes per 1,000 whites, 1900.
	Total.	White.	Colored.			Total.	White.	Colored.					
			Total.	Free.	Slave.			Total.	Negro.	Indian.	Mongolian.		
Morgan district	33,317	30,687	2,630	13	2,617	423,676	373,248	50,428	49,027	1,401		88	131
Burke [1]	8,106	7,497	609	9	600	150,376	134,633	15,743	15,057	686		81	112
Lincoln [2]	9,246	8,391	855		855	71,031	56,081	14,950	14,950			112	267
Rutherford [3]	7,808	7,197	611	2	609	138,676	124,212	14,464	13,758	706		85	111
Wilkes [4]	8,157	7,602	555	2	553	63,593	58,322	5,271	5,262	9		73	90
Newbern district	55,683	38,800	16,883	841	16,042	218,855	127,391	91,464	91,454		10	435	718
Beaufort [5]	5,405	3,655	1,750	128	1,622	27,372	16,002	11,370	11,368		2	479	710
Carteret [6]	3,734	2,932	802	93	709	11,344	9,297	2,047	2,047			274	220
Craven [7]	10,474	6,474	4,000	337	3,663	31,704	14,472	17,232	17,228		4	618	1,190
Dobbs [8]	6,994	4,936	2,058	46	2,012	30,677	16,852	13,825	13,824		1	417	820
Hyde [9]	4,204	3,024	1,180	37	1,143	10,265	6,132	4,133	4,133			390	674
Johnston [10]	5,691	4,298	1,393	65	1,328	35,003	25,678	9,325	9,325			324	363
Jones [11]	4,796	3,071	1,725	70	1,655	8,226	4,466	3,760	3,760			562	842
Pitt [11]	8,270	5,881	2,389	25	2,364	30,889	15,397	15,492	15,492			406	1,006
Wayne [12]	6,115	4,529	1,586	40	1,546	33,375	19,095	14,280	14,277		3	350	748
Salisbury district	66,927	58,425	8,502	249	8,253	388,126	286,716	101,410	101,392	6	12	146	354
Guilford [11]	7,300	6,657	643	27	616	39,074	27,969	11,105	11,103	1	1	97	397
Iredell [13]	5,430	4,559	871	3	868	34,310	26,508	7,802	7,802			191	294
Mecklenburg [14]	11,360	9,685	1,675	67	1,608	90,853	57,069	33,844	33,842		2	173	594
Montgomery [15]	5,039	4,191	848	11	837	29,417	23,936	5,481	5,481			202	229
Rockingham [11]	6,211	5,088	1,123	10	1,113	33,163	21,544	11,619	11,617		2	221	539
Rowan [16]	15,972	14,129	1,843	102	1,741	67,497	53,380	14,117	14,110	4	3	130	264
Stokes [17]	8,423	7,633	790	12	778	54,214	40,806	13,378	13,346		2	103	327
Surry [18]	7,192	6,483	709	17	692	39,598	35,504	4,094	4,091	1	2	109	115
Wilmington district	26,097	15,814	10,283	216	10,067	128,153	74,526	53,627	53,355	259	13	650	716
Bladen [19]	5,100	3,356	1,744	58	1,686	34,230	21,891	12,339	12,194	145		520	557
Brunswick [20]	3,070	1,556	1,514	3	1,511	18,548	10,512	8,036	7,922	114		973	726
Duplin [11]	5,663	4,274	1,389	3	1,386	22,405	13,877	8,528	8,528			325	615
New Hanover [21]	6,837	3,032	3,805	68	3,737	41,030	19,916	21,114	21,101		13	1,255	1,081
Onslow [11]	5,427	3,596	1,831	84	1,747	11,940	8,330	3,610	3,610			509	433

SOUTH CAROLINA.

COUNTY.	POPULATION IN 1790.					POPULATION IN 1900.						Number of colored persons per 1,000 whites, 1790.	Number of negroes per 1,000 whites, 1900.
	Total.	White.	Colored.			Total.	White.	Colored.					
			Total.	Free.	Slave.			Total.	Negro.	Indian.	Mongolian.		
The state	249,073	140,178	108,895	1,801	107,094	1,340,316	557,807	782,509	782,321	121	67	777	1,402
Beaufort district [22]	18,753	4,364	14,389	153	14,236	59,233	11,585	47,648	47,639		9	3,297	4,112
Camden district [23]	38,265	29,242	9,023	158	8,865	358,884	96,707	262,177	262,092	72	13	309	2,710
Charleston district [24]	66,985	15,402	51,583	950	50,633	166,955	50,266	116,689	116,639	14	36	3,349	2,320
Cheraw district [25]	10,706	7,418	3,288	59	3,229	94,015	41,990	52,025	52,023		2	443	1,239
Georgetown district [26]	22,122	8,878	13,244	113	13,131	129,214	58,833	70,381	70,347	31	3	1,492	1,196
Ninety-six district [27]	73,729	62,462	11,267	198	11,069	349,544	233,589	115,955	115,952		3	180	496
Orangeburgh district [28]	18,513	12,412	6,101	170	5,931	182,471	64,837	117,634	117,629	4	1	492	1,814

[1] Area covered in 1900 by Burke, Madison, Yancey, and Mitchell counties, and by parts of McDowell, Haywood, Swain, Buncombe, Caldwell, Watauga, and Alexander counties.

[2] Area covered in 1900 by Lincoln, Gaston, and Catawba counties, and by part of Cleveland county.

[3] Area covered in 1900 by Cherokee, Graham, Macon, Jackson, Transylvania, Henderson, Polk, Rutherford, and Clay counties, and by parts of Swain, Cleveland, Buncombe, Haywood, and McDowell counties.

[4] Area covered in 1900 by Ashe and Wilkes counties, and by parts of Alleghany, Watauga, Alexander, and Caldwell counties.

[5] Area covered in 1900 by Beaufort county, and by part of Pamlico county.

[6] Area covered in 1900 by part of Carteret county.

[7] Area covered in 1900 by Craven county, and by parts of Pamlico and Carteret counties.

[8] Area covered in 1900 by Lenoir and Greene counties.

[9] Area covered in 1900 by Hyde county, and by part of Dare county.

[10] Area covered in 1900 by Johnston county, and by part of Wilson county.

[11] Area covered in 1900 coextensive with that of 1790.

[12] Area covered in 1900 by Wayne county, and by part of Wilson county.

[13] Area covered in 1900 by Iredell county, and by part of Alexander county.

[14] Area covered in 1900 by Mecklenburg and Cabarrus counties, and by part of Union county.

[15] Area covered in 1900 by Montgomery and Stanly counties.

[16] Area covered in 1900 by Davie, Rowan, and Davidson counties, and by part of Forsyth county.

[17] Area covered in 1900 by Stokes county, and by part of Forsyth county.

[18] Area covered in 1900 by Yadkin and Surry counties, and by part of Alleghany county.

[19] Area covered in 1900 by Bladen county, and by parts of Cumberland and Columbus counties.

[20] Area covered in 1900 by Brunswick county, and by part of Columbus county.

[21] Area covered in 1900 by New Hanover and Pender counties, and by part of Sampson county.

[22] Area covered in 1900 by Beaufort and Hampton counties.

[23] Area covered in 1900 by Chester, Clarendon, Fairfield, Kershaw, Lancaster, Richland, Sumter, and York counties, and by part of Florence county.

[24] Area covered in 1900 by Charleston, Colleton, and Dorchester counties, and by part of Berkeley county.

[25] Area covered in 1900 by Chesterfield, Darlington, and Marlboro counties, and by part of Florence county.

[26] Area covered in 1900 by Georgetown, Horry, Marion, and Williamsburg counties, and by parts of Florence and Berkeley counties.

[27] Area covered in 1900 by Abbeville, Anderson, Cherokee, Edgefield, Greenville, Greenwood, Laurens, Newberry, Oconee, Pickens, Saluda, Spartanburg, and Union counties, and by part of Aiken county.

[28] Area covered in 1900 by Bamberg, Barnwell, Lexington, and Orangeburg counties, and by part of Aiken county.

TABLE **105.**—WHITE AND COLORED POPULATION OF EACH COUNTY REPORTED IN 1790, COMPARED WITH THAT OF THE SAME AREA IN 1900, TOGETHER WITH THE NUMBER OF COLORED PER 1,000 WHITES—Continued.

GEORGIA.

COUNTY.	POPULATION IN 1790.					POPULATION IN 1900.						Number of colored persons per 1,000 whites, 1790.	Number of negroes per 1,000 whites, 1900.
	Total.	White.	Colored.			Total.	White.	Colored.					
			Total.	Free.	Slave.			Total.	Negro.	Indian.	Mongolian.		
The state	82,548	52,886	29,662	398	29,264	640,538	297,007	343,531	343,421	1	109	561	1,156
Burke[1]	9,467	7,064	2,403	11	2,392	48,744	12,792	35,952	35,952			340	2,811
Camden[2]	305	221	84	14	70	12,126	5,933	6,193	6,193			380	1,044
Chatham[3]	10,769	2,456	8,313	112	8,201	74,299	31,414	42,885	42,833	1	51	3,385	1,364
Effingham[4]	2,424	1,674	750		750	19,546	9,601	9,945	9,945			448	1,036
Franklin[5]	1,041	885	156		156	119,324	76,394	42,930	42,927		3	176	562
Glyn[6]	413	193	220	5	215	19,443	9,118	10,325	10,312		13	1,140	1,131
Greene[7]	5,405	4,020	1,385	8	1,377	36,469	10,346	26,123	26,123			345	2,525
Liberty[8]	5,355	1,303	4,052	27	4,025	25,839	9,972	15,867	15,867			3,110	1,591
Richmond[9]	11,317	7,162	4,155	39	4,116	55,347	27,981	27,366	27,325		41	580	9.7
Washington[10]	4,552	3,856	696	2	694	132,968	69,470	63,498	63,498			180	9.4
Wilks[11]	31,500	24,052	7,448	180	7,268	96,433	33,986	62,447	62,446		1	310	1,8.7

KENTUCKY.

COUNTY.	POPULATION IN 1790.					POPULATION IN 1900.						Number of colored persons per 1,000 whites, 1790.	Number of negroes per 1,000 whites, 1900.
	Total.	White.	Colored.			Total.	White.	Colored.					
			Total.	Free.	Slave.			Total.	Negro.	Indian.	Mongolian.		
The state	73,677	61,133	12,544	114	12,430	2,147,174	1,862,309	284,865	284,706	102	57	205	153
Bourbon[12]	7,837	6,929	908		908	181,378	159,832	21,546	21,542		4	131	135
Fayette[13]	18,410	14,626	3,784	32	3,752	61,601	41,930	19,671	19,669		2	259	469
Jefferson[14]	4,765	3,857	908	5	903	297,723	243,250	54,473	54,470	1	2	235	224
Lincoln[15]	6,548	5,446	1,102	8	1,094	756,996	642,753	114,243	114,212	16	15	202	178
Madison[16]	5,772	5,035	737		737	82,798	73,882	8,916	8,916			146	121
Mason[17]	2,729	2,500	229		229	292,521	283,613	8,908	8,811	85	12	92	31
Mercer[18]	7,091	5,745	1,346	7	1,339	33,750	26,591	7,159	7,159			234	269
Nelson[19]	11,315	10,032	1,283	35	1,248	266,224	237,517	28,707	28,705		2	128	121
Woodford[20]	9,210	6,963	2,247	27	2,220	174,183	152,941	21,242	21,222		20	323	139

[1] Area covered in 1900 by Burke county, and by parts of Jefferson and Screven counties.
[2] Area covered in 1900 by Camden and Charlton counties, and by part of Wayne county.
[3] Area covered in 1900 by Chatham county, and by part of Bryan county.
[4] Area covered in 1900 by Effingham county, and by part of Screven county.
[5] Area covered in 1900 by Franklin, Banks, Jackson, Hart, and Elbert counties, and by parts of Oconee, Clarke, and Madison counties.
[6] Area covered in 1900 by Glynn county, and by part of Wayne county.
[7] Area covered in 1900 by parts of Greene, Hancock, Oconee, Oglethorpe, Taliaferro, and Baldwin counties.
[8] Area covered in 1900 by Liberty and McIntosh counties, and by part of Tattnall county.
[9] Area covered in 1900 by Richmond county, and by part of Jefferson county.
[10] Area covered in 1900 by Washington, Bulloch, Emanuel, and Johnson counties, and by parts of Baldwin, Bryan, Hancock, Jefferson, Laurens, Montgomery, and Tattnall counties.
[11] Area covered in 1900 by Wilkes, Columbia, Glascock, Lincoln, McDuffie, and Warren counties, and by parts of Clarke, Greene, Madison, Oglethorpe, and Taliaferro counties.
[12] Area covered in 1900 by Bourbon, Montgomery, Bath, Letcher, Powell, Wolfe, Menifee, and Knott counties, and by parts of Clark, Harrison, Pendleton, Floyd, Nicholas, Estill, Harlan, Perry, Pike, Morgan, Breathitt, Magoffin, Lee, and Leslie counties.
[13] Area covered in 1900 by Fayette and Jessamine counties, and by part of Clark county.
[14] Area covered in 1900 by Shelby, Henry, Oldham, Trimble, and Jefferson counties, and by parts of Franklin, Bullitt, Spencer, Carroll, and Anderson counties.
[15] Area covered in 1900 by Lincoln, Logan, Pulaski, Christian, Warren, Cumberland, Muhlenberg, Barren, Knox, Wayne, Casey, Livingston, Hopkins, Caldwell, Union, Allen, Whitley, Simpson, Todd, Monroe, Trigg, Hickman, Calloway, Graves, McCracken, Laurel, Russell, Clinton, Crittenden, Marshall, Ballard, Fulton, Lyon, Metcalfe, Webster, and Carlisle counties, and by parts of Green, Garrard, Henderson, Adair, Clay, Rockcastle, Butler, Hart, Edmonson, Boyle, Taylor, McLean, and Bell counties.
[16] Area covered in 1900 by Madison, Owsley, and Jackson counties, and by parts of Garrard, Clay, Estill, Rockcastle, Perry, Breathitt, Lee, Leslie, Harlan, and Bell counties.
[17] Area covered in 1900 by Mason, Bracken, Fleming, Greenup, Lewis, Lawrence, Carter, Johnson, Rowan, Boyd, Elliott, Martin, Robertson, and Campbell counties, and by parts of Floyd, Nicholas, Pike, Morgan, Magoffin, Pendleton, and Harrison counties.
[18] Area covered in 1900 by Mercer county, and by parts of Franklin, Anderson, Garrard, and Boyle counties.
[19] Area covered in 1900 by Nelson, Washington, Hardin, Ohio, Breckinridge, Grayson, Daviess, Meade, Hancock, Marion, and Larue counties, and by parts of Green, Bullitt, Butler, Hart, Spencer, Edmonson, Anderson, McLean, Taylor, Adair, and Henderson counties.
[20] Area covered in 1900 by Woodford, Scott, Boone, Grant, Gallatin, Owen, and Kenton counties, and by parts of Harrison, Franklin, Carroll, and Pendleton counties.

TABLE **106.**—WHITE POPULATION, CLASSIFIED BY SEX AND AGE, OF EACH STATE AND TERRITORY REPORTED IN 1790, COMPARED WITH THAT OF THE SAME AREA IN 1900, WITH PER CENT OF INCREASE.

STATE OR TERRITORY.	WHITE POPULATION IN 1790.			WHITE POPULATION IN 1900.					
				All ages.		16 years and over.		Under 16 years.	
	All ages.	16 years and over.	Under 16 years.	Number.	Per cent of increase over white population in 1790.	Number.	Per cent of increase over white population in 1790.	Number.	Per cent of increase over white population in 1790.
BOTH SEXES.									
Continental United States	3,172,444	1,619,184	1,553,260	[1]66,893,405	2,008.6	43,046,595	2,558.5	23,846,810	1,435.3
Area enumerated in 1790	3,172,444	1,619,184	1,553,260	29,564,821	831.9	19,474,777	1,102.8	10,090,044	549.6
New England	992,384	526,094	466,290	5,527,026	456.9	3,916,531	644.5	1,610,495	245.4
Maine	96,107	47,354	48,753	692,226	620.3	491,434	937.8	200,792	311.9
New Hampshire	141,112	72,548	68,564	410,791	191.1	297,804	310.5	112,987	64.8
Vermont	85,072	41,440	43,632	342,771	302.9	241,914	483.8	100,857	131.2
Massachusetts	373,187	203,318	169,869	2,716,096	627.8	1,929,747	849.1	786,349	362.9
Rhode Island	64,670	34,683	29,987	472,718	631.0	328,555	847.3	144,163	380.8
Connecticut	232,236	126,751	105,485	892,424	284.3	627,077	394.7	265,347	151.5
Middle states	954,003	482,608	471,395	15,264,839	1,500.1	10,292,527	2,032.7	4,972,312	954.8
New York	314,366	159,276	155,090	7,156,881	2,176.6	4,944,668	3,004.5	2,212,213	1,326.4
New Jersey	169,954	87,203	82,751	1,812,317	966.4	1,220,587	1,299.7	591,730	615.1
Pennsylvania	423,373	212,699	210,674	6,141,664	1,350.7	4,023,718	1,791.7	2,117,946	905.3
Delaware	46,310	23,430	22,880	153,977	232.5	103,554	342.0	50,423	120.4
Southern states	1,226,057	610,482	615,575	8,772,956	615.5	5,265,719	762.6	3,507,237	469.7
Maryland and District of Columbia	208,649	114,806	93,843	1,143,956	448.3	762,703	564.3	381,253	306.3
Virginia and West Virginia	442,117	222,459	219,658	2,108,088	376.8	1,263,882	468.1	844,206	284.3
North Carolina	289,181	139,239	149,942	1,263,603	337.0	723,060	419.3	540,543	260.5
South Carolina	140,178	67,016	73,162	557,807	297.9	324,751	384.6	233,056	218.5
Georgia	52,886	24,814	28,072	297,007	461.6	173,399	598.8	123,608	340.3
Kentucky	61,133	27,790	33,343	1,862,309	2,946.3	1,110,743	3,896.9	751,566	2,154.0
Tennessee	31,913	14,358	17,555	1,540,186	4,726.2	907,181	6,218.3	633,005	3,505.8
Added area	....	....	....	37,328,584	....	23,571,818	....	13,756,766	....
MALES.									
Continental United States	1,615,761	815,098	800,663	34,285,307	2,021.9	22,223,462	2,626.5	12,061,845	1,406.5
Area enumerated in 1790	1,615,761	815,098	800,663	14,831,668	817.9	9,738,805	1,094.8	5,092,863	536.1
New England	494,254	255,048	239,206	2,730,121	452.4	1,922,795	653.9	807,326	237.5
Maine	49,074	24,341	24,733	349,786	612.8	248,310	920.1	101,476	310.3
New Hampshire	70,929	36,074	34,855	204,931	188.9	148,474	311.6	56,457	62.0
Vermont	44,710	22,405	22,305	174,641	290.6	123,596	451.6	51,045	128.9
Massachusetts	182,712	95,433	87,279	1,323,178	624.2	931,082	875.6	392,096	349.2
Rhode Island	31,801	16,056	15,745	231,232	627.1	157,931	883.6	73,301	365.6
Connecticut	115,028	60,739	54,289	446,353	288.0	313,402	416.0	132,951	144.9
Middle states	490,153	251,408	238,745	7,665,449	1,463.9	5,165,431	1,954.6	2,500,018	947.1
New York	162,073	83,815	78,258	3,558,116	2,095.4	2,448,151	2,820.9	1,109,965	1,318.3
New Jersey	86,667	45,251	41,416	906,543	946.0	610,059	1,248.2	296,484	615.9
Pennsylvania	217,487	110,559	106,928	3,122,304	1,335.6	2,054,286	1,758.1	1,068,018	898.8
Delaware	23,926	11,783	12,143	78,486	228.0	52,935	349.2	25,551	110.4
Southern states	631,354	308,642	322,712	4,436,098	602.6	2,650,579	758.8	1,785,519	453.3
Maryland and District of Columbia	107,254	55,915	51,339	566,316	428.0	374,578	569.9	191,738	273.5
Virginia and West Virginia	227,071	110,936	116,135	1,076,009	373.9	645,869	482.2	430,140	270.4
North Carolina	147,825	70,172	77,653	632,155	327.6	356,589	408.2	275,566	254.9
South Carolina	73,298	35,576	37,722	281,147	283.6	161,778	354.7	119,369	216.4
Georgia	27,147	13,103	14,044	149,721	451.5	87,122	564.9	62,599	345.7
Kentucky	32,211	15,154	17,057	948,048	2,843.2	565,705	3,623.0	382,343	2,141.6
Tennessee	16,548	7,786	8,762	782,702	4,629.9	458,938	5,794.4	323,764	3,595.1
Added area	....	....	....	19,453,639	....	12,484,657	....	6,968,982	....

[1] Includes 84,209 persons in the military and naval service stationed abroad.

TABLE **106.**—WHITE POPULATION, CLASSIFIED BY SEX AND AGE, OF EACH STATE AND TERRITORY REPORTED IN 1790, COMPARED WITH THAT OF THE SAME AREA IN 1900, WITH PER CENT OF INCREASE—Continued.

STATE OR TERRITORY.	WHITE POPULATION IN 1790.			WHITE POPULATION IN 1900.					
	All ages.	16 years and over.	Under 16 years.	All ages.		16 years and over.		Under 16 years.	
				Number.	Per cent of increase over white population in 1790.	Number.	Per cent of increase over white population in 1790.	Number.	Per cent of increase over white population in 1790.
					FEMALES.				
Continental United States	1,556,683	804,086	752,597	32,608,098	1,994.7	20,823,133	2,489.7	11,784,965	1,465.9
Area enumerated in 1790	1,556,683	804,086	752,597	14,733,153	846.4	9,735,972	1,110.8	4,997,181	564.0
New England	498,130	271,046	227,084	2,796,905	461.5	1,993,736	635.6	803,169	253.7
Maine	47,033	23,013	24,020	342,440	628.1	243,124	956.5	99,316	313.5
New Hampshire	70,183	36,474	33,709	205,860	193.3	149,330	309.4	56,530	67.7
Vermont	40,362	19,035	21,327	168,130	316.6	118,318	521.6	49,812	133.6
Massachusetts	190,475	107,885	82,590	1,392,918	631.3	998,665	825.7	394,253	377.4
Rhode Island	32,869	18,627	14,242	241,486	634.7	170,624	816.0	70,862	397.6
Connecticut	117,208	66,012	51,196	446,071	280.6	313,675	375.2	132,396	158.6
Middle states	463,850	231,200	232,650	7,599,390	1,538.3	5,127,096	2,117.6	2,472,294	962.7
New York	152,293	75,461	76,832	3,598,765	2,263.1	2,496,517	3,208.4	1,102,248	1,334.6
New Jersey	83,287	41,952	41,335	905,774	987.5	610,528	1,355.3	295,246	614.3
Pennsylvania	205,886	102,140	103,746	3,019,360	1,366.5	1,969,432	1,828.2	1,049,928	912.0
Delaware	22,384	11,647	10,737	75,491	237.3	50,619	334.6	24,872	131.6
Southern states	594,703	301,840	292,863	4,336,858	629.2	2,615,140	766.4	1,721,718	487.9
Maryland and District of Columbia	101,395	58,891	42,504	577,640	469.7	388,125	559.1	189,515	345.9
Virginia and West Virginia	215,046	111,523	103,523	1,032,079	379.9	618,013	454.2	414,066	300.0
North Carolina	141,356	69,067	72,289	631,448	346.7	366,471	430.6	264,977	266.6
South Carolina	66,880	31,440	35,440	276,660	313.7	162,973	418.4	113,687	220.8
Georgia	25,739	11,711	14,028	147,286	472.2	86,277	636.7	61,009	334.9
Kentucky	28,922	12,636	16,286	914,261	3,061.1	545,038	4,213.4	369,223	2,167.1
Tennessee	15,365	6,572	8,793	757,484	4,829.9	448,243	6,720.5	309,241	3,416.9
Added area				17,874,945		11,087,161		6,787,784	

TABLE **107.**—WHITE POPULATION, CLASSIFIED BY SEX AND AGE, OF EACH OF THE COUNTIES REPORTED

MAINE.

| | COUNTY. | BOTH SEXES. | | | MALES. | | | | | |
| | | | | | All ages. | | | 16 years and over. | | |
		1790	1900	Per cent of increase.	1790	1900	Per cent of increase.	1790	1900	Per cent of increase.
1	The state	96,107	692,226	620.27	49,074	349,786	612.77	24,341	248,310	920.13
2	Cumberland [1]	25,351	175,364	591.74	12,832	84,282	556.81	6,208	60,524	874.94
3	Hancock [2]	9,504	161,503	1,599.32	4,964	83,137	1,574.80	2,435	58,334	2,295.65
4	Lincoln [3]	29,592	200,152	576.37	15,347	103,705	575.73	7,668	76,043	891.69
5	Washington [4]	2,740	79,126	2,787.81	1,462	40,684	2,682.76	754	26,187	3,373.08
6	York [5]	28,920	76,081	163.07	14,469	37,978	162.48	7,276	27,222	274.13

NEW HAMPSHIRE.

	COUNTY.	1790	1900	Per cent of increase.	1790	1900	Per cent of increase.	1790	1900	Per cent of increase.
1	The state	141,112	410,791	191.11	70,929	204,931	188.92	36,074	148,474	311.58
2	Cheshire [6]	28,665	48,255	68.34	14,575	24,241	66.32	7,008	17,618	151.40
3	Grafton [8]	13,419	74,673	456.47	7,079	39,115	452.55	3,768	28,354	652.49
4	Hillsborough [9]	32,707	128,881	294.05	16,537	62,542	278.19	8,145	43,968	439.82
5	Rockingham [10]	42,795	84,835	98.24	20,808	42,290	103.24	11,141	31,503	182.77
6	Strafford [11]	23,526	74,147	215.17	11,930	36,743	207.99	6,012	27,031	349.62

VERMONT.

	COUNTY.	1790	1900	Per cent of increase.	1790	1900	Per cent of increase.	1790	1900	Per cent of increase.
1	The state	85,072	342,771	302.92	44,710	174,641	290.61	22,405	123,596	451.64
2	Addison [12]	6,383	19,648	207.82	3,424	10,028	192.87	1,768	6,933	292.14
3	Bennington [13]	12,173	21,536	76.92	6,308	10,901	72.81	3,103	7,668	147.12
4	Chittenden [14]	7,264	106,724	1,369.22	4,012	54,082	1,248.01	2,251	37,300	1,557.04
5	Orange [15]	10,485	90,774	765.75	5,638	47,043	734.39	2,873	33,729	1,074.00
6	Rutland [16]	15,558	44,898	188.58	8,088	22,718	180.89	3,990	16,004	301.10
7	Windham [13]	17,514	26,593	51.84	9,088	13,411	47.57	4,416	9,866	123.41
8	Windsor [17]	15,695	32,598	107.70	8,152	16,458	101.89	4,004	12,096	202.10

MASSACHUSETTS.

	COUNTY.	1790	1900	Per cent of increase.	1790	1900	Per cent of increase.	1790	1900	Per cent of increase.
1	The state	373,187	2,716,096	627.81	182,712	1,323,178	624.19	95,433	931,082	875.64
2	Barnstable [13]	16,970	26,971	58.93	8,293	12,795	54.29	4,200	9,395	123.69
3	Berkshire [18]	29,940	94,400	215.30	15,146	46,363	206.14	7,356	31,910	333.80
4	Bristol [19]	30,966	194,556	528.29	14,895	94,557	534.82	7,956	64,925	716.05
5	Dukes [13]	3,230	4,256	31.76	1,534	2,023	31.88	823	1,543	87.48
6	Essex [20]	57,007	354,298	521.50	26,825	172,069	541.45	14,258	122,311	757.84
7	Hampshire [21]	59,205	273,043	361.18	30,118	132,699	340.60	15,109	91,357	504.65
8	Middlesex [22]	42,177	618,867	1,367.31	20,691	297,910	1,339.80	11,071	209,108	1,788.79
9	Nantucket [13]	4,521	2,958	[7] 34.57	2,218	1,287	[7] 41.97	1,201	1,020	[7] 15.07
10	Plymouth [23]	29,013	106,983	268.74	14,029	53,565	281.82	7,493	39,192	423.05
11	Suffolk [24]	43,803	695,047	1,486.76	20,699	336,741	1,526.85	11,366	239,655	2,008.53
12	Worcester [25]	56,355	344,717	511.69	28,264	173,164	512.67	14,600	120,666	726.48

RHODE ISLAND.

	COUNTY.	1790	1900	Per cent of increase.	1790	1900	Per cent of increase.	1790	1900	Per cent of increase.
1	The state	64,670	472,718	630.97	31,801	231,232	627.98	16,056	157,931	883.63
2	Bristol [13]	3,013	12,975	330.63	1,455	6,422	341.37	778	4,519	480.85
3	Kent [13]	8,439	29,634	251.16	4,286	14,706	243.12	2,158	9,869	357.32
4	Newport [26]	13,174	135,085	925.39	6,112	65,712	975.13	3,256	42,774	1,213.70
5	Providence [27]	23,518	271,817	1,055.78	11,641	132,905	1,041.70	6,155	92,382	1,400.93
6	Washington [13]	16,526	23,207	40.43	8,307	11,487	38.28	3,709	8,387	126.13

[1] Area covered in 1900 by parts of Franklin, Somerset, York, Cumberland, Androscoggin, and Oxford counties.
[2] Area covered in 1900 by Hancock county, and by parts of Waldo, Penobscot, Piscataquis, and Aroostook counties.
[3] Area covered in 1900 by Lincoln, Knox, Kennebec, and Sagadahoc counties, and by parts of Waldo, Androscoggin, Somerset, Piscataquis, Franklin, Aroostook, and Penobscot counties.
[4] Area covered in 1900 by Washington county, and by parts of Penobscot and Aroostook counties.
[5] Area covered in 1900 by parts of York, Cumberland, Oxford, and Franklin counties.
[6] Area covered in 1900 by Cheshire county, and by part of Sullivan county.
[7] Decrease.
[8] Area covered in 1900 by Grafton and Coos counties, and by parts of Carroll and Merrimack counties.
[9] Area covered in 1900 by Hillsboro county (except Pelham, which was in Rockingham county in 1790), and by parts of Merrimack and Sullivan counties.
[10] Area covered in 1900 by Rockingham county, and by part of Merrimack county, and the town of Pelham (now in Hillsboro county).
[11] Area covered in 1900 by Strafford and Belknap counties, and by parts of Carroll and Merrimack counties.
[12] Area covered in 1900 by part of Addison county.
[13] Area covered in 1900 coextensive with that of 1790.

IN 1790, COMPARED WITH THAT OF THE SAME AREA IN 1900, WITH PER CENT OF INCREASE.

MAINE.

| MALES—continued. | | | FEMALES. | | | | | | | | | |
| Under 16 years. | | | All ages. | | | 16 years and over. | | | Under 16 years. | | | |
1790	1900	Per cent of increase.	1790	1900	Per cent of increase.	1790	1900	Per cent of increase.	1790	1900	Per cent of increase.	
24,733	101,476	310.29	47,033	342,440	628.08	23,013	243,124	956.43	24,020	99,316	313.47	1
6,624	23,758	258.67	12,519	91,082	627.55	6,124	66,587	987.31	6,395	24,495	283.03	2
2,529	24,803	880.74	4,540	78,366	1,626.12	2,143	54,196	2,428.98	2,397	24,170	908.34	3
7,679	27,662	260.23	14,245	96,447	577.06	6,728	70,684	950.59	7,517	25,763	242.73	4
708	14,497	1,947.60	1,278	38,442	2,907.98	580	23,926	4,025.17	698	14,516	1,979.66	5
7,193	10,756	49.53	14,451	38,103	163.67	7,438	27,731	272.83	7,013	10,372	47.90	6

NEW HAMPSHIRE.

1790	1900	Per cent of increase.	1790	1900	Per cent of increase.	1790	1900	Per cent of increase.	1790	1900	Per cent of increase.	
34,855	56,457	61.93	70,183	205,860	193.32	36,474	149,330	309.41	33,709	56,530	67.70	1
7,567	6,623	7 12.48	14,090	24,014	70.43	7,323	17,570	139.93	6,767	6,444	7 4.77	2
3,311	10,761	225.01	6,340	35,558	460.85	3,295	25,092	661.52	3,045	10,466	243.71	3
8,392	18,574	121.33	16,170	66,339	310.26	8,404	47,492	465.11	7,766	18,847	142.69	4
9,667	10,787	11.59	21,987	42,545	93.50	11,427	31,618	176.70	10,560	10,927	3.48	5
5,918	9,712	64.11	11,596	37,404	222.56	6,026	27,558	357.32	5,570	9,846	76.77	6

VERMONT.

1790	1900	Per cent of increase.	1790	1900	Per cent of increase.	1790	1900	Per cent of increase.	1790	1900	Per cent of increase.	
22,305	51,045	128.85	40,362	168,130	316.56	19,035	118,318	521.58	21,327	49,812	133.56	1
1,656	3,095	86.90	2,959	9,620	225.11	1,364	6,764	395.89	1,595	2,856	79.06	2
3,205	3,233	0.87	5,865	10,635	81.33	2,820	7,478	165.18	3,045	3,157	3.68	3
1,761	16,782	852.98	3,252	52,642	1,518.76	1,458	36,104	2,376.27	1,794	16,538	821.85	4
2,765	13,314	381.52	4,847	43,731	802.23	2,241	30,879	1,277.91	2,606	12,852	393.17	5
4,098	6,714	63.84	7,470	22,180	196.92	3,463	15,450	346.14	4,007	6,730	67.95	6
4,672	3,545	7 24.12	8,426	13,182	56.44	4,128	9,771	136.70	4,298	3,411	7 20.64	7
4,148	4,362	5.16	7,543	16,140	113.97	3,561	11,872	233.38	3,982	4,268	7.18	8

MASSACHUSETTS.

1790	1900	Per cent of increase.	1790	1900	Per cent of increase.	1790	1900	Per cent of increase.	1790	1900	Per cent of increase.	
87,279	392,096	349.24	190,475	1,392,918	631.29	107,885	998,665	825.68	82,590	394,253	377.36	1
4,093	3,400	7 16.93	8,677	14,176	63.37	4,915	10,855	120.85	3,762	3,321	7 11.72	2
7,790	14,458	85.60	14,794	48,032	224.67	8,379	33,163	295.79	6,415	14,869	131.78	3
6,939	29,632	327.04	16,071	99,999	522.23	9,102	67,341	639.77	6,969	32,658	368.69	4
711	480	7 32.49	1,696	2,233	31.66	961	1,728	79.81	735	505	7 31.29	5
12,567	49,758	295.94	30,182	182,229	503.77	17,095	132,279	673.79	13,087	49,950	281.68	6
15,009	41,342	175.45	29,087	140,344	382.50	16,475	99,179	502.00	12,612	41,165	226.40	7
9,620	88,802	823.10	21,486	320,957	1,393.80	12,170	232,917	1,813.86	9,316	88,040	845.04	8
1,017	267	7 73.75	2,303	1,671	7 27.44	1,304	1,338	2.61	999	333	7 66.67	9
6,536	14,373	119.91	14,984	53,418	256.50	8,487	39,283	362.86	6,497	14,135	117.56	10
9,333	97,086	940.24	23,104	358,306	1,450.84	13,086	260,435	1,890.18	10,018	97,871	876.95	11
13,664	52,498	284.21	28,091	171,553	510.70	15,911	120,147	655.12	12,180	51,406	322.05	12

RHODE ISLAND.

1790	1900	Per cent of increase.	1790	1900	Per cent of increase.	1790	1900	Per cent of increase.	1790	1900	Per cent of increase.	
15,745	73,301	365.55	32,869	241,486	634.69	18,627	170,624	816.00	14,242	70,862	397.56	1
677	1,903	181.09	1,558	6,553	320.60	883	4,686	430.69	675	1,867	176.59	2
2,128	4,837	127.30	4,153	14,928	259.45	2,353	10,050	326.93	1,800	4,878	171.15	3
2,856	22,938	703.15	7,062	69,373	882.34	4,002	49,594	1,139.23	3,060	19,779	546.37	4
5,486	40,523	638.66	11,877	138,912	1,069.59	6,731	97,712	1,351.67	5,146	41,200	700.62	5
4,598	3,100	7 32.58	8,219	11,720	42.60	4,658	8,582	84.24	3,561	3,138	7 11.88	6

[14] Area covered in 1900 by Franklin, Grand Isle, Lamoille, and Chittenden counties, and by parts of Orleans, Addison, and Washington counties.
[15] Area covered in 1900 by Essex, Caledonia, and Orange counties, and by parts of Orleans and Washington counties.
[16] Area covered in 1900 by parts of Rutland and Addison counties.
[17] Area covered in 1900 by Windsor county, and by part of Rutland county.
[18] Area covered in 1900 by Berkshire county, and by part of Franklin county.
[19] Area covered in 1900 by parts of Bristol and Norfolk counties, and by part of Providence county, R. I.
[20] Area covered in 1900 by part of Essex county.
[21] Area covered in 1900 by parts of Hampshire, Hampden, Franklin, and Worcester counties.
[22] Area covered in 1900 by parts of Middlesex, Suffolk, and Worcester counties.
[23] Area covered in 1900 by parts of Plymouth and Bristol counties.
[24] Area covered in 1900 by parts of Suffolk, Norfolk, Essex, Plymouth, Middlesex, and Worcester counties.
[25] Area covered in 1900 by parts of Worcester, Hampden, Hampshire, and Middlesex counties.
[26] Area covered in 1900 by Newport county, and by part of Bristol county, Mass.
[27] Area covered in 1900 by part of Providence county.

TABLE 107.—WHITE POPULATION, CLASSIFIED BY SEX AND AGE, OF EACH OF THE COUNTIES REPORTED

CONNECTICUT.

| | COUNTY. | BOTH SEXES. | | | MALES. | | | | | |
| | | | | | All ages. | | | 16 years and over. | | |
		1790	1900	Per cent of increase.	1790	1900	Per cent of increase.	1790	1900	Per cent of increase.
1	The state...............	232,236	892,424	284.27	115,028	446,353	288.04	60,739	313,402	415.98
2	Fairfield [1]...............	35,173	180,839	414.14	17,543	89,245	408.72	9,149	62,724	585.58
3	Hartford [2]...............	37,498	191,776	411.43	18,652	97,444	422.43	9,808	69,606	609.69
4	Litchfield [3]...............	38,119	65,182	71.00	19,372	33,048	70.60	10,135	23,376	130.65
5	Middlesex [4]...............	18,492	40,405	118.50	8,870	19,743	122.58	4,730	14,318	202.71
6	New Haven [5]...............	29,882	262,050	777.52	14,684	131,923	798.41	7,843	90,852	1,058.38
7	New London [6]...............	31,605	79,421	151.29	15,337	38,893	153.59	8,189	27,443	235.12
8	Tolland [7]...............	13,111	22,130	68.79	6,587	10,978	66.66	3,449	7,682	122.73
9	Windham [8]...............	28,356	50,450	77.92	13,983	25,079	79.35	7,436	17,401	134.01

NEW YORK.

| | COUNTY. | BOTH SEXES. | | | MALES. | | | | | |
| | | | | | All ages. | | | 16 years and over. | | |
		1790	1900	Per cent of increase.	1790	1900	Per cent of increase.	1790	1900	Per cent of increase.
1	The state...............	314,366	7,156,881	2,176.61	162,073	3,558,116	2,095.38	83,815	2,448,151	2,820.90
2	Albany [9]...............	72,087	424,404	488.74	37,644	207,707	451.77	18,684	147,386	688.84
3	Clinton [10]...............	1,583	208,408	13,065.38	901	106,030	11,668.04	545	71,525	13,023.85
4	Columbia [1]...............	25,811	41,779	61.87	13,293	20,671	55.50	6,554	15,032	129.36
5	Dutchess [12]...............	42,981	93,093	116.59	22,041	46,253	109.85	10,972	33,972	209.62
6	Kings [1]...............	3,021	1,146,909	37,864.55	1,606	564,321	35,038.29	903	374,351	41,356.37
7	Montgomery [13]...............	28,223	1,119,761	3,867.55	15,071	557,272	3,597.64	7,866	404,176	5,038.27
8	New York city and county [14]...............	29,619	1,808,968	6,007.46	14,382	897,291	6,138.99	8,482	610,892	7,102.22
9	Ontario [15]...............	1,058	1,225,283	115,711.25	716	610,565	85,174.44	524	416,947	79,470.04
10	Orange [16]...............	17,315	137,256	692.70	8,930	68,533	667.45	4,596	47,731	938.53
11	Queens [17]...............	12,886	203,328	1,477.90	6,418	103,086	1,506.20	3,555	67,316	1,793.56
12	Richmond [1]...............	2,945	65,863	2,136.43	1,500	33,841	2,156.07	747	22,679	2,936.01
13	Suffolk [1]...............	14,310	74,298	419.20	7,081	37,042	423.12	3,787	26,288	594.16
14	Ulster [18]...............	26,295	155,638	491.89	13,833	78,854	470.04	7,050	54,122	667.69
15	Washington [19]...............	14,028	75,228	436.27	7,405	37,435	405.54	3,616	26,551	634.26
16	Westchester [20]...............	22,204	376,665	1,596.38	11,252	189,215	1,581.61	5,934	129,183	2,077.00

NEW JERSEY.

| | COUNTY. | BOTH SEXES. | | | MALES. | | | | | |
| | | | | | All ages. | | | 16 years and over. | | |
		1790	1900	Per cent of increase.	1790	1900	Per cent of increase.	1790	1900	Per cent of increase.
1	The state...............	169,954	1,812,317	966.35	86,667	906,543	946.00	45,251	610,059	1,248.17
2	Bergen [21]...............	10,108	497,571	4,822.54	5,164	250,904	4,758.71	2,865	164,390	5,637.87
3	Burlington [22]...............	17,270	100,586	482.43	8,789	50,883	478.94	4,625	35,029	657.38
4	Cape-May [1]...............	2,416	12,328	410.26	1,240	6,309	408.79	631	4,425	601.27
5	Cumberland [1]...............	7,990	48,785	510.57	4,113	24,491	495.45	2,147	16,417	664.65
6	Essex [23]...............	16,454	554,107	3,267.61	8,311	271,784	3,170.17	4,339	181,183	4,075.68
7	Gloucester [24]...............	12,830	168,239	1,211.29	6,598	83,970	1,172.65	3,287	57,486	1,648.89
8	Hunterdon [25]...............	18,661	74,415	298.77	9,345	36,991	295.84	4,966	25,775	419.03
9	Middlesex [26]...............	14,498	88,050	507.32	7,370	46,502	530.96	3,995	31,936	699.40
10	Monmouth [27]...............	14,969	85,636	472.09	7,521	42,542	465.64	3,843	29,292	662.22
11	Morris [1]...............	15,532	63,503	308.85	8,030	31,879	296.99	4,092	22,068	439.30
12	Salem [1]...............	9,891	22,493	127.40	5,075	11,493	126.46	2,679	7,962	197.20
13	Somerset [28]...............	10,339	35,225	240.70	5,209	17,619	238.24	2,819	12,401	339.91
14	Sussex [29]...............	18,996	61,379	223.11	9,902	31,176	214.84	4,963	21,695	337.13

PENNSYLVANIA.

| | COUNTY. | BOTH SEXES. | | | MALES. | | | | | |
| | | | | | All ages. | | | 16 years and over. | | |
		1790	1900	Per cent of increase.	1790	1900	Per cent of increase.	1790	1900	Per cent of increase.
1	The state...............	423,373	6,141,664	1,350.65	217,487	3,122,304	1,335.63	110,559	2,054,286	1,758.09
2	Allegheny [30]...............	10,032	1,186,717	11,729.32	5,269	612,496	11,524.52	2,524	407,947	16,062.72
3	Bedford [31]...............	13,052	195,203	1,395.58	6,727	102,954	1,430.46	2,887	63,849	2,111.60
4	Berks [32]...............	29,928	315,081	952.80	15,262	161,387	957.44	7,711	103,277	1,239.35
5	Bucks [1]...............	24,374	68,788	182.22	12,423	34,404	176.94	6,529	23,150	254.57
6	Chester [1]...............	27,141	86,391	218.30	14,076	43,398	208.31	7,486	29,668	296.31
7	Cumberland [33]...............	17,779	73,690	314.48	9,330	36,038	286.26	4,816	23,356	384.97
8	Dauphin [34]...............	17,886	161,579	803.33	9,085	81,088	792.55	4,651	53,845	1,057.71
9	Delaware [1]...............	9,133	84,815	828.67	4,639	42,279	811.38	2,530	28,508	1,026.80
10	Fayette [1]...............	12,990	105,442	711.72	6,835	58,000	748.57	3,415	37,861	1,008.67

[1] Area covered in 1900 coextensive with that of 1790.
[2] Population of Wolcott town added to, and that of Hartland town and Marlboro town subtracted from, 1900 figures to make areas comparable.
[3] Population of Southbury town, Hartland town and Middlebury town added to 1900 figures to make areas comparable.
[4] Population of Durham town subtracted from 1900 figures to make areas comparable.
[5] Population of Middlebury town, Southbury town, and Wolcott town subtracted from, and that of Durham town added to, 1900 figures to make areas comparable.
[6] Population of Columbia town and part of Marlboro town added to, and that of Lebanon town and Voluntown town subtracted from, 1900 figures to make areas comparable.
[7] Population of Columbia town and Mansfield town subtracted from, and part of Marlboro town added to, 1900 figures to make areas comparable.
[8] Population of Mansfield town, Lebanon town, and Voluntown town added to 1900 figures to make areas comparable.
[9] Area covered in 1900 by Albany, Rensselaer, Saratoga, and Schenectady counties, and by parts of Greene and Schoharie counties.
[10] Area covered in 1900 by Clinton, Franklin, Essex, and St. Lawrence counties.
[11] Decrease.
[12] Area covered in 1900 by Dutchess and Putnam counties.
[13] Area covered in 1900 by Chemung, Montgomery, Fulton, Herkimer, Hamilton, Otsego, Jefferson, Tioga, Broome, Chenango, Oneida, Lewis, Madison, Cortland, Oswego, Onondaga, Cayuga, Seneca, and Tompkins counties, and by parts of Delaware, Schoharie, Schuyler, and Wayne counties.
[14] Area covered in 1900 by Manhattan borough.
[15] Area covered in 1900 by Chautauqua, Cattaraugus, Allegany, Erie, Niagara, Wyoming, Genesee, Orleans, Monroe, Livingston, Ontario, Yates, and Steuben counties, and by parts of Wayne and Schuyler counties.
[16] Area covered in 1900 by Orange and Rockland counties.

IN 1790, COMPARED WITH THAT OF THE SAME AREA IN 1900, WITH PER CENT OF INCREASE—Continued.

CONNECTICUT.

MALES—continued.			FEMALES.									
Under 16 years.			All ages.			16 years and over.			Under 16 years.			
1790	1900	Per cent of increase.	1790	1900	Per cent of increase.	1790	1900	Per cent of increase.	1790	1900	Per cent of increase.	
54,289	132,951	144.89	117,208	446,071	280.58	66,012	313,675	375.18	51,196	132,396	158.61	1
8,394	26,521	215.95	17,630	91,594	419.53	9,929	64,907	553.71	7,701	26,687	246.54	2
8,844	27,838	214.77	18,846	94,332	400.54	10,614	66,517	526.69	8,232	27,815	237.89	3
9,237	9,672	4.71	18,747	32,134	71.41	10,558	22,504	113.15	8,189	9,630	17.60	4
4,140	5,425	31.04	9,622	20,662	114.74	5,419	15,079	178.26	4,203	5,583	32.83	5
6,841	41,071	500.37	15,198	130,298	757.34	8,559	89,999	951.39	6,639	40,299	507.10	6
7,148	11,450	60.18	16,268	40,528	149.13	9,162	28,924	215.70	7,106	11,604	63.30	7
3,138	3,296	5.04	6,524	11,152	70.94	3,674	7,895	114.89	2,850	3,257	14.28	8
6,547	7,678	17.28	14,373	25,371	76.52	8,095	17,850	120.51	6,278	7,521	19.80	9

NEW YORK.

Under 16 years.			All ages.			16 years and over.			Under 16 years.			
1790	1900	Per cent of increase.	1790	1900	Per cent of increase.	1790	1900	Per cent of increase.	1790	1900	Per cent of increase.	
78,258	1,109,965	1,318.34	152,293	3,598,765	2,263.05	75,461	2,496,517	3,208.35	76,832	1,102,248	1,334.62	1
18,960	60,321	218.15	34,443	216,697	529.15	17,066	156,473	816.82	17,377	60,224	246.59	2
356	34,505	9,592.42	682	102,378	14,911.44	338	68,588	20,192.31	344	33,790	9,722.67	3
6,739	5,639	[11]16.32	12,518	21,108	68.62	6,202	15,542	150.56	6,316	5,566	[11]11.86	4
11,069	12,281	10.95	20,940	46,840	123.69	10,376	34,432	231.84	10,564	12,408	17.46	5
703	189,970	26,922.76	1,415	582,588	41,072.30	701	392,286	55,860.91	714	190,302	26,552.94	6
7,205	153,096	2,024.86	13,152	562,489	4,176.83	6,517	412,217	6,225.26	6,635	150,272	2,164.84	7
5,900	286,399	4,754.22	15,237	911,677	5,883.31	7,550	629,967	8,243.93	7,687	281,710	3,564.76	8
192	193,618	100,742.71	342	614,718	179,642.11	169	424,972	251,362.72	173	189,746	109,579.77	9
4,334	20,802	379.97	8,385	68,723	719.59	4,155	48,242	1,061.06	4,230	20,481	384.18	10
2,863	35,770	1,149.39	6,468	100,242	1,449.81	3,205	65,229	1,935.23	3,263	35,013	973.03	11
753	11,162	1,382.34	1,445	32,022	2,116.06	716	21,556	2,910.61	729	10,466	1,335.67	12
3,294	10,754	226.47	7,229	37,256	415.37	3,582	26,776	647.52	3,647	10,480	187.36	13
6,783	24,732	264.62	12,462	76,784	516.15	6,175	52,772	754.61	6,287	24,012	281.93	14
3,789	10,884	187.25	6,623	37,793	470.63	3,282	26,958	721.39	3,341	10,835	224.30	15
5,318	60,032	1,028.85	10,952	187,450	1,611.56	5,427	120,507	2,120.51	5,525	66,943	1,111.64	16

NEW JERSEY.

Under 16 years.			All ages.			16 years and over.			Under 16 years.			
1790	1900	Per cent of increase.	1790	1900	Per cent of increase.	1790	1900	Per cent of increase.	1790	1900	Per cent of increase.	
41,416	296,484	615.87	83,287	905,774	987.53	41,952	610,528	1,355.30	41,335	295,246	614.28	1
2,299	86,514	3,663.11	4,944	246,667	4,889.21	2,490	160,064	6,328.27	2,454	86,603	3,429.05	2
4,164	15,854	280.74	8,481	49,703	486.05	4,272	34,536	708.43	4,209	15,167	260.35	3
609	1,884	209.36	1,176	6,019	411.81	592	4,204	610.14	584	1,815	210.79	4
1,966	8,074	310.68	3,877	24,294	526.61	1,953	16,535	746.65	1,924	7,759	303.27	5
3,972	90,601	2,180.99	8,143	282,323	3,367.06	4,102	191,115	4,559.07	4,041	91,208	2,157.07	6
3,311	26,484	699.88	6,232	84,269	1,252.19	3,139	57,757	1,739.98	3,093	26,512	757.16	7
4,379	11,216	156.13	9,316	37,424	301.72	4,692	26,161	457.57	4,624	11,263	143.58	8
3,375	14,566	331.58	7,128	41,548	482.88	3,590	27,212	657.99	3,538	14,336	305.20	9
3,678	13,250	260.25	7,448	43,094	478.60	3,752	30,023	700.19	3,696	13,071	253.65	10
3,938	9,811	149.14	7,502	31,624	321.54	3,779	22,032	483.01	3,723	9,592	157.64	11
2,396	3,531	47.37	4,816	11,000	128.40	2,426	7,655	215.54	2,390	3,345	39.96	12
2,390	5,218	118.33	5,130	17,606	243.19	2,584	12,319	376.74	2,546	5,287	107.66	13
4,939	9,481	91.96	9,094	30,203	232.12	4,581	20,915	356.56	4,513	9,288	105.81	14

PENNSYLVANIA.

Under 16 years.			All ages.			16 years and over.			Under 16 years.			
1790	1900	Per cent of increase.	1790	1900	Per cent of increase.	1790	1900	Per cent of increase.	1790	1900	Per cent of increase.	
106,928	1,068,018	898.82	205,886	3,019,360	1,366.52	102,140	1,969,432	1,828.17	103,746	1,049,928	912.02	1
2,745	204,549	7,351.69	4,763	574,221	11,955.87	2,363	373,362	15,700.34	2,400	200,859	8,269.13	2
3,840	39,105	918.36	6,325	92,249	1,358.48	3,138	54,470	1,635.82	3,187	37,779	1,085.41	3
7,551	58,110	669.57	14,666	153,694	947.96	7,275	96,918	1,232.02	7,391	56,776	668.28	4
5,894	11,254	90.94	11,951	34,384	187.71	5,929	23,414	294.91	6,022	10,970	82.17	5
6,590	13,730	108.35	13,065	42,993	229.07	6,482	29,801	359.75	6,583	13,192	100.39	6
4,514	12,682	180.95	8,449	37,652	345.64	4,192	25,257	502.50	4,257	12,395	191.17	7
4,434	27,243	514.41	8,801	80,491	814.57	4,366	53,407	1,123.25	4,435	27,084	510.69	8
2,109	13,771	552.96	4,494	42,536	846.51	2,229	29,172	1,208.75	2,265	13,364	490.02	9
3,420	20,139	488.86	6,155	47,442	670.79	3,053	27,934	814.97	3,102	19,508	528.88	10

[17] Area covered in 1900 by Queens and Nassau counties.
[18] Area covered in 1900 by Ulster and Sullivan counties, and by parts of Greene and Delaware counties.
[19] Area covered in 1900 by Washington and Warren counties.
[20] Area covered in 1900 by Westchester county, and by part of New York county.
[21] Area covered in 1900 by Bergen and Hudson counties, and by part of Passaic county.
[22] Area covered in 1900 by Burlington county, and by parts of Mercer and Ocean counties.
[23] Area covered in 1900 by Essex and Union counties, and by part of Passaic county.
[24] Area covered in 1900 by Gloucester, Atlantic, and Camden counties.
[25] Area covered in 1900 by Hunterdon county, and by part of Mercer county.
[26] Area covered in 1900 by Middlesex county, and by parts of Mercer and Monmouth counties.
[27] Area covered in 1900 by parts of Mercer, Monmouth, and Ocean counties.
[28] Area covered in 1900 by Somerset county, and by part of Mercer county.
[29] Area covered in 1900 by Warren and Sussex counties.
[30] Area covered in 1900 by Allegheny, Butler, Crawford, Erie, Mercer, and Lawrence counties, and by parts of Armstrong, Beaver, Venango, Warren, and Forest counties.
[31] Area covered in 1900 by Bedford, Somerset, and Fulton counties, and by parts of Cambria and Blair counties.
[32] Area covered in 1900 by Berks county, and by part of Schuylkill county.
[33] Area covered in 1900 by Perry and Cumberland counties.
[34] Area covered in 1900 by Dauphin county, and by part of Lebanon county.

TABLE **107.**—WHITE POPULATION, CLASSIFIED BY SEX AND AGE, OF EACH OF THE COUNTIES REPORTED

PENNSYLVANIA—Continued.

| | COUNTY. | BOTH SEXES. | | | MALES. | | | | | |
| | | | | | All ages. | | | 16 years and over. | | |
		1790	1900	Per cent of increase.	1790	1900	Per cent of increase.	1790	1900	Per cent of increase.
11	Franklin[1]	15,057	52,944	251.62	7,895	25,910	228.18	4,021	16,137	301.32
12	Huntingdon[2]	7,491	134,628	1,697.20	3,960	68,210	1,622.47	1,871	42,889	2,192.30
13	Lancaster[3]	35,192	156,761	345.44	17,781	76,695	331.33	9,714	50,004	414.76
14	Luzerne[4]	4,868	560,417	11,412.26	2,565	288,686	11,154.81	1,237	184,875	14,845.43
15	Mifflin[5]	7,461	81,387	990.83	3,909	40,883	945.87	1,954	25,621	1,211.21
16	Montgomery[1]	22,365	134,436	501.10	11,383	66,446	483.73	6,001	44,956	649.14
17	Northampton[6]	24,086	313,535	1,201.73	12,411	160,878	1,196.25	6,007	106,400	1,671.27
18	Northumberland[7]	16,971	694,059	3,989.68	8,920	358,044	3,913.95	4,191	229,013	5,364.40
19	Philadelphia[1]	51,916	1,229,673	2,268.58	25,393	604,268	2,279.66	14,497	417,013	2,776.55
20	Washington[8]	23,617	116,393	392.84	12,612	59,924	375.13	5,333	39,172	634.52
21	Westmoreland[9]	15,852	240,845	1,419.34	8,372	126,485	1,410.81	4,013	80,146	1,897.16
22	York[10]	36,182	148,880	311.48	18,640	73,831	296.09	9,171	46,599	408.11

DELAWARE.[11]

	COUNTY.	1790	1900	Per cent of increase.	1790	1900	Per cent of increase.	1790	1900	Per cent of increase.
1	The state	46,310	153,977	232.49	23,926	78,486	228.04	11,783	52,935	349.24
2	Kent	14,050	25,017	78.05	7,172	12,689	76.92	3,705	8,522	130.01
3	New-Castle	16,487	93,456	466.84	8,720	47,578	445.62	3,973	32,803	725.64
4	Sussex	15,773	35,504	125.09	8,034	18,219	126.77	4,105	11,610	182.82

MARYLAND.[12]

	COUNTY.	1790	1900	Per cent of increase.	1790	1900	Per cent of increase.	1790	1900	Per cent of increase.
1	The state	208,649	[12]1,143,956	448.27	107,254	[12]566,316	428.01	55,915	[12]374,578	569.91
2	Allegany[13]	4,539	69,594	1,433.25	2,351	35,215	1,397.87	1,068	20,911	1,857.96
3	Ann-Arundel[14]	11,664	36,545	213.31	5,992	19,182	220.13	3,142	12,522	298.54
4	Baltimore[15]	18,953	125,446	561.88	9,852	62,760	537.03	5,184	40,921	689.37
5	Baltimore town and precincts[16]	11,925	396,324	3,223.47	6,422	191,934	2,888.70	3,866	127,938	3,209.31
6	Calvert[1]	4,211	5,080	20.64	2,200	2,745	24.77	1,091	1,660	52.15
7	Caroline[18]	7,028	12,009	70.87	3,539	6,102	72.42	1,812	3,837	111.75
8	Cecil[1]	10,055	20,850	107.36	5,224	10,612	103.14	2,847	6,966	144.68
9	Charles[1]	10,124	8,014	[17]20.84	4,964	4,186	[17]15.67	2,565	2,530	[17]1.36
10	Dorchester[19]	10,010	18,476	84.58	4,971	9,503	91.17	2,541	5,906	132.43
11	Frederick[20]	26,937	64,193	138.31	14,026	31,902	127.45	7,010	20,359	190.43
12	Harford[1]	10,784	22,411	107.82	5,684	11,269	98.26	2,872	7,386	157.17
13	Kent[1]	6,748	11,343	68.09	3,423	5,938	73.47	1,876	3,934	109.70
14	Montgomery[21]	11,679	30,387	160.18	6,030	15,198	152.04	3,284	10,177	209.90
15	Prince Georges[22]	10,004	199,448	1,893.68	5,156	97,555	1,792.07	2,653	70,349	2,551.68
16	Queen Anns[1]	8,171	11,991	46.75	4,132	6,154	48.94	2,158	3,873	79.47
17	St. Marys[1]	8,216	8,926	8.64	4,043	4,652	15.06	2,100	2,719	29.48
18	Somersett[23]	8,272	26,126	215.84	4,093	13,151	221.30	2,185	8,265	278.26
19	Talbot[1]	7,231	12,875	77.91	3,650	6,564	79.84	1,938	4,300	121.88
20	Washington[1]	14,472	42,642	194.65	7,601	20,945	175.56	3,738	13,264	254.84
21	Worcester[24]	7,626	21,276	178.99	3,901	10,749	175.54	1,985	6,761	240.60

VIRGINIA.[25]

	COUNTY.	1790	1900	Per cent of increase.	1790	1900	Per cent of increase.	1790	1900	Per cent of increase.
1	The state	442,117	2,108,088	376.81	227,071	1,076,009	373.85	110,936	645,869	482.20
2	Accomack	8,976	20,743	131.09	4,474	10,617	137.30	2,297	6,522	183.94
3	Albemarle	6,835	21,969	221.42	3,493	11,005	215.06	1,703	6,711	294.07
4	Amelia (including Nottoway Co)	6,684	8,018	19.96	3,406	4,052	18.97	1,709	2,442	42.89
5	Amherst[26]	8,286	21,210	155.97	4,291	10,694	149.22	2,056	6,197	201.41
6	Augusta[27]	9,260	41,919	352.69	4,836	20,845	331.04	2,599	13,069	402.85
7	Bedford	7,725	20,617	166.89	4,051	10,294	154.11	1,785	6,021	237.31
8	Berkley[28]	16,650	34,218	105.45	8,800	17,065	93.92	4,253	10,703	151.66
9	Botetourt[29]	9,241	58,791	536.20	4,809	29,946	522.71	2,247	18,382	718.07
10	Brunswick	5,919	7,375	24.60	3,001	3,711	23.66	1,472	2,239	52.10
11	Buckingham[30]	5,496	10,599	92.85	2,811	5,310	88.90	1,274	3,100	143.33

[1] Area covered in 1900 coextensive with that of 1790.
[2] Area covered in 1900 by Huntingdon county, and by parts of Center, Cambria, Clearfield, and Blair counties.
[3] Area covered in 1900 by Lancaster county, and by part of Lebanon county.
[4] Area covered in 1900 by Luzerne, Susquehanna, Wyoming, and Lackawanna counties, and by part of Bradford county.
[5] Area covered in 1900 by Mifflin and Juniata counties, and by part of Center county.
[6] Area covered in 1900 by Northampton, Wayne, Lehigh, Pike, Monroe, and Carbon counties, and by part of Schuylkill county.
[7] Area covered in 1900 by Northumberland, Lycoming, Jefferson, McKean, Potter, Tioga, Columbia, Union, Clarion, Clinton, Elk, Sullivan, Montour, Snyder, and Cameron counties, and by parts of Armstrong, Center, Venango, Warren, Indiana, Clearfield, Bradford, and Forest counties.
[8] Area covered in 1900 by Washington and Greene counties, and by part of Beaver county.
[9] Area covered in 1900 by Westmoreland county, and by parts of Armstrong and Indiana counties.
[10] Area covered in 1900 by York and Adams counties.
[11] County boundaries same in 1790 as in 1900.
[12] Includes population of the District of Columbia in 1900.
[13] Area covered in 1900 by Allegany and Garrett counties.
[14] Area covered in 1900 by Anne Arundel and Howard counties.
[15] Area covered in 1900 by Baltimore county, and by parts of Carroll county and Baltimore city.

IN 1790, COMPARED WITH THAT OF THE SAME AREA IN 1900, WITH PER CENT OF INCREASE—Continued.

PENNSYLVANIA—Continued.

MALES—continued.			FEMALES.									
Under 16 years.			All ages.			16 years and over.			Under 16 years.			
1790	1900	Per cent of increase.	1790	1900	Per cent of increase.	1790	1900	Per cent of increase.	1790	1900	Per cent of increase.	
3,874	9,773	152.27	7,162	27,034	277.46	3,553	17,587	394.99	3,609	9,447	161.76	11
2,089	25,321	1,112.11	3,531	66,418	1,781.00	1,752	41,544	2,271.23	1,779	24,874	1,298.20	12
8,067	26,691	230.87	17,411	80,066	359.86	8,638	53,324	517.32	8,773	26,742	204.82	13
1,328	103,811	7,717.09	2,303	271,731	11,699.00	1,143	168,476	14,639.81	1,160	103,255	8,801.29	14
1,955	15,262	680.66	3,552	40,504	1,040.32	1,762	25,718	1,359.59	1,790	14,786	726.03	15
5,382	21,490	299.29	10,982	67,990	519.10	5,448	46,639	756.08	5.534	21,351	285.81	16
6,404	54,478	750.69	11,675	152,657	1,207.55	5,792	99,260	1,613.74	5,883	53,397	807.65	17
4,729	129,031	2,628.50	8,051	336,015	4,073.58	3,994	209,706	5,150.53	4,057	126,309	3,013.36	18
10,896	187,255	1,618.57	26,523	625,405	2,257.97	13,157	439,132	3,237.38	13,366	186,273	1,293.74	19
7,279	20,752	185.09	11,005	56,469	413.12	5,460	36,254	563.99	5,545	20,215	264.56	20
4,359	46,339	963.06	7,480	114,360	1,428.88	3,711	69,629	1,776.29	3,769	44,731	1,086.81	21
9,469	27,232	187.59	17,542	75,049	327.82	8,703	48,428	456.45	8,839	26,621	201.18	22

DELAWARE.[11]

12,143	25,551	110.41	22,384	75,491	237.26	11,647	50,619	334.61	10,737	24,872	131.65	1
3,467	4,167	20.19	6,878	12,328	79.24	3,579	8,391	134.45	3,299	3,937	19.34	2
4,747	14,775	211.24	7,767	45,878	490.68	4,041	31,287	674.24	3,726	14,591	291.60	3
3,929	6,609	68.21	7,739	17,285	123.35	4,027	10,941	171.69	3,712	6,344	70.91	4

MARYLAND.[12]

51,339	[12] 191,738	273.47	101,395	[12] 577,640	469.69	58,891	[12] 388,125	559.06	42,504	[12] 189,515	345.86	1
1,283	14,304	1,014.89	2,188	34,379	1,471.25	1,271	20,434	1,507.71	917	13,945	1,420.72	2
2,850	6,660	133.68	5,672	17,363	206.12	3,294	10,981	233.36	2,378	6,382	168.38	3
4,668	21,839	367.84	9,101	62,686	588.78	5,286	41,170	678.85	3,815	21,516	463.98	4
2,556	63,996	2,403.76	5,503	204,390	3,614.16	3,196	139,892	4,277.10	2,307	64,498	2,695.75	5
1,085	1,085	[17] 2.16	2,011	2,335	16.11	1,168	1,422	21.75	843	913	8.30	6
1,727	2,265	31.15	3,489	5,907	69.30	2,026	3,798	87.46	1,463	2,109	44.16	7
2,377	3,646	53.39	4,831	10,238	111.92	2,806	6,825	143.23	2,025	3,413	68.54	8
2,399	1,656	[17] 30.97	5,160	3,828	[17] 25.81	2,997	2,244	[17] 25.13	2,163	1,584	[17] 26.77	9
2,430	3,597	48.02	5,039	8,973	78.07	2,927	5,507	88.14	2,112	3,466	64.11	10
7,016	11,543	64.52	12,911	32,291	150.10	7,499	21,114	181.56	5,412	11,177	106.52	11
2,812	3,883	38.09	5,100	11,142	118.47	2,962	7,264	145.24	2,138	3,878	81.38	12
1,547	2,004	29.54	3,325	5,405	62.56	1,931	3,455	78.92	1,394	1,950	39.89	13
2,746	5,021	82.85	5,649	15,189	168.88	3,281	10,294	213.75	2,368	4,895	106.71	14
2,503	27,206	986.94	4,848	101,893	2,001.75	2,816	74,629	2,550.18	2,032	27,264	1,241.73	15
1,974	2,281	15.55	4,039	5,837	44.52	2,346	3,645	55.37	1,693	2,192	29.47	16
1,943	1,933	[17] 0.51	4,173	4,274	2.42	2,424	2,400	[17] 0.99	1,749	1,874	7.15	17
1,908	4,886	156.08	4,179	12,975	210.48	2,427	8,035	231.07	1,752	4,940	181.96	18
1,712	2,264	32.24	3,581	6,311	76.24	2,080	4,122	98.17	1,501	2,189	45.84	19
3,863	7,681	98.84	6,871	21,697	215.78	3,991	14,277	257.73	2,880	7,420	157.64	20
1,916	3,988	108.14	3,725	10,527	182.60	2,163	6,617	205.92	1,562	3,910	150.32	21

VIRGINIA.[25]

116,135	430,140	270.36	215,046	1,032,079	379.93	111,523	618,013	454.16	103,523	414,066	299.97	1
2,177	4,095	88.10	4,502	10,126	124.92	2,335	6,146	163.21	2,167	3,980	83.66	2
1,790	4,294	139.89	3,342	10,964	228.07	1,733	6,813	293.13	1,609	4,151	157.99	3
1,697	1,610	[17] 5.13	3,278	3,966	20.96	1,700	2,401	41.24	1,578	1,565	[17] 0.82	4
2,235	4,497	101.21	3,995	10,516	163.23	2,072	6,093	194.06	1,923	4,423	130.01	5
2,237	7,776	247.61	4,424	21,074	376.36	2,294	13,523	489.49	2,130	7,551	254.51	6
2,266	4,273	88.57	3,674	10,323	180.97	1,905	6,224	226.72	1,769	4,099	131.71	7
4,547	6,362	39.92	7,850	17,153	118.51	4,071	11,139	173.62	3,779	6,014	59.14	8
2,562	11,564	351.37	4,432	28,845	550.83	2,298	17,492	661.18	2,134	11,353	432.01	9
1,529	1,472	[17] 3.73	2,918	3,664	25.57	1,513	2,117	39.92	1,405	1,547	10.11	10
1,537	2,210	43.79	2,685	5,289	96.98	1,392	3,153	126.51	1,293	2,136	65.20	11

[16] Area covered in 1900 by part of Baltimore city.
[17] Decrease.
[18] Area covered in 1900 by Caroline county, and by part of Dorchester county.
[19] Area covered in 1900 by part of Dorchester county.
[20] Area covered in 1900 by Frederick county, and by part of Carroll county.
[21] Area covered in 1900 by Montgomery county, and by Georgetown, D. C.
[22] Area covered in 1900 by Prince Georges county, and by the District of Columbia, exclusive of Georgetown.
[23] Area covered in 1900 by Somerset county, and by part of Wicomico county.
[24] Area covered in 1900 by Worcester county, and by part of Wicomico county.
[25] Area covered in 1900 by Virginia and West Virginia. Independent cities are included in county totals for 1790 and 1900.
[26] Area covered in 1900 by Amherst and Nelson counties.
[27] Area covered in 1900 by Augusta county, and by parts of Bath, Pocahontas, and Highland counties.
[28] Area covered in 1900 by Berkeley and Jefferson counties, and by part of Morgan county.
[29] Area covered in 1900 by Botetourt, Alleghany, and Roanoke counties, and by parts of Craig, Monroe, and Bath counties.
[30] Area covered in 1900 by Buckingham county, and by part of Appomattox county.

TABLE **107.**—WHITE POPULATION, CLASSIFIED BY SEX AND AGE, OF EACH OF THE COUNTIES REPORTED

VIRGINIA[1]—Continued.

| | | BOTH SEXES. | | | MALES. | | | | | |
| | | | | | All ages. | | | 16 years and over. | | |
	COUNTY.	1790	1900	Per cent of increase.	1790	1900	Per cent of increase.	1790	1900	Per cent of increase.
12	Campbell [2]	4,946	25,871	423.07	2,583	12,765	394.19	1,236	7,768	528.48
13	Caroline	6,994	7,667	9.62	3,530	3,814	8.05	1,799	2,280	26.74
14	Charles-City	2,084	1,344	[3] 35.51	1,041	714	[3] 31.41	532	473	[3] 11.09
15	Charlotte [4]	5,199	7,116	36.87	2,664	3,658	37.31	1,285	2,124	65.29
16	Chesterfield	6,358	17,481	174.94	3,209	8,668	170.11	1,652	5,363	224.64
17	Culpeper [5]	13,809	20,885	51.10	7,127	10,244	43.74	3,372	6,217	84.37
18	Cumberland	3,577	2,791	[3] 21.97	1,799	1,336	[3] 25.74	885	847	[3] 4.29
19	Dinwiddie	6,039	16,931	180.36	3,186	8,365	162.55	1,790	5,433	203.52
20	Elizabeth-City	1,556	10,757	591.32	778	7,091	811.44	390	5,814	1,390.77
21	Essex	3,543	3,576	0.93	1,777	1,777	....	908	1,070	17.84
22	Fairfax [6]	7,611	20,465	168.89	4,010	10,528	162.54	2,138	7,112	232.65
23	Fauquier	11,157	15,074	35.05	5,657	7,418	31.01	2,674	4,488	67.84
24	Fluvanna	2,430	5,039	107.37	1,243	2,492	100.48	589	1,551	163.33
25	Franklin	5,735	20,005	248.82	2,895	9,868	240.86	1,266	5,157	307.34
26	Frederick [7]	15,315	26,342	72.00	8,005	12,915	61.34	3,835	8,062	110.22
27	Gloucester [8]	6,225	12,068	93.86	3,120	6,127	96.38	1,597	3,715	132.62
28	Goochland	4,140	3,961	[3] 4.32	2,087	2,034	[3] 2.59	1,028	1,283	24.80
29	Greenbrier (includes Kanawa) [9]	5,676	387,036	6,718.82	3,037	200,794	6,511.59	1,463	113,327	7,646.21
30	Greensville	2,530	3,402	34.47	1,296	1,759	35.72	669	1,064	59.04
31	Halifax	8,931	17,922	100.67	4,534	9,107	100.86	2,214	5,247	136.99
32	Hampshire [10]	6,879	26,116	279.65	3,618	13,346	268.88	1,662	8,088	386.64
33	Hanover	6,291	9,696	54.12	3,049	5,023	64.74	1,637	3,085	88.45
34	Hardy [11]	6,556	15,015	129.03	3,364	7,615	126.37	1,108	4,457	302.26
35	Harrison [12]	2,013	146,447	7,175.06	1,066	75,383	6,971.58	487	45,872	9,319.30
36	Henrico	5,600	70,044	1,150.79	2,993	34,562	1,054.76	1,823	23,031	1,163.36
37	Henry [13]	6,763	24,660	264.63	3,486	12,463	257.51	1,523	6,728	341.76
38	Isle of Wight	4,786	6,833	42.77	2,371	3,446	45.34	1,208	2,121	75.58
39	James City	1,519	2,712	78.54	754	1,424	88.86	395	1,015	156.96
40	King & Queen	4,159	4,006	[3] 3.68	2,021	1,941	[3] 3.96	995	1,183	18.89
41	King George	3,123	3,596	15.14	1,538	1,839	19.57	757	1,074	41.88
42	King William	2,893	3,266	12.96	1,455	1,672	14.91	723	1,013	40.11
43	Lancaster	2,259	4,058	79.64	1,077	2,094	94.43	535	1,271	137.57
44	Loudon [14]	14,749	23,139	56.82	7,669	11,256	46.77	3,677	7,274	97.82
45	Louisa	3,880	7,896	103.51	1,981	3,915	97.63	957	2,415	152.35
46	Lunenburg	4,547	5,133	12.89	2,295	2,614	13.90	1,110	1,568	41.26
47	Mecklenburg	7,555	10,353	37.04	3,872	5,126	32.39	1,857	3,057	64.62
48	Middlesex	1,531	3,684	140.63	777	1,887	142.85	407	1,145	181.33
49	Monongalia [15]	4,602	78,800	1,612.30	2,434	40,822	1,577.16	1,089	25,769	2,266.30
50	Montgomery [16]	12,394	152,327	1,129.04	6,590	77,286	1,072.78	2,846	42,807	1,404.11
51	Nansemond	4,713	10,115	114.62	2,382	5,017	110.62	1,215	3,065	152.26
52	New-Kent	2,391	1,660	[3] 30.57	1,192	877	[3] 26.43	605	528	[3] 12.72
53	Norfolk	8,928	57,212	540.81	4,637	29,228	530.32	2,650	19,847	648.94
54	Northampton	3,181	6,141	93.05	1,600	3,191	99.44	857	2,008	134.31
55	Northumberland	4,506	5,680	26.05	2,183	2,994	37.15	1,046	1,880	79.73
56	Ohio [17]	4,907	130,672	2,562.97	2,599	67,093	2,481.49	1,222	42,721	3,395.99
57	Orange [18]	5,436	11,833	117.68	2,743	5,790	111.08	1,317	3,385	157.02
58	Pendleton [19]	2,378	11,730	393.27	1,254	5,934	373.20	568	3,357	491.02
59	Pittsylvania	8,538	35,607	317.04	4,455	17,777	299.03	2,008	10,337	414.79
60	Powhatan	2,286	2,343	2.49	1,171	1,247	6.49	623	769	23.43
61	Prince Edward [20]	4,082	5,912	44.83	2,121	2,869	35.27	1,044	1,783	70.78
62	Prince George	3,387	2,886	[3] 14.79	1,787	1,483	[3] 17.01	965	942	[3] 2.38
63	Prince William	6,744	8,240	22.18	3,441	4,189	21.74	1,644	2,609	58.70
64	Princess Anne	4,527	5,505	21.60	2,320	2,944	26.90	1,169	1,900	62.53
65	Randolph [21]	932	47,292	4,974.25	491	25,596	5,113.03	221	15,961	7,122.17
66	Richmond	2,918	4,159	42.53	1,401	2,080	48.47	704	1,239	75.99
67	Rockbridge	5,825	19,693	238.08	3,069	10,042	227.21	1,517	5,961	292.95
68	Rockingham [22]	6,677	34,909	422.83	3,468	17,094	392.91	1,816	10,129	457.76
69	Russell [23]	3,143	108,258	3,344.42	1,703	55,981	3,187.20	734	30,431	4,045.91
70	Shannandoah [24]	9,979	31,209	212.77	5,188	15,349	195.85	2,409	9,235	283.35
71	Southampton	6,312	9,165	45.20	3,178	4,650	46.32	1,632	2,797	71.38
72	Spotsylvania	5,171	8,799	70.16	2,639	4,236	60.52	1,361	2,679	96.84
73	Stafford	5,465	6,489	18.74	2,696	3,270	21.29	1,341	1,980	47.65
74	Surry	2,762	3,286	18.97	1,383	1,718	24.22	732	1,107	51.23
75	Sussex	4,771	4,121	[3] 13.62	2,389	2,098	[3] 12.18	1,215	1,288	6.01
76	Warwick	667	13,948	1,991.15	334	8,097	2,324.25	176	6,004	3,311.36
77	Washington [25]	5,167	44,469	760.63	2,727	22,367	720.20	1,287	12,722	888.50
78	Westmoreland	3,183	4,381	37.64	1,569	2,301	46.65	815	1,414	73.50
79	York	2,115	3,401	60.80	991	1,770	78.61	530	1,037	95.66

[1] Area covered in 1900 by Virginia and West Virginia. Independent cities are included in county totals for 1790 and 1900.
[2] Area covered in 1900 by Campbell county, and by part of Appomattox county.
[3] Decrease.
[4] Area covered in 1900 by Charlotte county, and by part of Appomattox county.
[5] Area covered in 1900 by Culpeper, Madison, and Rappahannock counties.
[6] Area covered in 1900 by Alexandria county, and by part of Fairfax county.
[7] Area covered in 1900 by Frederick and Clarke counties, and by part of Warren county.
[8] Area covered in 1900 by Gloucester and Mathews counties.
[9] Area covered in 1900 by Greenbrier, Boone, Cabell, Clay, Fayette, Jackson, Kanawha, Lincoln, Logan, Mason, Mingo, Nicholas, Putnam, Raleigh, Roane, Wayne, and Wyoming counties, and by parts of Braxton, Calhoun, Gilmer, McDowell, Monroe, Pocahontas, Summers, Webster, Wirt, and Wood counties.
[10] Area covered in 1900 by Hampshire and Mineral counties, and by part of Morgan county.
[11] Area covered in 1900 by Hardy and Grant counties.
[12] Area covered in 1900 by Harrison, Doddridge, Lewis, and Ritchie counties, and by parts of Barbour, Braxton, Calhoun, Gilmer, Marion, Taylor, Upshur, Webster, Wirt, Wood, and Pleasants counties.

IN 1790, COMPARED WITH THAT OF THE SAME AREA IN 1900, WITH PER CENT OF INCREASE—Continued.

VIRGINIA[1]—Continued.

MALES—continued.			FEMALES.									
Under 16 years.			All ages.			16 years and over.			Under 16 years.			
1790	1900	Per cent of increase.	1790	1900	Per cent of increase.	1790	1900	Per cent of increase.	1790	1900	Per cent of increase.	
1,347	4,997	270.97	2,363	13,106	454.63	1,225	8,284	576.24	1,138	4,822	323.73	12
1,731	1,534	³11.38	3,464	3,853	11.23	1,796	2,406	33.96	1,668	1,447	³13.25	13
509	241	³52.65	1,043	630	³39.60	541	422	³22.00	502	208	³58.57	14
1,379	1,534	11.24	2,535	3,458	36.41	1,315	2,116	60.91	1,220	1,342	10.00	15
1,557	3,305	112.27	3,149	8,813	179.87	1,633	5,592	242.44	1,516	3,221	112.47	16
3,755	4,027	7.24	6,682	10,641	59.25	3,465	6,704	93.48	3,217	3,937	22.38	17
914	489	³46.50	1,778	1,455	³18.17	922	922	....	856	533	³37.73	18
1,396	2,932	110.03	2,853	8,566	200.24	1,480	5,677	283.58	1,373	2,889	110.42	19
388	1,277	229.12	778	3,666	371.21	404	2,372	488.59	374	1,294	245.07	20
869	707	³18.64	1,766	1,799	1.87	916	1,131	23.47	850	668	³21.41	21
1,872	3,416	82.48	3,601	9,937	175.95	1,868	6,598	253.40	1,733	3,339	92.56	22
2,983	2,930	³1.94	5,500	7,656	39.20	2,852	4,843	69.81	2,648	2,813	6.23	23
654	941	43.88	1,187	2,547	114.57	616	1,646	167.21	571	901	57.79	24
1,629	4,711	189.20	2,840	10,137	256.94	1,473	5,702	287.10	1,367	4,435	224.43	25
4,170	4,853	16.38	7,310	13,427	83.68	3,791	8,704	129.60	3,519	4,723	34.21	26
1,523	2,412	58.37	3,105	5,941	91.34	1,610	3,636	125.84	1,495	2,305	54.18	27
1,059	751	³29.08	2,053	1,927	³6.14	1,065	1,209	13.52	988	718	³27.33	28
1,574	87,467	5,456.99	2,639	186,242	6,957.29	1,369	102,811	7,409.93	1,270	83,431	6,469.37	29
627	695	10.84	1,234	1,643	33.14	640	953	48.91	594	690	16.16	30
2,320	3,860	66.38	4,397	8,815	100.48	2,280	5,157	126.18	2,117	3,658	72.79	31
1,956	5,258	168.81	3,261	12,770	291.60	1,691	7,789	360.62	1,570	4,981	217.26	32
1,412	1,938	37.25	3,242	4,673	44.14	1,681	2,977	77.10	1,561	1,696	8.65	33
2,256	3,158	39.98	3,192	7,400	131.83	1,655	4,328	161.51	1,537	3,072	99.87	34
579	29,511	4,996.89	947	71,064	7,404.12	491	42,931	8,643.58	456	28,133	6,069.52	35
1,170	11,531	885.56	2,607	35,482	1,261.03	1,352	24,143	1,685.72	1,255	11,339	803.51	36
1,963	5,735	192.15	3,277	12,197	272.20	1,699	6,846	302.94	1,578	5,351	239.10	37
1,163	1,325	13.93	2,415	3,387	40.25	1,252	2,043	63.18	1,163	1,344	15.56	38
359	409	13.93	765	1,288	68.37	397	913	129.97	368	375	1.90	39
1,026	758	³26.12	2,138	2,065	³3.41	1,109	1,238	11.63	1,029	827	³19.63	40
781	765	³2.05	1,585	1,757	10.85	822	1,037	26.16	763	720	³5.64	41
732	659	³9.97	1,438	1,594	10.85	746	1,009	35.25	692	585	³15.46	42
542	823	51.84	1,182	1,964	66.16	613	1,114	81.73	569	850	49.38	43
3,992	3,982	³0.25	7,080	11,883	67.84	3,672	7,838	113.45	3,408	4,045	18.69	44
1,024	1,500	46.48	1,899	3,981	109.64	985	2,561	160.00	914	1,420	55.36	45
1,185	1,046	³11.73	2,252	2,519	11.86	1,168	1,527	30.74	1,084	992	³8.49	46
2,015	2,069	2.68	3,683	5,227	41.92	1,910	3,156	65.24	1,773	2,071	16.81	47
370	742	100.54	754	1,797	138.33	391	1,050	168.54	363	747	105.79	48
1,345	15,053	1,019.18	2,168	37,978	1,651.75	1,124	23,557	1,995.82	1,044	14,421	1,281.32	49
3,744	34,479	820.91	5,804	75,041	1,192.92	3,010	42,098	1,298.60	2,794	32,943	1,079.06	50
1,167	1,952	67.26	2,331	5,098	118.70	1,209	3,228	167.00	1,122	1,870	66.67	51
587	349	³40.54	1,199	783	³34.70	622	492	³20.90	577	291	³49.57	52
1,987	9,381	372.12	4,291	27,984	552.13	2,225	18,542	733.35	2,066	9,442	357.01	53
743	1,183	59.22	1,581	2,950	86.59	820	1,805	120.12	761	1,145	50.46	54
1,137	1,114	³2.02	2,323	2,686	15.63	1,205	1,617	34.19	1,118	1,069	³4.38	55
1,377	24,372	1,669.93	2,308	63,579	2,654.72	1,197	39,961	3,238.43	1,111	23,618	2,025.83	56
1,426	2,405	68.65	2,693	6,043	124.85	1,397	3,731	167.07	1,296	2,312	78.40	57
686	2,577	275.65	1,124	5,796	415.66	583	3,396	482.50	541	2,400	343.62	58
2,447	7,440	204.05	4,083	17,830	336.69	2,117	10,613	401.32	1,966	7,217	267.09	59
548	478	³12.77	1,115	1,096	³1.70	578	711	23.01	537	385	³28.31	60
1,077	1,086	0.84	1,961	3,043	55.18	1,017	1,919	88.69	944	1,124	19.07	61
822	541	³34.18	1,600	1,403	³12.31	830	874	5.30	770	529	³31.30	62
1,797	1,580	³12.08	3,303	4,051	22.65	1,713	2,603	51.96	1,590	1,448	³8.93	63
1,151	1,044	³9.30	2,207	2,561	16.04	1,145	1,574	37.47	1,062	987	³7.06	64
270	9,635	3,468.52	441	21,696	4,819.73	229	12,471	5,345.85	212	9,225	4,251.42	65
697	841	20.66	1,517	2,079	37.05	787	1,176	49.43	730	903	23.70	66
1,552	4,081	162.95	2,756	9,651	250.18	1,429	5,895	312.53	1,327	3,756	183.04	67
1,652	6,965	321.61	3,209	17,815	455.16	1,664	11,098	566.95	1,545	6,717	334.76	68
969	25,550	2,536.73	1,440	52,277	3,530.35	747	27,616	3,596.92	693	24,661	3,458.59	69
2,779	6,114	120.01	4,791	15,860	231.04	2,485	9,869	297.14	2,306	5,991	159.80	70
1,546	1,853	19.85	3,134	4,515	44.06	1,625	2,732	68.12	1,509	1,783	18.16	71
1,278	1,557	21.83	2,532	4,563	80.21	1,313	2,984	127.27	1,219	1,579	29.53	72
1,355	1,290	³4.80	2,769	3,219	16.25	1,436	1,968	37.05	1,333	1,251	³6.15	73
651	611	³6.14	1,379	1,568	13.71	715	995	39.16	664	573	³13.70	74
1,174	810	³31.01	2,382	2,023	³15.07	1,235	1,216	³1.54	1,147	807	³29.64	75
158	2,093	1,224.68	333	5,851	1,657.06	173	3,756	2,071.10	160	2,095	1,209.38	76
1,440	9,645	569.79	2,440	22,102	805.82	1,265	12,790	911.07	1,175	9,312	692.51	77
754	887	17.64	1,614	2,080	28.87	837	1,301	55.44	777	779	0.26	78
461	733	59.00	1,124	1,631	45.11	583	939	61.06	541	692	27.91	79

[13] Area covered in 1900 by Henry and Patrick counties.
[14] Area covered in 1900 by Loudoun county, and by part of Fairfax county.
[15] Area covered in 1900 by Monongalia county, and by parts of Preston, Marion, and Taylor counties.
[16] Area covered in 1900 by Montgomery, Bland, Carroll, Floyd, Giles, Grayson, Mercer, Pulaski, and Wythe counties, and by parts of Craig, McDowell, Monroe, Smyth, Summers, and Tazewell counties.
[17] Area covered in 1900 by Ohio, Brooke, Hancock, Marshall, Tyler, and Wetzel counties, and by part of Pleasants county.
[18] Area covered in 1900 by Orange and Greene counties.
[19] Area covered in 1900 by Pendleton county, and by part of Highland county.
[20] Area covered in 1900 by Prince Edward county, and by part of Appomattox county.
[21] Area covered in 1900 by Randolph and Tucker counties, and by parts of Barbour, Pocahontas, Preston, Upshur, and Webster counties.
[22] Area covered in 1900 by Rockingham county, and by part of Page county.
[23] Area covered in 1900 by Russell, Buchanan, Dickenson, Lee, and Wise counties, and by parts of McDowell, Scott, and Tazewell counties.
[24] Area covered in 1900 by Shenandoah county, and by parts of Page and Warren counties.
[25] Area covered in 1900 by Washington county, and by parts of Scott and Smyth counties.

TABLE **107.**—WHITE POPULATION, CLASSIFIED BY SEX AND AGE, OF EACH OF THE COUNTIES REPORTED

NORTH CAROLINA.

	COUNTY.	BOTH SEXES.			MALES.					
					All ages.			16 years and over.		
		1790	1900	Per cent of increase.	1790	1900	Per cent of increase.	1790	1900	Per cent of increase.
1	The state..........	289,181	1,263,603	336.96	147,825	632,155	327.64	70,172	356,589	408.16
2	Edenton district...........	33,568	56,455	68.18	17,058	28,678	68.12	8,405	16,865	100.65
3	Bertie[1]............	6,963	8,717	25.19	3,521	4,440	26.10	1,719	2,610	51.83
4	Camden[1]..........	2,954	3,283	11.14	1,479	1,690	14.27	725	959	32.28
5	Chowan[1]..........	2,360	4,406	86.69	1,189	2,221	86.80	638	1,302	104.08
6	Currituck[3]........	4,002	6,409	60.14	2,042	3,302	61.70	1,018	1,940	90.57
7	Gates[1]............	3,076	5,609	82.35	1,562	2,825	80.86	790	1,773	124.43
8	Hertford[1].........	3,269	5,895	80.33	1,637	2,964	81.06	813	1,750	115.25
9	Pasquotank[1]......	3,790	6,630	74.93	1,986	3,396	71.00	951	2,000	110.30
10	Perquimans[1]......	3,519	5,088	44.59	1,805	2,557	41.66	884	1,466	65.84
11	Tyrrell[4]..........	3,635	10,418	186.60	1,837	5,283	187.59	867	3,065	253.52
12	Fayette district............	28,112	112,522	300.26	14,435	55,863	287.00	7,111	31,816	347.42
13	Anson[5]............	4,365	20,092	360.30	2,218	10,122	356.36	1,035	5,496	431.01
14	Cumberland[6]......	6,467	26,810	314.57	3,413	13,198	286.70	1,852	7,561	308.26
15	Moore[1]............	3,487	15,773	352.34	1,815	7,765	327.82	850	4,504	429.88
16	Richmond[7]........	4,415	13,801	212.59	2,301	6,802	195.61	1,096	3,992	264.23
17	Robeson[1].........	4,533	19,577	331.88	2,270	9,806	331.98	1,132	5,567	391.78
18	Sampson[8].........	4,845	16,469	239.92	2,418	8,170	237.88	1,146	4,696	309.77
19	Halifax district............	37,955	83,827	120.86	19,345	42,694	120.70	9,215	24,965	170.92
20	Edgecombe[9].......	7,028	16,904	140.52	3,541	8,576	142.19	1,663	5,087	205.89
21	Franklin[10]........	4,764	12,678	166.12	2,457	6,465	163.13	1,076	3,751	248.61
22	Halifax[1]..........	7,170	11,060	54.25	3,699	5,649	52.72	1,873	3,469	85.21
23	Martin[1]...........	4,085	8,056	97.21	2,077	4,170	100.77	1,067	2,353	120.52
24	Nash[11]............	5,189	18,887	263.98	2,568	9,653	275.90	1,134	5,542	388.71
25	Northampton[1].....	5,120	9,031	76.39	2,618	4,563	74.29	1,335	2,681	100.82
26	Warren[12].........	4,599	7,211	56.79	2,385	3,618	51.70	1,067	2,082	95.13
27	Hillsborough district.........	45,820	148,918	225.01	23,840	73,863	209.83	10,937	43,183	294.83
28	Caswell[13].........	7,288	16,491	126.28	3,911	8,311	112.50	1,801	4,679	159.80
29	Chatham[1].........	7,593	15,573	105.10	3,929	7,763	97.58	1,761	4,432	151.68
30	Granville[14].......	6,504	17,176	164.08	3,454	8,499	146.06	1,581	4,917	211.01
31	Orange[15]..........	10,055	43,593	333.55	5,142	21,463	317.41	2,433	12,697	421.87
32	Randolph[1]........	6,834	24,560	259.38	3,542	12,119	242.15	1,590	6,803	327.86
33	Wake[16]...........	7,546	31,525	317.77	3,862	15,708	306.73	1,771	9,655	445.17
34	Morgan district............	30,687	373,248	1,116.31	15,726	185,717	1,080.96	6,953	99,651	1,333.21
35	Burke[17]...........	7,497	134,633	1,695.82	3,813	67,212	1,662.71	1,705	36,120	2,018.48
36	Lincoln[18].........	8,391	56,081	568.35	4,350	27,427	530.51	2,057	14,955	627.03
37	Rutherford[19]......	7,197	124,212	1,625.89	3,695	62,193	1,583.17	1,576	33,438	2,021.70
38	Wilkes[20]..........	7,602	58,322	667.19	3,868	28,885	646.77	1,615	15,138	837.34
39	Newbern district............	38,800	127,391	228.33	19,471	64,610	231.83	9,595	37,510	290.93
40	Beaufort[21]........	3,655	16,002	337.81	1,834	8,138	343.73	910	4,816	429.23
41	Carteret[22]........	2,932	9,297	217.09	1,427	4,689	228.59	718	2,841	295.68
42	Craven[23]..........	6,474	14,472	123.54	3,248	7,259	123.49	1,710	4,342	153.92
43	Dobbs[24]...........	4,936	16,852	241.41	2,457	8,551	248.03	1,164	5,000	329.55
44	Hyde[25]............	3,024	6,132	102.78	1,506	3,176	110.89	792	1,828	130.81
45	Johnston[26]........	4,298	25,678	497.44	2,217	12,951	484.17	1,040	7,213	593.56
46	Jones[1]............	3,071	4,466	45.42	1,530	2,301	50.39	736	1,344	82.61
47	Pitt[1].............	5,881	15,397	161.81	2,969	7,925	166.92	1,461	4,600	214.85
48	Wayne[27]..........	4,529	19,095	321.62	2,283	9,620	321.38	1,064	5,526	419.36
49	Salisbury district............	58,425	286,716	390.74	29,935	143,234	378.48	14,003	80,790	476.95
50	Guilford[1].........	6,657	27,969	320.14	3,422	13,993	308.91	1,615	8,439	422.54
51	Iredell[28]..........	4,559	26,508	481.44	2,336	12,965	455.01	1,118	7,260	549.37
52	Mecklenburg[29]....	9,685	57,009	488.63	4,927	28,578	480.03	2,364	16,324	590.52
53	Montgomery[30].....	4,191	23,936	471.13	2,162	12,032	456.52	942	6,225	560.83
54	Rockingham[1]......	5,088	21,544	323.43	2,599	10,902	319.47	1,188	6,106	413.97
55	Rowan[31]..........	14,129	53,380	277.80	7,227	26,557	267.47	3,399	15,104	344.37
56	Stokes[32]..........	7,633	40,866	435.39	3,968	20,506	416.78	1,846	11,625	529.74
57	Surry[33]...........	6,483	35,504	447.65	3,294	17,701	437.37	1,531	9,707	534.03
58	Wilmington district.........	15,814	74,526	371.27	8,015	37,496	367.82	3,953	21,809	451.71
59	Bladen[34]..........	3,356	21,891	552.29	1,671	10,930	554.10	837	6,084	626.88
60	Brunswick[35]......	1,556	10,512	575.58	778	5,337	585.99	380	2,992	687.37
61	Duplin[1]...........	4,274	13,877	224.68	2,222	6,982	214.22	1,035	4,036	289.95
62	New Hanover[36].....	3,032	19,916	556.86	1,536	9,907	544.99	834	6,200	643.41
63	Onslow[1]..........	3,596	8,330	131.65	1,808	4,340	140.04	867	2,497	188.00

[1] Area covered in 1900 coextensive with that of 1790.
[2] Decrease.
[3] Area covered in 1900 by Currituck county, and by part of Dare county.
[4] Area covered in 1900 by Tyrrell and Washington counties, and by part of Dare county.
[5] Area covered in 1900 by Anson county, and by part of Union county.
[6] Area covered in 1900 by Harnett county, and by part of Cumberland county.
[7] Area covered in 1900 by Richmond and Scotland counties.
[8] Area covered in 1900 by Sampson county, with the exception of a small section.
[9] Area covered in 1900 by Edgecombe county, and by part of Wilson county.
[10] Area covered in 1900 by part of Franklin county.
[11] Area covered in 1900 by Nash county, and by part of Wilson county.
[12] Area covered in 1900 by Warren county, and by part of Vance county.
[13] Area covered in 1900 by Caswell and Person counties.
[14] Area covered in 1900 by Granville county, and by parts of Vance and Franklin counties.
[15] Area covered in 1900 by Orange and Alamance counties, and by part of Durham county.
[16] Area covered in 1900 by Wake county, and by part of Durham county.
[17] Area covered in 1900 by Burke, Madison, Yancey, and Mitchell counties, and by parts of McDowell, Haywood, Swain, Buncombe, Caldwell, Watauga, and Alexander counties.
[18] Area covered in 1900 by Lincoln, Gaston, and Catawba counties, and by part of Cleveland county.

IN 1790, COMPARED WITH THAT OF THE SAME AREA IN 1900, WITH PER CENT OF INCREASE—Continued.

NORTH CAROLINA.

MALES—continued.			FEMALES.									
Under 16 years.			All ages.			16 years and over.			Under 16 years.			
1790	1900	Per cent of increase.	1790	1900	Per cent of increase.	1790	1900	Per cent of increase.	1790	1900	Per cent of increase.	
77,653	275,566	254.87	141,356	631,448	346.71	69,067	366,471	430.60	72,289	264,977	266.55	1
8,653	11,813	36.52	16,510	27,777	68.24	8,067	16,314	102.23	8,443	11,463	35.77	2
1,802	1,830	1.55	3,442	4,277	24.26	1,682	2,559	52.14	1,760	1,718	²2.39	3
754	731	²3.05	1,475	1,593	8.00	721	931	29.13	754	662	²12.20	4
551	919	66.79	1,171	2,185	86.59	572	1,313	129.55	599	872	45.58	5
1,024	1,362	33.01	1,960	3,107	58.52	958	1,764	84.13	1,002	1,343	34.03	6
772	1,052	36.27	1,514	2,784	83.88	740	1,650	122.97	774	1,134	46.51	7
824	1,214	47.33	1,632	2,931	79.60	797	1,740	118.32	835	1,191	42.63	8
1,035	1,396	34.88	1,804	3,234	79.27	881	1,954	121.79	923	1,280	38.68	9
921	1,091	18.46	1,714	2,531	47.67	837	1,444	72.52	877	1,087	23.95	10
970	2,218	128.66	1,798	5,135	185.60	879	2,959	236.63	919	2,176	136.78	11
7,324	24,047	228.33	13,677	56,659	314.26	6,683	33,108	395.41	6,994	23,551	236.73	12
1,183	4,626	291.04	2,147	9,970	364.37	1,049	5,571	431.08	1,098	4,399	300.64	13
1,561	5,637	261.11	3,054	13,612	345.71	1,492	8,032	438.34	1,562	5,580	257.23	14
965	3,261	237.93	1,672	8,008	378.95	817	4,699	475.15	855	3,309	287.02	15
1,205	2,810	133.20	2,114	6,999	231.08	1,033	4,179	304.55	1,081	2,820	160.87	16
1,138	4,239	272.50	2,263	9,771	331.77	1,106	5,800	424.41	1,157	3,971	243.22	17
1,272	3,474	173.11	2,427	8,299	241.94	1,186	4,827	307.00	1,241	3,472	179.77	18
10,130	17,729	75.01	18,610	41,133	121.03	9,093	24,576	170.27	9,517	16,557	73.97	19
1,878	3,489	85.78	3,487	8,328	138.83	1,704	5,010	194.01	1,783	3,318	86.09	20
1,381	2,714	96.52	2,307	6,213	169.31	1,127	3,712	229.37	1,180	2,501	111.95	21
1,826	2,180	19.39	3,471	5,411	55.89	1,696	3,303	94.75	1,775	2,108	18.76	22
1,010	1,817	79.90	2,008	3,886	93.53	981	2,305	134.96	1,027	1,581	53.94	23
1,434	4,111	186.68	2,621	9,234	252.31	1,281	5,345	317.25	1,340	3,889	190.22	24
1,283	1,882	46.69	2,502	4,468	78.58	1,222	2,697	120.70	1,280	1,771	38.36	25
1,318	1,536	16.54	2,214	3,593	62.29	1,082	2,204	103.70	1,132	1,389	22.70	26
12,903	30,680	137.77	21,980	75,055	241.47	10,739	45,504	323.73	11,241	29,551	162.89	27
2,110	3,632	72.13	3,377	8,180	142.23	1,650	4,794	190.55	1,727	3,386	96.06	28
2,168	3,331	53.64	3,664	7,810	113.16	1,790	4,683	161.62	1,874	3,127	66.86	29
1,873	3,582	91.24	3,050	8,677	184.49	1,490	5,164	246.58	1,560	3,513	125.19	30
2,709	8,766	223.59	4,913	22,130	350.44	2,401	13,606	466.92	2,512	8,524	239.20	31
1,952	5,316	172.34	3,292	12,441	277.92	1,608	7,384	359.20	1,684	5,057	200.30	32
2,091	6,053	189.48	3,684	15,817	329.34	1,800	9,873	448.50	1,884	5,944	215.50	33
8,773	86,066	881.03	14,961	187,531	1,153.47	7,310	104,101	1,324.09	7,651	83,430	990.45	34
2,108	31,092	1,374.95	3,684	67,421	1,730.10	1,800	37,408	1,978.22	1,884	30,013	1,493.05	35
2,293	12,472	443.92	4,041	28,654	609.08	1,975	16,242	722.80	2,066	12,412	500.48	36
2,119	28,755	1,257.01	3,502	62,019	1,670.96	1,711	34,145	1,895.62	1,791	27,874	1,456.34	37
2,253	13,747	510.16	3,734	29,437	688.35	1,824	16,306	793.97	1,910	13,131	587.49	38
9,876	27,100	174.40	19,329	62,781	224.80	9,444	36,784	289.50	9,885	25,997	162.99	39
924	3,322	259.52	1,821	7,864	331.85	890	4,653	422.81	931	3,211	244.90	40
709	1,848	160.65	1,505	4,608	206.18	735	2,780	278.23	770	1,828	137.40	41
1,538	2,917	89.66	3,226	7,213	123.59	1,576	4,292	172.34	1,650	2,921	77.03	42
1,293	3,551	174.63	2,479	8,301	234.85	1,211	4,875	302.56	1,268	3,426	170.19	43
714	1,348	88.80	1,518	2,956	94.73	742	1,700	129.11	776	1,256	61.86	44
1,177	5,738	357.51	2,081	12,727	511.58	1,017	7,249	612.78	1,064	5,478	414.85	45
794	957	20.53	1,541	2,165	40.49	753	1,270	68.66	788	895	13.58	46
1,508	3,325	120.49	2,912	7,472	156.59	1,423	4,426	211.03	1,489	3,046	104.57	47
1,219	4,094	235.85	2,246	9,475	321.86	1,097	5,539	404.92	1,149	3,936	242.56	48
15,932	62,444	291.94	28,490	143,482	403.62	13,920	84,077	504.00	14,570	59,405	307.72	49
1,807	5,554	207.36	3,235	13,976	332.02	1,581	8,711	450.98	1,654	5,265	218.32	50
1,218	5,705	368.39	2,223	13,543	509.22	1,086	8,057	641.90	1,137	5,486	382.50	51
2,563	12,254	378.11	4,758	28,431	497.54	2,325	16,678	617.33	2,433	11,753	383.07	52
1,220	5,807	375.98	2,029	11,904	486.69	991	6,456	551.46	1,038	5,448	424.86	53
1,411	4,796	239.90	2,489	10,642	327.56	1,216	6,136	404.61	1,273	4,506	253.97	54
3,828	11,453	199.19	6,902	26,823	288.63	3,372	15,901	371.56	3,530	10,922	209.41	55
2,122	8,881	318.52	3,665	20,360	455.53	1,791	11,969	568.29	1,874	8,391	347.76	56
1,763	7,994	353.43	3,189	17,803	458.26	1,558	10,169	552.70	1,631	7,634	368.06	57
4,062	15,687	286.19	7,799	37,030	374.80	3,811	22,007	477.46	3,988	15,023	276.71	58
834	4,846	481.06	1,685	10,961	550.50	823	6,321	668.04	862	4,640	438.28	59
398	2,345	489.20	778	5,175	565.17	380	2,919	668.16	398	2,256	466.83	60
1,187	2,946	148.19	2,052	6,895	236.01	1,003	4,054	304.19	1,049	2,841	170.83	61
702	3,707	428.06	1,496	10,009	569.05	731	6,385	773.46	765	3,624	373.73	62
941	1,843	95.86	1,788	3,990	123.15	874	2,328	166.36	914	1,662	81.84	63

[19] Area covered in 1900 by Cherokee, Graham, Macon, Jackson, Transylvania, Henderson, Polk, Rutherford, and Clay counties, and by parts of Swain, Cleveland, Buncombe, Haywood, and McDowell counties.
[20] Area covered in 1900 by Ashe and Wilkes counties, and by parts of Alleghany, Watauga, Alexander, and Caldwell counties.
[21] Area covered in 1900 by Beaufort county, and by part of Pamlico county.
[22] Area covered in 1900 by part of Carteret county.
[23] Area covered in 1900 by Craven county, and by parts of Pamlico and Carteret counties.
[24] Area covered in 1900 by Lenoir and Greene counties.
[25] Area covered in 1900 by Hyde county, and by part of Dare county.
[26] Area covered in 1900 by Johnston county, and by part of Wilson county.
[27] Area covered in 1900 by Wayne county, and by part of Wilson county.
[28] Area covered in 1900 by Iredell county, and by part of Alexander county.
[29] Area covered in 1900 by Mecklenburg and Cabarrus counties, and by part of Union county.
[30] Area covered in 1900 by Montgomery and Stanly counties.
[31] Area covered in 1900 by Davie, Rowan, and Davidson counties, and by part of Forsyth county.
[32] Area covered in 1900 by Stokes county, and by part of Forsyth county.
[33] Area covered in 1900 by Yadkin and Surry counties, and by part of Alleghany county.
[34] Area covered in 1900 by Bladen county, and by parts of Cumberland and Columbus counties.
[35] Area covered in 1900 by Brunswick county, and by part of Columbus county.
[36] Area covered in 1900 by New Hanover and Pender counties, and by part of Sampson county.

TABLE **107.**—WHITE POPULATION, CLASSIFIED BY SEX AND AGE, OF EACH OF THE COUNTIES REPORTED

SOUTH CAROLINA.

| | COUNTY. | BOTH SEXES. | | | MALES. | | | | | |
| | | | | | All ages. | | | 16 years and over. | | |
		1790	1900	Per cent of increase.	1790	1900	Per cent of increase.	1790	1900	Per cent of increase.
1	The state..................	140,178	557,807	297.93	73,298	281,147	283.57	35,576	161,778	354.74
2	Beaufort district [1]............	4,364	11,585	165.47	2,321	6,018	159.28	1,266	3,596	184.04
3	Camden district [2]...........	29,242	96,707	230.71	15,635	48,564	210.61	6,941	28,469	310.16
4	Charleston district [3].........	15,402	50,266	226.36	8,237	24,901	202.31	5,060	15,489	206.11
5	Cheraw district [4]...........	7,418	41,990	466.06	3,772	21,072	458.64	1,779	12,058	577.80
6	Georgetown district [5]........	8,878	58,833	562.68	4,823	29,898	519.90	2,356	16,537	601.91
7	Ninety-six district [6].........	62,462	233,589	273.97	32,138	117,871	266.77	14,973	66,371	343.27
8	Orangeburgh district [7]........	12,412	64,837	422.37	6,372	32,823	415.11	3,201	19,258	501.62

GEORGIA.

	COUNTY.	1790	1900	Per cent of increase.	1790	1900	Per cent of increase.	1790	1900	Per cent of increase.
1	The state..................	52,886	297,007	461.60	27,147	149,721	451.52	13,103	87,122	564.90
2	Burke [8]......................	7,064	12,792	81.09	3,649	6,586	80.49	1,808	3,771	108.57
3	Camden [9]...................	221	5,933	2,584.60	125	3,103	2,382.40	81	1,668	1,959.26
4	Chatham [10]..................	2,456	31,414	1,179.07	1,326	15,981	1,105.20	846	10,910	1,189.60
5	Effingham [11].................	1,674	9,601	473.54	963	4,904	409.24	627	2,777	342.90
6	Franklin [12].................	885	76,394	8,532.09	468	38,010	8,021.79	225	21,048	9,254.67
7	Glyn [13].....................	193	9,118	4,624.35	106	4,751	4,382.08	70	2,833	3,947.14
8	Greene [14]...................	4,020	10,346	157.36	2,138	5,091	138.12	1,027	3,061	198.05
9	Liberty [15]..................	1,303	9,972	665.31	690	5,170	649.27	426	2,888	577.93
10	Richmond [16]................	7,162	27,981	290.69	3,819	13,556	254.96	1,894	8,904	370.12
11	Washington [17]..............	3,856	69,470	1,701.61	1,971	35,540	1,703.14	947	19,396	1,948.15
12	Wilks [18]...................	24,052	33,986	41.30	11,892	17,029	43.20	5,152	9,866	91.50

KENTUCKY.

	COUNTY.	1790	1900	Per cent of increase.	1790	1900	Per cent of increase.	1790	1900	Per cent of increase.
1	The state..................	61,133	1,862,309	2,946.32	32,211	948,048	2,843.24	15,154	565,705	3,633.04
2	Bourbon [19]	6,929	159,832	2,206.71	3,680	82,368	2,138.26	1,645	45,901	2,690.33
3	Fayette [20]	14,626	41,930	186.68	7,598	21,283	180.11	3,517	14,337	307.65
4	Jefferson [21]	3,857	243,250	6,206.72	2,098	120,984	5,666.63	1,057	80,827	7,546.83
5	Lincoln [22]	5,446	642,753	11,702.30	2,816	329,217	11,590.94	1,375	192,089	13,870.11
6	Madison [23]	5,035	73,882	1,367.37	2,652	37,820	1,326.09	1,231	20,087	1,531.76
7	Mason [24]	2,500	283,613	11,244.52	1,365	144,316	10,472.60	594	82,877	13,852.36
8	Mercer [25]	5,745	26,591	362.85	3,003	13,450	347.89	1,460	8,329	470.48
9	Nelson [26].................	10,032	237,517	2,267.59	5,303	121,167	2,184.88	2,508	71,472	2,749.76
10	Woodford [27]...............	6,963	152,941	2,096.48	3,696	77,443	1,995.32	1,767	49,786	2,717.54

[1] Area covered in 1900 by Beaufort and Hampton counties.
[2] Area covered in 1900 by Chester, Clarendon, Fairfield, Kershaw, Lancaster, Richland, Sumter, and York counties, and by part of Florence county.
[3] Area covered in 1900 by Charleston, Colleton, and Dorchester counties, and by part of Berkeley county.
[4] Area covered in 1900 by Chesterfield, Darlington, and Marlboro counties, and by part of Florence county.
[5] Area covered in 1900 by Georgetown, Horry, Marion, and Williamsburg counties, and by parts of Florence and Berkeley counties.
[6] Area covered in 1900 by Abbeville, Anderson, Cherokee, Edgefield, Greenville, Greenwood, Laurens, Newberry, Oconee, Pickens, Saluda, Spartanburg, and Union counties, and by part of Aiken county.
[7] Area covered in 1900 by Bamberg, Barnwell, Lexington, and Orangeburg counties, and by part of Aiken county.
[8] Area covered in 1900 by Burke county, and by parts of Jefferson and Screven counties.
[9] Area covered in 1900 by Camden and Charlton counties, and by part of Wayne county.
[10] Area covered in 1900 by Chatham county, and by part of Bryan county.
[11] Area covered in 1900 by Effingham county, and by part of Screven county.
[12] Area covered in 1900 by Franklin, Banks, Jackson, Hart, and Elbert counties, and by parts of Oconee, Clarke, and Madison counties.
[13] Area covered in 1900 by Glynn county, and by part of Wayne county.
[14] Area covered in 1900 by parts of Greene, Hancock, Oconee, Oglethorpe, Taliaferro, and Baldwin counties.
[15] Area covered in 1900 by Liberty and McIntosh counties, and by part of Tattnall county.
[16] Area covered in 1900 by Richmond county, and by part of Jefferson county.
[17] Area covered in 1900 by Washington, Bulloch, Emanuel, and Johnson counties, and by parts of Baldwin, Bryan, Hancock, Jefferson, Laurens, Montgomery, and Tattnall counties.

IN 1790, COMPARED WITH THAT OF THE SAME AREA IN 1900, WITH PER CENT OF INCREASE—Continued.

SOUTH CAROLINA.

MALES—continued.			FEMALES.									
Under 16 years.			All ages.			16 years and over.			Under 16 years.			
1790	1900	Per cent of increase.	1790	1900	Per cent of increase.	1790	1900	Per cent of increase.	1790	1900	Per cent of increase.	
37,722	119,369	216.44	66,880	276,660	313.67	31,440	162,973	418.36	35,440	113,687	220.79	1
1,055	2,422	129.57	2,043	5,567	172.49	960	3,270	240.63	1,083	2,297	112.10	2
8,694	20,095	131.14	13,607	48,143	253.81	6,397	28,882	351.49	7,210	19,261	167.14	3
3,177	9,412	196.25	7,165	25,365	254.01	3,368	16,293	383.76	3,797	9,072	138.93	4
1,993	9,014	352.28	3,646	20,918	473.72	1,714	12,342	620.07	1,932	8,576	343.89	5
2,467	13,361	441.59	4,055	28,935	613.56	1,906	16,324	756.45	2,149	12,611	486.83	6
17,165	51,500	200.03	30,324	115,718	281.61	14,256	66,821	368.75	16,068	48,897	204.29	7
3,171	13,565	327.78	6,040	32,014	430.03	2,839	19,041	570.69	3,201	12,973	305.28	8

GEORGIA.

MALES—continued.			FEMALES.									
14,044	62,599	345.73	25,739	147,286	472.23	11,711	86,277	636.72	14,028	61,009	334.91	1
1,841	2,815	52.91	3,415	6,206	81.79	1,554	3,560	129.09	1,861	2,646	42.18	2
44	1,435	3,161.36	96	2,830	2,847.92	44	1,505	3,320.45	52	1,325	2,448.08	3
480	5,071	956.46	1,130	15,433	1,265.75	514	10,277	1,899.42	616	5,156	737.01	4
336	2,127	533.04	711	4,697	560.62	323	2,650	717.90	388	2,047	428.94	5
243	16,962	6,880.25	417	38,384	9,104.80	190	21,691	11,316.32	227	16,693	7,253.74	6
36	1,918	5,227.78	87	4,367	4,919.54	39	2,537	6,242.50	48	1,830	3,793.62	7
1,111	2,030	82.72	1,882	5,255	179.22	856	3,228	277.10	1,026	2,027	97.56	8
264	2,282	764.39	613	4,802	683.36	279	2,579	824.37	334	2,223	565.57	9
1,925	4,652	141.66	3,343	14,425	331.50	1,521	9,736	540.11	1,822	4,689	157.35	10
1,024	16,144	1,476.56	1,885	33,930	1,700.00	858	18,414	2,046.15	1,027	15,516	1,410.81	11
6,740	7,163	6.28	12,160	16,957	39.45	5,533	10,100	82.54	6,627	6,857	3.47	12

KENTUCKY.

MALES—continued.			FEMALES.									
17,057	382,343	2,141.56	28,922	914,261	3,061.13	12,636	545,038	4,213.37	16,286	369,223	2,167.12	1
2,035	36,467	1,691.99	3,249	77,464	2,284.24	1,419	42,599	2,902.04	1,830	34,865	1,805.19	2
4,081	6,946	70.20	7,028	20,647	193.78	3,071	13,946	354.12	3,957	6,701	69.35	3
1,041	40,157	3,757.54	1,759	122,266	6,850.88	769	82,479	10,625.49	990	39,787	3,918.89	4
1,441	137,128	9,416.17	2,630	313,536	11,821.52	1,149	182,002	15,740.03	1,481	131,534	8,781.43	5
1,421	17,733	1,147.92	2,383	36,062	1,413.30	1,041	19,061	1,731.03	1,342	17,001	1,166.84	6
771	61,439	7,868.74	1,135	139,297	12,172.86	496	79,924	16,013.71	639	59,373	9,191.55	7
1,543	5,121	231.89	2,742	13,141	379.25	1,198	8,206	584.97	1,544	4,935	219.62	8
2,795	49,695	1,678.00	4,729	116,350	2,360.35	2,066	68,546	3,217.81	2,663	47,804	1,695.12	9
1,929	27,657	1,333.75	3,267	75,498	2,210.93	1,427	48,275	3,282.97	1,840	27,223	1,379.51	10

[18] Area covered in 1900 by Wilkes, Columbia, Glascock, Lincoln, McDuffie, and Warren counties, and by parts of Clarke, Greene, Madison, Oglethorpe, and Taliaferro counties.

[19] Area covered in 1900 by Bourbon, Montgomery, Bath, Letcher, Powell, Wolfe, Menifee, and Knott counties, and by parts of Clark, Harrison, Pendleton, Floyd, Nicholas, Estill, Harlan, Perry, Pike, Morgan, Breathitt, Magoffin, Lee, and Leslie counties.

[20] Area covered in 1900 by Fayette and Jessamine counties, and by part of Clark county.

[21] Area covered in 1900 by Shelby, Henry, Oldham, Trimble, and Jefferson counties, and by parts of Franklin, Bullitt, Spencer, Carroll, and Anderson counties.

[22] Area covered in 1900 by Lincoln, Logan, Pulaski, Christian, Warren, Cumberland, Muhlenberg, Barren, Knox, Wayne, Casey, Livingston, Hopkins, Caldwell, Union, Allen, Whitley, Simpson, Todd, Monroe, Trigg, Hickman, Calloway, Graves, McCracken, Laurel, Russell, Clinton, Crittenden, Marshall, Ballard, Fulton, Lyon, Metcalfe, Webster, and Carlisle counties, and by parts of Green, Garrard, Henderson, Adair, Clay, Rockcastle, Butler, Hart, Edmonson, Boyle, Taylor, McLean, and Bell counties.

[23] Area covered in 1900 by Madison, Owsley, and Jackson counties, and by parts of Garrard, Clay, Estill, Rockcastle, Perry, Breathitt, Lee, Leslie, Harlan, and Bell counties.

[24] Area covered in 1900 by Mason, Bracken, Fleming, Greenup, Lewis, Lawrence, Carter, Johnson, Rowan, Boyd, Elliott, Martin, Robertson, and Campbell counties, and by parts of Floyd, Nicholas, Pike, Morgan, Magoffin, Pendleton, and Harrison counties.

[25] Area covered in 1900 by Mercer county, and by parts of Franklin, Anderson, Garrard, and Boyle counties.

[26] Area covered in 1900 by Nelson, Washington, Hardin, Ohio, Breckinridge, Grayson, Daviess, Meade, Hancock, Marion, and Larue counties, and by parts of Green, Bullitt, Butler, Hart, Spencer, Edmonson, Anderson, McLean, Taylor, Adair, and Henderson counties.

[27] Area covered in 1900 by Woodford, Scott, Boone, Grant, Gallatin, Owen, and Kenton counties, and by parts of Harrison, Franklin, Carroll, and Pendleton counties.

A CENTURY OF POPULATION GROWTH.

TABLE **108.**—WHITE AND COLORED POPULATION OF THE AREA COVERED BY THE ENUMERATION

	STATE OR TERRITORY.	POPULATION IN 1790.					POPULATION IN 1820.				
		Total.	White.	Colored.			Total.	White.	Colored.		
				Total.	Free.[1]	Slave.			Total.	Free.	Slave.
1	United States......................	3,929,625	3,172,444	757,181	59,557	697,624	[2] 9,638,453	7,862,166	1,771,656	233,634	1,538,022
2	Area enumerated in 1790...................	3,929,625	3,172,444	757,181	59,557	697,624	[4] 8,293,869	6,733,497	1,556,591	214,873	1,341,718
3	New England...........................	1,009,206	992,384	16,822	13,059	3,763	1,660,071	1,638,652	20,927	20,782	145
4	Maine............................	96,643	96,107	536	536	....	298,335	297,340	929	929	....
5	New Hampshire...................	141,899	141,112	787	630	157	244,161	243,236	786	786	....
6	Vermont.........................	85,341	85,072	269	269	....	235,981	235,063	903	903	....
7	Massachusetts...................	378,556	373,187	5,369	5,369	....	523,287	516,419	6,740	6,740	....
8	Rhode Island....................	69,112	64,670	4,442	3,484	958	83,059	79,413	3,602	3,554	48
9	Connecticut.....................	237,655	232,236	5,419	2,771	2,648	275,248	267,181	7,967	7,870	97
10	Middle states.....................	1,017,087	954,003	63,084	17,874	45,210	2,772,594	2,662,529	107,264	84,899	22,365
11	New York........................	340,241	314,366	25,875	4,682	21,193	1,372,812	1,332,744	39,367	29,279	10,088
12	New Jersey......................	184,139	169,954	14,185	2,762	11,423	277,575	257,409	20,017	12,460	7,557
13	Pennsylvania....................	433,611	423,373	10,238	6,531	3,707	1,049,458	1,017,094	30,413	30,202	211
14	Delaware........................	59,096	46,310	12,786	3,899	8,887	72,749	55,282	17,467	12,958	4,509
15	Southern states...................	1,903,332	1,226,057	677,275	28,624	648,651	3,861,204	2,432,316	1,428,400	109,192	1,319,208
16	Maryland and District of Columbia...	319,728	208,649	111,079	8,043	103,036	[5] 440,389	282,837	157,552	43,778	113,774
17	Virginia and West Virginia...........	747,610	442,117	305,493	12,866	292,627	[5] 1,065,366	603,085	462,031	36,883	425,148
18	North Carolina..................	395,005	289,181	105,824	5,041	100,783	638,829	419,200	219,629	14,712	204,917
19	South Carolina..................	249,073	140,178	108,895	1,801	107,094	502,741	237,440	265,301	6,826	258,475
20	Georgia (eastern part)............	82,548	52,886	29,662	398	29,264	226,739	115,183	111,552	1,497	110,055
21	Kentucky........................	73,677	61,133	12,544	114	12,430	564,317	434,644	129,491	2,759	126,732
22	Tennessee.......................	35,691	31,913	3,778	361	3,417	422,823	339,927	82,844	2,737	80,107
23	Added to area of enumeration since 1790.....	....	....	....	....	....	[6] 1,344,584	1,128,669	215,065	18,761	196,304
24	Added to area of enumeration, 1790 to 1820.	....	....	....	....	....	[6] 1,344,584	1,128,669	215,065	18,761	196,304
25	Ohio............................	....	....	....	....	....	581,434	576,572	4,723	4,723	....
26	Indiana.........................	....	....	....	....	....	147,178	145,758	1,420	1,230	190
27	Illinois.........................	....	....	....	....	....	55,211	53,788	1,374	457	917
28	Michigan........................	....	....	....	....	....	7,452	7,295	26	26	....
29	Wisconsin.......................	....	....	....	....	....	1,444	1,296	148	148	....
30	Alabama.........................	....	....	....	....	....	127,901	85,451	42,450	571	41,879
31	Mississippi......................	....	....	....	....	....	75,448	42,176	33,272	458	32,814
32	Louisiana........................	....	....	....	....	....	153,407	73,383	79,540	10,476	69,064
33	Arkansas........................	....	....	....	....	....	14,273	12,579	1,676	59	1,617
34	Missouri........................	....	....	....	....	....	66,586	55,988	10,569	347	10,222
35	Georgia (western part)...........	....	....	....	....	....	114,250	74,383	39,867	266	39,601
36	Added to area of enumeration, 1820 to 1850.	....	....	....	....	....	....	....	....	....	....
37	Minnesota.......................										
38	Iowa............................										
39	Florida..........................										
40	Texas...........................										
41	New Mexico......................										
42	Arizona.........................										
43	Utah............................										
44	Washington......................										
45	Oregon..........................										
46	California.......................										
47	Added to area of enumeration, 1850 to 1880.										
48	North Dakota.................... South Dakota....................										
49	Nebraska........................										
50	Kansas..........................										
51	Montana.........................										
52	Idaho...........................										
53	Wyoming........................										
54	Colorado........................										
55	Nevada..........................										
56	Alaska..........................										
57	Added to area of enumeration since 1880.										
58	Indian Territory.................										
59	Oklahoma........................										
60	Hawaii..........................										
61	Persons stationed abroad.........										

[1] Reported as "all other free persons."
[2] Includes 4,631 persons reported as "all other persons except Indians not taxed."
[3] Includes only Indians taxed; no Federal enumeration in 1880 of Indians not taxed.
[4] Includes 3,781 persons reported as "all other persons except Indians not taxed."

OF 1790, AND OF THE ADDED AREA IN 1820, 1850, 1880, AND 1900, BY STATES AND TERRITORIES.

POPULATION IN 1850.					POPULATION IN 1880.					POPULATION IN 1900.					
		Colored.					Colored.					Colored.			
Total.	White.	Total.	Free.	Slave.	Total.	White.	Total.	Negro.	Indian and Mongolian.	Total.	White.	Total.	Negro.	Indian and Mongolian.	
23,191,876	19,553,068	3,638,808	434,495	3,204,313	50,189,209	43,403,400	6,785,809	6,580,793	³205,016	76,303,387	66,990,788	9,312,599	8,840,789	471,810	1
14,569,584	12,365,444	2,204,140	361,570	1,842,570	23,925,639	20,682,783	3,242,856	3,236,664	6,192	33,553,630	29,564,821	3,988,809	3,956,864	31,945	.2
2,728,116	2,705,095	23,021	23,021	....	4,010,529	3,968,789	41,740	39,925	1,815	5,592,017	5,527,026	64,991	59,099	5,892	3
583,169	581,813	1,356	1,356	....	648,936	646,852	2,084	1,451	633	694,466	692,226	2,240	1,319	921	4
317,976	317,456	520	520	....	346,991	346,229	762	685	77	411,588	410,791	797	662	135	5
314,120	313,402	718	718	....	332,286	331,218	1,068	1,057	11	343,641	342,771	870	826	44	6
994,514	985,450	9,064	9,064	....	1,783,085	1,763,782	19,303	18,697	606	2,805,346	2,769,764	35,582	31,974	3,608	7
147,545	143,875	3,670	3,670	....	276,531	269,939	6,592	6,488	104	428,556	419,050	9,506	9,092	414	8
370,792	363,099	7,693	7,693	....	622,700	610,769	11,931	11,547	384	908,420	892,424	15,996	15,226	770	9
5,990,267	5,843,163	147,104	144,578	2,526	10,643,486	10,425,215	218,271	215,934	2,337	15,639,413	15,264,839	374,574	356,618	17,956	10
3,097,394	3,048,325	49,069	49,069	....	5,082,871	5,016,022	66,849	65,104	1,745	7,268,894	7,156,881	112,013	99,232	12,781	11
489,555	465,509	24,046	23,810	236	1,131,116	1,092,017	39,099	38,853	246	1,883,669	1,812,317	71,352	69,844	1,508	12
2,311,786	2,258,160	53,626	53,626	....	4,282,891	4,197,016	85,875	85,535	340	6,302,115	6,141,664	160,451	156,845	3,606	13
91,532	71,169	20,363	18,073	2,290	146,608	120,160	26,448	26,442	6	184,735	153,977	30,758	30,697	61	14
5,851,201	3,817,186	2,034,015	193,971	1,840,044	9,271,624	6,288,779	2,982,845	2,980,805	2,040	12,322,200	8,772,956	3,549,244	3,541,147	8,097	15
634,721	455,884	178,837	84,782	94,055	1,112,567	842,699	269,868	269,826	42	1,466,762	1,143,956	322,806	321,766	1,040	16
1,421,661	894,800	526,861	54,333	472,528	2,131,022	1,473,395	657,627	657,502	125	2,812,984	2,108,088	704,896	704,221	675	17
869,039	553,028	316,011	27,463	288,548	1,399,750	867,242	532,508	531,277	1,231	1,893,810	1,263,603	630,207	624,469	5,738	18
668,507	274,563	393,944	8,960	384,984	995,577	391,105	604,472	604,332	140	1,340,316	557,807	782,509	782,321	188	19
272,151	120,662	151,489	2,000	149,489	441,659	198,328	243,331	243,266	65	640,538	297,007	343,531	343,421	110	20
982,405	761,413	220,992	10,011	210,981	1,648,690	1,377,179	271,511	271,451	60	2,147,174	1,862,309	284,865	284,706	159	21
1,002,717	756,836	245,881	6,422	239,459	1,542,359	1,138,831	403,528	403,151	377	2,020,616	1,540,186	480,430	480,243	187	22
8,622,292	7,187,624	1,434,668	72,925	1,361,743	26,263,570	22,720,617	3,542,953	3,344,129	198,824	42,749,757	37,425,967	5,323,790	4,883,925	439,865	23
7,945,146	6,610,891	1,334,255	70,009	1,264,246	18,612,142	15,841,519	2,770,623	2,755,230	15,393	26,741,195	22,855,727	3,885,468	3,863,065	22,403	24
1,980,329	1,955,050	25,279	25,279	....	3,198,062	3,117,920	80,142	79,900	242	4,157,545	4,060,204	97,341	96,901	440	25
988,416	977,154	11,262	11,262	....	1,978,301	1,938,798	39,503	39,228	275	2,516,462	2,458,502	57,960	57,505	455	26
851,470	846,034	5,436	5,436	....	3,077,871	3,031,151	46,720	46,368	352	4,821,550	4,734,873	86,677	85,078	1,599	27
397,654	395,071	2,583	2,583	....	1,636,937	1,614,560	22,377	15,100	7,277	2,420,982	2,398,563	22,419	15,816	6,603	28
305,391	304,756	635	635	....	1,315,497	1,309,618	5,879	2,702	3,177	2,069,042	2,057,911	11,131	2,542	8,589	29
771,623	426,514	345,109	2,265	342,844	1,262,505	662,185	600,320	600,103	217	1,828,697	1,001,152	827,545	827,307	238	30
606,526	295,718	310,808	930	309,878	1,131,597	479,398	652,199	650,291	1,908	1,551,270	641,200	910,070	907,630	2,440	31
517,762	255,491	262,271	17,462	244,809	939,946	454,954	484,992	483,655	1,337	1,381,625	729,612	652,013	650,804	1,209	32
209,897	162,189	47,708	608	47,100	802,525	591,531	210,994	210,666	328	1,311,564	944,580	366,984	366,856	128	33
682,044	592,004	90,040	2,618	87,422	2,168,380	2,022,826	145,554	145,350	204	3,106,665	2,944,843	161,822	161,234	588	34
634,034	400,910	233,124	931	232,193	1,100,521	618,578	481,943	481,867	76	1,575,793	884,287	691,506	691,392	114	35
677,146	576,733	100,413	2,916	97,497	5,685,176	5,015,085	670,091	539,386	130,705	10,572,181	9,518,893	1,053,288	887,898	165,390	36
6,077	6,038	39	39	....	780,773	776,884	3,889	1,564	2,325	1,751,394	1,737,036	14,358	4,959	9,399	37
192,214	191,881	333	333	....	1,624,615	1,614,600	10,015	9,516	499	2,231,853	2,218,667	13,186	12,693	493	38
87,445	47,203	40,242	932	39,310	269,493	142,605	126,888	126,690	198	528,542	297,333	231,209	230,730	479	39
212,592	154,034	58,558	397	58,161	1,591,749	1,197,237	394,512	393,384	1,128	3,048,710	2,426,669	622,041	620,722	1,319	40
61,381	61,359	22	22	....	119,565	108,721	10,844	1,015	9,829	195,310	180,207	15,103	1,610	13,493	41
166	166	....	....	....	40,440	35,160	5,280	155	5,125	122,931	92,903	30,028	1,848	28,180	42
⁷11,380	11,330	50	24	26	143,963	142,423	1,540	232	1,308	276,749	272,465	4,284	672	3,612	43
1,201	1,049	152	152	....	75,116	67,199	7,917	325	7,592	518,103	496,304	21,799	2,514	19,285	44
12,093	12,038	55	55	....	174,768	163,075	11,693	487	11,206	413,536	394,582	18,954	1,105	17,849	45
92,597	91,635	962	962	....	864,694	767,181	97,513	6,018	91,495	1,485,053	1,402,727	82,326	11,045	71,281	46
....	....	....	....	....	1,966,252	1,864,013	102,239	49,513	52,726	4,400,770	4,230,044	170,726	70,651	100,075	47
....	....	....	....	....	135,177	133,147	2,030	401	1,629	720,716	692,426	28,290	751	27,539	48
....	....	....	....	....	452,402	449,764	2,638	2,385	253	1,066,300	1,056,526	9,774	6,269	3,505	49
....	....	....	....	....	996,096	952,155	43,941	43,107	834	1,470,495	1,416,319	54,176	52,003	2,173	50
....	....	....	....	....	39,159	35,385	3,774	346	3,428	243,329	226,283	17,046	1,523	15,523	51
....	....	....	....	....	32,610	29,013	3,597	53	3,544	161,772	154,495	7,277	293	6,984	52
....	....	....	....	....	20,789	19,437	1,352	298	1,054	92,531	89,051	3,480	940	2,540	53
....	....	....	....	....	⁷194,327	191,126	3,201	2,435	766	539,700	529,046	10,654	8,570	2,084	54
....	....	....	....	....	⁷62,266	53,556	8,710	488	8,222	42,335	35,405	6,930	134	6,796	55
....	....	....	....	....	33,426	430	32,996	....	32,996	63,592	30,493	33,099	168	32,931	56
....	....	....	....	....	....	....	....	....	....	1,035,611	821,303	214,308	62,311	151,997	57
....	....	....	....	....	....	....	....	....	....	392,060	302,680	89,380	36,853	52,527	58
....	....	....	....	....	....	....	....	....	....	398,331	367,524	30,807	18,831	11,976	59
....	....	....	....	....	....	....	....	....	....	154,001	66,890	87,111	233	86,878	60
....	....	....	....	....	....	....	....	....	....	91,219	84,209	7,010	6,394	616	61

⁵ Alexandria county, which in 1820 formed part of the District of Columbia, is here included with Virginia for comparative purposes.
⁶ Includes 850 persons reported as "all other persons except Indians not taxed."
⁷ The figures for Utah territory in 1850 may include part of the area of the present states of Colorado and Nevada, but as the territory was not reported by minor civil divisions, the facts can not be ascertained.

TABLE 109.—FAMILIES, CLASSIFIED BY NUMBER OF MEMBERS, BY COUNTIES: 1790.

COUNTY.	Total number of families.	NUMBER OF MEMBERS.										
		1	2	3	4	5	6	7	8	9	10	11 or over.
United States	410,636	15,353	31,979	48,116	56,615	57,171	54,052	46,172	36,932	26,687	17,356	20,203
Maine	17,009	1,109	1,115	1,978	2,201	2,223	2,175	1,886	1,531	1,129	784	878
Cumberland	4,218	144	264	449	535	555	552	477	443	304	224	271
Hancock	1,794	194	116	234	204	253	196	186	143	119	68	81
Lincoln	5,324	541	329	584	671	614	649	569	449	370	252	296
Washington	563	112	27	67	62	62	79	41	31	37	21	24
York	5,110	118	379	644	729	739	699	613	465	299	219	206
New Hampshire	24,065	814	1,502	2,669	3,282	3,392	3,109	2,855	2,301	1,732	1,131	1,278
Cheshire	4,796	48	275	562	670	677	646	605	480	363	233	237
Grafton	2,463	270	163	265	330	319	274	275	199	145	101	122
Hillsborough	5,330	84	321	542	671	711	734	676	567	396	298	330
Rockingham	7,398	249	508	850	1,021	1,088	922	842	669	528	335	386
Strafford	4,078	163	235	450	590	597	533	457	386	300	164	203
Vermont	14,992	505	1,060	1,734	2,146	2,139	2,040	1,781	1,400	895	638	654
Addison	1,157	5	96	166	169	178	170	137	105	57	46	28
Bennington	1,997	32	137	209	247	279	266	246	191	146	120	124
Chittenden	1,380	104	95	176	199	204	185	131	136	63	43	44
Orange	1,889	57	147	225	281	273	248	223	170	108	68	89
Rutland	2,794	77	233	332	413	409	392	327	226	168	114	103
Windham	3,042	176	172	303	423	414	382	387	320	180	138	147
Windsor	2,733	54	180	323	414	382	397	330	252	173	109	119
Massachusetts	65,779	1,393	5,754	7,990	8,999	9,224	8,709	7,490	5,971	4,380	2,791	3,078
Barnstable	2,889	23	243	387	402	407	340	351	287	201	119	129
Berkshire	4,899	27	327	499	650	674	679	620	506	381	261	275
Bristol	5,541	78	447	720	773	797	804	640	493	318	210	261
Dukes	558	9	42	77	78	65	75	63	54	52	19	24
Essex	10,883	362	1,248	1,527	1,599	1,583	1,342	1,081	794	574	360	413
Hampshire	9,617	104	561	912	1,182	1,278	1,385	1,267	1,114	795	506	513
Middlesex	7,580	112	757	991	1,062	1,108	1,014	832	626	474	284	320
Nantucket	872	27	111	152	116	121	90	81	67	44	30	33
Plymouth	5,173	100	474	624	739	760	685	573	457	337	214	210
Suffolk	8,038	248	808	1,089	1,182	1,142	1,080	835	570	432	287	365
Worcester	9,729	303	736	1,012	1,216	1,289	1,215	1,147	1,003	772	501	535
Rhode Island	11,296	231	865	1,387	1,523	1,472	1,551	1,221	1,028	810	510	698
Bristol	567	18	64	80	67	74	79	62	44	47	13	19
Kent	1,387	11	71	164	185	189	176	164	128	106	80	113
Newport	2,448	69	251	313	364	307	335	226	201	151	92	139
Providence	4,016	63	294	488	540	532	544	441	363	314	192	245
Washington	2,878	70	185	342	367	370	417	328	292	192	133	182
Connecticut	40,876	1,082	3,268	4,670	5,706	5,790	5,663	4,711	3,748	2,654	1,688	1,896
Fairfield	6,412	116	543	783	998	992	910	733	553	372	202	210
Hartford	6,582	102	537	763	920	944	948	756	649	441	257	265
Litchfield	6,563	199	431	664	847	957	974	796	657	467	284	287
Middlesex	3,282	72	297	394	490	435	447	366	287	193	148	153
New Haven	6,012	444	640	807	855	849	738	643	440	286	174	136
New London	5,686	116	525	712	841	812	762	575	457	354	246	286
Tolland	2,139	18	127	221	278	291	314	283	215	155	112	125
Windham	4,200	15	168	326	477	510	570	559	490	386	265	434
New York	54,878	1,123	3,909	6,560	7,945	8,197	7,466	6,330	4,918	3,555	2,233	2,642
Albany	12,317	199	711	1,433	1,793	1,819	1,758	1,497	1,166	837	518	586
Clinton	374	67	42	50	54	54	41	25	19	9	7	6
Columbia	4,276	72	258	456	608	580	566	533	403	333	210	257
Dutchess	6,717	47	305	651	845	955	875	819	714	542	400	564
Kings	546	9	50	67	81	90	72	61	48	26	20	22
Montgomery	4,906	176	328	541	704	717	690	537	453	319	214	227
New York city and county	6,037	176	813	1,023	1,022	908	679	516	375	211	132	182
Ontario	204	5	35	28	34	20	21	17	17	11	9	7
Orange	2,890	25	151	319	391	450	425	374	264	217	129	145
Queens	2,548	143	181	301	369	395	368	301	211	123	71	85
Richmond	566	7	51	83	102	86	75	67	48	24	14	9
Suffolk	2,858	85	327	412	446	432	412	288	208	125	67	56
Ulster	4,354	47	214	427	607	716	602	536	426	354	214	211
Washington	2,488	40	192	303	356	418	345	291	219	146	85	93
Westchester	3,797	25	251	466	533	557	537	468	347	278	143	192
Pennsylvania	73,874	2,546	5,807	8,592	9,971	10,191	9,745	8,365	6,736	4,857	3,207	3,857
Allegheny	1,844	119	160	202	256	254	227	196	172	122	70	66
Bedford	2,232	53	135	282	305	334	272	250	214	156	116	115
Berks	5,244	79	493	636	685	750	702	635	453	351	223	237
Bucks	4,180	145	282	442	539	591	569	492	402	284	184	250
Chester	4,435	118	320	467	550	553	546	532	430	349	234	336
Cumberland	3,017	80	210	332	405	418	392	376	295	205	132	172
Dauphin	3,248	112	243	382	491	489	460	348	311	178	136	98
Delaware	1,724	167	134	201	239	231	200	171	123	85	81	92
Fayette	2,388	219	156	290	300	318	268	262	218	147	105	105
Franklin	2,528	59	198	260	315	355	332	301	234	189	121	164
Huntingdon	1,268	44	81	136	178	167	158	147	124	108	63	62
Lancaster	5,980	65	426	710	852	851	859	709	537	381	258	332
Luzerne	867	3	78	110	138	113	119	107	76	62	35	26

TABLE **109.**—FAMILIES, CLASSIFIED BY NUMBER OF MEMBERS, BY COUNTIES: 1790—Continued.

COUNTY.	Total number of families.	NUMBER OF MEMBERS.										
		1	2	3	4	5	6	7	8	9	10	11 or over.
Pennsylvania—Continued.												
Mifflin	1,259	41	78	134	166	142	182	166	134	105	60	51
Montgomery	3,803	143	268	378	465	480	567	458	378	276	170	220
Northampton	4,091	40	344	522	567	573	537	449	390	255	195	219
Northumberland	2,946	127	217	324	382	383	378	335	323	215	133	129
Philadelphia	9,504	429	927	1,333	1,343	1,317	1,162	904	659	491	320	619
Washington	3,944	44	206	405	554	616	582	482	396	303	170	186
Westmoreland	2,813	83	246	346	389	367	372	311	277	194	130	98
York	6,559	376	605	700	852	889	861	734	590	401	271	280
Maryland	33,294	1,687	2,696	3,890	4,619	4,588	4,204	3,640	2,827	1,952	1,326	1,865
Allegany [1]												
Ann-Arundel	2,122	116	176	260	305	274	232	226	154	100	58	221
Baltimore	3,497	105	253	394	501	442	464	388	309	253	154	234
Baltimore town and precincts	1,727	50	182	251	288	259	184	162	109	72	51	119
Calvert [1]												
Caroline	1,352	61	108	158	214	219	174	122	121	75	50	50
Cecil	1,906	188	157	232	239	228	244	196	144	104	80	94
Charles	2,029	216	182	236	263	252	244	207	172	109	61	87
Dorchester	654	43	60	93	90	109	82	66	45	28	15	23
Frederick	4,377	118	302	419	543	582	557	513	439	322	246	336
Harford	2,039	127	167	258	279	256	229	244	179	113	80	107
Kent	1,299	69	132	160	184	191	165	137	83	65	42	71
Montgomery	2,077	102	197	245	272	264	259	222	156	131	109	120
Prince Georges	1,820	82	153	230	265	246	232	186	162	120	66	78
Queen Anns	1,579	100	122	175	211	239	221	179	136	86	57	53
St. Marys	1,527	54	115	206	225	218	204	179	128	86	63	49
Somersett [1]												
Talbot	1,425	55	117	151	213	232	188	173	114	75	46	61
Washington	2,445	149	201	274	277	342	280	273	253	145	122	129
Worcester	1,419	52	72	148	250	235	245	167	123	68	26	33
North Carolina	48,701	3,519	3,754	5,483	6,482	6,491	6,083	5,162	4,326	3,134	2,038	2,229
Edenton district	6,829	762	561	840	963	982	843	634	503	327	217	197
Fayette district	5,403	529	451	612	725	680	626	577	463	334	193	213
Halifax district	7,033	630	507	749	831	933	897	748	647	438	306	347
Hillsborough district	3,721	212	252	359	432	465	441	431	395	295	206	233
Morgan district	5,120	117	373	598	677	667	644	555	492	412	269	316
Newbern district	7,596	634	652	946	1,108	1,031	965	774	605	396	225	260
Salisbury district	9,977	472	681	1,003	1,285	1,270	1,275	1,154	992	776	521	548
Wilmington district	3,022	163	277	376	461	463	392	289	229	156	101	115
South Carolina	25,872	1,344	2,249	3,163	3,741	3,464	3,307	2,731	2,146	1,589	1,010	1,128
Beaufort district	962	107	113	135	153	137	111	79	43	40	24	20
Camden district	5,074	177	338	527	701	669	768	620	489	339	211	235
Charleston district	3,709	509	562	583	609	428	346	245	172	102	61	92
Cheraw district	1,344	45	110	159	207	184	183	142	107	86	66	55
Georgetown district	1,837	135	191	243	288	278	217	188	118	91	46	42
Ninety-six district	10,578	283	739	1,198	1,427	1,423	1,357	1,198	1,022	807	519	605
Orangeburgh district	2,368	88	196	318	356	345	325	259	195	124	83	79

[1] Schedules destroyed.

TABLE 110.—FOREIGN BORN POPULATION OF CONTINENTAL UNITED STATES, AND OF THE AREA COVERED BY THE ENUMERATION OF 1790, BY COUNTRY OF BIRTH: 1850 TO 1900.

COUNTRY OF BIRTH.	CONTINENTAL UNITED STATES.						AREA COVERED BY THE ENUMERATION OF 1790.					
	1900	1890[1]	1880	1870	1860	1850	1900	1890[1]	1880	1870	1860	1850
All foreign countries....	[2]10,356,644	9,249,547	6,679,943	5,567,229	[3]4,138,697	[3]2,244,602	5,022,989	4,153,155	3,055,088	2,765,197	[3]2,264,121	[3]1,466,806
North America.............	1,314,152	1,083,239	802,664	547,770	285,022	166,941	672,492	505,999	356,521	261,235	137,487	104,092
Canada {English[4]........	785,958	678,442	717,157	493,464	249,970	147,711	352,510	267,021	348,117	254,727	132,866	100,338
Canada {French[4]........	395,297	302,496					305,963	229,662				
Mexico and Central America......	107,311	79,045	69,106	42,736	27,699	13,458	3,040	1,325	812	505	394	359
Cuba and West Indies[5]..	25,586	23,256	16,401	11,570	7,353	5,772	10,979	7,991	7,592	6,003	4,227	3,395
Europe.................	8,884,846	8,020,608	5,744,311	4,936,618	3,805,701	[6]2,031,867	4,310,037	3,623,023	2,686,125	2,495,974	2,120,729	[6]1,333,156
United Kingdom.........	2,788,304	3,122,911	2,772,169	2,626,241	2,199,079	1,340,812	1,799,596	1,961,182	1,742,284	1,707,038	1,491,960	1,024,214
Ireland...............	1,618,567	1,871,509	1,854,571	1,855,827	1,611,304	961,719	1,162,931	1,307,005	1,278,184	1,300,187	1,171,279	779,547
England (including Great Britain, not specified)..........	842,078	909,092	664,160	555,046	433,494	278,675	458,537	472,695	334,760	292,139	234,759	179,079
Scotland.............	233,977	242,231	170,136	140,835	108,518	70,550	127,989	127,670	87,237	74,345	61,515	47,767
Wales...............	93,682	100,079	83,302	74,533	45,763	29,868	50,139	53,812	42,103	40,367	24,407	17,821
German Empire[7]........	2,670,031	2,787,776	1,979,578	1,696,335	1,276,075	583,774	987,160	1,016,013	730,020	664,128	540,208	270,433
Scandinavian countries...	1,064,309	933,249	440,262	241,685	72,582	18,075	180,409	122,165	41,601	16,712	6,616	2,956
Sweden...............	573,040	478,041	194,337	97,332	18,625	3,559	135,719	89,540	30,106	11,134	3,357	1,427
Norway...............	336,985	322,665	181,729	114,246	43,995	12,678	22,472	16,726	4,095	1,836	1,011	586
Denmark.............	154,284	132,543	64,196	30,107	9,962	1,838	22,218	15,899	7,400	3,742	2,248	943
Austria-Hungary.........	579,042	303,812	135,550	74,534	25,061	946	309,910	125,147	29,970	12,762	4,569	354
Austria...............	276,249	123,271	38,663	30,508	[8]25,061	[8]946	175,588	64,131	11,415	7,329	4,569	354
Bohemia.............	156,991	118,106	85,361	40,289			25,411	14,028	12,075	4,088	(8)	(8)
Hungary.............	145,802	62,435	11,526	3,737			108,911	46,988	6,480	1,345	....	....
Italy.................	484,207	182,580	[9]44,535	[9]17,212	[10]11,677	[10]3,679	362,768	124,602	[9]25,116	[9]6,896	[10]4,608	[10]1,823
Russia (including Finland).............	486,907	182,644	35,722	4,644	3,160	1,414	309,270	99,527	7,953	2,315	1,598	973
Poland {Russian.........	154,424	147,440	48,557	14,436	7,298	(11)	39,288	59,497	18,967	6,230	3,359	(11)
Poland {German.........	150,232						39,492					
Poland {Austrian.......	58,503						114,001					
Poland {Not specified.....	20,351						10,855					
Switzerland............	115,851	104,069	88,621	75,153	53,327	13,358	34,910	28,807	25,582	19,993	14,389	3,938
Netherlands............	105,049	81,828	58,090	46,802	28,281	9,848	22,264	18,240	15,534	12,001	8,651	4,014
France................	104,341	113,174	106,971	116,402	109,870	54,069	45,710	44,701	40,066	41,763	39,325	21,834
Spain and Portugal.......	37,690	22,181	13,426	8,383	8,360	4,387	19,968	7,488	4,484	3,096	3,392	1,818
Portugal..............	30,618	15,996	8,138	4,542	4,116	1,274	17,337	4,804	[12]2,208	1,493	1,990	861
Spain................	7,072	6,185	[12]5,288	[12]3,841	4,244	3,113	2,631	2,684	[12]2,276	[12]1,603	1,402	957
Belgium...............	29,804	22,639	15,535	12,553	9,072	1,313	8,617	6,093	2,693	1,966	1,416	712
Turkey...............	9,933	1,839	1,205	302	128	106	6,932	1,183	526	197	92	47
Greece...............	8,564	1,887	776	390	328	86	4,892	747	251	147	111	40
Europe, not specified.....	17,304	12,579	3,314	1,546	1,403	(13)	13,995	7,631	1,078	730	435	(13)
Asia.................	120,862	113,383	107,630	64,565	36,796	1,135	24,700	9,965	3,473	1,258	725	261
China................	81,827	106,688	104,468	63,042	35,565	758	15,546	7,303	2,078	419	175	57
Japan................	25,077	2,292	401	73	1,231	377	683	437	145	34	....	....
India................	2,050	2,143	1,707	586			937	1,040	992	354	....	....
Asia, not specified........	11,908	2,260	1,054	864			7,534	1,185	258	451	550	204
Oceania.................	8,900	9,353	6,859	4,028	2,140	588	2,397	2,425	1,739	861	437	196
Sandwich Islands (Hawaii)................	....	1,304	1,147	584	435	588	....	202	397	135	199	196
All other[14]...............	8,900	8,049	5,712	3,444	1,705	(13)	2,397	2,223	1,342	726	238	(13)
South America..........	4,761	5,006	4,566	3,565	3,263	1,543	2,274	2,123	1,764	1,081	798	545
Africa.................	2,552	2,207	2,204	2,657	526	551	1,306	1,024	818	1,007	315	311
All other countries, and unknown..................	12,342	10,218	7,641	5,388	[15]5,249	[15]41,977	6,919	6,767	3,027	2,796	[15]3,630	[15]28,245
Born at sea..................	8,229	5,533	4,068	2,638	....	....	2,864	1,829	1,621	985	....	....

[1] Exclusive of Indian Territory and Indian reservations.
[2] Including (15,368) persons stationed abroad, in the military or naval service of the United States.
[3] Corrected total, as given in Ninth Census Report on Population, Table IV.
[4] Includes Newfoundland.
[5] Porto Rico included from 1850 to 1890.
[6] Total for specified countries only.
[7] Luxemburg included from 1870 to 1900, because probably reported as a German state in 1850 and 1860.
[8] Reported as Austria; but Hungary did not have a separate government until 1867, and Bohemia not until later.
[9] Including Malta, which was reported separately in 1870 and 1880.
[10] Including Sardinia, which was reported separately in 1850 and 1860.
[11] Not reported separately; either divided between Russia, Germany, and Austria, or included in "all other countries."
[12] Including Gibraltar, which was reported separately in 1870 and 1880.
[13] Included in "all other countries."
[14] Philippine Islands, Guam, and Samoa included from 1860 to 1890.
[15] Balance required to produce corrected totals given in Ninth Census Report on Population, Table IV.

TABLE **111.**—NOMENCLATURE, DEALING WITH NAMES REPRESENTED BY AT LEAST 100 WHITE PERSONS, BY STATES AND TERRITORIES, AT THE FIRST CENSUS: 1790.

NAME.	Average size of family.	TOTAL. Heads of families.	TOTAL. All other members.	HEADS OF FAMILIES. Maine.	New Hampshire.	Vermont.	Massachusetts.	Rhode Island.	Connecticut.	New York.	Pennsylvania.	Maryland.	Virginia.	North Carolina.	South Carolina.
Aaron, Ahron, Aran, Aron, Arons	5.3	19	82					1		6			3	5	4
Abbe, Abba, Abbay, Abbee, Abbey, Abby, Aby	6.2	59	308		2	5	8		35	5	2		2		
Abbot, Abbert, Abbet, Abbett, Abbit, Abbitt, Abbott, Abet, Abit, Abitts, Abot, Abott	5.7	380	1,799	53	86	15	106	4	39	22	13	6	13	11	12
Abell, Abbell, Abeal, Abeel, Abel, Abels, Able	5.3	99	425		3	5	7		30	12	14	15	8	1	4
Abernathy, Abanatha, Abbinatha, Abenatha, Abennathy, Abernatha, Abernathey, Abernethie, Abinathy, Ebenathy	6.1	38	195			1	1		3		1		3	24	5
Abrams, Abraham, Abrahams, Abraim, Abramse	5.4	75	331	1	1		10		1	35	17	2	1	3	4
Acker, Acre, Acres, Aiker, Aker, Akers, Akus	5.9	65	319	2	1		4			24	22	2	9		1
Ackerman, Ackman, Acreman, Akemon, Akerman, Akkerman	5.8	42	201		9		2			21	5	2		2	1
Ackerson, Acason, Ackuson, Akerson	5.3	24	103							21	2		1		
Ackley, Acerly, Acheley, Acherly, Achley, Ackerly, Ackly, Acley, Akeley, Akely	5.9	87	426	1		6	5		35	33	5			1	1
Adair, Adear	6.7	19	108							2	2	3		1	11
Adams, Adam, Adames, Addam, Addams, Adems, Adom	5.6	1,246	5,712	51	89	57	325	5	127	96	138	70	96	111	81
Addison, Adderson, Addisson, Aderson, Adison, Atterson, Attison	5.1	28	116		3				1	1	3	7	2	3	8
Agnew, Agner, Aighner, Aigner	6.0	24	119							2	16	2			4
Ainsworth, Ainesworth, Anesworth, Answorth, Aynesworth, Aynsworth	5.7	35	163		2	10	7		8	1	2	1		1	3
Akin, Aiken, Aikens, Aikin, Aikins, Aking, Akins	5.3	132	568		17	13	20		7	23	6	3	16	13	14
Albaugh, Ailabaugh, Alabagh, Albo, Albough, Alebough, Allebough, Allibough, Alsbaugh, Alsbauh, Aulabaugh	5.6	22	102								6	16			
Albe, Albee, Albey, Albie, Albree, Alby, Allbee	5.4	42	186	5	5	4	23		1	2	2				
Albert, Alberd, Alburt, Alleburt, Allebut	5.6	40	185				1	2	1	3	20	3	7	2	1
Albertson, Alberson	5.3	51	221				2	3	1	18	7			18	2
Albright, Albrijht, Albrite, Allbright, Allbrite, Allright, Alpright	4.5	58	201							2	30	4	1	21	
Albro, Alboro, Alborrow, Alsbro	6.0	28	139			2		22		4					
Alcock, Alcocke, Alicock, Allcock, Allscock	5.0	34	136				1		8	1	2	7	4	7	
Alden, Aldin, Allden	6.0	81	405	5	6	3	53		8	2	2	2			
Alderman	5.8	23	110				1		15	2	1			4	
Aldrich, Alderidge, Aldridch, Aldridg, Aldridge, Aldrige, Aldrish, Aledridge, Alridge, Altridge, Auldridge	5.7	231	1,092	2	38	13	57	57	5	17	2	9	1	21	9
Alexander, Alexandor, Alexandry, Alixander, Alixandrew, Alleckzander, Allexander, Eleckandrew, Elexander, Elixander	5.8	408	1,966	14	24	12	26	6	5	10	86	31	33	118	43
Alford, Allford	6.3	50	266	1			2		12	1	3	7	9	14	1
Alger, Algier, Algire, Alguiar, Alguire, Algur, Aulgur	6.1	59	300			5	16	4	6	15	1	3	9		
Allard, Alhurd, Allod, Allord	6.6	16	90	1	10	1			4						
Allen, Alan, Alean, Alen, Alent, Alin, Allan, Alland, Allein, Allien, Allin, Alline, Allins, Allon, Allyn, Allyne	5.7	1,563	7,331	88	49	77	402	83	184	173	95	69	134	166	43
Alley, Ally	4.8	48	184	7	2		21		2	2	3	4	1	5	1
Alling, Aalin	5.3	47	200						45	2					
Allis, Alice, Alies, Allice	6.0	33	165	1			28		1	1	1				1
Allison, Aleson, Alisen, Alison, Allason, Alleson, Alleston, Allisen, Allisson, Alliston	5.5	175	787		4					24	66	18	10	32	21
Allman, Aldman, Allmand, Allmond, Alman, Almon, Almond	5.2	40	168							1	8	2	16	11	2
Almey, Almy	6.6	29	161				9	17		3					
Alred, Aldred, Allred	6.5	17	94				1							15	1
Alsobrook, Allbrooks, Allsobrook, Alsbrook	5.9	18	89										1	16	1
Alsop, Alsup	5.7	18	85						2	7	1		6	1	1
Alston, Allston, Allstone	5.0	33	133							1	1	2		19	10
Alvord, Alvard, Alverd	6.1	41	208		1	7	21		11					1	
Aman, Amandt, Amend, Ament, Ammon, Ammond, Ammonds, Ammons, Amond, Amons, Arman, Armant, Arment, Armon, Armond, Armount	6.0	46	229			1				2	21	1	5	11	5
Amason, Amazeen, Amerson, Ameson, Amoson	4.8	27	103	5	8					1				11	2
Ambler, Ambly	5.2	28	117			3	1		10	8	4		2		
Ambrose, Ambros, Ambrous, Ambrow, Ambrus, Ambruse	4.8	28	107		6	1		1		3	5	2	10		
Ames, Aames, Aims	5.6	156	722	20	30	18	51		16	19	1			1	
Ammidown, Amadown, Amedown, Amesdown, Amidown, Ammedoun, Ammedown, Ammidon, Ammidoun	5.9	29	141		2	2	20		5						
Amos, Amas, Amies, Amis, Amoss, Amus, Amyst	6.5	45	248				20		2	2	4		5	10	2
Amsbury, Almsbury, Amesbury, Amsberry, Armberry, Armsberry, Armsbury	5.3	19	82		3	2	6	2		6					
Amsden, Armden	5.7	21	98			4	2		14	1					
Anders, Andes, Andis	5.6	20	91							2	3	5	1	8	1
Anderson, Andersen, Andersons, Andresen, Andrson	5.5	726	3,262	24	23	10	32	4	25	61	157	68	137	89	96
Andrews, Andre, Andrees, Andrew, Andrw, Andrws	5.6	593	2,711	33	23	15	107	34	104	64	69	25	37	65	17
Andrus, Andras, Andres, Andress, Andries, Andris, Andros, Androse, Andross, Andruss	5.3	147	631	8		23	14		80	6	6			5	5
Angel, Angell, Angill, Angle	5.9	106	516		4	5	2	50	5	6	2	10	11	10	1
Annis, Annas, Annes, Annies, Anors	5.8	31	150	9	9	6	2		1		1				2
Anthony, Anthoney, Antoney, Antony	5.5	129	576			1	20	32		22	20	5	4	18	7
Appleby, Abbleby, Apleby, Appelbe, Appelby, Applebe, Applebee, Appyby	5.4	36	157	5	6		1	3		12	3	3	3		
Appleton	6.3	36	189	4	4		23								5
Archer, Archur	5.5	106	481	1	4	2	14	1	7	25	11	1	25	9	6
Archibald, Archabald, Archabeld, Archbald, Archbill, Archbold, Archebd, Archebald	5.8	29	139	1	3		4			2	9	1		7	2
Armer, Armor, Armour	5.3	24	102		2		1		4	1	11		3		2
Armistead, Almsted, Armestead, Armisted, Armstad, Armstead	5.5	37	166							1	1	2	26	7	
Armitage, Armetig, Armetrage, Armitge, Armittage, Armontage, Armontiage	6.2	18	93				1			1	14	2			
Arms, Armes	6.8	30	175	3	1	1	18			1	2		6		1
Armstrong	5.4	311	1,367	3	1	14	6	8	21	51	91	33	22	38	23
Arnold, Arnal, Arnald, Arnauld, Arnel, Arnell, Arnild, Arnol, Arnolds, Arnull	5.9	483	2,381	4	3	12	36	166	43	44	51	34	27	38	25
Arnout, Arnat, Arnatt, Arnaught, Arnet, Arnett, Arnot, Arnott	4.7	25	92							7	2	2		9	5
Arrington, Arington, Arranton	5.5	41	186									8	11	20	2
Arthur, Arther, Arthers, Arthurs, Aurthers, Auther, Authur	5.1	52	214				3		1	6	19	3	2	13	5
Ash, Ashe	5.5	65	294	5	6	1	4	1	2	7	17	7	7	5	3
Ashby, Ashbee	6.4	33	177				4			2	3		20	2	2
Ashcraft, Ashcroft	7.1	17	103							4	7	1	2	1	2
Ashley, Ashly	6.1	115	584	1	6	14	41	1	7	9	2	9	2	13	10
Ashton	5.3	53	227				12	2	1	6	29	1	1		1
Askew, Askue, Askyou, Asque	5.3	44	190								3	4	8	25	4
Askins, Asken, Askens, Askin, Askrin	5.5	37	167	10			1			7	7	4	2	4	2
Aspinwall, Arspinwell, Aspanell, Aspenvall, Aspenwall, Aspenwell, Aspenwill, Aspinwell	6.3	18	95	1	1	2	5		4	4	1				
Astin, Asten, Astins, Aston, Astons	5.8	36	174	3	3	4			5	8	2		5	3	3
Atchison, Acheson, Achison, Aitchason, Aitcheson, Atchason, Atcherson, Atcheson, Atchinson, Aychinson	6.0	36	180		1	1	2		2	1	10	6	11		2
Atherton, Atherten, Autherton	6.1	51	259	1	6	2	26		3	1	7		4	1	
Atkerson, Adkerson, Adketson, Atcason, Atkertson, Atkeson, Atkison	5.5	26	118				2			4	3	8	5		4
Atkins, Adkin, Adkins, Aitken, Aitkens, Aitkin, Atkens, Atkin, Attkins	5.6	225	1,036	7	10	2	41	1	30	11	10	12	49	33	19
Atkinson, Adkinson, Aitkinson, Atkenson	5.0	142	569	8	9		11		1	6	21	13	22	39	16
Attwater, Atwater	5.4	74	322			1	4		61	6	1			1	

TABLE 111.—NOMENCLATURE, DEALING WITH NAMES REPRESENTED BY AT LEAST 100 WHITE PERSONS, BY STATES AND TERRITORIES, AT THE FIRST CENSUS: 1790—Continued.

NAME.	Average size of family.	TOTAL. Heads of families.	TOTAL. All other members.	Maine.	New Hampshire.	Vermont.	Massachusetts.	Rhode Island.	Connecticut.	New York.	Pennsylvania.	Maryland.	Virginia.	North Carolina.	South Carolina.
Atwell, Attwell, Atwall, Atwill	5.0	37	149		3		4	1	12	4	2	7	2	2	
Atwood, Adwood, Attwood	5.4	201	877	5	27	12	94	11	26	9		3	11	2	1
Auger, Arger, Argo, Argrue, Augar, Augur	4.5	30	104			1	4		19	1	2			2	1
Auld, Ahl, All, Alld, Alles, Alls, Allse, Allt, Alt, Altz, Aules, Ault, Awl, Awld, Awll	5.3	54	230	2	6		1			5	25	11		2	2
Austin, Austen, Austine, Austins, Auston, Awstin, Orston	5.8	370	1,792	12	26	21	63	43	65	56	9	18	21	23	13
Averill, Averal, Averall, Averel, Averell, Averhill, Averil, Averile, Avrill	6.4	53	287	11	10	12	7	1	4	8					
Averitt, Averat, Averatt, Averet, Averett, Averit, Averite, Avert, Avret	5.2	22	92						3		1		3	15	
Avery, Avera, Avory	5.8	260	1,248	12	24	14	36		109	34		1	6	23	1
Ayers, Aers, Aeyre, Aire, Aires, Airs, Ayer, Ayere, Ayr, Ayres, Ayrs, Eyers, Eyre, Eyres, Eyrs	5.5	250	1,117	16	47	14	59	3	20	22	25	11	9	16	8
Aylsworth, Ailworth, Aylesworth	6.5	27	149			13	2	9		3					
Babb, Bab, Babbs, Babs	5.6	53	245	11	13		3		1		7	2	5	6	5
Babbett, Babbet, Babbit, Babbitt, Babet, Babitt	5.3	49	210		3	6	30		7	1	2				
Babcock, Babcok, Babecock	6.0	196	976		5	7	41	76	16	51					
Bachman, Backman	6.5	19	104							3	16				
Backus, Bacchus, Baccus, Bachus, Backeus, Backhause, Backhouse, Backhus, Backis, Backuss, Barkus, Beckas, Beckus, Boccus	6.2	63	328	9	1	1	8		33	14	3		3		
Bacon, Bacom, Bacorn, Bakon, Bakoon	5.6	235	1,093	9	6	12	114	6	49	13	7	5	11	1	2
Badcock	6.2	63	326	5	1	5	7		39	4	1	1			
Badger, Badgor, Badjo	5.7	74	349		17	7	17	1	17	5	4	2			4
Bagg, Bag, Bagge, Baggs, Bags	6.3	37	195				19	2		1	8	3		2	2
Bagget, Baggett, Baggot, Baggott	5.6	20	91									1	1	15	3
Bagley, Baggesly, Bagly, Bagsley, Begley	5.5	76	344	4	13	4	20	2	2	9	2	1	5	13	1
Bailer, Bailor, Baler, Balers, Bayler, Baylor	5.4	21	93						1	2	13	1	1	1	2
Bailey, Baeley, Bailie, Baily, Baley, Baly, Bayley, Bayly, Beyly	5.9	881	4,225	39	65	49	145	29	86	93	92	46	111	90	36
Bails, Baighel, Bail, Bale, Bales, Bayel, Beyhal	5.8	53	255	1	2	1	1		4	3	23	2	5	8	3
Bain, Baen, Baens, Bagn, Baign, Baine, Baines, Bains, Bane, Banes, Bayan, Bayhan, Bayne, Baynes	5.3	72	310				2			9	17	14	16	11	3
Baird, Bayard, Bayerd, Biard, Byard, Byart, Byord	5.6	70	324	1						7	30	7	10	11	4
Baker	5.9	1,157	5,641	39	40	45	257	43	68	168	146	96	86	131	38
Balch	6.3	46	242	2	7	5	24	1	5			1		1	
Balcom, Balcam, Balcomb, Balcome, Balkum, Bolcem, Bolcom	5.5	41	186	1		3	25	2	6	3			1		
Balding, Ballding, Baulding	6.3	27	143			6	2		2	8		2	1	4	2
Baldwin, Balden, Baldin, Baldon, Baldwine, Baldwing, Balwin, Bauldin, Bauldwin, Bauldwine, Bawlden, Bawldin, Boldwin	5.9	446	2,177		20	28	58		187	59	32	12	22	24	4
Ball, Bal, Baul	5.8	303	1,467	3	17	20	65	6	17	25	30	30	55	20	15
Ballard, Ballerd, Ballord	5.5	168	764	5	11	6	40	7	2	13		3	26	43	12
Ballentine, Balantine, Balentine, Balintine, Ballandine, Ballantine, Ballindine	4.7	35	131	1			2	1		1	2	1	17	8	2
Ballou, Ballew, Baloo, Belew, Bellew, Bellue, Belue, Bilew, Billew, Billyou, Bolue, Bulloo	6.0	80	402		13		6	35		2	4	1	9	4	6
Bancroft, Bancraft	6.7	59	339	1	7	1	40		10						
Bangs, Bang, Bange, Banges	5.5	45	201	8		1	30		2	2			2		
Banister, Bannester, Bannister	6.8	30	174			5	14	1	1	1		3	1	1	3
Banker, Bancker, Baneker, Bankard, Bankart	6.0	27	136				2			20		5			
Banks, Bancke, Banckes, Bancks, Bank, Bankes, Benckes, Benkes	5.3	142	608	13	4		3		43	11	4	6	18	27	13
Barber, Barbar, Barbour	5.9	336	1,638	6	7	23	37	43	85	40	17	18	12	40	8
Bard, Beord	6.2	38	198				3		8	4	21	2			
Barden, Bardeen, Bardin, Bardine, Barding, Bardon	5.2	38	161		4		16	2	4	3	1		1	6	1
Bardwell, Boardwell, Bodwell, Bordwell	7.0	43	260	1	3		34		1	3					
Barfield, Barefield, Bearfield, Bierfield	6.4	38	207							1	2		2	24	9
Barham, Barrom, Berham, Borham	6.7	16	91							1		1	9	5	
Barker	5.6	418	1,921	28	38	12	107	28	34	55	16	15	36	37	12
Barkley, Barckley, Barclay, Barcley, Barcly, Barkelay, Barklay, Berckley, Berkeley, Berkley, Berkly, Burkley	6.0	76	382		1		1		1	18	23	9	10	8	5
Barksdale, Backsdale, Barkdoll, Barkesdale, Barksdill	4.6	29	104							1		1	15	3	10
Barlow, Barler	6.0	113	561		1	10	22		16	11	5	2	30	13	3
Barnard, Barnerd, Barnerds, Barnhard, Barnhart, Barnheart, Barnird, Bearnhart, Bernard, Bernerd, Bernhard, Bernhart, Bernherd, Bhenard, Bonord, Burnard	5.8	251	1,195	4	18	12	85		22	33	36	13	7	18	3
Barnes, Barn, Barne, Barns	5.7	700	3,258	10	19	27	95	12	136	72	69	81	42	116	21
Barnett, Barnet, Barnit, Barnits, Barnitt, Barnot, Barnutt, Bornet	5.3	207	888		4	9			13	42	29	21	60	29	
Barney, Baney, Barny, Boney, Bonney, Bonny, Bony	5.7	153	726	6	12	13	50	5	10	10	7	10	23	6	1
Barnhill, Barnald, Barnell, Barnhil, Barnihill	5.0	24	95		1		1		1	1		4		12	5
Barnum, Barnam, Barnham, Barnon	6.0	83	419	1		14	2		53	13					
Barr, Bahs, Bar, Barre, Barrs, Bars	5.7	111	524	1	2	5	12		1	7	48	2	10	19	4
Barrack, Barhick, Barick, Barrick, Barwick, Berwick	5.4	45	199	1					1	4	2	24	5	4	4
Barrell, Barhyel, Barral, Barrel, Barrels, Barrolls, Byrel	6.1	21	104	1		1	11		1	2		2	1	1	1
Barrett, Barett, Barott, Barrat, Barret, Barretts, Barrit, Barritt, Barrot, Barrott, Berret, Berrit	5.6	269	1,236	7	32	17	67		26	36	20	11	22	22	9
Barron, Baron, Barons, Barren, Barrons	5.4	69	303		11	5	14		4	4	9	6	2	4	10
Barrows, Barrer, Barrow	5.9	138	674	10	2	7	38	1	26	7	1	6		37	3
Barry, Barrey, Bary, Bearey	5.4	48	212	7	2	1	7		1	4	8	7	3	6	2
Barstow	5.5	21	94				19		1		1				
Bartholomew, Bartelmey, Bartholemew, Bartholemy, Bartholmew, Bartholumew, Bathlmey, Battleme	5.9	95	464			6			46	12	27	1		3	
Bartle, Bartall, Bartel, Bartell	5.4	25	111				2			11	6	1	4		1
Bartlett, Bartlet, Bartletts, Bartlit, Bartlot	5.7	422	1,981	46	72	27	175	14	38	23	4	7	4	8	4
Bartley, Bartly	5.5	24	107							1	10	2	3	7	1
Barton, Barten, Bartin, Bartine, Borton	5.8	190	908	10	2	10	34	16	6	46	16	14	5	12	19
Bartow, Barto, Bertow, Burtow	5.5	21	94			5			1	9	12	3			
Bartram, Bartrom, Bartron, Bartrum	6.4	19	102							9		10			
Bascom, Bascomb, Bascum	6.8	20	115		4	1	11		3	1					
Basford, Bashford	7.3	15	95		6					4	1	2		2	
Bass, Basse	5.3	149	636	2	3		30		18	2	2		28	53	9
Bassett, Basett, Basset, Bassitt, Bassot, Besset	5.8	196	940	2	5	10	80	1	64	12	4	3	11	3	1
Batchelder, Bachelder, Bacheldor, Bacheler, Bacheller, Bachellor, Bachelor, Bachlor, Baechellor, Batchador, Batchedor, Batcheldon, Batcheldor, Batcheller, Batchellor, Batchelor, Batchler, Batchoder	5.8														
Bateman, Batemen, Batesman, Batman, Battman	5.6	236	1,075	16	99	8	81	1	2	2	2	4	5	13	4
Bates, Baits, Bate, Baytes, Beates, Beats	5.9	72	350			4	6		2	2	5	17	7	28	1
Batten, Baton, Baton, Battan, Battin, Batton	5.7	384	1,703	16	4	36	136	22	55	36	20	1	19	22	17
Battle, Battels, Battles	5.8	49	233	2	3	1	25			1		1		16	
Batts, Bats, Batt, Batte, Batz	5.9	28	138				2			4	5	9	8		
Baugh, Beaugh, Bough, Bow, Bowe, Bowes, Bows	5.8	59	285		2	2	5		6	1	13	1	23	1	5
Baum, Bawham, Bawm	6.8	25	144				2		5		17	1	1	5	
Baxter, Backsster, Backster, Barkster, Baxto, Baxtor, Beckster, Beckstor, Bexter	5.4	151	668	1	2	5	43	1	16	26	20	10	3	15	9
Bay, Bayes, Bays, Bey	6.1	18	92						1	1	4	4	5	2	1

TABLE 111.—NOMENCLATURE, DEALING WITH NAMES REPRESENTED BY AT LEAST 100 WHITE PERSONS, BY STATES AND TERRITORIES, AT THE FIRST CENSUS: 1790—Continued.

NAME.	Average size of family.	TOTAL. Heads of families.	TOTAL. All other members.	Maine.	New Hampshire.	Vermont.	Massachusetts.	Rhode Island.	Connecticut.	New York.	Pennsylvania.	Maryland.	Virginia.	North Carolina.	South Carolina.
Baylis, Bailes Bailess, Bailies, Bailis, Baleas, Balis, Bayles, Bayless, Baylies, Bayliss	5.7	39	183				6	1		7	5	4	10	5	1
Beach, Beche, Beech	5.7	176	832			15	11		96	30	9	1	8	5	1
Beacham, Beachum Beachump, Becham, Beechem, Beechum	5.2	30	126		1		1				1	4	11	10	2
Beaker, Beeker	5.4	26	115				1				22		3		
Beall, Beal, Beale Beales, Beals, Beel, Beele Beels, Biehle, Biell	5.5	286	1,296	21	6	6	92	1		8	18	88	22	21	3
Beam, Beams, Beem, Beems, Beham, Behm	5.8	58	281							4	35	3	9	3	4
Beamer, Beemar, Beemer, Behmer, Bemmer, Beymer	5.2	25	104						2	2	11	9	1		
Bean, Beane, Beanes, Beans, Been, Beene, Behn, Bene, Bien	5.8	244	1,163	41	77	2	7			3	53	33	10	14	4
Bear, Baehr, Baer, Bahre, Baier, Bair, Bairs, Bare, Bayer, Bayers, Beahr, Beair, Beare, Bears	5.7	188	878		1	3	3		14	7	129	19	5	3	4
Beard, Beards	5.9	177	868	1	5	2	33		11	8	33	25	8	26	25
Beardslee, Bardsley, Beadsley, Beardley, Beardly, Beardsley, Beardsly, Bearsley, Beerdslee	5.7	112	531			5			94	13					
Bearse, Bearce, Bierce, Birse, Burse	6.1	40	202	3	2		25		7		3				
Beasley, Beasly, Beassly, Beazeley, Beazley, Beazly, Beesely, Beesley, Beesly, Beezley, Besley, Bezley, Bisely, Bisley	5.1	93	381							7	8	5	24	37	12
Beason, Beasom, Beesom	5.5	19	86				4							14	1
Beaty, Baety, Baettey, Baitey, Baity, Batey, Battey, Batty, Baty, Beatey, Beatie, Beatte, Beattey, Beatty	6.0	145	723	1	2		2	12		22	62	11	3	19	11
Beaver, Beaverd, Beavers, Beavert, Beavor, Beavours, Beever, Bevar, Bever, Bevers, Bevier, Biever	5.8	85	408							25	20	8	13	16	3
Beavin, Beavan, Beavans, Beaven, Beavens, Beavins, Beevans, Bevan, Bevans, Beven, Bevens, Bevin, Bevins, Bevvins, Bivans, Biven, Bivins	5.3	72	307		1	4			6	5	9	32	5	9	1
Bechtel, Bachtel, Bechtell, Bechtle, Bechtold, Becktill, Becktle, Bishtel	6.6	35	196								32	3			
Beck, Becht, Becks	5.4	118	522	1	15		3		1	3	37	22	6	22	8
Becker, Bacher, Backer, Becher, Beckers, Beker	5.9	110	543	4	3		5			63	27	7			1
Beckett, Becket, Beckit	6.2	20	103		1	1	7		1	2	2	2	2		2
Beckham, Beckum, Bickham	6.7	26	148								6	1	6	7	6
Beckwith, Backwith, Beckworth	5.6	117	538		11	1	2	1	72	11	1	10	4	4	
Beebe, Beba, Bebbe, Bebbee, Bebe, Bebee, Beeba, Beebee, Beeby, Beyby	5.3	166	721		2	14	15	2	94	34	2	1	1		
Beecher, Beacher, Beacherd	5.4	63	276						57	2	2	2			
Beedle, Badelle, Beadle, Beadles, Beatle, Bedale, Beddle, Bedel, Bedell, Bedle, Beedel, Beedles, Beetel, Beetle, Betle, Bettle	6.2	111	573	5	6	2	6		3	49	10	16	12	2	
Beekman, Beckman	5.5	38	172		1					34	1				2
Beeler, Bealer, Bealor, Behler, Beiler, Beleh, Beler, Belor, Bieler, Bieller, Bielor	5.7	21	98						1	1	12	2	2		3
Beeman, Beaman, Beamen, Beamon, Beamons, Behman, Beman, Bemon	6.2	71	370	7	1	7	9		9	5	5		6	14	
Beers, Beeher, Beer, Beere, Beher, Beir, Bere	5.0	91	363			1	4	1	69	6	8	2			
Belcher, Belsches, Belshas, Belshaw, Belsher, Belshower	5.8	77	369	1	1		33	1	12	5	4		15	1	4
Belding, Belden, Beldin, Beldon, Bellding	5.7	108	512	1	10	13	22		53	9					
Belknap, Bellknapp, Belnap	5.9	63	309		9	8	19	2	9	16					
Bell	5.6	540	2,489	1	19	9	28	1	17	64	96	27	76	148	54
Bellamy, Ballemy, Bellemu, Bellemy, Bellomy	5.0	22	87	1		2	1		6		2		5	1	4
Bellinger, Balanger, Balinger, Ballanger, Ballenger, Ballingeer, Ballinger, Beellinger, Belenjer, Belinger, Bellenger	5.3	64	272							23	3	1	15	8	14
Bellows, Bello, Bellough, Bellow, Below, Billow, Billows	6.6	50	281		8	5	16	3	7	5	4	1		1	
Belt, Belts, Beltz	5.9	39	191			1					6	30		1	1
Bement, Bamont, Beamont, Beaumond, Beemont, Bemont, Bemount, Beumount	5.5	34	153				11	1	21	1					
Bemis, Beamas, Beamis, Beamos, Beamus, Beemis, Beemus, Bemas, Bemes, Bemus	5.9	74	342	1	5	13	48		2	3				1	1
Bender	5.1	46	188	1			2			2	37	1		2	1
Benedict, Benadicts, Benedicks, Benedit, Benidick, Bennedick, Bennedict	5.4	197	864			10	6		113	60	8				
Benham, Bennams, Bennem, Bennham, Bennom, Benom	5.7	40	188			2			30	6			2		
Benjamin, Bengaman, Benjamins	5.5	102	461			5	17	4	27	40	7	1			1
Benner, Bena, Benard, Benear, Bener, Benna, Bennar, Bennerd, Benners, Benno, Bennor, Benor	6.0	64	318	7			4			7	38	5	1	1	1
Bennett, Bannet, Bannett, Benat, Benet, Benett, Benit, Bennatt, Bennett, Bennit, Bonnitt, Benntt, Binnitt	5.7	713	3,329	22	35	36	79	41	103	143	77	33	48	64	32
Benson, Bensen, Benston, Benzun	6.1	167	849	9	8	7	40	2	7	32	3	22	3	20	14
Bent	5.9	32	157		2		25	1		1		2		1	
Bentley, Bently	5.5	132	600	1		7	7	18	5	39	13	8	18	15	1
Benton, Benten, Bentin	5.7	136	638	1	3	10	12		45	9	1	9		37	9
Berger, Berga, Bergher, Burger, Burgers, Burgher, Burgur	5.7	100	467				4		1	39	37	2	11	5	1
Berringer, Baringer, Barriger, Barringer, Bearinger, Beringar, Beringer, Berriger, Birringer	6.3	32	170							10	12	3		6	1
Berry, Berrey, Bery, Berys, Burray, Burry, Bury	5.7	372	1,747	46	39	2	48	4	9	32	33	40	44	36	39
Berryman, Beeryman, Beriman, Berriman	5.1	20	82							1	3	8	8		
Berthol, Bertolph, Bullolph, Bulluph, Butolph, Buttolph	5.8	19	91			1			4	13	1				
Bessey, Bessa, Besse, Bessee, Bessy	5.8	27	129	6		2	14		2	3					
Best	4.9	62	241							9	7	1	12	30	3
Bester, Besto, Bestor, Bestow	7.3	14	88	5	1	1			7						
Betts, Bets, Bettz, Betz	5.3	126	548				5		47	32	24	2	11	4	1
Betty, Bettee, Bettes, Bettey, Betteys, Bettis, Bettys	6.3	36	191	1	3	2	5		5	6	2	1	4		6
Beverly, Beaverley, Beaverly, Bevely, Beverley, Bevilley, Bevilly	4.6	25	90	2	2		1	4		3	1	2	3	3	4
Bibb	6.8	15	87								1		13		1
Bicker, Beger, Begir, Bicher, Bickers, Biger, Bigers, Biggar, Biggars, Bigger, Biggers	5.7	39	184	1		1				6	14	2	9	3	3
Bickford, Beckford	5.1	89	367	20	49	1	16	1		1	1				
Bicknall, Bechnal, Bechnall, Becknal, Becknall, Becknell, Bicknal, Bicknel, Bicknell	6.1	34	175	3	1	2	14	5	4		1		4		
Bidleman, Bedelman, Beidelman, Beideman, Beitenman, Beyderman, Bidelman, Bideman, Bydleman	6.6	19	106							1	18				
Bidwell, Bidwel, Birdwell	6.3	54	285			1	2		43	6	1		1		
Bierly, Beyerly, Bierley, Birely, Byerley, Byerly, Byorly, Byrely	6.2	25	130								11	8	2	4	
Bigelow, Bigalow, Biggalow, Biggelow, Biggilow, Biglow	5.7	144	680	3	9	26	68		26	9	1		2		
Biggs, Big, Bigge, Bigs	5.3	49	209	1			1		2	8	5	10	6	15	1
Bigham, Bigam, Biggam, Bigem, Biggem, Bighams	6.0	31	155							2	15		1	11	2
Bigsby, Bigbea, Bigbie, Bigsbee, Bigsbey, Bigsbie	5.3	36	153	2	5	3	9		12	3					2
Biles, Bial, Bile	5.5	19	85	1						3	7		4	3	1
Bill, Bills	5.8	63	302		5	8	5		33	2	3		4	3	
Billings, Billing, Billins	5.7	178	833	17	4	14	76	5	30	13	5	1	4	8	1
Billups, Billips, Billop, Billops	5.3	22	94							1			11	1	1
Bingham, Bingam	5.8	97	463		17	12	9		34	6	11	1	4	2	1
Bird, Burd, Byrd	5.8	190	910	2	1	1	36	1	10	10	16	6	29	52	26
Birdsall, Birdsell	6.2	47	246							47					
Bisbee, Besbee, Bisbe, Bisbey, Bisbie, Bisbuy, Bisby, Bysbe	6.0	40	200	8		5	26			1					
Bishop, Byshop	5.9	394	1,746	11	7	19	44	14	106	59	28	24	26	24	32
Bissell, Bisel, Bissel, Bissills, Bizzel, Bizzell, Bysel	5.7	93	440			6	8	9	52	4	6			8	
Bixby, Bixbe, Bixbee, Bixsbey, Bixsby	5.5	39	174		9	14	15			1					
Black	5.4	306	1,342	20	3	8	25	2	1	13	97	16	26	57	38
Blackburn, Blackbern, Blackborn, Blackburne	5.7	66	313	1			2				20	5	11	18	9
Blackman, Blackmon, Blakeman	5.5	127	575	2		9	29	2	43	9	4			16	13

Table 111.—NOMENCLATURE, DEALING WITH NAMES REPRESENTED BY AT LEAST 100 WHITE PERSONS, BY STATES AND TERRITORIES, AT THE FIRST CENSUS: 1790—Continued.

NAME.	Average size of family.	TOTAL. Heads of families.	TOTAL. All other members.	Maine.	New Hampshire.	Vermont.	Massachusetts.	Rhode Island.	Connecticut.	New York.	Pennsylvania.	Maryland.	Virginia.	North Carolina.	South Carolina.
Blackmore, Blackamoor, Blackamore, Blackmar, Blackmare, Blackmer, Blackmor, Blacmore, Blakemore, Blakmore	5.5	45	201	1		5	19	4	4	5	3		3	1	
Blackston, Blackistone, Blackstone, Blackstons, Blakston, Blaxton, Blockstone	6.2	29	150	4					4		4	13		4	
Blackwell, Blacwell, Blacwill	6.8	48	278	4			7			4	2		2	14	15
Blades, Blade	6.1	24	122							1	17	5		1	
Blain, Blaine, Blane, Blean	7.4	24	154		1					4	12		6		1
Blair, Blaer, Blaher, Blaire, Blare, Blayer, Blear, Bleher, Bliar	5.8	160	765	5	4	5	35	1		11	47	8	12	13	19
Blake, Blak, Blakes, Bleake, Bleaks	5.5	273	1,227	35	68	7	74	1	9	12	9	10	18	16	14
Blakely, Blachley, Blackally, Blackley, Blackly, Blakelee, Blakeley, Blakley, Blakly, Bleakley, Bleakly	5.0	96	385			8	3		43	10	6	2	5	4	15
Blakesley, Blackesley, Blackslea, Blackslee, Blacksly, Blakesly	5.4	26	115			3	1		19	3					
Blanchard, Blancherd, Blanchord, Blanshard, Blenchard	6.1	206	1,041	16	32	30	77	8	7	13	5			14	4
Bland, Blan, Blann	5.2	36	150						1	2	1	2	11	14	5
Blankinship, Blackenship, Blankenship	6.1	35	178				6						26	2	1
Blanks, Blank	4.2	27	86							8	5		9	3	2
Blanton, Blantn	6.0	21	104										8	11	2
Blasdel, Blaisdel, Blaisdell, Blaizdell, Blasdal, Blasdale, Blasdell, Blasdle, Blazdel, Blazedell	5.4	84	373	28	37	2	5			1		11			
Blauvelt	5.1	57	232							57					
Bledsoe, Bledso	5.3	30	129										12	16	2
Bleeker, Blecher, Blecker, Bleecker	5.6	18	82							16	2				
Blevin, Bleven, Blevins, Bliven, Blivin	5.8	18	87					16	1				1		
Blin, Blinn, Blyn	5.6	34	155	4	1	3	2	1	15	8					
Bliss, Blis	5.9	185	915		11	24	95	8	33	11	2	1			
Blodget, Bladget, Blodgett, Bloget	5.6	106	491	4	31	19	31		13	7	1				
Blood, Blaad	5.6	105	480			32	7	65		1					
Bloom, Bloome, Blum	5.1	30	122							13	14	1		2	
Bloomer, Blumer	5.4	25	110						1	21	2			1	
Blossom, Blosom, Blosson	5.1	25	102	3		5	16			1					
Blount, Blunt	5.7	99	466	5	10	3	2		3	4	3	8	9	46	6
Blowers, Blewer, Bloore, Blorer, Bloyer	5.8	18	87			7				6	1	1			3
Bly, Bley, Blies, Bligh, Blye	5.7	21	99	1	4		2		2	4	3		5		
Blythe, Blith, Blithe, Blyth	5.0	24	97				1		1		6	2	1	4	9
Boardman, Boardsman, Boordman, Bordeman, Bordman	5.7	107	505	1	6	11	42		34	8	2		1	2	
Boarman, Booman, Boorman, Boreman, Borman	4.6	41	146	1	4	1	1			3	8	22	1		
Bobbit, Bobart, Bobbet, Bobbett, Bobbitt	5.0	25	100				1		3			1	3	16	1
Bochford, Botchford	6.3	18	96						18						
Bodine	6.9	17	100							6	5			6	
Bogardus, Bogardas	5.9	37	181							37					
Bogert, Bogard, Bogart, Boggard	5.3	71	308							56	10		5		
Boggs, Bogg, Bogges, Boggess, Bogs, Bogse	5.5	60	270	5						6	23	1	16	3	6
Bohannon, Bohanan, Bohannan, Bohonon, Buhanan, Buhannan	6.4	33	179	1	6					5	3	4	3	7	4
Boles, Boales, Boals, Bohall, Bole, Boll, Bolles, Bolts, Bols, Bowl, Bowles, Bowls	5.7	119	564	1	11		18	1	29	7	14	7	14	12	5
Bolinger, Belongee, Bolingar, Bollinger, Belongee, Bolongee, Bullenger, Bullinger	6.4	16	86							2	8			5	1
Bolling, Bohlen, Bolan, Boland, Bolen, Bolien, Bolin, Boling, Bolleyn, Bowlan, Bowland, Bowlen, Bowlin, Bowline, Bowling	5.5	89	398	4		2	2			7	10	10	27	15	12
Bolt, Bolts, Boltz, Boult	4.9	25	98				1		3	9	5	1	4		2
Bolton, Bolten, Boltin	5.8	70	333	8		1	17	1	2	9	5	5	6	10	6
Bond, Bonde, Bonds	5.9	223	1,099	4	13	9	44	1	3	16	19	47	20	34	13
Bone, Bohn, Bones	5.7	26	122							2	9	1	3	5	6
Bonner, Bona, Bonar, Boner, Bonnars, Bonneau, Bonnor, Bowner	5.5	68	309		1	1	5			1	19	7	6	15	13
Bonsall, Bonsal, Bonsel, Bonsil, Bonsill, Bonsle	4.6	22	80							2	17		1	1	1
Booker, Bewker, Boocher, Bucher, Buchers, Bucker, Buker	5.2	113	479	26		1	7				16	8	45	5	5
Boon, Boone, Boons	6.3	124	655				1	4	1	2	24	40	1	41	10
Boose, Boos, Booz, Booze, Bose	5.5	22	98							4	14	3		1	
Booth, Boothe, Booths	5.5	207	929		8	1	18		71	19	10	20	30	20	10
Boothby, Boothy	5.9	17	84	16										1	
Borden, Boarden, Bordin, Bordine, Bording, Bordon, Bourdin	5.6	54	251			3	7	21	4	5	2	1	8	3	
Borum, Boorham, Boram, Boran, Boren, Borin, Borram	6.1	28	144							1	1	3	15	3	5
Bosley, Bossley, Bozley	8.7	13	100							1	12				
Boss	5.2	26	110					16		3	2		4	1	
Boston, Bosston, Bostone	5.8	41	197	15			2		1	3	5	6	8	1	
Bostwick, Bawstick, Bosteck, Bostic, Bostick, Boswick	4.9	106	417			13	3		31	24	1	7	9	7	11
Boswell, Bosswell, Bosweell, Boswel, Boswells, Boswill, Bozwell, Buzwell, Buzwill	5.2	73	309	1	3		2			2	1	21	27	16	
Bosworth, Bozworth	5.9	79	390	3	3	1	39	15	9	8			1		
Botsford	5.9	18	89				1			13	2		1	1	
Bottom, Bottoms, Bottum	4.6	28	101			5			9			9	2	3	
Botts, Bote, Bots, Bott	7.5	25	163				3		1	1	6	3	10	1	
Boughton, Bowten, Bowton	5.4	46	201				7		10	26		3			
Bourn, Bourne, Bourns	5.9	62	305	4	1		44	4	3	1			4		1
Bousman, Bausman, Boasman, Boazman, Bodzman, Borseman, Boseman, Bosiman, Bosman, Bosserman, Bozman	5.6	32	148	1						2	7	5	6	7	4
Bouton, Booten, Boutain, Bouten, Boutton, Butin	5.5	30	136				2		13	12		3			
Bovee, Boovey, Boovy, Bouve, Bouvy, Bovey, Bovie	6.4	19	103				3			12		3		1	
Bowden, Bouden, Bowdin, Bowdoin, Bowdon, Bowdown	5.3	73	312	17			24			1	5	6	4	15	1
Bowen, Boan, Boen, Bohan, Boin, Bowan, Bowin, Bowins	5.7	278	1,316	6	9	6	63	51	12	6	33	29	22	26	15
Bowers, Bauer, Baugher, Bauher, Bouer, Boughar, Bougher, Bowa, Bowar, Bowars, Bower	5.6	281	1,302	2	7	1	44	3	9	19	125	32	14	18	7
Bowie, Bouie, Boy, Buie, Buoy, Buye	6.0	49	246							4	3	22		18	2
Bowker, Bauker, Bawker, Bouker	5.5	33	148		3	5	20			3	1		1		
Bowman, Baughman, Bauhman, Bauman, Bawman, Beauman, Boaman, Boeghman, Boghman, Bohman, Boman, Boughman, Bouman	5.9	284	1,402	9	1	9	28	1	3	19	108	19	52	16	19
Bowne, Bown, Bowns	6.2	21	109				1		1	17	2				
Bowtell, Boutell, Boutels, Boutle, Bowdle	6.5	30	164		13	2	6	1				8			
Box	5.0	22	89				1	1		1	1		2		15
Boyce, Boice, Boies, Bois, Boyes, Boys, Boyse	5.8	156	746	2	15	8	31	2		40	24	4	5	21	4
Boyd, Boid, Boyde, Boyds	5.8	309	1,498	9	14	1	14	3	3	29	102	29	25	41	39
Boyden, Boiden, Boydin, Boyton	5.4	52	228	1	1	13	35	1	1						
Boyer, Bawyer, Bawyers, Bowyer, Boyers, Buoyar	5.6	132	602							2	95	24	5	3	3
Boykin, Boyakin, Boyekin, Boyking	5.9	25	122											21	4
Boyle, Boil, Boiles, Boils, Boyl, Boyles, Boyls	5.1	68	276			2	6		1	2	34	11		10	2
Boynton, Boyanton, Boyenton, Boyinton, Boyonton	6.4	95	510	19	29	7	39							1	
Boyt, Boyte	5.2	31	129										6	20	5
Brackenridge, Brackenridg, Brackenrig, Brakenidge, Brakenridge, Brakeridge, Brakinredge, Breckenredge, Breckinridge, Brickinridge	5.9	27	132			4	8				12		1		2
Bracket, Brachet, Brackett, Braket	5.4	124	548	39	17	4	25		23	5			9	2	

TABLE **111.**—NOMENCLATURE, DEALING WITH NAMES REPRESENTED BY AT LEAST 100 WHITE PERSONS, BY STATES AND TERRITORIES, AT THE FIRST CENSUS: 1790—Continued.

NAME.	Average size of family.	TOTAL.		HEADS OF FAMILIES.											
		Heads of families.	All other members.	Maine.	New Hampshire.	Vermont.	Massachusetts.	Rhode Island.	Connecticut.	New York.	Pennsylvania.	Maryland.	Virginia.	North Carolina.	South Carolina.
Bradbury, Bradberry, Bradbery, Bradsberrey, Broadberry	6.1	67	343	37	6		8			1	5		1	8	1
Bradford	5.5	191	861	16	19	4	51	8	22	7	14	10	4	21	15
Bradish	5.3	20	86	1			19								
Bradley, Bradlee, Bradly, Braidly, Breadly	5.5	440	1,981	3	17	29	50	1	166	18	27	12	28	49	40
Bradshaw, Bradchaw, Bradsha, Bradsher, Bredshaw	5.3	79	343				9	1	1	9	12	5	8	26	8
Bradt, Bratt, Bredt	6.3	50	264							50					
Brady, Brada, Braddy, Bradey, Braidy, Braydey, Braydy, Bready, Bredy	5.2	88	370	1		1				9	27	9	5	27	9
Bragdon, Bragden	5.0	37	149	37											
Bragg, Brag	5.4	65	287	5	8	5	15		3	2			16	7	4
Brainard, Brainerd, Branard, Brannard, Braynard, Brenard	6.6	94	528	7	7	3	1		69	6		1			
Brake, Break, Breck	6.0	20	99				6				1	2	6	5	
Braley, Brailey, Braily, Braly	5.7	20	94		1	1	7				2	2		6	1
Bramin, Braemin, Braman, Bramen, Braumin, Brayman, Breaman, Breeman, Breman, Bremen	5.7	34	161			1	7	8	6	8	1	1	1		1
Branch	6.2	68	351	3		11	5	3	3	1	1	1	15	20	5
Brand, Brandt, Brant	5.5	69	309	2			1	6	3	9	36	7	1	3	1
Brandon, Brandan, Branden, Brandin, Brandun	5.8	38	181							7	7		1	15	8
Branham, Bramham, Branan, Branhan, Branin, Brannan, Brannen, Brannin, Brannion, Brannon, Brannum, Branon, Branum	6.3	55	291	1			1			4	18	8	13	6	4
Branson, Branison, Branizor, Bransom, Brenson	4.8	26	99								3	7	6	10	
Brantley, Brantly, Brently	5.2	40	167								1		13	25	1
Branton	5.8	18	87						1		6		2	7	2
Brashears, Brashear, Brasher, Brasheres, Brashers, Brassher	5.6	39	178							5	3	25	1	2	3
Brasure, Braser, Brasier, Brassure, Brazer, Brazier, Brazor	6.3	23	122	6			2			1				4	10
Braswell, Brasswell, Braswel, Braswill, Brazwell	5.4	22	97										2	14	6
Bratton, Braten, Braton, Bratten	6.0	43	214			3	3			4	14	9	1	2	7
Brau, Braugh, Brough, Brow	6.2	23	120	2	2	1	2		11	1	2			1	1
Brawn, Bran, Brann, Brauin, Brawon, Bron, Brond	6.6	21	117	13		1	1	1			2	2		1	
Brawner, Braner, Branner, Branor, Brauner	5.5	26	118							1	2	17	4		2
Bray	6.0	71	356	8			23		3		4	1		31	1
Brayton	6.5	31	169				5	19	2	5					
Brazel, Brasel, Brasill, Brassell, Brassil, Brassill, Brazeal, Brazeel, Brazell, Brazil	5.7	29	137			2								15	12
Breed, Bread	6.0	48	240		14		29		1	1	1	1			1
Breeding, Breding	6.3	18	95									1	17		
Brenneman, Branaman, Braniman, Brannaman, Brannamer, Brenman, Brennemon, Brinerman, Bruneman, Brunoman	6.1	27	139								20		6	1	
Brenner, Bregneer, Breighner, Breignu, Breiner, Breneer, Brenegh, Brener, Brennor	5.2	27	112							1	21	2	3		
Brent, Breant, Brend, Brents, Brint	5.6	38	174						1	4		7	26		
Bressac, Brassac	6.4	18	98							18					
Brevard, Brevoort	5.3	23	98			1				9	2	3		7	1
Brewer, Brewah, Brewor, Brua, Bruer, Bruyer	5.7	217	1,027	10	3	4	44		8	40	16	16	18	54	4
Brewster, Brewstur, Brouster, Brusstar, Bruster	6.0	142	710	4	17	13	21		42	36	5			2	2
Brice, Brise, Brises, Bryce	5.5	43	195						2	2	7	7	2	19	4
Bricker, Brickert, Bricket, Brickett, Brickhart, Brigah, Briger	5.7	33	155	1		1	9			1	13	6	1	1	
Bridges, Bridge, Briges	5.7	152	712	24	3	4	50		2	2	5	3	4	42	13
Bridgman, Bridgeman	6.4	17	91		4	2	4			2			1	4	
Brier, Bryar, Bryer, Bryers	5.4	19	83	6	4		1	2		1	2		3		
Briggs, Bregs, Brigg, Brigs	5.7	439	2,068	14	18	25	189	56	12	74	19	2	7	18	5
Brigham	6.0	115	579	6	14	6	82		5	2					
Bright, Breight, Brite	5.1	100	408				9			4	21	14	5	40	7
Brightman	5.1	35	142				23	7	2		1			1	1
Brinck, Brink, Brinks	5.7	37	174			1				24	10		2		
Brinckerhoff, Brenkenkoof, Brinckershoff, Bringolf, Brinkenhoof, Brinkerhoff	5.7	32	150							23	8				1
Brinkley, Brinklee, Brinkly	4.3	58	192			1							24	33	
Brinson, Brinsen	5.1	24	98							2	1		3	14	4
Briscoe, Bisco, Biscoe, Biscow, Brisco	5.6	49	223			1	1		3			35	8	1	
Brison, Bricen, Brisen, Bryson	5.9	43	212	2			1				14	6	1	6	13
Bristol, Bristole, Bristoll	5.5	67	301			10	2		35	14	5				1
Bristow, Brister, Bristo, Bristoe, Briscor	4.9	33	130						12	1	1	3	7	8	1
Britt, Brit, Britts, Britz	5.4	62	272		1		9		1	4	2	1	10	29	5
Britton, Britain, Brition, Briton, Brittain, Brittan, Britten, Brittn	5.4	113	494	1	11	3	14	3	1	11	32	5	3	21	8
Broad, Brod, Brode	6.6	16	90	2			10			2	2				
Brock, Broch, Brockes, Brocks, Brokes, Broks	5.7	96	447	9	3	7	9	2	3	2	2		26	14	19
Brockman, Brechman, Breckman, Broakman, Brookman	6.1	20	101							2	3		12	1	2
Brockway, Brockaway, Brockwey	5.8	60	286		8	1	2			30	19				
Brookins, Brookin, Brooking, Brookings	5.0	26	104	1		7	4			5		1	4	4	
Brooks, Broock, Brook, Brooke, Brookes	5.5	586	2,639	22	18	22	126		93	35	72	51	60	58	29
Broom, Broam, Broham, Broms, Broome, Brume	6.8	27	156			1			1	2	6	3	2	8	4
Brothers, Brother, Bruthers	5.1	42	173							2	3	8	4	23	2
Broughton, Braughton, Brawton, Broten, Brotin, Brotton, Brougton, Brouton, Broyhton	5.4	42	183		8	3	2		4		3	1	7	7	7
Brower, Brauer, Brougher	6.4	63	340				1			51	7	1		2	1
Brown, Bronn, Broons, Broun, Broune, Browne, Browns	5.7	3,358	15,827	112	292	87	563	182	297	407	429	195	248	334	212
Brownell, Bronell, Brownall, Brownel, Brownill	6.3	69	368				22	27		20					
Browning, Brownin	6.0	80	402			3	11	22	2	2	2	13	5	17	3
Brownley, Brounley, Brownlee, Brownlie	6.2	34	176						1		8	2	16		7
Brownson, Bronsan, Bronson, Bronston, Brounsen, Brounson, Brunson	5.6	150	687		1	15	6		101	12	2				13
Brubaker, Brewbaker, Broobeaker, Browbaker, Brubacher, Brubacker, Bruboker	6.1	42	213								36	1	4		1
Bruce, Bruse	5.2	138	580	1	3	9	44		1	6	8	10	31	18	7
Brumley, Brambly, Bramly, Brombly, Bromley, Bromly, Broomly, Brumly	5.1	38	154			6	1	2	11	3		1	10	2	2
Brundage, Brundige	5.4	45	196			1	1		3	38	2				
Bruner, Bronaugh, Brooner, Brunner	5.3	60	259								40	11	2	4	3
Brush	6.2	60	314			6			15	35	1	1		1	
Bryan, Brian, Brien, Briene, Brion, Brions, Bryen, Bryn, Bryon	5.2	238	1,010	1			1	1	7	12	29	50	19	101	17
Bryant, Briand, Briant, Brient, Bryand, Bryent	5.3	296	1,285	29	27	8	86		13	12	3		40	55	23
Buchanan, Bachanan, Bochonon, Bucannon, Buccannon, Bucchannon, Buchanen, Buchannan, Buchannen, Buchannon, Buchnon, Buckana, Buckanan, Buckannan, Buckanon, Buckhanan, Buckhanen, Buckhannan, Buckhannon, Buckhanon	5.8	126	599			2				13	53	16	6	17	19
Buck, Bucks	5.3	195	839	13	11	17	31		40	14	37	6	9	16	1
Buckingham, Beckingham, Birkingham, Buckenham, Buckhingham, Buckinham, Bukingham	5.3	59	256			3	1		35	2	2	13		3	
Buckley, Buchley, Buckly, Bukley	5.9	101	493	3		1	4		65	1	9	10	7	1	
Bucklin, Buckland	6.8	39	226	2		5	17	6	7	2					
Buckman, Birkman	6.2	61	316	7	6	5	18		1	1	20	3			
Buckner, Beckner, Buckners, Bucknor	5.1	23	95								1		16	5	1
Budd, Bud	5.8	34	162			1			1	18	9	2		2	1
Buell, Bewel, Bewell, Buel	6.1	98	503		11	8	7		58	12		1		1	

TABLE 111.—NOMENCLATURE, DEALING WITH NAMES REPRESENTED BY AT LEAST 100 WHITE PERSONS, BY STATES AND TERRITORIES, AT THE FIRST CENSUS: 1790—Continued.

NAME.	Average size of family.	TOTAL.		HEADS OF FAMILIES.											
		Heads of families.	All other members.	Maine.	New Hampshire.	Vermont.	Massachusetts.	Rhode Island.	Connecticut.	New York.	Pennsylvania.	Maryland.	Virginia.	North Carolina.	South Carolina.
Buffington, Buffenton, Buffinton	6.5	41	226				15		1	2	14	1	6		2
Buffum, Buffham, Buffom	6.3	30	158	5	9	1	6	8	1	1					
Bugbee, Buckbee, Bugbe, Bugbey, Bugbie, Bugby, Burkbee	6.7	61	348	1	2	10	10		22	16					
Bulkley, Bulkeley, Bulkly	5.6	39	181		2	3			32	2					
Bull, Bulls	5.1	120	590				10	6	3	36	30	6	14	8	6
Bullard	5.7	97	453		8	3	57		6	1		4	15		3
Bullen, Bullin	6.2	26	134	3		2	5		2	2	1	5	2	4	
Bullock, Bolock, Bulleck, Bulloch, Bulluck	5.6	129	598		6	7	34	5	1	12	6	4	16	28	10
Bumgarner, Bamgartner, Bombgardner, Bomgarner, Bonggarner, Bumbgardner, Bumgamer, Bumganer, Bumgardener, Bumgardner, Bumgarnar	4.8	27	103								9	5	8	5	
Bumpus, Bampus, Bumpas, Bumpass, Bumpuss	5.4	43	190	6		3	24		1	2			2	5	
Bunce, Bunch	4.9	51	201				1		17	9				22	2
Bundy	5.5	43	194		4	1	1	1	5	9				22	
Bunker, Bonker	5.8	100	480	10	21		33		1	31	2	1	1		
Bunn, Bun	5.7	26	123			1	1	1		7	3	1	1	10	1
Bunnel, Banell, Banil, Benel, Bonell, Bonnel, Bonnell, Bunel, Bunell, Bunill, Bunnell, Bunnels, Bunnil, Burnal, Burnel, Burnell	5.5	69	309	3	1	1	12		36	4	6	3	1	1	1
Bunting, Bunten, Buntin, Bunton, Buntoon	5.1	49	200			3				5	20	3	3	12	3
Burbank, Burbanck, Burbanks	5.7	77	364	10	24	6	29		3	5					
Burch, Birch, Burtch	5.5	128	577			11	2		6	44	9	25	8	20	3
Burchard, Birchard, Birchhead, Birchird, Birrchard, Burchart, Burchet, Burchhead, Burchid, Burchird	5.2	60	254			2	17		17	2	2	11	3	5	1
Burden, Bearden, Beardin, Bearding, Beardon, Borden, Berdine, Burdin, Burdine	5.9	72	355			2		29	15	8	2		4	4	10
Burdet, Badet, Bardet, Barditt, Berditt, Birdet, Burdett, Burdit, Burditt	5.8	28	133			1	16		3	1		2	4	1	1
Burdick, Birdich, Burdack, Burdec, Burdeck, Burdict	5.6	120	558				3	9	61	14	31		1	1	
Burford, Beauford, Beaufort, Beuford, Bufford, Buford, Burfoot	5.2	24	101	1							1	1	9	6	6
Burge, Berge, Birge, Birje	5.3	27	116		2	2	6			7		2		1	7
Burgess, Berges, Burgas, Burgase, Burgass, Burgees, Burges, Burghes, Burghess, Burgis, Burgiss, Burjis	5.9	225	1,095	8		3	50	10	16	21	13	40	29	29	6
Burgh, Berg, Bergh, Burg, Burgue	5.7	19	90			3			1	4	11	2			1
Burghardt, Birkhart, Buchert, Buckhart, Bughart, Burchert, Burckhart, Burghart, Burgort, Burkard, Burkart, Burkert, Burkhard, Burkhardt, Burkhart	7.1	39	215	2			10				22		1	4	
Burk, Berck, Berk, Berks, Birk, Birke, Birks, Bourk, Burck, Burke, Burkes, Burks	5.0	160	647	5	3	13	9	2	5	14	34	26	21	17	11
Burket, Berkit, Birquit, Bureckett, Burget, Burgit, Burgot, Burkett, Burkit, Burkitt, Burkout	5.4	64	283			2		1	4	7	19	9	6	10	6
Burkholder, Buchwalter, Buckhalte, Buckhalter, Buckholter, Buckolter, Buckwalter, Burchholder, Burkalter, Burkolder	6.0	58	292								55				3
Burley, Berley, Berly, Burleigh, Burlie, Burligh	6.1	59	302	1	36		2		6	6	6		1	1	
Burlingham, Burlingam, Burlingame	6.3	62	330		1	3	4	40	4	10					
Burnap	5.1	23	94			3	7	8	4	1					
Burnett, Bernet, Bernett, Bernitt, Bernot, Burnet, Burnit, Burnitt, Byrnett	6.5	109	596			10	11		1	4	18	8	5	26	7
Burney, Berney, Berny, Birney, Birnie, Burny	5.4	23	101	2							2	7	1	7	4
Burnham, Burnam, Burnum	5.7	260	1,208	27	50	22	76		59	11		4	2	8	1
Burns, Bearn, Bearnes, Bern, Berns, Burhans, Burn, Burne, Burnes, Byrn, Byrne, Byrnes, Byrns	5.3	276	1,186	6	13	4	16	3	8	45	69	29	13	38	32
Burpee, Burpe, Burpey, Burpy	4.8	22	83		9		13								
Burr, Bur, Burs	5.7	163	761	2	1	3	29	11	95	18	1			2	1
Burrell, Buril, Burral, Burrall, Burrel, Burril, Burrill, Burroll, Burwell	5.5	105	486	8	7	4	39	2	18	7	6	1	9	1	3
Burrit, Burret, Burrett, Burritt	5.9	33	162				5			25	1	2			
Burrows, Borough, Boroughs, Borow, Borroughs, Bouroughs, Buress, Buro, Burows, Burras, Burrass, Burres, Burrice, Burris, Burriss, Burrough, Burroughs, Burrous, Burrow, Burrowes, Burrus, Burruss	6.1	233	1,182	5	14	12	19	8	29	31	21	30	24	27	13
Burt, Bert, Berttes, Birt, Burts, Burttes, Burtz	6.0	172	864		8	16	86	1	6	13	7	4	8	18	5
Burtis, Burtiss	6.5	26	144							26					
Burton, Berton, Birton, Burten, Burtin	5.3	213	907	7	6	15	12	5	11	11	10	16	78	26	16
Busby, Busbee, Busbey, Busbie, Bushbee, Bushby, Buzbie, Buzby	6.3	51	272				1		1	2	9	2	5	18	13
Bush, Bouche, Boush	5.4	234	1,041		1	8	36		2	21	60	34	10	39	13
Bushnell, Bishnel, Bushnal, Bushneel, Bushnel, Bushnoll, Bushnul	5.9	80	389				6	5		65	3			1	
Buskirk	5.5	21	94							15	6				
Bussey, Busey, Busie, Busse, Bussy, Busy	6.0	35	176				6	3	1	2	1	10	3	2	7
Butcher, Butchers	6.2	22	114								8	3	2	1	
Butler, Butlar, Butlers, Butlor, Buttler	5.6	550	2,503	31	29	24	86	6	87	46	45	38	54	65	39
Butman, Buteman, Buttman	6.4	16	86				11	14	1						
Butt, But, Buts, Butts, Buttz, Butz	5.5	120	539	1		5	12	5	9	14	11	13	33	15	2
Butterfield, Buterfld	6.2	88	462	11	32	12	27		5		4	5	1		
Button, Boton, Botton, Bottons, Butten, Buttons	5.5	62	273		1		5	6	12	16	4	3		6	4
Buxton, Buckstone	5.3	59	254	6	5	2	19	6	6	2		1	3	4	3
Buzzard, Bazzard, Bozard, Busard, Busert, Bussard, Buzard	6.3	33	176						1		11	9	6	2	4
Buzzell, Bussel, Bussell, Bussells, Buzzel	5.4	29	129	8	13							2	4	2	
Byers, Bayeaux, Bayeux, Beya, Beyea, Beyer, Beyor, Beyres, Biars, Bias, Bierr, Biers, Bior, Buyer, Buyers, Buyhe, Byar, Byars, Byas, Byass, Byer, Byrar, Byre, Byres, Byrs, Byuers	6.2	106	546			1	2		2	10	65	5	5	7	9
Byington	6.4	17	92							12	5				
Bynum, Bainum, Banum, Binom, Binum, Bynam, Bynhame	5.1	24	99						1			1	5	14	3
Byram, Biram, Birem, Byrom, Byrum	4.8	31	119	5		2	4			1	1	2	5	11	
Cable, Cabel, Cabell, Cables	4.9	53	208			1	1		17	7	7	5	12	3	
Cadwallader, Cadwalader, Cadwaleder, Cadwalider, Cadwaliter	6.5	21	116								21				
Cadwell, Cadwel	5.5	46	206			6	10		27	3					
Cady, Cadey	6.1	104	526			23	13		33	29					
Cahoon, Cahoone, Cahown, Cohoon, Cohoun, Cohown	5.6	60	276	1	3		14	7	1	7	9		2	14	1
Cain, Caine, Caines, Cains, Cane, Kaign, Kain, Kane	5.2	161	674	14	1		6		6	16	23	19	19	33	24
Calahan, Calihan, Callahan, Callehan, Callichan, Callihan, Callyhan, Kalahan, Kallahan, Kellyhan	5.5	30	134	1		3					1	7	2	8	6
Caldwell, Caldwall, Callwell, Calwell, Coldwell, Colwell, Colwill, Culdwell	5.5	265	1,200	1	20	6	26	12	8	27	80	10	21	18	36
Cale, Cail, Cales, Caols, Cayle, Kahl, Kail, Kails, Kale	5.2	30	125	1					1	1	7	3	7	9	
Calf, Calfe	5.7	29	135		16	1	2				2	5	1	2	
Calhoon, Calhoone, Calhoun, Colhoon, Colquhoon, Coulhoun, Culhoun	5.6	70	323				4		8	4	18	5	1	14	16
Calkins, Calkin, Caukins, Caulkins, Colking, Colkins, Corkin, Corkings, Corkins	5.5	99	443		3	13	5		34	42	1	1			
Call, Coll	5.5	52	236	7	9	8	13			3	4		2	6	
Callender, Calender, Callander, Caloneder, Collender, Collinder	6.2	34	176			3	15	1	1	2	5	3	2	2	
Calley, Caley, Cally, Caly, Kaley	5.1	22	90	2	8		5			3		1	1	2	
Callis, Calis	5.0	20	80						1		2	16	1		
Calvert, Calvit, Colvert	4.8	29	110						3	7	3	4	4	4	8
Cameron, Cameran, Camerion, Cammeron, Camoran, Camron	5.5	85	384		1		1		1	17	15	1	9	24	16
Camp, Camps, Kamp	5.8	137	651			2	7	7	77	5	19	1	12	5	2

TABLE 111.—NOMENCLATURE, DEALING WITH NAMES REPRESENTED BY AT LEAST 100 WHITE PERSONS, BY STATES AND TERRITORIES, AT THE FIRST CENSUS: 1790—Continued.

NAME.	Average size of family.	TOTAL.		HEADS OF FAMILIES.											
		Heads of families.	All other members.	Maine.	New Hampshire.	Vermont.	Massachusetts.	Rhode Island.	Connecticut.	New York.	Pennsylvania.	Maryland.	Virginia.	North Carolina.	South Carolina.
Campbell, Cambel, Cambell, Cambill, Camble, Cambol, Cambpell, Cambple, Camel, Camell, Camil, Cammall, Cammel, Cammell, Campbel, Campbells, Campbels, Campbill, Campble. Campel, Campell, Cample, Camppell, Compbell, Kemel, Kemmel, Kemmell	5.5	778	3,533	22	32	21	46	1	20	109	206	33	74	143	71
Candie, Canda, Cande, Candy	7.1	16	97				2			13			1		
Canfield, Cantfield	6.5	69	377	1	3	3	2			39	21				
Cannie, Caney, Canney, Canny, Cantey, Canty	4.8	22	83		9		1				8				4
Cannon, Cannan, Cannen, Cannine, Canon, Kannon	5.6	148	681	3			14		8	10	26	14	10	29	34
Cantrel, Cantral, Cantrall, Cantrell, Cantril, Cantrill	5.5	23	103										5	8	10
Capen, Capin, Capon	6.0	43	213	3		6	33		1						
Capps, Cap, Capp, Caps, Kapp, Kappes	5.5	98	439				1				10	1	38	37	9
Capron, Capran	6.5	36	199		6	3	6	11	5	5					
Card	5.8	62	295	6	3	2	4	38		7				2	
Cargill, Cargal, Cargel, Cargell, Cargil	7.1	16	97	3	1				1	1	3			4	3
Carl, Carle, Carll, Carls, Corl	5.6	59	271	14			2		1		27	13	1	1	
Carlisle, Carlile, Carliles, Carlilse, Carlyle, Corlile	5.4	72	318	6	2	1	6	2	1		14	10	5	16	9
Carlton, Carleton, Carlston	5.9	121	594	13	26	5	51		1	4	6	2	4	8	1
Carman, Carmean, Carmine, Carmon, Carrmand, Corman, Cormon	6.5	82	448	2			1		1	45	9	13	1	10	
Carmichael, Carmical, Carmichal, Carmicheal, Carmichel, Cormichael, Kermichael	5.4	36	160							4	11	2	6	10	3
Carnahan, Carnachan, Carnahen, Carnahon, Carnehon, Karnahan	6.6	16	90								14	2			
Carnes, Cairns, Carn, Carne, Carns, Kahn, Kairns, Karnes, Karns	5.0	69	276	2	1		9		1	5	18	5	10	12	8
Carney, Carnay, Carni, Carny, Kearney, Kerney, Kerny, Kirny	5.0	46	186	2	1		1			8	4	5	6	18	1
Carpenter, Carpender, Carpentor, Carpinder, Carpinter	6.2	544	2,817	5	24	51	87	51	51	149	55	9	26	33	3
Carr, Car, Cars, Corr, Kar, Karr, Kehr, Ker, Kerr, Kerrs, Kierr, Korr	5.6	494	2,258	8	38	15	30	43	5	50	137	34	42	59	33
Carraway, Caraway, Carriway, Carroway, Corroway	5.1	35	144				1					1	3	29	
Carrier, Carier, Carriere	6.1	32	162		4	3	8		13		1	2		1	
Carrington, Carington, Charingten, Charrington, Corrington	5.1	50	204						26		4	3	5	7	5
Carrol, Caril, Carol, Caroll, Carrel, Carrell, Carriel, Carril, Carrill, Carriot, Carrold, Carrole, Carroll, Carryl, Caryl, Correl, Correll, Corril, Corrill, Karell, Kerril, Kerrol	5.3	236	1,026			6	30	3	7	7	37	47	27	50	22
Carruthers, Carithers, Carothers, Caruthers, Corithers, Correthers, Corruthers, Coruthers, Cruthers, Currathers, Currethers	5.7	72	340								36	7	4	23	2
Carson, Carsen	5.3	121	525	1	3	1		1	1	4	51	4	6	28	21
Carswell	5.6	20	92								17	1		2	
Carter, Carters, Cartor	5.7	651	3,050	23	40	14	93	6	63	33	34	37	132	117	59
Cartwright, Cartright, Cartthrite, Cortright, Cortwright, Curtright, Kortright, Kortwright	5.4	107	472		3		9	1	3	20	15	8	3	45	
Carty, Cartee, Cartey, Cartie	5.2	23	97		1		1		1		6	8	3	2	1
Caruth, Carroth, Carruth	6.7	16	91		1	1	7							5	2
Carver, Carrver, Carvar	5.6	120	549	10	1	7	23	2	12	6	34	5	5	15	
Cary, Cairry, Cairy, Carey, Carie	5.7	185	868	5	8	6	43	8	18	16	28	18	25	7	3
Case	6.0	254	1,272	1	6	10	25	12	113	59	9	6	1	10	2
Casey, Caisey, Cassee, Cassey, Casy, Caycey, Caycie	5.8	64	307	1			1	2	4	5	3	9	15	15	9
Cash	5.2	38	160	3			9			5	3	3	9	6	
Cason, Caison, Casaun, Cassin, Casson, Chasin, Chason, Kason, Kassan, Kasson	5.9	72	351				3	1	8	2	1	3	23	18	13
Cass, Kass	6.5	37	205	1	25	2			2	1	6				
Cassady, Casaty, Cashaday, Cashady, Cashiday, Casity, Cassaday, Cassaty, Cassdy, Cassiday, Cassidy, Cassity	5.4	36	158				2				8	4	4	15	3
Caster, Casteers, Casters, Castor, Kaster	6.3	30	160		2		1			1	18	2	1	5	
Castle, Casiell, Casle, Cassel, Cassell, Cassells, Cassels, Castel, Casteill, Castells, Castles, Castul, Kassel	5.9	116	571	6	2	14	12	3	17	13	25	8	2	5	9
Caswell, Casswell, Castwell	5.1	76	311		12	2	43		6	5	1			7	
Cate, Cates, Kate, Kates	4.4	74	252	8	32				2		1			23	8
Cathey, Cathery, Cathy	6.7	21	119				1						3	16	1
Catlin, Catline, Catling, Cattlen, Katlin	6.3	59	313	1		3	10		36	7	1	1			
Cato, Catoe	6.1	17	86	1							1	1	4	5	5
Caton, Caeton, Caiton, Caten, Catton, Katon, Keigten	5.3	27	116				1			2	2	2	7	10	1
Cauley, Caulley, Cawley, Cawlley, Corley, Cowley	5.6	47	217	1	3	2	3	1	1	4	4	5	7		16
Caverly, Calverley, Cavarly	6.4	19	103		10		3		5				1		
Chadbourne, Chadborn, Chadboun, Chadbourn, Chad Bourn, Chadburn	6.0	32	161	26	5		1								
Chadwick, Chadewick	5.3	97	415	10	10		49	2	11	4				11	
Chaffee, Chafee, Chafey, Chaffe, Chaffey, Chaffy	6.1	64	328			13	23	3	25						
Chaffin, Chafen, Chaffen, Chaffind, Chaffing, Chafin	5.4	39	170		4		10					9		11	5
Challis, Challice, Chelles, Chellis	5.1	21	87	3	6	1	9							2	
Chamberlain, Chaimberlin, Chamberlaine, Chamberlan, Chamberlane, Chamberlayn, Chamberlayne, Chamberlen, Chamberlin, Chamberline, Chamberling, Cheamberlain, Cheamberlin	5.6	324	1,501	18	50	54	76	4	42	20	28	12	7	13	
Chambers, Chaimbers, Chamber	5.4	201	884	2	3	3	5	1	4	15	56	29	16	48	19
Champion	5.7	43	204			1	2		20	1			3	13	3
Champlin	6.0	82	413				1	56	14	11					
Chance	5.3	24	103			1					2	9		11	1
Chancy, Chancey, Chanchey, Chansey, Chansy	4.8	23	88	1			1			2	10			5	4
Chandler, Chandlor, Chanler, Chanlor	6.0	317	1,588	29	43	28	82		22	10	10	9	25	22	37
Chaney, Chainey, Chany	6.4	32	172	1	2						4	9	6	7	3
Chapin, Chapen, Chapins	6.0	172	863		7	11	108		27	17	1			1	
Chaplin, Chaplain, Chapline	5.0	51	202	1	4	3	16		1	1		13	1	3	8
Chapman	5.7	449	2,109	17	32	17	54	9	174	41	37	14	30	24	
Chappel, Chapel, Chapell, Chaple, Chaples, Chappele, Chappell, Chappill, Chapple	5.4	150	664	1	1	2	11	11	53	12	4	4	28	18	5
Charles, Charls	5.3	56	239	3			8		2	2	16	7	4	10	4
Charlton, Charleton, Charlten, Chartlon, Charton	4.7	22	81		1	1		1	1		4	3	4	6	1
Chase, Chace, Chaise	5.8	599	2,884	44	142	29	268	33	13	59	3	5	1	2	
Chatfield, Chattfield	5.5	30	136				4		19	6			1		
Cheatham, Chatham, Chattam, Chattom, Chittam, Chittem, Chittim	6.1	48	247								2	2	38	5	1
Cheek	5.1	28	114	10									3	15	
Cheesborough, Cheesbrough, Cheesebrough	7.0	29	175				3	1	23	1					1
Cheeseman, Cheasman, Cheesman	5.7	23	107				1	9			10	2	1		
Cheney, Cheaney, Cheany, Cheene, Cheeney, Cheeny, Chenee, Chenney, Chenny, Cheny, Cheyney, Chiney, Chinney	5.6	132	601	2	26	13	46		11	7	10	12	2		1
Cherry, Cherrey, Chery	5.5	90	407		1				1	6	12	1	24	43	2
Cheshire, Cheser, Cheshure, Chesser, Chesshar, Chessheir, Chesshire, Chessire, Chessur	5.3	26	111						6			5	5	8	2
Chesley, Chesle	6.1	29	148	2	22	1			1				3		
Chesnut, Chesnet, Chesnutt, Chestnut	4.4	29	108								8			17	4
Chester	5.3	30	130			2	1	2	12		5	1		6	
Chever, Chaver, Cheaver, Cheever, Cheevers, Chevers	5.1	53	219		2		48		1	1					1
Chew	5.0	21	85								2	13	4	1	1
Chick, Check	5.7	18	84	8									2	5	3
Chilcoat, Chilcoate, Chilcot, Chilcote, Chilcott, Chillcoat, Chillcut	5.2	24	101								8	11	5		
Childress, Cheldres, Cheldress, Childers, Childres, Childries, Childris	4.6	71	324								1		38	15	17

Table 111.—NOMENCLATURE, DEALING WITH NAMES REPRESENTED BY AT LEAST 100 WHITE PERSONS, BY STATES AND TERRITORIES, AT THE FIRST CENSUS: 1790—Continued.

NAME.	Average size of family.	TOTAL.		HEADS OF FAMILIES.											
		Heads of families.	All other members.	Maine.	New Hampshire.	Vermont.	Massachusetts.	Rhode Island.	Connecticut.	New York.	Pennsylvania.	Maryland.	Virginia.	North Carolina.	South Carolina.
Childs, Child, Childes, Chiles	5.9	226	1,110	7	5	16	93	15	30	12	18	8	6	6	10
Chilton, Chelton, Chilleton	4.6	29	104			1				1	5	22			
Chipman	5.5	47	210	3		20	12		9	1		1		1	
Chisolm, Cheseham, Chesham, Cheshlom, Chesholm, Chisham, Chisholm, Chism, Chisom, Chissum, Chisum	6.0	28	141	2			8	8		2	2	4	9	6	3
Chittenden, Chitendon, Chittendon, Chittenten, Chittenton, Chittington	4.8	53	203			8	8		34	3					
Choate, Choat, Chote	5.5	52	232	5	8	3	32		3				1		
Christian, Christain, Christein, Christen, Christians, Christianse, Crestian, Crestianse, Cristian, Cristine	5.4	78	344				2	1		19	11	3	31	10	1
Christie, Christee, Christey, Christy, Criste, Cristee, Cristie, Cristy	5.2	71	296		7	1	3		2	13	33	2	5	4	1
Christopher, Christifor, Christophers, Cristopher	6.1	31	157	1					1	8	4	4	11	2	
Church	5.8	231	1,116	6	19	28	55	23	52	15	7	3	8	14	1
Churchill, Churchel, Churchell, Churchhill	5.6	124	571	7	5	17	53	1	29	8	1		2	1	
Cilley, Celley, Celly, Cilly, Selley, Sillea, Silley, Silly, Sily	5.4	39	172	3	23	1	1		2		7		1	1	
Cissell, Cecil, Cecill, Cissel, Cissil, Cissill, Coecil, Sissel, Sissell, Sissol	5.7	31	147					4		1	1	25			
Claflin, Cleffland	6.2	29	150		1	4	22			1				1	
Clagett, Clegit	5.5	32	144		2							29		1	
Clap, Clapp, Klapp	6.3	178	936	2	4	5	111	6	13	21	2	1		12	1
Clardy	5.5	19	86										13		6
Clark, Clarck, Clarke, Clarkes, Clarks, Cleark, Clerk, Clerke	5.6	2,442	11,324	124	152	129	483	128	400	217	209	137	171	178	114
Clarkson, Clackson, Clarkston, Clarkton	5.4	28	122		1		2			3	7	7	6	1	1
Clary, Clarey, Cleary, Cleery	5.1	48	198	3	2	1	11			3	1	9	4	8	6
Clawson, Clausen, Clauson, Clossen, Closson	5.4	28	124	2		4	1	3		8	9	1			
Clay, Clays	5.4	78	347	6	15	5	2		2	1	10	3	27	7	
Claypole, Claypool, Claypoole	5.5	25	112							7	1	14	3		
Clayton, Claton, Claytons, Cleaton, Cleton, Cleyton	5.1	101	418	1		2	1		1	3	17	10	22	23	21
Cleaver, Clever	5.7	25	117	2			1	3			18	1			
Cleaves, Claves, Cleavs, Cleeves, Cleves	5.8	32	155	15	1		8			3		2		3	
Cleland, Clayland, Clealand, Cleelan, Cleeland, Clelon, Cleyland	5.4	21	93				2			4	5	5	1	1	3
Clements, Clemence, Clemens, Clement, Clementz, Clemings, Clemins, Clemmans, Clemmence, Clemmens, Clemment, Clemments, Clemmings, Clemmins, Clemmon, Clemmons, Clemon, Clemonds, Clemons, Clemont, Clemonts	5.6	277	1,271	10	38	7	37	5	8	29	31	45	21	28	18
Clendenin, Clandennen, Clandenning, Clendenan, Clendenen, Clendening, Clendennan, Clendennin, Clendinan, Clendinen, Clendinnen, Clindinon, Clindinin, Clyndinnin	4.7	27	101		3					2	12	2	4	3	1
Cleveland, Clavland, Cleaveland, Cleavland, Cleeveland, Clevland	5.8	149	710	4	8	16	45	2	32	31			6	2	3
Clifford, Clefford, Cleford, Cliford	5.7	76	355	10	34	2	7	2	4		9	2	1	4	1
Clift, Cleft, Cliff	6.3	21	112			2	5		4	1	2	3	3	1	
Clifton, Cliffton	5.2	43	180			2	5				4	1	4	22	7
Climer, Climmer, Clymer, Klimer	5.4	29	128								23	4		2	
Cline, Clein, Clyn, Clyne, Klein, Klien, Kline, Klyn, Klyne	5.8	202	961				2	1		23	138	22	5	11	
Clinton, Clentan, Clenton, Clindon	4.9	35	135	1			5		11	7	2			6	3
Close, Clothes, Clowes, Clowse, Klose, Klosz	5.1	45	185			1	1		9	19	12	2		1	
Cloud	6.0	36	181							1	16	2	6	5	6
Clough, Clow	5.7	142	671	16	79		31			14		1	1		
Clute	5.1	35	145							35					
Coats, Coat, Coates, Cotes	5.9	105	510	1		1	9	3	17	5	30	4	12	9	14
Cobb, Cob, Cobbs, Cobs, Kob, Kobb, Kolb	5.8	311	1,497	35	13	19	115	6	14	5	11	2	23	51	17
Coble, Cobble, Cobill	4.7	29	106						1		7			21	
Coburn, Cobern, Coborn, Cobourn, Cobourne, Coburns	6.2	96	502	2	6	7	55		4	2	11	1		8	
Cochran, Cochrin, Cochron, Cockerin, Cockeron, Cockran, Cockrane, Cockrin, Cockron, Cocran, Cokron	6.1	192	970	4	36	4	7		2	14	49	18	13	26	19
Cock, Cocke, Cocks, Coks, Koch, Kock	5.5	125	559							33	26	2	54	8	2
Cockrell, Cocheril, Cochrell, Cockarill, Cockerill, Cockral, Cockril, Cockroll	5.4	21	92				1						9	4	7
Coe, Co	5.9	117	574		1		9	4	47	32	9	10	3	2	
Coffee, Coffe, Coffy, Corfey	5.5	44	200	1			1			4	7	2	4	21	4
Coffield, Cofield	5.0	22	89										7	15	
Coffin, Coffen, Coffins	5.8	212	1,024	22	19	4	130	2		20	2			13	
Coggin, Coggen, Coggins	5.3	21	91	4	1		2					1	5	8	
Cogswell, Coggeshal, Coggeshall, Coggshall, Coggswell, Coggwell, Coghill, Cogshall, Cogshell, Cogswill, Cogwell, Cogwill	6.0	131	653	1	11	9	42	36	19	6			3	3	1
Cohen, Cohan, Coheen, Cohn, Cohon, Cohone, Cohorn, Cohun, Koens, Koghen	4.8	29	110	1			1			2	12		2	6	5
Coil, Coile, Coils, Coyal, Coyel, Coyl, Coyle, Koil, Koils, Koyl, Koyle	5.2	31	130							3	16	1	1	6	4
Coit	6.2	30	155	1	1	2	2	1	22	1					
Coker, Cocah, Cocar, Cocker	5.4	32	140	1	1		1		1				2	16	10
Colbraith, Colbreath, Colbrith, Colebroth, Collbreath, Culbrath, Culbreath	4.7	31	116	5					1	1	1	1	8	12	2
Colburn, Colborn, Colbourn, Colburne, Colebourn, Coleburn, Coulburn	6.1	80	404	6	29	6	19		10	2		6		1	1
Colby, Colbee, Colbey, Coleby	5.5	153	687	15	97	6	33			2					
Colcord	6.3	19	100	1	18										
Cole, Coal, Coale, Coals, Coles, Cowle, Cowles, Cowls	5.6	793	3,657	48	23	43	155	47	105	139	41	65	47	51	29
Colegrove, Coldgrove, Colgrove, Coolgrove	5.4	29	129			3	3	8	4	11					
Coleman, Coalman, Coalsman, Colaman, Colemand, Colemen, Colemon	5.9	307	1,489		8	3	57	3	22	36	38	15	55	45	25
Coley, Coaley, Coalley, Colley, Colly, Coly	5.6	68	310	4	1	2			15	4	7	3	10	17	5
Coller, Coaler, Coallar, Cola, Coler, Collar, Collars, Collers, Collour, Colour, Kholer, Koller	5.6	60	276		1	1	12	1	7	8	19	8		1	2
Collier, Colier, Collear, Colliar, Collyer, Colyer, Cullier	5.4	107	466	3		1	9	1	5	17	10	14	23	17	7
Collins, Colene, Colens, Colin, Colings, Colins, Collans, Collens, Collien, Collin, Colling, Collings, Collons	5.4	625	2,778	7	36	26	101	21	65	39	72	56	54	100	48
Colman, Collman, Colmon, Coltman, Coolman	6.4	41	220	2	4	2	18			8	2	1	3	1	
Colson, Coleson, Collison, Collisson, Collson, Colsin, Coulson	5.6	48	219	5	1		12	1		3	12	3	9	2	
Colt, Coltes, Colts	6.6	18	100			2	1	8	2	5					
Colton, Calton, Coletin, Coletton, Colten, Coulton	5.3	77	339		7	3	42		6	2	1	2		13	1
Colvin, Caldvin, Calvan, Calvin, Colven	6.0	77	385			14	1	25	2	5	14	1	4	3	8
Combs, Comb, Combe, Combes, Combess	5.5	102	455	4	5	2	6		10	20	11	13	23	6	2
Comer, Comber, Commer	5.6	31	144								2	3	17	4	5
Comfort, Komfort	6.2	20	103							10	10				
Comley, Comely, Comly	7.1	17	103							1	16				
Compton, Campton, Kamptom, Komton	5.8	43	206						1	9	5	6	17	3	2
Comstock, Compstock, Comstach, Comstack, Comstalk, Comstolk, Cumstack, Cumstick	5.9	116	565		3	7	15	8	64	18	1				
Conant, Connant	5.5	122	551	5	17	5	83		8	2					2
Condall, Condal, Condle, Congdel, Congdell, Congdoll, Cundal, Cundell	6.3	19	101				1	7	7			4			
Cone, Cones, Kone, Kohn	5.9	100	488		2	2	7	9		50	7	2	5	15	1
Coney, Conee, Cony	5.7	20	93	2			11			1	1	4	1		
Congdon, Condan, Conden, Condine, Condon, Congden	5.6	71	327	3		5	3	44		1	8	2	3	1	1
Conger, Congo, Congor	6.2	21	109			6				2	8	1		4	
Conkey	6.2	18	93			2	12			4					

Table **111.**—NOMENCLATURE, DEALING WITH NAMES REPRESENTED BY AT LEAST 100 WHITE PERSONS, BY STATES AND TERRITORIES, AT THE FIRST CENSUS: 1790—Continued.

NAME.	Average size of family.	TOTAL. Heads of families.	TOTAL. All other members.	Maine.	New Hampshire.	Vermont.	Massachusetts.	Rhode Island.	Connecticut.	New York.	Pennsylvania.	Maryland.	Virginia.	North Carolina.	South Carolina.
Conklin, Conchlin, Concklin, Conckline, Conclin, Coneklin, Conklan, Conklen, Conkline, Conkling.	5.5	210	940	1		1	1		5	195	6			1	
Conn, Con, Cons.	5.4	42	185		1	1	5		1	2	10	9	7	2	4
Connel, Conals, Connal, Connell, Conniel.	5.4	29	128				1		1	2	7	4	3	6	5
Conner, Conar, Coner, Connar, Conners, Connor, Connows.	5.2	228	953	3	23		16		3	29	45	31	27	30	21
Connolly, Conaldy, Conally, Coneley, Conely, Conley, Conly, Connala, Connally, Connaly, Conneley, Connelley, Connelly, Connely, Connerley, Connerlly, Connerly, Connoley, Connollee, Connoly, Conolley, Conolly, Conoly.	5.7	107	508	1	1		5	1	2	9	25	29	9	15	10
Conrad, Conrade, Conradt, Conrod, Conrodt, Koonrod.	5.5	95	429							7	65	8	9	5	1
Converse, Conver, Convers.	5.9	53	258		5	2	31	2	8	4	1				
Convus, Conves, Convis.	6.4	16	86				1		13	2					
Conway, Canaway, Canoway, Canwey, Conaway, Conneway, Conoway.	4.9	57	221				2			5	9	17	16	3	5
Cook, Coock, Cooke, Cookes, Cooks.	5.5	1,065	4,747	29	59	59	172	60	147	127	95	44	66	134	73
Cookey, Cookseey, Cooksy.	6.3	20	106									11	2	1	6
Cool, Coole, Coul, Coule.	6.1	27	139	2						19	4			2	
Cooley, Coolle, Coollly, Coolly, Cooly.	5.7	119	564	1	2	9	54		11	21	3	8	2	6	2
Coolidge, Cooladge, Coolage, Cooledge, Cooleg.	5.9	46	225	2	3	3	35		1	1		1			
Coombes, Coombs, Coomes, Cooms.	5.5	56	254	26	3	2	12		1	1		7	2	1	1
Coomer, Coomber, Cumber, Cummer, Cummir.	6.8	17	98				4				4	1	6	2	
Coon, Coonce, Coone, Coones, Coons, Coonse, Coonts, Coontz, Koon, Koonce, Koone, Koons, Koonse, Koontz.	6.0	234	1,172	1			1	18	2	86	56	34	9	14	13
Cooper, Coopper.	5.6	568	2,635	14	20	6	41	12	30	84	106	50	50	102	53
Cope, Cop, Copes, Copp, Coppes, Copps, Cops.	5.6	66	304	4	17		2		3	2	26	5	2	3	2
Copeland, Copelan, Copelin, Copland, Coplen, Coplin.	5.7	122	574	8	4	2	28		3	4	10	4	9	37	13
Corbet, Carbit, Corbert, Corbett, Corbit, Corbite, Corbitt, Corbutt.	5.2	57	237	1	1		13		1	3	5	5	6	13	9
Corbin, Corban, Corben, Corborn.	5.9	84	408		2	3	17		15	13		13	14	5	2
Cordwell, Cardwell, Cordwall, Cordwill.	5.7	31	145	2			15		2				9	3	
Corey, Coery, Correy, Corrie, Corry, Cory.	5.7	147	684	1	10	11	33	37	2	19	21	2	3	6	2
Corless, Carlis, Carloss, Corlas, Corlies, Corlis, Corliss.	5.9	17	84	1	12		2	1						1	
Cornelius, Carnelus, Conelies, Corneilas, Corneleise, Corneli, Cornelias, Cornelies, Cornelios, Cornelious, Cornelis, Cornelus, Curnelus.	5.1	49	200							10	14	6	6	7	6
Cornell, Cornal, Cornale, Corneall, Cornel.	5.5	110	497	1			30	22	1	40	12	3		1	
Corning, Cornin.	5.0	25	101		7		3		14	1					
Cornish, Carnish, Cornis.	4.9	45	174	2		2	18		9	6	2	1	5		
Cornwell, Cornwal, Cornwall, Cornwel, Cornwill.	5.4	134	591			3	10		28	81	3		4	4	1
Corson, Coarson, Corsen, Corsson, Courson.	5.7	36	169	14	5					5	12				
Cottingham.	6.1	17	86									9		3	5
Cottle, Cotle, Cottel, Cottille.	5.6	39	180	4		6	22			2	1		2	2	
Cotton, Cottawn, Cotten, Cottin, Cottins, Cottons.	5.4	130	575	8	21	12	16		24	5	5		10	26	3
Cottrell, Cotral, Cotrall, Cotrel, Cotrell, Cotrill, Cottrel, Cottril.	5.9	35	170	2				17	1	4		2	6	2	1
Couch, Cauch, Coutch.	5.5	68	303	1	3		5		25	5	8			5	16
Coulter, Coalter, Colter.	5.2	41	172				1			2	26	4	3	3	2
Council, Councel, Councill, Counsel, Counsell, Counsil.	4.9	29	114							1	4	7	16	1	
Countryman, Counteryman, Countyman, Cuntreman, Cuntryman.	5.9	22	107							13	6		1		2
Courtney, Coatney, Coltney, Cortany, Cortney.	4.9	29	113						1	1	5	4	2	5	11
Cousins, Cosine, Cosins, Cousens, Cousines, Couzins, Cozen, Cozens, Cozine, Cozzens, Cozzins, Cussens.	5.7	58	275	18			3	13		7	5		10	1	1
Covell, Coval, Covall, Covalt, Covel, Covels, Covil, Covile, Covill.	6.1	56	285	1	1	2	17	1	15	16	2	1			
Covenhoven, Covenhaven.	6.0	18	90							17	1				
Covert.	5.6	31	142						2	27	2				
Covey, Covy.	6.0	27	134	1		2	1		6	7		3		5	2
Covington, Cooventon, Coventon, Covinton.	6.0	41	206				1					10	12	14	4
Cow, Cowe, Cowes, Cows, Kow, Kows.	6.2	18	93	1		2	1		1	4	5	3		1	
Coward.	6.1	18	91									3		10	5
Cowden, Cawden, Cowdin.	6.1	20	101				5			7	6			1	1
Cowdry, Caudry, Coudry, Cowdre, Cowdrey.	5.4	24	105			1	7	1	9	3		2			1
Cowell, Cowel, Cowels, Cowill.	6.0	23	114	4		1	5	1	2	2	5			2	1
Cowen, Cowan, Cowans, Cowens, Cowhan, Cowin, Cowing.	5.7	140	658	12	1		21	10	1	11	33	11	1	26	13
Cox, Coxe, Coxs.	5.7	503	2,339	16	13	10	35	1	2	32	74	48	68	144	60
Coy, Coye.	5.3	29	125	2		4	8	2	11	1		1			
Crabb, Crab, Crabbs, Crabe.	5.4	28	124	1						5	5			7	2
Craddock, Craddack, Cradock, Cradok.	6.9	30	176									5	16	4	5
Craft, Crafd, Crafft, Crafts, Krafft, Kraft.	5.6	121	556	5	3	1	32	1	6	27	24	5	3	9	5
Craig, Craag, Craeg, Crag, Crage, Cragg, Craggs, Crags, Crague, Craige, Craigg, Craigs, Creag, Creg, Cregg, Creig, Creigh, Kreig.	5.1	217	888	9	11	4	8	1	2	12	81	15	19	31	24
Cram, Crammes, Krams.	5.9	73	360	6	57	2	1		1	2	4				
Cramer, Crama, Crammer, Crammr, Cramor, Cramore, Creamer, Creamore, Cremer, Kraemer, Kraimer, Kramer, Kreamer, Kremer.	5.7	110	513	7	1				4	19	49	23	1	3	3
Crandal, Crandall, Crandel, Crandell, Crandle, Crandol.	5.8	172	828	2	1	9	8	68	20	52		5	4	3	
Crane, Crain, Craine.	5.8	197	942	5	8	16	56		41	28	18	6	6	8	5
Cranston, Cranstin, Cranton.	5.5	26	117					16	8	1	1				
Crary, Crairy, Creary.	6.3	27	144	1		8	3	1	8	2			1	3	
Craven, Cravens, Cravin, Cravins.	6.1	22	112							8	1			8	5
Crawford, Crafard, Craferd, Crafferd, Crafford, Craford, Craufurd, Crawfoot, Crawfort, Crofford, Crofoot, Croford, Crowfoot, Crowford, Crwford.	5.5	377	1,699	9	8	12	20	3	34	52	107	30	26	40	26
Creekmerr, Creekmore.	4.6	24	86										13	24	
Cregar, Craiger, Creager, Cregier, Creiger.	5.8	18	86							4		13	1		
Creighton, Cratens, Craton, Crayton, Creaton, Creiton, Cretin, Crieghton.	4.5	34	118	2	2					4	6	10	2	2	6
Crenshaw.	4.8	28	105										26	1	1
Cressey, Creasey, Creasy, Crecy, Creesey, Creesy, Cresee, Cresey, Cressy, Criessee.	5.7	44	206	5	8	4	18		2	3	2		1	1	
Crews, Crew, Croos, Cruise, Cruize, Cruse, Kruse.	4.9	70	271	1						3	5	8	26	17	10
Crisman, Chrisman, Chrismon, Christman, Crismond, Crissman, Cristman, Krisman, Kristman, Kritsman.	5.9	72	355							7	40	4	14	6	1
Crisp.	5.5	20	89	1						1		3	3	11	1
Crist, Christ, Crice, Crise, Krist.	6.3	59	315							13	33	10	1	1	1
Crittenton, Chrittenden, Chrittenton, Crittenden, Crittendon, Crittenten, Crittinden, Crittindon, Crittinton.	5.0	51	203			2	15		24				6	1	3
Crocker, Crocar, Croker.	5.5	169	754	9	9	2	82	2	37	11		1	4	2	10
Crocket, Crockett, Crockit, Croket.	6.0	44	222	24	6							4	3		3
Cromwell, Crommel, Crommell, Cromvell, Cromwel, Crumuell, Crumwell.	6.1	49	251	3	5					16	2	19	1	2	1
Cronk.	6.3	16	85							15			1		
Cronkhite, Cronkite.	6.4	23	125			1				22					
Crooks, Crook, Crooke.	5.8	68	324	1	4	1	5	6	1	17	10	4	3	8	
Crosby, Crosbay, Crosbe, Crosbea, Crosbee, Crosbey, Crosbie, Crossbay, Crozby.	5.8	208	990	13	22	6	72	2	20	37	11	4		1	18
Crosman, Crossman, Crossmen, Krosman.	5.6	54	247	3	3	1	32	3	2	6	4				

TABLE **111.**—NOMENCLATURE, DEALING WITH NAMES REPRESENTED BY AT LEAST 100 WHITE PERSONS, BY STATES AND TERRITORIES, AT THE FIRST CENSUS: 1790—Continued.

NAME.	Average size of family.	TOTAL. Heads of families.	TOTAL. All other members.	Maine.	New Hampshire.	Vermont.	Massachusetts.	Rhode Island.	Connecticut.	New York.	Pennsylvania.	Maryland.	Virginia.	North Carolina.	South Carolina.
Cross, Crose	5.9	237	1,159	9	33	12	38	7	10	27	22	22	25	24	8
Crouch, Croutch	5.7	50	237	1	....	6	5	....	3	2	3	13	11	4	2
Crouse, Crous, Kraus, Krause, Krauss, Krous, Krouse	5.9	47	230	....	....	....	....	....	....	6	22	8	1	10	....
Crow, Croe, Crowe, Crows	5.7	101	475	....	....	....	5	....	6	5	36	17	8	9	15
Crowder, Crouder	6.2	30	157	....	....	....	....	....	....	....	1	1	19	5	4
Crowell, Croel, Crowall, Crowel	5.7	123	581	10	2	2	82	....	12	4	3	1	....	7	....
Crowl, Craull, Crawl, Croll, Crouel, Croul, Krawl, Kroll, Krowl	5.5	31	138	....	....	....	1	....	....	2	12	9	3	2	2
Crowson, Croasen, Crosen, Crossan, Crossen, Crossin, Crosson, Crousan	5.3	19	81	....	....	....	....	1	....	2	8	2	....	2	4
Crozer, Croseir, Croser, Crozier	5.9	20	98	....	....	3	....	....	....	1	16	....	....	....	....
Crum, Crom, Cromb, Crome, Croom, Crooms, Crumb, Crume, Crumm, Krom, Krome, Krum	5.6	100	461	....	....	....	....	2	5	4	41	16	4	10	13	5
Crump, Crumpts	6.3	38	201	....	....	....	....	....	....	....	1	....	28	7	2
Cryder, Creider, Crider	5.8	40	193	....	....	....	....	....	....	....	26	4	2	6	2
Cudworth, Codworth	6.0	25	125	....	3	....	15	....	....	....	....	....	4	1	2
Culbertson, Calbertson, Colberson, Colbertson, Colbeson, Cubbertson, Culberson	7.1	50	304	....	....	....	....	....	....	2	36	2	....	8	2
Culley, Cullee, Cully	5.7	23	109	....	....	....	....	....	....	5	7	1	6	4	....
Cullins, Culen, Culin, Culins, Cullan, Cullen, Cullin, Cullings	4.4	25	84	....	....	....	....	....	....	3	8	8	1	3	2
Culp, Culpt, Kulp	5.8	50	240	....	....	....	....	....	....	1	32	5	1	2	9
Culpeper, Culpepeper, Culpepper	4.7	28	103	....	....	....	....	....	....	....	....	....	17	9	2
Culver	5.6	111	510	....	1	17	10	....	35	37	3	6	....	2	....
Cummings, Coming, Comings, Comins, Commings, Commins, Cumin, Cumine, Cuming, Cumings, Cumins, Cummen, Cummin, Cumming, Cummins	5.6	332	1,538	23	38	15	75	3	12	47	41	27	12	28	11
Cunningham, Coningham, Conygham, Conyngham, Cunengham, Cunhingham, Cunigam, Cunigan, Cuningham, Cuninghame, Cunnigam, Cunninghame, Cunninham, Kuningham, Kunningham	5.7	275	1,293	19	3	4	26	....	8	28	71	17	48	26	25
Curle, Curl, Kearl, Keerls, Keirle, Kerl, Kirl, Kurl	6.2	25	129	1	....	....	....	....	....	....	6	2	12	4	....
Currier, Courier	5.6	147	680	9	72	9	54	....	....	....	....	....	....	....	2
Curry, Curray, Currey, Currie, Cury	5.1	157	650	1	4	....	1	6	....	27	32	11	12	50	13
Curten, Certain, Certin, Curtain, Curtin, Curtins, Kerton	5.9	22	107	....	....	....	3	....	....	7	1	3	....	5	3
Curtis, Curtes, Curtess, Curtice, Curtise, Curtiss, Curtiz	5.8	592	2,812	42	26	35	165	7	205	43	4	12	19	27	7
Curwin, Curvin, Curwen	5.6	37	169	....	....	....	....	....	1	35	1	....	....	....	....
Cushing, Cushin, Cushion, Cushon	6.2	125	656	16	9	6	87	3	....	3	....	....	....	1	....
Cushman, Cusman, Kushman	6.3	103	541	13	3	11	51	....	18	4	2	....	....	....	1
Custard, Custerd, Custord, Kustard	5.4	27	120	....	....	....	....	....	....	....	22	2	2	1	....
Cutler, Cutlar, Cuttler	6.2	133	689	3	10	15	57	3	18	18	2	2	1	....	....
Cutt, Cuts, Cutts, Kutz	6.0	37	185	13	4	....	....	....	....	....	16	....	1	3	....
Cutter	5.4	63	280	2	15	....	40	1	....	2	1	....	....	2	....
Cutting, Cuting, Cuttin	5.4	54	238	....	13	5	30	....	2	2	....	....	....	2	....
Daggett, Dagett, Daggart, Dagget, Daggot	5.9	68	332	6	5	5	37	4	9	2	....	....	....	....	....
Dailey, Daily, Daley, Dailley, Dally, Daly, Dayley, Dayly	5.1	115	467	4	2	3	12	1	8	14	27	17	6	14	7
Dakins, Dakin	7.3	19	120	....	3	3	5	....	....	8	....	....	....	....	....
Daland, Dealand, De Land, Deland	5.1	20	82	....	1	1	14	....	....	3	1	....	....	....	....
Dale, Dail, Dails, Dales	5.4	53	232	....	8	1	8	....	1	5	8	5	11	4	2
Dalrymple, Dalrimple, Darumple, Dilrimple	5.3	23	99	....	....	2	9	....	....	....	2	2	....	2	6
Dalton, Dolton	5.4	41	182	2	8	....	4	....	3	4	2	....	13	4	1
Dame, Dames	5.0	43	171	7	30	1	....	....	....	2	1	1	1	....	....
Dameron, Damerin, Dammeron, Damron	4.0	26	79	1	....	....	....	....	....	....	....	....	19	6	....
Damon, Daman, Dammon, Dammons, Dammun, Damons, Dayman	5.1	76	315	3	2	1	63	....	1	4	1	1	....	....	....
Dana, Danee, Daner, Danna, Danner, Danor, Danow	6.4	52	281	2	2	3	25	1	8	3	4	2	....	2	....
Dane, Dain, Daine, Dains, Danes, Dayns	5.1	42	173	1	4	....	21	....	4	7	4	....	....	1	....
Danforth, Danford, Danfort, Dantforth	5.6	99	452	4	32	11	39	1	5	2	1	2	....	....	2
Daniels, Danele, Danels, Danial, Daniel, Daniell, Daniells, Danil, Daniles, Danils, Dannel, Dannels, Danniels, Dannold, Danolds	5.4	385	1,677	3	29	9	67	....	41	24	24	2	53	111	22
Dann, Dan	5.9	27	133	1	....	....	1	....	5	17	2	1	....	....	....
Darby, Darbay, Darbe, Darbey, Derbe, Derbey, Derby	4.8	110	422	3	12	13	32	....	11	14	2	7	1	5	10
Darden, Dardan, Dardin, Dardon, Dawden	5.0	47	190	....	....	....	....	....	....	....	4	....	26	17	....
Darling, Dorling	5.6	143	653	5	19	15	57	9	8	23	2	2	2	....	1
Darlington, Darlenton, Darlinton	7.3	15	94	....	....	....	....	....	....	....	10	1	1	1	2
Darnall, Darnal, Darnel, Darnell, Darnil, Darnull	5.5	28	127	....	....	....	....	....	....	1	2	15	....	8	2
Darrow, Darough, Darragh, Darrah, Darrar, Darro, Darrough, Dorrah, Dorrow	5.6	62	286	1	4	5	2	....	22	16	10	1	....	1	....
Dart	5.0	56	224	....	10	5	2	....	32	1	1	3	....	....	2
Davenport, Deavenport, Debenport, Devanport, Devanporte, Devenport, Devensport, Devinport, Devonport	6.1	207	1,049	8	3	9	32	13	20	33	9	2	33	33	12
David, Davids	5.6	41	188	....	....	....	1	....	4	11	9	1	3	2	9
Davidson, Daverson, Davinson, Davison, Davisson, Deverson, Dividson	5.7	263	1,241	1	18	12	23	....	21	19	58	20	36	42	13
Davie, Davey, Davy	4.3	26	86	....	....	....	3	....	....	4	7	3	1	5	3
Davis, Daves, Davice, Davies, Davise, Daviss	5.6	2,575	11,725	121	203	67	357	68	136	224	336	194	316	392	161
Dawes, Daugh, Daw, Daws, Dawse	5.5	45	204	3	....	....	13	....	1	1	3	8	2	13	1
Dawkins, Darkins	5.4	18	79	....	....	....	....	....	....	....	2	2	4	5	5
Dawley, Dawly, D'Orlie, Dowly	5.4	37	161	....	....	....	1	15	....	1	....	1	18	1	....
Dawson, Dauson, Dorsen, Dorson	5.7	175	823	....	1	....	4	....	4	4	25	46	47	27	17
Day, Days, Deay, Dey, Deye	5.5	373	1,691	41	24	25	99	1	40	38	31	18	15	21	20
Dayton, Daten, Daton, Datton	5.6	77	356	....	....	2	2	3	32	33	....	....	1	3	....
Deal, Deale, Deals, Deel, Deele, Dehl, Deihl, Deil, Deill, Diel	6.2	113	586	....	....	2	3	....	2	6	39	25	6	25	5
Dean, Deane, Deanes, Deans, Deen, Deens, Diens	5.6	484	2,229	17	16	21	149	5	46	69	33	35	36	35	22
Dear, Deare, Dears, Deer, Deir	5.3	23	98	....	....	....	....	....	5	1	1	1	11	3	1
Dearborn, Dearben, Dearbin, Dearbon, Dearborne, Derban, Derborn	6.2	74	382	10	64	....	....	....	....	....	....	....	....	....	....
Dearing, Dearen, Dearens, Dearran, Deering, Dering, Derrin, Derring	5.4	54	236	20	3	....	2	....	4	6	4	....	12	3	....
Deaver, Deavor, Deavour, Deever, Deevers, Dever, Devers, Deves, Devirs	5.4	41	181	....	....	....	....	....	....	1	5	23	6	6	....
Decker, Deckir, Dicker, Dickers	6.2	169	880	12	....	....	....	....	....	108	38	2	7	1	1
Dedrick, Deadrich, Deatrich, Dederick, Dedrich, Deedrick, Deedrik, Deidk, Deidrich, Deidrick, Derttrick, Detrick, Didrich, Didrick, Dietrich, Dietrick	6.1	41	207	....	....	....	....	1	1	22	16	....	1	....	....
Dees, Deas, Dee, Deess, Deis	5.5	39	176	....	....	1	1	1	4	2	3	1	....	11	15
Deford	5.1	20	81	....	....	....	....	....	....	....	....	15	5	....	....
Deforest, Defforrest, D'Forest, De Forest, Deforist, D'Forrest, De Forrest, Deforrest, Duforrest	5.4	31	136	....	....	1	....	....	24	3	1	1	....	....	....
De Grove	6.7	27	154	....	....	....	....	....	....	27	....	....	....	....	....
Dehaven, Deheaven	6.3	20	105	....	....	....	....	....	....	....	20	....	....	....	....
De La Mater, Delamater, De Le Mater	6.0	42	209	....	....	....	....	....	....	42	....	....	....	....	....
Delaney, Delahny, De Laney, Delanoy, Delaney, Deleney, Delony, Delonay, Delony, Deluney, Dulany, Du Launy	5.1	37	153	....	....	....	3	....	....	4	14	8	2	4	2
Delano, Delanna, De La Noix, Deleno, Delino, Dellano, Dellino, Djlano, Dileno, Dilenow, Dillano, Dillanoe, Dilleno, Dillenor, Dilliner, Dillino, Dillinor	6.2	93	481	15	5	7	46	....	7	11	2	....	....	....	....
Delinger, Delinges, Dellinger, Dillinger	5.9	20	97	....	....	....	....	....	....	1	4	1	8	6	....
Deloach, Deeloach, De Loach, Deloatch	5.6	20	91	....	....	....	....	....	....	....	....	....	1	10	9

TABLE **111.**—NOMENCLATURE, DEALING WITH NAMES REPRESENTED BY AT LEAST 100 WHITE PERSONS, BY STATES AND TERRITORIES, AT THE FIRST CENSUS: 1790—Continued.

NAME.	Average size of family.	TOTAL. Heads of families.	TOTAL. All other members.	Maine.	New Hampshire.	Vermont.	Massachusetts.	Rhode Island.	Connecticut.	New York.	Pennsylvania.	Maryland.	Virginia.	North Carolina.	South Carolina.
Delong, Delon, De Long	6.3	41	219	....	....	1	1	....	....	24	12	....	1	2	....
Demerist, Demarest, Dimrest	5.3	29	126	....	....	....	....	....	....	29	....	....	....	....	....
Demeritt, Demerit, Demerrit, Demerritt	5.7	19	89	....	15	1	....	....	....	....	....	....	1	2	....
Deming, Deman, Demen, Demman, Demmans, Demmen, Demming, Demmins, Demmon, Demon	5.2	159	673	....	4	14	43	1	82	15	....	....	....	....	....
Dempsey, Dempsay, Dempsy, Demsey, Demsy, Dimpsey, Dimsey, Dimsy, Dincy	5.0	28	113	1	....	....	1	....	....	1	9	4	2	6	4
Denison, Denerson, Deniston, Dennerson, Denneson, Dennison, Dennisson, Denniston, Denson, Dineston, Dinnison	6.0	157	792	7	6	10	5	....	68	24	8	4	5	18	2
Dennet, Dennett, Dennit	6.5	28	153	17	10	....	....	....	....	1	....	....	....	....	....
Denning, Deneen, Denin, Dening, Dennen, Dennin, Dinin, Dinnen, Dinning	5.2	25	106	3	....	....	3	....	....	3	7	4	....	4	1
Dennis, Denais, Deneas, Denis, Dennise, Denniss, Dennyce, Diness, Dinnis	5.1	174	705	2	2	5	30	10	12	42	17	19	6	20	9
Denny, Denney, Dennie, Deny, Dinny	5.7	98	465	....	....	2	7	....	....	19	15	15	12	24	4
Dent, Dentz	5.3	47	201	....	....	....	....	....	....	2	....	32	4	8	1
Denton	5.4	89	391	....	....	1	5	....	2	50	....	2	14	11	4
De Puy, Deepu, De Pew, Depew, Depue, Dupey, Dupois, Dupu, Dupuey, Dupuis, Dupuy, Duypuy	5.6	67	305	....	....	....	....	....	2	39	10	....	14	....	2
Derr, Durr	6.4	37	201	....	....	....	....	....	....	....	25	4	....	6	2
Deshon, Deshang, Deshaun, Deshong, Dishon, Dishong, Dishorn	4.7	22	82	5	....	....	....	....	4	....	8	1	....	4	....
Devane, Devan, Devans, Devaughan, Devaughn, Devons, Divan, Divans	6.1	19	97	....	....	....	....	1	....	3	6	1	1	7	....
Devereux, Davarax, Deaverix, Deavorix, Debereaux, Devereaux, Deverick, Devericks, Deverix, Deviro, Devorex, Devorix, Devreaux, Divorux	4.8	31	119	2	....	1	12	....	....	9	....	4	1	1	1
De Vine, Devine, Divine	4.5	22	78	....	....	1	1	....	....	12	....	3	1	1	3
Devoe, Defoe, Devaugh, Devaux, Devoo, Devooe, Devoux, De Vow	5.7	41	192	....	....	....	....	....	....	36	....	1	2	....	2
Devore, Devar, Devarr, Devoir, Devoor, Devor, Devour, Devoy, Devoyer, Dvoure	5.6	28	128	....	....	....	....	....	....	1	16	3	4	....	4
Dew, Dews, Doux, Due, Dues, Duess, Duse	4.7	35	128	....	....	....	....	....	....	....	3	6	9	9	8
Dewees, Deweese, Deweeze, Dewese, Duwees	5.1	17	70	....	....	....	....	....	....	....	12	....	....	1	4
Dewey, Deway, Dewe, Dewy, Duae, Duay, Duyee	6.0	130	646	....	7	30	39	2	32	14	2	....	....	4	....
De Witt, Dewett, Dewhit, Dewight, Dewit, De Wite, Dewitt, Duet, Duett, Duewit	5.9	79	387	....	....	....	....	1	3	45	12	1	2	....	15
Dexter, Dextar, Dextor	5.7	107	501	4	6	5	47	22	14	8	1	....	....	....	....
De Yoe, Deo, De Yeo, De Yo, Deyo, De Yos	6.0	34	170	....	....	....	....	....	....	34	....	....	....	....	....
Dibble, Dibbell, Dibbill, Dibol	6.0	73	363	....	1	3	4	....	46	19	....	....	....	....	....
Dick, Dicke, Dickes, Dicks, Dix	5.3	127	541	....	3	5	16	....	9	11	35	12	10	15	11
Dickens, Deckins, Dicken, Dickins, Diking, Dykins	4.5	42	146	....	....	2	....	4	1	15	....	....	3	17	....
Dickerman	5.2	32	144	....	1	4	11	....	15	1	....	....	....	....	....
Dickey, Dickie, Dickkey, Dicky	5.8	79	379	5	9	2	....	1	....	1	35	....	1	14	11
Dickinson, Deckarson, Deckerson, Deckison, Dicingson, Dickason, Dickenson, Dickernson, Dickerson, Dickeson, Dickison, Dickoson, Dikerson, Dikingson	5.8	351	1,702	2	4	14	96	....	57	50	34	17	32	35	10
Diehl, Dial, Diall, Dile, Diol, Dyal, Dyall, Dyel, Dyle	6.0	31	156	1	....	....	....	....	....	....	16	6	2	4	2
Dietz, Deats, Deetz, Deits, Deitz, Dits	5.4	23	102	....	....	....	....	....	....	6	14	1	....	2	....
Diggs, Degge, Degges, Deig, Digges	5.4	29	127	....	....	....	....	....	....	1	6	19	3	....	....
Dike, Dikes, Dyche, Dyches, Dyek, Dyke, Dykes	5.9	45	222	....	....	7	14	....	2	3	1	3	7	....	8
Dill, Dille, Dills	5.1	69	280	2	....	....	5	....	....	1	7	21	7	12	14
Dillard, Dilliard, Dilyard	5.7	45	210	....	....	....	....	....	....	....	....	....	17	24	4
Diller, Dellow, Dilla, Dillar, Dillo, Dilor	5.5	23	104	....	....	....	....	....	1	....	18	....	1	3	....
Dillingham, Delenham, Dellingham, Dilinham, Dillenham, Dillinham	6.0	39	194	9	....	1	20	1	....	4	....	....	....	....	4
Dillon, Dilion, Dillen, Dillin, Dillins, Dillion, Dillyen	5.4	48	210	....	....	....	2	....	1	5	8	9	11	9	3
Dilworth, Delworth, Dilsworth	6.0	27	135	....	....	....	....	....	....	....	20	2	....	4	1
Dimmick, Damock, Demick, Demmack, Demmich, Demmick, Demock, Dimack, Dimick, Dimmik, Dimmock, Dimmuck, Dimock, Dymock, Dymuck	5.9	65	316	....	7	5	17	....	29	5	....	1	1	....	....
Dimond, Diamen, Diamon, Diamond, Diman, Dimand, Diment, Dimmon, Dimon, Dymond	5.2	63	263	....	14	1	12	8	8	8	4	4	....	4	....
Dingman, Dinghman	6.1	21	107	....	....	....	....	....	....	17	4	....	....	....	....
Dinsmore, Densemore, Densmore	6.5	49	268	7	21	6	8	....	1	1	4	....	....	....	1
Disbrow, Desbrow, Deseborough	6.5	19	104	....	....	....	....	....	13	5	....	1	....	....	....
Ditwiler, Deatwiler, Dedwaller, Dettwiler, Detwaller, Detweiler, Detwiler, Detwiller, Ditviler	5.1	18	90	....	....	....	....	....	....	....	18	....	....	....	....
Diver, Divas, Divers, Dives, Divese	7.3	16	100	....	....	....	2	....	....	1	3	8	1	1	....
Dixon, Dickson, Dixcon, Dixson	5.3	376	1,614	10	1	8	13	5	18	35	83	46	41	93	23
Doane, Doan	5.7	83	391	6	....	....	41	....	11	7	13	....	....	5	....
Dobbins, Dobbin, Dobins, Dobions, Dobyns	5.4	56	245	....	....	....	1	....	....	6	10	1	11	20	7
Dobbs, Dob, Dobb, Dobs	7.1	17	103	....	....	....	....	....	....	7	2	1	2	3	2
Dobson, Dabson, Dobbson, Dobston	5.0	35	140	....	....	....	....	....	....	6	3	5	8	9	4
Dockstader	7.4	14	89	....	....	....	....	....	....	14	....	....	....	....	....
Dodd, Dod, Dodds, Dods	6.2	79	412	2	....	....	15	....	7	7	14	6	3	11	14
Dodge, Dauge, Dodg, Doge, Doudge, Douge	5.9	346	1,712	28	50	16	119	18	20	51	3	....	16	24	1
Dodson, Dotson, Dotsons, Dottson	6.1	83	421	....	....	....	2	....	....	1	6	14	44	12	4
Doe, Dough	5.7	35	163	17	13	2	....	....	....	....	....	....	2	1	....
Doggett, Dogget, Doggot	5.3	31	133	....	....	2	14	....	....	....	....	....	13	1	1
Dole, Doles	5.9	44	217	5	2	....	30	....	....	1	....	....	....	6	....
Dolson, Dallison, Dallson, Dolenson, Dolison, Dollarson, Dollasson, Dollison, Dolsen	5.9	22	107	....	....	....	2	....	....	12	4	....	....	4	....
Donald, Donalds, Donnald, Donnalds, Dornald	5.2	26	109	....	....	....	....	....	1	3	3	13	....	....	5
Donaldson, Donaleson, Donalson, Donelson, Donillson, Donnaldson, Donnalson, Donnelson	6.2	76	395	....	1	....	1	....	....	12	30	5	9	13	5
Donally, Donaldly, Donaley, Donaly, Donely, Donley, Donly, Donnalay, Donnally, Donelly, Donnely, Donolly	4.6	41	146	....	....	1	2	....	....	4	20	5	4	2	3
Donnal, Donals, Donell, Donnel, Donnell, Donnels	5.6	25	115	3	....	....	....	....	....	4	1	....	16	....	1
Donoho, Donaho, Donehew, Donehugh, Donnahough, Donnehow, Donnehue, Donnihue, Donohoe, Donoughue, Dunahoe, Dunayhew, Dunnaho, Dunnahoe, Dunnahoo, Dunnehoe, Dunoho	4.8	26	99	1	....	2	....	1	....	2	3	2	3	5	7
Donovan, Donavan, Donnovan	5.4	19	83	....	....	1	....	....	....	2	4	11	....	....	2
Doolittle, Dolittle	5.4	100	444	....	2	10	6	....	65	15	1	....	....	....	2
Door, Doar, Doer, Doerr, Doore, Dor, Dorr, Dors	5.4	51	222	19	10	....	5	2	2	5	2	1	....	3	2
Doran, Dorans, Doren, Dorin, Doron, Duran, Duren, Durene, Durin, Duron, Durran, Durren	5.9	29	141	1	1	3	3	....	4	3	4	3	3	1	3
Dorman, Dormon, Dormond	5.3	49	212	6	....	2	5	....	18	5	....	5	....	7	1
Dorrance, Dorrence	5.8	18	87	....	....	....	1	7	9	....	1	....	....	....	....
Dorsey, Darsey, Dawsey, Dorcey, Dossey	5.8	104	499	....	....	....	1	....	1	....	7	86	2	4	3
Doss, Doz	6.8	18	105	....	....	....	....	....	....	....	2	....	13	1	2
Doty, Doaty, Dody, Dota, Dote, Dotee, Dotey, Dotty	5.6	80	367	1	....	4	17	....	6	41	4	....	....	6	1
Doud, Dowd, Dowds	5.2	51	216	....	....	8	8	2	23	2	....	1	....	7	....
Dougherty, Daughaday, Daugherty, Daughity, Daughtery, Daughtrey, Daughtry, Dawterry, Dogharty, Dogherty, Dohartee, Doharty, Dohatey, Dohertie, Doherty, Dohetey, Dohoty, Doratha, Doraty, Dorety, Dorhordy, Dorithy, Dorothy, Dougharty, Doughety	5.3	162	698	2	1	....	2	1	1	5	59	14	27	40	10
Doughty, Doubty, Doughte, Doughtee, Doutey, Douty, Dowty	5.6	73	333	10	....	....	2	....	....	35	14	1	....	5	6
Douglass, Doughlas, Doughlass, Douglas, Dougles, Dougless, Douglis, Duglas, Duglass, Dugles, Dugless, Duglis, Dugliss	5.6	296	1,362	17	5	8	17	12	39	32	54	14	43	30	25
Dove	5.2	24	100	....	....	....	6	....	....	....	1	4	8	2	3
Dow, Douw, Dowe, Dowes, Dowse	5.7	200	944	20	107	5	35	1	14	12	3	....	2	1	....
Dowdy, Doudey, Doudy, Dowdey	5.3	35	151	....	....	....	....	....	....	....	....	....	4	28	3

TABLE 111.—NOMENCLATURE, DEALING WITH NAMES REPRESENTED BY AT LEAST 100 WHITE PERSONS, BY STATES AND TERRITORIES, AT THE FIRST CENSUS: 1790—Continued.

NAME.	Average size of family.	TOTAL.		HEADS OF FAMILIES.											
		Heads of families.	All other members.	Maine.	New Hampshire.	Vermont.	Massachusetts.	Rhode Island.	Connecticut.	New York.	Pennsylvania.	Maryland.	Virginia.	North Carolina.	South Carolina.
Downer	5.9	35	172		3	12	6	2	4	1	3		1	1	2
Downey, Douney, Doweney, Downy	5.3	43	.187			1	1		1		6	20	2	10	2
Downing, Downen, Downend	5.8	142	676	11	15	3	22	2	9	23	25	2	14	11	5
Downs, Douns, Down, Downe, Downes	5.2	178	743	25	10	2	24		45	10	8	33	1	11	9
Doxey, Docksey, Doxcey, Doxsey, Doxy	5.8	21	101			1			1	12		2	3	2	
Doyle, Doil, Doile, Doyal, Doyale, Doyel, Doy'l, Doyl	4.8	58	221	4			3	1	3	2	25	10	3	4	3
Drake, Drack, Dreack, Dreick	5.4	271	1,197	4	23	9	52	2	28	78	32	2	7	28	6
Draper	5.4	108	471		7	6	42	3	3	14	4	5	8	10	6
Dreadon, Drayton	5.0	21	85									11	1		9
Dresser, Dresher, Dressor	5.8	49	236	8	1		25			7		7		1	
Drew, Drue	6.3	119	636	7	44	7	27	1	4	9		3	1	14	2
Drinkwater, Drinkworter	7.0	17	102	11			2		1	2			1		
Driver	5.8	44	213				8		1	1	9	2	8	12	3
Drown, Drownd, Drowne	5.8	33	158	3	9		5	14	1		1				
Drum, Drom, Droom	5.1	20	82				1			11	8				
Drummond, Drummon	5.8	18	87	6						2	2	2	2	1	3
Drury, Drewery, Drewry, Drurey, Drurye	5.4	78	341		7	5	25			2	2	17	14	6	
Du Bois, De Bois, Debose, Dubois, Du Boise, Duboise, Dubos, Dubose	5.7	99	469							81	1			1	16
Duck	5.6	27	123				1				8		5	12	1
Dudley, Dudly	5.1	227	929	20	31	7	33		47	8		10	36	29	6
Duel, De Waal, Dewall, Dewel, Dewell, Duall	5.3	53	226			3				36		1	13		
Duff	4.8	25	94				1			1	14	1	3	2	3
Duffey, Duffee, Duffie, Duffy	4.6	29	104		1					4	11	3	3	6	1
Duffield, Duffeld, Dufield	6.6	20	112							1	17	1	1		
Dugan, Doogan, Dougan, Dugen, Duggan, Duggans, Duggen, Duggin, Duggins, Duging, Dugins	5.2	58	241	3			2			5	17	8	5	12	6
Duke, Duk, Dukes	6.0	73	367				1			1	5	8	10	36	12
Duley, Dooley, Dooly, Dule, Dulley, Duly	6.2	18	93	1						1	1	8	1	5	1
Dulin, Doolan, Dooland, Doolin, Dooling, Dulan, Dulen, Duling, Dullen, Dulon	4.8	22	83	1						1	2	3	7	7	1
Dull, Dul	6.4	25	134								15	5	4	1	
Du Mont, Damont, Demond, Demont, Du Mond, Dumond, Dumong, Dumont	5.0	24	96				3			19				1	1
Dunaway, Donaway, Dunneway, Dunneway, Dunway	4.8	24	90							1	1	5	14	1	2
Dunbar, Dunbarr, Dunber, Dunbough	5.2	121	509	7	2	4	47	3	10	12	14	6	8	4	4
Duncan, Dongan, Duncin, Dungan, Dunkan, Dunken, Dunkin, Dunking, Dunncan	5.9	249	1,210	2	17	6	8	1	4	18	76	19	16	41	41
Dunham, Denham, Dennim, Donham, Donnom, Dunam, Dunnam, Dunnem, Dunnom, Dunnum	5.4	189	825	13	2	13	68	6	39	30	3		3	2	10
Dunkle, Dunckle, Dungill, Dunkel, Dunkell	8.6	14	106		3					1	7		3		
Dunlap, Dunlop	5.9	148	732	11	9	4	2		3	18	55	2	6	10	28
Dunn, Done, Dones, Dun, Dune	5.4	272	1,199	7	1	2	27	4	5	33	51	26	38	56	22
Dunnavant, Dunaphant, Dunavant, Dunnivant	6.2	17	88										15		2
Dunning, Doning, Dunin, Duning, Dunnen, Dunnin, Dunnon	5.8	95	459	11		11	1		24	23	6	5	2	11	1
Dunton, Dundon, Duntan	6.9	30	176	7	2	3	12		2				2	2	
Dunwoody, Denwiddie, Denwidie, Dinwedoe, Dinwiddie, Dinwody, Dinwoody, Dunwiddee, Dunwiddy, Dunwody, Dunwooddy	4.3	28	91								12	3	10	3	
Dupree, Depray, Deupree, Dupré	5.3	27	116				1						10	12	4
Durant, Durand, Durants, Duront, Durrant	4.9	48	189		6		14		11	7			1	2	7
Durfey, Durfey, Durffee, Durfy	6.6	50	279			4	6	31	5	3			1		
Durgin, Durgan, Durgon, Durkin	4.9	56	220	6	41	2					1	1	1	2	2
Durham, Darum, Dearum, Derham, Derram, Doram, Dorham, Durhame, Durram, Durrom	5.6	70	324	2		2			2	5	7	8	10	21	13
Durkee, Derkee, Durke, Durkey	6.0	30	149		5	12			10	2	1				
Duryee, Deryea, Deyea, Duryea	4.6	40	145							38		2			
Dusenbury, Dosenberry, Dusenberry, Dusenbery, Duzenberry	6.6	30	169							28	1		1		
Dustin, Dustan, Duston	5.7	45	210	1	35	1	4			2	2				
Dutcher, Ducher	6.5	35	194			3	1		3	26					
Duttero, Detterer, Dettro, Ditterer, Dudrow, Dutero, Dutterow	4.7	13	89								2	9		2	
Dutton, Duton, Dutten, Duttin, Dutting	6.0	98	492	9	16	16	14		25	1	8	6	1		2
Duvall, Davalt, Deval, Devall, Devalt, De Vaul, Devaul, Devaull, Devault, Devawl, Devol, Divall, Divol, Divoll, Duval, Du Vall, Duvalt, Duvol	5.8	122	590	1		1	32	7		4	14	42	13	4	4
Dwight	7.8	25	169				15		7					1	2
Dwinnell, Dwinal, Dwinals, Dwinel, Dwinell, Dwinelle, Dwinells, Dwinnel, Dwinnels, Dwinnills, Dwynal	6.1	35	177	14	9	2	10								
Dyckman, Dikeman, Dikman, Dykeman, Dykman	6.0	28	139							8	20				
Dye, Die, Digh, Duy, Dyes	5.7	41	193			1		5	4	7	8		8	3	5
Dyer, Diar, Dier, Dire, Duyer, Dyar, Dyars, Dyre	6.0	244	1,222	47	5	12	55	26	15	5	16	18	34	9	2
Dyson, Diason, Disins, Dison	5.5	28	126				1				1	12	7	4	3
Eager, Eagar, Eger, Egir, Egirs, Igher	6.5	35	194		3	2	14			5	5	1		3	2
Eagle, Eagel, Eagles, Egle, Igle	5.3	27	115							5	9	5	4	3	1
Eames, Eams	5.5	66	297	2	5	2	38	1	15			2			1
Earl, Earle, Earles, Earll, Earls, Erl, Erle	5.6	130	597		1	6	30	12	2	38	15	7	2	11	6
Early, Earley	6.0	42	209				1			6	14	6	6	7	2
Earnest, Earness, Earnist, Earnst, Ernest, Ernise, Ernist, Ernst	5.3	44	187			1				3	21	5	2	5	7
Earp, Earpe	7.1	16	97										6	9	1
Easley, Easely, Easly, Esley, Isley	5.2	26	108	2			1				2		10	5	6
Eason, Easson, Esign	5.7	41	194			1	1		2		2	2	2	30	1
East, Easte	6.0	30	149				2	2			3		7	4	12
Easter, Easters, Eastir	6.6	20	111	2			1			4	4	1	3	4	1
Easterbrook, Easterbrooks, Estabroks, Estabrook, Estabrooks, Esta Brooks, Esterbrooks, Estherbrooks	5.5	64	291		12	8	28	12	4						
Eastman, Easthman, Eastmon, Estman	5.7	162	764	7	104	20	13		9	8				1	
Easton, Easten, Eastern, Eastin, Easting, Esten, Eston, Estton	5.9	72	354			1	11	24	8	3	5	6	4	5	5
Eastwood, Easterwood	6.0	25	123							8	1	1	5	7	3
Eaton, Eaten, Eatton, Eten, Eton, Etton	5.7	380	1,782	33	82	26	118		25	25	24	12	21	14	
Eberley, Eberly	5.3	19	82								16		2		1
Ebert, Eberts, Ebhart	5.6	18	84							1	12	4		1	
Eby, Eaby, Ebi, Ebie	6.0	20	99								20				
Echols, Eccles, Ecels, Echolles, Echolls, Eckle, Eckles, Eckols, Eichols, Ekel, Ekels	7.3	28	175						1		6	1	15	5	
Eckart, Earchart, Echart, Eckard, Eckert, Eckhard, Eckhart, Ecurt, Eghart, Eichart, Eickard, Eigert, Ekart, Ekert, Ekirt	6.9	63	370							25	28	8	1		1
Eddins, Eddens, Eddin, Eddings, Edings, Edins, Iddings	5.8	25	121				2				3		8	6	8
Eddy, Eadie, Eady, Edde, Eddey, Eddie, Edee, Edey, Edie, Edy	5.8	193	920	3	2	22	71	38	12	25	11	1	3	2	3
Edelen	5.1	33	136									33			
Eden, Edens	5.1	23	94	1			1		1	1	2	4		3	10
Edes, Eades, Eads, Eeds	5.6	44	203	4	2		20	1	1	1		5	5	4	1
Edgar, Edger, Edgir, Edgo	4.2	24	76		2		1			5	11	4	2	1	

TABLE **111.**—NOMENCLATURE, DEALING WITH NAMES REPRESENTED BY AT LEAST 100 WHITE PERSONS, BY STATES AND TERRITORIES, AT THE FIRST CENSUS: 1790—Continued.

NAME.	Average size of family.	TOTAL. Heads of families.	TOTAL. All other members.	Maine.	New Hampshire.	Vermont.	Massachusetts.	Rhode Island.	Connecticut.	New York.	Pennsylvania.	Maryland.	Virginia.	North Carolina.	South Carolina.
Edge, Ege	5.7	18	84		28				1		7	1	3	6	1
Edgerly	5.5	30	134	1	28				1						
Edgerton, Eagerston, Eagerton, Edgarton, Edgeton, Edgiton, Egerton, Egeton	5.4	50	221		1	8	4		28		1	1		7	
Edmonds, Edman, Edmans, Edmon, Edmond, Edmons, Edmund, Edmunds	5.8	98	475	1	9	9	17	5	6	16	6		20	5	4
Edmondson, Edmandson, Edmonsen, Edmonson, Edmonston, Edmonstone, Edmundson, Edmunson	5.2	62	261							4	2	16	16	18	6
Edson, Eadson, Edinson, Edison, Ediston, Eidson	5.9	74	362	1	3	14	37		7	1	4		5		2
Edwards, Edwads, Edward, Edword, Edwords	5.5	593	2,658	8	11	3	59	14	53	48	73	31	108	137	48
Eeghmy	8.0	14	98							14					
Egburt, Egbert, Egberts, Egbertse, Egbird	4.5	25	88			1				22	2				
Egleston, Eagleston, Eaglestone, Eagleton, Eccleston, Eceleston, Egelston, Eggleson, Eggleston, Egglestone, Eggleton Eggliston, Eglerton, Egleson, Eglestin, Eglestone, Egleton, Elggleston	6.0	87	436		3	2	12		20	27	3	6	8	6	
Elam	6.1	18	92					1					16		1
Elder, Elders	5.7	92	432	10			7			3	39	18		4	11
Eldred	6.3	29	154				16	3	5	4	1				
Eldridge, Eldredge, Eldrig, Eldrige, Elridge	5.7	147	694	4	3	6	66	10	22	28	3		1	2	2
Elkins, Elkin, Elkings	5.9	57	279	1	25	3	5				1		1	17	4
Ellenwood, Elenwood, Ellengwood, Ellingwood, Ellinwood	5.1	25	102	2	12	1	8			1		1			
Eller, Ela, Eler, Ellar, Ellers, Ilar, Iler, Iller, Ilor	5.9	42	204		7		3			2	7	9		14	
Ellicott, Elicott, Ellcott	10.2	10	92							2	5	3			
Ellington, Ellenton, Ellinton	6.7	22	125							1			14	5	2
Elliott, Elet, Eliot, Eliott, Ellet, Ellett, Elliatt, Elliot, Ellit, Ellitt, Ellot, Ellott, Ellyot	5.6	469	2,154	10	44	3	49	3	33	41	80	51	41	71	43
Ellis, Eles, Elies, Elis, Elles, Ellise	5.7	541	2,535	7	26	26	146	10	33	49	40	19	52	106	27
Ellison, Ellerson, Elliston, Ellyson	5.0	82	330		5		4			22		1	24	14	12
Elmendorph, Elmendorf, Elmendorff	5.0	22	87							22					
Elmore, Ellimore, Ellmore, Elmor, Elmoure, Elsmore	4.9	76	300	1		7	1		16	13		2	7	21	8
Elsworth, Elesworth, Ellsworth	5.5	93	409	1	10	5	5	1	24	42	2		2		1
Elwell, Ellwell, Ellwill, Elwel, Elwil	5.4	55	244	16		1	26		3	7			2		
Elwood, Ellwood	6.6	17	95					1	8	4	3	1			
Ely, Ealey, Ealy, Eley, Eli, Elly	6.2	145	750		2	3	28	4	35	10	33	3	20	5	
Emerson, Emberson, Emeson, Emison, Emmersen, Emmerson, Emrson	5.8	207	991	19	75	13	64	1	8	3	3	8	8	5	
Emery, Emeary, Emmerie, Emmery, Emmory, Emmry, Emory, Emrey, Emry, Imry	5.6	200	910	76	46	3	14			4	17	20	13	4	3
Emes, Emmes	5.3	24	103	1	10		11				2				
Emmit, Emet, Emit, Emmet, Emmitt, Emott	5.4	22	97				1			3	10	3	2	2	1
Emmons, Eaman, Emens, Emmans, Emmins, Emmonds, Emonds, Emons	5.4	79	346	11	6	3	15		22	12	4		6		
Emrich, Emerick, Emmerich, Emric, Emrick	5.8	31	150								30	1			
England, Ingland	6.8	35	203			1	1			1	8	8	3	11	2
English, Inglish	5.2	79	330	2	2	4	5		3	9	18	3	8	16	9
Ennis, Eanis, Enes, Eness, Enis, Ennice, Enniss, Ennist	6.2	31	160				3			5	5	8	2	3	5
Enochs, Enoch, Enock, Enox	6.3	23	121				2				10		4	7	
Enos, Eanos, Eno, Enus	6.0	45	225		1	5	1	6	17	7	2	1	5		
Ensign	6.9	28	166				7		14	5	2				
Epps, Epes, Eppes, Eps	6.0	22	110	1	5		2						10	4	
Erb	5.4	26	115								23	3			
Erhart, Earhart, Earheart, Ehart, Ehrhart, Erehard, Erehart, Erhrardt	6.4	26	141							1	15	2	5		3
Eshelman, Eshleman	7.0	17	102								17				
Essex, Essack, Esseck, Esseick, Essick	7.3	15	95					6		2	7				
Ester, Esters, Esther, Esthers, Estor	6.1	17	86	3						2	4			6	2
Estes, Eastes, Eastis, Estas, Estees, Estis	5.2	61	258	14	4		10	4	1	2	1		14	5	6
Esty, Eastey, Easty, Estee, Estey	5.0	25	101		6	1	18								
Etheridge, Eatheridge, Etherage, Etheredge, Etherege, Ethiredge, Ethridge, Etridge, Ettridge	5.6	90	417		2		4		1				28	48	7
Eubank, Eubanks, Ewbank	5.0	25	101									4	11	5	5
Evans, Eavans, Eavens, Eavins, Evan, Evanse, Evens, Evians, Evins, Ivens, Ivins	4.5	698	3,126	11	46	21	35	7	20	33	197	68	71	109	80
Everhart, Everhard, Everheart	5.4	39	170								27	7		2	3
Everitt, Evaritt, Everat, Everatt, Everet, Everett, Everetts, Everit, Everite, Everrett, Evert, Everts, Evirett, Evret, Evritt	6.0	206	1,021	1	4	12	37		13	30	21	16	20	45	7
Everly, Eveleigh, Eveley, Evely, Everley, Eversley	4.7	22	81	1			5		1		9	3	1	1	1
Eversole	11.0	21	210								19	2			
Everson, Everston, Evisten	5.1	20	81				7		1	8	3		1		
Eves, Eave, Eaves, Eve, Evegh	5.7	19	89				1				11		3	2	2
Evetts, Evet, Eveth, Evets, Evett, Evit, Evits, Evitts	5.3	42	181			3			24	3	2	5		2	3
Ewell, Ewel	5.4	29	128	1	1		7					2	10	8	
Ewers, Euers, Ewer	7.1	14	86	2	2		7				2		1		
Ewing, Ewen, Ewin, Ewinge, Ewings, Ewins	5.2	120	505	4	2	1	1	1	4	2	47	17	26	5	10
Fagan, Fagen, Fagin, Fagins, Feagan, Feagins, Fegan, Fegean, Phagan	4.9	30	116							2	9	2	3	9	5
Fair, Fairs, Fare	6.1	28	144				3				7	5	1	8	4
Fairbanks, Fairbank, Farbanks, Farebank, Farebanks, Ferbanks, Firbanks, Furbanks	5.8	119	574	7	9	5	78	4	3	3		10			
Fairchild, Fairchield, Fairchilds, Fearechiles	5.6	104	473			9	6	1	60	20	1			2	5
Faircloth	5.5	21	95								1			19	1
Fales, Fail, Faile	6.2	35	181	9	5	3	12	1	2		1	1		1	
Fall, Falls	7.0	44	264	7			24	6			4		1	2	
Fanning, Faning, Fannan, Fannin, Fannon	5.1	28	126	9	2		1			4	6	2		4	
Fanning, Faning, Fannan, Fannin, Fannon	5.1	45	186	1		1	6		16	10	2		2	5	2
Farley, Fareley, Farlee, Farly	6.5	58	318	2	10	2	10		2		6	2	10	13	1
Farmer, Farmar, Farmor	5.5	136	616		8	8	20		4	2	5	7	42	29	11
Farnham, Farnam, Farnum, Farnume, Fernam	5.7	127	598	19	27	8	41	3	29						
Farnsworth, Farmsworth, Farnswort, Fawnsworth	5.5	72	325	7	18	13	26		3	4	1				
Farr, Far	6.4	67	364	3	21	7	9			6	5	5		4	7
Farrar, Farer, Fariar, Farrer, Farrier, Farrior, Farror	5.2	77	324		19		24	1		1	1		12	11	8
Farrell, Farall, Farell, Farral, Farrall, Farrel, Pharrell	5.4	22	96	2					1	2	6	8			3
Farrington, Farington, Ferrington	5.5	80	363	7	9	3	34		1	24			2		
Farrow, Fara, Farra, Farrah, Farree, Farro	4.9	48	186	6		1	5			1	4	1	6	17	7
Farwell, Fairwell, Farewel, Farewell	6.1	55	282	4	19	9	18		1	1		2		1	
Fassett, Fassat, Fasset, Fassitt	7.0	29	174	4	3	7	3		3			8	1		
Faulkner, Falconer, Falkener, Falkenur, Falkernr, Falkner, Faukner, Faulconer, Faulkener, Folkner, Folknor, Forkenor, Forkner	5.8	122	584	1			20	1	1	18	14	23	16	24	4
Faunce, Fauns	5.8	19	91			1	13				5				
Fawcett, Faucett, Faucit, Fauset, Fausett, Fausset, Fawsett	4.4	23	79	1							4		8	9	1
Faxon, Faxen, Faxin, Faxson, Faxton	6.5	20	109		2		16	1	1						
Fay, Fays	6.4	88	476		6	15	54		6	4	1	1			
Fell, Fells	7.1	37	224					1		1	30	2		2	1
Fellows, Fellow	5.6	104	477	3	37	8	24		17	9	2			3	1
Felt, Feltch, Felteh, Felts, Feltz	5.8	41	195		10	2	22		2	2			1		2

TABLE **111.**—NOMENCLATURE, DEALING WITH NAMES REPRESENTED BY AT LEAST 100 WHITE PERSONS, BY STATES AND TERRITORIES, AT THE FIRST CENSUS: 1790—Continued.

NAME.	Average size of family.	TOTAL. Heads of families.	TOTAL. All other members.	Maine.	New Hampshire.	Vermont.	Massachusetts.	Rhode Island.	Connecticut.	New York.	Pennsylvania.	Maryland.	Virginia.	North Carolina.	South Carolina.
Felter	6.6	18	100							16	1	1			
Felton, Feltin	5.2	53	224		2	1	37			1	4	1		5	2
Fennell, Fenel, Fenell, Fenil, Fennel, Fennil	5.5	26	117			1					3	3	4	10	5
Fenner, Fener, Fennir	5.9	40	197				3	27			6	1		3	
Fenton, Fentons, Phenton	5.0	62	249		1	3	3		29	8	11	2	5		
Fentress, Fentriss	5.7	40	186											38	2
Fenwick	5.3	20	86								18				2
Ferguson, Fargurson, Fargusen, Farguson, Farguhaison, Fergason, Fergerson, Fergison, Fergueson, Fergusson, Forgason, Forgerson, Forgeson, Forgison, Forguson, Furgason, Furgerson, Furgeson, Furgesson, Furgison, Furguson, Furgusson	5.6	324	1,494	7	7	3	16	1	4	71	55	28	55	50	27
Ferrell, Fearal, Fearell, Ferel, Ferral, Ferrall, Ferrel, Ferril, Ferrile, Ferrill, Ferroll	5.4	65	289				3	1	1	2	5	10	9	32	2
Ferrin, Farran, Farrand, Farren, Farron, Ferran, Ferrand, Ferren, Ferrend, Ferring, Ferrins, Ferron, Pherrin	6.6	49	272	8	12	6	2		4			10	6	1	
Ferris, Faires, Fairis, Fairiss, Faris, Fariss, Farras, Farries, Farris, Farrise, Farrist, Fearis, Feris, Firris, Phares, Pharis	6.0	170	857	1	1	8	7		40	61	11	3	13	12	13
Ferry, Feree, Ferree, Ferrey, Ferrie, Ferrys	5.9	65	321			1	23		11	4	24			1	1
Fessenden, Fesenden, Fessedon, Fessendon, Feszenden	6.8	29	168	2	1	1	24		1						
Fetter, Fetters	6.1	18	91							2	15		1		
Field, Fealds, Feild, Feilds, Fialds, Fieldes, Fields	6.2	339	1,761	15	18	28	79	23	26	36	29	22	5	38	20
Fielder, Felder, Fieldar	6.1	20	101				2				1		10		7
Fife	5.8	21	101		3	1	3			1	7	3		2	1
Fifield, Fefield, Fifeld, Fiffeald, Fiffield	5.1	50	204	2	45	3									
Fight, Feight, Feit, Feits, Fite, Fites	5.5	23	102		1						15	4		3	
Fike, Fick, Fickes, Fik, Fikes	5.7	29	135		6						15			5	3
File, Files, Fills, Fils	5.0	27	107	5						3	2	2		10	5
Filley, Filey, Filly, Phili	5.2	24	100						16		8				
Finch	5.8	131	623		3	2	3	2	30	56	7		11	11	4
Fink, Finck	6.0	52	262							2	17	26	4	1	2
Finley, Findeley, Findlay, Findley, Findly, Finlay, Finly	5.4	111	489			2	2		6	3	53	6	7	13	19
Finn, Fin, Fine	6.1	40	202				3		15	8	3	4	5	1	1
Finney, Finey, Finne, Finnie, Finny, Phiney, Phinney, Phinny	5.6	129	587	16	2	8	38	4	16	5	23	1	7	6	3
Fish, Fich	5.9	222	1,092	7	3	16	85	25	38	29	7	5		6	1
Fisher, Fesher, Fischer, Fysher	5.6	570	2,626	10	27	25	106	6	9	61	189	55	33	40	9
Fisk, Fiskes	6.1	189	954	3	19	17	101	17	13	12	5		1		1
Fitch	5.9	191	943	7	6	18	34		86	26	6	3	1	3	1
Fitz, Fits, Fitt, Fitts	5.5	52	232	7	4	3	21		2	1	6	2	1	3	2
Fitzgerald, Fichgerrel, Fitchgearald, Fitchgerrel, Fitsgarrel, Fitsgerald, Fitsgerel, Fitsgorrel, Fitsjarald, Fitsjerald, Fitts Gerald, Fitzarrell, Fitzgarald, Fitzgarrold, Fitzgearld, Fitzgeral, Fitz Gerald, Fitzgerrald, Fitz Gerrald, Fitzgerrel, Fitzgerrold, Fitzjairald, Fitzjarald, Fitzjerald	5.4	71	311	6	4			1	2	7	18	12	11	5	5
Fitzpatrick, Fetzpattreck, Fichpatrick, Fitchpattareck, Fitspatrick, Fitzpaterick	5.0	39	154							3	8	4	12	6	6
Flack, Flacke	5.7	23	108					1		2	14		2	4	
Flagg, Flag, Flogg	5.5	91	409	3	10	8	59	1	5	2			1		2
Flanagan, Flanaghan, Flanagin, Flanakin, Flanegan, Flanigan, Flanigin, Flanikin, Flannagan, Flannagin, Flannegan, Flannegon, Flanningham	5.5	40	178							3	10	11	9	4	3
Flanders, Flander	5.9	71	346	2	60	2	3			2	2				
Fleck, Flaake, Flake, Fleak	5.6	24	111				1			1	13	1	2	4	2
Fleet	5.1	20	81				2				14		4		
Fleming, Fleeming, Fleman, Flemans, Flemen, Flemin, Flemmin, Flemming, Flemmings, Flemmon, Flemons, Flemyng, Fliming, Floming, Fluming	5.8	186	887	1		3	7			12	66	17	21	36	23
Fletcher, Flecher, Flitcher	5.6	240	1,094	23	33	17	81		9	6	19	11	15	20	6
Flinn, Flin, Flyn, Flynn, Phlyn	4.4	43	145	2	1		3		2	9	5	4	5	6	6
Flint, Flynt	6.1	134	683	7	14	7	51		19	17	1	6	4	5	3
Flood, Flod, Flud	4.8	43	163	5	11	1	11				3	3	4	5	
Flowers, Flours, Flower, Flowrah	5.8	100	480				2	10	5	7	25	9	4	27	11
Floyd, Ffloyd, Floid, Floyde	5.0	91	363	4			15			5	3	6	6	27	25
Fly, Phly	6.4	16	86	6							4			5	1
Fobes, Forbis, Forbus	5.5	53	240	2	1	1	21			14			3	4	4
Fogg	5.5	72	325	33	34		1		1				2	1	
Fogle, Fogal, Fogel, Foghel	6.5	22	120								11	9			
Folger, Folgor, Foulger	5.2	62	261				51			8		2	1		
Folk, Faulk, Faulks, Fawkes, Fawlkes, Foalks, Folke, Folks, Foulk, Foulke, Foulks, Fowke, Fowlkes	5.4	129	561							6	61	2	33	23	4
Follet, Follett	5.3	34	148	3	11	5	7	5	1	2					
Follinsbe, Fallansbe, Fallensbee, Folansbee, Folemsby, Folensbee, Folensby, Follambe, Follansbe, Follensbee, Follinsbee	6.3	28	147		6	1	18			3					
Folsom, Falsom, Folsome, Folsum	5.8	73	353	7	62	1	1							2	
Foltz, Folts	5.7	28	131				1				5	14	1	4	3
Fonda, Fonnada	6.1	33	168							31	1			1	
Foot, Foote, Fout, Fouts, Foutz	6.3	174	917	4	6	13	23		77	16	14	4	1	15	1
Forbes, Forbs	5.8	112	535	1	1	5	31		14	10	13	4	2	30	1
Ford, Foard, Foord, Foords, Forde, Fordes, Fords, Fourd	5.7	383	1,802	18	13	7	56	1	60	32	25	75	32	23	1
Fordham, Fordam, Fordom, Foredom	5.8	19	91				1			14	2			1	1
Fore, Foore	6.9	16	95							3			8	3	2
Foreman, Foremon, Forman, Fourman	6.2	92	479							17	20	20	15	17	3
Forrest, Forest, Forist, Forress, Forriss, Forust	4.6	84	299		5	3	9			3	7	6	29	13	9
Forrister, Forester, Forister, Forrester, Forristor	5.3	41	175				2	1	1	1	2	16	3	8	7
Forsythe, Foresyth, Forsaith, Forscyth, Forseyth, Forsight, Forsith, Forsithe, Forsyth, Forsythes	5.6	45	207		4		1			8	16	4	4	7	1
Fort, Fourt	5.4	52	230	2			1			20		1	1	26	3
Fosdick, Fosdike	5.1	23	95				12		7	2					
Foss, Fose	5.3	91	391	31	58		1			1					
Foster, Farster, Faustar, Fauster, Forster, Fosster, Fosters, Fostor	5.5	830	3,771	45	50	32	265	20	35	82	68	40	105	51	37
Fountain, Fontaine, Fontaines, Fountaine, Fountin, Founton	5.5	54	245	4		2			2	9		14	8	10	5
Foust, Foost	5.9	30	148								16			6	8
Fowle, Fowl, Fowles, Fowls	5.0	35	140	3	1		25	1	1				2		1
Fowler, Fauler, Fouler, Fowlar, Fowlers	5.6	447	2,061	13	27	10	72	21	63	85	30	46	22	28	30
Fox	5.6	323	1,476	6	16	10	20	1	73	39	84	26	20	20	8
Foy, Foye	4.8	32	121	10	4		4				1	3	2	3	2
Frame, Fraim, Frain	5.7	19	89							1	16	1	1		
France, Franch	5.7	45	211							7	18	1	3	1	
Francis, Frances, Francies, Franciss, Franses, Frauncis	5.1	137	562	1		7	25	2	31	9	27	8	15	6	6
Frank, Franch, Franck, Franke, Franks	5.5	77	347	3						1	13	33	5	5	5
Franklin, Frankling, Franklyn	5.6	189	870		6	9	9	19	7	10	8	31	42	24	24
Frary, Frairey, Frara, Frarey	6.1	22	111				2	18		1	1				

TABLE 111.—NOMENCLATURE, DEALING WITH NAMES REPRESENTED BY AT LEAST 100 WHITE PERSONS, BY STATES AND TERRITORIES, AT THE FIRST CENSUS: 1790—Continued.

NAME	Average size of family	TOTAL. Heads of families	TOTAL. All other members	HEADS OF FAMILIES. Maine	New Hampshire	Vermont	Massachusetts	Rhode Island	Connecticut	New York	Pennsylvania	Maryland	Virginia	North Carolina	South Carolina
Fratz, Frats, Fratts	7.0	16	96							4	12				
Frazier, Fraiser, Fraisor, Fraisyier, Fraizer, Fraizier, Fraser, Frasher, Frashier, Frasier, Frasior, Frasure, Frasyier, Frayser, Frayzier, Frazair, Frazer, Frazir, Frazire, Frazor	4.9	200	787	1	2	5	10	3	7	27	31	25	17	43	29
Frederick, Fredenrick, Frederic, Fredrick	6.9	61	361				3			17	34	2	1	2	2
Free	5.7	18	84				1			1	5	5			6
Freeland, Freelan, Freland	6.1	32	164				10		1	4	3	5	3	5	1
Freeman, Freemon, Freman	5.6	394	1,795	23	15	21	88	6	26	42	25	20	28	75	25
Freeze, Frease, Frees, Freese	5.5	34	152	6	4		1	1			12	1	3	5	1
French, Frentch	5.5	488	2,180	12	122	41	164	2	56	30	19	17	7	10	8
Frere, Freear, Freer	5.6	56	257							47	2				7
Frick, Fricke, Fricks	5.8	20	95								16	1		3	
Friend, Freind, Frend	5.9	36	176	3	1		7	1		1	11	2	8		2
Frink	6.1	51	258		3	1	13	1	25	6		1			1
Frisbie, Frisbe, Frisbee, Frisbey, Frisby	5.5	74	333			6	4		43	13	1	6		1	
Fritz, Frit, Frits	5.9	34	167							5	27			1	1
Frizell, Frisell, Frissel, Frissell, Frizel, Frizzel, Frizzell, Frizzle	5.5	36	161	3		3	6		1			6	9	5	3
Frost, Fraust, Frostt	5.7	237	1,124	43	18	8	66	1	26	50	2	7	5	5	6
Frothingham	6.1	27	138	1			21	1	3	1					
Fry, Frey, Frye, Phry	6.0	231	1,155	13	2	1	29	11	5	9	101	15	19	24	2
Fryer, Frair, Frairs, Freaer, Frear, Freyer, Friar, Frier, Fryar, Fryers, Fryor	5.5	51	231			1			1		12	15	3	2	10
Fulford	6.2	20	103						4			1	4	11	
Fuller, Fullar, Fullear, Fullier	5.6	586	2,685	22	38	50	210	13	116	70	8	9	4	30	16
Fullerton	4.5	43	152	3	2		6		1	4	18	2	1	3	3
Fulmer, Fullmer, Fulmore, Fulner	6.2	38	196							8	23				7
Fulton, Fullton, Fulten, Fultin	5.7	92	436	2	3		5			9	46	8	7	7	5
Funk, Funck	6.2	70	365							4	42	12	12		
Furber, Ferber, Ferebee, Furbur	6.2	20	104		12		2				1		2	3	
Furbush	5.5	42	190	12		1	22						7		
Furman, Fureman	5.7	33	156			1				28	3				1
Furnald, Fernald, Fernalld, Furnal, Furnall	5.4	63	275	42	20						1				
Furnass, Furnace, Furness, Furnis, Furnish, Furniss	5.8	21	101	1	3		8				2		5		2
Futrill, Futrall	5.1	21	85											21	
Gable, Gabbel, Gabble, Gabel	5.5	23	104							2	17	1			3
Gaddis, Gaddes, Gaddice, Gadis, Geddes, Geddis, Gedis	4.8	25	94							1	12	3		8	1
Gage	6.0	124	624	4	33	8	37		5	29				8	
Gains, Gain, Gaine, Gaines, Ganes, Geans	5.7	76	360			2	4	9		11	3	2	4	22	12
Gale, Gael, Gail, Gales, Gayle, Gayles	6.1	164	836			28	7	38		14	30	5	11	18	9
Gallaher, Galaher, Galeher, Galleher, Gallehew, Galliher, Galloher, Gelaher, Golhar, Gollerher, Golliher, Gollihor	5.2	34	143								25	1	3	3	2
Gallop, Gallep, Gallup, Galop	6.2	74	385		2	7	8		39	5	3	1		9	
Galloway, Galaway, Galiway, Gallaway, Galleway, Galliway, Gallowary, Galoway, Galway, Golaway	5.4	69	303	1			4			9	13	14	4	12	12
Galpin, Galpen, Galphin	5.6	20	91				2		15	2					1
Galusha, Gallusha, Gelashee, Goleshir, Gulishau	6.9	17	100			6	8			1	1	1			
Gamble, Gamball, Gambel, Gambell, Gambol, Gimbold	5.4	70	307		1	3	3			5	24	5	1	7	21
Gammon, Gamman, Gammons, Gamon, Gayman, Gehman, Geiman, Gimman, Gumans, Gymon	5.7	44	205	14	1		5		1	2	12		5	3	1
Gant, Gants, Gantt, Gantz, Gaunts, Gent, Gontz	5.1	52	213	1						3	16	15	3	10	4
Gardner, Gadner, Gardeneer, Gardener, Gardenor, Gardineer, Gardiner, Gardiners, Gardnier, Gardnir, Gardnor, Gardrr, Gartiner, Gartner, Guardner	5.6	706	3,239	23	17	14	188	84	27	128	56	58	20	75	16
Garey, Gairey, Gairy, Garry, Gary	5.4	43	201	4	3	3	3		9	2	5	7		2	5
Garfield, Gaffeild, Gaffield, Gaffill, Garfeild, Gearfield, Goffield	5.4	35	153		3	3	28			1					
Garland, Garlant, Garlind	5.5	76	343	5	37	1				2	3	6	15	6	1
Garlock, Garlach, Garleck, Garlic, Garlick, Gerlach	5.6	26	119			1	2		6	7	5	3		2	
Garner, Gamer, Garnier, Garnur	5.6	107	497			1	1		1	4	13	8	22	38	19
Garnett, Garnet	5.4	25	109				14			2	1	2	2	1	3
Garrett, Garett, Garit, Garrat, Garratt, Garret, Garrit, Garrot, Garrott, Gerrit, Gerritt	5.6	163	749			4	2		9	13	38	8	18	48	23
Garrison, Garison, Garisson, Garitson, Garretson, Garrettson, Garrisson, Garritson, Gerison, Gerrison, Gerritson	5.9	119	588			5	2	1		55	21	4	11	17	10
Garvin, Garven	5.4	23	101			5	2			1	6	1			8
Gaskins, Gasken, Gaskin, Gasking, Gaskings, Gaskinn, Geskin, Geskins	5.9	54	262			3				3	1		18	20	9
Gaston, Gasten, Gastin, Gesting, Gostin, Gusten, Gustin, Gustion, Guston	5.4	63	277	2	6	3	6		5	3	14	2	7	2	13
Gates, Gaites, Gate	6.0	250	1,242	6	19	18	90	5	56	21	6	13	12	2	1
Gatewood, Gatwood	5.7	24	113								1	18	4	1	
Gather, Gaither, Gathe, Gathir	5.3	36	154							1	2	26		4	3
Gatling, Gatlen, Gatlin	5.0	32	128											32	
Gault, Gald, Galt, Golt	6.6	33	184			1	1			5	12	7	5	1	1
Gavit, Gavett, Gavitt, Govett, Govit	6.1	23	118				5	14	1		3				
Gay	6.0	145	731	9	3	2	50	1	19	9	3	4	15	29	1
Gaylor, Gailer, Galler, Gallow, Galor, Gayler, Gealer, Geller, Geyler, Guellow	5.1	32	131			1	1		15	4	4	1		4	2
Gaylord, Gailard, Gailerd, Gaillard, Galard, Gallard, Galliard, Gallode, Gallord, Gaylard, Gilard, Gillard, Gilliard	6.2	74	382			2	8		35	8	3	2	1	8	7
Geary, Gerry, Gery, Guerry	4.7	48	179		2	4	15		2	5	10	2		1	7
Gebhart, Gibbart, Gibbet, Gibbut, Gibert	6.2	18	94								16				2
Gee, Gea, Gehe	5.2	44	185			5		2		3	20	1	1	4	7
Geer, Gear, Gears, Geers, Gehr, Geir, Geirs, Gier, Giers	5.9	92	451			8	4	9	1	49	7	8	2	2	2
Geiger, Geigar, Gieger, Gigar, Giger, Gigher, Guiger, Gyger, Gygir, Gygor	5.7	42	197								27	1	2	2	10
Gentry, Gentrey	6.2	31	160								1		14	11	5
George, Georg, Georges, Jorge	5.7	240	1,116	3	40	2	18	1	2	9	60	12	53	25	15
Gerhart, Garehart, Gearhart, Gearhert, Geerheart, Gehrhart	6.2	27	140								23	4			
German, Germain, Germaine, Germen	5.5	38	170					1	1		5	10	13	8	
Gerrard, Garrard, Georid, Gerard, Gerhard, Gerod, Gerrad, Gerred, Geurard, Girard, Giraud, Guerard	5.2	32	134			2			1	5	11	1	2	2	8
Gerrish, Garish, Garrish, Gerish	5.9	55	267	18	21		11			1		2	2	2	
Getty, Gattes, Gattis, Gettes, Gettess, Getteys, Gettis, Gettys	5.3	22	95							8	9	2		1	2
Geyer, Guyer, Gyer	5.8	49	234	1	1		10		1	2	20	6	1	4	2
Gibbons, Gibans, Gibbens, Gibbins, Gibbions, Gibbon, Gibeons, Giberne, Gibins	6.1	65	334		4		6		3	3	18	16	8	5	2
Gibbs, Gib, Gibb, Gibbes, Gibes, Gibs	5.4	271	1,197	5	3	17	75	11	31	14	15	11	22	43	24
Gibson, Gibsons	5.7	353	1,671	2	21	11	36	4	10	22	73	27	23	64	60
Giddings, Giddig, Gidings, Gittings, Gittins	5.8	37	179	1	5	1	14		2	1	1		10	2	
Gideons, Gedion, Giddeons, Gideon, Gidion, Gidions	7.6	20	132		1	1	1		1	1	1			3	3
Gidney	6.1	17	86							17					
Giffin, Giffen, Giffens, Giffins	6.6	20	112			2	2			1	14			1	
Gifford, Giffard, Giffords	6.4	145	783			5	76	13	8	35	4	1	1	2	

TABLE 111.—NOMENCLATURE, DEALING WITH NAMES REPRESENTED BY AT LEAST 100 WHITE PERSONS, BY STATES AND TERRITORIES, AT THE FIRST CENSUS: 1790—Continued.

NAME	Average size of family	TOTAL Heads of families	TOTAL All other members	Maine	New Hampshire	Vermont	Massachusetts	Rhode Island	Connecticut	New York	Pennsylvania	Maryland	Virginia	North Carolina	South Carolina
Gilbert, Gilbart, Gilberts, Gilbirt...	5.6	424	1,966	6	7	24	67		103	60	58	25	17	43	14
Gilbreath, Gailbraith, Galbraith, Galbreath, Galbraith, Gilbraith, Gilbreth, Gillbreath, Gill-breth, Gulbreath.	5.7	57	270							2	28	2		14	11
Gilchrist, Gelchrist, Gilchrest, Gilchriston, Gilchrust, Gilcrest, Gilcrist, Gillchriest, Gillchrist...	5.9	47	228	2	6	2	3		1	10	10	1	2	7	3
Gildersleave, Gilderslave, Gilderslea, Gildersleaves, Gildersleeve, Gildersleeves, Gildersleve, Gildeusleaf.	5.0	28	112						5	23					
Giles, Gile, Jiles.	5.3	107	465	8	20	7	22	2	6	8	4	5	6	13	6
Gilford, Gillford, Guilford, Gulliford.	5.5	28	127	3		1	17			2	2			3	
Gill, Gills, Guil, Guild, Guill.	5.6	199	917	2	5	6	63		7		24	19	34	17	22
Gilleland, Gellelan, Gileland, Gillalan, Gillaland, Gillelan, Gillelin, Gillerland, Gillilan, Gilli-land, Gillilen, Gillilin, Gilliling, Gillilon.	5.7	48	226							2	20	3	7	6	10
Gillet, Gillat, Gillett, Gillit, Gillitt, Jellet, Jillet, Jillitt.	5.8	156	745			13	10		92	33	1	1	3	1	2
Gilliam, Gilham, Gillam, Gillham, Gillim, Gillom, Gillum, Guiliams.	5.6	64	290						1	1	9	3	19	19	12
Gillis, Gillies, Guillis.	4.9	32	126		2		2			11	1	3		11	2
Gillispie, Galaspey, Galaspie, Galaspy, Galespe, Galespey, Galisba, Gallaspie, Gallespie, Gel-aspey, Gelaspy, Gellaspie, Gellaspy, Gellespee, Gellespie, Gelaspy, Gilasby, Gilaspey, Gilaspy, Gil-espie, Gillasby, Gillaspey, Gillaspie, Gillaspy, Gillesby, Gillespey, Gillespie, Gillespy, Gillispi, Gillospy, Glaspy, Golaspee.	5.3	120	515				2			16	28	11	19	25	19
Gilman, Gillman, Gilmon.	5.8	159	756	21	104	7	4		14	3	5			1	
Gilmore, Gillmoore, Gillmor, Gillmore, Gilmer, Gilmor, Gilmour.	5.6	150	688	8	14	7	24	1		22	28	5	10	17	14
Gil Patrick, Gelpatrick, Gillpatrick, Gilpatrick.	6.3	22	117	22											
Gilson, Gillson.	5.2	52	220		12	10	13		2	6	8		1		
Ginn, Gin, Gyn, Gynn.	6.0	18	90	2							3			7	6
Gipson.	5.5	24	107	4					2	1	4		1	6	6
Gist, Geist, Gesst, Gest, Gests, Geyst, Guest, Guist.	6.1	45	229						1	16	13	2	2		11
Gitchel, Gatchall, Gatchel, Gatchell, Getchell, Gitchell, Gotchiel, Gutchel.	6.0	55	275	33	2	2	7		1		5	5			
Givens, Gavan, Gaven, Gavin, Gaving, Gavon, Geven, Gevin, Givan, Givans, Given, Givenn, Givin, Givins, Givon, Givons, Givvins, Govan, Guivens.	5.6	73	339	8			2	1	1	2	8	9	2	26	14
Gladding, Gladden, Gladdin, Gladdon, Gladen, Glading, Gledden, Gloding.	5.9	45	221	2			3	18	9		2	5	1	1	4
Glasgow, Glasco, Glascoe, Glascow, Glasgo, Glassco, Glassgow.	5.0	32	127						1	12	6	1		8	4
Glass, Glas, Gloss.	5.4	81	352	2	3	4	3		3	3	15	7	25	11	5
Glazier, Glaizer, Glaser, Glasher, Glasier, Glasser, Glazer, Glisser, Glosher.	5.2	38	161			8	12	1	3	3	7	1	1	1	1
Gleason, Glason, Gleasson, Gleazen, Gleazon, Gleeson, Gleson, Glesson, Glezen, Glezon.	6.0	114	567		8	10	65		20	9		1		1	
Glenn, Glen, Gleyn, Glinn, Glins, Glynn.	5.2	116	484		1		2			7	36	13	12	19	26
Glidden, Gliddon, Gliden, Glidon.	8.1	29	205	8	21										
Glover.	5.6	156	721	4	8		42		14	14	10	5	17	18	24
Goddard, Godard, Goddart, Godderd, Godward, Goodard, Goodhard, Goodhart, Goodheart....	5.7	91	427	5	4	3	49	8	2	1	7	7		1	4
Godfrey, Godferey, Godfree, Godfry, Goodferrey, Goodfrey.	5.2	142	594	5	8	4	37	6	18	7	4	3	23	17	10
Godin, Godden, Goddin, Godding.	5.3	22	94	1	4		3					1	4	9	
Godshall, Godshal, Godshalk, Godshalt, Godshell, Goodshul.	6.1	30	153				1		1		28				
Goelett, Gallet, Gallott, Gelat, Gellet, Gellit, Gillott, Gollatt, Gullatt, Gullet, Gullit.	6.9	15	88				1		2	4	1		3	4	
Goes, Gose.	6.1	27	139							26					1
Goff, Gaaff, Gaff, Gaft, Gauff, Gaugh, Gawf, Goaff, Goffe, Goft, Goph, Gough, Goughf.	5.6	130	594	1	5	5	30		26	13	13	9	9	11	8
Going, Goan, Goans, Goin, Goings, Goins, Goinz.	5.8	35	169	5	1		1			1	1	1	16	3	6
Gold, Goald, Gole.	4.9	46	180	2			3		10	14	6	3	2	3	3
Golding, Gilden, Golden, Goldin, Goldon, Goulding.	6.7	66	377		1	1	13	1	1	14	9	8	6	7	5
Goldsmith.	5.7	62	292		5		9		7	26	1	8	1	3	2
Gooch, Gouch.	5.4	38	167	11	1	2	3						10	11	
Good, Goode, Goods.	6.2	131	676						1	52	10	40	17	11	
Goodale, Godall, Goodall, Goodals, Goodel, Goodell.	5.9	131	638	6	14	12	57	1	26	9		4		2	
Gooden, Goodan, Goodhan, Gooding.	5.4	50	219	2	3		9		1	1	12	7	4	10	1
Goodenow, Goodenough, Goodino, Goodner, Goodnow.	5.6	72	333		13	15	41			1		1		1	
Goodhue.	5.3	56	240	1	12	5			1	2		34		1	
Goodman, Goodmon.	5.6	101	462				8		6	6	20	7	10	33	11
Goodrich, Godridge, Goodredge, Goodrick, Goodridg, Goodridge, Goodrigde, Goodrige, Goodruch, Goodwich.	5.9	244	1,196	8	3	23	69		89	23	1	5	21	2	
Goodsell, Goodsale, Goodsall, Goodsel, Goodsile, Goodsill.	4.9	26	101				1		18	7					
Goodson.	5.6	21	97										6	6	9
Goodspeed, Goodspead.	5.6	34	155	1		3	24		2	4					
Goodwin, Godwin, Goodwine, Goodwinn, Goodwyn.	5.7	427	1,998	80	34	11	57	1	46	11	16	16	66	54	35
Googins, Gogens, Goggan, Goggens, Goggin, Goggins, Gogin, Googin, Googing, Googings, Guggins.	5.9	18	89	8	1	1	2			1	1				4
Gordon, Goadon, Goarding, Gordan, Gorden, Gordin, Gording, Gordins, Gorten, Gorton, Gour-din. Gourding, Guodan, Guoden.	5.6	397	1,811	25	46	5	11	31	27	28	66	28	32	47	51
Gore, Goar, Goare.	6.5	63	349	3		2	11		2		4	13	10	4	14
Gorham, Ghoram, Ghorum, Goram, Goreham.	5.0	87	344	3		6	37	2	34	3	1			1	
Gorman, Garman, Garmin, Garmon, Gormon.	5.0	40	158		1		1			1	21	4	1	4	7
Gorsuch, Garsoch.	6.0	28	140									28			
Goslin, Gaslin, Gauslin, Gausling, Gooslin, Gosline, Gosling, Gossling.	4.8	30	115						2	11	10	2	2	2	1
Goss, Gaus, Gause, Gaws, Ghoss, Gosse.	5.7	80	378	2	17	7	16		2	2	14	1		15	4
Gossett, Gasset, Gassett, Gisert, Gosset, Gossit, Gossitt, Guset.	5.6	19	88				3			1	1	4	5	5	
Gott, Got.	5.6	29	133	6	1	1	8	1	2	3		6		1	
Goudy, Gaudy, Gawdy, Gordy, Gowday, Gowdey, Gowdy.	5.5	24	108	2	3		2		6	1	6	1	1	1	1
Gould, Gool, Goold, Goul.	5.5	342	1,537	34	51	29	147	16	28	21	9	6		1	
Gove.	6.6	52	293	8	41	1	1		1						
Gowen, Gouen, Goun, Gowan, Gowin, Gowing, Gowns.	5.6	54	247	10	6	2	19		1		2		2	3	9
Gozzard, Gasserd, Gossart.	5.4	19	84						16		3				
Grace, Grase, Grass, Grauss, Grayce, Greas, Grees, Greese, Gres, Gress.	5.5	53	236	8	3		1		2	4	9	12	5	6	3
Grady, Gradey.	6.2	17	89							1	1		3	12	
Graff, Graeff, Graf, Graffe, Grauf, Greaf, Greaff.	6.0	38	188								35			1	2
Grafton.	5.3	21	91	3			6	4			8				
Gragg, Grag, Graig, Graige, Greege.	6.2	47	244				24	3	10		2	1	5	1	
Graham, Grahame, Grahams, Grahms, Grame, Grames, Grayham, Grayhams, Greham, Grey-ham.	5.4	327	1,430		5	12	17		9	60	87	20	18	56	43
Grandy, Grandee.	5.3	24	102	1	1	8	4			1				9	
Granger, Grainger, Graneger, Grenger.	5.1	84	343		1	1	22	2	28	14		7	1	4	4
Granis, Graniss, Grannis.	6.2	19	99				1		16	1				1	
Grant, Grante, Grants.	5.6	305	1,399	58	14	5	44	8	55	32	16	13	15	25	20
Grantham, Grantum.	4.9	21	82							1		4	16		
Graves, Grave, Gravs, Greave, Greaves, Greves, Grieves.	5.3	346	1,491	8	32	25	101	4	45	26	9	17	33	29	17
Gray, Gra, Greay, Grey.	5.7	668	3,130	64	26	24	91	16	47	53	97	65	40	95	50
Graybill, Grabble, Grabell, Grabill, Grable, Graybil, Grebble, Grebill, Greble, Greybill, Grobill, Grubble.	6.5	35	193								27	4	3	1	
Greeley, Grealea, Grealey, Greele, Greely, Greley, Grilley, Grilly.	6.4	52	281	15	24	1	8	2	2						
Green, Greene, Greens.	5.6	1,205	5,559	30	61	45	212	152	72	186	81	95	72	137	62

TABLE **111.**—NOMENCLATURE, DEALING WITH NAMES REPRESENTED BY AT LEAST 100 WHITE PERSONS, BY STATES AND TERRITORIES, AT THE FIRST CENSUS: 1790—Continued.

NAME.	Average size of family.	Heads of families.	All other members.	Maine.	New Hampshire.	Vermont.	Massachusetts.	Rhode Island.	Connecticut.	New York.	Pennsylvania.	Maryland.	Virginia.	North Carolina.	South Carolina.
Greenfield, Greenfeild	5.7	33	155		2				3	8	2	18			
Greenleaf, Greanleaf, Greanlief, Greeleaf, Greenlief	5.2	87	366	12	12	4	53		1	2	3				
Greenough, Greeneu, Greenhaugh, Greenhoe, Greenhow, Greeno, Greno, Grenough	6.2	32	165	2	6		18		1		2			1	2
Greenwell, Graniwolt, Greenawalt, Greenewall, Greenewalt, Greeniwolt, Greenwall, Greenwalt, Grenewalt, Grenwell	5.6	54	250							3	18	33			
Greenwood, Greenwod	5.7	75	354	1	10	2	26	2	1	3	1	13	8	4	4
Greer, Grear, Greere, Greir, Grere, Griar, Grier	5.8	104	503			1			1	6	51	5	2	20	18
Gregory, Gragary, Greegory, Gregary, Greggery, Greggory, Gregorey, Gregrey, Griggery, Grigory, Grigrey, Grgory	5.5	262	1,183	2	2	5	16		58	34	19	6	20	78	22
Grice, Gryce	4.4	24	81			1	1				4			13	5
Gridley	5.8	50	240				5	1	36	7	1				
Griffin, Griffan, Griffen, Griffing, Griffins, Griffn, Grifing	5.8	493	2,355	12	39	8	36	6	67	104	11	32	38	99	41
Griffis, Griffes, Griffiss	5.7	25	118				1			2	2	3	3	8	6
Griffith, Greffeth, Grifeth, Griffeth, Griffeths, Griffiths, Griffits, Griffitts, Grifith, Grifiths	5.4	233	1,021	1	7	9	9	3	7	18	82	60	9	18	10
Griggs, Greg, Gregg, Greggs, Gregs, Greigs, Grig, Grigg, Grigs	5.7	153	723		16	3	15		21	22	29	3	18	13	13
Grim, Grimm, Grims	5.2	42	176							6	18	8	7	3	
Grimes, Ghrimes, Grihams, Grymes	5.4	190	841		15	4	8	2	13	2	35	24	29	46	12
Grindall, Grandell, Grendell, Grindel, Grindle	6.0	17	84	7	1						3	3	1		2
Grinman, Greenman, Grinmon, Grinnum, Gronman, Grunman	4.9	32	125			1	2	12	1	13	2			1	
Grinnell, Greenill, Grenal, Grenell, Grinal, Grinall, Grinell, Grinnall, Grinnel, Grinnol, Grunnel	5.2	45	187	3		1	7	17	6	10		1			
Grisham, Grissam, Grissham, Grissom, Grissum	5.8	22	106								1		7	9	5
Griswold, Greswold, Griswald, Griswall, Griswell, Griswould	5.7	205	967		8	21	13		128	32	3				
Groat	6.8	22	127							22					
Groesbeck, Grossbeck, Grouisbeck, Grusbeck	6.6	21	117							21					
Groff, Grofe, Groffe, Groof	6.3	29	153							1	26	2			
Groom, Groome, Groomes, Grooms, Grumes	5.8	38	182				3			9	3	3	8	4	8
Gross, Groase, Groce, Gros, Grose, Grosse	5.5	109	487	18	2		12	1	2	9	44	4	5	11	1
Grosvenor, Grossvenor, Grosvener, Grovener, Grovenor, Grovner	7.5	23	150				3	3	15	1	1				
Grout, Groot, Grotz, Grouts, Grut	5.7	42	198	1	8	10	14			6	2			1	
Grove, Groves, Grovs	5.9	129	633	6	1		12			3	62	17	12	14	2
Grover, Groover, Grovier	5.5	110	499	18	3	7	26		9	21	14	7	2	2	1
Grow, Groh, Grows, Growse	6.1	27	137		2	9			4	1	10		1		
Grubb, Groobs, Grub, Grubbs, Grubs	5.6	56	257				1				38	4	6	3	4
Gruber, Graber, Greber, Greeber	6.7	17	97								15				2
Gubtail, Gabtale, Gubtale	5.7	18	85	18											
Guernsey, Garnsey, Garnsy, Guensey, Guirnsey, Gurnsey, Gurnsway	5.6	40	185		4	2	3		25	6					
Guile, Giehl, Gihal, Guiles, Guyle	4.9	25	98	1	2	1	3	2	5	10	1				
Guion, Gion, Guing, Guyon, Gyon	5.8	24	116					1	1	15	3		3	1	
Gulley, Gooly, Gully	6.5	16	88						2		2	1	4	7	
Gunn, Gun, Gunce, Guns	5.5	83	372		3	1	23		21	3	10	4	7	7	4
Gunter, Gonter	5.9	25	122								3	3	1	10	8
Gurley, Girley, Gourley, Gourly, Gurly	6.7	37	209							10	7			15	5
Gurney, Guerney, Gurnee	5.4	48	213	5			27	1		13	2				
Guthrie, Gooterie, Gutherey, Gutherie, Guthery, Guthired, Guthre, Guthrey, Guthry, Gutorey, Gutree, Gutrie, Gutroe, Gutry, Guttery, Gutthery, Guttree, Guttrey, Guttrie	5.7	83	388				1		5	6	24	6	19	16	6
Gutridge, Gutheridge, Guthridge, Gutrage, Gutridg, Gutterage, Gutterige, Guttridge	5.1	20	81	8		4	2		5	4				1	
Guy, Gie, Guay, Guiy	6.8	41	238			2	2		3		13	5	7	6	3
Guyton, Gathen, Gathin, Gathings, Gatoing, Gatton, Gayton	6.4	23	125									15	2	4	2
Gwin, Goowin, Guein, Guin, Guinn, Guyn, Guynn, Gween, Gwinn, Gwins, Gwyn, Gwyne, Gwynn, Gwynne	4.6	95	338				1	1		2	12	15	33	18	13
Hacket, Hacate, Hackett	5.5	70	315	4	15	4	15			3	8	15	3	3	
Hackney, Hakney	6.5	18	99							2	1	1	5	8	
Hadden, Haddan, Haddin, Haddon, Hedden, Heddin, Heddon, Heden	5.8	28	135							16	6		3	1	2
Hadley, Hadeley, Hadly, Headley, Headly, Hedley, Hedly	5.6	126	580	2	24	11	24	1	1	13	11	5	10	23	1
Hadlock, Hadlouk	6.2	17	89	1	7	4	3		1	1					
Hagan, Hagans, Hagen, Hagens, Hagon, Heagen, Heagon, Heagons	5.2	45	188						1	3	7	19	4		11
Hager, Haga, Hagar, Heaga, Heager	5.5	70	317		3	4	27			8	14	7		7	
Hagerman, Hagaman, Hagamen, Hagarman, Hageman, Hagirman, Hagman, Hegerman	5.8	49	233							38	8	1		1	1
Hagey, Haggey, Hagy, Hegey	7.5	14	91		1		1				10			2	
Hagget, Hagert, Haggard, Haggart, Haggat, Haggett	4.7	26	97	5	5		4				2		6	4	
Hague, Hage, Haig	5.5	19	85								9	4	3		3
Haight, Hait, Haite, Haitt, Hayt	6.5	121	668	1	2	1	1		21	95					
Halbert, Halbud, Hallbert, Helbert	5.8	18	86		1		1		1	6		2	3	2	1
Hale, Hael, Hail, Haile, Hailes, Hails, Hales, Hayle, Hayles, Hayls, Heyl	5.8	402	1,911	23	41	21	107	8	63	33	15	22	22	34	13
Haley, Haeley, Hailey, Hailley, Haily, Haly, Hayley, Hayligh, Hayly, Healey, Healy	5.4	138	608	19	14	7	20	11	15	1	8	8	18	13	4
Hall, Halle, Halls, Hawl	5.6	1,478	6,837	63	124	69	245	61	246	105	107	104	127	179	46
Hallenbeck, Halenbeck, Hallenbach, Hallenbeek, Holembeck, Holenbauch, Holerback, Hollenbach, Hollenback, Hollenbagh, Hollenbeck, Hollenbuk, Hollinback, Hollinbeck, Holloback, Hollowboh, Holmbeck	6.0	89	449			3	4		1	71	8		1		1
Hallet, Halet, Hallete, Hallett, Hallhet, Hawlet	5.8	67	324	2			36		4	23	1			1	
Hallock, Hallick, Halock, Hollick	5.7	69	327			3	1		3	60	1	1			
Hallowell, Hallowall, Hallowel, Hollawel, Hollawell, Hollowell, Hollwell, Hollywell	5.8	60	285	1			4				29			26	
Halsey, Hallsey, Halseey, Holsay, Holsey	5.7	71	337					1	4	51		3		10	2
Halstead, Halstad, Halsted	6.2	66	340							57	4		5		
Ham, Hamm, Hamn	5.9	154	752	18	56			3		22	7	4	16	18	10
Hamby, Hambey, Hembey, Hemby	5.0	22	88									1		7	14
Hamilton, Hambelton, Hambilton, Hambleton, Hamblton, Hameleton, Hamelten, Hamelton, Hamileton, Hammelton, Hammilton, Hemelton	5.5	477	2,153	26	5	16	67	6	20	39	113	51	36	45	53
Hamlet, Hamblet, Hamblett, Hamlett	5.0	29	116				8	1	2		1		8	9	
Hamlin, Hamblen, Hamblin, Hamlen	5.4	155	681	23		10	43	3	29	20	4	2	12	4	5
Hammel, Hamble, Hamel, Hamil, Hammell, Hammill, Hembell, Hempble, Hemple	6.3	30	159		1				1		6	20	1	1	
Hammer, Hama, Hamar, Hamarr, Hamer, Hammar, Hammers	5.5	45	204	2							21	10	2	6	4
Hammet, Hammat, Hammatt, Hammett, Hammit, Hammitt, Hammot, Hemmit	7.8	34	230	2			9	5	1		1	11		1	4
Hammond, Haman, Hamman, Hammand, Hammant, Hammen, Hammon, Hammonds, Hamons, Hamon, Hamond, Hamons	5.8	399	1,897	26	13	17	112	18	20	42	26	38	25	41	19
Hampton, Hamton, Hempton	5.8	77	370								3	18	3	17	28
Hanchett, Hanchet, Hantchet, Hantichet	6.6	16	89				3		12	1					
Hancock, Hancok, Handcock, Hankok, Hencock, Hendcock	5.4	156	692	6	5	1	28		14	4	7	18	33	30	10
Hand, Hands	5.4	73	324		2	1	3		11	26	9	8	6	3	4
Handy, Handey, Hendy	5.8	88	422	5	7	7	36	5	6	3	2	8	9		
Haner, Hannar, Hanner, Hanners	6.4	26	140				1			22			1	1	1
Hanford, Handford, Hansford	5.5	42	189		1				34	3			4		
Hanks	6.1	35	177				4	5		5	4		7	9	1

TABLE 111.—NOMENCLATURE, DEALING WITH NAMES REPRESENTED BY AT LEAST 100 WHITE PERSONS, BY STATES AND TERRITORIES, AT THE FIRST CENSUS: 1790—Continued.

NAME.	Average size of family.	TOTAL. Heads of families.	TOTAL. All other members.	Maine.	New Hampshire.	Vermont.	Massachusetts.	Rhode Island.	Connecticut.	New York.	Pennsylvania.	Maryland.	Virginia.	North Carolina.	South Carolina.
Hanley, Handily, Handley, Handly, Hanlly	5.4	32	140	3	1		3	1		3	4	5	3	7	2
Hannah, Hana, Hanah, Hanna, Hannahs, Hannoh	5.2	126	526	1			1		5	13	56	10	14	12	14
Hannon, Hanan, Hanen, Hanin, Hannan, Hannaon, Hannens, Hannin, Hanon, Hanoun	6.0	24	119				1	2		4	8	3	1	5	
Hannum, Hannam	7.2	17	105				11		1		5				
Hanscum, Hanscom, Hanscomb	5.3	20	85	20											
Hansill, Hancel, Hansal, Hansel, Hansell, Hansil, Hensal, Hensel, Hensell, Hensle	5.5	22	98				1			1	15			4	2
Hanson, Handson, Hansen, Hansson	5.3	120	518	24	51		1		3	9	3	24	2	3	
Hapgood, Habgood, Hobgood	6.0	29	145	2		2	20						2	3	
Harbison, Harbeson, Herbison	6.1	21	107							9			4	8	
Hardenbergh, Hardenberghe, Hardenburg, Hardenburgh	5.3	20	85					1		19					
Hardesty, Hadesty, Hardiesty, Hardistay, Hardister, Hardisty	5.7	18	84							2	11		5		
Harding, Harden, Hardin	5.6	318	1,464	26		5	78	10	8	20	32	23	55	49	12
Hardison, Hardiston	5.8	27	129	6							1	1	19		
Hardman, Hardeman, Hardemon, Hardiman, Herdman	5.7	20	93				1			3	11	2	2	1	
Hardwick, Hardewick, Hardick, Hardwich, Heartwick	6.0	25	125							10			7	3	5
Hardy, Hardee, Hardey, Hardie, Hardyes	5.7	199	933	5	36	8	45	1		9	19	19	16	32	9
Hare, Hair, Haire, Hairs, Hares, Heire	6.1	116	591				6		3	10	50	8	8	23	8
Hargrove, Hairgrove, Hairgroves, Haregrave, Haregrove, Hargrave, Hargraves, Hargreaves, Hargroves	5.2	53	223							1	1	20	21	10	
Harkins, Harkin, Harking, Herkin	5.5	19	85			2	2		2		8	1			4
Harkness, Hakness, Harkniss	6.3	30	159	1	3	2	8	6	1	1	2	1		1	4
Harley, Harllee, Harly	6.2	22	114	3			1			1	4	5	2	2	4
Harlin, Harlan, Harland, Harlen, Harling, Harlon	6.1	49	252	1		1	2		1	1	31	5		1	6
Harlow, Harloe, Harlowe	5.8	61	295	2	2	3	39		1	4			8	2	
Harmon, Harman, Harmann, Harmen, Harmin, Harmond	5.6	185	850	39		27	22		10	9	27	6	11	23	11
Harness, Harnes, Harniss	6.5	16	88				1				1		14		
Harold, Hareld, Harolt, Harrald, Harrold, Herold, Herrald, Herreld	5.8	32	152		1					2	8	1	1	15	4
Harp, Harpe	4.3	25	83							6	1	6	1	10	1
Harper, Harpar, Harpir, Harpur	5.8	207	994	5	8		1		1	18	41	19	40	44	30
Harrell, Harral, Harrel, Harril, Harrill, Herral	5.5	133	605		1								35	89	8
Harridan, Harradan, Harrenden, Harriden, Harridon, Heredin, Herriden	5.2	21	89	2		1	15	2	1						
Harrington, Harington, Hearington, Herington, Herrington	5.7	311	1,454	5	7	39	108	28	15	41	10	24		27	7
Harris, Haris, Hariss, Harrace, Harras, Harres, Harress, Harrise, Harriss	5.6	1,034	4,730	22	38	38	119	53	66	86	57	86	142	255	72
Harrison, Hareson, Harison, Harisson, Harreson, Harrisen, Harrisson, Herison, Herrison	5.3	374	1,617	1		3	14	4	45	18	35	54	37	84	29
Harrod, Harod, Harrad, Harrard, Harred, Herard, Herod, Herrad, Herred, Herrid, Herrod	5.7	38	180			1	8		1	1	13	1	3	10	
Harry, Harrey, Harrys, Hary	6.3	33	176		1						18	7		3	4
Hart, Harte, Harts, Hartt, Heart	5.4	468	2,043	11	24	8	42	18	106	52	73	29	21	53	31
Hartgrove, Hardgrave, Hardgrove, Hardgroves, Hartsgraves, Heartgrove	6.7	15	85									3	4	6	2
Hartley, Hartly, Heartley, Heartly	5.4	55	241				1			2	25	2	10	9	6
Hartman, Heartman	5.9	86	420				1			2	67	4	1	9	2
Hartsel, Hartsell, Hartzel, Hartzil, Hertsel, Hertzel, Herzel	6.5	34	186								33			1	
Hartshorn, Hartshorne, Heartshorn, Hortshorn	6.0	64	317		14	3	20		16	6	2	2	1		
Hartwell, Hartwill, Heartwell	5.6	76	346	3	7	7	46		4	5	1		2	1	
Harvey, Harveey, Harvie, Harvy, Hervey, Hervy	5.3	356	1,548	11	36	14	45	14	30	20	50	28	34	58	16
Harwood	6.3	75	394	1	4	7	28	2	1	2	1	13	13	2	1
Hasbrouck, Hasbrauck, Hasbrook	6.4	33	177							33					
Haskell, Hasceli, Haskal, Haskall, Haskcal, Haskel, Haskil, Haskill, Hasskall, Hoskell	6.0	175	872	46	7	12	99	4	5	2					
Haskins, Haskin, Haskings, Hasskins	6.2	61	316		1	7	29		2	3	2	2	10	3	2
Haslip, Haislep, Haselip, Hayslip, Hazelip, Heslip, Heyslip	5.7	25	118							2	5	7	5	6	
Hassell, Hasel, Hassell, Hassel, Hazzell, Hessel	5.2	30	126		2						3	1		23	1
Hastings, Hasting, Hastins, Haystings	5.6	153	705	3	22	7	82	1	8	1	10	1	5	13	
Hatch, Heatch	5.7	285	1,339	69	21	26	97	3	28	27	1	1		12	
Hatcher, Hetcher	5.1	36	146	1					1		1	2	14	9	8
Hatfield, Hotfield	6.0	29	146				5			11	6			7	
Hathaway, Hatheway, Hathway, Hathwey	6.2	199	1,041	2		13	140	8	12	7	5		5	7	
Hatton, Hatten, Hatting	4.5	33	117				1			2	12	6	8	4	
Haun, Haan, Hahn, Han, Hann, Hans, Hawn, Hohn, Hohne, Honn, Hons	5.7	86	407		1		1		2	5	39	21	6	9	2
Hauser, Hausser	5.0	23	92								6	2		14	1
Havens, Haven, Havins	5.8	120	578		10	8	36	8	8	47		1	2		
Haviland, Haveland, Haverland, Havlan, Heaviland, Hevelan, Heveland, Hevilin	6.1	47	238				1			4	40	2			
Havner, Havener, Havenor, Heavener, Heavner, Heevner, Hevener, Heviner, Hevner	5.5	24	107	2						2	6	3	2	9	
Hawes, Haas, Haase, Haass, Hass, Hasse, Haus, Hause, Hauze, Haws, Hawse, Hawses	5.8	137	656	9	1	3	44		4	12	40	9	6	7	2
Hawkins, Hawkens, Hawkin, Hawkings	5.7	303	1,423		9	10	9	28	29	49	23	32	43	49	22
Hawks, Hauck, Hauk, Hawk, Hawke, Hawkes	6.6	114	644	7		1	45	2		5	37	4	11	1	1
Hawley, Halley, Hally, Hawlley, Hawly, Holley, Holly	5.7	259	1,210	1	1	28	22		110	36	10	1	14	21	15
Hawthorn, Harthorn, Hathorn, Hathorne, Hauthorn	6.0	48	238	15			7			1	15		3	3	4
Haycock, Hacock, Heacock, Heacocks, Hecock, Hecox	6.1	29	147		1	1			11	5	9	1			1
Hayden, Haden, Hadin, Hading, Hadon, Haiden, Haydon, Henden, Headin, Headon, Heyden, Heydon	5.6	169	780	6	6	1	70		27	7	1	19	22	6	4
Hayford, Hafard, Hafford, Hoffard, Hoffart, Hoffert	5.5	23	104			2	6		5	1	8			1	
Hayman, Haymans, Haymond, Heyman	6.6	21	118		1		1				5	7	4	3	
Haynes, Hain, Hainds, Haine, Haines, Hainess, Hains, Hane, Hanes, Hayn, Hayns, Heains, Hean, Heans, Hehn, Hehns, Heyn, Heyns	5.8	342	1,632	17	35	10	32	1	7	57	82	21	36	38	6
Haynie, Hainey, Haney, Hanie, Hany, Heney	5.1	110	456	1			1		1		27	5	53	11	11
Hays, Haise, Haize, Hase, Hay, Haye, Hayes, Hayse, Haze, Hey, Heyes	5.6	529	2,431	13	51	11	22		50	53	112	37	53	96	31
Hayward, Haward, Heywad, Heyward	6.2	118	608		2	19	80		1	1			8		8
Haywood, Hawood, Heywood	5.9	135	668	4	25	11	72	3		3	1	5	7	4	
Hazard, Hassard, Haszard, Hazzard	6.0	94	473		1		6	55	2	14	2	3	6	3	2
Hazelton, Haseltine, Haselton, Hasleton, Hasseltine, Hazellton, Hazeltine, Hazletine, Hazleton, Heselton, Hesseltine, Hosselton, Husselton	5.3	95	409	3	35	22	19		4	3	5	3			1
Hazen, Hayson, Hazens, Hazon, Hazzen	6.3	43	230		3	20	5		8	6	1				
Hazle, Haysles, Hazel, Hazell	5.7	28	132	1			4			4	4	5	2	3	9
Hazlet, Haslet, Haslett, Hazelet, Hazlett, Heslet, Heslit	6.4	29	156		2		3				18	4			
Head, Heads	5.8	74	356	4	8		8	8		7	11	5	9	4	10
Heald, Heal, Heel	5.2	31	129	6	1	1	18				1		1	1	
Hearn, Hearne, Hern, Hyrne	5.9	35	170	3	1					4	1	6	1	14	5
Heath, Heathe, Heth	5.8	217	1,051	10	53	9	32	6	11	19	9	3	22	35	8
Heaton, Heaten	5.0	45	179	2	6	4	4		5		21				3
Hedges, Hedge	5.4	56	248			3	9		3	30	1	10			
Hedrick, Heddrick, Hederic, Hederick, Hedreck, Hedrich, Hedricks, Heterick, Heterik	6.1	24	123								11	6	3	4	
Heffner, Hefner, Hephner, Hifner	5.7	20	94								13	6		1	
Heist, Heiss, Hise, Hist, Hyst	5.0	23	92								18		2	3	
Heller, Heler, Hellor, Hellyer	7.0	19	114								17	1		1	
Helm, Helems, Hellem, Hellems, Hellims, Hellms, Hellums, Helme, Helmes, Helmn, Helms	5.4	88	387			1	1	14	3	18	24	5	5	14	3
Helmer	6.5	20	110							18		2			

Table **111.**—NOMENCLATURE, DEALING WITH NAMES REPRESENTED BY AT LEAST 100 WHITE PERSONS, BY STATES AND TERRITORIES, AT THE FIRST CENSUS: 1790—Continued.

NAME	Average size of family	TOTAL		HEADS OF FAMILIES.											
		Heads of families.	All other members.	Maine.	New Hampshire.	Vermont.	Massachusetts.	Rhode Island.	Connecticut.	New York.	Pennsylvania.	Maryland.	Virginia.	North Carolina.	South Carolina.
Hemmenway, Haminway, Heamonway, Hemenway, Hemingsway, Hemingway, Hemmemsway, Hemmingway, Hemminway.	6.3	61	326	1	3	4	41		8	3					1
Hemphill, Hamphell, Hamphill.	6.6	20	112		7						1	2	1	5	4
Hemstead, Hampstead, Hampsted, Hempstead, Hempsted, Hensted, Homestead.	6.0	23	115						16	5	1	1			
Henderson, Handerson, Hendorson, Hendreson.	5.7	322	1,510	9	8	6	12	1	4	21	90	30	50	45	46
Hendricks, Hendereck, Hendreck, Hendric, Hendrick, Hendrik, Hendrix, Hendryx, Hindricks.	5.3	184	791			2	5	5	24	26	29	2	35	29	27
Hendrickson, Henderrickson, Hendrexson, Hendrixson, Henrickson.	5.6	57	262							2	37	2	10	2	4
Hening, Henan, Henen, Henin, Henins, Henning, Henon, Hining, Hinnings.	5.7	27	128				1			2	7	4	11	1	1
Henley, Hendley, Hendly, Henely, Henly.	4.9	43	169	1					6	1	3	5	13	11	3
Henry, Henary, Henerey, Heneries, Henery, Hennary, Henneries, Hennery, Hennry, Henrey, Henri.	5.6	322	1,467	4	13	6	29	4	16	34	109	26	15	39	27
Henshaw, Hinshaw.	5.5	40	179	1		4	11	1	6	2	2	1		12	
Hensley, Hensely, Hensly, Hinesley, Hinsely, Hinsley, Hinsly, Hynsley.	5.0	30	121				1		1				10	15	3
Henson, Hindson, Hinson, Hinston, Hynsen, Hynson.	5.8	85	411			1			2	1	2	15	7	38	19
Herbert, Herbett, Hurbut.	5.5	36	161			1			1	2	3	3	11	12	3
Herder, Hireder, Hurder.	6.1	27	139							7	20				
Herman, Hermans, Hermanse, Hermin, Hermon, Herrman.	5.6	76	349		1	2	2		1	29	34	3			4
Herndon, Harnden, Harndon, Hearndon.	6.2	34	176	2				5					13	12	2
Herrick, Herick, Herrek, Herrik, Heryck.	5.7	155	723	14	14	12	48	1	25	39		1		1	
Herriman, Hariman, Harramond, Harriman, Hereman, Heriman, Herreman, Herryman, Hurriman.	5.4	67	297	10	25	3	11		3	6	5	1		3	
Herring, Haring, Harrin, Harring, Hearing, Hearon, Hearring, Heran, Herin, Hering, Heron, Herran, Herren, Herrin, Herron, Herrown.	5.7	181	847	2	2		12		2	13	38	12	17	63	20
Hersey, Harsey, Hearsay, Hearsey, Hearsy.	5.2	68	287	8	8		44		1	1		5		1	
Hershberger, Harsburger, Harshbarger, Harshberger, Harshburger, Hershbargar.	7.1	22	134								15	2	5		
Hershy, Harshey, Harshy, Herschy, Hershey.	6.3	22	116								22				
Hess, Hese, Hesse, Hest.	6.4	102	551							20	69	4	4	4	1
Hester, Hesters, Hesther.	4.6	44	159								6	1	8	24	5
Heston, Heastant, Heastin, Heaston, Heestand, Hestand, Hestant, Hestonm.	6.2	24	125								16		8		
Hewins, Hewen, Hewings, Huen, Hughen, Hughengs, Hughins.	5.4	19	84	2	1		12			1	2		1		
Hewit, Hewet, Hewett, Hewitt.	5.5	106	472	2		2	12		26	24	12	8	2	15	3
Hewlet, Hewlett, Hewlit, Hewlitt, Hughlett, Hughlitt, Hulet, Hulett, Hulit, Hullet, Hullit.	6.3	65	344			3	6		5	25	1	1	16	7	1
Hibbard, Hebard, Hebbard, Hebert, Hebot, Hibard, Hibbards, Hibbart, Hibberd, Hibbert, Hibbird, Hibbord, Hibert.	5.9	111	549	8	7	20	18		27	12	17	2			
Hibs, Hibbs.	5.0	21	83								19			2	
Hickman, Heckman.	5.8	88	426				2			1	31	17	9	18	10
Hicks, Heck, Hecks, Hick, Hickes, Hix, Hixs, Hyx.	5.1	355	1,458	7	9	13	38	17	8	69	44	24	35	71	20
Hickson, Hichson, Hickason, Hikson, Hixon.	4.8	29	111		1		7		5		7	3			6
Hicock, Hiccock, Hickcox, Hickock, Hickocks, Hickok, Hickoks, Hiccocks, Hicox.	5.8	72	347			7	8		48	9					
Higby, Higbe, Higbee, Higbey, Higbie.	6.0	46	230			3	2	2		14	23		2		
Higden, Higdon.	5.6	18	82										11	7	
Higgenbotham, Hegginbottom, Hickenbottom, Hickimbottom, Hickinbotom, Hickinbottom, Hickumbotham, Higembotham, Higginbotham, Higginbottom.	5.4	32	142							1	6	3	22		
Higgins, Heggins, Hegins, Higan, Higens, Higgans, Higgens, Higgin, Higings, Higins.	5.7	234	1,104	38	4	7	74		31	20	14	19	10	4	13
High, Huy, Huys, Hye.	6.3	50	267				3	3		2	29	2	1	9	1
Higley, Higly.	5.6	25	115				4	1	18	2					
Hildebrand, Haldebrand, Heldebrand, Hellebrant, Heltebran, Heltebrand, Hildebraund, Hildenbrand, Hildenbrant, Hildlebrand, Hillderbran, Hillebrand, Hillebrant, Hillibrant, Hiltebrand, Hilterbrand.	6.1	34	175							6	19	4		4	1
Hildreth, Hildrieth, Hildrith, Hilldreath.	6.0	67	336		22	5	28		1	9				2	
Hill, Hills, Hils.	5.6	1,284	5,878	57	105	44	207	40	156	113	127	72	114	183	66
Hiller, Hillar, Hillers.	6.3	29	154				5			3	17	1			3
Hilliard, Hilleard, Hilliad, Hillyard, Hilyard, Hilyerd, Hyliard, Hylyard.	5.1	71	294		11	5	11	2	17	4	4	1	5	10	1
Hilliker, Hiliker, Hilker, Hilleker, Hilligar.	5.8	18	87			1				16	1				
Hilman, Hilleman, Hilliman, Hillman, Hillsmon, Hilsman.	5.3	42	179				20			4	10	1	5	2	
Hilton, Hilten.	5.1	121	502	29	13		12		1	20	4	15	2	20	5
Hines, Heigns, Hein, Heins, Hind, Hinde, Hindes, Hinds, Hine, Hinnes, Hyans, Hynds, Hyne, Hynes, Hynn, Hyns.	5.5	230	1,030	6	4	8	33	2	46	14	29	14	18	48	8
Hinkle, Hinckel, Hinckle, Hinkel.	5.0	44	177								29	2		10	3
Hinkley, Henkley, Hinckley, Hinkly.	5.8	99	479	24	1	2	42		17	11				2	
Hinman, Heineman, Hindman, Hineman, Hinemon, Hyndman, Hyneman, Hynman.	5.3	101	430		1	10	1		44	8	24	10		3	
Hinsdale, Hensdale, Hindsdale, Hinsdal.	6.9	25	148			2	5		17	1					
Hinton, Henton.	4.8	67	257						2	2	2	15	14	29	3
Hiscock, Hiscox, Hisscock.	5.9	18	89	4		2	4	4	2	2					
Hiser, Heiser, Heisser, Highser, Hizer, Hyeser.	5.5	25	113	1		1				3	13	2	5		
Hitchcock, Hichcock, Hichcox, Hitchcocks, Hitchcox, Hitchkok, Hitcock.	5.6	213	974	1	2	14	52	8	85	38		10	2	1	
Hite, Height, Hight, Highth, Hights.	5.5	52	236				3	3			1	8	1	25	11
Hitt, Hit, Hitts.	5.6	21	97				1		2	1	5	2		3	7
Hoadly, Hoadley.	6.1	30	153				1	3	24	1	1				
Hoar, Hoars, Hoor, Hore.	5.6	57	265	1	4	2	38	3		6			3		
Hoard, Hord.	5.4	20	103				3			5	1		9	1	1
Hobart, Hobbard, Hobbart, Hobert, Hoburt.	5.3	51	217	1		5	30		1		11	1		1	1
Hobbs, Hobb, Hobbes, Hobes, Hobs.	5.5	157	699	19	19	5	25		1	4	4	35	6	33	6
Hobby, Hobbey, Hobey, Hoby.	6.4	33	179	3			4		17	4	1			4	
Hobson, Hobsen.	5.3	54	231	2	1		7			2	3			19	20
Hoch, Hock, Hocks, Hoke.	5.8	38	181	3						2	28	1	3	1	
Hodgdon, Hodgdan, Hodgden, Hodgedon, Hodgsden, Hodgsdon, Hodsden, Hodsdon, Hogden, Hogdon, Hogeden, Hogsdon.	4.8	84	320	45	27	1	1		2		1			6	1
Hodges, Hadges, Hodg, Hodge, Hodgis.	5.2	298	1,255	7	6	9	61	1	18	26	8	12	51	71	28
Hodgkins, Hodgekins, Hodgkin, Hodgkings, Hodgskin, Hodgskins, Hodkin, Hodkins, Hodskin, Hodskings, Hodskins, Hogekins, Hogskem.	4.8	64	245	15	10		23		1	5	1	8	1		
Hodgman, Hodgeman, Hogeman.	5.8	21	100	2	7	3	8				1				
Hodgson, Hodgeson, Hodson, Hogson, Hogston.	6.4	29	158		4					2	4	10	1	7	1
Hoffman, Hafman, Hoafman, Hofeman, Hofemen, Hoffeman, Hoffmon, Hofman, Hoofman, Huffman, Hufman.	6.0	285	1,426				1	1	1	52	147	33	30	12	8
Hogan, Hoaghan, Hogans, Hogean, Hogen.	5.1	59	243	2	3	1	2			10	6	3	8	16	8
Hogg, Hoag, Hoage, Hoeg, Hoege, Hog, Hoge, Hoges, Hogge, Hogges, Hogue.	5.9	150	738		31	4	2			45	22	3	18	9	16
Hogiboom, Hageboom, Hageboom, Hogeboom, Hoggeboom, Hogobone.	5.5	22	99				1			21					
Hogland, Hoagland, Hogeland, Hoglen, Hoglin, Hoogland, Houghland, Hougland, Houglend, Houglin.	6.1	28	144							11	14		2	1	
Holbrook, Halbrook, Hallbrook, Holbrock, Holbrooks, Holdbrook, Holebrook, Hollbrook, Hoolbrook.	5.9	176	862	12	11	20	90	1	18	5		3		13	3
Holcomb, Halcom, Halcomb, Halcombe, Holcom, Holcombe, Holcum, Holkum.	5.6	133	607			6	11		68	13	3		2	11	19
Holden, Holdan, Holdin, Holding.	5.1	155	641		11	12	65	15	4	5	6	9	1	23	4
Holder, Halder, Haldre, Holdare, Holdor.	5.7	36	168			3	1		1	5			6	16	4

Table 111.—NOMENCLATURE, DEALING WITH NAMES REPRESENTED BY AT LEAST 100 WHITE PERSONS, BY STATES AND TERRITORIES, AT THE FIRST CENSUS: 1790—Continued.

NAME.	Average size of family.	TOTAL. Heads of families.	TOTAL. All other members.	Maine.	New Hampshire.	Vermont.	Massachusetts.	Rhode Island.	Connecticut.	New York.	Pennsylvania.	Maryland.	Virginia.	North Carolina.	South Carolina.
Holdridge, Holdrich, Holdrige, Holerige	6.4	29	157		1	2	2	2	10	11					1
Holibard, Haleburd, Haliburt, Hallabutt, Hallebert, Holabard, Holabird, Holabut, Holeburd, Holibart, Holibert, Holibort, Holiburd, Holiburt, Hollebert, Hollebot, Holleburt, Hollebut, Holliburt, Holliburt	5.2	52	218			20	4		25	3					
Holland, Holand, Hollan, Hollands, Hollen, Hollin, Hollon, Hollond	5.1	262	1,073	5		6	31	3	1	5	16	49	73	52	21
Holler, Haller, Holer, Hollar, Honard, Hollear, Holor	6.1	23	118		1					1	15	1	3	1	1
Holliday, Haliday, Halliday, Halowday, Holaday, Holiday, Holidy, Holladay, Holleday, Hollida, Holloday, Hollowday, Hollyday, Holyday	5.5	96	434			5	4		5	12	20	10	19	15	6
Hollingsworth, Hallensworth, Holensworth, Holingsworth, Holinsworth, Hollandsworth, Hollinsworth, Hollondsworth	6.5	64	351						1	8	17	4	12	22	
Hollis, Halis, Hallas, Hollace, Hollas, Hollice, Holliss	5.8	53	257	1			20		1	2	7	7		7	8
Hollister, Hallester, Holister, Hollester, Hollistor	6.6	65	362			8	3		44	10					
Holloway, Hallaway, Halleway, Halloway, Holiway, Hollaway, Holleway, Holliway	5.7	110	522	3			5	18	2	7	9	14	20	21	11
Holman, Halliman, Hallman, Halman, Holdman, Holeman, Holleman, Holliman, Hollimon, Holmans, Holmen, Holmon	5.8	128	618	2	8	1	32		1		20	1	17	31	15
Holmes, Hohmes, Holemes, Holms, Hom, Home, Homes, Hooms	5.6	527	2,419	24	42	25	132	5	65	81	42	16	25	41	29
Holomon, Halomon, Holloman, Hollowman, Hollyman, Holoman	7.1	18	109									2	13	3	
Holston, Holson, Holsten, Holstone, Houlston	4.7	22	82								10	4		2	6
Holt, Hoalt, Holts, Holtz, Hoults	5.2	302	1,256	7	47	12	59	3	51	5	16	8	57	33	4
Holton, Holten, Holtin	6.1	53	270	2	2	7	11		2	1	8	7		13	
Homan, Homans, Hommon, Homon	5.8	46	221	2	4		15			16	5		3		1
Homer	4.9	24	94	1			12		2		4	4		1	
Honeywell, Honnowel, Honowell, Honywell	5.9	17	84	4				1		12					
Hood, Hoods	5.9	113	552	3	2	1	15		5	2	18	12	22	10	23
Hoof, Hooff, Hoofes, Hooft, Hufft	6.3	16	85			1	1			1	4	2	1	1	3
Hook, Hoock, Hooke, Hookes, Hooks	6.0	79	395		18		3			2	18	16	6	11	5
Hooker	6.1	68	345		5	9	10		15	2	1	4	1	16	5
Hooper	5.7	118	559	18	6		34	2	2	6	5	23	6	6	10
Hoops, Hoop	7.2	48	298								44	2	2		
Hoover, Hoofer, Houver, Hover, Hovers, Huver	5.8	147	709							4	73	27	15	18	10
Hope, Hopes	4.6	30	109			1	1			2	6	5	4	4	7
Hopkins, Hoopkins, Hopkens, Hopkin, Hopkings	5.7	471	2,205	25	17	33	57	75	42	48	28	59	27	34	26
Hopper	5.4	45	199							16	8	2	2	14	3
Hopson	5.1	35	142	1		1				12	3	2	13	2	1
Horn, Horne, Hornes, Hornn	5.8	177	857	14	34		2	1	1	7	36	6	8	58	10
Hornback, Hornbeck, Hornbecke	6.4	36	195							20		16			
Horner	5.7	42	196	1		4			1		24	6	3	3	
Horton, Horten	5.9	272	1,346	2	2	13	54	6	21	110	12		9	38	5
Hosford, Horseford, Horsford	6.6	25	139			8	4		7	3	1		2		
Hosier, Hoser, Hozier	5.8	20	95					1		7	3	5	4		
Hoskins, Horskin, Horskins, Hoskin	5.6	111	511		5	3	27		24	21	3	4	10	10	4
Hosley, Horseley, Horsley, Horsly, Hoseley	6.2	29	152			1	12			1	1	2	12		
Hosmer, Hosmore	5.6	51	236	4	3	1	16		22	4			1		
Hostater, Hastater, Hastetter, Hoastater, Horsetiter, Hosstater, Hostatler, Hostetler, Hostetter, Hotstetter	5.9	20	98							18	2				
Hotchkiss, Hochskiss, Hodgecase, Hodgekiss, Hodgkiss, Hotchkis	4.8	151	572				5		132	12	1	1			
Hough, Haff, Hauf, Hoff, Houghf, Huff, Huffe	5.7	193	914	14	6	5	3		33	32	56	4	13	17	10
Houghtalen, Hoaghteling, Hoghtesling, Hoghtuling, Hooghteling, Hooghtuling, Hoogteling, Hoophteling, Houghtalin, Huftailing	5.2	45	234							45					
Houghton, Haughton, Hauton, Houghten, Hougton, Howton	5.5	130	580	3	9	31	64		4	4	1		5	8	1
Houk, Houck, Houke	6.4	42	228							12	21	6		2	1
House, Hous, Howse	6.1	153	777	7	1	8	14		23	26	14	12	11	27	10
Houseman, Hausman, Housemon, Housman, Housmon	5.0	27	109							9	14	1	1	2	
Houser, Howser, Howsor	6.3	51	268							3	31	11	2		4
Hovey, Hovy	6.5	80	436	6	15	5	34		14	4	1			1	
How, Howe, Howes, Hows	5.8	477	2,281	13	58	46	215	2	58	39	17	10	4	8	7
Howard, Howart, Howerd, Howert	5.6	607	2,765	24	30	24	156	14	42	53	34	70	35	90	35
Howell, Hawel, Hawele, Hawell, Houell, Howal, Howel, Howl, Howle	5.5	314	1,414	1	1	1	4	1	10	96	31	15	46	78	30
Hower, Hour, Hourre	6.2	17	89			1				1	9	2	4		
Howland, Houland, Howlen, Howlind, Howling, Howlings	6.1	154	789	7	1	4	101	21	1	15				4	
Howlet, Howlett, Howlit	5.7	22	104		3	4			3		1	2	6	2	1
Hoxie, Hoxey, Hoxkey, Hoxsey, Hoxsie	6.0	58	292	5			12	34	1	6					
Hoyl, Hoile, Hoyel, Hoyle	7.3	15	94					1	2		5	2		5	
Hoyt, Hoiet, Hoit, Hoitt, Hoyet	5.8	302	1,435	5	83	18	53		100	39	2				2
Hubbard, Hubard, Hubart, Hubbart, Hubbat, Hubberd, Hubbert, Hubbirt, Hubboard, Hubbord, Hubert	5.8	410	1,976	29	31	22	89	3	125	32	4	18	33	16	8
Hubbell, Hubbel, Hubbill, Hubble, Hubill, Huble	6.0	106	527			8	6		68	21	2		1		
Huber	5.8	73	347								71		1	1	
Huckins, Huckens, Huckings	4.8	28	106	3	17		3		4					1	
Huddleston, Huddleson, Huddlestone, Hudelston, Hudleson, Hudleston, Hudliston	6.9	27	159				1	1		2	6		4	8	5
Hudson, Hutsen, Hutson	5.7	315	1,466	1	2	7	33	9	9	36	17	35	75	59	32
Huggins, Hugans, Hugens, Huggans, Huggens, Hugghen, Hugins	5.2	78	328		9	2	3		5	7	8	3	4	15	22
Hughes, Heugh, Hewes, Hews, Hues, Hugh, Hughe, Hughs, Huse, Huws	5.8	407	1,955	4	19	3	26	2	7	14	86	48	85	57	56
Hughey, Hewey, Huey, Hughy	6.1	41	208	6	1					2	13	1		11	7
Hulin, Hewlin, Hughlin, Hulan, Huling, Hulings, Huilin	5.9	21	103			3	1	2		2	7		2	3	1
Hull, Hul, Hulls	5.5	251	1,142		5	8	13	22	117	36	25	13	1	5	6
Hulse, Hulsa, Hulsea	6.4	25	135						1	15	3		1		5
Humes, Hume	4.9	27	105	2			5	1	1	1	11	4		2	
Hummel, Humel, Hummell	5.4	24	106							4	19		1		
Humniston, Humberstone, Humerston, Humestone	5.4	22	96						21		1				
Humphrey, Humfrey, Humfry, Humphery, Hunphes, Humphress, Humphreys, Humphries, Humphris, Humphriss, Humphrs, Humphs, Humphry, Humphryes, Humphrys, Humphys, Humpress, Humpris, Humprys, Umfrey, Umphres, Umphreys, Umphries, Umphry, Umphrys	5.8	290	1,378	9	9	8	38	6	59	25	29	3	35	50	19
Hundley, Hunley, Hunly	5.3	39	169							2	2		33	2	
Hungerford, Hungeford	6.6	42	234			1	4		29	4	1	3			
Hunnicutt, Honecut, Honeycut, Honeycutt, Huneycut, Hunnecut, Hunneycut, Hunnicut	4.4	27	91									9	12	6	
Hunsucker, Hoonsacker, Hunsaker, Hunseker, Hunsiker, Hunsiker, Huntsucker	7.6	16	106								9		1	5	1
Hunt, Hunte, Hunts	5.6	606	2,807	17	41	25	147	23	51	119	31	26	43	58	25
Hunter	5.5	350	1,591	7	7	9	23	2	4	41	100	18	34	73	32
Hunting, Huntting	4.8	21	80			2		16		3					
Huntington, Huntingdon, Hunttington	6.7	121	687	3	15	15	7	1	67	7		4		2	
Huntley, Huntly	5.0	63	255	3	13	6	3		24	11				3	
Huntoon, Hunten, Hunton	5.4	38	168	1	25					3	1		7		1
Hurd, Heard, Herd, Hurde	6.0	217	1,084	15	29	31	32		65	17	5	11	2	1	9
Hurlbut, Hurlbart, Hurlbert, Hurlburt, Hurlbutt	5.6	93	424		6	8	16		52	6	5				

TABLE **111.**—NOMENCLATURE, DEALING WITH NAMES REPRESENTED BY AT LEAST 100 WHITE PERSONS, BY STATES AND TERRITORIES, AT THE FIRST CENSUS: 1790—Continued.

NAME.	Average size of family.	TOTAL.		HEADS OF FAMILIES.											
		Heads of families.	All other members.	Maine.	New Hampshire.	Vermont.	Massachusetts.	Rhode Island.	Connecticut.	New York.	Pennsylvania.	Maryland.	Virginia.	North Carolina.	South Carolina.
Hurley, Herly, Hirley, Hurly	5.5	33	149	1			4				8	11		9	
Hurst, Herst, Hirst, Hursts	5.4	54	240							4	11	3	30	5	1
Hurt, Herts, Hertz	6.4	42	228							7	4	4	23	3	1
Huson, Hewson, Hughson, Husong, Husson	5.2	29	121				1			21	3		4		
Hussey, Husey, Hussee, Hussy, Huzey, Huzy, Huzzey, Huzzy	5.9	77	377	28	9		24			3	2	4	1	4	2
Husted, Hustead	7.5	38	247	1					13	22			2		
Huston, Housten, Houstin, Houston, Hueston, Hustain, Husten, Hustin, Hustine	5.7	177	840	12	12	2	5		1	6	62	13	7	40	17
Hutchins, Huchens, Huchings, Huchins, Hudgen, Hudgens, Hudgeons, Huddggens, Hudging, Hudgins, Hutchans, Hutchens, Hutchin, Hutchings, Hutchons, Hutcion, Hutshion	5.5	261	1,181	37	22	10	8	1	13	35	2	18	70	31	14
Hutchinson, Huchenson, Hucheson, Huchinson, Huchison, Hutchenson, Hutcherson, Hutcheson, Hutchingson, Hutchison, Hutchonson, Hutchusson	5.6	260	1,208	13	31	17	37	1	21	10	51	11	28	14	26
Hutton, Huton	4.9	55	213				1			9	28	10	5		2
Hyatt, Hiat, Hiatt, Hiet, Hiett, Highat, Highet, Hiot, Hiott, Huyet, Hyat, Hyet, Hyett, Hyette, Hyetts, Hyot, Hyott	5.9	104	511						12	28	5	10	10	32	7
Hyde, Heyd, Heyde, Hide	6.2	213	1,105	2	7	29	43	2	80	14	14	4	5	8	5
Hyer, Heyer, Higher, Hyar, Hyers	6.0	17	85				1			14	1		1	1	
Hyland, Highland, Highlands, Hiland, Hilands, Hilens, Hylan, Hylens	5.8	24	116	1	3		4				8	5	2	1	
Hymes, Heim, Heims, Hime, Himes, Hyme, Hyms	6.0	32	159		2	2		4	2	1	16	5			
Ide	6.6	29	163			6	17	2		4					
Ingalls, Engalls, Engel, Engle, Engles, Ingales, Ingall, Ingals, Ingels, Ingle, Ingles, Ingoles, Ingolls, Ingols	5.6	176	811	10	25	4	57		10	11	46	4	4	3	2
Ingersoll, Ingarsoll, Ingersal, Ingersall, Ingersol, Ingersole	5.7	72	341	5			39		11	15	2				
Ingham	6.1	19	97	3		1			9	3	2	1			
Ingram, Engram, Engrim, Ingraham, Ingrahm, Ingrime, Ingrm, Ingrom, Ingrum	5.8	192	918	8	4	9	29	14	27	8	21	8	16	35	13
Inman, Inmon	6.5	44	241	1			2	18	2	5	4		4	5	3
Insley, Endley, Endsley, Endsly, Ensley	5.8	25	120				2				9	5		5	4
Irby, Ireby	5.8	31	148					1					23	2	5
Ireland, Iresland, Iriland, Irland	4.6	57	208	4			6		2	18	5	11	4	7	
Irish, Ireish	5.6	66	303	17		11	1	11	1	21	2	1		1	
Irwin, Ervan, Erven, Ervewin, Ervin, Ervine, Erving, Ervwin, Ervwn, Erwin, Erwine, Erwinn, Erwyn, Irven, Irvin, Irvine, Irving, Irwen, Irwin, Irwine, Urvin	5.4	294	1,301	1	2	4	7	1	2	16	147	11	17	60	26
Isaacs, Isaac, Isaacks, Isaaks, Isacks	4.8	34	130		1			1	4	9	5	4	1	2	7
Isbell, Isabel, Isbale, Isbel	5.3	25	108		1		2		5	2		1	3	9	2
Isham	5.1	23	94		1	5			12					1	4
Ives	5.8	137	651		1	14	9		76	10	6		5	16	
Ivey, Ivay, Ivy	5.5	55	249								1	1	13	28	12
Jack, Jacks, Jakes	5.7	42	199	4	4		1	1			24	2		2	4
Jackman	6.0	39	195	1	15	3	16				4				
Jackson, Jackison, Jackston, Jacson, Jaxson	5.6	785	3,635	33	45	18	88	6	51	98	93	48	89	161	55
Jacobs, Jacbs, Jacob	5.5	248	1,112	9	9	12	46	4	16	25	55	36	14	12	10
Jacoby, Jacby, Jacobie, Jcoby	4.7	31	114							10	21				
Jagger, Jager, Jaggar, Jaggers	5.0	23	92				1		3	17					2
James, Jams, Jeames, Jemes	5.3	408	1,736	5	12	2	29	27	15	25	64	40	67	83	39
Jameson, Jamerson, Jameston, Jamison, Jammeson, Jammison, Jamson, Jemerson, Jemeson, Jemeyson, Jeminson, Jemison, Jemisson, Jemmison, Jimerson, Jimeson, Jimmison	5.1	140	568	12	9	2	3			6	49	14	22	12	11
Janes, Jane, Jayn, Jayne, Jean, Jeans	6.1	55	278			3	17		3	7	11	5	2	7	
Jansen, J'Anson	5.8	20	95							19			1		
Jaques, Jacques, Jacquess, Jaqua, Jaquays, Jaquess, Jaquis, Jaquish	6.1	35	178	3	1	4	7	8	1	6		3	2		
Jaquith, Jacquett, Jacwith, Jaquet, Jaqueth	5.6	42	193		7	2	30			1	1	1			
Jarrell, Garell, Garrald, Garrel, Garreld, Garrell, Gerald, Geralds, Gerauld, Gerrald, Gerrauld, Jarral, Jarrall, Jarrel, Jerols, Jerould, Jerrald, Jerrel, Jerrell, Jerrold, Jerroll, Jeruild	6.2	49	257		4	1	6	3	2	3	1		6	18	5
Jarrett, Jarat, Jarrat, Jarrate, Jarratt, Jarret, Jarrot, Jarrott, Jerret, Jerrett, Jerrit	5.9	41	201							4	12	5	11	9	
Jarvis, Garvis, Gervis, Jarvais, Jarves, Jervis	5.3	118	503			1	18		13	24	5	16	16	24	1
Jeacocks, Jacocks	6.8	16	92				1			12				3	
Jeffers, Jefers, Jeffirs	5.8	47	227	1	2		3	2	2	7	17	2	1	5	5
Jefferson, Jeffison	6.8	21	121				1	1		1	5	8	3	1	
Jeffery, Gaffery, Geffereys, Gefries, Geofroy, Jaffray, Jaffrey, Jafreys, Jeferes, Jeferis, Jefferies, Jefferis, Jefferys, Jeffiries, Jeffres, Jeffress, Jeffrey, Jeffreys, Jeffries, Jeffris, Jeffry, Jeffrys, Jefres, Jefreys, Jefries	5.4	96	427	4	1		10	1	8	4	19	18	13	12	6
Jellitson, Jealoson, Jealouson, Jeleson, Jelison, Jelleson, Jellison	5.8	19	91	19											
Jenkins, Genkins, Ginkens, Jainkens, Jencans, Jenckins, Jenken, Jenkens, Jenkin, Jenkings, Jinkens, Jinkings, Jinkins, Juncan, Juncans, Junken, Junkin, Junkins	5.6	455	2,083	25	18	5	66	6	1	40	62	45	65	75	47
Jenks, Ginks, Jenckes, Jencks, Jenkes, Jincks, Jinks	6.3	93	497	2	4	5	22	45	4	4	4		3		
Jenne, Jenney, Jenny	5.6	42	193			5	24	2		6	1	2	2		
Jenness, Janis, Janus, Jennes, Jennis	6.0	40	199	1	35		1		1		1			1	
Jennings, Gennings, Gennins, Ginning, Ginnings, Ginnins, Jenings, Jennens, Jenning, Jennis, Jining, Jinings, Jinnings, Jinnins	5.5	274	1,241	2	6	5	31	5	67	39	21	5	38	30	25
Jennison, Jenenson, Jenesin, Jeneson, Jenison, Jennerson, Jenneson, Jenson, Jenstone	5.5	34	152	2	2	4	24	1			1				
Jermond, Jereman, Jermain, Jerman, Jermin, Jermon	6.0	31	154						1	15		3	2	6	4
Jernigan, Jernagan, Jernian	7.1	15	91				3							11	1
Jerom, Jaroms, Jearom, Jearome, Jearoms, Jeroams, Jeroms	4.5	20	90				2		11	6		1			
Jessop, Jasup, Jeasup, Jesep, Jesop, Jessup, Jesup, Jesuph, Jezup, Jusup	6.5	39	213				1			10	11	4	2	11	
Jeter, Jetar, Jether, Jetter	6.6	16	89										11	2	3
Jewell, Jewel, Jewill	6.2	92	475	10	20	3	11	1	4	22	5	9		5	2
Jewett, Jewet, Jewit, Jewitt, Jouett, Juett, Juwet	5.8	150	716	18	40	9	58		18	6			1		
Jilson, Jillson, Jilsom	5.8	18	87		1	1	8	7		1					
Job, Jobb, Jobe, Jobes, Jobs	5.7	23	109							1	10	4	4	4	
Johns, John, Johnes, Johnns, Jon, Jonnes, Jons	5.7	113	530	5	2	3	4		7	1	41	18	23	4	5
Johnson, Jahnson, Jhonson, Johnsin, Johnsom, Johnston, Johnstone, Jonson, Jonston	5.7	2,646	12,358	63	146	101	290	61	297	236	388	173	259	419	213
Joiner, Joinor, Joyner	5.7	97	460			5	3			2	1	7	4	58	17
Jolly, Jolley, Jollys	6.3	40	212							2	2	9	3	13	8
Jones	5.6	2,561	11,739	87	104	59	287	20	173	210	289	239	345	558	190
Jordan, Jaudon, Jordain, Jordeen, Jorden, Jordin, Jordon, Jordone, Jourdain, Jourdan, Jourden, Jourdin, Jurdan, Jurden, Jurdon	5.5	372	1,662	79	5	1	19	2	7	12	47	14	63	100	23
Joslin, Jocelin, Joseylin, Josland, Joslen, Josling, Joslyn, Josselin, Josselyn, Josslyn, Josylin, Joyslin	6.2	97	505	6	8	6	41	13	9	6	1		6	1	
Joy, Joye, Joys	5.7	94	442	10	10	11	34		4	3	2	13		1	6
Joyce, Joice, Joyas	5.7	46	218	1			6		3	5	5	11		14	1
Judd, Jud	5.8	117	560		7	7	17		69	4		8		5	
Judkins, Judgkins	4.8	65	248	11	22								26	6	
Judson, Jutson	6.2	70	361			2	2		65	1					
Judy, Judey	6.0	21	104								4	5	10		2
June	5.2	33	139			2	2		12	14				1	2
Justice, Justes, Justese, Justis, Justiss, Justus	5.7	56	264							1	16	9	9	17	4

TABLE 111.—NOMENCLATURE, DEALING WITH NAMES REPRESENTED BY AT LEAST 100 WHITE PERSONS, BY STATES AND TERRITORIES, AT THE FIRST CENSUS: 1790—Continued.

NAME	Average size of family	TOTAL — Heads of families	TOTAL — All other members	Maine	New Hampshire	Vermont	Massachusetts	Rhode Island	Connecticut	New York	Pennsylvania	Maryland	Virginia	North Carolina	South Carolina
Karen, Caren, Carons, Caroon, Carren, Carrin, Carron, Corran, Corron, Karran	5.3	20	85				1			2	8			9	
Kauffman, Cauffman, Caufman, Caughman, Coafman, Coffman, Coffmon, Cofman, Coufman, Coughman, Cowfman, Kaufman, Koffman, Kofman, Koufman	6.1	134	689							1	96	4	29		4
Kay, Cay, Caye, Kayes, Kays	5.6	18	83		2				1		2		8	3	2
Kayler, Caler, Callar, Caller, Calor, Caylor, Kahler, Kailer, Kaler, Kalor, Kaylor	4.9	24	94	1						5	11	4		3	
Keater, Keator, Keeter, Ketor	5.0	25	101							18				7	
Keaton, Keetan, Keeting, Keeton	5.5	27	121	2		1			1	6			6	10	1
Keech, Keach, Keatch, Keetch, Ketch	6.2	31	161			1		1	13	8	1	5		2	
Keefer, Keafer, Keffer, Keifer, Keiffer, Kieffer	5.5	34	154	1						7	19	5	1	1	
Keel, Keal, Keale, Keall, Keele, Keels, Kehl, Keil, Kiehl, Kiel	5.3	44	189								17	4	2	12	9
Keeler, Kealer, Keelor, Keelur, Kehler, Keiler, Kelah, Keler, Keyler, Keylor	5.5	118	528	1		15	2		53	25	20			4	1
Keeling, Keelin, Keling	5.2	39	162	1					1		2	1	30	4	1
Keely, Keeley, Keelley, Keelly	6.1	17	87	1							11		2	2	1
Keen, Kean, Keane, Keene, Keens, Keign, Kein, Keine, Kene	5.5	162	735	27			30	2		13	45	9	17	14	5
Keith, Keath, Keeth, Keth, Keyth, Kieth	6.0	135	680	5	1	4	74		8	3	14	8	3	3	12
Kell, Kells, Kill	5.9	17	84								3	2		6	3
Keller, Kellar, Kellere, Kelloe, Kellough, Kellow, Kelugh, Killar, Killer	5.8	164	779	3			1			12	86	16	19	15	12
Kellogg, Keelogg, Kellagg, Kelleg, Kellegg, Kelloch, Kellock, Kellog, Kelogg	6.3	195	1,033				6	1	20	56		65	43	1	3
Kelly, Kehly, Keiley, Kele, Keley, Kelley, Kely, Kiely, Killey, Killy	5.5	550	2,460	13	43	10	77	15	15	54	115	59	26	75	48
Kelsey, Kehelsy, Kelcey, Kelcy, Kellce, Kellsey, Kelse, Kelsy, Killse, Kilsey, Kilsy	6.1	124	587	2	12	9	8		57	19	5	3			9
Kelso, Kelsoe, Killsa, Kilso	6.8	21	122	3	7		1			2	6	2			
Kelton, Kalton, Kilton	5.1	29	118				21	4			1			2	1
Kemp, Kempe, Kemps, Kimp	6.2	116	603	1	13	1	21		1	3	10	28	14	15	9
Kempton, Kimpton	6.2	26	136	2	1	2	16			2					3
Kendall, Kendal, Kendel, Kendele, Kendle, Kenndall, Kindal, Kindall, Kindel, Kindell, Kindle, Kindol, Kindrel, Kinnel, Kinnell	5.9	195	963	8	19	21	77		16	4	21	9	7	11	2
Kendrick, Keindrick, Kendricks, Kenrick, Kindreck, Kindrick	5.5	71	321	2	8	1	18			1	16	3	14	8	
Kennard, Kenard, Kenhard, Keniard, Kinard, Kindard, Kinhard, Kinnard, Kinnerd	5.5	42	191	7	1						12	15	2	3	2
Kennedy, Canada, Canaday, Canadey, Canady, Caneday, Canedy, Caniday, Cannada, Cannaday, Cannady, Canneday, Canniday, Cenedy, Ceniday, Kanada, Kanaday, Kanadey, Kanady, Kannedy, Kenada, Kenady, Kendy, Keneday, Kenedy, Kenerdy, Kennaday, Kennady, Kennedy, Kenneday, Kennerday, Kennidy	5.4	368	1,626	14	9	7	19	4	17	34	90	23	21	83	47
Kenniston, Kenison, Keniston, Kenistone, Kenneston, Kennison, Kineson, Kiniston, Kinistone, Kinnerson, Kinneston, Kinnison	5.0	48	191	3	34	2	2			2			5		
Kenny, Keaney, Keany, Keeney, Keeny, Keiny, Keney, Kenney, Kennie, Kenoy, Keny, Kiney, Kinne, Kinney, Kinny	6.0	182	910	14	17	15	29		46	19	22	2	11	5	2
Kent, Kint	5.7	180	843	13	10	14	53	6	23	10	5	6	27	12	1
Kern, Kearn, Kearns, Keern, Keirns, Kerne, Kernes, Kerns, Kirn	5.1	81	334							2	58	5	5	3	8
Kersey, Kearsey, Keersey, Kersy, Kirsey, Kursey	4.2	32	101				1				1	9	5	11	5
Kesler, Keasler, Keesler, Keisler, Keissler, Kessler, Kieslar, Kisiler, Kisler, Kysler	6.4	39	209	1			1			2	22	7		3	3
Kester, Keaster, Keester, Keister, Kestor, Kisster, Kister	5.2	20	84								9		9	1	1
Ketcham, Catchem, Ketchem, Ketchum, Kitcham, Kitchum	5.9	102	497		3	5	4		4	81	3			2	
Key, Keay, Kee, Kees, Keese, Kese, Keyce, Keyes, Keys, Keyse, Keze	6.1	182	929	9	18	11	32		12	8	18	19	23	16	16
Keykendall, Kikendal, Kikendall, Kinkendal, Kirkendal, Kirkendol, Kirkindol, Koukendal, Kuykendall	6.0	27	136							4	10		8	5	
Keyser, Kaiser, Kaisor, Kayser, Keiser, Keisser, Keysar, Kiaser, Kiesser, Kioser, Kisear, Kiser, Kisor, Kizer, Kizier, Kizor, Kysar, Kyser, Kysor, Kyzer	5.5	129	583	1	1					22	83	4	11	3	4
Kibbe, Kibbee, Kibbey, Kibby, Kiby	5.0	53	210		1	4	10		33	5					
Kidd, Kid, Kidde	5.6	53	242			1				7	10	5	25	1	4
Kidder, Kider	6.3	66	349	1	23	5	29		4	2	1				1
Kilbourn, Kilborn, Kilborne, Kilbourne, Kilburn, Kilburne	5.5	97	434		7	8	31	1	41	6				2	1
Kilgore, Kilgo, Killgore, Killgour, Killgow	5.6	36	164	7							11	4	7	3	4
Killam, Kellam, Kellem, Kellum, Kilham, Kilhem	5.5	30	136	1	5	2	7		2	5	2	4	1		1
Killian, Kellan, Kellen, Kellin, Kelling, Kellon, Killand, Killean, Killen, Killens, Killin	4.0	39	116	1	1		2				12	2	1	18	2
Killmor, Killmer, Killmore, Kilmer, Kilmor, Kilmore	7.0	22	133							18	4				
Kilpatrick, Kelpatrick, Killpatrick, Kilpartrick, Kilpatric, Kilpatrieck	5.9	47	228	5						1	18	5		11	7
Kimball, Kemball, Kembell, Kemble, Kimal, Kimbal, Kimbald, Kimbel, Kimbell, Kimbil, Kimble, Kimbler, Kimbol, Kimboll, Kimbrel, Kimbrell, Kimbril, Kimbull, Kimel, Kimell, Kimil, Kimmel	5.9	442	2,182	56	137	18	115	13	23	18	28	8	5	14	7
Kimberly, Kammerlae, Kemberly, Kemmerley, Kemmerly, Kimberley, Kimerly, Kimsberlly	5.3	30	128			1			23		3		1		2
King, Kings	5.7	877	4,095	11	21	24	150	38	71	112	115	61	77	145	52
Kingery	6.2	17	88								15	1	1		
Kingman, Kingsman	5.2	33	138	1	3	1	28								
Kingsbury, Kingbury, Kingsberry, Kingsborough, Kinsbury	5.7	117	555	7	18	7	51		29	2	1			2	
Kingsley, Kingley, Kingsly, Kinsley	6.2	120	618	2	1	18	47	5	27	5	13		1		1
Kinkaid, Kenkade, Kenkead, Kincade, Kincaid, Kincard, Kinkad, Kinkade, Kinkead	5.0	57	227	7						1	26	1	12	7	3
Kinner, Kenar, Keneer, Kener, Kenna, Kennear, Kenner, Kenough, Kinear, Kinnear	5.9	33	162		1		1			1	6	9	1	9	5
Kinsey, Kense, Kensy, Kincey, Kinsay, Kinsy, Kinzee, Kinzey	6.1	53	268								31	2	3	14	3
Kinsman, Kenman, Kinman, Kinneman, Kinnemon, Kinomon	6.1	31	159	2	3		15		2	2		4		3	
Kinyon, Keenan, Kenan, Kennan, Kennen, Kennens, Kennion, Kennon, Kenyan, Kenyon, Keonan, Kinian, Kinion, Kinnion, Kinnon	5.4	142	631		3		5	62	9	28	4	1	9	17	4
Kipp, Kip, Kipps, Kips	5.8	56	267			2			1	47	3		1		
Kirby, Curbey, Curbie, Curby, Kerbey, Kerby, Kirbey, Kurbee	5.6	155	714		1	1	20	2	9	16	8	42	16	30	10
Kirk, Kerk, Kirkes, Kirks	5.8	104	504		1	1	1		5	47	16	12	11	11	9
Kirkland, Kerkland, Kirtland	6.0	45	223			1	4		10	3	1		1	3	21
Kirkpatrick, Kirckpatrick, Kirkpattrick, Kirkpetreck, Kirkpetrick	5.1	48	198	2						4	22	3	4	7	6
Kirshner, Kershner, Kersner, Kirsener	8.2	18	129								10	7	1		
Kissinger, Keesinger, Kessinger, Kishinger, Kisinger	5.4	26	114								19	4	3		
Kitchen, Keachen, Ketchen, Ketchun, Kitchens, Kitchin	5.2	41	174						2		12	1	3	13	10
Kite, Kettell, Kettle, Kettles, Kitle, Kittles	4.5	25	88								8		7	9	1
Kittle, Kettell, Kettle, Kettles, Kitle, Kittles	6.0	49	245			2	13	3	2	18	1			4	3
Kittredge, Ketteredge, Ketteridge, Kithridge, Kitridge, Kitterage, Kitteridge, Kitterige, Kittridge, Kittredge	6.1	37	188	1	13	5	17			1					
Kitts, Kets, Ketz, Kits, Kitt, Kitze	6.2	18	94								5	12			1
Klaw, Claus, Clause, Claw, Clawes, Clou, Clous, Clouse, Klause	5.7	27	128	1		1			1	13	8		1	2	
Klock, Clock, Clocks	7.1	25	152						8	14	3				
Knapp, Knap, Nap, Napp	6.1	283	1,440	3	9	22	49	4	84	105	5			1	1
Kneeland, Neland	6.0	20	100	1			11		4	3	1				
Knickerbacker, Knickabacker, Knickabocker, Knickebacker, Knickerbacor	7.1	22	135			1				14					
Kniffin	6.1	34	174							34					
Knight, Knights, Night, Nights, Nite, Nites	5.6	424	1,960	63	37	17	80	31	14	13	45	21	24	47	32
Knott, Knot, Knots, Knotts, Knotz, Nots, Nott, Notts, Notz	5.1	88	359		2	1	2		15	5	8	32	7	12	4
Knouse, Knaus, Knauss, Knous, Knouss, Knows, Naus, Nous, Nouse	6.3	27	144								25			1	1

TABLE **111.**—NOMENCLATURE, DEALING WITH NAMES REPRESENTED BY AT LEAST 100 WHITE PERSONS, BY STATES AND TERRITORIES, AT THE FIRST CENSUS: 1790—Continued.

NAME.	Average size of family.	TOTAL. Heads of families.	TOTAL. All other members.	Maine.	New Hampshire.	Vermont.	Massachusetts.	Rhode Island.	Connecticut.	New York.	Pennsylvania.	Maryland.	Virginia.	North Carolina.	South Carolina.
Knowles, Knolds, Knoles, Knoll, Knowel, Knowell, Knowls, Noal, Noel, Noell, Nole, Noles, Noll, Nolles, Nool, Noul, Nowel, Nowell, Nowells, Nowels, Nowls	5.8	234	1,128	20	32	1	47	21	18	5	26	13	25	22	4
Knowlton, Knolton, Knoulton, Nolten, Nolton, Noulton	6.1	92	465	10	15	7	45	1	8	6	....	....	....	....	....
Knox, Knock, Noc, Noch, Nock, Nocks, Nox	5.5	171	765	19	10	3	15	....	8	15	37	15	3	27	19
Kreider, Kraider, Kreeder, Krider	6.0	24	121	....	....	....	....	....	....	....	24	....	....	....	....
Kuhn, Kughn, Kuhns	5.4	25	111	....	....	....	1	....	....	....	24	....	....	....	....
Kuntz, Counce, Counts, Countz, Cuntz, Cunze, Kunse, Kunts	5.3	37	158	2	....	....	....	....	....	2	20	....	9	1	3
Kurtz, Curts, Curtz, Kurts	6.6	36	200	....	....	....	....	....	....	....	29	5	2	....	....
Kyes, Kies, Kise	6.3	20	106	....	....	1	6	....	5	4	....	1	1	1	1
Kyger, Kigar, Kiger	6.3	16	85	....	....	....	....	....	....	....	6	3	4	3	....
Kyle, Kyles	5.8	18	86	....	....	2	....	....	....	....	14	....	1	1	....
Kyser, Kisear, Kisser, Kisz r, Kysar, Kysor, Kyzer	4.3	24	79	....	....	....	....	....	....	....	18	2	1	....	3
Labar, Labagh, Labaugh, Labgh	6.6	16	89	....	....	....	....	....	....	....	16	....	....	....	....
Lackey, Lachy, Lackay, Lacky, Lakey	5.1	47	192	1	....	1	4	....	1	....	10	2	11	13	4
Lacy, Lacey, Laicey, Lasey, Leacy	5.0	97	390	....	3	3	2	....	17	8	8	3	24	17	12
Ladd, Lad, Ladds	6.3	111	586	4	43	12	9	5	21	2	....	....	8	6	1
Laferty, Laefferty, Laffarty, Lafferty, Laffity, Laugherty, Laverty	4.6	28	101	....	....	1	....	....	....	1	17	3	1	4	1
Laird, Lard, Larde, Leaird, Leard, Leird	5.6	48	223	....	....	2	2	....	2	3	22	2	3	5	7
Lake, Llake	5.2	106	446	4	6	9	15	18	8	30	6	1	1	2	6
Lakeman	5.0	20	80	2	4	....	14	....	....	....	....	....	....	....	....
Lakin, Laiken, Lakins, Laykin, Leakins	5.2	28	118	1	5	1	12	....	....	....	2	5	2	....	....
Lamaster, Lamasters, Leemaster, Leimaster, Lemaster, Lumaster	7.5	20	129	....	....	....	1	....	....	....	2	3	6	....	8
Lamb, Lam, Lambs	5.9	229	1,126	4	2	19	57	....	18	24	17	14	19	46	9
Lambert, Lambart, Lampert, Lamput	5.7	107	506	8	1	....	17	....	6	14	9	8	20	18	6
Lamkin, Lambkin, Lamkins, Lampkins	6.2	22	114	....	....	3	1	2	....	....	....	....	10	2	4
Lamphear, Lamfier, Lampheer, Lampher, Lamphere, Lamphier, Lamphire, Lanpher, Leamphear, Leamphere, Lemphear	5.5	61	275	4	2	10	2	13	13	17	....	....	....	....	....
Lamson, Lambsen, Lambson, Lameson, Lampsen, Lampson	5.1	91	374	5	15	9	41	....	15	3	3	....	....	....	....
Lancaster, Lancastor, Lancester, Lancestor, Lanchester, Langcaster, Lankester, Lankister	6.4	84	453	10	4	....	4	....	1	5	6	10	15	19	10
Lance	5.3	22	94	....	....	....	....	....	....	....	6	5	1	7	3
Land, Lands, Lannd	5.0	55	220	....	....	2	....	1	....	1	....	....	32	8	11
Landers, Landa, Lander	5.7	48	226	8	....	1	11	....	2	1	9	1	6	5	4
Landes, Landess, Landice, Landis, Lantes, Lantis	6.4	58	314	....	....	....	....	....	....	....	57	1	....	....	....
Landt, Lant, Lantz, Lanz	6.5	17	94	....	....	....	....	....	....	8	6	2	1	....	....
Lane, Lain, Laine, Lains, Lanes, Layn, Layne	5.6	437	2,019	27	44	12	67	....	32	65	28	35	41	71	15
Lang, Lange, Langs	5.2	64	270	2	28	....	5	....	....	3	10	3	3	1	9
Langdon, Landen, Landing, Landon, Landown, Langdin, Langedon, Langsdon, Langsdown, Langston, Langton	5.7	152	718	4	6	11	11	....	40	24	7	6	10	24	9
Langford, Landford, Lanford, Langsford, Lansford, Lantford	5.4	45	202	....	....	1	6	5	....	1	....	1	13	13	5
Langley, Langlee, Langly, Langsley	5.2	86	360	3	18	1	2	4	....	....	1	9	12	28	8
Lanham, Langham, Lanman	5.5	46	208	....	....	....	6	....	1	....	....	31	5	3	....
Lanier, Laniere, Lennier	5.8	20	95	....	....	....	....	....	....	....	....	....	3	16	1
Lansing, Lencing, Lensing	5.6	55	251	....	....	....	....	....	....	53	1	....	....	....	1
Lapham, Lappam, Lappan, Lappum, Lapum, Lepham	6.3	49	258	1	....	2	26	11	1	8	....	....	....	....	....
Lapp, Lap, Lape, Laph	5.8	19	91	....	....	....	....	....	....	2	13	4	....	....	....
Lare, Lair, Laire, Layar, Layer	5.6	20	91	....	....	....	....	1	....	....	15	1	2	1	....
Larkin, Larking, Larkins, Learkin	5.4	70	306	....	1	3	12	27	5	2	4	2	3	11	....
Larned, Larnard	5.4	38	168	1	7	1	27	....	2	....	....	....	....	....	....
Larrabee, Laraba, Larabbi, Larabee, Larabie, Laraby, Larebe, Larrabb, Larrabe, Larrabi, Larrabu, Larraby, Larreby, Larribee, Larriby, Lorabee, Lorrabee	5.4	48	212	16	....	9	12	....	5	6	....	....	....	....	....
Larrimore, Laramare, Laremore, Larimer, Larimore, Laurimer, Lawremare, Lawrimor, Lawrimore, Loramore, Lorimer, Lorumor	5.3	31	134	....	....	....	....	....	....	....	14	12	1	3	1
Larue, Lareu, Larew, La Rieu, Lereaux, Lerew, Leru, Lerue, Lurue	5.6	23	106	....	....	....	....	....	....	3	10	1	7	....	2
Lary, Lairy, Larey, Larree, Larrey, Larry	4.6	25	91	5	7	....	1	....	1	....	1	4	....	3	3
Lasher	5.9	24	119	....	....	....	....	....	....	19	4	....	1	....	....
Lassiter, Lasiter, Lasitor, Lasseter, Lassetor, Lassitor, Laster	5.8	80	386	....	....	....	....	....	....	....	1	....	22	57	....
Latham, Lathem, Lathim, Lathom, Lathrom, Lathrum, Lathum	5.7	90	422	2	3	1	11	9	26	11	1	....	7	13	6
Lathrop, Latrop, Lauthrop, Lorthorp, Lothorp, Lothrop, Lotrop, Lowthorp	5.8	147	706	....	7	9	48	....	65	14	1	....	....	1	2
Latimer, Latamore, Latemore, Latimor, Latimore, Latiner, Lattamore, Lattemer, Lattemore, Lattimer, Lattimore, Lettimore	5.4	70	311	....	....	....	1	....	26	7	12	8	9	4	3
Latta, Lata, Later, Lator, Latoure, Latter, Lature	6.2	28	146	....	....	....	1	....	1	4	10	....	....	7	5
Laughlin, Lafflin, Laflin, Laughling, Lofland, Loflin	5.7	45	212	....	4	3	4	....	....	....	22	1	4	4	3
Law, Lahr, Laer, Lar, Lauer, Laur, Laws, Lehr, Loar, Loher, Lore, Lorr, Lours, Lowar, Lower, Lowers	5.3	104	448	1	1	3	11	2	8	10	40	14	1	9	4
Lawrence, Larance, Larence, Larince, Larrance, Larrence, Laurance, Laurence, Laurens, Lawrance, Lawrens, Lawrrance, Lewrance, Lorance, Lorrentz, Lowrance	5.7	517	2,413	14	30	32	94	3	36	126	51	20	29	68	14
Lawson, Lauson	5.5	122	549	....	....	2	5	....	5	28	9	5	40	17	11
Lawton, Laughton, Lauton, Lorton	5.7	89	418	....	....	11	18	45	....	2	1	1	2	5	4
Lawyer, Lawyers, Loyer, Loyers	5.4	21	92	....	....	....	....	....	....	14	2	....	5	....	....
Lay, Laigh, Lays	6.5	45	247	....	....	1	1	....	20	2	....	....	7	11	3
Lazell, Lacells, Lasell, Lassel, Lassell, Lassells, Lazall, Lazel, Lazelle, Lazil, Lazolle	5.7	29	141	....	1	4	15	4	1	2	....	1	....	1	....
Leach, Leatch, Leech, Leetch, Leicht, Leitch, Letch, Lietch, Litch	6.0	233	1,167	16	19	5	64	5	35	13	28	20	2	16	10
Leak, Leack, Leake, Leakes, Leek, Leeke, Leeks, Lekes, Lieke	5.3	62	268	....	....	....	....	....	8	18	8	9	9	7	3
Lear, Leer	5.0	40	177	1	10	....	1	....	....	2	19	3	2	2	....
Leary, Lerry	4.9	21	82	....	....	....	1	....	....	4	1	3	2	11	....
Leathers, Leather	5.7	38	179	1	21	....	2	....	....	....	4	3	3	4	....
Leavenworth, Lavensworth, Lavenworth, Leavensworth, Levensworth, Levenworth	5.6	27	124	....	....	3	1	....	19	3	....	....	....	....	1
Leavitt, Leavet, Leavett, Leavit, Leveit, Levet, Levit, Levite, Levitt	5.9	116	563	12	67	2	17	....	12	2	....	....	4	....	....
Ledbetter, Leadbetter, Letbetter	5.3	20	86	4	....	....	1	....	....	....	....	....	....	13	2
Lee, Lea, Leagh, Leah, Leigh, Ley	5.6	707	3,371	8	12	24	94	10	93	70	64	56	68	142	66
Leeds, Leads, Leed	5.3	25	107	....	....	1	13	....	10	....	1	....	....	....	....
Leeper, Leaper, Leiper	6.8	18	105	....	....	....	....	....	....	2	13	1	....	2	....
Lees, Leas, Leess, Leis, Leise, Leiss	5.6	24	111	....	....	1	....	....	....	2	20	....	1	2	....
Leeson, Leasen, Leason, Leasson, Leesen, Leeterson, Leson, Lesson	4.9	22	85	....	....	....	4	....	3	6	2	1	1	....	4
Leet, Leat, Leatt, Leeht, Leets, Leit	5.0	37	147	....	4	3	....	....	24	1	3	1	1	....	....
Lefever, Lafavour, Leefever, Lefavar, Lefavour, Lefeever, Le Fever	6.3	45	240	....	....	....	....	5	1	....	16	17	4	1	1
Lefferts, Leffort	5.3	20	86	....	....	....	....	....	....	....	16	4	....	....	....
Leffingwell, Leppinwell	6.5	26	143	....	....	1	....	....	24	....	....	1	....	....	....
Leg, Legg, Legge, Leggs	5.3	40	173	....	....	....	15	....	1	4	1	10	3	....	6
Leggett, Legate, Leget, Legett, Legget, Leggit, Leggitt, Leggott, Liget, Liggat, Liggatt, Ligget, Liggett, Liggit, Ligit	5.8	87	420	....	....	....	5	....	....	17	19	6	6	25	9
Leighton, Laghton, Laighton, Laiton, Laten, Latin, Laton, Latten, Lattin, Latton, Tayton, Leaton	5.8	125	603	33	26	3	8	....	6	19	6	7	4	9	4

TABLE **111.**—NOMENCLATURE, DEALING WITH NAMES REPRESENTED BY AT LEAST 100 WHITE PERSONS, BY STATES AND TERRITORIES, AT THE FIRST CENSUS: 1790—Continued.

NAME.	Average size of family.	TOTAL. Heads of families.	TOTAL. All other members.	Maine.	New Hampshire.	Vermont.	Massachusetts.	Rhode Island.	Connecticut.	New York.	Pennsylvania.	Maryland.	Virginia.	North Carolina.	South Carolina.
Leland, Lalan, Laland, Layland, Lealand, Leeland	6.1	68	344	4	1	3	47				2	2	9		
Lemar, La Mar, Lamar, Lemare, Lymar	6.2	23	119						1	1	1	11		1	8
Lemmon, Laman, Lammon, Lammonds, Lamon, Layman, Laymon, Laymond, Leaman, Leeman, Lehman, Leman, Lemane, Lemean, Lemman, Lemmond, Lemmonds, Lemmons, Lemon, Lemond, Lemonds, Lemons, Limmon	5.8	211	1,022	15	3		7		3	13	87	33	18	24	8
Lent, Lente, Lentz	5.5	33	147			1			1	20	10			1	
Leonard, Leanard, Leanhart, Leanord, Learnard, Learnd, Learned, Learnhart, Lehnhart, Lenard, Lenhart, Lenhert, Lennard, Lennerd, Lenord, Leonerd	6.5	348	1,757	2	6	21	162	3	20	31	56	14	5	17	11
Lesher, Leshier	5.6	36	167							8	28				
Lesley, Lasley, Lasly, Lassley, Leisley, Lesle, Leslie, Lesly, Lessley, Lesslie, Lessly	5.1	56	231	1	7					2	19	6	2	10	9
Lester, Leicester, Leister, Lestear, Lestoe, Lestor, Lestors, Lestre, Lister, Lyster, Lystor	5.4	145	635		2	1	3		41	34	10	13	15	16	10
Levis, Levise, Levist	7.6	16	106							2	11	1			2
Levon, Leavens, Leavin, Leaving, Leavins, Levaun, Levene, Levin, Levins	6.0	42	209			1	3		5	4	19			6	4
Levy, Levey	5.6	29	133	2						7	8	5	2		5
Lewelling, Lewallen, Lewelan, Leweling, Lewellin, Lewellying, Lewellyn, Lewillin, Llewellin, Lualin, Luvallin, Luvellin	5.5	35	159								7	2	16	7	3
Lewis, Leus, Lewes, Lewey, Liewes, Liwis, Louis, Lues, Luies, Luis	5.5	1,221	5,478	40	28	44	156	67	165	153	173	52	120	168	55
Libbey, Lebbey, Libbe, Libbee, Libby, Libe, Liby, Lybbey	5.8	171	820	135	31		1	1			2				1
Lieb, Leab, Leib	6.5	17	94							5	12				
Light, Leight, Leitz, Lighte, Lights, Lite	6.2	46	238	1						2	24	7	6		6
Lightfoot	6.8	18	104						1		5	1	8	2	1
Lightner, Leghtner, Leichtner, Leightner, Leitner, Litener, Litner	7.1	15	91								12	1			2
Ligon, Leggon, Legon, Liggon, Ligrand	5.3	28	119										24	1	3
Liles, Leysle, Lisle, Lisles, Lyle, Lyles, Lysle	5.9	66	333						3	17	4	3	20	19
Lillibridge, Lillebridge	5.6	20	92				16	3					1		
Lilly, Lille, Lilley, Lillie	5.7	86	404	1	1	8	17	1	9	5	17	6	7	14	
Lincoln, Lincon, Linkcon, Linken, Linkhorn, Linkkon, Linkon, Linnecon, Linnekon	5.7	210	987	14	11	11	144		11	6	11			1	1
Lindley, Lindly, Linley, Linly	5.2	55	233			7	3	1	18	6	11			6	3
Lindsey, Lindsay, Lindsy, Lindze, Lingsey, Linsay, Linsey, Linsy, Linzay, Linzee, Linzey, Lyndsay, Lyndsey	5.1	186	769	5	5	7	29	4	1	9	34	10	22	31	29
Lines, Line	5.5	44	199						21	4	17	1		1	
Link, Linck, Lynck, Lynk	5.0	46	186							7	24	3	7	4	1
Linn, Lin, Lind, Linde, Linds, Lins, Lyn, Lynd, Lynde, Lyndes, Lynds, Lyne, Lynes, Lynn	5.5	151	682	1	3	8	16	1	9	7	62	8	8	19	9
Linnel, Lanels, Lenel, Linnell	4.5	23	81	2			18		2						1
Linnen, Lenin, Lennon, Lenon, Linam, Linen, Linin, Linnin, Lynam	6.2	17	88	3	1				1	2	2	3		3	2
Linsley, Lenslee, Linsly	6.4	17	92						12	3	2				
Lint	5.7	40	189								38	2			
Linton	5.2	38	158								13	6	2	14	3
Lipscomb, Lascomb, Lascome, Lepscomb, Lescum, Liscomb, Liscombe, Liscum, Lisecomb, Lisscomb, Luscomb, Luscombe, Lyscom	5.6	48	222			3	16	3	1	6	2		11	2	4
Litchfield, Leachfield, Leechfield, Leichfield, Leitchfield, Litchfeld	5.6	54	248	6			31		5	1		7		4	
Little, Liddell, Liddle, Litle, Littel, Lytle, Lyttle	5.7	346	1,642	13	40	5	42	5	27	23	69	19	21	57	25
Littlefield, Littelfield	5.9	117	570	76	2	4	17	11	1	2					4
Littleton, Lettleton, Lyttleton	5.6	18	82						1	1		4		8	4
Lively, Levely, Liveley	6.0	17	85								1		13		3
Livermore, Livemore, Livermar, Livermoor	6.0	51	255	1	7	8	32			2					1
Livingston, Lavingston, Leavingston, Levestone, Levingston, Levinston, Libinston, Livenston, Livingstone, Livington, Livinston, Liviston	5.6	117	544		4	1	11		3	54	12	4	4	8	16
Lobdell, Labdell, Lebdell, Lobdol	5.6	20	92				4		5	9	2				
Lock, Loch, Locke, Loech, Lough	5.6	155	713	7	53	7	33	9		3	5	5	8	25	
Lockett	6.7	18	103										18		
Lockhart, Locard, Lochard, Lochart, Lockard, Lockart, Lockeart, Lockerd, Lockheart, Lukehart	4.9	54	208								24	1	8	12	9
Lockwood, Lackwood, Larkwood, Lorkwood	5.9	177	865			13	3	7	86	59	1	4	1	1	2
Lofton, Loften, Loftin	5.8	25	121									1	17	7	
Logan, Logans, Logen, Loggan, Loggans, Loggin, Loggins, Logon	5.4	121	536			6	2		4	3	44	14	16	12	20
Long	5.5	486	2,183	5	15	8	26	1	5	17	198	51	27	90	43
Longfellow, Longfelow	6.1	19	96	10		4					5				
Longley, Lengley, Longly	6.0	23	116	5		16					1				1
Longnecker, Longacre, Longinecker, Longnaker	6.4	30	162								28		2		
Loomis, Laumiss, Loamis, Lomes, Lomice, Lomis, Loomise, Loomiss, Lumas, Lumis, Lummas, Lummis, Lummos, Lummus	6.2	234	1,228	1	5	16	51		135	22	3		1		
Lord, Laud, Lawd, Lawed, Lords	5.8	269	1,289	83	18	10	45	1	72	15	5	4	1	10	5
Loring, Loreing, Lorin, Lowring	5.9	85	420	14		66		1	2	1	1				
Losee, Losa, Losey, Loshy, Losie, Losyee	8.4	23	170							20	3				
Lott, Lot, Lotts, Lotz	6.1	58	296			1	1		2	26	15	1	6		6
Loud, Lowd	5.0	26	104	2	12		8		1		2	1			
Loudon, Louden, Loudin, Lowdan, Lowden, Lowdon	4.8	31	117		1		10			5	13	2			1
Louks, Louck, Louk, Loux, Lowk, Lowks	5.1	33	157							26	5	1	1		
Loun, Lownes, Lowns	6.1	19	96							7	11				1
Lounsbury, Lounsberry, Lownbury, Lownsberry, Lownsburry, Lownsbury	5.8	45	215			1			19	23	1		1		
Love	5.4	128	560		1		3	7	3	6	26	20	8	34	20
Lovejoy, Lovijoy, Lovjoy	5.8	77	370	6	30	9	16		2	5	3	5			1
Lovelace, Lovlace, Luvlace	8.0	17	119							2		8	2	4	1
Loveland	5.8	41	195		1		12		24		1		4		
Lovell, Lovel	5.7	75	353	1		8	52	2	2	2	1		3	1	3
Lovering, Loveran, Loverein, Loverin, Lovran, Lovrin, Lovring	6.1	36	184		19	2	15								
Lovett, Loveit, Lovet, Lovit, Lovitt	5.7	88	415	8	4	2	24	3	2	6	13	2	18	6	
Loving, Loveing, Lovin	7.2	17	105				1						6	9	1
Low, Loe, Lowe	5.9	309	1,395	31	12	2	62	8		48	29	35	13	52	17
Lowell, Lowel	5.6	83	379	32	18	6	17		1		1			5	3
Lowman, Lauman, Loman, Lomon, Loreman, Lorman, Lorrman, Louman	5.7	31	145							2	14	10		4	1
Lowry, Lauhery, Laure, Laury, Lawrey, Lawry, Lohery, Lohry, Lorey, Lory, Loughrey, Louree, Lourey, Loury, Lowerry, Lowery, Lowre, Lowrey, Lowrie	5.5	177	794	2	2	3			6	21	56	19	17	27	24
Loyd, Lloyd, Lloyde, Lloyed, Loyde, Loyed	5.2	126	525			1	2	2	1	11	48	7	10	34	10
Lucas, Locas, Locust, Lucass, Luccus, Lucus, Lucust, Lukess	5.3	163	693	3	7	5	29		16·	4	24	18	26	20	11
Luce, Loos, Loose, Lose, Lous, Louse, Luice, Luse	5.6	111	509	6		7	61		11	13	10	2			1
Luckey, Luckie, Lucky	5.5	26	117							8	7	1		8	2
Luddington, Luddenton, Luddonton, Ludenton, Ludington, Ludinton	5.2	24	100		1	4		11	6		1		2		
Ludlow, Ledlo, Ledloe, Ledlow	6.3	20	106		1					15	2	1	2	1	
Ludlum, Ludlam, Ludlim, Ludlom	6.3	23	122							21	2				
Ludwig, Lodowick, Lodwich, Lodwick, Ludewick, Ludwick	6.2	33	173	1						4	23	2	1	2	
Lufkin, Luffkin, Luftkin	5.8	20	96	3	3		14								
Luke, Luk, Lukes	6.0	38	183	2		1	11			6	11	2	1	1	2

Table 111.—NOMENCLATURE, DEALING WITH NAMES REPRESENTED BY AT LEAST 100 WHITE PERSONS, BY STATES AND TERRITORIES, AT THE FIRST CENSUS: 1790—Continued.

NAME.	Average size of family.	TOTAL. Heads of families.	TOTAL. All other members.	Maine.	New Hampshire.	Vermont.	Massachusetts.	Rhode Island.	Connecticut.	New York.	Pennsylvania.	Maryland.	Virginia.	North Carolina.	South Carolina.
Lukins, Luken, Lukens	5.8	43	207			1					39	3			
Lull	5.4	19	83		3	6	6		1	3					
Lum, Lume, Lumm, Lumn	6.0	18	90				1		8	4	1	2	1	1	
Lumbard, Lumbarrd, Lumbart, Lumbert	6.4	31	167	1		4	25			1					
Lumber	5.4	25	111	2			22	1							
Lunsford, Lunceford, Lunesford, Lunisford	4.8	33	126										22	11	
Lunt, Lund	5.7	65	304	22	22		18	1	1						1
Lusk	5.8	34	165			2	3		7	5	8	2		5	2
Luther, Louther	5.2	111	471		1	6	51	28	4	7	7	3	1	3	
Lutz, Loots, Lute, Lutes, Luts, Lutse, Lutte, Lutts, Lutze	5.3	67	291							3	53	6		5	
Lyford, Leford, Lifard, Liferd, Liffard, Liford, Luyphard, Luyphord	4.9	21	102	1	14	2				4					
Lyman, Leiman, Liman, Lymans, Lymon, Lymond	6.7	114	650	2	5	20	36	1	48		2				
Lynch, Linch, Lynck, Lyntch	5.1	142	582			1		4		17	23	47	11	28	11
Lyon, Lion, Lions, Lyons	5.8	353	1,705	7	8	17	60	5	91	67	29	19	17	21	12
Mabee, Mabe, Mabie, Maybe, Maybee, Meabee, Meby	6.2	40	206	2						35	1			1	1
Mabry, Mabberry, Mabery, Mabrey, Maybary, Mayberry, Maybry, Mayburry, Maybury	6.4	59	318	11							9	1	11	21	6
Mace, Mase	5.3	50	213	3	9		7			5	6	3	12	5	
Machen, Machan, Mehan, Machian, Machine, Macken, Mackin, Mckin, Makens, Makins, Mekins	4.9	22	86							2	4	2	10	4	
Mack, Mac, Macks	5.4	58	254		7	6	7		12	10	10	1		2	3
Maclin, Macklin, McLen, McLin, McLinn	7.1	14	86	1						1	3	1	6	1	1
Macomber, McComber, Maccomber, McKumber, Macumber, McCumber	6.2	90	471	3	1		64	7	1	14					
Macy, Macey, Maisey, Masey, Masi	6.3	46	242				24		4	1	2		2	13	
Madden, Maddin, Madding, Maddon, Maden, Madens, Madin, Mading	5.4	49	214	3	1	1	6			4	5	12	6	6	5
Maddox, Maddax, Maddix, Maddock, Maddocke, Maddocks, Maddok, Maddux, Madocks, Madox, Madux	5.5	60	268	10							3	31	8	5	3
Madery, Madary, Maddera, Maddery, Madera	6.2	22	114								6	6	10		
Magoon, Magoone	5.4	27	120	3	2	5	16					1			
Magruder, Magruda	4.6	49	174								46	2	1		
Mahon, Mahan, Mahen, Mahone, Mayhon, Mehan	6.2	53	276				6		1	1	17	5	10	9	4
Mahony, Mahoney, Mahorney, Mehoney, Mohony	5.8	19	91	2						1	2	11		3	
Maine, Main, Maines, Mains, Mane, Manes, Mayne	5.2	90	381	9	1	2	2		33	19	5	6	1	5	7
Major, Majer, Majoir, Majors	7.1	34	207		1	1				2	9	4	4	7	6
Malbone, Malborn, Malbourn, Maulbone	6.0	21	104	1				3	1				15	1	
Malcom, Malcolm, Malcomb, Malcum	5.5	21	94	7		1	3			4	2	1	2		1
Mallery, Malaery, Malary, Malery, Mallary, Mallerey, Mallory, Maiory	5.6	109	504		1	9	9		52	11	1		21	5	
Mallet, Mallat, Mallett, Mellat, Mellet, Melot, Melott, Mollet, Mullatt, Mullet, Mullett	5.5	61	275	3		3	8		17	6	3	8	5	4	4
Malone, Melone, Milone	4.5	49	173			1			1	9		4	13	15	6
Manchester	6.0	82	412	4		1	10	57	1	9					
Manley, Manly	5.8	57	276			11	19	1	4	2	3	9	1	2	5
Mann, Man, Manns, Mans, Mantz	5.7	306	1,423	12	24	18	65	15	13	21	41	11	41	30	14
Manning, Maning, Mannan, Mannen, Mannin, Mannon, Mannun, Manon	5.2	190	800	3	3	5	48	2	20	18	13	10	18	33	17
Mansfield, Manesfield, Manfield, Mannifield, Mansfeild, Mansfeld	5.4	127	561	4	10	3	42		27	7	9	12	9	4	
Mapes	4.9	35	136							33	2				
Maples, Maple	6.5	23	126						7	1	5		2	5	3
Marble, Marbel	5.0	64	258	2	8	5	42		3	4					
Marchant, Marchants	4.9	24	94	1			9		11	1		1			1
Marcy, Marcey, Marsey	6.3	22	116		1		8		8	1	2		2		
Marden, Mardin	5.5	33	148		32		1								
Marion, Marien, Marrion, Maryaun, Merian, Merion, Merrean, Merrian, Merrion	5.6	20	91				2		5	1	4		1		7
Markham, Marckum, Marcom, Marcum, Markam, Markum	5.4	45	199		3	1	7		13	4	1		5	11	
Markley, Markly	7.1	23	140								18	3			2
Marks, Mark, Marke, Markes, Marx	5.3	112	477	1	1	6	4	1	14	20	38	7	9	1	10
Marlow	4.7	33	121							1	2	9	4	7	10
Marr, Mar, Marre, Marrs, Mars, Marss	4.8	46	177	13	1	1	2			2	7	3	11	3	3
Marriott, Marret, Marrett, Marritt, Marrot, Marrott, Merriott	4.8	30	113				4	1			8	13	4		
Marsh, March, Marshe	6.0	325	1,613	12	45	31	78	4	51	20	32	7	25	13	7
Marshall, Marchal, Marchall, Marchel, Marchle, Marshal, Marsheal, Marshel, Marshell, Marshill, Mershall, Mershel, Mershele	5.6	481	2,190	13	38	7	77	5	31	53	108	49	40	45	15
Marston, Marsden, Marsdin, Marsdon, Marsten, Marstin, Marstone, Marstons, Masden, Masdon, Masten, Mastin, Maston, Morston	5.9	150	733	21	52	5	28			32	5	2	2	2	1
Martin, Martain, Marten, Martine, Martins, Marton, Martten, Martyn	5.7	1,169	5,509	22	44	50	98	31	55	103	247	83	157	169	110
Martindale, Martindal, Martindil	6.1	34	175			3	6	1		3	8	5		3	5
Marvin, Marvine, Marvins	6.3	70	369		3	4	6	1	27	26	3				
Mash	5.7	53	249		2	10	16			1	3	11	1	6	3
Mason, Maison, Masen, Masons, Mayson	5.8	478	2,297	19	44	14	130	18	36	25	34	34	58	50	16
Massey, Massa, Massay, Masse, Massie, Massy	5.3	114	485	4	2	1	2			3	13	20	22	32	15
Masters, Master	5.1	73	296		1	1	5		4	12	24	6	6	13	1
Mather, Marther, Mathers, Mathes, Matheys	6.1	91	461	2	6	7	4		41	8	16	4			3
Mathewson, Mathison, Mathson, Matison, Matson, Mattason, Matterson, Matteson, Mattheson, Matthewson, Mattison, Mattson	6.8	176	1,012		1	34	1	75	17	17	22	1		6	2
Matlock, Madlock, Matlack, Matlocks, Meadlock, Medlock	5.3	31	134							1	2	9	7	8	4
Matthews, Matthew, Marthews, Mathew, Mathewes, Mathewis, Mathews, Mathis, Mathure, Mathuse, Matthes, Matthew, Matthewis, Matthis, Matthws	5.6	448	2,065	20	15	14	42	1	28	32	44	50	57	87	58
Matthias, Mathias, Mathies	5.8	50	239						1	2	17	2	22	5	1
Mattingley, Mattenley, Mattenly, Mattingly	5.8	24	114									19	5		
Mattock, Matocks, Mattickes, Matticks, Mattocks, Mattoks, Mattox, Mattuck	5.9	18	89	3			1				6	2	2	2	2
Mattoon, Matoon, Matune, Metune	6.1	20	102			1	11		6	2					
Maxey, Maxcy, Maxxie, Maxy, Moxie, Moxy	5.1	20	81	2				5	2				11		
Maxfield	5.1	46	187		3	6	10	2	2	3	12	4		1	3
Maxin, Maxen, Maxon	6.0	37	185					2	33		2				
Maxwell, Maxwel, Maxwill, Meixwill	6.0	138	692	19	2	3	8	4	3	8	46	10	7	17	11
May, Mais, Maise, Maize, Maye, Mayes, Mays, Mayse, Mayses, Mayze, Maze, Mey	5.4	279	1,232		3	7	43	4	20	8	42	11	59	57	25
Mayfield, Mafield, Mayfeild	5.2	32	134						1					6	25
Mayhew, Mahew, Mayew, Mayhue	5.6	68	316	6			43			4	1	13	1		
Maynard, Mainard, Mainhard, Mainyard, Manard, Maneyard, Maynerd, Maynord, Menard	6.2	105	546		7	4	61		10	4	3	9	2	3	2
Mayo, Maho, Mayho, Mayos	6.0	109	546	8	1		49		3	2		8	14	23	1
McAdams, McAdam, McAddams, McCaddams	5.2	29	121			5				3	6		2	8	5
McAfee, McAffee, McEfee	6.6	18	100							1	9	1		5	2
McArthur, McArther, McAuther, McCartha	6.0	33	164	1		1				17	3			10	1
McAuley, McCalley, McCally, Maccauley, Maccauly, McCauley, McCaulley, McCauly, McCawley, McCawly, McColley, McColly, McCulley, McculIey, McCully, Mecauley	4.7	91	339	1	6		2			6	32	12	3	23	6
McBride, Mcbride, Mcbrde	5.8	99	472				3			7	35	5	10	24	15
McCain, McCaain, McCane, McKain	5.2	32	135						1	1	13			11	6

TABLE **111.**—NOMENCLATURE, DEALING WITH NAMES REPRESENTED BY AT LEAST 100 WHITE PERSONS, BY STATES AND TERRITORIES, AT THE FIRST CENSUS: 1790—Continued.

NAME.	Average size of family.	TOTAL.		HEADS OF FAMILIES.											
		Heads of families.	All other members.	Maine.	New Hampshire.	Vermont.	Massachusetts.	Rhode Island.	Connecticut.	New York.	Pennsylvania.	Maryland.	Virginia.	North Carolina.	South Carolina.
McCall, M'call, M'calle, M'Caul, M'Caul, M'caule, McCawl, McColl, Mackaň	5.5	103	460				1		13	8	29	6	3	23	20
McCallister, McAlaster, McAlester, McAlister, McAllaster, McAllester, McAllister, McCalester, McCalister, McCallaster, McCallester, McCallestor, McColister, M'Colister, McCollester, McCollister, McCollistor, McOllister	5.1	111	460	4	15	3	1			5	33	16		21	13
McCammon, McCamon, McComman, McCommon, McComon, McKamman, Macomen	6.7	23	132								16	2		2	3
McCandless, McCandeless, McCandles, McCandlish, McCanless, McKanless, McKindles	5.7	20	94						1	13	3	2	1		
McCann, McAnn, McCaan, McCan, McCand, McConn, McKan, McKann, Macon	5.3	50	214		1		1		1	3	17	1	10	11	5
McCarter, McArter, McCartor, McKarter	5.2	27	114	1	1	2	2		1	2	4	3	3	1	7
McCartney, McArtney, McCartny, McCertney	5.3	45	194							3	29	3	1	3	6
McCarty, Macartey, McArthy, McCartee, McCartey, McCarthey, McCarthy, McCartie, Maccarty, Mccarty, McCortey	4.8	126	499	3		3	13	1		24	26	8	27	7	14
McCaslin, McAuslan, McCasland, MacCaslin, McCasslin, McCausland, McCauslen, McCauslin, McCoslin, MaCslin	4.9	27	105	7						1	7	4		7	1
McCleary, McClarey, McClary, McLarry, McLary, MaClayry, McClearey, McCleery, McClery, McLeary, McliRy	5.3	63	265	2	9		5			4	27	6	1	5	4
McClelland, McClaland, McClalen, McClalin, McClallan, McClallen, McClallin, McClayland, McClelan, McCleland, McClelean, McClellan, McClellen, McClelon, McLaland, McLallan, McLallen, McLeeland, McLeland, McleIand, McLelen, McLellan, McLellen, McLillan	5.9	178	873	16	2		7	1	1	12	90	13	17	11	8
McClenahan, McClanahan, McClanathan, McClangen, McClanihan, McClaningham, McClannan, McClannen, McClannon, McClathan, McClenaghan, McClenahen, McClenan, McClenethan, McClenhiham, McClennacan, McClennahan, McClennan, McClennen, McClennin, McClennon, McClinahan, McLanan, McLenahan, McLenan, McLennan, McLennen	5.3	72	308	1		2	8			7	22	1	10	15	6
McClintock, McClentick, McClentock, MClentock, McClentorick, McClintic, McClintick, McClintoc, McClintoch, McClintuck, McLintack, McLintock	5.6	54	251	1	6		5			2	27	2	2	2	7
McClure, McClewer, McclewEr, McClour, McCloure, McCluer, McLlewer, McLure	5.6	156	712	1	14	3	3	1	3	7	75	6	5	15	23
McCluskey, McClaskey, McClasky, McClesky, McClisky, McCloskey, McClosky, McClusky, McLoskey	5.2	24	100							1	13	1		2	7
McCollum, McAllum, McCallam, McCallum, McCollam, McCollom, McCollums, McColm, McColom, McCullum	5.5	66	299	1	2	2			1	14	3	4	2	28	9
McComb, McCombs, McCome, McCoom, McCoomb, McCoombe, McCooms, Macomb	5.7	44	208				1		2	5	20	4		5	7
McConnel, McConal, McConel, M'conell, McConell, McConnal, McConnald, McConnell, McConyell, McKonnell	5.6	124	565		2	6				13	76	3		7	17
McCord	6.0	46	231							10	20	1	5	3	7
McCorkle, McCorkel, McCorkhill, McCoskill, Mckorkle	5.1	22	91								5			11	6
McCormick, McCarmeck, McCarmick, McComick, McCommic, McCormac, McCormach, McCormack, M'Cormic, M'Cormuck	5.4	100	440	1	1	3				5	62	8	3	9	8
McCown, McCoun, McCowan, McCowen, McCowin, McKowan, McKowen, McKown, McOwen, Mcown	5.7	43	200	3			1			9	13	1		5	11
McCoy, McCoey, M'Coy, Maccoy, Macoy, McCoye, McKoy, McKoye	5.4	224	994		13	2	2		3	20	63	27	26	46	22
McCracken, McCrackin, McCracon, McCraken, Mccraken, McCrakin, McCrehen, McCreken, McKrakin, McKrakkin, Mecrakin	6.5	64	354						2	7	26	4	3	15	7
McCready, McCrady, McCredie, McCredy, McCreedy, Mceready, McReady, McRedy	6.9	24	141							10	11				3
McCreary, McCrary, McCrearea, McCrearey, McCreery, McCrery, McReary, McReary	7.5	37	240							6	10	5		8	8
McCulloch, McCalla, McCallah, McCallow, McCollah, M'Collah, McCollak, McCollegh, MacCollock, McColloch, McCollogh, McCollough, McColough, McCoulough, McCulla, M'Cullah, McCullegh, Mcculloch, McCullock, McCullogh, McCulloh, McCullouch, M'Cullough, M'Cullugh, McCullow	5.8	145	703	1		1	5			7	67	12	9	21	22
McCune, M'Cuen, McEuen, McEwen, McEwin, McEwn, McKewan, McKewn, McKewn, McKune, McQuown	5.5	78	354	1		2			7	8	39	6	2	6	7
McCurdy, McCurday, McCurdey, McCurdie	5.8	54	258	3	2			1	3	5	30	2		3	5
McCutchen, McCuchin, McCuchion, McCutcheon, McCutchin, McKutchen	6.1	18	92		1	1				3	9	1			3
McDaniel, McDanail, McDanald, McDanals, McDanel, Mac Daniel, Mcdaniel, McDaniels, McDanil, McDannel, McDannels, McDanniel, Macdanniels, McDannil, McDanold, McDanolds, McDoniel, McDonniells	5.2	206	858	5	5	4	4		3	8	29	26	35	61	26
McDonald, McDonal, Mcdonald, McDonais, McDonanald, McDoneld, McDonell, McDonnal, McDonnald, Macdonnald, McDonnel, McDonnell, McDonnold, McDonol, McDonold	4.9	330	1,291	13	7		4	2	5	52	96	21	16	65	49
McDowell, McDowal, McDowall, McDowel, MacDowell, M'Dowell, McDowill, McDowl	5.3	135	587		1	1	1			13	66	8	8	17	20
McDuffee, McDuffe, McDuffie, McDuffy	5.6	33	151			13				1	2			17	
McDugal, McDewgle, McDougal, McDougall, McDougel, McDougle, McDugald	4.8	66	250		1		1			22	5		6	31	
McElheney, McElhaney, McElhany, McElheany, McElheny, McIlhaney, McIlhenney, Muckelhaney, Muckelheney, Muckelkeney	5.8	32	155				1				27		1		3
McElroy, Maccleroy, Macelroy, McIlroy, Mckelroy, McLRoy, McLroy, Muccleroy, Muckelroy, Muckeroy, Muckle Roy, Muckleroy, Muckleroych, Mucklaroy, Muclroy	5.5	55	246				1		3	6	25	2	1	11	6
McElwain, McElvain, McElven, McElvene, McElvin, McElwaine, McElwane, McElwean, McIlvain, McIlvaine, McIlveen, McIlveene, McIlwain, McIlwaine, MacLevain, McLwain, Miklewane, Mucclewain, Mucclewane, Mucklewain	5.8	44	210				2				27	2	1	2	10
McFadden, McFadan, McFaddin, McFadding, McFaddon, McFaden, McFadian, McFadien, McFadion	5.7	48	225	7			1				18	8		3	11
McFall, McFalls, McFaul	4.6	30	107						1	8	9	1	2	7	2
McFarland, McFarlan, McFarland, Mcfarland, McFarlane, Mcfarlane, McFarlen, Mcfarlen, McFarlin, Mcfarlin, Macfarlin, McFarlind, McFarling, Mcfarling, Macfarling, McPharlen	5.5	162	721	14	5	4	17			32	53	2	8	21	6
McFerrin, McFarran, McFarren, McFarron, McFerren, McFerron, McPherrin	4.6	27	96		1					6	12	3	2		3
McGee, McGahee, McGahey, Mcgahey, McGahhy, McGahy, McGaighy, Mcgeahey, Mcgee, M'gee, McGeehee, McGees, McGehe, McGehee, McGehey, McGhee, Mage, Magee, Magehee, Megee, Megehee	4.8	154	585	2		1	7	1	1	19	30	12	18	53	10
McGill, M Gill, Mcgill, Macgill, MaGill, Magill, Meagill, Megil, Megill	5.5	86	388	2	1		1		2	8	21	11	5	22	13
McGinnis, McGinnes, McGinness, McGuinis, Magines, Maginis, Maginness, Maginnis, Megines, Meginnes, Meginnis	5.3	49	212			1				6	22	5	9	6	
McGowen, McGowan, McGowin, McGowns	5.4	34	151	1			1			5	11	3		9	4
McGraw, McGra, McGrah, Magraw, Megraw	5.5	34	150	3	1				1	6	6	5	3	2	7
McGregor, McGreeger, McGreger, McGregger, McGreggor, McGreoger, McGriger, McGrigger, McGriggir, McGriggor, McGrigor	5.5	38	172	1		1	1			6	15	3	4	4	3
McGrue, McGrew	6.9	18	107								13	1			4
McGuire, McGuier, M'Guir, Mcguire, Macguire, McGuyer, MaGuire, Maguire, Meguier	5.7	74	351	2					2	8	28	9	8	14	3
McHenry, McHenary, McHenery	6.0	28	141							2	14	5	2	5	
McIntire, Macantire, McEntire, McEntirs, McInteer, McIntier, McIntiere, Macintire, Mcintire, McIntyer, McIntyre, McKentire, Mackentire, Mackintire	5.2	204	851	21	7	3	65	2	2	25	37	5	3	29	5
McIntosh, McCintush, Macintosh, Mcintush, Mackendorsh, McKentush	4.8	78	297	4	5	3	8		1	12	4	3	6	23	9
McIver, McEver, McEvers, McIvair, McIvers	6.2	22	114							6	2	1	2	8	3
McKay, Macay, McCay, McHay, McKae, MacKay, Mackay, McKays	5.3	104	442				5		1	7	18	9	19	37	8
McKean, McKeand, McKeen, McKeene, McKein, McKeine	6.2	37	193	4	11	1	2		1	2	9	1	1	4	1
McKee, McCee, Macke, Mahie, McKea, Mckee, Mackee, MacKee, Mackey, Mckey, McKey, McKeys, Mackie, Mackkee, Macky, Makee, Makey	5.4	234	1,031	1	2	2	7		12	30	86	13	11	32	38
McKillip, McAlep, McAlup, McCalep, McCalop, Mckellip, McKellup, McKillop	5.8	19	92	1	2					6	5	1		5	
McKinley, McCinley, McCinly, McInley, McKindley, McKinlay, McKinly	5.7	47	220		1				1	6	29	1		8	1
McKinnen, McCinnan, McKennon, McKinnin, McKinnon	4.8	25	94							1	1			22	1

TABLE 111.—NOMENCLATURE, DEALING WITH NAMES REPRESENTED BY AT LEAST 100 WHITE PERSONS, BY STATES AND TERRITORIES, AT THE FIRST CENSUS: 1790—Continued.

NAME.	Average size of family.	TOTAL.		HEADS OF FAMILIES.											
		Heads of families.	All other members.	Maine.	New Hampshire.	Vermont.	Massachusetts.	Rhode Island.	Connecticut.	New York.	Pennsylvania.	Maryland.	Virginia.	North Carolina.	South Carolina.
McKinney, McCiney, McCinney, McCinny, McHeney, McHinney, McKeney, McKenney, Mckenney, McKenny, McKiney, McKinna, McKinne, MacKinney, M'Kinney, McKinnie, McKinny, Mckinny, McKiny	5.6	160	738	25	1	....	2	....	7	16	36	9	16	25	23
McKinsey, McCinsey, McCinzie, Mcinsey, McKensee, McKensey, McKensie, McKensy, McKenzie, Mackenzie, McKenzy, McKinsay, McKinseg, McKinsei, M'Kinsey, McKinsie, McKinssy, McKinsy, McKinzey, McKinzie	4.5	118	410	4	3	....	2	3	2	13	23	13	7	29	19
McKishock, McKessick, McKessuk, McKieseck, McKisick, McKisock, McKissack, McKisseck, McKissek, McKissick, McKissix, McKissock, McKissox	5.6	23	106	4	....	....	....	....	....	1	11	2	....	4	1
McKnight, McKneight, McKnite, McKnitt, McNeght, McNight, McNite	5.4	93	413	1	....	3	9	....	2	5	38	....	4	14	17
McLaughlin, McGlachland, Mcglachlond, McGlaghlin, McGlauchlin, McGlaughlan, McGlaughlin, McGlochlan, McGlochland, McGlochlen, McGlocklin, McGlohlan, McGlohlin, McGloughlan, McGloughlin, Mcgloughlin, McLachland, McLachlen, McLachlin, McLacklin, McLaghlin, McLaighlin, McLaughlan, McLaughland, McLaughlen, M'Laughlin, McLaughling, McLauglin, McLlaughlin, McLocklin, McLoughlin, McLughlin	5.4	128	566	2	10	3	....	....	....	10	57	18	10	16	2
McLean, McClaen, McClain, Mcclain, McClaine, McClane, McClean, McClene, Maclain, McLain, Mclain, McLaine, McLane, Mclane, McLean, Mclean, McLeane, McLeain, McLene	5.6	278	1,265	4	1	3	10	2	5	31	89	21	14	83	15
McLemore, McClemore, McLamar, McLamare, McLemoore, Maclemore	4.9	24	94	....	....	....	....	....	....	....	....	1	3	15	5
McLeod, McClaud, McCleod, McCload, McClode, McCloud, McLoad, McLoud, Macloud	4.6	132	477	1	3	....	5	1	1	9	24	2	3	79	4
McLerran, McClaran, McClaren, McClarin, McClaron, McClarren, McClerin, McClerran, McClerren, McClerron, McLaren, McLeran	5.7	32	151	....	1	2	....	....	....	1	4	....	2	20	2
McMahan, McMahen, McMahens, McMahhan, McMahin, McMahon, McMayan, McMehan	5.0	41	166	3	....	....	....	....	1	1	12	3	3	5	13
McMasters, McMarster, McMarsters, McMaster	6.4	50	272	1	5	1	7	....	....	7	15	5	....	6	3
McMichael, McMical, McMichal, McMicheal, McMichel, McMickle, McMihal, McMikel	6.6	30	167	1	....	....	....	....	....	8	19	....	....	1	1
McMillen, McMellen, McMellens, McMillan, Mcmillan, Mcmillen, McMillian, McMillin, McMillion, Mcmillion, Macmillion, McMillon	5.8	91	435	....	3	....	4	....	....	1	16	1	8	45	13
McMin, McMinn, McMins	6.4	17	91	....	....	....	....	....	....	1	11	2	....	3	....
McMullen, McMollen, McMullan, McMulland, Mcmullen, M'Mullen, McMullens, McMullin, McMullind, McMulling, McMullon, McMullun, McMulyen	5.4	164	723	2	7	1	7	....	....	24	87	14	3	9	10
McMurphy, McMurphey	5.5	20	89	2	15	1	....	....	....	....	1	....	....	1	....
McMurray, McMurey, McMurrey, McMurry	5.7	27	126	....	....	....	....	....	....	2	5	....	....	16	4
McNair, McNare, McNear, McNeer, McNeir, McNire	5.1	49	203	....	....	....	2	2	1	1	10	4	....	24	5
McNaughton, McNacton, McNattin, McNatton, McNaughtin, Macnaughton	4.8	21	80	....	....	....	....	....	....	11	4	....	1	5	....
McNeely, McKnelly, McNeally, McNealy, McNelly	5.9	22	108	....	....	....	1	....	....	1	4	1	2	9	4
McNiel, McKneal, McNeal, Macneal, McNeale, McNeall, Mcneel, McNeel, McNeele, McNeell, McNeil, MacNeil, McNeile, McNeill, McNiell	5.5	168	764	....	11	5	5	1	7	21	26	4	11	64	13
McPherson, McFarshen, McFarshon, McFarson, MacFashion, Macfason, McFawson, McFercin, McFershion, McFersin, McFersion, Mcfersion, McFerson, Mcferson, McPharson, Macpherson	5.0	121	489	1	6	1	4	....	1	10	21	18	11	33	15
McQueen, Mcquian	4.6	24	87	....	....	....	....	....	1	6	....	1	....	10	6
McRae, McCrae, McCray, McCre, McCrea, McKray, McRa, McRay, Mcray, McRea, McRee	5.8	105	506	....	1	....	1	....	4	5	14	5	4	59	12
McSwaine, McSwain, McSwane	4.6	22	78	....	....	....	....	....	....	....	1	....	....	20	1
Mctyre, McTeer, McTeere, McTere, McTier, McTiere, McTyer, McTyre	5.8	18	87	....	....	....	....	....	....	....	7	....	7	1	3
McVay, M Vay, McVea, M Vea, McVeagh, McVey, M Vey, McVie	4.9	35	137	....	....	....	....	....	1	....	15	9	2	3	5
McWhorter	5.5	19	86	....	....	....	....	....	....	4	1	....	....	7	7
McWilliams, McWilliam	5.1	44	179	....	1	....	....	....	....	8	18	4	3	3	7
Meach	7.1	15	91	....	....	2	3	....	10	....	....	....	....	....	....
Meacham, Meachem, Meachum, Mechem, Mechum, Meecham	5.2	48	248	....	....	9	12	....	19	3	....	....	1	4	....
Mead, Meade, Meades, Meads, Mede, Medes, Meed, Meeds, Meid	5.9	282	1,385	1	16	23	32	....	84	88	13	10	9	4	2
Meader, Meaders, Meador, Meadors, Meder, Meeder	6.2	41	212	2	19	....	6	....	....	....	2	....	12	....	....
Meadows, Madows, Meadow, Medows	4.6	43	154	....	....	....	1	....	....	....	....	....	9	27	6
Means, Meanes, Meeans, Meen, Meens, Mein	6.5	46	253	4	1	....	....	....	....	1	17	4	2	7	10
Mears, Meair, Mear, Meare, Meers, Meirs	5.0	38	152	1	1	3	14	....	....	4	5	2	....	7	1
Medlin, Medlen, Medleng, Medling, Medlong	5.4	20	87	....	....	....	....	....	....	....	....	....	....	20	....
Meeker, Meaker, Mecher, Mechur, Mecker, Meecker, Meker	4.5	44	153	....	....	1	....	....	32	8	3	....	....	....	....
Meeks, Meak, Meake, Meaks, Meeck, Meecke, Meek, Meeke	5.4	59	259	....	....	....	2	....	....	6	14	12	1	14	10
Meigs, Meggs, Meiggs	6.2	30	155	....	1	3	1	....	16	3	1	1	4	....	....
Melcher, Melchear, Melchoir, Meleher, Melker	6.0	23	114	4	12	....	....	....	....	....	5	1	....	1	....
Mellen, Mellin, Melling, Mellins, Mellon	4.7	31	114	....	2	4	7	....	....	1	11	....	1	5	....
Mellinger, Millenger, Millinger	6.8	16	92	....	....	....	....	....	....	....	16	....	....	....	....
Meloney, Melona, Melonay, Melony, Meloony, Melowney	5.0	26	103	1	2	....	2	1	2	....	9	2	2	5	....
Meloy, Malloy, Maloy, Melloy, Molloy, Mulloy	4.9	26	101	2	....	....	2	1	3	....	7	3	1	6	1
Melton	5.1	45	183	....	....	....	....	....	....	....	....	3	13	21	8
Melvin, Melven	5.4	30	132	....	10	2	11	....	....	1	1	2	....	2	1
Mendall, Mendal, Mendell	5.5	21	95	1	....	1	18	....	....	....	1	....	....	....	....
Mendingall, Mendenal, Mendenall, Mendenhall, Mendinall, Mendinghall, Mendinhall, Meninall, Meningall, Mondenall	5.8	44	255	....	....	....	....	....	....	....	22	....	....	22	....
Mercer	5.5	62	278	....	3	....	1	....	1	2	16	7	3	23	6
Merchant	5.2	56	237	1	....	....	15	2	3	5	7	6	8	8	1
Meredith, Meredeth, Merideth, Meridith	6.8	58	336	....	....	....	....	....	....	....	16	20	9	12	1
Merkel, Merckel, Mercle, Merkele, Merkell, Merkil, Merkle, Murkle	6.0	41	204	....	....	....	....	....	....	18	21	1	....	1	....
Merriam, Meriam, Miriam	5.8	81	386	2	9	1	48	....	18	1	....	....	....	2	....
Merrick, Merack, Meragh, Merick, Merricks, Merrik, Mirach, Mireck, Mirich, Mirick, Miriek, Mirrick, Myrick	5.6	143	659	8	3	3	56	....	7	18	16	9	2	15	6
Merrifield, Marafield, Marrifield, Maryfield, Merefeild, Merifield, Merryfield	6.0	23	116	3	1	3	11	....	2	1	1	....	....	1	....
Merrill, Merell, Meril, Merill, Merills, Merrel, Merrell, Merrells, Merrels, Merril, Merrille, Merrills, Merrils	6.0	375	1,870	81	98	11	77	1	62	22	1	7	1	13	1
Merriman, Meremon, Meriman, Merreman, Merryman, Merrymoon, Merrymoone, Miriman, Mirriman	5.8	107	513	8	....	3	9	....	39	6	3	19	10	10	....
Merritt, Merett, Merit, Meritt, Merratt, Merret, Merrett, Merrit, Merrits, Merrot, Mirrit, Mirritt	5.6	200	920	7	1	5	30	2	18	67	4	4	5	54	3
Merrow, Mero, Merow	5.9	24	118	9	3	....	2	3	3	....	2	....	....	....	2
Merry, Mairy, Marey, Marry, Mary, Marys, Merey, Merrey, Merrie	5.8	42	200	1	....	4	17	....	2	6	6	....	4	2	....
Meserve, Messerve	6.0	21	106	12	9	....	....	....	....	....	....	....	....	....	....
Messenger, Mesenger, Mesinger, Messinger, Misinger, Missinger	6.5	56	306	....	1	3	15	....	16	7	12	1	....	1	....
Messer, Meser, Mesier, Messar, Messers	6.2	50	259	1	12	....	9	....	....	1	9	....	1	9	8
Metcalf, Madcalf, Medcaff, Medcalf, Medkiff, Midcalf, Midcufs, Mitcalf	5.8	126	605	5	20	7	48	3	18	2	4	1	9	9	....
Metz, Mets, Mett, Metts	5.9	29	141	....	....	....	....	....	....	....	19	3	....	3	4
Metzgar, Matsger, Metsgar, Metsger, Metsker, Metzear, Metzer, Metzger, Metzker	5.7	27	127	....	....	....	....	....	....	....	23	3	1	....	....
Meyer, Maher, Mair, Maire, Maires, Mairs, Mare, Mares, Mayer, Mayers, Mayhr, Mayors, Meyers, Meyor, Meyors	5.8	157	752	....	....	....	1	....	1	4	119	4	1	9	18
Michael, Micael, Mical, Michaels, Michal, Michall, Michals, Michel, Michell, Michill, Michl, Mich[1], Michle, Mickel, Mickell, Mickle, Mickles, Mihael, Mikell	5.9	132	650	4	....	1	4	....	....	11	57	12	5	22	16
Micheau, Michaux, Micheaux	6.1	18	91	....	....	....	....	....	....	5	....	....	2	....	11
Middlebrook, Middlebrooks, Midlebrook	5.6	18	83	....	....	....	....	....	12	3	....	1	....	1	1
Middleton, Midelton, Midleton, Myddelton, Myddleton	5.1	72	297	....	....	....	1	....	2	1	14	9	10	9	26
Midgett, Midget	6.0	22	111	1	....	....	....	....	....	....	....	....	....	21	....
Milburn, Milbern, Milborn, Milbourn, Milbun, Millbourn, Millburn	5.0	24	96	....	....	....	....	....	....	1	1	15	5	2	....
Miles, Mial, Mials, Myles	5.5	200	905	2	7	8	23	....	36	9	29	30	9	15	32

TABLE **111.**—NOMENCLATURE, DEALING WITH NAMES REPRESENTED BY AT LEAST 100 WHITE PERSONS, BY STATES AND TERRITORIES, AT THE FIRST CENSUS: 1790—Continued.

NAME.	Average size of family.	TOTAL.		HEADS OF FAMILIES.											
		Heads of families.	All other members.	Maine.	New Hampshire.	Vermont.	Massachusetts.	Rhode Island.	Connecticut.	New York.	Pennsylvania.	Maryland.	Virginia.	North Carolina.	South Carolina.
Miley, Milie, Milley, Milly	5.9	17	84								13		3		1
Millard, Milerd, Millerd, Millord	5.4	52	228		1	2	5	1	8	21	8	1	1	4	
Miller, Milaw, Miler, Milla, Millar, Millare, Millers, Millir, Millor, Millr	5.7	2,225	10,469	34	35	40	138	31	101	356	889	172	152	167	110
Millet, Millett, Millit, Millott	5.6	37	171	6	1	1	22	1			4		1		1
Milligan, Milagin, Milegan, Milekin, Miligan, Miligin, Milikan, Miliken, Milikin, Millagan, Millegan, Millegen, Millican, Millicon, Milligen, Millikan, Milliken, Millikin	5.8	91	435	24			3	1	1	9	24	2	1	13	13
Millins, Millin, Milling, Millon	6.0	18	90			1	5		1	1	1			1	8
Mills, Mill, Mils	5.6	423	1,926	11	24	8	36		68	82	26	38	34	63	33
Millspough	6.7	17	97							17					
Milton, Milten	6.7	29	164				3			5		3	1	16	1
Miner, Miners, Minner, Minnor, Minor, Myner	5.3	200	868		8	14	7	2	123	16	4	5	13	5	3
Minich, Mineck, Minick, Minicks, Minnick	5.0	25	101							2	17	3			3
Minot, Minott	6.4	25	136	2		2	18		1						2
Minter, Mintor, Mintur	7.8	25	171							3	3		11	7	1
Mitchel, Micthel, Mischel, Mitchael, Mitchal, Mitchall, Mitchele, Mitchell, Mitchels, Mitchiell, Mitchil, Mittchel	5.6	704	3,201	59	20	7	65	27	56	42	117	73	83	109	46
Mix	5.1	48	195			1			38	7	2				
Mixon, Mixen	6.3	16	85											5	11
Mobley, Mobly	5.9	25	122							1	10		10	4
Mock	6.3	34	180				1			2	11	3	2	10	5
Mockbee, McAbee, McBee, McCaby, Mackabie, Mackaby, Mocbey, Mockabe, Mockbey	6.5	19	104							1	1	13	1		3
Moffat, Mafet, Maffet, Maffett, Maffit, Maffitt, Maffort, Moffatt, Moffet, Moffett, Moffit, Moffitt, Mofit, Morfet, Morfit, Morfits, Muffet	6.0	87	437	2	2	6	7	2	7	17	14	8	4	15	3
Moncrief, Moncrieff, Muncrief, Muncriep, Muncriffe	6.3	16	85				3			3				4	6
Money, Monee, Monnys, Mony, Muney, Munnie	6.1	34	172			1	1	4	2	4	5	8	3	5	1
Monk, Monks	5.4	33	146				9	1		5		3	4	8	3
Montague, Montaigue, Montauge, Montgue, Montigue, Mountague	5.6	47	215			5	18		5	1			13	5	
Montfort, Monford, Monfort, Montford, Mountford, Munford, Munfort, Muntford	6.0	32	160		1					17	1		8	4	1
Montgomery, Mongomary, Montgomary, Montgomeroy, Montgommery, Montgomorey, Montgomrey, Montgummary, Montg'y, Motgomery, Mountgomary, Mountgomery, Mountgumry	5.4	223	982	3	6	1	12	2	6	17	68	25	17	26	40
Moody, Mody, Moodey, Moodie, Mooty, Moudy	6.1	190	970	32	16	4	51		6	2	15	7	24	18	15
Moon, Moone	6.2	71	370	2		5	5	4		18	10	1	5	18	3
Mooney, Moonie, Moony	5.4	43	191		5		1			12	12	1	3	9	
Moore, Moers, Mohr, Moor, Moores, Moors, More, Mores, Moure	5.6	1,724	7,977	69	111	48	174	7	82	173	343	91	181	320	125
Moran, Morang, Morans	6.0	25	124							3	1	15	1	4	1
Morehead, Moorehead, Morehed, Morhead	5.5	33	149				1				19		5	4	4
Morehouse	5.3	82	354			4	2		52	23	1				
Moreland	6.1	38	195								9	17	5	6	1
Morey, Mauray, Maurey, Maury, Moorey, Moral, Moray, Morery, Morrey, Morrie, Morry, Mory, Mourey, Mowery, Mowra, Mowre, Mowrey, Mowry	5.9	164	806	4	11	17	27	52	5	30	15		3		
Morgan, Maughan, Maughon, Morgain, Morgen, Morggen, Morgin, Morgon, Moughan, Moughon	5.7	604	2,838	7	17	27	74	2	95	48	77	41	55	115	46
Morrill, Moirel, Moral, Morel, Morell, Morill, Morral, Morrall, Morrel, Morrell, Morril	6.1	188	952	30	65	7	42		1	33	4		1		5
Morris, Maurice, Moorits, Morece, Moress, Moris, Morish, Moriss, Morits, Moritz, Morres, Morress, Morrice, Morrise, Morriss	5.5	608	2,741	4	3	6	25	2	36	43	119	49	94	171	56
Morrison, Maurison, Morason, Morison, Morreson, Morrisson, Morriston, Morrosen, Morroson, Morrowson	5.7	337	1,581	21	50	2	11		5	36	102	14	24	60	12
Morrow, Moroe, Morow, Morraw, Morrows, Murrow	6.0	134	674	2	2			1		1	7	54	4	11	22	31
Morse, Moorse, Morss	5.9	435	2,112	19	59	32	239	1	49	15	1		9	9	2
Morton, Mortain, Morten, Mortin, Mortorn	5.5	262	1,170	22	2	5	98	1	8	5	42	13	41	19	6
Moseley, Mosely, Mosley, Mossley, Mossly	5.5	118	537	1		4	16		20	2	1	1	42	21	10
Moser, Moasser, Mosir, Mosser, Mossir	5.5	81	361							1	66	4	1	9	
Moses, Mosses	6.0	88	404	5	13	10	9		17	4	10	3	2	8	7
Mosier, Mosher, Moshier, Moshure, Mosure, Mosyer, Mozier	5.5	147	661	7	2	10	30	8	11	75	2				
Moss, Maus, Moess, Mosce	5.9	144	710	11	3	5	1	3	18	17	14	4	24	33	11
Motley, Mottley	5.9	18	89	3			1						7	6	1
Mott, Mot, Mote, Motes, Motte, Motts, Motz	5.6	159	729	1	1	9	9	8	13	72	12	4	11	7	12
Mouie, Moale, Mole, Moles, Moul	6.5	17	94							9	2	3			3
Moulton, Molten, Molton, Moulten	5.6	159	726	36	57	10	32	2	15	1		4			2
Mount, Mont, Montz, Mounce, Mounts, Mountz	5.8	24	115							7	10	1	1	2	3
Mourer, Mourir	5.9	18	89	3			1						7	6	1
Mower, Mowerer, Mowers, Mowrer	5.7	43	201	3			2			18	15	2	3		
Moxley, Muxley	6.1	19	96		1	2			3			3	9	1	
Moyer, Moier, Moir, Moires, Moirs, Moyar, Moyers, Moyr, Moyre	6.1	218	1,114							1	6	174	13	14	9	1
Mudd, Mud	5.6	24	110									24			
Mudge	6.4	24	129			1	8		1	14					
Mudget, Mudgett, Muget, Mugett, Mugget, Muggett	5.6	22	101	6	14	2									
Mulford	5.4	25	109				1		4	18	1		1		
Mull	5.8	19	91							4	10	1		4	
Mullen, Mullin, Mullinax, Mullon	4.8	59	223		1		1			3	18	6	4	20	6
Muller	6.2	28	146						1	24		1		2	
Mullican, Mulliken, Mullikin, Mullokin	6.3	20	106	1	3		5				11				
Mullins, Mullings	5.6	30	139				2					20	6	2
Mumford, Mumfoort, Mumpford	5.5	71	322	4		1	4	19	6	6		14	4	12	1
Munday, Monday, Munde, Mundy	5.6	30	137				2		1	5	4	2	8	8	
Mundin, Munden, Mundine	4.6	23	82				1			1			5	16	
Munger, Mungar	5.6	49	225			1	13		19	12		2	1	1	
Munn, Mun	5.9	36	176		1	1	11		10		6			7	
Munroe, McRow, Monro, Monroe, Monrow, Munro, Munrow	5.7	192	903	1	8	6	63	22	15	28	6	6	9	21	7
Munsell, Monsel, Muncil, Munsel, Munsil, Munsill	5.0	24	95		1	5	1		17						
Munson, Monsen, Monson	5.6	105	480	8	2	8	9		64	7	1		1	5
Murch, Merche	4.8	23	88	17	1	1	1			2	1				
Murden, Murdin	5.8	19	92										14	5	
Murdock, Moordock, Mordack, Mordoch, Mordock, Moredock, Moredocke, Murdeck, Murdick, Murdoch	5.5	110	498			11	22		10	13	23	11	3	12	5
Murphy, Morfey, Morphy, Murfee, Murfey, Murfree, Murfrey, Murfy, Murphey, Murphree, Murphrey, Murphry, Murprey, Murpry, Murpy	5.3	301	1,311	10			8	6	1	24	60	47	34	66	45
Murray, Muray, Murey, Murrah, Murree, Murrey, Murry	5.3	288	1,236	12	13	6	20	3	22	33	54	27	29	40	29
Murrell, Murrel, Murril, Murrill	4.5	41	145		1	1	1			2		1	10	14	11
Murrin, Murrain, Murran, Murren, Murrine, Murring	5.6	30	137				4		25		1				
Muse	5.0	20	80								2		11	5	2
Musgrove, Musgrave	6.3	21	112							4	8	1	5	3
Musselman, Moesselman, Muselman, Mussillman, Mussleman, Musslman, Mussulman	6.1	33	168							30	1	2			
Musser, Muser	6.9	23	135							21	1	1			
Muzzy, Muzy, Muzze, Muzzey	6.8	16	92		1	4	10	1							
Myers, Miars, Mier, Miers, Mire, Mires, Myars, Myas, Myer, Myor, Myre, Myres, Myrs	5.8	404	1,948	1		5	5	1	2	119	136	58	29	22	26

TABLE **111.**—NOMENCLATURE, DEALING WITH NAMES REPRESENTED BY AT LEAST 100 WHITE PERSONS, BY STATES AND TERRITORIES, AT THE FIRST CENSUS: 1790—Continued.

NAME.	Average size of family.	TOTAL. Heads of families.	TOTAL. All other members.	Maine.	New Hampshire.	Vermont.	Massachusetts.	Rhode Island.	Connecticut.	New York.	Pennsylvania.	Maryland.	Virginia.	North Carolina.	South Carolina.
Nace, Naess, Nase, Nass	6.9	18	106								17	1			
Nagle, Nagel, Naglee, Naigly	5.6	43	199						2		38	3			
Nail, Naile, Nails, Nale, Nayle	5.2	27	114						1		5	4	2	11	4
Nally, Naligh, Nalley	7.0	15	90								1	12	1		1
Nance, Nantz	5.2	34	143		1		1						16	14	2
Nash, Knash	5.6	221	1,020	19	1	7	83	5	27	15	11	8	32	8	5
Nason, Nasson, Nayson	6.4	55	299	42	8		4	1							
Nave, Knave, Kneaves, Neave	6.5	30	164								14	7	9		
Naylor, Nailer, Nailor, Naler	5.2	33	139						1		15	12	3	2	
Neaff, Knaaf, Kneaf, Kneff, Naaf, Nafe, Naff, Neaf, Neafs, Neff, Neiff	5.9	65	318			1	1		6	5	32	6	14		
Neal, Kneel, Knell, Neail, Neale, Neall, Neals, Neel, Neeil, Neil, Neill, Niel, Niele, Niell, Nielle, Niels	5.5	284	1,277	18	30		13		9	17	51	37	41	44	24
Needham, Neadham, Neadum, Nedom	5.8	53	255		1	1	29		2	7		3		10	
Neely, Kneely, Kniely, Nealey, Neally, Nealy, Neeley, Neelie, Neelly, Neiley, Neilley, Neilly, Neily, Neley, Nely, Nielie	6.2	83	433	1	6					7	33		1	13	22
Neer, Kner, Knerr, Near, Nears, Nier	6.3	27	144							17	9	1			
Nellis	7.2	17	106							17					
Nelms, Nell, Nelles, Nelmes, Nill	5.7	42	198	1			1			2	7	2	20	9	
Nelson, Nealson, Neelson, Neilson, Nellson, Nielson, Nillson, Nilson	5.8	370	1,762	9	24	14	54		8	48	55	24	37	56	41
Nesbitt, Neasbit, Neesbit, Neisbet, Neisbit, Neisbitt, Nesbet, Nesbett, Nesbit, Nisbet, Nisbett, Nisbit, Nisbitt	5.3	60	257				3		1	4	24	6	1	5	16
Nesmith, Neasmith, Ne-smith, Ne Smith	5.0	21	84	1	10	1					1	1			7
Nettles, Knettle, Knittels, Knittle, Nettle	6.0	25	126								6	4		3	12
Nettleton, Nittleton	5.3	33	143		2	1	1		28	1					
Nevill, Navel, Navill, Navle, Neavel, Nevel, Nevell, Nevels, Nevil, Neville	5.2	36	151								11	6	8	7	4
Nevins, Neven, Nevens, Nevin	7.4	18	116	1	8	1	1		2		1	1		3	
New, Knew, News, Nuse	6.1	22	112				3		1	2	5	1	7	2	1
Newbury, Newberry	5.1	42	173	1		1	4		15	4	3	3		10	1
Newby	4.4	46	155								2		19	25	
Newcomb, Newcam, Newcom, Newcombe, Newcome, Newcum, Newcumb, Nucomb, Nucum	6.0	108	538	10	1	2	49		11	16	1	9	4	5	
Newcomer, Newcumber, Newcumer, Newkomer, Nicomer, Niewcomer	6.9	30	176								25	5			
Newell, Newal, Newall, Newel, Newil, Newill, Nuel	5.9	184	904	5	5	16	61	7	34	9	21	3	8	14	1
Newhall	6.6	71	397	1	5	4	61								
Newkirk, Neukirk, Newkerk, Nikerk	5.4	44	192							35	6	1		2	
Newland, Newlan, Newlands, Newlen, Newlin, Newling, Nuland, Nulen, Nulin	5.2	40	166			1	8			6	18	1	1	5	
Newman, Neuman, Newmen, Newmon, Nieuman, Nouman, Numan, Numans, Numon	5.5	199	896	3	5	3	27	5	10	22	45	9	37	18	15
Newsom, Newsome, Newsum	4.6	23	83									9	14		
Newton, Neuton, Newtown, Nuton	5.6	304	1,412		18	34	117	2	45	14	5	25	11	26	7
Nice, Kneese, Kneisse, Knies, Neace, Nease, Neece, Nees, Neese, Neice, Neics, Neiss, Niece, Nise	5.8	57	271				1			7	33	4	6	4	2
Nicely, Kniceley, Knisely, Knissley, Neesley, Neesly, Neicely, Niceley, Nichley, Nisely	6.6	29	163							1	20		8		
Nicholas, Nichales, Nicholes, Nickolas, Nicolas, Nicolaus	5.5	83	397		1	1	3	5		3	38	4	15	11	2
Nichols, Neichols, Nichall, Nichalls, Nichals, Nichels, Nichol, Nichold, Nicholds, Nicholl, Nicholls, Nickals, Nickels, Nickle, Nickles, Nickless, Nickolds, Nickolls, Nickols, Nicles, Nicol, Nicole, Nicoll, Nicolls, Nicols	5.5	713	3,174	19	56	53	164	29	102	81	26	50	31	76	26
Nicholson, Nichalson, Nichelson, Nicholason, Nicholdson, Nicholsen, Nicholsin, Nickleson, Nickolson, Nicolson, Nicolsons	5.3	127	548				8		6	15	21	20	18	29	10
Nickerson, Niccoson, Nicherson, Nickirson, Nickison, Nikerson	5.6	121	553	9	2	4	79		9	14		2			2
Niles, Nile, Niols, Nyles	5.9	88	433	5	3	14	17	7	22	16	1		2	1	
Nims	6.6	19	107		4		15								
Nixon, Nickson, Nixen, Nixson	5.6	66	302		6	1		6	1	6	15	4	5	23	6
Noble, Knoble, Nobel, Nobels, Nobles	6.1	211	1,066	11	9	21	47	2	22	15	23	12	10	19	20
Noland, Knowland, Knowlon, Nolan, Nolen, Nolland, Nowlan, Nowland, Nowlen, Nowlin	5.0	60	241	1	1		6		1	1	6	17	2	18	7
Norcott, Norcut, Norcute, Norcutt, Northcut, Northcutt	4.8	22	83				5		5				5	6	1
Norcross	5.5	22	100	4	3	1	12			1	1				
Norfleet, Norflet, Norflett	4.3	25	83										13	12	
Norman, Normand, Normant, Normen, Norment	5.1	71	291	2		1	1	2	3		5	9	13	27	8
Norris, Narris, Noris, Norress, Norrice, Norrige, Norriss	5.7	245	1,146	14	34	9	9	3	6	14	23	61	28	26	18
North, Noth	6.4	92	493	1		3	3		33	18	16	2	7	3	6
Northrop, Northoop, Northorp, Northrope, Northroup, Northrup, Northup, Nortrip, Nortrup, Nothrop	5.6	153	710			4	10	33	64	38	4		10	10	15
Norton, Nortin, Nortine, Noten, Noton	5.8	359	1,722	28	15	28	90	1	107	38	12	5	10	16	15
Norwood	6.0	62	308	4	1		14			4		14	3	12	10
Nostrand, Nostrant	5.6	22	101							22					
Nourse, Nurse, Nurss	5.1	47	195	1	7	3	31			4	1				
Noyes, Noice, Nois, Noyce, Noye, Noys, Noyse	5.9	183	889	20	50	5	71	5	21	11					
Null, Knull	5.5	40	178								17	5	4	14	
Nunnally, Nunally, Nunley, Nunnelly	5.6	19	88										19		
Nutt, Knutt, Nut, Nute, Nutts	6.2	56	291	4	16	1	5		1	1	7	1	12	6	2
Nutter	5.0	58	230	6	39				1	1	1	2	8		
Nutting	5.9	53	261	5	3	3	41			1					
Nye, Nie, Nigh	6.3	135	721	5	1	10	86	8	7	2	14	1	1		
Oakley, Oakly, Okeley, Okely	5.9	70	344					2	5	47	4	2	2	8	
Oaks, Oachs, Oak, Oakes, Oakh, Ocks, Okes	5.8	72	349	4	2	7	26		6	5	6		12	2	2
Oaswald, Osswald, Ostwalt, Oswald, Oswalt, Oswell, Oswelt	5.1	21	87							2	5			1	13
Oats, Oat, Oates, Oatts	5.2	30	125	3						5	4	1		9	8
Ober, Obar	5.2	39	163		4	4	22				5	1			3
Oberholtzer, Oberholtz, Oberholzer, Overhobzer, Overholsa, Overholse, Overholser, Overholtzer, Overholzer	5.9	22	108								21	1			
O'Bryan, Obeion, Obirant, O'Boyen, O'Brian, Obrian, O'Briant, Obriant, O'Brien, O'brien, Obrien, O'Brient, Obrient, Obrion, Obriont, Obryan, OBryant, Obryant, O'Bryon	5.2	73	303	5	1	3	7		3	14	5	11	3	11	10
Odell, Oadell, Oddle, Odel, O'Dell, Odelle, Odil, Odle, O'Dle	6.0	128	642		7	6	3	1	10	69		3	14	12	3
Odom, Odam, Oddum, Odem, Odiom, Odum	5.4	56	247		1							1	35	19	
Offutt	7.5	19	124								17	2			
Ogden, Octdon, Ogdon	5.8	71	338		1				12	27	14	12	4	1	
Ogle	5.9	17	84								5	10			2
Oglesby, Ogelby, Ogely, Ogilby, Ogillby, Ogilsby, Oglebay, Oglebe, Ogleby, Oglesbey, Oglisbey	5.8	36	163				1		1	1	7		12	9	5
Olcott, Olcot, Olcut, Olcutt, Ollcott	6.0	47	234		4	7	5		27	4					
Oldham, Oaldham, Oaldhum, Oldam, Oldhane	5.0	50	201	3	1		8				1	13	14	5	5
Olds, Oalds, Old, Oles, Olts	5.3	82	353		3	8	29		12	5	10		13	1	1
Oliver, Olefer, Olifer, Olipher, Ollavor, Ollefer, Olliver, Ollivor, Olover, Olver	5.5	212	944	25	2	4	34			15	20	13	34	46	19
Olmsted, Olmested, Olmstead, Olmstord, Omstead, Omsted, Onstead, Ormsted, Ormstid, Ulmsted, Umpstead, Umstad, Umstead, Umsted	5.6	147	683		3	10	1		81	33	13	4		2	

TABLE **111.**—NOMENCLATURE, DEALING WITH NAMES REPRESENTED BY AT LEAST 100 WHITE PERSONS, BY STATES AND TERRITORIES, AT THE FIRST CENSUS: 1790—Continued.

NAME.	Average size of family.	TOTAL.		HEADS OF FAMILIES.											
		Heads of families.	All other members.	Maine.	New Hampshire.	Vermont.	Massachusetts.	Rhode Island.	Connecticut.	New York.	Pennsylvania.	Maryland.	Virginia.	North Carolina.	South Carolina.
Olney.	6.0	48	238			3	2	35	2	6					
Onderdunk, Onderdonck, Onderdonk, Onderkirk.	6.0	37	185							37					
O'Neal, O'Nail, Onail, Onailes, Onale, Oncale, Oneal, ONeale, Oneale, Oneales, ONeall, Oneall, O'Neals, ONeil, Oneil, O Neill, Oniel, Oniell, Orneal.	5.5	87	391	1	1		1			4	9	14	10	34	13
Orcutt, Orcott, Orcult, Orcut.	5.4	35	154	4	2	3	11		11	4					
Ordway, Orday, Ordeway.	5.5	46	209		27	4	14								1
Orme, Orem, Orm, Orms.	6.7	17	97		1				1	1		12	2		
Ormsby, Ormby, Ormsbe, Ormsbee, Ormsbey, Ormsbry, Ormsbury, Ornsbey, Ornsbough, Ornsby.	5.4	33	146			2	8	8	10	1	3		1		
Orne, Orn, Ornd, Orns.	5.9	22	108		1	1	18				2				
Orr, Oar, Ore, Ores.	5.9	101	490	10	7	4	4			12	27	8	6	17	6
Orton, Orten.	6.9	21	123			3	2		8		3			4	1
Orvis.	6.8	15	87				6	4	5						
Osborn, Orsbern, Orsborn, Orsborne, Orsbourn, Orsburn, Osban, Osbern, Osbon, Osbone, Osborne, Osbourn, Osbourne, Osburn, Osburne, Ossburn, Ozborn, Ozborne, Ozburn, Ozburne.	5.5	432	1,936	1	10	8	62	4	112	75	23	37	41	45	14
Osgood, Ossgood.	6.4	141	762	14	40	3	69		5	8				1	1
Osterhout, Oserhout, Oslerhout, Osterhant, Osterhont, Osterhoudt.	6.3	34	179			1				32	1				
Ostrander, Ostranda, Ostrandar, Ostronder.	7.0	62	373			1				60	1				
Ostrum, Ostram, Ostrom.	5.9	26	127					1		24	1				
Otis, Oties, Ottis.	5.6	70	325	5	13	6	25	3	15	3					
Ott, Ots, Otts.	5.5	51	232	2						2	23	14	1		9
Outlaw.	6.2	26	135											24	2
Overholt, Overholts, Overholtz, Overhults.	7.3	16	101								13	3			
Overman, Oberman.	5.5	32	145								2			30	
Overton, Overturn.	5.4	87	380		1				2	23			18	42	1
Owen, Oans, Oens, Oings, Owans, Owens, Owin, Owing, Owings, Owins, Owns.	5.6	466	2,152	9	1	11	22	6	24	51	45	56	95	87	59
Pace, Palce, Pase.	5.8	44	213								5		12	22	5
Packard, Packad, Parkard.	5.5	106	478	9	6	12	75	3		1					
Packer, Paca, Paceher, Pacehore, Paker.	5.9	47	229	5	3		2	1	17		6	2	2	8	1
Paddock, Paddack, Paddocks.	6.3	64	340				8	22		7	27				
Padgett, Padget, Padjet, Padjit, Paget, Pagett, Pagget, Paggett, Paggit, Paggot, Paghert, Pagit.	5.7	61	286							4	1	18	12	13	13
Padleford, Paddleford.	6.5	21	116		5	1	15								
Page, Paige, Peaige.	6.0	408	2,040	39	134	32	56	9	39	13	12	7	21	38	8
Painter, Panter, Payntar.	5.7	76	353			2	1		6	3	41	6	12	2	3
Palmer, Palmere, Palmor, Palmore, Palmour, Pamer, Parmar, Parmer, Parmor, Parmore, Polmer.	5.8	674	3,206	18	61	49	56	20	167	140	45	21	42	25	30
Pardy, Parde, Pardee, Pardey, Pardie.	5.2	61	258			1			1	48	11				
Paree, Parrey, Parry.	6.2	25	129	3	3				1	1	16			1	
Parham, Parram, Parrum, Perham, Perhum.	3.8	52	146	4	3	4	8						11	21	
Parish, Parrish, Perrish.	5.4	144	636	3		8	10	1	15	19	8	24	14	39	3
Parker, Parcher, Parkers.	5.7	1,118	5,221	51	96	71	276	15	78	66	76	48	89	200	52
Parkhurst, Parckhurst, Parkhast, Parkherst, Parkhurt.	5.7	69	326			9	18	31		7	2	2			
Parkinson, Parkenson, Parkison.	6.4	23	124			1				1	12	1	5	2	1
Parkman.	7.2	14	87			1	8				3				2
Parks, Parcks, Park, Parke, Parkes, Parkess, Parkis, Pearks.	6.0	369	1,852	4	10	16	61	2	54	62	47	20	25	54	14
Parmalie, Palmerly, Pamely, Pamerly, Parmala, Parmale, Parmalee, Parmela, Parmele, Parmelee, Parmeley, Parmella, Parmely, Parmerle, Parmerley, Parmerly, Parmile, Parmly.	5.4	109	476			2	15	6	78	3			1	2	2
Parmenter, Parmentor, Parminter, Permenter.	5.9	30	147				18							5	7
Parmeter, Palmater, Palmatier, Palmatus, Palmetier, Palmitter, Parmarter, Parmater, Parmerter, Parmeta, Parmiter, Permater.	5.6	63	291		2	5	35		3	18					
Parr.	4.9	29	113				1			4	7	2	3	12	
Parrott, Pairott, Paret, Parott, Parratt, Parret, Parrett, Parriott, Parrit, Parrot, Perret, Perrett.	5.4	74	327	1	2		3		6		1	19	27	10	5
Parsons, Parsins, Parson, Parston.	5.5	413	1,864	29	20	15	108		82	21	27	27	50	23	11
Partridge, Pardridge, Partaradge, Partrich, Partrige, Pateridge, Patridge, Patrige, Pattarige, Pattridge.	5.8	116	556	13	9	11	56		7	2	4	5	4	2	3
Paschael, Pascal, Pascall, Pascault, Paschal, Paschall, Paschcall, Pascheal, Paschel, Paskall.	5.8	22	106		1		3				4	2	1	10	1
Passmore, Pasmoore, Pasmore, Pasmour.	6.0	17	85								9	2		5	1
Patch.	5.8	70	333	9	9	4	40		4	1	2				1
Patchin, Patchen, Patching, Patchon.	5.3	28	120						12	16					
Pate, Paits, Pates.	5.1	46	187				3		1	1	1	1	7	27	5
Patrick, Partrick, Paterick, Patric, Patrich, Pattrick.	5.4	102	447	2	4	4	14		8	19	7	3	4	27	10
Patten, Paten, Paton, Pattan, Pattin, Patton.	5.8	212	1,008	23	22		18	3	6	13	62	9	9	38	14
Patterson, Paterson, Patison, Pattersen, Patteson, Pattison, Potterson.	5.6	541	2,499	28	20	15	29	2	18	66	148	29	24	115	47
Paul, Pall, Paules, Paull, Pauls, Pawl.	5.5	158	708	23	6	8	27	3	7	8	42	8	6	13	7
Paxton, Packeton, Packson, Packston, Peckston, Pexton.	6.7	56	320							2	3	45	4	2	
Payne, Pain, Paine, Paines, Pane, Payn, Pean, Peane, Peayne.	5.6	463	2,124	24	17	21	104	40	57	59	8	22	60	34	17
Payson, Pasons, Passon, Passons.	5.8	33	158	6	3		18			2				2	2
Payton, Peaton, Peten, Petten, Petton, Peyton.	4.8	27	102			1				2			21	2	
Peabody, Pabodie, Peabodie, Peebody.	5.4	86	380	6	20	2	39	8	5	5				1	
Peacock.	5.1	39	161		4					3	1	10	1	14	6
Peal, Peale, Peel, Peele, Peels, Peil.	5.8	48	231				8				6	2	4	28	
Pearl, Pearle.	5.8	21	100	1	7	4			8					1	
Pearsall, Parcel, Parcell, Parsells, Parsels, Parsill, Pearcall, Pearceall, Pearsel, Pearsell, Persall, Persel, Persell, Pershall, Perzel, Piercall, Pierceall, Piersall, Purcall, Purcel, Purcell, Purkell, Pursel, Pursell, Pussal.	6.1	94	478			1			3	40	20	2	17	6	5
Pearson, Pearsons, Peircoen, Peirson, Piercen, Pierson.	5.6	247	1,128	6	12	4	53		15	43	37	6	21	24	26
Pease, Peace, Peas, Pees, Peice, Peise.	5.6	199	916	13	9	7	58	1	86	10	6		2	5	2
Peasley, Peasle, Peaslee, Peasly, Pesley.	6.6	70	393	6	33	2	17			2	2		5	3	
Peck, Pecke, Pecks.	5.5	451	2,048	2	1	22	66	30	229	47	23	6	9	5	1
Peckham, Peckam.	6.0	95	470		1		5	21	58	5	5				
Pedan, Peaden, Peadon, Peden, Pedian, Pedien, Pedin, Pedon, Peedin.	6.2	29	151								13		3	4	9
Pedrick, Paddrick, Padrick, Pedrik, Pedruck, Pedwick.	5.0	24	95				10				3		7	4	
Peek, Peack, Peak, Peake, Peaks, Peke, Pique.	5.6	62	282		2	6	3	1	2	20	3	5	10	2	8
Peet, Peate, Peete, Peets, Peits, Piet, Piets.	5.6	47	218					1	2	25	4	10	1	4	
Peirpoint, Parepoint, Perpoint, Pierpoint, Pierpont, Purpoint.	5.4	30	131	1			4				17	1	6	1	1
Pell, Pels.	5.3	31	133	1		1				20	1	1	1	2	1
Pellet, Pellett, Pellit, Pelot, Pelott, Pillet.	6.7	17	97			1			6	4	1	2			3
Pelton.	5.7	43	201	1	2	3	8		22	7					
Pemberton.	4.6	38	138								7	2	11	6	6
Pence.	6.3	30	160								5	5	18	1	1
Pendergrass, Pendergast, Pendergrast, Prendergast, Prendergrast.	3.9	26	74			5	3		1	3	1			10	1
Pendleton, Penalton, Pendelton, Pendleston, Penelton, Pintleton.	6.4	68	370	14		2		15	5	5	1			10	21
Penfield, Penfold, Penifield.	5.8	29	138			2	2		19	5			1		
Penn, Pen.	7.3	33	208								2	20	8	3	

TABLE **111.**—NOMENCLATURE, DEALING WITH NAMES REPRESENTED BY AT LEAST 100 WHITE PERSONS, BY STATES AND TERRITORIES, AT THE FIRST CENSUS: 1790—Continued.

NAME.	Average size of family.	TOTAL.		HEADS OF FAMILIES.											
		Heads of families.	All other members.	Maine.	New Hampshire.	Vermont.	Massachusetts.	Rhode Island.	Connecticut.	New York.	Pennsylvania.	Maryland.	Virginia.	North Carolina.	South Carolina.
Pennel, Panel, Pannel, Pannell, Pannill, Penal, Penel, Penell, Pennell	6.3	44	233	8		4	1			3	19		8		1
Pennington, Penengton, Penenton, Peninton, Pennenton, Pinnington	6.1	65	328							1	16	26	10	8	4
Penny, Peney, Penie, Penney	5.5	80	360	11	2	1	5		2	33	4	5	2	14	1
Pennyman, Penaman, Pennaman, Penneman, Penniman	5.4	40	174	1	6		29	2	2						
Penrose, Pennrose	5.5	20	89								20				
Peoples, Pebbles, Pebles, Pebples, Peebles, Peeples, Peobels, Peobles, Peples, Pepple, Poebles	5.5	63	283	1		1	6			3	13	6	4	24	5
Pepper, Peper, Peppers	5.7	46	218	2		1	15		6	2	6	6	3	1	4
Percival, Parcevell, Parseval, Parsivell, Percivall, Percivel, Persivell, Pierciful, Purcival, Pursevell	6.3	29	155		3	4	10		6	2	1		3		
Percy, Parcy, Pearsy, Percey, Persy, Piercey, Piercy	4.8	25	94	3	3		1		5	5	1	2		4	1
Perdue, Pardieu, Pardiew, Pardue	6.2	22	114									6	6	8	2
Perkerson, Perkinson, Perkison	6.1	25	128		1								23	1	
Perkins, Perkens, Perkin, Pirkens, Pirkins, Purkins	5.8	588	2,791	73	76	28	152	12	88	18	16	16	36	48	25
Perley, Pearley, Pearly, Perlee, Perly, Purley	7.0	18	108	4	1	1	8			1		1	2		
Perrigo, Perigo, Perrige, Purigo	6.3	27	142				4	2	1	5	3		12		
Perrin, Perin, Perine, Perinne, Perrean, Perreen, Perrine	6.4	57	310		1		7	7	2	15	14	2	2	5	2
Perry, Pearee, Pearey, Peary, Peerey, Peery, Peiry, Perie, Perre, Perrey	5.5	628	2,814	26	23	39	155	30	56	56	26	52	23	107	35
Person, Persen, Persons	5.5	128	575	2	16	5	11		19	23	9		6	23	14
Peters, Peter, Petere, Petre, Petres, Petter, Petters	5.7	207	970	3	4	9	20	1	8	26	81	24	18	12	1
Peterson, Petersen, Petterson	5.3	104	451	4	4	1	13	8	2	22	11	3	15	14	7
Petrie, Petree, Petrey, Petry	5.6	32	148							17	6		1	5	3
Pettibone, Petibone, Pettebone, Pettiborn	6.6	33	185				5	4		21	2	1			
Pettigrew, Pedigrew, Pedigrue, Petegrew, Petegrow, Petigrow, Pettegrew, Pettegrow, Pettegrue, Petticrew, Pettigew, Pettycrew, Pittegrew	5.8	29	139	9		2				2	7			2	7
Pettingill, Patingale, Patingell, Pedengill, Petengall, Petengil, Petingill, Pettengal, Pettengill, Pettigill, Pettingal, Pettingale, Pettingall, Pettingell, Pettingil, Pettingle, Pittengill, Pittingill	5.6	90	410	16	17	6	39	1	3	8					
Pettis, Petiss, Pettes, Pettice, Petties, Pettiss, Pettus	5.8	57	271	3		2	15	13	5	7			8	1	3
Pettit, Pattit, Petit, Petitt, Pettet, Pettite, Pettitt, Petut	5.5	74	334						4	38	18	1	3	7	3
Petty, Pette, Pettee, Pettey	6.7	88	497	8	11	5	12			9	1	1	20	16	5
Pfeiffer, Peiffer, Pfeifer, Pfeiffer, Pfleffer, Pfifer, Pfyfer, Pifer, Piffers	5.4	30	132						1	2	24	2		1	
Phelps, Felps, Filps, Phelphes, Phelphs, Pheps	5.6	395	1,816		24	20	71		161	40	2	12	4	58	3
Philbrick, Filbrick, Philbrik, Phillbrick	5.7	44	208	9	35										
Philbrook, Filbrook, Fillbrook, Philbrock, Philbrok, Philbrooks, Phillbrook, Phillbrooks	5.4	44	195	22	20	1		1							
Phillips, Fillips, Philip, Philipps, Philips, Phillip, Philliph, Philliphs, Phillps, Phillups, Philps, Philips, Pilips	5.6	878	4,004	17	17	31	174	56	39	143	111	53	63	143	31
Philpot, Fillpot, Fillpott, Phillpot, Philpots, Philpott, Philput	6.0	24	121	2	3						2	6	1	3	7
Pickard, Pichart, Pickart, Pickerd	5.1	29	120	4			12			10	2			1	
Pickens, Pickin, Picking, Pickings, Pickins, Pikin	6.7	29	166							3	9	2	1	4	10
Pickering, Pickring	6.8	61	353	2		24	15				11	4	4		1
Pickett, Picket, Pickets, Pickit	4.6	89	323	1	2	1	13		18	7	2	3	7	31	4
Pickle, Pickel, Pickell	5.3	31	133			1	3			3	16		4	4	
Pier, Peer, Peers, Peher, Peir, Peire, Peirre, Peyre, Pierre	5.4	24	106			3	3		1	11		1	4		1
Pierce, Pearce, Pearse, Peerce, Peirce, Perce, Pierse	5.7	950	4,490	38	62	57	332	87	56	66	59	42	39	97	15
Pike, Pikes, Pyke	5.0	184	736	12	41	9	68	6	13	12	5	2	3	10	3
Pilsbury, Pillsbury, Pilsberry, Pilsbery	5.6	58	266	9	18	1	28	1						1	
Pinckney, Pinckny, Pinkney	6.2	25	130					1		15					9
Pine, Pines, Pyne	4.9	32	126		1		1		1	15	3	3	2	1	5
Pinkerton	6.4	23	124			3			1	2	14		1	1	1
Pinkham, Pinkam, Pinkhum, Pinkim, Pinkum	5.7	58	272	18	18	1	17			1				3	
Pinner, Piner, Pinnor, Pinor, Pynor	4.6	33	118			2					1	2	14	11	2
Pinney, Pinnee, Pinny	6.1	21	108				2	2	13	2				2	
Pinson, Pincen, Pinston, Pintson	6.0	18	90							1			2	3	12
Piper, Peiper, Pipers, Pipper	5.4	111	502	7	23	2	14		1	6	25	12	10	8	3
Pipkin, Pipkins	6.6	20	112				1							18	1
Pippen, Pippin	6.3	18	95							1		3		12	2
Pitcher, Pitchr	5.9	44	216	3	1	3	13	7	4	13					
Pitkin	5.6	27	125						27						
Pitman, Pittman	5.3	132	570		13		13	12	1	1	9		23	55	5
Pitts, Pits, Pitt	5.6	108	493	5	2	1	11	4	1	9	2	10	17	23	23
Pixley, Pixly	5.9	23	113			3	3		11	2	4				
Place, Playce	5.4	64	281	4	18	6			16	15	5				
Plank	5.8	24	114				2	1	4	7	8	1	1		
Plant, Plants, Plantz	5.2	21	88		1		1		7	5	4		1	1	1
Platt, Plat, Platts	6.0	144	726		7	2	9	2	59	50	8		2		1
Plumb, Plum	5.6	60	278			2	6		35	9	5		2		1
Plummer, Plomer, Plommer, Plumar, Plumber, Plumer, Plumor	6.0	180	898	26	27	2	39		6	1	15	38	9	13	4
Plunket, Plunckett, Plunkett, Plunkitt	5.4	20	88								6		4	4	6
Plympton, Plimpton, Plymton	6.3	27	142	2		1	24								
Poe, Po, Poh	5.7	34	158							9	5	4	14		2
Poindexter, Pendexter, Pendextor, Pindexter, Poindexters	5.9	24	117	3	4								13	4	
Poland, Polen, Polin, Poling, Polland, Pollen, Pollin, Polline, Polun	6.0	38	189	8	1		12			1	6	2	1	4	3
Polhemus	6.3	25	132							25					
Polk, Poake, Poke, Polke, Poque	5.7	54	254	1				1	2	1	20	4	2	10	13
Pollard	5.4	114	503	6	12	4	29			4	2	3	34	14	6
Pollock, Polick, Polluck, Polock	5.4	48	210	2				4	1	7	21	2	3	5	3
Polly, Polley	5.5	40	178	1		3	15		4	6	5		5		1
Pomeroy, Pomeray, Pomery, Pomoroy, Pomroy, Pumrey, Pumroy	6.4	84	454	5	5	3	39		21	7	2		2		
Pond, Pon, Ponds, Ponns, Pons	5.5	99	441	1	2	13	52		17	3	1		3	4	3
Pool, Poole, Pooles	5.9	201	992	5	5	3	54	1	11	20	11	23	15	41	12
Poor, Poore, Poores, Por, Pore	5.7	91	427	8	15	1	37		2		8	9	4	6	1
Pope	5.8	184	886	4	6	4	47	1	5		11	10	16	57	18
Porter, Portar, Portor, Portter, Portur	5.7	587	2,773	15	23	26	116		123	28	87	60	35	44	30
Posey, Poesey, Possey	5.1	46	188								1	23	6	1	14
Post, Poste	5.9	158	772	1	2	18	4		38	81	9	2	2		1
Potter, Poter, Potters, Pottor	5.8	439	2,117	15	14	19	80	136	66	57	22	5	7	19	8
Potts, Pots, Pott, Potte	5.7	93	435	1			1		1	10	40	5	7	19	8
Pounds, Pound	5.9	17	83								3	4	2	5	3
Powell, Poules, Powal, Powall, Powel, Powels, Powill, Powle, Powles	5.6	478	2,174		3	11	16		3	61	51	33	128	139	33
Powers, Pouers, Powars, Power, Powrs, Powurs	5.7	288	1,355	12	34	30	46	6	15	25	25	15	28	35	17
Prather, Praithers, Prethers	6.1	26	133							1	21	1	3		
Pratt, Prat, Prats, Pratts	5.6	520	2,408	20	15	51	246	6	91	42	16	12	3	13	5
Pray, Prey	5.9	46	225	25	2	1	4	6		6	2				
Preble, Prebble	6.0	31	155	31											
Prentice, Prentis, Prentiss, Printice	6.0	113	561	2	9	5	52	2	28	5	2		4	3	1

TABLE **111.**—NOMENCLATURE, DEALING WITH NAMES REPRESENTED BY AT LEAST 100 WHITE PERSONS, BY STATES AND TERRITORIES, AT THE FIRST CENSUS: 1790—Continued.

NAME.	Average size of family.	TOTAL.		HEADS OF FAMILIES.											
		Heads of families.	All other members.	Maine.	New Hampshire.	Vermont.	Massachusetts.	Rhode Island.	Connecticut.	New York.	Pennsylvania.	Maryland.	Virginia.	North Carolina.	South Carolina.
Prescott, Prescoat, Prescoot, Prescot, Prescut, Prescutt, Presscott, Priscot, Priscott	5.5	143	637	17	71	1	31	1	2	...	24	7	1	12	8
Preston, Preson, Presson	5.8	150	724	1	14	19	25	1	28	22	24		6	2	1
Prewett, Prewet, Prewit, Prewitt, Pruet, Pruett, Pruit, Pruitt	5.2	37	157									4	12	9	12
Price, Preice, Priece, Prise	5.5	466	2,071	2	3	...	23	7	12	32	61	116	68	111	31
Pride	5.7	27	127	6		1			4	5			7	3	1
Pridgen, Pidgeon, Pidgin, Pigen, Pigeon, Pigon, Pridgeon, Prigeon, Prigion	5.3	22	95				4			1	3			14	....
Priest, Preast, Preist, Prest, Priess	5.1	67	272	3	11	6	31		2	1	9	1		3	....
Prince	6.0	129	645	19	5	3	29		14	14	5	1	17	6	16
Prindle	5.8	44	211			6	1		29	5			1	2	....
Pringle	6.0	26	129						1	4	3	3	3	3	9
Prior, Prier, Prire, Pryar, Pryer, Pryor	5.5	90	409	2			3	8	2	20	16	12	1	11	8	7
Pritchard, Prechard, Pretchard, Prichard, Prichet, Prichett, Pritchet, Pritchett, Pritchit	5.1	146	597		3		10		20	4	10	20	21	47	11
Proctor, Prockter, Procktor, Procter, Proctter	5.6	168	775	9	19	7	73		1	1	11	4	11	24	8
Proper	6.3	16	84							15			1		....
Prosser, Procer, Proser, Prossar, Prossor	5.4	21	93					1		8	3	2	5		2
Prouty, Proty, Proutty, Prowtey, Prowty	6.2	33	170		6	4	20			3					....
Puckett, Pucket	5.3	34	146										20	5	9
Puffer, Puffers	5.1	37	151		3	2	26		1	5					....
Pugh, Pew, Pou, Pu, Pue, Pughe	5.5	127	577				1			5	30	5	37	31	18
Pulley, Pully	6.5	17	93										6	9	2
Pulliam, Pullam, Pullim, Pullom, Pullum	5.5	22	99										11	7	4
Pullin, Pulin, Puling, Pullen, Pulling, Pullins	5.4	39	173	2		1	6		4	1			21	4	....
Pulsifer, Pulcifer, Pulispher, Pullsifer, Pulsepher, Pulsipher	4.4	27	93	1	2		21		3						....
Pulver	7.4	20	127							20					....
Pumfery, Pomfrey, Pumfrey, Pumphry	6.1	17	86									13	1	2	1
Purdy, Purday, Purdea, Purdee, Purdey, Purdie	6.1	134	686				6			4	90	15	6	6	3	4
Purington, Purrington, Purrinton	6.1	32	164	9	12		11								....
Purnell, Parnal, Parnald, Parnall, Parnel, Parnell, Pernal, Pernel, Purnal, Purnall, Purnel	5.4	66	290							2			1	32	4	16	11
Pusey, Puse, Pussey	6.3	17	90								14	3			....
Putnam, Putman, Putnan, Puttman, Puttnem	6.4	229	1,226	3	30	24	103	3	8	40	5	2	2	2	7
Putney	5.7	31	147	1	13		8			4			4	1	....
Pyle, Pile, Piles	6.1	55	278					1			35	6	6	3	4
Quackenbuss, Quackenboss, Quackenbush, Quackinbush, Quakenbus, Quakenbush	5.5	47	213							45				2	....
Queen, Queene, Quehen	5.7	23	108					1			6	7	2	5	2
Quick	5.4	51	223							30	10		2	3	6
Quigley, Quigly, Quikley	5.5	32	143		2		5			1	22	1		1	....
Quimby, Quemby, Quimba, Quimbee, Quimbey, Quinby	6.0	80	403	6	46	1	5			17	1	1		2	1
Quinn, Quain, Quin, Quine, Quynn	4.8	42	159	2			2				12	4	8	9	5
Raby, Raba, Rabe, Rabey, Raiby	5.5	20	90				1						12	7	....
Race	5.6	24	110	1						22					....
Radford, Redford	6.4	18	98				4				3		6	4	1
Ragsdale, Ragsdel, Ragsdell, Ragsdil	4.5	30	105										11	14	5
Rainey, Rainy, Raney, Rany, Reanys	4.1	45	140				2		1	3	4		12	11	12
Rains, Raen, Rahn, Rain, Raines, Ranes, Rayn, Rayne, Raynes, Reyen	5.0	40	161	6	4					2	4	2	5	10	7
Ralph, Ralf	5.2	39	162	1	6	2	6	11	1	3	5	1		2	1
Ralston, Ralstone, Rawlston, Rolston, Rolstone, Roulstone, Rowlstone	5.6	42	194	1	1		2				27		9		2
Rambo, Rambough, Rambow	5.4	26	114								22				4
Ramey, Raimey, Rama, Ramay, Rame, Ramme, Ramy, Reamey	6.3	26	139							3		1	13	7	2
Ramsdell, Ramsdal, Ramsdale, Ramsdall, Ramsdel, Ramsdul, Ransdell, Ransel	5.2	77	323	12	1	7	46	2	1		1		7		....
Ramsey, Ramsay, Ramsy	5.8	191	920	1	11	1		1	1	10	79	7	22	41	17
Rand, Ran, Rands, Rann, Ranns, Ranse	5.6	105	485	11	36	5	42		2	4	2			3	....
Randall, Randal, Randale, Randalls, Randals, Randel, Randell, Randels, Randil, Randle, Randled, Randles, Randol, Randols, Rendols	5.9	348	1,713	13	37	20	82	34	30	46	31	27	5	15	8
Randolph, Randelph, Randolf, Randolfe	5.0	62	249							4	8	1	29	15	5
Rankin, Rancan, Ranckens, Ranken, Rankens, Rankines, Ranking, Rankins	5.3	79	342	9	2	2	3			5	36	7		9	6
Ranney, Rannie, Ranny	5.6	39	179			9	5		21	3	1				....
Ransom, Ransome, Ranson, Ransone	6.0	90	447		1	12	22		21	12	1		9	12	....
Rapelye, Rapalje, Rapalye, Rapelje, Rapelyee	5.3	24	104							24					....
Ratcliff, Rackleff, Rackliffe, Ractliff, Radcliff, Radcliffe, Radclift, Raddcliff, Radlif, Radliff, Ratclif, Ratcliffe, Ratclift	5.6	76	348	3	1		3			6	4	18	24	5	12
Rathbone, Rathbane, Rathbon, Rathborn, Rathbun, Rathburn, Rothbone, Rothburn	5.4	80	355			1	16	26	23	12	1			1	....
Ratliff, Ratleff, Ratlief, Ratlif, Ratluf	5.3	23	98								1	6	1	15	....
Rawlings, Raling, Rallins, Raulens, Raulings, Rawlins, Rollens, Rollin, Rolling, Rollings, Rollins	5.4	143	627	17	54	1	4		1	3	5	33	12	10	3
Rawls, Rall, Ralls, Rawles	5.7	56	264							4			23	21	8
Rawson, Rauson	5.8	56	267	1	1	4	35	1	4	3			6		1
Ray, Rae, Raes, Raies, Rais, Raye, Rea, Reah, Reay, Reigh, Rey, Rhea, Rhey, Wray	5.3	337	1,444	7	8	7	43	8	26	28	60	27	23	73	27
Rayborn, Raban, Rabon, Raborn, Raiben, Raibon, Raiborne, Raybon, Raybourn, Rayburn	5.4	19	83								1		3	7	8
Raymond, Raiment, Raimond, Raimont, Raman, Rament, Ramon, Ramond, Ramont, Rayman, Rayment, Raymon, Raymong, Raymont, Reaman, Reyman, Reymond	5.5	187	847	7	5	10	62	2	61	33	2	3		1	1
Raynor, Rainer, Rainor, Raner, Ranor, Rayner, Raynour, Reighnear, Reighner, Reiner, Rener, Renier, Reynear, Reyner, Reynor, Rhainer, Rhener	5.3	72	312				2			43	10	5		7	5
Razor, Raiser, Raizer, Rajor, Raser, Rasor, Razar, Razer, Reasor	6.5	29	159	1	1	1					19		3	2	2
Reader, Reador, Reder, Redor, Reeder, Reider	6.7	57	326						2	6	26	11	3		9
Ream, Reames, Reams, Rean, Reem, Reeme, Rehm, Rheam, Rheams, Rheem, Rhem, Rheme, Riehm	5.2	57	242							1	34	4	5	6	7
Reardon, Rairden, Rarden, Raredan, Raredom, Reardan, Rearden	5.3	24	102	3					1		6	4	5	3	2
Reasoner, Reasner, Reasnor, Reesner, Reisner, Resioner, Resner	6.2	15	78			1				3	6		3	1	1
Reber, Reeber, Reiber, Rieber	7.1	18	109								17	1			....
Records, Reccord, Rechard, Reckard, Record, Reecord	5.3	23	98	4	2	2	6	2	2	1	1	2		1	....
Redding, Raddan, Radden, Readen, Reddan, Redden, Reddin, Reding	5.0	47	189		4		13		2		1	3	5	18	1
Redfield, Radfield	5.3	38	162			3	1		30	4					....
Redman, Radman, Readman, Reaidman, Redmon, Redmond	5.4	56	249	3	4	1	3			4	9	14	11	4	3
Reed, Read, Reade, Reads, Rede, Reede, Reid, Reide, Rhead, Ried	5.7	1,201	5,696	51	57	46	304	19	86	88	253	71	65	105	56
Reel, Real, Reels, Rheel, Riehl	5.5	21	95							1	8	5	4	5	4
Reese, Reace, Rease, Reece, Rees, Reess, Reesse, Reice, Reis, Reiss, Rese, Rhease, Ries	5.9	148	731				2		1	14	80	18	4	10	19
Reeser, Reecer, Reesa, Reesers, Reeses, Reesor, Reester, Rieser, Riester	5.3	23	99								20	1		1	1
Reeves, Reave, Reaves, Reavs, Reeve, Reevs, Reives, Reve, Reves, Rieves, Rives, Ryves	5.5	202	905	1		2	12		6	49	10	15	20	54	33
Regan, Ragan, Ragen, Ragin, Ragon, Ragons, Raygan, Raygen, Raygin, Reagan, Reagin, Reagon, Regin, Regins	5.4	54	235							1	8	5	9	22	9
Register, Regester, Registee, Rejester	5.8	25	119								5	4		14	2
Reiff, Reefs, Refe, Reife, Rieff	4.7	23	84								17		5	1	....

TABLE 111.—NOMENCLATURE, DEALING WITH NAMES REPRESENTED BY AT LEAST 100 WHITE PERSONS, BY STATES AND TERRITORIES, AT THE FIRST CENSUS: 1790—Continued.

NAME.	Average size of family.	TOTAL. Heads of families.	TOTAL. All other members.	Maine.	New Hampshire.	Vermont.	Massachusetts.	Rhode Island.	Connecticut.	New York.	Pennsylvania.	Maryland.	Virginia.	North Carolina.	South Carolina.
Remer, Reamer, Reemer, Reemor, Rehmer, Reimer, Rhemar, Riehmer, Riemer	5.4	28	124		1					1	26				
Remick, Reamich, Reamick, Remach, Remmeck, Remmick, Remmock, Rhemack	4.4	31	106	20	4	1	3				3			2	
Remington, Ramington, Reminton, Remmington, Remonton, Rennington, Rumington	5.6	90	416		1	8	20	35	16	5	1	1		2	1
Remsen, Remson	5.7	39	184						2	37					
Rex, Rix	6.2	33	171		1	1	3	1	4	2	15			4	2
Reynolds, Ranal, Ranel, Ranells, Ranels, Raunal, Raunalls, Raunel, Raunells, Raunels, Raunold, Raynold, Raynolds, Raynols, Regnolds, Renholds, Rennalds, Rennals, Rennells, Rennels, Rennolds, Renold, Renolds, Renols, Reynalds, Reynals, Reynold, Reynols, Reynull, Rownald, Rownalds, Rownals, Ruenold, Rynolds	5.9	483	2,388	4	5	17	23	67	54	118	46	39	39	40	31
Rhodes, Rhoades, Rhoads, Rhode, Rhods, Road, Roades, Roads, Rode, Rodes, Rohds	4.5	401	1,805	6	2	7	44	25	10	43	108	25	23	85	23
Rice, Ryce	5.4	657	2,910	16	31	59	222	28	68	48	52	23	44	41	25
Rich, Reich, Riche, Riech, Ritch, Ritche	5.8	194	933	10	2	16	75		17	21	20	3	1	23	6
Richards, Reichard, Reichart, Richard, Richardes, Ritchard	5.4	490	2,164	27	23	16	108	4	58	27	90	46	49	39	3
Richardson, Richardison, Richarson, Richason, Richenson, Richerson, Richeson, Richison, Richisson, Ritchardson, Ritchersan, Ritcheson	5.8	773	3,723	39	82	38	253	7	35	22	42	81	81	56	37
Richey, Richee, Richie, Richy, Ritchey, Ritchie, Ritchy	5.5	111	502	1	3	1	2			4	61	6	11	8	14
Richmond, Richman, Richmon	5.2	125	629	3		7	56	16	12	13	6	2	3	5	2
Rickart, Reakert, Ricard, Ricaud, Richar, Richart, Richhart, Rickard, Rickards, Rickert, Rickhart, Righart, Righhart, Righkart, Rishart, Ryegirt, Rygert, Ryhart, Rykert	6.1	53	269				4			14	25	3		6	1
Ricker, Riker, Rycker	5.8	90	436	35	20	2				27	3	2			1
Ricketts, Ricket, Ricketh, Rickets, Rickett, Rickitts	6.1	49	252	2						3	9	24	4	7	
Rickman, Rickmann, Rickmon, Ryckman	4.8	22	84					2		13	1		3	3	
Ricks, Rick, Ricke	6.0	26	130		2					2	3	1	2	16	
Riddick, Raduck, Readick, Reddeck, Reddick, Rederick, Redic, Redick, Redig, Rhedick, Riddich, Riddish, Ridditt, Rideck, Ridyck	5.6	68	310							1	10	2	20	35	
Riddle, Riddel, Riddell, Riddels, Riddles, Ridie	5.9	83	409		7	2	5			2	31	10	7	13	6
Ridenour, Redenhour, Redinor, Reidenhour, Reidenower, Ridenaur, Ridenhower, Ridonour, Roadaimour, Roadarmer, Roadenhour, Rudennaner	6.7	33	185							3	5	16	8	1	
Rider, Ruyder, Ryder, Wrider	5.6	181	833	4	5	12	78	1	8	50	13	2	2	3	3
Ridge, Ridges, Rige	6.2	19	99								12	4		3	
Ridgley, Ridgeley, Ridgely, Ridgly	7.7	34	228							1	2	31			
Ridgway, Regerway, Ridgaway, Ridgeway, Ridgwa, Rigiway	6.1	44	224				7			3	5	16	8	1	4
Ridley, Ridly	4.2	28	89	15		1	1			1	3	2	4		1
Riegel, Regal, Regel, Regil, Regle, Reichle, Reigel, Riechel, Riegle, Rigel, Riggell	5.8	21	101							3	17			1	
Rife, Riff, Riffe	6.3	17	90								9	3	3	1	1
Riffle, Rifle	6.2	19	99								9	3	5	2	
Rigby, Rigbay, Rigbey, Rigbie, Rigsbee, Rigsbey, Rigsby	4.7	34	127						1		7	9	1	16	
Rigdon, Rigden	6.1	18	91								5	10		2	1
Riggan, Rigan, Riggans, Riggen, Riggin, Rigging, Riggins	5.4	29	128							1		4	6	16	2
Riggs, Rigg, Rigs	5.3	113	488	11	1	1	10	1	13	6	15	11	12	29	3
Riley, Reighly, Reihlee, Reiley, Reilley, Reily, Reyley, Rhyley, Righley, Righly, Rileas, Rilee, Rileigh, Rilley, Rily, Ryla, Ryle, Ryley, Rylie, Ryly	5.0	170	687	1	1	2	3	2	25	13	38	27	13	26	19
Rine, Rein, Reine, Reines, Reins, Rhine, Righn, Rihne, Rines, Ryne, Rynes	6.1	64	329	10	5	1	1		1	5	21	2	1	17	
Rinehart, Rainhart, Raneheart, Reenhart, Reihart, Reinard, Reinhard, Reinhart, Rhinehart, Rhineheart, Rienhart, Rignhart, Rinard, Rinehard, Rinehast, Rineheart, Rinehot, Rinert, Rinhart, Rynehart, Rynhot	5.5	87	394							9	56	9	4	7	2
Ring, Ringe	6.1	55	281	8	6	1	6		8	6	8	2		10	
Ringgold, Ringold, Rinold	5.9	21	103							1	18		2		
Rinker	6.3	17	90								11		6		
Ripley, Riply	6.1	80	406	3	4	6	40		10	4	3		5	2	3
Rising	5.4	27	118			6	6		13	1			1		
Risley	6.3	42	222			2	6		29	4			1		
Rittenhouse, Ritenhouse	5.7	24	113								22	2			
Ritter, Reihtar, Righter, Riter, Rittar	5.7	82	384				5		2	14	47	8	3	3	
Rivers, River, Rivor	4.4	47	158	3						1	6	1	5	2	29
Roach, Roache, Roch, Roche	4.8	85	321		2	1	4		2	8	6	14	21	17	10
Roan, Roam, Roane, Rohn, Rone	4.6	40	145						1		20		7	9	3
Roath, Roth	5.5	30	135						17	1	12				
Robb, Rob, Robbe, Robbs, Robe, Robs	5.7	49	228				8		3	3	3	22	2	5	2
Robbins, Robbin, Robens, Robin, Robins, Robons	5.8	354	1,690	27	24	6	129	1	53	40	18	7	10	36	3
Roberts, Robard, Robards, Robarts, Robbard, Robbards, Robbarts, Robbert, Robberts, Roberds, Robert	5.5	826	3,693	37	67	29	43	9	98	57	154	60	83	109	80
Robertson, Reberson, Robartin, Robartson, Robason, Robbertson, Robbirson, Robbison, Roberson, Reberton, Robertrson, Robibison, Robirson, Robisan, Robison, Robistone	5.7	681	3,177	18	45	9	21		22	77	117	29	94	168	81
Robinson, Rebenson, Rhobbinson, Robanson, Robbinsan, Robenson, Robinsone, Robnson	5.7	823	3,829	45	52	52	129	22	68	61	117	76	107	53	41
Robuck, Rabuck, Robic, Roeback, Roebuck, Roorbach, Roorback, Rorbach, Roreback	4.8	26	98			1				7	4		5	2	7
Roby, Robbie, Robey, Robie	6.3	81	426	1	30		8			1	31	9		1	
Rock, Rocks	5.1	22	90				2	1	1	4	6	7	1		
Rockefeller	6.4	16	86							16					
Rockwell, Rockwel	5.7	101	477		2	7	8		65	17	2				
Rockwood	6.3	34	181		5		28					1			
Rodman, Roadman, Rodaman, Rodeman, Rodimon	5.5	28	125		1		1	5		10	8		1	1	1
Rodruck, Roderick, Roderock, Rodrick, Rodroch, Rodrock, Rodroke, Rodtrock	5.8	28	133								17	8	2		1
Rogers, Ridger, Rodger, Rodgers, Rogars, Roger, Roggers	5.6	1,059	4,916	49	49	37	197	29	141	162	72	37	57	148	81
Rohrer, Rorer, Rorrer	7.0	25	149								13	12			
Roles, Roals, Role, Roll, Rols	5.7	18	85		1				2		3	9	1	1	1
Rolph, Roef, Roff, Roffe, Rolf, Rolff	5.6	36	164	7	4		6			9	1	6	3		
Romine, Rohrman, Romain, Romaine, Roman, Romans, Romeyn, Romin, Rommon, Romnam, Romyne, Ronan, Ronian	5.9	28	136			1			2	12	8	1	3	1	
Rood, Roode, Roods, Rudd, Rudde, Rude	5.9	113	554	1	3	18	10		32	12	18	1	13	3	
Rook, Rooke, Rooks, Ruke	5.0	29	117	2			1			2	3	5		14	2
Roop, Roupe, Rouph, Rup, Rupe, Ruph, Rupp	5.6	32	146				1			1	29	1			
Roosa, Ruser, Rusha, Rusher	5.7	33	154							28	4			1	
Root, Rootes, Roots, Rute	6.2	214	1,116		4	20	63		78	20	19	4	4	1	1
Roper	4.8	42	158				6		1		2	2	12	13	6
Ropes, Rop, Rope, Ropp	5.5	25	113				16				8		1		
Rose	5.5	300	1,350	14		2	10	30	18	35	44	16	25	36	13
Rosecrans, Rosecrantz, Rosecrons, Rosegrants, Rosegrantz, Rosekranse, Rosekrons, Rosencrantz, Rosengrantz	6.0	26	130							17	7		2		
Roseter, Rositer, Rosseter, Rossetter, Rossetur, Rossiter	6.1	24	123			1	4		11	2	4	2			
Ross, Rosse	5.6	441	2,016	21	12	4	49	17	8	45	110	31	35	66	38
Rosser, Rochure, Roshere, Rosier, Rosir, Rosor, Rossor	4.8	27	103			3				1	2	3	5	9	4
Rossman, Roseman, Rosemond, Rosman, Rosmond, Rossmon	5.2	21	88				1			14	1			2	3
Rounds, Round, Rouns	6.2	49	255	5			4	16	14	10					

TABLE 111.—NOMENCLATURE, DEALING WITH NAMES REPRESENTED BY AT LEAST 100 WHITE PERSONS, BY STATES AND TERRITORIES, AT THE FIRST CENSUS: 1790—Continued.

NAME.	Average size of family.	TOTAL.		HEADS OF FAMILIES.											
		Heads of families.	All other members.	Maine.	New Hampshire.	Vermont.	Massachusetts.	Rhode Island.	Connecticut.	New York.	Pennsylvania.	Maryland.	Virginia.	North Carolina.	South Carolina.
Rountree, Roundtree	4.2	30	97										3	18	9
Rouse, Rouce, Rous, Rouss	5.0	53	214			2	2	2	3	15	8	7	1	10	3
Rowan, Rouan, Rowand, Rowans, Rowen, Rowens, Rowin, Rown, Rownd, Rownds	5.1	49	203		2		1		1	8	16	7	1	5	8
Rowe, Rhoe, Rhoes, Roe, Row, Rowes, Rows, Wroe	5.9	347	1,693	19	34	3	37	2	30	88	36	29	19	34	16
Rowell, Roul, Rowall, Rowel, Rowl, Rowles	6.1	84	428	4	40	2	11		4	1	2	3	5	5	7
Rowland, Rolain, Rolan, Roland, Rolands, Rolen, Rolin, Roling, Rolings, Rolins, Rollande, Rollands, Rowlands, Rowlin, Rowling, Rowlins	5.9	153	754		4	1	2	1	20	18	27	15	15	32	18
Rowley, Raulee, Rawle, Rawlee, Rawley, Rawly, Rowly, Royley	5.4	105	468	2		10	7		24	45	7	3	1	2	4
Roy, Roye	5.4	27	119	1						3	·2	3	8	3	7
Royall, Royal, Royally, Royals	5.3	35	149	1			1		1		1		24	3	4
Royce, Roirce, Rorse, Roys, Royse	5.5	30	134		6				15	2			3	4	
Royer, Roya	6.0	22	111						2		18				2
R Smith	5.7	22	103							22					
Rudolph, Rudulph	5.3	21	91								15	4	2		
Rudy, Ruday, Rudey	6.4	27	145								24	1			2
Rue, Rew, Rewes, Roo, Roux	5.2	30	125	1			2		1		10	3		11	2
Ruff, Rough, Roughf, Rought, Rugh	5.6	48	223	1			1		2	9	21	9		1	4
Rugg, Rug	5.5	40	179		7	15	16		1		1				
Ruggles, Rugles, Rugols	6.0	59	294			3	35		18	1	2				
Rule, Rools, Ruel, Ruhl, Rul, Rull	5.9	22	108						1		17	1	3		
Rulin, Ruland, Ruling, Rulong	5.0	20	80							19	1				
Rumsey	6.1	30	153			9			3	9	2	4	3		
Rundlett, Rundlet, Runlett	5.8	24	114		24										
Runkle, Runkel, Runkles	7.0	16	96							2	11	2	1		
Runnels, Runalds, Rundel, Rundell, Rundle, Rundles, Runells, Runels, Runnalds, Runnals, Runnel, Runnelds, Runneles, Runnell, Runnelle, Runnells, Runnills, Runnils, Runnold, Runnolds	5.5	160	727	11	19	9	15		19	46	4	6	2	22	7
Runyan, Runion, Runnion, Runnions, Runyen, Runyon	5.7	23	108							5	4		9	5	
Rush, Roush, Ruash, Ruask	5.6	111	508			3	4		2	2	57	5	18	8	12
Rushing, Rushen, Rusing	6.2	22	115								1			16	5
Russ, Rus, Russe, Russee, Rusue	5.8	43	206	4		2	2		5	5	4		2	16	3
Russell, Rusel, Russall, Russel, Russels, Russil, Russill, Russle, Russull, Rustle	5.7	719	3,410	22	44	26	205	9	81	65	70	27	52	66	52
Rust	5.6	71	324	1	7	8	25		8	5	3		8	6	
Ruth	6.4	30	162								13	5	2	9	1
Rutherford, Ritherford, Rotherford, Rutherfurd	4.9	36	140			2	2		5	10		6	8	3	
Rutledge, Routledge, Rutchledge, Rutledg, Rutlege	5.8	43	206						1			13	4	16	9
Rutter, Rutta, Rutu	6.2	57	295			1	2		1	30	16	5	2		
Ryal, Rial, Riale, Rials, Ryall, Ryals	4.7	39	146	3					2	5	2		22	5	
Ryan, Rian, Rion, Rions, Ryanes, Ryann, Ryans, Ryen, Ryend, Ryon, Ryond, Ryons	5.2	117	495	6	3	1	6		5	12	35	23	10	10	6
Sabin, Saban, Sabens, Sabine, Sabins, Saybins	6.3	74	395	1	2	14	17	6	24	10					
Sacket, Sackett	5.9	76	373			5	23		19	23	6				
Sadler, Saddler, Saidler	5.7	68	319			1	13		2	12	5	18	4	13	
Safford, Saford	5.3	60	257	6	7	14	17		9	6			1		
Sage, Sages	6.3	76	404	1		4	13		41	10	1	1	4		1
Sailor, Sahler, Sailer, Sailors, Saiolor, Saler, Saller, Salor, Saylor, Saylors	5.9	45	221					1		4	21	9	2	1	7
St. John, Saint John, St. Johns	5.8	73	354			4	2		43	20			1		3
Salisbury, Sailsberry, Salesbury, Salisberry, Salisburry, Salsberry, Salsbery, Salsbury, Salusbury, Saulsberry, Saulsbury	6.0	113	562	3		16	13	36	2	20	6	7	5	2	3
Salmon, Sallmon, Salman, Salmond, Salmonds, Salmons, Salomon	6.6	47	262	1			4		3	9	4	3	14	5	4
Salter, Saltar, Salters, Saltzer, Salzer, Saulter	5.5	57	255	1	8	1	11		3	3	5	1	2	13	9
Sammis, Samis, Samnis	5.5	28	125							27					1
Sammons, Sammon, Sammonds, Samons	4.8	24	91							8	1		10	3	2
Sample, Sampel, Semple	6.9	48	284						2	36		3	2	4	
Samson, Sampson	5.0	170	682	17	3	10	94		3	7	10	8	10	4	4
Sanborn, Samborn, Sambourn, Samburn, Samburne, Sanbon, Sanbourn, Sanbourne, Sanburn, Sandborn, Sandbourn	5.5	219	987	28	179	7	1		1	3					
Sanders, Sander, Saunders, Sonders	5.6	518	2,372	6	35	10	57	50	28	14	29	30	60	139	60
Sanderson, Sandorson, Saunderson	6.2	104	543	2	6	12	44		1		15	3	5	16	
Sands, Sand, Sandes, Sandt, Sann, Sans, Sant, Sants	6.0	82	407	8			3	4		36	20	6	3	1	1
Sanford, Sandford, Sandfort, Sandiford, Santford	5.7	235	1,102	3		11	23	21	101	43	3	1	17	5	7
Sanger, Sangar, Sangor, Sangster, Senger	6.2	34	176		5	1	13		10	1	2		2		
Sargent, Sargant, Sargeant, Sarjant, Sarjants, Sarjent, Seargeant, Seargent, Sergant, Sergants, Sergeant, Sergeants, Sergent, Sergents, Serjant, Serjeant, Serjeants, Serjents	5.8	253	1,210	22	86	16	97		3	6	8	7	1	6	1
Sartwell, Sarltell, Sartel, Sartell, Sartle, Sartwell, Sawtel, Sawtell, Sawtwel, Sawtwell	5.3	53	229	7	10	11	24			1					
Saterfield, Sarterfield, Satterfield, Saturfield	4.6	24	86									6		12	6
Satterly, Saterley, Saterly, Satille, Sattaly, Satterlee, Sattille, Saturlee, Saturly, Settely, Setterlia	6.5	29	159			1	1		3	19	4		1		
Saul, Sall, Salle, Salls, Sauls	6.1	33	167			2	1			6	9		2	9	4
Savage, Savidge	5.3	176	755	16	7	9	18		26	16	13	6	25	25	15
Savery, Savory	6.7	27	154		2		19			4	2				
Sawin, Sawen, Sawing, Sawings, Sawins, Sawying	5.2	28	118				23		2	1	1				1
Sawyer, Sawyear, Sawyers, Sawyes	5.8	395	1,880	74	66	27	107	6	16	6	11	2	1	71	8
Sayles, Saile, Sails, Sale, Sales, Sayle	6.5	60	328		1	1	3	30	1	10	1		7	4	2
Sayre, Sayer, Sayers, Sayrs, Seayres, Seyer	6.9	40	237			1		5		1	27	4		1	1
Scales, Scale, Sceales, Schales	5.1	20	81	2	6		3			2			1	6	
Scarborough, Scarber, Scarbor, Scarbro, Scarbro, Scarbrough, Scarbrow, Scharborough	5.2	65	276				1		6		5	10	6	31	6
Schermerhorn, Scamehorn, Scermehorn, Schermerham, Schermerhorne	5.9	62	306						1	60	1				
Schnavely, Schnabely, Schnablely, Shavely	7.2	14	87									13	1		
Schoonmaker, Schonmaker	6.2	45	235							45					
Schrack, Shrack, Shrake, Shreck, Shrock	6.9	15	89								13	1	1		
Schuyler	5.4	22	97							22					
Scofield, Schofield, Scoffield, Scotfield	5.5	112	509	4	2	2			57	31	4	1	9	2	
Scott, Scoctt, Scot	5.5	791	3,520	12	30	30	71	18	69	71	181	69	95	88	57
Scouten, Scatton, Scotten, Scotton, Scoutan, Scouton	5.0	23	92				2			16	3		2		
Scovil, Schovel, Scoval, Scovel, Scovell, Scovile, Scovill	4.5	82	371		2	11	7	1	54	6	1				
Scranton, Scrinton	5.4	27	120				4	3	14	3	1		1	1	
Scribner	5.9	44	217	9	9	1	2		13	10					
Scrivner, Scrivener, Scrivenor	8.5	18	135		7					1		7	2	1	
Scruggs, Scrug, Scrughs, Scrugs	5.2	18	104									22	2	1	
Scudder, Skudder	4.5	33	114						18			4			
Seabury, Seaberry, Seaburry, Sebery, Seberrey	6.1	22	112	2			8	1	2	18					
Seal, Seale, Seales, Seals, Seele, Sele, Seles	5.3	37	160	3			3			1	5	3	6	10	6
Seaman, Seamman, Seamonds, Seamons, Sehman, Seighman, Seman, Semans, Semon	5.2	89	370	4		6			2	65	10		1	1	

TABLE 111.—NOMENCLATURE, DEALING WITH NAMES REPRESENTED BY AT LEAST 100 WHITE PERSONS, BY STATES AND TERRITORIES, AT THE FIRST CENSUS: 1790—Continued.

NAME.	Average size of family.	TOTAL.		HEADS OF FAMILIES.											
		Heads of families.	All other members.	Maine.	New Hampshire.	Vermont.	Massachusetts.	Rhode Island.	Connecticut.	New York.	Pennsylvania.	Maryland.	Virginia.	North Carolina.	South Carolina.
Searing	6.6	16	89							11	5				
Searls, Sarle, Sarles, Sarls, Searl, Searle, Searles, Serl, Serle, Serles, Serls, Surles, Surls	5.7	131	615	1	15	9	43	7	4	34	6	1		10	1
Sears, Sear, Seares, Seeres, Seers, Seirs	5.7	162	756	3		7	63	3	24	29	4	3	12	14	
Seat, Seates, Seats, Seets, Seits, Seitz, Siets	5.6	31	144	1						3	12	2	6	7	
Seawell, Seavil, Seval, Sevell, Sevills, Sevils, Siveal, Sivel, Sivils	4.9	22	85		1				1		2		7	10	1
Seay, Sea, Seas, See, Sehy	6.1	52	268							9	2	3	30	3	5
Sebree, Sebry	6.4	19	103	1		1				1			16		
Secord, Seacer, Secars, Secaur, Secor, Seeker	7.1	30	184	1						28	1				
Secrist, Sacrist, Seacrist, Secrest, Secrets, Secriss, Seechrist, Seegrist, Segrist, Seigrist, Sekris	6.4	22	119	1							12			6	3
Sedgwick, Sedgewick, Sedgick, Sedgwith, Sedvick, Sedwick	6.8	25	145					5	8	4	2	5	1		
Seely, Sealey, Sealy, Seeley, Seelly, Seelye, Seiley, Seley, Sely, Siely	5.7	134	636			7	4		46	63	3			5	6
Segar, Ceger, Seagar, Seager, Seagers, Seegar, Seegars, Seeger, Seegers, Segars, Seger, Seiger, Seyger	5.9	64	312	4		2	8	1	9	13	6	7	9	3	2
Selby, Selbe, Selbey	5.7	66	307					1	5			50	1	8	1
Selden, Seldin	4.6	26	93			3	7		11				5		
Self	5.5	32	144								1	1	17	11	2
Sell, Sells	6.0	31	154							4	18	2	1	6	
Selleck, Selick, Selig, Sellick, Silik, Sillick, Sillock	5.6	43	199				3		29	8	3				
Sellers, Cellars, Sellar, Sellars, Seller	5.8	116	556	3		2			1	1	50	12	4	28	15
Selman, Sellman, Selmonds, Selsman	5.2	22	93				4				1	16			
Senter, Center, Centre, Sentor	5.9	36	175		17	2	3	2	3	1				4	4
Sessions, Session, Sessoms, Sesson, Sessons, Sessums	6.3	62	331		1	5	3	3	15					23	12
Sever, Ceever, Cever, Seaver, Seavers, Seever, Seevers, Seveir, Severe, Severs	5.5	61	274	1	7	4	28	1			14	2	3	1	
Severance, Severnce	5.4	45	196	2	18	2	20				1				2
Sevey, Seavey, Seavy, Seve, Sevea, Sevoy, Sevy	5.3	67	288	24	42		1								
Sewall, Sewal, Sewel, Sewell, Sewill, Sowel, Sowell, Suel	5.4	95	417	25	3				6	2	5	29	3	21	1
Seward, Seaward, Seawood, Sewards, Seyward	5.0	61	241	1	11	1	13		12	7	2	4	7	2	1
Sexton, Saxton, Sexten, Sixton	5.6	77	355		1		10	12	17	13	5	2	2	14	1
Seymour, Saymore, Saymour, Seamer, Seamers, Seamore, Seamour, Seemore, Semour, Seymor, Seymore	4.9	128	500	1		2	6		67	25	1	3	12	10	1
Shackleford, Shackelford, Shackford, Shacklefoot, Shakford, Shaklefoot	6.0	49	244	4	6		2	1					22	7	7
Shade, Schade, Schaid, Shead	4.6	36	129	2		2	4			1	21	5	1		
Shaler, Shallor, Shavler	6.7	18	102				1		14		3				
Shank, Schanck, Schenck, Schenk, Schink, Shanck, Shanks, Shenck, Shenk	6.0	112	565	2						22	54	19	11	3	1
Shannon, Shanam, Shanan, Shannan, Shanon, Shennon, Shenon, Shinnan	6.0	86	433	1	14		2			4	45	4	4	6	6
Shapley, Shaplaw, Shapleigh	5.2	23	97	6	9		1		2	1	2			1	1
Sharp, Sharpe, Sherp	5.5	211	939		1	6	5			18	43	63	13	33	11
Sharpless, Sharples	8.5	24	179							1	20	1	1	1	
Shattuck, Shatock, Shattock, Shatuck	5.8	84	402	2	19	3	55		4	1					
Shaver, Schaeffer, Schaffer, Schaver, Scheffer, Schiffer, Shafer, Shaffer, Shavor, Shavours, Shavrer, Sheafer, Sheaffer, Sheaver, Sheavor, Shefer, Sheffer, Sheffor	5.8	368	1,774	1						73	212	44	25	9	4
Shaw, Shawe, Shaws	5.7	573	2,677	40	44	26	166	16	12	63	87	37	6	61	15
Shay, Shays, Shea, Shey	5.0	27	107	2	1	2	1				8	12	1		
Sheafe, Shaaf, Shaff, Shaft, Sharff, Sheaf, Sheafe, Sheaff	6.9	21	124	2	7		1				2	7	2		
Shearer, Scherer, Shara, Sharaw, Sharer, Sharier, Sharrer, Sheerer, Sheerir, Sherer, Sherra, Sherrar, Sherrer, Shierer, Shirer, Shirow, Shirror	6.0	107	532		4	1	5			6	74	4	4	4	5
Shearin, Sharan, Sharran, Sharron, Shearon, Sherin, Sheroon, Shiron	5.8	23	111				1				7	1		13	1
Shed, Shedd, Sheed	5.4	47	209		7	1	31				3				5
Sheer, Share, Shares, Shear, Shears, Sheers, Sheirs, Shier, Shiers	6.5	34	187				2		1	21	2	3	2	2	
Sheets, Sheats, Sheet, Sheetz, Shete	5.8	60	286				3		1		33	9	9	4	1
Sheffield, Sheficld, Shiffields, Shuffield	5.9	48	236			2	4	16	12	5			4	5	
Sheldon, Schelton, Shelden, Sheldin, Shelding, Sheldone, Sheldorn, Sheldron, Shelton	6.1	325	1,663	4	4	28	54	43	62	46	5	4	52	21	2
Shell	6.1	39	198							11	18	1	1	8	
Shelly, Schalley, Schelly, Shalley, Shally, Shealy, Sheeley, Sheely, Sheley, Shelley	5.4	89	392			1			6	11	13	35	4	5	9
Shepardson, Sheperdson, Shephensen, Shepherdson, Sheppardson, Shepperdson, Shepperson, Shipperson	5.4	27	118		1	13	8	2	2				1		
Shepherd, Schiperd, Shapard, Shappart, Shappert, Shepard, Sheperd, Shephard, Shephert, Sheppad, Sheppard, Shepperd, Shipard, Shiphard, Shipperd	5.6	429	1,979	10	35	22	66	2	88	41	28	21	35	65	16
Sherburne, Sherbone, Sherborn, Sherbourn, Sherbourne, Sherburn	5.4	46	204	5	33		4	1	1	2					
Sheredine, Sharadine, Sharadon, Shardon, Sheardon, Sheradin, Sherden, Sherdon, Sheredan, Sheridine, Sheridan, Sherriden, Shoridine	5.0	20	80				2	1	1	1	8	4		2	1
Sherk, Sherch, Sherck, Sherks, Shirk, Shirke, Shurk	7.4	19	121								19				
Sherman, Shareman, Sharman, Sharmon, Shearman, Sheerman, Shereman, Shermin, Shermon, Shermond, Shireman, Shirman, Shurman	5.9	424	2,079	7	5	29	130	68	65	68	17	9	20	6	
Sherrill, Sheiral, Sherrel, Sherrell, Sherril	8.1	18	128				2				2		1	12	1
Sherrod, Shard, Shared, Shered, Sheried, Sherod, Sherrad, Sherrads	6.2	20	104							1	3	1	1	11	3
Sherwin, Schirvin, Shervin, Shirvin	6.0	20	99	1		3							3	2	8
Sherwood, Shearwood, Sheerwood, Sherewood, Sherwod	5.5	187	839			2	9		75	64	1	24	5	5	2
Shields, Sheal, Shealds, Sheals, Sheilds, Sheiltz, Shelds, Shield	6.1	95	489			1		1	1	2	6	30	16	20	9
Shiffer, Shefert, Shefirt, Shefor, Shieffer, Shifer, Shifert, Shuffart, Shuffer, Shuford	4.7	24	89						2		19			3	
Shilling, Shillings	5.2	30	126	8						2	8	9			3
Shipley, Shepley, Shippley	6.3	45	240			2				2	7	25	7		
Shipman	6.3	44	231			7	1		19	5	4			8	
Shipp, Ship, Shipe, Shipes, Shippe, Ships	5.4	36	159							2	6		16	8	4
Shippey, Shipee, Shippay, Shippee, Shippy	5.6	28	129			1	8	14		4					1
Shirley, Sherley, Sherly, Shierly, Shirely, Shirly, Shurley	6.3	41	216	1	11		2				6	3	5	1	12
Shively, Sheibley, Shibley, Shiebley, Shively	6.2	18	93							1	13	4			
Shock, Shoch	5.5	28	127								22	3	3		
Shockley, Shockly, Shokey, Shokley	5.0	25	101						1			13	4		6
Shoemaker, Schoomaker, Shoamaker, Shoemake, Shomaker, Shoumaker, Shuemake, Shumake, Shumaker	5.7	156	726					1		20	108	5	11	6	5
Sholl, Shoals, Sholds, Sholes, Shoulds, Shoules, Shouls	5.5	40	178			5		2	1	7	10	14			
Shook, Shoakes, Shuke, Skok	6.0	40	208							6	14	1	16	2	1
Shores, Shoare, Shoars, Shore, Showar, Showars, Shower, Showers, Showrs	5.0	47	187	2		4	3			2	15	7	5	9	
Short, Shorte, Shorts	6.0	115	570			2	20	8	4	8	17	6	23	24	3
Shoup, Shoap, Shoop, Shop, Shope, Shopf	6.3	25	132							1	13	6		4	1
Shove	6.4	17	92				12		4	1					
Shrader, Schrader, Schreder, Schrider, Schroder, Schroeder, Shradur, Shrawder, Shreader, Shreder, Shroeder	5.0	29	117							1	21	5		1	1
Shreiner, Schreiner, Schriener, Shrener, Shriener, Shriner, Shrinner, Sriner	5.8	24	115						1						
Shriver, Schreiver, Schriver, Screver, Scriver, Shreiber, Shreiver, Sriver	5.6	59	269								22	26	9	1	1
Shuler, Shoeler	5.6	24	111								4	13		2	5
Shull, Shul	5.9	21	102								13	5		2	1
Shultz, Schuls, Schultz, Schulz, Sholt, Sholts, Sholtz, Sholz, Shoults, Shoultz, Shualts, Thuls, Shult, Shults, Shulz	5.9	103	507						1	28	56	8	4	5	1
Shuman, Shoeman, Shooman, Shouman, Showman, Shueman, Shumon	5.2	31	131	2					1		16	5	2	4	1

TABLE 111.—NOMENCLATURE, DEALING WITH NAMES REPRESENTED BY AT LEAST 100 WHITE PERSONS, BY STATES AND TERRITORIES AT THE FIRST CENSUS: 1790—Continued.

NAME.	Average size of family.	TOTAL. Heads of families.	All other members.	Maine.	New Hampshire.	Vermont.	Massachusetts.	Rhode Island.	Connecticut.	New York.	Pennsylvania.	Maryland.	Virginia.	North Carolina.	South Carolina.
Shumway	6.6	31	174			5	23		2	1					
Shurtliff, Shircleff, Shirtlef, Shirtleff, Shirtliff, Shirtliffs, Shirtlift, Shurtlif, Shurtlift	5.5	41	184	3	6	2	23		3	3		1			
Shurts, Sherts, Shertz, Shirt, Shirts, Shirtz, Shurt	5.4	28	124							15	12	1			
Shuster, Schuster, Shoester	5.2	21	88					1	2	16	2				
Shute, Schut, Schuts, Schutt, Shoot, Shoote, Shoots, Shootz, Shoutz, Shutes, Shuts, Shutt, Shutts, Shutz	5.6	92	424	7	10	2	11		1	40	9	1		6	5
Sibley, Cibley, Sibly	6.0	68	337	1	4		44		6	2	2	1	4	4	
Sickler, Sicklor, Sicler, Siklair, Syclear	6.0	17	85							7	9				1
Sickles, Sickels, Sickle, Sicles	5.7	39	184				1			24	10			3	1
Sidwell, Seidel, Seidle, Seydel, Sidal, Siddle, Sidell, Sidle, Sydle	4.8	32	121				1			2	19	6	1	2	1
Sigler, Seagler, Segaler, Segler, Siegler, Sighler, Siglar, Sigleer	6.5	24	133								15	1	1	3	4
Sikes, Sykes	5.3	102	435		1	9	13		9	5	2		22	40	1
Sill, Sile, Siles, Sills, Syles, Syll	5.1	64	262						21	10	25	2		4	2
Silliman, Sileman, Silemon, Siliman, Sillaman, Sillimon, Silloman	5.1	29	120						19	1	8		1		
Silsby, Silsbe, Sillsbie, Silsbe, Silsbee, Silsbey	5.9	22	108		7		7		3	2	3				
Silver, Siliver, Silvers	5.4	34	150		12		10			1	6	3		2	
Silvester, Sylvester	5.4	107	467	22	3	8	50	4		2	1	13	2		2
Simmerman, Cimermin, Simerman, Simermon, Simmermon	5.3	32	138							3	16	8		5	
Simmons, Cimmins, Simmans, Simmens, Simmins, Simmon, Simmond, Simmonds, Sinmons, Symmonds, Symmons	5.6	436	1,984	3	7	10	58	54	15	73	19	49	36	86	26
Simons, Ciman, Seimon, Siman, Simands, Simen, Simon, Simond, Simonds, Symon, Symond, Symonds, Symons	5.6	311	1,440	14	26	17	92		39	23	22	1	14	43	20
Simonson	6.8	21	121							19	2				
Simonton, Simenton, Simington, Symenton	5.9	31	152	12						2	10	1		6	
Simpson, Cempsen, Simeson, Simison, Simson, Sympson	5.4	371	1,638	38	27	2	14	3		37	55	40	48	65	42
Sims, Semmes, Sim, Simes, Simm, Simmes, Simms, Sym, Syme, Symes, Symmes, Symms, Syms	5.9	215	1,043	2	4	1	21	4	2	6	14	40	43	40	38
Sinclair, Saintclair, St. Clair, St. Clear, St. Clere, Senkler, Sinckler, Sinclar, Sinclare, Sinclares, Sinclear, Sincleer, Sincler, Sinclere, Sinclier, Singclair, Sinklar, Sinklear, Sinkler	5.1	97	399	5	21	4	5			7	20	14	3	9	9
Singer, Singars	5.6	31	144			1				2	24	3	1		
Singletary, Singeltary, Singletarry, Singleterry	5.2	25	105				1							16	8
Singleton, Singellton, Singelton, Singeltong, Singlton, Sinkleton	5.7	65	307		1		4				3	4	13	12	28
Sink, Sinck, Sinks	5.9	21	103								10	2	6	3	
Sipe, Seip, Seipe, Sipes, Sipps, Sips, Sype, Sypes, Syps	6.3	24	128								19	2		3	
Sisson, Scison, Scisson, Sisam, Sisem, Sison, Sissen, Sissom	6.0	87	438				20	35	4	10	4	1	7		6
Skelton, Skilton	5.5	26	117				5		2		9		3	1	6
Skidmore, Schedmore, Schidmore, Scidmore, Scudmore, Shidmore, Skedmore, Skidmer	5.7	43	204	1			2		5	23	1		9	2	
Skiff, Sciff, Skeff, Skiffe, Skift	6.3	18	95			1	7		6	3				1	
Skillings, Sceling, Skellen, Skelling, Skillen, Skillens, Skillern, Skillin, Skilling, Skillins	5.7	21	98	7			6				6			1	1
Skinner, Skiner, Skinnr	5.5	234	1,048	5	9	12	33		67	35	9	27	10	24	3
Skipper, Sciper, Seipper, Skipperd	5.9	22	107							1				10	11
Slack, Sleck	6.9	40	236	1	1	1	5	4	5	5	16	2			
Slade, Slades, Slaid, Slead	5.6	76	350		5	3	21		2	2		8	6	27	2
Slagle, Slagel, Slegel	6.0	20	103								11	2	3	1	
Slater, Sclater, Shlater, Slader, Slator, Slatter, Slayter, Slaytor, Sleater, Sleighter, Sleyhter	6.0	64	317		2	3	2		10	9	11	8	11	7	1
Slaughter, Slauter, Slauwter, Slawter	5.4	73	318			1	5	3	2	6	15	10	16	15	
Slawson, Slason, Slausen, Slauson, Slosson	6.2	38	196			1	3		13	20					1
Slayton, Slaten, Slaton, Slatten, Slayden, Sletten	6.3	25	133			3	6				3		9	1	3
Sleeper	5.7	42	198	1	35	2	1			3					
Sleght, Slate, Slates, Slats, Sleight	6.3	42	221			1	7		2	25	1	1	5		
Sloan, Sloane, Slon, Slone, Sloon, Slowan, Slown	5.8	108	520		6	1	14		5	13	29	2	4	26	8
Slocum, Sloakum, Slocom, Slocomb, Slocome, Slocumb, Slokum	6.3	80	425			4	21	32	1	13	3	3		3	
Sluyter, Slighter, Sliter, Slyter	5.8	24	115							21	1	1	1		
Sly, Schley, Sligh, Slye	6.2	33	172		2	5	1	2	2	6	2	7	3		3
Small, Smals, Smalts, Smaltz, Smalz, Smawl	5.6	139	640	44	11		22		1	5	15	9	4	25	3
Smalley, Smaley, Smally, Smawley, Smayley	5.1	47	195	7		10	9		3	7	4		2	4	1
Smallwood, Swallwood	4.6	43	154								7	23	7	5	1
Smart	5.3	60	260	6	24				2		3	4	1	13	7
Smead, Smedes, Smedis, Smee, Smeed	6.6	27	151		3	6	8			8			2		
Smedley, Smeadley, Smedly	6.1	23	118			1	4		3		13	1	1		
Smiley, Smilely, Smilie, Smilley, Smilly, Smily, Smyley	5.9	46	224	5	3	2	3			5	19	1	1	4	3
Smith, Schmidt, Shmit, Smidth, Smit, Smithe, Smitt, Smitz, Smyth	5.6	5,932	27,313	193	366	257	1,028	174	767	383	838	396	425	725	380
Smither, Smithers	6.9	15	89								4		7	2	2
Smock, Smoke, Smook	4.9	29	112								13	3	2	2	4
Smoot, Smutz	5.3	36	154									31	4	1	
Snead, Snede, Sneed	4.9	45	176								5	11	25		4
Snell, Schnell, Shnelle	5.9	117	574	4	5	2	38	6	2	15	10	9	4	14	8
Snipes, Snipe, Snips	5.4	19	84	1									1	11	6
Snively, Shnively, Sneveley, Snevely, Snivley	7.8	17	115								17				
Snodgrass, Snodgres, Snodgress, Snudgrass	6.7	23	130								22		1		
Snook, Snoke, Snouk, Snuke	6.0	19	95							13	2	4			
Snow, Snows	5.8	326	1,557	35	20	11	179	10	29	8	2	1	14	14	3
Snowden, Snoden, Snodon, Snoton	4.7	40	148				1				15	6		11	7
Snyder, Schneider, Schnider, Schnidor, Schnieder, Schnyder, Schnydore, Shneider, Shneydor, Shnider, Shnyder, Sneider, Sneyder, Snider, Snidere, Snydor	6.0	517	2,564			3				120	313	40	16	15	10
Solomon, Salamon, Solemons, Solmon, Soloman, Solomans, Solomons	5.5	31	141							8	4	2	4	8	5
Soper, Soaper	5.7	65	304	4	2	14	10		4	15		13	3		
Sorrell, Sarrell, Sorell, Sorrel, Sorrels, Sorrils	5.7	18	85							2	1		1	14	
Souder, Sooter, Sootor, Souders, Souter	6.6	37	207		1		6				25	2	2		1
Soule, Soal, Soale, Solds, Sole, Soles, Soll, Soul, Souls, Sowle	5.6	115	526	20	1	5	45	5	1	23	2	1	5	5	2
South, Soutch	6.6	16	89								5	3	1	2	2
Southerland, Sotherlin, Sotherline, Southerlin, Southerling, Southorlin, Surtherland, Sutherland	6.4	100	536			6	1		1	35	8	4	19	22	4
Southern, Sothoron, Southen	5.4	22	96						1		1	10	2	5	3
Southward, Southard, Southwark	5.8	59	281	3	1	7	3		14	27	1		1	2	
Southwick, Southwic	5.3	38	163			2	22	7		7					
Southworth	6.5	46	252	1	1		32	2	5	5					
Soward, Saward, Sayards, Sayward, Sowards, Sowart	5.1	28	114	12			9				2	1	3	1	
Sowers, Sauer, Saur, Souer, Sour, Sours, Sower, Sowrs	5.3	44	191						1	4	23	6	8	2	
Spafford, Spafard, Spofford	6.1	67	343	3	9	18	26		11						
Spain, Spane	6.8	16	93										5	11	
Spalding, Spaldan, Spalden, Spaldin, Spaldon, Spaldwin, Spaulding, Spolden, Spoldin	5.6	280	1,294	19	49	29	82	3	45	18	4	29			2
Spangler, Spengler	6.2	42	217								38	2	2		
Sparhawk, Sparahauk, Sparowhawk	5.5	21	95		6	2	12				1				
Sparks, Sparkes, Spearks	5.8	97	470	2		2	2	1	8	6	13	24	13	15	11
Sparrow	6.2	35	183	2			8		2		2	6	9	6	

TABLE **111.**—NOMENCLATURE, DEALING WITH NAMES REPRESENTED BY AT LEAST 100 WHITE PERSONS, BY STATES AND TERRITORIES, AT THE FIRST CENSUS: 1790—Continued.

NAME.	Average size of family.	TOTAL.		HEADS OF FAMILIES.											
		Heads of families.	All other members.	Maine.	New Hampshire.	Vermont.	Massachusetts.	Rhode Island.	Connecticut.	New York.	Pennsylvania.	Maryland.	Virginia.	North Carolina.	South Carolina.
Spatz, Spade, Spades, Spaght, Spaight, Spates	5.0	27	108							1	23	1	1	1	
Speaks, Speak, Speake, Speeks	5.5	19	85								7	2	8		2
Spears, Spear, Speare, Speares, Speer, Speers, Speir, Speirs, Spiears, Spier, Spiers, Spires	5.7	190	890	9	7	15	42	4	4	8	33	6	14	31	17
Spelman, Spealman, Speelman, Speilman, Spellman	5.6	25	116			1	11	1	3		2	3	4		
Spence	5.3	70	302		1				3	1	13	7	2	30	13
Spencer, Spenscer, Spenser, Spensor, Spincer	6.0	449	2,227	15	15	25	19	43	147	68	30	15	29	31	12
Sperry, Speerry, Sperey	5.8	72	349		2	4	5		54	1		1	5		
Spicer, Spicar, Spiser	5.5	47	2:3		2	3	2		15	3	3	11	2	6	
Spight, Speight, Spights	6.2	19	99											17	2
Spikeman, Speakman, Speekman, Spekman, Spickman	6.4	25	136							1	21				3
Spink, Spinck, Spinks, Spynk	6.2	31	160			3	1	12	2	4		1	3	5	
Spinney, Spinny	5.5	21	95	17	2		2								
Spivey, Spiva, Spive, Spivy	5.5	44	198								1		10	33	
Spooner	5.9	72	352		2	8	40	8	7	3	2		3		
Spoor, Spoar, Spoore, Spore	6.4	29	158			3	4			18	1		3		
Sprague, Sprage, Spraig, Sprauge, Spreague	5.8	242	1,163	16	13	18	92	38	14	48	3				
Sprigg, Sprggs, Sprig, Spriggs	6.0	21	104			1	1		1	4	10	2	1	1
Spring, Springs	5.9	61	298	5	3	1	17		7	8	4		3	9	4
Springer, Spranger	5.3	83	359	18	2		1	7	1	13	26	8		3	4
Springsteel	5.0	20	80							20					
Sproul, Spraul, Sprawls, Sprole, Sproull, Sprouls, Sprowl, Sprowls	5.9	22	108	7						2	9	1		1	2
Spruil, Spruell, Spruril	6.0	31	154											29	2
Spur, Spuir	5.6	18	83				2			1				15	
Spurling, Sparlin, Sparling, Spurlin	7.9	17	117	2	1	1	1			3		1	3	5	
Squire, Squair, Squeer, Squier, Squiers, Squires, Squirres, Squre	5.4	142	625		1	27	15		53	28	1	3	3	10	1
Staats, State, States, Stats, Statt, Statts, Stauts	5.7	45	210			1	1	1	1	21	14	1	5		
Stackhouse	5.6	35	162			1			1	1	27		3		2
Stacy, Stacey, Stacia, Stasey, Staycy	5.3	73	316	9	2	11	34	1	2	2	2	2	3	4	1
Stafford	5.7	104	493		3	16	2	19	2	10	2	7	5	26	12
Stagg, Stag, Stage, Staggs, Stags	5.3	19	81							8	4		4		3
Staggers, Stager, Stagers, Staggar, Staggart, Stagger, Stayger, Steger, Stegher, Steiger	6.3	22	117							2	14		3		3
Staley, Stally, Staly, Stehly	6.5	31	171							10	8	9		4	
Stall, Staal, Staals, Stahl, Stal, Stale, Stales, Stalls	6.4	58	314	2				1	1	16	31	4		3	
Stallings, Stalings, Stallens, Stallins	5.6	42	193								6	7	27	2
Stallions, Stallians, Stallion, Stallons	5.7	20	93								2	2	15	1
Standish, Standage, Stannish	5.3	38	164	2		1	16		9	4	1	1	1		3
Stanfield, Standfield, Stanfild, Stanfill, Stondfield	6.3	26	139								3	8	12	3
Stanford, Standerford, Standford, Standiford, Staniford, Stanniford	4.7	55	203	7	4		10		1	5	3	10		11	4
Stanley, Standley, Standly, Stanlay, Stanly	5.8	241	1,146	23	18	10	36	1	46	3	12	5	13	58	16
Stannard, Stanard, Standard, Standart, Stannert, Stanord, Stonnard	5.6	37	169			6	5		18	3	1		1		3
Stansbury, Stanburry, Stanbury, Stansbery	6.2	47	243					1	1	5	3	32		4	1
Stanton, Stantown, Staunton	5.9	176	864	4	9	14	14	18	51	30	5	4		25	2
Stanwood	5.5	37	165	8	1		27						1		
Staples, Stapels, Staple, Stapole	5.8	117	567	57	2	4	20	6	10	6	1	1	9	1
Starboard, Starberd, Starbird, Starbord	5.7	18	84	12	4						1			1
Starbuck, Starbrick	6.8	19	111				13			3			3	
Staring, Stauring	6.8	19	110							19				
Stark, Starck, Starke, Starkes, Starks, Steark	5.4	88	382		14	9	7		12	10	9	8	10	2	7
Starkey, Starky	5.0	37	148		4		5		5		7	6	4	6	
Starkweather, Stackweather, Starkwether, Stearkweather	5.7	34	159			1	6		16	6					5
Starling, Starlin	6.1	36	182	3						14		2		1	14	2
Starns, Starn, Starnes	5.3	19	82	1		1	4		1		3			5	4
Starr, Star, Starrs, Stars	6.2	142	734			3	8		79	9	35	2	1	4	1
Staton, Staten, Statten, Statton, Stattons, Stayton	5.7	28	131		1		2				6	1	7	9	2
Stauffer, Staufer, Stofer, Stoffer, Stopher, Stophor, Stoufer, Stouffer, Stoupher, Stowfer	6.2	67	349								65	1		1	
Steaman, Stayman, Steiman, Steman, Stemane, Stemon	6.7	16	91								15				1
Stearns, Stearn, Stearnes, Stern, Sterne, Sternes, Sterns	5.6	189	876	4	28	23	101	1	9	1	10	1	3	1	7
Stebbins, Stebbens, Stebbin, Stebens, Stebins, Stibbins	6.3	105	558		5	12	63		19	6				
Stedman, Steadman, Stedmon, Steedman, Steedmon	6.0	67	334	1	2	4	15	13	20	1	2			2	7
Steel, Steal, Steale, Steals, Steele, Steell, Steil, Stell, Stells	5.6	290	1,343	7	20	9	19	1	46	11	96	24	12	18	27
Steenbergh, Steenberg, Sternbergh, Sternburgh, Strenbergh	7.3	14	88							13	1			
Steer, Stear, Steere, Steers, Stehr, Stier, Stiers	6.3	43	227						25		2	14	1		1
Stein, Stean, Steen, Steine, Steines, Sticen	5.4	32	142								1	23		2	2	4
Stephenson, Stepenson, Stephensen, Stephensons, Stevenson, Steveson, Stevinson, Stivison, Stiveson	5.6	237	1,082	5	2	3	16	1	5	28	51	44	15	35	32
Sterling, Stirling	5.2	33	138	1	3	3	1	1	7		8	7		1	1
Sterret, Starart, Staret, Starit, Starrat, Starratt, Starret, Starrit, Starrot, Sterrett, Sterrit, Sterritt	6.4	46	250	3	3					1	27	4		5	3
Stetson, Steatson, Stedson, Stutson	5.9	73	361	3	1	3	62		1	2		1		
Stevens, Staphens, Stavans, Steavens, Steevens, Steephens, Steevens, Stephans, Stephanus, Stephen, Stephens, Stephins, Stephen, Stevans, Stevins, Stiven, Stivens, Stivin, Stvens	5.6	1,125	5,227	87	160	69	190	13	146	119	88	56	49	101	47
Stewart, Steuad, Steuard, Steuart, Steuet, Steward, Stewat, Stewerd, Stewert, Stewort, Stuard, Stuart, Stuert, Stwart	5.5	891	3,981	33	36	21	58	1	54	115	242	77	71	125	58
Stickney, Stickny	5.8	91	434	4	26	6	53		1	2				
Stiles, Stile, Styles, Styls	5.2	161	669	4	21	11	41	1	29	17	15	7	3	9	3
Still, Stil, Stille, Stilles	5.7	32	150				4	1		2	12	1	5	5	2
Stillman, Stilman	6.9	41	242	1	1	1	4	10	19	5				
Stillwell, Stelwill, Stillwill, Stilwell, Stilwill	4.9	71	280				2	2	2	42	10	2	3	6	2
Stilson, Stillson, Stiltson	5.4	30	131		1	3	1		21	3		1		
Stimpson, Stimpon, Stimson	5.3	57	247	8	4	3	32		2		2	1	4		1
Stiner, Steiner, Styner	6.1	23	117							1	17	3		2	
Stinson, Stanson, Steinson, Stenson, Stienson, Stinsen	5.5	70	316	18	6	2	2			6	9	5	3	11	8
Stiver, Stever, Stevers, Stivers	6.0	27	135							12	14		1	
Stock, Stocke, Stocks	4.8	23	87				1		1	1	10	1	1	6	2
Stockbridge	7.2	18	112	4	5		9							
Stocking, Stockin, Stockings	4.8	32	123	1		2	6		19	3			1	
Stockman, Stackman, Stockerman	6.0	22	109	3	1		6	1	1	3	3			3
Stockwell, Stockwel, Stokell	5.9	52	254		6	6	29		5	4	1	1		
Stocton, Stockden, Stockdon, Stockston, Stockton	5.3	23	99		2					1	7	2	6	7	
Stoddard, Stodard, Stoddar, Stodder, Stoddred, Stoddert, Stoddord, Studdard	5.4	181	790	5	13	17	56	12	62	7	1	5	1	1	1
Stoker, Stocker	5.3	44	191	1	2	1	14	1	2	2	11	3	4	1	2
Stokes, Stoakes, Stoke, Stoks, Stook	5.3	80	345		2		1	1	1	4	5	8	14	30	14
Stone, Stoan, Stones	5.7	719	3,372	35	50	41	207	33	99	27	43	32	62	26	54
Stoner	5.8	76	368							3	50	16	2	5	
Storer	6.2	35	183	19	2		8	1	3	1	1				

TABLE **111.**—NOMENCLATURE, DEALING WITH NAMES REPRESENTED BY AT LEAST 100 WHITE PERSONS, BY STATES AND TERRITORIES, AT THE FIRST CENSUS: 1790—Continued.

NAME.	Average size of family.	TOTAL. Heads of families.	TOTAL. All other members.	Maine.	New Hampshire.	Vermont.	Massachusetts.	Rhode Island.	Connecticut.	New York.	Pennsylvania.	Maryland.	Virginia.	North Carolina.	South Carolina.
Storm, Storme, Storms	5.9	62	305				2			40	6	12		2	
Storrs, Stoher, Stoore, Stoors, Stores, Stower, Stowers	7.0	46	275	1	5	7	9		15	3	2	2	1		1
Story, Storey, Storie, Storry, Stowre	5.9	128	629	4	9	12	24		15	13	18	10	1	14	8
Stott, Stoats, Stot, Stots, Stotts	6.2	22	115				1				6	1	14		
Stoudt, Staudt	8.6	12	91								12				
Stoughton, Stoton, Stougton	6.4	21	114			2	3		12	2	1			1	
Stout, Stought, Stouts, Stowt	5.7	72	338	20		1				9	23	2	9	7	1
Stoutenburgh, Stoughtenburgh, Stoutenbergh, Stoutenburg	5.7	18	85							18					
Stover, Steover, Stouver, Stovar	6.4	84	457	21						5	34	6	16		2
Stow, Stoe, Stowe	5.2	88	368	1	2	4	35		26	8	7		1	4	
Stowell, Stoel, Stoell, Stoll, Stols, Stowel	5.9	73	355	5	5	7	35		8	6	3			2	2
Straight, Strait, Strate, Streat, Streight	6.1	37	188		1	3	4	10		10	3	1	1	2	3
Strain, Stran, Strane, Strayn, Strean	5.4	32	140							3	11	1		6	11
Strange, Strang	6.2	44	229				5	3	2	9		1	13	5	6
Stratton, Straten, Stratin, Straton, Stratron, Strattan, Stratten, Strotten, Strutton	5.7	115	537	1	6	11	51	2	13	11	3		16	1	
Straw	6.1	34	175	3	21	2	1				7				
Strawn, Strahan, Strahon, Strahorn, Straughan, Straughn, Strawhan, Strughon	5.5	27	122							1	9	4	3	8	2
Street, Streates, Streets	5.3	66	286			1	1		15	3	12	9	14	11	
Streeter, Strater, Streater, Streator, Streetor, Streter, Struter	5.2	61	254	2	13	17	17	3		3		4		2	
Stricker, Strecker, Streeker	5.2	20	84							5	11	3		1	
Strickland, Stricklen, Stricklin, Strikeland	5.5	147	666	1		2	9		26	7	10	4	1	78	9
Strickler, Stricklar, Stricler	6.9	34	199								26		8		
Stringer	6.1	21	107		1		1			1	7	4	1	3	3
Strong, Stronge	6.0	212	1,061		6	32	30		88	30	6	6		7	7
Strother, Strauther, Strawther, Strothers	5.3	21	90								2		7	5	7
Stroud, Strode, Strowd	5.3	53	229			2			1	2	14	4	5	14	11
Stroup, Stroop, Stroupe	6.0	20	100							2	18				
Strouse, Straus, Strause, Strauss, Strous	5.4	33	144								32	1			
Strowbridge, Strawbrege, Strawbridge, Strobridge, Strowbridg	5.4	26	115		4		9			1	6	1	2	2	1
Stubbs, Stubb, Stubs, Stulbs	5.2	62	269	9			7			2	5	4	7	22	6
Studley, Stoodley, Stoodly, Studly	5.3	31	133	4	2		20		2			1			2
Stump, Stutmp	6.7	40	229							1	21	8	10		
Sturdevant, Sterdefent, Stertwant, Stirdivan, Studefent, Studerfent, Studifent, Studiphunt, Studvent, Sturdaphant, Sturdavant, Sturdefant, Sturdephant, Sturdevant, Sturdevent, Sturdifent, Sturdiphant, Sturtevant, Sturvant	5.8	96	458	11	4	5	31		14	6		2	11	10	2
Sturges, Stergis, Sturgis, Sturgus	5.8	89	424	1			10		36	7	9	17	2	2	5
Suber, Serber, Serfer, Subers, Surber	7.6	18	118								11		2		5
Sugg, Suggs, Sugs	5.1	30	122										1	28	1
Sullivan, Sewlovan, Sulavan, Sulaven, Sulifen, Sulifin, Sulivan, Sulivane, Suliven, Sullavant, Sullaven, Sullavent, Sullavin, Sulleven, Sullivane, Sullivant, Sulliven, Sullivent, Sullivern, Sylivan, Sylivan	5.0	162	651	8	4	1	3		1	10	16	25	29	42	23
Summerlin, Sumerland, Summerland	5.8	18	87								4			10	4
Summers, Somer, Somers, Sommer, Sommers, Sumers, Summer, Summere, Summors	5.5	177	800	2	1	5	2		29	11	29	35	23	22	18
Sumner, Sumnar, Sumners	5.5	128	582	2	6	9	54		17	2			8	29	1
Sunderland, Sunderlin	6.2	19	99			5		6		1	4	1		2	
Supple, Suplee, Supplee	7.1	14	86								14				
Sutton, Suton, Sutten	5.4	205	908	1	2	6	8		7	26	58	21	16	47	13
Suydam	6.0	21	106							21					
Swagart, Swaggert, Swegart, Sweigard, Swergart, Swigard, Swigart, Swigert	5.0	21	85								18	3			
Swan, Swain, Swaine, Swane, Swann, Swayne, Swon	5.7	332	1,557	11	44	7	93	5	27	19	33	35	8	43	7
Swartwout, Swarthout, Swartout, Swartwaut	6.8	25	144							24	1				
Swartz, Schwartz, Swart, Swarts, Swarz	5.8	114	551	3						34	73	4			
Swasey, Swaesy, Swazey, Sweasey, Sweesy, Sweesey, Swesey, Swesy, Swezey, Swezy	5.3	43	184		8	1	13	1		18	1		1		
Swearingen, Swaringen, Swaringim, Swaringin, Swearengen, Swearingem, Swearinggam, Swearinggame, Swearinggen, Swearingham, Swearingon, Swearnggen, Sweringam	6.4	28	152							8	8		5	5	7
Sweet, Sweat, Sweatt, Sweit, Swet, Swete, Swett, Swetz	5.9	286	1,408	31	30	13	42	65	9	76	4		1	5	10
Sweetland, Swatland, Sweatland, Swedeland, Sweitland, Swetland, Switland	5.8	41	196	6	2	2	9	2	14	4	2				
Sweetser, Sweitzer, Swetser, Switser, Switzer	6.2	64	330	5	1	1	27			1	22	5			2
Swift, Sweft, Swif	6.0	159	801	3	3	19	71		24	10	7	9	2	10	1
Swim, Swaim, Swimb, Swimm, Swims	5.8	18	87							3	3		3	9	
Swindall, Swendel, Swindell, Swindill, Swindle	4.8	21	80											20	1
Swinney, Swainey, Swainy, Swaney, Swany, Sweaney, Sweany, Sweeney, Sweeny, Sweney, Swenney, Swiney, Swinne, Swiny	4.7	64	237		1		2			3	19	10	19	6	4
Swisher, Swicher, Swicker, Switcher, Switchur, Swsher	6.6	22	124	4			3			1	7		7		
Tabor, Taber, Tabour	6.0	113	570	4	4	4	44	32	6	13	1		1	4	
Taft, Taaff, Taaffe, Taff, Taffs, Tafft, Tafts	5.8	108	517		8	15	74	4	2	2		5			
Taggart, Tagard, Tagart, Tagert, Taggard, Taggert, Tagget, Taggort, Taggot, Teegard, Tegart	6.1	54	274	1	13	5	5	2		19	2		5	2	
Tainter, Taintor	5.5	22	98		1	1	10		10						
Talbot, Talberd, Talbert, Talbott, Talbut, Talbutt, Tallbard, Tolbart, Tolbert, Tolbot, Tolbott, Torbatt, Torbert, Torbit, Torbutt	6.0	127	632	6	2	2	18	2	3	3	25	33	18	5	10
Talcott, Talckut, Talcot, Tolcot, Tolcott	6.3	52	278	1		3	7		39	2					
Talley, Taley, Tally	4.7	47	176								1		39	6	1
Talmage, Tallmadge, Talmadge, Tamage	5.6	38	176			2	2		15	19					
Talman, Taleman, Tallman, Tallmans, Talmon, Taulman	5.6	55	255			3	5	8	3	29	3	1	2		1
Tanner, Taner, Tanna, Tannar, Tannir, Tannor	5.5	126	573		1	3	5	18	7	26	16	8	26	10	6
Tappen, Tapin, Tappan, Tappin, Tapping	5.8	28	133	2	5		2		2	17					
Tarbell, Tarabell, Tarball, Tarbalt, Tarbble, Tarbel, Tarbil, Tarble	5.7	48	226	4	9	9	23		1		1	1			
Tarbox	5.8	46	212	16	5	1	11	3	7	1					2
Tarlton	5.6	30	144		10							14		6	
Tarr, Tar	5.4	56	248	10	1	2	20			9	13			1	
Tate, Tait, Taite	4.8	68	258	2		1	4	1		2	20	6	6	13	13
Tatom, Tatum, Teatum	4.4	29	99				1						2	24	2
Taylor, Tahler, Tailer, Taillor, Tailor, Talor, Tayler, Tayloe, Taylore, Taylour	5.5	1,709	7,738	38	98	62	228	43	139	165	207	141	190	294	104
Teague, Teag, Teage	6.3	30	159	1		4		1		1	2	1		15	5
Teal, Teale, Teel, Teele, Teels, Teil, Tiel	5.5	66	297	3	1		10	3	5	11	21	1		10	1
Telford, Tilford, Tolford, Tylford	4.8	23	88		4				1	11			2		5
Teller, Teler, Telier	6.9	19	113							16	1	1	2		
Temple, Tempele, Temples	5.3	99	421	7	10	4	38			5	9	2	3	18	3
Templeton, Tempelton	5.9	55	268		6	1	1			2	24	1	3	10	7
Tenant, Tenent, Tennant, Tennent	6.0	23	114				2	6	3	4	3	2			3
Ten Brock, Ten Broecek, Ten Broeck, Ten Broock, Ten Brook	5.3	25	113							25					
Ten Eyck, Tanich, Ten Eck, Tennick, Ten Nycke, Ten Tycke	5.3	47	200							43	4				
Tenney, Teney, Tenny	5.8	47	227		12	6	25		1			1		1	1
Terry, Terey, Terrey, Tery	5.8	188	898			2	20	4	30	51	14	3	33	19	12

TABLE 111.—NOMENCLATURE, DEALING WITH NAMES REPRESENTED BY AT LEAST 100 WHITE PERSONS, BY STATES AND TERRITORIES, AT THE FIRST CENSUS: 1790—Continued.

NAME	Average size of family	TOTAL — Heads of families	TOTAL — All other members	Maine	New Hampshire	Vermont	Massachusetts	Rhode Island	Connecticut	New York	Pennsylvania	Maryland	Virginia	North Carolina	South Carolina
Terwilliger, Terwilleger, Tewilleger, Tirwilleger, Truwilligar	5.7	51	239							51					
Teter, Teeter, Teetor, Teters, Tetter	7.0	27	162								3	16	2	5	1
Tew	6.9	20	117				5	8						5	2
Tewksbury, Teuksbury, Teuxbury, Tewkbury, Tewkesbury, Tueksbury, Tuexbury, Tukesberry, Tukesbury, Tuxbury	7.0	27	163	1	9	4	13								
Thacker, Thaker	5.9	20	97							1	1		12		5
Thatcher, Thacher, Thracher	5.6	70	322	2	5	7	35	1	9	1	8		1	1	
Thaxter, Thaxtor	4.9	23	90	2			19			1		1			
Thayer, Thair, Thare, Thayre, Their, Theyar	5.7	265	1,239	3	11	18	206	5	12	9					1
Theale, Theal	6.3	17	90							17					
Thomas, Thomes, Thommas, Tomas, Tomes, Tommas	5.7	1,142	5,374	47	33	27	144	18	82	71	235	147	126	137	75
Thompson, Thomason, Thomerson, Thomison, Thomsin, Thomson, Tomason, Tomison, Tompson, Tomson	5.6	1,672	7,718	107	90	46	188	10	157	147	285	155	139	215	133
Thorn, Thorne	6.1	124	631	6	7		2		2	61	15	11	4	11	5
Thornbury, Thornberry, Thornbery, Thornsberry, Thornsburry, Thornsbury	5.1	27	111									10	4	13	
Thorndike	6.1	18	92	6	2		10								
Thornton, Thaunton, Thonton, Thorton, Thronton	5.8	137	653		5	1	8	20	2	11	18	7	33	21	11
Thorp, Tharp, Tharpe, Thearp, Thorpe, Thrope	5.1	116	471	1	1	2	12	1	42	11	6	9	10	20	1
Thrall	5.6	24	111			3	1		16			2	2		
Thrasher, Thresher	5.2	49	208	5	4		15		7	3	1	4	2	7	1
Thrift, Thrith	4.9	22	85									1	17	3	1
Throckmorton, Throgmorton	6.0	18	90							1			17		
Throop, Thoop, Throope, Throp, Thrope, Throup, Tthroop	5.8	25	121			3	2	4	12	3		1			
Thurber, Thirbur	5.6	44	203		7	7	7	14	1	8					
Thurmond, Therman, Thermon, Thirman, Thurman, Thurmon	6.2	30	157				1			4			18	1	6
Thurston, Thirston, Thurstain, Thursten, Thurstin, Thurstone, Thusten, Thustin, Thuston	5.8	152	723	8	24	7	43	23	3	26	1		10	3	4
Tibbalds, Tebbalds, Tibballs, Tibbals, Tibbells, Tibbels, Tibble, Tibbles	5.5	23	104						16			5	2		
Tibbets, Tebbets, Tebbetts, Tebbits, Thibbett, Tibbats, Tibbet, Tibbett, Tibbetts, Tibbit, Tibbits, Tibbitts, Tibbots, Tibits	5.7	118	559	51	34	4	3	10	3	11		2			
Tice, Tyce	6.5	27	148							12	8	4		3	
Tidd	5.8	27	130				13			11	2				1
Tier, Tear, Tears, Teer, Tiers	5.9	18	88		1		1	1		6	1	5		1	2
Tiffany, Tifeny, Tiffeney, Tiffeny, Tiffiny	5.6	51	235	2	3	1	19	3	12	11					
Tift, Tiff, Tifft	6.0	64	321			3		42	5	13	1				
Tilden, Telden, Tildan	6.1	43	221	1	7	4	20		5	1		5			
Tileston, Tilestone, Tilston	6.0	17	85				16		1						
Tilley, Tiley, Tillie, Tilly, Tily, Tyly	5.0	44	174	1			9	2	6	4	3	4		11	4
Tillinghast, Tillenghast, Tillinghass, Tillinghurst	6.2	37	191				2	29		3	1	1			1
Tillotson, Tillerson, Tilleson, Tilletson, Tillisen, Tillitson, Tilloson, Tilloton, Tillson, Tillstron, Tilson	5.2	64	268	1	2	1	22		22	14			1	1	
Tilman, Tilghman, Tillman, Tilmon, Tiltman	6.4	54	289							6	6	16	3	12	11
Tilton, Tillton	6.2	96	496	5	53		29			5	3			1	
Timmons, Timmins, Timmonds, Timons	5.3	44	188						1	1	10	13	4	4	11
Timms, Tims	6.3	16	85								5			2	9
Tindale, Tindal, Tindall, Tindle, Tinsdale	6.1	18	91				1		1				4	9	3
Tinker	5.6	45	203	2			6		31	1		1		4	
Tinkham, Tinkam, Tinkum	5.8	44	211	3	1	4	33	3							
Tinney, Tinny, Tyney	4.9	47	181	9	14		12		3	2	2		3	1	1
Tinsley, Tinsly	5.9	35	170								1	1	24	1	8
Tippett, Tippet	5.4	28	122				4				2	15	7		
Tipton, Typton	6.0	27	135								4	19	4		
Tisdale, Teasdale, Tisdal, Tisdail, Tisdel, Tisdell, Trisdal, Twisdale	5.9	52	255		1	1	29	1	6	2			4	3	5
Titcomb	6.0	41	207	10	7		24								
Titus, Titas, Titis	6.3	112	588	2	4	7	16		13	58	11			1	
Tobey, Toby	6.4	81	441	17	1	3	46		7			3			
Tobias	7.2	17	106			2					5	6			4
Todd, Tod	5.6	226	1,029	10	8	3	27		49	19	29	22	7	35	17
Toler, Toaler, Tolar, Towler	5.0	21	83	1				1					6	13	
Tolman, Toleman, Tollman	5.5	59	267	7	5	2	34	3		5				3	
Tolsin, Tolson, Tolston, Toltson	5.3	23	100									7	4	12	
Tomlinson, Thomlinson, Tomberlinson, Tomblinson, Tomerlinson, Tomlindson, Tomlicon	5.9	99	485				1			37	27	3	10	15	6
Tompkins, Thomkin, Thompkins, Tomkins, Tompkin	5.9	126	622			3	8	8	8	70	12	2	9	8	6
Toms, Thom, Thomb, Thombs, Thome, Thoms, Toam, Tom, Tomm	6.0	49	246	7	3	1				14	7	11	2	4	
Toney, Tony	6.2	17	89				1			2			1	4	5
Tooley, Tooly	5.4	30	132			1			4					16	9
Toppan, Topham, Toppen, Toppens, Toppin	5.6	28	130	1	1		18	2		2	1			3	
Torrence, Torence, Torrance, Torrans, Torrens, Torrons	6.0	26	130			4	2		1	1	9	1		6	2
Torrey, Torey, Torry, Tory	5.5	93	417	6	1	5	58	1	13	3			4	1	
Totten, Torton, Toten, Totton	4.6	36	130					1	2	27	2	1	2	1	1
Tower, Towers	5.5	77	347	1	3	5	45	3	1	5	4	7	2		
Towle, Toal, Tole, Toles, Toll, Tolles, Towl, Towles, Towls	6.0	93	464	8	53	4		4		10	9	2	3		
Town, Toun, Toune, Townd, Towne, Townes, Towns	5.8	149	712	13	29	12	56		7	7	9		12	2	2
Towner, Touner	5.3	26	112		1	3	1		18	2				1	
Townsend, Tounsand, Tounsend, Tounshend, Towndserd, Townsand, Townsen, Townshand, Townshend, Townsin, Townson	6.0	322	1,594	13	11	8	49	11	24	105	27	43	6	11	14
Townsley, Townley, Townsly	4.6	24	87	2	1		2			1	7	5	2	3	1
Tracy, Tracey, Traicy, Trasee, Trasse, Trasy, Treacy	6.0	143	722	7	2	12	25		58	15	4	15	3	2	
Trail, Trale, Trall	7.0	20	119				2		2	2	1	6	4		3
Train, Traine	5.1	20	81	1	1	4	11				2		1		
Trask	5.8	93	451	17	4	1	65	5		1					
Traver, Travarse, Travers, Traverse	6.0	62	308							46	4	6	1	2	3
Travis	5.7	53	247		2		2			34	7		1	4	3
Traylor, Tralor, Trayler	5.7	23	199										18		5
Treadway, Treadaway, Tredaway, Treddiway, Tredway	6.1	25	128			1			16			1	1	4	2
Treadwell, Tradwell, Treadwel, Tredwell, Tredwill	5.8	66	318	4	7		15		17	15		1		3	3
Treat, Treatt, Treet	5.3	75	320	6		1	7		51	7	3				
Trent	7.0	15	90									1	1	11	2
Trickey	5.7	18	85	3	10					1	3			2	
Trimble, Trembel, Tremble, Trimbel, Trumbal, Trumball, Trumbel, Trumble, Trumbul, Trumbull	6.1	87	444	2	2	5	7		20	8	31	7	3		2
Tripp, Trip, Trippe, Trips	5.3	159	690	4	2	3	61	28	4	40	5	3		7	2
Trott, Trot, Trotts	6.0	25	125	5	1			5		1	2	2	3		1
Trotter	4.6	25	89	5	1					1	8		3	6	6
Trout	5.4	28	123							3	14	3	6	2	

TABLE 111.—NOMENCLATURE, DEALING WITH NAMES REPRESENTED BY AT LEAST 100 WHITE PERSONS, BY STATES AND TERRITORIES, AT THE FIRST CENSUS: 1790—Continued.

NAME.	Average size of family.	TOTAL. Heads of families.	TOTAL. All other members.	Maine.	New Hampshire.	Vermont.	Massachusetts.	Rhode Island.	Connecticut.	New York.	Pennsylvania.	Maryland.	Virginia.	North Carolina.	South Carolina.
Troutman	6.9	17	100								7	2		7	1
Trowbridge, Trobridge	5.9	73	359		1	6	20	1	35	10					
Troxall, Traxall, Traxel, Traxell, Traxil, Troxel, Troxell, Troxill	6.1	18	91								10	8			
Truax, Trueax	5.6	28	128						26	2					
True, Trew	5.4	62	271	20	29		9			1		1	2		
Truitt, Trueit, Truit	4.8	26	99						1			22	1	1	1
Truman, Trueman	6.1	28	144			1	4	1	3	4	9	4	1	1	
Trusdell, Trousdale, Truesdal, Truesdale, Truesdall, Truesdell, Trusdal, Trusdale, Trusdall, Trusedale	5.7	36	170		1	2	1		4	22	3			3	
Tryon	6.1	55	279	1		2	2		39	8	3				
Tubbs, Tubb, Tubs	5.8	65	311		1	5	14	1	14	16	4	3			7
Tuck, Tucke, Tuckes	6.1	30	153	3	12		9				1	1		3	1
Tucker, Tuckers, Tuker	5.7	501	2,350	21	50	17	107	22	44	30	16	33	71	67	23
Tufts, Tuffs, Tuffts, Tuft	5.5	80	362	7	4	1	62		3	3					
Tull	6.1	19	96								3	9		6	1
Tuller, Tullar	6.0	26	130				6		19	1					
Tupper, Tupir	5.3	37	160	4	2	10	12		6	2					
Turk, Terk	5.6	24	110							15	6	1	2		
Turner, Turnner, Turrner	5.6	738	3,412	31	15	22	129	14	65	70	39	80	89	123	61
Turney	5.3	26	111	1						17	1	3	4		
Turrel, Terral, Terrall, Terrel, Terrell, Terril Terrill, Terrol, Tirrel Tirrell, Turell, Turrell, Turril, Turrill, Tyrel, Tyrell, Tyrrall, Tyrrel, Tyrrell, Tyrrill	5.8	133	640	2	8	4	31		41	9	1	1	14	13	9
Tuttle, Tutal, Tutall, Tutill, Tutle, Tuttel	5.6	308	1,409	9	39	16	34		107	80	11	2		7	3
Twiss, Twisk, Twist	5.2	30	127				4	1	18	1	3	3			
Twitchel, Twitchell	6.2	26	134	4	12	1	9								
Twombly, Twambly, Twamley, Twombley	6.3	27	143	2	25										
Tyler, Teyler, Tiler, Tuyler, Tylar, Tylor	5.7	283	1,338	14	13	9	66	13	83	29	4	8	20	10	14
Tyree, Tire, Tyer, Tyre, Tyrer	5.9	30	148						2	4			13	12	3
Tyson, Tison	6.5	73	379							4	31	5		31	2
Ulrich, Uldrick, Ulerich, Ullirick, Ullrich, Ulrick	6.4	17	89							1	15				1
Underhill, Underhil, Undrill	6.4	88	472		9	3			1	63	2	5	2	3	
Underwood, Underwod	5.7	144	680	4	6	12	32	4	8	4	22	7	11	26	8
Upham, Upam, Upum	5.7	56	264	2	3	4	39		7	1					
Upson, Upsom	5.8	24	115						24						
Upton	6.1	76	390				6		46	2	3		3		2
Usher	5.5	31	141	1	4		4	7	3		2	4	1	3	2
Utley, Utly, Uttley	5.8	40	191			5				19	4		1	10	
Utter, Uttor	6.2	23	120					4	1	16	2		1		
Vail, Vaile, Vale, Vales, Veile	5.8	64	308		1	2	2		4	48	1			4	2
Valentine, Vallentine, Vallintine, Valuntine, Volentine, Volintine, Vollintine	5.8	132	637		69	1	8	1		3	14	5	15	9	7
Van, Vann, Vans	6.1	29	147			2	1			1	4		1	17	3
Van Aken, Van Aaken, Vanakin, Van Auken, Van Aukin, Van Awken	5.9	33	160							19	14				
V: Allen, Vn Allen, Van Allen, Van Aulen	5.6	35	161							35					
Van Alstine, V: Alstin, Van Alstin, V: Alstine	5.8	47	226							47					
Van Antwerp, V: Antwerp	5.9	22	108							22					
Van Atten, Van Autin	6.4	16	86							16					
V: Buren, Van Beuren, Van Bueren, Van Buren	5.6	55	252							55					
Van Buskirk, V: Buskirk	5.4	22	96							12	9	1			
Vance, Vanse, Vantz	5.2	82	341		2	3	1	1		4	35	3	10	12	11
Van Curen, V: Curen	5.9	28	136							28					
V: De Bergh, Vanbergh, V: De Bargh, V: D: Bergh, Vadebergh, Vandebergh, Vandeburgh, Vandenberg, V: Den Bergh, Vandenbergh, Vandenburgh, Van Der Bergh, Van Der Burgh, Ve De Bergh	5.9	63	309							63					
V: De Bogert, Van De Bogart, Van de Bogert, Vandenbogert, V: Der Bogart	5.2	21	89							21					
Vandegrift, Vandegriff, Vandegriffe, Vandegrist, Vandegruff, Vandergriff, Vandergrift, Vandigraft, Vandigrif, Vandigrift	5.2	33	140								24	2		2	5
Vanderbelt, Vandebelt, Vanderbilt, Van Dubelt	5.6	33	150							27	6				
Van Der Mark, Vandamark, Van den Mark, Van Der Marks	5.5	27	122							21	6				
V: Der Pool, Vanderpool	5.4	23	100							17	1			2	3
Vanderweir, Vandavour, Vandeavour, Vanderveer, Vanderwier, Vandever, Vandivear, Vandiver, Vandivere, Venderver, Venevere, Vindever	6.9	21	124							8			7	6	
Van De Water, Vanderwater, V: De Water, Vandwater	4.8	23	88							23					
Van Dusen, Van Deusan, Van Deusen, Van Deuson, Van Doosen, Van Drusen, Van Duesen, Vandusan, V: Dusen, Van Dusin, Vanduzzen	6.2	69	356				9		2	55	3				
Van Dyke, Vandike, V: Dyck, Van Dyck, Vandycke, V: Dyk, V: Dyke	6.0	52	258							32	16	1		3	
Van Horn, V: Horn, Van Horne	5.8	77	369							17	46	4		1	1
V: Hosen, Van Hoesen, Van Hosen, Van Husen, Van Husin	5.8	45	218							45					
Van Houten	6.1	23	117							23					
Van Kleeck, V: Kleck, Van Kleech, V: Kleek	6.6	20	111							20					
Van Loon, Van Leon, Vanloan, Vanlone	5.6	18	83							16					
Vanmeter, Vanmeeter, Vanmeetor, Vanmetre	6.4	19	103								2	8	11		
Van Ness, Van Est, V: Ness, V: Nest, Van Nest	6.0	30	150							29	1				
Van Nostrand, Van Nostrandt, Van Nostrant, Vanorstrain, Vanorstrand, Vanostan, Vanosten, Vanostran, Van Ostrandt, Van Ostrant	5.2	26	122						2	20	4				
Van Orden, Van Arden	5.4	20	87						1	19					
Van Patten, V: Patten, V: Potten	6.5	19	104							19					
Van Pelt	5.9	32	157							22	3		1	6	
V: Rensselaer, Ransalear, Van Renselaer, Van Rensselaer	6.2	17	87							16					
Vansant, Vansandt, Vansanst, V: Zandt, Van Zandt, Van Zant	5.4	62	274						1	18	28	14			1
Van Schaick, V: Scaack, Van Scaack, Van Schaack, Van Schaaick, Van Schyck, Van Shaack	4.9	23	89					1		22					
Van Slyke, V: Sleyk, V: Slyck, Van Slyck, V: Slyk, Van Slyk	5.8	35	168							35					
Van Steenbergh, V: Steenbergh	5.6	27	123							27					
Van Tassel, Van Tasal, Van Tasell, V: Tassel, Van Tassell	5.6	36	165							36					
V: Valkenburgh, Valkenburgh, V: Valkenbergh, Van Valkenburgh, Van Volkenbergh, Van Volkenburgh, Van Volkinburg, Van Volkinburgh, Volkenburgh	6.9	66	386			2				64					
Van Vliet, V: Vleck, Van Vleck, Van Vleeck, V: Vleek, V: Vleet, Van Vleet, Van Vliet	6.4	30	163							29	1				
Van Vrankin, V: Vranken	5.7	25	117							25					
Van Waggenen, Van Wagenen, Van Waggonon	6.3	39	208							39					
Van Wart, Van Warp, V: Woort, Van Woort, Van Wort	6.0	28	140							28					
Van Wyck, Van Wyche, Van Wyk	6.4	16	87							15			1		
Varnam, Varnhan, Varnum	5.9	37	182	12	2	3	14		1	3		1	1		
Varney, Varny	5.6	58	268	5	48				1	3	3				
Vaughn, Vaughan, Vaughen, Vaughon, Vaughown, Vaugon, Vaun, Vaune, Veaughn, Vowan	6.0	235	1,170	1		6	26	27	8	12	10	10	86	27	22

TABLE 111.—NOMENCLATURE, DEALING WITH NAMES REPRESENTED BY AT LEAST 100 WHITE PERSONS, BY STATES AND TERRITORIES, AT THE FIRST CENSUS: 1790—Continued.

NAME.	Average size of family.	TOTAL.		HEADS OF FAMILIES.											
		Heads of families.	All other members.	Maine.	New Hampshire.	Vermont.	Massachusetts.	Rhode Island.	Connecticut.	New York.	Pennsylvania.	Maryland.	Virginia.	North Carolina.	South Carolina.
Vaught, Voght, Voigt, Vooght, Voogt, Voought, Vought	5.5	20	90							3	11		4		2
Veal, Veale, Veall	5.9	63	310			3	2		7	32	3	1	9	5	1
Veazey, Veasey, Veasy, Veazie, Veazy, Veesy	5.8	18	86		4	1	3				1	6		2	1
Veeder, Vedder, Veder, Veider	6.0	56	281							56					
Venable, Veanible, Veanneble, Venables, Veneble	5.9	31	152									4	13	5	9
Vermilya, Vermillia	7.1	22	134							22					
Verner, Vernier, Vernor	4.8	22	83					1		4	12			1	4
Vernon, Vernam, Vernan, Vernom, Vernum	5.7	49	230		3	1	1	5		19	1	5	7	7	
Very, Varry, Vary, Verree, Verrie, Verry	5.7	21	99		2		17			1					1
Vick, Vicks	5.7	24	112											24	
Vickers, Vickars, Vicors	5.1	22	90				1			1	10			6	4
Vickery, Vicary, Viccory, Vickary, Vickere, Vickeree, Vickeroy, Vickory, Vickry, Vicory	5.4	49	217	2	7	1	19	2		8				7	3
Vinal, Vinall	4.9	28	109	1			25			1	1				
Vincent, Vencent, Venson, Vinceent, Vincient, Vinsant, Vinson, Vinzant	5.7	146	684		4	1	28	6	2	29	9	20	11	36	
Vining, Vinings	5.5	25	112	2			16		2	3				1	1
Vinton, Vinten, Vintin	5.8	26	124		1		18		4	1		2			
Voorhis, Van Voorheis, Van Voorhis, Van Vooris, Van Voorkiss, Voorhees, Voorheese, Voorhes, Voorhies, Voorhiis, Vooris, Voras, Voreese, Vores, Voris, Vorres	6.2	56	291							42	12	1		1	
Vosburgh, Vorburgh, Vosbury, Vossbergh, Vossburgh	5.6	57	264					3		1	53				
Vose, Voce, Vos, Voss, Vosst, Vowse	6.1	55	279	5	6	1	26	3	5	1	2	1		3	2
Vredenburgh, Van Vredenbergh, Van Vredenburgh, Vredenbergh, Vredenbugh, Vredonbagh, Vreedenburgh	5.6	36	166							36					
Vroman, Vrooman	5.6	46	212							43					
Waddle, Waddel, Waddell, Waddill, Wadle, Woddell, Wodle	6.2	59	306		3	1	3			4	14	5	12	11	6
Wade, Wades, Waid, Waide, Wayd, Wayde	5.3	180	773	7	1	4	33	10	15	6	13	18	32	30	11
Wadley, Wadleigh, Wadliegh, Wadlow, Wadly, Wodley	5.4	45	197	10	25		7				1	1	1		
Wadsworth, Wadworth, Wardsworth, Wardworth, Watsworth, Wodsworth, Woodworth, Woodsworth	5.8	188	896	6	10	16	37	1	69	34	6	1		6	2
Wager, Wagaer, Wagar, Wagers, Waigor, Weager	6.0	27	136		1	1				13	4	3	1	2	2
Waggoner, Wagener, Waggener, Wagginor, Waggner, Waggnor, Waggonner, Waggonor, Wagner, Wagnor, Wagoner, Wagonour, Wegner, Wiegner	5.6	222	1,032	2		2	1		3	26	132	15	14	21	6
Wait, Waight, Waite, Waites, Waits, Waitt, Wate, Wates, Wayt, Wayts, Waytt	6.0	230	1,155	9	9	22	111	12	10	31	6	5	3	1	11
Wakefield, Waikfield, Wakfield, Weakfield	5.6	74	344	14	9	5	20		6		6		6	4	4
Wakely, Wakelee, Wakeley, Wakley	5.8	19	92						17	2					
Wakeman, Wackman, Wakman	6.0	40	198				1		30	7		1	1		
Walbridge	6.6	22	124		1	10			8	3					
Walden, Waldim, Waldin, Walding, Waldon	5.2	59	244		7	5	11	2	6	6	3	1	10	3	5
Waldo, Waldow	6.1	38	195	2	4	4	8		16	4					
Waldron, Waldran, Waldren, Waldrom, Warldren	6.0	77	388	1	12		8	10	2	37	2		1	3	1
Waldrop, Waldrip, Waldroop, Waldrope, Waldrup	7.3	19	120										1	3	15
Wales, Wail, Waile, Wailes, Wails, Wale	6.4	68	369		1	8	38	1	8		2	6	4		
Walker, Wacher, Wacker, Waker, Warker, Wocker, Wockker	5.5	1,014	4,602	42	62	28	182	20	40	46	157	72	110	165	90
Wall, Wahl, Wahle, Walle, Walls, Wals, Walse, Waul, Wawl, Wawls	5.2	162	677	3	1	2	6	9	2	6	31	15	28	39	20
Wallace, Walice, Walls, Wallas, Walles, Wallice, Wallis	5.5	453	2,045	13	48	17	57	2	12	30	104	30	27	79	34
Wallen, Wallin, Walling, Wallon, Waln	5.5	34	153						10	8	2	7	2		3
Waller, Wallar, Wallaugh, Wallaw, Wallers, Wallier	5.1	69	284			1			6	4	12	7	17	19	3
Walmsley, Walmsbey, Walmslie, Wamsley, Warmsley, Womley, Wormley	5.4	26	115						1	2	9	8	4	2	
Walradt, Wolradt, Wolrodt	7.1	22	135							22					
Walter, Wallter, Wallters, Walters, Waltor, Waltour	5.6	228	1,043	1	1		2	2	6	11	125	24	25	18	13
Walthall, Walthal, Walthel	4.7	33	121										33		
Walton, Walten	6.1	156	795	5	15	6	9	1	5	5	57	5	36	11	1
Wanmaker, Wamamacher, Wanamaker, Wanemaker, Wanimaker, Wannemacher, Wannemaker, Winamaker	4.8	24	91							6	14				4
Wansor, Wanser, Wantzer, Wanzer	6.0	18	90						6	11	1				
Ward, Wards	5.5	694	3,134	17	26	17	121	8	67	100	31	51	69	147	40
Warden, Wardin, Warding	5.3	39	166		2	8	7		2	1	7	1	7	3	1
Wardwell, Wardell, Wardwel, Wordel, Wordwell	5.2	39	162	6	3		9	9	5	6		1			
Ware, Waeres, Wair, Wares, Wear, Weare, Wears, Weeir, Weer, Weere, Weir, Weirs, Wier, Wiere, Wiers	5.5	219	975	14	19	6	64	1	4	9	34	19	15	13	21
Warner, Worner, Wornor	5.7	483	2,246	2	23	24	102	21	152	56	71	15	4	10	3
Warren, Waren, Warin, Waring, Warran, Warrin, Warring, Warron, Worren, Worrin	5.6	511	2,338	42	31	20	125	3	59	45	15	29	51	58	33
Warriner, Warrener	6.0	24	121			2	20		1	1					
Warthen, Warthin, Warthing, Wathan, Wathen, Wotham	6.2	34	179		1		6					26		1	
Warwick, Warick, Warrick, Worrick	5.5	25	112				3			1	3	2	9	7	
Washburn, Wasburn, Washbane, Washbern, Washbon, Washborn, Washborne, Washboun, Washbourn, Washbun, Washburne	5.9	187	916	8	8	19	88		23	27	5		4	5	
Washington	4.9	23	89				1			1	1		12	3	5
Wason, Wasen, Wasson, Wauson, Wawson	5.9	41	202	4	8					2	10	3		12	
Waterbury, Waterberry	4.9	44	172						29	15					
Waterhouse, Waterous	6.4	58	311	17	5	5	1	2	23	5					
Waterman, Watermon, Watterman	6.3	158	841	8	2	11	37	39	25	22	8		5	1	
Waters, Waoters, Warters, Water, Wattar, Watter, Watters, Wauters, Worter, Worters, Woters	5.4	300	1,330	3	9	7	36		34	40	13	89	13	34	22
Watkins, Wadkins, Watkens, Watkin, Wodkins	5.6	248	1,130			8	10	24		14	12	14	26	72	54
Watrus, Watrous	4.5	24	85						23						
Watson, Watsen, Watston, Wattson, Wattsons, Whatson, Wotson	5.8	562	2,720	17	59	7	43	33	21	30	88	46	50	106	62
Wattles, Wattle	6.7	18	103						11	6					
Watts, Wats, Watt, Wattes, Wots, Wott	5.5	204	910	8	9		16	1		22	40	35	27	23	23
Waugh, Wagh, Wah, Waw	5.5	45	201	3	3		4		5	1	8	8	9	2	2
Way, Ways, Wey	5.5	102	461		4	2	4	1	32	24	18	1	3	4	9
Wayman, Weyman	5.6	28	130				2			7	4	11	1	2	1
Wayne, Waen, Wain, Waine, Wane	6.4	25	135				1			1	2	14	3		2
Weakley, Weackley, Weakly, Weekly	7.2	14	87							6	2	4		2	
Weatherford, Wetherford	5.8	19	92										12	3	4
Weatherley, Weatherley, Weathersley, Weathersly, Wetherly	4.6	22	80				2	4				1		3	10
Weathers, Wether, Wethers	4.6	27	98						3		3	1	6	7	7
Weaver, Weavor, Weavour, Weever, Wevar, Wever, Wheever	5.7	427	2,022			10	7	37	15	60	195	25	23	36	19
Webb, Web, Webbs	5.7	395	1,864	21	2	11	41	7	61	40	35	27	59	71	20
Webber, Webbers, Weber, Webor	5.7	143	679	38	15	2	47	1	5	11	13	3	6	1	2
Webster	6.1	329	1,663	19	78	15	46	7	65	33	21	14	18	11	2
Weed, Wead, Weeds, Weiad	5.5	154	691	3	18	6	11		89	18	4				5
Weeden, Weadon, Weaton, Wedon, Wedons, Weeding, Weedon, Weeton	5.7	48	225					2	3	22	2		9	2	
Weeks, Weakes, Weaks, Week, Weekes, Weik, Weiks	5.5	292	1,318	35	35	8	40	9	3	109	7	3	8	31	4
Weidner, Widener, Widner, Widnor, Wydner	5.2	36	150								29	3	2		2
Weiss, Weis, Weise	6.3	32	170								31	1			

TABLE 111.—NOMENCLATURE, DEALING WITH NAMES REPRESENTED BY AT LEAST 100 WHITE PERSONS, BY STATES AND TERRITORIES, AT THE FIRST CENSUS: 1790—Continued.

NAME.	Average size of family.	TOTAL.		HEADS OF FAMILIES.											
		Heads of families.	All other members.	Maine.	New Hampshire.	Vermont.	Massachusetts.	Rhode Island.	Connecticut.	New York.	Pennsylvania.	Maryland.	Virginia.	North Carolina.	South Carolina.
Welch, Welsh	5.6	390	1,782	43	26	13	26	5	26	52	79	49	21	32	18
Weldon, Welden, Welding	6.0	23	116			3	2		3	5	4	1	1	2	2
Weller, Wellar	6.5	44	240			6	14		4	7	9	4			
Wells, Well, Welles	5.9	640	3,140	15	41	24	105	29	137	91	79	36	19	34	30
Welman, Wellman	5.0	43	174		6	13	19					1	1	3	
Welton	5.8	34	164			1			26					1	6
Wendell, Wendall, Wendel, Wendle, Wendoll, Windall, Windell, Windle	5.6	54	249		1		6			24	5	1	15	2	
Wentworth, Wintworth	5.4	122	542	29	48	4	22		12	7					
Wentz, Went, Wents	7.1	21	128							2	18	1			
Werner, Wermer, Wernar, Wernor	5.4	27	118	6						6	10	5			
Wesson, Wessen	5.2	40	168	9	2	2	24			1			2		
West, Wests	5.6	518	2,358	12	13	24	79	33	30	52	37	44	77	83	34
Westbrook, Westbroke, Westbrooke	6.0	32	159							5	6		9	12	
Westcoat, Wescoat, Wescot, Wescots, Wescott, Wescut, Wescutt, Westcoot, Westcot, Westcott	5.3	113	489	19		6	12	38	7	15	4		3	4	5
Westfall, Westfal	6.1	42	216							10	8		24		
Weston, Western	5.8	124	593	12	5	5	45		10	3	11	4	8	15	6
Wetherbee, Weatherbee, Weatherby, Weathersby, Wetherbe, Wetherbie, Wetherby, Witherbe, Witherbee, Witherby	6.2	86	449	2	15	1	49		1	3	5	2		1	7
Wetmore	5.8	23	110				1		21	1					
Wetzel, Wetzell, Whetzel, Whitzel, Witesell, Witzel, Witzell	6.1	21	108							2	13	2	4		
Weymouth, Wamoth, Waymoth, Waymouth	5.6	21	97	16	5										
Whaland, Whalen, Whealand, Whealen, Whealin, Whealon, Wheelan, Wheeland, Wheelen, Wheelin, Whelan, Wheland, Whelen, Whelon	5.3	47	201	3	1	5	2			11	8	14	2	1	
Whaley, Waeley, Waley, Walley, Wayley, Waylie, Weyley, Weyly, Whalley, Whaly, Wheale, Whealey, Whealy, Wheely, Wheley, Whely	6.0	78	393	1		1	2	9	8	22	7	4	5	12	7
Wharton, Wharten, Whorten, Whorton	5.2	54	226		5	3	3	1		1	29	3	6	9	6
Wheat	6.8	29	167		5	3	3	1	4	6	1	4			2
Wheatley, Wheatly, Wheetly, Whetely	6.0	40	201		2	1	1				3	25		8	
Wheaton, Wheeton, Wheton	5.5	76	345	1	1	3	24	13	20	9	1			4	
Wheeler, Weeler, Whealer, Whealor, Wheelar, Wheelor, Whelar, Wheler, Whelor	5.7	743	3,479	14	93	37	200	5	150	87	19	71	23	30	14
Wheelock, Whelock, Whillock	5.4	89	392		11	12	61	1	1	2		1			
Whicher, Whicharre, Whicker, Whitcher	6.5	25	137	7	14									3	1
Whidbee, Whidby, Whitby, Whiteby	5.9	20	98									3	1	16	
Whidden, Whiddon	6.0	22	110	6	12		1						1		2
Whipple, Whiple, Whipples, Whippol	6.0	189	955	1	20	19	44	54	25	24	2				
Whitaker, Whitacer, Whitacker, Whitacre, Whitcker, Whiteaker, Whitecar, Whitecor, Whiteker, Whitiacre, Whiticor, Whitiker, Whittacar, Whittacker, Whittacre, Whittaker, Whittecoe, Whittekar, Whitteker, Whittikar, Whittiker, Witacer, Witaker, Wittaker	5.8	130	627	3	17		19	5	6	20	16	11		28	5
Whitcomb, Whetcomb, Whitcom, Whitcum, Whitcumb, Whitecomb, Whitecombe, Witcom, Witcome	5.1	119	485	8	27	17	56		1	7	3				
White, Whight, Whites, Whyte	5.6	1,699	7,824	53	79	77	384	30	103	168	201	110	116	268	110
Whitehead, Whitehad	5.1	94	382						5	7	6	2	15	52	7
Whitehouse, Whithous, Whithouse, Withouse	5.3	46	200	12	18				1	1		1		11	2
Whitehurst, Whithurst	5.5	90	409										88	2	
Whiteside, Whitesedes, Whitesid, Whitesides	5.7	36	168							5	16			7	8
Whitfield, Whitefield	4.1	27	83				1			2			17	5	2
Whitford, Whiteford	6.2	40	208			1	6	22	3		8				
Whiting, Whighting, Whiteing, Whitings, Witing	5.5	189	852	8	9	5	106	5	34	14		1	5		2
Whitley, Whitly	5.6	40	183			1			1	1	1	1	5	28	2
Whitlock, Whitelock, Whitlocke, Whitlocks	5.4	57	248			4			20	7	2	3	11	4	6
Whitman, Whiteman, Whitemon, Whitmon, Whitmond, Wightman, Witeman, Witman, Witmon	5.7	229	1,076	5	9	12	51	34	24	34	36	2	10	4	8
Whitmarsh, Whitemarsh, Whitmash, Witmarsh, Witmash	5.4	30	131		1	1	24	2		2					
Whitmore, Whitemore, Whitmar, Whitmor, Whittemore, Whittimore, Whittmore, Witmore, Wittemore	5.9	205	1,011	11	16	2	80	2	44	10	19	10	3	2	6
Whitney, Whitny, Witney	5.8	382	1,825	49	35	44	156	1	44	44	1			4	4
Whitten, Whettum, Whittam, Whittem, Whittin, Whitting, Whittom, Whitton, Whittum	4.8	85	327	29	4		29	1	1	1	4		6	6	4
Whittier, Whiteher, Whitiar, Whitier	5.7	40	189	7	11	5	16			1					
Whittington, Whettington, Whitington, Whittenton	5.0	29	116				1				1	11	2	6	8
Whittlesey, Whitlesey, Whittelsey, Whittlesery	5.3	25	107				3		22						
Whitworth, Whetworth, Whiteworth, Whittworth	6.5	17	94										10	7	
Wicker, Wicher	5.4	21	92			2				1	2	5		11	
Wickham, Wickam, Wicomb	6.6	34	192		1			2	4	22		2	2		1
Wicks, Wick, Wickes	6.1	35	177			1			6	16	2	9			1
Wiggins, Wigans, Wiggans, Wiggen, Wiggens, Wiggin, Wiggon, Wiggons, Wigins, Wigons	6.0	171	859	8	62	2	1		2	23	10	4	10	43	6
Wiggs, Wige, Wigg, Wigs	6.2	17	88			1				1	2		2	10	2
Wight, Wicht	5.6	21	96	1	1	2	5	1	2	1	1	6			1
Wilbore, Wilbar, Wilbare, Wilber, Wilbour, Wilbur, Wilburr	6.1	171	880	1	8	3	44	64	5	39			6	1	
Wilborn, Wilbon, Wilborne, Wilbourn, Wilburn	5.3	26	113	1						3		1	5	15	1
Wilcox, Wilcock, Wilcocks, Wilcoks, Willcock, Willcocks, Willcox	6.1	386	1,956		9	21	38	69	146	65	13	9	3	10	3
Wild, Wilde, Wilds, Wile, Wiles, Wyld, Wylds	5.3	109	485	8	1	4	47		2	9	13	10	7	1	7
Wilder, Wildair, Wildar, Wildder, Wildear, Wildeer, Wilders, Willder, Willdor, Wyldur	6.0	180	905	3	12	25	90	1	5	4	4	3	14	15	4
Wileman, Wildeman, Wilderman, Wildman, Wilemon	5.6	33	153						20	1	6	5		1	
Wiley, Weilley, Weily, Whiley, Whilley, Whyley, Wiely, Wighley, Wilee, Wilie, Willee, Willey, Willie, Williy, Wily, Wyley, Wylie, Wylly, Wyly	5.7	298	1,402	16	48	7	33	1	25	27	61	17	20	30	13
Wilhelm, Wellhilm, Wilkelm, Willhelm, Willholm	5.4	28	122								24	3	1		
Wilkerson, Wilkason, Wilkeson, Wilkison, Wilkson	5.3	111	473	5	1			3	6	8	13	6	27	36	6
Wilkey, Wilkaw, Wilkee, Wilkie, Wilky	5.6	23	105					5	4		6	2		3	3
Wilkins, Wilken, Wilkens, Wilkin, Wilkings, Willkins	5.4	205	910	1	32	5	29			19	28	7	46	31	7
Wilkinson, Wilkenson, Willkinson	5.4	144	633		4	2	4	18		14	15	6	39	34	8
Wilks, Wilkes, Willkes, Willks	5.3	39	166			1	2		3	10	1	4	3	8	7
Willard, Wilard, Williard, Willyard, Wilyard	6.7	183	1,045	4	19	32	90	1	12	3	6	7	4	2	3
Willer, Wieler, Wiler, Wilhear, Willars, Willers, Willor	5.1	23	94			4	2		2	1	7	7			
Willet, Willert, Willets, Willett, Willetts, Willirt, Willist, Willit, Willits, Willitts, Willt	6.3	72	378			1		3		4	25	18	14		7
Williams, Wiliams, Willams, William, Williame, Williems	5.6	2,283	10,434	36	52	55	303	58	245	209	240	169	231	536	149
Williamson, Wiliamson, Wilimson, Willanson, Williamsen, Willimson	5.3	285	1,225	5		2	4		7	35	53	9	70	64	36
Williford, Welford, Wellford, Whilford, Wilford, Willford, Willford, Willfred, Willifred	5.7	25	117			1	1		3		1		1	17	1
Willington	6.9	29	171			1	26		1				1		
Willis, Willace, Willas, Willes, Willise, Williss, Wyles, Wylis, Wyllis, Wyllys	5.8	323	1,429	2	9	17	69	2	25	39	28	23	37	62	10
Williston, Willeston	6.2	25	130		1	1	10	1	1					11	
Willoughby, Willoby, Willougheby, Willowbe, Willowby	5.1	44	181		7	3			9	5		10	4	6	
Wills, Will, Wille	5.8	152	729	2	20	4			8	15	36	11	33	17	6
Wilman, Williman, Willimans, Willman, Willmon	4.8	21	80	7		2			2	1	3	1		1	4
Wilmarth, Willmarth, Wilmoth, Wilmouth	5.3	39	166		1	1	26	2	1	1		1	1	4	1

TABLE 111.—NOMENCLATURE, DEALING WITH NAMES REPRESENTED BY AT LEAST 100 WHITE PERSONS, BY STATES AND TERRITORIES, AT THE FIRST CENSUS: 1790—Continued.

NAME.	Average size of family.	TOTAL. Heads of families.	TOTAL. All other members.	Maine.	New Hampshire.	Vermont.	Massachusetts.	Rhode Island.	Connecticut.	New York.	Pennsylvania.	Maryland.	Virginia.	North Carolina.	South Carolina.
Wilmot, Willmot, Wilmott, Wilmut	4.9	35	137			3	1		21	3		4	3		
Wilsey, Willsee, Wilse, Wiltsey, Wiltsie	6.1	27	139				1			15	1		9	1	
Wilsher, Welcher, Welcker, Welker, Welsher, Wilshire, Wiltcher, Wiltshire	5.6	26	119				1				15		9		1
Wilson, Willirson, Willison, Willisson, Willson, Willston, Wilsen, Wilsin	5.6	1,765	8,032	53	101	58	121	16	92	143	380	199	163	276	163
Wiltse, Wilt, Wilts, Wiltz	6.7	41	233							22	19				
Wimbely, Wimbelly, Wimberle, Wimberley, Wimberly	5.6	23	106											20	3
Wimer, Weimer, Werner, Wemmer, Wimire, Wimmer, Wimor, Wymer, Wymor, Wymore	5.1	22	91							2	13	3	3		1
Winants, Winant, Wynant, Wynants	5.6	28	129							25		1		2	
Winchel, Winchal, Winchall, Winchell, Winchels, Winshell	4.8	53	204	3			3	13		21	13				
Winchester, Winchest, Winchister, Winshester	5.4	52	229	1	3	7	17		7	1		8		5	3
Winder, Winders	4.5	23	80									10	3	7	3
Wines, Wine, Wynes	6.5	20	110			1		1			7	7	1	2	1
Winfield, Wingfield	5.4	49	214			1				13	1		20	14	
Wing, Wings	5.8	126	606	19	2	9	66	3	4	18	2	1			2
Wingate, Wengate, Wingat, Wingatt, Winget, Wingit	5.4	62	274	6	21		5				5	7	4	14	
Winger, Winegar, Wineger, Wingar, Wingars, Winnegar	5.5	22	99				1		3	3	15				
Winkler, Winckler, Winklar	5.1	23	94							1	2	2	1	14	3
Winn, Win, Winne, Wins, Winse, Wynn, Wynne, Wynns, Wyns	5.8	138	667	12	3	1	13			21	11	4	30	23	20
Winship, Windship, Winshop	5.4	35	155	4			23	4	4						
Winslow	6.0	171	857	37	13	10	76	4	3	4	2		4	18	
Winsor	7.3	30	189				9	18				2			1
Winstead, Wemstead	5.3	22	94									1	12	9	
Winston, Winson, Winstone	5.6	35	161							4	6		7	18	
Winter, Winters, Wintor, Wintr	5.5	129	559	1	2	6	15	7	17	17	38	15		8	3
Wire, Wyer, Wyers	5.9	42	204	6	3	2	16		5	1	1	3	2	3	
Wirick, Weirich, Werick, Whirick, Wireck, Wirich, Wyrich, Wyrick	6.3	20	106								18			2	
Wirt, Wert, Werts, Wertz, Wirts, Wirtz, Wurtz	5.7	45	211				1			7	34	2			1
Wise, Wiese	5.4	143	635	3	2	1	9	1	6	5	52	19	18	17	10
Wisel, Wescl, Wessel, Wesseils, Wessels, Wissel	5.5	26	116	1			1	3		1	10	8		1	1
Wiseman, Weissman	5.9	23	112					1	1		5	2	4	9	1
Wiser, Weeser, Weiser, Weisser, Wieser	6.5	31	169			1			1		2	21	1	3	2
Wisner, Wisener, Wissner	5.5	21	94							8	11	2			
Wissler, Whisler, Whistler	5.9	17	84						1		15		1		
Wister, Wistar, Wisters	5.6	18	82								12		1	5	
Wiswall, Wiswell	5.5	22	100	4	1	2	13			2					
Witbeck, Witback, Witbech, Witbeek	5.5	42	191							42					
Witham, Whitham, Withum	5.2	50	208	25	3	2	17					3			
Witherell, Weatherall, Weatherals, Wetherall, Whetherell, Witheral, Witherel, Witherill, Withrell	5.9	49	241		1	3	40		2			2			1
Withers, Wither, Witherias	5.0	25	100	3						1	6		2	5	8
Witherspoon, Watherspoon, Weatherspoon, Wetherspoon, Wetherspoonc, Witherspoone, Wotherspoon	5.2	43	179			7					1	3	3	11	18
Withington, Witherington, Witherinton, Withinton, Withrington	5.7	40	189			3	26				3	1		7	
Witmer, Whitmer, Whitmire, Whitmyer, Witmeyer, Witmyer	6.0	36	179								28	2	1		5
Witt, Wit, Wite, Witts, Wittse, Wittz, Witz	5.9	58	282	2	3	2	17			3	9		16	5	1
Wolcott, Walcot, Walcott, Walcutt, Walkcutt, Walket, Wallcott, Wolcot, Wolcutt, Wolket, Wollcot, Wollcott, Woolcot, Woolcutt, Woolcut	5.5	108	487	1	1	10	32	4	53	6				1	
Wolf, Wholf, Wolfe, Wolff, Wolph, Woolf, Woolfe	5.7	246	1,165			2	8		7	15	131	29	24	17	13
Womack, Wamack, Wammock, Wamock, Womac, Womach, Wommack, Wommoch, Wormack	6.1	35	179										22	11	2
Wombwell, Wamble, Womble	5.0	20	80										9	11	
Wood, Woode, Woods	5.7	1,437	6,726	28	64	88	345	47	76	254	121	68	121	147	78
Woodall, Woodal, Woodale, Woodel	5.2	23	96				1					10	1	9	2
Woodbridge, Woodbridg, Woodbrige, Woodredge, Woodridge	6.0	40	200	7		2	14		15	1	1				
Woodbury, Woodberry, Woodbery, Woodbrey	5.6	149	686	10	27	4	101	1	1	1					4
Woodcock, Woodcoalk, Woodcok	5.3	41	178	3	4	2	12		4	5	2	4	3		2
Wooden, Woodden, Woodham, Woodin, Wooding	5.8	51	243			1	2			23	11	1	8	4	1
Woodford	6.5	22	122			1				19	1	1			
Woodhouse	5.7	35	165	1	4					6	1	1	2	18	2
Woodhull, Woodhul	5.5	28	126						1	3	24				
Woodman	5.8	97	466	32	25	2	19	9	1		5	1		2	1
Woodruff, Woodroff, Woodroof, Woodrop, Woodrough, Woodruf	6.1	144	728	1		2	8		93	17	9		5	2	7
Woodside, Wodside, Woodsides	6.1	20	102	4							7			7	2
Woodson, Wooderson, Woodsom, Woodsum	5.6	54	248	9			1						36	2	6
Woodward, Wodword, Woodard, Woodards, Woodart, Wooddart, Wooderd, Woodjard, Woodword	5.8	399	1,907	14	38	30	76	7	49	33	34	19	38	48	13
Woody, Wooddy, Woodey	4.8	24	90										11	6	7
Woolard, Wollard, Wollerd, Woolart, Woollard, Woorlard	5.8	30	145								4	1	5	19	1
Woolford, Wolfard, Wolfart, Wolfaurd, Wolferd, Wolfert, Wolford, Wolfort, Woolfard, Woolfert, Woolfort	5.0	27	108						1	1	15	5	5		
Woolley, Woohley, Wooley, Woolly	5.8	46	220			2	10	1		22	5	2		1	3
Woolsey, Woollsey	5.5	34	152							33				1	
Woolworth, Wallworth, Walsworth, Walworth, Wolworth	5.4	25	110					9		4	11	1			
Wooster, Woorster, Worcester, Worster, Worsters, Woster	5.3	96	414	17	12	5	14		35	5	6	1			
Wooton, Wootan, Wooten, Wootin, Wootten, Wootton	5.0	57	226									9	11	25	12
Word, Werd, Wooard, Words	5.9	19	93							1	3	5	3	5	2
Worden, Woorden, Wordin, Wording, Wordon	5.3	67	288			3	3	9	13	36	1	1		1	
Worell, Warrell, Whorrel, Worral, Worrel, Worrell	4.7	67	249							1	47	9		10	
Worfield, Warefield, Warfeild, Warfield, Wharfield	5.3	62	264					9			2	51			
Work, Woork, Works	6.0	51	256	2	3		5		6		25	5		4	1
Workman	6.1	17	86						1		10	1		2	3
Worley, Worldly, Worly	6.2	20	103								9	1	2	7	
Wormwood, Warmwood	5.2	21	89	12	2						7				
Worsham, Warsham, Washam	5.5	32	145										30	2	
Worth, Wirth	6.1	48	243	1	5		20				11	5	1	5	
Worthen, Worthin, Worthing	5.7	19	89			12		2					5		
Worthington, Worthinton, Wothington	5.9	66	322						9	14	1	5	17	17	3
Wren, Ren, Renn, Wrenn	5.1	50	207								6	3	28	10	3
Wright, Right, Rights, Rite, Rites, Wrights, Write, Writes	5.6	1,135	5,171	10	67	60	201	7	111	143	129	92	120	123	72
Wyatt, Wiart, Wiat, Wiatt, Wiet, Wiott, Wyart, Wyat, Wyatts, Wyet, Wyett	5.2	81	341		5		14	2	1	5	2	4	25	15	8
Wykoff, Wickoff, Wickoffe, Wikoff, Wychoff, Wyckoff, Wycoff, Wycoffe	5.8	23	110								15	7		1	
Wyman, Wiman, Wymon	5.5	135	612	24	29	12	64		2		3			1	
Wynkoop, Winecoop, Winekoop, Winkoop	5.6	35	160							3	20	11	1		
Wynner, Winar, Winnah, Winner	6.0	22	110								15	7			

A CENTURY OF POPULATION GROWTH.

TABLE 111.—NOMENCLATURE, DEALING WITH NAMES REPRESENTED BY AT LEAST 100 WHITE PERSONS, BY STATES AND TERRITORIES, AT THE FIRST CENSUS: 1790—Continued.

NAME.	Average size of family.	TOTAL. Heads of families.	TOTAL. All other members.	Maine.	New Hampshire.	Vermont.	Massachusetts.	Rhode Island.	Connecticut.	New York.	Pennsylvania.	Maryland.	Virginia.	North Carolina.	South Carolina.
Yale, Yales	5.1	41	167			4	3		26	5	3				
Yarborough, Yarber, Yarbro, Yarbrough	5.4	39	172											31	8
Yarnall, Yarnal, Yarnell, Yarnold	7.2	20	124								15	2	1	2	
Yates, Yate, Yeates, Yeats	5.6	137	634	3		1	3	3	6	34	2	21	24	35	5
Yeager, Yagar, Yager, Yarger, Yeagar, Yeauger, Yeger	5.8	43	205							7	32		3		1
Yeaton	6.1	32	164	7	24						1				
Yeoman, Yeamans, Yeamons, Yeomans, Yoeman, Yomans, Youmans, Yumans	5.6	46	211		1	2	3	2	6	19	1	1	2	3	6
Yergar, Yerger	6.8	17	99								17				
Yerkes, Yerk, Yerkas, Yerks	5.9	32	156							7	25				
Yocom, Yeocom, Yeokim, Yoakam, Yoakum, Yocam, Yocham, Yochum, Yocum, Yokem, Yokim, Yokom, Yokum, Youcum	4.9	37	146								23		14		
Yoder, Yodder	5.3	25	108								25				
York, Yark, Yorke, Yourk	5.5	109	494	26	22	2	1	1	10	10	4	6	2	22	3
Yost, Yhost, Yoast, Yobst, Yoest, Youst	6.7	44	252							2	29	7	4	2	
Young, Yong, Yonge, Yongs, Yongue, Younges, Youngs, Yung	5.7	1,022	4,825	69	72	10	89	39	40	165	236	82	54	89	77
Youngblood, Younblood, Youngblud	5.8	25	121								1	2		4	18
Younger, Yougher	5.8	19	91				3		1				4	8	3
Yount, Yant, Yont	6.9	20	118								9	1		10	
Ziegler, Zeegler, Zeggler, Zegler, Zeiger, Zeigler, Zigler	6.3	55	294				1		*		41	5	1		7
Zimmerman, Zemerman, Zemmerman, Zimerman, Zimmermon, Zimmormon	5.7	65	303							1	44	6	4		10
Zuck, Zook, Zuke	7.5	16	104								13	3			

Table 112.—WHITE POPULATION, CLASSIFIED ACCORDING TO NATIONALITY AS INDICATED BY NAMES OF HEADS OF FAMILIES, BY COUNTIES: 1790.

MAINE.

COUNTY.	All nationalities.	English and Welsh.	Scotch.	Irish.	Dutch.	French.	German.	Hebrew.	All other.
The state	96,107	89,515	4,154	1,334	279	115	436	44	230
Cumberland	25,351	23,974	954	180	63	45	20	2	113
Hancock	9,504	9,012	318	94	5	31	32		12
Lincoln	29,592	26,849	1,670	435	151	27	359	29	72
Washington	2,740	2,427	162	80		12	25	6	28
York	28,920	27,253	1,050	545	60			7	5

NEW HAMPSHIRE.

COUNTY.	All nationalities.	English and Welsh.	Scotch.	Irish.	Dutch.	French.	German.	Hebrew.	All other.
The state	141,112	132,726	6,648	1,346	153	142			97
Cheshire	28,665	27,329	1,115	95	62	16			48
Grafton	13,419	12,830	476	37	20	51			5
Hillsborough	32,707	29,917	2,368	390	32				
Rockingham	42,795	40,426	1,687	615	18	21			28
Strafford	23,526	22,224	1,002	209	21	54			16

VERMONT.

COUNTY.	All nationalities.	English and Welsh.	Scotch.	Irish.	Dutch.	French.	German.	Hebrew.	All other.
The state	85,072	81,149	2,562	597	428	153	35		148
Addison	6,383	6,035	170	70	53	16	21		18
Bennington	12,173	11,466	398	110	163	34			2
Chittenden	7,264	6,824	292	52	62	6	5		23
Orange	10,485	9,905	441	99	20	13			7
Rutland	15,558	14,911	411	120	48	23	9		36
Windham	17,514	16,858	499	75	64	3			15
Windsor	15,695	15,150	351	71	18	58			47

MASSACHUSETTS.

COUNTY.	All nationalities.	English and Welsh.	Scotch.	Irish.	Dutch.	French.	German.	Hebrew.	All other.
The state	[1] 370,264	351,698	13,375	3,793	428	700	53	49	168
Barnstable	16,970	16,187	159	549	9	14		17	35
Berkshire	29,940	28,514	845	271	203	30	6		71
Bristol	30,966	29,522	932	239		235			38
Dukes	3,230	2,900	51	273					6
Essex	57,007	53,915	2,143	753	3	136	36	17	4
Hampshire	[1] 56,282	53,268	2,437	504	57	3	3		10
Middlesex	42,177	40,340	1,500	213		120	4		
Nantucket	4,521	4,426	62	33					
Plymouth	29,013	27,394	1,053	396	135	35			
Suffolk	43,803	42,062	1,366	253	1	113	4		4
Worcester	56,355	53,170	2,827	309	20	14		15	

RHODE ISLAND.

COUNTY.	All nationalities.	English and Welsh.	Scotch.	Irish.	Dutch.	French.	German.	Hebrew.	All other.
The state	64,670	62,079	1,976	459	19	88	33	9	7
Bristol	3,013	2,777	144	39	15	31	7		
Kent	8,439	8,027	362	43					7
Newport	13,174	12,567	428	146		24		9	
Providence	23,518	22,469	842	144	4	33	26		
Washington	16,526	16,239	200	87					

CONNECTICUT.

COUNTY.	All nationalities.	English and Welsh.	Scotch.	Irish.	Dutch.	French.	German.	Hebrew.	All other.
The state	232,236	223,437	6,425	1,589	258	512	4	5	6
Fairfield	35,173	34,116	676	162	41	173		5	
Hartford	37,498	36,239	956	234	21	42			6
Litchfield	38,119	36,453	1,174	325	122	45			
Middlesex	18,492	17,763	574	97	26	32			
New Haven	29,882	28,591	780	381	22	104	4		
New London	31,605	30,593	799	142	16	55			
Tolland	13,111	12,650	411	50					
Windham	28,356	27,032	1,055	198	10	61			

[1] Exclusive of 2,923 persons for whom no data are available.

TABLE 112.—WHITE POPULATION, CLASSIFIED ACCORDING TO NATIONALITY AS INDICATED BY NAMES OF HEADS OF FAMILIES, BY COUNTIES: 1790—Continued:

NEW YORK.

COUNTY.	All nationalities.	English and Welsh.	Scotch.	Irish.	Dutch.	French.	German.	Hebrew.	All other.
The state	314,366	245,901	10,034	2,525	50,600	2,424	1,103	385	1,394
Albany	72,087	54,925	2,518	644	13,563	193	92		152
Clinton	1,583	1,354	66	43	33	64	14		9
Columbia	25,811	20,183	521	143	4,710	118	102	8	26
Dutchess	42,981	32,996	624	458	7,393	577	465	2	466
Kings	3,021	1,531	23	20	1,380	67			
Montgomery	28,223	22,052	1,100	96	4,630	63	142		140
New York	29,619	24,340	1,445	244	2,846	425	88	106	125
Ontario	1,058	948	64	16	27				3
Orange	17,315	13,754	395	102	2,831	119	16		98
Queens	12,886	10,908	171	88	1,562	22		110	25
Richmond	2,945	2,075	38	14	582	157			79
Suffolk	14,310	12,915	231	182	844	74		40	24
Ulster	26,295	16,222	1,412	191	7,902	304	134	69	61
Washington	14,028	11,986	1,140	213	528	12	50	44	55
Westchester	22,204	19,712	286	71	1,769	229		6	131

PENNSYLVANIA.

COUNTY.	All nationalities.	English and Welsh.	Scotch.	Irish.	Dutch.	French.	German.	Hebrew.	All other.
The state	423,373	249,656	49,567	8,614	2,623	2,341	110,357	21	194
Allegheny	10,032	6,621	2,501	418	11	15	454	6	6
Bedford	13,052	9,954	1,064	191	20	24	1,784	15	
Berks	29,928	6,983	319	143	16	32	22,435		
Bucks	24,374	17,515	1,821	475	544	153	3,866		
Chester	27,141	20,905	3,646	707	38	200	1,645		
Cumberland	17,779	10,576	4,575	534	21	131	1,939		3
Dauphin	17,886	10,491	1,480	222	22	100	5,571		
Delaware	9,133	7,544	1,034	155	21	32	347		
Fayette	12,990	9,317	2,110	592	114	99	758		
Franklin	15,057	9,992	3,178	491	45	55	1,296		
Huntingdon	7,491	5,522	1,494	136	15	12	312		
Lancaster	35,192	18,092	2,950	339	71	290	13,449		1
Luzerne	4,868	4,088	268	91	179	21	221		
Mifflin	7,461	4,856	2,044	289	22	34	216		
Montgomery	22,365	14,677	766	197	285	68	6,284		88
Northampton	24,086	11,295	648	106	603	127	11,250		57
Northumberland	16,971	9,504	2,431	467	169	29	4,371		
Philadelphia	51,916	29,897	4,560	1,331	190	680	15,232		26
Washington	23,617	16,103	5,278	656	76	117	1,374		13
Westmoreland	15,852	9,301	3,559	616	62	71	2,243		
York	36,182	16,423	3,841	458	99	51	15,310		

MARYLAND.

COUNTY.	All nationalities.	English and Welsh.	Scotch.	Irish.	Dutch.	French.	German.	Hebrew.	All other.
The state	[1] 191,627	161,011	12,441	4,550	254	1,336	11,246	599	190
Ann-Arundel	11,664	10,915	571	150		18	6		4
Baltimore	18,953	16,375	1,096	464	44	53	627	180	114
Baltimore town	11,925	9,871	893	273	25	183	444	203	33
Caroline	7,028	6,286	353	270		65	49	5	
Cecil	10,055	7,915	1,705	271	9	82	57	16	
Charles	10,124	8,980	744	296		85	12		7
Dorchester	10,010	9,588	234	128	7	50		3	
Frederick	26,937	19,525	1,337	468	15	265	5,137	167	23
Harford	10,784	9,024	1,253	369	28	41	69		
Kent	6,748	5,946	453	143	56	13	128	9	
Montgomery	11,679	10,156	783	481		33	226		
Prince Georges	10,004	8,781	719	297		161	46		
Queen Anns	8,171	7,403	379	230	30	103	20	6	
St. Marys	8,216	7,682	392	126	5	9	2		
Talbot	7,231	6,529	466	170	7		59		
Washington	14,472	9,118	641	260	28	59	4,356	10	
Worcester	7,626	6,917	422	154		116	8		9

VIRGINIA.[2]

COUNTY.	All nationalities.	English and Welsh.	Scotch.	Irish.	Dutch.	French.	German.	Hebrew.	All other.
The state	128,112	108,859	9,114	2,591	247	773	6,277		251
Albemarle	4,341	3,665	464	104		93	15		
Amelia	3,941	3,448	319	92	3	25	41		13
Amherst	4,530	3,813	484	125		40	68		
Charlotte	3,790	3,449	228	64		2			47
Chesterfield	4,885	4,276	440	65		59	45		
Cumberland	2,415	2,145	185	31		13	23		18
Essex	2,489	2,250	119	12		80			28
Fairfax	3,687	3,177	369	99		14	20		8
Fluvanna	1,985	1,810	103	63					9
Frederick	4,786	4,126	483	100	7	16	34		20

[1] Exclusive of 17,022 persons for whom no data are available.   [2] State enumerations of 1782 and 1783.   Data incomplete.

TABLE **112.**—WHITE POPULATION, CLASSIFIED ACCORDING TO NATIONALITY AS INDICATED BY NAMES OF HEADS OF FAMILIES, BY COUNTIES: 1790—Continued.

VIRGINIA [1]—Continued.

COUNTY.	All nationalities.	English and Welsh.	Scotch.	Irish.	Dutch.	French.	German.	Hebrew.	All other.
Gloucester	3,348	3,081	143	5		62	48		9
Greensville	1,845	1,685	94	12		54			
Halifax	6,486	5,803	391	129	16	55	79		13
Hampshire	7,182	5,669	524	136	74	35	734		10
Hanover	3,707	3,370	244	93					
Harrison	1,507	1,242	156	51	7	14	29		8
Isle of Wight	3,760	3,603	90	67					
Lancaster	1,726	1,547	122	41			16		
Mecklenburg	6,397	5,803	387	159	20		28		
Middlesex	1,167	1,048	80	23		8	8		
Monongalia	2,302	2,019	192	91					
Nansemond	357	340	17						
New Kent	1,621	1,468	113	33		3			4
Norfolk	5,273	4,771	418	75			9		
Northumberland	3,370	3,100	178	58	25	9			
Orange	4,020	3,574	235	168		32	4		7
Pittsylvania	5,851	5,093	568	158	6	15	11		
Powhatan	1,468	1,256	123	44	12	22			11
Prince Edward	3,425	2,913	403	58		51			
Princess Anne	3,995	3,666	190	97	5	7	1		29
Richmond	2,947	2,740	115	68	7	7			10
Rockingham	3,657	2,484	228	63		19	863		
Shenandoah	6,460	2,027	294	26			4,113		
Stafford	2,483	2,197	133	70		5	71		7
Surry	2,667	2,454	169	29		10	5		
Sussex	2,923	2,576	217	56	65	3	6		
Warwick	597	529	48	14			6		
Williamsburg, city of	722	642	48	12		20			

NORTH CAROLINA.

COUNTY.	All nationalities.	English and Welsh.	Scotch.	Irish.	Dutch.	French.	German.	Hebrew.	All other.
The state	[2]265,334	220,566	29,829	6,206	405	751	7,422	1	154
Edenton district	33,568	30,472	2,371	527	63	34	90		11
Fayette district	28,112	19,699	7,462	817	28	34	65		7
Halifax district	37,955	34,573	2,081	947	48	227	74		
Hillsborough district	21,973	19,751	1,631	328	25	7	231		
Morgan district	30,687	24,405	3,560	730	47	31	1,884		30
Newbern district	38,800	34,009	3,223	1,146	73	199	56		94
Salisbury district	58,425	43,751	8,160	1,277	118	151	4,960	1	7
Wilmington district	15,814	13,901	1,341	434	3	68	62		5

SOUTH CAROLINA.

COUNTY.	All nationalities.	English and Welsh.	Scotch.	Irish.	Dutch.	French.	German.	Hebrew.	All other.
The state	140,178	115,480	16,447	3,576	219	1,882	2,343	85	146
Beaufort district	4,364	3,793	328	120	10	67	36		10
Camden district	29,242	23,843	4,517	709	15	121	27		10
Charleston district	15,402	12,334	1,522	478	62	817	126	13	50
Cheraw district	7,418	6,313	575	260	30	161	62		17
Georgetown district	8,878	7,052	1,282	127		365	42	10	
Ninety-six district	62,462	52,890	7,468	1,419	99	263	244	27	52
Orangeburgh district	12,412	9,255	755	463	3	88	1,806	35	7

[1] State enumerations of 1782 and 1783. Data incomplete.　　　[2] Exclusive of 22,847 persons for whom no data are available.

TABLE **113.**—NUMBER OF WHITE FAMILIES, SLAVEHOLDING AND NONSLAVEHOLDING, CLASSIFIED ACCORDING TO NATIONALITY AS INDICATED BY NAME OF HEAD, TOGETHER WITH THE NUMBER OF WHITE PERSONS AND OF SLAVES REPORTED FOR SUCH FAMILIES, BY STATES AND TERRITORIES: 1790.

MAINE.

NATIONALITY.	WHITE FAMILIES.				WHITE PERSONS.		SLAVES.		
	Total number.	Slave-holding.	Nonslave-holding.	Per cent slaveholding families form of all families.	Total number.	Average number per family.	Total number.	Average number per slaveholding family.	Number per 100 of all families.
All nationalities	16,972	....	16,972	....	96,107	5.7	....	....	....
English and Welsh	15,807	....	15,807	....	89,515	5.7			
Scotch	721	....	721	....	4,154	5.8			
Irish	240	....	240	....	1,334	5.6			
Dutch	49	....	49	....	279	5.7			
French	23	....	23	....	115	5.0			
German	83	....	83	....	436	5.3			
Hebrew	10	....	10	....	44	4.4			
All other	39	....	39	....	230	5.9			

NEW HAMPSHIRE.

NATIONALITY.	WHITE FAMILIES.				WHITE PERSONS.		SLAVES.		
	Total number.	Slave-holding.	Nonslave-holding.	Per cent slaveholding families form of all families.	Total number.	Average number per family.	Total number.	Average number per slaveholding family.	Number per 100 of all families.
All nationalities	23,982	123	23,859	0.5	141,112	5.9	157	1.3	1
English and Welsh	22,574	118	22,456	0.5	132,726	5.9	152	1.3	1
Scotch	1,107	5	1,102	0.5	6,648	6.0	5	1.0	(1)
Irish	234	....	234	....	1,346	5.8			
Dutch	28	....	28	....	153	5.5			
French	23	....	23	....	142	6.2			
German									
Hebrew									
All other	16	....	16	....	97	6.1			

VERMONT.

NATIONALITY.	WHITE FAMILIES.				WHITE PERSONS.		SLAVES.		
	Total number.	Slave-holding.	Nonslave-holding.	Per cent slaveholding families form of all families.	Total number.	Average number per family.	Total number.	Average number per slaveholding family.	Number per 100 of all families.
All nationalities	14,969	....	14,969	....	85,072	5.7			
English and Welsh	14,282	....	14,282	....	81,149	5.7			
Scotch	441	....	441	....	2,562	5.8			
Irish	105	....	105	....	597	5.7			
Dutch	76	....	76	....	428	5.6			
French	29	....	29	....	153	5.3			
German	5	....	5	....	35	7.0			
Hebrew									
All other	31	....	31	....	148	4.8			

MASSACHUSETTS.

NATIONALITY.	WHITE FAMILIES.				WHITE PERSONS.		SLAVES.		
	Total number.	Slave-holding.	Nonslave-holding.	Per cent slaveholding families form of all families.	Total number.	Average number per family.	Total number.	Average number per slaveholding family.	Number per 100 of all families.
All nationalities	65,149	....	65,149	....	[2] 370,264	5.7			
English and Welsh	61,846	....	61,846	....	351,698	5.7			
Scotch	2,392	....	2,392	....	13,375	5.6			
Irish	661	....	661	....	3,793	5.7			
Dutch	78	....	78	....	428	5.5			
French	118	....	118	....	700	5.9			
German	11	....	11	....	53	4.8			
Hebrew	12	....	12	....	49	4.1			
All other	31	....	31	....	108	5.4			

RHODE ISLAND.

NATIONALITY.	WHITE FAMILIES.				WHITE PERSONS.		SLAVES.		
	Total number.	Slave-holding.	Nonslave-holding.	Per cent slaveholding families form of all families.	Total number.	Average number per family.	Total number.	Average number per slaveholding family.	Number per 100 of all families.
All nationalities	10,854	461	10,393	4.2	64,670	6.0	958	2.1	9
English and Welsh	10,401	437	9,964	4.2	62,079	6.0	910	2.1	9
Scotch	339	16	323	4.7	1,976	5.8	25	1.6	7
Irish	79	6	73	7.6	459	5.8	20	3.3	25
Dutch	5	....	5	....	19	3.8			
French	19	2	17	10.5	88	4.6	3	1.5	16
German	9	....	9	....	33	3.7			
Hebrew	1	....	1	....	9	9.0			
All other	1	....	1	....	7	7.0			

CONNECTICUT.

NATIONALITY.	WHITE FAMILIES.				WHITE PERSONS.		SLAVES.		
	Total number.	Slave-holding.	Nonslave-holding.	Per cent slaveholding families form of all families.	Total number.	Average number per family.	Total number.	Average number per slaveholding family.	Number per 100 of all families.
All nationalities	40,457	1,557	38,900	3.8	232,236	5.7	2,642	1.7	7
English and Welsh	38,844	1,488	37,356	3.8	223,437	5.8	2,543	1.7	7
Scotch	1,178	47	1,131	4.0	6,425	5.5	67	1.4	6
Irish	288	13	275	4.5	1,589	5.4	18	1.4	6
Dutch	49	1	48	2.0	258	5.3	5	5.0	10
French	95	7	88	7.4	512	5.4	8	1.1	8
German	1	....	1	....	4	4.0			
Hebrew	1	1	....	100.0	5	5.0	1	1.0	100
All other	1	....	1	....	6	6.0			

[1] Less than 1 per hundred.　　　　[2] Exclusive of 2,923 persons for whom no data are available.

Table **113.**—NUMBER OF WHITE FAMILIES, SLAVEHOLDING AND NONSLAVEHOLDING, CLASSIFIED ACCORDING TO NATIONALITY AS INDICATED BY NAME OF HEAD, TOGETHER WITH THE NUMBER OF WHITE PERSONS AND OF SLAVES REPORTED FOR SUCH FAMILIES, BY STATES AND TERRITORIES: 1790—Continued.

NEW YORK.

NATIONALITY.	WHITE FAMILIES.				WHITE PERSONS.		SLAVES.		
	Total number.	Slave-holding.	Nonslave-holding.	Per cent slaveholding families form of all families.	Total number.	Average number per family.	Total number.	Average number per slaveholding family.	Number per 100 of all families.
All nationalities........................	54,185	7,787	46,398	14.4	314,366	5.8	21,178	2.7	39
English and Welsh........................	42,543	4,883	37,660	11.5	245,901	5.8	11,861	2.4	28
Scotch...................................	1,773	154	1,619	8.7	10,034	5.7	336	2.2	19
Irish....................................	461	28	433	6.1	2,525	5.5	83	3.0	18
Dutch....................................	8,494	2,537	5,957	29.9	50,600	6.0	8,357	3.3	98
French..................................	433	102	331	23.6	2,424	5.6	286	2.8	66
German..................................	189	36	153	19.0	1,103	5.8	130	3.6	69
Hebrew..................................	70	10	60	14.3	385	5.5	19	1.9	27
All other...............................	222	37	185	16.7	1,394	6.3	196	2.9	48

PENNSYLVANIA.

NATIONALITY.	Total number.	Slave-holding.	Nonslave-holding.	Per cent slaveholding families form of all families.	Total number.	Average number per family.	Total number.	Average number per slaveholding family.	Number per 100 of all families.
All nationalities........................	73,322	1,851	71,471	2.5	423,373	5.8	3,698	2.0	5
English and Welsh........................	43,026	1,123	41,903	2.6	249,656	5.8	2,277	2.0	5
Scotch...................................	8,552	428	8,124	5.0	49,567	5.8	875	2.0	10
Irish....................................	1,555	59	1,496	3.8	8,614	5.5	127	2.2	8
Dutch....................................	465	29	436	6.2	2,623	5.6	58	2.0	12
French..................................	377	8	369	2.1	2,341	6.2	13	1.6	3
German..................................	19,307	204	19,103	1.1	110,357	5.7	348	1.7	2
Hebrew..................................	3	....	3	....	21	7.0	....	....	....
All other...............................	37	....	37	....	194	5.2	....	....	....

MARYLAND.

NATIONALITY.	Total number.	Slave-holding.	Nonslave-holding.	Per cent slaveholding families form of all families.	Total number.	Average number per family.	Total number.	Average number per slaveholding family.	Number per 100 of all families.
All nationalities........................	32,012	12,142	19,870	37.9	[1] 191,627	6.0	84,769	7.0	265
English and Welsh........................	26,524	10,633	15,891	40.1	161,011	6.1	74,936	7.0	283
Scotch...................................	2,271	876	1,395	38.6	12,441	5.5	5,824	6.6	256
Irish....................................	863	246	617	28.5	4,550	5.3	2,072	8.4	240
Dutch....................................	44	23	21	52.3	254	5.8	124	5.4	282
French..................................	247	112	135	45.3	1,336	5.4	719	6.4	291
German..................................	1,935	221	1,714	11.4	11,246	5.8	944	4.3	49
Hebrew..................................	101	16	85	15.8	599	5.9	85	5.3	84
All other...............................	27	15	12	55.6	190	7.0	65	4.3	241

VIRGINIA.[2]

NORTH CAROLINA.

NATIONALITY.	Total number.	Slave-holding.	Nonslave-holding.	Per cent slaveholding families form of all families.	Total number.	Average number per family.	Total number.	Average number per slaveholding family.	Number per 100 of all families.
All nationalities........................	48,021	14,945	33,076	31.1	[3] 265,334	5.5	91,730	6.1	191
English and Welsh........................	39,920	12,421	27,499	31.1	220,566	5.5	79,696	6.4	200
Scotch...................................	5,369	1,764	3,605	32.9	29,829	5.6	8,458	4.8	158
Irish....................................	1,172	397	775	33.9	6,206	5.3	2,297	5.8	196
Dutch....................................	70	22	48	31.4	405	5.8	71	3.2	101
French..................................	144	90	54	62.5	751	5.2	601	6.7	417
German..................................	1,314	240	1,074	18.3	7,422	5.6	556	2.3	42
Hebrew..................................	1	....	1	....	1	1.0	....	....	....
All other...............................	31	11	20	35.5	154	5.0	51	4.6	165

SOUTH CAROLINA.

NATIONALITY.	Total number.	Slave-holding.	Nonslave-holding.	Per cent slaveholding families form of all families.	Total number.	Average number per family.	Total number.	Average number per slaveholding family.	Number per 100 of all families.
All nationalities........................	25,552	8,798	16,754	34.4	140,178	5.5	106,787	12.1	418
English and Welsh........................	20,884	7,043	13,841	33.7	115,480	5.5	86,309	12.3	413
Scotch...................................	3,107	1,072	2,035	34.5	16,447	5.3	11,980	11.2	386
Irish....................................	627	213	414	34.0	3,576	5.7	1,961	9.2	313
Dutch....................................	41	13	28	31.7	219	5.3	291	22.4	710
French..................................	405	268	137	66.2	1,882	4.6	4,937	18.4	1,219
German..................................	446	170	276	38.1	2,343	5.3	1,101	6.5	247
Hebrew..................................	14	6	8	42.9	85	6.1	52	8.7	371
All other...............................	28	13	15	46.4	146	5.2	156	12.0	557

[1] Exclusive of 17,022 persons for whom no data are available.   Schedules destroyed.   [3] Exclusive of 23,847 persons for whom no data are available.

TABLE 114.—NUMBER OF FAMILIES REPORTED AT THE FIRST CENSUS, CLASSIFIED AS SLAVEHOLDING AND NON-SLAVEHOLDING, WHITE, AND FREE COLORED, TOGETHER WITH THE TOTAL AND AVERAGE NUMBER OF SLAVES, BY COUNTIES AND MINOR CIVIL DIVISIONS: 1790.

NEW HAMPSHIRE.

COUNTY AND TOWN.	Total number.	Slaveholding. Number.	Slaveholding White. Number of families.	Slaveholding White. Members Total.	Slaveholding White. Average per family.	Slaveholding Free colored.[1]	Nonslaveholding. Number.	Nonslaveholding White. Number of families.	Nonslaveholding White. Members Total.	Nonslaveholding White. Average per family.	Nonslaveholding Free colored.[1]	Pct Slaveholding White.	Pct Slaveholding Free colored.[1]	Pct Nonslaveholding White.	Pct Nonslaveholding Free colored.[1]	Slaves Total number.	Slaves Average per slaveholding family.
The state	24,065	123	123	760	6.2	......	23,942	23,859	140,428	5.9	83	0.5	......	99.1	0.3	157	1.3
Cheshire county	4,796	16	16	107	6.7		4,780	4,766	28,569	6.0	14	0.3	......	99.4	0.3	18	1.1
Acworth	117						117	117	705	6.0				100.0			
Alstead	188						188	188	1,111	5.9				100.0			
Charlestown	160	1	1	3	3.0		159	158	1,099	7.0	1	0.6		98.8	0.6	1	1.0
Chesterfield	315						315	315	1,901	6.0				100.0			
Claremont	240	2	2	21	10.5		238	238	1,398	5.9		0.8		99.2		2	1.0
Cornish	161	1	1	4	4.0		160	160	976	6.1		0.6		99.4		1	1.0
Croydon	94						94	93	533	5.7	1			98.9	1.1		
Dublin	157						157	156	895	5.7	1			99.4	0.6		
Fitzwilliam	187						187	187	1,038	5.6				100.0			
Gilson	54						54	54	298	5.5				100.0			
Hinsdale	86	2	2	12	6.0		84	84	508	6.0		2.3		97.7		4	2.0
Jeffrey	203						203	201	1,227	6.1	2			99.0	1.0		
Keene	208	2	2	15	7.5		206	205	1,285	6.3	1	1.0		98.6	0.5	2	1.0
Langdon	42						42	42	242	5.8				100.0			
Lempster	72						72	71	412	5.8	1			98.6	1.4		
Marlborough	138						138	138	786	5.7				100.0			
Marlow	64						64	64	319	5.0				100.0			
New Grantham	60	1	1	4	4.0		59	59	327	5.5		1.7		98.3		1	1.0
Newport	132	1	1	7	7.0		131	130	767	5.9	1	0.8		98.5	0.8	1	1.0
Packersfield	123						123	122	721	5.9	1			99.2	0.8		
Plainfield	190						190	190	1,022	5.4				100.0			
Protectworth	46	1	1	7	7.0		45	45	202	4.5		2.2		97.8		1	1.0
Richmond	221						221	221	1,380	6.2				100.0			
Rindge	188						188	187	1,136	6.1	1			99.5	0.5		
Stoddard	123	1	1	6	6.0		122	122	694	5.7		0.8		99.2		1	1.0
Sullivan	37						37	37	219	5.9				100.0			
Surry	79						79	79	448	5.7				100.0			
Swanzey	192						192	191	1,149	6.0	1			99.5	0.5		
Unity	88						88	87	537	6.2	1			98.9	1.1		
Walpole	195	2	2	13	6.5		193	193	1,238	6.4		1.0		99.0		2	1.0
Washington	97						97	97	545	5.6				100.0			
Wendell	51						51	51	267	5.2				100.0			
Westmoreland	299	1	1	7	7.0		298	297	1,988	6.7	1	0.3		99.3	0.3	1	1.0
Winchester	189	1	1	8	8.0		188	187	1,196	6.4	1	0.5		98.9	0.5	1	1.0
Grafton county	2,463	13	13	107	8.2		2,450	2,446	13,315	5.4	4	0.5		99.3	0.2	21	1.6
Alexandria	54						54	54	297	5.5				100.0			
Bartlett	51	1	1	3	3.0		50	50	244	4.9		2.0		98.0		1	1.0
Bath	85	1	1	10	10.0		84	84	482	5.7		1.2		98.8		1	1.0
Bridgewater	61	1	1	4	4.0		60	60	276	4.6		1.6		98.4		1	1.0
Burton	23						23	23	141	6.1				100.0			
Cambridge (not inhabited)																	
Campton	75	1	1	15	15.0		74	74	379	5.1		1.3		98.7		1	1.0
Canaan	87						87	87	483	5.6				100.0			
Chatham	12						12	12	58	4.8				100.0			
Cockburn	4						4	4	26	6.5				100.0			
Cockermouth	70						70	70	373	5.3				100.0			
Colburne	7						7	7	29	4.1				100.0			
Concord (alias Gunthwaite)	65						65	65	313	4.8				100.0			
Coventry	17						17	17	88	5.2				100.0			
Dalton	2						2	2	14	7.0				100.0			
Dame's Location	3						3	3	21	7.0				100.0			
Dartmouth	21						21	21	111	5.3				100.0			
Dorchester	37						37	37	175	4.7				100.0			
Dummer (not inhabited)																	
Enfield (alias Relham)	124						124	124	722	5.8				100.0			
Errol (not inhabited)																	
Franconia	16						16	16	72	4.5				100.0			
Grafton	69						69	69	403	5.8				100.0			
Hale's Location	2						2	2	9	4.5				100.0			
Hanover (including 152 students at Dartmouth College)	212	1	1	5	5.0		211	210	1,364	6.5	1	0.5		99.1	0.5	2	2.0

[1] Includes families of Indians taxed.

TABLE **114.**—NUMBER OF FAMILIES REPORTED AT THE FIRST CENSUS, CLASSIFIED AS SLAVEHOLDING AND NON-SLAVEHOLDING, WHITE, AND FREE COLORED, TOGETHER WITH THE TOTAL AND AVERAGE NUMBER OF SLAVES, BY COUNTIES AND MINOR CIVIL DIVISIONS: 1790—Continued.

NEW HAMPSHIRE—Continued.

COUNTY AND TOWN.	Total number.	Slaveholding.					Nonslaveholding.					Per cent families of each class form of all families.				SLAVES.	
		Number.	White.			Free colored.¹	Number.	White.			Free colored.¹	Slaveholding.		Nonslaveholding.		Total number.	Average number per slaveholding family.
			Number of families.	Number of members.				Number of families.	Number of members.			White.	Free colored.¹	White.	Free colored.¹		
				Total.	Average per family.				Total.	Average per family.							
Grafton county—Continued.																	
Hart's Location	3						3	3	12	4.0				100.0			
Haverhill	101	2	2	25	12.5		99	99	522	5.3		2.0		98.0		4	2.0
Kilkenny (not inhabited)																	
Lancaster	27						27	27	161	6.0				100.0			
Landaff	55						55	55	292	5.3				100.0			
Lebanon	225						225	223	1,172	5.3	2			99.1	0.9		
Lincoln	5						5	5	22	4.4				100.0			
Littleton	19						19	19	96	5.1				100.0			
Lyman	43						43	43	202	4.7				100.0			
Lyme	175						175	174	815	4.7	1			99.4	0.6		
Millfield (not inhabited)																	
New Chester	50						50	50	312	6.2				100.0			
New Holderness	62						62	62	329	5.3				100.0			
Northumberland	16						16	16	117	7.3				100.0			
Orange	22	1	1	5	5.0		21	21	125	6.0		4.5		95.5		1	1.0
Orford	91	1	1	10	10.0		90	90	527	5.9		1.1		98.9		3	3.0
Peeling (not inhabited)																	
Percy	8						8	8	48	6.0				100.0			
Piermont	72	3	3	20	6.7		69	69	402	5.8		4.2		95.8		3	1.0
Plymouth	131	1	1	10	10.0		130	130	611	4.7		0.8		99.2		4	4.0
Rumney	71						71	71	411	5.8				100.0			
Senter's Location	3						3	3	8	2.7				100.0			
Shelburne	6						6	6	35	5.8				100.0			
Stark's Location	6						6	6	29	4.8				100.0			
Sterling's Location	2						2	2	9	4.5				100.0			
Stratford	25						25	25	144	5.8				100.0			
Success (not inhabited)																	
Thornton	70						70	70	385	5.5				100.0			
Trecothick (not inhabited)																	
Wales's Location	1						1	1	6	6.0				100.0			
Warren	35						35	35	202	5.8				100.0			
Wentworth	42						42	42	241	5.7				100.0			
Hillsborough county	5,330						5,330	5,317	32,706	6.2	13			99.8	0.2		
Amherst	384						384	384	2,351	6.1	1			100.0			
Andover	111						111	111	645	5.8				100.0			
Antrim	97						97	97	526	5.4				100.0			
Bedford	141						141	141	890	6.3				100.0			
Boscawen	178						178	178	1,107	6.2				100.0			
Bradford	45						45	45	217	4.8				100.0			
Campbell's Gore	23						23	23	120	5.2				100.0			
Dearing	148						148	148	936	6.3				100.0			
Derryfield	58						58	58	362	6.2				100.0			
Derryfield Gore	4						4	4	30	7.5				100.0			
Dunbarton	134						134	131	901	6.9	3			97.8	2.2		
Dunstable	115						115	115	633	5.5				100.0			
Duxbury Mile-slip	27						27	27	169	6.3				100.0			
Fishersfield	60						60	60	325	5.4				100.0			
Francestown	173						173	173	983	5.7				100.0			
Goffstown	201						201	200	1,241	6.2	1			99.5	0.5		
Hancock	117						117	116	631	5.4	1			99.1	0.9		
Heniker	177						177	177	1,116	6.3				100.0			
Hillsborough	141						141	141	797	5.7				100.0			
Hollis	242						242	242	1,441	6.0				100.0			
Hopkinton	269						269	269	1,714	6.4				100.0			
Kersarge Gore	18						18	18	103	5.7				100.0			
Litchfield	57						57	54	352	6.5	3			94.7	5.3		
Lyndborough	219						219	219	1,280	5.8				100.0			
Lyndborough Gore	8						8	8	38	4.8				100.0			
Mason	145						145	145	919	6.3				100.0			
Merrimac	135						135	135	809	6.0				100.0			
New Boston	177						177	177	1,194	6.7				100.0			
New Ipswich	176						176	176	1,237	7.0				100.0			
New London	50						50	50	311	6.2				100.0			
Nottingham West	188						188	187	1,051	5.6	1			99.5	0.5		
Peterborough	136						136	136	857	6.3				100.0			
Raby	60						60	59	335	5.7	1			98.3	1.7		

¹ Includes families of Indians taxed.

TABLE **114.**—NUMBER OF FAMILIES REPORTED AT THE FIRST CENSUS, CLASSIFIED AS SLAVEHOLDING AND NON-SLAVEHOLDING, WHITE, AND FREE COLORED, TOGETHER WITH THE TOTAL AND AVERAGE NUMBER OF SLAVES, BY COUNTIES AND MINOR CIVIL DIVISIONS: 1790—Continued.

NEW HAMPSHIRE—Continued.

		FAMILIES										Per cent families of each class form of all families				SLAVES	
		Slaveholding					Nonslaveholding					Slaveholding		Nonslaveholding			
			White					White									
COUNTY AND TOWN.	Total number.	Number.	Number of families.	Members Total.	Members Average per family.	Free colored.[1]	Number.	Number of families.	Members Total.	Members Average per family.	Free colored.[1]	White.	Free colored.[1]	White.	Free colored.[1]	Total number.	Average number per slaveholding family.
Hillsborough county—Cont'd.																	
Salisbury	215						215	215	1,360	6.3				100.0			
Sharon	45						45	45	260	5.8				100.0			
Society Land	57						57	57	329	5.8				100.0			
Sutton	90						90	90	520	5.8				100.0			
Temple	116						116	114	741	6.5	2			98.3	1.7		
Warner	148						148	148	863	5.8				100.0			
Weare	286						286	286	1,924	6.7				100.0			
Wilton	159						159	158	1,088	6.9	1			99.4	0.6		
Rockingham county	7,398	76	76	438	5.8		7,322	7,275	42,419	5.8	47	1.0		98.3	0.6	97	1.3
Allenstown	46						46	46	254	5.5				100.0			
Atkinson	79						79	79	478	6.1				100.0			
Bow	94						94	94	566	6.0				100.0			
Brintwood	156	1	1	2	2.0		155	154	967	6.3	1	0.6		98.7	0.6	1	1.0
Candia	167						167	167	1,039	6.2				100.0			
Canterbury	160	1	1	6	6.0		159	159	1,038	6.5		0.6		99.4		3	3.0
Chester	340						340	340	1,898	5.6				100.0			
Chichester	82						82	82	492	6.0				100.0			
Concord	278	4	4	20	5.0		274	273	1,707	6.3	1	1.4		98.2	0.4	4	1.0
Deerfield	299	2	2	9	4.5		297	297	1,601	5.4		0.7		99.3		2	1.0
East Kingston	58						58	58	356	6.1				100.0			
Epping	223	5	5	29	5.8		218	218	1,219	5.6		2.2		97.8		5	1.0
Epson	131						131	131	830	6.3				100.0			
Exeter	287	1	1	2	2.0		286	273	1,637	6.0	13	0.3		95.1	4.5	2	2.0
Gosport (on Star Island)	20						20	20	93	4.7				100.0			
Greenland	105	2	2	21	10.5		103	102	599	5.9	1	1.9		97.1	1.0	2	1.0
Hampstead	121	1	1	9	9.0		120	119	713	6.0	1	0.8		98.3	0.8	1	1.0
Hampton	154	1	1	6	6.0		153	152	842	5.5	1	0.6		98.7	0.6	1	1.0
Hampton Falls	91						91	90	537	6.0	1			98.9	1.1		
Hawke	75	1	1	3	3.0		74	74	418	5.6		1.3		98.7		1	1.0
Kensington	146						146	146	804	5.5				100.0			
Kingston	167						167	167	902	5.4				100.0			
Londonderry	422	5	5	42	8.4		417	415	2,588	6.2	2	1.2		98.3	0.5	5	1.0
Loudon	166	2	2	18	9.0		164	163	1,052	6.5	1	1.2		98.2	0.6	2	1.0
Newcastle	94						94	94	534	5.7				100.0			
Newington	89	9	9	51	5.7		80	80	475	5.9		10.1		89.9		14	1.6
Newmarket	194	1	1	4	4.0		193	192	1,125	5.9	1	0.5		99.0	0.5	1	1.0
Newtown	99	1	1	3	3.0		98	98	526	5.4		1.0		99.0		1	1.0
Northampton	99						99	99	655	6.6				100.0			
Northfield	114						114	114	604	5.3				100.0			
Northwood	124	1	1	5	5.0		123	123	745	6.1		0.8		99.2		1	1.0
Nottingham	178	7	7	34	4.9		171	170	1,020	6.0	1	3.9		95.5	0.6	11	1.6
Pelham	131						131	131	794	6.1				100.0			
Pembrook	155	2	2	6	3.0		153	153	954	6.2		1.3		98.7		2	1.0
Pittsfield	147						147	146	868	5.9	1			99.3	0.7		
Plaistow	94						94	94	516	5.5				100.0			
Poplin	78	1	1	2	2.0		77	77	489	6.4		1.3		98.7		1	1.0
Portsmouth	893	21	21	121	5.8		872	856	4,497	5.3	16	2.4		95.9	1.8	26	1.2
Raymond	128						128	125	719	5.8	3			97.7	2.3		
Rye	152	2	2	12	6.0		150	150	841	5.6		1.3		98.7		3	1.5
Salem	207	1	1	4	4.0		206	205	1,203	5.9	1	0.5		99.0	0.5	2	2.0
Sandown	105						105	105	562	5.4				100.0			
Seabrook	132						132	132	713	5.4				100.0			
South Hampton	73						73	73	448	6.1				100.0			
Stratham	113	1	1	3	3.0		142	140	870	6.2	2	0.7		97.9	1.4	1	1.0
Windham	102	3	3	26	8.7		99	99	631	6.4		2.9		97.1		5	1.7
Strafford county	4,078	18	18	108	6.0		4,060	4,055	23,419	5.8	5	0.4		99.4	0.1	21	1.2
Barnstead	128	1	1	4	4.0		127	127	802	6.3		0.8		99.2		1	1.0
Barrington	420						420	420	2,479	5.9				100.0			
Conway	98						98	98	574	5.9				100.0			
Dover	314	6	6	33	5.5		308	308	1,937	6.3		1.9		98.1		8	1.3
Durham	225	3	3	19	6.3		222	222	1,222	5.5		1.3		98.7		3	1.0
Eaton	44						44	44	254	5.8				100.0			
Effingham	31	1	1	4	4.0		30	30	148	4.9		3.2		96.8		1	1.0
Gilmantown	441	1	1	9	9.0		440	436	2,578	5.9	4	0.2		98.9	0.9	1	1.0
Lee	180						180	180	1,034	5.7				100.0			
Madbury	98						98	98	588	6.0				100.0			

[1] Includes families of Indians taxed.

TABLE **114.**—NUMBER OF FAMILIES REPORTED AT THE FIRST CENSUS, CLASSIFIED AS SLAVEHOLDING AND NON-SLAVEHOLDING, WHITE, AND FREE COLORED, TOGETHER WITH THE TOTAL AND AVERAGE NUMBER OF SLAVES, BY COUNTIES AND MINOR CIVIL DIVISIONS: 1790—Continued.

NEW HAMPSHIRE—Continued.

COUNTY AND TOWN.	FAMILIES. Total number.	Slaveholding. Number.	Slaveholding White. Number of families.	Slaveholding White. Members Total.	Slaveholding White. Members Average per family.	Slaveholding Free colored.[1]	Nonslaveholding. Number.	Nonslaveholding White. Number of families.	Nonslaveholding White. Members Total.	Nonslaveholding White. Members Average per family.	Nonslaveholding Free colored.[1]	Per cent Slaveholding White.	Per cent Slaveholding Free colored.[1]	Per cent Nonslaveholding White.	Per cent Nonslaveholding Free colored.[1]	SLAVES. Total number.	SLAVES. Average number per slaveholding family.
Strafford county—Continued.																	
Merideth	153						153	153	878	5.7				100.0			
Middleton	107						107	107	617	5.8				100.0			
Moultonborough	91	1	1	5	5.0		90	90	559	6.2		1.1		98.9		1	1.0
New Durham	104						104	104	554	5.3				100.0			
New Durham Gore	74						74	73	438	6.0	1			98.6	1.4		
New Hampton	111						111	111	650	5.9				100.0			
Ossipee	69						69	69	339	4.9				100.0			
Rochester	507	1	1	8	8.0		506	506	2,843	5.6		0.2		99.8		1	1.0
Sanborntown	293						293	293	1,587	5.4				100.0			
Sandwich	155						155	155	905	5.8				100.0			
Somersworth	164	3	3	21	7.0		161	161	919	5.7		1.8		98.2		4	1.3
Stark's Location	2						2	2	3	1.5				100.0			
Sterling's Location	9						9	9	48	5.3				100.0			
Tamworth	47	1	1	5	5.0		46	46	260	5.7		2.1		97.9		1	1.0
Tuftonborough	20						20	20	109	5.5				100.0			
Wakefield	115						115	115	646	5.6				100.0			
Wolfborough	78						78	78	448	5.7				100.0			

RHODE ISLAND.

COUNTY AND TOWN.	FAMILIES. Total number.	Slaveholding. Number.	Slaveholding White. Number of families.	Slaveholding White. Members Total.	Slaveholding White. Members Average per family.	Slaveholding Free colored.[1]	Nonslaveholding. Number.	Nonslaveholding White. Number of families.	Nonslaveholding White. Members Total.	Nonslaveholding White. Members Average per family.	Nonslaveholding Free colored.[1]	Per cent Slaveholding White.	Per cent Slaveholding Free colored.[1]	Per cent Nonslaveholding White.	Per cent Nonslaveholding Free colored.[1]	SLAVES. Total number.	SLAVES. Average number per slaveholding family.
The state	11,296	461	461	2,993	6.5		10,835	10,393	61,590	5.9	442	4.1		92.0	3.9	958	2.1
Bristol county	567	53	53	318	6.0		514	504	2,694	5.3	10	9.3		88.9	1.8	98	1.8
Barrington	115	8	8	40	5.0		107	103	599	5.8	4	7.0		89.6	3.5	12	1.5
Bristol	252	34	34	221	6.5		218	213	1,074	5.0	5	13.5		84.5	2.0	64	1.9
Warren	200	11	11	57	5.2		189	188	1,021	5.4	1	5.5		94.0	0.5	22	2.0
Kent county	1,387	32	32	221	6.9		1,355	1,309	8,228	6.3	46	2.3		94.4	3.3	63	2.0
Coventry	394	4	4	23	5.8		390	385	2,420	6.3	5	1.0		97.7	1.3	5	1.3
East Greenwich	296	8	8	67	8.4		288	281	1,674	6.0	7	2.7		94.9	2.4	13	1.6
Warwick	397	16	16	88	5.5		381	350	2,156	6.2	31	4.0		88.2	7.8	35	2.2
West Greenwich	300	4	4	43	10.7		296	293	1,978	6.8	3	1.3		97.7	1.0	10	2.5
Newport county	2,448	180	180	1,157	6.4		2,268	2,141	12,024	5.6	127	7.4		87.5	5.2	372	2.1
Jamestown	79	8	8	44	5.5		71	63	379	6.0	8	10.1		79.7	10.1	16	2.0
Little Compton	260	12	12	84	7.0		248	246	1,400	5.7	2	4.6		94.6	0.8	23	1.9
Middleton	128	8	8	65	8.1		120	119	734	6.2	1	6.3		93.0	0.8	15	1.9
New Shoreham	90	20	20	139	7.0		70	70	438	6.3		22.2		77.8		48	2.4
Newport	1,242	109	109	648	5.9		1,133	1,054	5,447	5.2	79	8.8		84.9	6.4	226	2.1
Portsmouth	243	10	10	81	8.1		233	231	1,472	6.4	2	4.1		95.1	0.8	19	1.9
Tiverton	406	13	13	96	7.4		393	358	2,154	6.0	35	3.2		88.2	8.6	25	1.9
Providence county	4,016	54	54	391	7.2		3,962	3,840	23,023	6.0	122	1.3		95.6	3.0	81	1.5
Cranston	315	7	7	50	7.1		308	295	1,744	5.9	13	2.2		93.7	4.1	10	1.4
Cumberland	313						313	311	1,958	6.3	2			99.4	0.6		
Foster	363	3	3	27	9.0		360	357	2,222	6.2	3	0.8		98.3	0.8	4	1.3
Glocester	620	1	1	12	12.0		619	617	3,981	6.5	2	0.2		99.5	0.3	1	1.0
Johnstown	219	3	3	20	6.7		216	204	1,226	6.0	12	1.4		93.2	5.5	3	1.0
North Providence	183	4	4	30	7.5		179	171	986	5.8	8	2.2		93.4	4.4	5	1.3
Providence	1,127	29	29	208	7.2		1,098	1,029	5,592	5.4	69	2.6		91.3	6.1	47	1.6
Scituate	382	3	3	24	8.0		379	376	2,257	6.0	3	0.8		98.4	0.8	6	2.0
Smithfield	494	4	4	20	5.0		490	480	3,057	6.4	10	0.8		97.2	2.0	5	1.3
Washington county	2,878	142	142	906	6.4		2,736	2,599	15,621	6.0	137	4.9		90.3	4.8	344	2.4
Charleston	295	4	4	21	5.3		291	271	1,584	5.8	20	1.4		91.9	6.8	12	3.0
Exeter	423	24	24	154	6.4		399	384	2,218	5.8	15	5.7		90.8	3.5	37	1.5
Hopkinston	404	6	6	35	5.8		398	393	2,350	6.0	5	1.5		97.3	1.2	7	1.2
North Kingston	454	42	42	262	6.2		412	382	2,348	6.1	30	9.3		84.1	6.6	96	2.3
Richmond	290	2	2	9	4.5		288	285	1,682	5.9	3	0.7		98.3	1.0	2	1.0
South Kingston	653	60	60	386	6.4		593	535	3,258	6.1	58	9.2		81.9	8.9	180	3.0
Westerly	359	4	4	39	9.8		355	349	2,181	6.2	6	1.1		97.2	1.7	10	2.5

[1] Includes families of Indians taxed.

A CENTURY OF POPULATION GROWTH.

TABLE 114.—NUMBER OF FAMILIES REPORTED AT THE FIRST CENSUS, CLASSIFIED AS SLAVEHOLDING AND NON-SLAVEHOLDING, WHITE, AND FREE COLORED, TOGETHER WITH THE TOTAL AND AVERAGE NUMBER OF SLAVES, BY COUNTIES AND MINOR CIVIL DIVISIONS: 1790—Continued.

CONNECTICUT.

COUNTY AND TOWN.	Total number.	Slaveholding. Number.	Slaveholding White. Number of families.	Slaveholding White. Number of members. Total.	Slaveholding White. Number of members. Average per family.	Slaveholding. Free colored.[1]	Nonslaveholding. Number.	Nonslaveholding White. Number of families.	Nonslaveholding White. Number of members. Total.	Nonslaveholding White. Number of members. Average per family.	Nonslaveholding. Free colored.[1]	Per cent Slaveholding. White.	Per cent Slaveholding. Free colored.[1]	Per cent Nonslaveholding. White.	Per cent Nonslaveholding. Free colored.[1]	Slaves. Total number.	Slaves. Average number per slaveholding family.
The state	40,876	1,563	1,557	9,769	6.3	6	39,313	38,900	222,372	5.7	413	3.8	(²)	95.2	1.0	2,648	1.7
Fairfield county	6,412	470	470	2,798	6.0		5,942	5,899	32,376	5.5	43	7.3		92.0	0.7	799	1.7
Brookfield	189	2	2	5	2.5		187	186	997	5.4	1	1.1		98.4	0.5	3	1.5
Danbury	563	18	18	130	7.2		545	541	2,859	5.3	4	3.2		96.1	0.7	23	1.3
Fairfield	707	96	96	540	5.6		611	609	3,253	5.3	2	13.6		86.1	0.3	203	2.1
Greenwich	527	49	49	308	6.3		478	476	2,748	5.8	2	9.3		90.3	0.4	82	1.7
Huntington	476	67	67	400	6.0		409	398	2,174	5.5	11	14.1		83.6	2.3	120	1.8
New Fairfield	277	9	9	44	4.9		268	268	1,515	5.7		3.2		96.8		9	1.0
Newtown	445	47	47	297	6.3		398	397	2,410	6.1	1	10.6		89.2	0.2	71	1.5
Norwalk / Stamford	} 1,628	67	67	420	6.3		1,561	1,547	8,190	5.3	14	4.1		95.0	0.9	117	1.7
Reading	264	20	20	131	6.6		244	242	1,321	5.5	2	7.6		91.7	0.8	32	1.6
Ridgefield	351	5	5	26	5.2		346	346	1,912	5.5		1.4		98.6		5	1.0
Stratford	548	67	67	376	5.6		481	478	2,699	5.6	3	12.2		87.2	0.5	98	1.5
Weston	437	23	23	121	5.3		414	411	2,298	5.6	3	5.3		94.1	0.7	36	1.6
Hartford county	6,582	157	157	1,020	6.5		6,425	6,372	36,494	5.7	53	2.4		96.8	0.8	256	1.6
Berlin	452	2	2	14	7.0		450	449	2,469	5.5	1	0.4		99.3	0.2	2	1.0
Bristol	440	1	1	4	4.0		439	434	2,445	5.6	5	0.2		98.6	1.1	2	2.0
East Hartford	473	15	15	93	6.2		458	457	2,879	6.3	1	3.2		96.6	0.2	31	2.1
East Windsor	480	8	8	49	6.1		472	470	2,498	5.3	2	1.7		97.9	0.4	8	1.0
Enfield	317	10	10	47	4.7		307	307	1,745	5.7		3.2		96.8		13	1.3
Farmington	439	6	6	42	7.0		433	426	2,598	6.1	7	1.4		97.0	1.6	7	1.2
Glastenbury	468	14	14	70	5.0		454	442	2,565	5.8	12	3.0		94.4	2.6	27	1.9
Granby	489						489	489	2,602	5.3				100.0			
Hartford	663	30	30	212	7.1		633	625	3,733	6.0	8	4.5		94.3	1.2	47	1.6
Simsbury	424	2	2	23	11.5		422	422	2,659	6.3		0.5		99.5		2	1.0
Southington	389	9	9	69	7.7		380	376	2,006	5.3	4	2.3		96.7	1.0	11	1.2
Suffield	407	14	14	99	7.1		393	388	2,330	6.0	5	3.4		95.3	1.2	28	2.0
Wethersfield	685	37	37	246	6.6		648	641	3,432	5.4	7	5.4		93.6	1.0	59	1.6
Windsor	456	9	9	52	5.8		447	446	2,533	5.7	1	2.0		97.8	0.2	19	2.1
Litchfield county	6,563	119	119	776	6.5		6,444	6,400	37,392	5.8	44	1.8		97.5	0.7	203	1.7
Bethlem	179	4	4	39	9.8		175	175	1,012	5.8		2.2		97.8		4	1.0
Cornwall	255	12	12	70	5.8		243	239	1,357	5.7	4	4.7		93.7	1.6	19	1.6
Harwinton	230	3	3	17	5.7		227	227	1,345	5.9		1.3		98.7		6	2.0
Kent	215	4	4	37	9.3		211	210	1,263	6.0	1	1.9		97.7	0.5	6	1.5
Litchfield	3,358	47	47	290	6.2		3,311	3,292	19,755	6.0	19	1.4		98.0	0.6	89	1.9
New Milford	555	12	12	96	8.0		543	536	3,010	5.6	7	2.2		96.6	1.3	25	2.1
Southbury	307	9	9	50	5.6		298	294	1,652	5.6	4	2.9		95.8	1.3	21	2.3
Warren	146	5	5	24	4.8		141	139	740	5.3	2	3.4		95.2	1.4	6	1.2
Washington	268	5	5	33	6.6		263	261	1,628	6.2	2	1.9		97.4	0.7	5	1.0
Watertown	574	9	9	61	6.8		565	564	3,068	5.4	1	1.6		98.3	0.2	11	1.2
Woodbury	476	9	9	59	6.6		467	463	2,562	5.5	4	1.9		97.3	0.8	11	1.2
Middlesex county	3,282	114	113	685	6.1	1	3,168	3,145	17,790	5.7	23	3.4	(²)	95.8	0.7	192	1.7
Chatham	563	12	12	72	6.0		551	549	3,109	5.7	2	2.1		97.5	0.4	16	1.3
East Haddam	472	10	10	68	6.8		462	457	2,619	5.7	5	2.1		96.8	1.1	19	1.9
Haddam	356	3	3	11	3.7		353	352	2,170	6.2	1	0.8		98.9	0.3	3	1.0
Killingworth	390	5	5	37	7.4		385	384	2,088	5.4	1	1.3		98.5	0.3	11	2.2
Middletown	942	60	60	371	6.2		882	870	4,755	5.5	12	6.4		92.4	1.3	109	1.8
Saybrook	559	24	23	126	5.5	1	535	533	3,049	5.7	2	4.1	0.2	95.3	0.4	34	1.4
New Haven county	6,012	241	241	1,306	5.4		5,771	5,684	28,478	5.0	87	4.0		94.5	1.4	387	1.6
Branford	386	29	29	149	5.1		357	353	1,990	5.6	4	7.5		91.5	1.0	47	1.6
Cheshire	445	9	9	47	5.2		436	428	2,241	5.2	8	2.0		96.2	1.8	13	1.4
Derby	558	23	23	151	6.6		535	525	2,718	5.2	10	4.1		94.1	1.8	43	1.9
Durham	209	7	7	9	1.3		202	201	998	5.0	1	3.3		96.2	0.5	9	1.3
East Haven	169	20	20	121	6.1		149	148	873	5.9	1	11.8		87.6	0.6	35	1.8
Guilford	728	23	23	99	4.3		705	701	3,293	4.7	4	3.2		96.3	0.5	25	1.1
Hamden	291	4	4	22	5.5		287	286	1,391	4.9	1	1.4		98.3	0.3	4	1.0
Milford	447	45	45	244	5.4		402	387	1,709	4.4	15	10.1		86.6	3.4	65	1.4
New Haven city	919	45	45	264	5.9		874	849	4,028	4.7	25	4.9		92.4	2.7	71	1.6
North Haven	238	4	4	16	4.0		234	233	1,205	5.2	1	1.7		97.9	0.4	6	1.5
Wallingford	656	19	19	99	5.2		637	630	3,183	5.1	7	2.9		96.0	1.1	45	2.4
Waterbury	552	4	4	28	7.0		548	545	2,817	5.2	3	0.7		98.7	0.5	10	2.5
Woodbridge	414	9	9	57	6.3		405	398	2,032	5.1	7	2.2		96.1	1.7	14	1.6

[1] Includes families of Indians taxed. [2] Less than one-tenth of 1 per cent.

TABLE 114.—NUMBER OF FAMILIES REPORTED AT THE FIRST CENSUS, CLASSIFIED AS SLAVEHOLDING AND NON-SLAVEHOLDING, WHITE, AND FREE COLORED, TOGETHER WITH THE TOTAL AND AVERAGE NUMBER OF SLAVES, BY COUNTIES AND MINOR CIVIL DIVISIONS: 1790—Continued.

CONNECTICUT—Continued.

COUNTY AND TOWN.	Total number.	Slaveholding White Number.	Slaveholding White Number of families.	Slaveholding White Members Total.	Slaveholding White Average per family.	Slaveholding Free colored.[1]	Nonslaveholding White Number.	Nonslaveholding White Number of families.	Nonslaveholding White Members Total.	Nonslaveholding White Average per family.	Nonslaveholding Free colored.[1]	Per cent Slaveholding White.	Per cent Slaveholding Free colored.[1]	Per cent Nonslaveholding White.	Per cent Nonslaveholding Free colored.[1]	Slaves Total number.	Slaves Average number per slaveholding family.
New London county[2]	5,686	329	325	2,173	6.7	4	5,357	5,231	29,397	5.6	126	5.7	0.1	92.0	2.2	581	1.8
Tolland county	2,139	35	34	246	7.2	1	2,104	2,104	12,857	6.1	......	1.6	(³)	98.4	......	46	1.3
Bolton	228	2	2	14	7.0	......	226	226	1,340	5.9	......	0.9	......	99.1	......	2	1.0
Coventry	336	4	4	24	6.0	......	332	332	2,078	6.3	......	1.2	......	98.8	......	7	1.8
Ellington	171	3	2	19	9.5	1	168	168	1,020	6.1	......	1.2	0.6	98.2	......	4	1.3
Hebron	345	14	14	116	8.3	......	331	331	2,151	6.5	......	4.1	......	95.9	......	19	1.4
Somers	200	3	3	23	7.7	......	197	197	1,190	6.0	......	1.5	......	98.5	......	5	1.7
Stafford	315	2	2	2	1.0	......	313	313	1,849	5.9	......	0.6	......	99.4	......	2	1.0
Tolland	236	5	5	35	7.0	......	231	231	1,430	6.2	......	2.1	......	97.9	......	5	1.0
Union	100	1	1	8	8.0	......	99	99	621	6.3	......	1.0	......	99.0	......	1	1.0
Willington	208	1	1	5	5.0	......	207	207	1,178	5.7	......	0.5	......	99.5	......	1	1.0
Windham county	4,200	98	98	765	7.8	......	4,102	4,065	27,588	6.8	37	2.3	......	96.8	0.9	184	1.9
Ashford	393	4	4	30	7.5	......	389	387	2,524	6.5	2	1.0	......	98.5	0.5	7	1.8
Brooklyne	177	6	6	60	10.0	......	171	168	1,227	7.3	3	3.4	......	94.9	1.7	10	1.7
Canterbury	288	2	2	12	6.0	......	286	284	1,855	6.5	2	0.7	......	98.6	0.7	2	1.0
Hampton	201	1	1	7	7.0	......	200	198	1,315	6.6	2	0.5	......	98.5	1.0	1	1.0
Killingley	326	7	7	35	5.0	......	319	317	2,098	6.6	2	2.1	......	97.2	0.6	9	1.3
Lebanon	573	19	19	142	7.5	......	554	549	3,910	7.1	5	3.3	......	95.8	0.9	51	2.7
Mansfield	393	4	4	31	7.8	......	389	389	2,586	6.6	......	1.0	......	99.0	......	7	1.8
Plainfield	238	8	8	55	6.9	......	230	227	1,586	7.0	3	3.4	......	95.4	1.3	10	1.3
Pomfret	244	15	15	141	9.4	......	229	229	1,581	6.9	......	6.1	......	93.9	......	19	1.3
Thompson	333	2	2	18	9.0	......	331	330	2,238	6.8	1	0.6	......	99.1	0.3	7	3.5
Voluntown	290	7	7	58	8.3	......	283	281	1,772	6.3	2	2.4	......	96.9	0.7	21	3.0
Windham	414	14	14	103	7.4	......	400	388	2,569	6.6	12	3.4	......	93.7	2.9	28	2.0
Woodstock	330	9	9	73	8.1	......	321	318	2,327	7.3	3	2.7	......	96.4	0.9	12	1.3

NEW YORK.

COUNTY AND TOWN.	Total number.	Slaveholding White Number.	Slaveholding White Number of families.	Slaveholding White Members Total.	Slaveholding White Average per family.	Slaveholding Free colored.[1]	Nonslaveholding White Number.	Nonslaveholding White Number of families.	Nonslaveholding White Members Total.	Nonslaveholding White Average per family.	Nonslaveholding Free colored.[1]	Per cent Slaveholding White.	Per cent Slaveholding Free colored.[1]	Per cent Nonslaveholding White.	Per cent Nonslaveholding Free colored.[1]	Slaves Total number.	Slaves Average number per slaveholding family.
The state	54,878	7,796	7,787	47,495	6.1	9	47,082	46,398	265,430	5.7	684	14.2	(³)	84.5	1.2	21,193	2.7
Albany county	12,317	1,474	1,467	8,881	6.1	7	10,843	10,830	63,051	5.8	13	11.9	0.1	87.9	0.1	3,722	2.5
Albany city	573	332	331	1,689	5.1	1	241	238	1,210	5.1	3	57.8	0.2	41.5	0.5	571	1.7
First ward	267	140	140	746	5.3	......	127	125	646	5.2	2	52.4	......	46.8	0.7	214	1.5
Second ward	160	88	87	404	4.6	1	72	72	359	5.0	......	54.4	0.6	45.0	......	100	1.1
Third ward	146	104	104	539	5.2	......	42	41	205	5.0	1	71.2	......	28.1	0.7	257	2.5
Ballstown	1,232	35	35	238	6.8	......	1,197	1,196	6,986	5.8	1	2.8	......	97.1	0.1	69	2.0
Cambridge	792	23	23	169	7.3	......	769	769	4,792	6.2	......	2.9	......	97.1	......	43	1.9
Catskill	280	143	143	876	6.1	......	137	137	771	5.6	......	51.1	......	48.9	......	305	2.1
Coxsackie	535	87	87	522	6.0	......	448	448	2,545	5.7	......	16.3	......	83.7	......	302	3.5
Duanesburgh	281	5	5	26	5.2	......	276	276	1,437	5.2	......	1.8	......	98.2	......	5	1.0
Easton	399	12	12	89	7.4	......	387	387	2,401	6.2	......	3.0	......	97.0	......	57	4.8
Freehold	331	5	5	26	5.2	......	326	326	1,741	5.3	......	1.5	......	98.5	......	5	1.0
Halfmoon	607	55	55	314	5.7	......	552	551	3,165	5.7	1	9.1	......	90.8	0.2	123	2.2
Hoosick	505	17	17	124	7.3	......	488	486	2,867	5.9	2	3.4	......	96.2	0.4	27	1.6
Pittstown	378	15	15	106	7.1	......	363	363	2,319	6.4	......	4.0	......	96.0	......	33	2.2
Rensselaerville	499	11	11	57	5.2	......	488	488	2,666	5.5	......	2.2	......	97.8	......	13	1.2
Rensselaerwick	1,266	171	171	1,160	6.8	......	1,095	1,095	6,586	6.0	......	13.5	......	86.5	......	562	3.3
Saratoga	527	19	19	135	7.1	......	508	507	2,875	5.6	1	3.6	......	96.2	0.2	53	2.8
Schaghticoke	254	47	47	298	6.3	......	207	207	1,209	5.8	......	18.5	......	81.5	......	143	3.0
Schenectady	113	27	27	194	7.2	......	86	86	484	5.6	......	23.9	......	76.1	......	78	2.9
Schenectady south of the Mohawk	582	141	136	734	5.4	5	441	441	2,333	5.3	......	23.4	0.9	75.8	......	381	2.7
Schoharie	305	55	55	369	6.7	......	250	249	1,544	6.2	1	18.0	......	81.6	0.3	152	2.8
Stephentown	1,255	10	10	96	9.6	......	1,245	1,245	7,087	5.7	......	0.8	......	99.2	......	26	2.6
Stillwater	508	27	27	200	7.4	......	481	479	2,807	5.9	2	5.3	......	94.3	0.4	61	2.3
Watervliet	1,091	236	235	1,457	6.2	1	855	853	5,205	6.1	2	21.5	0.1	78.2	0.2	707	3.0
Island in the river not included in any town	4	1	1	2	2.0	......	3	3	21	7.0	......	25.0	......	75.0	......	6	6.0
Clinton county	374	6	6	39	6.5	......	368	368	1,531	4.2	......	1.6	......	98.4	......	16	2.7
Champlain	126	2	2	6	3.0	......	124	124	552	4.5	......	1.6	......	98.4	......	2	1.0
Crown Point	45	......	......	......	......	......	45	45	202	4.5	......	......	......	100.0	......	......	......
Plattsburgh	86	3	3	29	9.7	......	83	83	416	5.0	......	3.5	......	96.5	......	13	4.3
Wellsburgh	117	1	1	4	4.0	......	116	116	361	3.1	......	0.9	......	99.1	......	1	1.0

[1] Includes families of Indians taxed. [2] Not returned by towns. [3] Less than one-tenth of 1 per cent.

TABLE 114.—NUMBER OF FAMILIES REPORTED AT THE FIRST CENSUS, CLASSIFIED AS SLAVEHOLDING AND NON-SLAVEHOLDING, WHITE, AND FREE COLORED, TOGETHER WITH THE TOTAL AND AVERAGE NUMBER OF SLAVES, BY COUNTIES AND MINOR CIVIL DIVISIONS: 1790—Continued.

NEW YORK—Continued.

COUNTY AND TOWN.	Total number.	Slaveholding. Number.	Slaveholding White. Number of families.	Slaveholding White. Members Total.	Slaveholding White. Members Average per family.	Slaveholding Free colored.[1]	Nonslaveholding. Number.	Nonslaveholding White. Number of families.	Nonslaveholding White. Members Total.	Nonslaveholding White. Members Average per family.	Nonslaveholding Free colored.[1]	Per cent Slaveholding White.	Per cent Slaveholding Free colored.[1]	Per cent Nonslaveholding White.	Per cent Nonslaveholding Free colored.[1]	Slaves Total number.	Slaves Average per slaveholding family.
Columbia county	4,276	528	528	3,076	5.8	......	3,748	3,736	22,453	6.0	12	12.3	......	87.4	0.3	1,633	3.1
Canaan	1,018	23	23	175	7.6	......	995	994	6,272	6.3	1	2.3	......	97.6	0.1	36	1.6
Claverack	470	109	109	685	6.3	......	361	359	2,224	6.2	2	23.2	......	76.4	0.4	341	3.1
Clermont	131	37	37	208	5.6	......	94	94	542	5.8	......	28.2	......	71.8	......	112	3.0
Germantown	81	16	16	108	6.8	......	65	65	354	5.4	......	19.8	......	80.2	......	40	2.5
Hillsdale	754	20	20	135	6.8	......	734	733	4,283	5.8	1	2.7	......	97.2	0.1	33	1.7
Hudson	380	63	63	418	6.6	......	317	310	1,947	6.3	7	16.6	......	81.6	1.8	199	3.2
Kinderhook	698	174	174	789	4.5	......	524	523	3,033	5.8	1	24.9	......	74.9	0.1	639	3.7
Livingston	744	86	86	558	6.5	......	658	658	3,798	5.8	......	11.6	......	88.4	......	233	2.7
Dutchess county	6,717	670	670	4,740	7.1	......	6,047	5,990	38,234	6.4	57	10.0	......	89.2	0.8	1,864	2.8
Amenia	441	22	22	188	8.5	......	419	416	2,809	6.8	3	5.0	......	94.3	0.7	52	2.4
Beekman	510	46	46	358	7.8	......	464	462	3,125	6.8	2	9.0	......	90.6	0.4	106	2.3
Clinton	696	67	67	524	7.8	......	629	624	3,877	6.2	5	9.6	......	89.7	0.7	176	2.6
Fishkill	885	195	195	1,275	6.5	......	690	686	4,023	5.9	4	22.0	......	77.5	0.5	601	3.1
Frederickstown	914	36	36	270	7.5	......	878	872	5,557	6.4	6	3.9	......	95.4	0.7	63	1.8
Northeast	500	33	33	261	7.9	......	467	464	3,034	6.5	3	6.6	......	92.8	0.6	80	2.4
Pawling	676	20	20	181	9.1	......	656	642	4,022	6.3	14	3.0	......	95.0	2.1	42	2.1
Philipstown	331	12	12	91	7.6	......	319	319	1,961	6.1	......	3.6	......	96.4	......	25	2.1
Poughkeepsie	370	80	80	537	6.7	......	290	284	1,745	6.1	6	21.6	......	76.8	1.6	207	2.6
Rhinebeck	514	121	121	771	6.4	......	393	385	2,404	6.2	8	23.5	......	74.9	1.6	421	3.5
Southeast	141	6	6	36	6.0	......	135	134	869	6.5	1	4.3	......	95.0	0.7	13	2.2
Washington	759	32	32	248	7.8	......	707	702	4,808	6.8	5	4.3	......	95.0	0.7	78	2.4
Kings county	546	333	332	1,896	5.7	1	213	211	1,128	5.3	2	60.8	0.2	38.6	0.4	1,482	4.5
Brooklyn	218	104	103	602	5.8	1	114	114	585	5.1	......	47.2	0.5	52.3	......	455	4.4
Bushwick	74	49	49	239	4.9	......	25	24	128	5.3	1	66.2	......	32.4	1.4	171	3.5
Flatbush	99	73	73	402	5.5	......	26	26	149	5.7	......	73.7	......	26.3	......	378	5.2
Flatlands	48	32	32	184	5.8	......	16	16	102	6.4	......	66.7	......	33.3	......	137	4.3
Gravesend	48	31	31	203	6.5	......	17	17	83	4.9	......	64.6	......	35.4	......	135	4.4
New Utrecht	59	44	44	266	6.0	......	15	14	81	5.8	1	74.6	......	23.7	1.7	206	4.7
Montgomery county	4,906	300	299	1,754	5.9	1	4,606	4,603	26,300	5.7	3	6.1	(2)	93.8	0.1	588	2.0
Canajoharie	1,047	60	60	366	6.1	......	987	987	5,646	5.7	......	5.7	......	94.3	......	96	1.6
Caughnawaga	721	71	71	391	5.5	......	650	650	3,690	5.7	......	9.8	......	90.2	......	133	1.9
Chemung	405	5	5	31	6.2	......	400	400	2,357	5.9	......	1.2	......	98.8	......	7	1.4
Chenango	12	......	......	......	......	......	12	12	45	3.8	......	......	......	100.0	......	......	......
German Flatts	225	11	11	64	5.8	......	214	214	1,217	5.7	......	4.9	......	95.1	......	20	1.8
Harpersfield	319	6	6	32	5.3	......	313	312	1,688	5.4	1	1.9	......	97.8	0.3	6	1.0
Herkimer	274	5	5	28	5.6	......	269	269	1,488	5.5	......	1.8	......	98.2	......	8	1.6
Mohawk	791	61	60	318	5.3	1	730	730	3,957	5.4	......	7.6	0.1	92.3	......	111	1.8
Otsego	304	4	4	22	5.5	......	300	299	1,640	5.5	1	1.3	......	98.4	0.3	8	2.0
Palatine	474	72	72	475	6.6	......	402	402	2,718	6.8	......	15.2	......	84.8	......	192	2.7
Whites	334	5	5	27	5.4	......	329	328	1,854	5.7	1	1.5	......	98.2	0.3	7	1.4
New York city and county	6,037	1,115	1,115	6,673	6.0	......	4,922	4,753	22,277	4.7	169	18.5	......	78.7	2.8	2,373	2.1
New York city	5,926	1,067	1,067	6,421	6.0	......	4,859	4,695	21,953	4.7	164	18.0	......	79.2	2.8	2,184	2.0
Dock ward	325	115	115	641	5.6	......	210	208	975	4.7	2	35.4	......	64.0	0.6	234	2.0
East ward	586	235	235	1,471	6.3	......	351	349	1,699	4.9	2	40.1	......	59.6	0.3	514	2.2
Montgomery ward	1,377	210	210	1,188	5.7	......	1,167	1,108	4,979	4.5	59	15.3	......	80.5	4.3	373	1.8
North ward	805	154	154	871	5.7	......	741	705	3,459	4.9	36	17.2	......	78.8	4.0	311	2.0
Out ward	1,087	130	130	833	6.4	......	957	927	4,372	4.7	30	12.0	......	85.3	2.8	268	2.1
South ward	380	58	58	298	5.1	......	322	313	1,299	4.2	9	15.3	......	82.4	2.4	115	2.0
West ward	1,276	165	165	1,119	6.8	......	1,111	1,085	5,170	4.8	26	12.9	......	85.0	2.0	369	2.2
Harlem division	111	48	48	252	5.3	......	63	58	324	5.6	5	43.2	......	52.3	4.5	189	3.9
Ontario county	204	4	4	4	1.0	......	200	200	1,036	5.2	......	2.0	......	98.0	......	10	2.5
Canandaigua	88	1	1	1	1.0	......	87	87	454	5.2	......	1.1	......	98.9	......	1	1.0
Erwin	31	2	2	2	1.0	......	29	29	147	5.1	......	6.5	......	93.5	......	7	3.5
Genesee	69	1	1	1	1.0	......	68	68	336	4.9	......	1.4	......	98.6	......	2	2.0
Jerusalem	16	......	......	......	......	......	16	16	99	6.2	......	......	......	100.0	......	......	......
Orange county	2,890	415	415	2,627	6.3	......	2,475	2,453	14,688	6.0	22	14.4	......	84.9	0.8	961	2.3
Goshen	343	87	87	609	7.0	......	256	250	1,567	6.3	6	25.4	......	72.9	1.7	212	2.4
Haverstraw	810	114	114	650	5.7	......	696	693	3,920	5.7	3	14.1	......	85.6	0.4	238	2.1
Minisink	370	21	21	135	6.4	......	349	347	2,013	5.8	2	5.7	......	93.8	0.5	51	2.4
New Cornwall	605	62	62	475	7.7	......	543	542	3,544	6.5	1	10.2	......	89.6	0.2	167	2.7
Orange	190	78	78	400	5.1	......	112	109	539	4.9	3	41.1	......	57.4	1.6	198	2.5
Warwick	572	53	53	358	6.8	......	519	512	3,105	6.1	7	9.3	......	89.5	1.2	95	1.8

[1] Includes families of Indians taxed.   [2] Less than one-tenth of 1 per cent.

TABLE **114.**—NUMBER OF FAMILIES REPORTED AT THE FIRST CENSUS, CLASSIFIED AS SLAVEHOLDING AND NON-SLAVEHOLDING, WHITE, AND FREE COLORED, TOGETHER WITH THE TOTAL AND AVERAGE NUMBER OF SLAVES, BY COUNTIES AND MINOR CIVIL DIVISIONS: 1790—Continued.

NEW YORK—Continued.

| COUNTY AND TOWN. | Total number. | Slaveholding. | | White. | | | | Nonslaveholding. | | White. | | | | Per cent families of each class form of all families. | | | | Slaves. | |
		Number.	Number of families.	Number of members. Total.	Average per family.	Free colored.[1]	Number.	Number of families.	Number of members. Total.	Average per family.	Free colored.[1]		Slaveholding. White.	Slaveholding. Free colored.[1]	Nonslaveholding. White.	Nonslaveholding. Free colored.[1]	Total number.	Average number per slaveholding family.
Queens county	2,548	775	775	4,698	6.1	......	1,773	1,468	8,143	5.5	305		30.4	......	57.6	12.0	2,308	3.0
Flushing	256	104	104	602	5.8	......	152	97	536	5.5	55		40.6	......	37.9	21.5	340	3.3
Jamaica	265	85	85	487	5.7	......	180	154	889	5.8	26		32.1	......	58.1	9.8	221	2.6
Newtown	295	141	141	806	5.7	......	154	127	695	5.5	27		47.8	......	43.1	9.2	533	3.8
North Hempstead	386	153	153	963	6.3	......	233	172	1,055	6.1	61		39.6	......	44.6	15.8	507	3.3
Oyster Bay	683	158	158	1,042	6.6	......	525	430	2,364	5.5	95		23.1	......	63.0	13.9	381	2.4
South Hempstead	663	134	134	798	6.0	......	529	488	2,604	5.3	41		20.2	......	73.6	6.2	326	2.4
Richmond county	566	238	238	1,290	5.4	......	328	324	1,695	5.2	4		42.0	......	57.2	0.7	755	3.2
Castleton	121	39	39	229	5.9	......	82	81	435	5.4	1		32.2	......	66.9	0.8	114	2.9
Northfield	158	46	46	251	5.5	......	112	111	640	5.8	1		29.1	......	70.3	0.6	135	2.9
Southfield	125	72	72	360	5.0	......	53	51	236	4.6	2		57.6	......	40.8	1.6	234	3.3
Westfield	162	81	81	450	5.6	......	81	81	384	4.7	......		50.0	......	50.0	......	272	3.4
Suffolk county	2,858	496	496	2,632	5.3	......	2,362	2,310	11,577	5.0	52		17.4	......	80.8	1.8	1,105	2.2
Brookhaven	566	103	103	524	5.1	......	463	450	2,195	4.9	13		18.2	......	79.5	2.3	233	2.3
Easthampton	249	43	43	243	5.7	......	206	206	1,056	5.1	......		17.3	......	82.7	......	99	2.3
Huntington	572	102	102	563	5.5	......	470	462	2,509	5.4	8		17.8	......	80.8	1.4	219	2.1
Islip	106	9	9	45	5.0	......	97	83	459	5.5	14		8.5	......	78.3	13.2	35	3.9
Shelter Island	35	5	5	23	4.6	......	30	28	131	4.7	2		14.3	......	80.0	5.7	24	4.8
Smithtown	155	51	51	248	4.9	......	104	101	397	3.9	3		32.9	......	65.2	1.9	166	3.3
Southampton	582	90	90	521	5.8	......	492	489	2,454	5.0	3		15.5	......	84.0	0.5	146	1.6
Southold	593	93	93	465	5.0	......	500	491	2,376	4.8	9		15.7	......	82.8	1.5	183	2.0
Ulster county	4,354	878	878	5,535	6.3	......	3,476	3,464	20,761	6.0	12		20.2	......	79.6	0.3	2,914	3.3
Hurley	104	56	56	298	5.3	......	48	48	303	6.3	......		53.8	......	46.2	......	245	4.4
Kingston	534	210	210	1,255	6.0	......	324	324	1,938	6.0	......		39.3	......	60.7	......	721	3.4
Mamakating	284	15	15	107	7.1	......	269	269	1,600	5.9	......		5.3	......	94.7	......	51	3.4
Marbletown	304	89	89	541	6.1	......	215	213	1,260	5.9	2		29.3	......	70.1	0.7	374	4.2
Middletown	172	4	4	29	7.3	......	168	168	983	5.9	......		2.3	......	97.7	......	6	1.5
Montgomery	524	97	97	675	7.0	......	427	427	2,635	6.2	......		18.5	......	81.5	......	236	2.4
New Marlborough	368	23	23	173	7.5	......	345	344	2,004	5.8	1		6.3	......	93.5	0.3	58	2.5
New Paltz	336	78	78	483	6.2	......	258	256	1,507	5.9	2		23.2	......	76.2	0.6	302	3.9
New Windsor	280	42	42	276	6.6	......	238	237	1,409	5.9	1		15.0	......	84.6	0.4	117	2.8
Newburgh	387	28	28	179	6.4	......	359	358	2,096	5.8	1		7.2	......	92.5	0.3	57	2.0
Rochester	223	76	76	452	5.9	......	147	146	881	6.0	1		34.1	......	65.5	0.4	281	3.7
Shawangunk	277	102	102	683	6.7	......	175	174	1,070	6.1	1		36.8	......	62.8	0.4	349	3.4
Wallkill	392	47	47	322	6.9	......	345	344	2,138	6.2	1		12.0	......	87.8	0.3	102	2.2
Woodstock	169	11	11	62	5.6	......	158	156	937	6.0	2		6.5	......	92.3	1.2	15	1.4
Washington county	2,488	24	24	209	8.7	......	2,464	2,464	13,819	5.6	......		1.0	......	99.0	......	46	1.9
Argyle	400	9	9	71	7.9	......	391	391	2,265	5.8	......		2.3	......	97.8	......	14	1.6
Granville	392	......	......				392	392	2,242	5.7	......		......	......	100.0	......		
Hampton	75						75	75	463	6.2					100.0			
Hebron	306						306	306	1,703	5.6					100.0			
Kingsbury	178						178	178	1,119	6.3					100.0			
Queensbury	183	1	1	17	17.0	......	182	182	1,062	5.8	......		0.5	......	99.5	......	1	1.0
Salem	395	10	10	78	7.8	......	385	385	2,098	5.4	......		2.5	......	97.5	......	21	2.1
Westfield	407	3	3	30	10.0	......	404	404	2,072	5.1	......		0.7	......	99.3	......	9	3.0
Whitehall	152	1	1	13	13.0	......	151	151	795	5.3	......		0.7	......	99.3	......	1	1.0
Westchester county	3,797	540	540	3,441	6.4	......	3,257	3,224	18,737	5.8	33		14.2	......	84.9	0.9	1,416	2.6
Bedford	420	20	20	150	7.5	......	400	399	2,273	5.7	1		4.8	......	95.0	0.2	38	1.9
Cortlandt	328	33	33	194	5.9	......	295	293	1,646	5.6	2		10.1	......	89.3	0.6	66	2.0
Eastchester	102	32	32	216	6.8	......	70	70	438	6.3	......		31.4	......	68.6	......	75	2.3
Greenburgh	208	46	46	311	6.8	......	162	162	918	5.7	......		22.1	......	77.9	......	121	2.6
Harrison	152	26	26	185	7.1	......	126	118	730	6.2	8		17.1	......	77.6	5.3	54	2.1
Mamaroneck	65	15	15	89	5.9	......	50	48	288	6.0	2		23.1	......	73.8	3.1	57	3.8
Morrisania	13	5	5	48	9.6	......	8	8	53	6.6	......		38.5	......	61.5	......	30	6.0
Mt. Pleasant	303	38	38	230	6.1	......	265	264	1,599	6.1	1		12.5	......	87.1	0.3	84	2.2
New Rochelle	112	38	38	236	6.2	......	74	70	340	4.9	4		33.9	......	62.5	3.6	87	2.3
North Castle	397	18	18	129	7.2	......	379	376	2,264	6.0	3		4.5	......	94.7	0.8	29	1.6
North Salem	177	11	11	73	6.6	......	166	166	943	5.7	......		6.2	......	93.8	......	28	2.5
Pelham	31	11	11	66	6.0	......	20	20	95	4.8	......		35.5	......	64.5	......	38	3.5
Poundridge	186	......	......				186	185	1,055	5.7	1		......	......	99.5	0.5		

[1] Includes families of Indians taxed.

TABLE **114.**—NUMBER OF FAMILIES REPORTED AT THE FIRST CENSUS, CLASSIFIED AS SLAVEHOLDING AND NON-SLAVEHOLDING, WHITE, AND FREE COLORED, TOGETHER WITH THE TOTAL AND AVERAGE NUMBER OF SLAVES, BY COUNTIES AND MINOR CIVIL DIVISIONS: 1790—Continued.

NEW YORK—Continued.

COUNTY AND TOWN.	FAMILIES.														SLAVES.	
	Total number.	Slaveholding.					Nonslaveholding.					Per cent families of each class form of all families.				Total number.	Average number per slaveholding family.
		Number.	White.			Free colored.[1]	Number.	White.			Free colored.[1]	Slaveholding.		Nonslaveholding.			
			Number of families.	Number of members.				Number of families.	Number of members.			White.	Free colored.[1]	White.	Free colored.[1]		
				Total.	Average per family.				Total.	Average per family.							
Westchester county—Cont'd.																	
Rye	182	49	49	270	5.5	......	113	112	579	5.2	1	30.2	......	69.1	0.6	123	2.5
Salem	260	11	11	50	4.5	......	249	246	1,370	5.6	3	4.2	......	94.6	1.2	19	1.7
Scarsdale	33	8	8	59	7.4	......	25	25	183	7.3	......	24.2	......	75.8	......	28	3.5
Stephen	189	19	19	150	7.9	......	170	170	1,102	6.5	......	10.1	......	89.9	......	38	2.0
Westchester	170	62	62	358	5.8	......	108	107	554	5.2	1	36.5	......	62.9	0.6	242	3.9
White Plains	75	24	24	140	5.8	......	51	50	310	6.2	1	32.0	......	66.7	1.3	49	2.0
Yonkers	152	51	51	352	6.9	......	101	100	591	5.9	1	33.6	......	65.8	0.7	170	3.3
York	262	23	23	135	5.9	......	239	235	1,406	6.0	4	8.8	......	89.7	1.5	40	1.7

PENNSYLVANIA.

COUNTY AND TOWN.	Total number.	Number.	Number of families.	Total.	Average per family.	Free colored.[1]	Number.	Number of families.	Total.	Average per family.	Free colored.[1]	White.	Free colored.[1]	White.	Free colored.[1]	Total number.	Average per slaveholding family.
The state	73,874	1,858	1,851	12,942	7.0	7	72,016	71,471	408,690	5.7	545	2.5	(²)	96.7	0.7	3,707	2.0
Allegheny county	1,844	66	66	429	6.5	......	1,778	1,775	9,603	5.4	3	3.6	......	96.3	0.2	159	2.4
Depreciation tract	37	......	......	......	......	......	37	37	206	5.6	......	......	......	100.0	......	......	......
Elizabeth	255	10	10	80	8.0	......	245	245	1,397	5.7	......	3.9	......	96.1	......	21	2.1
Pitt	266	19	19	123	6.5	......	247	245	1,303	5.3	2	7.1	......	92.1	0.8	40	2.1
Pittsburgh town	77	......	......	......	......	......	77	76	375	4.9	1	......	......	98.7	1.3	......	......
Plum	70	1	1	13	13.0	......	69	69	388	5.6	......	1.4	......	98.6	......	1	1.0
Versailles	67	2	2	18	9.0	......	65	65	393	6.0	......	3.0	......	97.0	......	3	1.5
That part of Allegheny county taken from Washington county	1,072	34	34	195	5.7	......	1,038	1,038	5,541	5.3	......	3.2	......	96.8	......	94	2.8
Bedford county[3]	2,232	24	24	165	6.9	......	2,208	2,204	12,887	5.8	4	1.1	......	98.7	0.2	46	1.9
Berks county	5,244	31	31	209	6.7	......	5,213	5,209	29,717	5.7	4	0.6	......	99.3	0.1	60	1.9
Albany	132	......	......	......	......	......	132	132	773	5.9	......	......	......	100.0	......	......	......
Alsace	152	......	......	......	......	......	152	151	831	5.5	1	......	......	99.3	0.7	......	......
Amity	147	1	1	4	4.0	......	146	146	853	5.8	......	0.7	......	99.3	......	1	1.0
Bern	360	2	2	18	9.0	......	358	358	2,230	6.2	......	0.6	......	99.4	......	2	2.0
Bethel	164	......	......	......	......	......	164	164	949	5.8	......	......	......	100.0	......	......	......
Brecknock	60	......	......	......	......	......	60	60	324	5.4	......	......	......	100.0	......	......	......
Brunswick and Manheim	241	1	1	10	10.0	......	240	240	1,493	6.2	......	0.4	......	99.6	......	1	1.0
Caernarvon	91	2	2	12	6.0	......	89	89	488	5.5	......	2.2	......	97.8	......	4	2.0
Colebrookdale	100	......	......	......	......	......	100	100	549	5.5	......	......	......	100.0	......	......	......
Cumru	245	......	......	......	......	......	245	245	1,440	5.9	......	......	......	100.0	......	......	......
Douglass	89	1	1	11	11.0	......	88	88	462	5.3	......	1.1	......	98.9	......	1	1.0
Earl	101	1	1	10	10.0	......	100	99	514	5.2	1	1.0	......	98.0	1.0	1	1.0
East District	120	......	......	......	......	......	120	120	629	5.2	......	......	......	100.0	......	......	......
Exeter	151	2	2	12	6.0	......	149	149	871	5.8	......	1.3	......	98.7	......	7	3.5
Greenwich	133	......	......	......	......	......	133	133	724	5.4	......	......	......	100.0	......	......	......
Heidelberg	362	3	3	21	7.0	......	359	358	2,044	5.7	1	0.8	......	98.9	0.3	6	2.0
Hereford	173	1	1	9	9.0	......	172	172	956	5.6	......	0.6	......	99.4	......	1	1.0
Longswamp	129	......	......	......	......	......	129	129	738	5.7	......	......	......	100.0	......	......	......
Maiden Creek	120	......	......	......	......	......	120	120	726	6.1	......	......	......	100.0	......	......	......
Manheim. (See Brunswick and Manheim.)																	
Maxatany	177	......	......	......	......	......	177	177	1,013	5.7	......	......	......	100.0	......	......	......
Oley	161	2	2	9	4.5	......	159	159	944	5.9	......	1.2	......	98.8	......	4	2.0
Pinegrove	145	......	......	......	......	......	145	145	900	6.2	......	......	......	100.0	......	......	......
Reading borough	435	5	5	27	5.4	......	430	430	2,186	5.1	......	1.1	......	98.9	......	9	1.8
Richmond	109	3	3	17	5.7	......	106	106	624	5.9	......	2.8	......	97.2	......	4	1.3
Robeson	199	1	1	6	6.0	......	198	198	1,073	5.4	......	0.5	......	99.5	......	1	1.0
Rockland	142	......	......	......	......	......	142	142	741	5.2	......	......	......	100.0	......	......	......
Ruscomb	94	......	......	......	......	......	94	94	468	5.0	......	......	......	100.0	......	......	......
Tulpehocken	389	4	4	29	7.3	......	385	385	2,250	5.8	......	1.0	......	99.0	......	15	3.8
Union	119	2	2	14	7.0	......	117	116	671	5.8	1	1.7	......	97.5	0.8	3	1.5
Windsor	204	......	......	......	......	......	204	204	1,253	6.1	......	......	......	100.0	......	......	......
Bucks county[3]	4,180	134	134	905	6.8	......	4,046	3,985	23,449	5.9	61	3.2	......	95.3	1.5	261	1.9

[1] Includes families of Indians taxed.　　　[2] Less than one-tenth of 1 per cent.　　　[3] Not returned by townships.

TABLE **114.**—NUMBER OF FAMILIES REPORTED AT THE FIRST CENSUS, CLASSIFIED AS SLAVEHOLDING AND NON-SLAVEHOLDING, WHITE, AND FREE COLORED, TOGETHER WITH THE TOTAL AND AVERAGE NUMBER OF SLAVES, BY COUNTIES AND MINOR CIVIL DIVISIONS: 1790—Continued.

PENNSYLVANIA—Continued.

COUNTY AND TOWN.	FAMILIES. Total number.	Slaveholding. Number.	Slaveholding White. Number of families.	Slaveholding White. Members Total.	Slaveholding White. Members Average per family.	Slaveholding Free colored.[1]	Nonslaveholding. Number.	Nonslaveholding White. Number of families.	Nonslaveholding White. Members Total.	Nonslaveholding White. Members Average per family.	Nonslaveholding Free colored.[1]	Per cent Slaveholding. White.	Per cent Slaveholding. Free colored.[1]	Per cent Nonslaveholding. White.	Per cent Nonslaveholding. Free colored.[1]	SLAVES. Total number.	SLAVES. Average number per slaveholding family.
Chester county	4,435	88	88	618	7.0	......	4,347	4,289	26,263	6.1	58	2.0	......	96.7	1.3	144	1.6
Birmingham	35						35	35	220	6.3	.....			100.0	0.8		
Brandywine	127						127	126	735	5.8	1			99.2	0.8		
Charlestown	209	5	5	45	9.0		204	200	1,167	5.8	4	2.4		95.7	1.9	7	1.4
Coventry	195	1	1	11	11.0		194	193	1,106	5.7	1	0.5		99.0	0.5	1	1.0
East Bradford	125						125	121	825	6.8	4			96.8	3.2		
East Caln	107	1	1	11	11.0		106	105	666	6.3	1	0.9		98.1	0.9	3	3.0
East Fallowfield	85						85	85	516	6.1	.....			100.0			
East Marlborough	144						144	138	797	5.8	6			95.8	4.2		
East Nantmill	170	2	2	18	9.0		168	166	976	5.9	2	1.2		97.6	1.2	[2]8	4.0
East Nottingham	123	2	2	14	7.0		121	121	792	6.5	.....	1.6		98.4		2	1.0
East Town	75	1	1	2	2.0		74	74	419	5.7	.....	1.3		98.7		2	2.0
East Whiteland	75	2	2	16	8.0		73	72	453	6.3	1	2.7		96.0	1.3	2	1.0
Fallowfield	124	6	6	40	6.7		118	118	732	6.2	.....	4.8		95.2		9	1.5
Goshen	204	2	2	19	9.5		202	198	1,194	6.0	4	1.0		97.1	2.0	4	2.0
Honeybrook	118	5	5	30	6.0		113	113	713	6.3	.....	4.2		95.8		13	2.6
Kennet	99	2	2	13	6.5		97	96	629	6.6	1	2.0		97.0	1.0	2	1.0
London Britain	43	4	4	25	6.3		39	39	202	5.2	.....	9.3		90.7		8	2.0
Londonderry	96	5	5	32	6.4		91	91	545	6.0	.....	5.2		94.8		7	1.4
Londongrove	110	4	4	40	10.0		106	106	736	6.9	.....	3.6		96.4		5	1.3
New Garden	126	1	1	9	9.0		125	121	717	5.9	4	0.8		96.0	3.2	1	1.0
New London	120	13	13	80	6.2		107	107	628	5.9	.....	10.8		89.2		20	1.5
Newlin	89						89	88	527	6.0	1			98.9	1.1		
Oxford	148	10	10	76	7.6		138	138	891	6.5	.....	6.8		93.2		20	2.0
Pennsbury	86						86	83	581	7.0	3			96.5	3.5		
Pikeland	142						142	138	798	5.8	4			97.2	2.8		
Sadsbury	89	5	5	38	7.6		84	84	554	6.6	.....	5.6		94.4		7	1.4
Thornbury	26						26	25	118	4.7	1			96.2	3.8		
Trediffrin	157	3	3	25	8.3		154	153	931	6.1	1	1.9		97.5	0.6	3	1.0
Uwchland	165	4	4	29	7.3		161	157	915	5.8	4	2.4		95.2	2.4	4	1.0
Vincent	182	1	1	4	4.0		181	181	1,218	6.7	.....	0.5		99.5		1	1.0
West Bradford	117						117	114	714	6.3	3			97.4	2.6		
West Caln	133						133	133	837	6.3	.....			100.0			
West Marlborough	121	1	1	2	2.0		120	117	659	5.6	3	0.8		96.7	2.5	1	1.0
West Nantmill	147	3	3	13	4.3		144	144	814	5.7	.....	2.0		98.0		7	2.3
West Nottingham	69	2	2	6	3.0		67	66	403	6.1	1	2.9		95.7	1.4	3	1.5
West Town	60						60	58	348	6.0	2			96.7	3.3		
West Whiteland	72	3	3	20	6.7		69	68	417	6.1	1	4.2		94.4	1.4	4	1.3
Willistown	122						122	117	770	6.6	5			95.9	4.1		
Cumberland county	3,017	117	117	931	8.0		2,900	2,896	16,849	5.8	4	3.9		96.0	0.1	223	1.9
Hopewell, Newton, Tyborn, Westpensboro	} 1,281	57	57	433	7.6		1,224	1,221	6,976	5.7	3	4.4		95.3	0.2	98	1.7
Eastern portion of county	1,736	60	60	498	8.3		1,676	1,675	9,873	5.9	1	3.5		96.5	0.1	125	2.1
Dauphin county	3,248	92	92	602	6.5		3,156	3,098	17,281	5.6	58	2.8		95.4	1.8	210	2.3
Harrisburgh town	184	12	12	77	6.4		172	171	777	4.5	1	6.5		92.9	0.5	25	2.1
Lebanon town	180	1	1	6	6.0		179	179	950	5.3	.....	0.6		99.4		2	2.0
Remainder of county	2,884	79	79	519	6.6		2,805	2,748	15,554	5.7	57	2.7		95.3	2.0	183	2.3
Delaware county	1,724	24	22	192	8.7	2	1,700	1,670	8,951	5.4	30	1.3	0.1	96.9	1.7	49	2.0
Ashton	75						75	75	431	5.7	.....			100.0			
Bethel	39	1	1	5	5.0		38	36	211	5.9	2	2.6		92.3	5.1	1	1.0
Birmingham	64	4	4	38	9.5		60	59	371	6.3	1	6.3		92.2	1.6	4	1.0
Chester	154						154	152	651	4.3	2			98.7	1.3		
Concord	108	1	1	11	11.0		107	100	622	6.2	7	0.9		92.6	6.5	6	6.0
Darby	141	2	2	18	9.0		139	138	600	4.3	1	1.4		97.9	0.7	8	4.0
Edgmont	63	1	1	7	7.0		62	61	416	6.8	1	1.6		96.8	1.6	5	5.0
Haverford	102	4	4	31	7.8		98	97	419	4.3	1	3.9		95.1	1.0	9	2.3
Lower Chichester	97						97	96	486	5.1	1			99.0	1.0		
Lower Providence	52						52	52	215	4.1	.....			100.0			
Marple	82						82	82	460	5.6	.....			100.0			
Middletown	99	2	2	22	11.0		97	92	537	5.8	5	2.0		92.9	5.1	3	1.5
Newtown	73	1	1	13	13.0		72	72	432	6.0	.....	1.4		98.6		1	1.0

[1] Includes families of Indians taxed. [2] Includes 5 slaves in an institution.

TABLE 114.—NUMBER OF FAMILIES REPORTED AT THE FIRST CENSUS, CLASSIFIED AS SLAVEHOLDING AND NON-SLAVEHOLDING, WHITE, AND FREE COLORED, TOGETHER WITH THE TOTAL AND AVERAGE NUMBER OF SLAVES, BY COUNTIES AND MINOR CIVIL DIVISIONS: 1790—Continued.

PENNSYLVANIA—Continued.

COUNTY AND TOWN.	Total number.	Slaveholding. White. Number.	Slaveholding. White. Number of families.	Slaveholding. White. Members. Total.	Slaveholding. White. Members. Average per family.	Slaveholding. Free colored.[1]	Nonslaveholding. White. Number.	Nonslaveholding. White. Number of families.	Nonslaveholding. White. Members. Total.	Nonslaveholding. White. Members. Average per family.	Nonslaveholding. Free colored.[1]	Per cent Slaveholding. White.	Per cent Slaveholding. Free colored.[1]	Per cent Nonslaveholding. White.	Per cent Nonslaveholding. Free colored.[1]	Slaves. Total number.	Slaves. Average number per slaveholding family.
Delaware county—Continued.																	
Radnor	112	2	2	14	7.0	......	110	110	661	6.0	......	1.8	......	98.2	......	2	1.0
Ridley	112	1	1	8	8.0	......	111	110	464	4.2	......	0.9	......	98.2	......	1	1.0
Springfield	63	1	1	8	8.0	......	62	59	295	5.0	3	1.6	......	93.7	4.8	4	4.0
Thornbury	61	......	......	......	......	......	61	60	399	6.7	1	......	......	98.4	1.6	......	......
Tinicum	41	2	......	......	......	2	39	35	131	3.7	4	......	4.9	85.4	9.8	3	1.5
Upper Chichester	45	1	1	10	10.0	......	44	44	251	5.7	......	2.2	......	97.8	......	1	1.0
Upper Darby	85	......	......	......	......	......	85	85	559	6.6	......	......	......	100.0	......	......	......
Upper Providence	56	1	1	7	7.0	......	55	55	340	6.2	......	1.8	......	98.2	......	1	1.0
Fayette county	2,388	100	100	630	6.3	......	2,288	2,286	12,354	5.4	2	4.2	......	95.7	0.1	282	2.8
Bullskin	138	5	5	33	6.6	......	133	133	701	5.3	......	3.6	......	96.4	......	19	3.8
Franklin	316	17	17	113	6.6	......	299	298	1,694	5.7	1	5.4	......	94.3	0.3	31	1.8
Georges	258	3	3	17	5.7	......	255	255	1,350	5.3	......	1.2	......	98.8	......	4	1.3
German	234	2	2	14	7.0	......	232	232	1,282	5.5	......	0.9	......	99.1	......	3	1.5
Luzerne	196	7	7	37	5.3	......	189	188	1,043	5.5	1	3.6	......	95.9	0.5	27	3.9
Menallen	296	20	20	139	7.0	......	276	276	1,479	5.4	......	6.8	......	93.2	......	43	2.2
Springhill	253	13	13	86	6.6	......	240	240	1,195	5.0	......	5.1	......	94.9	......	38	2.9
Tyrone	132	6	6	35	5.8	......	126	126	674	5.3	......	4.5	......	95.5	......	21	3.5
Union	289	13	13	76	5.8	......	276	276	1,425	5.2	......	4.5	......	95.5	......	28	2.2
Washington	206	14	14	80	5.7	......	192	192	1,082	5.6	......	6.8	......	93.2	......	68	4.9
Wharton	70	......	......	......	......	......	70	70	429	6.1	......	......	......	100.0	......	......	......
Franklin county	2,528	163	162	1,174	7.2	1	2,365	2,357	13,887	5.9	8	6.4	(2)	93.2	0.3	326	2.0
Fannet, Hamilton, Letterkenney, Montgomery, Peters	} 1,160	75	74	569	7.7	1	1,085	1,083	6,372	5.9	2	6.4	0.1	93.4	0.2	148	2.0
Remainder of county	1,368	88	88	605	6.9	......	1,280	1,274	7,515	5.9	6	6.4	......	93.1	0.4	178	2.0
Huntingdon county[3]	1,268	24	24	154	6.4	......	1,244	1,243	7,302	5.9	1	1.9	......	98.0	0.1	43	1.8
Lancaster county	5,980	193	193	1,507	7.8	......	5,787	5,771	33,579	5.8	16	3.2	......	96.5	0.3	347	1.8
Bart	137	5	5	37	7.4	......	132	132	816	6.2	......	3.6	......	96.4	......	5	1.0
Brecknock	120	......	......	......	......	......	120	120	629	5.2	......	......	......	100.0	......	......	......
Caernarvon	131	11	11	56	5.1	......	120	119	645	5.4	1	8.4	......	90.8	0.8	29	2.6
Cocalico	538	......	......	......	......	......	538	537	2,991	5.6	1	......	......	99.8	0.2	......	......
Colerain	113	......	......	......	......	......	113	113	662	5.9	......	......	......	100.0	......	......	......
Conestogo	169	......	......	......	......	......	169	168	1,084	6.5	1	......	......	99.4	0.6	......	......
Donegal	90	4	4	36	9.0	......	86	86	477	5.5	......	4.4	......	95.6	......	10	2.5
Drumore	156	13	13	102	7.8	......	143	143	870	6.1	......	8.3	......	91.7	......	34	2.6
Earl	539	11	11	63	5.7	......	528	528	2,830	5.4	......	2.0	......	98.0	......	20	1.8
Elizabeth	86	1	1	35	35.0	......	85	85	510	6.0	......	1.2	......	98.8	......	[4]1	1.0
Elizabeth town	30	......	......	......	......	......	30	30	196	6.5	......	......	......	100.0	......	......	......
Heidelberg	12	......	......	......	......	......	12	12	69	5.8	......	......	......	100.0	......	......	......
Hempfield	270	2	2	14	7.0	......	268	268	1,580	5.9	......	0.7	......	99.3	......	4	2.0
Lampeter	238	1	1	10	10.0	......	237	236	1,523	6.5	1	0.4	......	99.2	0.4	1	1.0
Lancaster	54	1	1	13	13.0	......	53	53	282	5.3	......	1.9	......	98.1	......	1	1.0
Lancaster borough	678	37	37	294	7.9	......	641	638	3,375	5.3	3	5.5	......	94.1	0.4	57	1.5
Leacock	213	11	11	82	7.5	......	202	201	1,292	6.4	1	5.2	......	94.4	0.5	18	1.6
Little Britain	196	19	19	144	7.6	......	177	177	1,073	6.1	......	9.7	......	90.3	......	42	2.2
Manheim	126	1	1	7	7.0	......	125	125	772	6.2	......	0.8	......	99.2	......	1	1.0
Manheim town	82	......	......	......	......	......	82	82	367	4.5	......	......	......	100.0	......	......	......
Manor	267	......	......	......	......	......	267	264	1,592	6.0	3	......	......	98.9	1.1	......	......
Martick	220	3	3	23	7.7	......	217	216	1,245	5.8	1	1.4	......	98.2	0.5	9	3.0
May town	194	12	12	111	9.3	......	182	181	980	5.4	1	6.2	......	93.3	0.5	23	1.9
Mountjoy	136	4	4	33	8.3	......	132	132	805	6.1	......	2.9	......	97.1	......	7	1.8
Rapho	255	8	8	70	8.8	......	247	246	1,499	6.1	1	3.1	......	96.5	0.4	11	1.4
Sadsbury	108	8	8	60	7.5	......	100	100	634	6.3	......	7.4	......	92.6	......	11	1.4
Salisbury	207	32	32	233	7.3	......	175	175	1,038	5.9	......	15.5	......	84.5	......	46	1.4
Strasburg	263	6	6	64	10.7	......	257	257	1,603	6.2	......	2.3	......	97.7	......	6	1.0
Warwick	352	3	3	20	6.7	......	349	347	2,140	6.2	2	0.9	......	98.6	0.6	11	3.7
Luzerne county[3]	867	7	7	31	4.4	......	860	859	4,847	5.6	1	0.8	......	99.1	0.1	11	1.6
Mifflin county	1,259	39	39	264	6.8	......	1,220	1,220	7,194	5.9	......	3.1	......	96.9	......	59	1.5
That portion south of the river Juniata	360	8	8	51	6.4	......	352	352	2,132	6.1	......	2.2	......	97.8	......	9	1.1
Remainder of county	899	31	31	213	6.9	......	868	868	5,062	5.8	......	3.4	......	96.6	......	50	1.6

[1] Includes families of Indians taxed.
[2] Less than one-tenth of 1 per cent.
[3] Not returned by townships.
[4] In an institution.

TABLE 114.—NUMBER OF FAMILIES REPORTED AT THE FIRST CENSUS, CLASSIFIED AS SLAVEHOLDING AND NON-SLAVEHOLDING, WHITE, AND FREE COLORED, TOGETHER WITH THE TOTAL AND AVERAGE NUMBER OF SLAVES, BY COUNTIES AND MINOR CIVIL DIVISIONS: 1790—Continued.

PENNSYLVANIA—Continued.

County and town	Total number	SH Number	SH White families	SH White members Total	SH White members Avg per family	SH Free colored[1]	NSH Number	NSH White families	NSH White members Total	NSH White members Avg per family	NSH Free colored[1]	Per cent SH White	Per cent SH Free colored[1]	Per cent NSH White	Per cent NSH Free colored[1]	Slaves Total number	Slaves Avg per SH family
Montgomery county	3,803	72	72	458	6.4		3,731	3,696	21,912	5.9	35	1.9		97.2	0.9	113	1.6
Abington	163	2	2	16	8.0		161	160	850	5.3	1	1.2		98.2	0.6	5	2.5
Cheltenham	101	2	2	14	7.0		99	95	559	5.9	4	2.0		94.1	4.0	2	1.0
Manor of Moreland	224	10	10	67	6.7		214	210	1,140	5.4	4	4.5		93.8	1.8	17	1.7
Springfield	88						88	87	438	5.0	1			98.9	1.1		
Remainder of county	3,227	58	58	361	6.2		3,169	3,144	18,925	6.0	25	1.8		97.4	0.8	89	1.5
Northampton county	4,091	16	16	97	6.1		4,075	4,059	23,623	5.8	16	0.4		99.2	0.4	20	1.3
Allen	241						241	241	1,451	6.0				100.0		1	
Bethlehem	156	1	1	11	11.0		155	155	729	4.7		0.6		99.4		1	1.0
Chestnut Hill	107						107	107	709	6.6				100.0			
Cosikton District	56						56	55	326	5.9	1			98.2	1.8		
Delaware	77						77	77	415	5.4				100.0			
Easton town	134	5	5	31	6.2		129	127	661	5.2	2	3.7		94.8	1.5	5	1.0
Forks	116	1	1	2	2.0		115	115	733	6.4		0.9		99.1		2	2.0
Hamilton	95						95	95	594	6.3				100.0			
Heidelberg	166						166	166	962	5.8				100.0			
Lehigh	106						106	106	626	5.9				100.0			
Lower Mount Bethel	149	1	1	5	5.0		148	148	889	6.0		0.7		99.3		1	1.0
Lower Saucon	179						179	175	979	5.6	4			97.8	2.2		
Lower Smithfield	235	4	4	24	6.0		231	224	1,346	6.0	7	1.7		95.3	3.0	7	1.8
Lowhill	75						75	75	418	5.6				100.0			
Lynn	169						169	169	1,016	6.0				100.0			
Macunge	210	1	1	9	9.0		209	209	1,252	6.0		0.5		99.5		1	1.0
More	127						127	127	752	5.9				100.0			
Nazareth	150						150	149	735	4.9	1			99.3	0.7		
Penn	110						110	110	605	5.5				100.0			
Plainfield	146						146	146	886	6.1				100.0			
Salisbury	170						170	170	1,009	5.9				100.0			
Towamensink	74	1	1	8	8.0		73	73	386	5.3		1.4		98.6		1	1.0
Upper Milford	202						202	202	1,149	5.7				100.0			
Upper Mount Bethel	168	1	1	3	3.0		167	167	1,030	6.2		0.6		99.4		1	1.0
Upper Saucon	144						144	144	851	5.9				100.0			
Upper Smithfield	63	1	1	4	4.0		62	62	347	5.6		1.6		98.4		1	1.0
Wallen Papack	30						30	30	169	5.6				100.0			
Weisenbergh	101						101	101	625	6.2				100.0			
Whitehall	203						203	203	1,253	6.2				100.0			
Williams	132						132	131	720	5.5	1			99.2	0.8		
Northumberland county [2]	2,946	48	48	352	7.3		2,898	2,897	16,315	5.6	1	1.6		98.3	(2)	87	1.8
Philadelphia county	9,504	220	216	1,542	7.1	4	9,284	9,082	49,822	5.5	202	2.3	(3)	95.6	2.1	373	1.7
Blockley	148	4	3	16	5.3	1	144	143	841	5.9	1	2.0	0.7	96.6	0.7	4	1.0
Bristol	124	2	2	18	9.0		122	120	683	5.7	2	1.6		96.8	1.6	3	1.5
Byberry	95	2	2	14	7.0		93	92	553	6.0	1	2.1		96.8	1.1	6	3.0
Germantown town	555	3	3	7	2.3		552	549	2,732	5.0	3	0.5		98.9	0.5	5	1.7
Kingsessing	107	4	4	29	7.3		103	97	452	4.7	6	3.7		90.7	5.6	7	1.8
Lower Dublin	228	15	15	92	6.1		213	209	1,099	5.3	4	6.6		91.7	1.8	19	1.3
Manor of Moreland	65	2	2	13	6.5		63	60	340	5.7	3	3.1		92.3	4.6	8	4.0
Moyamensing and Passyunk	259	7	7	48	6.9		252	250	1,296	5.2	2	2.7		96.5	0.8	8	1.1
Northern Liberties town	2,169	32	31	195	6.3	1	2,137	2,106	9,430	4.5	31	1.4	(3)	97.1	1.4	61	1.9
Oxford	175	9	9	63	7.0		166	165	873	5.3	1	5.1		94.3	0.6	17	1.9
Passyunk. (See Moyamensing and Passyunk.)																	
Roxborough	134	1	1	5	5.0		133	133	770	5.8		0.7		99.3		1	1.0
Southwark	984	15	14	103	7.4	1	969	945	5,335	5.6	24	1.4	0.1	96.0	2.4	24	1.6
Philadelphia city: Northern district (between Vine and Race streets from the Delaware to the Schuylkill)	872	18	18	113	6.3		854	842	3,712	4.4	12	2.1		96.6	1.4	27	1.5
Middle district (from the north side of Chestnut street to the south side of Race street from the Delaware to the Schuylkill)	2,095	34	34	267	7.9		2,061	2,011	12,814	6.4	50	1.6		96.0	2.4	71	2.1

[1] Includes families of Indians taxed. [2] Not returned by townships. [3] Less than one-tenth of 1 per cent.

Table 114.—NUMBER OF FAMILIES REPORTED AT THE FIRST CENSUS, CLASSIFIED AS SLAVEHOLDING AND NON-SLAVEHOLDING, WHITE, AND FREE COLORED, TOGETHER WITH THE TOTAL AND AVERAGE NUMBER OF SLAVES, BY COUNTIES AND MINOR CIVIL DIVISIONS: 1790—Continued.

PENNSYLVANIA—Continued.

		FAMILIES.														SLAVES.	
		Slaveholding.					Nonslaveholding.					Per cent families of each class form of all families.					
			White.			Free colored.[1]		White			Free colored.[1]	Slaveholding.		Nonslaveholding.			
COUNTY AND TOWN.	Total number.	Number.	Number of families.	Number of members.			Number.	Number of families.	Number of members.			White.	Free colored.[1]	White.	Free colored.[1]	Total number.	Average number per slaveholding family.
				Total.	Average per family.				Total.	Average per family.							
Philadelphia county—Cont'd. Philadelphia city—Cont'd. Southern district (from the south side of Chestnut street to the north side of South street from the Delaware to the Schuylkill)	1,494	72	71	559	7.9	1	1,422	1,360	8,892	6.5	62	4.8	0.1	91.0	4.1	112	1.6
Washington county[2]	3,944	123	123	875	7.1	......	3,821	3,820	22,741	6.0	1	3.1	......	96.9	(3)	263	2.1
Westmoreland county	2,813	53	53	349	6.6	......	2,760	2,721	15,422	5.7	39	1.9	......	96.7	1.4	128	2.4
Armstrong	272	3	3	10	3.3	......	269	261	1,420	5.4	8	1.1	......	96.0	2.9	5	1.7
Derry	287	4	4	20	5.0	......	283	277	1,591	5.7	6	1.4	......	96.5	2.1	6	1.5
Donegal	142	......	......	......	......	......	142	141	721	5.1	1	......	......	99.3	0.7	......	......
Fairfield	118	3	3	21	7.0	......	115	112	607	5.4	3	2.5	......	94.9	2.5	8	2.7
Franklin	141	......	......	......	......	......	141	140	777	5.6	1	......	......	99.3	0.7	......	......
French Creek	16	......	......	......	......	......	16	16	93	5.8	......	......	......	100.0	......	......	......
Hempfield	383	4	4	31	7.8	......	379	372	2,156	5.8	7	1.0	......	97.1	1.8	6	1.5
Mount Pleasant	174	5	5	44	8.8	......	169	169	1,006	6.0	......	2.9	......	97.1	......	9	1.8
North Huntingdon	262	5	5	39	7.8	......	257	256	1,524	6.0	1	1.9	......	97.7	0.4	17	3.4
Rostraver	191	16	16	87	5.4	......	175	175	951	5.4	......	8.4	......	91.6	......	49	3.1
Salem	144	2	2	19	9.5	......	142	138	768	5.6	4	1.4	......	95.8	2.8	4	2.0
South Huntingdon	271	7	7	51	7.3	......	264	260	1,513	5.8	4	2.6	......	95.9	1.5	14	2.0
Unity	205	3	3	20	6.7	......	202	201	1,216	6.0	1	1.5	......	98.0	0.5	9	3.0
Washington	134	1	1	7	7.0	......	133	132	697	5.3	1	0.7	......	98.5	0.7	1	1.0
Wheatfield	73	......	......	......	......	......	73	71	382	5.4	2	......	......	97.3	2.7	......	......
York county	6,559	224	224	1,458	6.5	......	6,335	6,334	34,692	5.5	1	3.4	......	96.6	......	503	2.3
Chanceford	295	12	12	73	6.1	......	283	283	1,555	5.5	......	4.1	......	95.9	......	27	2.3
Codorus	239	5	5	17	3.4	......	234	234	1,439	6.1	......	2.1	......	97.9	......	12	2.4
Dover	253	......	......	......	......	......	253	253	1,461	5.8	......	......	......	100.0	......	......	......
Fawn	230	14	14	78	5.6	......	216	216	1,173	5.4	......	6.1	......	93.9	......	43	3.1
Hellam	128	2	2	15	7.5	......	126	126	709	5.6	......	1.6	......	98.4	......	7	3.5
Hopewell	210	6	6	36	6.0	......	204	204	1,110	5.4	......	2.9	......	97.1	......	11	1.8
Manchester	297	7	7	40	5.7	......	290	290	1,604	5.5	......	2.4	......	97.6	......	13	1.9
Monaghan	254	6	6	36	6.0	......	248	248	1,354	5.5	......	2.4	......	97.6	......	12	2.0
Newberry	402	......	......	......	......	......	402	402	2,203	5.5	......	......	......	100.0	......	......	......
Paradise	214	3	3	18	6.0	......	211	211	1,127	5.3	......	1.4	......	98.6	......	4	1.3
Reading	178	9	9	46	5.1	......	169	169	855	5.1	......	5.1	......	94.9	......	25	2.8
Shrewsbury	220	10	10	59	5.9	......	210	210	1,141	5.4	......	4.5	......	95.5	......	15	1.5
Warrington	262	2	2	13	6.5	......	260	260	1,405	5.4	......	0.8	......	99.2	......	8	4.0
Windsor	250	3	3	30	10.0	......	247	247	1,406	5.7	......	1.2	......	98.8	......	3	1.0
York	257	3	3	23	7.7	......	254	254	1,314	5.2	......	1.2	......	98.8	......	10	3.3
York borough	388	15	15	109	7.3	......	373	373	1,812	4.9	......	3.9	......	96.1	......	30	2.0
Huntington, Manallen, Manheim, and Tyrone	829	20	20	148	7.4	......	809	808	4,460	5.5	1	2.4	......	97.5	0.1	38	1.9
Berwick, Cumberland, Franklin, Germany, Hamiltonban, Heidelberg, Mount Pleasant, Mountjoy, and Straban	1,653	107	107	717	6.7	......	1,546	1,546	8,564	5.5	......	6.5	......	93.5	......	245	2.3

MARYLAND.

COUNTY AND TOWN.	Total number.	Number.	Number of families.	Total.	Average per family.	Free colored.[1]	Number.	Number of families.	Total.	Average per family.	Free colored.[1]	White.	Free colored.[1]	White.	Free colored.[1]	Total number.	Average number per slaveholding family.
The state	33,294	12,226	12,142	71,168	5.9	84	21,068	19,870	109,577	5.5	1,198	36.5	0.3	59.7	3.6	[4]103,036	7.5
Allegany county[5]																258	....
Ann-Arundel county	2,122	1,096	1,084	5,672	5.2	12	1,026	962	4,910	5.1	64	51.1	0.6	45.3	3.0	10,130	9.2
Baltimore county	3,497	1,029	1,029	6,553	6.4	......	2,468	2,400	13,595	5.7	68	29.4	......	68.6	1.9	5,877	5.7
Back River hundred	287	135	135	859	6.4	......	152	140	682	4.9	12	47.0	......	48.8	4.2	1,052	7.8
Mine Run hundred	241	83	83	535	6.4	......	158	157	975	6.2	1	34.4	......	65.1	0.4	358	4.3
Two Deleware hundreds	255	78	78	480	6.2	......	177	177	1,099	6.2	......	30.6	......	69.4	......	410	5.3
County not separated	2,714	733	733	4,679	6.4	......	1,981	1,926	10,839	5.6	55	27.0	......	71.0	2.0	4,057	5.5
Baltimore town and precincts	1,727	389	388	2,601	6.7	1	1,338	1,293	6,704	5.2	45	22.5	0.1	74.9	2.6	1,255	3.2
Calvert county[5]																4,305	....

[1] Includes families of Indians taxed.
[2] Not returned by townships.
[3] Less than one-tenth of 1 per cent.
[4] Includes 11,633 slaves not distributed in families.
[5] Schedules destroyed, therefore no detail can be given.

TABLE **114.**—NUMBER OF FAMILIES REPORTED AT THE FIRST CENSUS, CLASSIFIED AS SLAVEHOLDING AND NON-SLAVEHOLDING, WHITE, AND FREE COLORED, TOGETHER WITH THE TOTAL AND AVERAGE NUMBER OF SLAVES, BY COUNTIES AND MINOR CIVIL DIVISIONS: 1790—Continued.

MARYLAND—Continued.

DISTRICT, COUNTY, AND TOWN.	Total number.	Slaveholding. White. Number.	Slaveholding. White. Number of families.	Slaveholding. White. Number of members. Total.	Slaveholding. White. Number of members. Average per family.	Slaveholding. Free colored.[1]	Nonslaveholding. White. Number.	Nonslaveholding. White. Number of families.	Nonslaveholding. White. Number of members. Total.	Nonslaveholding. White. Number of members. Average per family.	Nonslaveholding. Free colored.[1]	Per cent. Slaveholding. White.	Per cent. Slaveholding. Free colored.[1]	Per cent. Nonslaveholding. White.	Per cent. Nonslaveholding. Free colored.[1]	Slaves. Total number.	Slaves. Average number per slaveholding family.
Caroline county	1,352	418	417	2,424	5.8	1	934	861	4,613	5.4	73	30.8	0.1	63.7	5.4	2,057	4.9
Cecil county	1,906	539	538	3,337	6.2	1	1,367	1,175	6,449	5.5	192	28.2	0.1	61.6	10.1	3,407	6.3
Back Creek hundred	109	37	37	242	6.5	.....	72	65	377	5.8	7	33.9	.....	59.6	6.4	160	4.3
Bohemia hundred	123	84	84	458	5.5	.....	39	35	188	5.4	4	68.3	.....	28.5	3.3	791	9.4
Bohemia Manor hundred	103	51	51	315	6.2	.....	52	49	264	5.4	3	49.5	.....	47.6	2.9	315	6.2
Charles town	58	10	10	47	4.7	.....	48	42	186	4.4	6	17.2	.....	72.4	10.3	23	2.3
East Nottingham	141	21	21	166	7.9	.....	120	114	689	6.0	6	14.9	.....	80.9	4.3	58	2.8
Elk Neck hundred	167	45	45	283	6.3	.....	122	114	609	5.3	8	26.9	.....	68.3	4.8	215	4.8
Middle Neck hundred	20	10	10	62	6.2	.....	10	8	37	4.6	2	50.0	.....	40.0	10.0	89	8.9
North Milford hundred	300	76	75	505	6.7	1	224	212	1,096	5.2	12	25.0	0.3	70.7	4.0	313	4.1
North Sassafras hundred	59	27	27	145	5.4	.....	32	30	154	5.1	2	45.8	.....	50.8	3.4	204	7.6
North Susquehannah hundred	154	43	43	299	7.0	.....	111	104	594	5.7	7	27.9	.....	67.5	4.5	349	8.1
Octoraro hundred	191	26	26	154	5.9	.....	165	45	243	5.4	120	13.6	.....	23.6	62.8	117	4.5
South Milford hundred	100	14	14	99	7.1	.....	86	85	483	5.7	1	14.0	.....	85.0	1.0	49	3.5
South Susquehannah hundred	149	26	26	162	6.2	.....	123	116	626	5.4	7	17.4	.....	77.8	4.7	164	6.3
West Nottingham hundred	133	19	19	128	6.7	.....	114	110	682	6.2	4	14.3	.....	82.7	3.0	55	2.9
West Sassafras hundred	99	50	50	272	5.4	.....	49	46	221	4.8	3	50.5	.....	46.5	3.0	377	7.5
Charles county	2,029	1,221	1,218	6,636	5.4	3	808	680	3,505	5.2	128	60.0	0.1	33.5	6.3	10,085	8.3
Dorchester county	654	296	293	1,688	5.8	3	358	334	1,559	4.7	24	44.8	0.5	51.1	3.7	5,337	18.0
Frederick county	4,377	678	677	4,572	6.8	1	3,699	3,681	22,331	6.1	18	15.5	(2)	84.1	0.4	3,641	5.4
Harford county	2,039	586	586	3,645	6.2	.....	1,453	1,312	7,139	5.4	141	28.7	.....	64.3	6.9	3,417	5.8
Kent county	1,299	781	747	4,149	5.6	34	518	432	2,156	5.0	86	57.5	2.6	33.3	6.6	5,433	7.0
Montgomery county	2,077	933	933	5,384	5.8	.....	1,144	1,111	6,194	5.6	33	44.9	.....	53.5	1.6	6,030	6.5
Prince Georges county	1,820	978	977	5,364	5.5	1	842	833	4,608	5.5	9	53.7	0.1	45.8	0.5	11,176	11.4
Queen Anns county	1,579	828	819	4,875	6.0	9	751	651	3,269	5.0	100	52.4	0.6	41.2	6.3	6,674	8.1
St. Marys county	1,527	892	890	4,939	5.5	2	635	597	3,246	5.4	38	58.3	0.1	39.1	2.5	6,985	7.8
Somersett county[3]	.....	.....	.....	.....	.....	.....	.....	.....	.....	.....	.....	.....	.....	.....	.....	7,070	.....
Talbot county	1,425	651	635	3,887	6.1	16	774	626	3,303	5.3	148	44.6	1.1	43.9	10.4	4,777	7.3
Washington county	2,445	269	269	1,784	6.6	.....	2,176	2,165	12,031	5.6	11	11.0	.....	88.5	0.4	1,286	4.8
Worcester county	1,419	642	642	3,658	5.7	.....	777	757	3,965	5.2	20	45.2	.....	53.3	1.4	3,836	6.0

NORTH CAROLINA.

DISTRICT, COUNTY, AND TOWN.	Total number.	Slaveholding. White. Number.	Slaveholding. White. Number of families.	Slaveholding. White. Number of members. Total.	Slaveholding. White. Number of members. Average per family.	Slaveholding. Free colored.[1]	Nonslaveholding. White. Number.	Nonslaveholding. White. Number of families.	Nonslaveholding. White. Number of members. Total.	Nonslaveholding. White. Number of members. Average per family.	Nonslaveholding. Free colored.[1]	Per cent. Slaveholding. White.	Per cent. Slaveholding. Free colored.[1]	Per cent. Nonslaveholding. White.	Per cent. Nonslaveholding. Free colored.[1]	Slaves. Total number.	Slaves. Average number per slaveholding family.
The state	48,701	14,973	14,945	87,121	5.8	28	33,728	33,076	178,077	5.4	652	30.7	0.1	67.9	1.3	[4]100,783	6.7
Edenton district	6,829	2,917	2,915	15,926	5.5	2	3,912	3,783	17,666	4.7	129	42.7	(2)	55.4	1.9	19,153	6.6
Bertie county	1,415	607	606	3,447	5.7	1	808	782	3,486	4.5	26	42.8	0.1	55.3	1.8	5,121	8.4
Camden county	583	201	201	1,128	5.6	.....	382	377	1,889	5.0	5	34.5	.....	64.7	0.9	1,038	5.2
Chowan, excluding Edenton town	376	205	205	1,000	4.9	.....	171	171	760	4.4	.....	54.5	.....	45.5	.....	1,646	8.0
Edenton town	176	108	108	433	4.0	.....	68	58	130	2.2	10	61.4	.....	33.0	5.7	941	8.7
Currituck county	793	257	256	1,479	5.8	1	536	516	2,653	5.1	20	32.3	0.1	65.1	2.5	1,103	4.3
Gates county	626	344	344	1,887	5.5	.....	282	268	1,193	4.5	14	55.0	.....	42.8	2.2	2,217	6.4
Hertford county	649	359	359	1,910	5.3	.....	290	259	1,259	4.9	31	55.3	.....	39.9	4.8	2,448	6.8
Pasquotank county	798	299	299	1,622	5.4	.....	499	481	2,165	4.5	18	37.5	.....	60.3	2.3	1,600	5.4
Perquimans county	708	322	322	1,787	5.5	.....	386	381	1,733	4.5	5	45.5	.....	53.8	0.7	1,883	5.8
Tyrrell county	705	215	215	1,233	5.7	.....	490	490	2,398	4.9	.....	30.5	.....	69.5	.....	1,156	5.4
Fayette district	5,403	1,229	1,225	7,053	5.8	4	4,174	4,074	20,940	5.1	100	22.7	0.1	75.4	1.9	5,673	4.6
Anson county	789	174	174	1,066	6.1	.....	615	608	3,196	5.3	7	22.1	.....	77.1	0.9	829	4.8
Cumberland county, excluding Fayetteville town	1,066	313	313	1,811	5.8	.....	753	750	3,669	4.9	3	29.4	.....	70.4	0.3	1,666	5.3
Fayetteville town	280	110	110	490	4.5	.....	170	161	497	3.1	9	39.3	.....	57.5	3.2	514	4.7
Moore county	639	88	88	525	6.0	.....	551	550	2,961	5.4	1	13.8	.....	86.1	0.2	371	4.2
Richmond county	829	142	141	848	6.0	1	687	679	3,570	5.3	8	17.0	0.1	81.9	1.0	583	4.1
Robeson county	866	163	160	961	6.0	3	703	660	3,555	5.4	43	18.5	0.3	76.2	5.0	533	3.3
Sampson county	934	239	239	1,352	5.7	.....	695	666	3,492	5.2	29	25.6	.....	71.3	3.1	1,177	4.9
Halifax district	7,033	3,260	3,249	19,015	5.9	11	3,773	3,608	18,839	5.2	165	46.2	0.2	51.3	2.3	25,529	7.8
Edgecombe county	1,259	491	491	2,900	5.9	.....	768	757	4,128	5.5	11	39.0	.....	60.1	0.9	3,167	6.5
Franklin county	802	388	388	2,430	6.3	.....	414	409	2,334	5.7	5	48.4	.....	51.0	0.6	2,701	7.0
Halifax county, including Halifax town	1,417	734	731	4,259	5.8	3	683	630	2,912	4.6	53	51.6	0.2	44.5	3.7	6,697	9.1
Martin county	794	277	277	1,607	5.8	.....	517	503	2,376	4.7	14	34.9	.....	63.4	1.8	1,829	6.6
Nash county	852	328	328	2,093	6.4	.....	524	510	3,096	6.1	14	38.5	.....	59.9	1.6	2,008	6.1
Northampton county	1,109	583	576	2,979	5.2	7	526	464	2,141	4.6	62	51.9	0.6	41.8	5.6	4,414	7.6
Warren county	800	459	458	2,747	6.0	1	341	335	1,852	5.5	6	57.3	0.1	41.9	0.8	4,713	10.3

[1] Includes families of Indians taxed.
[2] Less than one-tenth of 1 per cent.
[3] Schedules destroyed, therefore no detail can be given.
[4] Includes 8,959 slaves not distributed in families.

TABLE 114.—NUMBER OF FAMILIES REPORTED AT THE FIRST CENSUS, CLASSIFIED AS SLAVEHOLDING AND NON-SLAVEHOLDING, WHITE, AND FREE COLORED, TOGETHER WITH THE TOTAL AND AVERAGE NUMBER OF SLAVES, BY COUNTIES AND MINOR CIVIL DIVISIONS: 1790—Continued.

NORTH CAROLINA—Continued.

DISTRICT, COUNTY, TOWN, AND PARISH.	Total number.	Slaveholding. Number.	Slaveholding White. Number of families.	Slaveholding White. Members Total.	Slaveholding White. Members Average per family.	Slaveholding Free colored.[1]	Nonslaveholding. Number.	Nonslaveholding White. Number of families.	Nonslaveholding White. Members Total.	Nonslaveholding White. Members Average per family.	Nonslaveholding Free colored.[1]	Per cent Slaveholding White.	Per cent Slaveholding Free colored.[1]	Per cent Nonslaveholding White.	Per cent Nonslaveholding Free colored.[1]	Slaves Total number.	Slaves Average per slaveholding family.
Hillsborough district	3,721	841	841	5,465	6.5	......	2,880	2,858	16,510	5.8	22	22.6	......	76.8	0.6	13,449	16.0
Caswell county²																2,736	......
Chatham county	1,270	314	314	1,959	6.2	......	956	956	5,634	5.9	......	24.7	......	75.3	......	1,558	5.0
Granville county²																4,163	...
Orange county²																2,060	
Randolph county	1,161	137	137	911	6.6	......	1,024	1,023	5,925	5.8	1	11.8	......	88.1	0.1	460	3.4
Wake county	1,290	390	390	2,595	6.7	......	900	879	4,951	5.6	21	30.2	......	68.1	1.6	2,472	6.3
Morgan district	5,120	751	751	4,971	6.6	......	4,369	4,367	25,712	5.9	2	14.7	......	85.3	......	2,617	3.5
Burke county	1,253	173	173	1,162	6.7	......	1,080	1,080	6,332	5.9	......	13.8	......	86.2	......	600	3.5
Lincoln county	1,409	283	283	1,847	6.5	......	1,126	1,126	6,547	5.8	......	20.1	......	79.9	......	855	3.0
Rutherford county	1,181	164	164	1,122	6.8	......	1,017	1,017	6,072	6.0	......	13.9	......	86.1	......	609	3.7
Wilkes county	1,277	131	131	840	6.4	......	1,146	1,144	6,761	5.9	2	10.3	......	89.6	0.2	553	4.2
Newbern district	7,596	2,725	2,720	15,018	5.5	5	4,871	4,743	23,731	5.0	128	35.8	0.1	62.4	1.7	16,042	5.9
Beaufort county	780	290	289	1,470	5.1	1	490	469	2,187	4.7	21	37.0	0.1	60.1	2.7	1,622	5.6
Carteret county	579	155	155	870	5.6	......	424	404	2,062	5.1	20	26.8	......	69.8	3.5	709	4.6
Craven county, including Newbern town	1,440	576	572	2,836	5.0	4	864	806	3,638	4.5	58	39.8	0.3	56.0	4.0	3,663	6.4
Dobbs county	913	336	336	1,895	5.6	......	577	574	3,001	5.2	3	36.9	......	62.9	0.3	2,012	6.0
Hyde county	625	247	247	1,306	5.3	......	378	372	1,718	4.6	6	39.5	......	59.5	1.0	1,143	4.6
Johnston county	776	249	249	1,460	5.9	......	527	522	2,815	5.4	5	32.1	......	67.3	0.6	1,328	5.3
Jones county	583	217	217	1,279	5.9	......	366	358	1,792	5.0	8	37.2	......	61.4	1.4	1,655	7.6
Pitt county	1,095	401	401	2,316	5.8	......	694	693	3,565	3.1	1	36.6	......	63.3	0.1	2,364	5.9
Wayne county	805	254	254	1,586	6.2	......	551	545	2,953	5.4	6	31.6	......	67.7	0.7	1,546	6.1
Salisbury district	9,977	2,023	2,023	13,021	6.4	......	7,954	7,878	45,507	5.8	76	20.3	......	79.0	0.8	8,253	4.1
Guilford county	1,095	179	179	1,175	6.6	......	916	913	5,480	6.0	3	16.3	......	83.4	0.3	616	3.4
Iredell county	768	232	232	1,478	6.4	......	536	536	3,081	5.7	......	30.2	......	69.8	......	868	3.7
Mecklenburg county	1,742	423	423	2,591	6.1	......	1,319	1,253	7,100	5.7	66	24.3	......	71.9	3.8	1,608	3.8
Montgomery county	701	180	180	1,234	6.9	......	521	518	2,958	5.7	3	25.7	......	73.9	0.4	837	4.7
Rockingham county	840	212	212	1,405	6.6	......	628	628	3,683	5.9	......	25.2	......	74.8	......	1,113	5.3
Rowan county, including Salisbury town	2,429	432	432	2,700	6.3	......	1,997	1,995	11,429	5.7	2	17.8	......	82.1	0.1	1,741	4.0
Stokes county	1,329	202	202	1,311	6.5	......	1,127	1,125	6,421	5.7	2	15.2	......	84.7	0.2	778	3.9
Surry county	1,073	163	163	1,127	7.0	......	910	910	5,355	5.9	......	15.2	......	84.8	......	692	4.2
Wilmington district	3,022	1,227	1,221	6,652	5.4	6	1,795	1,765	9,172	5.2	30	40.4	0.2	58.4	1.0	10,067	8.2
Bladen county	634	237	237	1,291	5.4	......	397	388	2,065	5.3	9	37.4	......	61.2	1.4	1,686	7.1
Brunswick county	318	116	116	592	5.1	......	202	202	975	4.8	......	36.5	......	63.5	......	1,511	13.0
Duplin county	723	255	255	1,631	6.4	......	468	468	2,646	5.7	......	35.3	......	64.7	......	1,386	5.4
New Hanover county, including Wilmington town	626	341	337	1,685	5.0	4	285	276	1,348	4.9	9	53.8	0.6	44.1	1.4	3,737	11.0
Onslow county	721	278	276	1,453	5.3	2	443	431	2,138	5.0	12	38.3	0.3	59.8	1.7	1,747	6.3

SOUTH CAROLINA.

DISTRICT, COUNTY, TOWN, AND PARISH.	Total number.	Slaveholding. Number.	Slaveholding White. Number of families.	Slaveholding White. Members Total.	Slaveholding White. Members Average per family.	Slaveholding Free colored.[1]	Nonslaveholding. Number.	Nonslaveholding White. Number of families.	Nonslaveholding White. Members Total.	Nonslaveholding White. Members Average per family.	Nonslaveholding Free colored.[1]	Per cent Slaveholding White.	Per cent Slaveholding Free colored.[1]	Per cent Nonslaveholding White.	Per cent Nonslaveholding Free colored.[1]	Slaves Total number.	Slaves Average per slaveholding family.
The state	25,872	8,859	8,798	48,097	5.5	61	17,013	16,754	92,310	5.5	259	34.0	0.2	64.8	1.0	107,094	12.1
Beaufort district	962	578	576	2,746	4.8	2	384	364	1,584	4.4	20	59.9	0.2	37.8	2.1	14,236	24.6
Camden district	5,074	1,369	1,367	8,283	6.1	2	3,705	3,683	21,101	5.7	22	26.9	(³)	72.6	0.4	8,865	6.4
Chester county	1,041	230	230	1,447	6.3	......	811	810	4,463	5.5	1	22.1	......	77.8	0.1	938	4.1
Claremont county	400	170	170	1,129	6.6	......	230	230	1,362	5.9	......	42.5	......	57.5	......	2,110	12.4
Clarendon county	330	79	79	484	6.1	......	251	251	1,398	5.6	......	23.9	......	76.1	......	602	7.6
Fairfield county	1,048	254	254	1,520	6.0	......	794	794	4,498	5.7	......	24.2	......	75.8	......	1,485	5.8
Lancaster county	861	222	221	1,282	5.8	1	639	632	3,685	5.8	7	25.8	0.1	73.4	0.8	1,370	6.2
Richland county	480	187	186	945	5.1	1	293	279	1,537	5.5	14	38.8	0.2	58.1	2.9	1,437	7.7
York county	914	227	227	1,476	6.5	......	687	687	4,158	6.1	......	24.8	......	75.2	......	923	4.1
Charleston district	3,709	2,538	2,487	10,959	4.4	51	1,171	1,054	4,249	4.0	117	67.1	1.4	28.4	3.2	50,633	20.0
Berkley county	186	123	119	495	4.2	4	63	48	196	4.1	15	64.0	2.2	25.8	8.1	5,170	41.2
Colleton county	187	176	176	563	3.2	......	11	10	21	2.1	1	94.1	......	5.3	0.5	4,705	26.7
Dorchester county	236	140	140	746	5.3	......	96	95	506	5.3	1	59.3	......	40.3	0.4	3,022	21.6
Christ Church parish	144	114	113	474	4.2	1	30	29	95	3.3	1	78.5	0.7	20.1	0.7	2,377	20.9
St. Andrews parish	112	106	106	351	3.3	......	6	6	19	3.2	......	94.6	......	5.4	......	2,546	24.0
St. Bartholomes parish	503	277	270	1,157	4.3	7	226	198	976	4.9	28	53.7	1.4	39.4	5.6	10,338	37.4
St. James Goose Creek parish	112	93	92	347	3.8	1	19	19	92	4.8	......	82.1	0.9	17.0	......	2,333	25.1
St. James Santee parish	119	83	81	337	4.2	2	36	30	100	3.3	6	68.1	1.7	25.2	5.0	3,345	40.3

[1] Includes families of Indians taxed. ² Schedules destroyed, therefore no detail can be given. ³ Less than one-tenth of 1 per cent.

TABLE 114.—NUMBER OF FAMILIES REPORTED AT THE FIRST CENSUS, CLASSIFIED AS SLAVEHOLDING AND NON-SLAVEHOLDING, WHITE, AND FREE COLORED, TOGETHER WITH THE TOTAL AND AVERAGE NUMBER OF SLAVES, BY COUNTIES AND MINOR CIVIL DIVISIONS: 1790—Continued.

SOUTH CAROLINA—Continued.

DISTRICT, COUNTY, AND PARISH.	Total number.	Slaveholding. Number.	Slaveholding White. Number of families.	Slaveholding White. Number of members. Total.	Slaveholding White. Number of members. Average per family.	Slaveholding Free colored.[1]	Nonslaveholding. Number.	Nonslaveholding White. Number of families.	Nonslaveholding White. Number of members. Total.	Nonslaveholding White. Number of members. Average per family.	Nonslaveholding Free colored.[1]	Per cent Slaveholding. White.	Per cent Slaveholding. Free colored.[1]	Per cent Nonslaveholding. White.	Per cent Nonslaveholding. Free colored.[1]	Slaves Total number.	Slaves Average number per slaveholding family.
Charleston district—Cont'd.																	
St. Pauls parish	65	62	61	207	3.4	1	3	3	9	3.0	......	93.8	1.5	4.6	......	3,202	51.6
St. Phillips and St. Michaels parish	1,866	1,220	1,185	5,763	4.9	35	646	581	2,132	3.7	65	63.5	1.9	31.1	3.5	7,684	6.3
St. Stephens parish	57	49	49	198	4.0	......	8	8	27	3.4	......	86.0	......	14.0	......	2,506	51.1
St. Thomas parish	122	95	95	321	3.4	......	27	27	76	2.8	......	77.9	......	22.1	......	3,405	35.8
Cheraw district	1,344	382	382	2,284	6.0	......	962	952	5,192	5.5	10	28.4	......	70.8	0.7	3,229	8.5
Georgetown district	1,837	842	842	4,224	5.0	......	995	976	4,801	4.9	19	48.5	......	53.1	1.0	13,131	15.6
All Saints parish	95	64	64	289	4.5	......	31	30	136	4.5	1	67.4	......	31.6	1.1	1,795	28.0
Prince Fredericks parish	718	380	380	1,900	5.0	......	338	333	1,512	4.5	5	52.9	......	46.4	0.7	4,685	12.3
Prince Georges parish	1,024	398	398	2,035	5.1	......	626	613	3,153	5.1	13	38.9	......	59.9	1.3	6,651	16.7
Ninety-six district	10,578	2,418	2,418	15,470	6.4	......	8,160	8,112	46,869	5.8	48	22.9	......	76.7	0.5	11,069	4.6
Abbeville county	1,338	331	331	2,040	6.2	......	1,007	998	5,428	5.4	9	24.7	......	74.6	0.7	1,665	5.0
Edgefield county	1,751	599	599	3,627	6.1	......	1,152	1,123	5,962	5.3	29	34.2	......	64.1	1.7	3,619	6.0
Greenville county	964	162	162	1,090	6.7	......	802	801	4,808	6.0	1	16.8	......	83.1	0.1	606	3.7
Laurens county	1,394	300	300	1,989	6.6	......	1,094	1,090	6,221	5.7	4	21.5	......	78.2	0.3	1,120	3.7
Newberry county	1,377	302	302	1,874	6.2	......	1,075	1,073	6,283	5.9	2	21.9	......	77.9	0.1	1,144	3.8
Pendleton county	1,433	251	251	1,687	6.7	......	1,182	1,182	7,074	6.0	......	17.5	......	82.5	......	834	3.3
Spartanburgh county	1,264	242	242	1,643	6.8	......	1,022	1,019	6,159	6.0	3	19.1	......	80.6	0.2	866	3.6
Union county	1,057	231	231	1,520	6.6	......	826	826	4,934	6.0	......	21.9	......	78.1	......	1,215	5.3
Orangeburgh district	2,368	732	726	4,131	5.7	6	1,636	1,613	8,514	5.3	23	30.7	0.3	68.1	1.0	5,931	8.1
North part	1,290	473	473	2,560	5.4	......	817	817	4,161	5.1	......	36.7	......	63.3	......	4,529	9.6
South part	1,078	259	253	1,571	6.2	6	819	796	4,353	5.5	23	23.5	0.6	73.8	2.1	1,402	5.4

[1] Includes families of Indians taxed.

TABLE **115.**—SLAVEHOLDING FAMILIES, CLASSIFIED ACCORDING TO NUMBER OF SLAVES HELD, BY COUNTIES AND MINOR CIVIL DIVISIONS: 1790.

NEW HAMPSHIRE.

COUNTY AND TOWN.	Total number of slaveholding families.	1 slave.	2 to 4 slaves.	5 to 9 slaves.	COUNTY AND TOWN.	Total number of slaveholding families.	1 slave.	2 to 4 slaves.	5 to 9 slaves.
The state	123	97	24	2	Rockingham county—Continued.				
					Deerfield	2	2		
Cheshire county	16	14	2		Epping	5	5		
					Exeter	1		1	
Charlestown	1	1			Greenland	2	2		
Claremont	2	2			Hampstead	1	1		
Cornish	1	1			Hampton	1	1		
Hinsdale	2		2		Hawke	1	1		
Keene	2	2			Londonderry	5	5		
New Grantham	1	1			London	2	2		
Newport	1	1			Newington	9	5	4	
Protectworth	1	1			Newmarket	1	1		
Stoddard	1	1			Newtown	1	1		
Walpole	2	2			Northwood	1	1		
Westmoreland	1	1			Nottingham	7	5	2	
Winchester	1	1			Pembrook	2	2		
					Poplin	1	1		
Grafton county	13	9	4		Portsmouth	21	17	4	
					Rye	2	1	1	
Bartlett	1	1			Salem	1		1	
Bath	1	1			Stratham	1	1		
Bridgewater	1	1			Windham	3	2	1	
Campton	1	1							
Hanover	1		1		Strafford county	18	13	3	2
Haverhill	2	1	1						
Orange	1	1			Barnstead	1	1		
Oxford	1		1		Dover	6	5	1	
Piermont	3	3			Durham	3		1	2
Plymouth	1		1		Effingham	1	1		
					Gilmantown	1	1		
Rockingham county	76	61	15		Moultonborough	1	1		
					Rochester	1	1		
Brintwood	1	1			Somersworth	3	2	1	
Canterbury	1		1		Tamworth	1	1		
Concord	4	4							

RHODE ISLAND.

COUNTY AND TOWN.	Total number of slaveholding families.	1 slave.	2 to 4 slaves.	5 to 9 slaves.	COUNTY AND TOWN.	Total number of slaveholding families.	1 slave.	2 to 4 slaves.	5 to 9 slaves.
The state	461	255	160	[1] 46	Newport county—Continued.				
					Tiverton	13	6	7	
Bristol county	53	30	18	5					
					Providence county	54	36	17	1
Barrington	8	5	3						
Bristol	34	20	10	4	Cranston	7	4	3	
Warren	11	5	5	1	Foster	3	2	1	
					Glocester	1	1		
Kent county	32	21	7	4	Johnston	3	3		
					North Providence	4	3	1	
Coventry	4	3	1		Providence	29	19	9	1
East Greenwich	8	5	3		Scituate	3	1	2	
Warwick	16	11	2	3	Smithfield	4	3	1	
West Greenwich	4	2	1	1					
					Washington county	142	74	46	22
Newport county	180	94	72	[1] 14					
					Charlestown	4	1	2	1
Jamestown	8	4	4		Exeter	24	18	5	1
Little Compton	12	5	7		Hopkinton	6	5	1	
Middletown	8	3	5		North Kingstown	42	20	17	5
New Shoreham	20	11	5	4	Richmond	2	2		
Newport	109	59	41	[1] 9	South Kingstown	60	25	21	14
Portsmouth	10	6	3	1	Westerly	4	3		1

[1] Includes 1 family holding 13 slaves.

CONNECTICUT.

COUNTY AND TOWN.	Total number of slaveholding families.	1 slave.	2 to 4 slaves.	5 to 9 slaves.	10 to 19 slaves.	COUNTY AND TOWN.	Total number of slaveholding families.	1 slave.	2 to 4 slaves.	5 to 9 slaves.	10 to 19 slaves.
The state	1,563	980	505	66	[1] 12	Fairfield county—Continued.					
						Stratford	67	43	24		
Fairfield county	470	299	150	20	1	Weston	23	17	5	1	
Brookfield	2	1	1			Hartford county	157	101	44	10	2
Danbury	18	14	4								
Fairfield	96	50	37	9		Berlin	2	2			
Greenwich	49	35	12	2		Bristol	1		1		
Huntington	67	40	23	4		East Hartford	15	6	7	2	
New Fairfield	9	9				East Windsor	8	8			
Newtown	47	33	13	1		Enfield	10	7	3		
Norwalk	67	37	27	2	1	Farmington	6		1	3	2
Stamford						Glastenbury	14	9	4	1	
Reading	20	15	4	1		Hartford	30	21	8	1	
Ridgefield	5	5				Simsbury	2	2			

[1] Includes 1 family holding 28 slaves.

TABLE **115.**—SLAVEHOLDING FAMILIES, CLASSIFIED ACCORDING TO NUMBER OF SLAVES HELD, BY COUNTIES AND MINOR CIVIL DIVISIONS: 1790—Continued.

CONNECTICUT—Continued.

COUNTY AND TOWN.	Total number of slave-holding families.	NUMBER OF FAMILIES HOLDING—				COUNTY AND TOWN.	Total number of slave-holding families.	NUMBER OF FAMILIES HOLDING—			
		1 slave.	2 to 4 slaves.	5 to 9 slaves.	10 to 19 slaves.			1 slave.	2 to 4 slaves.	5 to 9 slaves.	10 to 19 slaves.
Hartford county—Continued.						New Haven county—Continued.					
Southington	9	8	1			Milford	45	32	12	1	
Suffield	14	8	4	2		New Haven city	45	27	16	2	
Wethersfield	37	24	13			North Haven	4	2	2		
Windsor	9	6	2	1		Wallingford	19	9	7	3	
						Waterbury	4	2	1	1	
Litchfield county	119	70	41	6	2	Woodbridge	9	6	3		
Bethlem	4	4				New London county [1]	329	193	127	9	
Cornwall	12	9	3								
Harwinton	3	1	2			Tolland county	35	27	7	1	
Kent	4	3	1								
Litchfield	47	24	21	1	1	Bolton	2	2			
New Milford	12	5	6	1		Coventry	4	2	2		
Southbury	9	5	2	2		Ellington	3	2	1		
Warren	5	4	1			Hebron	14	11	3		
Washington	5	1	1	2	1	Somers	3	2	1		
Watertown	9	7	2			Stafford	2	2			
Woodbury	9	7	2			Tolland	5	5	••		
						Union	1	1			
Middlesex county	114	71	38	4	1	Willington	1				1
Chatham	12	9	3			Windham county	98	68	25	3	2 2
East Haddam	10	6	3	1							
Haddam	3	3				Ashford	4	2	2		
Killingworth	5	2	3			Brooklyne	6	4	2		
Middletown	60	36	20	3	1	Canterbury	2	2			
Saybrook	24	15	9			Hampton	1	1			
						Killingley	7	6	1		
New Haven county	241	151	73	13	4	Lebanon	19	14	4		2 1
						Mansfield	4	2	2		
Branford	29	19	10			Plainfield	8	6	2		
Cheshire	9	6	3			Pomfret	15	12	3		
Derby	23	11	8	1	3	Thompson	2	1		1	
Durham	7	1	2	4		Voluntown	7	3	3		1
East Haven	20	11	7	1	1	Windham	14	9	3	2	
Guilford	23	21	2			Woodstock	9	6	3		
Hamden	4	4									

[1] Not returned by towns.   Includes 1 family holding 28 slaves.

NEW YORK.

COUNTY AND TOWN.	Total number of slave-holding families.	NUMBER OF FAMILIES HOLDING—						COUNTY AND TOWN.	Total number of slave-holding families.	NUMBER OF FAMILIES HOLDING—					
		1 slave.	2 to 4 slaves.	5 to 9 slaves.	10 to 19 slaves.	20 to 49 slaves.	Un-known slaves.			1 slave.	2 to 4 slaves.	5 to 9 slaves.	10 to 19 slaves.	20 to 49 slaves.	Un-known slaves.
The state	7,796	3,088	2,867	1,165	181	1	494	Columbia county—Cont'd.							
								Clermont	37	15	17	2	3		
Albany county	1,474	422	428	197	23		404	Germantown	16	7	7	2			
								Hillsdale	20	14	6				
Albany city	332	53	81	26	4		168	Hudson	63	27	21	12	3		
First ward	140	29	32	9	1		69	Kinderhook	174	59	64	38	13		
Second ward	88	10	17	4	2		55	Livingston	86	45	33	5	2	1	
Third ward	104	14	32	13	1		44								
Ballstown	35	23	8	4				Dutchess county	670	281	265	110	14		
Cambridge	23	14	7	2											
Catskill	143	25	23	14	2		79	Amenia	22	9	11	2			
Coxsackie	87	21	21	18	2		25	Beekman	46	26	12	8			
Duanesburgh	5	2					3	Clinton	67	31	24	11	1		
Easton	12	1	5	5	1			Fishkill	195	73	75	42	5		
Freehold	5	5						Frederickstown	36	23	11	2			
Halfmoon	55	24	26	5				Northeast	33	17	12	4			
Hoosick	17	8	9					Pawling	20	9	8	3			
Pittstown	15	8	5	2				Philipstown	12	8	3	1			
Rensselaerville	11	9	1				1	Poughkeepsie	80	29	43	7	1		
Rensselaerwick	171	64	69	28	10			Rhinebeck	121	38	50	27	6		
Saratoga	19	9	8	2				Southeast	6	3	2	1			
Schaghticoke	47	18	17	12				Washington	32	15	14	2	1		
Schenectady	27	10	15	2											
Schenectady (south of the Mohawk)	141	34	35	24			48	Kings county	333	67	129	112	25		
Schoharie	55	10	14	8			23	Brooklyn	104	25	38	34	7		
Stephentown	10	3	6	1				Bushwick	49	15	20	13	1		
Stillwater	27	17	4	6				Flatbush	73	12	22	30	9		
Watervliet	236	64	74	37	4		57	Flatlands	32	4	15	12	1		
Island in the river not included in any town	1			1				Gravesend	31	6	12	11	2		
								New Utrecht	44	5	22	12	5		
Clinton county	6	4	1	1				Montgomery county	300	114	79	16	1		90
Champlain	2	2						Canajoharie	60	24	11	1			24
Plattsburgh	3	1	1	1				Caughnawaga	71	27	19	1			24
Wellsburgh	1	1						Chemung	5	3			1		1
								German Flatts	11	5	6				
Columbia county	528	218	202	84	23	1		Harpersfield	6	4					2
								Herkimer	5	2	3				
Canaan	23	18	3	2				Mohawk	61	24	12	4			21
Claverack	109	33	51	23	2			Otsego	4	2		1			1

TABLE 115.—SLAVEHOLDING FAMILIES, CLASSIFIED ACCORDING TO NUMBER OF SLAVES HELD, BY COUNTIES AND MINOR CIVIL DIVISIONS: 1790—Continued.

NEW YORK—Continued.

COUNTY AND TOWN.	Total number of slave-holding families.	NUMBER OF FAMILIES HOLDING—					
		1 slave.	2 to 4 slaves.	5 to 9 slaves.	10 to 19 slaves.	20 to 49 slaves.	Unknown slaves.
Montgomery county—Con.							
Palatine	72	20	28	9	.....	.....	15
Whites	5	3	.....	.....	.....	.....	2
New York city and county	1,115	553	479	78	5	.....	.....
New York city	1,067	543	461	59	4	.....	.....
Dock ward	115	54	54	7			
East ward	235	107	112	16			
Montgomery ward	210	126	76	8			
North ward	154	75	74	5			
Out ward	130	71	50	8	1		
South ward	58	30	25	3			
West ward	165	80	70	12	3		
Harlem division	48	10	18	19	1		
Ontario county	4	3	.....	1			
Canandaigua	1	1	.....	.....			
Erwin	2	1	.....	1			
Genesee	1	1	.....				
Orange county	415	195	177	37	6		
Goshen	87	42	35	8	2		
Haverstraw	114	58	47	7	2		
Minisink	21	9	9	3	.....		
New Cornwall	62	25	28	7	2		
Orange	78	26	42	10			
Warwick	53	35	16	2			
Queens county	775	312	289	156	18		
Flushing	104	31	48	23	2		
Jamaica	85	37	36	11	1		
Newtown	141	41	53	44	3		
North Hempstead	152	54	54	38	6		
Oyster Bay	159	82	53	20	4		
South Hempstead	134	67	45	20	2		
Richmond county	238	81	86	68	3		
Castleton	39	13	17	9	.....		
Northfield	46	12	27	7	.....		
Southfield	72	26	16	28	2		
Westfield	81	30	26	24	1		
Suffolk county	496	272	168	49	7		
Brookhaven	103	65	26	8	4		
Easthampton	43	24	13	6	.....		
Huntington	102	53	37	12	.....		
Islip	9	2	4	3	.....		
Suffolk county—Continued.							
Shelter Island	5	1	2	1	1		
Smithtown	51	14	26	9	2		
Southampton	90	62	24	4	.....		
Southold	93	51	36	6	.....		
Ulster county	878	302	357	177	42	.....	
Hurley	56	11	23	18	4		
Kingston	210	66	91	41	12		
Mamakating	15	5	6	4	.....		
Marbletown	89	16	37	31	5		
Middletown	4	3	1	.....			
Montgomery	97	38	49	9	1		
New Marlborough	23	9	11	3	.....		
New Paltz	78	20	36	15	7		
New Windsor	42	23	11	6	2		
Newburgh	28	14	12	2	.....		
Rochester	76	23	29	18	6		
Schwangunk	102	39	34	25	4		
Wallkill	47	26	15	5	1		
Woodstock	11	9	2	.....			
Washington county	24	14	8	2	.....		
Argyle	9	5	4	.....			
Queensbury	1	1	.....	.....			
Salem	10	5	4	1			
Westfield	3	2	.....	1			
Whitehall	1	1	.....				
Westchester county	540	250	199	77	14	.....	
Bedford	20	13	5	2	.....		
Cortlandt	33	19	12	2	.....		
Eastchester	32	10	19	3	.....		
Greenburgh	46	21	17	8	.....		
Harrison	26	17	7	1	1		
Mamaroneck	15	5	5	4	1		
Morrisania	5	2	1	1	1		
Mt. Pleasant	38	20	13	5	.....		
New Rochelle	38	16	18	4	.....		
North Castle	18	13	3	2	.....		
North Salem	11	7	1	3	.....		
Pelham	11	3	5	3	.....		
Rye	49	22	20	5	2		
Salem	11	5	6	.....	.....		
Scarsdale	8	3	3	1	1		
Stephen	19	11	6	2	.....		
Westchester	62	16	24	17	5		
White Plains	24	12	10	2	.....		
Yonkers	51	20	17	11	3		
York	23	15	7	1	.....		

PENNSYLVANIA.

COUNTY AND TOWN.	Total number of slave-holding families.	NUMBER OF FAMILIES HOLDING—					
		1 slave.	2 to 4 slaves.	5 to 9 slaves.	10 to 19 slaves.	20 to 49 slaves.	Unknown slaves.
The state	1,858	1,031	667	145	12	1	2
Allegheny county	66	33	26	6	1	.....	.....
Elizabeth	10	4	5	1	.....		
Pitt	19	8	10	1	.....		
Plum	1	1	.....				
Versailles	2	1	1	.....			
That part of Allegheny county taken from Washington county	34	19	10	4	1	.....	
Bedford county[1]	24	11	13	.....			
Berks county	31	18	11	2	.....		
Amity	1	1	.....				
Bern	2	2	.....				
Brunswick and Manheim	1	1	.....				
Caernarvon	2	1	1	.....			
Douglass	1	1	.....				
Earl	1	1	.....				
Exeter	2	1	.....	1			
Heidelberg	3	1	2	.....			
Hereford	1	1	.....				
Oley	2	1	1	.....			
Reading borough	5	2	3	.....			
Richmond	3	2	1	.....			
Robeson	1	1	.....				
Tulpehocken	4	1	2	1			
Union	2	1	1	.....			
Bucks county[1]	134	71	56	7	.....		
Chester county	88	53	35	.....	.....		
Charlestown	5	4	1	.....			
Coventry	1	1	.....				
East Cain	1	.....	1	.....			
East Nantmill	2	1	1	.....			
East Nottingham	2	2	.....				
East Town	1	.....	1	.....			
East Whiteland	2	2	.....				
Fallowfield	6	4	2	.....			
Goshen	2	1	1	.....			
Honeybrook	5	.....	5	.....			
Kennet	2	2	.....				
London Britain	4	1	3	.....			
Londonderry	5	3	2	.....			
Londongrove	4	3	1	.....			
New Garden	1	1	.....				
New London	13	7	6	.....			
Oxford	10	4	6	.....			
Sadsbury	5	4	1	.....			
Trediffrin	3	3	.....				
Uwchland	4	4	.....				
Vincent	1	1	.....				
West Marlborough	1	1	.....				
West Nantmill	3	1	2	.....			
West Nottingham	2	1	1	.....			
West Whiteland	3	2	1	.....			
Cumberland county	117	61	50	6	.....		
Hopewell, Newton, Tyborn, Westpensboro	57	33	21	3	.....		
Eastern portion of county	60	28	29	3	.....		

[1] Not returned by townships.

TABLE **115.**—SLAVEHOLDING FAMILIES, CLASSIFIED ACCORDING TO NUMBER OF SLAVES HELD, BY COUNTIES AND MINOR CIVIL DIVISIONS: 1790—Continued.

PENNSYLVANIA—Continued.

COUNTY AND TOWN.	Total number of slave-holding families.	NUMBER OF FAMILIES HOLDING—					
		1 slave.	2 to 4 slaves.	5 to 9 slaves.	10 to 19 slaves.	20 to 49 slaves.	Unknown slaves.
Dauphin county	92	49	34	7	2		
Harrisburgh town	12	6	5	1			
Lebanon town	1		1				
Remainder of county	79	43	28	6	2		
Delaware county	24	16	6	2			
Bethel	1	1					
Birmingham	4	4					
Concord	1			1			
Darby	2	2					
Edgemont	1			1			
Haverford	4	1	3				
Middletown	2	1	1				
Newtown	1	1					
Radnor	2	2					
Ridley	1	1					
Springfield	1		1				
Tinicum	2	1	1				
Upper Chichester	1	1					
Upper Providence	1	1					
Fayette county	100	41	43	13	2	1	
Bullskin	5		4	1			
Franklin	17	9	8				
Georges	3	2	1				
German	2	1	1				
Luzerne	7		4	3			
Menallen	20	12	6	2			
Springhill	13	7	2	3	1		
Tyrone	6		4	2			
Union	13	6	6	1			
Washington	14	4	7	1	1	1	
Franklin county	163	95	53	15			
Fannet, Hamilton, Letterkenney, Montgomery, Peters	75	46	21	8			
Remainder of county	88	49	32	7			
Huntingdon county[1]	24	14	8	2			
Lancaster county	193	107	79	7			
Bart	5	5					
Caernarvon	11	5	4	2			
Donegal	4	1	2	1			
Drumore	13	3	9	1			
Earl	11	6	5				
Elizabeth	1	1					
Hempfield	2		2				
Lampeter	1	1					
Lancaster	1	1					
Lancaster borough	37	23	14				
Leacock	11	6	5				
Little Britain	19	8	10	1			
Manheim	1	1					
Martick	3	1	1	1			
May town	12	4	8				
Mountjoy	4	1	3				
Rapho	8	5	3				
Sadsbury	8	5	3				
Salisbury	32	24	8				
Strasburg	6	6					
Warwick	3		2	1			
Luzerne county[1]	7	4	3				
Mifflin county	39	25	10	2			2
That portion south of the river Juniata	8	3	3				2
The remainder	31	22	7	2			
Montgomery county	72	47	22	3			
Abington	2		2				
Cheltenham	2	2					
Manor of Moreland	10	4	6				
Remainder of county	58	41	14	3			
Northampton county	16	12	3	1			
Bethlehem	1	1					
Easton town	5	5					

COUNTY AND TOWN.	Total number of slave-holding families.	NUMBER OF FAMILIES HOLDING—					
		1 slave.	2 to 4 slaves.	5 to 9 slaves.	10 to 19 slaves.	20 to 49 slaves.	Unknown slaves.
Northampton county—Con.							
Forks	1						
Lower Mount Bethel	1			1			
Lower Smithfield	4	2	2				
Macunge	1	1					
Towamensink	1	1					
Upper Mount Bethel	1	1					
Upper Smithfield	1	1					
Northumberland county[1]	48	32	11	5			
Philadelphia county	220	126	75	15	4		
Blackley	4	4					
Bristol	2	1	1				
Byberry	2		2				
Germantown town	3	2	1				
Kingsessing	4	2	2				
Lower Dublin	15		6	5	4		
Manor of Moreland	2			2			
Moyamensing and Passyunk	7	6	1				
Northern Liberties town	32	17	13	2			
Oxford	9	6	2	1			
Roxborough	1	1					
Southwark	15	10	5				
Philadelphia city:							
Northern district (between Vine and Race streets from the Delaware to the Schuylkill)	18	12	6				
Middle district (from the north side of Chestnut street to the south side of Race street from the Delaware to the Schuylkill)	34	21	8	5			
Southern district (from the south side of Chestnut street to the north side of South street from the Delaware to the Schuylkill)	72	44	28				
Washington county[1]	123	68	41	12	2		
Westmoreland county	53	25	17	11			
Armstrong	3	2	1				
Derry	4	3	1				
Fairfield	3	1	1	1			
Hempfield	4	2	2				
Mount Pleasant	5	4		1			
North Huntingdon	5	2	1	2			
Rostraver	16	6	5	5			
Salem	2		2				
South Huntingdon	7	3	4				
Unity	3	1		2			
Washington	1	1					
York county	224	123	71	29	1		
Chanceford	12	8	2	2			
Codorus	5	2	3				
Fawn	14	7	3	4			
Hellam	2		1	1			
Hopewell	6	4	2				
Manchester	7	5	1	1			
Monaghan	6	3	3				
Paradise	3	2	1				
Reading	9	5	2	2			
Shrewsbury	10	6	4				
Warrington	2	1		1			
Windsor	3	3					
York	3		1	1			
York borough	15	10	3	2			
Huntington, Manallen, Manheim, and Tyrone	20	11	8	1			
Berwick, Cumberland, Franklin, Germany, Hamiltonban, Heidelberg, Mountjoy, Mount Pleasant, and Straban	107	55	37	14	1		

[1] Not returned by townships.

TABLE **115.**—SLAVEHOLDING FAMILIES, CLASSIFIED ACCORDING TO NUMBER OF SLAVES HELD, BY COUNTIES AND MINOR CIVIL DIVISIONS: 1790—Continued.

MARYLAND.

COUNTY, TOWN, AND HUNDRED.	Total number of slave-holding families.	NUMBER OF FAMILIES HOLDING—									
		1 slave.	2 to 4 slaves.	5 to 9 slaves.	10 to 19 slaves.	20 to 49 slaves.	50 to 99 slaves.	100 to 199 slaves.	200 to 299 slaves.	300 slaves and over.	Unknown slaves.
The state	12,226	2,841	3,617	2,807	1,796	713	96	16	3	1	336
Allegany county [1]											
Ann-Arundel county	1,096	146	216	221	158	86	13	4		1	251
Baltimore county	1,029	304	305	232	126	39	3	1			19
Back River, Upper hundred	135	29	37	34	27	8					
Mine Run hundred	83	25	34	16	7	1					
Two Deleware hundreds	78	14	36	15	11	2					
County not separated	733	236	198	167	81	28	3	1			19
Baltimore town and precincts	389	154	178	51	5	1					
Calvert county [1]											
Caroline county	418	126	149	87	43	12	1				
Cecil county	539	146	172	132	57	29	3				
Back Creek hundred	37	9	13	13	2						
Bohemia hundred	84	16	19	23	16	8	2				
Bohemia Manor hundred	51	8	18	14	9	2					
Charles town	10	5	4	1							
East Nottingham hundred	21	9	9	3							
Elk Neck hundred	45	17	13	11	3	1					
Middle Neck hundred	10	1	3	5		1					
North Milford hundred	76	24	32	12	6	2					
North Sassafras hundred	27	8	4	8	4	3					
North Susquehannah hundred	43	14	10	12		6	1				
Octoraro hundred	26	7	8	7	4						
South Milford hundred	14	7	3	3	1						
South Susquehannah hundred	26	6	13	2	3	2					
West Nottingham hundred	19	7	8	3	1						
West Sassafras hundred	50	8	15	15	8	4					
Charles county	1,221	247	317	295	243	107	11	1			
Dorchester county	296	72	99	58	43	24					
Frederick county	678	214	234	129	73	26	1	1			
Harford county	586	148	194	150	71	20	3				
Kent county	781	142	219	192	125	38	1				64
Montgomery county	933	203	257	277	159	35	2				
Prince Georges county	978	156	265	208	197	122	24	4	2		
Queen Anns county	828	180	230	209	140	58	9		2		
St. Marys county	892	199	265	204	149	61	12	1	1		
Somersett county [1]											
Talbot county	651	181	195	136	97	29	9	2			2
Washington county	269	90	98	55	20	4	2				
Worcester county	642	133	224	171	90	22	2				

[1] Schedules destroyed.

NORTH CAROLINA.

DISTRICT, COUNTY, AND TOWN.	Total number of slave-holding families.	NUMBER OF FAMILIES HOLDING—								
		1 slave.	2 to 4 slaves.	5 to 9 slaves.	10 to 19 slaves.	20 to 49 slaves.	50 to 99 slaves.	100 to 199 slaves.	200 to 299 slaves.	Unknown slaves.
The state	14,973	4,040	4,959	3,375	1,788	701	90	11	2	7
Edenton district	2,917	703	961	684	399	154	10	2	1	3
Bertie county	607	109	185	163	98	49	3			
Camden county	201	53	69	46	28	5				
Chowan county, excluding Edenton town	205	38	68	49	30	17	3			
Edenton town	108	30	39	18	11	4	1	1	1	3
Currituck county	257	74	89	71	18	5				
Gates county	344	91	98	82	52	21				
Hertford county	359	76	120	78	61	24				
Pasquotank county	299	86	100	64	40	7	2			
Perquimans county	322	88	110	67	41	15	1			
Tyrrell county	215	58	83	46	20	7		1		
Fayette district	1,229	412	408	265	114	28	2			
Anson county	174	55	49	51	16	3				
Cumberland county, excluding Fayetteville town	313	92	102	74	36	8	1			
Fayetteville town	110	35	42	18	11	4				
Moore county	88	28	31	19	8	2				
Richmond county	142	52	51	26	11	1	1			
Robeson county	163	72	56	26	8	1				
Sampson county	239	78	77	51	24	9				

TABLE **115.**—SLAVEHOLDING FAMILIES, CLASSIFIED ACCORDING TO NUMBER OF SLAVES HELD, BY COUNTIES AND MINOR CIVIL DIVISIONS: 1790—Continued.

NORTH CAROLINA—Continued.

DISTRICT, COUNTY, AND TOWN.	Total number of slave-holding families.	NUMBER OF FAMILIES HOLDING—								
		1 slave.	2 to 4 slaves.	5 to 9 slaves.	10 to 19 slaves.	20 to 49 slaves.	50 to 99 slaves.	100 to 199 slaves.	200 to 299 slaves.	Unknown slaves.
Halifax district	3,260	696	1,002	800	478	243	35	6		
Edgecombe county	491	84	186	117	78	25	1			
Franklin county	388	79	116	113	51	27	2			
Halifax county, including Halifax town	734	165	178	184	124	66	16	1		
Martin county	277	84	86	66	27	12	1	1		
Nash county	328	77	117	77	42	14	1			
Northampton county	583	125	189	133	85	46	4	1		
Warren county	459	82	130	110	71	53	10	3		
Hillsborough district	841	234	292	181	105	27	2			
Chatham county	314	91	106	75	35	6	1			
Randolph county	137	60	48	21	6	2				
Wake county	390	83	138	85	64	19	1			
Morgan district	751	289	256	148	51	7				
Burke county	173	67	63	31	10	2				
Lincoln county	283	117	94	54	17	1				
Rutherford county	164	63	54	35	10	2				
Wilkes county	131	42	45	28	14	2				
Newbern district	2,725	747	899	603	335	119	17	1		4
Beaufort county	290	79	105	65	29	9	3			
Carteret county	155	49	62	25	14	5				
Craven county, including Newbern town	576	161	188	120	73	26	6	1		1
Dobbs county	336	82	117	86	35	14	2			
Hyde county	247	70	84	67	19	6				1
Johnston county	249	76	77	50	36	9	1			
Jones county	217	56	61	44	32	20	2			2
Pitt county	401	99	134	91	59	16	2			
Wayne county	254	75	71	55	38	14	1			
Salisbury district	2,023	691	751	412	136	28	4	1		
Guilford county	179	69	64	33	12	1				
Iredell county	232	80	81	57	11	3				
Mecklenburg county	423	145	167	83	24	3	1			
Montgomery county	180	54	64	39	19	4				
Rockingham county	212	48	88	45	24	7				
Rowan county, including Salisbury town	432	153	168	80	22	7	1	1		
Stokes county	202	86	59	42	12	2	1			
Surry county	163	56	60	33	12	1	1			
Wilmington district	1,227	268	390	282	170	95	20	1	1	
Bladen county	237	50	81	48	37	19	2			
Brunswick county	116	21	33	21	20	17	3		1	
Duplin county	255	71	84	61	29	10				
New Hanover county, including Wilmington town	341	66	103	69	53	35	14	1		
Onslow county	278	60	89	83	31	14	1			

SOUTH CAROLINA.

DISTRICT, COUNTY, AND PARISH.	Total number of slave-holding families.	NUMBER OF FAMILIES HOLDING—									
		1 slave.	2 to 4 slaves.	5 to 9 slaves.	10 to 19 slaves.	20 to 49 slaves.	50 to 99 slaves.	100 to 199 slaves.	200 to 299 slaves.	300 slaves and over.	Unknown slaves.
The state	8,859	1,930	2,603	1,853	1,201	859	285	96	21	6	5
Beaufort district	578	73	91	91	86	150	66	18	2	1	
Camden district	1,369	349	471	297	158	78	11	5			
Chester county	230	76	82	51	18	3					
Claremont county	170	20	47	39	35	23	4	2			
Clarendon county	79	19	16	24	13	7					
Fairfield county	254	65	90	65	25	9					
Lancaster county	222	68	83	39	20	8	2	2			
Richland county	187	30	60	33	34	25	4	1			
York county	227	71	93	46	13	3	1				
Charleston district	2,538	315	607	527	495	356	156	58	17	4	3
Berkley county, St. Johns parish	123	14	18	15	16	23	28	7	2		
Colleton county, St. Johns parish	176	11	23	24	27	67	19	5			
Dorchester county, St. Georges parish	140	16	36	21	25	21	14	3	1		3
Christ Church parish	114	4	21	24	31	21	11	2			
St. Andrews parish	106	3	8	25	24	38	5	2	1		
St. Bartholomes parish	277	23	50	44	55	61	27	11	4	2	
St. James Goose Creek parish	93	10	18	12	18	25	5	4	1		
St. James Santee parish	83	3	7	22	15	16	12	3	4	1	

TABLE 115.—SLAVEHOLDING FAMILIES, CLASSIFIED ACCORDING TO NUMBER OF SLAVES HELD, BY COUNTIES AND MINOR CIVIL DIVISIONS: 1790—Continued.

SOUTH CAROLINA—Continued.

DISTRICT, COUNTY, AND PARISH.	Total number of slave-holding families.	NUMBER OF FAMILIES HOLDING—									
		1 slave.	2 to 4 slaves.	5 to 9 slaves.	10 to 19 slaves.	20 to 49 slaves.	50 to 99 slaves.	100 to 199 slaves.	200 to 299 slaves.	300 slaves and over.	Un-known slaves.
Charleston district—Continued.											
St. Pauls parish	62	2	8	6	13	19	7	5	1	1	....
St. Phillips and St. Michaels parish	1,220	219	398	321	244	38	....	....	....	....	....
St. Stephens parish	49	3	3	4	5	11	15	8	....	....	....
St. Thomas parish	95	7	17	9	22	16	13	8	3	....	....
Cheraw district	382	92	113	87	48	34	6	1	....	....	1
Georgetown district	842	125	182	195	162	133	32	10	2	1	....
All Saints parish	64	10	11	13	9	12	5	2	1	1	....
Prince Fredericks parish	380	43	71	89	98	68	10	1	....	....	....
Prince Georges parish	398	72	100	93	55	53	17	7	1	....	....
Ninety-six district	2,418	794	890	494	177	59	3	....	....	....	1
Abbeville county	331	87	134	72	24	13	1	....	....	....	....
Edgefield county	599	148	199	155	68	27	2	....	....	....	....
Greenville county	162	55	66	30	9	2	....	....	....	....	....
Laurens county	300	129	107	54	8	2	....	....	....	....	....
Newberry county	302	102	113	62	23	2	....	....	....	....	....
Pendleton county	251	101	106	27	15	2	....	....	....	....	....
Spartanburgh county	242	95	90	45	9	2	....	....	....	....	1
Union county	231	77	75	49	21	9	....	....	....	....	....
Orangeburgh district	732	182	249	162	75	49	11	4	....	....	....
North part	473	103	160	108	51	39	8	4	....	....	....
South part	259	79	89	54	24	10	3	....	....	....	....

INDEX.

Adults of self-supporting age, ratio of, to children, 103; for principal countries, 104; for states and territories, 105.

Africa, per cent distribution of foreign population born in, 130; number born in, 226.

Age, classification used in First Census returns, 93; method of obtaining proportions used in this report, 93; white population classified according to sex and, 94, 208.

Agriculture, rank as an industry, 26; acres of improved land and value of farm property, 145.

Albany, N. Y., population at the First and at the Twelfth Census, 78.

Allegheny, Pa., population at the First and at the Twelfth Census, 78.

Apportionment, congressional, primary object of census taking, 2; changes in, during the century, 92.

Area, in square miles, at First Census, 17, 51; at each enumeration, 54, 145; growth in population compared with, 56.

Asia, foreign population born in, 226.

Atlanta, Ga., population at the First and at the Twelfth Census, 78.

Austria, date of first census in, 2; increase in population in nineteenth century, 85; foreign population born in, 226. *See also* Austria-Hungary.

Austria-Hungary, ratio of adults of self-supporting age to children, 104; foreign population born in, per cent distribution, 130; number, 226. *See also* Austria

Baden, date of first census in, 2.

Baltimore, Md., preconstitutional population, 11, 13; exports and imports, 30; population at the First and at the Twelfth Census, 78; by color, 84.

Bancroft, Mr., estimates of colonial population, 8; by color, 8; rule of increase of population given by (*note*), 10.

Banks, names of those in existence in 1790, 21.

Bavaria, date of the first census in, 2.

Belgium, increase in population in nineteenth century, 85; rate of increase in, applied to native population in United States, 90; foreign population born in, per cent distribution, 130; number, 226.

Birth, area of, compared with area of residence for native white population of native parentage, 125, 126, 127.

Birth rate, changes in, 95.

Bohemia, foreign population born in, 226.

Boston, Mass., preconstitutional population, 11, 13; exports and imports, 30; population at the First and at the Twelfth Census, 78; by color, 84.

Boundaries, at First Census, 17.

Bridgeport, Conn., population at the First and at the Twelfth Census, 78.

Bridges, erection of, 21.

British Board of Trade, enumeration of population demanded by, 3.

British race, growth of population due to, 91.

Buffalo, N. Y., population at the First and at the Twelfth Census, 78.

Burnett, Governor, difficulties in making colonial enumerations outlined, 3.

Cambridge, Mass., population at the First and at the Twelfth Census, 78.

Camden, N. J., population at the First and at the Twelfth Census, 78.

Canada and Newfoundland, foreign population born in, per cent distribution, 130; number, 226.

Capital of the United States, provisions for making permanent, 16.

Census, First. *See* First Census.

Census act, provisions of, for taking First Census, 43.

Census taking, attitude of nations toward, 1; of states, 1; in preconstitutional period, 2, 4; influence of superstitions against, 3.

Censuses, colonial. *See* Colonial censuses.

Central America. *See* Mexico and Central America.

Charleston, S. C., population in preconstitutional period, 11, 13; at the First and at the Twelfth Census, 78; exports and imports, 30.

Chickering, Doctor, early estimates of population in Massachusetts and Maine, 5.

Children (white population under 16 years of age), method of obtaining proportions for classifying by age and sex, 93; number and proportion of population formed by, classified by sex, 94, 208, 210; effect of immigration on proportions, 95; average number per family, 100, 101; number per 1,000 of all ages, by specified years, 103; ratio of adults of self-supporting age to, 103, 105; in principal foreign countries, 104; ratio of, to adult females, 105; changes in ratios, during eighteenth and nineteenth centuries, 107; ratio of, to females 16 years of age and over, 106; in New York census of 1712, 107; in the native and the foreign stock, 107; in two counties shown by nationality for the First and for the Twelfth Census, 108; in principal foreign countries, 109; number in 1790 according to 1900 proportions and in 1900 according to those of 1790, 107; conditions effecting changes in proportions, 109.

China, foreign population born in, per cent distribution, 130; number, 226.

Cities, specified, population of, during preconstitutional period, 11; at the First and at the Twelfth Census, 78; increase in population, 79; proportion white and colored in, 84.

Coins, kinds in circulation, 20.

Colleges, list of, 32.

Colonial censuses, population, of New Hampshire, 149; Massachusetts, 156, 158; Rhode Island, 162; Connecticut, 164; New York, 170; New Jersey, 184; Maryland, 185.

Colonial period, census taking during, 3, 4; De Bow's estimates of population, 8; compilation of estimates of population, by decades, 9, 10.

Color, population classified according to, for each census, 80, 81; by states and territories, 82, 201; by counties, 201; white and negro, 83; by nativity of parents, 86; families classified by, according to slave ownership, for minor civil divisions, 276.

Columbia county, N. Y., population at the First and at the Twelfth Census distributed by nationality, 123; and ratio of adult females to children, 108.

Commerce, conditions and restrictions under colonial government, 29; tonnage of incoming vessels classified by ports of entry, 29; by country owning vessel, 30, 31; classes and value of imports and exports, 29; extent and character of trade with West Indies, 31.

Congress, number of members at the time of the First Census, 16; at each census, 92; provision in Constitution for representation in, 92.

Connecticut, population in preconstitutional period, 4, 5, 164, 165; Indian tribes, number and place of residence, 39; surnames classified according to number of families recorded under each, 113; number of members in such households, 114; population classified, by nationality, 116, 271; by counties and minor civil divisions, 193; according to color, 202; by sex and age, 212; slaves, number of, 132; families, classified by slave ownership and nationality, 274; and color, 280; by number of slaves held, 292. *See also* States and territories.

Continental period, census taking during, 3; estimated population of each state during, 9.

Counties, population of, classified according to increase or decrease, 60; number reaching maximum population prior to Twelfth Census, 71; population as returned on schedules, 188; families classified by number of members, 224.

Cuba and West Indies, foreign population born in, 226.

Currency, establishing system of, 20.

De Bow, Mr. J. E. D., estimates of colonial population, 8.

Debt, national, a factor in census taking, 4.

Declaration of Independence, signatures of signers, 115.

Delaware, population in preconstitutional period, 4, 6; list of minor civil divisions, 74; population, computed distribution of, by nationality, 119, 121; by counties and minor civil divisions, 198; by color, 203; by sex and age, 214; number of slaves in, 132. *See also* States and territories.

Denmark, tonnage of vessels from, entering ports, 30; increase in population in nineteenth century, 85; foreign population born in, per cent distribution, 130; number, 226.

Density of population, for states and territories, 58; in specified areas, 59; in certain European countries, 59; increase in United States compared with Europe, 85.

Dexter, Prof. Franklin Bowditch, estimates of colonial population, 8.

Dutch, population classified as, by states, 117; by counties, 271.

Dwellings, number, in colonial Philadelphia, 13; in Massachusetts, 101; definition in Twelfth Census, 101; computations on basis of Massachusetts data, 102; estimated average number of persons per, 102.